The Rou [barcode] D0976639

Argentina

written and researched by

**Danny Aeberhard, Andrew Benson,
Rosalba O'Brien and Lucy Phillips**

with additional contributions by
Ed Stocker and Clemmy Manzo

ROUGH
GUIDES

www.roughguides.com

Contents

Criollo culture
colour section
following p.168

The legendary Ruta 40
colour section
following p.312

◀◀ Tango dancers, Buenos Aires ◀ Iguazú Falls

Introduction to

Argentina

Argentina is a vast land: even without the titanic wedge of Antarctica that the authorities like to include in the national territory, it ranks as one of the world's largest countries. The mainland points down from the Tropic of Capricorn like a massive stalactite, tapering towards the planet's most southerly extremities. Consequently, the country encompasses a staggering diversity of landscapes, ranging from the hot and humid jungles of the Northeast and the bone-dry highland steppes of the Northwest, via the fertile Pampas and windswept Patagonia, to the end-of-the-world archipelago of Tierra del Fuego.

Argentina is, for the most part, less obviously "exotic" than most of its neighbours to the north, and its inhabitants will readily, and rightly, tell you how great an influence Europe has been on their nation. It was once said that Argentina is actually the most American of all European countries, but even that clever maxim is wide of the mark. It's a country with a very special character all of its own, distilled into the national ideal of **Argentinidad** – an elusive identity that the country's utopian thinkers and practical doers have never really agreed upon.

In terms of identity, there are lots of sweeping generalizations about the people of Argentina, who generally get bad press in the rest of the continent for being loud and arrogant. Though such a characterization isn't entirely without merit, it's more the exception than the rule – you're bound to be wowed by Argentines' zeal for so many aspects of their own culture and curiosity about the outside world. On this score there is a lot of truth in the

5

clichés – their passions are dominated by **football**, politics and living life in the fast lane (literally, when it comes to driving) – but not everyone dances the **tango**, or is obsessed with **Evita** or gallops around on a horse. The locals will help to make any trip to their country memorable.

There are loads of other reasons to visit Argentina, not least the great metropolis of **Buenos Aires**, one of the most fascinating of all Latin American capitals. It's an immensely enjoyable place just to wander about, people-watching, shopping or simply soaking up the unique atmosphere. Its many barrios, or neighbourhoods, are startlingly different – some are decadently old-fashioned, others thrustingly modern – but all of them ooze character. Elsewhere in the country, cities aren't exactly the main

Pre-Columbian Argentina

Of all South American countries, superficially, at least, Argentina has the least marked pre-colonial culture. During the nineteenth century in particular, whole indigenous peoples were wiped out by various waves of newcomers, their superior weapons and their deadly diseases. Yet drinking *mate* – now a quintessentially Argentine custom – was learned from the native peoples, while a good many traditional festivals and prevailing superstitious beliefs were inherited from those who lived on Argentine soil long before the Europeans arrived. Though no Machu Picchu, the pre-Columbian – and mostly pre-Inca – ruins at Quilmes, Tilcara and Shinkal are nevertheless marvellous archeological sites, while fine rock drawings can be admired at accessible locations across the country.

draw, with the exception of beautiful **Salta** in the Northwest, beguiling **Rosario** – the birthplace of Che Guevara – and **Ushuaia**, which, in addition to being the world's most southerly city, enjoys a fabulous setting on Tierra del Fuego.

The vastness of the **land** and the varied **wildlife** inhabiting it are the country's real attractions outside the capital. In theory, by hopping on a plane or two you could spot howler monkeys and toucans in northern jungles in the morning, then watch the antics of penguins tobogganing into the icy South Atlantic in the afternoon. There are hundreds of bird species – including the Andean Condor and three varieties of flamingo – plus pumas, armadillos, llamas, foxes and tapirs, to be found in the country's forests, mountainsides and the dizzying heights of the altiplano, or *puna*. Lush tea plantations

Fact file

• Argentina is the world's eighth-largest nation by area, with 2.8 million square kilometres, though with a population of just over 40 million – one-third of whom live in Greater Buenos Aires – it is one of the least densely populated countries in the world (India's density is 26 times greater, Singapore's over 500 times).

• Argentina not only produces the finest beef on earth, but it also is one of the world's leading producers of lemons, wheat, wine and genetically modified soya. Around half of the country's arable land is planted with the latter crop.

• Five Argentines have been honoured with Nobel Prizes, including three in the sciences: Bernardo A. Houssay (Medicine and Physiology, 1947), Luis F. Leloir (Chemistry, 1970) and César Milstein (Medicine and Physiology, 1984). Two Argentines have been awarded the Nobel Peace Prize: Carlos Saavedra Lamas (politician, 1936) and Adolfo Pérez Esquivel (architect, sculptor and human-rights activist, 1980).

• Argentina has one of the world's most vibrant film industries and has twice carried off an Oscar for best foreign language film: *La historia oficial* (The Official Story) in 1985 and *El secreto de sus ojos* (The Secret in Their Eyes) in 2010.

• Just over two-fifths of Argentina's lower house of parliament (following 2009 elections) is female – the sixth-highest ratio in the world, according to Inter-Parliamentary Union figures.

▶ Ruins at Quilmes

and parched salt-flats, palm groves and icebergs, plus the world's mightiest waterfalls, are just some of the sights that will catch you unawares if you were expecting Argentina to be one big cattle ranch. Dozens of these biosystems are protected by a network of national and provincial **parks and reserves**.

As for **getting around** and seeing these wonders, you can generally rely on a well-developed infrastructure inherited from decades of domestic tourism. Thanks in part to an increasing number of boutique hotels, the range and quality of **accommodation** have improved noticeably in recent years. Among the best are the beautiful ranches known as **estancias** – or *fincas* in the north – that have been converted into luxury resorts. In most places, you'll be able to rely on the services of top-notch tour operators, who will not only show you the sights but also fix you up with all kinds of **outdoor adventures**: horse-riding, trekking, white-water rafting, kayaking, skiing, hang-gliding, along with more relaxing pursuits such as wine-tasting, bird-watching or photography safaris. Argentina is so huge and varied it's hard to take in all in one go – don't be surprised if you find yourself longing to return to explore the areas you didn't get to see the first time around.

Where to go

Argentina has many attractions that could claim the title of natural wonders of the world: the majestic waterfalls of **Iguazú**; the spectacular **Glaciar Perito Moreno**; fascinating whale colonies off **Península Valdés**; or the mountains around the holiday resort of **Bariloche** – indeed, **Patagonia** in general. Yet many of the country's most noteworthy sights are also its least known, such as the **Esteros del Iberá**, a

Tango

Tango is not only a dance, or even an art form, but it is also a powerful symbol, perhaps what people associate with Argentina more than anything else. Essentially and intrinsically linked to Buenos Aires and its history, it nonetheless has fans all around the country. Rosario and to a lesser extent, Córdoba, the country's two biggest cities after the capital, have a strong tango culture, complete with *milongas* (dance halls) and shops to buy the right footwear. And don't be surprised to find humble folk in some remote village, hundreds of miles from Buenos Aires, listening to a scratchy recording of Carlos Gardel – still the leading figure of tango as song. Perhaps it is because tango depicts the Argentine psyche so well: a unique blend of nostalgia, resignation and passion.

huge reserve of floating islands offering close-up encounters with all sorts of birds and mammals; or **Antofagasta de la Sierra**, a remote village set amid frozen lagoons mottled pink with flamingoes; or **Laguna Diamante**, a high-altitude lake reflecting a wondrous volcano. In any case, weather conditions and the sheer size of the country will rule out any attempt to see every corner; it's more sensible and rewarding to concentrate on a particular section of the country.

Unless you're visiting Argentina as part of a South American tour, **Buenos Aires** is likely to be your point of entry, as it has the country's only *bona fide* international airport, Ezeiza. Only inveterate city-haters will be able to resist the capital's charms. Buenos Aires is one of the world's greatest urban experiences, with an intriguing blend of architecture and a vernacular flair that includes houses painted in the colours of a legendary football team. The city's museums are eclectic enough to suit all interests – Latin American art, colonial silverware, dinosaurs and ethnography are just four subjects on offer – and you can round off a day's sightseeing with a tango show, a bar tour or a meal at one of the hundreds of fabulous restaurants.

Due north stretches the **Litoral**, an expanse of subtropical watery landscapes that shares borders with Uruguay, Brazil and Paraguay. Here are the photogenic **Iguazú waterfalls** and Jesuit missions whose once-noble ruins are crumbling into the jungle – with the exception of well-preserved **San Ignacio Miní**. Immediately west of the Litoral stretches the **Chaco**, one of Argentina's most infrequently visited regions, a place for those with

an ardent interest in **wildlife**. Be prepared for fierce heat and a poor tourism infrastructure here. Up in the country's landlocked **Northwest** is the **Quebrada de Humahuaca**, a fabulous gorge lined with rainbow-hued rocks; it winds up to the oxygen-starved altiplano, where llamas and their wild relatives graze. In the **Valles Calchaquíes**, a series of stunningly scenic valleys, high-altitude vineyards produce the delightfully flowery *torrontés* wine along with some subtle reds.

Stretching across Argentina's broad midriff to the west and immediately south of Buenos Aires are **the Pampas**, arguably the country's most archetypal landscape. Formed by horizon-to-horizon plains interspersed with low sierras, this subtly beautiful scenery is punctuated by small towns, the odd ranch and countless clumps of pampas grass (*cortaderas*). Part arid, part wetland, the Pampas are grazed by millions of cattle and planted with soya and wheat fields of incomprehensible size. The Pampas are also where you'll glimpse signs of traditional **gaucho culture**, most famously in the charming town of **San Antonio de Areco**. Here, too, are some of the classiest estancias, offering a combination of luxury and horseback adventures. On the Atlantic Coast are a string of fun beach resorts, including longstanding favourite **Mar del Plata**.

The further west you go, the larger the Central Sierras loom: the mild climate and bucolic woodlands of these ancient mountains have attracted Argentine tourists since the late nineteenth century, and within reach of **Córdoba**, the country's vibrant second city, are some of the oldest resorts on the continent. In the **Cuyo**, further west still, with the highest Andean peaks as a backdrop, you can discover one of Argentina's most enjoyable cities, the regional capital of **Mendoza**, also the country's **wine capital**. From here, the scenic **Alta Montaña** route climbs steeply to the Chilean border, passing **Cerro Aconcagua**, now well established as a fantasy challenge for mountaineers. Just south, **Las Leñas** is a winter resort where celebrities are out in force, while the nearby black-and-red lava wastes of **La Payunia**, one of the country's hidden jewels, are all but overlooked. Likewise, **San Juan** and **La Rioja** provinces

Península Valdés

The Patagonian headland, **Península Valdés**, offers unrivalled opportunities for seeing the world's most endangered large cetacean, the **southern right whale**. Every year as many as a thousand of these gigantic mammals come to breed and give birth in the sheltered waters nearby. Nineteenth-century whalers named them "right whales" because their curious nature meant they swam close to passing ships, making them the right whales – in other words, the easiest – to harpoon. That same curiosity leads them to approach whale-watching boats – sometimes so close you can smell their breath. You don't even need to go out in a boat: take an evening stroll along the beaches of Golfo San José or Golfo Nuevo and you'll often see and hear the creatures.

are relatively uncharted territories, but their marvellous mountain and valley landscapes reward exploration, along with their underrated wineries. Their star attractions are a brace of parks: **Parque Nacional Talampaya**, with its giant red cliffs, and the nearby **Parque Provincial Ischigualasto**, usually known as the **Valle de la Luna** on account of its intriguing moonscapes.

Argentina has the lion's share of the wild, sparsely populated expanses of **Patagonia** (shared with Chile) and boasts by far the more interesting half of the remote archipelago of **Tierra del Fuego**. These are lands of seemingly endless arid steppe hemmed in for the most part by the southern leg of the Andes, a series of volcanoes, craggy peaks and deep glacial lakes. An almost unbroken chain of national parks along these Patagonian and Fuegian cordilleras makes for some of the best trekking anywhere on the planet. You should certainly include the savage granite peaks of the FitzRoy massif in **Parque**

▶ Southern right whale, Península Valdés

Nacional Los Glaciares in your itinerary, but also the less frequently visited araucaria, or monkey puzzle, forests of **Parque Nacional Lanín** or the trail network of **Parque Nacional Nahuel Huapi**. For wildlife enthusiasts, **Peninsula Valdés** is a must-see (see box, p.11). If you have a historical bent, you may like to trace the region's associations with FitzRoy and Darwin in the beautiful **Beagle Channel** off Ushuaia, or track down the legacy of Butch Cassidy, who lived near Cholila, or of the Welsh settlers whose influence can still be felt in communities like **Gaiman** and **Trevelin**.

When to go

Given the size of Argentina, you're unlikely to flit from region to region, and, if you can, you should try and visit each area at the optimal time of year. Roughly falling from September to November, the Argentine **spring** is perfect just about everywhere, although in the far south icy gales may blow. Avoid the southern half of the country in the coldest months (May–Oct), when deep snow can cut off towns and villages; likewise with the Chaco and most other lowland parts of the North in the height of summer, as temperatures can be scorching and roads flooded by heavy storms. The only time, however, to climb the highest Andean peaks, such as Aconcagua, is **midsummer** (Dec to Feb) – also the most reliable time of year to head for Tierra del Fuego, though it has been known to snow there even in December.

▲ Lake Belgrano, Parque Nacional Perito Moreno

24 **Football** Page **47** • It wouldn't be a stretch to say that nothing else quite holds a grip on Argentine society like football – for some no trip to the country is complete without attending a match.

25 **Estancias** Pages **38, 186, 192, 225–261, 300, 332, 526** & **545** • Try your hand at cattle-herding or sheep-shearing at a working estancia – one of the great Argentine institutions – and get an authentic taste of the gaucho way of life.

26 Tigre and the Paraná Delta Page 156 •

Take a boat or paddle a kayak around the swampy islets and muddy creeks of Tigre – a subtropical Venice right on the capital's doorstep.

27 The Pampas Page 180 •

Rugged gauchos, nodding pampas grass and herds of contented cattle are the famous inhabitants of Argentina's most archetypal landscape – fertile plains stretching for as far as the eye can see.

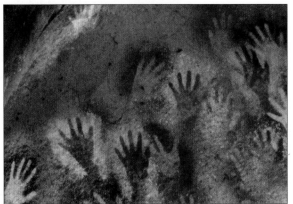

28 Cueva de las Manos Pintadas Page 552 •

A prehistoric mural, an early finger-printing exercise or ancient graffiti? Whatever it is, this delicate tableau of many hands is one of the continent's most enchanting archeological sites.

Basics

Basics

Getting there

Though some visitors reach Argentina overland from a neighbouring country and a tiny handful arrive by boat, the overwhelming majority of travellers first set foot on Argentine soil at Buenos Aires' international airport, Ezeiza.

In general, airfares to Argentina still tend to be quite high, but they do vary widely depending on the routing and the **season**. The highest fares are between December and February, around Easter and in July and August. You'll get the best prices during the low season: March to June and September to November. Note also that flying on weekends often hikes return fares; price ranges quoted in this section assume midweek travel. You can often reduce costs by going through a **discount flight agent** (see p.29).

Flights from the UK and Ireland

Several airlines offer regular scheduled flights **from the UK** to Buenos Aires, via another European city, São Paulo or the US (the latter trips can be marginally less expensive, but are usually longer). British Airways is currently the only airline to fly direct from London, refuelling in Sao Paulo. It's nearly always cheaper to book your flight through a specialized or discount flight agent. It's also worth checking the travel sections of London's *Time Out* and the national Sunday newspapers, or phoning the Air Travel Advisory Bureau (☏020/7636 5000) for a list. Adult **fares** from London to Buenos Aires usually start at around £700 in the low season, rising to over £1000 in the high season.

There are no direct flights **from Ireland** to Argentina. If you're trying to keep costs down, consider flying to London with an economy airline and making a connection there. For less hassle, though, and only a fraction more money, you're better off flying direct to New York or Miami and catching an onward flight from there.

In addition to fares, it's worth paying attention to the **routes** used by different airlines. The shortest and most convenient routes from London, often via São Paulo or Madrid, entail a total travelling time of around sixteen hours. Apart from minimizing the length of the flight, another reason to check the routes is that many airlines allow you to take **stopovers** on the way — sometimes for free, sometimes for a surcharge of around ten percent. Potential stopovers include Bogotá, Rio and São Paulo in South America; Boston, Chicago, Dallas, Houston, Miami, Newark and Washington DC in the US; and Frankfurt, Madrid, Milan, Paris and Rome in Europe.

Flights from the US and Canada

Several airlines, including American Airlines, United and Aerolíneas Argentinas, offer daily nonstop **flights from the US** to Buenos Aires. Typical **fares** start at US$900 from New York in low season or US$1000 from Chicago or Washington, rising to US$1600 in the high season. Flying times to Buenos Aires are around eleven hours from New York and Chicago, and nine from Miami.

There's less choice if you're flying **from Canada**, with Air Canada offering the only direct flight into the country – from Toronto via São Paulo (with connections from other major Canadian cities). You'll be able to put together a considerably more flexible itinerary if you look for connecting flights with a US carrier. Direct flights from Toronto take around thirteen hours and **prices** start at Can$1000 in low season; from Vancouver the journey time is at least eighteen hours, and fares start from around Can$1100.

Flights from Australia, New Zealand and South Africa

The best flight deals to Argentina from Australia and New Zealand are offered by Aerolíneas Argentinas and LAN in conjunction

with Qantas and Air New Zealand, either direct to Buenos Aires or via a stopover in Santiago. **In Australia**, flights to Argentina leave from Sydney, plus a couple a week that depart from Brisbane and Melbourne. The most direct route to Buenos Aires **from New Zealand** is via Auckland and takes about seventeen hours. Flights **from South Africa** to Argentina leave from Cape Town and Johannesburg and go via São Paulo, taking sixteen or seventeen hours. Malaysia Airlines flights between Kuala Lumpur and Buenos Aires stop over in Cape Town, from where the last leg takes around ten hours direct; South African Airways has slightly longer direct flights from Johannesburg.

Airfares depend on both the season and duration of stay. Fares from Australia normally start around Aus\$1800 in low season, with flights from New Zealand costing around NZ\$1600. The lowest return fares from Cape Town or Johannesburg cost around ZAR7500.

Round-the-world flights

If Argentina is only one stop on a longer journey, you might want to consider buying a **round-the-world (RTW)** ticket. Some travel agents can sell you an "off-the-shelf" RTW ticket that will have you touching down in about half a dozen cities (Buenos Aires is on many itineraries). Alternatively, you can have a travel agent assemble a RTW ticket for you; in this case the ticket can be tailored to your needs but is usually more expensive.

Airlines, agents and operators

Airlines

Aerolineas Argentinas Ⓦ www.aerolineas.com
Air Canada Ⓦ www.aircanada.com
Air Europa Ⓦ www.aireuropa.com
Air France Ⓦ www.airfrance.com
Air New Zealand Ⓦ www.airnz.co.nz
Alitalia Ⓦ www.alitalia.com
American Airlines Ⓦ www.aa.com
Avianca Ⓦ www.avianca.com
British Airways Ⓦ www.ba.com
Continental Airlines Ⓦ www.continental.com
Delta Ⓦ www.delta.com
Iberia Ⓦ www.iberia.com
LAB (Lloyd Aereo Boliviano) Airlines
Ⓦ www.labairlines.co.uk
LanChile Ⓦ www.lan.com

Lufthansa ⓦ www.lufthansa.com
Malaysia Airlines ⓦ www.malaysiaairlines.com
Qantas Airways ⓦ www.qantas.com
South African Airways ⓦ www.flysaa.com
Swiss ⓦ www.swiss.com
United Airlines ⓦ www.united.com
Varig ⓦ www.varig.com

Discount agents

Adventure World Australia ☎ 02/8913 0755,
ⓦ www.adventureworld.com.au; New Zealand
☎ 09/524 5118, ⓦ www.adventureworld.co.nz.
Agents for a vast array of international adventure
travel companies that operate trips to South America.
Bridge the World UK ☎ 0870/443 2399, ⓦ www
.bridgetheworld.com. Specializing in RTW tickets,
with good deals aimed at backpackers.
North South Travel UK ☎ 01245/608 291,
ⓦ www.northsouthtravel.co.uk. Friendly,
competitive travel agency, offering discounted fares
worldwide. Profits are used to support projects in
the developing world, especially the promotion of
sustainable tourism.
South American Experience UK ☎ 020/7976
5511, ⓦ www.southamericanexperience.co.uk.
Mainly a discount flight agent, but also offers a range
of tours, plus a very popular "soft landing package",
designed to make arrivals pain-free.
STA Travel UK ☎ 0871/2300 040, US
☎ 1-800/781-4040, Australia ☎ 134 782, New
Zealand ☎ 0800/474 400, South Africa ☎ 0861/781
781; ⓦ www.statravel.com. Worldwide specialists in
independent travel; also student IDs, travel insurance,
car rental, rail passes and more. Good discounts for
students and under-26s.
Trailfinders UK ☎ 0845/058 5858, Ireland
☎ 01/677 7888, Australia ☎ 1300/780 212;
ⓦ www.trailfinders.com. One of the best-informed
and most efficient agents for independent travellers.
Travel Cuts Canada ☎ 1-866/246-9762, US
☎ 1-800/592-2887; ⓦ www.travelcuts.com.
Canadian youth and student travel firm.
USIT Ireland ☎ 01/602 1906, Northern Ireland
☎ 028/9032 7111; ⓦ www.usit.ie. Ireland's main
student and youth travel specialist tour operator.

Specialist tour operators

Adventure Center US ☎ 1-800/228-8747,
ⓦ www.adventurecenter.com. Hiking and "soft
adventure". Offers a few Argentina tours, including
a 23-day "Patagonian Dreaming" Buenos Aires to
Ushuaia trip.

Six steps to a better kind of travel

At Rough Guides we are passionately committed to travel. We feel strongly that only
through travelling do we truly come to understand the world we live in and the
people we share it with – plus tourism has brought a great deal of **benefit** to
developing economies around the world over the last few decades. But the
extraordinary growth in tourism has also damaged some places irreparably, and of
course **climate change** is exacerbated by most forms of transport, especially flying.
This means that now more than ever it's important to **travel thoughtfully** and
responsibly, with respect for the cultures you're visiting – not only to derive the
most benefit from your trip but also to preserve the best bits of the planet for
everyone to enjoy. At Rough Guides we feel there are six main areas in which you
can make a difference:

• Consider what you're contributing to the **local economy**, and how much the
services you use do the same, whether it's through employing local workers and
guides or sourcing locally grown produce and local services.
• Consider the **environment** on holiday as well as at home. Water is scarce in many
developing destinations, and the biodiversity of local flora and fauna can be
adversely affected by tourism. Try to patronize businesses that take account of this.
• Travel with a purpose, not just to tick off experiences. Consider **spending longer**
in a place, and getting to know it and its people.
• Give thought to how often you **fly**. Try to avoid short hops by air and more harmful
night flights.
• Consider **alternatives to flying**, travelling instead by bus, train, boat and even
bike or on foot where possible.
• Make your trips "**climate neutral**" via a reputable carbon offset scheme. All Rough
Guide flights are offset, and every year we donate money to a variety of charities
devoted to combating the effects of climate change.

Adventures Abroad US & Canada ☎1-800/665-3998, ⓦwww.adventures-abroad.com. Adventure specialist offering two-week tours to Patagonia.

Contours Australia ☎1300/135 391, ⓦwww.contourstravel.com.au. Specialists in tailored city stopover packages and tours, including self-drive tours through the Lake District and a ten-day budget tour of Patagonia.

Destination Argentina ☎011/5218-2820, ⓦwww.destinationargentina.com. Luxury travel and tourism website covering accommodation for the whole country and all manner of useful services.

Dragoman UK ☎0870/499 4478, ⓦwww.dragoman.co.uk. Extended overland journeys; shorter camping and hotel-based safaris, too.

Thirty-day mostly camping trip from Santiago to Rio de Janeiro via Bariloche, Buenos Aires.

Exodus UK ☎0870/240 5550, ⓦwww.exodus.co.uk. Adventure-tour operator taking small groups for specialist programmes, including walking, biking, overland, adventure and cultural trips. Among its tours is a three-week Fitz Roy and Torres del Paine trip.

Explore Worldwide UK ☎01252/760 000, ⓦwww.explore.co.uk. Small-group tours, treks, expeditions and safaris. Offers three-week tours of the fjords and Patagonia.

Journey Latin America UK ☎020/8747 3108, ⓦwww.journeylatinamerica.co.uk. Specialist in flights, packages and tailor-made trips to Latin America. Two-week Salta hiking and biking trip.

Tailored Expeditions in Argentina ⓦwww.tailoredexpeditions.com. Organizes custom packages and local excursions with emphasis on the Northwest, cultural activities and luxury accommodation.

Tucan Travel UK ☎020/8896 1600, ⓦwww.tucantravel.com. Group holidays in Argentina, plus a range of overland expeditions in the rest of South America.

Wilderness Travel US ☎1-800/368-2794, ⓦwww.wildernesstravel.com. Specialist in hiking, cultural and wildlife adventures. Offers an eleven-day tour in the Lake District.

Wildlife Worldwide UK ☎020/8667 9158, ⓦwww.wildlifeworldwide.com. Tailor-made trips for wildlife and wilderness enthusiasts. Seventeen-day southern Patagonia and Iguazú trip.

World Expeditions UK ☎020/8870 2600, ⓦwww.worldexpeditions.co.uk; Australia ☎1300/720 000, ⓦwww.worldexpeditions.com.au. Australian-owned adventure company offering a two-week Jesuit-route trip and fifteen days in Torres del Paine. Challenging trips, such as a three-week Aconcagua ascent, available for hardcore adventurers. Special offers for travellers over 50.

Getting around

Distances are immense in Argentina, and you are likely to spend a considerable portion of your budget on travel. Ground transport (mostly bus) is best for giving a true impression of the scale of the country and for appreciating the landscape. However, you may want to cover some big legs, particularly to and around Patagonia, in which case travelling by domestic flights can often save a day or more. The inter-city bus network is extensive but services in remote areas can be poor and infrequent; in these places, it is worth considering car rental.

By bus

By far the most common and straightforward method of transport in Argentina is the **bus** (*omnibus, bus* or *micro*). There are hundreds of private companies, most of which concentrate on one particular region, although a few, such as TAC and Cruz del Sur, run essentially nationwide.

Many buses are modern, plush Brazilian-built models designed for long-distance travel. Breakdowns do happen, but in general your biggest worry will be what movie the driver has chosen to "entertain" you with (usually subtitled Hollywood action flicks of the Stallone/Seagal/Schwarzenegger type, played with the sound either turned off or at thunderous volume). On longer journeys, snacks and even hot meals are served (included in the ticket price), although these vary considerably in quality and tend towards sweet-toothed tastes. *Coche cama, ejecutivo* and *pullman* services are the luxury services, with wide, fully reclinable seats; *semi-cama* services are not far behind in terms of seat comfort. These services usually cost twenty to forty percent more than the *común* (regular) services, but are well worth the extra, particularly over long distances. On minor routes, you'll have less choice of buses, though most are decent with plenty of legroom. Many services turn the air conditioning up beyond most people's levels of endurance; take a sweater on board.

Buying tickets (*boletos*) is normally a simple on-the-spot matter, but you must plan in advance if travelling in the high season (mid-Dec to Feb), especially if you're taking a long-distance bus from Buenos Aires or any other major city to a particularly

popular holiday destination. In these cases you should buy your ticket two to three days beforehand; note that prices rise during peak times. Some destinations have both direct (*directo* or *rápido*) and slower services that stop at all intermediary points, and though most services call into the bus terminal (*terminal de omnibus*), this is not always the case: some drop you on the road outside the centre. Similarly, when heading to Buenos Aires, check that the bus goes to **Retiro**, the central bus terminal (see p.80).

There's usually some kind of **left-luggage office** (*guardamaleta* or *guardaequipaje*) at terminals, or, if you have a few hours to kill between connections, the company with whom you have your onward ticket will usually store your pack free of charge, enabling you to look around town unencumbered.

If you are planning to travel a lot by bus, it may be worth investing in a **South Pass**, which allows unlimited travel in the Southern Cone and Andean countries over a set number of days, though you will have to be clocking up quite a few miles to make it worthwhile, with prices starting at US$160 for 10 days (T011/4724-7878, Wwww .argentinabybus.com).

By air

Argentina's most important domestic **airport** is Buenos Aires' Aeroparque Jorge Newbery, which has **flights** to all the country's provincial capitals and major tourist centres. People who want to get an overview of Argentina's tremendous variety in a limited time may rely heavily on domestic flights to combat the vast distances involved – what takes twenty or

more hours by bus might take only one or two by plane. As a rule, you'll find **prices** are the same whether you buy your ticket direct from the airline office or from the plentiful travel agencies in most towns and cities. Availability can be a problem on tourist routes such as those around Patagonia or at popular times (the summer), and if these feature in your itinerary you are advised to book as far in advance as possible. Some deals booked in advance are good value, although non-residents usually pay a considerably higher tariff than Argentines. Domestic **departure taxes** are usually only $20 or so, sometimes included in the price of the ticket.

Aerolíneas Argentinas (☎0810/222-86527, Ⓦwww.aerolineas.com.ar) is the national flag carrier, with the biggest destination network. The company has faced many problems for the past decade or so and its once excellent reputation has been tarnished, but in many places it will be your only option. Its main rival in Argentina these days is Chilean flag carrier **LAN** (☎0810-9999-526, Ⓦwww.lan.com), which has an Argentine subsidiary (LAN Argentina)

operating flights to the country's major tourist destinations.

The military also provides civilian services – the Air Force's **LADE** (☎0810/810-5233, Ⓦwww.lade.com.ar) is one of the cheapest methods of travel in the country and flies to isolated, often unexpected places, mostly destinations in Patagonia. However, routings can be convoluted, and you might find a flight stops four or five times between its original departure point and final destination. Timetables change frequently (up to once a month) and services can be cancelled at the last moment if the Air Force needs the plane. That said, it's worth asking at LADE offices as you travel round just in case they've something useful.

Other small airlines in operation are Salta-based Andes (☎0810-777-26337, Ⓦwww.andesonline.com), which connects the city with several destinations, including Buenos Aires and Iguazu, and Sol (☎0810-444-765, Ⓦwww.sol.com.ar), a Rosario-based low-cost airline that serves destinations in the centre of the country such as Córdoba and Santa Fe, as well as some coastal and Uruguayan destinations.

By car

You are unlikely to want or need a **car** for your whole stay in Argentina, but you'll find one pretty indispensable if you want to explore some of the more isolated areas of Patagonia, Tierra del Fuego, the Northwest, Mendoza or San Juan. If possible, it makes sense to get a group together, not just to keep costs down but also to share the driving, which can be arduous and potentially dangerous, especially on unsealed roads. Approximately thirty percent of roads are paved in Argentina, but some of the less important of these routes are littered with potholes. Unsealed roads can be extremely muddy after rain, and may be impassable, even to 4WDs, after prolonged wet spells. A 4WD is not usually necessary, but can be useful on minor roads in mountainous areas, when you're likely to encounter snow, or on Ruta 40 in Patagonia. Outside major cities, most accidents (often the most serious ones) occur on unsurfaced gravel roads (*ripio*) – for information about safe driving on these, see *The legendary Ruta 40* colour section.

Altitude can also be a problem in the high Andes – you may need to adjust the fuel intake. One thing worth noting: flashing your lights when driving is a warning to other vehicles *not* to do something, as opposed to the British system, where it is used to signal concession of right of way. You can be fined for not wearing **seatbelts** (both in the front and back), although many Argentines display a cavalier disregard of this law.

To **rent a car**, you need to be over 21 (25 with some agencies) and hold a driver's licence – an international one is not usually necessary. Bring a credit card and your passport for the **deposit**. Before you drive off, check that you've been given insurance, tax and ownership papers, check carefully for dents and paintwork damage and get hold of a 24-hour emergency telephone number. Also, pay close attention to the small print, most notably what you're liable for in the event of an accident: the list of people with grievances after renting a car and spending considerably more than they intended is a long one. Your insurance will not normally cover you for flipping the car, or

smashed windscreens or headlights – a particularly common occurrence if driving on unsurfaced roads. Another frequent type of damage is bent door hinges – be careful when opening doors that they're not wrenched off by high winds.

Car rental **costs** are relatively high in Argentina, though rates between different agencies can vary considerably. Small, local firms often give very good deals – up to half the price of the global rental names – and it doesn't necessarily hold that the local branch of an international agency will be up to the standards you expect. The main cities offer the most economical prices, while costs are highest in Patagonia; **unlimited mileage** deals are usually your best option, as per-kilometre charges can otherwise exceed your daily rental cost many times over. Unfortunately, there are relatively few places in Argentina where you can rent a vehicle and drop it in another specified town without being clobbered with a high relocation fee. Book as early as possible if you're travelling in high season to popular holiday destinations, as demand usually outstrips supply. It's fairly straightforward to take a vehicle into **Chile** but it is essential to have

Addresses

Addresses are nearly always written with the street name followed by the street number – thus, San Martín 2443; with avenues (avenidas), the abbreviation "**Av**" or "**Avda**" appears before the name – thus, Av San Martín 2443. The relatively rare abbreviation "**c/**" for calle (street) is used only to avoid confusion in a city that has streets named after other cities: thus c/Tucumán 564, Salta or c/Salta 1097, Tucumán. If the name is followed by "**s/n**" (sin número), it means the building is numberless, frequently the case in small villages and for larger buildings such as hotels or town halls. Sometimes streets whose names have been officially changed continue to be referred to by their former names, even in written addresses. In most cities, **blocks** (*cuadras*) go up in 100s, making it relatively easy to work out on a map where a hotel at no. 977 or a restaurant at no. 2233 is located.

the correct paperwork from the rental firm. Many provide this free of charge, particularly those in towns near the border.

If you plan to do a lot of driving, consider a membership with the **Automóvil Club Argentino (ACA)**, which has a useful **emergency breakdown** towing and repair service and offers discounts at a series of lodges across the country (many of which are in need of an overhaul). You can join in Buenos Aires at Av del Libertador 1850 (Mon–Fri 10am–6pm; ☎011/4808-4000, ⓦwww.aca.org.ar), or at any of the ACA service stations.

Taxis

There are two main types of taxi in Argentina: regular **urban taxis** that you can flag down in the street; and **remises**, or minicab radio taxis, that you must book by phone or at their central booking booth. Urban taxis are fitted with meters – make sure they use them – and each municipality has its own rates. *Remises* operate with rates fixed according to the destination and are less expensive than taxis for out-of-town and long-distance trips. Often, it makes more sense to hire a *remise* for a day than to rent your own car: it can be more economical, you save yourself the hassle of driving and you'll normally get the sights pointed out for you along the way.

In some places, **shared taxis** (*taxis colectivos*) also run on fixed routes between towns: they wait at a given collection point, each passenger pays a set fee and the *colectivos* leave when full (some carry destination signs on their windscreen, others

don't, so always ask around). They often drop you at a place of your choice at the other end. *Taxis colectivos* also drive up and down fixed routes within certain cities: flag one down and pay your share (usually posted on the windscreen).

By boat

Boat services in Argentina fall into two broad categories: those that serve as a functional form of transport, and (with some overlap) those that you take to enjoy tourist sights. The two **ferry services** you are most likely to use are the comfortable ones from Buenos Aires to Colonia del Sacramento in Uruguay (also served by the speedier hydrofoil) and the much more spartan Chilean ones that transport foot passengers and vehicles across the Magellan Straits into Tierra del Fuego at Punta Delgada and Porvenir. There are also several practical river crossings throughout the Litoral region, connecting towns such as Concordia with Salto in Uruguay and Goya in Corrientes with Reconquista in Santa Fe, as well as numerous crossings from Misiones to neighbouring Paraguay and Brazil. Tigre, just northwest of the capital, tends towards the pleasure-trips end of the market, and offers boat trips around the Delta and to Isla Martín García.

In Patagonia, most **boat trips** are designed purely for their scenic value, including ones that give access to the polar scenery of the Parque Nacional Los Glaciares, and the Three Lakes Crossing from Bariloche to Chile, a trip that can be truncated so as to access the Pampa Linda area of Parque Nacional Nahuel Huapi.

By rail

Argentina's **train network**, developed through British investment in the late nineteenth century and nationalized by the Perón administration in 1948, collapsed in 1993 when government subsidies were withdrawn. The railways are now in a pitiful state, with very little in the way of long-distance services – just a handful in Buenos Aires Province (see p.80, p.154 & p.173), which are cheaper than the bus but considerably less savoury. The government has announced a plethora of measures and licences intended to reinvigorate the system and introduce new, modern services, most notably a controversial US$4 billion bullet train connecting Buenos Aires, Rosario and Córdoba, the licence for which has been awarded but which is on hold indefinitely at the time of writing.

You're far less likely to want to use Argentine trains as a method of getting from place to place, however, than you are to try one of the country's **tourist trains**, where the aim is simply to travel for the fun of it. There are two principal lines: *La Trochita* (see p.466), the Old Patagonian Express from Esquel; and the *Tren a las Nubes* (see p.334), one of the highest railways in the world, climbing through the mountains from Salta towards the Chilean border. At the time of writing the latter was out of action, but due to be reactivated at any time.

Cycling

Most towns with a tourist infrastructure have at least one place that rents out **bicycles** for half- or full-day visits to sights at very reasonable prices. These excursions can be great fun, but remember to bring spare inner tubes and a pump, especially if you're cycling off sealed roads, and check that the brakes and seat height are properly adjusted. There are almost no places that rent out **motorbikes**.

Argentina is also a popular destination for more serious cyclists, and expeditions along routes such as the arduous, partly unsurfaced RN-40 attract mountain-biking devotees who often value physical endurance above the need to see sights (most points of interest off RN-40 lie a good way west along branch roads, which deters most people from visiting more than one or two). Expeditions such as these need to be planned thoroughly. You should buy an extremely robust mountain bike and the very best **equipment** you can afford. Bring plenty of high-quality spares with you, as they can be hard to come by out of the major centres; punctures and broken spokes are extremely common on unsealed roads. Be prepared to get very dusty, and pay particular attention to how much **water** you're going to need per stage. Wind is a big problem in places like Patagonia, and if you get the season wrong, your progress will be cut to a handful of kilometres a day. High altitude can have a similar effect. Keep covered as best you can to protect yourself from wind and sun (especially your face), and do not expect much consideration from other vehicles on the road.

For more **information**, see *Latin America by Bike: A Complete Touring Guide*, by Walter Sienko.

Hitchhiking

Hitchhiking always involves an element of risk, but it can also be one of the most rewarding ways to travel, especially if you can speak at least elementary conversational Spanish. It is getting trickier to hitchhike in Argentina: some truck drivers are prohibited by company rules from picking you up, others are reluctant as it often invalidates car insurance or you become the liability of the driver. And in general, it is not advisable for women travelling on their own to hitchhike, or for anyone to head out of large urban areas by hitchhiking: you're far better off catching a local bus out to an outlying service station or road checkpoint and trying from there. In the south of the country, hitching is still generally very safe. In places such as Patagonia, where roads are few and traffic sparse, you'll often find yourself part of a queue, especially in summer. If you do try to hitchhike, always travel with sufficient reserves of water, food, clothes and shelter; you can get stranded for days in some of the more isolated spots.

Accommodation

Accommodation in Argentina runs the gamut from campsites and youth hostels to fabulously luxurious estancias (ranches) and opulent hotels offering every conceivable amenity. Between these two extremes you'll find a whole variety of establishments, including charming old colonial houses with balconies and dark and seedy hotels that lack so much as a window. Informal room rental is also common in towns with seasonal influxes of tourists but too few hotels to cope.

Prices vary considerably depending on where you are in the country. Areas receiving large numbers of foreign visitors, particularly Buenos Aires and Patagonia, have seen prices rise sharply in recent years; less-visited areas offer less variety but also much better bargains. Even in the capital, however, you can expect to pay slightly less for comparable accommodation than you would in most European countries or North America. Single travellers on a budget and seeking more privacy than is available at a youth hostel will find things harder, although the number of places offering per-person prices appears to be on the rise, especially at resorts and estancias where meals or activities are included. Discounts can sometimes be negotiated, particularly if you are staying for a longer period. Bear in mind the practice of dual pricing, and that taxes are often not included in quoted prices (see "Costs", p.56).

Hotels

Most towns in Argentina will have at least one **hotel**, though in many places these are unimaginative, rather drab places. If you are on a budget, and the option is available, you might do better to head for a hostel, most of which provide good value private rooms as well as dorms. Posadas and bed and breakfasts can be more attractive in the middle of the range, while small boutique or designer hotels – which have popped up in significant numbers in Argentina in the last few years – often have a lot more individuality than the standard plush but monotonous five-star places aimed at business travellers.

Posadas, hosterías and B&Bs

The use of the term **posada** usually denotes a fairly characterful place, often with a slightly rustic feel, but generally comfortable or even luxurious. In a similar vein, the term **hostería** is frequently used for smallish, upmarket hotels – oriented towards tourists rather than businessmen.

A similar type of accommodation, particularly common around Buenos Aires, are **B&Bs** (the English term is used), which tend to be

---

Accommodation price codes

All the accommodation listed in this guide has been sorted according to the **price codes** below, which account for the cost of the **least expensive double or twin room in high season**, in Argentine pesos. Prices of beds in shared hostel dorms are specified in the text; they tend to cost about $25-45. As a general rule, categories ❶ and ❷ will be a budget hotel in a less visited area; ❸ and ❹ a private hostel room or budget hotel in a more visited area; ❺ and ❻ more comfortable, mid-range hotels; ❼ and ❽ upmarket rooms with modern conveniences and attractive decor; and category ❾ will take in most luxury hotels, estancias and boutique hotels.

❶ $50 and under	❹ $151–200	❼ $301–400
❷ $51–100	❺ $201–250	❽ $401–600
❸ $101–150	❻ $251–300	❾ $601 and over

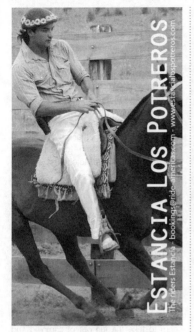

chic, converted townhouses with an exclusive but cosy atmosphere – price-wise they tend to be mid-range to top-range options, and generally offer far more attractive surroundings than standard hotels at the same price.

Hostels

Youth hostels are known as *albergues juveniles* or *albergues de la juventud* in Argentina, though the term "*(youth) hostel*" is frequently used instead – *albergue* is normally taken to mean *albergue transitorio* (short-stay hotels where rooms are rented by the hour). There is an extensive chain of mostly reliable hostels in Argentina affiliated with Hostelling International, as well as a good number of independent hostels, which vary more in quality, but when they are good – particularly in Buenos Aires, Mendoza and Salta – they are among the country's best. Accommodation is generally in **dormitories**, though most places also have several double **rooms**, often en suite. Facilities vary, too, from next to nothing to swimming pools, internet access, washing machines, cable TV and patios with barbecue equipment.

Note you sometimes see the term **"hostal"** used as a seemingly general term for hotels – both youth hostels and high-rise modern hotels call themselves *hostales*.

Youth hostel associations

The local office of Hostelling International is in Buenos Aires, at Florida 835 (☎011/4511-8723, ⓦwww.hihostels.com /argentina). Associated hostels give discounts – usually a few pesos a night – to holders of HI cards but they rarely require that you possess a card in order to stay there.

Residenciales and hospedajes

Basic **hospedajes** and **residenciales** have low prestige in Argentina and often are not recommended by tourist offices, but they can be far more welcoming, clean and secure than one-star hotels; a few of them stand out as some of Argentina's best budget accommodation. Furnishings tend to be basic, with little more than a bed, perhaps a desk and chair and a fan in each room – though some are far less spartan than others and there is

37

even the odd one with cable TV. Most places offer private bathrooms. There's little difference between *residenciales* and *hospedajes* – indeed, the same establishment may be described in different accommodation lists as both, or even as a hotel or hostel. The only real difference is that *hospedajes* tend to be part of a family house.

Estancias

A very different experience to staying in a hotel is provided by Argentina's many **estancias** (ranches, or **fincas** as they are known in the North) that are open to visitors. Guests usually stay in the *casco*, or farmhouse, which can be anything from a simple family home to an extravagant castle-like residence. Estancias are nearly always family-run, the income from tourism tending to serve as a supplement to the declining profits earned from the land itself. Accommodation is generally luxurious, with bags of character, and a stay is a mini-vacation in itself; for about US$200–500 a day you are given four meals, invariably including a traditional *asado,* with activities such as horse-riding and swimming also usually part of the price. Many places offer experiences that reflect the local area, from cattle herding and branding in the pampas to wine tasting at Mendoza to observing caymans in the Litoral.

You can **book** your estancia accommodation either by approaching them directly or through certain travel agencies; a comprehensive one in Buenos Aires is Estancias Argentinas, at Roque Sáenz Peña 616, 9th floor (☎011/4343-2366, ⓦwww .estanciasargentinas.com).

Cabañas

Popular in resort towns, self-catering *cabañas* are small, chalet-style buildings that can vary from miniature suburban villas with cable TV and microwaves to pleasingly simple and rustic wooden constructions. If you have been staying in a lot of hotels or doing some hardcore camping, *cabañas* can be fun and relaxing places to take a break for a few days. They are often very good value for money for small groups, although a few of the simpler ones can also be surprisingly affordable options for couples or even single travellers. They are usually grouped together in outfits of between two and ten cabins; many campsites also offer basic ones as an alternative to tents.

Camping

There are plenty of places to camp throughout Argentina, with most towns and villages having their own municipal **campsites** (*campings*), but standards vary wildly. At the major resorts, there are usually plenty of privately owned, well-organized sites, with facilities ranging from provisions stores to volleyball courts and TV rooms. Some are attractive, but mostly they seem to take the fun out of camping and you're more likely to wake up to a view of next door's 4WD than the surrounding countryside. They are, however, good places to meet other travellers and generally offer a high degree of security. There are also simpler campsites, though at nearly all of them showers, electric light and barbecue facilities are standard. A campsite with no, or very limited, facilities is referred to as a *camping libre*. Municipal sites can be rather desolate and sometimes not particularly safe: it's usually a good idea to check with locals as to the security of the place before pitching a tent. Expect to pay around $15 per person plus $15 per tent; more in touristy locations.

Food and drink

Argentine food can be summed up by one word: beef. And not just any beef, but the best in the world – succulent, cherry-red, healthy and certainly not mad, meat raised on some of the greenest, most extensive pastures known to cattle. The asado, or barbecue, is an institution, every bit a part of the Argentine way of life as football, fast driving and tango.

Where to eat

Apart from generic *restaurantes* (or *restoranes*), you will come across *parrillas* (for steak and beef), *marisquerías* (for seafood), *confiterías* (cafés for coffee, cakes, snacks or simple meals), *comedores* (simple local eateries), *pizzerías, bodegones* (unpretentious restaurants that theoretically serve a house wine) and *cantinas* (neighbourhood places often dishing up Italian food, such as home-made pasta). By South American standards the quality of restaurants is high, and by international standards the exchange rate makes them unbelievable value – albeit less than in the post-crisis years. If you're on a tight budget make lunch your main meal, and take advantage of the **menú del día** or **menú ejecutivo** – usually good-value set meals for about $50 – and in the evening try **tenedor libre** restaurants where you can eat as much as you like for a set price (about $60) at self-service buffets. Up your budget to $100 or so a head and you can dine à la carte at most mid-range restaurants, wine included. Argentina also has a fair sprinkling of gourmet *locales* (*restaurantes de autor*), concentrated in, but by no means limited to, Buenos Aires. In these your per-head bill will be more like $200 or even more, though this still compares well with cities in other industrialized countries and you get fabulous food, wine, ambience and service. You should try and splash out at least once during your visit.

When to eat

Breakfast is usually served up until around 10am, and **lunch** from around noon until 3pm. Hardly any restaurant opens for **dinner** before 8pm, and in the hotter months – and all year round in Buenos Aires – few people turn up before 10 or even 11pm. Don't be surprised to see people pouring into restaurants well after midnight: Argentines, and Porteños in particular, are night owls. If you think you're going to be starving by 7pm, do like the locals and either have a hearty lunch or take **merienda** – tea and snacks – at a café or *confitería* in the late afternoon.

What to eat

While beef is the most prominent feature on many menus, it's by no means the whole story. In general, you seldom have a bad meal in Argentina. That said, imagination, innovation and a sense of subtle flavour are sometimes lacking, with Argentines preferring to eat the wholesome but often bland dishes their immigrant forebears cooked. At the other end of the spectrum, there is some very (some might say overly) inventive *cordon bleu* cooking being concocted by daring young chefs across the country. Fast food is extremely popular, but you can also snack on delicious local specialities such as empanadas or home-made pizza if you want to avoid the ubiquitous multinational chains.

Snacks

If you're feeling peckish during the day there are plenty of **minutas** (snacks) to choose from. The **lomito** (as opposed to *lomo* – the name of the steak cut itself) is a nourishing sandwich filled with a juicy slice of steak, often made with delicious **pan árabe** (pitta bread); the **chivito** (originally Uruguayan) refers to a similar kind of sandwich made with a less tender cut, though it literally means "kid", or baby goat. Other street food includes the **choripán**, a local version of the hot dog made with natural meaty sausages (*chorizos*), while at cafés a popular snack is the **tostado** (or *tostado mixto*), a toasted cheese and ham sandwich, often daintily thin and sometimes (in the provinces) called a *carlitos*. **Barrolucas** are beef and cheese sandwiches, a local variant on the cheeseburger, and very popular around Mendoza. **Milanesas**, in this context, refer to breaded veal escalopes served in a sandwich, hamburger-style. **Empanadas** are small pastries with savoury fillings, usually stuffed with beef, cheese and/or vegetables, although the fillings are as varied as the cook's imagination.

Parrillas, pizza and pasta

Parrillas, pizza and pasta are the mainstays of Argentine cuisine, both at home and in restaurants. **Parrillas** are simply barbecues (or the restaurants that employ them) where you can try the traditional *asado* (see box, p.41). Usually there's a set menu (the **parrillada**), though the establishments themselves vary enormously. At many, especially in big cities, the decor is stylish, the staff laidback, the crockery delicate and the meat served tidily. Elsewhere, especially in smaller towns, *parrillas* are more basic, and you're likely to be served by burly, sweaty grill men who spend all their time carving hunks of flesh and hurling them onto wooden platters. Traditionally, you eat the offal before moving on to the choicer cuts, but don't be put off – you can choose to skip these delicacies and head straight for the steaks and fillets.

Mass immigration from Italy since the middle of the nineteenth century has had a profound influence on Argentine food and drink – the abundance of **fresh pasta** (*pasta casera*) is just one example. The fillings tend to be a little unexciting (lots of cheese, including ricotta, but seldom meat), the sauces are not exactly memorable (mostly tomato and onion) and the pasta itself cooked beyond *al dente*, yet it's a reliable staple and rarely downright bad. **Pizzas** are very good on the whole, though the toppings tend to lack originality, especially away from the capital. One popular ingredient regularly used as a garnish may be unfamiliar to visitors: the **palmito**, a sweet, crunchy vegetable resembling something between asparagus and celery. Argentine pizzas are nearly always of the thick-crust variety, wood-oven baked and very big, meant to be divided between a number of diners.

Other cuisines

In addition to the authentic Italian cooking available all over the country, **Spanish** restaurants serve tapas and familiar dishes such as *paella*, while specifically Basque restaurants are also fairly commonplace; these are often the places to head for fish or seafood. **Chinese** and, increasingly, **Korean** restaurants are found in many Argentine cities, but they rarely serve anything remotely like authentic Asian food and specialize in *tenedor libre* buffet diners. **Japanese**, **Indian** and **Thai** restaurants have become fashionable in Buenos Aires, where nearly every national cuisine from Armenian to Vietnamese via Mexican, Peruvian, Polish and Thai is also available, but such variety is rare in the provinces.

Arab and **Middle Eastern** food, including specialities such as kebabs and *kepe*, seasoned ground raw meat, is far more widespread, as is **German** fare, such as sauerkraut (*chucrút*) and frankfurters, along with Central and Eastern European food, often served in *choperías*, or beer-gardens. **Welsh tearooms** are a speciality of Patagonia.

For more on other Argentine (*criollo*) cooking, see the *Criollo culture* colour section.

Vegetarian food

Your experience as a **vegetarian** in Argentina will depend on where in the country you are. You shouldn't have too many problems in the capital, the larger cities or the Patagonian resorts, all of which are relatively cosmopolitan. While there aren't many **restaurants** completely dedicated to non-meat eaters, they do exist and many places have a few good non-meat alternatives. The exceptions are the *parrillas*, though the sight and smell of entire animals roasting on the grill is unlikely to appeal to vegetarians anyway.

In the smaller provincial towns, however, vegetarian fare tends to be a lot simpler and you will likely have to adjust to a diet of pizza, pasta, empanadas and salads, with

Asado basics

The term **asado** (from *asar*, to roast) originally referred specifically to a particular cut of beef, the brisket, meant to be slowly grilled or roasted, but now is applied to any **barbecued meat**. Since barbecues are an integral part of life in Argentina, it's good to know your way around the vocabulary of beef-eating, especially as beef in Argentina isn't cut in the same way as in the rest of the world – cuts are sliced through bone and muscle rather than across them.

Argentines like their meat **well done** (*cocido*), and indeed, some cuts are better cooked through. If you prefer your meat medium, ask for *a punto*, and for rare – which really requires some insistence – *jugoso*. Before you get to the steaks, you'll be offered **achuras**, or offal, and different types of sausage. **Chorizos** are excellent beef sausages, while **morcilla**, blood sausage, is an acquired taste. Sometimes **provoletta**, sliced provolone cheese, grilled on the barbecue till crispy on the edges, will be on the menu. Otherwise, it's beef all the way.

After these "appetizers" – which you can always skip, since Argentine *parrillas* are much more meat-generous than their Brazilian counterparts – you move on to the **asado** cut, followed by the **tira de asado** (ribs; also called *costillar* or *asado a secas*). There's not much meat on them, but they explode with a meaty taste. Next is the muscly but delicious **vacío** (flank). But save some room for the prime cuts: **bife ancho** is entrecôte; **bife angosto** or **lomito** is the sirloin (referred to as **medallones** when cut into slices); **cuadril** is a lump of rumpsteak, often preferred by home barbecue masters; **lomo**, one of the luxury cuts and often kept in reserve, is fillet steak; **bife de chorizo** (not to be confused with *chorizo* sausage) is what the French call a *pavé*, a slab of meat, cut from either the sirloin or entrecôte. The **entraña**, a sinewy cut from inside the beast, is a love-it-or-hate it cut; aficionados claim it's the main delicacy. Rarely barbecued, the **peceto** (eye round steak) is a tender lump of flesh, often braised (*estufado*) and served on top of pasta, roasted with potatoes (*peceto al horno con papas*) or sliced cold for *vittel tonne* – a classic Argentine starter made with tuna and mayonnaise.

Mustard (*mostaza*) may be available, but the lightly salted meat is usually best served with nothing on it but the traditional condiments of **chimichurri** – olive oil shaken in a bottle with salt, garlic, chilli pepper, vinegar and bayleaf – and **salsa criolla**, similar but with onion and tomato as well; everyone jealously guards their secret formulas for both these "magic" dressings.

very little variety in the toppings and fillings. The good news is that these fillings are often options such as spinach, **acelga** (Swiss chard – similar to spinach, but slightly more bitter) and ricotta. Other foods to keep an eye out for are **fainá**, a fairly bland but agreeable Genovese speciality made with chickpea dough, and **milanesas de soja** (breaded and fried soya) – **a la napolitana** means it comes with cheese and tomato – while *milanesas* of vegetables like **berenjena** (aubergine) and **calabaza** (pumpkin) are also quite popular.

When all the cheese gets a bit much, look out for the popular Chinese-ish *tenedor libres*, which usually feature a good smattering of veggies, as do Middle Eastern restaurants. Another possibility would be to self-cater – supermarkets are usually fairly well stocked with vegetables, seasonings and soy products.

You should always check the ingredients of a dish before ordering, as the addition of small amounts of meat is not always referred to on menus. Don't be surprised if your "*no como carne*" (I don't eat meat) is dismissed with a glib "*no tiene mucha*" (It doesn't contain much) and be particularly on your guard for the seemingly ever-present **jamón** (ham).

Vegans will have a hard time outside of Buenos Aires, as pretty much everything that doesn't contain meat contains cheese or pastry. Waiters will rarely be familiar with veganism, but will usually try to accommodate your requests.

Desserts

Argentines have a fairly sweet tooth and love anything with sugar, especially *dulce de leche* (see box below). Even breakfast tends to be dominated by sweet things such as sticky croissants (*medialunas*) or **chocolate con churros**, Andalucian-style hot chocolate with fritters, sometimes filled with *dulce de leche*. All kinds of cakes and biscuits, including *alfajores* (maize-flour cookie sandwiches, filled with jam or *dulce de leche*, sometimes coated with chocolate), pastries called **facturas** and other candies and sweets are popular with Argentines of all ages.

However, for dessert you'll seldom be offered anything other than the tired trio of **flan** (a kind of crème caramel, religiously served with a thick custard or *dulce de leche*), **budín de pan** (a syrupy version of bread pudding) and fresh fruit salad (*ensalada de fruta*). In Andean regions, or in *criollo* eateries, you'll most likely be served **dulce vigilante**, a slab of neutral, pallid cheese called *quesillo* eaten with candied fruit such as sweet potato (*batata*), quince (*membrillo*), (*al*)cayote (a kind of spaghetti squash), pumpkin (*zapallo*) or lime (*lima*). *Panqueques*, or crepes, are also popular.

With such a large Italian community it is not surprising that superb *helado* (**ice cream**) is easy to come by in Argentina. Even the tiniest village has at least one *heladería artesanal*. If you're feeling really self-indulgent you might like to have your cone dipped in chocolate (*bañado*). Some of the leading ice-cream makers offer an overwhelming range of flavours (*sabores*). Chocolate chip (*granizado*) is a favourite, and raspberry mousse (*mousse de frambuesa*) is also delicious.

Drinks

Fizzy drinks (*gaseosas*) are popular with people of all ages and often accompany meals. All the big brand names are available, along with local brands such as Paso de los Toros, which makes tonic water and fizzy grapefruit (*pomelo*) drinks. You will often be asked if you want **mineral water** – either still (*agua sin gas*) or carbonated – (*agua con gas* or *soda*) – with your meal, but you can ask for **tap water** (*agua de la llave*), which is safe to drink in most places, though this may raise eyebrows. Although little is grown in the country, good **coffee** is easy to come by. You will find very decent espressos, or delicious *café con leche*, in most cafés. **Tea** is usually made from teabags; Argentine tea is strong rather than subtle, and is served with either milk or lemon. **Herbal teas** (*infusiones*) are all the rage, camomile (*manzanilla*) being the most common. **Mate** is a whole world unto itself and is explained, along with the etiquette and ritual involved, on p.263. **Fruit juices** (*jugos*) and **milkshakes** (*licuados*) can be excellent, though freshly squeezed orange juice is often sold at ridiculously high prices.

Argentina's **beer** is more thirst-quenching than alcoholic and mostly comes as fairly bland lager, with Quilmes dominating the market and Heineken producing a frequently sold beer in the country; imported brands are

see p.263

Dulce de leche

Dulce de leche, a sticky, sweet goo made by laboriously boiling large quantities of vanilla-flavoured milk and sugar until they almost disappear, is claimed by Argentines as a national invention, although similar concoctions are made in Brazil, France and Italy. Something called *manjar* is produced in Chile, but Argentines rightly regard it as far inferior. The thick caramel is eaten with a spoon, spread on bread or biscuits, used to fill cakes, biscuits and fritters or dolloped onto other desserts. Some of the best flavours of ice cream are variations on the *dulce de leche* theme. Although some people still make their own, most people buy it ready-made, in jars. While all Argentines agree that *dulce de leche* is fabulous, there is no consensus on a particular brand: the divisions between those who favour Havanna and those who would only buy Chimbote run almost as deep as those between supporters of Boca Juniors and River Plate. Foreigners are advised to maintain a diplomatic neutrality on the issue.

fairly common in the cities, though more expensive. Regional brews are sometimes worth trying: in Mendoza, the Andes brand crops up all over, while Salta's own brand is also good, and a kind of stout (*cerveza negra*) can sometimes be obtained in the Northwest. **Home-brewed beer** (*cerveza artesanal*) is increasingly available, often coming in a surprising array of flavours. Usually when you ask for a beer, it comes in large litre bottles, meant for sharing; a small bottle is known as a *porrón*. If you want draught beer ask for a *chopp* (or a *liso* in Santa Fe province).

The produce of Argentina's **vineyards,** ranging from gutsy plonk to some of the world's prize-winning **wines**, is widely available both in the country and abroad. Most vintages are excellent and not too expensive. Unfortunately, many restaurants still have limited, unimaginative wine lists, which don't reflect Argentina's drift away from mass-produced table wines to far superior single or multi-varietals (for more on wine, see box, p.378 & pp.390–391). It is also quite difficult to get wine by the glass, and half-bottles too are rare. Cheaper wine is commonly made into **sangria** or its fruitier, white wine equivalent, **clericó.**

Don't be surprised to see home-grown variants (*nacionales*) of whisky, gin, brandy, port, sherry and rum, none of which is that good; familiar imported brands (*importados*) can be very dear, however. It's far better to stick to the locally distilled **aguardientes**, or firewaters, some of which (from Catamarca, for example) are deliciously grapey. **Fernet Branca** is the most popular, a demonic-looking brew the colour of molasses with a medicinal taste, invariably combined with Coke and consumed in huge quantities – it's generally regarded as the gaucho's favourite tipple.

The media

In terms of newspaper circulation, Argentina is Latin America's most literate nation, and it has a diverse and generally high-quality press. Its television programming is a rather chaotic amalgam of light-entertainment shows and sports, and its radio services tend to fall into one of two categories: urban mainstream commercial channels or amateur ones designed to serve the needs of local rural communities.

Newspapers and magazines

In the past, the fortunes of the print **press** in Argentina have varied greatly, depending on the prevailing political situation. Overbearing state control and censorship characterized much of the twentieth century, but the current situation is much more dynamic, and a resilient streak of investigative journalism provides a constant stream of stories revolving around official corruption. Self-censorship, though, is fairly widespread, and deep criticism of the country's institutions is pretty muted in favour of a generally patriotic stance.

The *Buenos Aires Herald* (Ⓦwww .buenosairesherald.com) is South America's most prestigious **English-language daily** and dates back to 1876. Although the quality of the writing and editing is a little inconsistent, the *Herald* is useful for getting the low-down on current events in Argentina and for catching up on international news and sports, as it features stories from the wires as well as syndicated articles from the likes of the *New York Times* and Britain's *Independent*. It is still associated in many minds with the old-style Anglo-Argentine elite, but it won international plaudits for its stand on human rights issues in the years of the military dictatorship. The *Herald* is easily available in the capital, but don't expect to find it outside major cities and tourist centres. Look out also for the *Argentimes* (🕸www .theargentimes.com), a free monthly English language publication written by and aimed at young expats and visitors, with articles on aspects of life and travel in Argentina – an agenda of upcoming events – the website is also useful.

If you have some Spanish, the most accessible of the **national dailies** is *Clarín* (🕸www.clarin.com.ar), the paper with the highest circulation. Despite its mass-market appeal, it is surprisingly highbrow, with politics on page three, followed by a fair-sized economics section, with celebrities usually kept in their place – that is, the "*Espectáculos*" supplement, which also has good listings of what's on. The country's major **broadsheet** is *La Nación* (🕸www .lanacion.com.ar), the favoured reading of the upper and educated classes. It is conservative in some ways, but is also the most international, outward-looking and arguably best written of the Spanish-language newspapers. At the other extreme, the unabashedly anti-establishment *Página 12* (🕸www.pagina12.com.ar) is a left-leaning paper popular with students and intellectuals that requires a pretty good knowledge of the Spanish language and Argentine politics.

Argentina's **regional press** is also strong, though the quality varies enormously across the country. A handful of local dailies, such as Mendoza's *Los Andes* (🕸www.losandes .com.ar), Córdoba's *La Voz del Interior* (🕸www.lavozdelinterior.com.ar) and Rosario's *La Capital* (🕸www.lacapital .com.ar), are every bit as informative and well-written as the leading national newspa-pers, and they contain vital information about tourist attractions, cultural events and travel news. Outside Buenos Aires, you pay a supplement for the nationals, and dailies often don't arrive till late in the day.

International publications such as *Time*, *Newsweek*, *The Economist,* the *Miami Herald* and the *Daily Telegraph* are sold at the kiosks on Calle Florida and in Recoleta in Buenos Aires, and at the capital's airports, as are some imported European and US magazines. However, check the cover as they can often be long past their publication date; they are also usually so expensive that unless you're really desperate you're probably better off with the *BA Herald.*

Radio

Argentina's most popular **radio** station, La 100 (99.9FM), plays a fairly standard formula of Latin pop, whereas Rock & Pop (95.9FM) veers, as its name would imply, toward rock and blues. Classical can be heard on on Radio Clasica (96.7FM). Neither the **BBC World Service** nor the Voice of America now broadcast on shortwave to Argentina. Towns are blessed with a remarkable number of small-time radio stations, which are listened to avidly by locals, though they're rarely likely to appeal to foreign visitors. In rural areas, local amateur radio stations form a vital part of the community fabric, providing a message service that relays every conceivable type of salutation, appeal and snippet of gossip. Messages normally go out twice a day and it is sometimes amazing how effective this seemingly rudimentary system can be. Should you ever lose anything or have documents stolen, these services are normally all too pleased to put out an appeal for you; indeed, this is usually your best chance of recovering your property.

Television

There are five national **television stations**, mostly showing a mix of football, soap operas (*telenovelas*) and chat shows.There have been Argentine versions of international hits such as *Big Brother* and *Popstars,* although on the whole there is less interest in "reality TV" than in Europe or the US. The channels also show syndicated foreign programmes, but they are almost always dubbed. Even if you can't understand much, however, Argentine TV can provide a fasci-nating glimpse into certain aspects of society, from the almost freakish plastic surgery of some presenters to the bouncy Saturday afternoon cumbia show *Pasion de Sabado*. There are also some worthwhile news documentary shows, such as *Punto Doc*. Cable TV is common in many mid-range and even budget hotels; the channels you get depend on the cable provider, but they generally include CNN and BBC World in English, with a myriad of channels playing movies and (mostly American) TV shows, usually subtitled. Where they are dubbed, you can sometimes turn the dubbing off by pressing the SAP (Second Audio Protocol) button on your remote. Fox and ESPN cover worldwide sports, including baseball, the NBA and English Premiership football. Argentine cable news channels include Clarín's TN (*Telenoticias*) and the unique Crónica, a budget Buenos Aires-based news channel that provides live, unedited coverage of anything that happens in the city; indeed, it is said that the Crónica vans often arrive before the police do.

Festivals

Festivals of all kinds, both religious, celebrating local patrons, and secular, showing off produce such as handicrafts, olives, goats or wine, are good excuses for much partying and pomp in Argentina, particularly the closer you get to the country's northern neighbours, with their strong festival traditions.

Although carnival in Argentina cannot quite compete with Brazil, the nearer you approach that country the more gusto you will see **Carnaval** celebrated with: Argentina's premier parades are found at Gualeguaychú (see p.245), while a boisterous time can also be had in Salta (see p.317) and all along the Quebrada de Humahuaca. Other major festivals are November's celebration of pampas culture, the **Fiesta de la Tradición**, in San Antonio de Areco and elsewhere (see p.184), September's religious **Fiesta del Milagro** in Salta (see p.323) and Mendoza's wine-inspired **Fiesta de la Vendimia** in March (see p.389).

Owing to its attachment to tradition and its high proportion of ethnic communities, the Northwest has maintained or revived more **pre-Hispanic festivals** than any other Argentine region – nearly every village seems to have one. There are also many religious and secular celebrations observed here that are a blend of indigenous and imported customs, so subtly melded that the elements are indistinguishable: carnival, Holy Week and saints' days predominate among the latter. **January 6** is the date of processions in Belén (see p.366) in honour of the Virgin Mary. In the **second half of January**, Tilcara (see p.348) holds its annual bean-feast, followed by Humahuaca's (see p.351) tribute to the Virgen de Candelaria on **February 2**. Pachamama, the Mother Earth deity dear to the indigenous peoples, is feted on **February 6** in Purmamarca (see p.346) and Amaicha (see p.365), where festivities last a whole week. Cheese fans should head for Tafí del Valle (see p.364), where the **Fiesta Nacional del Queso** takes place in early February. The **Serenata Cafayateña** is a folk jamboree held on the weekend following Shrove Tuesday in Cafayate (see p.339). Londres (see p.367) hosts a lively walnut festival in early February, while Fiambalá's **Festival del Camino Hacia el Nuevo Sol** takes place on **February 18 and 19**. The third Wednesday of the month sees the **Fiesta Nacional del Aguardiente** in Valle Viejo, and the third Thursday the hangover. In **March**, the **Feria Artesanal y Ganadera de la Puna** transforms normally quiet Antofagasta de la Sierra (see p.371). **March 19**, St Joseph's Day, is a red-letter day in Cachi (see p.336), while a major pilgrimage, with night vigils and processions, converges on the tiny village of

Puerta de San José, near Belén, on **March 18 and 19**.

Holy Week is a serious affair throughout the region but the highlights are Maundy Thursday at Yavi (see p.355), the pilgrimage to El Señor de la Peña at Aimogasta, in northern La Rioja Province, and the procession of the Virgen de Punta Corral, from Punta Corral to Tumbaya (see p.346). A week after Easter sees a minor performance of the momentous rituals in honour of the Virgen del Valle, in Catamarca. **May** kicks off with Santa Cruz celebrations at Uquía (see p.351), on **May 4**, while **May 25** is celebrated in El Rodeo, in Catamarca Province, by a *destreza criolla* – or rodeo – and St John's Day, **June 24**, is a major feast throughout the region. **Late July** is when Catamarca stages one of the country's biggest folk and crafts festivals, the **Festival Nacional del Poncho**. St James' Day, **July 25**, is a major holiday in Humahuaca.

Argentina's only **bullfight**, an unusually bloodless tradition, is the main event at Assumption celebrations held at Casabindo (see p.355) on **August 15**. Santa Rosa de Lima is honoured at Purmamarca (see p.346) on **August 30**. Salta's (see p.323) big feast thanks God for the Virgin of the Miracle during the nine days leading up to **September 15** while Iruya (see p.353) holds a highly photogenic feast for **Our Lady of the Rosary** on the first Sunday in October. In early October, it's Cafayate's (see p.338) turn to honour the Virgin. Two Sundays later (usually around October 20), La Quiaca (see p.355) holds its Fiesta de la Ollas, or "Manca Fiesta". All Souls' Day and the Day of the Dead, **November 1 and 2**, are important feasts all along the Quebrada de Humahuaca and especially in Antofagasta de la Sierra (see p.371). The city of Catamarca attracts thousands of pilgrims for processions involving the Virgen del Valle, on **December 8**. Angastaco hosts a gaucho festival in honour of the Virgin around the same time.

On the whole, **holidays** such as Christmas and Easter are more religious, family-focused occasions than they are in Europe and the US. Although some traditions – such as the European custom of eating chocolate eggs at Easter – are starting to take off, the festivals are generally a lot less commercial, and the run-up to them doesn't start two months beforehand. Christmas is celebrated more on Christmas Eve evening than during Christmas Day – midnight on December 24 (and again on December 31) is a great time to be in Buenos Aires, particularly if you have a high vantage point from which to watch the sky explode with fireworks. Imported festivals such as St Valentine's and Halloween are also becoming increasingly popular, while more home-grown festivals include the **Día de las Malvinas** (June 10), the day the South Atlantic conflict ended, remembered with ceremonies, and the **Día de la Primavera** (September 21), when young people gather in parks to picnic and drink cheap wine.

For a list of public holidays, see the box on p.67.

Sports

Argentines suffer an incurable addiction to sport; many go rigid at the thought of even one week without football (soccer), and you'll hear informed and spirited debate in bars on subjects as diverse as tennis, rugby, basketball and the uniquely Argentine equestrian sport of pato.

Football

Ever since two teams of British merchants lined up against each other at the Buenos Aires Cricket Club for a kick-about in 1867, *futból* has been an integral part of Argentine identity. The incredible atmosphere generated by the passion of the fans makes attending a match one of the highlights of many people's visits to Argentina, and it is certainly worth setting aside time to do so, even if you're not normally a fan. There are twenty teams in the Primera División, the country's top flight, including the "Big Five": River Plate, Boca Juniors, Independiente, San Lorenzo and Racing Club (all based in Buenos Aires but supported around the country). If you can catch the *superclásico*, the derby between Boca and River, then you're in for a real treat.

The domestic league's year is split into two **seasons** – allowing for two champions and two sets of celebrations. The first season runs from August to December and is known as the *apertura* (opening); the second, from February to June, the *clausura* (closing); fixtures are mostly played on Sunday afternoons. In addition, there are two South American club championships – the Copa Libertador and Copa Sudamericana, roughly equivalent to Europe's UEFA Champions League and Europa Cup, respectively. These are generally dominated by teams from Argentina, Brazil and Colombia, with a leg played in each country, usually a midweek fixture. If you're lucky, you may even get the chance to see the national side (*la selección*) strutting their stuff in a friendly or World Cup qualifier.

You can usually buy **tickets** at the grounds on match day, although some games sell out in advance, notably the matches between the big five and top-of-the-table clashes. For these, you can get tickets two days before the game at the stadium (be prepared for a scrum) or further in advance for some games from Ticketek (☎011/5237-7200, ⓦwww .ticketek.com.ar). Many Buenos Aires-based tour agencies, hotels and hostels have caught on to visitors' interest in attending games and, for a premium, provide a service of ticket and transfer.

Tickets for spectators are either in the *popular* or the more expensive *platea*, with the price depending on your vantage point and the game's importance, although it always compares favourably with the cost of European match tickets. The *popular* are the standing-only **terraces**, where the young men, the hardcore home fans, sing and swear their way through the match. This is the most colourful part of the stadium, but it's also the area where you're most likely to be pickpocketed, charged by police or faced with the wrath of the equally hardcore away fans (in the *visitantes* section, where you can often buy the cheapest tickets, though it's standing room only). Unless you're pretty confident, or with someone who is, you may be better off heading to the relative safety of the *platea* **seats**, from where you can photograph the *popular* and enjoy the match sitting down. Don't be surprised if someone's in the seat allocated to you on the ticket – locals pay scant regard to official seating arrangements. After major wins, the Obelisco in central Buenos Aires is the epicentre of raucous **celebrations**.

It's advisable to turn up forty minutes or so before the match in order to avoid the rush, and not to hang around the stadium afterwards, when trouble sometimes brews. Dress down, avoid flaunting the colours of either side and take the minimum of valuables.

Polo and pato

Although it's mainly a game for *estancieros* and wealthy families from Barrio Norte, **polo** is nonetheless far less snobbish or exclusive in Argentina than in Britain or the US; there are some 150 teams and five thousand club members nationwide. You don't need an invitation from a member or a double-barrelled surname to see the world's top polo players; simply turn up and buy a ticket during the open championship in November and December, played at the **Campo de Polo** in Palermo, Buenos Aires. Even if the rules go over your head, the game is exciting and aesthetically pleasing, with hooves galloping over impeccably trimmed grass.

The sport is at least as hard as it looks, but if you're confident on horseback and determined to have a go, many estancias (listed throughout the text) offer lessons as part of their accommodation and activity packages. Alternatively, contact the Asociación Argentina de Polo at Arévalo 3065, Buenos Aires (☎011/4777-6444, ⓦwww.aapolo .com), which can also provide match information.

Less glamorous, the curious sport of **pato** has been played by gauchos since the early 1600s. Named after the trussed duck that once served as the "ball" – a leather version with six handles is now used – pato is a sort of lacrosse on horseback, which also has its national tournament in November and December each year, played at the **Campo Argentino de Pato** in San Miguel, just outside the city limits. For more information on pato and a fixture list, see the national federation's website, ⓦwww.fedpato.com.ar.

Rugby

Argentina's national **rugby** squad, the Pumas, is currently ranked fifth in the world and the country's recent success in the sport has seen its popularity rise significantly. By 2012, it should be taking part in the southern hemisphere Tri Nations tournament, to be renamed the Four Nations. In the meantime, you can catch the burly Pumas playing test series at home (all over the country) or in World Cup qualifiers. See the website of the Unión Argentina de Rugby (ⓦwww.uar.com .ar) for upcoming fixtures.

Outdoor activities

Argentina is a highly exciting destination for outdoors enthusiasts: world-class fly-fishing, horse-riding, trekking and rock-climbing opportunities abound, as do options for white-water rafting, skiing, ice climbing and even – for those with sufficient stamina and preparation – expeditions onto the Southern Patagonian Icecap.

Nature tourism

Argentina's network of national and provincial parks offers wonderful opportunities for nature tourism across this country's range of ecosystems (see pp.609–616). **Highlights for wildlife viewing** include the Península Valdés, a superb destination for marine wildlife and fauna of the Patagonian steppe (see p.502), the humid swamplands of

Esteros de Iberá (see p.257), and the subtropical jungles of Iguazú (see p.269).

For an overview of the national park system, visit the **National Park Headquarters** in Buenos Aires at Santa Fe 690 (Mon–Fri 10am–5pm; ☎011/4311-0303, ⓦwww .parquesnacionales.gov.ar). There is an underfunded and not terribly helpful information office on the ground floor that may be able to provide some introductory leaflets, and they can give you tips if you're intending to visit some of the more isolated places like Baritú, Perito Moreno, San Guillermo and Santiago del Estero's Copo, which have limited infrastructure and require some prior planning. A wider range of free material is available at each individual park, but these are of variable quality – many only have a basic map and a brief park description. Each national park has its own **intendencia**, or park administration, although these are often in the principal access town, not within the park itself. An information office or visitors' centre is often attached. Argentina's **guardaparques**, or national park rangers, are some of the most professional on the continent: generally friendly, they are well trained and dedicated to jobs that are demanding and often extremely isolated. All have a good grounding in the wildlife of the region and are happy to share their knowledge, although don't expect them all to be professional naturalists – some are, but ranger duties often involve more contact with the general public than the wildlife.

A good port of call in the capital for nature enthusiasts is the **Fundación Vida Silvestre**, located at Defensa 251, 60 (1065) Buenos Aires (Mon–Fri 10am–1pm & 2–6pm; ☎011/4343-4086 or 4331-3631, ⓦwww.vidasilvestre.org.ar), a committed and highly professional environmental organization, and an associate of the WWF. Visit its shop for back issues of its beautiful magazine (in Spanish) and for books and leaflets on wildlife and ecological issues, as well as for information on its nature reserves.

Argentina has an incredible diversity of birdlife – you can see some ten percent of all the world's bird species here. **Birdwatchers** should visit the headquarters of the country's well-respected birding organization, **Aves Argentinas/Asociación Ornitológica del Plata**, at Matheu 1246/8 y Av San Juan (C1249 AAB) Buenos Aires (nearest Subte station is Pichincha on Linea E; Mon–Fri 3–8pm; ☎011/4943-7216, ⓦwww.avesargentinas.org.ar). It has an excellent library and a shop, and organizes regular outings and **birding safaris**. The \$120 annual membership (US\$75 outside Argentina) entitles you to its high-quality quarterly magazine, discounts on bird safaris, free access to the library and the possibility of getting involved in scientific and conservation work.

Trekking

Argentina offers some truly marvellous **trekking**, and it is still possible to find areas where you can trek for days without seeing a soul. Trail quality varies considerably, and many are difficult to follow, so always get hold of the best **map** available (see p.65) and ask for information as you go. Most of the best treks are in the national parks – especially the ones in

---

Trekking routes

Please refer to the following pages in the guide for further information on specific treks and trails:

Protecting Argentina's natural wonders

When visiting natural parks and wild areas, always try to be **environmentally responsible**. Stick to marked trails, camp only at authorized sites, take all litter with you (don't burn it), bury toilet waste at least 30m away from all water sources and use detergents and toothpastes as sparingly as possible, choosing biodegradable options such as glycerine soap. Above all, pay particular respect to the fire risk. Every year, fires destroy huge swathes of forest, and virtually all of these are started by hand: some deliberately, but most because of unpardonable negligence. As ever, one of the prime culprits is the cigarette butt, often casually tossed out of a car window, but just as bad are campfires, both those that are poorly tended and those that are poorly extinguished. Woodland becomes tinder-dry in summer droughts, and, especially in places such as Patagonia, it is vulnerable to sparks carried by the strong winds. Once started, winds, inaccessibility and limited water resources can turn fires into infernos that blaze for weeks on end, and much fire-damaged land never regenerates its growth. Many parks have a complete ban on lighting campfires and trekkers are asked to take stoves on which to do their cooking; please respect this. Others ban fires during high-risk periods. The most environmentally responsible approach is to avoid lighting campfires at all: even dead wood has a role to play in often-fragile ecosystems. If you do need to light one, never choose a spot on peaty soil, as peat, once it has caught, becomes virtually impossible to put out. Choose a spot on stony or sandy soil, use only fallen wood and always extinguish the fire with water, not earth, stirring up the ashes to ensure all embers are quenched.

Patagonia – but you can often find lesser-known but equally superb options in the lands bordering them. Most people head for the savage granite spires of the **Fitz Roy** region around El Chaltén, an area whose fame has spread so rapidly over the last ten years that it now holds a similar status to Chile's renowned Torres del Paine. Tourist pressures are starting to tell, however, at least in the high season (late Dec to Feb), when campsites are packed. The other principal trekking destination is the mountainous area of **Parque Nacional Nahuel Huapi**, south of Bariloche. This area has the best infrastructure, with a network of generally well-marked trails and mountain refuges. In the north of the country, some of the best trekking is in **Jujuy Province**, especially in Calilegua, where the habitat ranges from subtropical to bald, mountain landscape. **Salta Province** also offers a good variety of high mountain valley and cloudforest trails.

Camping is possible in many national parks, and sites are graded according to three categories: *camping libre* sites, which are free but have no or very few services (perhaps a latrine and sometimes a shower block); *camping agreste* sites, which are run as concessions and usually provide hot water, showers, toilets, places for lighting a campfire and some sort of small shop; and *camping organizado* sites, which have more services, including electricity and often some sort of restaurant.

You should always be well prepared for your trips, even for half-day hikes. Good quality, **water- and windproof clothing** is vital: temperatures plummet at night and often with little warning during the day. Keep spare dry layers of clothing and socks in a plastic bag in your pack. **Boots** should provide firm ankle support and have the toughest soles possible (Vibram soles are recommended). Gore-Tex boots are only waterproof to a degree: they will not stay dry when you have to cross swampland. A **balaclava** is sometimes more useful than a woollen hat. Make sure that your **tent** is properly waterproofed and that it can cope with high winds (especially for Patagonia). You'll need a minimum of a three-season sleeping bag, to be used in conjunction with a solid or semi-inflatable foam mattress (essential, as the ground will otherwise suck out all your body heat). Also bring high-factor **sunblock** and lipsalve, plus good **sunglasses** and headgear.

Park authorities often require you to carry a **stove** for cooking. The Camping Gaz models that run on butane cylinders (refills are fairly widely available in *ferretería* hardware shops) are not so useful in exposed areas, where you're better off with a high-pressure petrol stove such as an MSR, although these are liable to clog with impurities in the fuel, so filter it first. Telescopic hiking poles save your knees from a lot of strain and are useful for balance. Miner-style head **torches** are preferable to regular hand-held ones, and gaffer tape makes an excellent all-purpose emergency repair tool. Carry a **first-aid kit** and a **compass**, and know how to use both. And always carry plenty of **water** – aim to have at least two litres on you at all times. Pump-action **water filters** can be very handy, as you can thus avoid the hassle of having to boil suspect water.

Note also that, in the national parks, especially on the less-travelled and overnight routes, you should inform the **park ranger** (*guardaparque*) of your plans, not forgetting to report your safe arrival at your destination – the ranger will send a search party out for you if you do not arrive. You'd be advised to buy all your camping equipment before you leave home: quality gear is relatively expensive in Argentina, and there are still relatively few places that rent decent equipment, even in some of the key trekking areas.

Climbing

For **climbers**, the Andes offer incredible variety. You do not always have to be a technical expert, but you should always take preparations seriously. You can often arrange a climb close to the date – though it's best to bring as much high-quality gear with you as you can. The climbing season is fairly short – November to March in some places, though December to February is the best time. The best-known challenge is South America's highest peak, **Aconcagua** (6962m), accessed from the city of Mendoza (see pp.398–400). Not considered the most technical challenge, this peak nevertheless merits top-level expedition status, as the altitude and storms claim several victims a year. Only slightly less lofty are nearby Tupungato (6750m), just to the south; Mercedario (6770m), just to the north; Cerro Bonete (6872m) and Pissis (6793m) on the provincial border between La Rioja and Catamarca; and Ojos del Salado, the highest active volcano in the world (6885m), a little further north into Catamarca. The last three can be climbed from Fiambalá, but Ojos is most normally climbed from the Chilean side of the border. The most famous volcano to climb is the elegant cone of **Lanín** (3776m), which can be ascended in two days via the relatively straightforward northeastern route. Parque Nacional Nahuel Huapi, near Bariloche, offers the **Cerro Catedral** massif and **Cerro Tronador** (3554m). Southern Patagonia is also a highly prized climbing destination. One testing summit is **San Lorenzo** (3706m), which, from the Argentine side, can best be approached along the valley of the Río Oro, although the summit itself is usually climbed from across the border in Chile. Further south are the inspirational granite spires of the Fitz Roy massif and Cerro Torre, which have few equals on the planet in terms of technical difficulty and scenic grandeur.

On all of these climbs, but especially those over 4000m, make sure to acclimatize thoroughly, and be fully aware of the dangers of *puna*, or altitude sickness (see p.61).

Useful climbing contacts

In Argentina

Centro Andino Buenos Aires Rivadavia 1255, Buenos Aires ☎011/4381-1566, ⊛www.caba .org.ar. Offers climbing courses, talks and slideshows. Their website has a useful page of links to other Argentine climbing clubs.

Club Andino Bariloche (CAB) 20 de Febrero 30, Bariloche, Río Negro ☎02944/422266, ⊛www .clubandino.com.ar. The country's oldest and most famous mountaineering club, with excellent specialist knowledge of guides and Patagonian challenges.

In the US

American Alpine Club 710 Tenth St, Suite 100, Golden, CO 80401 ☎303/384-0110, ⊛www .americanalpineclub.org. Annual membership includes a limited global rescue policy, and access to its comprehensive library.

In the UK

British Mountaineering Council 177–179
Burton Rd, Manchester M20 2BB ☎0161/445-
6111, ⓦ www.thebmc.co.uk. Produces regularly
updated expedition reports. Excellent insurance
services and book catalogue.

Fishing

As a destination for **fly-fishing** (*pesca con mosca*), Argentina is unparalleled, with Patagonia drawing in professionals from around the globe. Trout, introduced in the early twentieth century, is the sport's mainstay, but there is also fishing for landlocked and even Pacific salmon. The most famous places to go are those where the world's largest sea-running brown trout (*trucha marrón*) are found: principally the **Río Grande** and other rivers of eastern and central Tierra del Fuego, and the Río Gallegos on the mainland. The reaches of the Río Santa Cruz near Comandante Luis Piedra Buena have some impressive specimens of steelhead trout (sea-running rainbows, or *trucha arco iris*), and the area around Río Pico is famous for its brook trout. The Patagonian **Lake District** – around Junín de los Andes, San Martín de los Andes, Bariloche and Esquel – is the country's most popular trout-fishing destination, offering superb angling in delightful scenery.

The **trout-fishing season** runs from mid-November to Easter. Regulations change slightly from year to year, but **permits** are valid countrywide. They can be purchased at national park offices, some *guardaparque* posts, tourist offices and at fishing equipment shops, which are fairly plentiful – especially in places like the north Patagonian Lake District. With your permit, you are issued a **booklet** detailing the regulations of the type of fishing allowed in each river and lake in the region, the restrictions on catch-and-release and the number of specimens you are allowed to take for eating. Argentine law states that permit holders are allowed to fish any waters they can reach without crossing private land. You are, in theory at least, allowed to walk along the bank as far as you like from any public road, although in practice you may find that owners of some of the more prestigious beats try to obstruct you from doing this.

For more **information** on fly-fishing in Argentina, contact the Asociación Argentina de Pesca con Mosca, Lerma 452 (1414) Buenos Aires (☎011/4773 0821, ⓦ www .aapm.org.ar).

Skiing

Argentina's **ski resorts** are not on the same scale as those of Europe or North America and attract mainly domestic and Latin American tourists (from Chile and Brazil), as well as a smattering of foreigners who are looking to ski during the northern summer. However, infrastructure is constantly being upgraded and it's easy to hire gear. The main **skiing season** is July and August (late July is peak season), although in some resorts it is possible to ski from late May to early October. Snow conditions vary from year to year, but you can often find excellent powder.

The most prestigious resort for downhill skiing is modern **Las Leñas** (see p.406), which also offers the most challenging skiing and once hosted World Cup races. Following this are **Chapelco**, near San Martín de los Andes (see p.473), where you also have extensive cross-country options, and the Bariloche resorts of **Cerro Catedral** and **Cerro Otto** (see p.454), which are the longest-running in the country, with wonderful panoramas of the Nahuel Huapi region, albeit with rather too many people. **Ushuaia** (see p.567) is an up-and-coming resort, with some fantastic cross-country possibilities and expanding – if still relatively limited – downhill facilities; the resort's right by the scenic town, so it's a good choice if you want to combine skiing with sightseeing. Bariloche and Las Leñas are the best destinations for those interested in après-ski.

Rafting

Though it does not have the same range of extreme options as neighbouring Chile, Argentina nevertheless has some beautiful **white-water rafting** possibilities, ranging from grades II to V. Many of these are offered as day-trips, and include journeys through enchanting monkey puzzle tree scenery on the generally sedate Río Aluminé (see p.448); along the turbulent and often silty Río Mendoza (p.393) or the wild Rio Diamante (see p.405); on the Río Manso (p.448) in the Alpine-like country south of Parque Nacional Nahuel Huapi (p.448); and along the similar but less-visited Río Corcovado, south of Esquel (p.463). Esquel can also be used as a base for rafting on Chile's fabulous, world-famous Río Futaleufú, a turquoise river that flows through temperate rainforest and tests rafters with rapids of grade V. Salta too has some fine options – for example, the Ríos Lipeo and Iruya (p.329). You do not need previous rafting experience to enjoy these, but you should obviously be able to swim. Pay heed to operators' safety instructions, and ensure your safety gear (especially helmets and life-jackets) fits well.

Culture and etiquette

Argentina's mores reflect its overwhelmingly European ancestry, and, apart from the occasional language barrier, most travellers from the West will have little trouble fitting in.

Argentine society generally displays a pleasing balance between formal politeness and casual tolerance. When it comes to dress, Argentines are quite conservative, and take great pride in their appearance, but in the bigger cities in particular you will see examples of many different styles and subcultures. Particularly outlandish clothing might raise eyebrows out in the provinces, but probably no more than it would in, say, deepest Wisconsin or Wiltshire.

Rules, regulations and bureaucracy

Argentines' rather cavalier attitude towards **rules** and considerations of health and safety is probably the biggest culture shock many foreigners have to deal with; the most obvious example of this is the anarchy you'll see on the roads, but you will also likely come across things such as loose wiring in hotels or wobbly cliff-top fencing. A complaint will probably get you no more than a shrug of the shoulders, though there are signs of a change in attitudes. Many visitors actually find the lack of regulations liberating.

Another difference is the Kafka-esque **bureaucracy** that you will encounter if you're in the country for any length of time – when obtaining a visa, say, or picking up a parcel from the post office. Do not lose your temper if faced with red tape – it will have absolutely no benefit.

Sexual harassment and discrimination

Women planning on travelling alone to the country can do so with confidence. Some **machista** attitudes do persist – men usually pay in restaurants, and it is relatively unusual for groups of girls to go out drinking the way they might in Europe or the US – but the next generation seems to be shedding these inhibitions with alacrity and few people will find it strange that you are travelling unaccompanied. You will probably find you are the target of comments in the street and chat-up lines more frequently than you are accustomed to, but those responsible will not persist if you make it clear you're not interested. Such attentions are almost never hostile or physical – Italian-style bottom pinching is very rare here.

Greetings

When **greeting** people or taking your leave, it is normal to kiss everyone present on the cheek (just once, always the right cheek), even among men, who may emphasize their masculinity by slapping each other on the back. Shaking hands tends to be the preserve of businessmen or formal situations; if in doubt, watch the locals. One area of etiquette that will probably be new to you is the very Argentine custom of drinking *mate*, which comes with its own set of rules (see box, p.263), but foreigners will be given lots of leeway here, as in other areas of social custom – *faux pas* are more likely to cause amusement than offence.

Drinking and smoking

Argentine attitudes to **drinking** tend to be similar to those in southern Europe: alcohol is fine in moderation, and usually taken with food. Public drunkenness remains rare and frowned upon, though it occurs more frequently among the young than it used to. **Smoking** is fairly common among both sexes and all classes, although a number of areas, including Buenos Aires and Córdoba, have recently passed statutes making it illegal to smoke in enclosed public areas, including restaurants. Whether enforcement

of this will be strict remains to be seen – Argentine history is littered with laws that are obeyed patchily at best before being quietly disposed of.

Shopping

You will find no real tradition of **haggling** in Argentina, although you can always try it when buying pricey artwork, antiques, etc. Expensive services such as excursions and car rental are also obvious candidates for bargaining, while hotel rates can be beaten down off season, late at night or if you're paying cash (*efectivo*). But try and be reasonable, especially in the case of already low-priced crafts or high-quality goods and services that are obviously worth every centavo.

Tipping

Tipping is not widespread in Argentina, with a couple of exceptions. It's normal to round up taxi fares to the nearest 50 centavos (though not expected), and you should add a small gratuity to restaurant bills if service is not included. The kids who hang around taxi ranks to open and close doors also appreciate a coin, as do hotel porters and the people who load and unload long-distance bus luggage.

Travelling with children

Argentines love children and you will generally find them helpful and understanding if you're travelling as a family. In terms of **accommodation**, most hotels have triple rooms or suites with connecting rooms to accommodate families. Apartment hotels and *cabañas*, which also contain small kitchens, are particularly good. Many hotels will be able to provide a cot if you have a small child (ask when you reserve), but be aware that though perfectly

adequate these may be pretty old and are unlikely to conform to European or US safety standards. Top hotels will often provide babysitting services. On the other hand, some boutique and upmarket **hotels** have a no-child rule; these are fairly few and far between, but check when you reserve.

When it comes to **eating out**, only the very snotty top-of-the-range restaurants will turn children away or look pained when you walk in; the vast majority will do their best to make sure you and your offspring are comfortable and entertained. Highchairs are sometimes, but not always, provided. It is quite normal to see children out with their parents until late – you may well see families strolling home at 1 or 2 am, especially in summer.

Argentina's **natural attractions** may be your best bet for entertaining your kids – the country has little in the way of amusement parks or specific family destinations, and the ones that do exist are generally rather poor. Consider the waterfalls and jungle critters at Iguazú, the boat rides and glaciers of Parque Nacional Los Glaciares or the whales and penguins near Península Valdés. Buenos Aires' somewhat sophisticated attractions will mostly appeal more to adults, but there is enough to keep younger ones amused for a couple of days, including a zoo (p.125), a planetarium (p.126) and a natural history museum (p.128). Rosario (p.288) is unusual among Argentine cities for the amount of child-centred attractions it has – and it's fun for their parents too. Wherever you go,

remember the distances in Argentina are vast and travel times can be lengthy – do not be too ambitious in planning your itinerary. Avoid the summer heat unless you will be spending most of your time in Patagonia.

International brands of **nappies** (diapers), **wipes** and **baby milk** are widely available, as are **dummies** (pacifiers). Bring any **children's medicine** with you that you are likely to need, as it can be difficult to work out what the local equivalent is. Many people who work in pharmacies have little medical training so if your child does get sick, go to a private hospital, preferably in one of the larger cities, where you will be attended by a paediatrician rapidly and professionally. **Baby food** is usually only sold in large supermarkets, and the range is very limited, but waiters will usually be happy to provide mashed potatoes, pumpkin and so on. Discreet **breastfeeding** in public is fine. Changing facilities are practically non-existent (large city malls being the only exception), so you will have to get used to changing on the move.

Travel essentials

Costs

The **Argentine peso** has remained relatively stable at between three and four to the US dollar for nearly a decade. Continual high inflation has eroded many of the exchange gains that the 2001 devaluation first gave and it can no longer really be described as a cheap destination. But the quality of what is on offer is mostly pretty good, and certain things can represent particularly smart value – notably eating out and transport – and outside Buenos Aires and the main tourist destinations you can find real bargains in shops and hotels.

Adhering to a reasonable **daily budget** is not impossible, but there are considerable

regional variations. As a rule of thumb, the further south you travel the more you will need to stretch your budget. Roughly speaking, on average you'll need to plan on spending at least $1000/US$260/£160 a week on a tight budget (sharing a dorm, eating snacks, limiting other spending), double that if staying in budget accommodation but not stinting, while to live in the lap of luxury you could easily burn through $10000/US$2600/£1600 in a week.

Camping and self-catering are good ways of **saving money**, though the now-extensive network of youth hostels enables you to pay little without sleeping rough. Out of season, at weekends and during slow periods it is a good idea to bargain hotel

Student cards

These are not as useful as they can be in some countries, as museums and the like often refuse to give **student discounts**. Some bus companies, however, do give a ten- to fifteen-percent discount for holders of **ISIC cards**, as do certain hotels, laundries and outdoor gear shops, and even one or two ice-cream parlours. ASATEJ, Argentina's student travel agency, issues a booklet that lists partners throughout the country. The international student card often suffices for a discount at youth hostels in the country, though membership of the Youth Hostelling Association may entitle you to even lower rates.

prices down. You can save money on **food** by having your main meal at lunch time – especially by opting for the set menu (usually called *menú ejecutivo*). Picnicking is another option; local produce is often world-class and an alfresco meal of bread, cheese, ham or salami with fresh fruit and a bottle of table wine in a great location is a match for any restaurant feast.

Long-distance **transport** will eat up a considerable chunk of your expenses, particularly if you use internal flights; buses are obviously much cheaper if you have the time. They vary greatly in condition and price from one category to another, though you may find the cheaper fares are a false economy – the better companies usually give you free food and drink (of varying quality) on lengthy journeys, while spacious *coche cama* comfort overnight enables you to save the price of a room and is worthwhile for covering the longest distances over less interesting terrain. City transport – including taxis and *remises* (radio taxis) – is inexpensive, but then most cities are compact enough to walk around anyway.

Hotels, restaurants and big stores may ask for a hefty handling fee for credit-card payments (as high as twenty percent), while many businesses – and hotels in particular – will give you a fair-sized **discount for cash payments** (*efectivo* or *contado*) on the quoted price, though they may need prompting. Be aware that many services, especially air travel and hotels, operate **dual pricing** – one price for Argentine residents (including foreigners) and another, often as much as three times more, for non-residents. Hotels and other types of commerce, especially at the luxury end of the market, may charge foreigners in US dollars, rather than Argentine pesos, as a covert but perfectly legal way of charging more. This practice is mostly found in more touristy locations such as Ushuaia and Bariloche, as well as the capital.

All prices in this book are quoted in Argentine pesos ($) unless noted otherwise.

Crime and personal safety

With the effects of economic crises in 2001 and 2009 still lingering, Argentina has lost the reputation it enjoyed for many years as a totally safe destination. However, any concern you have should be kept in perspective – the likelihood of being a victim of crime remains small, because most of the more violent crime (concentrated in the big cities) is directed at wealthy locals rather than foreign visitors.

The usual precautions should be taken, particularly in the capital, cities like Rosario and Córdoba, and some of the northern border towns (near the frontiers with Paraguay and Brazil). In Buenos Aires, highly publicized incidents of violence and armed robbery have increased over the years but the vast majority of visitors have no problems. Some potential pitfalls are outlined here – not to induce paranoia, but on the principle that to be forewarned is to be forearmed.

There are some **basic precautions** you should take to reduce the likelihood of being a victim of crime. A basic rule is to carry only what you need for that day, and conceal valuable items such as cameras and jewellery. Be cautious when withdrawing cash from ATMs. If you're not sure about the wisdom of walking somewhere, play it safe and take a cab – but call radio taxis or hail

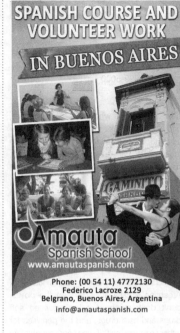
them in the street, rather than taking a waiting one. Remember that pickpockets most commonly hang around subte stations and bus terminals (particularly Retiro in the capital), and on crowded trains and buses.

Theft from **hotels** is rare, but do not leave valuables lying around. Use the hotel safe if there is one. Compared with other Latin American countries, you're unlikely to have things stolen on long-distance **buses** (luggage Is checked in and you should get a ticket for each item), but it makes sense to take your daypack with you when you disembark for meal stops, and, particularly at night, to keep your bag by your feet rather than on the overhead rack. Pilfering from checked-in luggage on **flights** is quite common – don't leave anything of value in outside pockets, and lock your bag where possible. **Car theft** has become a very common occurrence; if you are renting a car, check that the insurance will cover you, and always park in a car park or where someone will keep an eye on it. When driving in the city, keep windows closed and doors locked.

As elsewhere in Latin America, you should be aware of the possibility of **scams**. A popular one, especially in the tourist areas of Buenos Aires, is having mustard, ice cream or some similar substance "spilt" over you. Some person then offers to help clean it off – cleaning you out at the same time. If this happens to you, push them off, get away from them fast and make as much noise as possible, shouting "thief!" ("*ladrón*!"), "police!" ("*policía*!") or for help ("*socorro*!"). Another well-worked scam involves a regular cab picking you up from the taxi rank outside Aeroparque Jorge Newbery, driving off the airport grounds (so they're no longer on CCTV), then the driver taking a call on his mobile phone and suddenly saying that he has to drop you off and can't take you to your destination. He leaves you stranded at the side of the road to be picked up by a "random" cab he's in league with, who'll fleece you. Easily avoided: always make sure you take an official, booked *remise* rather than waiting for a regular cab.

Note, too, that, though the police are entitled to check your documents, they have no right to inspect your money or travellers' cheques: anyone who does is a con artist, and you should ask for their identification or offer to be taken to the police station (*gendarmería*). If you ever do get "arrested", never get into a vehicle other than an official police car.

Drugs are frowned upon, although perhaps not as much as in other parts of South America. Drug use, particularly of marijuana and cocaine, is fairly common among the younger generation, and quite openly celebrated in some popular song lyrics. Despite court rulings in 2009 interpreted as a step towards decriminalization, Argentine society at large, and the police, don't draw much of a line between soft drugs and hard drugs, and the penalties for either can be stiff if you get caught. As everywhere else, there are many slang words for drugs: common ones for marijuana include *porro, maconia* and *yerba;* for cocaine, *merca* and *papa.*

If you are unlucky enough to be the victim of a **robbery** (*asalto*) or lose anything of value, you will need to make a report at the nearest police station for insurance purposes. This is usually a time-consuming but fairly straightforward process. Check that the report includes a comprehensive account of everything lost and its value, and that the police add the date and an official stamp (*sello*). These reports do not cost anything.

Electricity

220V/50Hz is standard throughout the country. Two different types of sockets are found: two-pronged with round pins, but which are different to the two-pin European plugs; and three-pronged, with flat pins, two of which are slanted. **Adapters** will probably be needed and can be bought at a string of electrical shops along Calle Talcahuano, in Buenos Aires. Some, but not all, of the multi-adaptors on sale at airports will do the trick, so check the instructions.

Entry requirements

Citizens of the US, Canada, the UK, Ireland, Australia and New Zealand do not currently need a **visa** for tourist trips to Argentina of up to ninety days. In the past entry fees (some quite hefty) have been introduced on a reciprocal basis for the citizens of certain countries such as the US. All visitors need a valid **passport** and will have to fill in a landing card (*tarjeta de entrada*) on arrival, when you will be given a stamp. In theory, this could be for thirty, sixty or ninety days, but in practice it's almost always ninety. If you are travelling alone with a child you may be requested to show a notarized document certifying both parents' permission for the child to travel. Keep your landing card safe, as you'll need to show it to leave the country. If you do lose it, it's rarely a serious problem, but you'll have to fill in a new form at the border control.

On entering the country, you will also be given a **customs declaration form**. Duty is not charged on used personal effects, books and other articles for non-commercial purposes, up to the value of US$300. Make sure you declare any valuable electronic items such as laptop computers or fancy mobile phones.

You can **extend your stay** for a further ninety days by paying a reasonable fee and presenting your passport at the main immigration department, Dirección de Migraciones in Buenos Aires, at Av Antártida Argentina 1350, Retiro (☏011/4317-0237 or 0238). This costs $100 and must be done on weekdays between 8am and 1pm; be prepared for a possible lengthy wait. You can do this extension, called a *prórroga,* once only. Alternatively, you could try leaving the country (the short hop to Colonia del Sacramento in Uruguay is a good option) and returning to get a fresh stamp. This usually works, but may be frowned upon if done repeatedly, and the provision of an extra stamp is totally at the discretion of the border guards. If you do overshoot your stay, you pay a moderate fine at Migraciones, who will give you a form that allows you to leave the country within ten days. This was a fairly common practice at the time of publication, but bear in mind that if you do this your stay in the country will be illegal and could potentially cause you problems. If you are crossing into **Chile**, make sure your papers are in order, as Chilean officials are considerably more scrupulous.

When leaving the country, you must obtain an **exit stamp**. At certain border controls, particularly in the north of the country, it is often up to you to ensure that the bus driver stops and waits while you get this – otherwise drivers may not stop, assuming that all passengers are Argentine nationals and don't need stamps. In some places (for example, Clorinda) your Argentine exit stamp is actually given on the far side of the border, but check this with the driver beforehand.

Visas for work or study must be obtained in advance from your consulate. Extensive paperwork, much of which must be translated into Spanish by a certified translator, is required; allow plenty of time before departure to start the process. The websites listed below have details of what documentation is needed, or contact the consulate directly.

Although checks are rare, visitors are legally obliged to carry their passport as ID. You might get away with carrying a photocopy, but don't forget to copy your entrance stamp and landing card as well. In the majority of cases, this is acceptable to police, but getting a copy certified by a public notary increases its credibility.

Argentine embassies and consulates abroad

Australia

Embassy John McEwan House, Level 2, 7 National Circuit, Barton ACT 2600 ☏02/6273-9111, ⓦwww.argentina.org.au.
Consulate 44 Market St, Piso 20, Sydney, NSW ☏02/9262-2933, ⓦwww.argentina.org.au /consulado.

Canada

Embassy 90 Sparks St, Suite 910, Ottawa, Ontario K1P 5B4 ☏613/236-2351, ⓦwww .argentina-canada.net.

Consulates 2000 Peel St, 7th floor, Suite 600, Montréal, Québec H3A 2W5 ☏514/842-6582, ⓦwww.consargenmtl.com; 5001 Yonge St, Suite 201, Toronto, Ontario M2N 6P6 ☏416/955-9190, ⓦwww.consargtoro.ca.

New Zealand

Embassy Sovereign Assurance Building, Level 14, 142 Lambton Quay, PO Box 5430, Wellington ☏04/472-8330, ⓦwww.arg.org.nz.

UK

Embassy 65 Brook St, London W1K 4AH ☏020/7318 1300, ⓦwww.argentine-embassy-uk .org.
Consulate 27 Three Kings Yard, London W1K 4DF ☏020/7318 1340, ⓔfclond@mrecic.gov.ar.

US

Embassy 1600 New Hampshire Ave, NW, Washington DC 20009 ☏202/238-6401, ⓦwww.embajadaargentinaeeuu.org.
Consulates 245 Peachtree Center Ave, Suite 2101, Atlanta, Georgia 30303 ☏404/880-0805, ⓦwww.consuladoargentinoatlanta.org; 205 N Michigan Ave, Piso 42, Suite 4209, Chicago, IL 60601 ☏312/819-2610, ⓔargchic@aol.com;

3050 Post Oak Blvd, Suite 1625, Houston, TX 77056 ⓣ713/871-8935, ⓔchous_ar@hotmail.com; 5055 Wilshire Blvd Suite 210, Los Angeles, CA 90036 ⓣ323/954-9155, ⓦwww.consuladoargentino -losangeles.org; 800 Brickell Ave, Penthouse 1, Miami, FL 33131 ⓣ305/373-1889, ⓦwww .consuladoargentinoenmiami.com; 12 West 56th St, New York, NY 10019 ⓣ212/603-0400, ⓦwww .congenargentinany.com.

Embassies in Argentina

Australia

Buenos Aires Villanueva 1400, C1426BMJ ⓣ011/4779-3500.

Canada

Buenos Aires Tagle 2828, C1425EEH ⓣ011/4808-1000.

New Zealand

Buenos Aires Carlos Pellegrini 1427, 5th floor, CP1011 ⓣ011/4328-0747.

UK

Buenos Aires Dr Luis Agote 2412, C1425EOF ⓣ011/4808-2200.

US

Buenos Aires Av Colombia 4300, C1425GMN ⓣ011/5777-4533.

Gay and lesbian travellers

Despite remarkable progress in recent years, the attitude in Argentina towards homosexuals is generally ambivalent. **Discreet relationships** are tolerated, but in this overwhelmingly Roman Catholic nation any "deviance", including any explicit physical contact between members of the same sex (let alone transvestism or overtly intimate behaviour) will be almost universally disapproved of, to say the least. Violent manifestations of **homophobia** are rare, however, especially now that the Church and the military exert less influence; homosexual acts between consenting adults have long been legal.

Gay and lesbian **associations** are springing up in the major cities, notably in Buenos Aires, where nightlife and meeting places are increasingly open (see p.139), but rural areas still do their best to act as if homosexuality

doesn't exist. Yet one of the first pieces of legislation passed by parliament in 2003 afforded all citizens protection from discrimination, making a specific reference to sexual orientation. In the same year, the city of Buenos Aires legalized non-marriage unions for heterosexuals and homosexuals alike, with several gay couples tying the knot in highly publicized ceremonies. At the end of 2009 two men were given permission to marry in Ushuaia, having failed to do so in their home city of Buenos Aires, following a legal struggle that won national and international press coverage.

Contacts for gay and lesbian travellers

Listed below are some of the main companies and organizations catering for gay and lesbian travellers.

In Argentina

Bue Gay Argentina Pueyrredón 2031, 1st floor, B, Buenos Aires ⓣ011/4805-1401, ⓦwww .buegay.com.ar. Young company concentrating on city tours and activity vacations around the country, accompanied by gay tour guides.
Pride Travel Paraguay 523, 2nd floor, E, Buenos Aires ⓣ011/5218-6556, ⓦwww.pride-travel.com. Argentine travel agent offering air tickets, day-trips, tours and adventure tourism aimed at gay and lesbian travellers.

Gay resources online

Ba4uapartments Santa Fe 2630, 7th floor, E, Buenos Aires ⓣ011/4827-5293, ⓦwww .ba4uapartments.com.ar. In addition to a variety of excellent apartments for rent (usually 3 nights minimum), this dynamic team also offers other services including Spanish classes, massages, etc.
Gay Places to Stay ⓦwww.gayplaces2stay .com. Information about gay-friendly accommodation worldwide.
Gay Travel ⓦwww.gaytravel.com. The most helpful site for trip planning, bookings and general information about international travel.
Nexo ⓦwww.nexo.org. The best site for finding out latest news and venues in Argentina.

Health

Travel to Argentina doesn't raise any major **health** worries and with a small dose of precaution and a handful of standard vaccinations or updates (tetanus, polio, typhoid and hepatitis A) you are unlikely to encounter any serious problems. There have been highly publicized outbreaks of **dengue fever** in the far north and there were a large number of (again, much publicized) cases of swine flu in mid-2009. Yet a bout of **travellers' diarrhoea**, as your body adjusts to local micro-organisms in the food and water, is the most you're likely to have to worry about. The **tap water** in Argentina is generally safe to drink, if sometimes heavily chlorinated, but you may prefer to err on the side of caution in rural areas in the north of the country. Mineral water is good and widely available.

Argentine **pharmacies** are plentiful, well-stocked and a useful port of call for help with minor medical problems; the staff may offer simple diagnostic advice and will often help dress wounds, but if in doubt consult a doctor. Medicines and cosmetic products are fairly expensive, however, as they are mostly imported, so if you have room, take plenty of supplies.

The easiest way to get treatment for more serious ailments is to visit the outpatient department of a **hospital**, where treatment will usually be free. In Buenos Aires, the Hospital de Clínicas, at José de San Martín, Av Córdoba 235l (☎011/4961-6001), is a particularly efficient place to receive medical advice and prescriptions; you can simply walk in and, for a small fee, make an on-the-spot appointment with the relevant specialist department – English-speaking doctors can usually be found. For a list of English-speaking doctors throughout the country, contact your embassy in Buenos Aires. For **emergencies or ambulances** in Argentina, dial ☎107.

Among the nasty complaints that exist on Argentine territory are Chagas' disease, cholera, malaria, dengue, hantavirus, yellow fever and rabies, though are all rare, mostly confined to remote locations off the tourist trail. That said, each is sufficiently serious that you should be aware of their existence and of measures you should take to avoid infection. For up-to-date information on current health risks in Argentina check ⓦwww.cdc.gov and ⓦwww.medicineplanet.com.

The incidence of HIV/AIDS is similar to that in most developed countries. As some of the condoms sold in Argentina are of pretty poor quality, it's wise to bring a reliable brand with you.

Puna (altitude sickness)

Altitude sickness is a potentially – if very rarely – fatal condition encountered at anything over 2000m, but likeliest and most serious at altitudes of 4000m and above. It can cause severe difficulties, but a little preparation should help you avoid the worst of its effects. In many South American countries it is known by the Quichoa word *soroche*, but in Argentina it is most commonly, and confusingly, called *puna* (the local word for altiplano, or high Andean steppes). You'll also hear the verb *apunar* and the word *apunamiento*, referring to the state of suffering from *puna*, whether affecting humans or vehicles (which also need to be adjusted for these heights).

First, to avoid the effects of the *puna*, don't rush anywhere – walk slowly and breathe steadily – and make things easier on yourself by not smoking. Whenever possible, **acclimatize**: it's better to spend a day or two at around 2000m and then 3000–3500m before climbing to 4000m or more rather than force the body to cope with a sudden reduction in oxygen levels. Make sure you're fully **rested**; an all-night party isn't the best preparation for a trip up into the Andes. Alcohol is also best avoided both prior to and during high-altitude travel; the best thing to **drink** is plenty of still water – never fizzy because it froths over and can even explode at high altitudes – or tea. **Eating**, too, needs some consideration: digestion uses up considerable quantities of oxygen, so snacking is preferable to copious meals. Carry supplies of high-energy cereal bars, chocolate, dried fruit (the local raisins, prunes and dried apricots are delicious), walnuts or cashews, crackers and biscuits, and avoid anything that ferments in the stomach, such as milk, fresh fruit and juices, vegetables or acidic food – they're guaranteed to make you throw up if you're affected. The best form of sugar to ingest is honey, because it's the least acidic. Grilled meat is fine, so *asados* are all right, but don't over-indulge. If you're **driving** into the altiplano make sure that your vehicle's engine has been properly adjusted. All engines labour because of the low oxygen levels, so don't try to force the pace: stay in low gears and go easy on the air conditioning. Take care also with items such as ink pens and screw-top tubes and bottles of shampoo or creams – the low pressure at these altitudes may cause them to burst or leak.

Minor symptoms of the *puna*, such as headaches or a strange feeling of pressure inside the skull, nausea, loss of appetite, insomnia or dizziness, are nothing to worry about, but more severe problems, such as persistent migraines, repeated vomiting, severe breathing difficulties, excessive fatigue and a marked reduction in the need to urinate are of more concern. If you suffer from any of these, return to a lower altitude and seek out medical advice at once. Severe respiratory problems should be treated immediately with oxygen, carried by tour operators on excursions to 3000m or more as a legal requirement, but you're unlikely ever to need it (see more information relating to Aconcagua on p.400).

Sunstroke and sunburn

You should take the sun very seriously in Argentina. The north of the country, especially the Chaco region and La Rioja Province, is one of the hottest regions of Latin America in summer – temperatures regularly rocket above 40°C; the extended siestas taken by locals are wise precautions against the debilitating effects of the midday heat. Where possible, avoid excessive activity between about 11am and 4pm and when you do have to be out in the sun, wear sunscreen and a hat. You should also drink plenty of liquids – but not alcohol – and always make sure you have a sufficient supply of water when embarking on a hike. Throughout the country, the sun can be extremely fierce and even people with darker skin should use a much higher factor sunscreen than they might normally: using factor 15 or above is a sensible precaution. Remember that the cooler temperatures in the south are deceptive – ozone depletion and long summer days here can be more hazardous than the fierce heat of the north.

Medical resources for travellers

US and Canada

Canadian Society for International Health ☏613/241-5785, ⊛www.csih.org. Extensive list of travel health centres.
CDC ☏1-800/232 4636, ⊛www.cdc.gov/travel. Official US government travel health site.
International Society for Travel Medicine ☏1-770/736-7060, ⊛www.istm.org. Has a full list of travel health clinics.

Australia, New Zealand and South Africa

Travellers' Medical and Vaccination Centre ☏1300/658 844, ⊛www.tmvc.com.au. Lists travel clinics in Australia, New Zealand and South Africa.

UK and Ireland

Hospital for Tropical Diseases Travel Clinic ☏0845/155 5000, ☏020/7388 9600 (Travel Clinic), ⊛www.thehtd.org.
MASTA (Medical Advisory Service for Travellers Abroad) ☏0870/606 2782, ⊛www.masta.org for the nearest clinic.
Travel Medicine Clinic ☏028/9031 5
Tropical Medical Bureau ☏1850/487 674, ⊛www.tmb.ie. Ireland

Insurance

It is a good idea to take out an **insurance policy** before travelling, though always check first to see whether you are already covered by your home insurance, provincial health plan or student/employment insurance. In Argentina, insurance is more important to cover theft or loss of belongings and repatriation than medical treatment – the country has a state medical system that is free for emergencies. It is perfectly adequate, though the technology is not the latest and waits can be long. Most well-off Argentines use private healthcare, which is very good and far cheaper than the equivalent in the US or Europe. Make sure your travel insurance policy includes coverage for any adventure sports you may be planning, such as scuba-diving, white-water rafting, or skiing – you will probably have to pay a premium to have this included. If you need to make a claim, you should keep all receipts, and in the event you have anything stolen, you must obtain an official statement from the police.

Internet

All towns and most villages in Argentina have public places where you can access the **internet**, either in internet cafés, or in *locutorios* (see p.67). Rates vary considerably, from $1 to $10 an hour, with the highest rates in Patagonia. In most decent-sized places there will be broadband, but out in the sticks internet connections can still be painfully slow, sometimes down for days, or non-existent. Virtually all upmarket hotels in towns and cities offer wi-fi, and increasingly hostels and mid-market hotels do as well. The ones that don't often have a PC with broadband access you can use. Cafes with wi-fi are common in Buenos Aires, less so in the interior – try ⓦwww.navegawifi.com for a hotspot list.

The Spanish keyboard is prevalent; if you have problems locating the "@" symbol (called *arroba* in Spanish), try holding the "Alt" key down and type 64.

Laundry

Most towns and cities have a plentiful supply of **laundries** (*lavanderías* or *lavaderos*), especially since not everyone has a washing machine. Some also do dry-cleaning, though you may have to go to a *tintorería*. Self-service places are almost unheard of; you normally give your name and leave your washing to pick it up later (the service is fast by European standards); some places will deliver to wherever you're staying. Laundry is either charged by weight or itemized, but **rates** are not excessive, especially compared with the high prices charged by most hotels. Furthermore, the quality is good and the service is usually reliable. One important word of vocabulary to know is **planchado** (ironed).

Living and working in Argentina

More and more foreigners are choosing to stay in Argentina long-term, and if you want to take the plunge you will be in good company, particularly if you settle in Buenos Aires or one of the key travel destinations such as Ushuaia or Mendoza. **Organizations** that cater to expats include the South American Explorers' Club, which has a Buenos Aires clubhouse (see p.81), the lively internet forum ⓦbaexpats.org and the website ⓦwww.livinginargentina.com.

Tourist **visas** are valid for ninety days. You are usually allowed to renew your visa once, although this does mean an encounter with the bureaucratic immigration services. Many medium-term residents simply leave the country every three months (usually hopping across to Colonia, in Uruguay), to get a new stamp, but this approach might not be tolerated over many years. Obtaining a **residence permit** is time-consuming and is usually granted only if you have an Argentine spouse or child, or make a sizeable investment in the national economy.

As far as **working** is concerned, remember Argentines themselves compete for the few jobs on offer and your entry into the employment market may not be looked on kindly; also, unless you are on a contract with an international firm or organization, you will be paid in pesos, which will inevitably add up to a pretty low salary by global standards, though of course it will stretch further in Argentina. If you're determined anyway, many English-speaking foreigners do the obvious thing and **teach English**. Training in this is an advantage but by no means necessary; the demand for native English-speaking teachers is so high that many soon build up a roster of students via the odd newspaper ad and word of mouth. **Working in tourism** is another possibility – a fair proportion of agencies and hotels are run by foreigners. Consider also translation if you have the language ability.

If you just want to **volunteer**, contact the South American Explorers' club, which matches potential volunteers and organizations that need help, and doesn't charge a hefty fee for doing so, although you do need to be member.

If you need a **place to live**, there are plenty of agencies aimed at foreigners – one is ⓦwww.alojargentina.com – offering accommodation in apartments, university residences and B&B-type establishments; more are listed on the forums mentioned above, or you could try ⓦwww.craigslist .com. Apartments aimed at locals are advertised in newspapers or rented by *inmobiliarías* (estate agents) and are cheaper, but you will need somebody who owns property to be your guarantor and be prepared to sign a two-year contract.

Mail

Argentina's rather unreliable **postal service**, Correo Argentino (☎011/4891-9191) is the *bête noire* of many a hapless expat. Not only is it costly to send post to North America or Europe (starting at $5.50 for a postcard), but many items also never arrive. If you want to **send mail abroad**, always use the *certificado* (registered post) system, which costs about $11 for a letter, but increases chances of arrival. Safer still is Correo Argentino's *encomienda* system ($110 or $140 for a package with 1kg to North America or Europe respectively), a **courier-style** service; if you are sending something important or irreplaceable, it is highly recommended that you use this service or a similar international one such as UPS (☎0800/2222-877) or DHL (☎0810/2222-345). Packets over 2kg need to be examined by the customs (*Aduana*) at the Centro Postal Internacional at Antártida Argentina 1900 y Comodoro Py

in Retiro, Buenos Aires (Mon–Fri 10am–5pm). For regular airmail, expect delivery times of one to two weeks – the quickest deliveries, unsurprisingly, are those out of Buenos Aires. You are not permitted to seal envelopes with sticky tape: they must be gummed down (glue is usually available at the counter). The good news is that as well as post offices, many *locutorios*, lottery kiosks and small stores deal with mail, which means you don't usually have to go very far to find somewhere open.

Receiving mail is generally even more fraught with difficulties than sending it. Again, a courier-style service is your best bet; if not, make sure the sender at least registers the letter or parcel. All **parcels** go to the international post office at Antártida Argentina 1900 in Retiro, and you will receive a card informing you that it is there; you will have to pay customs duties and should expect a long wait. If you are elsewhere in the country you must find out where your nearest customs office is. All post offices keep **poste restante** for at least a month. Items should be addressed clearly, with the recipient's surname in capital letters and underlined, followed by their first name in regular script, then "Poste Restante" or "Lista de Correos", Correo Central, followed by the rest of the address. Buenos Aires city is normally referred to as Capital Federal to distinguish it from its neighbouring province. Bring your passport to collect items ($4.50 fee per item).

To send **packages within Argentina**, your best bet it to use the *encomienda* services offered by bus companies (seal boxes in brown paper to prevent casual theft). This isn't a door-to-door service like the post: the recipient must collect the package from its end destination (bring suitable ID). By addressing the package to yourself, this system makes an excellent and remarkably good-value way of reducing the weight in your pack while travelling, but be aware that companies usually keep an *encomienda* for only one month before returning it to its original sender. If sending an *encomienda* to Buenos Aires, check whether it gets held at the Retiro bus station (the most convenient) or at a bus depot elsewhere in the capital.

Maps

There are a number of **country maps** available outside Argentina, including the **Rough Guides'** detailed, indestructible Argentina map. Other than that and the maps in this book, the best city map of Buenos Aires is the brilliant Insight Fleximap, which is clear, reliable and easy to fold.

Within Argentina, **road maps** can be obtained at bookshops and kiosks in all big towns and cities or at service stations. Many maps aren't up to date: it's often a good idea to buy a couple of maps and compare them as you go along, always checking with the locals to see whether a given road does exist and is passable, especially with the vehicle you intend to use. The most reliable maps are those produced by **ACA** (Automóvil Club), which does individual maps for each province, to varying degrees of accuracy. These are widely available at ACA offices, kiosks on Calle Florida in the capital and service stations. Glossy and fairly clear – but at times erratic – regional road maps (Cuyo, Northwest, Lake District, etc) are produced by **AutoMapa** and are often available at petrol stations and bookshops. Slightly more detailed but a tad less accurate is the mini-atlas *Atlas Vial* published by **YPF**, the national petrol company, which is sold at their service stations. There's a good series by **Mapa de Dios** (ⓦwww.dediosonline.com), sold in bookshops, with themes such as restaurants, tango and shopping in Buenos Aires, plus other country and regional maps.

For 1:100,000 ordnance survey-style maps, the Instituto Geográfico Nacional at Av Cabildo 381 in Buenos Aires is the place to go (Mon–Fri 8.30am–4pm; ☏011/4576-5576 ext 152, ⓦwww.igm .gov.ar). These topographical and colour satellite maps are great to look at and very detailed, but they are only really of practical for those like trekkers who are used to maps of this type.

Internet

Country maps can be found at the University of Texas's Perry-Castañeda Library: ⓦwww .lib.utexas.edu/maps/argentina.html.

A good interactive map of Buenos Aires capital can be found at ⓦmapa.buenosaires .gov.ar/.

Money

After dollar–peso parity lasting a pipedream decade, from 2002 to 2008 the exchange rate against the US dollar fluctuated slightly around or just above the three-peso mark. Then, as the worldwide value of the greenback recovered and Argentina slid into a new recession, the rate drifted towards 3.80 or even 4 to the dollar by the end of 2009. Notes come in 2, 5, 10, 20, 50 and 100 denominations, while (rare), 1 peso and 1 5, 10, 25 and 50 centavo coins are in circulation. Sometimes people are loath to give change, as coins can be in short supply, so it's a good idea to have plenty of loose change on your person. Ask for small denomination notes at banks if possible, break bigger ones up at places where they obviously have plenty of change (busy shops, supermarkets and post offices), and withdraw odd amounts from ATMs ($190, $340, etc) to avoid getting your cash dispensed in $100 bills only – trying to buy a drink, an empanada or a postcard with a crisp $100 note can be a frustrating ordeal and won't make you many friends. Argentine money is difficult to change outside the country, other than just across the border, where it may even be used as legal tender.

You can check current **exchange rates** and convert figures on ⓦwww.xe.com.

Taxes

IVA (*Impuesto de Valor Agregado*) is the Argentine equivalent of VAT or **sales tax** and is usually included in the price for goods and

---

Currency notation

When you see the $ sign in Argentina – and throughout this book – you can safely assume that the currency being referred to is the Argentine peso. Where a price is quoted in US dollars, the normal notation in Argentina – and the notation we use – is US$.

services except food or medicines. The major exceptions are some hotels, which quote their rates before tax, plus airfares and car rental fees. IVA is currently a hefty **21 percent** and is added to everything except food and medicines. It is worth knowing that foreigners can often get IVA reimbursed on many purchases, though this is practical only for bigger transactions (over $100) and subject to all kinds of limits and complications. Shops in the more touristy areas will volunteer information and provide the necessary forms, but finding the right place to go to have the final paperwork completed, signed and stamped and to get your money back, at your point of exit (international airports), is a much taller order; ask for instructions when you check in, as you must display your purchases before check-in and then go through the often frustratingly slow formalities once you've been given your boarding pass.

ATMs and credit and debit cards

ATMs (*cajeros automáticos*) are plentiful in Argentina. It's rare that you'll find a town or even a village without one, though you can sometimes be caught out in very remote places, especially in the Northwest, so never rely completely on them. Most machines take all credit cards or display those that can be used: you can nearly always get money out with Visa or Master-Card, or with any cards linked to the Plus or Cirrus systems. Most ATMs are either Banelco or LINK – test the networks to see which works best with your card. Machines are mostly multilingual though some of them use Spanish only, so you might need to have a phrase book or a Spanish-speaker handy.

Credit cards (*tarjetas de crédito*) are a very handy source of funds, and can be used either in the abundant ATMs (note that this can be expensive) or for purchases. Visa and MasterCard are the most widely used and recognized, with American Express and Diners Club less likely to be accepted. Be warned that you might have to show your ID when making a purchase with plastic, and, especially in small establishments in remote areas, the authorization process can take ages and

may not succeed at all. Using your **debit card**, which is not liable to interest payments like credit cards, is usually the best method to get cash and the flat transaction fee is generally quite small – your bank will be able to advise on this. Make sure you have a card and PIN that are designed to work overseas.

Opening hours

Most **shops and services** are open Monday to Friday 9am to 7pm, and Saturday 9am to 2pm. Outside the capital, they may close at some point during the afternoon for between one and five hours. As a rule, the further north you go, the longer the siesta – often offset by later closing times in the evening. Supermarkets seldom close during the day and are generally open much later, often until 8 or even 10pm, and on Saturday afternoons. Large shopping malls don't close before 10pm and their food and drink sections (*patios de comida*) may stay open as late as midnight. Many of them open on Sundays too. *Casas de cambio* more or less follow shop hours. However, **banks** tend to open only on weekdays: opening times depend on the region. In hotter regions, banks open as early as 7am or 8am, but close by noon or 1pm; whereas in many other areas, including Buenos Aires, they're open from 10am to 3 or 4pm.

The opening hours of **attractions** are indicated in the text; however, bear in mind that these often change from one season to another. If you are going out of your way to visit something, it is best to check if its opening times have changed. **Museums** are a law unto themselves, each one having its own timetable, but all commonly close one day a week, usually Monday. Several Buenos Aires museums are also closed for at least a month in January and February. **Tourist offices** are forever adjusting their opening times, but the trend is towards longer hours and opening daily. **Post offices'** hours vary; most should be open between 9am and 6pm on weekdays, with siestas in the hottest places, and 9am to 1pm on Saturdays. Outside these hours, many *locutorios* will deal with mail.

Public holidays

On the most important national **public holidays**, such as Christmas Day, just about everything closes. On the other holidays you will find lots of places stay open. Bear in mind that some of these holidays (marked with an *) move to the nearest Monday, and that there are several local public holidays, specific to a city or province, throughout the year, and ones specific to certain communities and non-Christian faiths. Many offices close for the whole of Semana Santa (Holy Week), the week leading up to Easter, while the Thursday is optional, as is New Year's Eve. Oddly, Easter Monday is not a holiday.

January 1	New Year's Day
Good Friday	Friday before Easter
March 24	Truth and Justice Day, in commemoration of the 1976 coup
April 2	Malvinas Veterans' Day
May 1	Labour Day
May 25	Day of the Revolution
June 20*	Day of the Flag (anniversary of General Belgrano's death)
July 9	Independence Day
August 17*	Liberator San Martín Day
October 12*	Day of Race (Columbus Day)
December 8	Immaculate Conception
December 25	Christmas Day

Phones

Argentina operates a GSM 850/1900 **mobile phone** network, in common with much of Latin America. Most modern mobile phones are tri- or quad-band so should work fine, but if yours is older you should check with your phone provider to confirm it will work. Local mobile numbers are prefixed by the area code, like fixed lines, and then 15. If you are dialling an Argentine mobile number from abroad, omit the 15 and dial 9 before the area code. If you're likely to use your phone a lot, it may be worth getting an **Argentine SIM card** to keep costs down. These can be obtained before you travel from various providers, or, cheaper still – though you'll need some Spanish here – is to get a pre-paid SIM (*chip*) from a local operator such as Movistar (🌐 www.movistar .com.ar) or Personal (🌐 www.personal .com.ar). Movistar is preferable as it will activate your service straight away, whereas you may have to wait a day or two with other providers. They have a large customer service centre in Buenos Aires at Santa Fe 1844 (Mon–Fri 9am–6pm).

In many ways it's just as cheap and straight-forward to make calls from the public call centres known as **locutorios**. Although they are not as ubiquitous as they once were, they are still widely found throughout the country. You'll be assigned a cabin with a meter, with which you can monitor your expenditure. Make as many calls as you want and then pay at the counter. You can get significant discounts on international calls with pre-paid phonecards, available at the *locutorios*.

Photography

Digital memory cards are widely available, although generally more expensive than in places like the US and Europe, especially in the more remote locations and for the larger-memory cards. Most mid-size towns have places where you can burn photos onto DVDs or CDs. Standard photographic **film** is also still available, but you're advised to bring specialist films (eg. slide film, black-and-white, low-light ASA ratings) from home. The same goes for all camera spares and supplies. **Developing** and printing are usually of decent quality but are also quite expensive and outside Buenos Aires the situation is erratic. A constant, however, is that you should watch out where you take photos: sensitive border areas and all military installations, including many civilian airports, are camera **no-go areas**, so watch out for signs and take no risks.

Calling home from abroad

Note that the initial zero is omitted from the area code when dialling the UK, Ireland, Australia and New Zealand from abroad.

Australia international access code + 61
New Zealand international access code + 64
UK international access code + 44
US and Canada international access code + 1
Ireland international access code + 353
South Africa international access code + 27

Time

Argentina hasn't – it seems – settled on a stable pattern of **time zones. Officially**, there's supposed to be a unified national time zone (3 hours behind GMT), but in reality – and according to changing local policies – some provinces operate separate systems. Some parts of the country, mainly in the east, have recently adopted a mid-Oct to mid-March daylight saving time (2 hours behind GMT). Other parts of the country (eg San Luís) are four hours behind GMT from mid-March to mid-Oct. For the latest information you're best off checking on ⓦen .wikipedia.org/wiki/Time_in_Argentina and the official government site at ⓦwww.hidro .gov.ar.

Tourist information

The main **national tourist board** (ⓦwww .turismo.gov.ar) is in Buenos Aires (see p.80) and is a fairly useful stop for maps and general information. Piles of leaflets, glossy brochures and maps are dished out at provincial and municipal **tourist offices** (*oficinas de turismo*) across the country, which vary enormously in quality of service and quantity of information. Don't rely on staff speaking any language other than Spanish, or on the printed info being translated into foreign languages. In addition, every province maintains a **casa de provincia** (provincial tourist office) in Buenos Aires.

Casas de provincias in Buenos Aires

Buenos Aires Av Callao 237 (Mon–Fri 9am–5pm; ☎011/4371-3587 or 7045).
Catamarca Av Córdoba 2080 (Mon–Fri 8am–6pm; ☎011/4374-6891 ext 30).

Córdoba Av Callao 332 (Mon–Fri 8am–6pm; ☎011/4372-8859).
Corrientes San Martín 333, 4th floor (Mon–Fri 8am–2pm; ☎011/4394-7418).
Chaco Av Callao 328 (Mon–Fri 9am–3pm; ☎011/4372-0961 ext 1029).
Chubut Sarmiento 1172 (Mon–Fri 10am–5.30pm; ☎011/4383-7458).
Entre Ríos Suipacha 844 (Mon–Fri 9am–5pm; ☎011/4326-2573).
Formosa H. Yrigoyen 1429 (Mon–Fri 9am–3pm; ☎011/4381-2037).
Jujuy Av Santa Fe 967 (Mon–Fri 10am–7pm; ☎011/4393-6096).
La Pampa Suipacha 346 (Jan & Feb Mon–Fri 9am–3pm; rest of year same days 8am–6pm; ☎011/4326-0511).
La Rioja Callao 745 (Mon–Fri 9am–6pm; ☎011/4813-3417).
Mendoza Av Callao 445 (Mon–Fri 9am–5pm; ☎011/4371-0835).
Misiones Santa Fe 989 (Mon–Fri 9am–6pm; ☎011/4317-3722).
Neuquén Maipú 48 (Mon–Fri 9.30am–4pm; ☎011/4343-2324).
Río Negro Tucumán 1916 (Mon–Fri 10am–4pm; ☎011/4371-7273).
Salta Av Pte Roque S. Peña 933 (Mon–Fri 10am–6pm; ☎011/4326-2456).
San Juan Sarmiento 1251 (Mon–Fri 9am–5pm; ☎011/4382-9241).
San Luis Azcuénaga 1087 (Mon–Fri 9am–6pm; ☎011/5778-1665).
Santa Cruz Suipacha 927 (Mon–Fri 10am–5pm; ☎011/4313-4880).
Santa Fe 25 de Mayo 178 (Mon–Fri 9.30am–6pm; ☎011/4342-0408).
Santiago del Estero Florida 274 (Mon–Fri 10am–6pm; ☎011/4326-7739).
Tierra del Fuego Esmeralda 783 (Mon–Fri 9am–5pm; ☎011/4328-7040 ext 108).
Tucumán Suipacha 140 (Mon–Fri 9am–5pm; ☎011/4322-0010 ext 124).

Useful websites

Argentina – LANIC ⓦ lanic.utexas.edu/la
/argentina. The most complete resource of links to
every imaginable aspect of life in Argentina, invaluable
both to travellers and researchers.
Argentina Parques Nacionales ⓦ www
.parquesnacionales.gov.ar. Spanish-only site for the
country's national park system, with information and
news on all the parks.
Ciudad de Buenos Aires ⓦ www.bue.gov.ar.
The official city site, with listings for bars, clubs,
restaurants, shops, theatres, all searchable by
genre and area. A good section on tours, including
suggested circuits designed around famous
literary, cultural and historical figures linked to
the capital.
Directorio de Museos Argentinas ⓦ www
.museosargentinos.org.ar. Useful searchable
database of most of the country's museums, including
practicalities.
Literatura Argentina Contemporánea ⓦ www
.literatura.org. Site dedicated to Argentine writers,
with a biography and bibliography for all the major
authors, plus extracts of their work. Mostly Spanish,
but with some English links.
Planeta Argentina ⓦ www.planeta.com
/argentina.html. Articles and advice relating to
ecotourism in Argentina.
El Portal del Tango ⓦ www.elportaldeltango.com.
Lots of background on the national dance.
South American Explorers ⓦ www.saexplorers
.org. Useful site set up by the experienced nonprofit
organization South American Explorers aimed at
scientists, explorers and travellers to South America.
Includes travel-related news, descriptions of individual
trips, a bulletin board and links to other websites, and
information about their clubhouse in central Buenos
Aires.
Travel Blog ⓦ www.travelblog.org/South-America
/Argentina/ and **Travel Pod** ⓦ www.travelpod.com
/travel-blog-country/Argentina/tpod.html. Two good
travel sites with forums, photos, hotel options etc.

Travellers with disabilities

Argentina does not have a particularly
sophisticated infrastructure for travellers
with disabilities, but most Argentines are
extremely willing to help anyone
experiencing problems and this helpful
attitude goes some way to making up for
deficiencies in facilities. There are also a
couple of organizations based in the capital
that can help you once you arrive, and

several that can help you plan your trip
before you leave home.

Things are beginning to improve, and it is
in Buenos Aires that you will find the most
notable changes: a recent welcome innovation has been the introduction of wheelchair
ramps on the city's pavements – though
unfortunately the pavements are not great.
Public transport is less problematic, with
many of the new buses that now circulate in
the city offering low-floor access. Laws
demand that all new hotels now provide at
least one room that is accessible for those
in wheelchairs, but the only sure-fire option
for those with severe mobility problems is at
the top end of the price range: many
five-star hotels have full wheelchair access,
including wide doorways and roll-in
showers. Those who have some mobility
problems, but do not require full wheelchair
access, will find most mid-range hotels are
adequate, offering spacious accommodation and lifts.

Outside Buenos Aires, finding facilities for
the disabled is pretty much a hit-and-miss
affair, although there have been some
notable improvements at major **tourist
attractions** such as the Iguazú Falls, where
new ramps and catwalks have been
constructed, making the vast majority of the
falls area accessible by wheelchair. The
hostel associations Red Argentina de
Albergues Juveniles and the Asociación
Argentina de Albergues de la Juventud, can
offer information on access at their respective hostel networks.

Useful contacts

In the US and Canada

Directions Unlimited 720 N. Bedford Rd, Bedford
Hills, NY 10507 ⓣ 914/241-1700. Travel agency
specializing in customized tours for people with
disabilities.
Mobility International USA PO Box 10767,
Eugene, OR 97440. Voice and TDD: ⓣ 541/343-
1284. Information and referral services, access
guides, tours and exchange programmes.
Twin Peaks Press Box 129, Vancouver, WA 98666
ⓣ 360/694-2462 or 1-800/637-2256. Publisher
of the Directory of Travel Agencies for the Disabled,
listing more than 370 agencies worldwide; Travel for
the Disabled; and Wheelchair Vagabond, loaded with
personal tips.

In the UK and Ireland

Disability Action Group 2 Annandale Ave, Belfast BT7 3JH ☎ 01232/491011. Information about access for disabled travellers abroad.

RADAR (Royal Association for Disability and Rehabilitation) 12 City Forum, 250 City Rd, London EC1V 8AF ☎ 020/7250 3222, minicom ☎ 020/7250 4119, ⊛ www.radar.org. Provides brief lists of accommodation in Argentina; also offers good general advice for travellers with disabilities.

In Australia and New Zealand

ACROD (Australian Council for Rehabilitation of the Disabled) PO Box 60, Curtin, ACT 2605 ☎ 02/6282-4333, and 24 Cabarita Rd, Cabarita, NSW 2137 ☎ 02/9743-2699. Provides lists of travel agencies and tour operators for people with disabilities.

Barrier Free Travel 36 Wheatley St, North Bellingen, NSW 2454 ☎ 02/6655-1733. Independent travel consultant, who will draw up individual itineraries catering for your particular needs.

Disabled Persons Assembly PO Box 10, 138 The Terrace, Wellington ☎ 04/472-2626. Provides lists of travel agencies and tour operators for people with disabilities.

Websites

⊛ **www.access-able.com** US-based site with scant information on Argentina but good general tips for travellers, plus a forum where travellers can exchange information. Also links to other organizations and specialist tour operators.

⊛ **www.sath.org** The homepage of the US-based Society for Accessible Travel and Hospitality has plenty of tips on specific issues such as wheelchair access, visual impairment and arthritis, though no specific information on Argentina.

Guide

Guide

Guide

Buenos Aires

CHAPTER 1   # Highlights

✱ **San Telmo** Of all the city's barrios, San Telmo is perhaps the most traditional – tango is the backdrop to antique stores and laidback cafés. See p.102

✱ **Bombonera** Whether playing host to the mighty national side or the Boca v River *superclásico*, the passion and the footwork on display at this soccer stadium is worth 90 minutes of anyone's time. See p.106

✱ **Recoleta Cemetery** Wander around one of the world's most exclusive cemeteries, where Evita's resting place is hidden away among ostentatious tombs and elaborate sculptures. See p.116

✱ **MALBA** The best of contemporary Latin American art showcased in cutting-edge architecture. See p.123

✱ **Palermo Viejo** Borges loved it, the glitterati flock to it and you can enjoy this district's tree-lined streets, fashionable boutiques and fantastic restaurants and guesthouses. See p.123

✱ **Tango** Listen to *bandoneón* players, choose between showcase extravaganzas or humble *milongas* – and maybe learn the basic steps. See p.140

▲ Boca Juniors versus River Plate at the Bombonera

Buenos Aires

Of all South America's capitals and major cities, **Buenos Aires** – aka Capital Federal, Baires, BsAs or simply **BA** – has by far the most going for it. Seductive and cultured, beguilingly eclectic and in constant flux, it never bores, seldom sleeps and invariably exerts a mesmerizing power over its visitors. Though clearly influenced by the great European capitals, it is a city that nonetheless has it own distinct personality, thanks partly to its deeply entrenched **traditions**, such as drinking tea-like *mate*, partly to its proud and hospitable, extravagant and attractive inhabitants – known as **Porteños** – and partly to its location. To the north and east of the city flows the caramel-hued **Río de la Plata** (River Plate), the world's widest river estuary, while to the south and west extends the verdant grassy plain of the **Pampas**, punctuated by sleepy towns, clumps of pampas grass (*cortaderas*) and the odd ombú tree, in whose broad shade the gauchos traditionally rested. Away from its extensive **harbour** facilities, stacked high with containers, and ever-busier cruise-ship docks, the city has tended to shun the river, while its outer suburbs seem to meld seamlessly into the Pampas beyond.

Buenos Aires also enjoys an incomparable **lifestyle**. Restaurants, bars, cafés and nightclubs to suit every taste and pocket, a world-class opera house, myriad theatres, cinemas and galleries and splendid French-style palaces underscore both its attachment to the arts and its sense of style. Another boon are its countless **parks and gardens** and the abundance of **trees** lining the streets – around one-fifth of which are still picturesquely cobbled – and providing shade in the many lively **plazas** that dot the huge conurbation; they add welcome splashes of colour, particularly when they blaze with yellow, pink and mauve blooms in spring and early summer. The squadrons of squawky parrots that populate them help visitors forget that this is the world's twelfth-largest city: there are nearly fourteen million inhabitants in the Greater Buenos Aires (**Gran Buenos Aires**) area, which spills beyond the **Ciudad Autónoma**'s defining boundary of multi-lane ring roads into Buenos Aires Province.

Indeed, on the map and from the air, the metropolis looks dauntingly huge, stretching over 40km from north to south and more than 30km from west to east. Yet BA's compact centre and the relative proximity of all the main sights mean that you don't have to travel that much to gain a sense of knowing the city. Of the city's 47 **barrios** (neighbourhoods) you will most probably be visiting only the half-dozen most central. The **city centre** – comprising the tiny, historic neighbourhoods of San Nicolás and Monserrat – is a hectic place, particularly during the week, but from the bustle of pedestrianized Calle Florida, to the *fin-de-siècle* elegance of **Avenida de Mayo** and the café culture of **Corrientes**, the area is surprisingly varied in both architecture and atmosphere. Providing a quiet counterpoint, the converted dock area of **Puerto Madero** runs alongside it to the east, beyond which is the unexpectedly wild **Reserva Ecológica**, one of the city's most unusual green spaces.

The **south** of the city, containing its oldest parts, begins just beyond Plaza de Mayo. Its narrow, often cobbled streets are lined with some of the capital's finest architecture, typified by late nineteenth-century townhouses with ornate Italianate facades, sturdy but elegant wooden doors and finely wrought iron railings. Once seedy, but increasingly gentrified, **San Telmo** is primarily known for its avant-garde artists, its antiques fair and its tango haunts, while resolutely working-class **La Boca**, further south still, is so inextricably and fanatically linked with its football team, Boca Juniors – whose main rivals, River Plate, have their stadium in middle-class **Belgrano** – that many of its buildings are painted blue and yellow. The **north** of the city is the leafiest and wealthiest part of Buenos Aires. You may well opt to stay in one of the boutique hotels or guesthouses of **Retiro**, **Recoleta** and **Palermo**, head there to shop or dine, or just to wander the labyrinth cobbled streets so beloved of the great Argentine short story writer Jorge Luis Borges. The bulk of the city **museums** lie within their boundaries, too, with themes as varied as science and Spanish-American art, immigration and Eva Perón.

Buenos Aires lends itself perfectly to aimless wandering, and its mostly ordered grid pattern makes it fairly easy to orient yourself. The boundaries of the Capital Federal are marked by the **Río de la Plata** to the northeast and by its tributary, the **Riachuelo**, to the south, while **Avenida General Paz** forms a semicircular ring around the west of the city, connecting the two. Cutting right across the middle, **Avenida Rivadavia**, an immensely long street runs east–west for nearly two hundred blocks from Plaza de Mayo to Morón, outside the city limits. The other main east–west thoroughfares are avenidas Corrientes, Córdoba and Santa Fe, while north–south the major routes are Avenida L. N. Além – which changes its name to Avenida del Libertador as it swings out to the northern suburbs – Avenida Callao and **Avenida 9 de Julio** – a car-oriented conglomeration of four multi-lane roads.

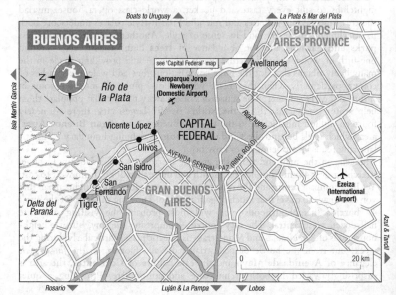

Some history

Buenos Aires was named in honour of **Nuestra Señora de Santa María del Buen Aire**, provider of the good wind, the patron saint of the Spanish sailors who first landed on the banks of the Río de la Plata estuary in 1516. The first successful settlement came in 1580 but, though the **Spanish found the** horses and cattle that they brought over from Europe thrived, the fertility of the land made little impression on them. They were more interested in precious metals, and named the settlement's river the **Plata** (silver) in the belief that it flowed from the lands of silver and gold in the Andes.

Expansion was slow, however, and Buenos Aires remained a distant outpost of the Spanish-American empire for the next two centuries, with **smuggling** being the mainstay of the local economy. In 1776, in an attempt to shore up its empire, Spain gave the Argentine territories **Viceroyalty status**, with Buenos Aires as the capital. It was too little, too late: boosted by the defeat of two attempted British invasions, the Viceroyalty declared **independence** in 1810, freeing the area from the last vestiges of colonial hindrance.

But it was the industrial revolution some half century later that gave the capital of the new republic the opportunity to exploit and export the great riches of the Pampas, thanks to technological advances such as railways and refrigeration – which enabled Europeans to dine on Argentine beef for the first time. Few cities in the world have experienced a period of such astonishing **growth** as that which spurred Buenos Aires between 1870 and 1914. Massive foreign investment – most notably from the British – poured into the city and Buenos Aires' stature leapt accordingly. European **immigrants**, over half of whom were Italians, flocked to the capital, and the city's population doubled between 1880 and 1890. Most of the old town was razed and an eclectic range of new buildings went up in a huge grid pattern. The standard of living of Buenos Aires' middle class equalled or surpassed that of many European countries, while the incredible wealth of the city's elite was almost without parallel anywhere. At the same time, however, much of the large working-class community endured appalling conditions in the city's overcrowded *conventillos*, or tenement buildings.

But by the mid-twentieth century the period of breakneck development had come to a close as the country slid into a long period of political turmoil and economic **crisis**. In September 1945, Buenos Aires saw the first of what was to become a regular fixture – a massive **demonstration** that filled the city centre. Rallies of almost religious fervour in support of Perón and his wife **Evita**, who came out onto the balcony of the Casa Rosada to deliver their speeches, followed at regular intervals until Evita's death and Perón's deposition.

In the last thirty years, Buenos Aires has been the most visible face of the country's economic rollercoaster. The temporary stabilization of the currency in the 1990s brought a new upsurge in spending by those who could afford it – and an infrastructure to match. Smart new shopping malls, restaurants and cinema complexes sprung up around the city. But Buenos Aires entered the twenty-first century in retreat, as a grinding **recession** led to weeks of protests and looting that came to a horrendous head in December 2001, when widespread rioting led to dozen of deaths. Demonstrations and roadblocks by unemployed *piqueteros* became part of the fabric of everyday life in the city during the messy recovery that followed, with the sad sight of *cartoneros* rooting through rubbish the most obvious example of the economic problems, and growing crime an inevitable offshoot of this rise in poverty.

However, with the country celebrating its **bicentennial** in 2010 – and despite some backwash from the global financial crisis – Buenos Aires is looking in good shape. Long overdue repairs have been carried out, welfare plans have reduced (though not eradicated) the worst poverty, and **international tourism** has been an engine of recovery, leading to dozens of new gourmet restaurants and boutique hotels. Problems remain – traffic, crime, shantytowns and the still frequent roadblocks – but, from the perspective of its 200th birthday, Buenos Aires has cause to look forward with cautious confidence at the next hundred years.

Arrival

Buenos Aires is well served by numerous international and domestic **flights**. It is also a transport hub for the rest of the country, with frequent daily **bus** services to and from most towns and cities. Limited **train** services join the capital to the provinces, while **ferries** arrive from neighbouring Uruguay.

By air

All **international flights**, with the exception of a few from neighbouring countries, arrive 22km southwest of the city centre at Ministro Pistarini Airport or – as it is actually referred to by everyone – **Ezeiza**, in reference to the outlying

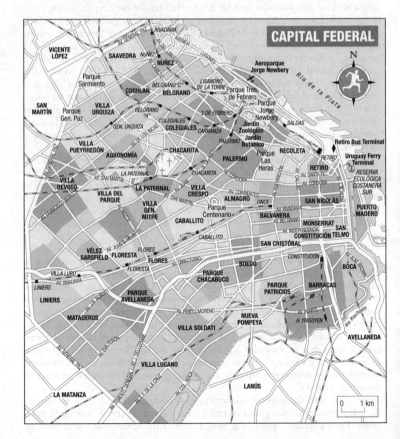

neighbourhood in which it is situated. In comparison with some Latin American airports, arriving at Ezeiza is relatively stress-free: touting for taxis is banned inside the airport and the tourist information stand (daily 8am–8pm) has good information on accommodation in the city. Ignore the privately run exchange booths strategically placed before you exit arrivals – **change money** instead at the small branch of Banco Nación in the airport arrivals hall, where you may face longer lines at busy times but will get a much better rate. ATMs are also available.

If you want to take a **taxi** into the city ($100 and up), ask at one of the official taxi stands immediately outside the arrivals exit. Unofficial taxi drivers congregate outside the terminal and, while these offer cheaper rates, they are less secure and scams of various descriptions have been reported. Alternatively, **express buses** are operated by Manuel Tienda León (℡011/4314-3636, Ⓦwww.tiendaleon.com.ar). Running nonstop between Ezeiza and the centre every thirty minutes during the day and hourly at night, these cost $40 and take approximately forty minutes, making them fair value for solo travellers. They drop you at the company's main terminal at San Martín and Madero; for an extra $5 you can get a transfer from there to anywhere downtown or in Barrio Norte. If you are transferring to a domestic flight (for some destinations these also leave from Ezeiza; check first), you could get a Manuel Tienda León bus ($45; 9am–midnight) to the Aeroparque Metropolitano Jorge Newbery. If you are staying in a part of the city near the domestic airport, such as Palermo or Belgrano, you might consider using this service and taking a taxi for the final stretch, though be aware that queues for taxis at Aeroparque can be long at busy arrival times. Finally, there's the **local bus** #86 ($1.75), which runs between Ezeiza and Boca, entering the city via Rivadavia and continuing past Congreso, Plaza de Mayo and San Telmo; it takes about two hours, and leaves just beyond the entrance to the airport. Make sure you have change for the ticket machines, as notes are not accepted, and be warned that it can become very full.

Buenos Aires' other airport is **Aeroparque Metropolitano Jorge Newbery**, usually known as Aeroparque, on the Costanera Norte, around six kilometres north of the city centre. Most **domestic flights** and some flights from Brazil and Uruguay arrive here. Manuel Tienda Léon also runs a bus service from here to the centre ($15; 9am–midnight); a taxi will set you back about $25 (again, it's better to go with an official, booked car rather than take one from the rank outside), or you could catch the local bus ($1.20; the #33 will take you to Paseo Colón). Aeroparque also has a tourist information booth (daily 8am–8pm).

By bus

If you are travelling to Buenos Aires by **bus** from other points in Argentina, or on international services from neighbouring countries, you will arrive at Buenos Aires' huge long-distance bus terminal (℡011/4310-0700, Ⓦwww.tebasa .com.ar), known as **Retiro**, located in the barrio of that name at the corner of Avenida Antártida and Ramos Mejía. There are good facilities at the terminal, including toilets, shops, cafés and left luggage. Retiro is very centrally placed and nobody with a reasonable amount of energy will find it too strenuous to walk to hotels in the Florida/Retiro area of the city (although at night this is not recommended – there is a shantytown close by and robberies are fairly common). Taxis are plentiful and the Retiro subte station is just a block away, outside the adjoining train station (see p.80 & p.111). There are also plenty of local buses leaving from stands along Ramos Mejía, though actually finding the one you want might be a rather daunting first taste of local bus transport. Buses #5 or #50 will take you to Congreso and the upper end of Avenida de Mayo, a promising hunting ground for accommodation if you haven't booked ahead.

If you are **departing** from Retiro, you can call the general number for information – it takes you to a recorded message that will ask for your province and destination and provide you with the numbers of the appropriate companies (Spanish only). The website will also let you check companies, destinations and timetables. You can then call the individual companies to check times and, in most cases, make a reservation. Alternatively, visit the terminal itself, where the 150 or so companies all have ticket booths and there is a useful information booth.

By train

Few tourists arrive in Buenos Aires by **train** these days; although plans are afoot to reinstate long-distance services (possibly with high-speed connections), currently most trains are suburban only. The main exceptions are trains from the Atlantic coast, Tandil and Carmen de Patagones, which arrive at **Constitución**, in the south of the city at General Hornos 11 (Ferrobaires ✆011/4304-0028, ⓦwww.ferrobaires.gba.gov.ar); and trains from Rosario, which arrive at **Retiro** on Avenida Ramos Mejía (TBA ✆0800/3333-822, ⓦwww.tbanet.com.ar). Both terminals have subte stations and are served by numerous local bus routes.

By boat

Cruise ships aside, it is still possible to arrive in Buenos Aires by **boat**. Ferries and faster catamarans (✆011/4316-6500, ⓦwww.buquebus.com or ✆011/4317-4100, ⓦwww.coloniaexpress.com.ar) cross the Río de la Plata estuary from Uruguay, both from the capital Montevideo and the historic town of Colonia. Boats arrive at a gleaming new **terminal** at Dársena Norte at the bottom of Avenida Córdoba. Although within walking distance of downtown, the route involves jay-walking across a rather bewildering skein of busy roads and overgrown rail-tracks, so it is advisable to take a taxi from the rank outside. The terminal is not connected to the public transport system.

Information and tours

For **information**, head to one of the city's numerous tourist kiosks; the staff do not generally have much specialist knowledge but they can usually provide maps and a few leaflets. The most central kiosk is just off the Plaza de Mayo at Avenida Diagonal Roque Sáenz Peña and Florida (Mon–Fri 10am–6pm, Sat 10am–4pm). There are other kiosks at the Retiro bus terminal, at Calle 10 local 83 (Mon–Sat 7.30am–1pm); in Recoleta, on avenidas Quintana and Ortíz, near the cemetery (daily 10am–6pm); in Puerto Madero, by dock 4, also offering information on Montevideo (daily 10am–7pm); and in San Telmo at Defensa 1250 (Sat & Sun 10am–6pm only). There's also a general telephone line (✆011/4313-0187; daily 7.30am–7pm; English spoken) and a comprehensive **website** with ideas of where to go and what to do (ⓦwww.bue.gov.ar).

The city government runs daily **bus tours with audio** in a variety of languages, including English, beginning in Roque Sáenz Peña and Suipacha (9am–5.30pm, every 30 mins; tickets must be bought from the tourist info kiosk on Roque Sáenz Peña and Florida) and stopping at various points of interest, such as Monserrat, Boca, the Reserva Ecológica and the Rosedal in Palermo. It costs $25 per day and you can get on and off as many times as you like, so if you're planning to cover a lot of ground in a day it represents good value compared to taxis. The tourism secretariat also organizes free walking tours, in English and Spanish, usually around a given barrio, but sometimes with themes such as Evita or Carlos Gardel – ask for the current schedule.

An excellent source of **English-language information** is the ever-reliable South American Explorers, which has its clubhouse at Chile 557, San Telmo (Mon–Fri 9.30am–5pm, Sat 9.30am–1pm; Ⓦwww.saexplorers.org). Membership of US$60 a year gets you access to this and all their other clubhouses, where you can store gear, use their computers, consult trip reports, chat with their knowledgeable staff, borrow books, find out about local volunteer opportunities, obtain discounts on hostels and other services and generally chill out. The clubhouse also holds events such as movie showings, Spanish classes and wine tastings, and produces a newsletter – sign up at the website.

If you are planning to stay in the city a while and make use of the public transport, a combined **street map and bus atlas** such as *Guía Lumi* or *Guía "T"* is a useful accessory. Both are widely available from central kiosks and occasionally at knockdown prices, from hawkers on the buses or trains.

City transport

Buenos Aires may seem like a daunting city to get around, but it's actually served by an extensive, inexpensive and generally efficient **public transport** service – albeit not the world's cleanest, quietest or most modern. The easiest part of this system to come to grips with is undoubtedly the underground rail system, or **subte**, which serves most of the city centre and the north of the city. You may also want to familiarize yourself with a few bus routes, as **buses** are the only form of public transport that serve the outlying barrios and the south of the city. That said, with **taxis** being plentiful and relatively cheap, you'll likely find them the most convenient means to get you where you want to go.

The subte

Buenos Aires' underground rail system, or **subte** (short for *subterráneo*) was inaugurated in 1913, making it the oldest in the Spanish-speaking world. It's a reasonably efficient system – you shouldn't have to wait more than a few minutes during peak periods – and certainly the quickest way to get from the centre to outlying points such as Caballito, Plaza Italia (Palermo) or Chacarita. Many of the stations are beautifully decorated with tile murals, depicting anything from famous battles to Gaudí masterpieces, but they are also often dirty and very hot in the summer. The main flaw in the subte's design is that it's shaped like a fork, meaning that journeys across town involve going down one "prong" and changing at least once before heading back up to your final destination. However, the network is being gradually extended, with work underway on new north–south lines as well as extensions to the existing lines.

Using the subte is a fairly straightforward business. There are **six lines**, plus a "premetro" system which serves the far southwestern corner of the city, linking up with the subte at the end of line E. Lines A, B, D and E run from the city centre outwards, while line C, which runs north–south between Retiro and Constitución, connects them all. Line H is a new north–south line running south from Once. Check the name of the last station on the line you are travelling on in order to make sure you're heading in the right direction; directions to station platforms are given by this final destination. Tickets can be purchased from the *boleterías* (ticket booths) at each station. A single trip (*viaje*) ticket ($1.10) will take you anywhere on the system. The ticket booths usually have good, free maps of the system, available on request.

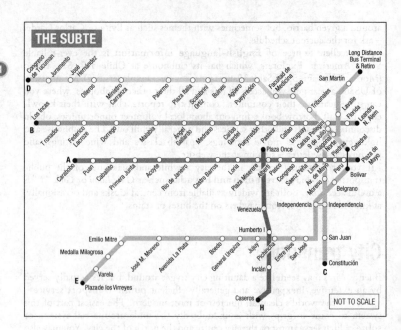

Even if you use the subte only once during your stay in Buenos Aires, you really shouldn't miss the chance to travel on **Line A**, which runs between Plaza de Mayo and the residential neighbourhood of Flores. It's the only line to preserve the network's original carriages, and travelling in one of the rickety and elegantly lit wood-framed interiors is like being propelled along in an antique wardrobe.

Buses

Peak hours aside, when traffic is increasingly gridlocked, Buenos Aires' **buses** (*colectivos*) are a useful way of getting to many of the outlying barrios for those on a limited budget. Unfortunately, they are also noisy, prone to belching out clouds of exhaust and are driven with scant regard for traffic laws – standing, or even sitting, can be an ordeal, and is certainly an experience. From a visitor's point of view, possibly the most daunting thing about them is the sheer number of routes – almost two hundred wend their way around the vast capital. Invest in a combined street and bus-route map (see p.81), however, and you shouldn't have too much trouble. Trips within the city cost $1.20; once beyond the centre and into Gran Buenos Aires, fares increase slightly. Tickets are acquired on board from a machine, which gives change for coins, though not for notes. Do not expect the driver to be helpful if you're not sure where you're going, or to wait for you to take your seat before accelerating away.

Despite accidents involving buses, the system is a generally safe way of getting around the city – though, as always, keep your eyes on your belongings, especially when buses are crowded.

Taxis and remises

The sheer volume of black and yellow **taxis** touting their business on Buenos Aires' streets is one of the city's most characteristic sights and – other than during sudden downpours or in the outer barrios – it's rare that it takes more than a few minutes, or even seconds, to flag down a cab. The meter starts at $3.80 and clocks up 38 centavos every couple of blocks, making it an affordable way of getting around the central neighbourhoods, though it starts to add up if your journey takes you across several barrios. Note also that, thanks to Argentina's rampant inflation, the price goes up every few months. Taxi rides are sometimes white-knuckle affairs – drivers range from amiable characters who drive carefully and like to chat to maniacs who seem to want to involve you and others on the streets in some road-borne suicide pact. Regardless of road skills, drivers are generally trustworthy, despite occasional reports of their using accomplices to rob passengers. **Radio taxis** are regarded as more secure and better quality than the unaffiliated type – they are distinguished by the company name on the side and can be hailed in the street or ordered by telephone. Premium (℡011/4374-6666, ⓦwww.taxipremium.com) has good-quality cars, all with air conditioning, at the same price as other taxis.

Remises are plain cars that can be booked through an office. They're cheaper and usually more comfortable than taxis for getting to the airport (and they tend to have larger boots). Remise companies include Reminor (℡011/4639-1101) and Tres Sargentos (℡011/4311-4832).

Driving

Make no mistake, **driving** in Buenos Aires demands nerves of steel: traffic hurtles around like in a Formula One race, with high-speed weaving common and even split-second hesitation punished by a fusillade of honking. The good news is that the city is simple to navigate once you've got the hang of the street system. With a few exceptions – notably avenidas 9 de Julio and Del Libertador – the streets are one way, with the direction (which mostly alternates street by street) marked on the street signs with an arrow. Some streets within the centre, mostly around the financial district, are closed to private traffic during the day.

The local technique for crossing the city's numerous traffic-light-less intersections at night is to slow down and flash your lights to warn drivers of your approach. In theory the vehicle coming from the right has the right of way, at all times, but be prepared to give way if the other driver looks more determined and never take it for granted that a speeding bus will respect your trajectory: accidents involving buses regularly make the headlines. Parking in the street, wherever the curb is not painted yellow, is allowed. However, car theft has risen sharply in recent years and you may prefer the relative security of an *estacionamiento* (car park) – look out for the large "E" signs.

A number of both international and national **car rental** companies (see "Listings", p.149) operate in Buenos Aires. Be prepared to book some time ahead if you're planning to rent a car over a long weekend or holiday period. Given the comprehensive public transport system and the abundance of taxis, however, there's really little point in renting a car simply to tour the city.

Accommodation

Buenos Aires' popularity with international visitors means that many of the city's best **accommodation** – at all levels – is frequently full. With around half of all the country's hotels in the capital, you will always be able find somewhere to stay, but if you are fussy about where you lay your head, you are advised to reserve in advance. At the budget end, there are dozens of **hostels**, mostly cheerful, well-run places in converted nineteenth-century mansions. If you baulk at dormitory living, consider a private room at a hostel or a costlier but homely **B&B,** which tend to be a better deal than the city-centre budget and mid-market **hotels**, many of which can be rather grim. The city has also seen a surge in upmarket **boutique hotels**, altogether more pleasant (though naturally more expensive) places to stay, catering principally to international visitors and scattered throughout the central neighbourhoods. Wherever you spend the night, a fan or air conditioning is really a requirement in summer, and heating a big plus in winter. **Discounts** can sometimes be negotiated, particularly if you are staying for more than a few days, but note that credit cards may entail a surcharge. **Breakfast** is not always included at the budget hotels, but in any case you'll probably get a better start to the day in a nearby *confitería*.

For advice on long-term accommodation, see "Living in Argentina", p.63.

The city centre

The biggest concentration of accommodation is to be found in the **city centre**, mostly hostels and budget to mid-range hotels on and around Avenida de Mayo and Congreso, plus a sprinkling of top-range places in the streets surrounding busy but pedestrianized Florida. It is not a laidback area in which to stay, and in many of the more traditional hotels you face a choice of internal windowless rooms, or front rooms where it can be hard to escape the noise of the city-centre traffic. However, there are plenty of exceptions, and the area has excellent transport links and is handy for its abundance of shopping and banks.

All the following places are marked on the Central Buenos Aires map.

725 Buenos Aires Roque Sáenz Peña 725 ⊕011/4131-8000, ⓦwww.hotel725buenosaires .com. A swish bar, trendy restaurant, spa and swimming pool are just some of the attractions at this fabulous hotel, in an equally remarkable 1920s building; the decor combines dark wood with vibrant colour schemes, with gorgeous results. ⑨

Castelar Av de Mayo 1152 ⊕011/4383-5000, ⓦwww.castelarhotel.com.ar. A Buenos Aires institution, this pleasant, old-fashioned hotel, where Spanish poet Federico García Lorca stayed when he was in town, offers attractive and soundproof, if slightly over-priced, rooms with big comfortable beds. There's also a glamorous bar downstairs and a sauna/spa. ❼

Chile Av de Mayo 1297 ⊕011/4383-7877. Well-known Art Deco hotel; some rooms have balconies overlooking a side street and others have great views of Av de Mayo. All are spacious, with central heating, a/c and TV. ❸

Esplendor San Martín 780 ⊕011/5256-8800, ⓦwww.esplendorbuenosaires.com. In this boutique hotel 52 rooms, including very spacious suites, are arranged around a luminous atrium, on a corner of the beautiful late-nineteenth-century building mostly occupied by *Galerías Pacífico* (see p.97). Avant-garde works adorn the immaculate walls and each room has its own luxurious decor. ⑨

Gran Hotel España Tacuarí 80 ⊕011/4343-5541. Good budget option in central yet quiet location,

with clean, basic rooms, helpful staff and a lovely antique, manually operated elevator. It's worth paying a few pesos more for the front rooms with little balconies. ❸

Hotel de los Dos Congresos Rivadavia 1777 ⊕011/4371-0072, ⓦwww.hoteldoscongresos .com. Well-maintained hotel in a late-nineteenth-century building. The best rooms at the front overlook the Congreso building and have a spiral staircase and mezzanine within them. All are decorated in a clean, modern style with a/c, TV and mini-bar, although the interior rooms can be on the stuffy side. ❹

Ibis Buenos Aires Hipólito Yrigoyen 1592 ⊕011/5300-5555, ⓦwww.ibishotel.com. Part of the Accor chain, the *Ibis* is a good-value hotel, offering clean, simple comfort and a friendly welcome in the city centre, near the Congreso building. ❺

Jousten Av Corrientes 280 ⊕011/4321-6750, ⓦwww.nh-hoteles.com. High-end accommodation in a beautiful early twentieth-century building popular with business travellers but with appeal for all; also has an excellent restaurant serving modern Spanish cuisine. One of several central hotels ran by the Spanish NH designer hotel chain. ❼

Milhouse Hipólito Yrigoyen 959 ⊕011/4345-9604, ⓦwww.milhousehostel.com. Large, popular hostel, part of the HI chain, in a three-storey nineteenth-century house a block from Av de Mayo. The hostel arranges daily entertainment, both in-house events such as tango lessons and trips to football matches and nightclubs, and has expanded to a second locale at Av de Mayo 1245. Dorms US$11, attractive doubles with private bath. ❹

O'Rei Lavalle 733 ☏011/4393-7186 ⓦwww .hotelorei.com.ar. The high-ceilinged rooms are a bit gloomy and basic, but the O'Rei has two things really going for it – it's very central, and very cheap. ❸

Sportsman Rivadavia 1425 ☏011/4381-8021, ⓦwww.hotelsportsman.com.ar. Popular budget hotel in a rambling old building with lots of character, though the interior is beginning to show its age. There's a range of rooms available, all with fans and some with shared bathrooms; the nicest ones are the en-suite doubles at the front, which have balconies. US$8 for a dorm, ❸ for a double with private bath.

V&S Youth Hostel Viamonte 887 ☏011/4322-0994, ⓦwww.hostelclub.com. The most luxurious hostel in Buenos Aires, the V&S is centrally located in a 1910 French-style mansion. A bar and giant TV top the list of amenities, as well all kinds of interesting organized excursions to keep you occupied. In addition to dormitory accommodation (US$12 per person) there are three great-value double rooms (❺) with private bathrooms and balconies.

San Telmo, Monserrat, Puerto Madero and Constitución

Most accommodation in the south is in the barrio of **San Telmo**, a magnet for travellers as much for its cobbled streets and prettily crumbling buildings as for its budget hotels and youth hostels. **Puerto Madero** has a handful of upmarket places to stay, while the area around **Constitución** station has some interesting accommodation options, as well as plenty of less salubrious budget joints.

Axel Venezuela 649, Monserrat. ☏011/4136-9393, ⓦwww.axelhotels.com; see Central Buenos Aires map. The first gay hotel in Latin America, *Axel* is also hetero-friendly. It's all built and decorated in a markedly contemporary style – the grey and white bedrooms are minimalist and hi-tech, while the top-floor deck features a glass-bottom pool, a sauna, a hammam and jacuzzis. There's another outdoor pool with a deck-bar, and a restaurant open to the public. Book well in advance. ❽

Boquitas Pintadas Estados Unidos 1393, Constitución ☏011/4381-6064, ⓦwww .boquitas-pintadas.com.ar; see Central Buenos Aires map. An ordinary-looking building in a rather run-down neighbourhood is the surprising home to a small offbeat hotel, where each of the five rooms is decorated differently (and comes at a different price), with an artist's touch. All guests have use of the flower-filled sun terrace, and there's a bar downstairs that hosts DJ nights and art happenings. ❹–❼

La Cayetana México 1330, Monserrat ☏011/4383-2230, ⓦwww.lacayetanahotel .com.ar; see Central Buenos Aires map. Beautifully renovated nineteenth-century townhouse, with a huge sun-lit central patio and much of the original furniture worked harmoniously into the rooms, each of which is individually decorated. The only drawback is the location near Constitución – a good seven blocks away from anywhere of interest – but taxis are always available. Reservations essential; the hotel won't accept anyone who just turns up. ❼

Circus Hostel Chacabuco 1020, San Telmo ☏011/4878-7786, ⓦhostelcircus.com. Circus successfully bridges the gap between hostel and hotel, offering the ambience and friendliness of the former with the comforts of the latter – the beds have decent mattresses, each room has its own bathroom, and there is even a smart decked pool.The street has other hostels, so is a good place to try your luck if you haven't anything booked. Dorm bed US$14, ❹

Faena Hotel & Universe Marta Salotti 445, Puerto Madero Este ☏011/4010-9000, ⓦwww .faenahotelanduniverse.com; see Central Buenos Aires map. Buenos Aires' hotel for the in-crowd, this former grain-storage building has been given a serious Philippe Starck makeover and now has a *belle époque* jazz bar, a café stuffed with kitsch antiques, a floor-to-ceiling white restaurant with unicorn heads on the walls, an oriental spa and, of course, swish rooms. It's the kind of place that's too cool for a reception – you get an "experience manager" – and where the movie producers and celebrities that stay here certainly don't talk about anything as crude as money; count on US$400 and up for a room. ❾

Gran Hotel América Bernardo de Irigoyen 1608, San Telmo ☏011/4307-8785, ⓦwww .granhotelamerica.com.ar. A stone's throw from Constitución station, this reasonably priced hotel was where famous tango composer Angel Villoldo entertained his lady friends. Some of the rooms are a bit gloomy and noisy but the large, airy triples are a good deal. ❷

Moreno Moreno 376, Monserrat ☎ 011/6091-2000, ⓦ www.morenobuenosaires.com; see Central Buenos Aires map. The stunning Art Deco façade tells you this is something special – the forty sumptuous rooms inside range from large room to the jazuzzi loft. There is also a tango lounge and a wonderful deck terrace, offering amazing views. ❽

Retiro and Recoleta

These two barrios, jointly known as Barrio Norte, are where the city's top-flight luxury hotels tend to be located, although some cheaper options exist too. Recoleta is the perfect location, with plenty to offer *per se* – restaurants, bars and shops – but is still within walking distance (about 20min) of the microcentro, but with less hustle and bustle.

Alvear Palace Hotel Av Alvear 1891, Recoleta ☎ 011/4804-7777, ⓦ www.alvearpalace.com. Once the choice of wealthy landowners and now the favourite of politicians and royalty, the Alvear is still BA's luxury hotel par excellence, despite the trendy new upstarts. It offers fabulously decorated rooms in Louis XV style and all the extras you would expect, including a personal butler. Excellent restaurants, too. If you can't afford the US$400 price tag, you can still enjoy the (indoor) pool for $70 during the day. ❾

Ayacucho Palace Ayacucho 1408, Recoleta ☎ 011/4806-1815, ⓦ www.ayacuchohotel.com.ar. Housed in a smart French-style building, the rooms in this hotel are clean, comfortable and come with a/c in a good location near the centre of Recoleta. ❻

Four Seasons Posadas 1086, Retiro ☎ 011/4321-1200, ⓦ www.fourseasons.com/buenosaires. Part of the international chain, this fantastically luxurious hotel is divided between a modern block and the *belle époque* Alazaga Unzué mansion (see p.115), which looks like a French chateau inside and out. Sun brunch, open to the public, is served in the latter; rates around US$400. ❾

Guido Palace Guido 1780, Recoleta ☎ 011/4812-0341, ⓦ www.guidopalace.com.ar. Not exactly a palace, more a functional, typical mid-range hotel. Its big advantage is its location in the heart of Recoleta. ❺

Lion d'Or Hotel Pacheco de Melo 2019, Recoleta ☎ 011/4803-8992, ⓦ www.hotel-liondor.com.ar. Homely and friendly place, with a variety of appealing rooms mercifully free of the tasteless decor found in similar places nearby. Rooms vary considerably in size, style and price, ranging from an internal single with shared bath to a lovely, spacious triple with a fireplace and balcony. ❸–❼

Palacio Duhau-Park Hyatt Av Alvear 1661, Recoleta ☎ 011/5171-1234, ⓦ www.buenosaires.park.hyatt.com. The Duhau family home on the city's most desirable street (see p.115) is now a hyper-luxury hotel, with huge rooms decorated with soothing woods and marble baths; the top floor Duhau suite has a wrap-around terrace, among its many enticing features. The giant, superbly lit swimming pool, restaurant, vinoteca and *Oak Bar* mean you never need to leave the building. Rooms around US$480. ❾

Palermo

Away from the blasting horns and spluttering buses of the centre, **Palermo** is a greener, more relaxed neighbourhood in which to stay. There are some fabulous, if expensive, small hotels, extremely agreeable B&Bs and some fun hostels, all with the added benefit of being close to the city's most interesting bars, restaurants and boutiques. A taxi to the centre costs about $25 from here.

Casa Esmeralda Honduras 5765 ☎ 011/4772-2446, ⓦ www.casaesmeralda.com.ar. Wonderful Franco–Argentine-run guesthouse smack in the middle of Palermo Hollywood, with a green garden and friendly service. Shared rooms for $45, doubles ❸.

Costa Petit Hotel Costa Rica 5141 ☎ 011/4776-8296, ⓦ www.costapetithotel.com. An outdoor swimming pool sets this stunning Palermo Soho establishment apart from its rivals; the hotel can also arrange activities such as polo or shopping. Just four handsomely decorated rooms, all with a retro look but modern conveniences. ❾

Craft Nicaragua 4583 ☎ 011/4833-0060, ⓦ www.crafthotel.com. Overlooking the beautiful Plaza Armenia at the heart of Palemo Viejo, this trendy little hotel revels in its minimalistic decor, that includes functional shower cubicles divided from the bedroom by a curtain. The cheapest room, Song, includes a vinyl record player (choose from a collection at reception). The excellent self-service breakfast is served on the top floor, where a sunny roof-terrace includes four-poster beds. ❽

Home Honduras 5860 ☎011/4778-1008, ⓦwww .homebuenosaires.com. Owned and run by a British record producer and his Irish–Argentine wife, this masterpiece of modern architecture and hotel design is simply incredible: from the wallpaper in each room to the swimming pool and deck, the attention to detail is breathtaking. Every Fri night a DJ adds further coolness to the restaurant-bar. ❼

Legado Mítico Gurruchaga 1848 ☎011/4833-1300, ⓦwww.legadomitico.com. Like its sister hotel in Salta (see p.320), this remarkable boutique hotel goes in for themed rooms. You can choose between Argentine heroes like San Martín and Evita or arty types like Borges and Tita Merello. Each is spacious and stylishly decorated and furnished, with all manner of memorabilia recalling each historical figure. The breakfast room resembles the library of a gentleman's club. ❾

Nuss El Salvador 4916 ☎011/4833-6222, ⓦwww .nusshotel.com. This utterly classy boutique hotel in a converted convent at the corner of Serrano houses a range of 22 beautiful rooms, ranging from spacious superior category to sizeable suites. The convent's inner courtyard has been preserved, adding to the sense of space and airiness, while the top floor deck with its plunge pool and a small gym and spa is refreshed by the majestic plane trees in the neighbouring street. US$270

La Otra Orilla Julián Álvarez 1779 ☎011/4867-4070, ⓦwww.otraorilla.com.ar. Lovely, quiet little B&B in Palermo Viejo, with seven rooms of varying sizes, all comfortably, brightly and tastefully decorated, and some with balconies. Prices, including buffet breakfast and free internet, range from ❸ for the smallest single with shared bath to ❻ for the suite with a/c and TV.

Posada Palermo Salguero 1655 ☎011/4826-8792, ⓦwww.posadapalermo.com. Wonderful B&B in a more residential corner of Palermo, away, but not far, from the nerve centre of Soho; this typical *casa chorizo* (kind of elongated townhouse found in most Argentine cities), offers smart rooms, a homely atmosphere and a great breakfast, including home-made preserves. ❼

Tailor Made Hotel Arce 385 ☎011/4774-9620, ⓦwww.tailormadehotels.com.ar. Located in trendy Las Cañitas, the exquisite suites of this unusual hotel are organized according to the concept of its name – every personal whim is answered for, from an ipod lease to the wines in your cooler. Extras such as laundry and phone calls are free. ❾

The city centre

A sometimes chaotic mix of cafés, grand nineteenth-century public edifices, high-rise office blocks and tearing traffic, Buenos Aires' **city centre** exudes both energy and elegance. Its heart is the spacious, palm-dotted **Plaza de Mayo**, a good place to begin a tour of the area, perhaps more for its historical and political connections than for its somewhat mismatched collection of buildings, which includes the famous **Casa Rosada**, or government house. An amble westwards from the plaza will take you along **Avenida de Mayo**, the city's major boulevard, with an impressive selection of Art Nouveau and Art Deco architecture. At its western end, Avenida de Mayo opens onto the **Plaza del Congreso**, presided over by the **Congreso Nacional** building, the seat of the senate.

From Plaza del Congreso, the route north along Avenida Callao will take you to **Avenida Corrientes**. Now a busy shopping street, Corrientes was famous in the past as the hub of the city's left-leaning café society. Though there's less plotting going on here today, it's still the place to get some culture, lined as it is with bookstores, music shops, cinemas, theatres and cafés. A short detour north from Corrientes will take you to **Plaza Lavalle**, a long grassy square most notable for the opera house along its western edge, the regal **Teatro Colón**.

East from Plaza Lavalle, you'll hit the jarring and enormous **Avenida 9 de Julio** – the city's multi-lane central nerve. Presiding at its heart is the stark white **Obelisco**, a 67m stake through the intersection between 9 de Julio and Corrientes.

Crossing east over the avenue, you head into a densely packed and busy block known as the **microcentro**, whose two main streets are pedestrianized **Lavalle** and **Florida**, where you'll be swept along by a stream of human traffic past elegant *galerías* (arcades) and stores of every kind. Buenos Aires' small financial district – called, in homage to London, **"La City"** – makes up the southeast corner of the microcentro, while its northeast contains the quieter **"El Bajo"**, home to some good bars and restaurants.

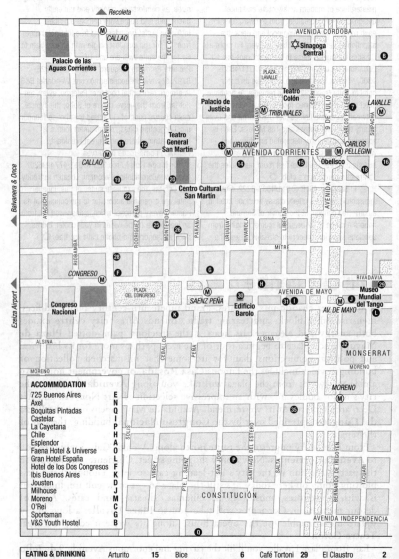

EATING & DRINKING		Arturito	15	Bice	6	Café Tortoni	29	El Claustro	2
A222	17	Asia de Cuba	37	Brasserie Petanque	38	Celta Bar	22	Confitería Ideal	18
Alsina Buenos Aires	32	Bahrein	9	Cabaña Las Lilas	23	Chiquilín	20	Las Cuartetas	16
La Americana	28	El Baqueano	39	Cadore	11	La Cigale	3	Estadio Luna Park	8

Plaza de Mayo

The one place that can lay claim to most of Buenos Aires' historical moments and monuments is the **Plaza de Mayo**. It's been bombed, filled by Evita's *descamisados* (literally "the shirtless ones", or manual workers) and was for many years the site of the Madres de Plaza de Mayo's weekly demonstration (see box, p.91). Although it still often attracts small, noisy protests, more often than not these days it's

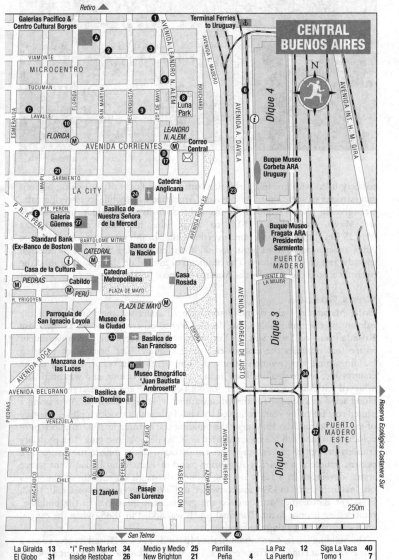

CENTRAL BUENOS AIRES

Retiro

Galerías Pacífico & Centro Cultural Borges

Terminal Ferries to Uruguay

VIAMONTE

MICROCENTRO

TUCUMAN

ESMERALDA

LAVALLE

FLORIDA

AVENIDA CORRIENTES

Luna Park

LEANDRO N. ALEM

Correo Central

SARMIENTO

LA CITY

Catedral Anglicana

PTE. PERON

Galería Güemes

Basílica de Nuestra Señora de la Merced

Standard Bank (Ex-Banco de Boston)

BARTOLOME MITRE

CATEDRAL

Banco de la Nación

Casa de la Cultura

PIEDRAS

Cabildo

PERÚ

Catedral Metropolitana

PLAZA DE MAYO

Casa Rosada

H. YRIGOYEN

Parroquia de San Ignacio Loyola

Museo de la Ciudad

Basílica de San Francisco

AVENIDA ROCA

Manzana de las Luces

Museo Etnográfico 'Juan Bautista Ambrosetti'

AVENIDA BELGRANO

Basílica de Santo Domingo

VENEZUELA

MEXICO

CHACABUCO

CHILE

El Zanjón

Pasaje San Lorenzo

San Telmo

Buque Museo Corbeta ARA Uruguay

Buque Museo Fragata ARA Presidente Sarmiento

PUERTO MADERO

PUENTE DE LA MUJER

Dique 4

Dique 3

Dique 2

PUERTO MADERO ESTE

Reserva Ecológica Costanera Sur

0   250m

La Giralda	13	"i" Fresh Market	34	Medio y Medio	25
El Globo	31	Inside Restobar	26	New Brighton	21
Granix	27	Laurak-Bat	35	Nsalad	5
Güerrín	14	Maluco Beleza	19	Palacio Barolo	30

Parrilla		La Paz	12	Siga La Vaca	40
Peña	4	La Puerto		Tomo 1	7
Patio San		Rico	33	La Trastienda	36
Ramón	24	Richmond	10	Winery	1

89

▲ Plaza de Mayo

sedately filled with gossiping old men batting away flocks of squawking pigeons and hawkers selling candied peanuts and Argentine flags, while its towering palm trees give the plaza a wonderfully tropical feel. At its centre stands the **Pirámide de Mayo**, erected in 1811 to mark the first anniversary of the May 25 Revolution, when a junta overthrew the Spanish viceroy, declared Buenos Aires' independence from Spain and set about establishing the city's jurisdiction over the rest of the territory. The headscarves painted on the ground around the pyramid echo those worn by the **Madres** (see box, p.91).

Casa Rosada

Evita, Maradona, Galtieri and Perón have all addressed the crowds from the balcony of the unmissable **Casa de Gobierno**, otherwise known as the **Casa Rosada** (tours on Sat & Sun at 11am; take your passport), the pink government palace that occupies the eastern end of the square. The practice of painting buildings pink was common during the nineteenth century, particularly in the countryside, where you'll still see many estancias this colour, and was originally achieved with the use of ox blood, for both decorative and practical reasons – the blood acted as a fixative for the whitewash to which it was added. After being a muted rose for many years, followed by a brief phase in a shocking pink – a legacy of the flamboyant Menem years – the building was restored in 2007 to a deep puce colour, a shade which has been patented as "Casa de Gobierno pink" in a probably fruitless attempt to prevent any more tampering with the tone in the future. The present structure, a typically Argentine blend of French and Italian Renaissance styles, developed in a fairly organic fashion. It stands on the site of the city's original fort, begun in 1594 and converted in 1776 to the viceroy's palace. In 1862, President Bartolomé Mitre moved the government ministries to the building, remodelling it once again. The final touch was added in 1885, when the central arch was added, unifying the facade.

The building has its own museum, the **Museo de la Casa Rosada,** accessed via a side entrance at Hipólito Yrigoyen 219. This was closed at the time of writing while renovation work was being carried out but is in any case a rather staid collection of official photographs, medals and the like. Behind the Casa Rosada, the Plaza Colón features a gigantic Argentine flag and a Carrara marble statue of **Cristóbal Colón** (Christopher Columbus), looking out to the river and towards the Old World.

Cabildo

At the far end of the square from the Casa Rosada is the **Cabildo**, the only colonial-era civil construction that managed to survive the rebuilding craze of the 1880s. Its simple, unadorned lines, green and white shuttered facade and colonnaded front stand in stark contrast to the more ornate buildings around it. The Cabildo houses a small **museum** (Mon–Fri 10am–5pm, Sat & Sun 11am–6pm; $1) whose modest collection includes standards captured during the 1806 British invasion, some delicate watercolours by Enrique Pellegrini and original plans of the city and the fort. Though the exhibits themselves are of only minor interest, the interior of the building is worth a visit, in particular the upper galleries lined with an assortment of relics from the colonial period onwards, such as huge keys and sturdy wooden doors. Behind the Cabildo, a patio area houses a café and small artisans' fair (Thurs & Fri 11am–4pm).

Catedral

The **Catedral Metropolitana** (daily 9am–7pm; free guided tours Mon–Fri 11.30am & 4pm, Sat & Sun 4pm; Ⓦ www.catedralbuenosaires.org.ar), with its rather severe Neoclassical facade, is not, in truth, a particularly beautiful or

---

Madres de Plaza de Mayo

Many of those arrested – and, in many cases, tortured and executed – during the **1976–83 dictatorship** (see Contexts, p.600) were young people in their teens and 20s who were kidnapped from their homes and streets with no acknowledgement from the authorities as to their whereabouts. Some of their mothers, frustrated by the intimidating silence they were met with when they tried to find out what had happened to their children, in 1976 started what would become the **Madres (Mothers) movement**.

At first just a handful of women, the Madres met weekly in the **Plaza de Mayo**, the historical centre of the city, as much to support each other as to embarrass the regime into providing answers; the wearing of white headscarves emerged as a means of identification. As their numbers grew, so did their defiance – standing their ground and challenging the military to carry out its threat to fire on them in front of foreign journalists, for instance. Some disappeared themselves after the notorious torturer known as the "Angel of Death" Alfredo Astiz infiltrated the group, posing as the brother of a *desaparecido* (disappeared).

In 1982, during the Malvinas/Falklands crisis, the Madres were accused of being anti-patriotic for their stance **against the war**, a conflict that they claimed was an attempt by the regime to divert attention away from its murderous acts. With the return to democracy in 1983, the Madres were disappointed by the new government's reluctance to delve too deeply into what had happened during the "Dirty War", as well as by the later granting of immunity to many of those accused of kidnap, torture and murder. The group rejected economic "compensation" and both the Madres and the respect in which they are held were key in finally getting the amnesty laws overturned in 2005. The Madres continued to protest at the Pirámide de Mayo weekly until January 2006, when, after around 1500 protests, the Madres finally brought their long vigil to an end, citing confidence in President Néstor Kirchner. Now some of the Madres have branched into other areas of social protest: the emblem of the white headscarf was at the forefront of the movement to demand the **non-payment of the country's foreign debt**, among other issues.

impressive church. However, it is assured a steady stream of visitors, partly due to its location, partly due to its status as Buenos Aires' foremost cathedral and partly due to the **mausoleum** to Independence hero General San Martín (see Contexts, p.591) inside, solemnly guarded and usually mobbed by school-children on history trips.

The cathedral assumed its final form over many years; built and rebuilt since the sixteenth century, the present building was completed in the mid-nineteenth century, complete with Venetian mosaic floors, gilded columns and a silver-plated altar. The twelve columns that front the entrance represent the twelve apostles; above them sits a carved tympanum whose bas-relief depicts the arrival of Jacob and his family in Egypt.

Avenida de Mayo

Heading west from Plaza de Mayo takes you along one of the capital's grandest thoroughfares, **Avenida de Mayo**, a wide, tree-lined boulevard flanked with ornamental street lamps and offering a stunning ten-block vista between Plaza de Mayo and Plaza del Congreso. Part of an 1880s project to remodel the city along the lines of Haussmann's Paris, Avenida de Mayo is notable for its architectural melange; many of its buildings are topped with decorative domes and ornamented with elaborate balustrades and sinuous caryatids. Unimpressed with the city's European pretensions, Borges called it one of the saddest areas in Buenos Aires, yet even he couldn't resist the charm of its **confiterías** and traditional restaurants, a handful of which remain open.

Casa de la Cultura and around

Just half a block west of Plaza de Mayo, at Avenida de Mayo 567, there's the magnificent, French-influenced **La Prensa** building, with grand wrought-iron doors, curvaceous lamps and a steep mansard roof. The building – now housing the city's culture secretariat and renamed the **Casa de la Cultura** – was originally built as the headquarters of the national newspaper *La Prensa*. You can pop in to take a peek at the opulent interior – all ornamental glass and elaborate woodwork – or take advantage of one of the free guided tours organized by the city govern-ment (Sat 4pm & 5pm, Sun hourly 11am–4pm). A little further on, the corner of Perú is home to **London City**, a typical Buenos Aires café of black and white tiles, smart waiters and wooden tables, less known – but also less crowded – than the famous *Tortoni* (see below).

Café Tortoni and the Museo Mundial del Tango

At Avenida de Mayo 829, you'll find the **Café Tortoni** (℡011/4342-4328, Ⓦwww.cafetortoni.com.ar). Its presence on every tourist's must-visit list – some days you even have to line up to get in – has spoilt the atmosphere a little and hiked the prices a lot, but the *Tortoni*, which has existed in some form for over 150 years, is still worth stopping by for a *cafecito*. Famous for its literary and artistic connec-tions – notable habitués included poets Alfonsina Storni and Rubén Darío – its heavy brown columns and Art Nouveau-mirrored walls create an elegant ambience.

Next door, at Avenida de Mayo 833, the fine **Palacio Carlos Gardel** is home to the Academia Nacional del Tango and the **Museo Mundial del Tango**, on the first floor and accessed from the building's back entrance at Rivadavia 830 (Mon–Fri 2–6pm; $5). The museum traces the history of tango (in Spanish, though an English-speaking guide may be available) through displays such as Tita Merello's glittering dress and a photo of men dancing tango together in 1910 – women were rarely available to dance in those days, except in brothels.

Edificio Barolo

Continuing down Avenida de Mayo will take you over the wide Avenida 9 de Julio and past a clutch of old-fashioned hotels, cafés and government institutions dressed in *belle époque* Art Deco splendour. On the south side of the street, at no. 1370, stands the avenue's most fantastical building, the **Edificio Barolo** – named after the extremely wealthy farmer of Italian origin who had it built. Designed by the Italian architect Mario Palanti and constructed between 1919 and 1923, its unusual top-heavy form is an example of the eclectic style popular at the time. Created as a monument to Dante's *Divine Comedy* (of which Barolo was a great admirer) it is full of references to the epic poem – its different sections represent Hell, Purgatory and Heaven, its height in metres equals the number of songs (one hundred) and it has 22 floors, the same as the number of stanzas in each canto. Moreover, in early June, the roof's tip aligns with the Southern Cross constellation – the "entrance to heaven". Rather prosaically, the building is used mostly for offices, but there is also a sumptuous ground-floor café-restaurant, *Palacio Barolo* (see p.131). There are fascinating guided tours of the building, explaining its details and symbolism, on Mondays and Thursdays (2pm & 7pm; $20; Ⓦ www.pbarolo.com.ar/visitasguiadasin.htm).

Plaza del Congreso

At its western extremity, Avenida de Mayo opens up to encircle the **Plaza del Congreso**, a three-block-long wedge of grass dotted with statues, a fountain, swooping pigeons and a number of benches. Its western end is presided over by the Greco-Roman **Congreso Nacional** building (guided visits in English Mon, Tues, Thurs & Fri 11am & 4pm at Hipólito Yrigoyen 1846; Ⓣ 011/4959-3006; free), inaugurated in 1906 and designed by Vittorio Meano, who was also the architect of the Teatro Colón (see p.95). The northern wing is where the Lower Chamber sits, while the southern wing is used by the Upper Chamber of senators. The tours include a visit to the marble Salon Azul, right in the centre of the building under the copper cupola; look up to see the giant 2000kg chandelier featuring figures representing the Republic and its provinces.

The square's most striking monument is the exuberant **Monumento a los dos Congresos**, a series of sculptural allegories atop heavy granite steps and crowned by the triumphant figure of the Republic, erected to commemorate the 1813 Assembly and the 1816 Declaration of Independence. The plaza has traditionally been the final rallying point for many political demonstrations – it was the site of a mass illegal encampment of farmers protesting the government's increase in export taxes in 2008 – and the sculpture has now been surrounded by a high fence to try to prevent the constant reappearance of fresh graffiti. You'll also see a greening bronze statue in the square, a somewhat rain-streaked version of Rodin's *The Thinker*. Next to it, a white block marks *kilómetro cero* – the point from which all roads that lead from Buenos Aires are measured.

Avenida Corrientes

Running parallel to Avenida de Mayo, four blocks north of Plaza Congreso, **Avenida Corrientes** is another of the city's principal arteries, sweeping down to the lower grounds of El Bajo. Unlike other thoroughfares, it's not the architecture along here that is of note – rather, it's the atmosphere generated by its mix of cafés, bookstores, cinemas, theatres and pizzerias. For years, **cafés** such as *La Paz*, on the corner of Corrientes and Montevideo, and the austere *La Giralda* two blocks west, have been the favoured meeting places of left-wing intellectuals and bohemians – and good places to spot the Porteño talent for whiling away hours over a single tiny coffee.

The Bicentennial

In 2010 Argentina observed its bicentennial: two hundred years ago, on May 25, 1810, locals gathered in the **Plaza de Mayo** to demand the withdrawal of the viceroy and to form the **Primera Junta** – the first move in throwing off the yoke of Spanish rule and creating an independent nation.

The centennial in 1910 was cause for great celebration: in its first hundred years Argentina had gone from being a fairly small colonial backwater to one of the world's richest countries, still in the throes of an unprecedented immigration and building boom, and bursting with confidence that it was destined to be a great country, perhaps even challenging US hegemony in the Western Hemisphere. Several foreign nations gifted **monuments**, many of which are still standing in Buenos Aires, including the Torre Monumental (Britain; see p.111) and the Monumento de los Españoles (Spain; see p.126).

Now, one hundred years further on, Argentina has failed to live up to its original heady promise, but its citizens nonetheless passionately celebrated their two hundredth birthday. In Buenos Aires, lasting legacies of the party include a new **Casa del Bicentenario**, at Riobamba 983 (℡011/4129-2400, ⒲www.bicentenario.gov.ar), which holds exhibitions on different aspects of Argentine identity; while the main post office, the Correo Central, at Sarmiento 189, near the beginning of Avenida Corrientes, was at the time of writing being restored and transformed into a cultural centre. It is to be the seat of the national symphony orchestra, and host more exhibitions.

Corrientes' **bookstores**, many of which stay open till the wee hours, have always been as much places to hang out in as to buy from – in marked contrast to almost every other type of shop in the city, where you'll be accosted by sales assistants as soon as you cross the threshold. The most basic places are simply one long room open to the street with piles of books slung on tables and huge handwritten price labels. There are more upmarket places, too, such as the very swish Gandhi at no. 1743 and the leftish, alternative Liberarte at no. 1555. Almost as comprehensive as the bookstores are the street's numerous pavement kiosks, proffering a mind-boggling range of newspapers, magazines and books on subjects from psychology to sex to tango.

Teatro General San Martín

At Corrientes 1530, you'll find the glass front of the **Teatro General San Martín** (see p.144 for booking details), one of the city's most important cultural spaces. As well as the theatre itself, there's an arthouse cinema and a small free gallery that often has worthwhile exhibitions showcasing Argentine photographers, among other subjects. Adjoining the theatre at the back is a large and rather shabby 1960s building that is home to the eclectic **Centro Cultural General San Martín** (see p.144), a space for cutting-edge art, theatre and dance and also a major venue for conventions and academic debates. Its front entrance is at Sarmiento 1551, but it can also be accessed via the Teatro San Martín.

Obelisco

The centrepiece of Buenos Aires' cityscape, the iconic 67-metre tall **Obelisco** dominates the busy intersection between Corrientes and Avenida 9 de Julio. Erected in 1936 in just 31 days, it commemorates four key events in the city's history: the first and second foundings; the first raising of the flag in 1812; and the naming of Buenos Aires as Capital Federal in 1880. Its giant scale and strategic location also make it a magnet for carloads of celebrating fans after a major football victory. The obelisk stands on the Plaza de Republica, where you will also see representations in bronze of the country's provinces and the flags of Buenos Aires and Argentina, raised in 2008 to commemorate 25 years since the return to democracy.

Plaza Lavalle

A short walk northwest from the Obelisco along Avenida Roque Sáenz Peña takes you past a pretty row of fountains and patio cafés – popular places to take a coffee break or eat lunch – to **Plaza Lavalle**. Stretching for three blocks, the plaza is a pleasant green space at the heart of the city, notable for its fine collection of native and exotic trees, many of them over a hundred years old. Among the pines, magnolias and jacarandas stands an ancient *ceibo*, a tall tree with a twisted trunk whose bright red spring blossom is Argentina's national flower.

The plaza began life as a public park, inaugurated in 1827 by British immigrants, and thirty years later was the departure point for the first Argentine train journey, made by the locomotive *La Porteña* to Floresta in the west of the capital; the original locomotive can still be seen in the Complejo Museográfico in Luján (see p.189). Nowadays the plaza is practically synonymous with the law courts that surround it; the whole area is often referred to as **Tribunales**. The western end of the square is dominated by the grimy **Palacio de Justicia**, which houses the Supreme Court. In a loose and heavy-handed interpretation of Neoclassicism, heavily adorned with pillars, the building stands as something of a monument to architectural uncertainty. The needs of the lawyers who rush to and from the court are catered for by numerous stallholders who set up tables spread with pamphlets and secondhand books explaining every conceivable aspect of Argentine law.

At the northeastern end of the plaza, at Libertad 785, lies the **Sinagoga Central de la Congregación Israelita de la República Argentina**, the central synagogue of Argentina's Jewish population; visits are possible (Tues & Thurs 3–6pm only; $15) but security is strict – take your passport. Guides (English speakers available) will take you around the synagogue and small museum of religious artefacts, many imported from Europe, and explain the history of the Jewish community in Argentina. Just over the road, at Libertad 815, the **Teatro Nacional Cervantes** is a fine theatre (see p.144 for booking details) whose intricately ornamentated exterior reflects Spanish Plateresque architecture, a style common in the early sixteenth century and named for its supposed similarity to fine silversmith's work.

Teatro Colón

On the eastern side of Plaza Lavalle, between Viamonte and Tucumán and with its back entrance on the plaza, resides the handsome **Teatro Colón**, with its grand but restrained French Renaissance exterior. Most famous as an opera house – though it also hosts ballet and classical recitals – the Teatro Colón is undoubtedly Argentina's most prestigious cultural institution and is considered to have some of the best acoustics in the world. Most of the twentieth century's major opera and ballet stars appeared here, from Caruso and Callas to Nijinsky and Nureyev, while classical music performances have been given by the likes of Toscanini and Rubinstein. The interior features an Italian Renaissance-style central hall, the beautiful gilded and mirrored Salón Dorado (allegedly inspired by Versailles) and the stunning auditorium itself, whose five tiers of balconies culminate in a huge dome decorated with frescoes by Raúl Soldi.

The theatre was closed for an extensive refurbishment in 2006, with plans to reopen put back repeatedly – at the time of writing the hope was that it should be

1

Jewish Buenos Aires

Argentina is home to one of the largest **Jewish communities** in the world, currently estimated at around 200,000, although this is around half the size it was at its peak in the mid-twentieth century. The majority live in Buenos Aires; the more well-to-do in Belgrano, and the lower middle classes in Once. The latter is where you'll find most of the city's kosher restaurants, especially on the streets around Pueyrredón between Córdoba and Corrientes. Approximately eighty synagogues dot the city, including the huge non-Orthodox Central Synagogue (see p.95), along with more than seventy Jewish educational institutions.

The first Jewish **immigrants** arrived in Argentina from Western European countries around the middle of the nineteenth century; Jewish refugees later fled here in large numbers from pogroms and persecution in Russia and Eastern Europe, and were commonly known as "rusos", a term still often used erroneously to refer to all Jews. Perón's government was one of the first to recognize the State of Israel, but he also halted Jewish immigration and infamously allowed Nazi war criminals to settle in Argentina, including Adolf Eichmann, the SS officer who masterminded the systematic massacre of Jews. Eichmann was later abducted from a Buenos Aires suburb by Israeli secret agents and whisked off for trial and execution in Jerusalem. Jews suffered particularly harshly during the 1976–83 dictatorship, often because they were artists, intellectuals, left-wing sympathizers or anti-junta militants rather than for overtly religious reasons, although many junta members and torturers were openly anti-Semitic; it is estimated that over 1000 of the disappeared were Jewish.

More recently, the Jewish community was the target of two of the country's most murderous **terrorist attacks**: a bomb explosion at the Israeli Embassy in 1992, in which around thirty people died, and another at the headquarters of AMIA, the Argentine Jewish association, in 1994, which killed at least 86 people. Despite a long-running investigation, the perpetrators have yet to be found, with locals who had been accused of complicity, including police, cleared in 2004. In 2006, Argentine prosecutors officially accused the Iranian government and Hezbollah of the crime, a charge Teheran adamantly denies. A monument in Plaza Lavalle remembers those who lost their lives.

ready in time for the 2010 bicentennial. Once the theatre does reopen, check the website (⊕www.teatrocolon.org.ar) or enquire at the box office for both guided visits and tickets for performances; it's in the passageway, formerly used for carriages, that cuts sideways through the building.

The microcentro

The **microcentro** – bounded by Avenidas Corrientes, Além, de Mayo and 9 de Julio – is the core of downtown, the central nerve system of the modern city, a fast-moving, noisy, traffic-filled district packed with offices, banks, bars, hotels and stores. Even if you're not staying here, you're bound to come here frequently during your stay to eat or drink, make travel arrangements, shop and take in the sights. The microcentro's key thoroughfares are pedestrianized **Calle Florida**, which runs from Plaza de Mayo to Plaza San Martín in Retiro (see p.111), and partly pedestrianized cheap and cheerful **Calle Lavalle**, which bisects Florida halfway along its length.

Calle Florida

At the beginning of the last century, **Florida** was one of the city's most elegant streets – the obligatory route for a stroll following tea at its very own branch of Harrods. Nowadays over one million people a day tramp its length, and cutting your way through its stream of foot traffic requires considerable determination. But this traffic is probably Florida's most appealing quality; there's always a lively buzz about the place, and a handful of street performers doing their best to charm a few pesos from the passers-by.

Florida commences at Plazo de Mayo and, save for the elegant facade of the Standard Bank (formerly the **Banco de Boston**) at no. 99, which is particularly impressive when lit up at night, its initial blocks are mostly taken up with bookstores, clothes stores, exchange offices and fast-food outlets, packed with office workers at lunch time. Vestiges of Florida's more sophisticated past remain in its **galerías**, or shopping arcades, such as the Art Nouveau **Galería Güemes** at no. 165, which features a series of beautiful glass cupolas, or in certain cafés, such as the almost anachronistic **Richmond confitería** at Florida 468, famed for its cakes, hot chocolate and large leather armchairs.

Towards the northern end of Florida, the crowds become thinner and the stores more upmarket – at no. 877 you'll see there was once a Harrods. Until the 1960s, this operated as the South American branch of the famous department store, with visitors flocking to marvel at its full-size London bus and live Indian elephant. Despite occasional rumblings that it is to be reopened, and its intermittent use as an exposition hall and arts venue, it has been sadly shuttered for years, and is no longer linked to the London store. At Florida 753 you'll find the most notable of Florida's *galerías* – the **Galerías Pacífico**, which offers a glitzy bit of retailing within a vaulted and attractively frescoed building constructed by Paris department store Bon Marché at the end of the nineteenth century. The first floor is also home to the Centro Cultural Borges (see p.144), a large space offering a worthwhile selection of photography and painting exhibitions from both Argentine and foreign artists. Florida's last two blocks before it spills into Plaza San Martín are filled with leather and handicraft stores; look out also for the fine decorative facade and door of the Centro Naval on the corner of Córdoba.

La City

La City, Buenos Aires' financial district, takes up the southeastern quarter of the microcentro's grid of streets. Its atmosphere serves as a barometer of the country's economic ups and downs – from frantic money changing during hyperinflation in the 1980s, to the noisy pot-banging demonstrations that followed the savings withdrawal freeze in 2001–2002; you can still see the scars of these protests on the battered bank shutters. The tight confines and endless foot traffic make it difficult to look up, but if you do you'll be rewarded with an impressive spread of grand facades crowned with domes and towers.

La City was once known as the *barrio inglés*, in reference to the large number of British immigrants who set up business here. Indeed, the first financial institutions were built in a rather Victorian style; it seems that the Porteño elite thought their houses should be French and their banks British. The barrio is also home to one of the most beautiful and least visited churches in Buenos Aires, the **Basílica de Nuestra Señora de la Merced** at Reconquista and Perón, which has been favoured by important political and military figures through the ages. The main structure dates from 1783, while the sandy coloured façade – the tympanum shows General Belgrano after he defeated the Spanish in battle in 1812 – was added in 1905. Every inch of the sombre interior is ornamented with gilt or tiles. Attached to the basilica, at Reconquista 269, is one of the city's best-kept secrets, the **Convento de San Ramón** (Mon–Fri 10.30am–6pm; free; Ⓦwww .conventosanramon.org.ar). At its heart is a charming courtyard where you can eat in the restaurant under the arches, or just take a break from elbowing your way through the crowds outside.

Puerto Madero

Almost more water than land, **Puerto Madero**, Buenos Aires' newest and glossiest barrio, centres on a defunct port directly to the east of the historical centre. Here four enormous *diques*, or docks, run along the Río de la Plata, connecting on either side to the Dársena Sur (Southern Harbour), near Boca, and the Dársena Norte (Northern Harbour), near Retiro, from where ferries depart for Uruguay. Lining these docks – which officially number one to four, Dock One being the most southerly – are a series of preserved and restored brick and iron warehouses, originally used to hold grain from the Pampas before it was shipped around the world. By 1898, before the port was even fully finished, it was already insufficient in scale to cope with the volume of maritime traffic, and a new port was constructed to the north. For most of the twentieth century, Puerto Madero sat as an industrial relic, but in the 1990s private money was injected and it began to be converted into a

▲ Puente de la Mujer, Puerto Madero

voguish mix of restaurants, luxury apartments and offices. While this dockside development is upmarket and somewhat lacking in colour, it's nonetheless a pleasant place to stroll, and there are far worse ways to spend a lazy summer afternoon than sitting on a verandah here, sipping a *clericó*, watching the yachts bob on the water and enjoying the gentle breeze off the river.

Puerto Madero is within easy walking distance from downtown – just head east along Avenida Belgrano, calle Juan Domingo Perón or calle Viamonte – though the train tracks that run their length, sandwiched between Avenida Alicia Moreau de Justo and Avenida Eduardo Madero, can be awkward to cross on foot. For the last four decades these lines were used only by freight trains, but in 2007 the **Tranvía del Este**, a shiny, silent and smooth passenger tram, began operating along these old tracks, connecting Avenida Córdoba with Avenida Independencia (approximately every 10 min; Mon–Sat 8am–11pm, Sun 9am–10pm; $1). With stops where it crosses avenidas Corrientes and Belgrano, it's an excellent way to give your legs a break if they begin to falter midway along the barrio's 24-block length; note that you will need change to use the ticket machines.

The docks

It's logical to begin your tour of Puerto Madero on the western (or city) side of the docks, which is flanked by a walkway the entire length. Docks four and three host the pick of the restaurants, and are also home to two well-maintained **museum ships** – the *Buque Museo Corbeta ARA Uruguay* (daily 10am–7pm; $2), built at the Cammell Laird shipyard in Liverpool in 1874 and the Argentine navy's first training ship, and the *Buque Museo Fragata ARA Presidente Sarmiento* (daily 10am–7pm; $2), also built in British shipyards, and the Argentine navy's flagship from 1899 to 1938. However, the area's focal point is Spanish architect Santiago Calatrava's striking white bridge known as the **Puente de la Mujer** (the "women's bridge"). Unveiled in 2001, its graceful curve – which echoes the outstretched leg of a tango dancer – is an intriguing blend of the modern and traditional.

Crossing over one of the several road and footbridges that span the docks will bring you to the shiny and rather soulless sub-barrio known as **Puerto Madero Este**, a compact grid of streets that has seen frantic development in recent years and now consists of elegant apartments, less elegant but equally expensive high-rise monoliths, chi-chi restaurants and a few neighbourhood stores. The landmark site here is the **Faena Art District**, an ongoing cultural, retail and residential development that marries cutting edge design with rather pretentious ambitions about reinventing the city concept.

Running along Puerto Madero Este's eastern edge, the **Costanera Sur** is a sweeping avenue flanked by elegant balustrades, originally built as a riverside promenade at the beginning of the twentieth century. The avenue essentially lost its *raison d'être* in the 1970s when the government devised a project to reclaim land from the river. Dykes were constructed and the water drawn off but the project was never completed, leaving the suddenly inaptly named Costanera cut off from the river. However, the drained land unexpectedly became a haven for wildlife – now the Reserva Ecológica (see below).

Reserva Ecológica

The **Reserva Ecológica** (Tues–Sun: April–Oct 8am–6pm, Nov–March 8am–7pm; free; ☎011/4315-4129, ⓦwww.buenosaires.gov.ar/areas/med_ambiente/reserva) is a strange and wonderful place, a fragment of wild and watery grassland stretching for 2km alongside the Costanera. Having self-seeded with grassland after the landfill project was abandoned in 1984, the reserve offers a juxtaposition of urban and natural scenes, whether factory chimneys glimpsed through fronds of pampas or the city skyline over a lake populated by ducks and herons.

Just outside the reserve, it's worth pausing to see the flamboyant **Fuente de las Nereidas**, a large and elaborate marble fountain created by Tucumán sculptress Lola Mora in 1902. The fountain depicts a naked Venus perched coquettishly on the edge of a shell supported by two straining sea nymphs. The fountain was originally destined for the Plaza de Mayo, but its seductive display was thought too risqué to be in such proximity to the cathedral.

Inside the reserve, near the entrance, the visitors' centre displays panels explaining the park's development and serves as the starting point for ranger-guided walks along the park's many trails (Sat & Sun 10.30am & 3.30pm). Full-moon nocturnal tours (weather permitting; dates are listed on the website) allow you to spot all manner of creatures, mainly birds, that keep a low daytime profile. There is a surprising diversity of flora and fauna in the park, with over two hundred species of birds visiting during the year. Aquatic species include ducks, herons, elegant black-necked swans, skittish coots, the common gallinule and the snail hawk, a bird of prey that uses its hooked beak to pluck freshwater snails out of their shells. The park is also home to small mammals, such as the easily spotted coypu, an aquatic rodent, and reptiles such as monitor lizards. The reserve's vegetation includes the bright red *ceibo*, but the most dominant plant is the *cortadera*, or pampas grass.

The south

Described by Borges as "an older, more solid world", **the south** is Buenos Aires' most traditional quarter. Immediately south of the Plaza de Mayo lies the barrio of **Monserrat**, packed with historic buildings, churches and a couple of noteworthy museums. Heading south through Monserrat, you'll emerge among the cobbled streets and alleyways of **San Telmo**, where grand nineteenth-century mansions testify to the days when the barrio was home to wealthy landowners. San Telmo is most commonly visited on a Sunday, when its central square, Plaza Dorrego, is the scene of a fascinating **antiques fair**, although there are plenty of antiques stores also open during the week. At the southern end of the barrio, there's the tranquil **Parque Lezama** – a good spot for observing local life, and home to an important history museum. Beyond Parque Lezama, and stretching all the way to the city's southern boundary, the Río Riachuelo, the quirky barrio of **La Boca** is a great place to spend a morning, wandering its colourful streets and soaking up its idiosyncratic atmosphere.

Monserrat

Monserrat, also known as Barrio Sur, is the city's oldest district and, together with neighbouring San Telmo, is one of the most beguiling areas to explore on foot. A good starting point for delving into its grid of narrow streets and historic buildings is along **Calle Defensa**, named in honour of the barrio's residents, who, during the British invasions of 1806 and 1807, impeded the British troops by pouring boiling water on them as they marched down the street.

On the corner of Alsina and Defensa stands the neo-Baroque **Basílica de San Francisco** (Mon–Fri 8am–7pm). Dating from 1754, it was one of a number of churches burnt by angry Peronists in March 1955 in reaction to the navy's bombing of an anti-Church, pro-Perón trade union rally in the Plaza de Mayo. The basilica was eventually restored, reconsecrated and reopened in 1967. An oak column from the original altarpiece, destroyed by the fire, is preserved in the adjoining Franciscan monastery, where monks sell bee-derived products, including honey and soap.

Half a block west of the church at Defensa 219, on the first floor of a handsome private residence, is the imaginative **Museo de la Ciudad** (daily 11am–7pm; $1; ⓦwww.museodelaciudad.buenosaires.gov.ar). About half the museum is given over to a permanent display of children's toys through the ages, making it particularly worth a visit if you have youngsters to entertain. Look out for the toy farm reinvented as an Argentine estancia – dancing gauchos, bucking broncos and all. The rest of the museum is devoted to regularly changing exhibitions designed to illustrate everyday aspects of Porteño life, such as holidays or football. The objects are accompanied by witty descriptions, sadly in Spanish only. Downstairs, a salon open to the street holds larger items, such as rescued doors and a traditional barrow from which an *ambulante* (hawker) would have sold his or her wares, decorated in the *filete* style (see box, p.102). Just by the museum on the corner, it's worth popping into the **Farmacia de la Estrella**, a beautifully preserved old pharmacy. Founded in 1834, it boasts an opulent interior of heavy walnut fittings, quirky old-fashioned medical murals and mirrors, finished off with a stunning frescoed ceiling.

Continuing south along Defensa, you'll find the **Basílica de Santo Domingo**, an austere twin-towered structure on the corner of Avenida Belgrano, whose glory is somewhat overshadowed by the elevated mausoleum to General Belgrano that dominates the tiled patio at its front. The square on which the basilica stands was taken by the British on June 27, 1806, on which date Catholicism was outlawed. In the corner to the left of the altar as you enter you can see the flags from British regiments captured by General Liniers when the city was retaken two months later.

Manzana de las Luces

Taking up the block bounded by Alsina, Perú, Moreno and Bolívar – the latter one block west of Defensa – is the complex of buildings known as the **Manzana de las Luces**, or "block of enlightenment" (guided visits Mon 1pm & 3pm, Tues–Fri 3pm, Sat & Sun 3pm, 4.30pm & 6pm; from entrance at Perú 272; $6 except Mon 1pm free; ⓦwww.manzanadelasluces.gov.ar). Dating from 1662, the complex originally housed a Jesuit community, and has been home to numerous official institutions throughout its history. The forty-minute tour (in Spanish, with summary explanations given in English) generally visits the inner patio, tunnels constructed to connect the churches (and later used for smuggling), some of the surrounding chambers – including one that hosted a nineteenth-century political assassination – and the reconstructed **Sala de Representantes**, a semicircular chamber where the first provincial legislature sat. Opposite the statue of General Roca at Av Julio Roca 600, the **Mercado de las Luces** (Mon–Fri 10.30am–7.30pm, Sun 2–7.30pm) has stalls set up in one of the Jesuit corridors, selling antiques, crystals, candles and other artisan products.

The block also encompasses the elite Colegio Nacional, where the nation's future politicians are schooled, and Buenos Aires' oldest church, **San Ignacio**, on the corner of Bolívar and Alsina, which dates from 1675. Apart from the rather Baroque Altar Mayor, the church's interior is fairly simple, an arrangement that makes one of its most notable icons, the beautiful seventeenth-century Nuestra Señora de las Nieves, all the more arresting.

Museo Etnográfico Juan Bautista Ambrosetti

Part of the Universidad de Buenos Aires, the fascinating **Museo Etnográfico Juan Bautista Ambrosetti** lies at Moreno 350 (Tues–Fri 1–7pm, Sat & Sun 3–7pm, guided visits Sat & Sun 4pm; closed Jan; $3 voluntary; ⓦwww.museoetnografico.filo.uba.ar). Although the museum has some international anthropological exhibits, its real interest lies in its well-displayed collection from pre-Columbian South America.

The ground-floor rooms display the impressive jewellery, pots and tools of the few native groups who lived on what is now Argentine territory, such as the Mapuche, whose territory reached from modern Chile as far as the pampas. For hundreds of years the Mapuche successfully resisted both Inca and Spanish attempts to conquer their territory; their textiles and jewellery are particularly noteworthy, with distinctive headbands and chest pieces featuring heavy silver frills. There are also exhibits on the Yámana and other peoples of Tierra del Fuego, whose societies were less developed (see box, p.579). Panels (and pamphlets in English) give context to the exhibits.

The upper floor deals with different themes relating to the culture, religion and trade of various other pre-Columbian South American peoples, including the Inca. Of particular note are a fine Huari tunic covered in the symbols that they used in place of a written language and religious costumes from Bolivia made of jaguar skin, an animal that represented power and wisdom. There are many fascinating examples of the gradual Hispanicization of the indigenous people, where Christian motifs and European materials were melded with native American beliefs – look out for the wooden statue of Jesus wearing a jaguar pelt.

San Telmo

It's impossible not to be seduced by the romantically crumbling facades and cobbled streets of **San Telmo**, a neighbourhood that is proud of its reputation as the guardian of the city's traditions. A small, almost square-shaped barrio, San Telmo is bounded to the north by Avenida Chile, six blocks south of Plaza de Mayo, to the west by **Calle Piedras**, to the east by Paseo Colón and to the south by Parque Lezama. Like neighbouring Monserrat, its main artery is **Calle Defensa**, once the road from the Plaza de Mayo to the city's port.

The barrio's appearance of decaying luxury is the result of a kind of reverse gentrification. When the city's grand mansions were abandoned by their patrician owners after a yellow fever epidemic in 1871, they were soon converted into *conventillos* (tenements) by landlords keen to make a quick buck from newly arrived immigrants. This sudden loss of cachet preserved many of the barrio's original features: whereas much of the north, centre and west of the city was variously torn down, smartened up or otherwise modernized, San Telmo's inhabitants simply adapted the neighbourhood's buildings to their needs. It's still largely a

---

Filete art

As you wander around Monserrat, San Telmo and Boca, look out for examples of **filete art**, particularly on shop signs. Characterized by ornate lettering, heavy shading and the use of scrolls and flowers entwined with the azure and white of the national flag, this distinctive art form first made its appearance on the city transport system in the early twentieth century. Often associated with tango, its actual origins are a little murky, but it seems to have been introduced by Italian immigrants. Banned from public transport in 1975 – the authorities felt bus destinations and numbers should be unadorned – it moved onto signs above stores and cafés as well as more traditional canvases. Today it is synonymous with Porteño identity, particularly in the south. As well as tango stars, a popular subject is the pithy saying, including the classic *si bebe para olvidar paga antes de tomar* ("if you drink to forget, pay first") and the more obscure *si querés la leche fresca, atá la vaca a la sombre* ("if you want fresh milk, tie the cow up in the shade").

CHILE

El Zanjón

Pasaje
San Lorenzo

AVENIDA INDEPENDENCIA

(M) INDEPENDENCIA

ESTADOS UNIDOS

Mercado
Municipal

CARLOS CALVO

PLAZA
DORREGO

Iglesia San
Pedro Telmo

HUMBERTO

Pasaje de
la Defensa

AVENIDA SAN JUAN

(M) SAN JUAN

COCHABAMBA

Russian
Orthodox
Church

AVENIDA JUAN DE GARAY

Parque
Lezama

ACCOMMODATION
Circus Hostel **A**
Gran Hotel América **B**

BRASIL

Centro Cultural
Torquato Tasso

Museo
Histórico
Nacional

CASEROS

EATING & DRINKING

Abuela Pan	2	Gibraltar	5
Bar Sur	4	Mitos Argentinas	7
Bar Británico	9	Plaza Dorrego Bar	6
Café San Juan	8	La Poesía	1
El Desnivel	3		

0   250 m

SAN TELMO

▼ Boca

working-class area, and well-heeled Palermo-dwellers may warn you off coming here, but the area's superb architecture also attracts bohemians, students, backpackers and artists. Together with rising rents, the recent appearance of designer clothing and homewares stores among the traditional antiques shops is an indication that San Telmo may once again be going up in the world – and this new gentrification is not a development that everyone welcomes.

The barrio is one of Buenos Aires' major tourist attractions, particularly due to its Sunday antiques market, the **Feria de San Telmo**, which takes place in the neighbourhood's central square, Plaza Dorrego; there is also a smaller version on Saturdays. It's also the barrio most associated with **tango**, and the place where many of the best-known tango shows and bars have their home. At the southern end of the barrio, the small, palm-lined Parque Lezama, containing the city's well-organized **Museo Histórico Nacional**, makes a restful spot to end a tour of the neighbourhood.

Along Calle Defensa

Leading south from Plaza de Mayo, Defensa runs through Monserrat (see p.100) and then straight on through San Telmo to Parque Lezama. On weekends, vehicles are replaced with human traffic as visitors wend their way past performance artists and buskers to visit the cobbled lane's antiques stores and bars. A stroll along here is more about soaking up the atmosphere than visiting specific sites, though there are a couple. At no. 755, **El Zanjón** (guided visits Mon–Fri hourly 11am–2pm, $36; shorter tours Sun every 30 mins 1–6pm, $15; reservations advisable on ☎011/4361-3002, Ⓦwww.elzanjon.com.ar) was the site of both a pre-yellow-fever-era mansion and a *conventillo*. The visits take you underground through layers of history to see the reconstructed and tastefully lit tunnels where the city's water once flowed, and the cisterns the inhabitants used, though the tour price is a bit steep to see what are essentially little more than foundations and old water tanks. Don't, however, miss the **Mercado Municipal** (Mon–Sat 7am–2pm & 4.30–9pm, Sun 7am–2pm) on Defensa between Carlos Calvo and Estados Unidos, a thriving city-centre food market, and one of the few of its kind left in the city.

Plaza Dorrego

At the heart of San Telmo on the corner of Defensa and Humberto 1°, **Plaza Dorrego** is a tiny square surrounded by elegant mansions, most of them now converted into bars and antiques shops. During the week, cafés set up tables in the square, and on Sunday it becomes the setting for the city's long-running antiques market, the **Feria de San Pedro Telmo** (10am–5pm; Ⓦwww.feriadesantelmo .com). Overflowing with antique *mates*, jewel-coloured soda syphons, watches and old ticket machines from the city's buses, the stalls make for fascinating browsing, albeit through occasionally heavy crowds. There are no real bargains to be had – the stallholders and habitués are far too canny to let a gem slip through their fingers – but among the jumble you may find your own souvenir of Buenos Aires. The market's pickpockets are also very canny – one famously swiped the bag of former US President Bush's daughter despite the presence of six security guards – so be careful with your belongings.

After the stallholders pack away their wares on Sunday evenings, Plaza Dorrego becomes – weather permitting – the setting of a free outdoor **milonga** (tango dance; see box, p.143). There's a refreshing informality to this regular event, frequented by tourists, locals and tango fanatics alike, which might encourage even those with only a rudimentary knowledge of tango to take the plunge.

Parque Lezama and the Museo Histórico Nacional

Continuing south along Defensa will take you through a slightly more run-down though more authentic part of San Telmo, with its own neighbourhood cafés and stores. Four blocks on from Plaza Dorrego, you will reach the classic 24-hour café *Bar Británico* (see p.136), overlooking the **Parque Lezama**, an inviting green expanse. On a bluff towering over Paseo Colón, the park is generally regarded as the site of Buenos Aires' founding by **Pedro de Mendoza** in 1536. The conquistador's statue looms over you as you enter the park from the corner of Defensa and Brasil; a bronze of Mendoza thrusts his sword into the ground, while behind him a bas-relief shows an indigenous man, throwing up his hands in surrender. The park is best visited in early evening, when the sun filters through its trees, children run along its paths and groups of old men play cards or chess at stone tables. Opposite the north end of the park, look out for the exotic **Iglesia Ortodoxa Rusa** (☎011/4361-4274; Sat 5–8pm, Sun 10am–12.30pm; women must wear long skirts to be allowed entry) at Brasil 313. A mass of bright blue curvaceous domes, it was built in 1899 and contains many valuable icons donated by Tsar Nicolas II just as his empire was falling into decline.

Within the park, though entered via Defensa 1600, the **Museo Histórico Nacional** (Tues–Sun noon–6pm; free), founded in 1887, is housed in a magnificent colonial building painted a startling deep red and covered with elaborate white mouldings that resemble piped icing. The museum takes a tour through Argentina's history, concentrating mainly on the tumultuous nineteenth century, featuring portraits of all the big names from Argentina's formative years as well as maps and a number of important paintings of historical, rather than artistic, interest. But the high point of the collection is the stunning **Tarja de Potosí**, an elaborate silver and gold shield given to General Belgrano in 1813 by the women of Potosí (a silver-mining town in Upper Peru, now Bolivia) in recognition of his role in the struggle for independence from Spain. Over a metre tall, it's a delicately worked and intricate piece complete with tiny figures symbolizing the discovery of America.

Boca

More than any other barrio in Buenos Aires, **Boca** (or "La Boca") and its inhabitants seem to flaunt their idiosyncrasies. Located in the capital's southeastern corner, this working-class riverside neighbourhood has been nicknamed the "República de la Boca" since 1882, when a group of local youths declared that the barrio was seceding from the country. Even today, its residents – many new immigrants from other South American countries – have a reputation for playing by their own rules and are most famous for their brightly coloured wooden and corrugated-iron houses. The district was originally the favoured destination for Italian immigrants, and the colours of the houses derive from the Genoese custom

▲ San Telmo & Blues Special Club

of painting homes with the paint left over from boats. Boca's other most characteristic emblem is its football team, **Boca Juniors**, the country's most popular club and probably the most famous one abroad.

Named after the *boca*, or mouth, of the Río Riachuelo, which snakes along its southern border, Boca is an irregularly shaped barrio, longer than it is wide. Its main thoroughfare is Avenida Almirante Brown, which cuts through the neighbourhood from Parque Lezama to the towering iron **Puente Transbordador** that straddles the Riachuelo. Apart from some excellent pizzerias, there's little to detain you along the avenue: the majority of Boca's attractions are packed into the grids of streets on either side. Even then, there's not a great deal to see as such, and unless you plan to visit all the museums an hour or two will suffice; morning is the ideal time to go, when the light best captures the district's bright hues and before the tour buses arrive.

Be warned that Boca remains a poor neighbourhood and has an unfortunate reputation for crime, with muggings a fairly common occurrence. There's no need to be paranoid, but it is advisable to stick to the main tourist district and follow the advice of the police who patrol the area. The barrio is easily reached on foot from Parque Lezama or by bus #86 from Plaza de Mayo or #53 from Constitución; it's also on the route of the city government's tour bus (see p.80).

La Bombonera

The true heart of Boca is Boca Juniors' stadium, **La Bombonera**, at Brandsen 805. Built in 1940, it was remodelled in the 1990s and the name – literally "the chocolate box" – refers to its compact structure; although Boca has more fans than any other Argentine team, the stadium's capacity is less than several of its rivals. This is the place where many of the country's best young players cut their teeth before heading to Europe on lucrative deals – the Bombonera's most famous veteran is Diego Maradona (see box, p.107), who retains a VIP seat at the stadium. Seeing a game here is an incredible experience, even for non-soccer fans, and it's worth arranging your itinerary around one – see Basics, p.47, for more details.

If you don't get the opportunity to watch a match, at least head for the **Museo de la Pasión Boquense** and its **stadium tour** (daily 10am–6pm; $20 for museum

▲ Kids playing football, Boca

El Diego

Few people have captured the imagination of the Argentine public as much as **Diego Armando Maradona**. The diminutive no. 10 was the finest footballer of his generation, and arguably of all time – a bull of a player with exceptional close control, balance and on-field vision. Born in a poor neighbourhood on the outskirts of Buenos Aires, Maradona's playing career (1976–97) was peerless. He made his first-team, first-division debut for club **Argentinos Juniors** in 1976, when he was just 15 years old. Maradona wore the colours of seven clubs in total, including **Boca Juniors**, **Barcelona** and, most famously, **Napoli**, where he is still venerated as the player who brought southern Italy's poorer brother glory and silverware. He also led Argentina to win the World Cup in 1986, a campaign that included one of the most celebrated of all World Cup games, the quarter-final played against England, just four years after the South Atlantic conflict. Maradona scored two goals, including the infamous "Hand of God" goal, in which he tapped the ball in with his hand, and a second, legitimate goal considered to be one of the finest ever scored.

Like many geniuses, though, Maradona was flawed – in his case, by the excesses of alcohol and, particularly, drugs. He was suspended in 1991 for testing positive for cocaine, and then again for the banned substance ephedrine during the 1994 World Cup. After a low point in 2004 where he was hospitalized following a cocaine-induced heart attack, he bounced back to host his own talk show in 2005, where guests included Pele and Maradona's friend Fidel Castro. In 2008 he surprised many when he took over as coach of the Argentine national side and during qualifications for the 2010 World Cup was strongly criticized for his tactics (or lack of them) – which led him to more notoriety, this time when he launched an obscenity-laden tirade against the press following Argentina's qualification.

visit only or tour only, $30 for both; ⓦ www.museoboquense.com). The museum is a modern audiovisual experience, with a 360-degree film that puts you in the boots of a Boca player, and a charming model of how the barrio would have looked and sounded in the 1930s. The tour not only includes the stands, pitch and press conference room, but even the players' jacuzzi and dressing room, complete with statues of the Virgin Mary. Just inside the stadium entrance, there's a large painting by famous local artist Benito Quinquela Martín (see below) entitled *Orígen de la bandera de Boca* ("the origin of Boca's flag"), which illustrates one of the club's most famous anecdotes. Though the exact date and circumstances of the event are disputed, all agree that Boca chose the colours of its strip from the flag of the next ship to pass through its then busy port. The boat was Swedish, and thus the distinctive blue and yellow strip was born.

Around the stadium, a huddle of stalls and shops sell Boca souvenirs while, on the pavement outside the stadium, stars with the names of Boca players past and present, some featuring their footprints, were laid as part of the club's centenary celebrations in 2005. Some of the neighbouring houses have taken up the blue and yellow theme, too, with facades painted like giant football shirts. From the stadium it's a short walk southwards to La Boca's other nerve centre: Caminito.

Caminito and around

A former train siding now transformed into a pedestrian street and open-air art museum, **Caminito**, which runs diagonally between the riverfront and Calle Lamadrid, is the barrio's most famous street. Lined with the most pristine examples of Boca's coloured houses, it's very photogenic but not very lived-in – a life-size museum or a tourist trap, depending on your point of view. The street was "founded" by the barrio's most famous artist, **Benito Quinquela Martín**, who painted epic and expressive scenes of the neighbourhood's daily life. Quinquela Martín rescued the old siding from oblivion after the rail company removed the tracks in 1954. He encouraged the immigrants' tradition of painting their houses in bright colours and took the name for the street from a famous 1926 tango.

There's something of the pastiche about the Caminito these days, but, nonetheless, the bold blocks of rainbow-coloured walls, set off with contrasting window frames and balconies, are still an arresting sight. Down the middle of the street, there's an **arts and crafts fair**, dominated by garish paintings of the area. Tango musicians frequently perform along the street, too, accompanied by the sound of cameras clicking. At the western end of Caminito, Calle Garibaldi runs past and on south, a charmingly ramshackle street with a slew of coloured corrugated iron buildings, less done up than those of Caminito.

The eastern end of Caminito leads to Avenida Pedro de Mendoza and the Riachuelo, which bulges dramatically at this point, creating an inlet known as the **Vuelta de Rocha**. The view from Pedro de Mendoza is of a jumbled but majestic mass of boats, factories and bridges: directly south, across the river, there's the working-class suburb of Avellaneda while to your left there's one of Buenos Aires' major landmarks, the massive iron **Puente Transbordador**, or transport bridge, built in the early years of the twentieth century and now out of use. Next to the transport bridge is Puente Nicolás Avellaneda – a very similar construction built in 1939. This functioning bridge is one of the major causeways in and out of the city. Far below it, small rowing boats still ferry passengers to and from Avellaneda.

Fundación Proa and Museo de Bellas Artes de La Boca

Avenida Pedro de Mendoza is lined with cafés catering to the gangs of visiting tourists, plus two excellent **art museums**. The first is the **Fundación Proa** (Tues–Sun 11am–7pm, guided visits Sat & Sun noon–6pm in Spanish; $10; ☎011/4104-1000, ⓦwww.proa.org), at no. 1929. Set inside a converted mansion – all Italianate elegance outside and modern, angular galleries within – Proa has no permanent collection but hosts some fascinating and diverse exhibitions, usually with a Latin American theme, ranging from 1980s Argentine art to pre-Columbian Aztec sculptures.

Further east along Pedro de Mendoza at no. 1835 there's the long-established **Museo de Bellas Artes de La Boca** (Tues–Sun 10am–6pm; free). It was founded in 1938 by Benito Quinquela Martín on the site of his studio (now also a school) and houses many of his major works, as well as those of contemporary Argentine artists. It's the perfect setting for a display of Quinquela Martín's work, since you can actually see much of his subject matter simply by peering out of the windows of the gallery or climbing up to the viewpoint on the roof. More than anyone, Quinquela Martín conveyed the industrial grandeur of La Boca, dedicating himself to painting scenes of everyday life. Indeed, he was so associated with the city's least salubrious neighbourhood that, like the tango, he only garnered respect at home once he had become famous abroad.

The north

A combination of extravagant elegance and an authentic lived-in feel pervades **the north** of Buenos Aires, where the four residential barrios of most interest to visitors – Retiro, Recoleta, Palermo and Belgrano – each retain a distinctive character. Nearest to the centre, **Retiro** and **Recoleta** – known jointly as **Barrio Norte** – have chic streets lined with boutiques, art galleries and smart cafés, although the dockside fringes and the highly insalubrious bits near the city's biggest train station, also called Retiro, are just as down at heel as parts of the southern barrios, if not more so. Recoleta is associated primarily with its magnificent **cemetery** where, among other national celebrities, Evita is buried. Both barrios also share an extraordinary concentration of French-style **palaces**, tangible proof of the obsession of the city's elite at the beginning of the twentieth century with established European cities. Many of these palaces can be visited and some of them house the area's opulent museum collections, but they are also sights in themselves.

Palermo and **Belgrano**, further north, are large districts composed of a mixture of tall apartment buildings, tree-lined boulevards, little cobbled streets and grandiose neocolonial houses. Many of Buenos Aires' best **restaurants** and **shops** are here, so you should plan a visit in this direction at least once. It's worth making a day of it to check out the beautiful **parks** and **gardens**, attend a game of polo (see p.48), or to see another beguiling side of the city in, for example, Palermo Soho, a district of lively cafés-cum-art galleries.

Retiro

Squeezed between the city centre to the south, Recoleta to the west and mostly inhospitable docklands to the north and east, **Retiro** gets its name from a hermit's *retiro* (retreat) that was hidden among dense woodland here in the sixteenth century, when Buenos Aires was little more than a village. Today it's surprisingly varied for such a small barrio: commercial **art galleries** and airline offices outnumber other businesses along the busy streets around the end of Calle Florida near the barrio's focal point, Plaza San Martín, while west of busy Avenida 9 de Julio lies a smart, quiet residential area.

The rather sleazy northernmost swathe of the barrio is chiefly of interest for the **Museo Nacional de Inmigración**, a sort of Argentine equivalent of New York's Ellis Island. Lying at Retiro's aristocratic heart, meanwhile, **Plaza San Martín** is one of the city's most enticing green spaces, flanked by opulent patrician buildings. More outstanding examples of the barrio's palaces, which reflect how wealthy Porteños of the late nineteenth century yearned for their city to be a New World version of Paris, are clustered around **Plaza Carlos Pellegrini**, one of the city's most elegant squares. For most Porteños, the barrio's name has become synonymous with the once grand but now mostly decrepit train terminal, the **Estación Retiro**, on Avenida Dr Ramos Mejía, which still retains original Edwardian features, such as porcelain tiles and wrought-iron lamps. Next to it is the city's major bus terminal, a modern and fairly efficient complex, and beyond that urban wasteland and a shantytown. Retiro is easily reached on foot from the city centre, and is connected to the subte via San Martín and Retiro stations, both on Line C.

Museo Nacional de Inmigración

Between 1911 and 1920 just under half a million immigrants passed through the Gran Hotel de los Inmigrantes, Av Antártida Argentina 1355, now home to the **Museo Nacional de Inmigración** (Mon–Fri 10am–5pm, Sat & Sun 11am–6pm; free; ☏011/4317-0285), next to the Dársena Norte. They were encouraged to come by an Argentine government keen to populate the country's vast territory with "industrious" Europeans. For many, the state-run hotel was their first taste of life in the New World. The *microcine* room is most interesting, with its collection of photos and descriptions of daily life. Writ large are the words of a pamphlet given to Italian immigrants, informing them of the rules of social etiquette – don't spit, walk on the pavement so you're not taken for a beggar, take your hat off at the theatre and, whatever you do, don't call a lady *donna*. Modern

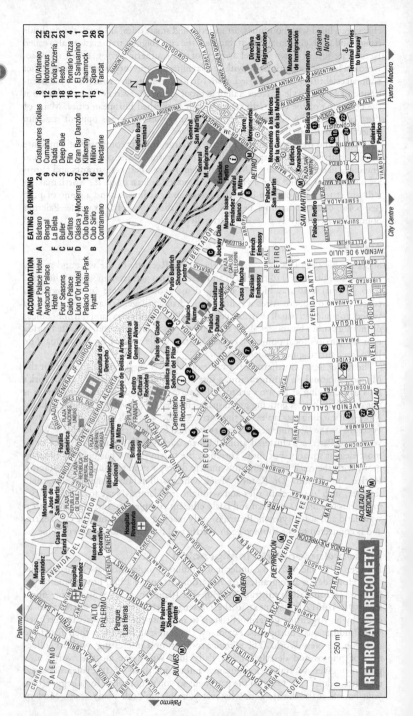

RETIRO AND RECOLETA

ACCOMMODATION
Alvear Palace Hotel	A
Ayacucho Palace Hotel	F
Four Seasons	C
Guido Palace	E
Lion d'Or Hotel	D
Palacio Duhau-Park Hyatt	B

EATING & DRINKING
Bárbaro	24	Costumbres Criollas	8
Bengal	9	Cumaná	12
La Biela	2	Dadá	19
Buller	3	Deep Blue	18
Carlitos	5	Filo	16
Clásica y Moderna	27	Gran Bar Danzón	11
Club Danés	13	Kilkenny	17
Club Sirio	6	Million	15
Contramano	B	Nectarine	14

ND/Ateneo	22
Notorious	25
Piola Pizzería	21
Restó	23
Romario Pizza	4
El Sanjuanino	10
Shamrock	1
Sipan	26
Tancat	20

0   250 m

Argentines can check their surname against the computer database of immigration records. A panel states: "Argentina gave them lodging and they bequeathed us their children and their children's children." Indeed, given the bearing immigration has had in shaping Argentina, it's a shame that more hasn't been done with the displays. The building is in the port area, behind the modern Migraciones headquarters, so it's advisable to take a taxi rather than negotiate the labyrinth of roads and their heavy traffic on foot.

Estación Retiro

A massive complex of rail terminals looming to the west of the museum, **Estación Retiro** is in fact three train stations in one: General San Martín, General Belgrano and General Mitre. The third of these is also by far the most impressive, a massive stone and metal structure completed in 1915 by Charles John Dudley, a British constructor based in Liverpool. Decorated with Royal Doulton porcelain tiles, it is a majestic, airy edifice with an iron roof that, at the time, was the largest of its kind in the world. Recently restored to its former glory, it's worth a visit for its splendid café, *Café Retiro*. This is also the place to come if you plan to take the train to Tigre (see p.154).

Plaza San Martín

Immediately southeast of the stations, the leafy **Plaza San Martín** plays many roles: romantic meeting-place, picnic area for office workers, children's playground and many people's arrival point in downtown Buenos Aires, owing to the main train and bus terminals nearby. Plaza San Martín was designed by Argentina's most important landscape architect, Frenchman **Charles Thays** (see box, p.113), and created especially for a monument to **General San Martín** that was moved to its southwestern corner in 1910 for the country's centenary. Aligned with Avenida Santa Fe, the imposing bronze equestrian statue stands proudly on a high marble pedestal decorated with scenes representing national liberation. The Libertador points west, showing the way across the Andes. The plaza's lush lawns are a favourite sunbathing spot in the warmer months, but when it gets baking hot you can always cool down on a bench beneath the luxuriant palms, *ceibos*, monkey puzzles, lime trees and acacias.

Monumento a los Héroes de la Guerra de las Malvinas

The more open, northern half of Plaza San Martín slopes down to Avenida del Libertador, which runs through northern Buenos Aires all the way to Tigre. The **Monumento a los Héroes de la Guerra de las Malvinas** stands on the brow of the slope, a sombre cenotaph comprising 28 black marble plaques inscribed with the 649 names of the country's fallen during the conflict, its eternal flame partly symbolizing Argentina's persistent claim over the South Atlantic islands. It is permanently guarded by a rotation of the army, navy and air force, and is the scene of both remembrance ceremonies and demonstrations on April 2 each year, the day on which Argentina began its brief occupation of the islands in 1982. The monument was deliberately placed opposite the former Plaza Británica – called the Plaza Fuerza Aérea Argentina since 1982.

Torre Monumental (Torre de los Ingleses)

At the centre of the Plaza Fuerza Aérea Argentina there are echoes of London's Big Ben in the 76-metre high **Torre de los Ingleses** (Mon–Fri 10am–5pm, Sat & Sun 10am–6.30pm; free), the Anglo-Argentine community's contribution to the 1910 centenary celebrations. During and after the 1982 conflict there was talk of demolishing the tower, and it was officially renamed Torre Monumental, though no one calls it that. The lift that used to carry visitors to the top for great views has been out of operation for some years, but it is still worth going inside to see the collections of interesting old photos of Retiro or to chat to the tower's caretaker – a fount of knowledge on local history and museums throughout the city.

Basílica del Santísimo Sacramento

The **Basílica del Santísimo Sacramento**, at San Martín 1039, lurks east of the Plaza San Martín, at the end of a narrow *pasaje* and rather dwarfed by the skyscrapers surrounding it. It was built with some of the vast fortune of Mercedes Castellanos de Anchorena, a matriarchal figure who married into one of Argentina's wealthiest and most influential landowning clans (hence the Argentine expression "as rich as an Anchorena"). Consecrated in 1916, the basilica is still regarded as the smartest place to get married in Buenos Aires. Not surprisingly, it was designed by French architects, with a white marble dome and five slender turrets; it's no coincidence that it looks so much like Paris's Sacré Coeur. Inside, no expense was spared: red onyx from Morocco, marble from Verona and Carrara, red sandstone from the Vosges, glazed mosaic tiles from Venice and bronze from France were imported to decorate her monument to devotion. Down in the crypt and behind a protective grille is Mercedes Castellanos de Anchorena's **mausoleum**, an ostentatious yet doleful concoction of marble angels guarded by a demure Virgin Mary.

Edificio Kavanagh

The **Edificio Kavanagh**, next to the basilica at San Martín and Florida 1065, similarly sums up the social – and architectural – evolution in twentieth-century Buenos Aires. It is rumoured that Corina Kavanagh sold most of her property in the country to erect what, when it went up in 1935, was to be the tallest building (120m) in South America. It is also rumoured that she deliberately built it in front of the basilica to conceal her bitter rival's masterpiece. The two facades of its distinctive flat-iron shape – it's built in a wedge formed by the two streets – were hailed at the time by the American Institute of Architects as the world's best example of Rationalist architecture, and the building was inhabited in the early years by many of the city's rich and famous.

Palacio Retiro

Press baron José Paz, founder of daily newspaper *La Prensa* and related by marriage to the Anchorenas, wanted his Buenos Aires home to look like the Louvre in Paris, so he commissioned the **Palacio Retiro** (guided visits only, in English Wed & Thurs 3.30pm, $34; in Spanish Tues–Fri 11am & 3pm, Sat 11am, $18; Ⓦwww .palaciopaz.com.ar) – previously known as the Palacio Paz – to be built by a French architect between 1902 and 1914. Sadly, however, Paz died in 1912, without ever seeing the finished product. The palace runs along the southwest side of Plaza San Martín, and access is via magnificent wrought-iron gates at Av Santa Fe 750. It remains the largest single house ever built in Argentina, and its main facade is an uncanny replica of the Sully wing of the Louvre, with steeply stacked slate roofs, a double row of tiny windows and a colonnaded ground floor.

Inside, the eighteen rooms open to the public – less than one-sixth of the whole building – are decorated in an eclectic range of French styles, from Gothic to Empire, including a scaled-down copy of the Hall of Mirrors in Versailles, but the *pièce de résistance* is the great Hall of Honour, a cavernous, circular room lined with several types of European marble and crowned with a stained-glass dome from which the Sun King beams down. Artur Rubinstein entertained guests in the little

Charles Thays: Buenos Aires' landscape artist

In the 1880s, French botanist and **landscape architect Charles Thays** (1849–1934) travelled to South America to study its rich flora, particularly the continent's hundreds of endemic tree species. He initially settled in Argentina, where his services were in great demand as municipal authorities across the country sought to smarten their cities up. They, like their European and North American counterparts, were spurred by the realization that the country's fast-growing urban sprawls needed parks and gardens to provide vital breathing spaces and recreational areas.

In 1890, Thays was appointed director of parks and gardens in Buenos Aires, in no small part due to his adeptness at transforming open plazas formerly used for military parades, or *plazas secas*, into shady *plazas verdes*, or green squares, such as Plaza San Martín. He also designed the capital's botanical garden and the zoo – which he planted with dozens of *tipas* (also known as *palo rosa*, or rosewood) – as well as Palermo's Parque 3 de Febrero, Belgrano's Barrancas, Córdoba's Parque Sarmiento and Parque San Martín, Tucumán's Parque 9 de Julio and, most impressive of them all, Mendoza's Parque General San Martín. Thays received countless private commissions, too, including the garden of Palacio Hume, on Avenida Alvear in Recoleta, and the layout of the exclusive residential estate known as Barrio Parque, in Palermo Chico.

Despite his French origins, he preferred the informal English style of landscaping, and also experimented with combinations of native plants such as jacarandas, tipas and *palo borracho* (a spiky-trunked relative of the *ceibo* with handsome pink flowers) with Canary Island palms, planes and lime trees. Oddly enough, given the high regard in which he was held and his contributions to the greening of Buenos Aires, the lone plaza named in his honour, Plaza Carlos Thays, in Palermo, is disappointingly barren, and definitely not the best example of landscaping the city has to offer.

---

music room and the Prince of Wales dined here during his visit to the city in 1925, but the Paz family fell on hard times in the late 1930s, most of the original furniture was sold off and the palace was divided between the Círculo Militar, an officers' club, and the **Museo de Armas de la Nación** (Tues–Fri 1–6.30pm; $6). The latter now houses an exhibition of armour, weapons and military uniforms, some dating back to the Wars of Independence.

Palacio San Martín

Just north of the Palacio Retiro and northwest of Plaza San Martín, at Arenales and Esmeralda, **Palacio San Martín** (free guided visits in English and Spanish Mon & Wed 2.30pm; ☎011/4819-8092) is a particularly extravagant example of the city's ostentatious palaces. Built in 1905 for the **Anchorena** family, it was originally known as the Palacio Anchorena. Mercedes Castellanos de Anchorena (see opposite) lived here with her family for twenty years, until the Great Depression left them penniless. The enormous building is actually divided up into three subtly different palaces, all sharing a huge Neoclassical entrance and ceremonial courtyard. Its overall structure is based on a nineteenth-century Parisian banker's mansion, with slate mansard roofs, colonnades and domed attics, while the neo-Baroque interior is inspired by the eighteenth-century Hotel de Condé, also in Paris. Fashionable Art Nouveau details, such as ornate stained-glass windows and wrought-iron staircases, were also incorporated.

After the palace and its accumulated treasures were hurriedly sold off in 1927, the government turned it into the Ministry of Foreign Affairs, International Trade and Worship, and renamed it Palacio San Martín. Since the 1980s, when the ministry moved into the larger plate-glass building across Calle Esmeralda, the palace has been reserved for state ceremonies, and is open to the public for tours. Some of the original furniture and paintings have been recovered, but the guided visits are above all a rare opportunity to witness the opulent interior of a Porteño palace. The gilt mirrors, marble fireplaces and chandeliers are all on a grandiose scale, yet they still look lost in the cavernous rooms, with their polished parquet floors, inlaid wooden panelling and ceilings richly decorated with oil paintings.

Museo de Arte Hispanoamericano Isaac Fernández Blanco

Two blocks north and one west of Palacio San Martín, at Suipacha 1422, the **Museo de Arte Hispanoamericano Isaac Fernández Blanco** (Tues–Fri 2–7pm, Sat & Sun 11am–7pm; $1; ⊤011/4327-0228, ⓦwww .museofernandezblanco.buenosaires.gov.ar), is one of the city's undisputed cultural highlights. The museum occupies the **Palacio Noel**, a stunning Neocolonial house built in the 1920s by architect Martín Noel, who later donated it to the city. Its style imitates eighteenth-century Lima Baroque, a backlash against the slavish imitation of Parisian palaces fashionable at the time. With plain white walls, lace-like window-grilles, dark wooden bow windows and wrought-iron balconies, it's the perfect residence for the superb collection of **Spanish–American art** on display inside. Most of the artefacts on display, all favourably presented, were produced in the seventeenth and early eighteenth centuries, in Peru or Alto Peru (present-day Bolivia).

The collection is spread across three floors and divided into three principal parts – the influence of the Conquest in the Andes, Buenos Aires as the port to the continent and the mix of Jesuit and indigenous cultures in the jungle. One of the most striking pieces is a fantastic eighteenth-century silver sacrarium, embellished with a portrait of Christ on a copper plaque. Other high points of this huge and varied collection include a Luso-Brazilian silver votive lamp, polychrome furniture – the work of Bolivian craftsmen – and fine Jesuit/Guaraní statues, all carved from wood. There's also an extensive display of anonymous paintings from the **Cusqueña School** – one of the most prodigious in colonial South America. Its masters, based in the Peruvian city of Cusco and especially active in the eighteenth century, produced subtle oil paintings, mostly of religious, devotional subjects, which combined sombre understatement with a startling vitality and mixed traditional Catholic imagery with indigenous motifs.

Plaza Carlos Pellegrini and around

The elegant triangle of **Plaza Carlos Pellegrini** is a centre of Retiro's well-heeled residential streets west of Avenida 9 de Julio, and near it you'll find a variety of spectacular buildings that share a common theme: their meticulous French style. Between 1910 and 1925, the obsession with turning Buenos Aires into the "Paris of the South" reached a fever pitch in this part of the city, making this neighbourhood one of the more exclusive, something it remains to this day. The many feats of **Carlos Pellegrini**, president in the 1890s and the plaza's namesake, include founding both the Banco Nación and Argentina's influential **Jockey Club**; the latter's national headquarters occupies the massive honey-coloured **Palacio Unzué de Casares**, on the north side of the plaza at Av Alvear 1345. Built in the severely unadorned *style académique*, it's alleviated only by its delicate wrought-iron balconies. Opposite, on the south side of the plaza, stands the **Palacio Celedonio Pereda**, named after a member of the oligarchy who wanted a carbon copy of the Palais Jacquemart-André in Paris. The Porteño palace, now occupied by the Brazilian Embassy, is a uniformly successful replica, classical columns and all.

Directly east of the plaza, at the corner of Calle Cerrito, ivy-clad **Casa Atucha** presides, a soberly stylish Second Empire mansion by René Sergent, a French architect who never set foot in Argentina but designed dozens of houses here. Half a block north, at Cerrito 1455, the **Mansion Alzaga Unzué** now forms a luxurious annexe of the *Four Seasons* hotel (see p.86). It's a faultless duplicate of a Loire chateau, built in attractive red brick and cream limestone and topped with a shiny slate mansard roof. Back up on the other side of Arroyo, the Louis XIV-style **Palacio Ortiz Basualdo** has been the location of the French Embassy since 1925. This magnificent palace with slightly incongruous detailing, including Art Nouveau balconies, monumental Ionic pilasters and bulging Second Empire corner turrets, mercifully escaped demolition in the 1950s when Avenida 9 de Julio was widened, though it did have to be altered considerably to accommodate the highway. From Plaza Carlos Pellegrini, Avenida Alvear leads due northwest to Recoleta.

Recoleta

Northwest of Retiro and stretching all the way to Avenida Coronel Díaz, the well-heeled barrio of **Recoleta** is, for most Porteños, intrinsically tied to the magnificent **La Recoleta Cemetery** at its heart. Recoleta wasn't always a prestigious place, though: until the end of the seventeenth century, its groves of Barbary figs were hideouts for notorious brigands. It wasn't until the cholera and yellow fever epidemics of 1867 and 1871 that the city's wealthy moved here from hitherto fashionable San Telmo. Although many of its residents have left for the northern suburbs in recent years, a Recoleta address still has cachet. **Avenida Alvear** is Buenos Aires' swankiest street: along it you'll find stately **palaces**, plus designer **boutiques**, swish art galleries and one of the city's most prestigious hotels. Scattered throughout the barrio are a host of **restaurants** and bars, ranging from some of the city's most traditional to trendy joints that come and go.

Recoleta's other notable attractions include one of the capital's few remaining colonial buildings, the gleaming white **Basílica Nuestra Señora del Pilar**; the **Centro Cultural de Recoleta**; and the country's biggest and richest collection of nineteenth- and twentieth-century art at the **Museo Nacional de Bellas Artes**.

The subte skirts the southern edge of Recoleta, but the barrio is walking distance (or a short cab ride) from the city centre.

Avenida Alvear

Only five blocks in length, stretching from Plaza Carlos Pellegrini to Plaza San Martín de Tours, Avenida Alvear is one of the city's shortest but most exclusive avenues, lined with expensive **art galleries** – selling mostly conventional portraits and landscapes but also some avant-garde pieces – and international designer **fashion boutiques** like Louis Vuitton and Emporio Armani. At the corner of Ayacucho lies the city's most famous and traditional luxury hotel, the French Art Deco **Alvear Palace** (see p.86), built in 1932.

Two blocks south, opposite elegant apartment buildings between Montevideo and Rodriguez Peña, are three palaces that were home to some of Argentina's wealthiest families at the beginning of the twentieth century. Although none is open to the public, the exteriors are worth a peek for their splendid architecture. The northernmost, behind a Charles Thays-designed garden, is the **Palacio Hume**. This perfectly symmetrical Art Nouveau creation, embellished with intricate wrought-iron work, now looks a little the worse for wear. It was originally built for British rail-engineer Alexander Hume, but was sold to the Duhau family in the 1920s, who staged the city's first-ever art exhibition inside. The Duhau family also built the middle palace, the **Palacio Duhau**, now the *Park Hyatt* (see p.86). This austere imitation of an eighteenth-century French Neoclassical *palais* has been converted into another of the city's leading hotels. The third palace, the severely Neoclassical **Nunciatura Apostólica** on the corner of Montevideo, was designed by a French architect for a member of the Anchorena family. Nowadays it's the seat of the Vatican's Argentina representative, and was used by Pope John Paul II during his visits to the country.

La Recoleta Cemetery

In around 1720, drawn to the area's tranquillity, which was deemed perfect for meditation or "recollection" (hence the name), Franciscan monks set up a monastery in present-day Recoleta. A hundred years later, after the monks had been ejected by the city governor, **La Recoleta Cemetery**, at Avenida Quintana and Junín (daily 7am–6pm; guided tours in English Tues & Thurs 11am; free), was created in the monastery's gardens. One of the world's most remarkable burial grounds, it presents an exhilarating mixture of architectural whimsy and a panorama of Argentine history. The giant vaults, stacked along avenues inside the high walls, resemble the rooftops of a fanciful Utopian town from above. The necropolis is a city within a city, a lesson in architectural styles and fashions, and a great place to wander, exploring its narrow streets and wide avenues of yews and cypress trees.

The **tombs** themselves range from simple headstones to bombastic masterpieces built in a variety of styles including Art Nouveau, Art Deco, Secessionist, Neoclassical, neo-Byzantine and even neo-Babylonian. The oldest monumental grave, dating from 1836, is that of **Juan Facundo Quiroga**, the much-feared La Rioja *caudillo* (local leader) immortalized in the Latin American classic *Facundo* by Argentine statesman and writer Domingo Sarmiento, also buried here. Facundo's tomb stands straight ahead of the gateway. Next to it, inscribed with a Borges poem, stands the solemn granite mausoleum occupied by several generations of the eminent Alvear family. The vast majority of tombs in Recoleta belong to similar patrician families of significant means – but not all. Perhaps the most incongruous statue in the cemetery is that of a boxer, in the northwest sector – the final resting place of **Angel Firpo**, who fought Jack Dempsey for the world heavyweight title in 1923. Military heroes, many of them Irish or British seafarers who played a key part in Argentina's struggle for independence, are also buried here, such as **Admiral William Brown**. An Argentine hero of Irish origins, at the beginning of the nineteenth century Brown decimated the Spanish fleet in the River Plate estuary. An unusual monument decorated with a beautiful miniature of his frigate, the *Hercules*, is a highlight of the cemetery's central plaza.

Evita's final resting place

Recoleta cemetery's most famous resident is undoubtedly **Evita Perón**, second wife of President Juan Perón and one of Argentina's most enduring figures (see box, p.597), who died in 1952. Given the snobbishness surrounding the cemetery – the authorities who preside over it treat it more like a gentlemen's club than a burial ground – it's hardly surprising that Porteño high society tried to prevent Evita's family from laying her to rest here. Nevertheless, her family's plain, polished black granite vault, pithily marked **Familia Duarte** and containing poignant quotes on bronze plaques from her speeches, has been her resting place since the 1970s – with the coffin supposedly inside concrete to prevent it from disappearing. Unlike many other graves, it's not signposted (the cemetery authorities are still uneasy about her presence) but you can locate it by following the signs to Sarmiento's, over to the left when you come in, then counting five alleyways farther away from the entrance, and looking out for the pile of bouquets by the vault.

Basílica Nuestra Señora del Pilar

Just north of the cemetery gates is the stark white silhouette of the **Basílica Nuestra Señora del Pilar** (Mon–Sat 10.30am–6.15pm, Sun 2.30–6.15pm; free; @www.basilicadelpilar.org.ar). Built in the early eighteenth century by Jesuits, it's the second oldest church in Buenos Aires and effectively the parish church for the Recoleta elite. The sky-blue Pas-de-Calais ceramic tiles atop its single slender turret were restored in the 1930s, along with the plain facade. The interior was also remodelled, and the monks' cells turned into side chapels, each decorated with a gilded reredos and polychrome wooden saints. These include a statue of San Pedro de Alcántara, the Virgen de la Merced and the Casa de Ejercicios, all attributed to a native artist known simply as "José". The magnificent Baroque silver altarpiece, embellished with an Inca sun and other pre-Hispanic details, was made by craftsmen from Alto Peru. Equally admirable is the fine altar crucifix allegedly donated to the city by King Carlos III of Spain. It is possible to visit the cloisters above the church (same hours as church; $2) via the staircase three altars to the left. The rooms, once home to the Franciscan monks, now hold a collection of religious paintings and artefacts, including some impressive colonial and *criollo* silverware. From the windows you get a good view over Recoleta Cemetery.

Centro Cultural Recoleta and around

Immediately north of Basílica Nuestra Señora del Pilar, at Junín 1930, the **Centro Cultural Recoleta** (Mon–Fri 2–8pm, Sat & Sun 10am–9pm; free) is one of the city's leading **arts centres**, a good deal bigger and more impressive inside than its modest front suggests. The building, which dates from the 1730s, is one of Buenos Aires' oldest, and originally housed the area's Franciscan monks. The building was extensively, but tastefully, remodelled in the 1980s and retains its former cloisters. These cool, white, arched hallways and simple rooms make an excellent setting for the changing art, photography and audiovisual exhibitions that the centre hosts. There are also a number of auditoriums for theatre, dance and music, including the **Sala Villa Villa**, the occasional home of the internationally renowned anarchic theatre troupe De La Guarda/Fuerza Bruta.

Opposite the centre, grassy **Plaza San Martín de Tours** is shaded by three of the biggest rubber trees in the city, an impressive sight with their huge buttress-roots, contorted like arthritic limbs. A one-hundred-year-old rubber tree, the famous *Gran Gomero*, shelters the terrace of nearby *La Biela*, on the corner of Avenida Quintana. One of the city's most traditional *confiterías*, *La Biela* gets its name, which means "connecting-rod", from being the favourite haunt of racing drivers in the 1940s and 50s, and was a frequent guerrilla target in the 1970s, owing to its conspicuously wealthy patrons. On the other side of the cultural centre in Plaza Francia, buskers, jugglers and groups practising the fluid Brazilian martial art of *capoeira* entertain crowds during the **Fería Plaza Francia**, also known as the Feria Hippy, at weekends (11am–8pm; free), while artisans sell hand-crafted wares including *mate* gourds, jewellery and ceramics at stalls arranged along the wide paths.

Museo Nacional de Bellas Artes

Argentina's principal art museum, the **Museo Nacional de Bellas Artes** (Tues–Fri 12.30–8.30pm, Sat & Sun 9.30am–8.30pm; free; @www.mnba.org.ar) occupies an unassuming, slightly gloomy, brick-red Neoclassical building at Av del Libertador 1473, half a kilometre due north of Recoleta Cemetery. Like the barrio's architecture, the museum's contents, comprising mostly nineteenth- and twentieth-century paintings and some sculpture, are resoundingly European, while the Old World influences on the Argentine art on display are clearly evident.

Only about a tenth of the museum's collection of 11,000 exhibits is on display at any time. The whole of the ground floor is given over to **international art**, dominated by French, Dutch and Italian masters such as Degas and Rubens. Later masters as varied as Pollock, Picasso and Italo-Argentine Lucio Fontana also feature. In a room by itself, the wide-ranging **Hirsch bequest** – left to the nation by the wealthy Belgrano landowners and art-collectors – includes some fabulous European paintings, sculptures, furniture and other art objects spanning several centuries, including a Spanish retable (an ornamental screen behind the altar) and a portrait by Rembrandt of his sister.

The upper-floor galleries are an excellent introduction to **Argentine art**, containing a selection of the country's major artists. The works span from pre-Columbian terracotta and textiles, through nineteenth-century European imitators such as Prilidiano Pueyrredón and Eduardo Sívori to the Argentine artists in the twentieth century who managed to break away from this imitative tendency and create a movement of their own, like Guillermo Kuitca and Xul Solar (who has a museum dedicated to his works in Recoleta; see below).

Floralis Genérica

Behind the Museo Nacional de Bellas Artes lurks the massive Doric columns of the Facultad de Derecho (Law Faculty), next to which it's hard to miss the 25-metre-high aluminium and steel bloom named **Floralis Genérica**, one of the city's newest sculptures. Argentine architect **Eduardo Catalano** donated this work to the city as a tribute to all flowers and a symbol of "hope for the country's new spring". A system of light sensors and hydraulics closes the petals at sunset and opens them again at 8am, but they stay open on May 25, September 21 (the beginning of spring), Christmas Eve and New Year's Eve.

Museo Xul Solar

The **Museo Xul Solar** (Tues–Fri noon–8pm, Sat noon–7pm, closed Jan; $10; guided visits Tues & Thurs 4pm, Sat 3.30pm; Ⓦwww.xulsolar.org.ar) is at Laprida 1212, deep in residential Recoleta. The museum is in the "Fundación Pan Klub", an early twentieth-century townhouse where, for the last twenty years of his life, eccentric Porteño artist Xul Solar (1888–1963) lived. The house was remodelled in the 1990s, and its award-winning design is as exciting as the display of Solar's paintings and other works. The space contains work spanning nearly five decades and is on several different levels, built of timber and glass, each dedicated to a specific period in the artist's career. As well as paintings, there's a set of "Pan Altars", multicoloured mini-retables designed for his "universal religions" – Solar once told Borges that he had "founded twelve new religions since lunch". Other curiosities include a piano whose keyboard he replaced with three rows of painted keys with textured surfaces, created both for blind pianists and to implement his notion of the correspondence of colour and music.

Palermo

Much of **Palermo**, Buenos Aires' largest barrio, is vibrantly green and appealingly well kempt: ornate balconies overflow with jasmine and roses, grand apartment blocks line wide avenues, and plane trees, palms and jacarandas shade older, cobbled streets; its beautifully landscaped parks, some of the biggest in the world, come alive with locals practising in-line skating, playing football or walking their dogs.

Palermo takes its name from an Italian farmer, Giovanni Palermo, who in 1590 turned these former flood plains into vineyards and orchards. The barrio began to take on its present-day appearance when large parks and gardens were laid out at the end of the nineteenth century; the process of gentrification continued and Palermo is now regarded as a distinctly classy place to live.

Given its sizeable proportions – it stretches all the way from Avenida Coronel Díaz, on the border with Recoleta, to Colegiales and Belgrano, to the north – it's not surprising that the barrio isn't completely homogeneous. The bit of Palermo around Plaza República de Chile that juts into Recoleta is known as **Palermo Chico** and contains some significant museums, including the **Museo de Arte Decorativo**. Nearby, the **Museo de Arte Latinoamericano de Buenos Aires (MALBA)** is a must for fans of modern art. About ten blocks west, **Palermo Viejo** is a traditional neighbourhood with lovely old houses along cobbled streets, but it's become such a trendy place, full of funky cafés and avant-garde art galleries, that the area around Plaza Cortázar is now known as **Soho**. Across the rail tracks, people in the media work, eat and drink in a cluster of TV studios, restaurants and bars that have been christened **Hollywood**. Much of the north of Palermo is taken up by parks and gardens, such as the grand **Parque 3 de Febrero**, giving the area its soubriquet the "**bosques de Palermo**" (Palermo woods). At the barrio's northern edge is **Las Cañitas**, a zone of upmarket bars and restaurants, focused on the corner of Báez and Arévalo.

Part of subte Line D runs underneath Avenida Santa Fe, one of Palermo's main arteries, and where appropriate the nearest station is indicated in the text. Otherwise, take one of the many buses that go up avenidas Las Heras and Del Libertador, such as #10 or #38.

Museo de Arte Decorativo

There's no finer example of the decadent decor money could buy in early twentieth-century Buenos Aires than that on display in the **Museo de Arte Decorativo**, Av del Libertador 1902 (Tues–Sun 2–7pm; $2, free Tues; guided visits in English 2.30pm Tues–Sat; ⓦwww.mnad.org.ar), with its remarkable collection of art and furniture. The museum is housed in **Palacio Errázuriz**, one of the city's most original private mansions, albeit of typically French design. The two-storey palace was built in 1911 for a Chilean diplomat and his patrician Argentine wife, and was turned into a museum in 1937. Designed by René Sergent, a French architect and proponent of the Academic style, it has three contrasting facades. The western one, on Sanchez de Bustamante, is inspired by the Petit Trianon at Versailles; the long northern side of the building with its Corinthian pillars, on Avenida del Libertador, is based on the palaces on Paris's Place de la Concorde; and the eastern end, near the entrance, is dominated by an

Dog walkers

Along the wide avenues and in the many parks of Barrio Norte and Palermo, you'll often be treated to one of Buenos Aires' more characteristic sights: the *paseaperros*, or professional **dog walkers**. Joggers holding seven or eight prized pedigrees on leashes are surprising enough, but these dilettantes are rightly held in contempt by the beefy specialists who confidently swagger along towed by twenty to thirty dogs – you can't help wondering how it is they don't get tangled up or lose one of the pack. These invariably athletic young men (or, occasionally, women) are not paid just to take all manner of aristocratic breeds for a stroll, with the inevitable pit stops along the way, but must brush and groom them and look out for signs of ill health; many dog walkers have veterinary training. They perform these vital duties every weekday – the dogs' owners usually manage such chores themselves on the weekends.

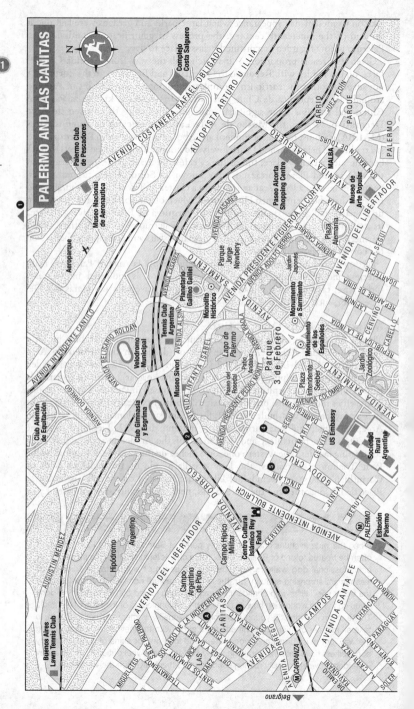

PALERMO AND LAS CAÑITAS

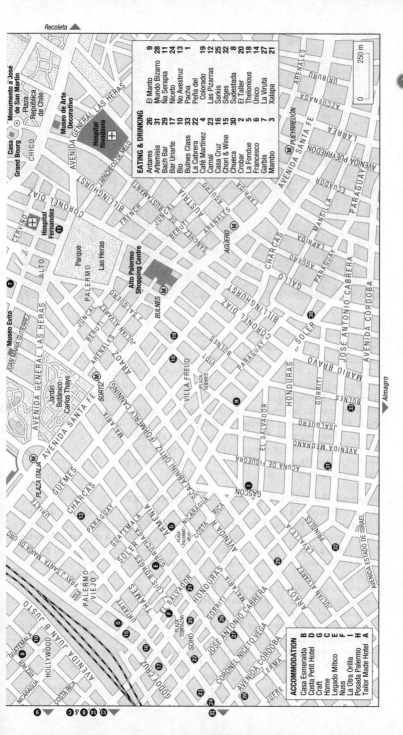

BUENOS AIRES

Recoleta ▲

Casa Grand Bourg
Monumento a José de San Martín
Plaza República de Chile
Museo de Arte Decorativo
Hospital Rivadavia

Museo Evita

Alto Palermo Shopping Centre

Jardín Botánico Carlos Thays

Almagro ▼

EATING & DRINKING

Antares	26
Artemisia	31
Bach Bar	29
Bar Uriarte	17
Bio	10
Bulnes Class	33
La Cabrera	22
Café Martínez	4
Carnal	23
Casa Cruz	16
Chori & Wine	15
Chueca	30
Crobar	2
La Fondue	5
Francesco	6
Garbis	7
Mambo	3
El Manto	9
Mundo Bizarro	28
Ña Serapia	11
Niceto	24
No Avestruz	13
Pacha	1
Peña del Colorado	19
Las Pizarras	12
Sarkis	25
Sitges	32
Sudestada	8
El Taller	20
Thelonious	18
Único	14
La Viruta	27
Xalapa	21

ACCOMMODATION

Casa Esmeralda	B
Costa Petit Hotel	D
Craft	G
Home	E
Legado Mítico	F
Nuss	I
La Otra Orilla	H
Posada Palermo	A
Tailor Made Hotel	C

0   250 m

121

▲ Exhibition Hall, Museo de Arte Decorativo

enormous semicircular stone porch, supported by four Tuscan columns. The coach house, now a restaurant and tearoom, *Croque Madame*, sits just beyond the monumental wrought-iron and bronze gates, in the style of Louis XVI.

The interior is as French as the exterior, especially the Regency ballroom, lined with gilded Rococo panels and huge mirrors, all stripped from a Parisian house. The couple's extravagant taste in **art** – Flemish furniture and French clocks, Sèvres porcelain, bronzes by Bourdelle, and paintings, old and modern, ranging from El Greco (*Christ Bearing the Cross*) to Manet (*The Sacrifice of the Rose*) – is reflected and preserved. In the basement resides a Gothic chapel, transferred from the Château de Champagnette in France. Temporary exhibitions of ancient and contemporary art are also held down here, or in the garden in the summer, as are classical concerts.

Museo de Arte Popular José Hernández

A very different kind of art from that on display at the Museo de Arte Decorativo can be found further along Avenida del Libertador in a rambling Neocolonial house at no. 2373, home to the small **Museo de Arte Popular José Hernández** (Wed–Fri 1–7pm, Sat & Sun 10am–8pm; $1, free Sun; guided tours on request; Ⓦ www.museohernandez.org.ar). José Hernández wrote the great gaucho classic *Martín Fierro* (1872), a revolutionary epic poem that made *campo* (peasant) culture respectable, and in this vein the museum's purpose is to highlight the value of **popular crafts**. It has a permanent exhibition about Argentine folk heritage housed in two buildings separated by a shady patio. The first section is an impressive but unimaginatively presented display of mostly nineteenth-century rural silverware; spurs, stirrups, saddles, knives and gaucho weaponry stand side by side with a large collection of fine silver *mate* ware, including a particularly splendid and unusual *mate* vessel in the shape of an ostrich. The second part, across the courtyard, comprises a number of beautiful Mapuche hand-woven ponchos displayed alongside factory-made competition.

Museo de Arte Latinoamericano de Buenos Aires (MALBA)

One of the city's best museums, the **Museo de Arte Latinoamericano de Buenos Aires** (MALBA; Thurs–Mon noon–8pm, Wed noon–9pm; $15, Wed $5; Ⓦ www.malba.org.ar) is at Avenida Figueroa Alcorta 3415, two blocks north of the Museo de Arte Popular. The modern, glass-fronted, purpose-built building is an attraction in its own right and its airy, spacious galleries contrast with the dark nooks and crannies of the city's more traditional art museums.

The permanent **Constantini collection**, on the first floor up, concentrates on the best Latin American art of the twentieth century. It is arranged chronologically, beginning around 1910, when the Modernist movement in Latin America heralded the start of a real sense of regional identity. This is exemplified in paintings such as a series by Argentine master Xul Solar, a Frida Kahlo self-portrait and Brazilian Tarsila Do Amaral's Mexican-influenced *Abaporu*. Dark political undercurrents run through the 1930s to 1950s and the work of Antonio Berni and the Chilean Roberto Matta, while Catholic traditions are given a Surrealist twist in Remedios Varo's votive box *Icono*. Things get more conceptual from the 1960s on, with the moving installations of Julio Le Parc and the LSD-splashed "end of art" collages by the "Nueva Figuración" movement.

Upstairs, temporary exhibitions generally feature the collected works of a prominent modern or contemporary artist, often an Argentine. MALBA also has its own small art house cinema (see website for programme), a café open until midnight, a bookstore and a fun gift shop.

Palermo Viejo

Palermo Viejo, bounded by avenidas Santa Fe, Córdoba, Juan B. Justo and Raúl Scalabrini Ortíz, is the city's most fashionable place to live, shop or have an evening out. The part of the city most closely linked to Borges, where he lived and began writing poetry in the 1920s, its architecture has changed little since then. It's a compact oblong of narrow streets, most of them still cobbled and lined with brightly painted one- or two-storey Neocolonial villas and townhouses, many of them recently restored, some of them hidden behind luxuriant gardens full of bougainvillea and jasmine. Part run-down, part gentrified, it's a leafy district with a laidback bohemian ambience, and many of its stylish houses have been converted into bars, cafés and boutiques. Large communities from Poland, Ukraine, Lebanon and Armenia live here, alongside a larger Italian contingent and some old Spanish families, and they all have their shops, churches and clubs, adding to the district's colour. The area also boasts a dazzling blend of outstanding **restaurants**, serving cuisines as varied as Armenian and Vietnamese, and has succeeded in luring the city's residents and visitors alike away from more superficial districts such as Puerto Madero and Las Cañitas.

Palermo Viejo's official epicentre is **Plaza Palermo Viejo**, a wide, park-like square dominated by a children's playground and some huge lime trees, but the barrio's cultural and social focal point is nearby **Plaza Serrano**. The plaza's official name (used on maps but unknown by most taxi drivers) is Plaza Cortázar, after Argentine novelist Julio Cortázar, who frequented this part of the city in the 1960s and set his Surrealist novel *Hopscotch* here. The plaza centre becomes the site of a crafts fair at weekends (Sat & Sun 10am–8pm), while more permanently it is surrounded by trattorias, cafés and bars, some of them doubling as arts centres and galleries. Among them, a rash of independent designer shops sell upmarket bohemian clothes, jewellery and furnishings – hence the **Soho** nickname. The nearest subte stations to Palermo Viejo are Scalabrini Ortíz and Plaza Italia.

Borges and Buenos Aires

This city that I believed was my past,
is my future, my present;
the years I have spent in Europe are an illusion,
I always was (and will be) in Buenos Aires.

Jorge Luis Borges, "Arrabal", from *Fervor de Buenos Aires* (1921)

There's no shortage of literary works inspired by Argentina's capital city, but no writer has written so passionately about it as **Jorge Luis Borges**. Though he was born in the heart of Buenos Aires, in 1898, it was the city's humbler barrios that most captivated Borges' imagination. His early childhood was spent in **Palermo**, now one of Buenos Aires' more exclusive neighbourhoods, but a somewhat marginal barrio at the start of the twentieth century. Borges' middle-class family inhabited one of the few two-storey houses on their street, **Calle Serrano** (now officially renamed Calle J. L. Borges), and, though his excursions were strictly controlled, from behind the garden wall Borges observed the colourful street life that was kept tantalizingly out of his reach. In particular, his attention was caught by the men who gathered to drink and play cards in the local *almacén* (a sort of store-cum-bar) at his street corner. With their tales of knife fights and air of lawlessness, these men appeared time and again in Borges' early short stories, and, later, in *Doctor Brodie's Report*, a collection published in 1970.

Borges' writing talent surfaced at a precocious age: at 6 he wrote his first short story and when he was 11, the newspaper *El País* published his translation of Oscar Wilde's *The Happy Prince*. However, it was not until he returned from Europe in 1921, where he had been stranded with his family during World War I, that Borges published his first book, *Fervor de Buenos Aires*, a collection of **poems** that attempted to capture the essence of the city. Enthused by his re-encounter with Buenos Aires at an age at which he was free to go where he wanted, Borges set out to explore the marginal corners of the city. His wanderings took him to the outlying barrios, where streets lined with simple one-storey buildings blended with the surrounding Pampas, or to the poorer areas of the city centre with their tenement buildings and bars frequented by prostitutes. With the notable exception of La Boca, which he appears to have regarded as too idiosyncratic – and perhaps, too obviously picturesque – Borges felt greatest affection for the **south** of Buenos Aires. His exploration of the area that he regarded as representing the heart of the city took in not only the traditional houses of San Telmo and Monserrat, with their patios and decorative facades, but also the humbler streets of Barracas, a largely industrial working-class neighbourhood, and Constitución, where, in a gloomy basement in Avenida Juan de Garay, he set one of his most famous short stories, *El Aleph*.

For a writer as sensitive to visual subtlety as Borges – many of his early poems focus on the city's atmospheric evening light – it seems particularly tragic that he should have gone virtually blind in his 50s. Nonetheless, from 1955 to 1973, Borges was **Director of the National Library**, then located in Monserrat, where his pleasure at being surrounded by books – even if he could no longer read them – was heightened by the fact that his daily journey to work took him through one of his favourite parts of the city, from his apartment in Maipú along pedestrianized Florida. As Borges' fame grew, he spent considerable periods of time away from Argentina, travelling to Europe, the US and other Latin American countries – though he claimed always to return to Buenos Aires in his dreams. Borges died in 1986 in Geneva, where he is buried in the Plainpalais cemetery. Borges pilgrims in Buenos Aires will find a commemorative plaque at no. 2108 on Calle Serrano, inscribed with a stanza from his *Mythical Foundation of Buenos Aires*.

Jardin Botánico

The entrance to Buenos Aires' charming **botanical garden** (daily 8am–6pm; free; guided visits Sat, Sun 10.30am & 3pm; ⓦ www.jardinbotanico.gov.ar) is at Plaza Italia, east of Palermo Viejo and near the Plaza Italia subte station. Established at the end of the nineteenth century, the layout was completed by Charles Thays in 1902. He divided the garden into distinct areas representing the regions of Argentina and further afield. Most of the trees are labelled with their Latin and common names, as well as where they are found.

On entering, you'll be greeted by a lush waterlily pool around an elegant stone statue of *Ondina de Plata*, a demure river-nymph from a legend about the Río de la Plata. This Italianate section is dotted with a number of sculptures, including a white marble Venus copied from a Roman statue in the Louvre, a bronze she-wolf suckling Romulus and Remus – a centenary gift to the city from its Italian community – and *Saturnalia*, an enormous, fun ensemble of a Roman orgy, intended to warn cityfolk against debauchery. Inside the garden, you'll find a large glasshouse brought back from the 1900 Universal Exhibition in Paris, where it was part of Argentina's pavilion: this ethereal Art Nouveau construction of wrought-iron and crystal shelters the garden's less hardy specimens such as orchids and cacti. Sadly, its age is beginning to show.

Jardín Zoológico

Next door to the botanical garden on Plaza Italia, Buenos Aires' **zoo** (Tues–Sun 10am–5pm; $12, or $22 for a "*pasaporte*", entitling you to all the attractions and activities, under-12s free; ⓦ www.zoobuenosaires.com.ar) was also landscaped by Thays and is of considerable architectural, as well as zoological, interest. Its monumental pavilions and cages, built around 1905, include a fabulous replica of the temple to the goddess Lakshmi in Mumbai, a Chinese temple, a Byzantine portico and a Japanese pagoda. A popular place for kids, especially during the school holidays, it's home to an aquarium, a mock rainforest and some 2500 animals. The big cat area – pumas, lions, jaguars – is a highlight. Borges fondly wrote that the zoo "smelled of toffee and tiger", a description that still holds true. It's also the place to learn the difference between guanacos, llamas, vicuñas and alpacas – the four camelids native to South America.

Outside the zoo, traditional **mateos** (horse and carriages), decorated with the ribbons and swirls of *filete* art (see box, p.102), cart off the romantically minded on trips around Palermo's parks ($30–50, depending on trip length).

Museo Evita

A block east from the zoo, at Lafinur 2988, the **Museo Evita** (Tues–Sun 11am–7pm; $12; ⓦ www.museoevita.org), was, for many Argentines, a long time coming. Located in an attractive early twentieth-century building that was once a hotel, it was bought in 1948 by Evita's Social Aid Foundation to be set up as emergency temporary accommodation for homeless families. The well-laid-out museum traces Evita's life and passions, as well as the daily life of the families who were given shelter here, with helpful info sheets in English in each room. The walls are adorned with quotes from her speeches and autobiography *La Razón de mi Vida* (My Mission in Life), such as the succinct and apt: "The two greatest conditions to which a woman of the people can aspire: love of the humble and the hatred of the oligarchs." Despite its uncritical stance and glossing over of the less salubrious facts in Evita's life, including her Nazi sympathies, the museum has some interesting pieces, including magazines featuring her when she was Eva Duarte the radio star, and videos of the extraordinary scenes in the city after she died.

Parque 3 de Febrero and around

A short way northwest, at the corner of Avenida del Libertador and Avenida Sarmiento, **Parque 3 de Febrero** is one of the biggest and most popular parks in the city. Another Palermo fixture designed by Thays, it was originally envisioned by President Sarmiento, who believed that parks were a civilizing influence and wanted something for Buenos Aires that would be on the scale of New York's Central Park or London's Hyde Park. Named in honour of the date in 1852 when his arch rival General Rosas was defeated, the park is a wonderful place to stroll on a sunny afternoon. With its beautifully tended trees, lawns and patios, it's at its most serene during the week. Although the wide pathways running along the banks of the boating lake become rather crowded with joggers, cyclists and in-line skaters on weekends and public holidays, that's also the time to see Porteños at play. You'll see typical scenes of families drinking *mate* under the shade of palms or rubber trees, but perhaps also less expected sights, such as tai chi classes, or transvestite volleyball games.

The park's features include an **Andalucian patio**, decorated with vibrant ceramic tiles and donated by the city of Seville, and a **Rosedal** (rose garden) that showcases new and colourful varieties of the flower. The far northeastern tip of the park, at Avenida Sarmiento, serves as the setting for the UFO-shaped **Planetario Galileo Galilei** (Mon–Fri 10am–4pm, Sat & Sun 4–7pm; free, shows $6; Ⓦwww.planetario.gov.ar). In the entrance hall, you can see an alarmingly huge metal meteorite, discovered in the Chaco in the 1960s (see p.308) and every Saturday and Sunday at 7.30pm (weather permitting) local astronomy enthusiasts cluster around telescopes to peer at the night sky. To the east, and with its own entrance on Plaza de la República Islámica de Irán, the **Jardín Japonés** (daily 10am–6pm; $5; Ⓦwww.jardinjapones.org.ar) was donated to the city by Buenos Aires' small Japanese community in 1979 and contains beautifully landscaped gardens, including a bonsai section, a lake of huge koi carp kissing the air with their pouting mouths, and a temple-like café. It is at its best in the springtime, when the almond trees are in blossom and the azaleas are out.

The busy rotunda to the park's southeast, at the junction of Avenida del Libertador and Avenida Sarmiento, is taken up by the most glorious monument in the city, the **Monumento de los Españoles**, whose fine bronze sculptures symbolize the Andes, the Chaco, the Pampas and the Río de la Plata. Its allegorical figures, including the dainty angel at the top, are sculpted from Carrara marble.

Belgrano

North of Palermo, leafy **Belgrano** is largely residential, apart from the lively shopping streets on either side of its main artery, Avenida Cabildo. Named after General Manuel Belgrano, hero of Argentina's struggle for independence, it was founded as a separate town in 1855. Over the next decade or two lots of wealthy Porteños built their summer or weekend homes here, and it was incorporated into Buenos Aires during the city's whirlwind expansion in the 1880s. Many Anglo-Argentines settled in the barrio in those years, and it became popular with the city's sizeable Jewish community in the 1950s. More recently Taiwanese and Korean immigrants have settled in **Barrio Chino**, Buenos Aires' small Chinatown, which stretches along Arribeños between Juramento and Olazába.

Belgrano C is the central part of the barrio, whose nucleus lies at the junction of avenidas Cabildo and Justamento. As well as stores, cafés and galleries, there's a clutch of minor museums here, with the most impressive being the **Museo de Arte Español** at Juramento 2291 (Mon–Fri 2–8pm, Sat & Sun 10am–8pm; $1, free Thurs; Ⓦwww.museolarreta.buenosaires.gov.ar). This well-restored, whitewashed colonial building is home to a priceless collection of **Spanish art** amassed by an aristocratic Uruguayan exile, **Enrique Larreta**. From around 1900 to 1916, the dandyish Larreta spent many of his days in Spain; during that time he visited churches and monasteries, buying up artwork for his Belgrano home, most of them from the Renaissance – statues and paintings of saints, but also furniture, porcelain, silverware and tapestries, all of which are displayed in this house, which he bequeathed to the city.

Juramento station, one stop before the end of subte Line D, is a block from the museum, while plenty of buses run along Avenida Cabildo.

El Monumental

Out on the eastern edge of Belgrano, on the border with residential barrio Nuñez at Avenida Pte Figueroa Alcorta 7597, rise the huge concrete stands of **El Monumental** (☎011/4323-7600). Home to Boca Juniors' bitter rivals, **River Plate** football club, it can seat 70,000 and is the country's largest stadium, remodelled for the 1978 World Cup. Matches at the Monumental are a glorious riot of red and white shirts, banners and streamers.

In 2009 a new **museum** (daily 9am–7pm, closes early on match days; $45 museum and tour or $30 museum only) was opened, an audiovisual experience that makes every effort to be bigger and better than the Boca museum in the Bombonera (see p.106), although it's less tourist-friendly – both the tour and museum are in Spanish only. Highlights are a "time machine" that takes you with whizzes and bangs through a tunnel that relates the history of the club through the twentieth century, with plenty of fascinating historical and cultural context, and era-appropriate TVs that show you River's greatest goals. On site there is also a comprehensive souvenir shop, and a café that's surprisingly upmarket for a football stadium.

The west

West of central Buenos Aires a vast, mostly residential area spreads out for over a dozen kilometres towards Avenida General Paz. Northwest of Palermo, the barrio of **Chacarita** is best known for its namesake **cemetery**, where tango singer Carlos Gardel is buried. **Caballito**, right in the heart of the city, has an entertaining natural history museum. Architecture fans shouldn't miss the stunning **Palacio de las Aguas Corrientes** in the barrio of **Balvanera**, the neighbourhood just west of Congreso and Avenida Callao. Finally, right at Buenos Aire's fringes, the hugely enjoyable gaucho fair, the **Feria de Mataderos**, is held on Sundays in the barrio of the same name and provides one of the best days out in the city.

Chacarita

Dominated by railway lines, **Chacarita** takes its name from the days when the barrio was home to a small farm (*chacra*) run by Jesuits. Nowadays, the neighbourhood is synonymous with the enormous **Cementerio de Chacarita** (daily 7am–6pm; free). Less aristocratic than Recoleta's cemetery, but impressive nonetheless, it contains the city's other most-visited tomb, that of **Carlos Gardel**, the greatest of all tango singers (see p.618–619).

Lying at the northern end of Avenida Corrientes (subte station Federico Lacroze, Line B), with the monumental main entrance at Avenida Guzmán 780, the cemetery covers a good third of the barrio; at one square kilometre, it's Argentina's largest. Immediately facing the entrance, a section of grand mausoleums comes quite close to the Baroque splendour of Recoleta. By far the best sight in the cemetery, however, is **Gardel's tomb**, on the corner of streets 6 and 33, a brisk five-minute walk to the left of the entrance and a little towards the middle. It is topped by a life-sized statue of the singer in typical rakish pose: hand in pocket, hair slicked back and characteristic wide grin. Every inch of the surrounding stonework is plastered with plaques of gratitude and flowers placed there by the singer's devotees. There is a pilgrimage to his graveside every year on the anniversary of his death (June 24). Many visitors also light a cigarette and place it between the statue's fingers; you will often see a dog-end still dangling between his index and forefinger.

Not far from Gardel's grave, slightly nearer the entrance, is one of the most majestic mausoleums in the whole cemetery, that of aviation pioneer **Jorge Newbery**, after whom Buenos Aires' domestic airport is named. He died near Mendoza while preparing for the first flight across the Andes and is honoured with a tomb that somehow manages to be magnificent, sinister and camp all at once: four hungry-looking condors overlook a supine nude male form who is outstretched in a melodramatic pose like some latter-day Prometheus. At the centre of the graveyard, the **Recinto de Personalidades** is a collection of rather kitsch statues adorning the graves of some of Argentina's most popular figures, including tango composer Aníbal Troilo, pianist Osvaldo Pugliese, poet Alfonsina Storni and painter Quinquela Martín. You may be able to pick up a free map of the grounds at the cemetery's administrative offices, to the right of the entrance.

Caballito

An unassuming, mostly middle-class barrio, **Caballito** lies at the very centre of the metropolis. Narrow Plaza Primera Junta, on Line A of the subte, is the barrio's core, while Avenida Rivadavia, flanked by high-rise apartment blocks and shopping malls, runs east–west through it. Its main attraction is the natural science museum, the **Museo Argentino de Ciencias Naturales**, at Angel Gallardo 490 (daily 2–7pm; $3; ⓦwww.macn.secyt.gov.ar) in the circular Parque del Centenario. The museum is of note for its impressive **paleontological** collection – you can see a spiky-necked amargasaurus from Neuquén and a fifteen-metre patagosaurus sauropod from Chubút. There is also a host of **megafauna** – giant herbivorous mammals that evolved in South America when the region broke away from other continents – such as giant sloths and creepy glyptodonts, a forerunner of today's armadillo. These megafauna were wiped out around three million years ago, after South America reconnected with North America and more successful fauna such as the sabre-toothed tiger and, later, humans arrived.

Balvanera

Just west of the city centre, **Balvanera** is a commercial, somewhat downmarket barrio, home to many of the city's recent South American immigrants. It has two focal points: **Once**, a noisy shopping area around the Once (de Septiembre) train station, traditionally patronized by the city's less well-heeled Jewish community and a good place to pick up bargains, including football shirts, *chamamé* CDs and carnival gear; and **Abasto**, focused on what is now the Abasto shopping centre (see p.146).

Other than for shopping, the main point of interest is the spectacular **Palacio de las Aguas Corrientes**, right on the Recoleta border at Córdoba and Riobamba. Every bit as palatial as the name suggests, it has been described quite accurately as a cross between London's Victoria and Albert Museum and the Uffizi in Florence. Somewhat incongruously, it is home to twelve giant tanks that supplied Buenos Aires with water from 1894 until 1978. An impressive feat of engineering, it was

For all its parks and tree-lined avenues, Buenos Aires is nonetheless predominantly urban, and it can be nice to get away from the hectic tumult for a day or two. Immediately surrounding the city limits as you cross the Avenida General Paz ring road, the Capital Federal spreads into greater Buenos Aires. Largely residential, the most appealing suburbs are those to the city's north – the **Zona Norte**, an affluent suburban world of riverine villas where the subtropical heart that lies beneath Buenos Aires' European veneer starts to show through. Most worth visiting is San Isidro, which preserves a villagey charm and worthwhile historic quarter that can be accessed via the Tren de la Costa (see p.154) or taxi (about $50). Further on but still easily in day-trip territory you will reach **Tigre**, a kind of cross between Venice and the Everglades, at the edge of the verdant **Paraná Delta** (see pp.154–160).

To the east of the city, meanwhile, boats cross the Río de la Plata to the small **Isla Martín García**, a steamy island that appears to have walked off the pages of a children's adventure story. Once used as a penal colony, it is now mostly given over to a nature reserve (visits via Cacciola Turismo in Tigre; ℡011/4749-0931, ⓦwww.cacciolaviajes.com). You can also reach the Portuguese colonial historic town of **Colonia** in Uruguay, or even visit pleasant **Montevideo**, the capital of Argentina's *rioplatense* neighbour – both destinations are served by Buquebus, whose ferries and catamarans depart regularly from Puerto Madero (℡011/4316-6500, ⓦwww.buquebus.com).

Go a little further beyond the city in any other direction and you will swiftly emerge in the emerald green **pampas**, Argentina's heartlands. Magnificent estancias (farmsteads or ranches) and traditional Pampean villages are close enough to reach as a day-trip, though if possible they really warrant at least one overnight stay. The capital of Buenos Aires province, **La Plata**, an orderly city with a large, old-fashioned natural history museum, is also only an hour or so on the bus from Retiro. For more on La Plata and the pampas, see chapter 2.

planned and built in Europe, down to the glazed coloured ceramics that dot the facade, all manufactured by Royal Doulton of London, but painted in Buenos Aires. Inside, there is a small museum (Mon–Fri 9am–1pm; free) explaining the building's history.

Mataderos

Lying just inside the boundary of Capital Federal, around 6km southwest of Caballito, **Mataderos** is a barrio with a gory past. For many years, people came to Mataderos to drink the fresh blood of animals killed in the slaughterhouses from which the area takes its name, in the belief that this would cure such illnesses as tuberculosis. The slaughterhouses have long gone, but Mataderos is still home to the **Mercado Nacional de Hacienda**, or livestock market, set back from the intersection of Lisandro de la Torre and Avenida de los Corrales, whose faded pink walls and arcades provide the backdrop for one of Buenos Aires' most fabulous events: the Sunday **Feria de Mataderos** (11am–8pm; buses #92 & #126; ⓦwww.feriademataderos.com.ar). A celebration of Argentina's rural traditions, this busy fair attracts thousands of locals and tourists for its blend of folk music, traditional crafts and regional food such as *locro*, empanadas and *tortas fritas*, mouthwatering fried cakes. You can also try your hand at regional dances such as the *chamamé* and *chacarera*. The undoubted highpoint, however, is the display of **gaucho skills** in which riders participate in events such as the *sortija*, in which, galloping at breakneck speed and standing rigid in their stirrups, they attempt to spear a small ring strung on a ribbon. Take plenty of cash – the artisan wares here

▲ Traditional folk dancers, Feria de Mataderos

are good quality and considerably cheaper than in the central stores – and make sure the fair is actually on before setting out, as it sometimes closes or changes its day and opening hours, especially during the summer months; the city's tourist kiosks (see p.80) should be able to advise.

Eating

Buenos Aires is Latin America's **gastronomic capital** and, with many places offering excellent quality for the price, eating out here must count as a highlight of any visit to Argentina. In addition to the ubiquitous **pizza** and **pasta** restaurants common to the country as a whole, the capital offers a number of **cosmopolitan** cuisines, ranging from Armenian and Basque to Thai and Vietnamese. Foodie fashions are enthusiastically adopted; Peruvian haute cuisine and mini-gourmet restaurants in the intimate space of someone's house are currently all the rage. The city's crowning glory, however – though you have to be a meat eater – are its **parrillas**, whose top-end representatives offer the country's choicest beef cooked on an *asador criollo* – staked around an open fire. There are plenty of humbler places, too, where you can enjoy a succulent *parrillada* in a lively atmosphere.

Though most restaurants open in the evening at around 8pm, it's worth bearing in mind that Porteños don't normally go out to eat until a couple of hours later; many restaurants suddenly go from empty to full between 9.30pm and 10pm. Most kitchens close around midnight during the week, though at weekends many keep serving till the small hours. There are also plenty of *confiterías* and pizzerias open throughout the night, so you shouldn't have trouble satisfying your hunger at any time.

Restaurants

Excellent meals can be had throughout Buenos Aires but, with some exceptions, the **centre** and the **south** are best for the city's most traditional restaurants, while the **north** is the place for more innovative or exotic cooking. **Puerto Madero**, the recently renovated port area, is knee-deep in big, glitzy themed restaurants, though – a couple of decent places notwithstanding – these are hardly the capital's most exciting eating options. You'll find a far more original crop of restaurants in **Palermo**, in three clusters – Soho around Plaza Cortázar/Serrano; Hollywood around Honduras and Fitzroy; and Las Cañitas around Báez and Chenaut.

The city centre

The following are all on the Central Buenos Aires map.

Arturito Corrientes 1124 ☎011/4382-0227. An old-fashioned haven reigned over by courteous white-jacketed waiters, *Arturito* is a Corrientes landmark, and its *bife de chorizo con papas* (rump steak and chips) is an unquestionably good deal. Daily lunch and dinner.

Brasserie Petanque Defensa and Mexico, Monserrat ☎011/4342-7930. Classic French food such as *boeuf bourguignon*, *moules*, steak tartare and *crème brûlée*, with a particularly good value lunch-time *menu du jour*; at times, slightly uppity classic French service to match. Sat eve, Sun–Fri lunch and dinner.

Chiquilín Sarmiento 1599 ☎011/4373-5163. A classic Porteño restaurant, popular with tourists, serving traditional dishes in a friendly and stylish atmosphere. The *pollo al verdeo* (chicken with spring onions) is good, but it's the revered *bife* ($40) that brings most people in. Daily lunch and dinner.

El Claustro San Martín 705 ☎011/4312-0235. The vaulted dining room was part of the Santa Catalina convent, making it a haven of peace and quiet amid the frantic financial district. Considering the inventiveness of the cuisine – such as a tajine-like lamb dish or pears with lemongrass – the two-course lunch served every weekday is quite reasonably priced.

Las Cuartetas Corrientes 838. A pared-down pizza and empanada joint where you can grab a slice of their delicious and cheap pizza at the counter and while away a few hours after the cinema over a cold Quilmes. Sun eve, Mon–Sat lunch and dinner.

El Globo Hipólito Yrigoyen 1199 ☎011/4381-3926. One of several Spanish restaurants in the area, *El Globo* has a gorgeously old-fashioned interior and serves generous portions of classic dishes such as *gambas al ajillo* (spicy prawns) and *puchero*. About $70 for a two-course meal; daily lunch and dinner.

Granix Florida 165, Galería Güemes, Entrada Mitre, 1st floor. You pay a small fixed charge on entry at this large, airy, self-service vegetarian restaurant located in one of Florida's magnificent shopping arcades, and then eat as much as you want. Salads are straight-from-the-market fresh and the variety of soft drinks, warm dishes and delicious desserts, including some unusual options, is overwhelming. Weekdays lunchtimes only.

Güerrín Corrientes 1368. A quintessential Porteño pizza experience, the traditional order here is a portion of *muzzarella* and *fainá* eaten at the counter and accompanied by a glass of sweet moscato. Some locals hold that the pizzas served in the proper dining area are a notch above the counter versions; however, all are inexpensive. Daily, noon until late.

Laurak-Bat Belgrano 1144, Monserrat ☎011/4381-0682. A moderately priced Basque restaurant within *Club Vasco* boasting specialities such as *bacalao al pil-pil* (salt cod in a garlic sauce). Mon–Sat lunch and dinner; closed Sun.

Palacio Barolo Av de Mayo 1380. *Confitería*-cum-restaurant on the ground floor of the emblematic Barolo building (see p.93) that oozes atmosphere. Unusual meals using native ingredients are served – you can eat creatures such as ñandú (rhea), capybara, cayman, and llama, which come in sauces flavoured with herbs, mustard and red berries. About $80 for a two-course meal; open from 8am until midnight daily.

Parrilla Peña Rodríguez Peña 682. Knowledgeable liveried waiters serve up some of the juiciest meat in town, as well as fine wines and mouth-watering salads at this great-value, no-nonsense *parrilla*. Lunch and dinner; closed Sun eve.

Patio San Ramón Reconquista 269. Generously portioned, well-cooked and inexpensive food with daily specials such as *pollo al horno con puré de batata* (roast chicken with sweet potato puree). The real attraction, however, is the stunning location – the patio of an old convent where, among palm trees and birdsong, you might even forget that you're at the heart of Buenos Aires' financial district. Lunch only, closed weekends.

Tomo 1 Carlos Pellegrini 525, in Hotel Panamericano ☎011/4326-6695. Considered by many to be Buenos Aires' best haute cuisine restaurant, this is an elegant but refreshingly unpretentious place where the emphasis is squarely placed on the exquisitely cooked food, such as chilled melon soup and quail with pistachios. Not cheap, but good value, particularly if you go for the set menus (around $180). Mon–Fri lunch and dinner, Sat dinner only, Sun closed.

Winery Av Alem 880 ⊕011/4314-2639. As well as a store that holds regular tastings of all the best Argentine wines, *Winery* – a growing BA chain – has a restaurant serving cheeses, gourmet sandwiches and unusual specialities such as braised goat. About $100 for two courses; open all day Mon–Sat.

Puerto Madero

The following are all on the Central Buenos Aires map.

Bice Av Alicia M. de Justo 192 ⊕011/4315-6216. Style often triumphs over content in Puerto Madero, but the excellent pasta and gnocchi at this highly regarded, if expensive, Italian restaurant will not disappoint. Daily lunch and dinner.

Cabaña Las Lilas Av Alicia M. de Justo 516 ⊕011/4313-1336. The place to head if you want to splurge on just about the finest steak around; an *ojo de bife*, best savoured from a shaded veranda on the waterfront, will set you back what it would cost to eat for a week in a standard *parrilla*. Very popular with tourists; reservations advisable. Daily lunch and dinner.

"i" Fresh Market Azucena Villaflor and Olga Cossenttini. By Dique 3, the pick of the chic new places in Puerto Madero Este. A great place for lunch or merienda, with a selection of inventive sandwiches, salads and bruschettas, plus a range of yummy *licuados* (fruit shakes) and herbal teas to accompany; meals such as pasta and steak are also available. Slightly pricey but not outrageous; daily lunch and dinner.

Siga La Vaca Av Alicia M. de Justo 1714 ⊕011/4315-6801. At this upmarket *tenedor libre* you can eat till you drop for a reasonable sum; the fixed rate (about $70, less at lunchtime) includes a carafe of wine, a dazzling choice of salads and, of course, a mountain of meat. As with all *tenedor libres*, go for quantity, variety and speed, rather than quality. Daily noon until late.

San Telmo and Boca

El Baqueano Boliver and Chile, San Telmo ⊕011/4342-0802. Unusual restaurant that uses local ingredients, particularly indigeneous animals, to create gourmet dishes such as provençale cayman tails and ñandú stuffed with liquor-soaked fruit. Relatively normal meats such as pheasant are also served, but it's not a place for vegetarians or the squeamish. Tasting menu with five dishes $105. Tues–Sat evenings only.

Café San Juan Av San Juan 450, San Telmo ⊕011/4300-1112. A small, good-value, family-run joint whose huge portions and fresh-from-the-market meals mean it's always full. Try the "hunter's-style" rabbit. Lunch and dinner; closed Mon.

El Desnivel Defensa 855, San Telmo ⊕011/4399-9081. The backpackers pile in to this no-frills *parrilla*, which offers meat-laden dishes at rock-bottom prices. Tues–Sun lunch and dinner, Mon dinner only.

El Obrero Caffarena 64, Boca ⊕011/4362-9912. With Boca Juniors souvenirs decorating the walls and tango musicians sauntering from table to table at weekends, the atmosphere at the hugely popular and moderately priced *El Obrero* is as much a part of its appeal as the simple home-cooked food, including great *milanesas*. Lunch and dinner; closed Sun.

Retiro and Recoleta

Bengal Arenales 837 ⊕011/4314-2926. Although, as the name suggests, this smart restaurant offers Indian specialities, including a perfectly passable *rogan josh*, it really excels in its Mediterranean Italian dishes, with a strong focus on fish. The decor and ambience are decidedly posh but the highly attentive service is not snobbish, and the wine and food, albeit not budget-priced, are impeccable, down to all the nibbly bits they serve before and after. Closed Sat dinner & Sun.

Club Danés Alem 1074 12th floor ⊕011/4312-9266. This lunch-only Danish restaurant serves a mean *smörrebrod* – lots of herrings, anchovies and blue cheese – and other specialities in a suitably airy dining room with great river views, with change from $50. Brown ale brewed in Buenos Aires Province is available. Closed Sat & Sun.

Club Sírio Ayacucho 1496 ⊕011/4806-5764. Every major Argentine city has its Syrian club-restaurant, and this palatial place is one of the best, with an excellent and varied menu of starters. About $100 for 2 courses; daily from 8.30pm.

Filo San Martín 975 ⊕011/4311-0312. Some of the centre's best salads, if not the cheapest, featuring less common ingredients such as rocket, radishes and sultanas soaked in wine, in addition to imaginative pizzas, pastas and other Italian-inspired fusion dishes such as Venetian mussel soup with Patagonian clams. Daily from noon.

Milion Paraná 1048 ⊕4815-9925. A beautifully converted mansion, with dozens of candlelit rooms. Cocktails and modern Argentine cuisine served, such as *pacu* river fish with orange and parsley sauce, or pasta with goats cheese and sweet pumpkin, for around $60. It's really more about the very cool ambience than the gastronomy, though. Daily lunch and dinner.

Nectarine Vicente López 1661 011/4813-6993. A classical dining room painted in a suitable peachy hue is the setting for what some locals say is the city's best cordon bleu food: pheasant and duck grace the menu, with expensive wines to accompany them. Closed Sat lunch & Sun.

Piola Pizzeria Libertad 1078. You'll find dozens of toppings to choose from at this huge, hip, gay-friendly pizza joint, where thin crusts meet the city's upper crust. Prices higher than usual for pizza; Mon–Fri lunch and dinner, Sat & Sun dinner only.

Restó Montevideo 938. Set back from the street in the building housing the Sociedad Central de Arquitectos, this elegant and expensive little French restaurant serves quail, duck and other less common ingredients, while puddings include the likes of candied kumquat tartlets with peanut frangipane and muscovado sugar ice cream. Lunch Mon–Fri, dinner Thurs & Fri (a set menu; bring your own wine).

Romario Pizza Vicente López 2102. A young crowd savours *Romario's* great, reasonably priced pizzas in a small, outdoor seating area from where Recoleta in full swing can be observed; part of an excellent chain famed for its roller-skating delivery boys and girls. Daily lunch and dinner.

El Sanjuanino Posadas 1515 011/4805-2683. The place to try *empanadas*, this inexpensive restaurant also has other regional fare such as *locro* and *humitas*, as well as more exotic dishes like pickled *vizcacha*. Closed Mon.

Sipan Paraguay 624 011/4315-0763. Stylish and pricey Peruvian–Japanese fusion cooking, offering ultra-fresh ceviche and sushi, as well as a number of delicious takes on the classic Peruvian sauteed beef dish *lomo saltado* – try the one with calamari. Mon–Sat lunch and dinner; closed Sun.

Tancat Paraguay 645 011/4312-5442. A beautifully decorated and lit Spanish–Catalan tasca, where the *cañas* (small glasses of draft beer), varied tapas and other mainstays, like grilled baby squid, are totally genuine; the service is brisk, it gets very busy at lunch times (bookings recommended) and can be noisy, but that only adds to the authenticity. Moderately priced, unless you opt for seafood. Also open for dinner; closed Sun.

Palermo

The following are all marked on the Palermo and Las Cañitas map.

Artemisia Cabrera 3877 011/4863-4242. Probably BA's best non-meat restaurant, the vegetarian and fish dishes (around $40

each) here make no sacrifices flavour-wise. Even die-hard carnivores will enjoy *Artemisia*'s twist on polenta lasagne or lime and cilantro spiked *abadejo* (pollock). The food is freshly cooked, so it's not the place to go if you're in a hurry – but it's worth the wait. Tues–Sat from 8.30pm.

Bar Uriarte Uriarte 1572 011/4834-6004. This luxurious and pricey restaurant serves tasty food, mostly with a Mediterranean touch, in a bright, airy dining room, decorated with ethnic art and dominated by a northern-style adobe oven used to cook meat- and dough-based dishes. Daily lunch and dinner.

Bio Humboldt 2199 011/4774-3880. Stylish, moderately priced vegetarian restaurant, more inventive than most but still wholesome, with dishes incorporating ingredients such as quinoa and tofu, with of course lots of vegetables. Organic wine and beer are also served. Closed Mon dinner & Sun.

La Cabrera Cabrera 5099 & 5127 011/4831-7002. This fabulous down-to-earth *parrilla* serves hard-to-beat *bifes de chorizo* (the half portion can feed two) with an array of delicious tapa garnishes; it's so popular the owners had to open a second restaurant just up the road. Reservations aren't accepted, so go early and grit your teeth until a table is free. Tues–Sun lunch and dinner, Mon dinner only.

Casa Cruz Uriarte 1658 011/4833-1112. The glossy red mahogany panelling and perfect portions at this trendy restaurant make you feel as if you are dining inside a Chinese lacquered box, while the food is eclectic, sumptuously presented and absolutely delicious – try the warm oysters served with tapioca caviar and a pear salad. Faultless service, but the bill is steep by local standards. Mon–Sat from 8.30pm.

Chori & Wine Costa Rica 5198 esq. Godoy Cruz, Palermo Soho 011/4773-0954. A clear step above most *parrillas*, this intimate restaurant serves truly exceptional, export-quality meat, cooked to perfection by an internationally trained chef. The wine list and desserts are excellent, complemented by attentive, friendly service. Mon–Sat from 8pm; no credit cards.

La Fondue J.F. Segui 4674 011/4778-0110. A small, friendly side-street bistro that uses home-made ingredients to make unbeatable pasta and fondue. Fairly expensive; daily lunch and dinner.

Francesco Sinclair 3096 011/4878-4496. Classy Peruvian cuisine with an emphasis on fish, including several different ceviches and *parihuela* – a wonderful soup filled with all kinds of seafood. About $100 for two courses; Mon–Sat lunch and dinner.

Garbis Scalabrini Ortiz 3190 ⊕011/4511-6600. A stand-out diner in the local Armenian community, *Garbis* prepares a delicious and very different *picada*, as well as a range of shish-kebabs. Moderately priced; daily lunch and dinner.

El Manto Costa Rica 5801 ⊕011/4774-2409. Lamb, yogurt and mint dominate the menu at this authentic Armenian restaurant, where a Carrara marble statue of the Virgin presides over dinner. About $90 for two courses; daily dinner only.

Ølsen Gorriti 5870 ⊕011/4776-7677. This large, modern restaurant serves exciting cuisine with a Scandinavian touch, such as salmon pizza or goat-cheese ravioli. There are around forty different kinds of vodkas and all manner of cocktails to kick things off, as well as an admirable wine cellar. About $120 for two courses; Tues–Sat lunch and dinner, Sun from 10.30am, closed Mon.

Ña Serapia Las Heras 3357 ⊕011/4801-5307. An unexpectedly traditional and rustic restaurant in the heart of upmarket Palermo, *Ña Serapia* styles itself as a *pulpería* and bar and serves delicious regional dishes including *locro* and *tamales* at very reasonable prices. Daily lunch and dinner.

Las Pizarras Thames 2296 ⊕011/4775-0625. Informal restaurant that's all about the fabulous (and reasonably priced) food. Run by a chef who has worked in top London restuarants, the menu varies according to what is available and is written up on blackboards (*pizarras*), so it's a bit of a lottery – but that's all part of the fun. Tues–Sun dinner only.

Sarkis Thames 1101 ⊕011/4772-4911. Spartan decor, but excellent tabbouleh, *keppe crudo* (raw meat with onion – much better than it sounds) and falafel at this popular budget restaurant serving a fusion of Armenian, Arab and Turkish cuisine. Daily lunch and dinner.

Sudestada Guatemala & Fitzroy ⊕011/4776-3777. Smart noodle bar with a Vietnamese chef who prepares tasty curries and other Southeast Asian food at reasonable prices, all in modern, minimalist surroundings. The same owners run *Standard*, diagonally opposite. Lunch and dinner; closed Sun.

Xalapa Gurruchaga and El Salvador ⊕011/4833-6102. Argentines usually shy away from hot and spicy food, but this place, which has the most authentic and tasty Mexican fare in the city, is packed even mid-week. Proceed with caution, lest you torch your taste buds, especially when sampling the stuffed chiles. About $60 for two courses; Mon–Fri dinner only, Sat & Sun lunch and dinner.

Cafés, confiterías and snacks

You can learn a lot about Porteños from a little discreet people-watching in the city's **cafés**. People stream through all day, from office workers grabbing a quick *medialuna* in the morning to ladies of leisure taking afternoon tea to students gossiping over a beer or juice in the evenings. They're not quite the hotbed of revolutionary activity they were in the 1970s, but they're still in many ways where you'll find authentic Buenos Aires – over an excellent espresso, usually served with a welcomingly hydrating glass of water. **Confiterías** are traditional tearooms that also specialize in biscuits, cakes and pastries to accompany the tea and coffee, although the dividing line between these, regular cafés and even restaurants (many serve full-blown meals, at very reasonable prices) can be quite blurred. Most are open from about noon to 8pm; places open at other times are indicated in the text.

A222 Corrientes 222, 19th floor; see Central Buenos Aires map. For breathtaking views of Puerto Madero and its surroundings have a tea or coffee at one of the window tables; stay for a glass of wine and watch the same scene turn into a sea of lights as dusk turns to night. Pass on dinner though: it is overpriced and the service is poor.

Abuela Pan Bolívar 707, San Telmo. Homely vegetarian café and whole-food store offering a daily menu with options such as tofu burgers, stuffed aubergines and vegetarian sushi. Mon–Fri 8am–7pm.

La Americana Callao 83–99; see Central Buenos Aires map. A Callao landmark, serving up juicy empanadas – some say they're the city's best – to be consumed standing up at metal counters.

La Biela Quintana 600, Recoleta. Institutional *confitería* famed for its *lomitos* and coffee, served in the elegant bistro interior or, with a surcharge, in the shade of a gigantic gum tree on the terrace. Also open for breakfast.

Café Martínez Libertador 3598, Palermo. One of several branches of this seventy-year-old, upmarket café. Its enticing speciality drinks include iced cappuccino with *dulce de leche*, while its *cappuccino miel* is a rich mix of chocolate, honey, steamed milk, cream, cinnamon – and a little coffee. Also open for breakfast.

Café Tortoni Av de Mayo 825 ☏011/4342-4328; see Central Buenos Aires map. Buenos Aires' most famous café (see p.92) exudes pure elegance, but it is in grave danger of turning into a tourist trap. Some evenings it hosts live jazz or tango in *La Bodega* downstairs, but there are many far more authentic venues around.

Carlitos Guido 1962, Recoleta. Classic neighbourhood café that's BA's branch of the famous *Carlitos*, "king of the pancakes" in Villa Gesell (see p.170). Choose from over one hundred different generous savoury and sweet fillings for their signature pancakes, from the expected (mozzarella, tomato and basil) to the less so (sauteed apple and ham).

Confitería Ideal Suipacha 384; see Central Buenos Aires map. It's not quite as famous as the *Tortoni*, and therefore less frequented, though it is just as beautiful, if a little worn at the edges. The main reason to go here is to see a *milonga* in the upstairs tango salon (see p.143). Do not be put off by the dusty, smelly entrance.

Costumbres Criollas Libertador 308, Retiro. A small restaurant specializing in excellent *empanadas tucumanas* and regional dishes such as *locro* and *tamales*. Worth seeking out for a snack if you have an hour or two to kill in the vicinity of Retiro. Daily 11am–4pm and 7pm–midnight.

Cumaná Rodriguez Peña 1149, Retiro. Popular with students and office workers, this is a good place to try *mate*, served from 4pm to 7.30pm with a basket of crackers. There's also a selection of provincial food, such as empanadas and *cazuelas* (casseroles), on the menu.

La Giralda Corrientes and Uruguay, in the city centre; see Central Buenos Aires map. Brightly lit and austerely decorated Corrientes café famous for its *chocolate con churros*. A perennial hangout for students and intellectuals and a good place to experience the Porteño passion for conversation.

Medio y Medio Montevideo and Perón; see Central Buenos Aires map. Named after Montevideo market's famous drink, *Medio y Medio* serves *chivitos* (Uruguayan beef sandwiches) and, of course, *mate* from behind its ornate facade.

New Brighton Sarmiento 645; see Central Buenos Aires map. The classic Anglo–Porteño *Brighton*, which first opened its doors in 1908, was recently renovated and reopened, retaining many of its original features. Wood panelling and stained glass help recreate a *belle époque* atmosphere, with a café area at the front and expensive restaurant at the back. Open for lunch and dinner.

Nsalad Tucumán 269; see Central Buenos Aires map. A great option for a quick and healthy lunch, to eat in or take away. *Nsalad* does, as you might expect, a variety of healthy salads, as well as filled tortillas and – a rarity in BA – bagels. Mon–Fri 9am–5pm.

La Paz Av Corrientes 1599; see Central Buenos Aires map. The classic Corrientes (and Porteño) café; less sumptuous but also with fewer tourists than the *Tortoni. La Paz* was once the favourite hangout of left-wing intellectuals and writers and it's still a good place to meet a friend or read a book over a coffee, especially when it's raining outside and the windows steam up.

La Poesía Bolivar and Chile, San Telmo. Self-consciously traditional San Telmo café bar with wooden tables and a mind-boggling choice of sandwiches and *picadas*. Tango is the usual backdrop.

La Puerto Rico Alsina 420; see Central Buenos Aires map. Simple and elegant, one of the city's classic *confiterías*, famous for its outstanding espressos; now serving meals too. Daily until late.

Las Violetas Av Rivadavia 3899, Almagro. Nearest subte is Castro Barros. Rescued from closure by popular demand, this *confitería*-restaurant is a monument to the Porteño heyday of the 1920s, with its fine wood panelling, gorgeous stained glass, Carrara marble table-tops and impressive columns; it was a favourite hangout of writers such as Roberto Arlt. The *confitería* is justly famed for its breads, cakes and pastries, while the restaurant combines attentive service with copious and refined cuisine – try the delicious *agnelottis* (pasta) filled with ricotta, ham and walnuts.

Heladerías

More than anything else, one institution in Buenos Aires, and indeed the rest of the country, serves as a constant reminder of Argentina's strong Italian inheritance: the **heladería**, or ice-cream parlour. Ubiquitous, varied, extremely popular and the subject of fierce debate as to which is the best, these minefields of temptation serve millions of cones and cups daily, and dispatch hundreds of boys on motorbikes to satisfy the needs of those who cannot be bothered to go and out and buy in person.

Cadore Corrientes 1695; see Central Buenos Aires map. Some experts have declared this the best place for ice cream in the city – despite much competition – and the *dulce de leche* flavour above all.

Freddo Guido and Junín, Recoleta. Arguably Buenos Aires' best ice-cream chain – *dulce de leche* aficionados will be in heaven, and few will fail to be seduced by the banana split or *sambayon*. You get to choose two flavours with your cone, but almost inevitably you'll want to try more. One of many branches throughout the city (see Ⓦwww .freddo.com.ar for others).

 Persicco Salguero 2591 and Cabello (Palermo), plus other branches. This small,

family-run chain of stylish parlours – part modern, part retro – dish out fabulous ice creams and sorbets, with emphasis on chocolate flavours; they also serve excellent cakes, croissants, coffees, while the toast and jam served for breakfast are delicious.

Un'Altra Volta Libertador 3060 (Palermo Chico), Ayacucho and Quintana (Recoleta), plus others. Fighting it out with *Freddo* and *Persicco* to be the city's number-one ice-cream chain, *Volta*, as it is usually known, produces delicious desserts rivalling those in Italy, clearly the inspiration for its gourmet *gelato*; fabulous cakes, pastries and coffee, too.

Drinking and nightlife

If you've come to Buenos Aires eager to experience the city after dark you will not leave disappointed. Porteños are consummate night owls and though nightlife peaks from Thursday to Saturday, you'll find plenty of things to do during the rest of the week too. Worthwhile venues are spread all over the city, but certain areas offer an especially large selection of night-time diversions. The city's young and affluent head to Palermo's **Soho** and **Hollywood** to strut their stuff year-round, and the **Costanera Norte** as well in the summer. **El Bajo**, as the streets around Reconquista and 25 de Mayo are known, offers a walkable circuit of bars and restaurants as well as the odd Irish pub, while **San Telmo** harbours some eclectic and charismatic bars in amongst the tango spectacles. Though some bars open all day, most don't really get going until around midnight. Increasingly, the smoother bars run so-called *after offices* on weekdays to fill the early evening slot, but these are almost invariably rather sleazy. Websites with worthwhile **listings** include Ⓦwww.adondevamos.com and www.wipe.com.ar; for dance clubs, the best listings website is Ⓦwww.buenosaliens.com.

Bars and pubs

Buenos Aires has no shortage of great **bars**, ranging from noisy Irish **pubs** to eminently cool places where the young and chic sip wine, cocktails and imported beers. Most of the former and their ilk are clustered in El Bajo or in San Telmo; while the latter variety are easiest to find – there are dozens – in any part of Palermo Viejo, Soho or Hollywood. Note that smoking is banned in public spaces, including bars and restaurants.

Antares Armenia 1447, Palermo. Home-brewed kölsch, porter, stout and barley beer, to name just a few, to accompany tapas and simple dishes, in a roomy, converted storehouse; jazz, blues and Irish music add to the ambience.

 Bar Británico Defensa & Brasil, San Telmo. Long-established bohemian bar overlooking Parque Lezama, reopened in 2007 after a sustained neighbourhood campaign to save it from closure. Freshly renovated, it retains both the table where Ernesto Sábato wrote *On Heroes and Tombs* and its 24-hour opening policy.

Bárbaro Tres Sargentos 415, Retiro. This cosy bar, a long-standing institution tucked down a side street, regularly puts on live jazz.

Buller Pres. Ortíz 1827, Recoleta. The shiny stainless-steel vats and whiff of malt tell you that this brasserie brews its own excellent beer, which runs the gamut from pale ale to creamy stout.

Carnal Coronel Niceto Vega 5511, Palermo. This bar, right opposite *Niceto* (see p.139), has a large upstairs terrace that fills quickly during the warmer months, when a DJ plays laidback dance grooves for a young, trendy crowd.

Celta Bar Sarmiento 1702; see Central Buenos Aires map. Popular with a friendly and relaxed crowd, this attractive bar with big wooden tables is a good place for an early-evening drink. There's often live music, including Argentine rock and Brazilian MPB (Música Popular Brasileira) in the basement.

La Cigale 25 de Mayo 722; see Central Buenos Aires map. Renowned for its happy hours (6–9 pm week nights) when it offers cocktails at ridiculously cheap prices, this lounge style bar is particularly popular with students and backpackers.

Dadá San Martín 941, Retiro. Small, hip and attractive bar, playing jazz soundtracks, serving reasonable food and offering a laidback alternative to the nearby Irish joints.

Deep Blue Reconquista 920, Retiro. A popular, modern bar, done out in vibrant blue, with the funkiest pool tables in the city downstairs; also has a branch at Ayacucho 1240.

Gibraltar Peru 895, San Telmo. Popular both with expats and locals who like to hang out with expats, *Gibraltar* is a British-style pub that's a bit more relaxed than *Kilkenny*, with a friendly atmosphere, bar service and great bar food, including fish and chips and Thai curry.

Gran Bar Danzón Libertad 1161, 1st floor, Retiro. Fashionable after-office bar and restaurant with sharply dressed staff and a very comprehensive wine list. Elegant and popular, even mid-week.

Kilkenny Reconquista and Paraguay, Retiro. The boisterous *Kilkenny* is one of the few bars heaving well before midnight and is an established favourite of both visiting foreigners and Guinness-drinking

Porteños, though it can be a bit on the sleazy side. The bar – one of several Irish-themed pubs in the area – is the focus for the uproarious St Patrick's Day celebrations in the microcentro.

Mundo Bizarro Serrano 1222, Palermo. The name means "strange world" and this bar is definitely a bit different for super-trendy Palermo: expect low lighting, good cocktails and a relaxed crowd.

Notorious Av Callao 966, Recoleta ☎011/4816-2888. Friendly bar selling CDs that you can listen to on headphones. There's also a great garden at the back where you can chill out over a cold beer. Interesting small-scale concerts given – blues, jazz, tango, Latin – throughout the year.

Plaza Dorrego Bar Defensa 1098, San Telmo. Most traditional of the bars around Plaza Dorrego, a sober wood-panelled place where the names of countless customers have been etched on its wooden tables and walls, and piles of empty peanut shells adorn the tables.

Shamrock Rodríguez Peña 1220, Recoleta. Irish bar with a Porteño touch. A good place to meet foreigners, with a small club downstairs.

El Taller Borges 1595, Palermo ☎011/4831-5501. Bars and restaurants have sprouted around it, but *El Taller* still has the best outside seating in one of Buenos Aires' liveliest evening plazas. It also hosts regular jazz events.

Único Honduras and Fitzroy, Palermo. At the very centre of Hollywood, a lively crowd is always guaranteed at this well-known bar, which also does reasonable food; it fills early but is more laidback after 1am or so.

Live music

Places offering **live music**, including folk, jazz, tango and rock, are scattered all over the city and differ enormously in style and ambience, though the quality is invariably high. For recitals by local bands, check the *Sí* supplement in *Clarín* on Fridays (ⓦ www.si.clarin.com) and the oppositionally named *No* supplement in *Página 12* on Thursdays; ⓦ www.atconcert.net is a useful web-based source on what bands are coming to town. As well as the larger venues like *Luna Park*, international stars often play at the football stadiums, particularly River Plate's Monumental – these gigs are widely advertised and are usually best booked through a ticket agency (see p.140). Tickets are generally sold on the door at the smaller venues. Prices vary from around $10 for a local band at a small venue to $400 or more to see a big name at one of the stadiums. If folk music is your thing, check out ⓦ www.folkloreclub.com.ar. Classical music and opera are accounted for on p.145.

Blues Special Club Av Almirante Brown 102, Boca ☎011/4854-2338 The name says it all: special blues acts, including those from the US, perform Fri–Sun, while most Fridays there is also a *zapada blusera*, or jam session. It's also a venue for *rock nacional* acts.

Estadio Luna Park Bouchard 465, in the city centre. ☎011/5279-5279, ⓦ www.lunapark.com.ar. Wonderful Art Deco edifice whose huge capacity lends itself to big sell-out events like boxing fights, the Chinese state circus and acts ranging from well-known international names like the Pet Shop Boys to big Argentine folk stars like Horacio Guarany. Make sure you don't get a "poor visibility" seat.

Mitos Argentinos Humberto 1° 489, San Telmo ☏011/4362-7810, 🌐www.mitosargentinos .com.ar. The main attraction of this old mansion is the offbeat nature of the bands playing Fri–Sun, with Argentine tribute bands often the star act. The format is *cena show*, starting at around $55.

ND/Ateneo Paraguay 918, Retiro ☏011/4328-2888, 🌐www.ndateneo .com.ar. Folk, rock, tango, jazz, modern classical – all the big national and South American names play here at some point. The medium-sized theatre also hosts film screenings and recitals.

No Avestruz Humboldt 1857, Palermo Viejo ☏011/4777-6956, 🌐www.noavestruz.com .ar. Outstanding venue hosting emerging and established artists focusing on jazz and Latin sounds from Buenos Aires and further afield. Delicious food too.

Pan y Teatro Muñiz and Las Casas, Boedo ☏011/4924-6920, 🌐www.panyteatro.com.ar. This beautifully restored grocer's shop serves an original blend of Italian and *criollo* food and puts on shows, including tango, classical music and jazz. Closed Mon.

Peña del Colorado Güemes 3657, Palermo ☏011/4822-1038, 🌐www.delcolorado .com.ar. Famed for its past-midnight *guitarreadas* (bring your guitar, play and sing) that "finish when the candles burn out", the Colorado is the city's most traditional folk venue – there is also a *mate* bar, a restaurant and occasional folk and even tango shows.

Thelonious Salguero 1884, Palermo 🌐www .thelonious.com.ar. The odd soul or blues concert is given here, but as the name implies, this is a jazz club, and generally regarded as the top; the music is always mesmerizing, the acoustics are faultless and the food isn't bad.

La Trastienda Balcarce 460, Monserrat ☏011/4342-7650, 🌐www.latrastienda.com. Trendy live music in a late nineteenth-century mansion, with a wide-ranging roster of acts including rock, jazz, salsa and tango.

Vaca Profana Lavalle 3683, Balvanera ☏011/4867-0934, 🌐www.vacaprofana.com.ar. Groundbreaking joint serving a delicious vegetarian *picada* (mixed platter) and all manner of food and drinks, but more interesting for its avant-garde music and occasionally theatre – new South American sounds including neo-ethnic.

Nightclubs

In terms of **nightclubs**, Buenos Aires stands head and shoulders above any other city in Argentina. Traditionally clubs don't get going until around 3am but – to the relief of those who like to get at least some sleep, perhaps – there has been a tendency in BA to go out a bit earlier in recent times, with closing hours now quite strictly controlled. Drunkenness and drug-taking are frowned up on by wider society but pretty common in clubs.

Music in dance clubs varies from the cheesiest commercial house and Eighties pop to cutting-edge tunes mixed by DJs of international standing. Although Buenos Aires has some great home-grown DJs, trends in dance music tend to follow those of Europe and the US (particularly London) and clubbers are almost always young and affluent. If you're in town, don't the miss big annual shindigs such as the South American Music Conference (Oct) or Creamfields (Nov). At the other end of the spectrum, *bailantas* are events where the predominant music is *cumbia villera* – a version of Colombia's famous, repetitive *cumbia* rhythm that's the Argentine equivalent of gangsta rap, glorifying drugs and crime. Cheap, alcoholic and rowdy, *bailantas* can be fun but are not really recommendable unless you go in the company of a regular.

Admission prices range wildly from free (particularly for women) to $100 or more, with prices sometimes including a drink. For more information and listings on gay nightlife, see p.139.

Asia de Cuba Pierina de Alessi Cossentini 750, Puerto Madero 🌐www.asiadecuba.com.ar. Famous for its fashion model and VIP crowd, this place starts off the night as a sushi bar and then turns into an exclusive disco.

Bahrein Lavalle 345, in the city centre 🌐www .bahreinba.com. Uber-cool club in a beautifully renovated townhouse dripping with antique furnishings. Drum 'n' bass on Tues, house and techno on Fri and Sat.

Crobar Paseo de la Infanta Isabel, Palermo ⓦwww.crobar.com.ar. Large and flashy complex of bars and dancefloors playing mainstream dance music that attracts a smartly dressed clientele.

Fantástico Bailable Rivadavia and Sánchez de Loria, Once (Loria subte) ⓦwww.fantasticodeonce .com. The best known *bailanta* – and a good place to try the heady mix of non-stop dancing and full-on flirting that goes with the territory.

Maluco Beleza Sarmiento 1728, in the city centre ☏011/4372-1737 ⓦwww .malucobeleza.com.ar. Long-running Brazilian club, playing a mix of lambada, afro, samba and reggae to a lively crowd of Brazilians and Brazilophiles. Wed is Brazilian music only, with a *feijoada* (traditional stew) served; book ahead.

Mambo Báez 243, Las Cañitas ☏011/4252-0492 ⓦwww.mambobar.com.ar. Extravagantly tropical

Club Latino with dinner-shows – the shows are fun, the food not great – and disco; book ahead. Salsa classes also held at various times.

Niceto Niceto Vega 5510, Palermo ⓦwww .nicetoclub.com. *Niceto* is the club to hit to for a friendly, diverse crowd, outlandish podium dancers and house music played by the city's most acclaimed resident DJs. The jewel in Niceto's crown is the infamous hedonistic *Club 69* party on Thursdays (ⓦclub69.wordpress.com).

Pacha Costanera Norte and La Pampa ⓦwww .pachabuenosaires.com. The club scene in Buenos Aires changes fast but "Clubland" nights at *Pacha* just keep on going. Big and glitzy like its Ibiza namesake, Pacha attracts a lively crowd, including a sprinkling of Argentine celebrities. Dance DJs of international standing often play here. Sat from midnight.

Gay and lesbian nightlife

Buenos Aires is increasingly considered the major urban **gay tourist destination** in Latin America. Although the scene can be a disappointment for those looking for specifically gay and lesbian locales, for a lot of gay and lesbian tourists the very attraction is a lack of any "ghetto", with San Telmo the nearest the city comes to such a phenomenon. As in many Latin American cities, exclusively gay places are not always the best places to go out in any case, especially when it comes to restaurants; anywhere fashionable, with a "mixed" crowd, will most likely prove a better option.

There is also an increasing open-mindedness on the part of its inhabitants and authorities – in 2009 Buenos Aires became the first place in Latin America to sanction gay marriage. The streets, plazas and parks of Buenos Aires can be very cruisy, making them likelier places to meet people than bars or discos, where people tend to go out in groups of friends. *Gay Buenos Aires* (ⓦwww.gay-ba.com) is a booklet and website in English and Spanish; it carries comprehensive details of meeting-points, clubs, restaurants, hotels, travel agencies, gay-friendly shops and so forth. Most venues will also hand out a free gay city map, *BSASGay* (ⓦwww.mapabsasgay.com.ar), with all the latest locales. Women are far less well catered for than men, but information about events and venues for lesbians can be found at the website ⓦwww .lafulana.org.ar.

The long-established heart of gay Buenos Aires is the corner of avenidas Pueyrredón and Santa Fe, where nondescript *Confitería El Olmo* is still the place to hang out on Friday and Saturday evenings for free entrance flyers or discount vouchers, and to find out where to go. Palermo has increasingly become the main magnet, especially Palermo Hollywood, while San Telmo has ambitions to become the Porteño "Village", or Chueca. For gay *milongas*, try *La Marshall* (☏011/4912-9043, ⓦwww.lamarshall.com.ar), which holds one at Maipú 444 in the centre at 10pm on Wednesdays – though, as with all *milongas*, you should check it hasn't moved on before setting out.

Alsina Buenos Aires Alsina 934, in the city centre ⓦwww.alsinabuenosaires .com.ar. This palatial converted industrial building stages gay nights on Fridays and Sundays, usually

starting around midnight and attracting some of the most beautiful people in the city. All ages and tastes come to dance to varied music, everything from house to 1970s disco.

Amerika Gascón 1040, Almagro ⓦwww.ameri-k
.com.ar. One of the biggest and best-known gay
discos. Three dancefloors playing house and Latin
music. Open Thurs–Sun.

Bach Bar Cabrera 4390, Palermo ⓦwww
.bach-bar.com.ar. Fairly mixed bar, with shows on
Fri and Sat and karaoke on Sun, all starting very
late, even though it is a pre-disco venue.

Bulnes Class Bulnes 1250, Palermo. Laidback bar
with singers, frequented by professional types and
open late Fri & Sat.

Chueca Soler 3283, Palermo. Arguably the city's
best gay restaurant, doubling up as a bar, and
staging shows and events. The food tends towards
the nouvelle cuisine, to match the trendy decor.
Open Wed–Sun from 9pm.

Contramano Rodríguez Peña 1082, Recoleta
ⓦwww.contramano.com. One of the longest-
running discos, attracting an older crowd, with
bears night on Sun and shows on Sat.

Inside Restobar Bartolomé Mitre 1571,
in the city centre ⓦwww.restaurantinside.com.ar.
Located in a beautiful setting in the Pasaje
de la Piedad. Functions as a restaurant,
wine bar and show, hosting strippers, singers
and dancers.

Sitges Av Córdoba 4119, corner of Pringles,
Palermo ⓦwww.sitgesonline.com.ar. Large,
bright trendy bar, frequented by a mixed but
invariably young crowd. Bursting at the seams
from 6pm Thurs to Sun, with late-night weekend
shows.

The arts and entertainment

There's a superb range of **cultural events** on offer in Argentina's capital, ranging
from avant-garde theatre to blockbuster movies and grand opera with a wealth of
options in between. One of the best features of Porteño cultural life is the strong
tradition of free or very cheap events, including film showings at the city's
museums and cultural centres, tango and a series of enthusiastically attended
outdoor events put on by the city government every summer; street performers
are also of very high quality.

A plethora of **listings** are given in the entertainment sections of both
Clarín and *La Nación*. Numerous independent listings sheets are also available in
bars, bookshops and kiosks throughout the city; it's always worth trying
the tourist kiosks for pamphlets and magazines. *Arte al Día* (ⓦwww
.artealdia.com) is a monthly newspaper with details of art exhibitions, available
from newspaper stands. The website ⓦwww.mundoteatral.com.ar is an
excellent source of info on shows going on around the city, with a focus on
off-beat stuff.

You can buy **tickets** at discounted prices for theatre, cinema and music events at
the various centralized *carteleras* (ticket agencies) in the centre, such as Cartelera
Baires, Av Corrientes 1382, local 24 (Mon–Thurs 10am–10pm, Fri 10am–11pm,
Sat 10am–midnight, Sun 2–10pm; ⓣ011/4372-5058, ⓦwww.cartelerabaires
.com). Alternatively Ticketek (ⓣ011/5237-7200, ⓦwww.ticketek.com.ar) sells
tickets to many upcoming concerts, plays and sporting events, bookable over the
phone or online with a credit card. The most central of their outlets is at Viamonte
560 (Mon–Sat 9am–8.30pm).

Tango

Tango is so strongly associated with Buenos Aires that a visit to the city really
isn't complete unless you immerse yourself in it at least once. The most accessible way for visitors to experience tango is via the *tango espectáculos*. These
generally rather expensive *cena shows* (dinner followed by a show) are performed
by professionals who put on a highly skilled and choreographed display. Many
hotels and hostels offer excursions to them, and they're mostly attended by
foreign visitors, though there's usually a smattering of locals too. Porteños who
are tango fans tend to prefer to go either to music recitals – with no dancing – or

to *milongas* (see box, p.143) to dance themselves. A *milonga* refers to a moveable event rather than a specific venue, so the days, times and locations of these change frequently; many are situated in the city's outer barrios, with entry usually around $10 to $20. *El Tangauta* (Ⓦ www.eltangauta.com) is a free magazine with listings, which can generally be picked up at tourist kiosks, hotels, cultural centres and record stores.

There are also regular tango festivals, with a host of free shows and hundreds of classes and *milongas* – the biggest is the Tango World Championship and Festival, held in August in recent years, and the **Día del Tango**, celebrated on and around December 11 (Carlos Gardel's birthday).

Bar Sur Estados Unidos 299, San Telmo ☎ 011/4362-6086, Ⓦ www.bar-sur.com.ar. One of San Telmo's more reasonably priced tango shows (about $220 with dinner). The quality of the shows can vary but it's an intimate space where audience participation is encouraged towards the end of the evening. Daily 8pm–2am.

Centro Cultural Torquato Tasso Defensa 1575, San Telmo ☎ 011/4307-6506, Ⓦ www .torquatotasso.com.ar. Friendly San Telmo neighbourhood cultural centre with top quality tango recitals, some of them free.

El Chino Beazley 3566, Pompeya ☎ 011/4911-0215. This bar and *parrilla* in traditional Pompeya in the southwest of the city is probably the most authentic place to hear tango sung by the talented staff and a crowd of locals and regulars. It's even been the subject of a movie, *Bar El Chino*. Fri and Sat from 10pm.

Clásica y Moderna Callao 892, Recoleta Ⓦ www .clasicaymoderna.com. The dark, brick interior was converted from a bookstore into a café-restaurant with great food and live tango and other acts, including many top names (daily from around 9.30pm).

Club Gricel La Rioja 1180, San Cristóbal (Urquiza subte) ☎ 011/4957-7157. Small, friendly, authentic club holding *milongas* on Fri and Sat from 11pm and Sun from 9pm. Also daily classes.

🏃 Confitería Ideal Suipacha 384, 1st floor, in the city centre ☎ 011/5265-8069, Ⓦ www.confiteriaideal.com. An oasis of elegance just a few blocks from busy Corrientes, the *Ideal* has a stunning salon, which is undoubtedly one of the most traditional and consistently popular places to dance. There is an exhaustive programme of classes and *milongas* in both the afternoons and evenings every day; see the website for details.

Niño Bien Centro Región Leonesa, Humberto 1° 1462, Constitución (San José subte) ☎ 011/4305-7310. Popular *milonga* with both locals and foreign "tango tourists", and with a great atmosphere. Thurs from 11.30pm.

🏃 Parakultural Ⓦ www.parakultural.com.ar. Young, bohemian organization that puts on the coolest *milongas* and shows in town at a rotating and eclectic set of venues, including the huge Salón Canning at Scalabrini Ortiz 1331, Palermo. See the website for schedule; classes also offered.

Piazzola Centro de Artes Galería Güemes, Florida 165, in the city centre ☎ 011/4344-8201, Ⓦ www.piazzollatangoshow.com. In a renovated theatre in the lovely Galería Güemes, this is one of the most central tango show locations, with a dinner and exciting programme daily at 8.30pm for around $280.

Señor Tango Vieytes 1655, Barracas ☎ 011/4303-0231, Ⓦ www.senortango.com.ar. Large and very professional *tanguería* in the quiet southern barrio of Barracas. Daily dinner and a real spectacle of a show that traces the history of tango and incorporates trapezes, 1980s tango fusion and even horses. From 8.30pm; $350 for dinner, drinks and show, or $90 for the show only.

Taconeando Balcarce 725, San Telmo ☎ 011/4307-6696, Ⓦ www.taconeando.com. Smaller, more informal *tango cena* show; a good option if you want to see a show rather than a *milonga* but also want to avoid the larger, more commercial options; $180 with dinner, $140 without.

El Viejo Almacén Av Independencia and Balcarce, San Telmo ☎ 011/4307-6689. Probably the most famous of San Telmo's *tanguerías*, housed in an attractive nineteenth-century building. Occasionally hosts nationally famous tango singers, otherwise slickly executed dinner and dance shows daily from 8pm. $300 with dinner, $180 without.

🏃 La Viruta Armenia 1366, Palermo ☎ 011/4779-0030, Ⓦ www.lavirutatango .com. Huge, long-running institution with *milongas* (Sat & Sun) and shows (Thurs & Fri) that mix tango with folklore, salsa and even rock 'n' roll. The action begins at midnight, with classes during the afternoon and evening.

▲ Tango in La Boca

Cinema and theatre

Porteños are keen and knowledgeable cinema-goers and there are dozens of **cinemas** in the city showing everything from the latest Hollywood releases to Argentine films and art house cinema. Foreign films are usually subtitled. Traditionally, cinemas showing purely mainstream stuff were concentrated on Calle Lavalle, while art house flicks were more common on Avenida Corrientes. However, both are increasingly losing out to the multiplex cinemas in the city's various shopping malls, which offer excellent visuals and acoustics, though in a blander atmosphere. Tickets normally cost around \$20, though you can find free or very cheap showings at museums and cultural centres.

Theatre is also very strongly represented, with Avenida Corrientes standing up well in comparison to New York's Broadway and London's West End – although obviously almost all plays are in Spanish. Away from the major theatrical venues – where you'll find a good spread of international and Argentine theatre, both classic and contemporary, ranging from serious drama to reviews and musicals – the city

Milongas

Tango has gained a whole new audience in recent times, with an increasing number of young people filling the floors of social clubs, *confiterías* and traditional dancehalls for regular events known as **milongas**. Even if you don't dance yourself, it's still worth going to see one: the spectacle of couples slipping almost trance-like around the dancefloor, as if illustrating the oft-quoted remark "tango is an emotion that is danced", is a captivating sight. Apart from the understated skill and composure of the dancers, one of the most appealing aspects of the *milonga* is the absence of class – and, especially, age – divisions; indeed, most younger dancers regard it as an honour to be partnered by older and more experienced dancers.

While the setting for a *milonga* can range from a sports hall to an elegant salon, the structure – and etiquette – of the dances varies little. In many cases, classes are given first. Once the event gets underway, it is divided into musical sets, known as *tandas*, which will cover the three subgenres of tango: tango "proper"; *milonga* – a more uptempo sound; and waltz. Each is danced differently and occasionally there will also be an isolated interval of salsa, rock or jazz. The invitation to dance comes from the man, who will nod towards the woman whom he wishes to partner. She signals her acceptance of the offer with an equally subtle gesture and only then will her new partner approach her table. Once on the dancefloor, the couple waits eight *compases*, or bars, and then begins to dance, circulating in a counter-clock-wise direction around the dancefloor. The woman follows the man's lead by responding to *marcas*, or signs, given by her partner to indicate the move he wishes her to make. The more competent she is, the greater number of variations and personal touches she will add. Though the basic steps of the tango may not look very difficult, it entails a rigorous attention to posture and a subtle shifting of weight from leg to leg, essential to avoid losing balance. The couple will normally dance together until the end of a set, which lasts for four or five melodies. Once the set is finished, it is good tango etiquette for the woman to thank her partner who, if the experience has been successful and enjoyable, is likely to ask her to dance again later in the evening.

Watching real tango danced is the kind of experience that makes people long to do it themselves. Unfortunately, a *milonga* is not the best place to take your first plunge; unlike, say, salsa, even the best partner in the world will find it hard to carry a complete novice through a tango. In short, if you can't bear the thought of attending a *milonga* without dancing, the answer is to take some classes – you should reckon on taking about six to be able to hold your own on the dancefloor. There are innumerable places in Buenos Aires offering dance classes, including cultural centres, bars and *confiterías* and, for the impatient or shy, there are private teachers. If you're going to take classes, it's important to have an appro-priate pair of shoes with a sole that allows you to swivel (no rubber soles). For women, it's not necessary to wear heels but it is important that the shoes support the instep. At a *milonga*, however, a pair of well-polished heels is the norm, and will act as a signal that you are there to dance. Any woman going to a *milonga*, but not intending to dance, should make that clear in her choice of dress and footwear; go dressed to kill and you'll spend the night turning down invitations from bemused-looking men.

is dotted with innumerable independent venues, with stages in bars and tiny auditoriums at the back of shopping centres; the terms "Off Corrientes" and "Off Off Corrientes" found in press listings are based on those used in New York and London. Tickets tend to cost around $50; some theatres will do a half-price show mid-week.

Some of the more noteworthy cinemas and theatres are listed below; for what's on, consult the listings sections of *Clarín* or *La Nación*.

Abasto Shopping Av Corrientes 3200, Balvanera Ⓦwww.abasto-shopping.com.ar. Enormous modern cinema at the Abasto shopping centre, featuring a good mix of international and local movies; usually one of the main hosts of April's enthusiastically attended international film festival.

Arteplex Centro Av Corrientes 1145, city centre Ⓦwww.cinesarteplex.com. The most central of a small local chain of art-house cinemas, and one of the last remaining cinemas on Corrientes; there's a bar and DVD store inside too.

Gaumont Rivadavia 1633, Balvanera Ⓣ011/4371-3050. One of several "Espacio INCAA" showcase cinemas run by the Instituto Nacional de Cine y Artes Audiovisuales, the Argentine national cinema institute. If your Spanish is up to it, this is the place to catch the best examples of the country's strong national film industry.

Teatro General San Martín Corrientes 1500, city centre Ⓣ011/4371-0111, Ⓦwww.teatrosanmartin.com.ar. Excellent modern venue with several auditoriums and a varied programme that usually includes one or two Argentine plays as well as international standards such as Pinter or Brecht. Also hosts contemporary dance events, ballet, children's theatre and art-house cinema in the Sala Leopoldo Lugones, while a cultural centre with free exhibitions is tucked behind.

Teatro Nacional Cervantes Libertad 815, city centre Ⓦwww.teatrocervantes.gov.ar. This grand old-fashioned theatre, superb inside and out, presents a broad programme of old and new Argentine and foreign works, with a particular emphasis on plays from Spain.

Teatro Ópera Corrientes 860, city centre. Fabulous Art Deco theatre, which in its heyday billed Edith Piaf and Josephine Baker, has undergone a recent revival focusing on a music and dance programme, usually of a very high quality.

Cultural centres and art galleries

Buenos Aires' numerous **cultural centres** are one of the city's greatest assets. Every neighbourhood has its own modest centre – good places to find out about free tango classes and generally offering a mixture of art exhibitions, film and cafés – while the major institutions such as the Centro Cultural Borges and the Centro Cultural Recoleta put on some of the city's best exhibitions. Buenos Aires also has some prestigious commercial **art galleries**, the majority of which are based in Retiro and Recoleta, particularly around Plaza San Martín and nearby Suipacha and Arenales. During May or June, the art fair **ARTE BA** (Ⓦwww.arteba.com), held in La Rural exhibition centre in Palermo, showcases work from Buenos Aires' most important galleries.

British Arts Centre (BAC) Suipacha 1333, Retiro Ⓣ011/4393-6941, Ⓦwww.britishartscentre.org.ar. The place to head for if you're nostalgic for a bit of Hitchcock or Monty Python – regular English-language film and video showings, as well as plays by playwrights such as Harold Pinter. Tues–Fri 3–9pm.

Centro Cultural Borges Viamonte and San Martín, Retiro Ⓣ011/5555-5359, Ⓦwww.ccborges.org.ar. Large space above the Galerías Pacífico shopping centre. Excellent photography exhibitions such as World Press Photo in spacious galleries, as well as painting, theatre, dance, and art-house cinema. Mon–Sat 10am–9pm, Sun noon–9pm; $10.

Centro Cultural Recoleta Junín 1930, Recoleta Ⓣ011/4803-1040, Ⓦwww.centroculturalrecoleta .org. One of the city's best cultural centres – see p.117.

Centro Cultural Ricardo Rojas Corrientes 2038 Ⓣ011/4954-5521, Ⓦwww.rojas.uba.ar. Affiliated with the University of Buenos Aires, this friendly cultural centre and gallery space offers free events including live music and bargain film showings, usually alternative or art house.

Espacio Fundación Telefónica Arenales 1540, Recoleta Ⓣ011/4333-1300, Ⓦwww.fundacion .telefonica.com.ar/espacio. A high-tech art centre that lays emphasis on communications media, as you would expect for a foundation run by a telecoms company. This sleek, modern space stages small, mostly avant-garde exhibitions of work by contemporary Argentine artists, and houses an excellent media library. Mon–Sat 2–8.30pm; free.

Fundación Federico J. Klemm Marcelo T. de Alvear 626, Retiro Ⓦ www.fundacionfjklemm.org. The late Argentine art maverick Federico Klemm was a kind of self-fashioned Andy Warhol, producing bizarre portraits of modern-day Argentine celebrities in mythic and homoerotic poses. Klemm was also a collector of modern art and on a display here there is a serious collection of works by Picasso, Dali, Mapplethorpe and Warhol himself – to name just a few – as well as

major Argentine artists such as Berni and Kuitca. Mon–Fri 11am–8pm; free.

Goethe Institut Corrientes 319, city centre ☎ 011/4318-5600, Ⓦ www.goethe.de/hs/bue. Smart German cultural institute that has a good library for German and English books, as well as German movies and plays on offer. Mon–Fri 9am–6pm; closed during summer.

Ruth Benzacar Gallery Florida 1000, Retiro ☎ 011/4313-8480, Ⓦ www.ruthbenzacar.com. Rather unexpectedly reached through an underground entrance at the end of Florida, this prestigious gallery has temporary exhibitions featuring international artists as well as Argentines. Mon–Fri 11.30am–8pm.

Classical music, opera and ballet

Argentina has a number of excellent classical performers, including **opera** singers, such as tenors Marcelo Álvarez and soprano María Cristina Kiehr, ballet dancers like Iñaki Urlezaga, and classical **musicians** such as pianist and conductor Daniel Barenboim. Keeping a much lower media profile, but equally acclaimed, is concert pianist and multiple Grammy Award winner Martha Argerich; she presides over her own international piano competition in Buenos Aires.

Classical performances in Buenos Aires have seen something of a revival in recent years, boosted by frequent free and outdoor performances, especially in the summer. Some of the best concerts are small-scale affairs held at museums, churches and the like, such as those held at the **Museo de Arte Hispanoamericano Isaac Fernández Blanco** (see p.114), though the larger venues are also exciting, and none is more spectacular than the Teatro Colón. For news of concerts, consult Ⓦ www.musicaclasicaargentina.com.

Casa de la Cultura Av de Mayo 575. Free classical concerts, mostly chamber music, are given from time to time in the marvellous Salón Dorado in the La Prensa building (see p.92); look out for flyers and posters.

La Scala de San Telmo Pasaje Giuffra 371 (Defensa 800), San Telmo ☎ 011/4362-1187, Ⓦ lascala.org.ar. Not Milan, but this sumptuous bijou theatre hosts tango, jazz and other music genres, plus some excellent operas and classical concerts.

Teatro Avenida Avenida de Mayo 1222, city centre ☎ 011/4381-0662, Ⓦ www.balirica.org.ar. This stylish theatre, opened only a few months

after the Colón in 1908, is the home to Buenos Aires Lírica, which puts on a number of operas here every season.

Teatro Coliseo Marcelo T. de Alvear 1125, Retiro ☎ 011/4816-3789. The most important venue for ballet, musicals and classical music after the Colón, which it has replaced during the latter's renovation; also offers occasional free recitals.

Teatro Colón Libertad 621, in the city centre Ⓦ www.teatrocolon.org.ar. Buenos Aires' most glamorous night out and one of the world's great opera houses – acoustically on a par with La Scala in Milan, showcasing opera, ballet and classical music. See p.95.

Shopping

Shopping in Buenos Aires is a pleasure unmatched elsewhere in South America. While goods tend to be more Western and familiar than those you will come across in, say, Bolivia or Peru, you can nonetheless count on finding some highly original items to take home.

Palermo Soho is the place to head for independent **designer clothing** stores, while malls scattered throughout the city house both Argentine and international chains. Shops selling **books and music** are strung along Avenida Corrientes between 9 de Julio and Callao. Others stretch out on Florida north of Avenida Córdoba, together with a bevy of **craft**, T-shirt and leather stores aimed at tourists, many of them in covered arcades or *galerías*. Contemporary **art** is on sale at the scores of smart galleries that line Retiro, with several along Avenida Alvear, while anyone looking for colonial paintings and **antiques** should head for San Telmo. The best **handicrafts** are found in their home provinces rather than in Buenos Aires, but the next best alternative are the craft markets. Other typically Argentine goods include *mate* paraphernalia, polo wear, wine and world-class leatherware. A box of widely available Havanna *alfajores* (see p.42) makes a good present, or take a jar or two of *dulce de leche* away with you to satisfy cravings. For outdoor gear, there is a whole row of **camping** and **fishing** shops along the 100 to 200 block of Calle Paraná, just off Corrientes. If you're heading south, bear in mind Ushuaia and many Patagonian towns are just as well stocked as Buenos Aires, although prices may be higher down there.

Shopping malls

Over the past decade or two, **shopping malls** have partly superseded small shops and street markets, but those in Buenos Aires are among the most tastefully appointed in the world. Several of the malls, like Abasto, are housed in revamped buildings of historical and architectural interest in their own right. On a practical level, the malls are air-conditioned and the places where you'll find that rarity in Buenos Aires, public toilets.

Abasto Avenida Corrientes 3200, Balvanera. This grand building, dating from the 1880s, was once the city food market; now it's the daddy of all the central malls. As well as a ten-screen cinema, it has hundreds of designer and cheaper stores, an enormous food hall, an amusement arcade and a hands-on museum for children, the Museo de los Niños (museum Tues–Sun 1–8pm; $10 for adults, $15 for children).
Bond Street Avenida Santa Fe 1670, Recoleta. The alternative mall, full of local teenagers skulking around skate stores and tattoo parlours; there's also a few surf shops in the surrounding streets. A good place to pick up flyers for live music and clubs.

Buenos Aires Design Center Plaza Intendente Alvear, Recoleta. Right next to the Centro Cultural de Recoleta, this mall is dedicated to shops selling the latest designs, mostly for the home, from Argentina and elsewhere.
Galerías Pacífico Florida 750, in the city centre. Fashion boutiques and bookshops in a beautiful building decorated with murals by leading Argentine artists, plus the Centro Cultural Borges at the top and a food court and children's play area in the basement. The most central mall.
Patio Bullrich Libertador 750, Retiro. Once a thoroughbred horse market, this is one of the most upmarket malls, and a good place to find designer clothes and leather.

Clothing and accessories

With inventive designers aplenty, Buenos Aires is a good place to expand your wardrobe. **Fashions** tend to echo those of Europe, albeit a season behind, but you can also find plenty of stores selling fairly unique off-the-peg designs, both in the malls and the streets, where they rub shoulders with stores selling more classic attire. On the downside, prices have rocketed in recent years, and the quality of domestic goods, except at the highest end, is not always the best – do not expect your nifty Buenos Aires outfits to hold together for long. Unsurprisingly, **leather** is an exception – a frequently used material at all price levels, you can find high quality and excellent value boots, jackets and wallets – and bags to take it all home in.

Bailarín Porteño Suipacha 251, city centre. Everything a tango dancer needs, from head to toe – hats, shirts, jackets, shoes, and even jewellery with a *milonga* touch. One of a number of tango-ware stores in the same street.

Bolivia Gurruchaga 1581, Palermo ⓦwww .boliviaonline.com.ar. Hip mens' clothes, perfect for all-night dancing. Floral shirts, grungy tops, zipped jackets and other clothes for guys who prefer not to take things too seriously.

Cardón Sante Fe 1399, Recoleta; Honduras 4755, Palermo; Abasto; Galerías Pacífico ⓦwww.cardon .com.ar. With the slogan "*cosas nuestras*" ("our things") Cardón, beloved of the Argentine land-owning classes, sells smart khaki and white clothing and *carpincho* (capybara) leather shoes, jackets and belts. Perfect for polo matches or estancia stays – just don't get too muddy.

Casa López Marcelo T. de Alvear 640, Retiro ⓦwww.casalopez.com.ar. Regarded as the city's very best exporter of classic leather goods – bags, wallets, briefcases and clothing – the quality is excellent but it has prices to match.

Centro del Cuero Murillo 500–700, Villa Crespo (Malabia subte). A three-block stretch known as the "Centro del Cuero" (leather centre), this is actually a clustering of around thirty warehouse stores and some boutiques selling leather clothing both wholesale and direct to the public. This is the place to go for a bargain, but prices are mostly unmarked so be prepared to haggle.

Deporcamping Santa Fe 4830, Palermo ⓣ011/4772-0534, ⓦwww.deporcamping.com.ar. Limited but decent quality range of trekking clothes and boots, as well as other camping gear such as tents, mats, sleeping bags and stoves.

Jazmin Chebar El Salvador 4702, Palermo; Patio Bullrich ⓦwww.jazminchebar.com.ar. One of the country's best-known designers, creating clothes for women that are simultaneously voguish yet soft and feminine. Expensive but top quality.

JM Cueros Marcelo T. de Alvear 628; Paraguay 616; Santa Fe 1240, all Retiro ⓦwww.jmcueros .com. Traditional *tabalartería* (leatherware shop) selling shoes, bags and accessories, some leather and some made from the soft, attractively mottled skin of the *carpincho*. Many items also feature the geometric designs characteristic of the Pampas region.

Kosiuko Santa Fe 1779, Recoleta; Abasto; Patio Bullrich ⓦwww.kosiuko.com.ar. Very cool shop where affluent young Porteños go to get gear for the weekend's hanging out. Lots of individual items made with a real flair – you're bound to find something irresistible. Women's, men's and children's ranges.

La Martina Paraguay 661, Retiro; Galerías Pacífico ⓦwww.lamartina.com. Well-established Argentine polo brand that sponsors the national teams. As well as polo equipment, stores carry the kind of clothes that people wear to matches (think pastel blouses and lozenge-patterned sweaters). The floor spaces are laid out beautifully, with the polo boots and piles of cashmere set off by dark wood fittings and leather sofas.

Palermitana Diseño Plaza Serrano, Palermo. This salon (and next door's *Escaparate*) provides a home for dozens of market stalls that sell t-shirts with cheeky slogans, beaded flip-flops, tie-dye tops and the like.

Rapsodia Andrés Arguibel 2899, Palermo; Abasto; Galerías Pacífico; Patio Bullrich ⓦwww.rapsodia .com.ar. Although it markets a variety of clothes, many with a bohemian twist, *Rapsodia* is most famous for its range of jeans, which are cut in ways that seem to flatter all shapes and sizes.

Books and music

Corrientes is the traditional place to head for **books and music**, though there are also a number of antique bookstores housed on the ground floors of Avenida de Mayo's Art Nouveau concoctions. Upmarket bookstores, with good foreign-language and glossy coffee table sections, can be found around Florida, Córdoba and Santa Fe.

Ateneo Grand Splendid Santa Fe 1860, Recoleta. Easily the largest bookshop in Latin America and surely a strong contender for the most beautiful bookshop in the world, this store is housed in a former cinema, built in 1919 and inspired by the Opéra Garnier in Paris. A branch of the Ateneo/Yenny chain, it is particularly strong on art and architecture books, with an array of collectable albums of photos of Buenos Aires and the rest of the country. There is a small café on the ground floor, from where you can admire the sumptuousness of it all and browse before you buy.

Kel Ediciones Marcelo T. de Alvear 1369, Recoleta. This long-running all-English bookstore has mostly fairly mainstream stock but it's big enough for anyone to find that perfect accompaniment to a long-distance bus journey; they also stock *Rough Guides*.

Liberarte Avenida Corrientes 1555, in the city centre. An emporium of the assorted interests of the Porteño left-wing intelligentsia. Loads of offbeat periodicals.

Librería de Ávila Alsina 500, Monserrat. Allegedly the site of the city's first bookshop, this wonderful sprawling antique bookshop is worth a visit as much for the ambience as the books – which include a great selection on Argentina.

Musimundo Florida 267, in the city centre, and branches throughout the city. Argentina's major record chain, stocking everything from techno to tango. Online delivery also possible via ⓦwww .musimundo.com.

Walrus Books Estados Unidos 617, San Telmo. Excellent English-language new and secondhand bookstore, with the emphasis on quality literature and non-fiction from around the world. Tues–Sun noon–8pm. Restricted opening hours during the summer.

Zival's Av Callao 395, in the city centre ⓦwww .tangostore.com. Small but well-stocked music store, particularly good for tango. There's a strong selection of CDs and DVDs as well as books and sheet music, and the staff are very knowledgeable on the best tango recordings.

Arts and crafts

The city's markets – such as the Sunday fairs in Recoleta, San Telmo and Mataderos, along with some of the *casas de provincia* (see p.68), are where you'll find **handicrafts**, including unique ceramics, wooden masks or alpaca-wool items, usually at far better value than the mass-produced alternatives. Local **arts and crafts** are also available at a number of central stores.

Arte Etnico Argentino El Salvador 4656, Palermo ⓦwww.arteetnicoargentino.com. Mostly pricey rugs and tapestries from the North, plus rustic furniture made from native wood. A fantastic shop – just go and look at the chairs hanging from the main ceiling like wooden bats – in every sense.

El Boyero Florida 953, Retiro; Galerías Pacífico. Usual leather and *campo* (countryside) artefacts including wine bottle holders, horse whips and *mate* gourds, and with some more interesting, less garish designs than in many of the surrounding stores.

El Gauchito Carabelas 306, city centre. A stone's throw from the Obelisco, this reassuringly

long-running store is an authentic vendor of gaucho clothing, artwork, antique and modern crafts for the home and many other goods emanating from Argentina's pampas heartlands.

Kelly's Paraguay 431, Retiro. Colourful store that sells a variety of ponchos from different provinces, ceramics and, of course, *mates*.

Plata Lappas Florida 740, in the city centre. The city's most renowned silverware and kitchenware have been sold here for years. Some of it is imported, but there's still plenty of local stuff, including gorgeous goblets.

Listings

Airlines Aerolíneas Argentinas, Perú 2 ☎011/4340-7777 or 0810/222-86527; Air Canada, Av Córdoba 656 ☎011/4327-3640; Air France, San Martín 334, 23rd floor ☎011/4317-4711; Alitalia, Suipacha 1111, 28th floor ☎011/4310-9999; American Airlines, Santa Fe 881 ☎011/4318-1111; Andes, Av Córdoba 966, 8th floor ☎0810/1222-6337; Avianca, Carlos Pellegrini 1163, 4th floor ☎011/4322-2731; British Airways, Libertador 498, 13th floor ☎0800/666-1459; Delta, Reconquista 737, 3rd floor ☎011/4312-1200; Gol ☎0810/266-3131; Iberia, Carlos Pellegrini 1163, 1st floor ☎011/4131-1000; KLM, Suipacha 268, 9th floor ☎0880/122-3014; LADE, Perú 714 ☎011/5129-9001; LAN, Cerrito 866 ☎0810/999-9526; Lloyd

Aéreo Boliviano (LAB), Carlos Pellegrini 137 ☎011/4323-1900; Lufthansa, Marcelo T. de Alvear 636 ☎011/4319-0600; Qantas, Av Córdoba 673, 13th floor ☎011/4114-5800; Sol ☎0810/444-4765; South African Airways, Suipacha 1067, 2nd floor ☎011/4319-0099; TAM, Cerrito 1026 ☎011/4819-6950; United Airlines, Av Madero 900, 9th floor ☎0810/777-8648.

Airport enquiries Ezeiza and Aeroparque ☎011/5480-6111.

Banks and exchange There is an entire street of bureaux de change in the financial district, near the corner of San Martín and Sarmiento – rates are similar and opening hours are generally Mon–Fri 9am–6pm. This is also where you'll find the central bank branches, with similar hours. At other times, look out for the branches of exchange company Metropolis at Corrientes 2557, Florida 506 and Quintana 576, which are also open at weekends. Buenos Aires is the only city in the country where you will find it relatively easy to change travellers' cheques, though it can still be difficult. ATMs are widespread.

Car rental Dollar, San Martín 945 ☎011/4315-8800, ☒www.dollar.com.ar; Thrifty, Carlos Pellegrini 1576 ☎011/4326-0338, ☒www.grupoexpress.com.ar.

Embassies and consulates Australia, Villanueva 1400 (☎011/4779-3500); Brazil, Carlos Pellegrini 1363, 5th floor (☎011/4515-6500); Canada, Tagle 2828 (☎011/4808-1000); Chile, San Martín 439, 9th floor (☎011/4394-6582); Ireland, Suipacha 1380, 2nd floor (☎011/5787-0801); New Zealand, Carlos Pellegrini 1427, 5th floor (☎011/4328-0747); Peru, Florida 165, 2nd floor (☎011/4334-0970); South Africa, Marcelo T. de Alvear 590, 8th floor (☎011/4317-2900); UK, Dr Luis Agote 2412 (☎011/4803-7070); Uruguay, Las Heras 1907, 4th floor (☎011/4807-3045); US, Av Colombia 4300 (☎011/5777-4533).

Hospitals Consultorio de Medicina del Viajero, Hospital de Infecciosas F.J. Muñiz, Uspallata ☎011/4304-2180; Hospital Británico, Perdriel 74 ☎011/4309-6400; Hospital Italiano ☎011/4959-0200. The Argentine medical emergency number is ☎107.

Language learning There are a number of organizations which provide Spanish immersion programmes, often with cultural and social activities as part of the language learning. These include EleBaires, Av de Mayo 1370, 3rd floor office 10 (☎011/4383-7706, ☒www.elebaires.com) and Amauta, Federico Lacroze 2129 (☎011/4777-2130, ☒www.amautaspanishschool.com).

Laundry Laverap, Suipacha 722 ☎011/4322-3458 or Av Córdoba 466 ☎011/4312-5460, plus many others across the city. Most Laveraps will also pick up and deliver free of charge.

Pharmacies Farmacity, Lavalle 919 or Corrientes 1820 (24 hours). For more branches see ☒www.farmacity.com.ar.

Police Tourist police Corrientes 436 ☎011/4346-5748, emergencies ☎101. There's a special number that visitors can call if they have been robbed or need other emergency assistance – ☎0800/999-2838.

Post office Correo Central, Sarmiento 189 (Mon–Fri 10am–8pm). There are numerous smaller branches throughout the city, open from 10am to 6pm. Outside these hours, there are many post office counters within stationery shops (*papelerías*), at *locutorios* and at kiosks.

Travel agents Say Hueque, Viamonte 749, 6th floor (☎011/5199-2517/20, ☒www.sayhueque.com), is a highly commendable outfit with English-speaking staff, geared to the independent traveller and offering trips all over the country. Tangol, Florida 971 ground floor (☎011/4312-7276, ☒www.tangol.com), in a similar vein, helps independent travellers with their plans in BA and further afield; it produces a useful free guide *Buenos Aires Day & Night* and works with SA Explorers (see p.81), via whom you can get a discount. Fuegos del Sur, Maipú 812 1°K (☎011/4311-1376, ☒www.fuegosdelsur.com), run by the dependable Tomás Lorenz, is good for deals on domestic and Brazilian trips. ASATEJ, Florida 835, 2nd floor (☎011/4114-7595, ☒www.asatej.com) offers cheap flight deals, particularly for students and young travellers – be prepared to wait as the office gets very busy.

Travel details

Buses

Buenos Aires to: Asunción, Paraguay (hourly; 18–22hr); Bahía Blanca (every 2hr; 9hr); Bariloche (7 daily; 21–23hr); Carmen de Patagones (4 daily; 12hr); Catamarca (8 daily; 15hr); Clorinda (3 daily; 17hr); Comodoro Rivadavia (8 daily; 26hr); Córdoba (hourly; 11hr); Corrientes (6 daily; 12hr); Formosa (5 daily; 14–15hr); Jujuy (hourly; 22hr); La Rioja (4 daily; 17hr); Lima, Peru (2 daily; 72hr); Mar del Plata (hourly; 7hr); Mendoza (hourly; 17hr); Merlo (6 daily; 12hr); Neuquén (4 daily; 15hr); Paraná (8 daily; 7hr); Posadas (8 daily; 13hr); Puerto Iguazú (7 daily; 14hr 30min–19hr); Resistencia (every 2hr; 13hr); Rio de Janeiro, Brazil (2 daily; 40hr); Rio Gallegos (5 daily; 36hr); Rosario (hourly; 4hr); Salta (hourly; 22hr); San Juan (10 daily; 16hr); San Luis (9 daily; 12hr); San Rafael (4 daily; 13hr); Santa Rosa (every 2hr; 8–10hr); Santiago de Chile, Chile (daily; 19hr); Santiago del Estero (11 daily; 13hr); Trelew (twice weekly; 20hr); Tucumán (every 2hr; 15hr); Zapala (3 daily; 17–18hr).

Ferries

Buenos Aires to: Colonia, Uruguay (4–5 daily; 55min–2hr 45min); Montevideo, Uruguay (2 daily; 2hr 35min); Punta del Este, Uruguay (2 daily; 2hr with bus).

Trains

Buenos Aires to: La Plata (every 30min; 1hr); Mar del Plata (3 daily; 6hr); Rosario (1 daily; 4hr).

Flights

Buenos Aires to: Bariloche (10 daily; 2hr 20min); Catamarca (1 daily; 2hr 30min); Comodoro Rivadavia (2 daily; 2hr 30min); Córdoba (10 daily; 1hr 15min); Corrientes (2 daily; 1hr 20min); El Calafate (10 daily; 3hr 20min); Formosa (1 daily; 1hr 45min); Jujuy (2 daily; 2hr 10min); La Rioja (1 daily; 3hr); Mar del Plata (5 daily; 1hr 15min); Mendoza (7–9 daily; 1hr 50min); Neuquén (4 daily; 1hr 40min); Posadas (3 daily; 1hr 30min); Puerto Iguazú (10–12 daily; 1hr 50min); Resistencia (1–2 daily; 1hr 30min); Rio Gallegos (3 daily; 3hr 15min); Salta (3 daily; 2hr); San Juan (1 daily; 1hr 50min); San Luis (1 daily; 1hr 30min); San Martín de los Andes (3 weekly; 2hr 20min); San Rafael (1 daily; 2hr 35min); Santiago del Estero (1 daily; 1hr 40min); Trelew (4 daily; 2hr); Tucumán (5 daily; 1hr 50min); Ushuaia (6 daily; 3hr 40min).

Buenos Aires
Province

CHAPTER 2   # Highlights

✳ **Tigre and the Paraná Delta**
The equivalent of having the Everglades on the doorstep of Manhattan – a vivid reminder that Buenos Aires is a subtropical city. See p.156

✳ **Small beach resorts** The small and fashionable resorts of Cariló, Mar de las Pampas and Mar del Sud have an intimate feel as well as quiet sands, pine forests and long walks. See p.167, p.170 & p.178

✳ **San Antonio de Areco** An attractive riverside pampas town that's a magnet for those interested in gaucho culture and crafts. See p.181

✳ **Estancias** The fertile pampas are home to many of the country's best-appointed and best-known estancias, easily accessible from Buenos Aires for a taste of country living. See p.186 & p.192

✳ **Luján** Home to Argentina's patron saint, with an enormous basilica and thousands of pilgrims that are a testimony to the country's Catholic traditions. See p.186

✳ **Sierra de la Ventana** The flat pampas fold into the craggy Sierra de la Ventana range in the west of the province, an area known for good walking, pretty chalets and delicious *picada* platters. See p.196

▲ Beach at Pinamar

Buenos Aires Province

As attractive a city as Buenos Aires is, you may wish to escape the urban mêlée for a few days. Stretching for hundreds of kilometres south and west of the capital, the flat expanse of Buenos Aires province is the country's agricultural heartland. Less visited than some of the country's big-ticket destinations further afield, the **Pampas** (plains) offer a fascinating window into traditional gaucho culture and small-town life. The country's beaches are less renowned, but some thirty resorts fringe the **Atlantic coast** of the province, stretching from San Clemente in the north to Bahía Blanca, nearly 700km south of the capital. They are generally characterized by wide, sandy beaches edged by dunes, and little else, although Mar del Plata has some interesting historical buildings and is a thriving city in its own right. In January and February much of the capital pulls down its shutters and heads en masse for the coast; if crowds and 24-hour parties aren't your thing, head out of season when hotel prices can drop by half. Mostly visited by domestic tourists, the beaches are not, in truth, the continent's most fabulous – if it's white sands and warm seas you're after, you'd be better off heading north to Brazil.

The coastal route south starts after **La Plata**, often visited as a day-trip from Buenos Aires. Another 260km southwest, the Río de la Plata flows out into the cool waters of the Atlantic Ocean, and the **resorts** that line the coast – all popular with local families in the summer – begin. **Pinamar** and **Villa Gesell** are the younger destinations, while **Mar del Plata** is the liveliest, with crowds that pack its beaches by day, then move to the city's numerous clubs and restaurants at night. If you hanker after peace and quiet, there are more isolated spots, though, such as exclusive **Cariló**, forested **Mar de las Pampas** or sleepy **Mar del Sud**.

Moving inland, the landscape is dominated by grain and cattle farmland – the source of much of the country's exports – and pretty gaucho settlements. **San Antonio de Areco**, lying just over 100km west of the capital, is a charmingly old-fashioned town of cobbled streets and well-preserved nineteenth-century architecture and a must if you're interested in the Pampas' distinctive culture; **Tandil**, further south, is another noted centre of pampas culture, with some great little cafés and museums, and is a worthwhile detour if you're headed to Patagonia overland. The quiet and attractive town of **Mercedes** is less visited but has an authentic *pulpería* (a traditional bar-cum-store) that also offers a glimpse into Argentina's gaucho past. On the way to Mercedes, the small city of **Luján** exposes the country's spiritual heart, with a mass display of religious devotion in honour of Argentina's patron saint, the Virgin of Luján. And throughout the province, you'll find some of Argentina's most traditional and luxurious **estancias** – great places to spend a night or two.

To reach anything approaching a mountain, you will need to head for the west of the province, where you'll find the Pampas' most dramatic, the **Sierra de la Ventana** range, 580km southwest of Buenos Aires and offering a welcome change of scenery from the surrounding flat farmlands.

Buenos Aires is probably Argentina's easiest province to get around: it is crisscrossed with roads and railways, making it pretty straightforward to negotiate using **public transport**. Bear in mind, though, that services to the coast are greatly reduced out of season.

The Paraná Delta

One of the world's most beautiful and unusual landscapes, the exotic **Paraná Delta** lies just a few kilometres north of Buenos Aires' Avenida General Paz. Constantly changing due to sediment deposits by the Río Paraná, the Delta region is a wonderfully seductive maze of lush, green islands separated by rivers and streams. Lining the banks, traditional houses on stilts peep out from behind

Tren de la Costa

The **Tren de la Costa** (daily; $12 for a *boleto turístico* one way, which means you can get off and on as many times as you like – tickets can be bought on board; every 30min 7.20am–9pm; ☏011/4794-9159, ⓦwww.trendelacosta.com.ar) runs north from Olivos to Tigre, a 25-minute trip if you do it in one go. It's one of the most attractive options for getting to Tigre – it runs parallel to the waterfront, mostly through green parkland and past grandiose suburban mansions and villas – and also presents a number of enticing stopoffs, with eleven restored or purpose-built stations along the route. Originally part of the state-run Tren del Bajo line, which was built in 1891, the service fell into disuse in the 1960s. In 1995 the northernmost section reopened as this privately run scenic railway, with luxurious mock-Victorian carriages running smoothly and silently along electrified tracks.

To get to the Olivos terminus, known as **Estación Maipú**, first take a commuter train from Retiro (see p.111) to Olivos's Estación Mitre, a thirty-minute journey. From here, take the walkway across Avenida Maipú to the red-brick station (many of the stations are modelled on those of the British Victorian era).

As well as hopping-off points for Olivos and San Isidro, many of the Tren de la Costa's stations hold their own appeal. **Estación Borges**, the nearest to Olivos's marina, is referred to as the "station of the arts" – it's home to an art café with open-air sculptures. **Libertador** station has a shopping centre comprised of outlets for many of the most popular Argentine designer stores, while **Anchorena** station has been christened "Estación Tango" and sits alongside a cultural centre that puts on tango shows and classes; it's also the station closest to the river, and borders a riverside park. **Estación Barrancas** hosts an antiques fair (Sat & Sun 10am–6pm) and provides access to a cycling path, which runs north to San Isidro. **Estación San Isidro**, with its upmarket shopping mall, is located conveniently near the suburb's historic quarter. North of here, you pass through four more riverside stations – Punta Chica, Marina Nueva, San Fernando and Canal – before arriving at the northern terminus, **Estación Delta**, close to Tigre's fruit market and opposite the entrance to the Parque de la Costa.

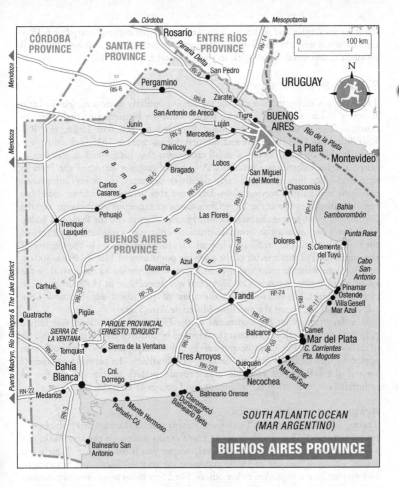

CÓRDOBA PROVINCE

SANTA FE PROVINCE

ENTRE RÍOS PROVINCE

Córdoba

Mesopotamia

Rosario

Paraná Delta

San Pedro

RN-3

Pergamino

RN-8

RN-8

Zarate

San Antonio de Areco

Tigre

Luján

Junín

RN-7

Mercedes

BUENOS AIRES

URUGUAY

Río de la Plata

Chivilcoy

Lobos

La Plata

Montevideo

Bragado

RN-5

RN-205

San Miguel del Monte

Carlos Casares

Las Flores

Chascomús

Bahía Samborombón

Pehuajó

RN-3

Trenque Lauquén

BUENOS AIRES PROVINCE

Humeda

Dolores

RP-11

Punta Rasa

S. Clemente del Tuyú

Carhué

Olavarría

Azul

RP-30

Cabo San Antonio

Guatrache

Pigüe

RP-76

Tandil

RP-74

RN-2

Pinamar Ostende Villa Gesell Mar Azul

SIERRA DE LA VENTANA

PARQUE PROVINCIAL ERNESTO TORQUIST

RN-226

RN-3

Bahía Blanca

Tornquist

Sierra de la Ventana

Tres Arroyos

Balcarce

RP-55

Camet Mar del Plata C. Corrientes Pta. Mogotes

RN-22

Cnl. Dorrego

RN-228

Quequén

Miramar Mar del Sud

Medanos

RN-3

Monte Hermoso

Ciaromecú Duramar Balneario Reta

Balneario Orense

Necochea

SOUTH ATLANTIC OCEAN (MAR ARGENTINO)

Pehuén-Co

Balneario San Antonio

BUENOS AIRES PROVINCE

0   100 km

N

Mendoza

Mendoza

Puerto Madryn, Río Gallegos & The Lake District

screens of subtropical vegetation. The Delta actually begins at the port of Diamante in Entre Ríos Province, some 450km to the northwest of the city, and its one thousand square kilometres are divided into three administrative sections. By far the most visited area, is the first section, most of which lies within a 90min boat trip from the picturesque town of **Tigre**, around 25km northwest of Capital Federal. Travel beyond here into the wide Río Paraná de las Palmas, however, and you may be forgiven for thinking that you've stumbled onto a tributary of the Amazon. At this point the Delta widens, inhabitants and amenities are much more dispersed and isleños rely on electric generators and kerosene lamps.

The Delta can be visited on a day-trip, but it's worth taking it in on at least an overnight break from the hectic pace of Buenos Aires. Though for many the Delta's biggest attraction is that it offers the chance to do not much at all, its numerous waterways are also popular with watersports enthusiasts, as well as devotees of rowing and fishing. **Isla Martín García**, a former penal colony close to the Uruguayan coast some 40km to the northeast of Tigre, is accessible by a regular boat service and makes for an interesting day or overnight trip (see p.159). Lots of water and a warm climate unfortunately mean that mosquitoes are a real problem in and around the Delta, so come prepared.

Tigre and around

TIGRE owes its poetic name to the jaguars – popularly known as *tigres* in Latin America – that inhabited the Delta region until the beginning of the twentieth century. The town sits on an island bounded by the Río Luján, the Río Reconquista and the Río Tigre and was first documented in 1635 under the name of El Pueblo de las Conchas, a small settlement that functioned as a defensive outpost against Portuguese invasions. A favoured summer retreat of the Porteño elite in the late nineteenth and early twentieth centuries, the town's sumptuous mansions and palatial rowing clubs date from this period. Back then social life revolved around events at the Tigre Club, home to Argentina's first casino, and the grand *Tigre Hotel*, whose clientele included Enrico Caruso and the Prince of Wales. The town's decline as a glamorous destination was in part a result of the closure of the casino (shut in 1933 through a law which prohibited casinos in the vicinity of the capital) and in part a result of the growing popularity of Mar del Plata, 400km south on the Atlantic coast and ever more accessible thanks to the arrival of the railway and improved roads. The *Tigre Hotel* was demolished in 1940, although the elegant Tigre Club still stands at the apex of the island and has now been reinvented as the site of the excellent Museo de Arte Tigre.

As a departure point for excursions to the Delta and Isla Martín García (see p.159), the town itself is sometimes overlooked by tourists. At first glance, it's a bit of a hodgepodge but don't be put off by initial impressions – Tigre offers an appealing mix of faded glamour and day-trip brashness. Its bars and restaurants around the refurbished riverside area provide perfect vantage points for an unhurried contemplation of the comings and goings of Delta life.

Arrival and information

Trains depart regularly for Tigre from Retiro station (Línea Mitre); the hour's journey costs $1.35 and terminates at Tigre's train station on the riverbank, just a block south of the **Estación Fluvial**, where you'll find one of Tigre's five tourist offices, a number of kiosks representing assorted hotels and restaurants, and various boat companies' ticket offices. For a few pesos more, you can transfer to the Tren de la Costa at Olivos, which drops you at the portals of the Parque de la Costa. There are so many ways of seeing the Delta that it can seem slightly bewildering, and not surprisingly the excellent Estación Fluvial **tourist office** (daily 8am–6pm; ☎011/4512-4498, ⓦ www.tigre.gov.ar) is often busy, especially at weekends. They have good maps and can help you find your way through the labyrinth of trips available.

Accommodation

There are some attractive accommodation options both in Tigre and on the Delta itself. However, getting to most Delta destinations requires a bit of forward planning, so you should ring ahead to make a reservation and obtain transport details. One of the most accessible places to stay is the area known as **Tres Bocas**, a thirty-minute boat trip from the Estación Fluvial. To really appreciate the wild charm of the Delta, you should head further out to its more isolated areas like Arroyo Las Canas. In addition to the hotels detailed below, there are plenty of houses and *cabañas* available to rent for weekends or longer stays – see ⓦ www .tigre.gov.ar or www.vivitigre.gov.ar for a list.

La Becasina ⊤011/4728-1253, ⓦwww.labecasina
.com.ar. In the second, quieter section on Arroyo Las
Canas, these thoroughly luxurious bungalows are the
Delta's closest approximation to a jungle lodge. ❾
Bonanza Deltaventura ⊤011/4728-1674,
ⓦwww.deltaventura.com. At an isolated spot on
the Carapachay river, *Deltaventura* is the place to
go for serious peace and quiet, with only three
rooms and around 3km worth of trails, where you
can trek, birdwatch and canoe. It can also be
visited as a day-trip ($142, including lunch). ❾
  Casona La Ruchi Lavalle 557, Tigre
  ⊤011/4749-2499, ⓦwww.casonalaruchi
.com.ar. A fabulous old family house with enormous
wood-floored bedrooms, huge balconies, a swimming
pool in the garden and exceptionally friendly owners,
though only shared bathrooms are available. ❺
Hotel Fundación Agustín García Av Liniers 1547,
Tigre ⊤011/4749-0140, ⓔfundaciongarcia
@yahoo.com.ar. Simple, old-fashioned town hotel,

with rooms sleeping one to five people. Also has its
own restaurant. ❹
l'Marangatu ⊤011/4728-0752, ⓦwww
.i-marangatu.com.ar. Well-known place on the
Río San Antonio close to the Tres Bocas part of
the Delta, complete with swimming pool, sports
pitches and even a heliport. ❺
Los Pecanes ⊤011/4728-1932, ⓦwww
.hosterialospecanes.com. An appealing, family-
run *hostería* out on the Arroyo Felicaria in the
second section of the Delta, away from the roar
of the jet skis. ❼
  Villa Julia Paseo Victorica 800
  ⊤011/4749-0242, ⓦwww.villajuliaresort
.com.ar. A 1910 house carefully converted into a
luxury hotel, using many of the original floors,
fittings and furniture alongside modern comforts
such as soft pillows and air conditioning. The
suites' wide balconies look out over the river, and
the hotel has its own elegant restaurant. ❼

The Town

Tigre lies along the western bank of the Río Luján, one of the Delta's main
arteries, and the town is divided in half by the smaller Río Tigre, which runs
north–south through its centre. Riverside avenues flank both sides of the Río
Tigre, while the broad Paseo Victorica runs along the Río Luján on the western
side of town. A good place to begin a tour of the area is around the **Estación
Fluvial**, immediately north of the bridge over the Río Tigre. The point of
contact between island and mainland life, the Estación bustles with activity,
particularly at weekends.

On the same side of the river as the Estación Fluvial you'll find the **Parque de la
Costa**, at Vivanco 1509 (summer Tues–Sun 11am–9pm; winter Sat & Sun
11am–7pm; $40–55; ⊤011/4002-6000), one of Latin America's largest amusement
parks, with roller coasters, carousels and arcades. A couple of blocks to the west,
alongside the Río Luján, there's a rather more serene attraction, the **Puerto de
Frutos** (Mon–Fri 10am–6pm, Sat & Sun 10am–7pm). A Tigre institution, the
Puerto de Frutos – or fruit port – has declined somewhat in importance since the
days when fruit cultivation was the region's main source of income, but it is still a
working port, and you can watch boats being unloaded with wood, wicker –
which grows in abundance in the Delta – and other goods in the small harbours.
The Puerto also operates as a craft market, with country-style furniture and
wickerwork the market's chief products.

The most enjoyable part of Tigre to explore on foot is on the western side of the
Río Tigre. Once over the bridge, follow riverside Avenida Lavalle north to the
confluence of the river with the Río Luján, where Lavalle merges with **Paseo
Victorica**, a delightful riverside road with plenty of bars and restaurants. The
Museo Naval, at Paseo Victorica 602 (Mon–Fri 8.30am–5.30pm, Sat & Sun
10.30am–6.30pm; $3), is housed in the old naval workshops and holds exhibits
relating to general maritime history, as well as to Argentine naval history from the
British invasions of 1806 to the Malvinas conflict. At the end of Paseo Victorica is
the **Museo de Arte Tigre** (Wed–Fri 9am–7pm, Sat & Sun noon–7pm; guided
tours hourly; ⊤011/4512-4528, ⓦwww.mat.gov.ar; $5). A vast turreted and
balustraded structure dating between 1910 and 1927, the building (formerly the
Tigre Club casino) was influenced by grand European hotels of the same period.

Inside, the opulent mansion – with its marble staircase, wrought-iron bannisters, gigantic chandaliers and delicate ceiling frescoes – is a setting to rival any of the capital's art museums. The art itself – mostly by Argentines or on Argentine themes, with many gauchos in evidence – is arranged into themes such as Tigre, the human figure and architecture.

From the end of Victorica, the road curves round, merging with Avenida Liniers, which leads back towards the bridge. The avenue is flanked by fine, if sometimes slightly decaying, examples of the town's grand nineteenth-century mansions, interspersed with equally luxurious modern residences. At no. 818, you'll find reconstructed colonial **Casa de Goyechea**, housing the **Museo de la Reconquista** (Wed–Sun 10am–6.30pm; free), surrounded by a lovely veranda and garden. The building was used as a base by General Liniers and his troops before they launched their counterattack against the British invasions in 1806. The museum has an interesting display of documents and objects relating to the recapture of Buenos Aires, such as a number of British caricatures from the time satirizing the poor performance of British troops.

Eating and drinking

There are plenty of **restaurants** in Tigre; the pick of them are along Paseo Victoria. The best options include *La Terraza* at no. 134, a classy *parrilla* with an outside seating area both on the pavement and on the first floor; and *Novo Maria* at no. 611, Tigre's most upmarket restaurant, situated in an elegant dining room on the riverbank. *Via Toscana* at no. 470, meanwhile, has a lovely Victorian-style garden area from where you can enjoy its ice cream and watch river life. There are lots of cheap and cheerful *parrillas* near the entrance to the Parque de la Costa, while the above-average café at the Estación Fluvial prepares imaginative sandwiches.

On the Delta itself, there are a number of eating options, including the rather swanky *Gato Blanco*, on the Río Capitán (T011/4728-0390); and the Germanic *Alpenhaus* (T011/4728-0422, Wwww.alpenhaus.com.ar) at Rama Negra. The simple and pretty *La Riviera* (T011/4728-0177, Wwww.la-riviera.com.ar), just by the jetty at Tres Bocas, is also a *hosteria* and is one of the Delta's oldest restaurants, with a typical *parrilla* menu. There's not much in the way of **nightlife** in the Delta – which is kind of the point – although some restaurants, including *La Riviera*, double up as a bar if you fancy a contemplative beer or two.

Boat trips and activities

There are many ways to go messing about on the river delta, but you should plan ahead and make reservations. The summer months see more options and also more visitors.

In the capital, various tour companies organize day-trips, including Tangol (T011/4312-7276, Wwww.tangol.com). In Tigre itself there are companies offering **paseos**, or round-trip tours. They generally last around an hour and inevitably don't go far into the Delta, but if you're pressed for time they do at least give a taste of river life. Rather touristy catamarans as well as the better, smaller *lanchas* (launches) run regular *paseos* (11am–5pm; from $20), some from the Estación Fluvial and some from around the international terminal opposite at Lavalle 520. A second option is the frequent **passenger services**, known as *lanchas colectivas*, run by three companies – Interisleña, Delta and Jilgüero. These are used by Delta residents to go about their daily business – picking up supplies, taking children to school – and go to all points in it. If you have a specific destination in mind, phone the tourist office (not the companies themselves) for the timetable. Most routes are one way, but all three companies also do round trips to the Paraná de las Palmas in the second section, lasting about four hours (Delta 10.30am; Jilgüero 12.30pm; Interslefia 2.30pm). All cost $20–30; it is advisable to confirm the timetable with the tourist office in Tigre and, if possible, avoid the weekends, when the boats are packed and the trips take much longer. If you want to do some **walking**, you will need to take one of the regular services to Rama Negra and/or Tres Bocas ($19 & $17 return), where you can disembark and wander for a considerable distance thanks to a public riverside path and wooden footbridges that cross from island to island.

As far as activities are concerned, there are various places around Tigre where you can practise **watersports**. Buenos Aires Outdoors (☎011/5258-5383, ⑩www.buenosairesoutdoors.com) offers guided tours in **kayaks** which can be organized from their offices in Capital Federal, while Puro Remo, at Lavalle 945 (☎15/5808-2237, ⑩www.puroremo.com.ar), gives you the choice of kayaks or rowing boats with wooden oars. Note that you must take a guide or instructor with you for safety reasons and should ring ahead and reserve. There's also a **wake-boarding** school run by South American champion Gabriela Díaz (☎011/4728-0031, ⑩www.wakeschool.com.ar).

Isla Martín García

With its quirky historical buildings, abandoned prison, uninhabited forest and permanent population of only two hundred, **ISLA MARTÍN GARCÍA** seems to have walked off the pages of a children's adventure story. First discovered by Portuguese navigator Juan de Solís – and named after one of his sailors – on his pioneering trip to the Río de la Plata in 1516, the island has a rich history and unexpectedly varied terrain that make it a compelling excursion from Buenos Aires.

The island is best known for being used as a **prison**, principally as the place where Perón was kept before he was president by members of the military who were jittery about his popularity. Other presidents incarcerated here include Hipólito Yrigoyen, Marcelo T. de Alvear, and, most recently, Arturo Frondizi in 1962. In the winter, which is bleak, the island's former role seems appropriate, but in the summer its green plazas and lush vegetation make it seem more of a tropical retreat than a place for punishment. Though only a few kilometres from the Uruguayan coast, Martín García is separated from the mainland by a channel known as the **Canal del Infierno** (Hell's Channel), whose seven currents would have been a daunting prospect for any prisoner foolhardy enough to try to swim to freedom.

Martín García's location between Uruguay and Buenos Aires has also given it an important strategic role historically. Most notably, it was used as a source of supplies by forces loyal to the Spanish crown in Montevideo in 1814. The loyalists were finally defeated by a naval squadron commanded by William Brown, an Irish-born lieutenant-colonel. In 1886, the island came under the jurisdiction of the Argentine Navy, who remained in control until 1974. A pact signed by the Argentine and Uruguayan governments agreed that, despite being much closer to the Uruguayan coast, Martín García should remain Argentine on the condition that it functioned as a **nature reserve** rather than a military base.

The island

With a surface area of less than two square kilometres, Martín García can easily be seen in a day or two. Many of Buenos Aires' cobbles came from the old *canteras*, or quarries, in the southwest of the island. Given the island's small size, the terrain is surprisingly varied, ranging from sandy beaches and reed beds to jungly areas of thick subtropical vegetation. Of the island's equally varied fauna, which includes herons, deer and coypu, the most surprising inhabitants are perhaps the large monitor lizards that amble lazily about, occasionally losing a tail in scraps with local dogs.

Walking up from the dock, the unsealed road leads straight to the sloping, leafy **Plaza Almirante Brown**. Here you'll find the island's civic centre, a small collection of attractive buildings housing administrative offices and a tiny post office. On the northeastern corner of the square are the crumbling ruins of a prison building. Along the street to the east of the square, the **Cine Teatro** is a gem of decorative architecture with an original and elaborate facade. Opposite it, the **Museo Histórico** (Tues, Thurs, Sat & Sun 9am–5pm; free), which relates the island's history through displays and in-character testimonials, is housed in an old *pulpería*. Down the street and to the left is the **Casa de Rubén Darío**, where the Nicaraguan poet stayed for a short time when the building functioned as a hospital in the early part of the twentieth century. This was also where Argentine doctor **Luis Agote**, who developed modern blood transfusion techniques just in time for World War I, worked for a while; it now houses a modest ecological exhibition.

Practicalities

Boats and tours to Isla Martín García are operated by Cacciola Turismo (Tues, Thurs, Sat & Sun at 9am, return 5pm; journey time 3hr; $104 for standard return, $131 including guided tour; $170 for the full tour and lunch). Boats depart from the international terminal at Tigre, Lavalle 520 – arrive at least half an hour ahead of departure. Tickets are best bought in advance from their Buenos Aires office at Florida 520, 1st floor (T011/4393-6100, W www.cacciolaviajes.com). The first part of the journey to the island passes through the Delta region and is a highlight of the trip. For most people, a day-trip will probably be enough, but if you want to enjoy the island at a more relaxed pace you can spend the night at the island's **hostería** (packages arranged through Cacciola; $339 per person including return trip and all meals). There's also a campsite where you can pitch a tent ($30 for 2 people per night), and some basic cabins – you'll need your own sheets and towels (reservations advisable during busy periods; T011/4728-1808).

Note that Martín García's **mosquitoes** are possibly even more ferocious than the Delta's and a good repellent is a must, particularly if you venture into the forested region around the Barrio Chino.

La Plata

With the declaration of Buenos Aires as the federal capital in 1880, Buenos Aires Province – already by far the wealthiest and most powerful in the republic – was left without a centre of government. A year later, the province's newly named governor, Dardo Rocha, proposed that a provincial capital be created 50km east of the federal capital. The new city's layout, based on rationalist concepts and characterized by an absolutely regular numbered street plan sitting within a 5km square, was designed by the French architect Pedro Benoit. An international competition was held to choose designs for the most important public buildings, and the winning architects included Germans and Italians as well as Argentines, a mix of nationalities reflected in the city's impressive civic architecture.

The country's first entirely planned city, **La Plata** was officially founded on November 19, 1882. Electric streetlights were installed in 1884 – the first in Latin America. Unfortunately, much of La Plata's carefully conceived architectural identity was lost during the twentieth century, as anonymous modern constructions replaced many of the city's original buildings. On a brighter note,

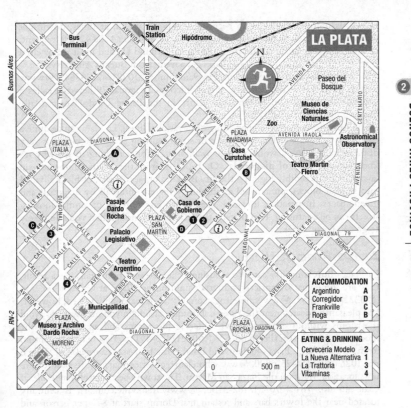

there have been some successful attempts to preserve what's left – most notably the old train station, now the wonderful setting for the **Pasaje Dardo Rocha** arts centre – and the 1990s saw the final completion of the city's grandiose Neo-Gothic cathedral, over a dentury after its foundation stone was laid.

La Plata was essentially conceived as an **administrative centre**, and one might argue that it shows: indeed, for many Argentines the city is little more than a place you visit to carry out the dreaded and complicated *trámites*, bureaucratic procedures in which Argentine public bodies seem to specialize. In terms of identity, the city suffers somewhat through its proximity to Buenos Aires, whose seemingly endless sprawl now laps at its outskirts, practically turning the city that was created as a counterbalance to the capital into its suburb. But it has a rich cultural life, partly because it is an important **university town**, with three major institutes that attract students from all over the country. La Plata's chief attractions are its pleasant park, the **Paseo del Bosque**, and – even though it is struggling to live up to its self-proclaimed reputation as one of the world's major natural history museums – the **Museo de Ciencias Naturales**. Note that several of the city's museums and galleries are closed throughout January.

Arrival and information

Theoretically, the nicest place to arrive in La Plata is at the beautiful *fin-de-siècle* **train station**, on the corner of avenidas 1 and 44, around ten blocks northwest of the town centre; the train itself, however, which leaves from Constitución in the capital, is unfortunately not so beautiful, being dirty and, at times, downright dangerous. The nearby **bus terminal**, on the corner of calles 4 and 42, has frequent, quicker and safer buses to and from the capital (around $9) and most major cities throughout the country. You could also get a *remise* from Buenos Aires city.

La Plata's **tourist office** (Mon–Fri 9am–5pm; ☎0221/422-9764, ⓦwww .laplata.gov.ar) is in the Palacio Campodónico on Diagonal 79 between calles 5 and 56; there's also an information centre in the Pasaje Dardo Rocha (daily 10am–5pm; ☎0221/427-1535).

Ironically (for a place designed along ultra-rational lines), La Plata can be quite a challenge to navigate. The prevalence of streets cutting across the blocks is very disorienting, and you won't need to walk around for very long to see why it's known as the "**city of diagonals**". On paper, or from the air, its numbered grid layout looks incredibly logical – the city is a kind of *mega cuadra*, or block divided into smaller blocks, punctuated at absolutely regular intervals by diagonals and green spaces. In practice, however, the sudden convergence of similar-looking streets can be confusing. Fortunately, the city is small enough that you're unlikely to go too far off track.

Accommodation

La Plata's **hotels** mostly cater to a business clientele and politicians. As a result, they are somewhat overpriced and rather uninspiring. *Roga*, at Calle 54 no. 334 (☎0221/421-9553, ⓦwww.hotelroga.com.ar; ⑤), is reasonably priced, however, and pleasantly located near the Paseo del Bosque, although you may want to avoid the rooms without external views. Offering big rooms and apartments is the modern *Argentino*, at Calle 46 no. 536 (☎0221/423-4111, ⓦwww.hotelargentino .com; ⑥), while La Plata's highest-end hotel is the four-star *Corregidor*, at Calle 6 no. 1026 (☎0221/425-6800, ⓦwww.hotelcorregidor.com.ar; ⑦). Its best feature is its location, right on the Plaza San Martín. The town's best **hostel**, *Frankville*, at Calle 46 no. 781 (☎0221/482-3100, ⓦwww.frankville.com.ar), is centrally located near the town's bars and restaurants. Dorms start at $41 per person and there are some doubles (③).

The City

La Plata's major points of interest lie along avenidas 51 and 53. At the very centre of the city, **Plaza Moreno** is dominated by the city's monumental **cathedral**, while ten blocks northeast the **Paseo del Bosque** hosts the city's zoo, planetarium and the **Museo de Ciencias Naturales**. Cultural activity centres around **Plaza San Martín**, halfway between the two; on the eastern side of this plaza, the city's arts centre, the **Pasaje Dardo Rocha**, is notable not only for its contemporary art museum but also for its stunning interior.

Plaza Moreno and around

La Plata's official centre is **Plaza Moreno**, a vast open square covering four blocks. The city's foundation stone was laid in the centre of the square in 1882, together with a time capsule containing documents and medals relating to the founding of the city. Over the years, a handful of theories circulated claiming the buried documents offered proof that La Plata was founded according to a secret Masonic scheme. When the capsule was unearthed on the city's centenary, however, the papers were too damaged to bear out the theory. The contents of the exhumed time capsule can be viewed in the **Museo y Archivo Dardo Rocha** (Mon–Fri 9am–5pm, Sat & Sun 3–6pm; free; ☎0221/427-5591), which is housed in the residence once occupied by La Plata's founder on the western side of the square at Calle 50 no. 933.

On the northeastern end of the square is the Germanic **municipalidad**, a broad white edifice dominated by a lofty central clock tower and elegant arched stained-glass windows. At the southwestern end you can't miss the gigantic, slightly forbidding **Catedral de la Inmaculada Concepción** (daily 9am–7pm, closed 1–4pm in summer), South America's largest Neo-Gothic church. Designed by Pedro Benoit, it features a pinkish stone facade and steep slate roofs. The foundation stone was laid in 1884 but the cathedral was not finally completed until 1932, with its two principal towers not finished until 1999. If the cathedral doesn't strike you as exactly beautiful, it is certainly tremendously imposing, with its soaring, vertigo-inducing interior punctuated by austere ribbed columns, while its high windows make it surprisingly light and airy. The **museum in the crypt** (daily 10am–7pm; $10) has some excellent photographs documenting the cathedral's construction; the entrance fee also allows you to visit the crypt and a *mirador* (viewpoint), 63m high and accessed by a lift, which gives a good view of La Plata's distinctive city plan.

Two blocks northeast of Plaza Moreno is the site where the grand Italianate **Teatro Argentino**, second in national importance after Buenos Aires' Teatro Colón, once stood. Sadly, it was razed to the ground after a suspicious fire in the 1970s and has been rebuilt as an octagonal concrete monolith. However, the structure is still impressively big inside and puts on a decent selection of operas and plays – contact the box office (Tues–Sun 10am–8pm; ☎0221/429-1732, ⓦwww .teatroargentino.ic.gba.gov.ar) for details of the current programme.

Plaza San Martín and around

Avenidas 51 and 53 lead from Plaza Moreno to **Plaza San Martín**, the real hub of city life. This square is smaller and less stately than Plaza Moreno, though it too is flanked by government buildings. At the northeastern end there's the **Casa de Gobierno**, a sturdy Flemish-Renaissance building with a central slate-roofed dome; to the southwest you'll find the **Palacio Legislativo**, designed in the style of the German Renaissance – its grand Neoclassical entrance sitting slightly awkwardly on a more restrained facade. More interesting than these civic edifices, however, is the **Pasaje Dardo Rocha**, on the northwestern side of the square. This elegant pitched-roof building, whose three-storey facade mixes French and Italian influences, was built in 1883 as the city's first train station. After the station moved to its current site, the Pasaje was remodelled and it now functions as an important **cultural centre** comprising a small cinema and various art museums, including the very worthwhile **Museo de Arte Contemporáneo Latinoamericano**, or MACLA (Tues–Fri 10am–8pm, Sat & Sun 2–10pm; free). The galleries are located around a stunning Doric-columned central hall, in which natural light (enhanced by a discreet modern lighting system) filters down through a high glass roof onto a vast sweep of black-and-white tiled floor.

Paseo del Bosque and around

From Plaza San Martín, Avenida 53 heads northeast past the Casa de Gobierno. After four blocks you come to Plaza Rivadavia, next to the **Paseo del Bosque**, La Plata's major green space. Before entering the park, take a small detour along Boulevard 53, a short diagonal road branching off to the right of the plaza. Halfway along the street at no. 320 stands the angular **Casa Curutchet**, the only Le Corbusier-designed residence built in Latin America. Commissioned by local surgeon Pedro Curutchet in 1949, the house is a typical Le Corbusier construction, combining functionality with a playful use of colour and perspective. The building, also housing the Colegio de Arquitectos of Buenos Aires Province, is open to visitors (Tues–Thurs 10am–2.30pm; ☎0221/482-2631; $40).

The park itself covers just over half a square kilometre. It's an attractive open space, dissected by various roads and with a pretty artificial lake. Aside from the famous Museo de Ciencias Naturales (see below), the park's attractions include the city's old-fashioned **zoo** (Tues–Sun 10am–6pm; T0221/427-3925; $5), complete with original enclosures dating from its foundation in 1907. These enclosures are a little small for the larger exotic species like the rhinoceros, but seem more appropriate for smaller native fauna such as the endangered grey fox. Within the zoo, a **botanical garden** offers examples of most of Argentina's most typical trees, such as the ombú, the araucaria (monkey puzzle) and the ceibo.

Museo de Ciencias Naturales

The first purpose-built museum in Latin America, and something of a relic in itself, the **Museo de Ciencias Naturales** (Tues–Sun 10am–6pm; $6), housed in the Universidad Nacional de La Plata's natural science faculty, is a real treat for anyone with a fondness for old-fashioned museums. It is gradually being remodelled, and modern audio-visuals make a brief appearance in the first rooms. However, later rooms, such as the six dedicated to zoology, are being preserved to look just as they did when the museum was first opened in 1888, with the embalmed animals exhibited in glass cases with hard-to-read labels.

The museum has 21 rooms, all chronologically ordered, including a **paleontological section** that contains a reproduction of a diplodocus skeleton, and the original skeleton of a neuquensaurus, a herbivorous dinosaur common in northern Patagonia towards the end of the Cretaceous Period. Room VI is dedicated to the beginnings of the **Cenozoic Period**, also known as the Age of Mammals, which extends from around 65 million years ago to the present day. It houses the museum's most important collection: the megafauna, a group of giant herbivorous mammals that evolved in South America at the time when the region was separated from the other continents. The room's striking collection of skeletons includes the creepy gliptodon, forerunner of today's armadillo; the enormous megatherium, largest of the megafauna, which, when standing upright on its powerful two hind legs, would have reached almost double its already

▲ Museo de Ciencias Naturales, La Plata

impressive six metres. Upstairs, a **Latin American archeology** section showcases items used by the main indigenous groups that once inhabited Argentine territory, from the colourful, feathered headdresses of the Amazonicos to the simple wood and leather articles of Tierra del Fuego's Onas.

Eating and drinking

La Plata is large and cosmopolitan enough to have a bit of culinary breadth. There are some quite decent **restaurants**, mostly aimed at businessmen, although you'll find local hangouts more convivial – the bulk of these are located around the intersection of calles 10 and 47, such as *La Trattoria*, a restaurant and café that gives great views of the to and fro of La Plata life. The city's best-known and most appealing bar and restaurant is the ⅍ *Cervecería Modelo*, at calles 5 and 54, whose vast wood-panelled interior is hung with hams; the seemingly endless menu includes everything from hamburgers and liverwurst sandwiches to *bife de chorizo* and seafood. Diagonally opposite, *La Nueva Alternativa* is a smart *parrilla*, set up as an alternative to the *Modelo* (hence the name). Nearby *Vitaminas*, on Diagonal 74 between 49 and 50, is a colourful restaurant and bar, serving healthy vegetarian dishes and good value lunchtime specials.

Listings

Banks and exchange Banco de Galicia, Av 7 no. 875.
Hospital Hospital Italiano, Av 51 between calles 29 and 30.

Internet access There is a *locutorio* in the bus terminal with internet and wi-fi.
Laundry Marva, at calle 2 on the corner with calle 54.
Post office At the corner of calles 4 and 51.

The Interbalnearia

The many resorts in this section are connected by the RP-11, or the **Interbalnearia**, lined with resorts, including the trendy pair **Pinamar** and **Villa Gesell** and their smaller, but rapidly growing, satellites **Cariló** and **Mar de las Pampas**. The route from La Plata runs southeast along the RP-36, which takes you through flat pampas landscape, dotted with cows and divided at intervals by tree-lined drives leading to estancias. Tall metal wind pumps, which extract water from beneath the surface of the land, inject a little drama into the scene, while giant cardoon thistles – a desiccated brown in summer – sprout in clusters like outsize bouquets. The RP-36 joins up with the RP-11 around 90km southeast of La Plata. As you hit **Pinamar** and **Villa Gesell**, where sand dunes predominate, you will encounter in many ways Argentina's most attractive beach destinations, now growing fast and encompassing several smaller places on their outskirts.

Pinamar

PINAMAR takes its name from the surrounding pine forests that were planted among dunes by the town's founder, Jorge Bunge, in the 1930s. This attractive setting is now somewhat overwhelmed, however, by the town's mix of high-rise buildings and ostentatious chalet-style constructions. Long the favourite resort of the Porteño elite, in the 1990s the town became almost synonymous with the high-living lifestyle of the Menem era, and the exploits of the politicians and celebrities who holidayed here were staples of the gossip mags. Pinamar fell out of popularity for a while following the high-profile murder of a journalist here in

1997 and the economic recession, but it has bounced back with a vengeance, and it remains a hugely popular summer holiday spot, although it's lost out to some of the smaller satellite resorts in the race to be crowned the most exclusive.

To the south, Pinamar stretches out along the coast, swallowing up the neighbouring resorts of **Ostende** and **Valeria del Mar**, tranquil places that can be easily reached as a day-trip, though they also have their own, interesting accommodation options.

Arrival and information

All long-distance **buses** arrive at the terminal at Jason 2250, several blocks west of the town centre, just off Avenida Bunge. The **train station**, served by Ferrobaires (℡011/4305-0157), which runs trains from Buenos Aires (Constitución), is a couple of kilometres west of town, a short taxi ride away. The closest **airport** to Pinamar is at Villa Gesell (see p.169). With glossy brochures advertizing golf courses, spas and estate agencies, the **tourist office**, at Avenida Shaw 18 (Jan & Feb daily 8am–9pm; March–Dec Mon–Sat 8am–8pm, Sun 10am–6pm; ℡02254/491680, Ⓦwww.pinamar.gov.ar), is heavily geared towards Pinamar's wealthy visitors, but also provides decent maps and guides.

Accommodation

Hotels in Pinamar and its satellite resorts are plentiful, if generally expensive, with little in the way of decent budget accommodation. As in all resorts, reservations are advisable in high season. There are only a handful of **campsites**: *Quimey Lemú*, just 250m north of the entrance to town along the RP-11 (℡02254/484949, Ⓦwww.quimeylemu.com.ar; ❶), is set in attractive wooded grounds with plenty of facilities. It also has some basic cabins for rent (❸). More convenient if you don't have your own transport is the small but well-located *Camping Saint Tropez* (℡02254/482498, Ⓦwww.sainttropezpinamar.com.ar; ❷), on the border with Ostende at Quintana 138, which also rents out apartments.

Algeciras Hotel Av del Libertador 75
℡02254/485550, Ⓦwww.algecirashotel.com.ar. A large and rather ugly building houses this luxurious, top-of-the-range place, which has a swimming pool, sauna and nursery. ❽
Las Calas Hotel Boutique Av Bunge 560
℡02254/405999, Ⓦwww.lascasashotel.com.ar. Predominantly designed from wood, this deisgner hotel has an intimate interior courtyard and spacious rooms. ❽
Hotel Casablanca Av de los Tritones 258
℡02254/482474, Ⓦwww.casablancapinamar .com.ar. A block from the beach, the *Casablanca* offers light, airy rooms, some with balconies. Open Dec–Mar and Semana Santa. ❺
Playas Hotel Av Bunge 250 ℡02254/482236, Ⓦwww.pinamarsa.com.ar. Pinamar's longest-established hotel, attracting an older clientele, with

elegant rooms and bar as well as its own swimming pool. ❽
Posada Pecos Odiseo and Silenios
℡02254/484386, Ⓦwww.posadapecos.com.ar. Charming *hostería*-style place, whose tiled floors and whitewashed walls lend it an attractive, slightly rustic feel. ❻
Viejo Ostende Biarritz 799, Ostende
℡02254/486081, Ⓦwww.hotelostende.com.ar. A beautifully preserved reminder of the days when this pioneer resort hosted literary figures such as Argentine author Adolfo Bioy Casares and French writer Antoine de St-Exupéry. The rooms are quite simple and you do pay over the odds for the ambience, but the price includes breakfast and dinner, access to the hotel swimming pool, a beach tent at the *balneario* and a nursery. ❽

The Town

With its burgeoning popularity, Pinamar is no longer quite as exclusive as it once was, although by Argentine standards it remains fairly expensive. Its main street, **Avenida Bunge**, is a wide avenue flanked by restaurants and branches of the same boutiques that make up most of the capital's malls. Bunge runs east to west through the town centre, ending at beachfront Avenida del Mar. Though the town itself has little to detain you, the **beach** is attractive, its pale sands dotted with delicate shells and, to the north and south of the centre, bordered by high dunes. Various companies offer excursions by jeep to the most dramatic section of dunes, where, during the summer, you can try **sandboarding**; ask at the tourist office for details.

Eating, drinking and nightlife

The majority of Pinamar's **restaurants** are around Avenida Bunge and along the seafront. Several of them specialize in fresh seafood, such as the sea-facing *Viejo Lobo* at Avenida del Mar and Bunge. *Tulumei*, at Bunge 64, is a small and friendly place with a laidback atmosphere, good music and imaginative seafood dishes. Nearby, *Paxapoga* offers good-value traditional Argentine food, including excellent squid. The best of Pinamar's cooking is undoubtedly found at the teahouse and restaurant *Tante*, at De las Artes 35 (℡02254/482735). The wide-ranging menu offers elaborate, mostly Germanic, dishes, including some good vegetarian options, and at *merienda* time there's a number of exotic tea blends with which to wash down some exceptionally good cakes. There's also a smaller sister café on Bunge 400.

Nightlife is mostly centred on a handful of bars along Avenida Bunge and the seafront. One of the most consistently cool, *UFO Point*, on the beachfront at Avenida del Mar and Tobías, is where you'll find the best DJs, while **Paco Bar**, at Avenida de las Artes 156, is a more traditional place, its walls and counters stuffed with memorabilia. Pinamar's biggest nightclubs are *Ku* and *El Alma*, on Quintana and Nuestras Malvinas respectively, which play everything from dance to rock and salsa.

Cariló

Pinamar merges seamlessly with **Ostende**, **Valeria del Mar** and finally **CARILÓ**, the area's most exclusive resort. While Ostende and Valeria del Mar effectively act as quieter barrios of Pinamar, Cariló has more of a separate personality, a fact made clear as Calle Bathurst, the paved main street of Valeria del Mar, abruptly turns to a sand track with a sign announcing the entrance to Cariló's exclusive "parque" on Calle Divisadero. An idyllic pine forest full of luxury hotels, spas and designer shops, this is where Argentina's rich and powerful come to get pampered, hidden away from the rest of society. While apart hotels and rental homes are a tasteful distance from each other, and development in the village is controlled by tight laws, the amount of new construction has spiralled in recent years – too fast for some locals – and you're likely to hear the distance noise of building work among the tweeting birds.

Cariló nevertheless remains a tranquil place, albeit one significantly more expensive than other resorts nearby. If you can afford it, and don't mind the rather snooty attitude of some of its regulars, its varied and thick vegetation, quiet, sandy streets and gourmet restaurants can make it a very agreeable destination. Stressed-out professional Porteños come to Cariló to *desenchufarse* (literally, unplug themselves), but if you fancy some activity, **horseriding** and **polo** lessons are possible at the Estancia Dos Montes (℡02254/480045), just west of the village. Alternatively you can organize **sandboarding** on the plentiful dunes through Turismo Aventura (℡02267/15676835) or whizz around the sand on a 4WD buggy with Buggycar (office in Pinamar; ℡02254/492809).

Practicalities

Cariló is connected by the local Montemar **bus** to Valeria del Mar, Ostende and Pinamar, where the nearest long-distance bus terminal is located. Alternatively you can simply stroll along the beach, which runs for 10km or so without interruptions past all of them. Cariló's tourist board, a small wooden hut on the corner of calles Boyero and Castaño, has minimal information, probably since the main office in Pinamar covers all the satellite resorts.

Accommodation is all high-end luxury, with nothing near a budget option in sight. While most options – whether hotel, self-catering apartment or *cabaña* – include a wide range of excellent services, *La Hosteria Carilo*, at Jacarandé 7167 (☎02254/570704; ⑨) stands out. Decorated with the owner's photography, the hotel puts on film screenings in its small underground cinema and there are thousands of DVDs behind reception. Other options include the stylish boutique rooms at *La Estación* (☎02254/570829; ⑨), where breakfast is served in your room, and *Marcin Hotel* (☎02254/570888; ⑨), with a decent range of services and lovely sea views.

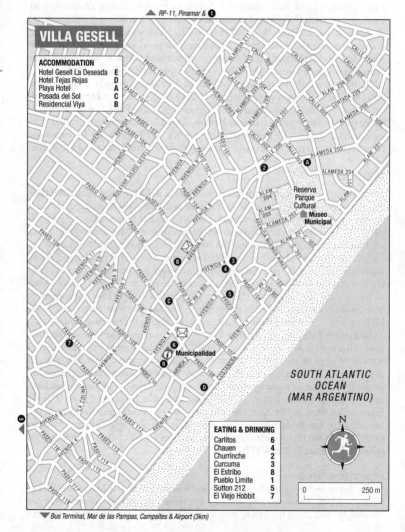

▲ RP-11, Pinamar & ❶

VILLA GESELL

ACCOMMODATION
Hotel Gesell La Deseada	E
Hotel Tejas Rojas	D
Playa Hotel	A
Posada del Sol	C
Residencial Viya	B

Reserva Parque Cultural

Museo Municipal

Municipalidad

SOUTH ATLANTIC OCEAN (MAR ARGENTINO)

EATING & DRINKING
Carlitos	6
Chauen	4
Churrinche	2
Curcuma	3
El Estribo	8
Pueblo Limite	1
Sutton 212	5
El Viejo Hobbit	7

N

0   250 m

▼ Bus Terminal, Mar de las Pampas, Campsites & Airport (3km)

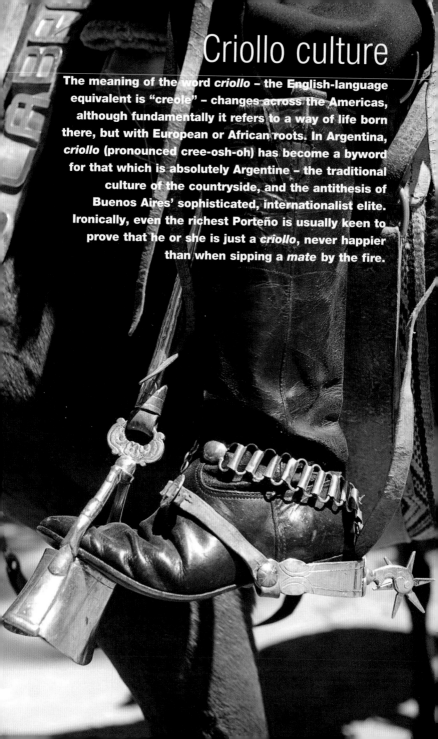

Criollo culture

The meaning of the word *criollo* – the English-language equivalent is "creole" – changes across the Americas, although fundamentally it refers to a way of life born there, but with European or African roots. In Argentina, *criollo* (pronounced cree-osh-oh) has become a byword for that which is absolutely Argentine – the traditional culture of the countryside, and the antithesis of Buenos Aires' sophisticated, internationalist elite. Ironically, even the richest Porteño is usually keen to prove that he or she is just a *criollo*, never happier than when sipping a *mate* by the fire.

Bowl of locro ▲

An asado ▼

Mate gourd and straw (bombilla) ▼

Criollo cuisine

The distinctive *criollo* **cuisine** has developed over the years, as indigenous ingredients such as maize, beans, peppers and squash have been added to the country's ever-present beef, and adapted by the Spanish and other immigrant groups. This is not food you will find in elegant city restaurants – it's cheap and filling peasant fare, served in humble *pulperías*, stores and cafés. Classics include the **empanada**, a small pasty either baked or fried, and filled with anything at hand, often minced beef or cheese; **humita**, steamed creamed sweetcorn, sometimes served in neat parcels made from the husk of corn cobs; and **locro**, a substantial stew based on maize, with onions, beans and meat thrown in. Then, of course, there's the **asado** – the barbecue that takes place year-round, come sunshine or snow (or, as the *criollo* saying would have it, *llueve o truene* – rain or thunder). Usually held on Sunday, the *asado* is a sacrosanct male preserve, the pride of the true host and a chance to show off his *criollo* credentials. For more on *asados*, see p.41.

Time with your mate

Over ninety percent of Argentines regularly drink **mate**. Bitter, and with a sort of grassy aftertaste, it has been used in rituals since pre-Hispanic times, although today it's more of a spontaneous act that brings people together. The word *mate* (spelled *maté* in English) comes from the Quechua *mati*, or "vessel", referring to the calabash from which it's traditionally drunk. Banned in early colonial times, *mate* – like most prohibited substances – only grew in popularity. For more on *mate* and how to drink it, see the box on p.263.

Gaucho gear

Clothing is another important indicator of *criollo* status. The basic gaucho uniform include **bombachas** and a **poncho**. The former are flared trousers, buttoned at the bottom (ideal for riding); the latter was originally an all-purpose garment, used for shielding the wearer from wind and rain, as a blanket and, wrapped around the arm, as a shield in knife fights. *Bombachas* are still worn in the pampas, ponchos less so, although you will probably see them on sale. The outfit is finished off with **alpargatas** – canvas and rope-sole shoes, similar to espadrilles. The gaucho's wide **belt** (*tirador*), usually decorated with coins and used as a tool belt, his **knife** (*façon*), his ornate spurs and riding **whips**, and his **boleadoras** – a sort of lasso finished with heavy balls designed to trip running game – do not have much practical application today but are used for decorative purposes.

▲ A gaucho façón

▼ Men watching jineteadas at the Fiesta de la Tradición

The gaucho personality

A profound attachment to *criollo* culture affects daily life at all levels of Argentine society, characterized by a great **pride** – gauchos, despite suffering poverty and discrimination, were never humble, and mocked city dwellers and immigrants for their lack of equestrian and other countryside skills. Come crisis or catastrophe, this pride is rarely dented and today is sometimes perceived – particularly in other Latin American countries – as arrogance. Other gaucho qualities include a fierce **independence** and a decidedly **anti-authoritarian** streak: Argentine politicians win popular plaudits by thumbing their noses at other countries and international institutions.

▼ Gauco in traditional attire, drinking mate

A kingdom for a horse

Introduced by the Spanish in the early years of the colonial period, **horses** flourished on the pampas' pastures and quickly became crucial as a means of covering the region's vast distances and for working the developing cattle ranches. The beast was as common and disposable as fallen fruit, to the astonishment of nineteenth-century European travellers, who considered horses high-value goods. They reported that everybody – Porteños included – did practically all tasks on horseback, with even beggars asking for alms from the saddle. Today the horse is not so omnipresent as it once was, but it remains a key feature of *criollo* culture. You'll find evidence of this all over Argentina: in the world-class polo ponies for the wealthy, the popular *hipódromos* (racecourses) that skirt many towns, and the estancia workers trotting home at the end of the day, alone except for their dog, cattle and mount-still a common sight in the countryside, from Salta to Patagonia.

A gaucho foreman selects horses for work ▲

Rounding up sheep on an estancia near El Calafate ▼

Horseman, San Antonio de Areco ▼

The criollo experience

Though you can find evidence of *criollo* culture throughout Argentina, certain places – particularly in and around the pampas – are focal points:

▶▶ **San Antonio de Areco** Self-designated centre of pampas tradition ringed by estancias, its pretty buildings are filled with artisan workshops, museums and old-fashioned bars. See p.181.

▶▶ **Mercedes** The country's finest salami and one of its last *pulperías* are found in this modest pampas town. See p.190.

▶▶ **El Gauchito** Small, rather dingy but utterly authentic store selling antique and modern *façons* and *boleadoras*, in the centre of the capital. See p.148.

Eating and **drinking** is centred on the main strip of Avenida Divisadero and the *centros commerciales* that branch off it. *Cattalina*, in the Feria del Bosque shopping centre, has excellent Italian pasta dishes while *Hemingway*, on the beach by calle Lambertiana, serves up sushi during summer months and has a downstairs spa.

Villa Gesell and around

Separated from Cariló by a strictly off-limits nature reserve, **VILLA GESELL** is reached by taking the RP-11 a further 10km or so south. The town is named after its founder, Carlos Gesell, a mildly eccentric outsider of German descent. In 1931, Gesell bought a stretch of coastal land, largely dominated by still-moving sand dunes. After some experimentation, Gesell managed to stabilize the dunes by planting a mixture of vegetation including tamarisks, acacias and esparto grass. He sold lots, many of which were bought by Germans and Central Europeans escaping World War II. Gesell has a more laidback feel than some of its smarter neighbours, and it teeters on the edge of being run-down. The resort remains popular with the middle and working classes, plus teenage groups enjoying holidays away from their parents. Now largely developed, something of the bohemian feel that once distinguished it can be discerned in the small but fast-growing double resort of **Mar de las Pampas** and **Mar Azul**, 14km down the coast.

Arrival and information

The town's main **bus terminal** is around 3km south of the centre, at Avenida 3 and Paseo 140; you'll probably want to get a local bus (#504, which will drop you off close to Avenida 3) or taxi to the centre. Villa Gesell's **airport** (☏02255/458345) is 3km south from the turn-off to town on the RP-11, with regular flights during the summer from Buenos Aires with Sol (☏ 011/50314212, ⓦwww.sol.com.ar). A shuttle runs from the airport to the town, dropping off at central hotels.

The popularity of Gesell is reflected by its five **tourist offices**. The most central one is at Avenida 3 no. 820 (summer daily 8am–midnight; winter daily 9am–8pm; ☏02255/478042, ⓦwww.gesell.gov.ar). Other useful ones are at the bus terminal (summer only 6am–1pm & 5pm–1am), and further out on the road towards Mar de las Pampas at Avenida 3 and Paseo 174 (Fri–Sun 10am–5pm).

Accommodation

As with the other coastal resorts, the cost of **accommodation** varies considerably according to the season. Many places cut prices by up to fifty percent out of season; others close altogether. It is easier to find budget accommodation here than it is in Pinamar and the tourist office holds a complete list of these as well as Villa Gesell's numerous **campsites**, all of which are some distance from the centre. Some of the nicest sites lie among the dunes at the southern end of town: try *Mar Dorado*, at Avenida 3 and Paseo 170 (☏02255/470963, ⓦwww.mardorado.com.ar; $35).

Hostel Gesell La Deseada Av 6 no.1183 ☏02255/473276, ⓦwww.ladeseadahostel.com.ar. Newly built hostel with six shared dorms at $65 per person and some doubles outside high season (❹). Great views of woodland and a spacious communal living room.

Playa Hotel Alameda 205 and 303 ☏02255/458027, ⓦwww.gesell.com.ar/playahotel. Villa Gesell's oldest hotel is set in wooded grounds near the nature reserve, far from the bustle of the centre. The pretty whitewashed building has pleasant, simply decorated rooms. Closed April–Oct. ❺

Posada del Sol Av 4 no. 642 ☏02255/462086, ⓦwww.gesell.com.ar/posadadelsol. Definitely the most unusual place in town, this very friendly posada has a mini-zoo in its garden in which parrots, flamingos and rabbits wander freely. Rooms are small but comfortable and well equipped. Closed April–Nov. ❻

Residencial Viya Av 5 no. 582 ☏02255/462757, ⓦwww.gesell.com.ar/viya. The best of the town's budget places, this charming *residencial* has a pleasant garden and seating area, along with plain but very well-kept rooms. ❸

Tejas Rojas Costanera no. 848
℡ 02255/462565, ⓦ www.hoteltejasrojas.com.ar.
This beachfront hotel is in a cool, tiled and

spacious building and has a swimming pool.
Rooms with sea views cost slightly more. Closed
Easter–Oct. ❽

The Resort

Villa Gesell is an amiable resort whose winding streets – many of them unsealed –
do their best to defeat the order imposed by a complex system of numbered avenidas
(which run parallel to the sea), paseos, calles and alamedas, designed by Gesell to
follow the natural course of the land. The town's main street is Avenida 3, the centre
of its lively nightlife. At the northern end of town, and entered from Alameda 202,
lies the **Reserva Parque Cultural**. Also designed by Gesell, the park's wooded
walkways offer welcome shade on hot days, and the dunes that separate it from the
beach to the east are particularly good for sunbathing or picnicking. The house used
by Gesell has been turned into a small **Museo Municipal** (summer daily 10am–8pm;
winter Wed–Sat 10am–4pm; $1) dedicated to this pioneering family, who also own
a famous Argentine chain of baby equipment.

If you fancy something a bit livelier, head for one of Villa Gesell's popular
balnearios spread out along the length of the beach, such as *Amy*, *AfriKa* or *13 al
Sur*, which vie with each other every year to become the season's in spot. There are
also various places to rent **bikes** in town; try Casa Macca, on Avenida Buenos Aires
between Paseo 101 and Avenida 5 (℡02255/468013), or Rodados Luis, on Paseo
107 between avenidas 4 and 5 (℡02255/463897).

Eating

Carlitos Av 3 no.184 ℡ 02255/464611. The self-
styled "King of Pancakes" makes them with an
exhaustive range of savoury and sweet fillings. A
super-sweet *dulce de leche* pancake will set you
back $14, while a fully loaded hamburger costs
$17. Open daily 11am–11pm.
Churrinche Alameda 205. European-style
teahouse with a beautiful garden and delicious
cakes. Also sells jars of artisanal *dulces*. Open
summer daily 8am–4pm, winter Fri–Sun
3pm–midnight.
Curcuma Paseo 104 with Av 4 ℡ 02255/473989.
A homely restaurant serving everything from beef
brochettes ($31) to chop suey ($25) on its menu,
as well as an exhaustive range of desserts. Open
daily noon–3pm & 8pm–midnight.

El Estribo Av and Paseo 109 ℡ 02255/466357.
The best traditional *parrilla* in town, serving
delicious cuts of *bife de chorizo* ($28) and fish,
including sole with boiled potatoes ($28), for the
meat-shy. Open daily noon–3.30pm &
7.30pm–1am.
Sutton 212 Paseo 105 no.212
℡ 02255/460674. Funky decor that gives it
the feeling of a laidback bar, but the kitchen serves
up great mid-priced food. Open summer daily
10–5am, winter Fri & Sat 5pm–5am.
El Viejo Hobbit Av 8 between paseos 111
and 112. Pints of home-brew and delicious
platters of farmhouse cheeses in enjoyable
faux-Middle Earth surroundings. Open Jan–March
from 6pm.

Drinking and nightlife

You'll have no problem finding **nightlife** in Gesell; just follow the crowds to the
area around Avenida 3 and paseos 104 and 105, where bars such as *Chauen* are
clustered. And no self-respecting Argentine beach resort would be without its
disco complex: Gesell's, called *Pueblo Límite*, is out on Avenida Buenos Aires,
opposite the Secretaría de Turismo.

Mar de las Pampas and Mar Azul

The evocatively named **MAR DE LAS PAMPAS**, just south of Villa Gesell, is a
haven of tranquil pine forests and pampas grass. The beach is not as deserted as you
might expect, since it is easily accessible from Gesell, but inland you can lose yourself
along sandy tracks that meander around dunes and woody valleys. The pine forest

setting is not dissimilar to Cariló, although the resort retains a less snobby, more down-to-earth feel – for now. There is no real gap between it and **MAR AZUL**, distinguished from its neighbour only by its more regular lanes and lesser development. The two are currently enjoying a reputation for maintaining the bohemian spirit of Villa Gesell, with blues musicians playing at local pub *Mr Gone* on Mar Azul's main drag, Avenida Mar del Plata, and *Blue Beach*, a *balneario*, cultivating a chilled-out atmosphere, although the resorts are all a bit too VIP to be truly counterculture.

Accommodation in Mar de la Pampas is mostly in small, luxurious *cabaña* outfits distributed among the trees, such as *Aqui me Quedo* (℡02255/479884, Ⓦwww.aquimequedonet.com.ar; ❽ with a heated pool and solarium). *Hostal de las Piedras* (℡02255/454220, Ⓦwww.hostaldelaspiedras.com; ❼) on Cuyo e/ Virazón y Roca, has large rooms with private outdoor spaces.

Mar Azul's only hotel is the friendly *Hostería Alamos*, at Avenida Mar del Plata and Calle 35 (℡02255/479631, Ⓦwww.alamoshosteria.com.ar; ❽), although there are several *cabaña* options, including *Poetas del Bosque*, at Copacabana y Calle 45 (℡011/48226686, Ⓦwww.poetasdelbosque.com.ar; ❼), with rooms for two to six people. There are also a couple of **campsites**, the best of which is *Camping del Sur*, on Avenida Mar del Plata and Calle 47, two blocks from Mar Azul's beach (℡02255/479502, Ⓦwww.campingdelsur.com.ar; $35 for camping and dorm rooms from $37.50 per person).

The resorts can be reached on foot from Villa Gesell, either along the beach or via Avenida 3, but it's a pretty hefty walk. Alternatively, take the local **bus**, which leaves every half-hour from behind the bus terminal on Avenida 4 and passes through both villages. Gesell's tourist offices have maps and accommodation information for both Mar de las Pampas and Mar Azul.

Mar del Plata and around

Big, busy and brash, **MAR DEL PLATA** towers above all other resorts on Argentina's Atlantic coast. Around six million tourists holiday here every year, drawn by its bustling beaches and lively entertainment. If the thought of queuing for a restaurant or seeking an unoccupied scrap of sand makes you shudder, you're better off avoiding the resort in the height of summer, but if you prefer to mix your trips to the beach with a spot of culture, nightlife or shopping, you may find this seaside town has a certain cheeky charm for you. Despite some haphazard development, Mar del Plata is favoured by the gentle drama of a sweeping coastline and hilly terrain, and while its rather urban beaches may lack the wild charm of less developed strips of sand, they are fun places to hang out and good for people-watching.

Mar del Plata is also the only resort really worth visiting out of season – while the city may breathe a sigh of relief when the last of the tourists leave at the end of the summer, it certainly doesn't close down. The city has around 600,000 inhabitants, a rich cultural life that includes a number of modest but interesting **museums** and **galleries**, and one of Argentina's most important **ports**, appealing not only for its colourful traditional fishing boats and seafood restaurants, but also for a close encounter with the area's noisy colony of sea lions.

Some history

Founded in 1874, the settlement of Mar del Plata was developed three years later into a European-style bathing resort, following the vision of Pedro Luro, a Basque merchant. As the railway began to expand into the province, Mar del Plata became accessible to visitors from the capital, with the first passenger train arriving from Buenos Aires in September 1886. The subsequent opening of the town's first hotel in 1888 – the luxurious, long-gone **Hotel Bristol** – was a great occasion for the Buenos Aires elite, many of whom travelled down for the opening on an overnight train.

The town's initial success aside, the richest of Argentina's very rich continued to make their regular pilgrimages to Europe. It took the outbreak of World War I in Europe to dampen Argentine enthusiasm for the journey across the Atlantic and to firmly establish Mar del Plata as an exclusive resort. **Mass tourism** began to arrive in the 1930s, helped by improved roads, but took off in the 1940s and 1950s, with the development of union-run hotels under Perón finally putting the city within the reach of Argentina's middle and working

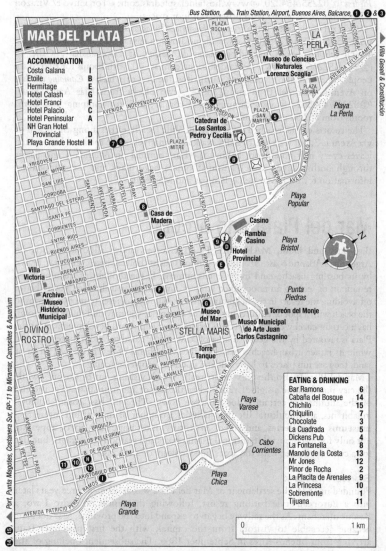

Bus Station, ▲ Train Station, Airport, Buenos Aires, Balcarce, ❶, ❷ & ❸

MAR DEL PLATA

ACCOMMODATION
Costa Galana — I
Etoile — B
Hermitage — E
Hotel Calash — G
Hotel Franci — F
Hotel Palacio — C
Hotel Peninsular — A
NH Gran Hotel
  Provincial — D
Playa Grande Hostel — H

EATING & DRINKING
Bar Ramona — 6
Cabaña del Bosque — 14
Chichilo — 15
Chiquilin — 7
Chocolate — 3
La Cuadrada — 5
Dickens Pub — 4
La Fontanella — 8
Manolo de la Costa — 13
Mr Jones — 12
Pinor de Rocha — 2
La Placita de Arenales — 9
La Princesa — 10
Sobremonte — 1
Tijuana — 11

Museo de Ciencias Naturales 'Lorenzo Scaglia'

Catedral de Los Santos Pedro y Cecilia

Casa de Madera

Casino

Rambla Casino

Hotel Provincial

Villa Victoria

Archivo Museo Histórico Municipal

DIVINO ROSTRO

Museo del Mar

Museo Municipal de Arte Juan Carlos Castagnino

STELLA MARIS

Torre Tanque

Torreón del Monje

Punta Piedras

Cabo Corrientes

Playa La Perla
Playa Popular
Playa Bristol
Playa Varese
Playa Chica
Playa Grande

▶ Villa Gesell & Constitución

◀ Port, Punta Mogotes, Costanera Sur, RP-11 to Miramar, Campsites & Aquarium

0 — 1 km

classes. The horrified rich subsequently abandoned it for more chic resorts such as Pinamar and Uruguay's Punta del Este.

Today, with the notable exception of its landmark seafront **casino** and the building housing the **Gran Hotel Provincial**, the resort's coastline is dominated by modern developments. However, scattered here and there are wonderfully quirky buildings, built in a decorative – even fantastical – style known as **pintoresquista**, an eclectic brew of mostly Norman and Tudor architecture. Above all, it's a place where the Argentine working classes go to forget the daily grind and have fun, and it would be hard not to be affected by the atmosphere.

Arrival, information and city transport

Mar del Plata is well connected by public transport to most points in Argentina, particularly during the summer, when services increase dramatically. Its **airport** lies around 8km northwest of the city centre along Autovía 2; from here local bus #542 will take you into town. **Trains** from Buenos Aires (Constitución) arrive at Estación Norte, to the northwest of the town centre at Luro and Italia; services are operated by Ferrobaires (℡011/4306-7919). The new **bus** terminal opened at the end of 2009 beside the train station on San Juan 152. From the combined bus and train terminal bus #511 gets you into the centre of town. If you are travelling **by car** from Buenos Aires, you have a choice of three routes. Mind-numbingly straight Autovía 2 is the most direct of these, but is also by far the busiest route during the summer. The RP-29 via Balcarce and the coastal RP-11 are quieter, have lower tolls and meander through more attractive landscape, but add 80km or so to your journey.

The main office for Emtur, Mar del Plata's **tourist information** service, is centrally located on Belgrano 2740 (summer daily 8am–10pm; winter daily 8am–8pm; ℡0223/494-4140, ⓦwww.turismomardelplata.gov.ar). There's also a useful office by the coast, on the northwest corner of the old *Hotel Provincial* on the Boulevard Marítimo, on the inland side by Avenida Colón (summer daily 8am–10pm, winter daily 8am–8pm; ℡0223/495-1777).

Taxis are easy to come by and cheap; **local buses** are efficient and routes are well marked at bus stops. Useful routes include #551, #552 and #553, all of which run between Avenida Constitución – the centre of the city's nightlife – downtown and the port. Some buses only accept cards, with prepaid credit on them ($1.70 a journey; card $1 available at most kiosks), so check before boarding.

Accommodation

It's advisable to book ahead if you plan to stay in Mar del Plata during high season. Most of the **budget accommodation** is around the bus terminal, although you can also find some good deals in La Perla, a pleasant barrio with hilly streets just to the north of the town centre. There are numerous **campsites**, many of them just out of town along the Costanera Sur/RP-11 that heads south to Miramar. The pick of these is the large *Del Faro*, at Costanera Sur 400, near the lighthouse and some of the best beaches (℡0223/467-1168, ⓦwww.autocampingdelfaro.com.ar; camping $27.50 per person per day). The site is well equipped with pool, store, laundry, restaurant and shower blocks, and there are also simple *cabañas* (④) and bungalows (⑥). You can reach the Costanera Sur via bus #511, which passes by the bus and train terminals.

Calash Falucho 1355 ℡0223/486-2354, ⓦwww .entodalacosta.com.ar/calash. On a quiet street near the centre, this friendly, mock-Tudor hotel has rambling hallways, a wooden staircase and simple but light and attractive rooms. There's also a café and a shady seating area outside. ⑤

Costa Galana Blvd Marítimo 5725 ℡0223/410-5000, ⓦwww.hotelcostagalana.com. Modern luxury hotel overlooking Playa Grande, with a private tunnel running to the beach. Large, attractively decorated rooms with a/c; all with sea views. ⑨

Etoile Santiago del Estero 1869 ☎0223/493-4968, ✉hoteletoile@hotmail.com. Three-star hotel with five-star pretensions. The comfortable, spacious, if slightly dog-eared rooms are very reasonably priced. In a central spot; facilities include a gym. ⑥

Franci Sarmiento 2742 ☎0223/486-2484, ✉info@hotelfranci.com. Right by the bus terminal, this is a good-value hotel. Rooms have TV and private bathroom, and there's a 24hr bar. ③

Hermitage Av Colón 1643 ☎0223/451-9081, ⓦwww.hermitagehotel.com.ar. A classically elegant hotel, almost lost amid the surrounding modern buildings. Popular with visiting celebrities, the *Hermitage* has suitably luxurious rooms, a pool and spa, and an excellent location. ⑧

🏃 NH Gran Hotel Provincial Av Peralta Ramos 2502 ☎0223/499-5900, ⓦwww.nh-hotels.com. The city's swishest hotel recently reopened in the original 1946 building beside the casino, overlooking the seafront. Services include massages, cable

TV, 24-hour room service, cocktail bar and swimming pool. ⑧

Palacio Alberti 2056 ☎0223/495-6546, ⓦwww.hotelpalacio.com.ar. This pretty hotel, with its colourful artefacts the owner has collected from around the world, stands out from its rather dingy neighbours near the bus terminal. Private bathrooms and breakfast are included. ③

Peninsular 9 de Julio 2987 ☎0223/495-4151, ⓦwww.hotelpeninsular.com.ar. Colourful hotel located in La Perla neighbourhood. Rooms are functional but comfortable. Discounts offered when paying in cash. ⑤

Playa Grande Hostel Quintana 168 ☎0223/451-7307, ⓦwww.hostelplayagrande.com.ar. In a large, bright house a couple of blocks from the sea, this is one of Mar del Plata's most reliable hostels. Shared dorms ($75 per person) are decent, and there's an on-site surf school. Private doubles (③) available as well. Open Dec–Mar although sister establishment Playa Grande Suites (at Alem 3495) is open all year.

The City

Mar del Plata's centre is **Plaza San Martín** but on summer days its true heart lies further south in the area surrounding central **Playa Bristol** and the **Rambla Casino**, a pedestrian promenade flanking the grand casino and *Hotel Provincial*. Aside from the beach itself, there's little in the way of sightseeing in the city centre, other than the quietly attractive neighbourhood of **La Perla**. Culture vultures will want to head south to the steep streets of **Loma Stella Maris**, where they'll find the Museo Municipal de Arte Juan Carlos Castagnino, or to the quiet residential area of **Divino Rostro**, where the main attractions are the Villa Victoria cultural centre and the Archivo Museo Histórico Municipal. South along the coast, a visit to the **port** makes a fine way to end the day – both for the lively bustle of returning fishermen and for the majestic sea lions who have made their home at the port's southern end.

Plaza San Martín and the microcentro

Plaza San Martín, Mar del Plata's spacious central square, covers four blocks. The square's statue of San Martín, created by sculptor Luis Perlotti, is slightly unusual in that it shows the general in his old age. At the southern end of the square, the **Catedral de los Santos Pedro y Cecilia** was designed by Pedro Benoit, chief architect of La Plata (see p.160).

Immediately south of the square lies the hectic **microcentro**, dominated by pedestrianized Calle San Martín, which becomes so packed on summer evenings that it can be difficult to weave your way through the assembled mass of holiday-makers and street performers. Alternatively, follow Avenida Luro eight blocks north of Plaza San Martín to reach **Plaza Rocha**, where there is a small **green fair** (Tues & Sat 9am–1pm) selling organic vegetables, honey, jams and other goods from local orchards.

La Perla

Heading north from Plaza San Martín takes you through the much quieter neighbourhood of **La Perla**. Just one block from the plaza on Mitre and 9 de Julio, you'll find the lovely *La Cuadrada* café (see p.177), and following Mitre another two blocks will bring you to La Perla **beach**, almost as busy as the central beaches but regarded as slightly more upmarket. Inland is La Perla's main square, the Plaza España, where you can visit the **Museo de Ciencias Naturales Lorenzo Scaglia** (Tues–Fri 9am–4.30pm, Sat & Sun 3–6.30pm; $4), which has a good collection of fossils from all over the world, including Patagonian dinosaurs, as well as a salt- and fresh-water aquarium.

Playa Bristol and around

Playa Bristol, Mar del Plata's most famous beach, is nine blocks south of Plaza San Martín. Together with neighbouring Playa Popular, just to the north, these are the city's busiest beaches and in high season their blanket coverage of beach tents and shades suggests a strange nomadic settlement. Follow the bay round to the southeast and you will come to a promontory known as Punta Piedras, crowned by another of the city's landmark buildings, the **Torreón del Monje**. This "monk's tower" is a perfect example of Mar del Plata's peculiar brand of fantasy architecture, which at times makes the city look like a toy village. Built as a folly in 1904 by Ernesto Tornquist, the tower is a little overwhelmed by its neighbours these days, but you can still get a great view of Playa Bristol and the Rambla Casino from its restaurant.

Loma Stella Maris

One block inland from Playa Bristol, wide Avenida Colón begins to climb to the hill known as **Loma Stella Maris**. The area provides some good views over the city, particularly from the crest of the hill back down the impeccably straight Avenida Colón, while Güemes, which branches off Colón, has some of the city's most upmarket **shopping**. The barrio is also a pleasant place to wander if you're interested in Mar del Plata's *pintoresquista* architecture. At Colón 1189, the imposing Villa Ortiz Basualdo, an exuberantly turreted and half-timbered Anglo-Norman mansion, houses the **Museo Municipal de Arte Juan Carlos Castagnino** (summer daily 5–10pm; winter daily noon–6pm; closed Tues; $4). Local artist Castagnino was born in 1908 and painted colourful Expressionist scenes of Mar del Plata. His work forms the basis of the permanent collection, which has also been boosted in recent years by a growing number of contemporary Argentine works.

Opposite, the **Museo del Mar**, at Colón 1114 (daily 10am–9pm; $18; Ⓦwww .museodelmar.org), is a modern complex built around the sea-shell obsession of Benjamin Sisterna, who spent over sixty years amassing thirty thousand shells, which the museum claims is one of the world's largest such collections on display.

Three blocks south, you can climb to the top of the bizarre, castle-like **Torre Tanque**, at Falucho 995, an Anglo-Norman water tower, from where there are great views over the city (Mon–Fri 8am–3pm; free).

Divino Rostro

Some 3km southwest of Plaza San Martín is the leafy and well-heeled neighbourhood of **Divino Rostro**. The area is almost exclusively residential, with little in the way of cafés or bars, but is worth the detour to Matheu 1851 to see the **Villa Victoria**, which houses the **Centro Cultural Victoria Ocampo** (summer daily 10am–1pm & 5–9pm; winter Mon & Wed–Sun noon–6pm; $3; Ⓣ0223/492-0569). The site of some lively exhibitions and events, the villa is an architectural curiosity in its own right. Built of Norwegian wood, it is a fine example of the prefabricated housing that the English took with them to their colonial outposts. It was shipped to the country in 1912 by the great-aunt of one of Argentina's most famous authors, Victoria Ocampo.

The excellent **Archivo Museo Histórico Municipal** (Mon–Fri 8am–5pm, Sat & Sun 2–6pm; $4; ☎0223/495-1200), at Lamadrid 3870, one block southwest of Villa Victoria, has plenty of interesting information on Mar del Plata's history. Within the archives are some wonderful photos of the resort's early days when the cognoscenti from Buenos Aires flocked to the *Hotel Bristol*, as well as copies of the strict rules enforced on bathers: single men could be fined or arrested for approaching within thirty metres of women bathers or for using opera glasses.

To reach the Archivo Histórico and Villa Victoria, take bus #511 from Avenida Luro or the Boulevard Marítimo and get off on the corner of Alsinas and Formosa.

The Port and Costanera Sur

After the Rambla Casino, Mar del Plata's favourite postcard image is the striking orange fishing boats that depart daily from its **port**, about 3km south of the city centre. In the early evening you can watch them returning to the Banquina de Pescadores full of crates bursting with bass, sole and squid, which are hauled onto the quayside by the fishermen. At the far end of the wharf there is a colony of around eight hundred **sea lions** – all males, with their distinctive giant manes and loud bark. These can be observed from an incredibly close (and smelly) distance – only one metre or so – all year round, though the colony is much smaller in summer, as large numbers head for the Uruguayan coast to mate. There are also a number of good **seafood restaurants** around the port, mostly grouped around the Centro Comercial. Various buses head to the area, including #551 and #553, which can be caught along Avenida Luro.

Following the coastal road round southeast of the port will take you along the **Costanera Sur**, via an area known as **Punta Magotes** – easy to locate, with the city's red-and-white striped lighthouse, the Faro de Punta Magotes, at its head. Here you'll find quieter beaches and *balnearios*, including several popular with the surf crowd and a naturist beach, as well as most campsites. It's also home to the **Mar del Plata Aquarium**, at Avenida Martínez de Hoz 5600 (Jan & Feb daily 10am–9pm, March daily 10am–7pm, April–Nov Fri–Sun 10am–6pm, Dec daily 10am–6pm; $65; ☎0223/467-0700, ⊛www.mdpaquarium.com.ar). There are the inevitable sea lion and dolphin shows, but the aquarium's foundation carries out conservation and educational work to try and ensure it's not just a theme park. If you won't be heading to Patagonia you may want to take this opportunity to see Magellanic and Emperor penguins.

Eating, drinking and nightlife

There are a huge number of reasonable **restaurants** in the microcentro, though in high season if you want to avoid standing in line you may prefer to head for the otherwise quiet streets around Castelli and Yrigoyen, southwest of the micro-centro, where there are some attractive small bars and restaurants.

For many visitors, Mar del Plata's summer **nightlife** is at least as important as its beaches – and if you want to keep up with the locals, you'll need both stamina and transport. The densest concentration of **bars** is along lively Calle Além, which also has a good selection of late-night restaurants and is swamped by a young crowd, intent on showing off their tan during the summer. Their next port of call is likely to be Constitución, an enormous avenue 4km north of the town centre, housing numerous **clubs**, none of which really gets going until well after 2am.

Restaurants and cafés

🏃 **Cabaña del Bosque** El Cardenal s/n, Bosque Peralta Ramos ☎0223/467-3007, ⊛www .lacabanadelbosque.com.ar. Mar del Plata's most

famous café is in a wooden building set in lush grounds within a residential district around 10km south of the city centre. The wildly exotic and rambling interior, decorated with fossils, carved wooden sculptures and stuffed animals, is worth a visit on its own, though the café's fantastic cakes are a pretty enticing attraction too. Bus #521 or #522 will get you there. Open daily in summer 2–9pm.

Chichilo Centro Comercial Puerto, Local 17 ☏0223/489-6317. One of a clutch of cheap and excellent seafood restaurants that serve up the fresh catch of the day in the port's Centro Comercial; try local *rabas* (squid rings), *lenguada* (sole) or *langostinos* (shrimp). Open daily 11am–midnight.

Chiquilin Castelli and H. Yrigoyen 2899. Attractive oak-panelled pub with an eclectic menu that gives an inventive twist to standard dishes. The dish of the day costs $30–40, while beef goulash for two costs $57. There's live music some evenings too. Open daily 8am–2am.

La Fontanella Rawson 2302 ☏0223/494-0533. Named for its pretty fountain, *La Fontanella* specializes in *pizza a la piedra* as well as fish and pasta.

Manolo de la Costa Castelli 15. Offering good sea views, *Manolo de la Costa* is a Mar del Plata institution that does upmarket fast food such as pizzas and a delicious *brochette mixto* (kebab), but it is for its fabulous range of filled *churros* (fried dough) that it is best known. The sister branch at Rivadavia 2371 is busy, too, and a popular spot for *chocolate con churros* after a hard night's clubbing.

La Placita de Arenales Arenales 2184 ☏0223/493-2794. Cosy pizza restaurant with photos of the owner with local celebrities hanging from the walls. Serves twelve different types of empanadas ($4.50) and specializes in delicious *calzones*. Open daily 8pm–1am.

Bars and nightclubs

Bar Ramona Castelli 291 and H. Yrigoyen. A slightly posey but attractive bar, popular with the young and well-to-do.

Chocolate Constitución 4445. Large, glossy club, consistently one of Mar del Plata's most highly rated dance destinations.

La Cuadrada 9 de Julio and Mitre. A café-bar and theatre that's worth a visit for its decor alone. The interior is covered with paintings, sculptures and antiques, and with a basement that is a rabbit warren of tiny rooms filled with wooden tables and stone seats. It's a mesmerizing place to while away an hour over a beer or a cup of their extensive range of teas. The food is also excellent and served with great style.

Dickens Pub Diagonal Pueyrredón 3017. Pub that holds regular jazz evenings; popular with foreign visitors.

Mr Jones Além, between Matheu and Quintana. One of Além's most popular bars, heaving with bronzed bodies on summer evenings. Next to it is the softer lit, sit-down *Mr Lounge*.

Pinar de Rocha Av Constitución 5470. One of the city's big dance clubs, with two floors, featuring different styles of music, and a *cena-show* (dinner with show).

La Princesa B. de Irigoyen 3820. Long-running surfer bar and restaurant, with a good range of *milanesas* (both meat and soya), pizzas and salads to accompany your margarita.

Sobremonte Av Constitución 6690. Constitución's most popular club complex, featuring bars and dancefloors ranging from a mock-Mexican *cantina* to the laidback Velvet chillout room. The music is generally mainstream dance, although international DJs of the stature of Sasha and Deep Dish have played here.

Tijuana B. de Irigoyen 3966. Alternative hangout to *Mr Jones* around the corner – and in a very similar vein.

Entertainment

Mar del Plata is also well catered for as far as **theatres** and **cinemas** are concerned; most of them are in the downtown area, such as the Teatro Colón, at H. Yrigoyen 1665 (☏0223/499-6555), and the Cine Ambassador, at Córdoba 1673 (☏0223/495-7271). In March (some years November), Mar del Plata hosts a major international **film festival** (ⓦwww.mardelplatafilmfest.com), one of South America's most important, in which movies from around the world compete, with an emphasis on Latin American works. **Live music** concerts are a part of the fabric of summer too, with some popular national acts playing outdoors at the *balnearios*, as well as indoors in the theatres. Regular **folk music shows** take place at the Casa de Folklore, San Juan 2543 (☏0223/472-3955).

In addition, Mar del Plata is the host of a **football** mini-tournament during the summer, in which the country's five major teams – Boca Juniors, River Plate, San Lorenzo, Racing and Independiente – decamp from their Buenos Aires homes to battle it out by the sea. Other sports tournaments are held throughout the season, including everything from backgammon to surfing – the tourist office can provide you with details.

Listings

Airlines Aerolíneas Argentinas, Moreno 2442 (☏0223/496-0101); LADE, Rambla Casino Loc. 5 (☏0223/491-1484).

Banks and exchange There are many banks on avenidas Independencia, Luro and San Martín. Jonestur, at Luro 3185 (Mon–Fri 10am–7pm, Sat 10am–1pm), exchanges currency and travellers' cheques.

Bike rental Madrid, at H. Yrigoyen 2249 ☏0223/494-1932.

Hospitals Hospital Interzonal Mar del Plata, Juan B. Justo 6800 ☏0223/477-0265.

Laundry Laverap, Av Libertad 5519 ☏0223/474-6884.

Post office The main office is at Luro 2460, on the corner of Santiago del Estero, offering all the usual facilities ☏0223/499-1839; there are numerous other offices throughout the city.

Taxis Mar del Plata ☏0223/483-1111; Tele Taxi ☏0223/475-8888.

Travel agents and tour operators You'll find several travel agents in Galería de las Américas at San Martín 2648. Surf school: Playa Grande Balneario 8 ☏0223/154554829. Paragliding: Arcángel ☏0223/463-1167, suitable for beginners.

Miramar and Mar del Sud

Heading south from Mar del Plata, the first resort you come to is **MIRAMAR**, 45km further down the RP-11. A largely modern town, it sells itself very much as a family-oriented resort and consequently most visitors tend to have children in tow. Miramar's beachfront is dominated by some rather grim high-rise buildings, although it's not a bad place to entertain children for a couple of days, and has a tranquil vibe outside the peak months of January and February.

A more interesting choice than Miramar if you want a complete break from the bustle of places like Mar del Plata is tiny **MAR DEL SUD**, a further 16km southeast. One of Argentina's least-developed beach resorts, Mar del Sud is in many ways one of its most appealing. It is becoming increasingly popular with in-the-know Porteños looking for something a little different, but the atmosphere remains tranquil, with a friendly, community feel and the occasional party. Its beaches are far less frequented than those further north, and if you venture a few hundred metres away from the small clutch of beachgoers grouped around the bottom of Avenida 100, you won't have much trouble finding a stretch of soft sand to yourself. The town's pleasantly unassuming buildings are dominated by the crumbling faded-pink walls and steeply pitched roof of the ex-**Boulevard Atlantic Hotel**, an elegant, French-influenced construction built in 1886. It's now a wonderfully creepy old building, its once glamorous rooms taken over by doves and scattered with chunks of plaster. Guided visits are possible during the day on request from Eduardo Gambo, who runs the place and is something of a local personality, and also rents out bungalows (see opposite).

Practicalities

Buses to Miramar arrive at different terminals/offices in the town centre – most are along Diagonal Fte de la Plaza, which leads south to Plaza General Alvarado. El Rápido del Sur, which serves Mar del Plata, and Expreso Mar del Sud, for Mar del Sud, leave from Avenida 23 and Calle 34, three blocks northwest of the plaza. There's a helpful **tourist office** (summer daily 7am–11pm; winter 8am–8pm; ☏02291/420190, ⓦwww.miramar-digital.com.ar) on Calle 12 between 19 and 21, which also covers Mar del Sud. **Accommodation** is easy to find, with a wide choice of places in the streets surrounding Plaza General Alvarado. The seafront is taken up by apartment buildings; the closest hotel to the sea is the *Marina*, at Avenida 9 no. 744 (T 02291/420462, W www.miramar-digital.com/hotelmarina; ●), one block back from the beach, which has some attractive rooms with balconies and sea views; these cost a few pesos more than the internal rooms but are worth it. Further out of town, *Las Camelias* on RP-77 at Km10.5 (T 011/1550236642, W www.posadalascamelias .com.ar; ●) is a stunning posada set in large grounds. The hotel has a gym, swimming pool and can organize horseriding. **Eating** options are plentiful, too, with most places again around Plaza General Alvarado and the seafront.

In Mar del Sud, though the main section of the *Boulevard Atlantic* is uninhabitable, there are some slightly musty but well-equipped apartments run by Gambo adjoining the hotel, with a definite Gothic appeal as well as cooking facilities (T 02291/491135; ●). The only **hotel** on the seafront itself is the *Hostería Villa del Mar* on the corner of Avenida 100 (T 02291/491141; ●; open Jan & Feb only), which has small rooms overlooking the sea and a lovely breakfast area with a hearth. *La Posada*, at calles 15 and 98 (T 02291/491274; ●), is two blocks from the beach and has comfortable, simple rooms with shared bath; it's one of the few places open year round. **Campsite** *La Ponderosa*, five blocks from the beach and to the west of the town centre, on the corner of Avenida La Playa (T 02291/491118), is well equipped, with showers, a restaurant and shops. Camping costs $16 per person per night. The town's few **places to eat** are mostly around the bottom of Avenida 100; the best is Croat restaurant *Makarska*, which does goulash as well as a tasty vegetable and ricotta strudel. The *JR Café* is a family-friendly bar that also houses the town's *locutorio*.

Balcarce and the Museo Fangio

Around 60km northwest of Mar del Plata on RN-226, the agricultural town of **BALCARCE**, near the tabletop foothills of the Tandilia Range, does not, at first glance, appear to have much to distinguish it from other provincial towns. This modest place, however, was the home town of legendary Formula One driver **Juan Manuel Fangio**, and it now houses a spectacular museum that is certainly worth the detour if cars and racing are your thing. The **Museo Fangio** (daily Jan–Mar 10am–7pm; Apr–Dec Mon–Fri 10am–5pm, Sat & Sun 10am–6pm; $25; T 02266/425540, W www.museofangio.com) was built to honour the man who won the Formula One World Championship five times in the 1950s, a record not equalled until the twenty-first century. The five floors of the museum are connected by a spiral ramp and tell Fangio's story in words, pictures and trophies. There are also displays on other prominent drivers, but the car's the star here – around fifty of them, in fact, including a red 1954 Maserati 250 and the Brabham BT36 driven by Argentine ex-Formula One driver Carlos Reutemann, now a politician. The most impressive, though – and saved for the top floor – is the Mercedes-Benz Silver Arrow that Fangio drove to victory in 1954.

Buses run between Mar del Plata and Balcarce every two hours and take ninety minutes; you will need to take a taxi (Teletaxi: T 02266/425076) from the terminal to the museum. If you need to spend the night in the town, there's a basic **hotel**, the *Alberghini* (T 02266/431397; ●), at Avenida Kelly 688, near the museum.

Necochea

NECOCHEA is a sprawling resort town popular with families, thanks to its much-publicized wide beaches, as well as surfers – it is home to some of the country's best waves. The town has a disjointed layout: the town centre proper, known as the **centro viejo**, sits 3km inland, but most tourist activity is packed into a grid of streets down by the seafront known as the **centro nuevo**. The enormous **Parque Miguel Lillo** lies immediately west of the centro nuevo, alongside Calle 89, and contains, among other things, a lake, an amphitheatre, an amusement train and a small regional history museum. Necochea's beachfront is a typically regimented and busy stretch of sand dominated by tents and sunshades, and lined with restaurants. To the north, close to the mouth of the Río Quequén, lies the quieter **Playa de los Patos**, flanked by low dunes and popular for fishing and surfing. To the south, the beaches extend for over 30km; the most accessible of these undeveloped rocky stretches is known as **Las Grutas**, backed by low cliffs and lying around 7km from the centre.

Practicalities

Necochea's **bus terminal** is at Avenida 58 and Jesuita Cardiel, in the centro viejo. The **tourist office** (daily: summer 8am–8pm; winter 8am–2pm; ℡02262/425983), in a cabin on the seafront at the corner of Avenida 79 and Avenida 2, has limited information. Accommodation-wise, at all but the height of the summer season it shouldn't be difficult to find somewhere to stay in Necochea – and prices are generally lower here than they are further north. Most hotels are in the centro nuevo, with the pick being the ⚜ *Hostería del Bosque*, at Calle 89 no. 350 (℡02262/420002, ⓦwww.hosteria-delbosque.com.ar; ❼), a charming *hostería* with elegantly decorated rooms, big, comfortable beds and a lovely shady courtyard that is set with tables and chairs for breakfast. The best of the town's budget options is *La Casona*, at Calle 6 no. 4356 (℡02262/423345, Ⓔlacasonahlc@yahoo.com.ar; closed Apr–Nov; ❷), a friendly place with rooms around a central garden, while the new, upmarket *Nikén*, at Calle 87 no. 335 (℡02262/432323, ⓦwww.hotelniken .com.ar; ❼), is one of the few to offer a pool. There are many **campsites**; the nicest, at nearby Quequén on Avenida 502 and 529, is *Monte Pasubio* (℡02262/451482, ⓦwww.montepasubio.com.ar; camping $25), named after a nearby shipwreck and sited right by the sea. Equipped with a restaurant, it offers shady camping spots on the beach and has a laidback atmosphere. It's popular with surfers and has a surf school. Tents and bungalows (❼) are also available to rent.

When it comes to **eating**, Necochea is the place to take a break from beef and try some fish. Many restaurants are centred on Plaza San Martín and the surrounding streets, the best one being the friendly *Taberna Española*, at Calle 89 no. 366, opposite the park. A nice spot to sit on a summer evening, it has a menu including paella and *cazuela de mariscos*. Fish is also available in the port, for example at long-established and popular *Cantina Venezia*, at Calle 59 no. 259. The majority of **bars** are on the pedestrianized streets between Plaza San Martín and the seafront; many have outdoor seating and the area fills with musicians, performance artists and artisan stalls in the evening.

The Pampas

The vast expanse of flat pampas grassland that radiates out from Buenos Aires is one of the country's most famous features, just as the **gaucho** who once roamed on horseback, knife clenched between teeth, leaving a trail of broken hearts and gnawed steak bones behind him, is as important a part of the collective romantic imagination as the Wild West cowboy is in the US. The popular depiction of this splendid, freedom-loving figure – whose real life must actually have been rather lonely and brutal – was crystallized in José Hernández's epic poem *Martín Fierro*, from which just about every Argentine can quote. It's a way of life whose time has passed, but the gaucho's legacy remains. You're not likely to witness knife fights over a woman, but you can still visit well-preserved *pulperías* (traditional bars), stay at estancias and watch weather-beaten old *paisanos* (countrymen) playing cards and chuckling behind their huge handlebar moustaches. Shrines to the semi-mythical Gauchito Gil (see box, p.255), one of the most famous gauchos of all, are often seen by the roadside in the Pampas.

The best area for this kind of visit is the **Eastern Pampas**, in a radius of a couple of hundred kilometres around Buenos Aires city. This is where you'll find the *pampa húmeda* (wet pampa), land that is the country's most fertile – and most valuable. There are several sites of interest here, most notably **San Antonio de Areco**, which has retained a remarkably authentic feel despite its popularity. As you move into the **Western Pampas**, and towards the border with La Pampa Province, the scenery starts to change. The unremitting flat landscape is given welcome relief by the modest mountain range of **Sierra de la Ventana**, while the drier, more desert-like features of the *pampa seca* (dry pampa) herald the start of the long route south through Patagonia.

The Eastern Pampas

The closest places are potential day-trips from the capital, although spending a night – perhaps at a nearby estancia – will give you a better feel for the much slower pace of life in the interior. Others are useful as stopping-off points. The charming town of **San Antonio de Areco** is the main site of interest to the capital's northwest, on the RN-8; if you visit only one pampas town during your stay in Argentina, this is the one to head for. The recognized centre of pampas tradition, San Antonio puts on a popular gaucho festival in November and has some highly respected artisans and an extremely attractive and unusually well-preserved town centre. At the very beginning of the RN-5, **Luján**, 61km west of the capital, is Argentina's most important religious site, thanks to its vast basilica, built to house the country's patron saint, the Virgin of Luján. Further along the RN-5, **Mercedes** stands out thanks to its authentic *pulpería*, largely untouched since the nineteenth century, and the small town of **Lobos**, to the capital's southwest, is a popular weekend destination for Porteños, primarily for its lakeside setting. **Tandil** is also an appealing town of cobbled streets and traditional pampas culture.

San Antonio de Areco

Delightful **SAN ANTONIO DE ARECO** is considered the home of gaucho traditions and hosts the annual **Fiesta de la Tradición** (see box, p.184), the country's most important festival celebrating pampas culture. Despite its modest promotion as a tourist destination, San Antonio has retained a surprisingly genuine feel, augmented by its setting on the banks of a tranquil river, the Río Areco. You may not find the town full of galloping gauchos outside festival week, but you still have a good chance of spotting estancia workers on horseback, sporting traditional berets and rakishly knotted scarves, or of coming across *paisanos* propping up the bar of a traditional *boliche* establishment. San Antonio has a prestigious literary connection: the town was the setting for Ricardo Güiraldes' Argentine classic *Don Segundo Sombra* (1926), a novel that was influential in changing the image of the gaucho from that of an undesirable outlaw to a symbol of national values.

The town's only real sights are a couple of museums, the most important of which is the **Museo Gauchesco Ricardo Güiraldes**. But what really makes San

▲ Gauchos at La Fiesta de la Tradición, San Antonio de Areco

Antonio memorable is the harmonious architectural character of the town's centre: all cobbled streets and faded Italianate and colonial facades punctuated by elaborate wrought-iron grilles and delicately arching lamps. There are also some excellent **artisans** working in the town in *talleres* (workshops). Weaving and leatherwork are well represented, but the silversmiths are the highlight.

The town's traditional gaucho atmosphere also extends to the surrounding area, where you will find some of Argentina's most famous **estancias**, offering a luxurious accommodation alternative to staying in Areco itself.

Arrival and information

Most **buses** from Buenos Aires and Rosario stop at the pink Chevallier terminal at General Paz and Avenida Dr Smith, six blocks east of Areco's town centre. It's an easy and enjoyable stroll into town along Calle Segundo Sombra, which brings you to Areco's main square, Plaza Ruiz de Arellano. If you're carrying a lot of luggage – or heading for an estancia – take a *remise* (℡02326/456225).

The **tourist office** on the corner of Arellano and Zerboni (daily 8am–7pm; ℡02326/453165) has useful information, including maps, lists of hotels and artisan workshops. There's also a small office in the municipalidad building (Sat & Sun 9am–8pm) on Plaza Ruiz de Arellano, to cope with the extra influx of Porteños on weekends.

Accommodation

San Antonio is easily visited as a day-trip from Buenos Aires, but many museums and workshops close during the afternoon, so this can be a frustrating experience. Staying overnight gives you the chance to explore the town at a more leisurely pace and enjoy it as its best, in the morning and evening. Several cafés also double up as simple *hospedajes* – see p.186 for details. If you plan on visiting during the Fiesta de la Tradición celebrations, book at least two weeks in advance; once the hotels are full, the tourist office can provide information on staying with families. There are one or two **campsites** within easy reach of San Antonio, the best being *Club River* (℡02326/453590; $40 a tent), reached by following Zerboni west out of town. It includes a swimming pool.

Los Abuelos Zapiola and Zeboni
①02326/456390. A decent option if you're after a more modern type of hotel, and reasonably priced. Rooms have TV and fans (extra for a/c) with balconies looking out over the Río Areco. ④

Antigua Casona Segúnda Sombra 495 ①02326/456600, ⓦwww.antiguacasona.com. A B&B with a rustic edge and a lovely patio where a good breakfast is served. ⑤

Hostal de Areco Zapiola 25 ①02326/456118, ⓦwww.hostaldeareco.com.ar. One of the most attractive accommodation options in town: a traditional rose-coloured building with farmhouse style decor. The hotel has a bar and comfortable communal area with a fireplace. ④

Hostel Gaucho Zerboni 308 ①02326/453625 ⓦwww.hostelgaucho.com.ar. Hostel with decent

communal area and a garden equipped with *parrilla*. Dorms cost $50 per person and there are also doubles (③).

🏃 Patio de Moreno Moreno and San Martín ①02326/455197, ⓦwww.patiodemoreno .com. Stylish, centrally located boutique hotel with modern rooms, most of which have views onto a pretty garden. There's also a heated swimming pool and a wine bar serving local produce. ⑧

Solar del Pago Hipólito G. Fiore 232 (Acceso Dr Duran) ①02326/15410252, ⓦwww.solardelpago .com. Located out of town on the RP-41 in the direction of San Andres de Giles, this hotel affords stunning views of the nearby pampas. The hotel has a restaurant and spa, as well as disabled access. ⑦

The Town

Areco's main square, the leafy **Plaza Ruiz de Arellano**, six blocks west of the bus terminal, is named after José Ruiz de Arellano, whose estancia stood on the site now occupied by the town and who built San Antonio's founding chapel, the **Iglesia Parroquial San Antonio de Padua**, on the south side of the square. The original chapel, a simple adobe construction, was declared a parish

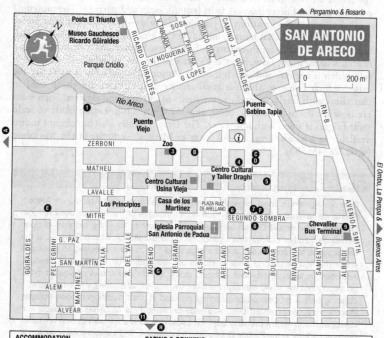

ACCOMMODATION				EATING & DRINKING					
Los Abuelos	C	Hostal de Areco	D	Almacén de Ramos		Café de las Artes	5	La Olla de Cobre	4
Antigua Casona	F	Hostel Gaucho	B	Generales	7	La Costa	3	Puesto La Lechuza	2
La Cinacina	E	Patio de Moreno	G	Bar San Martin	11	La Esquina de Merti	6	Tragame Tierra	1
Club River	A	Solar del Pago	H	Boliche de Bessonart	8	Gualicho	9	La Vieja Sodería	10

church in 1730, and was rebuilt in 1792 and then again in 1870 in keeping with the town's growing importance. Of no great architectural note, the current version is nonetheless a pleasingly simple white construction, with clear Italian influences. The exterior is dominated by a sculpture of San Antonio himself, who stands within a niche clad with blue-and-white tiles that echo those of the church's small bell-shaped dome. The inside is impressive, with a high vaulted ceiling.

Among the elegant *fin-de-siècle* residences that flank the plaza, there is the Italianate **municipalidad**, to the north, painted a particularly delicate version of the pink that characterizes so many of Areco's buildings. On the northwest corner of the square stands a typically colonial two-storeyed construction known as the **Casa de los Martínez**, after the local family who once inhabited it. The building's handsome but rather plain green-and-white exterior is dominated by the original railings of a balcony, which runs all the way around the first floor.

Centro Cultural y Museo Taller Draghi

Right opposite the church, at Lavalle 387, one of San Antonio's most renowned silversmiths runs the **Centro Cultural y Taller Draghi** (Mon–Sat 9am–1pm & 3.30–7.30pm, Sun 10am–1pm; free guided visits 11am, 5pm & 6pm; $10). The centre displays pieces made in the style of *platería criolla*, which first emerged around 1750 when local craftsmen, who had previously been working according to Spanish and Portuguese tradition, began to develop their own style. Fantastically ornate yet sturdy, in keeping with the practical use to which the items are – at least in theory – put, the style is still commonly used to produce gaucho knives (*facones*), belts (*rastras*), *mates* and stirrups. The museum/workshop mixes the creations of Juan José Draghi – who has produced pieces for various international figures, including the king and queen of Spain – with a collection of nineteenth-century silver spurs, bridles and swords that have been his inspiration; however, there's little in the way of labels, so it's hard to tell which is antique and which modern. Among Draghi's finest work are the *mates*, which come in their original chalice shape (based on those used in churches) with finely wrought silver stems of cherubs and flowers. Such *mates* are now for decoration only, being expensive – not to mention likely to scald your fingers if filled with hot water. The Draghi family also has elegant rooms available in a *parador* (inn) a block away in Matheu – enquire at the workshop (☎02326/455583).

The Fiesta de la Tradición

One of Argentina's most original and enjoyable festivals, San Antonio de Areco's **Fiesta de la Tradición** began in 1939 on an initiative of then-mayor José Antonio Güiraldes. The actual Día de la Tradición is November 10 – the birthday of José Hernández, author of Argentina's gaucho text par excellence, *Martín Fierro* – but the celebrations last for a week and are organized to run from weekend to weekend, either the first or second week in November, depending on the weather forecast. Activities, including exhibitions, dances, music recitals and shows of gaucho skills, go throughout the week, although the highpoint is the final Sunday, which begins with dancing and a procession of gauchos dressed in their traditional loose trousers (*bombachas*), ornamented belts and wide-brimmed hats or berets. An *asado con cuero*, at which meat – primarily beef – is cooked around a fire with its skin on, takes place at midday in the Parque Criollo ($25 for gauchos, $35 for everyone else) and is followed by an extensive display of gaucho skills, including *jineteadas*, or Argentine bronco riding.

Centro Cultural Usina Vieja

A block north of Plaza Ruiz de Arellano, at Alsina 66, is the **Centro Cultural Usina Vieja** (Tues–Sun 11.15am–4.45pm; $1.50). The restored building originally housed Areco's first electrical generator and has been declared a national industrial monument. Now housing a cultural centre, the building also contains the **Museo de la Ciudad**, an eclectic collection – mainly supplied through local donations – of everyday items, from clothing to record players and even the town's old telephone switchboard, plus occasional temporary exhibitions, focusing mainly on subjects related to rural Argentine life. There's also a good display of the famous gaucho cartoons of Florencia Molino Campos, first published in almanacs and now adorning hotel walls the length of the country.

Beyond the cultural centre, wide Calle Zerboni separates the town centre from the grassy banks of the Río Areco, popular for picnics and *asados* during good weather. Zerboni is home to a small **zoo** (summer Mon–Fri 3–7pm, Sat & Sun 11am–1pm; winter Mon–Fri 1–5pm, Sat & Sun 11am–5pm; $5), chiefly of interest for its pleasant green surroundings.

Parque Criollo and Museo Gauchesco Ricardo Güiraldes

Crossing the simple brick **Puente Viejo** opposite leads to the rather scrubby **Parque Criollo**, less a park than a kind of exhibition ground, used during the Fiesta de la Tradición as the setting for the main displays of gaucho skills. It also houses the **Museo Gauchesco Ricardo Güiraldes** (Wed–Mon 11am–5pm; $4). The entrance to the park and the museum is via the *Pulpería La Blanqueada*, once a staging post on the old Camino Real, which linked Buenos Aires with Alto Peru. It was the setting for the first encounter between Fabio, the young hero of Güiraldes' novel – a sort of South American Huckleberry Finn – and his mentor, Don Segundo Sombra. The *pulpería* was closed in the 1930s but its original features have been retained, including the traditional grille that separated the owner from his customers and their knives and light fingers. For a *pulpería* that's still serving, head to Moreno and Mitre, where you'll find *Los Principios*, an authentic store that also sells groceries to locals from its high wooden shelves.

The museum is housed in a 1930s reproduction of an old estancia. Its collection mixes gaucho paraphernalia – *mate* gourds, silverware and *boleadoras* (lasso balls) – with objects deemed to be interesting largely because of their famous owners – General Rosas' bed, W.H. Hudson's books, and so on. Of particular interest are the black-and-white photos of the original gauchos who were the inspiration for Güiraldes, and the branding irons they used – each landowner had his own, somewhat cabalistic symbol, worn in various forms as a badge of pride by his men as well as his cattle.

Eating

Almacén de Ramos Generales Zapiola 143 ☎ 02326/456376, ⓦ www.ramosgeneralesareco .com.ar. Serves *parrilla*, *picadas* ($25 for two) and specials such as trout in Roquefort sauce with potatoes ($55). Open daily noon–3.30pm & 8.30pm–midnight.

Café de las Artes Bolivar 68. Does tasty handmade pasta from all over the world ($23–28) and delicious pork in blackberry sauce ($32). Open summer daily noon–4pm & 8pm–midnight; winter Wed–Sun same hours.

La Costa Corner of Zerboni and Belgrano. *Parrilla* that is popular with the locals.

La Esquina de Marti On the main plaza at Lavalle and Arellano ☎ 02326/456705, ⓦ www .esquinademerti.com.ar. Has walls adorned with old signs, ads and bottles and is a tasteful recreation of a *pulpería* serving straightforward Argentine classics and a set lunch for $35.

La Olla de Cobre Matheu 433 ☎ 02326/453105, ⓦ www.laolladecobre.com.ar. A small chocolate factory and sweet shop where you can try handmade chocolates and particularly delicious *alfajores* before buying. Open Sun–Mon 10am–1pm & 3.30–8.30pm.

Tragame Tierra On the riverside at the far end of Calle Martínez. Does *panchos* and *picadas*, has basic rooms available and also rents out *piraguas* (boats) and mountain bikes.

🏃 **La Vieja Sodería** Bolivar and General Paz. The pick of San Antonio de Areco's old-style establishments. The walls here are lined with coloured soda bottles; serves a wide range of teas and beers, and snacks including sandwiches and *picadas*. Open every day.

Drinking and nightlife

The best **bars** in Areco are *boliches* – traditional places where estancia workers drink Fernet and play cards. Some of the best include *Bar San Martín*, on Moreno and Alvear, and *Puesto La Lechuza*, near the river at Victorino Althaparro 423, both of which are good places to catch folklore music and dancing. *Barril 990*, at San Martín 381, is a more modern pub, where there is occasional live music. *Boliches* in the modern sense of the word – **nightclubs** – are out on Avenida Dr Smith, such as *Gaulicho* next to the bus terminal (Fri & Sat only).

Estancias in and around San Antonio de Areco

The countryside around San Antonio is home to a couple of the province's most traditional **estancias**. Arguably the most luxurious is **El Ombú**, at Ruta 31 (☎02326/492080, ⓦwww.estanciaelombu.com; ⑨, or US$70 as a day visit). Its rooms are sumptuously decorated and a lovely tiled and ivy-covered verandah runs round the exterior of the building. As well as offering horseriding, the estancia has a small but well-maintained swimming pool and a games room. Other activities include helping out with – or at least observing – farm tasks and, of course, eating delicious *asados*, sometimes served under the shade of the large ombú tree that gives the estancia its name. Directions are on the website; the estancia will arrange a transfer from Buenos Aires for around US$105.

Around 12km from town, **La Bamba** (☎011/1553161200, ⓦwww.la-bamba .com.ar; ⑨, or day-trips at US$121) was used in Maria Luisa Bemberg's film *Camila* – the story of the ill-fated romance between Camila O'Gorman and a priest – and is one of Argentina's most distinctive estancias. The Río Areco runs through the grounds, so guests can fish as well as ride, although the "shows" in the recently built *pulpería* and immaculate living rooms make the place seem a bit like a Disney version of an estancia experience at times.

La Sofía Polo (☎011/6091-9266, ⓦwww.lasofiapolo.com.ar; ⑨), run by a German and Argentine couple, is for those wanting to improve their polo game. Husband Marcos Antin has taught polo around Argentina and Europe and is also a qualified referee. Lessons cater to all levels. It costs US$140 per person per night to stay at the estancia, located 14km from San Antonio de Areco, and the price includes food, drink and one horseride a day. There are additional costs for polo lessons and playing matches.

La Cinacina estancia in Areco itself (☎02326/452773, ⓦwww.lacinacina .com.ar; ⑨) has more affordable "days in the country"; follow Bartolomé Mitre five blocks west of the main plaza to the end of the street. It offers a full day of *asado*, horseriding and a display of gaucho skills for $114, or $180 with transport from the centre of town included (Tues, Fri & Sun). Staying the night (④) is also possible, in pretty, light, country-style rooms.

Luján

Officially founded in 1756 on the site of a shrine containing a tiny ceramic figure of the Virgin Mary, **Luján**, about 70km west of Buenos Aires, is now one of the major religious centres in Latin America. The **Virgin of Luján** is the patron saint of

Argentina and the epic basilica erected in her honour in 1887 in Luján attracts around eight million visitors a year. This Neo-Gothic edifice is one of the most memorable – though not really the most beautiful – churches in Argentina. The town's other major attraction, the vast **Complejo Museográfico Enrique Udaondo**, is a multiplex museum with an important historical section, as well as Argentina's largest transport museum. Away from the museums and the basilica, all grouped around the central square, Luján is pretty much like any other provincial town, with elegant, early twentieth-century townhouses and slightly less elegant modern buildings.

If you want to get a real flavour of Luján in full religious swing, you should visit at the weekend, when seven or eight Masses are held a day – but, unless you want to take part, try to avoid visiting during the annual **pilgrimages**, when the town becomes seriously full. These take place on the last Sunday of September for the Gaucho pilgrimage, when up to a million gauchos come to honour the Virgin of Lujan; the first Sunday of October, when young people walk here from Buenos Aires; May 8, the day of the Coronation of the Virgin; and December 8, when smaller, informal pilgrimages mark the Day of the Immaculate Conception.

Arrival and information

Regular **buses** to Luján from Buenos Aires arrive at the bus terminal on Avenida Nuestra Señora de Luján 600 (℡02323/420044), a couple of blocks north of the town's central square, Plaza Belgrano. There are also frequent **trains** from the capital (Once station), changing at Moreno and terminating at Luján's train station, a couple of kilometres southeast of the centre at Avenida España and Belgrano. The **tourist office** (Mon–Fri 9am–5pm, Sat & Sun 10am-6pm; ℡02323/427082,

A tiny miracle: the Virgin of Luján

In 1630, a Portuguese ship docked in Buenos Aires on its way back from Brazil. Among its cargo was a simple terracotta image of the **Virgin** made by an anonymous Brazilian craftsman. The icon had been brought to Argentina at the request of a merchant from Sumampa, Santiago del Estero, and, after unloading, it was transported by cart towards the estancia of its new owner. The cart paused on the outskirts of **Luján**, from where, the story goes, it could not be moved. Various packages were taken down from the cart in an attempt to lighten the load – all to no avail, until the tiny package containing the Virgin was removed. In the time-honoured tradition of miracles, this was taken as a sign that the Virgin had decided on her own destination. A small chapel was built and the first pilgrims began to arrive.

The Virgin has actually been moved over the centuries, although according to legend it took three attempts and several days of prayer the first time. In 1872, Luján's Lazarist order – a religious body founded in Paris in 1625 with the emphasis on preaching to the rural poor – was entrusted with the care of the Virgin by the archbishop of Buenos Aires. In 1875, a member of the order, **Padre Jorge María Salvaire**, was almost killed in one of the last Indian raids on Azul. Praying to the Virgin, he promised that if he survived he would promote her cult, write her history and, finally, build a huge temple in her name. He survived, and the foundation stone to the basilica was laid on his initiative in 1887.

The original terracotta Virgin is now barely recognizable: a protective bell-shaped silver casing was placed around the image in the late nineteenth century. Sky-blue and white robes were also added, reflecting the colours of the Argentine flag, as well as a Gothic golden surround, in keeping with the style of the basilica. The face of the original statue can now just about be seen, peering out a small gap in the casing. Even if you don't visit Luján itself, you're likely to have seen the Virgin: she is the patron saint of roads and paths, and stickers with her image can be seen on almost every bus rear windscreen in Argentina.

Ⓦwww.lujanargentina.com) is in a building known as La Cúpula, which stands in a park area on the riverbank between Lavalle and San Martín, one block west of Plaza Belgrano. In addition to maps and hotel lists, it has detailed info on the phenomenon of the Virgin and the basilica's history and importance.

Accommodation

There is plenty of accommodation in the city – mostly fair, mid-range **hotels**. The ones around the bus terminal are on the whole pretty seedy and not a very good deal. An exception is the *Biarritz*, on Lezica and Torrezuri 717 (Ⓣ02323/435988; ❸), one block south of the terminal. The simple but reasonable rooms all have air conditioning and cable TV; breakfast is included. In general, though, you're probably better off heading to the streets to the east of the basilica. At 9 de Julio 1054, *La Paz* (Ⓣ02323/424034; ❹) is one of Luján's oldest hotels, offering airy rooms and a pretty garden overlooked by the basilica's towers. Two blocks east of Plaza Belgrano is *Los Monjes*, at Francia 981 (Ⓣ02323/420606, Ⓦwww.hotellosmonjes.com.ar; ❹), with attractive decent-sized air-conditioned rooms and a good breakfast.

▲ Basílica de Nuestra Señora de Luján

Some visitors set up camp informally around the river, but there are also a couple of organized **campsites** on the way out of town. Just outside the town, *El Triángulo*, on the RN-7 at Km69.50 (℡02323/430116; $35 for 2 people), is a reasonable wooded site that has showers, security and a picnic area. Follow Avenida Nuestra Señora de Luján out of town and turn left at the main access point – the campsite is just over the bridge, on the banks of the Río Luján.

The Town

At busy times, all you need to do to visit the Virgin is go with the flow. The town's main drag, Avenida Nuestra Señora de Luján, rolls up like a tarmac carpet to the door of the **Basílica de Nuestra Señora de Luján** (daily 8am–8pm; Mass Mon–Sat 8am, 9am, 10am, 11am, 5pm & 7pm, Sun also at 12.30pm & 3.30pm), at the far end of Luján's main square, Plaza Belgrano. Begun in 1887 but not actually finished until 1937, the basilica is a mammoth edifice, built using a pinkish stone quarried in Entre Ríos. In true Neo-Gothic style, everything about the basilica points heavenwards, from its remarkably elongated twin spires, which stand 106m tall, to the acute angles of the architraves surrounding the three main doors. At the very centre of the facade there is a large circular stained-glass window depicting the Virgin. The basilica's nineteen bells were cast in Milan from the bronze of World War I cannons. One of the two heavy crosses on the spires fell from a height of 100m at midnight on June 13, 2000. Luckily no one was harmed, but both crosses were replaced for safety reasons.

Despite its grand exterior, it's what goes on inside the basilica that's most likely to catch your attention. On busy days, entering the place through one of the heavy bronze doors is a bit like stepping onto a religious conveyor belt, as you get caught up in a seemingly endless stream of pilgrims, some on their knees, others in wheelchairs, making their way to the **Camarín de la Virgen**. To take a closer look at the Virgin, head up the stairs to the chamber behind the main altar, where you will see her from the back. Positioned on a marble pedestal and swathed in robes and adornments, the statue at the centre of all the fuss is rather hard to see; most people just gather around the replica in front of the altar below. On the outside wall of the chamber are dozens of plaques of all shapes and sizes – including heart-shaped – thanking the "Virgencita" for prayers answered. The **crypt** (Mon–Fri 10am–5pm, Sat & Sun 10am–6.30pm; $3) below the basilica also holds a replica and explains the history. It harbours reproductions of Virgins from all over the world, but particularly from Latin America and Eastern Europe.

West of the plaza in a cluster of mustard-and-white colonial buildings is the **Complejo Museográfico Enrique Udaondo** (Nov–Mar Wed–Fri 12.30–6pm, Sat & Sun 10.30am–6pm; Apr–Oct Wed–Fri 11.30am–5pm, Sat & Sun 10.30am–6pm; $1). It claims to be the most important museum complex in South America; this is debatable, but it's certainly one of the continent's biggest. Its principal collections are those within the Museo Histórico Colonial, housed in the Casa del Virrey and the cabildo on the western side of Plaza Belgrano, and the Museo de Transportes, on the northern end of the plaza, between Avenida Nuestra Señora de Luján and Lezica y Torrezuri.

The **Museo Histórico Colonial** is rather misleadingly named, since its exhibits actually cover a much wider period. The main collection is accessed via the **Cabildo** next door, a two-storey galleried building dating from 1772. The leaders of the short-lived British invasion, General William Beresford and Colonel Dennis Pack, were held here after their surrender in August 1806. Trophies captured during the quashing of the invasion, notably the staff of the 71st Highland Regiment, are prominently displayed. An internal door leads onto a pretty courtyard with a marble well in the centre and an elegant wooden balustrade around the first floor of its green-and-white walls. Other rooms here feature displays on the gaucho – including some fine silver *mate* vessels – nineteenth-century fashion and the disastrous and bloody War of the Triple Alliance.

The **Museo de Transportes**, Argentina's largest transport museum, offers less a chronology of the evolution of transport than a display of some of Argentina's most historically significant planes, trains and carriages. The museum's two most important exhibits are *La Porteña*, Argentina's first steam locomotive, whose maiden journey between Plaza Lavalle and Floresta in Buenos Aires took place in 1857, and *Plus Ultra*, the hydroplane with which Ramón Franco, brother of General Franco, made the first crossing of the South Atlantic in 1926.

Eating and drinking

There are plenty of **eating** options, mainly *parrillas* geared up to feed hungry pilgrims, on Avenida San Martín and Calle 9 de Julio, while next to the tourist office you'll find *La Recova*, a restaurant offering pleasant outdoor seating and a simple, reasonably priced menu that focuses on pasta. Luján's most famous restaurant is a long way out of the centre: *L'Eau Vive* at Constitución 2112 (☎02323/421774; open for lunch and dinner Tues–Sat) is fifteen blocks east along Avenida San Martín from Plaza Colón and most easily reached by taxi. The restaurant's main claim to fame is that it is run exclusively by nuns. The cooking – a traditional European menu with an emphasis on rich meat dishes – is generally excellent.

Mercedes

Tranquil and cultured **MERCEDES**, 37km southwest of Luján along the RN-5, was founded in 1752 as a fortress to protect that city from Indian attacks. It's a well-preserved provincial town and easy to find your way around – the main drag is Avenida 29, which crosses central **Plaza San Martín**. The plaza houses the grand Italianate **Palacio Municipal** and large Gothic **Basílica Catedral Nuestra Señora de Mercedes** and is a real hub of activity – especially in the evening, when locals fill the tables that spill out of its various inviting *confiterías*.

Mercedes' main draw is its unmissable **pulpería**, over twenty blocks north of Plaza San Martín, at the end of Avenida 29. *Pulperías*, essentially provisions stores with a bar attached, performed an important social role in rural Argentina and enjoy an almost mythical status in gaucho folklore. The sign outside 🛪 **Mercedes' pulpería**, known locally as "*lo de Cacho*" (Cacho's place), claims it to be the last *pulpería*, run, until his death in 2009, by the last *pulpero*, Cacho Di Catarina. The gloomy interior, which has hardly changed since it opened its doors in 1850, harbours a collection of dusty bottles, handwritten notices – included an original wanted poster for the biggest gaucho outlaw of them all, Juan Moreira – and gaucho paraphernalia: it doesn't require much imagination to conjure up visions of the knife fights that Cacho claimed to have witnessed in his youth. His family still runs the bar in his name and musicians frequently drop in for a glass of Vasco Viejo and impromptu singing and guitar playing, much of it dedicated to the sorely missed Cacho. To get to the *pulpería*, best visited in the evening for a beer and a *picada* featuring some of the renowned local salami, take the local bus that runs towards the park from Avenida 29. A couple of blocks beyond the last stop, the road becomes unsealed and on the left-hand corner you'll see the simple white building, a sign saying "*pulpería*" painted on its side.

Practicalities

Mercedes' **bus terminal**, served by regular buses from the capital, is south of the town centre, from where it's a twenty-minute walk to Plaza San Martín. There's an infrequent local bus from the terminal to the centre, so if you don't fancy the walk you may be better off taking one of the terminal **taxis** (℡02324/420651). There are also regular trains from Once station in the capital; the **train station** is along Avenida España, eight blocks north of the centre. The **tourist office**, on the corner of Avenida 29 and Calle 26 (Mon 7am–1pm, Tues–Fri 7am–6pm, Sat & Sun 10am–5pm; ℡02324/421080, ⓦwww.mercedes.gba.gov.ar), doesn't have much in the way of printed information, but the staff are enthusiastic and knowledgeable, and can provide you with a map of the town.

Accommodation is not plentiful, and what exists is rather lacking in character. The *Gran Hotel Mercedes*, on the corner of Avenida 29 and Calle 16 (℡02324/425987; ⑤), looks stern and unpromising from the outside, but inside the rooms are quite comfortable and have air conditioning and TV, while facilities include a restaurant and bar area. Otherwise, try the *Hostal del Sol*, on the western edge of town at avenidas 2 and 3 (℡02324/433400, ⓦwww.hotelhostaldelsol.com; ⑤), which has large rooms in a tranquil setting. There's a free municipal **campsite** in the park on the edge of town; take any local bus from Avenida 29. Note that Mercedes hosts a motorbike rally at the end of March, which is the only time you might have trouble finding space to pitch your tent here.

Eating and **drinking** options in the centre include 🍴 *La Vieja Esquina*, a charming traditional bar on the corner of calles 25 and 28, which also sells deli produce and serves excellent *picadas*. Mercedes is the national capital of **salami** and even hosts a salami festival in September. You should certainly try some while you are here – the *picado grueso* is favoured by locals, although its high fat content might be off-putting. Of the *confiterías* around the plaza – good for coffee, sandwiches and snacks – one of the nicest is *La Recova*, the only building in the square to retain an old-fashioned arcade.

Lobos

About 100km southwest of the capital on the RN-205 – you can also reach it from Mercedes via the RP-41 – **LOBOS** is an old-fashioned country town with pretty, slightly crumbling houses and a famous son – Juan Domingo Perón, who was born here in 1895 at the house which now bears the address Perón 482, and where an archive of his letters and photos is stored (Wed–Sun 10am–noon & 3–6pm; ℡02227/422843).

Lobos sits on a series of lakes known as the **Lagunas Encadenadas** ("chained lakes"), the area's main attraction. To get to Lobos's quiet lakeside area, around 15km southwest of town – where there are picnic spots shaded by pines and eucalyptus – take the local bus that runs every couple of hours from the corner of Além and 9 de Julio, opposite the train station. Fishing, boating and windsurfing are all possible; equipment can be rented from several spots around the lake.

Those who fancy something more active will find Lobos is something of a centre for **parachuting** and **polo**. For the former, there is a large and well-equipped skydiving school, CEPA (℡02227/1561-3722, ⓦwww.paracaidismolobos .com.ar), on the RP-205 at Km105, just outside Lobos. All levels are catered for, and tandem jumps with instructors are available. Polo is taught at a number of ranches that also double as estancias. The most notable is **La Martina Polo Ranch** (℡02226/430777, ⓦwww.lamartinapolo.com.ar), a prestigious school attended by Argentina's top players, although they will also teach beginners. La Martina is about 40km northeast of Lobos just outside the tiny settlement of Vicente Casares, off the RN-3 just past the RN-205 junction. You can visit it as a day-trip or stay in the comfortable rooms of the nineteenth-century estancia building (⑨, full board). For more on estancias around Lobos see p.192.

Practicalities

Lobos's smaller **bus** terminal faces the **train** terminal on the corner of 9 de Julio and Além, around six blocks east of the town's central square, Plaza 1810. The new main bus station is on the corner of Heroes de Malvinas and Perón. Lobos's useful **tourist office** (Mon–Fri 8am–2pm) is in the Edificio Bicentenario, by the train station on Avenida Além 149. Smaller information centres that are open on weekends only (9.30am–6.30pm) can be found by the entrance of the Lagunas, and in the train station (℡02227/422275, Ⓦwww.lobos.gov.ar).

There's not much **accommodation** in town; in the centre is the *Class Hotel*, at Belgrano and Almafuerte (℡02227/430090; ❹), which has large rooms, an all-hours café and includes a buffet breakfast. The best of the many **campsites** around the lake is the *Club de Pesca* (℡02227/494089; ❶), where you can rent boats or fish from the jetty. For eating, there are many *parrillas* on the road by the lake, or try *La Tapera*, at the corner of Buenos Aires and Hiriart. The town has a surprisingly lively nightlife – one good bar is *La Porteña*, at Salgado and Junín – and there are regular *peñas* (folklore shows); ask at the tourist office for a schedule.

Estancias around Lobos

Upmarket accommodation is provided by nearby **estancias**, most notably ⚑*Santa Rita* (℡02227/495026, Ⓦwww.santa-rita.com.ar; ❾ with activities included), just beyond the tiny village of Carboni. Its faded pink *casco* has been renovated with great taste by its owners. The rooms are gorgeous – choose between fresh, clean Caribbean decor or darker Old World antique elegance; all have views over the estate. You can arrive at the estancia by train from Buenos Aires (Constitución); the train tracks run right past it and, with prior notice, you can arrange to get off in Carboni, from where the estancia's friendly, English-speaking owners will pick you up.

Tandil and around

TANDIL, 70km southeast of Azul, is set among the central section of the range of hills known as the **Sistema de Tandilia**. The range begins around 150km northwest of Tandil, running across the province to Mar del Plata, on the coast, and only rarely rising above 200m. Around Tandil, however, there are peaks of up to 500m. This is not wild trekking country, but Tandil's hills are good for **horse-riding** and **mountain-biking**. The town itself is well geared for the holidaymakers that come all year on weekend breaks, with some very good delicatessens and restaurants and a lively, bustling feel in the evening. Tandil is particularly popular during Holy Week, when the Via Crucis (Stations of the Cross) processions take place, which end at Monte Calvario, a small hillock topped by a giant cross to the east of the town centre.

Arrival and information

Tandil's **bus terminal** (℡02293/432092) is around fifteen blocks east of the main square, at Buzón 650; there are usually plenty of taxis (℡02293/422466) waiting at the terminal to take you into town, or you could take local bus #501. The **train station** (℡0800/2228736) is at Avenida Machado and Colón, around twenty blocks northeast of the main square – trains leave weekly from Buenos Aires on Fridays and return on Sundays, taking seven hours. The main **tourist office** is east of the city centre, on the main route in at Avenida Espora 1120 (summer Mon–Fri 8am–7pm, Sat 10am–7pm, Sun 9am–1pm; winter Mon–Fri 8am–6pm, Sat 10am–6pm, Sun 9am–1pm; ℡02293/432073, Ⓦwww.tandil.gov.ar), but there are also smaller, helpful offices at the bus terminal and on the Plaza Independencia.

▲ Train Station   ▲ ⓘ

TANDIL

Museo
Tradicionalista

Bus
Terminal

ACCOMMODATION
Albergue Casa Chango   E
Camping Chacra El
  Centinela   G
Hostería Casa Grande   F
Hostería Lo de Olga
  Gandolfi   A
Hotel Austral   B
Plaza Hotel   D
Viñas del Rosario   C

N

Iglesia
del Santisimo ⓘ
Sacramento

PLAZA
INDEPENDENCIA

🅿 ACA Parking

Museo de
Bellas Artes Ⓔ

Danish Lutheran
Church

EATING & DRINKING
Epoca de Quesos   5
Eulogia   6
La Giralda   7
Golden   4
Liverpool   1
Lo de Martín   3
Paca Bar   2

Parque
Independencia

0   500 m

▼ Reserva Natural Sierra del Tigre

Accommodation

Popular for short breaks throughout the year, Tandil is absolutely inundated in January and even more so at Easter, when most **hotels** substantially increase their prices and are often fully booked up to a month beforehand; otherwise, there is generally a good choice of mid-range accommodation. There are also numerous **cabañas** on the outskirts of the town (the tourist office has plenty of leaflets), although you'll need your own transport to reach most of them. Tandil has plenty of **campsites**: *Camping Chacra El Centinela* (●) lies 4km west of town along Avenida Estrada (℡02293/433475, ⓦwww.chacraelcentinela.com.ar); it's a quiet and attractive wooded site on the road out towards Cerro El Centinela, with hot water round the clock and firepits. Log cabins are also available.

Albergue Casa Chango 25 de Mayo 451 ℡02293/422260, ⓦwww.casa-chango .com.ar. Youth hostel in a large, attractive house, colourfully decorated with an artistic touch. Scattered throughout the house are a series of pretty patios perfect for playing chess or chatting with one of the many Argentine students who make up the bulk of the guests. Decent dormitories ($50 per person) or double rooms (●).

Hostería Casa Grande Bolívar 557 ℡02293/431719, ⓦwww.hosteriacasagrande .com.ar. Very comfortable *hostería* in a one-storey stone building, with its own decent-sized pool.

There's a recreation area with a bar, pool table and even a darts board. ●

Hostería Lo de Olga Gandolfi Chacabuco 977 ℡02293/440258, ⓦwww.lodeolgagandolfi.com.ar. A lovely rambling old building with a garden and *parrilla*. The furniture's a bit old and creaky, but the rooms are still good value; there's only a few of them and the place is particularly popular with families, so try to reserve in advance. ●

Hotel Austral 9 de Julio 725 ℡02293/425606, ⓦwww.hotelaustraltandil.com.ar. A friendly hotel in a modern building. The en-suite rooms are equipped with TV and telephone; the hotel does

193

not offer breakfast but there is an adjoining *confitería*. ❸

Plaza Hotel Gral Pinto 438 ☏ 02293/427160, ⓦ www.plazahoteldetandil.com.ar. A three-star hotel with slightly sterile but comfortable a/c rooms and restaurant; rooms at the front overlook the plaza. ❼

Viñas del Rosario Paz 625 ☏ 02293/444776, ⓦ www.vinasdelrosario.com. An attractive boutique hotel in the centre of town, decorated in Spanish colonial style, with jacuzzis and a garden. Extras include massages. ❼

The Town

Many of the streets in Tandil's attractive town centre are cobbled with stones quarried from the surrounding sierra. Its central square, **Plaza Independencia**, on the site of the old fort, is overlooked by the rather grand municipalidad and the **Iglesia del Santísimo Sacramento**. Neo-Romanesque in style, it was inspired by Paris's Sacré Coeur – hence the unusual elongated domes that top the three towers. The streets surrounding the plaza, especially 9 de Julio, have a pleasant bustling feel, particularly in the evenings, when they are filled with people out for a stroll, or sitting outside the cafés and ice-cream parlours.

Northwest of the plaza, on the corner of San Martín and 14 de Julio, is one of Tandil's oldest buildings, a simple, white construction which originally functioned as a staging post and which now houses the *Epoca de Quesos* (daily 9am–11pm; ⓦ www.epocadequesos.com) – a delicatessen and bar where you can buy local specialities, including every conceivable kind of salami, delicious garlic and herb cheeses, strong whisky cheddar, berry conserves and artisan dark stout. The house behind the deli has been as beautifully preserved as the jams and you can wander its tiny, antique rooms, with their homely little hearths straight out of a Hans Christian Andersen tale.

To the south, Tandil's streets slope down towards **Parque Independencia**. The park's entrance, on Avenida Avellaneda, is marked by the twin towers of a mock-Venetian palazzo, while its central wooded hill is topped by a kitsch Moorish castle. A road snakes around to the summit of the hill, from where there's a clear view over the city and an equally kitschy Moorish bar and restaurant, the *Luz de Luna*, complete with belly dancers.

North of the town centre, at 4 de Abril 845, the **Museo Tradicionalista** (Tues– Sun 2–6pm; $5) is in a handsome old building and consists of a staggeringly large collection of artefacts donated by locals. Slightly disorganized, the museum is still a pleasant place to wander and boasts some interesting curiosities, including photos of the enormous **Piedra La Movediza** (literally "the moving stone"), which rested at an inconceivably steep angle on one of the town's many rocky outcrops, before finally smashing to the valley floor in 1912. The stone is so nationally famous that many Argentines are disappointed to arrive and find that it's no longer there; however, a cement replica stands in the place where the original once hovered. Outdoors in the museum's warehouses there are many valuable examples of the huge carts, or *chatas*, used to transport cereals around Argentina; the enormous wheels in the courtyard, the largest in the country, come from a *chata* that needed fifteen horses to pull it. Look out also for the *materas* – huge country hearths – where the gaucho and his clan would take their *mate*, roast their *asado*, stay warm, wash their clothes and just about everything else in between.

Eating, drinking and nightlife

There are plenty of good **restaurants** in Tandil, most of them within a few blocks of Plaza Independencia. *La Giralda* and *Eulogia*, on opposite sides of the intersection of Constitución and General Rodríguez, are attractive, old-fashioned places that both do classic, well-priced *parrilladas*, while the ever-popular *Lo de Martín*, an upmarket *tenedor libre*, serves an impressive range of meats, salads and international dishes. On warm evenings, you'll find plenty of people sitting outside **bars** such as *Golden*, on the corner of 9 de Julio and Pinto, or *Liverpool*, on 9 de Julio and San Martín; the latter's Anglo-inspired interior comes complete with a red phone box and photos of England. For late night drinking, try the centrally located *Paca Bar* on San Martín 775, which sometimes hosts karaoke nights.

The sierras

Opportunities for independent trekking in **Tandil's sierras** are somewhat limited, as much of the area is privately owned. The highest peak here is the **Sierra Las Animas** (504m), southeast of the town centre, not far from the end of Avenida Brasil. It's a two to three-hour scramble over rocks to the top, but the peak lies on private land and to access it you must go with a guide – the tourist office has a list. Much more visited, and more accessible, is **Cerro El Centinela**, a small peak in the sierras topped by **El Centinela**, an upright seven-metre rock balanced on an unfeasibly tiny base. Head southwest along Avenida J.M. Estrada, the continuation of Avenida Avellaneda. The signposted track to the Cerro lies to the left, about 6km out of town. The Cerro has been turned into a *complejo* (complex) with all kinds of attractions, and consequently is perhaps a bit too developed for some tastes. The road now stops just a few metres short of El Centinela, and – should all that driving make you hungry – there's a *parrilla* here, too. Nearby is the base of the *aerosilla*, or chairlift (noon–dusk; $20 return), a fifteen-minute ride over the pines of the valley to another, higher peak from where you can enjoy views over the hills as well as waffles and milkshakes at the *Salon de Cumbre*, a *confitería*. Short walks are possible in the vicinity of the chairlift.

Perhaps the best way to explore the region is with the growing number of companies offering **adventure tourism** opportunities, embracing a range of activities including trekking, abseiling, canoeing and mountain-biking, such as Nido de Condores, at Necochea 166 (☎02293/426519, ⓦ www.nidodecondores .com.ar). If you fancy getting to know the sierras on horseback, contact Gabriel Barletta, at Avellaneda 673 (☎02293/427725, ⓔ cabalgatasbarletta@yahoo.com .ar), who organizes adventurous half-day rides, and regularly takes groups swimming. Mountain bikes can be rented at Av Alvear 121 (☎02293/434313).

Several blocks south of town, on the corner of Don Bosco and Suiza, the **Reserva Natural Sierra del Tigre** (daily: summer 9am–6pm; winter 9am–5pm; $5) is a privately run stretch of sierra where you can see indigenous species such as guanacos as well as exotic deer and antelope. The sierra is also home to the tiny striped *marí marí* frog, barely the size of a thumb and only found here and in Córdoba.

The reserve's highest point is **Cerro Venado** (389m), an easy walk along the unsealed road that winds to the top, from where there are good views over the surrounding sierra. Near the entrance to the reserve there is a small zoo housing pumas, grey foxes and ñandús (a breed of Argentine ostrich).

The Western Pampas

Moving west across the province, you'll cross an unbroken stretch of pampas with little except farmland, homesteads and the odd market town for several hundred kilometres. Increasingly popular with domestic visitors, the mountains of the **Sierra de la Ventana** range offer good trekking near two pretty villages – Sierra de la Ventana and Villa Ventana – and their many well-equipped *cabañas*, perfect to use as a base for exploring the area.

Sierra de la Ventana and around

The rugged **Sierra de la Ventana** mountain range, 550km southwest of Buenos Aires, is the principal attraction of southern Buenos Aires Province. Running from northeast to southwest for 100km or so, the sierras' craggy spine forms an unlikely backdrop to the serene pampas and provides the best opportunities in the province for walking and climbing. The range is named after one of its highest points, the **Cerro de la Ventana**, a 1136m peak pierced by a small "window", or *ventana*; it's located within the **Parque Provincial Ernesto Tornquist**, bisected by the RP-76, the main highway through the sierras. There are plenty of options for accommodation in the area: as well as a base camp within the park, there are two villages within striking distance of the range, with **Sierra de la Ventana** being the best set-up for visitors, around 30km southeast of the park entrance. **Villa Ventana** is a quiet wooded village south of the park, just 5km from the park entrance; it has a more laidback atmosphere than Sierra village.

Formed principally from sedimentary rock during the Paleozoic period, the range is notable for its intensely folded appearance and for its subtle grey-blue and pink hues. Though the harsh, somewhat threatening, peaks may appear rather barren, the area also supports a surprising range of **wildlife**, including pumas, foxes, guanacos, armadillos, vizcachas and copper iguanas, which are named for their distinctive colour and are one of over forty species endemic to the region.

The province's highest peak, **Cerro Tres Picos** (1239m), sits on private land 6km south of Villa Ventana. It is less dramatic-looking than Cerro de la Ventana, but its height, combined with its distance from the nearest base, makes it a more substantial hike. It is usually done as a two-day trek, overnighting in a cave on the way up. The route passes through the **Estancia Funke** (℡0291/494-0058, ⓦwww.funketurismo .com) and you must go with a guide provided by them. The estancia has a campsite and *albergue*; rooms in the nineteenth-century homestead are reserved for German-speakers only, in keeping with the estancia's Germanic origins. Rock-climbing and mountain-biking are also possible. The easiest way of **getting around** the sierras is with your own transport; if you're relying on public transport you'll need to plan carefully: a local service by La Estrella runs along the RP-76, stopping more or less everywhere along the route, including at both park entrances, the turn-off to Villa Ventana and Sierra de la Ventana. Buses go two times a day in either direction. Alternatively, you could take a *remise* (℡0291/491-5517).

Parque Provincial Ernesto Tornquist

The majority of walking and climbing activities take place within a relatively small stretch of the sierras, mostly contained within the **Parque Provincial Ernesto Tornquist**, which covers about 65 square kilometres. There are two **entrances** to the park (summer 8am–6pm; winter 9am–5pm; $10), both just off the RP-76. The Bahia Blanca entrance is around 22km from Sierra de la Ventana village, signposted "Acceso a Reserva Provincial". This is where you'll find the **Centro de Visitantes**, with a good display of photos of the region's flora and fauna and a useful 3D topographical map. From the Centro de Visitantes you can also visit the **Reserva Natural Integral**, a strictly controlled sector of the park where you can see herds of wild horses or explore caves, including one with ancient paintings. Visits to the reserve are in your own vehicle accompanied by a guide ($40) and generally take place twice a day in high season and weekends only in low season – enquire at the Centro.

The rest of the park's treks are in the **Monumento Natural**, an area of the park that includes the national monument of Cerro Ventana; the entrance is around 5km west of the main entrance. There is a helpful *guardaparques*' post (℡0291/491-0039) here, which can usually provide you with a sketchy map of the main attractions, as well as indications of distance, direction and estimated duration of the walks. A well-marked trail to the summit of 1134m **Cerro Ventana** leads northeast from the post. Though the climb to the summit (5hr return trip; access 8am/9am–11am; $10) is not difficult, you need to be basically fit. Follow the park keepers' guidelines, and be aware that conditions can change dramatically. *Campamento Base* (T 0291/494-0999, E rhperrando@yahoo.com.ar), a few minutes' walk west of the *guardaparques'* post, and recognizable from the road by its iron gate, is the best **place to stay** if you want to start out early for the park; as well as a shady campsite ($18 per person per day), the site provides dormitory accommodation and some cabins with wood-burning stoves for up to six people (both $30 per person). You'll need to bring sleeping bags for all accommodation options. Cooking facilities and hot showers are provided and there is a small shop with a few basics. For more luxurious accommodation, head for *Hotel El Mirador* (T 0291/494-1338, W www.complejoelmirador.com.ar; ⑥ with breakfast, half and full board also available), just outside the park; it has some pleasant rooms overlooking the sierras as well as attractive and well-equipped wooden cabins that hold from four to eight people (⑧ with breakfast). The hotel also has a good restaurant and swimming pool. A few kilometres west along the RP-76 good home cooking is on offer at the *Ich-Hutu* **restaurant**, whose specialities include rabbit with peppers and onions in *escabeche*, a delicious sour-sweet vinaigrette.

Sierra de la Ventana village

Away from its rather drab main street, Avenida San Martín, **SIERRA DE LA VENTANA** is a pretty, quiet little village with sandy lanes encircled by streams. Divided into several barrios and dissected by both a railway line and the Río Sauce Grande, the village has a rather disjointed layout. Its centre is really **Villa Tivoli**, which lies west of the railway tracks; here you'll find most shops and restaurants. By following San Martín east over the rail tracks, you'll come first to **Barrio Parque Golf**, a mostly residential area of curving streets and chalet-style buildings. More appealing is quiet **Villa Arcadia** to the north, separated from Barrio Parque Golf by a bridge over the Río Sauce Grande (note that, technically, Villa Arcadia is in a different district, so the tourist office has no information on it). There are various swimming spots throughout the village, mostly to the north of Avenida San Martín, along the banks of the Río Sauce Grande.

Practicalities

Buses from Buenos Aires, La Plata and Bahía Blanca drop you at the small bus terminal on Avenida San Martín. For return journeys to the capital, it's best to buy tickets in advance. The **train station**, also with services from Buenos Aires, is at the intersection of Avenida Roca and San Martín. Right by it, on Avenida del Golf, s/n, you'll find the busy **tourist office** (daily 8am–8pm, although hours may vary slightly according to the season; T 0291/491-5303, W www.sierradelaventana.org.ar).

There's a good range of **accommodation** in and around Sierra de la Ventana village. One option is the enormous and attractive 🏃 *Pillahuincó Parque Hotel*, at Avenida Raíces 161, Villa La Arcadia (T 0291/491-5423, W www.hotelpillahuinco .com.ar), which is set in beautiful grounds with a swimming pool (⑥, half board ⑦). It organizes trekking and biking excursions in the area. There are many **campsites** around the village, though the most popular form of accommodation on both sides of the river is the area's **cabañas**, which can represent good value for money, and are usually quite cosy and come fully equipped. The tourist office has a complete list, or you could try the friendly *Balcón del Golf* (T 0291/491-5222, W www .balcondelgolf.com; ⑦), which has comfortable cabins with all mod cons as well as a sauna and pool. To get there, head over the bridge into Villa Arcadia and follow the road straight for about 300m.

There are few **restaurants** in the village, although there's one very good *parrilla*, the *Rali-Hue*, at San Martín 307, which does an excellent *parrillada* for two people. Other than this, it's mostly typical pizza and empanada joints. A good alternative, especially if you're staying in a *cabaña*, is to visit the popular deli 🍴 *La Rueda*, at San Martín 250, and arm your own *picada* from its range of delicious salamis and cheeses. Alternatively, the smaller and more laidback Villa Ventana – 18km northwest of Sierra de la Ventana village and just off the RP-76 – is also a good base.

Travel details

Buses

La Plata to: Buenos Aires (every 30min; 1hr).
Lobos to: Buenos Aires (every 30min; 2hr).
Mar del Plata to: Bahía Blanca (5 daily; 6hr); Bariloche (1 daily; 20hr); Buenos Aires (hourly; 7hr); Córdoba (3 daily; 18hr).
Miramar to: Buenos Aires (7 daily; 8hr); Mar del Plata (every 30min; 1hr); Necochea (2 daily; 2hr).
Necochea to: Bariloche (2 daily; 18hr); Buenos Aires (hourly; 9hr); Mar del Plata (hourly; 3hr); Tandil (4 daily; 3hr); Tres Arroyos (5 daily; 3hr).
Pinamar to: Buenos Aires (10 daily; 5hr); Mar del Plata (hourly; 2hr).
Sierra de la Ventana to: Azul (Mon–Fri & Sun 1 daily; 4hr); Buenos Aires (Mon–Fri & Sun 1 daily; 8hr).
Tandil to: Azul (6 daily; 2hr); Buenos Aires (hourly; 5hr); Mar del Plata (hourly; 3hr); Necochea (4 daily; 3hr); San Miguel del Monte (3 daily; 3hr).
Villa Gesell to: Bariloche (1 daily; 22hr); Buenos Aires (hourly; 6hr); Córdoba (1 daily; 17hr); Mar del Plata (5 daily; 2hr).

Trains

Azul to: Buenos Aires (1 daily; 7hr).
Bahía Blanca to: Buenos Aires (1 daily; 13hr); Sierra de la Ventana (5 weekly; 2hr 30min).
La Plata to: Buenos Aires (every 30min; 1hr 15min).
Lobos to: Buenos Aires (every 2hr; 2hr 30min).
Mar del Plata to: Buenos Aires (3 daily; 6hr).
Pinamar to: Buenos Aires (3 weekly; 5hr 15min).
Sierra de la Ventana to: Buenos Aires (5 weekly; 9hr 45min).
Tandil to: Buenos Aires (1 weekly; 8hr).

Flights

Mar del Plata to: Buenos Aires (2 daily; 1hr 15min).
Villa Gesell to: Buenos Aires (4 daily, summer only; 1hr).

3

Córdoba and the Central Sierras

CHAPTER 3 # Highlights

* **Córdoba city** Argentina's second city is home to important colonial architecture and one of South America's oldest universities. See p.204

* **Jesuit architecture** Beautifully preserved estancia museums offer an insight into early colonial Argentina. See p.217

* **Cerro Colorado** Fascinating pre-Columbian pictures etched onto the side of a cliff. See p.219

* **Hang-gliding** The region's rugged sierras and professional infrastructure make it a great place for adventure sports. See p.223

* **Estancias** Ride on handsome horses, swim or just relax and enjoy breathtaking views in the unspoilt countryside. See p.225

* **Parque Nacional de la Quebrada del Condorito** Spectacular mountain views and a major condor breeding ground. See p.234

▲ Cathedral and cabildo, Córdoba city

Córdoba and the Central Sierras

The **Central Sierras** are the highest mountain ranges in Argentina away from the Andean cordillera. Their pinkish-grey ridges and jagged outcrops alternate with fertile valleys, wooded with native carob trees, and barren moorlands, fringed with pampas grass – a patchwork that is one of Argentina's most varied landscapes. Formed more than four hundred million years before the Andes and gently sculpted by the wind and rain, the sierras stretch across some 100,000 square kilometres, peaking at **Cerro Champaquí**.

Colonized at the end of the sixteenth century by settlers heading south and east from Tucumán and Mendoza, **Córdoba** was the region's first city. The Society of Jesus and its missionaries played a pivotal part in its foundation, establishing it at a strategic point along the Camino Real ("Royal Way"), the Spanish route from Alto Peru to the Crown's emerging Atlantic trading posts on the Río de la Plata. From that point on, the Jesuits dominated every aspect of life in the city and its hinterland, until King Carlos III of Spain had them kicked out of the colonies in 1767. You can still see their handsome temple in the city centre, among other examples of **colonial architecture**. Further vestiges of the Jesuits' heyday, **Santa Catalina** and **Jesús María**, are two of Argentina's best-preserved **Jesuit estancias**, located between Córdoba city and the province's northern border, just off the Camino Real, promoted locally as the **Camino de la Historia**. Slightly north of Santa Catalina is one of the country's most beguiling archeological sites, **Cerro Colorado**, where hundreds of pre-Columbian petroglyphs decorate open-air galleries of red sandstone at the foot of cave-riddled mountains.

Northwest from Córdoba city is the picturesque **Punilla Valley**, along which are threaded some of the oldest, most traditional holiday resorts in the country, such as **La Falda** and **Capilla del Monte**, sedate towns with genteel hotels. At the southern end of the valley, close to Córdoba city, are two nationally famous resorts: noisy, crowded **Villa Carlos Paz** and slightly quieter **Cosquín**, the latter known for its annual folk festival. By way of contrast, the far north of the province, particularly a stunningly unspoilt area roughly between Capilla del Monte and Santa Catalina, remains little visited: the dramatic rock formations at **Ongamira** and the lovingly restored hamlet of **Ischilín** are just two of the secret marvels hereabouts. Directly south of Córdoba, the **Calamuchita Valley** is famed for its two popular holiday spots, sedately Germanic **Villa General Belgrano** and much rowdier **Santa Rosa de Calamuchita**, from where alpine trails climb into

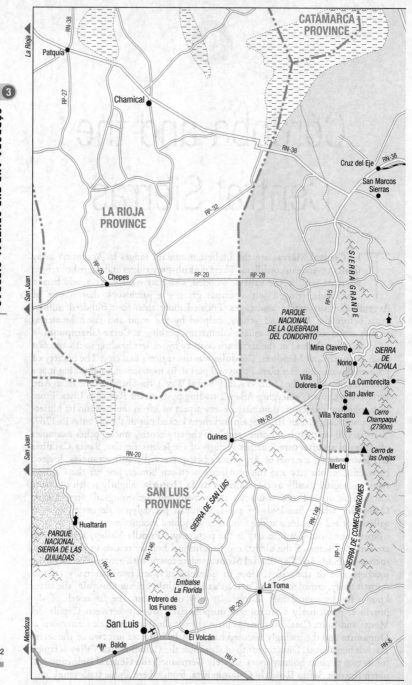

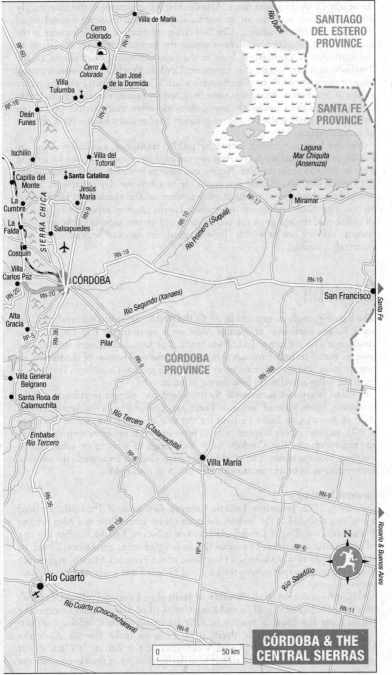

SANTIAGO DEL ESTERO PROVINCE

SANTA FE PROVINCE

CÓRDOBA PROVINCE

Río Dulce

Villa de María

Cerro Colorado

Cerro Colorado ▲

San José de la Dormida

Villa Tulumba

Deán Funes

Ischilín

Capilla del Monte

La Cumbre

La Falda

Cosquín

Villa Carlos Paz

CÓRDOBA

Alta Gracia

Pilar

Villa General Belgrano

Santa Rosa de Calamuchita

Embalse Río Tercero

Villa del Totoral

Santa Catalina

Jesús María

Salsapuedes

Laguna Mar Chiquita (Ansenuza)

Miramar

Río Primero (Suquía)

Río Segundo (Xanaes)

San Francisco

Villa María

Río Tercero (Ctalamochita)

Río Cuarto

Río Cuarto (Chocancharava)

Río Saladillo

RP-60

RP-16

RN-9

RN-9

RN-9

RP-10

RP-17

RN-19

RN-19

RN-20

RN-20

RP-5

RN-36

RN-36

RN-9

RN-168

RN-158

RP-6

RP-6

RP-4

RN-11

RN-8

SIERRA CHICA

Santa Fe

Rosario & Buenos Aires

N

0   50 km

CÓRDOBA & THE CENTRAL SIERRAS

the nearby Comechingones range. **Alta Gracia**, at the entrance to this increasingly urbanized valley, is home to an outstanding historical museum housed in an immaculately restored estancia; Che Guevara spent much of his adolescence in the town. A high mountain pass cuts through the natural barrier of the sierras to the southwest of Córdoba. It leads to the generally more placid resorts of the **Traslasierra**, a handsome valley in western Córdoba Province, and some stunning scenery in the lee of Cerro Champaquí, which is easily climbed from the pretty village of **San Javier**. Along this route lies Córdoba Province's only national park, the **Quebrada del Condorito**, whose dramatic, often misty ravines provide an outstanding breeding site for the magnificent condor and a habitat for a number of endemic species.

Córdoba Province is well served by **public transport**, especially along the Punilla and Calamuchita valleys, but you can explore at your own pace by renting a car or even a mountain bike. Nearly everywhere is within striking distance of the city of Córdoba, which you could use as a base for day excursions, but it would be a shame to miss out staying at some of the estancias in the Central Sierras. The whole region gets overcrowded in the summer, especially in January, so you should try and go in the cooler, drier and quieter months; although night temperatures are low in winter (June–August), the days can be mild, sunny and extremely pleasant.

Córdoba

The bustling, modern metropolis of **CÓRDOBA**, Argentina's second city, sits some 700km northwest of Buenos Aires, on a curve in the Río Suquía, at its confluence with the tamed La Cañada brook. The jagged silhouettes visible at the western end of its broad avenues announce that the cool heights of the **sierras** are not far away, and it's here that many of the 1.25 million Cordobeses take refuge from the valley's sweltering heat during summer.

Córdoba is reputed nationwide for its hospitable, elegant population and its caustically ironic sense of humour. These days Córdoba lacks the dynamism and style of Rosario, its Santa Fe rival for the title of Argentina's second city (see p.282), and many people spend only an hour or two here before sprinting off to the nearby resorts. But Córdoba has a wide range of services on offer, and its excellent location makes it an ideal base for exploring the area, while the colonial architecture at its heart remains an attraction in its own right.

Some history

On July 6, 1573, **Jerónimo Luis de Cabrera**, Governor of Tucumán, declared a new city founded at the fork in the main routes from Chile and Alto Peru to Buenos Aires, calling it Córdoba la Llana de la Nueva Andalucía, after the city of his Spanish ancestors. The Monolito de la Fundación, on the north bank of the Río Suquía nearly a kilometre northeast of the Plaza San Martín, supposedly marks the precise spot where the city was founded and commands panoramic views.

Almost from the outset the **Society of Jesus** played a crucial role in Córdoba's development (see box, p.217), and King Carlos III of Spain's order to expel the Jesuits from the Spanish empire in 1767 inevitably dealt Córdoba a serious body blow. That, plus the decision in 1776 to make Buenos Aires the headquarters of the newly created Viceroyalty of the Río de la Plata, might well have condemned the city to terminal decline had it not then been made the

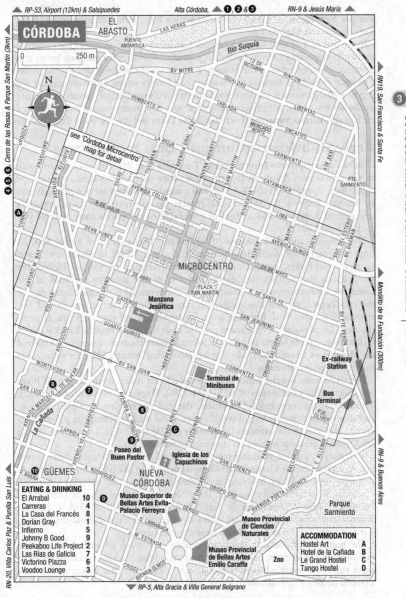

CÓRDOBA

EL ABASTO

LAS HERAS

PUENTE ANTARTICA

Rio Suquía

BV MITRE

12 DE OCTUBRE

RINCON

IGUALDAD

0   250 m

N

HUMBERTO I°

TABLADA

LIBERTAD

MERCADO NORTE

ONCATIVO

SARMIENTO

6 DE JULIO

LA RIOJA

TUCUMAN

AVENIDA GRAL PAZ

RIVERA INDARTE

SAN MARTIN

CATAMARCA

RIVADAVIA

PTE. SARMIENTO

see 'Córdoba Microcentro' map for detail

SUCRE

AVENIDA COLON

LIMA

MAIPU

SGO. DEL ESTERO

BV GUZMAN

9 DE JULIO

AVENIDA F. ALCORTA

DEAN FUNES

AVENIDA OLMOS

SALTA

25 DE MAYO

MICROCENTRO

27 DE ABRIL

BELGRANO

PLAZA SAN MARTIN

R. DE SANTA FE

CASEROS

Manzana Jesuítica

DUARTE QUIROS

SAN JERONIMO

ENTRE RIOS

OBISPO SALGUERO

BV PTE. PERÓN

MONTEVIDEO

CORRIENTES

Ex-railway Station

BV SAN JUAN

INDEPENDENCIA

BUENOS AIRES

BV A. ILLIA

Terminal de Minibuses

Bus Terminal

PJE OLIVER

SAN LUIS

La Cañada

⑦

AVENIDA H. IRIGOYEN

⑧

RONDEAU

PARANA

BALCARCE

L. C. ALLENDE

⑨

Paseo del Buen Pastor

Iglesia de los Capuchinos

SAN LORENZO

ITUZAINGO

A. RODRIGUEZ

⑩ GÜEMES

F. RIVERA

NUEVA CÓRDOBA

OBISPO ORO

AVENIDA CHACABUCO

Museo Superior de Bellas Artes Evita-Palacio Ferreyra

DERQUI

O. LARRAÑAGA

M. ESTRADA

Museo Provincial de Ciencias Naturales

AVENIDA POETA LUGONES

Parque Sarmiento

Museo Provincial de Bellas Artes Emilio Caraffa

Zoo

CRISOL

AVENIDA OLMOS

RN19, San Francisco & Santa Fe ▶

Monolito de la Fundación (300m) ▶

RN-9 & Buenos Aires ▶

3

CÓRDOBA AND THE CENTRAL SIERRAS | Córdoba

RP-53, Airport (12km) & Salsipuedes ▲

URQUIZA

FRAGUEIRO

CORRO

ARTURO M. BAS

BOLIVAR

AYACUCHO

SAN LUIS

AVENIDA MARCELO T. DE ALEAR

LAPRIDA

AVENIDA VELEZ SARSFIELD

RN-20, Villa Carlos Paz & Punilla San Luis ◀

◀ ❹ ❺ ❻ Cerro de las Rosas & Parque San Martín (3km)

EATING & DRINKING

El Arrabal	10
Carreras	4
La Casa del Francés	1
Dorian Gray	8
Infierno	5
Johnny B Good	9
Peekaboo Life Project	2
Las Rías de Galicia	7
Victorino Piazza	6
Voodoo Lounge	3

ACCOMMODATION

Hostel Art	A
Hotel de la Cañada	B
Le Grand Hostel	C
Tango Hostel	D

administrative centre of a huge *Intendencia*, or viceregal province, stretching all the way to Mendoza and La Rioja. Like so many Argentine cities, Córdoba benefited from the arrival of the railways in 1870 and a period of prosperity followed, still visible in some of the city's lavishly decorated banks and theatres. By the close of the nineteenth century, Córdoba had begun to spread south, with European-influenced urban planning on a huge scale, including the

205

Parque Sarmiento. This all coincided with a huge influx of immigrants from Europe and the Middle East.

In the first half of the twentieth century Córdoba emerged as one of the country's main manufacturing centres. Sadly, the post-2001/2001 crisis economic boom that occurred in other parts of the country never reached Córdoba, and the industries that once ruled here are now shadows of their former selves. However, despite the recent global downturn, the local government has invested heavily in arts and culture in the last few years, with the opening of several new museums and cultural spaces, such as the **Museo Superior de Bellas Artes Evita** and the Paseo del Buen Pastor.

Arrival, information and city transport

Córdoba's **Aeropuerto Internacional Taravella** is at Pajas Blancas, 11km north of the city centre. A **tourist information office** operates in the main concourse (daily 8am–8pm; ℡0351/434-8390), and a regular **minibus** service privately run by Transfer Express (℡0351/475-3083) takes passengers to the city centre and a selection of hotels for $53. A **taxi** or *remise* ride to the microcentro will set you back at least $70.

The long-distance **bus station** (℡0351/428-4141) is at Blvd Perón 380. Its impressive array of **facilities** includes banks and ATMs, a pharmacy, travel agency, telephones, restaurants, showers and dozens of shops. Tickets for destinations throughout the region and rest of the country are sold in the basement – advance booking is advisable. The terminal is several blocks east of the city centre, so you might need to take a bus or a taxi to get to and fro, especially if laden with luggage; stops for city buses and taxi ranks are close to the exit. Local buses serving some provincial destinations such as Santa Rosa de Calamuchita, Jesús María and Cerro Colorado leave from the cramped **Terminal de Minibuses** behind Mercado Sur on Boulevard Arturo Illia, between calles Buenos Aires and Ituzaingó.

The city's main **tourist office** is in the Cabildo on Independencia, just off Plaza San Martín (daily 8am–8pm; ℡0351/434-1200, ⓦwww.cordobaturismo.gov.ar). Though not the most helpful of offices, the staff nonetheless have piles of maps and flyers, and there are useful weekly events and walking-tour lists pinned on a board. The staff at the **information centre** (℡0351/433-1982) in the bus station tend to be more helpful, though they cannot book rooms.

Informative, guided **walking tours** of selected downtown sights, lasting two hours, start from the Oratorio del Obispo Mercadillo (daily: summer 9.30am & 4.30pm; winter 10am & 4pm; in English upon request; ℡0351/428-6500, extension 9244). Privately run City Tour (Mon 4pm & 6pm, Tues & Thurs 6pm, Fri 10am, 4pm & 6pm, Sat & Sun 10am & 6pm; $30; ℡0351/424-6605, ⓦwww.cordobacitytour.com.ar) offers sightseeing in a red double-decker bus, starting from the Plaza San Martín near the cathedral.

The majority of the city sights are within easy reach of each other, in the microcentro; to venture further afield you are advised to take a taxi rather than brave the city's terrible **buses**. If you do take a bus, note that you must first buy a **token** (*cospel*; $2), available at kiosks and newsstands.

Accommodation

Córdoba has plenty of centrally located **hotels**. The more expensive establishments tend to cater to a business clientele, lacking much charm or finesse. Demand at the **budget** end of the market is improving, with several new **youth hostels** cropping up to join a sometimes squalid bunch of cheap hotels at the eastern end of calles Entre Ríos and Corrientes, towards the bus station.

There's a passable **campsite**, offering free parking and a range of facilities, at Parque San Martín, behind the Fair Complex, on the banks of the Río Suquía 10km northwest of the city centre. The #E1 bus from Plaza San Martín runs there.

Hostels

Hostel Art Corro 112 ☏0351/423-0071, ⍟www .hostelart.com.ar. Recently given a refurb by friendly French owner Maty, the ambience in the large, comfy common area is bohemian, with the hostel favoured by visiting artists and musicians. Regular concerts and events also arranged. Beds $35 per person, and some double rooms (❸).

Le Grand Hostel Buenos Aires 547 ☏0351/422-7115, ⍟www.legrandhostel.com. The city's newest, biggest and brashest hostel in a French-style building. Clean and spacious with large communal area. Dorms from $37 and several doubles (❸).

Palenque Hostel General Paz 371 ☏0351/423-7588, ⍟www.palenquehostel.com.ar. Noisy but fun hostel in a prettily converted nineteenth-century townhouse that has retained such features as a black- and white-tiled floor, stained-glass windows and wrought-iron banisters. The elegant wood-panelled common areas are great for meeting fellow backpackers. Dorm beds $35 and a few doubles (❷).

Tango Hostel Fructuoso Rivera 70 ☏0351/425-6023, ⍟www.latitudsurtrek.com.ar. Well located, near the Paseo de las Artes, and organizes decent evening meals that make you feel part of the extended family. Dorms $37 per person and some doubles (❷).

Hotels

Azur Real Hotel Boutique San Jerónimo 243/257 ☏0351/424-7133, ⍟www .azurrealhotel.com. A touch of boutique class in Córdoba's microcentro. Stylish norteño decor in a beautifully converted building, with a small outdoor splash pool and sun lounge. ❻

Dorá Entre Ríos 70 ☏0351/421-2031, ⍟www.hoteldora.com. Centrally located but old-fashioned, offering a wide range of facilities including a swimming pool and garage, and large bedrooms. ❻

Hotel de la Cañada Marcelo T. de Alvear 580 ☏0351/421-4649, ⍟www.hoteldelacaniada .com.ar. Comfortable hotel geared towards a business clientele in a modern tower with swimming pool, garage, sauna and gym. ❼

NH Panorama Marcelo T. de Alvear 251 ☏0351/410-3900, ⍟www.nh-hotels.com. As the name suggests, the hotel enjoys fine views from its pleasant bedrooms and en-suite bathrooms, roof garden and small pool. Another establishment of the stylish Spanish NH chain, the *Urbano*, is on the same street at no. 363 (☏0351/410-3960). ❽

Quetzal San Jerónimo 579 ☏0351/422-9106, ⍟www.hotelquetzal.com.ar. Appealing, bright, summery decor throughout, with en-suite bathrooms and friendly staff. Avoid the street-facing bedrooms and you'll be able to sleep at night. ❸

Royal Blvd Reconquista 180 ☏0351/422-7155. The freshest-looking, least squalid of all the hotels near the bus terminal. Rooms are plain but comfortable and breakfasts are generous. ❸

Windsor Buenos Aires 214 ☏0351/422-9164, ⍟www.windsortower.com. One of the few hotels with charm in this category, going for a resolutely British style. Rooms in the classy new wing are more expensive, and the bathrooms are more modern. Sauna, heated pool and gym, plus pretentious restaurant. ❼

The Centre

You can see most of the sights in Córdoba's compact centre in a couple of days. The city's **historic core**, or microcentro, wrapped around leafy **Plaza San Martín**, contains all the major **colonial buildings** that sealed the city's importance in the seventeenth and eighteenth centuries. Its elegant **Cabildo** (colonial headquarters), now houses the city museum, which sits conveniently adjacent to the **cathedral**, one of the oldest in the country. Nearby, beyond a handsome Baroque convent, the **Monasterio de Santa Teresa** is a group of several well-preserved Jesuit buildings, including the temple and university, that form the **Manzana Jesuítica** ("Jesuits' Block"). East of the Plaza San Martín, the eighteenth-century home of Governor Sobremonte (and the city's oldest standing residential building) has been turned into the **Museo Histórico Provincial**, and contains some outstanding colonial paintings, while some interesting examples of nineteenth- and twentieth-century

Argentine art are on display in a splendid French-style house, the **Museo Municipal de Bellas Artes**, a couple of blocks northwest of the plaza.

The city's regular Hispano-American grid, centred on Plaza San Martín, is upset only by the winding **La Cañada** brook a few blocks west of the centre, on either side of which snakes one of the city's main thoroughfares, acacia-lined Avenida Marcelo T. de Alvear, which becomes Avenida Figueroa Alcorta after crossing Deán Funes. Street names change and numbering begins level with the Cabildo.

Plaza San Martín

The **Plaza San Martín** has always been the city's focal point. The square is at its liveliest during the *paseo* hour in the early evening, although it becomes a less appealing place to wander after dark, when it fills with homeless people. Originally used for military parades, the shady square was granted its recreational role in the 1870s when the Italianate marble fountains were installed and semi-tropical shrubberies planted: lush palm-fronds, the prickly, bulging trunks of the *palo borracho* and, in the spring, blazing pink *lapacho* and purple jacaranda blossoms. Watching over all the activity is a monumental bronze **sculpture** of the Liberator himself, victorious on a splendid mount and borne aloft on a huge stone plinth, which was unveiled in 1916 to mark the centenary of the declaration of independence.

The square's southern edge is dominated by the dowdy Banco Nación and the Teatro Real; more banks sit along the eastern edge. Wedged between shops and the modern municipal offices on the pedestrianized northern side is the diminutive **Oratorio del Obispo Mercadillo**, all that remains of a huge colonial residence built for Bishop Manuel Mercadillo. He had the seat of Tucumán diocese moved from Santiago del Estero to Córdoba at the beginning of the eighteenth century, before becoming the city's first bishop.

The Cabildo

On the traffic-free western side of the square is the **Cabildo**, or colonial headquarters, a sleekly elegant two-storey building whose immaculate white facade dates to the late eighteenth century. Fifteen harmoniously plain arches, enhanced at night by lighting, alleviate the otherwise sober exterior. Old-fashioned lamps hang in the **Recova**, a fan-vaulted colonnade held up by slender pillars, in front of a row of wooden doors alternating with windows protected by iron grilles. On the pavement in front of the Cabildo, as elsewhere in the historic centre, a clever *trompe-l'oeil* device of mock shadows has been incorporated into the flagstones.

The original Cabildo was built on the same spot at the end of the sixteenth century, but the present facade was added when the Marqués de Sobremonte became governor-mayor in 1784. Put to many different uses throughout its long history – law court, prison, provincial parliament, government offices and police headquarters – nowadays the building and its inner courtyards are mainly used for exhibitions and official receptions. The Recova, meanwhile, houses the tourism office and Tienda de la Ciudad (daily 8am–8pm), a shop selling books postcards and Córdoban souvenirs.

The cathedral

Immediately south of the Cabildo, and completing the plaza's western flank, is Córdoba's eighteenth-century **cathedral**. One of Argentina's oldest if not its most beautiful cathedrals, it is part Baroque, part Neoclassical – its most imposing external feature, the immense **cupola**, is surrounded by stern Romanesque turrets that contrast pleasingly with its Baroque curves. However, the building's highly porous, cream-coloured stone has suffered badly from ambient pollution and its sooty black facade required extensive cleaning in 2009.

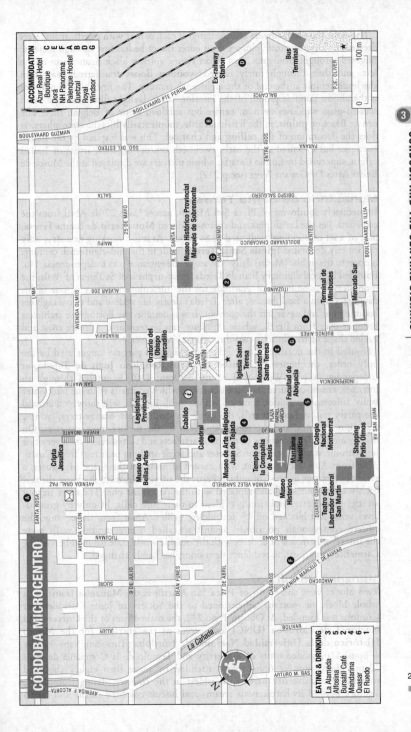

CÓRDOBA MICROCENTRO

ACCOMMODATION
Azur Real Hotel Boutique — C
Dorá — E
NH Panorama — F
Palenque Hostel — A
Quetzal — B
Royal — D
Windsor — G

EATING & DRINKING
La Alameda — 3
Alfonsina — 5
Bursátil Café — 2
Mandarina — 4
Quasar — 6
El Ruedo — 1

Bus Terminal

Ex-railway Station

BOULEVARD PTE PERON

BOULEVARD GUZMAN

Museo Histórico Provincial Marqués de Sobremonte

Terminal de Minibuses

Mercado Sur

Oratorio del Obispo Mercadillo

PLAZA SAN MARTIN

Iglesia Santa Teresa

Monasterio de Santa Teresa

Facultad de Abogacia

Legislatura Provincial

Cabildo

Catedral

Museo de Arte Religioso Juan de Tejada

Templo de la Compañía de Jesús

Manzana Jesuítica

Museo Histórico

Colegio Nacional Montserrat

Shopping Patio Olmos

Teatro del Libertador General San Martín

Museo de Bellas Artes

Cripta Jesuítica

La Cañada

0   100 m

The cathedral's **bell towers** are decorated at each corner with angelic trumpeters dressed in skirts of exotic plumes. You enter the cathedral first through majestic filigreed wrought-iron gates, past Deán Funes' solemn black mausoleum to the left, and then through finely carved **wooden doors** transferred here from the Jesuit temple at the end of the eighteenth century. The first thing you notice is the almost tangible gloom of the interior: scant daylight filters through small stained-glass windows onto an ornate but subdued **floor** of Belgian tiles. The ornate Baroque **pulpit**, in the left-hand aisle, momentarily lifts the atmosphere, as does the decoration of the **ceiling** and **chancel**. This was inspired by the Italian Baroque, but executed in the early twentieth century by local artists of Italian origin, supervised by Emilio Caraffa, whose pictures are displayed at the Museo de Bellas Artes Dr Genaro Pérez (see p.212).

Monasterio de Santa Teresa

Immediately southwest of Plaza San Martín, across Calle 27 de Abril from the cathedral, lies the lavish pink and cream-coloured **Monasterio de Santa Teresa**, part of a set of buildings dedicated to St Teresa. As it is a working nunnery, only the soberly decorated **Iglesia Santa Teresa**, built in the mid-eighteenth century, is open to the public (Matins daily 7.30am) – the entrance is at Independencia 146. Founded by local dignitary Juan de Tejeda, great-nephew of St Teresa of Ávila, the monastery was built out of gratitude for the miraculous recovery of one of his daughters from a fatal disease; after Tejeda's death, his widow and two daughters became nuns and never left the convent. It was designed by Portuguese architects brought over from Brazil, whose influence can be seen in the ornate cross and gabled shape of the church's two-dimensional bell tower.

Housed in the northern side of the complex, in a part no longer used by the holy order, the impressive **Museo de Arte Religioso Juan de Tejeda**, at Independencia 122 (Wed–Sat 9.30am–12.30pm; $10), is entered through an intricate, cream-coloured Baroque doorway, which contrasts with the pink outer walls. Informative guides, some of whom speak English, will show you around the partly restored **courtyards**, the garden of hydrangeas, orange trees, jasmine and pomegranates, and the rooms and cells of the former nuns' quarters. On display alongside all manner of religious artefacts and sacred relics are a very fine polychrome wooden statue of St Peter and some striking paintings from Cusco. Also from Alto Peru is a seat with carved armrests in the shape of jaguars, a symbol of power in pre-Columbian Peru; the original Spanish shield on the seat back was later removed and replaced with the Argentine one. The nuns' devout asceticism and utter isolation is evident in their bare **cells**, lit only by ground-level vents and blocked off by forbidding grilles. Apart from these vents, the austere confessionals positioned against so-called communicating walls were the sisters' only means of contact with the outside world. Life for members of the Carmelite Order, still in residence next door, has barely changed.

Manzana Jesuítica

Two blocks west and south of Plaza San Martín is the **Manzana Jesuítica**, a whole block, or *manzana*, apportioned to the Society of Jesus a decade after Córdoba was founded. At Obispo Trejo 242, the main offices of the **Universidad Nacional de Córdoba (UNC)** also serves as the entrance for the **Museo Histórico de la Universidad Nacional de Córdoba** (Tues–Sun 9am–1pm & 4–8pm; $10; guided tours of university and Templo de la Compañía de Jesús 10am, 11am, 5pm & 6pm). Now attended by more than eighty thousand students, the university here is the oldest in the country, dating from 1610. Venture beyond its harmonious cream- and biscuit-coloured facade and take a look around its shady patios, ablaze with bougainvilleas for much of the year. The **libraries** contain a priceless collection of maps, religious works and late fifteenth-century artefacts, while a ceiling fresco in the **Salon de Grados** shows naked students reaching out to the Muses. Fittingly, this was where applicants for doctorates were quizzed for eight hours a day for three days by their seniors – one wrong answer and they were out.

To the north is Argentina's oldest surviving Jesuit temple, the **Templo de la Compañía de Jesús**, built by Felipe Lemaire between 1640 and 1675. The almost rustic simplicity of its restored facade, punctuated only by niches used by nesting pigeons, is a foretaste of the severe, single-naved interior, with its roof of Paraguayan cedar in the shape of a barrel. Fifty painted canvas panels huddled around the ceiling and darkened by time depict the figures and legends of the Society of Jesus – at ten metres above ground level they're hard to make out without the aid of binoculars. Even more striking is the handsome **Cusqueño altarpiece** and the floridly decorated pulpit. The chapel to the side is dedicated to Our Lady of Lourdes and was known as the Capilla de los Naturales: it was a roofless structure where indigenous churchgoers were graciously allowed to come and pray until the nineteenth century, when it was covered and lined with ornate marble.

Around the corner on Calle Caseros is the **Capilla Doméstica**, the residents' private chapel and "gateway to heaven" – at least according to the inscription over the doorway. Its intimate dimensions, finely painted altarpiece and remarkable ceiling are in total contrast with the grandiose austerity of the main temple. The ceiling is a primitive wooden canopy, decorated with rawhide panels that have been painted with natural vegetable pigments. While the main temple is easily accessible, you have to ask the concierge to let you into the chapel.

South of the UNC, and rounding off the trio of Jesuit buildings, is the prestigious **Colegio Nacional de Nuestra Señora de Montserrat**, founded at a nearby location in the city in 1687 but transferred to its present site in 1782, shortly after the Jesuits' expulsion; the building had been their living quarters, arranged around quadrangles. This all-male bastion of privilege finally went co-ed in 1998 despite fierce opposition. The building's studiously Neocolonial appearance – beige-pink facades, a highly ornate doorway, grilled windows and a pseudo-Baroque clock tower looming at the corner with Calle Duarte Quirós – dates from remodelling in the 1920s. Through the embellished doors and the entrance hall with its vivid Spanish majolica floor tiles are the original, seventeenth-century Jesuit cloisters.

Teatro del Libertador General San Martín
The austere building a block southwest of the Colegio Nacional Montserrat, at Av Vélez Sarsfield 365, is the Neoclassical **Teatro del Libertador General San Martín** (℡0351/433-2323). Of world-class calibre, with outstanding acoustics and an elegant, understated interior, it was built in 1887 and inaugurated four years later, making it the oldest of its kind in the country. Its creaking wooden floor, normally steeply tilted for performances, can be lowered to a horizontal position and the seats removed for dances and other social events.

Museo Histórico Provincial Marqués de Sobremonte
East of Plaza San Martín, at Rosario de Santa Fe 218, the **Museo Histórico Provincial Marqués de Sobremonte** (Mon–Fri 8.30am–2pm; $2; ℡0351/433-1661) is a well-preserved and carefully restored showpiece residence and the city's last private colonial house. Built at the middle of the eighteenth century, it was the home of Rafael, Marqués de Sobremonte, between 1784 and 1796. As governor

of Córdoba he was responsible for modernizing the city, securing its water supplies and extending it westwards beyond La Cañada.

The building's unassuming exterior, sturdily functional with thickset walls, is embellished by a wrought-iron balcony resting on finely carved wooden brackets, while delicate whitewashed fan-vaulting decorates the simple archway of the entrance. Guarding the door are two monstrous creatures, apparently meant to be lions, made of *piedra sapo*, a relatively soft stone quarried in the nearby sierras. The leafy **patio** is shaded by a pomegranate tree, supposedly planted when Sobremonte lived here.

Downstairs, the first rooms to the right house collections of silver and arms, while the rest have been arranged to reflect a nineteenth-century interior; each has an information sheet in English narrating how a typical day there may have passed. Best of all is the museum's outstanding set of paintings of the **Cusco School**, scattered throughout the house. Some of them, such as the *Feast of King David* and *Santa Rita de Cascia*, both downstairs, have been recently and very successfully restored, but others are still in dire need of attention. The portrait of Bishop Salguero de Cabrera displayed in the chapel, dated 1767 and painted at Arequipa, Peru, is a minor masterpiece, while upstairs there is a *Descent from the Cross* featuring a wonderfully contrite Mary Magdalen. Also upstairs, the relentless religious imagery is given a more secular counterpoint by a huge map of South America from 1770 that gives an idea of perceptions of regional geography in the era, and a surprisingly irreverent, scarlet four-poster bed in the "female" bedroom.

Museo de Bellas Artes Dr Genaro Pérez

To take in Argentine art from the nineteenth and twentieth centuries, head for the **Museo de Bellas Artes Dr Genaro Pérez**, a block west of the Legislatura Provincial at Av General Paz 33 (daily 8am–6pm; free). The municipal art gallery is housed in a handsome early twentieth-century building, designed in a French style for the wealthy Dr Tomás Garzón, who bequeathed it to the city in his will. Impeccably restored in the late 1990s, and with fine iron and glass details including an intricate lift, the museum is worth a visit for its interior alone, an insight into how the city's prosperous bourgeoisie lived a century ago. Most of the paintings on permanent display belong to the **Escuela Cordobesa**, a movement whose leading master was **Genaro Pérez** – after whom the museum is named – mostly brooding portraits and local landscapes, some imitating the French Impressionists. Other names to watch out for are those of the so-called **1880s Generation** such as Fidel Pelliza, Andrés Piñero and Emilio Caraffa, the last famous for his supervision of the paintings inside Córdoba Cathedral. The **1920s Generation**, markedly influenced by their European contemporaries including Matisse, Picasso and de Chirico, is represented by Francisco Vidal, Antonio Pedone and José Aguilera.

Cripta Jesuítica

One block east and one north of the Museo de Bellas Artes, where pedestrianized Calle Rivera Indarte intercepts noisy, traffic-infested Avenida Colón, steps lead down into one of the city's previously hidden treasures. Beneath the hectic street lies the peaceful and mysterious **Cripta Jesuítica** (Mon–Fri 10am–3pm; $2), all that remains of an early eighteenth-century Jesuit noviciate razed to the ground in 1928 during the enlargement of Avenida Colón, and rediscovered by accident in 1989 when telephone cables were being laid under the avenue. The rough-hewn **rock walls** of its three naves, partly lined with bare brick, are a refreshing counterpoint to the cloying decoration of some of the city's other churches, and the space is used to good effect for exhibitions, plays and concerts.

Nueva Córdoba and around

South of the historic centre and sliced diagonally by Avenida Hipólito Yrigoyen, **Nueva Córdoba** was laid out in the late nineteenth century. It was designed as an exclusive residential district, but many of Nueva Córdoba's villas and mansions were taken over by bars, cafés, restaurants and offices after the prosperous middle classes moved to the northwestern suburb of Cerro de las Rosas in the 1940s and 1950s. Architectural styles here are eclectic, to say the least: Neo-Gothic churches, mock-Tudor houses, Georgian facades and Second Empire mini-palaces. Today, Nueva Córdoba's bars are frequented by the city's large student population.

Due east of the Plaza España stretches **Parque Sarmiento**, the city's breathing space. The centre of the park occupies high ground, affording it panoramic views of otherwise flat Nueva Córdoba and the surrounding city. Designed by French landscape architect **Charles Thays** (see box, p.113), work was completed by 1900, and included the boating lake and the planting of several thousand native and European trees. This huge open area, crisscrossed by avenues of plane trees, is where the city's main **sports facilities** are located, including tennis courts, jogging routes and an Olympic-sized swimming pool.

Paseo del Buen Pastor and Iglesia de los Capuchinos

Heading along Hipólito Yrigoyen towards Plaza España you reach the **Paseo del Buen Pastor,** a two-storey cultural centre made of stone and glass on the site of a former women's prison, in between the Independencia and Buenos Aires street intersections. A source of much civic pride, the building houses a small art gallery (Mon–Sun 10am–10pm; free), temporary exhibitions on the walls of the covered passage that winds around the building's upper level, and several cafés and restaurants. There are also much hyped "dancing water" displays (Mon–Thurs 5pm, 7pm, 9pm & 10pm, Fri & Sat 5pm, 7pm, 9pm, 10pm & 11pm) when the fountains around the centre's northern end are lit up in garish colours, set to a musical accompaniment. The area around the fountains is the hangout of choice for lovestruck teenage couples. The chapel (Tues–Sun 9am–6pm; free guided tours) is perhaps of most interest, hosting regular music concerts and film screenings. Designed by José Montbanch and completed in 1906, its lavishly decorated interior, with murals depicting religious scenes, is a fine example of Italian-influenced *neomanierismo*.

Opposite the Paseo on calles Buenos Aires and Obispo Oro towers the **Iglesia de los Capuchinos**, an impressive church mixing Neo-Gothic and Romanesque styles, built between 1927 and 1933, that dominates the Nueva Córdoba skyline. Designed by Italian architect Augusto Ferrari, the church's most interesting features adorn its exterior, in particular images of spiders, scorpions and other animals carved out of stone at the base of the columns beside the main entrance. Most notable are statues of hunched men, representing earthly sin, struggling to support the weight of the godly apostles above them. Above the church's central rose window a statue of Saint Francis keeps watch over the city.

Museo Provincial de Bellas Artes Emilio Caraffa and Museo Provincial de Ciencias Naturales

On the eastern side of the busy Plaza España roundabout is the **Museo Provincial de Bellas Artes Emilio Caraffa** (Tues–Fri 10am–8pm; Sat & Sun 10.30am–7pm; $3), a ponderous Neoclassical pile inaugurated in 1916, and recently enlarged with the addition of a modernist new block. It was designed by Johan Kronfuss, architect of the Legislatura Provincial, and is named for the influential 1880s Generation artist who oversaw the decoration of the cathedral interior. Its airy galleries and shady gardens are used for temporary exhibitions, mostly featuring local artists. Next to it on Avenida Poeta Lugones stands the newly opened **Museo Provincial de Ciencias Naturales** (Mon–Fri 9am–6pm, Sat & Sun 11am–7pm; $2). Geared up for children, the museum has rooms on South American megafauna and Córdoba Province's varied topography.

Museo Superior de Bellas Artes Evita

Housed in the Palacio Ferreyra, one of Nueva Córdoba's finest buildings, the **Museo Superior de Bellas Artes Evita** (Tues–Sun 10am–8pm; $3) is set in large French-influenced gardens, designed by Charles Thays, at the southern end of Avenida Hipolito Yrigoyen. Until recently the private residence of the Ferreyra family, the Palacio was built between 1912 and 1916 in an opulent Neo-Bourbon style fashioned by French architect Paul-Ernest Sanson. The building passed into public ownership in 2004 and the new museum, which gutted most of the impressive interior of the house – amid much controversy at the time – opened in 2007, mixing original features like the grand central staircase with new flooring, lighting and a third floor that feels more chic bar than major art gallery, with cowhide adorning the walls and stair banisters. The result is a bold mix of old and new with spacious rooms featuring five hundred works of art, covering an ambitious range of artists and styles.

The ground floor focuses on local artists and nineteenth century Spanish painters while the upper two floors house portrait collections, local landscapes painted between 1920 and 1950 and the eclectic modernist period that followed. Heading up the staircase to the second floor, you pass a silver sculpture of **Evita's head**, a replica made by local artist Juan Carlos Pallarols of the death mask ordered by General Perón following his wife's death in 1952. Other museum highlights include two graphic sketches by Picasso on the top level, as well as a very powerful and moving exhibition about the abuses of the 1970s military dictatorship by Carlos Alonso, entitled Manos Anónimas (Anonymous Hands).

Güemes and the Paseo de las Artes

Bordering the lively commercial area of Nueva Córdoba, the tranquil barrio of Güemes has an altogether different feel. The oldest part of town, it's here that Córdoba's mainly Italian population first settled in the 1860s, originally naming the neighbourhood Pueblo Nuevo. Today many of the old low-rise buildings still stand, although some are in desperate need of restoration work. Lined with antique shops and restaurants, Güemes is Córdoba's bohemian neighbourhood, comparable to San Telmo in Buenos Aires. Every weekend it hosts the **Paseo de las Artes** (Sat, Sun & public holidays, from 5pm), when the streets around calles Belgrano and Archaval Rodriguez are overtaken by an excellent evening market, with handicraft stalls selling everything from *mate* holders to jewellery. It's the best time to visit the neighbourhood and when its bars and restaurants are at their liveliest.

Cerro de las Rosas and Chateau Carreras

The fashionable and prosperous northwestern suburbs of **Cerro de las Rosas** and **Chateau Carreras**, some 3km from the microcentro, are home to many of Córdoba's trendiest nightclubs. Avenida Figueroa Alcorta leads out of the El Abasto area, on the northern bank of the Río Suquía, becomes Avenida Castro Barros and eventually turns into **Avenida Rafael Núñez**, the wide, main street of Cerro de las Rosas, lined with shops, cafés and restaurants. Otherwise, it's a mainly residential area of shaded streets and large villas, built on the relatively cool heights of a wooded hill.

From the northern end of Avenida Rafael Núñez another avenue, Laplace, swings southwest and crosses a loop in the Río Suquía. On the peninsula formed by the river is the leafy district known as Chateau Carreras, named after a Neo-Palladian mansion built in 1890 for the influential Carreras family. This picturesque building, painted the colour of Parma violets, save for a row of slender white Ionic columns along the front portico, houses the **Centro de Arte Contemporáneo** (Tues–Sun 3pm–7pm; free), which stages temporary exhibitions of contemporary paintings and photographs. The mansion is tucked away in the landscaped woods of **Parque San Martín**, another of the city's green spaces, which, like Parque Sarmiento, was designed by Charles Thays. Incidentally, the area immediately around the museum is regarded as unsafe and it's best not to linger here alone or after dusk. Just to the north of the park is the city's **Fair Complex**, while across Avenida Ramón J. Cárcano to the east is Córdoba's massive football stadium, built for the 1978 World Cup finals. Along the avenue, just south of here, are clustered a number of the city's most popular nightclubs (see p.216).

Eating, drinking and nightlife

Interesting **restaurants** and cafés are disappointingly thin on the ground in Córdoba, although the city cranks up a gear during university term time. With a couple of notable exceptions, the city centre has little to offer in the evenings, even becoming rather seedy. Nueva Córdoba and the cooler heights of the Cerro de las Rosas feel safer and have a number of eating places, but they can also be rather colourless. Most of the nightlife has moved to two outlying areas: El Abasto, a revitalized former warehouse district close to the centre on the northern banks of the Río Suquía that buzzes with **bars**, **discos** and **live music venues**, many along Boulevard Las Heras and the even trendier Chateau Carreras area, just south of Cerro de las Rosas, which has a number of more upmarket **nightclubs** to choose from. One of Argentina's best **theatres**, the Teatro del Libertador General San Martín, puts on excellent dance and music shows.

Restaurants and cafés

Alfonsina Duarte Quirós 66. Lively, colourfully decorated café that offers a wide range of typical Argentine fare including *locro* and *humitas* (both $18) and *picadas* (cheese and meat platters) from $50, along with the chance to sip *mate* and listen to the occasional live folklore performance. Open Mon–Sat 8am–2pm & Sun 7pm–2am.

El Arrabal Belgrano 899, at Fructuoso Rivera ☎0351/460-2990, ⓦwww.elarrabal.com.ar. Good-value meals – featuring excellent steaks – but the main reason to come is for the brilliant tango and milonga shows, different each night of the week; a three-course meal and tango show costs $89, far less than in Buenos Aires. Open daily 12.30–3.30pm & 9pm–1am.

Bursátil Café Ituzaingo and San Jeronimo ☎0351/571-9971, ⓦwww.bursatilcafe.com.ar. In Córdoba's small financial district, this lunchtime café takes its name from the Spanish for "stock exchange", and names its main dishes for international exchanges. Food includes classics like *locro* (stew) or international dishes including Caesar salad, with a set lunch menu for $35. Open Mon–Fri 7am–8pm.

La Casa del Francés Independencia 512 ☎0351/425-4258. Attractively decorated in the style of a French bistro, with black and white pictures on the walls. This popular parrilla offers juicy *milanesas* and other excellent value traditional fare; the *budín de pan* is especially memorable. Steaks around $35 and pasta $18.50. Open daily 12.30–3.30pm & 8.30–midnight (shut Sun night and Mon lunch).

Mandarina Obispo Trejo 171 ☎0351/426-4909. Along with *La Alameda* directly opposite (see p.216), this coolly decorated restaurant is one of the few decent places to eat out in the city centre. The menu has plenty of meat, fish and vegetarian dishes, including *rabas a la marinera* ($46), gnocchi ($27) and chop suey ($34). Open daily 8–12.30am.

Quasar Corrientes 141. No-nonsense vegetarian café that does a roaring lunchtime trade. Choose from a range of delicious veggie salads and stir-fries priced by the kilo at the self-service bar if you fancy a break from pasta, pizza and parrilla. Open daily noon–4pm.

Las Rías de Galicia Montevideo 271 ☎0351/428-1333. You can choose from top-quality, Spanish-influenced seafood, fish and meat dishes at this swish restaurant; the weekday

3

lunch-time *menú ejecutivo* is great value at $23. Open daily noon–3pm & 8.30pm–midnight.

Victorino Piazza Av Rafael Núñez 4005, Cerro de las Rosas ☎0351/481-8127. A rusty locomotive on the forecourt serves as a landmark for this café-bar, which prepares hearty meals, including pasta and fast food, plus huge cocktails. The set lunch is great value at $31. Open daily 7am–midnight.

Bars and nightclubs

🏃 **La Alameda** Obispo Trejo 170. With a great bohemian ambience, *Alameda* serves reasonably priced food including empanadas and *humitas* alongside its beers. Patrons leave scribbled notes and minor works of art pinned to the wall. Closed Sun.

Carreras Av Cárcano and del Piamonte, Chateau Carreras. Large disco with "beach" decor plus an eclectic music selection that ranges from country to golden oldies via salsa and Argentine rock. Open Fri–Sun.

Dorian Gray Las Heras and Roque Saenz Peña, El Abasto. Currently one of Córdoba's most popular clubs, playing techno and house on Fridays and pop on Saturdays.

Listings

Airlines Aerolíneas Argentinas, Av Colón 520 ☎0351/410-7676; LAN, San Lorenzo 309 PB, esquina Boulevard Chacabuco ☎0351/425-3030.

Banks and exchange The best for exchanging money are: Citibank, at Rivadavia 104, and BBVA, at 9 de Julio 450. ATMs are everywhere, especially around Plaza San Martín.

Car rental Avis, Av Colón 540 ☎0351/424-6185; Localiza, Av Entre Rios 70 ☎0351/422-4867.

Consulates Bolivia, Bellas Artes 56 ☎0351/411-4489; Chile, Calle Buenos Aires 1386 ☎0351/469-2010; Germany, Elíseo Canton 1870 ☎0351/4489-0900; Uruguay, San Jeromino 167, piso 20 ☎0351/424-1028.

Infierno Av del Piamonte and Cárcano, Chateau Carreras ⚛www.infiernocordoba.com. Large, popular, commercial dance venue, featuring a slightly odd mix of cutting-edge house and fashion parades. Open Sat only.

Johnny B Good Av Hipólito Yrigoyen 320, Nueva Córdoba, and Av Rafael Núñez 4791, Cerro de la Rosas ⚛www.jbgood.com. These identical twins are trendy cocktail bars-cum-restaurants and popular meeting places, with live rock music most weekends. Open Mon–Thurs 7.30–2am, Fri 7.30–4am, Sat 11–4am & Sun 6pm–3am.

🏃 **Peekaboo Life Project** Tillard 1255, El Abasto. Boasts regular appearances by the country's best DJs, as well as the occasional set spun by international stars.

El Ruedo Obispo Trejo and 27 de Abril ☎0351/422-0347. Lively café-bar with music and a mixed clientele, serving fast-food snacks. Open Sun–Thurs 7–2am, Fri 7–3am, Sat 7–4am.

Voodoo Lounge Jerónimo Luis de Cabrera 565, Alta Córdoba ⚛www.voodoocba.com.ar. Billing itself as a "glamour bar", this sleek venue plays everything from rock and pop, to 1980s crowd pleasers and salsa. Open Fri & Sat 10pm–5am.

Internet access CyberUNO, at Duarte Quiros 201.

Laundry Laverap at Chacabuco 313 and Belgrano 76.

Post office Av General Paz 201.

Taxis Tala Car Remis ☎0351/494-7000; Taxi-Com ☎0351/464-4444.

Telephones Telecom, Av Colón 771 & 4880 and 27 de Abril 458, and *locutorios* everywhere.

Tour operators Nativo Viajes, 27 de Abril 11 ☎0351/424-5341, ⚛www.cordobanativoviajes.com.ar.

Travel agents Asatej, Shopping Patio Olmos, Av Bellas Artes 361 ☎0351/426-2005.

The Camino de la Historia

The first 150km stretch of **RN-9** that runs north from Córdoba city towards Santiago del Estero is promoted by the provincial tourist authority as the **Camino de la Historia** ("Historical Route"), as it coincides with part of the colonial Camino Real ("Royal Way"), the Spanish road from Lima and Potosí to present-day Argentina. This was the route taken, albeit in the opposite direction, by the region's first European settlers – the founders of Córdoba city – and the **Jesuit missionaries** who quickly dominated the local economy and culture. Eastwards from the road stretch some of Argentina's most fertile cattle ranches;

to the west the unbroken ridge of the Sierra Chica runs parallel to the highway. One of the country's finest Jesuit estancias, now host to the well-presented **Museo Jesuítico Nacional**, can be visited at **Jesús María**, while beautiful **Santa Catalina**, lying off the main road to the north in a bucolic hillside setting, is still inhabited by direct descendants of the family who moved here at the end of the eighteenth century. Further north, in **Villa Tulumba**, a timeless little place well off the beaten track, the nondescript parish church houses a masterpiece of Jesuit art, the altarpiece that once adorned the Jesuits' temple and, later, Córdoba Cathedral, until it was moved up here in the early nineteenth century. As they developed their intensive agriculture, the Jesuits all but wiped out the region's pre-Hispanic civilizations, but some precious vestiges of their culture, namely intriguing rock paintings, can be seen in the far north of the province, just off RN-9 at **Cerro Colorado**, one of Argentina's finest pre-Columbian sites.

Jesús María

Lying just off the busy RN-9 50km north of Córdoba, **JESÚS MARÍA** is a sleepy little town that comes to life for the annual Festival Nacional de la Doma y el Folklore, a gaucho fiesta with lively entertainment held every evening during the first fortnight of January. On the town's northern outskirts, near the amphitheatre where the festival takes place, is the **Museo Jesuítico Nacional** (Tues–Fri 8am–7pm, Sat & Sun 10am–noon & 2/3–6/7pm winter/summer; $5), housed in the former residence and the bodega, or wineries, of a well-restored **Jesuit estancia**. Next to the missionaries' living quarters and the adjoining eighteenth-century church are a

The Jesuits in Córdoba Province

Even today the city of **Córdoba** owes its importance largely to the **Jesuits** who founded a college here in 1613. It would later become South America's second university, the Universidad San Carlos, in 1621, making Córdoba the de facto capital of the Americas south of Lima. In 1640, the Jesuits built a temple (see p.210) at the heart of the city, and for the next 120 years the Society of Jesus dominated life there. Their emphasis on education earned the city the nickname *La Docta* ("the Learned"), and even today Córdoba is still regarded as an erudite kind of place – albeit politically radical.

But while the Jesuits and other missionaries turned Córdoba into the cultural capital of this part of the empire, their presence elsewhere resulted in the decline in numbers of the native population. The indigenous Sanavirones, Comechingones and Abipones resolutely defended themselves from the invaders. Finally conquered, they thwarted attempts by the Spanish to "civilize" them under the system of *encomiendas*, a forced labour system in which indigenous populations were taught Catholicism and Spanish in "exchange" for their toil. Nonetheless, devastated by influenza and other imported ailments, the indigenous population dwindled from several thousand in the late sixteenth century to only a few hundred a century later. Apart from a few archeo-logical finds, such as rock paintings, the only signs of their former presence are the names of villages, rivers and the mountain range to the south of the city, and discern-ible indigenous features in the *serranos*, or rural inhabitants of the sierras.

Despite their profound effect on the area's original inhabitants, the Jesuits were relatively enlightened by colonial standards, educating their workforce and treating them comparatively humanely. In addition to various monuments in the city itself, you can still visit their estancias, whose produce sustained communities and boosted trade in the whole empire. The Jesuit buildings in Córdoba and four of the remaining estancias around the province – including **Santa Catalina** (see p.218), **Alta Gracia** (see p.228), **Jesús María** (see p.217) and **Caroya**, near Jesús María – have all been declared UNESCO World Heritage Sites.

colonial *tajamar*, or reservoir, and apple and peach orchards – all that remain of the estancia's once extensive territory, which in the seventeenth and eighteenth centuries covered more than a hundred square kilometres.

In contrast to the bare, rough-hewn granite of the outside walls of the complex, a whitewashed courtyard lies beyond a gateway to the right of the church. Its two storeys of simple arches on three sides set off the bright red roofs, which are capped with the original ceramic tiles, or *musleros*. These slightly convex tiles, taking their name from *muslo*, or thigh, because the tile-makers shaped the clay on their legs, are common to all the Jesuit estancias. The U-shaped *residencia* contains the former missionaries' cells, storehouses and communal rooms, now used for temporary exhibits and various permanent displays of archeological finds, colonial furniture, sacred relics and religious artwork from the seventeenth and eighteenth centuries, along with farming and wine-making equipment. The local wine, Lagrimilla, is claimed to be the first colonial wine served in the Spanish court – Argentina's earliest vineyards were planted here at the end of the sixteenth century. Much newer vintages accompany first-rate *parrillas* at the excellent *El Faro* **restaurant**, on the RN-9 at Juan Bautista Alberdi 245 (℡03525/466258) in neighbouring Colonia Caroya, effectively a suburb of Jesús María; try the succulent goat.

Santa Catalina and Villa Tulumba

West of Jesús María, the RP-66 leads to Ascochinga, from where an easily passable trail heads north through thick forest to **SANTA CATALINA**, 20km to the northwest. Almost completely hidden among the hills, Santa Catalina is the biggest, and undoubtedly the finest, Jesuit **estancia** (summer Tues–Sun 10am–1pm & 3–7.30pm; winter Tues–Sun 10am–1pm & 2–6pm; $3) in the region, an outstanding example of colonial architecture in the Spanish Americas. A sprawling yet harmonious set of early eighteenth-century buildings, it is dominated by its church, whose elegant silhouette and symmetrical towers suddenly and unexpectedly appear as you emerge from the woods. Whitewashed to protect the porous stone from the elements, the brightness of the building almost dazzles you when you approach. The **church** is dedicated to St Catherine of Alexandria, whose feast day is celebrated with pomp every November 25; the sternly imposing facade is reminiscent of the Baroque churches of southern Germany and Austria. Inside, the austere single nave, whitewashed like the exterior, is decorated with a gilded wooden **retable** that houses an image of St Catherine, and a fine carob-wood pulpit. On the right-hand flank of the church is an overgrown little cemetery, whose outer wall bears a plaque commemorating the Italian composer and organist Domenico Zípoli, who died here in 1726.

Accessible through a narrow passageway to the right of the church is the stylish *La Ranchería*, a small restaurant-*confitería*, plus a shop selling high-quality local crafts; someone should be on hand to serve you some delicious home-cured ham, a platter of cheese or cooked meals before showing you around the estancia. The charm of this place is that it looks and feels so lived-in: it's still the residence of direct descendants of Antonio Díaz, a mayor of Córdoba who acquired it in the 1770s, following the Jesuits' expulsion from the Spanish empire. Although you can't stay at the estancia itself, **accommodation** in the area can be found at the modern *Posada Camino Real* (℡0351/6134287, ⓦwww.posadacaminoreal.com.ar; ⓻), 10km north from Santa Catalina. The rooms are extremely comfortable; riding and other activities in the unspoilt countryside are laid on and a swimming pool and massages provide welcome relaxation. It's also worth visiting for the beautifully presented gourmet food served in the restaurant (also open to non-guests).

▲ Jesuit estancia, Santa Catalina

The winding track that leads to Santa Catalina continues northeast for some 20km, to where the RN-60 forks left from the RN-9. Another 50km north along the RN-9, at San José de la Dormida, a signposted road heads west to **VILLA TULUMBA**, 25km beyond, a tiny hamlet that's home to a Baroque masterpiece: a subtly crafted seventeenth-century **tabernacle**, complete with polychrome wooden cherubs and saints, and decorated with just a hint of gold, inside the otherwise nondescript parish church. Soon after Argentina's independence, Bishop Moscoso, a modernizing anti-Jesuit bishop of Córdoba, decided that the city's cathedral should have a brand new altarpiece, and asked all the parishes in his diocese to collect funds for it. The citizens of Villa Tulumba were the most generous, and were rewarded with this tabernacle, which had been transferred to the cathedral from the city's Jesuit temple after the Society of Jesus was expelled from the Spanish empire by King Carlos III in 1767.

Cerro Colorado

Nearly 120km north of Jesús María, at the far northern end of the Camino de la Historia, is the **Reserva Cultural Natural Cerro Colorado** (guided tours 11.30am, 2pm & 4pm; $2), home to some fascinating vestiges of pre-Columbian culture. It's located next to Cerro Colorado village, 10km down a meandering dirt track off the RN-9 to the west of Santa Elena. Drivers beware: there's a deep ford lurking round a bend, 1km before you enter the village, followed by another in the village itself.

CERRO COLORADO village, no more than a few houses dotted along a riverbank, nestles in a deep, picturesque valley, surrounded by three looming peaks, the Cerro Colorado (830m), Cerro Veladero (810m) and Cerro Inti Huasi (772m), all of which are easily explored on foot and afford fine views of the countryside. The main attraction, though, is one of the country's finest collections of **petroglyphs**, several thousand drawings that were scraped and painted by the indigenous inhabitants onto the pink rock face at the base of the mountains and in caves higher up between 1000 and 1600 AD; compulsory **guided tours** leave four to five times daily from the *guardería* at the entrance to the village. Nearby is the diminutive **Museo Arqueológico** (Tues–Fri 11am–5pm, Sat–Sun 9am–6pm; free), with some photographs of the petroglyphs and native flora, though it is made slightly redundant by the guide who takes you round the petroglyphs, pointing out the many plant varieties along the way. Some of the glyphs depict horses, cattle and European figures as well as native llamas, guanacos, condors, pumas and snakes, but few of the abstract figures have been satisfactorily or conclusively interpreted – though your guide will offer convincing theories. The deep depressions, or *morteros*, in the horizontal rock nearby were caused over the centuries by the grinding and mixing of paints. Of the different **pigments** used – chalk, ochre, charcoal, oils and vegetable extracts – the white and black stand out more than the rest, but climatic changes, especially increased humidity, are taking their toll, and many of the rock paintings are badly faded. The petroglyphs are best viewed very early in the morning or before dusk, when the rock takes on blazing red hues and the pigments' contrasts are at their strongest.

Direct buses from Córdoba to Cerro Colorado are scheduled on weekends only, but several **buses** a day run from Córdoba to Santa Elena, 11km from Cerro Colorado village; the only practical way to get to Cerro Colorado from here is by *remise*, costing around $25–30. There are **camping** facilities with river bathing in the village, and many *cabañas*, including the friendly, rustic *La Italiana* (℡0351/4246598; ❸). Alternatively, *Hotel Cerro Colorado* has clean, simple rooms and a restaurant (℡03522/15648990; ❸). Of the **places to eat**, the best is *Purinqui Huasi*, opposite the agencia Córdoba Cultural and Museo Arqueologico, serving reasonably priced grilled meats and sandwiches.

The Punilla Valley

Squeezed between the continuous ridge of the Sierra Chica to the east, and the higher peaks of the Sierra Grande to the west, the peaceful **Punilla Valley** is Argentina's longest-established inland tourist area, drawing a steady stream of visitors with its idyllic mountain scenery and fresh air, family-friendly resorts and numerous top-class outdoor pursuits.

The RN-38 to La Rioja bisects the valley, which stretches northwards for about 100km from horrendously noisy **Villa Carlos Paz**, the self-styled "Gateway to the Punilla", some 35km along the RP-34 west of Córdoba. Tens of thousands of Cordobeses and Porteños migrate to this brash inland beach resort every summer in an insatiable quest for sun, sand and socializing – the town is renowned for its mega-discos and crowded bars. A short distance north and overlooked by a sugar-loaf hill, El Pan de Azúcar, is **Cosquín**, a slightly calmer place famed for its once-prestigious annual folk festival. The further north you go, the more tranquil the resorts become: **La Falda**, **La Cumbre** and **Capilla del Monte** have all retained their slightly old-fashioned charm while offering a mixture of high-quality services and a propensity for New Age pursuits. Relatively less crowded, they make for better bases from which to explore the mountains on foot, on horseback or in a vehicle, or to try out some of the adventurous sports on offer. Anyone looking for remote locales to explore should head for the dirt roads between Capilla del Monte and Santa Catalina, where from **Ongamira** and **Ischilín** you can discover some of the region's most remarkable landscapes.

Buses between Córdoba and Villa Carlos Paz are fast and frequent, running around the clock; many of them continue up the valley towards La Rioja and San Juan, stopping at all the main resorts along the way. Naturally, the hinterland is best visited with your own transport.

Villa Carlos Paz and Cosquín

The brash resort of **VILLA CARLOS PAZ** lies at the southern end of the Punilla Valley, on the southwestern banks of a large, dirty reservoir, the Lago San Roque. It sits at a major junction, that of the RP-34, which heads south to Mina Clavero, and the RN-38 toll-road, which goes north through the valley towards Cruz del Eje and La Rioja. Nationally famous, but now spoilt by chaotic construction, pollution and overcrowding, the resort is frequently compared with Mar del Plata (see p.171), only without the ocean. It started out in the 1930s as a holiday centre for well-off Cordobeses, with sandy beaches created along the lakeside. Nowadays people whiz around the lake in catamarans and motorboats, or on water skis. In the town centre, dozens of amusement arcades and entertainment theme parks blare music, while most of the bars and *confiterías* show video clips or offer karaoke. The town sprawls in a disorderly way around the lake – the western districts are generally greener, airier and more attractive. The local population of 72,000 more than doubles at the height of summer, when accommodation gets booked up well in advance.

Some 25km north of Villa Carlos Paz, and barely more appealing, the small but bustling town of **COSQUÍN** nestles in a sweep of the river of the same name and in the lee of the 1260m **Pan de Azúcar**. It's one of the region's oldest settlements – dating from colonial times – and has been a holiday resort since the end of the nineteenth century. The summit of the sugar-loaf mountain, which affords panoramic views of the valley and mountains beyond, can be reached by a chairlift, or *aerosilla* (daily 10am–7pm; $18 return), from the well-signposted Complejo Aerosilla, which sits about 8km north of town and also houses a bronze monument to **Carlos Gardel**, the legendary tango singer, as well as the inevitable *confitería*. Alternatively, you can skip the chairlift and use your legs – from the Complejo Aerosilla it's about half an hour up a steep path. Cosquín has always been associated nationwide with the **Festival Nacional de Folklore** (Ⓦ www.aquicosquin.org), held every year in the second half of January and attended by folk artists, ballet troupes and classical musicians from across the country, although it has declined in quality in recent years. The festival takes place in the so-called Plaza Nacional del Folklore (actually the Plaza Próspero Molina) just off RN-38, which threads through the centre of town.

Practicalities

With services to dozens of local, regional and national destinations, including Buenos Aires and Córdoba, Villa Carlos Paz's busy and cramped **bus terminal** is on Avenida San Martín, between calles Belgrano and Maipú. Right in front of it is the main **tourist information office**, Av San Martín 400 (Jan & Feb daily 7am–10.30pm; rest of year 7am–9pm; ☎03541/421624). During peak periods finding a **place to stay** can be difficult, even though there are many hotels, but residents often stand by the road advertising rooms for rent. There are dozens of **places to eat**, mostly pizzerias. Six blocks east from the centre on Av. Illia 675 is popular *Pueblo Mio*, serving up the usual parrilla and pasta as well as some great fish dishes. In the centre, many restaurants are clustered around Avenida General Paz.

Cosquín's **bus station**, with half-hourly services to and from Córdoba and other Punilla resorts, lies one block west of Plaza San Martín at Presidente Perón s/n. The poor **tourist information office** is at San Martín 560 (summer daily 7am–10pm; winter Mon–Fri 7am–2pm & 2.30pm–7pm, Sat & Sun 10am–1pm & 3pm–7pm; ☎03541/454644, Ⓦ www.aquicosquin.org), five blocks north opposite Plaza Próspero Molina. You can eat very well at two **restaurants** in particular: *Saint Jeans parrilla* at Avenida San Martín and Soberanía Nacional, or *San Marino*, at Avenida San Martín 715, which serves excellent seafood.

La Falda and around

Twenty kilometres north of Cosquín and a little more peaceful still, **LA FALDA** serves as a base from which to explore the nearby mountains – a taste of the far finer scenery to come some way up the valley. Today the town is best known for its annual three-day tango festival (Ⓦwww.festivaldetangolafalda.com) in July, but in the early twentieth century, La Falda was an exclusive resort, served by the newly built railway and luring the great and the good from as far afield as Europe. A major advertising campaign was conducted here by a German-run luxury hotel, **Hotel Edén**, a magnificent holiday palace built in the 1890s, now a dilapidated and unusual tourist attraction (guided visits daily 10am–6pm; $20; Ⓦwww .hoteledenlafalda.com). Nearly all of Argentine high society stayed here in the 1920s and 1930s, as well as such famous international guests as the Prince of Wales and Albert Einstein, and some say even Adolf Hitler. The state confiscated it from its German owners in the 1940s, after which it fell into decline, but its grandiose design and opulent decor are still discernible, especially in the newly renovated lobby, wine cellar and *confitería*. The guided tours take you around the faded

▲ Ex-Hotel Edén, La Falda

③

rooms; night tours, which are good, creepy fun, are also run during the summer and Easter (Jan, Feb & Holy Week 10pm & 11pm), though you'll need decent Spanish if you want to understand the ghost stories.

The RN-38 winds through the western side of the town as Avenida Presidente Kennedy; from it, Avenida Edén heads straight towards the mountainside to the east. For exhilarating views of the valley, head for nearby **Cerro Banderita**; go to the far end of Avenida Edén and take Calle Austria as far as El Chorrito, a small waterfall among lush vegetation. This is the starting-point of the steep one-hour climb to the peak, which many people do on horseback, before riding along the mountaintop. Of the longer routes, one of the most impressive takes you east over the Sierra Chica towards **Río Ceballos**; the views into the Punilla Valley from the peak at **Cerro Cuadrado**, 2km from La Falda, are stunning.

Practicalities

La Falda's **bus station** is on Avenida Buenos Aires, just north of the intersection of avenidas Presidente Kennedy and Edén; all buses from Córdoba and Carlos Paz to San Juan and La Rioja stop here. Several blocks south at España 50, the **tourist office** (summer daily 10am–10pm; winter Mon–Sat 8am–9pm, Sun 10am–5pm ⓣ03548/423007) has stacks of information on accommodation and services, including where to hire horses or rent motorbikes or mountain bikes. There are a number of agencies running **tours** in the surrounding area, including Carlitur at Diagonal San Martín 38 (ⓣ03548/423448).

Accommodation ranges from the beautifully located *cabañas* of *Las Ardillas*, at Las Lomas y El Rodeo (ⓣ03548/426254, ⓦwww.lasardillas.net; ❼), to the very comfortable *Hotel Ollantay*, at La Plata 236 (ⓣ03548/422341, ⓦwww.hotelollantay .com.ar; ❹), and the inexpensive but pleasant *El Hostal de Ana Clara*, at Avenida Argentina 239 (ⓣ03548/422450, ⓦwww.hostaldeanaclara.com.ar; ❸). *Hostal L'Hirondelle*, at Av Edén 861 (ⓣ03548/422825, ⓦwww.lhirondellehostal.com; ❾), has bright rooms, clean bathrooms and a pool. The best-equipped **campsite** is the *Club del Lago,* 500m from the *Siete Cascadas* waterfalls (ⓣ03548/428011, ⓦwww .campingclubdel-lago.com), due west of the bus terminal. Places to **eat** include the excellent *La Parrilla de Raúl*, a Calle Buenos Aires 111, while simple vegetarian fare can be found at *Pachamama*, at Av Edén 127.

La Cumbre and around

LA CUMBRE, a small, leafy town just east of the RN-38, 14km north of La Falda, is a great spot for fishing, exploring the mountains, participating in adventure pursuits or just relaxing. Over 1140m above sea level, it enjoys mild summers and cool winters, and has been known to be blanketed in snow. Several trout-rich streams rush down the steep mountains and gurgle through town, among them the Río San Gerónimo, which runs past the central Plaza 25 de Mayo. A British community was established here when the railways were built in the nineteenth century, and La Cumbre's prestigious golf club, its predominantly mock-Tudor villas and manicured lawns testify to a long-standing Anglo-Saxon presence. But despite the resort's genteel appearance it has become synonymous with **hang-gliding**; every March international competitions are held here. Cerro Mirador, the cliff-top launching-point for hang-gliding and parasailing, is near the ruined colonial estancia and chapel of **Cuchi Corral**, 8km due west of La Cumbre and worth visiting for the views alone, whether or not you join in the lemming-like activities.

Anyone with a literary bent will enjoy the small museum at **El Paraíso**, in Cruz Chica, over 2km to the north of La Cumbre as you head towards Los Cocos (guided daily visits Jan & Feb 10.30am–1pm & 4–8pm, April–Sept 2–6pm; March & Oct–Dec 3–7pm; $10). The handsome Spanish-style house, built in 1915 and with an exquisite garden designed by Charles Thays (see box, p.113), was home to hedonistic writer Manuel "Manucho" Mujica Laínez, whose novel *Bomarzo* is regarded as an Argentine classic. Written in 1962, it was turned into an opera whose premiere at the Teatro Colón in Buenos Aires in 1967 was banned by the military dictatorship. The house, where it is said he held frequent orgies – he and his wife kept separate lovers, his mostly men – contains a delightful collection of his personal effects, including 15,000 books, paintings, photographs and all manner of objects. Look out in particular for the "Gate to Heaven", an ornate iron door decorated with erotic figures; a small gallery in the basement hosts exhibitions of mainly local artists.

Running roughly parallel to the RN-38 as it heads south to Villa Giardino is the winding **Camino de los Artesanos**, along which you'll find over two dozen establishments selling all manner of crafts – silver- and pewterware, macramé, ceramics, woollens – along with breweries, shops serving *dulce de leche* and home-made cakes and even places offering yoga and massages.

One of the province's most spectacular scenic routes, ideal for mountain bikes and strong calf muscles, takes you east along the **Camino del Pungo**. Beyond **Estancia El Rosario** (daily 8.30am–7pm), a farmhouse selling its own jams, *dulce de leche*, *alfajores* and other goods to delight a sweet tooth, signposted from La Cumbre golf course to the southeast of La Cumbre's town centre, it climbs the mountainside and plunges into dense pine forest, before fording the Río Tiu Mayu. It then passes through luxuriant forest – eucalyptus, cacti, palms, firs and osiers – and crosses the summit of the Sierra Grande, before reaching Ascochinga, 41km away, and Santa Catalina (see p.218). A right-hand fork immediately before the Río Tiu Mayu takes you south along a roughly surfaced but spectacular road. At the end of the road, some 45km from La Cumbre, is the old **Estancia Santa Gertrudis** (Wed–Fri 11.30am–7.30pm, Sat & Sun 11.30am–8.30pm; ☏0351/155294778, ⒲www.candonga.com.ar), whose most interesting feature is the splendid eighteenth-century Jesuit chapel of **Candonga** – a historic national monument – with its pristine walls, ochre-tiled roof and rough-hewn stone steps. The majestic curve of its porch, the delicate bell tower and lantern-like cupola fit snugly into the bucolic valley setting, set off by a fast-flowing brook that sweeps through the pampas fields nearby. The estancia serves lunch and tea at the remodelled *casco* (farmhouse), with many of the ingredients coming from the estancia's own orchards.

Practicalities

La Cumbre's **tourist office** (summer daily 8.30am–11pm; winter daily 8.30am–8.30pm; ☏03548/452966, ⒲www.lacumbre.gov.ar) is in the former train station where Avenida San Martín intersects Avenida Caraffa, 300m southwest of the central square. Immediately to the south, the **bus station** is at Caraffa and General Paz; services to and from Córdoba and Capilla del Monte (see opposite) are half-hourly. La Cumbre has a good choice of upmarket **accommodation**, including the *Posada San Andrés*, at Benitz and Monteagudo (☏03548/451165, ⒲www .posadasanandres.com; ⑥), which has excellent breakfasts and a swimming pool; the very comfortable *Posada Los Cedros*, at Argentina 837 (☏03548/451028, Ⓔposadaloscedros@arnet.com.ar; ⑥); and the *Gran Hotel La Cumbre*, near the golf course at Posadas s/n (☏03548/451550, ⒲www.granhotellacumbre.com; ⑦) – a rather old-fashioned but cosy place, with great views. There's less choice at the budget end – *Posada de la Montaña*, at 9 de Julio 753 (☏03548/451867, ⒲www .posadadelamontania.com.ar; ④), is probably your best bet. La Cumbre's top campsite is the *El Paso*, up near the Cristo Redentor statue at Monseñor Pablo Cabrera s/n (℡03548/452545). The finest **restaurant** for trout and other regional specialities is *La Casona del Toboso*, at Belgrano 349. Delicious cakes are on offer at *Dani Cheff*, opposite the tourist office at Avenida Caraffa and Belgrano.

Should you be tempted by the prospect of something a bit adventurous, try Escuela de Montaña George Mallory (℡03548/492271) for **rock-climbing**, or Aero Club La Cumbre (℡03548/452544) for **hang-gliding**. **Horses** can be hired from El Rosendo at Juan XXIII s/n (℡03548/15565150).

Capilla del Monte and around

Lively **CAPILLA DEL MONTE**, 17km north of La Cumbre, sits at the confluence of the rivers Calabalumba and Dolores against the bare-sloped Cerro Uritorco, at 1979m the highest peak of the Sierra Chica. It was a resort for Argentina's bourgeoisie at the end of the nineteenth century, as testified by the many luxurious villas, some of them slightly or very dilapidated. These days it attracts more alternative vacationers, as you can tell from the number of hotels and restaurants calling themselves *naturista*, or back to nature. The town has little to offer in the way of sights, but it serves as an appealing base along the valley for treks into the mountains or for trying out hang-gliding and other pursuits. Central Plaza San Martín lies only a couple of blocks east of the RN-38, which runs through the west of the town, parallel to the Río de Dolores. From the plaza, Diagonal Buenos Aires, the busy commercial pedestrian mall, runs southeast to the quaint former train station on Calle Pueyrredón; it's claimed to be South America's

Estancias around the Sierra Chica

Although the Jesuit **estancias** in the Sierra Chica do not generally allow the opportunity to stay the night, there are a number of estancias around Santa Catalina and in the Punilla Valley that have opened their doors to visitors. These places can make excellent spots to laze away a few days in the countryside, horse-riding and swimming; they can also be used as a base for visiting the area's other attractions.

An hour's drive northwest of Córdoba, ⚲ *Estancia Los Potreros* (℡011/48782692, Ⓦwww.estancialospotreros.com; Ⓞ) is an authentic working estancia that has been owned by the same Anglo-Argentine family for four generations. This is the place to come if you want to do some horseriding – the friendly owners will take you on trips around the area, organize polo lessons and tournaments, and even allow you to observe or help with farm activities. The animals are so well looked after and trained that even reluctant riders usually end up happily on horseback. Accommodation is in the attractive adobe *casco*, and you dine with the family; the price of US$360 per person per night (Jan–April; Oct–Dec) & US$290 per person per night (May–Sept) includes all activities and facilities, transport from Córdoba and delicious food and drink. **Trail rides**, staying at local homesteads, also take place throughout the year, but must be arranged in advance.

A different kind of stay can be had at *Estancia La Paz* (℡03525/492073, Ⓦwww .estancialapaz.com; Ⓞ), near Ascochinga. In the nineteenth century, this was the beloved homestead of President Roca (see p.594) where he entertained many of the powerful men of his day. In many ways resembling a country hotel, with a spa, putting green, rowing lake and large, comfortable rooms, it's the place to head for if you'd rather feel like a pampered politician than a pioneer. Meals are served on a tiled verandah that offers great views over the estancia's extensive, manicured grounds, landscaped by the omnipresent Charles Thays. Day visits possible (US$120), including breakfast, lunch and snack; otherwise, half-board stays are US$165 per person per night, excluding drinks and transfers.

only roofed street, an assertion nowhere else has rushed to contend. A number of safe bathing areas, or *balnearios*, can be found along the Río Calabalumba, including *Balneario Calabalumba*, at the northern end of General Paz, and *Balneario La Toma*, at the eastern end of Avenida Sabattini.

In addition to the fresh air, unspoilt countryside and splendid opportunities for sports pursuits, such as trekking and fishing, many visitors are also drawn to the area by claims of **UFO sightings**, "energy centres" and numerous local **legends**. One such legend asserts that when Calabalumba, the young daughter of a witch-doctor, eloped with Uritorco, the latter was turned into a mountain while she was condemned to eternal sorrow, her tears forming the river that flows from the mountainside. Incidentally, the **Cerro Uritorco**, the focus for Capillo del Monte's supposed paranormal activity, is well worth the climb (about 4hr to the top; $20; register at the base of the mountain) for the grandiose views across the valley to the Sierra de Cuniputo to the west. The steep clamber up a well-trodden path starts 3km from the *Balneario Calabalumba*, northeast of Plaza San Martín, and cuts through private property. Only part of the climb is shaded, so take water with you. You must set off between 8am and noon and start your return by 3pm in winter and 5pm in summer, which rather rules out opportunities for UFO-hunting.

Fifteen kilometres out of Capilla del Monte is the entrance to **LOS TERRONES** (Ⓦwww.losterrones.com; daily 9am–dusk; $14), an amazing formation of multi-coloured rocks on either side of a 5km dirt track. You can drive through the privately owned park quickly enough, but it's far better to walk along the signposted path that winds in between the rocks (a 1.5hr circuit), to more clearly admire the strange shapes, all gnarled and twisted, some of them resembling animals or human forms. To get here head 8km north of town, along the RN-38, then head east at Charbonier along a small track towards Sarmiento.

Practicalities

Capilla del Monte's **bus station** is at the corner of Corrientes and Rivadavia, 200m south of Plaza San Martín; there are regular bus services down the valley to Córdoba and up to the transport hub of Cruz del Eje. The old railway station, in the centre, houses the dynamic **tourist information centre**, at Pueyrredón s/n (daily 8am–8pm; Ⓣ03548/481903, Ⓦwww.capilladelmonte.gov.ar), whose eager staff have the details of dozens of guides and operators offering treks, horseriding and hang-gliding in the nearby mountains. The town's **hotel** options include the clean and smart *Hotel Petit Sierras*, at Pueyrredón 622 and Salta (Ⓣ03548/481667, Ⓔhotelpetitsierras@estaciondelcerro.com.ar; ❹); and the plain but tidy *Hostería Las Gemelas*, at L.N. Além 967 (Ⓣ03548/481186, Ⓔhosterialasgemelas@yahoo .com.ar; ❹). The town's youth hostel, *Los 3 Gómez* (Ⓣ03548/482647, Ⓦwww .hosterialos3gomez.com.ar), has a laidback atmosphere and a decent outdoor area with dorm rooms from $38 and some doubles (❸). The best **campsite** is the *Calabalumba*, on the riverbank, near the bridge at the end of General Paz (Ⓣ03548/489601, Ⓔcamping@capilladelmonte.gov.ar). Most of the **cafés and restaurants** are strung along Diagonal Buenos Aires: *Valpisa*, at Buenos Aires 102, specializes in pizzas and pasta while at *Ongamira*, at Paseo La Cascada, you can build your own veggie salads.

Ongamira and Ischilín

ONGAMIRA, some 25km northeast of Capilla del Monte and 1400m above sea level, is a remote hamlet. It famed for its **Grutas**, strange caves amid rock formations sculpted by wind and rain in the reddish sandstone, and painted with black, yellow and white pigments by indigenous tribes some six hundred years ago. The drawings depict animals, human figures and abstract geometric patterns, and must be surveyed from a special viewpoint (daily 9.30am–6.30pm; $8), as the extremely fragile stone is gradually crumbling away and many of the paintings have already been lost. Nearby is the **Parque Natural Ongamira** (daily 9am–8pm, weekends only in winter; $8), a private park affording breathtaking views of the cerros Pajarillo, Áspero and Colchiquí; you can see condors and go on horseback rides. The road, with magnificent panoramas all the way, eventually leads on to Santa Catalina and Cerro Colorado. Lying discreetly off this road in extensive grounds, 🕱 *Estancia Dos Lunas* (☏011/5032-3410, Ⓦwww.doslunas.com.ar; Ⓞ) is one of the best places to stay in northern Córdoba. Simple but comfortable rooms are housed in English-style long houses, while the large pool offers views of the dramatic surroundings, including the peak of Cerro Uritorco (1949m). Gourmet cooking, excellent horse rides (including full-moon outings), massages and a professional touch are the estancia's major assets.

A dirt road immediately west of Ongamira snakes through mesmerizing rocky landscapes and past an unexpected polo ground to the once-abandoned village of **ISCHILÍN**, some 20km further north. A couple of kilometres before you reach the village is the signposted **Casa Museo Fernando Fader** (Thurs–Sun noon–5pm; free), a brick house built by the painter Fernando Fader, an adoptive Argentine born of German parents who settled here in the vain hope of curing his chronic tuberculosis. His paintings, well executed if strongly influenced by Van Gogh and at times Monet, are best seen at the provincial fine-arts museum near Mendoza (see p.394). Only one is on show at this museum, alongside various personal effects and furniture, but the mock-Italianate garden is worth a visit. In the village itself, the charming 🕱 *Hostería La Rosada* (☏03521/423057, Ⓦwww.ischilinposada.com.ar; Ⓞ) is run by the artist's grandson and family; you can stay the night or just enjoy the fine food and swimming pool. Don't miss the chance of being taken around the village, devotedly renovated by Carlos Fader himself, including the ancient school, now in use once more, the recreation of a traditional *pulpería* and the old police station. Ischilín's spectacular **Plaza de Armas**, not unlike an English village green, is dominated by a venerable algarrobo tree, its gigantic gnarled trunk host to epiphytic cacti and skeins of moss, and by the early eighteenth-century Jesuit church, **Nuestra Señora del Rosario**, its facade painted mustard yellow. Ask around for the key to visit the delightfully primitive interior, with its rickety choir balcony made of algarrobo wood, bearing a pithy Latin inscription.

The Calamuchita Valley

Long established as one of Córdoba Province's major holiday destinations, and where many cityfolk have weekend or summer homes, the green **Calamuchita Valley** begins 30km south of Córdoba city at the Jesuit estancia town of **Alta Gracia** – a popular day-trip destination from Córdoba – and stretches due south for over 100km, between the undulating Sierra Chica to the east and the steep Sierra de Comechingones to the west. The varied vegetation that covers the valley's sides provides a perfect habitat for hundreds of species of birds and other fauna. Two large and very clean reservoirs, Embalse Los Molinos in the north and Embalse Río Tercero in the south, both dammed in the first half of the twentieth century for water supplies, electricity and recreational angling, give the valley its alternative name, sometimes used by the local tourist authority: **Valle Azul de los Grandes Lagos** ("Blue Valley of the Great Lakes"). It's believed that the area's **climate** has been altered by their creation, with noticeably wetter summers than in the past.

The valley's two main towns could not be more different: **Villa General Belgrano** is a chocolate-box resort with a predominantly Germanic population, whereas **Santa Rosa de Calamuchita**, the valley's rather brash capital, is youthful and dynamic but far less picturesque. Both, however, are good bases for exploring the beautiful Comechingones mountains, whose Camiare name means "mountains and many villages". One of these villages, the quiet hamlet of **La Cumbrecita**, would not look out of place in the Swiss Alps, and is the starting-point for some fine highland walks. All the villages offer a wide range of accommodation and high-quality places to eat, making them ideal for anyone wanting to avoid big cities like Córdoba. Frequent **buses** and *trafics* run along the arterial RP-5 between Córdoba and Santa Rosa de Calamuchita, some stopping at Alta Gracia en route.

Alta Gracia

Less than 40km south of Córdoba and 3km west of busy RP-5, historic **ALTA GRACIA** lies at the northern entrance of the Calamuchita Valley. It is now rather nondescript, but in the 1920s and 1930s its location between the city and the mountains made it popular with the wealthy bourgeoisie of Buenos Aires and Córdoba, who built holiday homes in the town – Che Guevara, surprisingly, spent some of his youth here, and revolutionary composer Manuel de Falla fled here from the Spanish Civil War. The original colonial settlement dates from the late sixteenth century, but in 1643 it was chosen as the site for a **Jesuit estancia** around which the town grew up. After the Jesuits' expulsion in 1767, the estancia fell into ruin but was inhabited for a short time in 1810 by Viceroy Liniers, forced to leave Córdoba following the Argentine declaration of independence. The **Museo Casa del Virrey Liniers** is housed in the Residencia, the Jesuits' original living quarters and workshops (summer Tues–Fri 9am–8pm, Sat & Sun 9.30am–8pm; winter Tues–Fri 9am–1pm & 3–7pm, Sat & Sun 9.30am–12.30pm & 3.30–6.30pm; $4; guided tours in English upon request; Ⓦwww.museoliniers.org.ar). Entered through an ornate Baroque doorway on **Plaza Manuel Solares**, the town's main square, the beautifully restored Residencia, with its colonnaded upper storey, forms two sides of a cloistered courtyard. Exhibits consist mainly of furniture and art dating from the early nineteenth century, but there are also some magnificent examples of colonial religious paintings and sculptures. Perhaps the most interesting sections of the museum are the painstakingly recreated kitchen and the *herrería*, or forge, the oldest part of the estancia. The church adjoining the Residencia, though in pitifully poor repair, is used regularly for Mass; it lies immediately to the south.

Directly north of the estancia are the peaceful waters of the **Tajamar**, or estancia reservoir, one of Argentina's earliest hydraulic projects, dating from 1659; it both supplied water for the community and served as a millpond. In its mirror-like surface is reflected the town's emblematic **clock tower**, erected in 1938 to mark 350 years of colonization in the area. Avenida Sarmiento leads up a slope from the western bank of the Tajamar into **Villa Carlos Pellegrini**, an interesting residential district of quaint timber and wrought-iron dwellings, dating from when rich Porteños built summerhouses here in the fashionable so-called *estilo inglés*, a local interpretation of mock-Tudor. Many of them are sadly dilapidated, but one, Villa Beatriz, at Avellaneda 501, was for several years in the 1930s home to the family of **Che Guevara**. His doctor recommended the dry continental climate of the sierras, and his family rented various houses in Alta Gracia during his adolescence in the vain hope of curing his debilitating asthma. Homage is paid to the young revolutionary-to-be here in the **Museo Casa de Ernesto "Che" Guevara** (Jan & Feb daily 9.30am–7pm; March–Dec daily

▲ Museo Casa de Ernesto "Che" Guevara

9am–7pm except Mon from 2pm; $5), where photographs, correspondence and all manner of memorabilia are lovingly displayed.

Another villa, Los Espinillos, nearby at Av Carlos Pellegrini 1011, was Spanish composer **Manuel de Falla's home** for four years until his death in 1946; like Che Guevara, he came to the sierras for health reasons, in his case because he suffered from chronic tuberculosis. Now the **Museo Manuel de Falla** (Jan & Feb daily 9am–7pm; March–Dec until 8pm; $3), exhibiting his piano and other personal effects, the well-preserved house affords fine views of the nearby mountains. Piano and other music recitals are given, normally on Saturday evenings, in the small concert hall in the garden.

Practicalities

Regular **buses** from Córdoba use the omnibus terminal on Calle P. Butori and Avenida Presidente Perón , around eight blocks west of the Tajamar, while the **tourist office** is in the landmark clock tower at the corner of Avenida del Tajamar and Calle del Molino (Dec–Feb daily 8am–11pm; Mar–Nov Mon–Thurs 8am–8pm & Fri–Sun 8am–9pm; ☎03547/428128, ⓦwww.altagracia.gov.ar). Of the town's several, mostly uninspiring **restaurants**, you are best off at *Morena*, occupying a fine Neocolonial house at Sarmiento 417, heading towards the Manuel de Falla museum; the rabbit, trout, pasta and pizza are all excellent, as is the service.

Villa General Belgrano

Just over 50km south of Alta Gracia, reached along attractive corniches skirting the blue waters of the **Embalse Los Molinos**, and less than a couple of kilometres west of the RP-5, is the demure resort of **VILLA GENERAL BELGRANO**.

Despite being one of Argentina's most famous sons, **Ernesto "Che" Guevara** is little celebrated in his homeland, with nothing like the number of monuments and museums and the amount of fanfare you might expect for such as international icon. This is no doubt at least in part due to Che fighting his battles elsewhere – primarily, of course, in Cuba, where he is idolized, but also in places like Bolivia, where he finally met his end. It is hard to know whether Argentine authorities ignore his legacy because he was, well, anti-authoritarian, or whether they feel offended that he had the cheek to go and instigate revolution outside of *la gran Argentina*. Whatever his claims to supra-nationality may be, though, Che was certainly Argentine – a fact reflected even in his nickname ("che" being a common interjection, more or less meaning "hey", and very characteristic of the River Plate region). He was born to a middle-class family in **Rosario** (see p.282 & p.290) in 1928, and moved to **Alta Gracia** with his family at the age of 5, going to Deán Funes college in Córdoba before moving on to the Universidad de Buenos Aires to study medicine. Three years later, he set off on his famous **motorbike trip** around South America, during which he was exposed to the continent's poverty and inequalities, as well as the cultural similarities that led him to believe in the need to foster a sense of regional rather than national identity. He did return to Buenos Aires to finish his studies, but a month after graduating he was back on the road, this time heading to Guatemala and a meeting with local radicals which eventually led him to Fidel Castro, Cuba and his status as one of the great revolutionary figures of the twentieth century.

The unspoiled alpine scenery of its back country, the folksy architecture and decor and the Teutonic traditions of the local population all give the place a distinctly alpine feel. Many of the townspeople are of German, Swiss or Austrian origin, some of them descended from escapees from the *Graf Spee*, the pocket battleship scuttled by its captain off the Uruguayan coast on December 13, 1939, after it was surrounded by Allied cruisers during World War II's landmark Battle of the River Plate. The older generations still converse in German, maintain a Lutheran outlook and read the local German-language newspaper, while souvenir shops sell cuckoo clocks, tapes of oompah music and other such curios. Whether or not the place's kitsch cosiness holds appeal, Villa General Belgrano is a decent base for the region if you'd rather avoid Córdoba itself, with plentiful and varied accommodation choices. However, if adventure sports or nightclubs are what you're after, you're better off heading for Santa Rosa de Calamuchita, a short way to the south (see p.231).

Essentially a sedate place favoured by families and older visitors attracted by its creature comforts and hearty food – especially welcome during winter snow – Villa General Belgrano shifts up a gear or two during one of its many **festivals**. While the Feria Navideña, or Christmas festival, the Fiesta de Chocolate Alpino, in July, and the Fiesta de la Masa Vienesa, a Holy Week binge of apple strudel and pastries, are all eagerly awaited, the annual climax, during ten days at the beginning of October, is the nationally famous **Oktoberfest**, Villa General Belgrano's answer to Munich's world-renowned beer festival. Stein after stein of foaming Pilsener is knocked back, after which merry revellers stagger down Villa Belgrano's normally genteel streets to their hotels.

Two streams, Arroyo del Molle and Arroyo La Toma, trickle through the town before joining Arroyo del Sauce, 1km to the south. **Avenida Julio Roca**, the town's main drag, is lined with shops, cafés, restaurants, hotels and other amenities, many of them located in replicas of Swiss chalets or German beer-houses, and runs south from oval Plaza José Hernández, where the Oktoberfest takes place. Frankly, the town's museums are not worth your time. The real attraction of Villa General Belgrano is its proximity to the great Sierra de Comechingones, looming to the west.

Practicalities

Regular services from Buenos Aires, Córdoba and Santa Rosa de Calamuchita arrive at the small **bus terminal** on Avenida Vélez Sarsfield, five minutes northwest of Plaza José Hernández. Pájaro Blanco runs a shuttle minibus service several times a day to and from La Cumbrecita and Córdoba; its bus stop is on Avenida San Martín, 100m north of Plaza José Hernández. The **tourist office**, in the German town hall at Avenida Julio A. Roca 168 (daily 8.30am–8.30pm; ☏03546/461215, Ⓦwww.elsitiodelavilla.com), has been doing its best in recent years to give the town a younger, more modern image. Banks and **ATMs** can be found along Avenida Julio A. Roca.

You're spoilt for choice when it comes to accommodation, although if you're planning to attend the popular Oktoberfest you should book well ahead and be prepared for steeper prices. Most of the **hotels** are on the expensive side, but they're nearly all of a high standard, spotlessly clean and comfortable. Try *Tantra Posada,* at Vicente Palotti 36, with spacious rooms and an attractive pool (☏03546/462142, Ⓦwww.posadatantra.com.ar; ❻); or the centrally located but old-fashioned *Posada Nehuen*, at San Martín 17 (☏03546/461412, Ⓦwww .elsitiodelavilla.com/nehuen; ❺). The laidback **youth hostel** *El Rincón*, at Calle Alexander Fleming 347, fifteen minutes' walk northwest of the bus station (☏03546/461323, Ⓦwww.calamuchitanet.com.ar/elrincon), has dorms ($30), rooms with private bathroom (❷) and a place to pitch your tent ($10). There are a number of **campsites** out along the RP-5 a short way out of the town centre: the best is ecofriendly *Rincón de Mirlos* (☏03546/155164254, Ⓦwww .rincondemirlos.com.ar), signposted 7km west of the centre on the road towards La Cumbrecita; from there it is another 2km through handsome farmland and woods to the bucolic riverside setting, where there are clean dorms from $47, isolated pitches (from $26) among the trees, a bar and restaurant, and long stretches of sandy beach.

Not surprisingly, many of the town's plentiful **places to eat** offer German and Central European dishes such as goulash, sauerkraut, sausages and tortes. *Ciervo Rojo*, at Avenida Julio A. Roca 210, serves schnitzels and wurst, washed down with tankards of home-brewed beer, while *Café Rissen*, at Avenida Julio A. Roca 36, is the place to go for Black Forest gâteau, strudel and fruit crumbles, served on floral tablecloths. *Krems*, an excellent ice-cream parlour, is opposite.

Santa Rosa de Calamuchita and around

In 1700, a community of Dominicans built an estancia and a chapel dedicated to the patron saint of the Americas, Santa Rosa of Lima, after which nothing much else happened in **SANTA ROSA DE CALAMUCHITA**, 11km south of Villa General Belgrano, until the end of the nineteenth century. Then, thanks to its mountainside, riverbank location and its mild climate, the place suddenly took off as a holiday resort, an alternative to its more traditional neighbour to the north. Now it's a highly popular destination, swamped by thousands of visitors from many parts of the country in the high season, and makes an excellent base for exploring the relatively unspoilt **mountains** nearby. Many of Santa Rosa de Calamuchita's visitors use it as a springboard to experience all kinds of **outdoor activities**, from diving and kayaking to jet-skiing and flying, all located at **Villa del Dique**, 17km away. Noticeably less sedate than Villa General Belgrano but more bearable than Villa Carlos Paz, from Christmas until Easter Santa Rosa throbs with disco music blaring from convertibles packed with holiday-makers.

The town's compact centre is built in a curve of the Río Santa Rosa, just south of where the Arroyo del Sauce flows into it. There's no main plaza, but a number of busy streets run off the main Calle Libertad. You can take refuge from the hullabaloo at the northern end of Libertad in the beautifully restored **Capilla Vieja** – the ruined estancia was demolished at the beginning of the twentieth century. It houses the **Museo de Arte Religioso** (Jan & Feb daily 10am–1pm; March–Aug Wed–Sun 10am–1pm; Sept–Dec Thurs–Sun 10am–1pm; free), where you can see a superb late seventeenth-century wooden Christ, crafted by local Jesuit artisans, and other works of colonial religious art.

Practicalities

Regular **bus** services from Córdoba and Villa General Belgrano drop and pick up passengers at stops along Avenida Gómez. The staff at the **tourist information office**, at Córdoba y Entre Rios (daily 8am–11pm; ℡03546/429654, ⓦwww.starosacalamuchita.com.ar), dish out brochures on accommodation, activities and tour operators.

Accommodation tends to be less expensive here than in Villa General Belgrano, and includes the stylish 1930s *Hotel Yporá*, 1km outside town on the RP-5 (℡03546/421233, ⓦwww.hotelypora.com; ⑥); the slightly run-down, family-oriented *Hotel Santa Rosa*, at Entre Ríos and Córdoba (℡03546/420186; ④); and the *Hostería Ana Mar*, at Libertad 594 (℡03546/420248; ④), which has small but pleasant rooms with private bathrooms and cable TV. The best **campsite** is *Miami* (℡03546/499613, ⓦwww.campingmiami.com.ar; $25 camping per person; $60 for a dorm bed), on the road up to Yacanto. The town's best **restaurants** are the reliable *La Pulpería de los Ferreyra*, a *parrilla* at Libertad 578, and *El Gringo*, an inexpensive pizzeria at Libertad 270.

One- or three-day **treks** and 4WD **safaris** into the Comechingones range are arranged by Naturaleza y Aventura (℡03546/464144, ⓦwww.elsitiodelavilla.com/naturaleza). **Motorcycles** and **buggies** can be rented all along Playa de Santa Rita, and it is also possible to hire **horses** or **mountain bikes** in town.

La Cumbrecita

Around 35km northwest of Villa Belgrano along a winding scenic track, **LA CUMBRECITA** is a small, peaceful alpine-style village in the foothills of the Comechingones range. Benefiting from a mild microclimate and enjoying views of wild countryside, it has developed as a relatively select holiday resort ever since it was built in 1934 by Swiss and Austrian immigrants. From Villa Belgrano, take Avenida San Martín, which leads north from Plaza José Hernández, and keep going until you reach the edge of town; from here the dirt road swings in a westerly direction and climbs through hills that open to views of the Río Segundo Valley.

Two paths wind their way through the village, parallel to the Río del Medio that cuts a deep ravine below. **Paseo Bajo**, the lower of the two, passes several cafés and hotels and the mock-medieval Castillo, on the way to the Río Almbach, which flows into the Río del Medio north of the village; the upper trail climbs the hill to the west of the village, cutting through a well-tended cemetery from where you can enjoy wonderful views of the Lago Esmeralda and the fir-wooded mountains

Nature's medicine in the Central Sierras

A bewildering variety of vegetation grows on the mountainsides of the Central Sierras and is representative of three of the country's principal phytogeographic zones – the Andes, the Pampas and the Chaco. Many of these plant species are reputed to possess remarkable **medicinal properties**. Perhaps best known is the *peperina*, of which there are two varieties: *Mintostachys verticillata* and *Satureja parvifolia* (the latter often known as *peperina de la sierra*). Both are highly aromatic and extremely digestive but, in men, diminish sexual potency. The *yerba del pollo* (*Alternanthera pungens*), on the other hand, is a natural cure for flatulence, while ephedrine, a tonic for heart ailments, is extracted industrially from *tramontana* (*Ephedra triandra*), a broom-like bush found all over the highlands at altitudes of 800–1300m. Anyone suffering from problems of the gall bladder might do well to drink an infusion of *poleo* (*Lippia turbinata*), a large shrub with silvery foliage and an unmistakable aroma. Appropriately enough, since Santa Lucia is the patron saint of the blind, the *flor de Santa Lucia* (*Commelina erecta*), whose intense blue or lilac blooms carpet the ground to astonishing effect, exudes a sticky substance that can be used as effective eye drops. The *cola de caballo* (*Equisetum giganteum*) – or "horsetail" – is used to control arterial pressure thanks to its diuretic powers; its ribbed, rush-like stems grow alongside streams and are crowned with hairy filaments that give it its popular name. Whatever you do, however, steer clear of *revienta caballos* (*Solanum eleagnifolium* or *S. sisymbrifolium*), a distant relative of the deadly nightshade. Its pretty violet flowers give way to deceptively attractive yellow berries, but the whole plant is highly toxic.

Obviously, you should **seek expert advice** before putting natural cures to the test, and they should not be used instead of conventional medicine for the severest of complaints. Pharmaceutical herbs, known as *yuyos*, are sold (usually in dried form) in pharmacies and in stores selling dietetic products throughout the region.

behind. Private motor vehicles are banned from the whole village during the day (summer 9am–7pm; winter 10am–6pm), but many people rent electric buggies to get around – distances are walkable, however, and visitors are allowed to drive to their hotel's car park.

To cool off in hot weather, head for one of the **balnearios** along the clean Río Almbach, such as *Lago de las Truchas* or *Confluencia* – the former named for the plentiful trout in the stream and the latter renowned for its caves – both with bucolic settings and views up the craggy mountaintops. La Cumbrecita is also a perfect base for some of the region's most rewarding mountain walks, including some well-trodden but uncrowded trails going up to 2000m or more. Signposted treks lasting between one and four hours each way head off to the eyrie-like *miradores* at Casas Viejas, Meierei and Cerro Cristal, while one of the most popular trails climbs from El Castillo, past *Balneario La Olla*, with its very deep pools of crystal-clear water created by the gushing waterfalls, to the 1715m-summit of Cerro Wank.

Practicalities

Pájaro Blanco runs a **shuttle bus** service six times daily to La Cumbrecita from Villa General Belgrano. The **tourist office** is across the bridge over the Río del Medio (summer daily 9am–9pm; winter 10am–6pm; ℡03546/481088, Ⓦwww.lacumbrecita.gov.ar).

Accommodation in La Cumbrecita is pretty much all faux-alpine and includes the recently renovated *Hotel Solares Cumbrecita*, with an excellent range

of facilities and several self-catering apartments (☎03546/481019, ⓦwww
.solarescumbrecita.com; ❼). The town's basic but comfortable hostel *El Viaje*
(☎0351/155735085, ⓦwww.elviajelacumbrecita.com) has dorm rooms at $45
and one double (❸). The string of generally excellent *confiterías* and **restaurants**
along La Cumbrecita's Paseo Bajo mostly offer fondues, strudels and other
Central European specialities, plus the odd steak. For meals, *Bar Suizo*, near the
river end of the village, leads the way, serving a hearty range of Germanic
pork-dominated dishes and tarts, while the village's best cakes and pastries are
at *Conditorei Liesbeth*, in a quaint little cabin with a garden right at the far end of
the Paseo Bajo, across the Arroyo Almbach.

The Traslasierra

By far the most rewarding route from Córdoba to San Luis, capital of the
neighbouring province of the same name, is by the RP-34 and then the RN-20
beyond Villa Carlos Paz. The winding **Nueva Ruta de las Altas Cumbres**
climbs past the **Parque Nacional de la Quebrada del Condorito**, a deep
ravine where condors nest in cliffside niches, climbing over a high mountain-
pass before winding back down a series of hairpin bends. The serene, sunny
valleys to the west of the high Sierra Grande and Sierra de Achala, crisscrossed
by gushing streams and dotted with oases of bushy palm trees, are known
collectively as the **Traslasierra**, literally "across the mountains". The self-
appointed capital of the sub-region, **Mina Clavero**, is a popular little riverside
resort and minor transport hub, but not the best place to stay, owing to the
hordes of holiday-makers who spend the summer here. Several **buses** a day run
between Córdoba and Mina Clavero, and some can drop you at the national
park entrance.

Near **Nono**, a tiny village at the foot of the northern Comechingones to the
south of Mina Clavero, is the oddball **Museo Rocsen**, an eclectic jumble of
artefacts, archeological finds and endless miscellanea. In a long valley parallel to
the Sierra de Comechingones lies the picturesque village of **San Javier**, from
where you can climb the highest summit in the Central Sierras, the majestic
Cerro Champaquí.

Parque Nacional de la Quebrada del Condorito

About 65km from Villa Carlos Paz, just to the south of the RP-34, is the
PARQUE NACIONAL DE LA QUEBRADA DEL CONDORITO
(☎03541/433371, ⓦwww.condoritoapn.com.ar), which takes its name from the
Quebrada de los Condoritos, a misty canyon eroded into the mountains that, in
turn, gets its name from the baby condors reared in its deep ravines.

To get here, take the RP-34 that sweeps across the **Pampa de Achala**, an eerily
desolate landscape, ideal for solitary treks or horse rides. For the first 15km or so,
this road, which starts southwest of crowded Villa Carlos Paz, is quite narrow, but
several viewpoints have been built at the roadside. From them, you have
unobscured vistas of the Icho Cruz and Malambo valleys to the northwest, the
distant peak of **Cerro Los Gigantes** (at 2374m the highest mountain in the Sierra
Grande) to the north, and the **Sierra de Achala** to the south; the views are framed
by nodding pinkish *cortaderas*, or pampas grass. Some 20km further on, the bleak
granite moorlands of the Pampa de Achala, reaching just over 2000m above sea

level, are barren save for thorny scrub and a few tufty alpines. Condors, some with wingspans exceeding three metres, can be seen circling majestically overhead.

Travelling along the RP-34 you reach the **Fundación Cóndor** (daily 9am–6pm; Ⓦwww.fundacion-condor.com.ar) an independently run centre specializing in information on condors and a striking photo exhibition of the park's flora and fauna. They also have a café, organize condor-feeding spectacles in the evenings and can organize transport to the park.

The park's **Interpretation Centre** (summer 8am–8pm, winter 9am–4pm; free entry) is situated 1.5km from the main road entrance along a winding dirt track (if arriving by bus, ask the bus driver to drop you off at the entrance, La Pampilla). Despite the eerily empty vista, persevere and you'll reach a small building where *guardaparques* encourage registering before setting out on a hike. They can also provide useful information on the best walks depending on length and fitness levels, the park's flora and fauna, and weather advice. Be warned, there's little shade and currently no food or drink on sale within the park boundaries, so bring a hat, sun-cream and sustenance. If you're travelling in your own vehicle, and haven't stopped off at the Fundación, the nearest restaurant, *Parador La Pampilla* (not to be confused with the name of the park entrance), is located 3.5km away on the RP-34 towards Villa Carlos Paz.

Hikes take between two hours and several days, and there are designated areas in the park where camping is permitted. The hike route is clearly marked with numbered posts, getting steadily more difficult after you pass number ten, which takes you down steep and sometimes slippery paths towards the bottom of the canyon. All kinds of trees, shrubs and ferns can be spotted, even some endemic species such as rare white gentians, while the plentiful fauna includes various wild cats, frogs, foxes and lizards. Birdlife is prolific but the stars are the condors themselves, especially their young; if you're lucky you might see condors and their chicks bathing in the water at the bottom of the gorge. **Guides** can be hired in advance from the park's main office, the Intendencia del Parque Nacional Quebrida del Condorito (Resistencia 30 ☎03541/15631727) in Villa Carlos Paz.

The best **accommodation** in the area can be found at *La Posta del Qenti* (☎03544/472532, Ⓦwww.qenti.com; ⑨), a tastefully converted nineteenth-century post house located 17km from the park entrance on the RP-34 towards Carlos Paz, where salt convoys on the way to Córdoba used to stop for a change of horses. Its remote location on the barren pampas lends it an almost eerie atmosphere, offset by the designer-magazine interior, snug rooms, fully equipped gym and good food. You can hire **horses** to explore the surrounding countryside, dominated by unbeatable views of Cerro Champaquí, and a whole range of other activities are available, including trekking, mountain-biking and rock-climbing.

Mina Clavero and around

Some 15km west of the Quebrada de los Condoritos, the RP-34 begins to snake along narrow corniche roads, which offer stunning views of the Traslasierra valley and a cluster of extinct volcanic cones in the distance; the sheer cliffs and fissured crags look as if they might crumble at any moment into the wide plains below. Just 1.5km up the RP-15 north of the junction with the the RP-34 is **MINA CLAVERO**, wedged between the Sierra Grande and the much lower Sierra de Pocho, to the west. A transport hub for routes between Córdoba, San Luis, Merlo and Cruz del Eje, at the northern end of the Punilla Valley, it's also a boisterous riverside resort. The place is noteworthy for little else, though, other than its attractive black ceramics, made at various workshops in and around the town; the metallic glaze on the vases, pots and animal figures, with a bluish sheen, is made from cow dung.

Mina Clavero is packed during January and February, when people come to relax at the many *balnearios* along the three rivers – Los Sauces, Mina Clavero and Panaholma – that snake through the small town. Of all the bathing areas, the cleanest is the Nido de Aguila, set among beautiful rocks on the Río Mina Clavero 1km east of the centre, along Calle Urquiza. The nearby mountains lend themselves to a number of pursuits, such as mountain-biking, horse-riding, trekking and climbing, while trout-fishing is possible in the many brooks.

A compact place, it's not difficult to find your way around; the two main streets are Avenida San Martín and Avenida Mitre, which forks off it at the southern end of the village. From the town's central plaza take Jorge Raúl Recalde street and follow the signs to the **Camino de los Artesanos**, a stretch of road about 18km along that is lined with excellent **ceramics workshops**, with little stalls set up on the roadside; the pick of the lot belongs to Atilio López, whose clearly signposted house is set among a lush garden some 12km east of town.

Practicalities

Mina Clavero's **bus terminal** is along Avenida Mitre, next to the municipalidad; there are regular services from Córdoba, Merlo, San Luis, Mendoza and Buenos Aires. Seven blocks south, in the cleft of the fork with Avenida San Martín, is the **tourist information centre** (daily Dec–Easter 7am–midnight; Easter–Nov 9am–9pm; ℡03544/470171, ⊛www.minaclavero.gov.ar); as well as helping you with accommodation, the staff can provide information on local activities.

Owing to its popularity and despite its diminutive size, Mina Clavero has a wide choice of **hotels**; out of season, prices can be half the cost of the high summer season ones quoted below. Options include the comfortable *Panaholma Sierras*, at Avenida San Martín 1840 (℡03544/472181, ⊛www.traslasierra.com /panaholmasierras; ⓺) and the French-run *Du Soleil* motel, with a good restaurant and smart rooms with modern bathrooms, at Ruta 14 s/n (℡03544/470066, ⊛www.dusoleil.com.ar; ⓺). The town's best **hostel**, the colourful, family run *Oh La La Hostel*, at J.B. Villanueva 1192 (℡03544/472634, ⊛www.ohlalahostel.com.ar), has a new pool and large garden. Dorm rooms start at $45 and there is one double (❸). There are a dozen or so **campsites** in and around Mina Clavero, with the best ones at Villa Cura Brochero, 2km to the north: *Los Serranitos*, at Avenida Cura Gaucho 350 (℡03544/470817, ⊛www.losserranitos.com.ar), offers pitches (from $20 per person), dorm rooms from $30 per person and simple cabins (❸). Restaurants selling the usual Argentine trio of pasta, pizza and *parrilla* line avenidas San Martín and Mitre; the pick is *Lo de Jorge*, at Poeta Lugones 1417, known for its excellent meat.

Nono and Museo Rocsen

From the junction with the RP-15, the RN-20 heads due south through rolling countryside, in the lee of rippling mountains, whose eroded crags change colour from a mellow grey to deepest red, depending on the time of day. Their imposing peak, Cerro Champaquí, lurks to the southeast at the northern end of the Comechingones range. Some 10km south of Mina Clavero you reach the sleepy village of **NONO**, a huddle of picturesque brick buildings around a little plaza. Its name is a corruption of the Quichoa *ñuñu*, meaning breasts, an allusion to the bosom-shaped hills poking above the horizon. For good, reasonably priced food, snacks or a drink with a fabulous valley vista, head to *La Terraza*, on the main road next to the YPF service station.

Some 5km from the village centre, a well-maintained dirt road leads eastwards to one of the country's weirdest museums, the hallucinatory **Museo Rocsen** (daily 9am–sunset; ℡03544/498218, Ⓦwww.museorocsen.org; $14). Its imposing pink sandstone facade is embellished with a row of 49 statues – from Christ to Mother Teresa and Buddha to Che Guevara – representing key figures who, according to the museum's owner and curator, Juan Santiago Bouchon, have changed the course of history. After many years as cultural attaché at the French embassy in Buenos Aires, Bouchon opened his museum in 1969, with the intention of offering "something for everybody". The result is an eclectic collection of more than thirty thousand exhibits, from fossils and mummies to a two-headed calf, clocks and cars.

Another 3km towards the mountains along a signposted track is the French-run 𝕏 *Estancia La Lejanía* (℡03544/498960, Ⓦwww.lalejania.com; ◐), an outstanding **hotel** with comfortable rooms and all amenities in a secluded setting with a private riverside beach and delicious French cuisine on offer, accompanied by select Argentine champagnes and wines from the cellar. The hotel also conducts treks and horseriding in the nearby mountains. Also signposted off the road to the museum, *Hostería La Manantial* (℡03544/498179, Ⓦwww.hosteriamanantial .com.ar; ◐) provides a very acceptable alternative in terms of accommodation. Its huge grounds stretch across to another river beach, while a swimming pool and delicious food are further bonuses.

San Javier

Some 35km south of Mina Clavero, the RP-148 branches off the RN-20 and heads due south towards **SAN JAVIER**, another 12km away. The tree-lined road, which takes you through some of the province's most attractive scenery and traditional settlements, offers outstanding views of the northern Comechingones mountains to the east. If you're driving, though, watch out for the often treacherous *badenes*; these are very deep fords that suddenly flood after storms, and even when dry their sudden drop and rough surface can damage a car's undercarriage or tyres.

San Javier is a pretty little place, set amid peach orchards, and serve as bases for climbing to the 2884m summit of **Cerro Champaquí**, directly to the east. It has developed swiftly as an exclusive tourist centre in recent years, offering a variety of services including massages, reiki and even solar shamanism. Ask at the municipalidad on the main square with its oddball church (℡03544/482077, Ⓦwww.sanjavieronline.com.ar) for information about **guides** to accompany you on the seven-hour hike to the top of Champaquí. For **accommodation**, secluded *Hostería San Javier* (℡03544/482006; ◐) is set among pastoral grounds and blessed with the inexpensive French restaurant *L'Hibou*. It's 3km up the bumpy dirt road towards the mountain peak, leading up from the main square past a number of interesting **crafts workshops**. Another 4km beyond is the superb *Estancia-Hostería La Constancia* (Ⓦwww.laconstancia.net; ◐ full board), a designer-built hotel set in stunning environs. The road to get there is through the sierras, so although it's only 7km from San Javier, the slow drive will take around forty minutes. The hotel can arrange transfers from Villa Dolores. A couple of blocks from the main square, *Amelie* is a charming teahouse and restaurant, serving an unusual combination of Asian and local cuisine to lift jaded tastebuds.

Travel details

Buses

Córdoba to: Alta Gracia (every 15min; 1hr); Buenos Aires (hourly; 11hr); Capilla del Monte (every 1hr; 1hr 30min); Catamarca (11 daily; 6hr); Cerro Colorado (1 Mon, Fri & Sat; 3hr 30min); Chilecito (2 daily; 7hr); Jesús María (every 30min; 1hr 30min); La Rioja (5 daily; 6hr); Mendoza (7 daily; 10hr); Mina Clavero (5 daily; 3hr); Rosario (every 30min; 5hr); Salta (6 daily; 11hr); San Juan (5 daily; 8hr); Santa Rosa de Calamuchita (19 daily; 2hr 20min); Santiago del Estero (10 daily; 6hr); Villa General Belgrano (6 daily; 2hr).

Flights

Córdoba to: Buenos Aires (10 daily; 1hr 15min).

The Litoral and the Gran Chaco

CHAPTER 4 # Highlights

✻ **Colón** This picturesque riverside resort has it all: sandy beaches, hot springs, and even a winery. See p.248

✻ **Esteros del Iberá** Glide in a boat across a mirror-like lagoon where capybaras splash, deer trampoline on spongy islets and thousands of birds fly overhead. See p.253

✻ **Estancia Santa Inés** A splendid colonial-style mansion, near its own *yerba mate* plantation, offering hospitality, relaxation, delicious food – and a monkey colony. See p.261

✻ **San Ignacio Miní** The best preserved of all the Jesuit settlements is set among impeccably mown lawns worthy of a cricket pitch. See p.268

✻ **Garganta del Diablo** Of the 250 waterfalls at Iguazú, the "Devil's Throat" is the most powerful, most dramatic – and wettest. See p.271

✻ **Fogón de los Arrieros** Visited over the years by leading artists and artistes, Resistencia's top culture club offers tango, folk and poetry recitals. See p.307

▲ The ruins, San Ignacio Miní

The Litoral and the Gran Chaco

The defining feature of northeastern Argentina is water. Dominated by two of the continent's longest rivers, plus several of the country's other major waterways, it's a land of powerful cascades and gushing streams, blue-mirrored lagoons and rippling reservoirs, vast marshes and fertile wetlands. The riverine landscapes of the **Litoral** (meaning "Shore" or "Coastline") – a term generally used to refer to the four provinces of **Entre Ríos**, **Corrientes**, **Misiones** and **Santa Fe** – range from the caramel-coloured maze of the Paraná Delta, just north of Buenos Aires, via the gentle sandy banks of the Río Uruguay and the jungle-edged Río Iguazú to the wide translucent curves of the upper Río Paraná. All of them exude a seductive subtropical beauty enhanced by the unhurried lifestyle of the locals and a warm, humid climate. To Argentines, however, the Litoral above all means two things: **mate** and **chamamé**. Litoraleños, as the inhabitants are called, are fanatical consumers of Argentina's national drink, while the infectiously lively chamamé music is most reliably heard in the highly traditional province of Corrientes.

The **Iguazú Falls**, shared with Brazil, in the far north of Misiones Province, are the region's major attraction by a long chalk: Iguazú's claim to the title of the world's most spectacular waterfalls has few serious contenders. Running a remote second, in terms of the number of visitors, **San Ignacio Miní** is one of the best-preserved ruins in the huge Jesuit Mission region – though some may find picking their way through nearby gothically overgrown **Loreto** and **Santa Ana** a more magical experience. Less well known than Iguazú and San Ignacio, but increasingly visited as the infrastructure improves, are two of Argentina's most unusual attractions: the strange and wonderful – but capricious – **Saltos del Moconá**, the world's most extensive longitudinal waterfalls; and the **Esteros del Iberá**, a vast wetland reserve stretching across the centre of Corrientes Province.

Further south, the region's biggest city, and Argentina's third largest, is **Rosario**. It is home to a vibrant cultural life, including its own laidback version of **tango**, fabulous restaurants and some exquisite late nineteenth- and early twentieth-century architecture.

Bordering the Litoral, the **Gran Chaco** is a vast, little-visited area of flatlands forming the central watershed of South America and lying predominantly in western Paraguay and the far north of Argentina. Varying from brutally desiccated

THE LITORAL AND THE GRAN CHACO

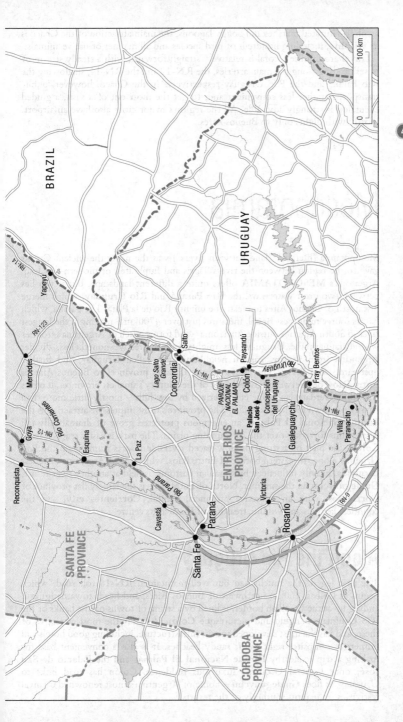

scrub to saturated marshes and boggy lagoons, the main attraction of the Chaco is its **wildlife**, including hundreds of bird species and all manner of native animals.

Travel around the Litoral is relatively straightforward, with a steady stream of buses heading along the main arteries, the RN-12 and the RN-14, shadowing the Río Paraná and the Río Uruguay respectively. In the Chaco, however, public transport is rather less convenient and, to get the most out of a visit, a guided excursion is strongly advisable. All the region's major cities also have an airport, mostly with flights only to Buenos Aires.

Mesopotamia

Mesopotamia (literally, "land between rivers") was the name the ancient Greeks gave to the region between the rivers Tigris and Euphrates, or modern-day Iraq. Argentina's **MESOPOTAMIA** offers quite a different landscape, but it too lies between two great waterways, the **Río Paraná** and **Río Uruguay**, which merge just north of Buenos Aires to create the mighty Río de la Plata. The Paraná, which has its source in deepest Brazil, measures just over 4700km – making it the longest river in South America outside Amazonia – and forms much of Argentina's frontier with Paraguay; the Uruguay, less mighty but impressive nonetheless, divides Argentina from its tiny eastern neighbour, also called Uruguay, and further upstream, from Brazil. The closest of the Litoral's provinces to Buenos Aires is **Entre Ríos**, or "Between Rivers": one of the country's smallest provinces, it offers a soothing verdant landscape characterized by low hills – mostly little more than ripples – known locally as *cuchillas*. The province's most impressive attraction is the **Parque Nacional El Palmar**, an enormous protected grove of dramatically tall *yatay* palms towering over the surrounding plains. The park is easily reached from **Colón**, the pick of a string of slow-paced riverside resorts running up the Río Uruguay along the eastern border of Entre Ríos, while one of Argentina's liveliest **carnivals**, heavily influenced by Brazilian customs, is held at another river resort, **Gualeguaychú**, in the summer. North of Entre Ríos is the largely flat province of **Corrientes**, with an attractive provincial capital, **Corrientes city**, and the countless lagoons and wildlife treasures of **Iberá** at its centre.

Along the Río Uruguay

The first leg of the much-used but well-maintained RN-14 toll road, which begins at Ceibas, 160km northwest of Buenos Aires, and heads towards Iguazú, ending up at the Brazilian border, is lined by a string of towns on the banks of the Río Uruguay. Languid and picturesque **Colón** is by far the most attractive of these, and has the most developed tourist infrastructure, including good hotels and numerous campsites right by its sandy beaches. It is also a convenient base for making a trip to nearby **Parque Nacional El Palmar** and the **Palacio de San José**, once General Urquiza's luxurious residence. Colón has road links to Uruguay, as does **Gualeguaychú** – home of Argentina's most renowned carnival festivities – the most southerly of the resorts.

Gualeguaychú

Apart from having a name that sounds like a tongue-twister followed by a sneeze, **SAN JOSÉ DE GUALEGUAYCHÚ**, or just plain Gualeguaychú (its name is possibly derived from the Guaraní words for "tranquil waters"), is most notable for its **Carnival**, generally regarded as Argentina's most important; during the months of January and February, the town is mobbed with people, particularly at weekends. Gualeguaychú's passion for processions is given further vent in October, when local high-school students take part in the **desfile de carrozas**, in which elaborate floats, constructed by the students themselves, are paraded around the streets. During the rest of the year – with the exception of long weekends, when it still attracts holiday-makers from Buenos Aires – Gualeguaychú is a tranquil town with some handsome old buildings and a pleasant *costanera* (riverfront) and park, plus decent accommodation and numerous campsites.

In recent years, the building of **paper-pulp plants** by European companies on the Río Uruguay, including one just opposite Gualeguaychú, on Uruguay's side of the river, has caused great anger here. Argentines claim the plant is polluting their air and water, and the spat has seriously soured diplomatic relations between the two countries. Argentine protestors have completely cut off the General San Martín International Bridge, which connects the city with Fray Bentos in Uruguay – currently, if you want to cross, you'll need to travel 100km upriver to Colón (see p.248). Feelings run very high in town about the plant – you'll see *"No a las papaleras"* signs everywhere – and the roadblock, which not everyone approves of; it is a topic of conversation that should not be lightly entered into.

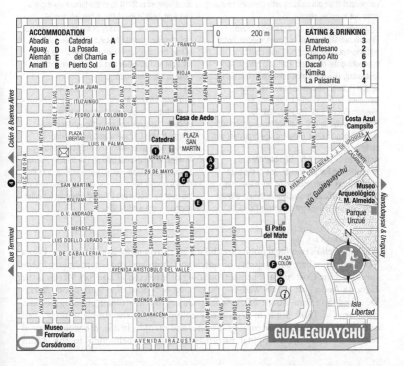

245

Arrival and information

Gualeguaychú's **bus terminal** (T03446/427987) is at the corner of Bulevard Pedro Jurado and Avenida General Artigas, 2km from the centre – taxis into town cost about $6. Tourist information is available at the bus terminal (daily 8am–8/10pm; T03446/440706), but the main **tourist office** (same hours; T03446/423668, Wwww.gualeguaychuturismo.com) is on the Plazoleta de los Artesanos, Paseo del Puerto, down by the port; it keeps a list of families who rent rooms, plus an up-to-date price list of cabins and bungalows in the area. The staff can also offer information on excursions on the Río Gualeguaychú – such as regular catamaran trips and canoe rental – and on the *jineteadas*, or rodeo events, held in the vicinity throughout the year.

Accommodation

Gualeguaychú has a good selection of mostly budget **accommodation**. You'll need to book in advance if you plan to stay during Carnival, and probably on long weekends, too, when most places also raise their prices. At these times, a number of impromptu notices spring up around town offering rooms to rent. There are numerous **campsites** in Gualeguaychú and the surrounding area; most are along the banks of the Río Gualeguaychú, or out towards the Río Uruguay. One of the best is *Ñandubaysal* (T03446/423298; $50 per tent plus $10 per person) on the banks of the Río Uruguay, 15km east of the town. It's an extensive site forested with *ñandubay*, a thorny plant typical of the region whose fruit is a favourite of the ñandú (rhea) – hence the name.

Abadía San Martín 588 T03446/437502 Wwww.milashoteles.com.ar. An attractive residencial in an old building with pleasant rooms done out in pastel shades. ④

Aguay Av Costanera 130 T03446/422099, Wwww.hotelaguay.com.ar. Smart, modern hotel with top-floor swimming pool and *confitería* overlooking the river, and a reliable ground-floor restaurant, *Di Tulia*, that specializes in fish dishes. Spacious, bright rooms all have river-view balconies. Copious buffet breakfasts. ⑧

Alemán Bolívar 535 T03446/426153. Professionally run and centrally located hotel with well-equipped rooms. Rates include breakfast and parking. ⑥

Amalfi 25 de Mayo 571 T03446/426818, Eamalfihotel@yahoo.com.ar. One of the best of the budget hotels, located on the main drag, with some particularly spacious – though slightly dark – rooms at the front and cable TV. ⑤

Catedral Mitre 25 T03446/425469, Wwww.hotelcatedralgchu.com.ar. Guale's first boutique hotel, opened in 2010, is in the former governor's mansion, built in the1870s. It has a beautiful Italianate façade, and many of the original features, including the marble staircase, tiled floors and ceiling frescoes, have been preserved. The rooms are light and spacious and it's in a good location close to the main plaza. ⑧

La Posada del Charrúa Av del Valle 250 T03446/426099. A rustic name somewhat belied by the hotel's appearance, which is bland and modern. It is spick and span, though, and well located by the Costanera, and with parking. ④

Puerto Sol San Lorenzo 477 T03446/434017, Wwww.hotelpuertosol.com.ar. The friendly *Puerto Sol* has comfortable rooms, some looking onto the hotel's interior patio. You can also be taken across the river by boat to Isla Libertad opposite, for quiet relaxation and a drink. ④

The Town

Gualeguaychú's two focal points are the streets surrounding its main square, **Plaza San Martín**, where the majority of hotels and shops are, and – particularly in the summer – the **Costanera**. The main building of interest on Plaza San Martín is the **Casa de Aedo** (Jan & Feb Wed–Sat 9am–noon & 5–8pm, Sun 9am–noon; April–Dec Wed–Sun 9am–noon; $2); officially Gualeguaychú's oldest building, it dates from around 1800. Built in a primitive colonial style, the simple whitewashed building opens onto a garden of grapevines and orchids. Inside, the wood-floored rooms are filled with original furniture and objects belonging to the Aedos

▲ Carnival, Gualeguaychú

(sometimes written Haedos), one of Gualeguaychú's early patrician families. Among other exhibits, there's a beautiful Spanish representation of the Virgen del Carmen, made of silver and real hair, and a number of fine pieces of French porcelain. The house is also notable for having been occupied by Italian hero Giuseppe Garibaldi in 1845, when he ransacked Gualeguaychú for funds and provisions to assist General Oribe, who was under siege in Montevideo.

The **Costanera J.J. de Urquiza**, quiet during the day and out of season, heaves with life on summer evenings, when locals and holiday-makers indulge in an obligatory evening stroll or simply while away the hours on a bench, sipping a *mate*. The southern end of the Costanera leads to the **old port** and if you head down this way just before the October *desfile de carrozas* you will come across scenes of frenetic activity as students – many of whom barely sleep for the last few days – put the finishing touches to their floats, which are assembled in huge riverside warehouses. The port was the termination point for the old railway tracks, which reached Gualeguaychú in 1873. If you follow the tracks round along Avenida Irazusta, you will come to the old train station, now the open-air **Museo Ferroviario**, or railway museum, where an old steam locomotive is displayed along with other relics; access is unrestricted. Just next door is the **Corsódromo**, where up to 30,000 spectators pile in to watch Gualeguaychú's *comparsas*, or processions, during Carnival. Though not as spectacular as Río de Janeiro's carnival, the processions here are still well worth a detour to see – a lot of effort is put into the costumes, music and floats and the crowd is always enthusiastic. Carnival **tickets** can be bought on the door, or beforehand via

Ticketek (@www.ticketek.com.ar), and vary in price from $15 on wooden benches at the back to $500 for a seat in the VIP area with the best view.

Gualeguaychú's most original retailing experience is provided by **El Patio del Mate** (open daily until late), on Gervasio Méndez down by the Costanera: a shrine to Litoraleños' most pervasive habit, it sells *mates* carved out of every material imaginable – from simple and functional calabazas or gourds (generally regarded as the best material for *mates*) to elaborate combinations of hoof and hide, best described as gaucho kitsch.

Eating, drinking and nightlife

Gualeguaychú is a town with a split personality – in the summer (Dec–March) all life is centred on the Costanera, while the rest of the year the action gravitates to the town centre, around 25 de Mayo. The Costanera is lined with parrillas – the best being the consistently good *Dacal*, on the corner of Andrade, whose wide-ranging menu includes river fish. Another Costanera classic at San Lorenzo and Concordia, *Campo Alto* specializes more in meat than fish, with seating in a roomy *quincho*-style building or outside in a secluded garden-terrace. Downtown, sample good pizza at *El Artesano*, on the corner of 25 de Mayo and Mitre, while down-to-earth *La Paisanita*, 25 de Mayo 1176, is popular with locals for *parrilla* and pasta.

The town centre is somewhat lacking in enticing **bars**; *Kimika*, on Urquiza and Pellegrini, is where most locals go to dance the night away outside summer. In summer, the names of the bars and clubs that buzz with *cumbia* and commercial dance on the Costanera change every season, though *Amarelo*, at the junction of Costanera and 25 de Mayo, is a relatively long-running favourite.

Colón and around

Thanks to its setting, variety of activities and attractive hotels and restaurants, **COLÓN** is easily the most appealing of Entre Ríos' resorts. It also makes a good base for visiting the wonderfully exotic-looking **Parque Nacional El Palmar**, just 50km north, or the European-style splendour of **Palacio San José**, about 40km southwest. Moreover, Colón is linked to the major Uruguayan city Paysandú, 15km southeast, via the Puente Internacional General Artigas. Closer by, you can take memorable boat trips on the enticing **Río Uruguay**, swim at a riverine **beach**, hunt for semi-precious stones, taste wine at the region's only commercial **vineyard**, or tour the abandoned **Liebig meat-processing plant**, a vestige of the area's once-thriving beef export industry. A day's exploration is well rewarded with a soak in the city's thermal springs, or with a visit to the **Termas Villa Elisa**, only a short distance north. Every February Colón hosts an important craft fair, the **Fiesta Nacional de la Artesanía**, with over five hundred exhibitors from Argentina and further afield. The rest of the year, there's no shortage of stores selling **artesan goods** ranging from *mates* and *asado* tableware to local cheese and salami.

Arrival and information

Colón's **bus terminal** (@03447/421716) lies fifteen blocks or so northwest of Plaza San Martín, on the corner of Paysandú and 9 de Julio. The busy and mostly helpful **tourist office** (daily 6am–10pm high season, 6am–8pm out of season; @03447/421233, @www.colon.gov.ar) is in an attractive mansion down in the port area, two blocks north of the plaza, on the corner of Avenida Costanera and Gouchón: it provides useful accommodation information, plus details of the sights around Colón and ways of exploring the river.

Villa Elisa, Paraná, El Palmar & Liebig

Arroyo | Artalaz

Complejo Termal

COLÓN

ACCOMMODATION
Bodega Vulliez Sermet — D
Cabañas del Urú — A
Hostería del Puerto — C
Hotel Costarenas — F
Hotel Paysandú — B
Hotel Plaza — E

EATING & DRINKING
La Cantina — 3
La Cosquilla del Angel — 2
Mediterráneo — 1
Moments — 5
Plaza — 6
Verde Gourmet — 4
Viejo Almacén — 7

M VIOLLAZ

BA DE CEPEDA

TRATADO DEL PILAR

LAVALLE

COMB DE MALVINAS

GENERAL PAZ

SOURIGUES

MARINO LIMA

MARINO LIMA

ALVEAR

PAYSANDÚ

Bus Terminal

MAIPÚ

PAYSANDÚ

3 DE FEBRERO

BELGRANO

PEYRET

ROCAMORA

ROCAMORA

BVARD GAILLARD

BVARD GAILLARD

AVENIDA PTE PERÓN

PASO DE LOS ANDES

PASO DE LOS ANDES

ALBERDI

ALBERDI

CHACABUCO

CHACABUCO

GOUCHÓN

GOUCHÓN

BOLÍVAR

BOLÍVAR

SAN MARTIN

SAN MARTIN

SARMENTO

12 DE ABRIL

12 DE ABRIL

PLAZA SAN MARTÍN

PLAZA WASHINGTON

URQUIZA

URQUIZA

PLAZA ARTIGAS

M MORENO

M MORENO

GRAL NOAILLES

GRAL NOAILLES

BROWN

PASO

TUCUMÁN

ALEM

LAPRIDA

LUGONES

AVENIDA COSTANERA QUIRÓS

PBRO COT

AVENIDA GÜEMES

HERNÁNDEZ

GRAL MITRE

25 DE MAYO

ANDRADE

E BERGA

BOULEVARD FERRARI

Balneario Piedras Coloradas

0   500 m

Parque Quirós

Piedras Coloradas

Río Uruguay

RN-14, Gualeguaychú & Buenos Aires

Camping Agueste

249

Accommodation

Colón has a fine range of accommodation at all budget levels, though it does become severely overstretched on summer weekends, when bookings should be made weeks ahead. There are also plenty of **campsites**, spread out along the length of Colón's waterfront, starting with the organized – and sometimes noisy – *Piedras Coloradas* (℡03447/423548; $10 per tent), reached via the southern end of Calle General Belgrano; it has volleyball and basketball courts plus the usual facilities. Beyond this site, the campsites have a slightly more rustic feel. The last of them, *Camping Agreste* (℡03447/15457787; $20 per tent), is an attractive wooded site popular for fishing.

Cabañas del Urú Mauricio Viollaz 330 ℡03447/424029, ⓦwww.cabanasdeluru.com.ar. Six-bed thatched *cabañas* in a small garden with an equally small swimming pool; well-appointed "rustic chic" and in quiet away-from-it-all location, but a shame they are crammed into a tiny plot. ⑦

Hostería del Puerto Gouchón and Alejo Peyret 158 ℡03447/422698, ⓦwww.hosteriadecolon.com.ar. Remarkably good value, this *hostería*, housed in a pink colonial building just one block from the port, has a refreshing swimming pool. The mostly large, attractively decorated rooms are arranged around a central courtyard with an unusual well; some rooms have a river view, but try and avoid the noisy street-side ones. ⑤

Hotel Costarenas Av Quirós and 12 de Abril ℡03447/425050, ⓦwww.hotelcostarenas.com.ar. Undoubtedly Colón's most luxurious hotel, enjoying a prime location overlooking the river. The spa is enticing, the indoor pool a mini-oasis, the gym functional and the restaurant bright and efficient. The rooms are spacious, comfortable and decorated tastefully, though the place lacks character. ⑦

Hotel Paysandú Maipú and Paysandú ℡03447/421140, ⓦwww.hotelpaysandu.com.ar. A good option near the bus terminal, this spruce modern place has clean, comfortable rooms, parking and very friendly owners; breakfast is included. ④

Hotel Plaza Belgrano and 12 de Abril ℡03447/421043, ⓦwww.hotel-plaza.com.ar. A hotel with a split personality – the older side, which has been a hotel since 1913, has small, fairly run-of-the-mill but perfectly acceptable rooms (⑥), while the newer part of the building has much larger, smartly furnished rooms with LCD TVs and private jacuzzis (⑥). All guests can use the outdoor pool and communal jacuzzi and there's a good breakfast served.

The Town

Colón spreads along the Río Uruguay, with a narrow strip of beach running for several kilometres alongside its alluring riverside avenue, the **Costanera Gobernador Quirós**. The town's central square, **Plaza Washington**, where you will find the municipalidad, covers four blocks and lies ten blocks inland; far more elegant, however, is smaller **Plaza San Martín**, east of Plaza Washington along Colón's main commercial street, Avenida 12 de Abril – named after the town's foundation date in 1863. The most distinctive district is the sleepy **port area**, a small but charming cobbled quarter lined with a clutch of handsome colonial-style buildings which slopes down to the riverbank, immediately to the north of Plaza San Martín; if you are driving, watch out for the huge toads that often hop across the street here.

A few hundred metres from Colón's "coast", in the middle of the Río Uruguay, are some lush **islands** flanked with dense vegetation and pristine sandbanks: both offer opportunities for observing local flora and fauna, especially birdlife, and for sunbathing on a private beach. Excursions to the islands in motorized dinghies (1–3hr; take sunscreen, bathing clothes, insect repellent and a sweater on cool evenings) can be made with Ita-i-Corá (℡&ⓕ03447/423360, ⓦwww.itaicora .com), a wonderfully dynamic outfit whose co-owner, Charlie Adamson, speaks excellent English. Their office is at San Martín 97, on the corner of Plaza San Martín, but they also have an information stand on the corner of the Costanera and General Noailles, three blocks south. The same operator runs land-based trips

(2–3hr) to see petrified tree trunks, a display of locally discovered semi-precious stones and the sadly disused **Pueblo Liebig** (open to public every afternoon), a former meat-packing plant 12km north of town, where beef extract was invented. The surprisingly interesting stones are on display at the **Reservorio de Piedras Semipreciosas** (daily 9am–8pm; $2), RP-130 Km3.5; Selva, queen of the agates, is always delighted to show visitors the collection.

Although there's a thermal spa complex right in the middle of town, the best place hereabouts for a relaxing, therapeutic soak is at **Villa Elisa** (daily 8am–10pm; ☏03447/480687, ⓦwww.termasvillaelisa.com; $37), about 30km northwest, 15km off the fork of the RN-14 and the RN-130. This huge, spacious, state-of-the-art **thermal complex** has seven pools with mineral waters especially good for sufferers from rheumatism, with massages and refreshments available; the restaurant is decent. You can also stay on site at the comfortable, modern *Hotel Vertientes* (ⓦwww.hotelvertientes.com.ar; ❹), or you can **camp** (❷) or stay in *cabañas* (❻).

Eating, drinking and nightlife

There are some very good **restaurants** in Colón, most of which are within a few blocks of Plaza San Martín. The best place is the enticingly decorated ✦*La Cosquilla del Angel*, Peyret 186, down at the old port (☏03447/423711); fish, meat and delicious salads are on the menu, prices are moderate and the wine list is commendable. Another excellent choice is the *Viejo Almacén* (☏03447/422216), on the corner of calles Urquiza and J.J. Paso, one block southeast of the plaza, a stylishly old-fashioned place that does excellent river fish – try the grilled *surubí* or *pacú*. For something a bit different, ✦ *Verde Gourmet* (☏03447/15-453354, ⓦwww.verdegourmet.com; booking essential) at Belgrano 75, is a small, informal restaurant space, based in the living room of Martín and his family, who lovingly prepare delicious three-course tailor-made vegetarian meals at a very reasonable price. Alternatively, you can get good, cheap pasta at the long-established and homely *La Cantina*, on Alejo Peyret 79, which also does decent freshwater fish and has tables outside on a quiet street.

As far as **bars** go, the main hub of activity is Avenida 12 de Abril, an obligatory stop for locals on their evening stroll. Nicest of the slew of bars along here is the

Colón's unique winery

In defiance of Colón's subtropical climate, usually regarded as totally hostile to wine grapes, in 1857 a Swiss immigrant named **Joseph Favre** planted a few **vines** from his homeland just outside the city. Seventeen years later, with his vines not only succeeding, but thriving, he added a handsome **bodega** (winery) in the Piedmontese style – an Italianate villa with ochre walls that would not look out of place in the countryside around Turin. In 1936, the national government banned the commercial production of wine anywhere outside the Cuyo and the Andean Northwest, but Favre's descendants continued making wine for their own consumption. When the law was finally repealed in 1998, Jesús Vulliez, a local descendant of other Swiss immigrants, bought the nineteenth-century bodega and began producing wine for commercial distribution under the label **Vulliez Sermet**, planting five hectares with chardonnay, malbec, merlot, cabernet sauvignon, tannat, syrah and sangiovese vines. If you call ahead, you can visit the beautiful bodega, with its impeccably restored interior and cool cellars, taste the fine red and white wines, and eat at the bodega restaurant (closed Tues). The attractive grounds nearby house a large swimming pool and three luxurious **cabañas** sleeping up to six (☏03447/156-45925, ⓦwww.bodegavulliezsermet.com.ar; ❻). To reach the complex from the RN-14, take the RP-135 Colón–Paysandú road and stay on it for another 200m after the turn-off to Colón.

modern and lively *Moments*, between Lavalle and 3 de Febrero. Colón's main **nightclub** is *Mediterráneo*, housed in a distinctive white building along Alejo Peyret between Alberdi and Chacabuco. Just about all of Colón ends up here at weekends.

Palacio San José

When it was built in the middle of the nineteenth century for General Justo José de Urquiza, the **Palacio San José** (Mon–Fri 8am–7pm, Sat & Sun 9am–6pm; Jan & Feb also Fri 9pm–12.30am; 1hr guided visits, in Spanish, at 10am, 11am, 3pm & 4pm, plus noon & 2pm at weekends; $5; ⓦwww.palaciosanjose.com.ar), 40km southwest of Colón and a short way off the RP-39, was Argentina's most luxurious private residence. *Caudillo* of Entre Ríos Province in the early nineteenth century and its governor from 1841, Urquiza was also the province's largest and wealthiest landowner, possessing a huge *saladero* (meat-salting plant). Restrictions imposed by Buenos Aires on the provinces' freedom to trade led Urquiza to revolt against dictator General Rosas, finally defeating him at the Battle of Caseros, outside Buenos Aires, in 1853. The lavishness of the palace seems clearly intended as a challenge to the Buenos Aires elite's idea of provincial backwardness – it had running water before any building in the capital. The architect was Pedro Fosatti – who also designed the Italian hospitals in Buenos Aires and Montevideo – and, despite the colonial watchtowers that dominate its facade, it shows a strong Italian influence in its elegant Tuscan arches.

The entrance to the palace is at the back of the building, now painted the deep pink of national monuments; to your right as you enter stands a tiny **chapel** lined with spectacular frescoes by nineteenth-century Uruguayan academic painter Juan Manuel Blanes and an imposing three-metre high baptismal font, entirely carved from Carrara marble, a gift from Pope Pius IX (who kept a copy in the Vatican). The palace's 38 rooms are laid out around two vast courtyards. The first of these, the **Patio del Parral**, is named for its grapevines, many of which were brought for Urquiza from France. The rooms in the second courtyard, the **Patio de Honor**, were occupied by Urquiza's most immediate family and important guests. Its most significant room is the dramatically named **Sala de la Tragedia** (Room of Tragedy), Urquiza's bedroom where, on April 11, 1870, he was assassinated by followers of rival *caudillo* López Jordán. It was turned into a shrine by Urquiza's widow, and traces of blood can still be seen on the door, along with bullets embedded in the wall. Beyond the Patio de Honor extends a small French-style **garden**, from where the Palacio's harmonious facade appears to best advantage.

During the high season (January, February and Easter), various **tour** companies offer trips from Colón, such as LDL, 12 de Abril 119 (☏03447/422222). Otherwise, a *remise* will cost around $50, or you can take a bus from Concepción del Uruguay (just south of Colón) to Caseros or Paraná and ask to be let off at the turn-off to the Palacio San José, from where it's a three-kilometre walk.

Parque Nacional El Palmar

As you head north from Colón along the RN-14, the first sign that you are approaching **PARQUE NACIONAL EL PALMAR** is a sprinkling of tremendously tall palm trees towering above the flat lands that border the highway. The 85-square-kilometre park was set up in 1966 to conserve examples of the **yatay palm**, which once covered large areas of Entre Ríos Province, Uruguay and southern Brazil. Intensive cultivation of the region almost wiped out the palm, and the national park is now the largest remaining reserve of the *yatay*; it is also one of the southernmost palm groves in the world. Though the terrain itself is nondescript rolling grassland, the sheer proliferation of the majestic *yatay* – with many examples over three hundred years old and up to eighteen metres in height – makes for a wonderfully exotic-looking landscape. Bordering the Río Uruguay along its eastern fringe, the park is composed of **gallery forest**, dense pockets of subtropical vegetation formed when seeds and sediment are borne downstream from Brazil and Misiones. It is best appreciated on an overnight stay – the extensive acres of palm forest are absolutely stunning in the late afternoon light, when their exotic forms sing out against the deepening blue sky and reddish gold of the earth.

There are a number of well-signposted trails in the park, taking you along the streams and through palm forests; the longer of these are designed for vehicles, though if you don't mind trekking along several kilometres of gravel road, there's nothing to stop you doing them on foot. There are great views from **La Glorieta**, a gentle bluff from where you can take in the surrounding sea of palms. Wildlife in the park includes ñandús, armadillos, foxes and capybaras and, particularly around the campsite, vizcachas and monitor lizards.

Practicalities

The **entrance** to the park lies 50km north of Colón, along the RN-14. There is a *guardaparques'* post at the entrance where you pay a $25 entrance fee and can pick up a map and information leaflet. It's a hefty ten-kilometre or so walk from the entrance to the visitors' centre and campsite, though at all but the quietest times it should be possible to get a lift with someone else entering the park. Alternatively, you can take an organized trip – usually half-day tours – from Colón with a company such as LDL. The only place to stay within the park is *Camping El Palmar* (☏03447/423378; $12 per tent, plus $14 per person), a spacious and shady site with showers and a provisions store; the best pitches have a great view over the Río Uruguay. There is also a decent restaurant in the park, next door to the visitors' centre.

You can stay near the park, though, at the ecology-minded ⚘ *Aurora del Palmar* complex (☏03447/15-431689, Ⓦwww.auroradelpalmar.com.ar; ❻–❼), set well back from the RN-14 at Km202, on the opposite side to the park entrance. The 1.5 square kilometres of preserved land host a grove of *yatay* palms, plus a set of disused train carriages that have been converted into **accommodation**; there are also more spacious rooms in a colonial-style building nearby, overlooking citrus orchards and a large swimming pool. Guests and non-guests can eat simple meals here and go on excursions such as horse rides, canoe trips, birdwatching and treks into the Palmar. Even as you have lunch on the terrace you are treated to a bucolic scene and effortless sightings of several bird species. **Camping** is also allowed, for $12 per person.

Central Corrientes: the Esteros del Iberá

Covering nearly 13,000 square kilometres (one-sixth of Corrientes Province), the delicate ecosystem of the **ESTEROS DEL IBERÁ** is a magical landscape that offers some of the best opportunities in the country for close-up observation of wildlife. An elongated sliver of land running through the centre of Corrientes Province, the *esteros* (marshes) are bordered to the north by the RN-12, to the east by tributaries of the Aguaypey and Miriñay rivers and to the west by tributaries of the Paraná. The southern tip touches the RN-123, which runs east–west from the border town of Paso de los Libres, joining the RN-12 150km south of Corrientes city. In addition to the *esteros* that give the area its name, you will see a good many lakes, ponds, streams and wonderful floating islands, formed by a build-up of soil on top of intertwined waterlilies.

For many years this was one of Argentina's wildest and least-known regions – a local legend even had it that a tribe of pygmies lived on the islands – harbouring an isolated community who made their living from hunting and fishing the area's wildlife. Since the **Reserva Natural del Iberá** was created in 1983, hunting has been prohibited in the area and many locals have been employed as highly specialized guides, or *baqueanos*, and park rangers, thus helping to preserve the unique environment. The ban on hunting has led to an upsurge in the region's abundant bird and animal population, with an amazingly diverse range of species thriving here (see box, p.258).

In the heart of the reserve, beside the ecosystem's second largest lake, the Laguna del Iberá, is the spread-out village of **Colonia Carlos Pellegrini** ("Pellegrini"). The main gateway to the *esteros*, though is **Mercedes**, a picturesque traditional town 120km southwest of Pellegrini. If **driving**, note that the road linking Pellegrini to Posadas in a northeasterly direction is not always viable, especially after rain (in any case, best in a 4WD); whatever you do, enquire about its current state before attempting it.

Mercedes

Approximately 200km southeast of the city of Corrientes, **MERCEDES** is unlikely to impress at first sight. Set among the flatlands of central Corrientes Province, it appears as a sprawling modern settlement with little to tempt you into staying. Head into the centre, though, and you'll find an appealing agricultural town given a distinctive flavour by a mix of old-fashioned adobe and galleried-roof buildings plus some elegant nineteenth-century architecture. The town is a real hub of country life, too: horses and carts are a common sight on its streets and on Saturdays gauchos come to town, traditionally dressed Corrientes-style, with shallow, wide-brimmed hats, ornate belts and wide *bombachas* (trousers) and accompanied by their wives, who wear frilly, old-fashioned dresses. Around 9km west of town, along the RN-123, there is a roadside shrine to a popular local hero, **Gauchito Gil** (see box opposite).

The town, built on a regular grid pattern, is centred on **Plaza 25 de Mayo**, a densely planted square with little fountains. At its southern end stands the rather unusual **Iglesia Nuestra Señora de las Mercedes**, a lofty, late nineteenth-century red-brick church whose towers are topped with Moorish domes. Along the southern side of the square runs Juan Pujol, an attractive street lined with some fine buildings.

Three blocks east of the square, on the corner of San Martín and Batalla de Salta, there's a beautifully preserved example of the local building style: a low whitewashed adobe-walled construction with a gently sloping red-tiled roof which overhangs the pavement, supported on simple wooden posts. This building houses the **Fundación Manos Correntinas**, a nonprofit enterprise that functions as an outlet for locally produced crafts. The small but superior collection of goods includes basketwork, simple gourd *mates*, heavy woollens and hand-turned bone and horn buttons. There are various other craft outlets throughout town: try the shops along San Martín and Juan Pujol selling belts, gaucho knives, *mates* and the like – all with a sturdy utilitarian feel and far less gimmicky than the pieces on sale in more touristy towns.

Practicalities

Mercedes' **bus terminal** is six blocks west of Plaza San Martín, on the corner of Avenida San Martín and El Ceibo, with a left luggage and general information office (open 24hr). The **tourist office** (daily 8am–noon & 4–8pm;

Gauchito Gil

Along roadsides throughout Argentina you'll see mysterious **shrines** of varying sizes, smothered in red flags, red candles, empty bottles and other miscellaneous bits and pieces. These are erected in homage to the semi-mythical **Gauchito Gil**, a kind of nineteenth-century gaucho Robin Hood – one of those folkloric figures whose story has some basis in reality yet has undoubtedly been embellished over the years.

Born – perhaps – in 1847 in Corrientes, Antonio Gil refused to fight in that province's civil war and fled to the mountains, robbing from the rich, helping the poor and healing with his hands. Captured by the police, he claimed that he had deserted from the army as he had been told in a dream by a Guaraní god that brothers shouldn't fight each other. An unimpressed sergeant took him out to a spot near Mercedes to execute him. Gil told the sergeant that when he returned to town he would find that his son was seriously ill, but as Gil's blood was innocent it could perform miracles, so the sergeant must pray for his intervention. Unmoved, the sergeant cut Gil's throat. When he returned to town, he found that the situation was indeed as the gaucho had described, but – after fervent prayer – his son made a miraculous recovery.

The sergeant put up the first shrine to thank him, and Gauchito Gil has since been credited with numerous **miracles** and honoured with many **shrines**, all bedecked in the distinctive **red flags** – which may represent his neck scarf soaked in blood – making the shrine look like the aftermath of a left-wing political demonstration after all the protesters have gone home. The shrine erected near **Mercedes**, on the place where he was killed, presumably began life as a simple affair, but such is the popularity of **Gauchito Gil** that the site has mushroomed over time into a vast *villa* of humble restaurants, makeshift sleeping areas and souvenir stalls; there is even a kind of museum exhibiting the offerings made to the Gauchito, such as football shirts, wedding dresses and children's bicycles, along with more conventional rosaries. Simpler offerings, often made by passing motorists to ensure a safe journey, include ribbons and candles. January 8 sees Gauchito Gil pilgrims flock to the main shrine from the whole country. There is a close parallel with the folk-saint shrines to the Difunta Correa, whose main pilgrimage site lies near San Juan (see p.419) but is also honoured by smaller versions nationwide.

T03773/15414384), inconveniently located in an isolated building at the western entrance to town, can provide useful information and a map. There's an **ATM** at the Banco de Corrientes, on the corner of Pedro Ferre, three blocks west of Plaza San Martín; stock up here if you are heading to Pellegrini, in the heart of the *esteros*, as it has no banking facilities or decent stores.

Accommodation options in Mercedes are surprisingly good for a small provincial town, though there aren't that many beds available. The best place is *La Casa de China* (T03773/156-27269, Wwww.corrientes.com.ar/lacasadechina; ❹), a fabulous B&B at Fray Luis Beltrán 599 and Mitre; the tastefully furnished, quiet, patrician villa has four double rooms, a private botanical garden behind, and China herself will prepare delicious meals if given notice. If it's full, a good fall-back is the quaint *Hotel Sol*, San Martín 519, a few blocks east of the plaza (T03773/420283, Wwww .corrientes.com.ar/hotelsolmercedes; ❸); it is in a lovely old building with spotless if dingy rooms – all of them en suite with TV and fans – set around an attractive flower-filled courtyard. The best budget option is the *Hostel Delicias del Iberá*, Dr Rivas 688 (T03773/423167, Wwww.corrientes.com.ar/deliciasdelibera; $35 per person); the rooms are a little small and tatty but the ambience is ultra-friendly. For **meals**, *Pizza Libre*, on the plaza, dishes up passable pizzas, while *Sal y Pimienta*, at Gómez 665, near the bus terminal, does good *supremas* (breaded chicken) and pasta.

Colonia Carlos Pellegrini and the esteros

COLONIA CARLOS PELLEGRINI lies at the heart of the Reserva Natural del Iberá, 120km northeast of Mercedes, and is mainly accessed via the unsealed but well-maintained RP-40. The journey there takes you through flat, unremarkable land, reminiscent of the African savannah, but with little to prepare you for the wonderfully wild, watery environment of the *esteros* themselves. The village sits on a peninsula on the edges of the Laguna del Iberá, a 53 square-kilometre expanse of water. The banks of the sparkling lake (*iberá* means "shining" in Guaraní) are spread with acres of waterlilies, most notably the striking lilac-bloomed *camalotes* and yellow *aguapés*, and dotted with bouncy floating islands formed of matted reeds and grass, known as *embalsados*.

If you come from Mercedes by bus or with your own transport, access to the village is over a temporary-looking – and sounding – narrow bridge constructed of earth and rock. There's a small **visitors' centre** (open daily during daylight hours) immediately to the left just before you cross the bridge, where you can see a small display on the *esteros* and their wildlife. Short trails on either side of the road lead through a small forested area south of the visitors' centre; the densely packed mix of palms, jacarandas, *lapachos* and willows here is a good place to spot and hear black howler monkeys who typically slouch in a ball shape among the branches or swing from tree to tree on lianas. Easiest to see are the yellowish young, often ferried from tree to tree on the backs of their mothers. Birds and butterflies abound, while capybaras often graze on the grass.

The village itself is composed of a small grid of sandy streets, centred on grassy **Plaza San Martín**. There are few services, and no banking facilities, so make sure you bring enough cash with you for your stay (nobody takes credit cards).

Accommodation

The best **accommodation** is provided by various posadas, most of which offer full board with at least one **boat trip** to the lagoon included and other activities laid on. For those on a budget, there are a couple of hostels and a municipal **campsite** immediately to the left as you enter the village from the bridge; it's a pleasant riverside site with showers but is almost entirely bereft of shade.

Don Justino ☏ 03773/499415, ⊛ www.corrientes .com.ar/donjustinohostel. Decent hostel in an attractive converted house overlooking the lake, with simple rooms and a basic restaurant; the friendly staff will help arrange excursions and onward travel. US$14–20 per person for a dorm bed and breakfast.

Estancia Rincón del Socorro ☏ 03782/497073, ⊛ www.rincondelsocorro.com. Five kilometres from the main road, this converted working estancia is efficiently run by the hospitable Cook family. The traditional main building and luxurious rooms are all decorated with handsome furnishings and splendid photos of Iberá flora and fauna. Food includes home-grown, organic fruit, vegetables and herbs. A small plane can take you to a sister estancia, *San Alonso*, on the shores of Laguna Paraná, bang in the middle of the *esteros*, where it is also possible to spend the night. ❾ full board including activities.

Irupé Lodge ☏ 03773/154-402193, ⊛ www .irupelodge.com.ar. Handsome wooden *hostería*

with five down-to-earth, brightly decorated rooms overlooking the lagoon, with its own jetty and launch. ❼ full board with some activities.

Posada Aguapé ☏ 03773/499412, ⊛ www .iberaesteros.com.ar. A traditional building set in spacious grounds with twelve appealing en-suite rooms overlooking the lake. There's also a swimming pool and a cosy bar area. ❹ full board including two trips.

Posada de la Laguna ☏ 03773/499413 or 156-29827, ⊛ www.posadadelalaguna.com. Particularly well situated in a quiet lakeside spot at the eastern edge of the village, this pioneering posada offers pared-down luxury with a rustic feel. The elegant and spacious but simple en-suite rooms are in a galleried building whose verandah provides a good vantage point for observing the birds that gather around the lake; food and service are top-notch and the swimming pool is another great spot for some laidback birdwatching. ❼ full board.

Posada Rancho de los Esteros ☎03773/154-93041, ⓦwww.ranchodelosesteros.com.ar. Just two handsomely decorated suites in a wonderful ranch with a traditional gallery. ⑧ full board including some activities.

Puerto Valle just off the the RN-12 between Posadas and Corrientes city ☎03786/425700, ⓦwww.hotelpuertovalle.com. Not in Carlos Pellegrini but allowing access to the northern reaches of the *esteros*, this small luxury hotel is on a large timber estate. The spacious, very comfortable rooms in a single storey building – all overlooking trimmed lawns that run down to the

edge of the Paraná river – are perfect for those who don't like their rural encounter to be too rustic, and there is a lovely pool and boat trips on the river and into the *esteros* included in the price. ⑧ full board.

Rancho Inambú Yeruti and Peguajó ☎03773/436159, ⓦwww.ranchoinambu.com.ar. Recently converted from a hostel to a budget posada, Inambú is a typical mudbrick house, with attractive rooms of various sizes, an airy breakfast room and a bar with a pool table. Packages including boat and horse riding excursions can be arranged for around $300 per person. Double room including breakfast ⑤

The Esteros del Iberá

Wildlife-spotting excursions are organized through the posadas, which take visitors out in their small motorboats, with the boatmen acting as guides. After speeding across the centre of the lake, the boats dip under the causeway bridge, calling in at the visitors' centre to register, before cutting their engines to drift through the narrow streams that thread between the islands on the other side of the Laguna. This silent approach allows you an incredibly privileged view of the *esteros'* wildlife (see box, p.258); turning a corner you suddenly find yourself among a wonderful landscape of water lilies and verdant floating islands, the whole of it teeming with bird and animal life. Sometimes guides will take you onto the floating islands themselves; it's a particularly bizarre experience to feel the ground vibrating beneath your feet as you move. Another trip takes you along the Río Miriñay, home to slightly different varieties of flora and fauna to the lake. Enquire also about **horse rides** in the nearby marshes, another excellent way to see birds and the like, especially in the morning.

▲ Capybaras

Home to well over three hundred species of **birds** and a mindblowing variety of **reptiles** and **mammals**, the Esteros del Iberá are a paradise for any visitor with an interest in animals. Armed with binoculars and a guidebook to South American species, you stand an excellent chance of observing dozens of different varieties in just an hour or two; a good guide will help, too.

A common sight and sound around the Laguna del Iberá are *chajás* (**Southern Screamers**), large grey birds with a patch of red around the eyes and a look of bashful nervousness. They frequently perch on the trees on the lakeside, nonchalantly chanting "aha-aha" but occasionally emitting a piercing yelp (hence the English name) similar to the sound a dog makes when trodden on. Other large birds include sleek, black **Olivaceous cormorants**; **Maguari storks**, with striking black and white plumage, and a tendency to soar on the thermals above the lake; and **Striated Herons**, characterized by a black crown and a lazy disposition. A particularly impressive sight during the spring nesting period is that of the *garzales*, where hundreds of normally solitary herons unite in a spectacular mass gathering. Another magical, if rarer, sight is the elegant *jabirú*, a long-legged relative of the stork with a white body, bright crimson collar and a black head and beak. Different species of **kingfisher** also put on a show of aviation prowess, swooping across the water and diving into it. **Wattled jacanas**, on the other hand, prefer to scuttle over waterlilies and floating weeds, seldom showing off their lemon-tipped wings. Another strange-moving bird is the **Giant Wood-Rail**, or *ipacaá*, whose Guaraní name is onomatopoeic; it croaks plaintively as it tiptoes around near houses, grabbing any food left out for it and scampering off to peck away at it.

Birds are not the only wonders around the *esteros*. Among the reedbeds at the edges of the lake you may catch sight of large **snakes**, such as the handsome **yellow anaconda**, its golden skin dotted with black patches; they can reach up to three metres in length. As you approach the edges of the floating islands, in particular, charcoal-grey **caymans**, or *yacarés*, freeze, often with their ferocious-looking jaws stuck open, or else they suddenly slither into the water, where they observe you with only their eyes peeking above the surface. Another startling spectacle is provided by creepily large **spiders**, which lurk in huge webs among bushes and reeds, waiting for their helpless insect prey. Some guides delight in making it look as though the boat is heading straight for them, so arachnophobes be warned. Rather more appealing are the hundreds of **butterflies**, in every colour imaginable, an enchanting sight you will see all over the region.

Mammals are well represented, too. **Howler monkeys** – which really growl rather than howl – are much easier to hear than to see, but you might, if you are patient, observe their antics near the visitors' centre or in other tall trees in the area. Listen, too, for the sudden splash of a **capybara**, or *carpincho*, diving into the water. On land, this guinea-pig-like mammal, the world's largest rodent, looks almost ungainly, but they are incredibly graceful as they glide through the water. The floating islands are where the capybaras go to sleep and graze. There, and on the marshy lands and pastures around the more isolated extremes of the lake, you may also spot the rare **marsh deer**, South America's largest, equally at home in the water and on dry land. If you approach them gently, these astonishingly beautiful animals seem to accept your presence and continue grazing lazily on aquatic plants. Rarest of all of the *esteros'* wildlife, and certainly the hardest to spot, is the endangered *aguara-guazú*, or **maned wolf**, a reddish long-legged creature that awkwardly lopes through the vegetation, moving first its two left legs and then the two right ones – or so they say.

Misiones Province

The proboscis-shaped territory of **Misiones**, in the extreme northeast of the country, is one of Argentina's smallest, poorest but most beautiful provinces. **Posadas**, the relaxed capital, is usually bypassed by most travellers, but the province has a lot more to offer than the juggernaut that is **Iguazú Falls**, the only place most visitors ever see, zipping in and out by plane. What looks odd on the map makes perfect sense on the ground: Misiones' borders are almost completely defined by the wide Paraná and Uruguay rivers and one can even imagine that the province's sierras have been formed through the land being compressed by neighbouring Brazil and Paraguay. Even the province's distinctive iron-rich **red earth** ends abruptly just over the border with Corrientes, while the torrent of water that hurtles over the waterfalls at Iguazú must surely mark one of world's most dramatic and decisive frontiers.

The territory was named for the Jesuit settlements that flourished in the region – also across the present-day borders in Paraguay and Brazil – in the seventeenth and eighteenth centuries; the most impressive mission on Argentine soil is the much photographed ruins of **San Ignacio Miní**. Along the Brazilian frontier, formed by the upper reaches of the Río Uruguay, you can see one of the world's most unusual, if not most powerful, sets of cascades, the **Saltos del Moconá**, weather conditions permitting. The province's wildlife-filled **jungle** and its emerald fields and orchards – pale tobacco, vivid lime trees, darker manioc and neatly clipped tea plantations, painting the landscape endless shades of green – are further attractions that make wandering off the beaten tracks that are the RN-12 and the RN-14 infinitely rewarding. Misiones was also the centre of considerable immigration in the early twentieth century: throughout the province you'll find the descendants of Ukrainians, Swedes, Japanese and Germans. A Guaraní influence is also obvious, with scattered small native communities. This cross-cultural phenomenon is echoed in the speech of inhabitants in the more rural areas, where a mix of Guaraní and Spanish can be heard; throughout the Litoral, Guaraní words are a common feature of speech: you may hear a child referred to as a "*gurí*" or a woman as a "*guaina*". Although away from Iguazú tourist facilities are few and far between, a number of **estancias** and **lodges** make for some of the country's most enjoyable accommodation experiences.

Posadas and around

If you arrive in **Posadas** expecting your first taste of the jungle, you'll be disappointed: the provincial capital sits on a rather bare patch of land bordering the Río Paraná, which – bar the red earth – has more in common with northern Corrientes than with the luscious emerald sierras of central and northern Misiones Province. However, while not exactly postcard-worthy, Posadas is a pleasant and prosperous place with a lively feel, some attractive buildings tucked away among the centre's mostly modern constructions, and a revamped Costanera, or riverside esplanade, a wonderful place for a stroll on a summer's evening.

The first recorded settlement in the vicinity of modern-day Posadas was a **Jesuit Mission**, founded in 1615. In 1879, the fledgling city was named after **José Gervasio de Posadas**, who, in 1814, had become the first Supreme Director of the Provincias Unidas del Río de la Plata – a title that rather outdid his reign, which lasted only until January of the following year. In 1884 Posadas, by far the most important settlement in the region, became Misiones' provincial capital. Since then it has largely been a quiet backwater, whose fortunes in recent years have been tied to its proximity to the massive **Yacyretá Dam** and the linked construction of a road to Paraguay via the **Puente Roque González de Santa Cruz**. The dam has led to a significant rise in the water level of the Paraná, submerging beaches, campsites and docks in Posadas (and further afield) in 2009, while the link with Paraguay has dramatically swelled the town's population.

Posadas is primarily a **stopover city** and appears to do little to reap any benefit from the modest but steady stream of tourists who pass through. While there's a handful of mildly interesting **museums** here, there is little – bar the odd craft shop – specifically aimed at the holiday-maker. The town hosts a lively provincial festival, known as the **Estudiantina**, which runs over three weekends in September. During the festival local schools prepare and perform dance routines – all with a strong Brazilian influence.

Arrival and information

The quiet **airport** is around 7km southwest of the centre; bus #28 runs into town from here, or you could take a taxi (around $30). Posadas' **bus terminal** (☏03752/454887 or 454888) is about 4km south of the centre at the intersection

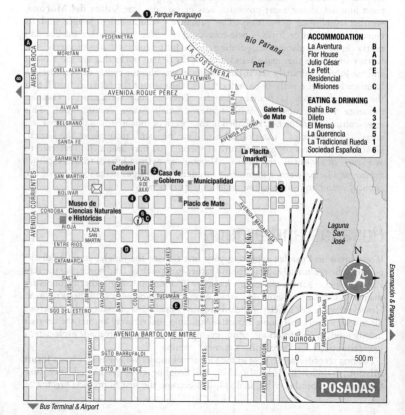

of Avenida Santa Catalina and the RN-12. It's a modern building with good facilities, though no ATM machine. From the terminal there are numerous local buses (including #24, #25 and #21) heading into the centre; the taxi ride will cost about $20.

Posadas' well-stocked **tourist office**, at Colón 1985 (Mon–Fri 7am–8pm, Sat & Sun 8am–noon & 4.30–8pm; ℡03752/447539, ⓦwww.posadas.gov.ar), has fairly decent maps of both the town and the province, though it doesn't have an awful lot of information on anything beyond the well-worn Posadas/San Ignacio/Iguazú groove. Posadas' streets were renumbered in the 1990s but, confusingly, both systems are still in use. You will generally find that the address will be written as the new number (usually four digits), with the old number (usually three digits) in brackets, while either may be used on the building itself – where necessary, we have followed this custom.

Accommodation

The majority of people seeking **accommodation** in Posadas are businessmen, so many of the hotels are fairly bland with a couple of worthy exceptions. There's also a very pleasant **cabin and camping complex**, *La Aventura*, on the riverbank towards the outskirts of town. Note that Posadas can be extremely hot and sticky during the summer, so plan on spending more than your normal budget in order to get air conditioning. Alternatively, if you have your own transport, consider staying at one of the excellent **estancias** in the surrounding countryside, where you can get to know the locals and enjoy the province's flora and fauna; booking ahead is vital.

In town

La Aventura Av Urquiza and Av Zapiola ℡03752/465555, ⓦwww.complejoaventura .com. Swish camping and cabin complex on the outskirts of town, complete with good recreational facilities – including tennis courts and a swimming pool. Dorm beds cost around $50 per person. Buses #3 and #13 go from the corner of San Lorenzo and Sarmiento. ❻.

Flor House Av Roca 962 ℡ 03752/438053, ⓦwww.florhouse.com.ar. Charming, traditional B&B in a lovely family house – the larger rooms are immaculate and spacious, with mountains of frilly pillows and balconies. The breakfasts are top notch and there is an outdoor pool set in a garden filled with birdsong. ❸–❹

Julio César Entre Ríos 1951 ℡03752/427930, ⓦwww.juliocesarhotel.com.ar. Posadas' most upmarket hotel – four-star comfort including a swimming pool and gym. ❼

Le Petit Santiago del Estero 1630 ℡03752/436031, ⓔlepetithotel@ciudad.com.ar. On a quiet, tree-lined street away from the centre, this small, prettily decorated place has light and spacious rooms. Facilities include TV, telephone and a/c, and breakfast is provided. The friendly owner is also a good source of tourist information. Reservations advisable. ❸

Residencial Misiones Félix de Azara 1960 (382) ℡03752/430133. This is just about the cheapest

recommendable place in the centre of town: an old-fashioned hotel with rooms around a central patio. The whole family mucks in with the running of the hotel and there's a friendly atmosphere, although some of the rooms are in serious need of an overhaul. ❷

Estancias around Posadas

Estancia Santa Cecilia Candelaria, 30km northeast of Posadas ℡03752/493018, ⓦwww .santa-cecilia.com.ar. Built in 1908 on a bluff overlooking the Río Paraná, this patrician house has six delightful rooms full of colonial charm, with a refined but not snobbish atmosphere. It provides horses for rides along the riverbanks, puts on impressive displays of gaucho horsemanship and horse-related crafts and serves traditional regional cuisine. The grounds are subtly landscaped, but the general feeling is one of open space – the swimming pool is fabulous. ❾ full board.

Estancia Santa Inés 20km southeast of Posadas (℡03752/156-60456, ⓦwww .estancia-santaines.com.ar). With a lovely, old-fashioned interior, displaying a marvellous collection of silver mate paraphernalia, the estancia's trump card is its exotic setting within a mini-jungle of luxuriant vegetation. You can ride through the mate plantations to the huge outdoor pool, 5 km away, fed by a natural spring, or visit the family's private chapel, containing handsome Jesuit carvings. Prices range from $40 for an afternoon visit, including tea (or mate), to $150 per person (⑤) for an overnight stay, including all activities and meals.

The City

The centre of Posadas is demarcated by four main avenues – Sáenz Peña, Guacurarí, Corrientes and B. Mitre, the last of which leads towards the inter-national bridge. Within this area you will find the majority of hotels and points of interest. The main reason for heading further northeast is to visit the **Parque Paraguayo**, where there is a crafts market and the Museo Regional Aníbal Cambas, and the **Costanera**, a popular hangout in the evenings.

Plaza 9 de Julio and around

Posadas' central plaza, the **Plaza 9 de Julio**, is flanked to the north by the early twentieth-century **Iglesia Catedral**, a work by super-prolific Alejandro Bustillo, who designed Buenos Aires' Banco Nación, among many other buildings. The plaza's best-looking building, however, is the **Casa de Gobierno**, a sugar-pink Rococo construction on Félix de Azara. The building sits perfectly alongside the manicured splendour of the square, where there's a healthy selection of local vegetation, including *pindó* palms and *lapacho*, neatly displayed in densely packed flowerbeds that are like little urban squares of jungle. Throughout the town you will find examples of the bright red and yellow *chivato* tree, originally imported from Madagascar, together with ficus or rubber trees, whose enormous leaves provide welcome shade.

The city's **commercial centre** is concentrated on the streets west of the plaza, with Calle Bolívar in particular forming the hub of the clothes shops that make up much of the town's retail activity. There's usually a huddle of street traders, too, though for a real market atmosphere, you should head for the **Mercado Paraguayo** (daily 8am–6pm), towards the port on the intersection of San Martín and Avenida Presidente Roque Sáenz Peña. Known locally as **"La Placita"**, it sells a vast range of electronic goods, toys, clothes and shoes, all imported from Paraguay.

At Rivadavia 1846, two blocks east of Plaza 9 de Julio, the rather grandly named **Palacio de Mate** (daily 9am–6pm) houses temporary exhibitions by local artists, alongside a permanent collection of small wooden carvings of laidback Chaco life by Juan de Dios Mena – look out for *Empleado Publico* (public employee) asleep, with his feet up on his desk. On the patio in front of the building, check out the scrap metal sculpture of a *cebador* preparing his mate (see box, p.263).

The port and Costanera

Just beyond Avenida Roque Penez, Calle Fleming, more commonly known as the **Bajada Vieja**, is one of Posada's most picturesque streets, lined with original nineteenth-century houses. The street leads down to the **port**, where boats formerly departed to Paraguay and Brazil, though the rising level of the Paraná has put all ferry services on hold for the immediate future. Nearby, at Roque Saenz Peña 1405, the **Galería de Mate** is worth browsing for its dizzying array of *yerba* as well as all the accompanying equipment, and other local handicrafts.

From here, the riverside walkway known as the **Costanera** is lined with bars and restaurants and is a lovely spot to watch the sunset or wonder about life in Encarnacíon, Paraguay, clearly visible on the opposite bank. Currently stretching about twenty blocks from north to east, it has been much improved in recent years, and is popular with joggers and dog-walkers; plans are in place to extend it as far as the international bridge.

Mate: more than just a drink

The herby leaves used in making **mate**, Argentina's national beverage, come from an evergreen tree, *Ilex paraguayensis*, a member of the holly family that grows in north-eastern Argentina, southern Brazil and Paraguay. Its leaves and buds are harvested with machetes in the dry southern winter (June–Aug) and used to make the *yerba* or *mate* herb. The **preparation** process for good *yerba* is complex and subtle: first comes the *zapecado*, literally "opening of the eyes", when the *mate* leaves are dry-roasted over a fire, to prevent fermentation and keep the leaves green. They are then coarsely ground, bagged and left to mature in dry sheds for nine months to a year, though this is sometimes artificially accelerated to two months or even less. A milling process then results in either coarse *caá-guazú* "big herb", or the more refined *caá-mini*.

The **vessel** you drink it out of is also called a *mate*, or *matecito*, originally a hollowed-out gourd of the climbing species *Lagenaria vulgaris*, native to the same region. It's dried, hollowed out and "cured" by macerating *yerba mate* inside it overnight. These gourds are still used today and come in two basic **shapes**: the pear-shaped *poro*, traditionally used for *mate* sweetened with sugar, and the squat, satsuma-shaped *galleta*, meant for *cimarrón*, literally "untamed", or unsweetened *mate*. Many *mates* are **works of art**, intricately carved or painted, and often made of wood, clay or metal – though connoisseurs claim gourds impart extra flavour to the brew. The *bombilla* – originally a reed or stick of bamboo – is the other vital piece of equipment. Most are now straw-shaped tubes of silver, aluminium or tin, flattened at the end on which you suck, and with a spoon-shaped protruberance at the other; this is perforated to strain the *mate* as you drink it. Optional extras include the *pava hornillo*, a special kettle that keeps the water at the right temperature. A thermos-flask is the modern-day substitute for this kettle, and can be replenished at shops and cafés; "hot water available" signs are a common sight all over Argentina but especially in the Litoral.

Mateine is a gentler **stimulant** than the closely related caffeine, helping to release muscular energy, pace the heartbeat and aid respiration without any of the side-effects of coffee. In the 1830s it even met with the approval of a wary Charles Darwin, who wrote that it helped him sleep. It's a tonic and a **digestive agent**, and by dulling the appetite can help you lose weight. Its laxative, diuretic and sweat-making proper-ties also make it very effective at purging toxins, perfect after excessive *asado* binges.

If find yourself in a **group** drinking *mate*, it's just as well to know how to avoid gaffes. The *cebador* – from *cebar* "to feed" – is the person who makes the *mate*. After half-filling the *matecito* with *yerba*, the *cebador* thrusts the *bombilla* into the *yerba* and trickles very hot – but not boiling – water down the side of the *bombilla*, to wet the *yerba* from below. The *cebador* always tries the *mate* first – the "fool's *mate*" – before refilling and handing it round to each person present, in turn – always with the right hand and clockwise. Each drinker drains the *mate* through the *bombilla*, without jiggling it around, sipping gently but not lingering, or sucking too hard, before handing it back to the *cebador*. Sucking out of the corner of the mouth is also frowned upon. A little more *yerba* may be added from time to time but there comes a moment when the *yerba* loses most of its flavour and no longer produces a healthy froth. The *matecito* is then emptied and the process started afresh. Saying *"gracias"* means you've had enough, and the *mate* will be passed to someone else when your turn comes round.

Parque Paraguayo and the Museo Regional Aníbal Cambas

Ten blocks northwest of the Plaza 9 de Julio, the small Parque Paraguayo hosts a **crafts market** in the mornings and late afternoons, where you can see examples of Guaraní basketwork made from local wild cane and carved wooden animals, among other items. By the park at Alberdi 600, the **Museo Regional Aníbal**

Regional food specialities

The food you find around Argentina is remarkably homogeneous for such a huge country. However, there are **regional variations** that reflect the culinary influence of neighbouring nations more than most Argentines realize or care to admit. The most notable of these cross-border gastronomic influences can be found in the northern reaches bordering **Paraguay**. In the Chaco, northern Corrientes and much of Misiones you will find dishes that are part of the staple diet in Asunción and the rest of Paraguay. **Chipas** – savoury cheese-flavoured lumps of manioc-flour dough – are extremely popular snacks sold on the street, served in restaurants instead of bread and cooked in people's homes. **Sopa paraguaya** is actually not a soup at all, but a hearty maize and cheese dish, said to have been invented during the War of the Triple Alliance, when the beleaguered Paraguayan soldiers needed more sustenance than was provided by their traditional chicken broth, so army cooks thickened it with corn flour. **Borí borí**, on the other hand, is a soup, made from chicken, with little balls of maize and cheese floating in it. Last but not least, **tereré**, or cold *mate*, is hugely popular in Paraguay, but can also be tasted in the borderlands of northeast Argentina, and is wonderfully refreshing on a hot summer's day.

Cambas (Tues–Fri 7.30am–noon & 3–7pm, Sat 9am–noon; free) is housed in a handsome century-old brick building and loyally maintained by its friendly staff in the face of an obvious shortage of funds. There are some interesting and well-labelled exhibits in the **historical and ethnographical collection**, such as objects culled from the ruins of Jesuit missions and artefacts produced by the region's indigenous populations: the Guayaquí, the Chiripá, the Mbyá and the Guaraní. The last are particularly strongly represented, with a large collection of clay funerary urns, known as *yapepo*, meaning "handmade" in Guaraní. There are also a number of musical instruments, notably the *mimby*, a kind of wooden flute used by men and the *mimby reta*, similar but much smaller and used by women. The importance of music to the Guaraní is documented as far back as Alvar Núñez Cabeza de Vaca's first incursion into the Paraná region, when he noted that the Indians "received them covered in many-coloured feathers with instruments of war and music". You can reach the museum on local buses, including #4 and #14 from Colón and Catamarca.

Eating, drinking and nightlife

Although the Costanera is lively at night there aren't that many interesting places to **eat** or **drink**, though a couple of places do great things with river fish. Posadas has a thriving **nightlife**, however, which from Thursday to Saturday goes on until around 7am. In addition to home-grown rock and *cumbia*, the musical mix usually includes a bit of *marcha* (commercial dance) and Brazilian music. Popular nightspots include *Pan y Manteca*, on Buenos Aires 1857, and *Complejo Power*, an enormous complex of restaurants and ten dancefloors on Avenida Corrientes.

Bahía Bar Bolívar 1911. Centrally located café-bar, good for reasonably priced snacks such as hamburgers and *lomos*.

Dileto Bolívar 1929. Sophisticated à la carte restaurant specializing in fish – try the delicious grilled *surubí* and the reasonably priced pasta and steaks. Occasional live music. Closed Mon.

El Mensú Coronel Reguera and Fleming ☏03752/434826. Regarded by some locals as the best restaurant in Posadas, *El Mensú* specializes in excellent home-made pasta and seafood and has a very good wine list – plus the bonus of being on the corner of Posadas' prettiest street. Open every evening and also midday at weekends.

La Querencia Bolívar 1849. A bustling place that's a surprisingly good deal, particularly as you can easily share some of the dishes. Try their juicy *bife de chorizo* – shipped in from Buenos Aires

Province, as local beef is of poorer quality – and accompany it with fried manioc for a local touch, or go for the excellent *galetos*, a kind of chicken and vegetable kebab. Closed Sun eve.

Sociedad Española Córdoba between Colón and Félix de Azara. Very popular lunchtime spot – not surprising, as the basic two-course menu, which goes for next to nothing, could possibly feed a small family. There are also more Spanish – and more expensive – dishes available à la carte.

La Tradicional Rueda Costanera and Arrecha. This two-storey wooden building, decorated with facsimiles of historic photos of the city, does a mean, moderately priced *parrilla* and good river fish. There are great views of the Río Paraná across to Paraguay from the upstairs dining room.

The Jesuit missions

After Iguazú Falls, the province's major tourist attractions are the **Jesuit missions**, north of Posadas. The largest, **San Ignacio Miní**, is also the best preserved in the whole of the missions region, which extended beyond the Paraguay and Uruguay rivers to Paraguay and Brazil, and also into Corrientes Province. Far less well preserved – and much less visited – are the ruins of **Santa Ana** and **Loreto**, south of San Ignacio; these crumbling monuments, set amid thick jungle vegetation, are less dramatic but appealing if only because they attract fewer visitors. All three missions can be visited on a day-trip from Posadas, though it's well worth spending a night in San Ignacio, visiting the ruins in the morning light – the best time for photographs, when the low light enhances the buildings' deep reddish hues – and again at night. In addition to the attractive village, there's a stunning area of forest with perhaps the finest stretch of river scenery in the whole region. A ticket can be bought at the mission entrances ($30), which gives you entry to all the missions and is valid for two weeks.

Santa Ana and Loreto

Heading northeast from Posadas along the RN-12, the first mission site you come to, after approximately 40km, is **Santa Ana** (daily 7am–7pm). A signposted, unsealed road just south of Santa Ana village leads to the mission entrance and a small visitors' centre. Originally founded in the Tapé region in 1633, Santa Ana was refounded, with a population of two thousand Guaraní, on its present site after the *bandeirante* attacks of 1660 (see box, p.266). Like all the *reducciones*, Santa Ana is centred on a large square, to the south of which stand the crumbling walls of what was once one of the finest of all Jesuit churches, built by the Italian architect Brazanelli, whose body was buried underneath the high altar. A lot of work has been carried out on the site, yet the roots and branches of trees are still entangled in the reddish sandstone of the buildings around the plaza, offering a glimpse of the way the ruins must have appeared when they were rediscovered in the late nineteenth century. North of the church, on the site of the original orchard, you can still make out the channels from the *reducción*'s sophisticated irrigation system.

Around 12km north of Santa Ana, the ruins of **Loreto** (daily 7am–7pm) are even wilder than those of Santa Ana. This site, founded in 1632, was one of the most important of all the Jesuit missions, housing six thousand Guaraní by 1733 and noted not only for its production of cloth and *yerba mate* but also for having the missions' first printing press. Like Santa Ana, Loreto has a small visitors' centre at its entrance, reached via a six-kilometre stretch of unsealed road (impassable after heavy rain), which branches off the RN-12. Restoration work is being carried out with the assistance of the Spanish government. When you head out from the visitors' centre to the *reducción* itself, it's actually difficult at first to work out where

The Jesuits and their missions

The first Jesuit **missions** in Argentina were established in 1609, three decades after the order founded by San Ignacio de Loyola first arrived in the region. Known in Spanish as **reducciones**, these missions were largely self-sufficient settlements of Guaraní Indians who lived and worked under the tutelage of a small number of Jesuit priests. Missions were initially established in three separate zones: the **Guayrá**, corresponding mainly to the modern Brazilian state of Paraná; the **Tapé**, corresponding to the southern Brazilian state of Río Grande do Sul, present-day Misiones Province and part of Corrientes Province; and the **Itatín**, lying between the Upper Paraná and the sierras to the north of the modern Paraguayan city of Concepción.

If the Jesuits were essentially engaged in "civilizing" the natives, they did at least have a particularly enlightened approach to their task – a marked contrast to the harsh methods of procuring native labour practised elsewhere in Latin America. Work was organized on a co-operative basis, with those who could not work provided for by the rest of the community. **Education** and culture also played an important part in mission life, with Guaraní taught to read and write not only in Spanish but also in Latin and Guaraní, and music and artisanship actively encouraged.

The early growth of the missions was impressive, but in 1660 *bandeirantes*, slave traders from São Paulo, attacked, destroying many of the missions, and carrying off their inhabitants, leading the Jesuits to seek more sheltered areas to the west, away from the Guayrá region in particular. The mission population soon recouped – and then surpassed – its former numbers, and also developed a strong standing **army**, making it one of the most powerful military forces in the region. Their most important crop proved to be *yerba mate*, which had previously been gathered from the wild but was now grown on plantations for export; other products sold by the missions included cattle and their hides, sugar, cotton, tobacco, textiles, ceramics and timber. They also exported musical instruments, notably harps and organs from the Reducción de Trinidad in Paraguay.

By the end of the seventeenth century, the *reducciones* were among the most populous and successful areas of Argentina. By the 1730s, the larger missions such as Loreto (see p.265) had over six thousand inhabitants – second only to Buenos Aires. Nonetheless, the mission enterprise was beginning to show cracks: a rising number of epidemics depleted the population, and the Jesuits were becoming the subject of **political resentment**. Settlers in Paraguay and Corrientes were increasingly bitter at the Jesuit hold over the "supply" of Guaraní labour and domination of the market for *yerba mate* and tobacco. Simultaneously, the previous climate of Crown tolerance towards the missions' almost complete autonomy also began to change, with the Jesuits' power and loyalty questioned. Local enemies of the missions took advantage of this, claiming that the Jesuits were hiding valuable silver mines and that foreign Jesuit priests were agents of Spain's enemies. In 1750, an exchange treaty between Spain and Portugal was proposed, according to which Spain would give up its most easterly mission. The Jesuits and Guaraní put up considerable military resistance and the treaty was abandoned. The victory proved a double-edged sword, however; the resistance against the Crown only reinforced their image as dangerous rebels and, following earlier expulsions in France, Portugal and Brazil, the Jesuits were **expelled from Argentina** in 1767. Their magnificent buildings fell into disuse – lumps of stone were used for other constructions and the jungle did the rest – resulting in the ruins that can be visited today.

the buildings are. After a while, though, you begin to see the walls and foundations of the settlement, heavily camouflaged by vegetation and lichen, on which tall palms have managed, fantastically, to root themselves.

San Ignacio

Considering it's home to such a major attraction, the grand Jesuit ruins of San Ignacio Miní, **SAN IGNACIO**, 60km northeast of Posadas via the RN-12, is a remarkably low-key place – away from the restaurants and souvenir stands around the ruins themselves, the town has little in the way of tourist facilities. There are, however, a few worthwhile attractions southwest of the village.

Casa de Horacio Quiroga and Puerto Nuevo

The western extremity of San Ignacio is bounded by Avenida Horacio Quiroga, and if you head south along here for a kilometre or so, you'll come to the **Casa de Horacio Quiroga** (daily 8am–7pm; $4; ☎03752/470130), a museum to the Uruguayan writer, who made his home here in the early twentieth century. Quiroga, famed for his rather Gothic short stories and Kipling-inspired jungle tales for children (see Contexts, p.628) first visited the region in 1903, taking some of the earliest pictures of the then little-known ruins. He moved to San Ignacio in 1910, where the tropical setting further fired his imagination, inspiring stories of sunstroke and giant snakes. The museum is composed of two houses – a replica of the first wooden house built by the writer, containing many of his possessions, and a later stone construction also built by him. Though the buildings are pleasant to wander around, much of the museum's charm is derived from its wonderful setting, amid thick vegetation. At the back of the wooden house there's a small swimming pool built by the writer for his second wife (the first committed suicide, as would Quiroga himself in 1937, and his children after his death). She later left him, at which point Quiroga filled the pool with snakes.

Continuing south past the museum, the unsealed road winds down for another 2km or so to the **Puerto Nuevo**, where there's a fantastic view across the curves of the Paraná to the Paraguayan side of the river – all rolling wooded slopes tumbling down to the water.

Parque Provincial Teyú Cuaré and Osununú

The **Parque Provincial Teyú Cuaré**, 10km south of the village via a good unsealed road, is accessed from the southern end of Bolívar. It's a small but stunning park of less than a square kilometre, notable for its golden-hued rocky formations, which jut out over the Paraná, and dense vegetation. The name Teyú-Cuaré, meaning "the lizard's cave", refers to a local legend that tells of a giant reptile that inhabited the region, attacking passing boats. The park's most publicized feature is its high rocky cliff, the **Peñón Reina Victoria**, named for its supposed similarity to the profile of the British monarch. There is a wild **campsite** within the park. En route to the park, a small **private reserve**, the **Osununú**, is a wonderful wild patch of forest with some fantastic views over the river and islands and to the Parque Provincial.

Practicalities

Buses to San Ignacio all arrive at the western end of Avenida Sarmiento. It's not a terminal, but there's a kiosk where you may be able to leave luggage for a few hours. The **tourist office** (daily 7am–7pm) is at the main entrance road, the turn-off from the RN-12.

Accommodation options in the town are limited but cheap and agreeable enough. The largest hotel is the *San Ignacio* (☎03752/470042, ⓔhotelsanignacio @arnet.com.ar; ②), on the corner of San Martín and Sarmiento 823. It's a slick modern place with comfortable en-suite rooms, all with air conditioning. There's also an adjoining restaurant. Several kilometres south, signposted from the centre, is *Club de Río* (☎03755/15-570843, ⓦhttp://clubderiosanignacio.com.ar; ③), with comfortable *cabañas* set around a huge swimming pool, at a quiet location. There are several hostels in the village, including the *Adventure Hostel San Ignacio* at Independencia 469 (☎03752/470955, ⓦwww.sihostel.com.ar; ❸). Run by the same outfit behind *La Aventura* in Posadas (see p.261) the hostel has a pool and hammocks – very welcome after a day tramping round ruins – and charges $40 for a dorm bed. The best **campsite** in town is at the *Club de Pesca y Deportes Acuáticos*, down at Puerto Nuevo (☎03752/156-83411); tents can be pitched here on a bluff with a great view over the river to Paraguay.

At the village entrance *Lo de Lenguaza* provides a variety of **food and drink**, including pizza and river fish, while there's a clutch of very similar large restaurants geared up for day-trippers around the entrance to the ruins, all of which serve snacks plus some more substantial dishes such as *parrilla*. One of the most popular is *Carpa Azul*, with a swimming pool and shower facilities, at Rivadavia 1295.

San Ignacio Miní

The most famous of all the *reducciones*, **San Ignacio Miní** (daily 7am–7pm) was originally founded in 1610 in the Guayrá region (see box, p.266), in what is now Brazil. After the *bandeirantes* attacked the mission in 1631, the Jesuits moved thousands of miles southwards through the jungle, stopping several times en route at various temporary settlements before finally re-establishing the *reducción* at its present site in 1696.

The ruins occupy six blocks at the northeastern end of the village of San Ignacio: from the bus stop head east along Avenida Sarmiento for two blocks and turn left onto Rivadavia. Follow Rivadavia, which skirts around the ruins, for six blocks and then turn right onto Alberdi, where you'll find the entrance to the site. At the entrance, there's a small but worthwhile museum with a series of themed rooms depicting various aspects of Guaraní and mission life, plus a detailed maquette of the entire *reducción*. The site itself is dotted with panels lending context to the ruins, with audio provided in various languages, including English. Free, more detailed tours in rapid-fire Spanish depart regularly from the museum. There are also popular **sound and light shows** each evening (8pm in summer, 6pm rest of year).

The settlement

On entering the settlement itself, you'll come first to rows of simple *viviendas*, or living quarters, a series of six to ten adjoining one-roomed structures, each of which housed a Guaraní family. Like all the mission settlements, these are constructed in a mixture of basaltic rock and sandstone. Passing between the *viviendas*, you arrive at the spacious Plaza de Armas, whose emerald grass provides a stunning contrast with the rich red hues of the sandstone. At the southern end of the plaza, and dominating the entire site, stands the magnificent facade of San Ignacio's **church**, designed, like Santa Ana's, by the Italian architect Brazanelli. The roof and much of the interior have long since crumbled away, but two large chunks of wall on either side of the entrance remain, rising out of the ruins like two great Baroque wings. Though somewhat eroded, many fine details can still be made out: two columns flank either side of the doorway and much of the walls' surface is covered with decorative bas-relief sculpture executed by Guaraní craftsmen; most striking are the pair of angels that face each other high up on either side of the entrance, while a more austere touch is added by the prominent insignia of the Jesuit order on the right-hand side of the entrance.

To the left of the main entrance, you can wander around the **cloisters** and **priests' quarters**, where a number of other fine doorways and carvings remain. Particularly striking is the doorway connecting the cloisters with the church baptistry, flanked by ribbed columns with heavily moulded bases and still retaining a triangular pediment over the arched doorway.

Iguazú Falls and around

Poor Niagara!

Eleanor Roosevelt

Composed of over 250 separate cascades, and straddling the border between Argentina and Brazil, the **Iguazú Falls** (or "Cataratas", as they are known locally) are quite simply the world's most dramatic waterfalls. Set among the exotic-looking subtropical forests of **Parque Nacional Iguazú** in Argentina, and **Parque Nacional do Iguaçu** in Brazil, the Falls tumble for a couple of kilometres over a complex set of cliffs from the Río Iguazú Superior to the Río Iguazú Inferior below. At their heart is the dizzying **Garganta del Diablo**, a powerhouse display of natural forces in which 1800 cubic metres of water per second hurtle over a 3km semicircle of rock into the boiling river canyon 70m below.

The first Europeans to encounter the Falls, in 1542, were members of a Spanish expedition led by Cabeza de Vaca, who named them the Saltos de Santa María. For nearly five hundred years, however, they remained practically forgotten in this remote corner of Argentina, and it wasn't until the early twentieth century that tourism began to arrive, encouraged by the then governor of Misiones, Juan J. Lanusse. The first hotel was constructed in 1922, right by the Falls, and by the mid-twentieth century Iguazú was firmly on the tourist map. Today, the Falls are one of Latin America's major tourist attractions, with around two million visitors each year.

The Falls are not the only attraction in the parks, though. The surrounding subtropical **forest** is packed with animals, birds and insects, and opportunities for spotting at least some of them are good. Even on the busy catwalks and paths that skirt the edges of the Falls you've a good chance of seeing gorgeously hued bright blue butterflies as big as your hand (just one of over 250 varieties that live around the Falls) and – especially on the Brazilian side – you will undoubtedly be pestered for food by greedy coatis (a raccoon relative). For a real close-up encounter with the parks' varied wildlife, though, head for the superb **Sendero Macuco**, a tranquil nature trail that winds through the forest on the Argentine side. Commonly spotted species along here include various species of toucans and shy capuchin monkeys.

The vast majority of the **Iguazú Falls** lie on the **Argentine side** of the border, within the **Parque Nacional Iguazú**. This side offers the most extensive experience of the *cataratas*, thanks to its well-planned system of trails and catwalks taking you both below and above the waters – most notably to the Garganta del Diablo. The surrounding forest also offers excellent opportunities to explore the region's wildlife. The main settlement on this side, **Puerto Iguazú**, lies approximately 18km northwest of the park entrance with a slightly sleepy, villagey feel, though its popularity with backpackers has livened it up a bit in recent years.

To complete your trip to Iguazú, you should also try and visit the **Brazilian side**. Though it offers a more passive experience, the view is more panoramic and the photo opportunities are amazing. If you want to stay in Brazil, the city of **Foz do Iguaçu** lies a good 20km northwest of the access to the park. Much larger than **Puerto Iguazú** and with a modern, urban feel, Foz is neither the most beautiful nor most exotic of Brazilian cities, but if you've been travelling in Argentina for a while it'll give you the chance to hear another language, try some different food and sample some lively nightlife. Foz definitely feels less safe than its Argentine counterpart – a fact much exaggerated by Argentines, but nonetheless you should be on your guard in the city.

The Argentine side

The **Parque Nacional Iguazú** lies 18km southeast of Puerto Iguazú, along the RN-12. A bus (30min) runs to the park every hour from the bus terminal in town, with the first one leaving at 7.30am and the last one returning at 8pm. The bus takes you to the visitors' centre, but stops first at the entrance to the park, where you have to get off and pay an entrance fee of $85 (for foreigners); keep your ticket and its stamp, which will entitle you to a 50 percent discount the following day.

As you get off the bus, you're greeted by the sound of rushing water from the Falls, the first of which lies just a few hundred metres away. There's a **visitors' centre** to the left of the bus stop, where you can pick up maps and information leaflets. There's also a small but interesting museum here with photographs and stuffed examples of the park's wildlife. Various operators, such as Iguazú Jungle Explorer (☎03757/421696, Ⓦwww.iguazujungle.com), will accost you and tempt you with different trips and tours, involving trucks, boats and walks, ranging from $50 to $230, depending on their length and the transport involved. The jeep rides are a little too noisy to allow for much wildlife observation, but the boat rides (around $100) are a thrill – albeit somewhat short-lived – not to be missed, providing the exhilarating experience of coming close up to the gush of the Falls.

AROUND THE IGUAZÚ FALLS

ACCOMMODATION
Aldea de la Selva   **B**
Hotel das Cataratas   **E**
Hostel Inn   **C**
Iguazú Grand Hotel   **A**
Sheraton Iguazú   **D**

Posadas, El Dorado & Las Mercedes

▲ Iguazú Falls

The trails

From the visitors' centre, the so-called *Sendero Verde* ("Green Path") leads to the Estación Cataratas, from where two well-signposted trails, formed by a series of catwalks and paths, take you past the Falls. A recommended approach is probably to tackle the **Paseo Superior** first, along a short trail through the forest above the first few waterfalls. For more drama, segue into the **Paseo Inferior**, which winds down through the forest before bringing you within metres of some of the smaller but still spectacular waterfalls – notably **Saltos Ramírez** and **Bossetti** – which run along the western side of the river. Around the waterfalls, look out for the swallow-like *vencejo*, a remarkable small bird that, seemingly impossibly, makes its nest behind the gushing torrents. As you descend the path, gaps in the vegetation offer great views across the Falls: photo opportunities are numerous. Note that new catwalks have made **wheelchair access** to all of the Paseo Superior and much of the Paseo Inferior possible, although there is little room to turn round in many sections.

Another signposted trail leads down to the jetty from where the boat rides depart, including a regular free boat service (suspended when the river is high) for **Isla San Martín**, a gorgeous high rocky island in the middle of the river. More trails circumnavigate the island, through thick vegetation and past emerald green pools. There's a small sandy beach at the northern end of the island, though bathing is allowed only in summer.

Heading west from the visitors' centre, a well-marked trail leads to the start of the **Sendero Macuco**, a 4km nature trail down to the lower banks of the Río Iguazú, past a waterfall, the **Salto Arrechea**, where there is a lovely secluded bathing spot. The majority of the trail is along level ground, through a dense wood, and is one of the best places to spot the area's fauna (see p.272), especially early in the morning, before the helicopters on the Brazilian side get going.

Garganta del Diablo

To visit the **Garganta del Diablo** ("Devil's Throat"), you must take the *Tren de la selva* ("Jungle Train"), which leaves regularly from Estación Cataratas for the Estación Garganta del Diablo, 3km southeast (fare included in entrance fee). From here a catwalk with a small viewing platform takes you to within just a few metres of the staggering, sheer drop of water formed by the union of several immensely powerful waterfalls around a kind of horseshoe. As the water crashes over the edge, it plunges into a dazzling opaque whiteness in which it is impossible to distinguish mist from water. The *vencejos* often swirl around the waterfall in all directions, forming giant swarms that sometimes swoop up towards you and perform miraculous acrobatic twists and turns – quite a sight. If you're bringing your camera, make sure you've an airtight bag to stash it in, as the platform is invariably showered with a fine spray.

Puerto Iguazú

PUERTO IGUAZÚ, just under 300km northeast of Posadas, is a strange place. Originally a rather dull, backwater town, its popularity with Falls visitors has increasingly given it the feel of a lively resort in recent years, and though it has little in the way of notable architecture, it has a certain simple charm that can grow

Flora and fauna around the Falls

Despite appearances, the jungle landscape around the Falls is not virgin forest. In fact, it is in a process of recuperation: advances in the navigation of the Upper Paraná – the section of the river that runs along the northern border of Corrientes and Misiones – in the early twentieth century allowed access to these previously impenetrable lands and economic exploitation of their valuable timber began. In the 1920s, the region was totally exploited and stripped of its best species and traversed by roads. Only since the creation of the park in 1943 has the forest been protected.

Today, the forest is composed of several layers of **vegetation**. Towering above the forest floor is the rare and imposing *palo rosa*, which can grow to 40m and is identifiable by its pale straight trunk that divides into twisting branches higher up, topped by bushy foliage. At a lower level, various species of palm flourish, notably the *pindó* palm and the palmito, much coveted for its edible core, which often grows in the shade of the *palo rosa*. Epiphytes, which use the taller trees for support but are not parasitic, also abound as does the *guaypoy*, aptly known as the strangler fig, since it eventually asphyxiates the trees around which it grows. You will also see lianas, which hang from the trees in incredibly regular plaits and have apt popular names such as *escalera de mono*, or "monkey's ladder". Closer still to the ground there is a stratum of shrubs, some of them with edible fruit, such as the pitanga. Ground cover is dominated by various fern species.

The best time to spot **wildlife** is either early morning or late afternoon, when there are fewer visitors and the jungle's numerous birds and mammals are at their most active: at times the screech of birds and monkeys can be almost cacophonic. At all times, you have the best chance of seeing wildlife by treading as silently as possible, and by scanning the surrounding trees for signs of movement. Your most likely reward will be groups of agile **capuchin monkeys**, with a distinctive black "cowl", like that of the monks they are named after. Larger, lumbering **black howler monkeys** make for a rarer sight, though their deep growl can be heard for some distance. Along the ground, look out for the tiny **corzuela deer**. Unfortunately, you've little chance of seeing the park's most dramatic wildlife, large cats such as the puma and the jaguar or the tapir, a large-hoofed mammal with a short, flexible snout. **Toucans**, however, are commonly spotted; other birds that can be seen in the forest include the solitary **Black Cacique**, which makes its nest in the *pindó* palm; various species of woodpecker and the striking Crested Yacutinga. Of the forest's many butterflies, the most striking are those of the *Morphidae* family, whose large wings are a dazzling metallic blue.

ACCOMMODATION
Hostería La Cabaña   C
Hostería San Fernando   D
Hotel Esturión   B
Iguazú Jungle Lodge   A
Lilian   F
Residencial Noelia   G
Saint George   E
La Strada   H

EATING & DRINKING
La Barranca   1
Boca Mora   2
Maria Preta   3
Pizza Color   5
La Rueda   6
El Quincho del Tío Querido   4

on you. Its tropical vegetation and quiet streets seem more in keeping with the region than the high-rise concrete of the Brazilian city of Foz, and of the three border towns (the commercial settlement of Ciudad del Este in Paraguay, notoriously unsavoury and unsafe, is definitely best avoided) Puerto Iguazú is the only one to have a really secure and accessible riverfront area from which you can take in the surrounding panorama.

Arrival and information

Puerto Iguazú's international **airport** lies around 20km southeast of the town, along the RN-12 just past the entrance to the park; a taxi to town or one of the nearby lodges will cost around $80. The recently modernized **bus terminal** is central, on the corner of avenidas Córdoba and Misiones. There's no official tourist information kiosk here, though there are plenty of private companies who tout for your custom as you get off the bus. The most helpful of the numerous kiosks offering **information** is probably friendly Agencia Noelia (☎03757/422722), which also sells the tickets for the bus to the national park. There's a restaurant in the terminal, a *locutorio* and a **left-luggage** service.

Puerto Iguazú's **tourist office** is at Av Aguirre 311 (Mon–Fri 7am–1pm & 2–9pm, Sat & Sun 8am–noon & 4–8pm, sometimes open longer in high season; ☎03757/420800). They have some good maps and information, though most answers to practical transport and accommodation queries can just as easily be answered by the kiosks in the bus terminal.

Accommodation

Puerto Iguazú's budget **accommodation** tends to be located in town, while the more upmarket places are found set back among jungle vegetation on the road to the park and in the surrounding area. The government has recently auctioned off an eye-watering 42 lots for new hotels to be built, including a *Hyatt*, a *Hilton*, and others. You may get a better deal at some of the more expensive hotels by booking a package, with flight, from a travel agency in Buenos Aires. There are about a dozen **youth hostels** in town: the best is 🐾 *Hostel Inn* (℡03757/421823, ⊛www.hostel-inn.com; dorms $45 per person; ④), a large, well-run place with different sized dorms, doubles and triples, in enormous grounds with a large swimming pool, at Km5 on the RN-12; see map on p.270. The best-organized **campsite** is the large and well-equipped *Camping Americano* (℡03757/420190, ⊛www.complejoamericano.com.ar), about 5km out of town along the RN-12 towards the national park, with showers, store, telephone and swimming pool; see map on p.270. Camping inside the park is forbidden.

In town

The accommodation listed below is shown on the map on p.273.

Hostería La Cabaña Av Tres Fronteras 434 ℡03757/420564, ⊛www.lacabanahotel.com.ar. Quiet, motel-style place with comfortable if slightly musty rooms. ④

Hostería San Fernando Av Córdoba and Guaraní ℡03757/421429. Friendly hotel opposite the bus terminal. Simple, pleasant rooms all with fan, much improved following renovation. Breakfast included. ④

Hotel Esturión Av Tres Fronteras 650 ℡03757/421429, ⊛www.hotelesturion.com. With fine river views, a large swimming pool, spacious, cool rooms and decks and gardens brimming with native flora, this extremely professional hotel has a definite tropical feel to it. ⑨

Hotel Saint George Av Córdoba 148 ℡03757/420633, ⊛www.hotelsaintgeorge.com. A courteous hotel and one of the most comfortable in town, with some exceptionally light and attractive first-floor rooms with balconies overlooking the swimming pool. Good restaurant downstairs and buffet breakfast with fresh fruit included in room rate. ⑧

🐾 **Iguazú Jungle Lodge** Hipólito Irigoyen and San Lorenzo ℡03757/420600, ⊛www.iguazujunglelodge.com. Simply fabulous *cabañas* sleeping up to seven – plus a couple of doubles – in a landscaped plot overlooking the jungle at the edge of the village. Extremely well equipped and tastefully appointed, they are really luxurious houses, with ample verandahs, a huge kitchen and barbecue facilities. Large swimming pool and decent breakfasts served either poolside or in the *cabañas*. ⑨

Lilian Fray Luis Beltrán 183 ℡03757/420968, ⓔhotellilian@yahoo.com.ar. Spotless, light and airy rooms with good fans and modern bathrooms. ④

Residencial Noelia Fray Luis Beltrán 119 ℡03757/420729, ⓔresidencialfamiliarnoelia @yahoo.com.ar. The best deal in Iguazú, this friendly, family-run place largely caters to backpackers. Scrupulously maintained three- and four-bed rooms with fans and private bathroom and breakfast of toast, fruit and coffee brought to your room or the shady patio. ②

La Strada Pombero 166 ℡03757/427156, ⊛www.lastradaresidencial.com.ar. Simple but tasteful bungalows with wooden floors, a/c and TVs, set around a pool and garden; friendly staff. ④

Out of town

The accommodation listed below is shown on the map on p.270.

Aldea de la Selva Selva Iriapú ℡03757 425777, ⊛www.laaldeadelaselva.com. Wooden *cabañas* that are comfortable but retain a rustic, jungle lodge feel, with much creative use of local woods and tree roots such as *quebracho* and *loro negro*. All have verandahs with hammocks from where you can listen to the noises of the forest, and there's also a tiered pool and good restaurant that does river fish served with local ingredients such as manioc and palm hearts. ⑧

Iguazú Grand Hotel The RN-12 Km1460 ℡03757/498050, ⊛www.iguazugrandhotel.com. This is the place to stay for film-star glamour – a fabulously luxurious hotel with enormous suites boasting everything from CD players to glossy picture books on Misiones. Landscaped outdoor pool and two very good restaurants. Weekends are reserved for high-rolling gamblers whom the hotel flies in from São Paulo and Buenos Aires to play at the adjoining casino. Rates start at US$360. ⑨

Sheraton Iguazú Parque Nacional Iguazú ℡03757/491800, ⊛www.starwoodhotels.com. Big, ugly modern hotel inside the national park. The crime of its construction is compounded by the fact that you only get a decent view of the Falls from a few of its rooms (for which you pay more), but it has to be admitted it is well located from the guests' viewpoint, with the Falls in walking distance and the possibility of exploring the jungle before most visitors arrive. Rates start at US$275 for jungle view, US$335 for Falls view. ⑨

Estancias and lodges around Iguazú

Las Mercedes, just outside El Dorado, 100km south of Iguazú ☏03751/420939, ⓦwww .estancialasmercedes.com. A 1920s property founded as a ranch by a family of British origin and now both a working farm and an ecotourism resort. The five charming rooms, delicious food (call ahead if you just want to visit lunch or tea) and beautiful swimming pool, set among immaculate lawns, make this a superb spot for a few days' relaxation. You can also go horse-riding and canoeing on the nearby river. ⑥

Panambí Lodge 50km east of Puerto Iguazú within the National Park ☏03757/497418, ⓦwww .panambilodge.com.ar. On the jungle-clad banks of the Río Iguazú, this rugged stone-and-timber lodge has five large rooms with picture windows and all mod cons, and offers birdwatching opportunities along with horse-drawn carriage rides. ⑨

🔭 **Yacutinga** 60km east of Iguazú airport via a dirt road that runs parallel to the Río Iguazú ⓦwww.yacutinga.com. This ecolodge is a great place to stay while visiting the Falls, tucked away amid one of the last remaining patches of unspoilt jungle. The main building is beautifully designed, while the rooms are in twenty well-camouflaged cabins. Expert multilingual guides take you on walks, pointing out all kinds of wildlife, including an astounding array of birds and butterflies. US$450 per person, full board, for a three-day, two-night package only. ⑨

The Town

A small town of around 30,000 inhabitants, Puerto Iguazú sits high above the meeting of the Paraná and Iguazú rivers, at the most northern extremity of Misiones Province. The town is bisected diagonally by **Avenida Victoria Aguirre**, which runs from Puerto Iguazú's modest **port** out towards the RN-12 and the national park. You wouldn't exactly call Iguazú's **town centre** bustling, but most of its activity takes place around the intersection of Avenida Aguirre, Calle Brasil and Calle Ingeniero Gustavo Eppens. From here the Avenida Tres Fronteras runs west for 1.5km to the **Hito Argentino de las Tres Fronteras**, a vantage point over the rivers with views over to Brazil and Paraguay that is marked by an obelisk painted in the colours of the Argentine flag; similar markers across the rivers in the neighbouring countries are painted in their national colours, too. An alternative route to the Hito is via Avenida Aguirre, which forks right just before the town's triangular grassy plaza. From here, Avenida Aguirre snakes down through a thickly wooded area of town to the port area; you can then follow the pleasant Avenida Costanera, popular with joggers and cyclists, left uphill towards the Hito.

There is an unusual attraction on the outskirts of town: 4km along the RN-12 towards the national park, rustic signposts direct you to **La Aripuca** (8am–7pm; ⓦwww.aripuca.com.ar; $10, children free). An *aripuca* is an indigenous wooden trap used in the region to catch birds; La Aripuca is a giant replica of the trap, standing over 10m high and constructed out of 29 species of trees native to Misiones Province (all obtained through unavoidable felling or from victims of thunderstorms). Above all, La Aripuca is a kind of eco-symbol: the friendly German- and English-speaking family who constructed the strange monument hope to change visitors' conscience about the environment through tours designed to explain the value and significance of these trees.

Eating, drinking and nightlife

The development of Puerto Iguazú has seen some fairly sophisticated **eating** places appear alongside the standard greasy spoons serving *milanesas* with loud TV as a backdrop. A couple of good *parrillas* that also do river fish are *El Quincho del Tío Querido*, next door to the *Libertador* hotel on Calle Bompland, and 🔭 *La Rueda*, a short walk along Avenida Cordoba towards its junction with Avenida V. Aguirre, in especially congenial surroundings – all rustic wood and old photos. Alternatively, *Maria Preta*, at Brasil 39, is a stylish bar-restaurant with outdoor seating and a comprehensive menu that includes *yacaré* (cayman) as well as more conventional pasta and *parrilla*; it also has live Brazilian music some evenings. The bright and modern *Pizza Color*, Av Córdoba 135, does excellent *pizza a la piedra* and good salads.

For **drinking** and **nightlife**, many locals head over to Brazil for a good night out. In town itself, there's a handful of bars-cum-nightclubs on Calle Brasil just before the junction with Aguirre. There's an older, more relaxed crowd at *La Barranca* pub on Perito Moreno, while the town's main disco is *Boca Mora* on the Costanera.

Listings

Airlines Aerolíneas Argentinas/Austral, Av Aguirre and B. Brañas ℗03757/420168 and at the airport ℗03757/420915.
Banks and exchange There are several ATMs in Puerto Iguazú.
Car rental Rent a Car/Europcar, Av Aguirre 211 ℗03757/420289.
Consulates Brazil, Córdoba 264 ℗03757/421348 (Mon–Fri 8am–1pm).
Internet access Cybercafé at Aguirre and Alvar Nuñez.

Post office Av San Martín 780.
Telephones Cybercafé at Aguirre and Alvar Nuñez
Travel agents and tour Aguas Grandes, Entre. Ríos 66 ℗03757/425500, ⓦwww.aguasgrandes .com; Cuenca del Plata, Paulino Amarante 76 ℗03757/421062, ⓦwww.cuencadelplata.com; Sol Iguazú Turismo, Av Aguirre 316 ℗03757/421147, ⓦwww.soliguazu.com.ar; Turismo Dick, Av Aguirre 226 ℗03757/420778, ⓦwww.dickturismo.com.ar.

The Brazilian side

You'll only need a few hours on the **Brazilian side**, but it's worth crossing in order to take photos of the Falls – particularly in the morning – as it provides you with a superb panorama of the points you will have visited close up in Argentina, as well as its own close encounter with the Garganta del Diablo.

The **Parque Nacional do Iguazú** lies around 20km southeast of Foz. There is a visitor centre at the entrance with a restaurant and other facilities, where you pay an entrance fee of R\$37 (pesos or dollars accepted). Shuttle buses, included in the price, pass drop-off points for boat and trail tours (see below) before stopping at the head of the waterfalls trail, just opposite the *Hotel das Cataratas*. From here a walkway takes you high along the side of the river; it is punctuated by various viewing platforms from where you can take in most of the Argentine Falls, the river canyon and Isla San Martín. The one-and-a-half-kilometre path culminates in a spectacular walkway offering fantastic views of the Garganta del Diablo and of the Brazilian Santo Salto Maria, beneath the viewing platform and surrounded by an almost continuous rainbow created by myriad water droplets. You are likely to get soaked here – enterprising locals sell ponchos, for what they're worth; carry a plastic bag to protect your camera. At the end of the walkway you can take an elevator to the top of a cliff for more good views. A little further along, the Porto Canoas complex has a shuttle bus stop, souvenir stores and restaurants, plagued by stripe-tailed coatis that accost visitors, begging for food.

From near the visitor centre, you can get helicopter flights over the Falls. The view from the helicopters is of course superb, but they're a noisy and intrusive presence in the surrounding area and seriously disruptive to local wildlife: Argentina has banned them from flying over its side. Less controversial **excursions** are offered by Macuco Safari (℗(0055)45/3574-4244, ⓦwww.macucosafari .com.br) and Macuco Ecoaventura (℗(0055)45/3529-9627), which run a variety of jeep, boat and trekking tours in the Parque Nacional do Iguazú; these can also be booked at an information kiosk at the visitor centre.

If you've not been lucky enough to see some of Iguazú's exotic birds at the Falls themselves, head for the **Parque Das Aves**, 300m north of the park entrance (daily 8.30am–5.30pm; ℡(0055)45/3529-8282, Ⓦwww.parquedasaves.com.br; US$12), where walk-through aviaries allow for close encounters with some of the most stunning. The first of these is populated with various smaller species such as the noisy Bare-throated Bellbird, with a weird resonant call, the bright blue Sugar Bird and the Blue-black Grosbeak. For most people, though, the highlight is a sighting of the bold toucans – almost comically keen to have their photo taken.

Practicalities

You will need to cross to Brazil via the Ponte Presidente Tancredo Neves, the bridge that crosses the Río Iguazú between the two towns and where immigration formalities take place. Certain nationalities may need **visas** to enter Brazil, which can be obtained (for a fee) at the consulate in Puerto Iguazu; check beforehand. When returning to Argentina make sure you have enough days to continue your journey, as passport control often gives only thirty days here – though you can ask for the normal ninety.

If you are staying in Puerto Iguazu, the most convenient **buses** are run by Crucero del Norte, which go direct from Puerto Iguazu's bus terminal to the Brazilian falls and back (every 45min; $35 either one way or return; approx one hour). Cheaper ($5) but more time consuming are the international buses that depart regularly from Puerto Iguazú to Foz do Iguaçu, from where you can take the local bus (see p.278). You should be able to get by with pesos or dollars if you are just using the buses and visiting the park, but if you want to do any more in Foz you'll need a supply of the Brazilian currency, the real – change can be obtained from various kiosks at Foz's terminal. There's also a change facility and an ATM at the Falls visitor centre. Note that between November and February Brazil is one hour ahead of Argentina – this **time difference** could be vital for making sure you catch the last bus back into town.

Foz do Iguaçu (Brazil)

The modern city of **FOZ DO IGUAÇU** faces its Argentine counterpart, Puerto Iguazú, across the Río Iguazú and is separated from the unappealing Paraguayan city of Ciudad del Este, 7km northwest across the Río Paraná, by the Ponte da Amizade/Puente de la Amistad. Until the 1970s, Foz had only around 30,000 inhabitants, but its population soared with the construction of the titanic Itaipú Dam. Today, the city has over 400,000 residents and though the dam is still an important source of employment, the vast majority of them are involved in the tourism industry. In addition to servicing the hundreds of thousands of tourists who pass through every year on their way to the Falls, Foz gains a lot of business as a retail outlet for Argentines and Brazilians in search of bargain clothes and shoes. The town's growth is evident around its sprawling outskirts and in its scattering of high-rise buildings, but the city centre remains a modest and compact area.

Foz is laid out on a fairly regular grid, with the main access route from Argentina being via the **Avenida das Cataratas**, which heads into town from the southeast, joining up with Avenida Jorge Schimmelpfeng, off which the town's main drag, Avenida Juscelino Kubitschek (often referred to as Avenida JK – *jota ka*) runs north towards Paraguay. The main shopping centre, where you'll also find plenty of banks, is Avenida Brasil, which runs parallel to Avenida Juscelino Kubitschek, one block east.

You'll hear a lot about the supposed dangers of Foz on the Argentine side, but the central area around the local bus terminal and shops is normally safe during the day, and the vast majority of people are welcoming and friendly in a way that belies the volume of tourists they are accustomed to seeing. You should, however, avoid heading down to the river below the bus terminal, where there is a shantytown whose inhabitants may be less hospitable.

Practicalities

Foz's local **bus terminal**, the arrival point for buses from Argentina, is at the intersection of avenidas Juscelino Kubitschek and República Argentina. From here, Transbalan buses leave approximately every 20–30 minutes for the airport and Falls (7am–6pm; $7). The city centre is easy to walk around, though a taxi is a good idea at night if you feel cautious. There are various tourist information offices throughout the town but the best is on the corner of Avenida Jorge Schimmelpfeng and Rua Benjamin Constant (Mon–Fri 8am–2pm; T(0055)45/574-2196, or toll free 0800/451516, Wwww.iguassu.tur.br).

Accommodation, ranging from campsites and youth hostels to five-star hotels, is abundant in Foz but the strength of the Brazilian real makes it expensive compared with Argentina. Close to the terminal, the decent *Hotel del Rey*, at Rua Tarobá 1020 (T(0055) 45/3523-2027, Wwww.hoteldelreyfoz.com.br; R$120), offers clean, uncluttered en-suite rooms with good air conditioning and a tiny outdoor swimming pool; an excellent buffet breakfast is included. There's a good youth hostel, *Paudimar Campestre*, at Rua Rui Barbosa 634 (T(0055) 45/3529-6061, Wwww.paudimar.com.br; $90 or R$25 dorm bed with breakfast), near the local bus terminal; it's a secure and very friendly place with hotel-style bedrooms, a kitchen and internet facilities. Modern *Foz Presidente*, at Rua Xavier da Silva 1000 (T(0055)45/3572-4450, Wwww.fozpresidentehoteis.com.br; US$80), has spacious rooms with big comfortable beds and an attractive outdoor swimming pool and sunbathing area. For location, however, you can't beat the fabulous *Hotel das Cataratas* (T(0055)45/3521-7000, Wwww.hoteldascataratas.com; rates from US$300), inside the national park itself, just metres from the Falls. A charming old building run by the Orient Express group, with cool tiled floors and elegantly decorated rooms, it packs in all the style that the *Sheraton* on the Argentine side lacks. There's also a great outdoor swimming pool and an excellent restaurant.

Back in town, there are plenty of inexpensive buffet-style **restaurants** along central Rua Marechal Deodoro, while the route out to the Cataratas is lined with *churrascarias*, Brazil's version of the *parrilla*. If you've been travelling in Argentina, you're less likely to be impressed by the meat, much of it from the zebu – a kind of humped ox, originally from India, and far less appetizing than Argentina's beef – than by the buffet accompaniment of fresh salads, rice, beans and plantain: a good place to sample it is at *Rafain*, on Avenida das Cataratas, Km6.5.

The Saltos del Moconá

The quiet village of **El Soberbio** lies in one of Missiones province's most striking areas, with some of the finest scenery in the whole region; at this border Brazil and Argentina sit like plumped-up cushions on either side of the curvaceous Río Uruguay. The village is the point of access for the **Saltos de Moconá**, an unusual but decidedly uncooperative set of waterfalls. One of Argentina's strangest sights, the **Saltos del Moconá** are made up of nearly 3km of immensely powerful waterfalls which spill down the middle of the Río Uruguay, tumbling from a raised riverbed in Argentina into a 90m river canyon in Brazil. The split-level waterfalls – the longest of their kind in the world – are formed by the meeting of the

Uruguay and Pepirí-Guazú rivers just upstream of a dramatic gorge. As the waters encounter this geological quirk, they "split" once again, with one branch flowing downstream along the western side of the gorge and the other plunging down into it. This phenomenon is visible only under certain conditions: if water levels are low, all the water is diverted into the gorge, while if water levels are high the river evens itself out. At a critical point in between, however, the Saltos magically emerge, as water from the higher level cascades down into the gorge running alongside, creating a curtain of rushing water between three and thirteen metres high. The incredible force of the water as it hurtles over the edge of the gorge before continuing downstream explains its Guaraní name – *moconá* means "he who swallows everything".

El Soberbio

EL SOBERBIO, the main gateway to the Saltos del Moconá, is perched on the banks of the Río Uruguay, about 322km south of Iguazú. The village's charm is derived not so much from its buildings, which are unassuming modern constructions, but from its gorgeous riverside setting, amid lush undulating sierras. There's also an intriguing **mix of cultures** – sunburnt, blond-haired Polish and German immigrants rub shoulders with Argentines of Spanish and Italian descent, all with a hefty dose of Brazilian culture thrown in. Locals have a refreshingly cavalier attitude to the idea of national boundaries, popping over to Brazil for Saturday-night dances and listening to Brazilian country music on the radio; indeed, in many homes Portuguese is often the main language.

El Soberbio's modest **bus terminal** is right in the village centre at the intersection of Avenida San Martín and Avenida Rivadavia. There's a sporadically open **tourist information** kiosk on Avenida Rivadavia as you head into the centre. You're best off staying at one of the posadas and lodges deep in the nearby jungle (see box, p.280); otherwise, the least offensive of the poor **accommodation** in the village itself is the run-down *Hostería Puesto del Sol*, sited high above the village at the southern end of Calle Suipacha (℡03755/495161, ⓦwww.h-puestadelsol .com.ar; ④). The rustic rooms with very noisy air conditioning have French windows opening onto a verandah from where there are great views over the valley and the river, its only saving grace. At Av San Martín 800, on the way to the Saltos, the *Cabañas Saltos del Moconá* (℡03755/495179, ⓔsaltosdelmocona @gmail.com.ar; ④), offers fairly plain but comfortable *cabañas* for up to four people. There's a good municipal **campsite** around 3km northwest of the village off RP-13 towards San Vicente; in a lovely riverside spot, the low-priced site has toilets, electricity and barbecue facilities. There is no ATM in the village, so bring enough money to cover all your expenses.

The Parque Provincial Moconá and the waterfalls

The **Saltos del Moconá** themselves lie just over 80km northeast of El Soberbio in the **Parque Provincial Moconá**, currently accessed via a partly unsealed road, although the paved the RN-2 is being gradually extended all the way to the Falls. They can be seen from both Argentina and Brazil (where they are known as Yucumã), the latter only by taking a boat trip from El Soberbio (unless you make arrangements on the Brazilian side directly). As with Iguazú, the better view is from Brazil, while the Argentine side wins out in the adventure stakes.

The first 40km of the road north takes you through tobacco plantations and communities of Polish and German immigrants clustered around numerous

Posadas and lodges in the Selva Misionera

To experience the awe-inspiring beauty of this area of remote, virgin jungle at its best, it is worth treating yourself to a couple of days being pampered at one of the lodges or posadas tucked away in the forest. Access is difficult, even in a 4WD, so you're advised to fork out the extra for a transfer to and from your accommodation; if you have a vehicle they will arrange for its safekeeping while you are away.

Don Enrique Lodge (℡011/4723-7020 or 011/155-9326262, Ⓦwww .donenriquelodge.com.ar; ◐), just beyond La Bonita on the aptly named Río Paraíso, took up the concept of its neighbour and perfected it. Hospitable hostess Bachi and her family run this place with dedication and affection, offering fabulous service, delicious meals and, above all, peace and quiet. The individual wooden lodges, each with a balcony and sundeck, are furnished with impeccable taste. You can explore the jungle with a guide – on one side of the river up to a lookout, on the other to a waterfall to admire tree-ferns and all manner of flora and fauna

Posada La Bonita (℡011/154-4908386 or 03755/156-80380, Ⓦwww .posadalabonita.com.ar; ◐ half board), 30km north of El Soberbio, is a fabulous construction smack in the middle of the jungle. Built from stone and timber, and furnished with rustic pieces made of dead wood, it sets the trend for the other lodges in the region. The three isolated units stand apart from the main house and have their own little verandahs.

Posada La Misión (℡03755/155-20783, Ⓦwww.posadalamision.com.ar; ◐ full board, two night minimum) at Ruta Costera 2, Km40, Puerto Paraíso, 45km north of El Soberbio on the banks of the Río Uruguay, is extremely convenient for visits to the falls; you can use their mountain bikes or kayaks, or go fishing. The six *cabañas* are handsome cedar and stone constructions, the food is good, the welcome warm and the views of the river and jungle are fantastic.

simple wooden Lutheran, Adventist and Evangelical churches. Despite the incredible lushness of the landscape, this is a region afflicted by considerable poverty, and local small farmers carry out much of their work using old-fashioned narrow wooden carts, pulled by oxen. Various side-trips can be made en route, including to the **Salto El Paraíso**, a gentle waterfall with swimming spots and camping facilities, and to the simple **perfume distilleries** (*alambiques*) where locals extract essential oils from native plants. If you are taking a **boat trip**, your guide will drive you down to the river and you will complete the journey by water – a fabulous experience in itself. Having surveyed the waterfalls from the spectacular Brazilian side, you will be transferred to land on the Argentine side, where you can look across the apparently "normal" river from the shore, swim in the shallows and admire the butterflies, and, if possible, wade over to view the waterfalls from above.

Forty kilometres from El Soberbio the road strikes into the heart of an area of secondary forest, the last stretch of which is protected as the park, which was created in 1988. As yet, little work has been done on registering the park's flora and fauna; sighted species of birds include the condor and the peculiarly noisy Bare-throated Bellbird. It is thought (despite no recent sightings) that the park is one of the last refuges in Argentina of the rare *yaguareté*, or jaguar, whose presence has been registered on the Brazilian side. The Brazilian park is far older (created in 1947) and larger (its total area is approximately seventeen square kilometres) and the degree of protection is higher – surveys of its wildlife have confirmed the presence not only of the *yaguareté*, but also the capuchin monkey, the tapir and over two hundred species of birds, including various toucans. After another 40km or so, you arrive at the *guardaparques'* post, from where there are a number of short trails through the forest. A trail of just over a kilometre leads to the edge of the Río Uruguay, from where – compulsorily accompanied by a *guardaparque* or local guide, and conditions permitting – you can embark on an adventurous wade across 300m of knee-high water to reach the edge of the waterfalls.

Practicalities

Before setting out for the Saltos, you should check the state of the river with the police, who maintain a post nearby (☎03755/441001), and with locals in El Soberbio as to the condition of the road and for precise directions. For the current road a 4WD is best, and the only option for periods when sections of the road are flooded, but once the the RN-2 extension is complete it should be straightforward to drive there in an ordinary car – check at the tourist information office in El Soberbio or Posadas. Without your own transport, the easiest option for seeing the falls is to arrange an **organized tour**: some companies in Posadas and Puerto Iguazú offer packages to the waterfalls, involving at least an overnight stay, but these are expensive and only really worthwhile for a group. Better value is to make your own way to El Soberbio and then arrange a tour from there. The *Hostería Puesto del Sol* (see p.279) does packages including accommodation and excursions (from \$200), while a number of agencies in El Soberbio, such as Yabotí Jungle, at Av Corrientes 481 (☎03755/495266), offer 4WD and boat tours to the waterfalls for around \$130 per person. Otherwise, if you are prepared to hang around in El Soberbio for a few days, it may be possible to catch a lift to the waterfalls; vehicles do travel regularly to and from the site, taking provisions and sometimes school parties.

Up the Río Paraná: Rosario to Corrientes

The mighty **Río Paraná** is an attraction in itself, with its lush islands, delicious fish and relaxing aquatic landscapes. Anyone looking for urban pleasures should head for **Rosario**, the country's third largest city, whose famously handsome people, active cultural life and fascinating architecture make it one of Argentina's most attractive cities. Nearby **Santa Fe**, the much-overshadowed provincial capital, is at first sight less enticing, but its faded grandeur and revived dock area merit a stopover. Opposite, the dynamic city of **Paraná** shares not only its name with the river, but also its slow pace and a certain subtropical beauty. To the south, since it was linked to Rosario by a splendid bridge, the traditional town of **Victoria**, famous for its monastery, has been opening itself up to tourism. Some way to the north is the provincial capital of **Corrientes**, named for the strong currents in a sweeping loop of the Paraná. One of the region's oldest and most dynamic cities, it is also the gateway to the Gran Chaco (see p.304).

Rosario and around

I've always said that Rosario has beautiful women and good football. What more could an intellectual ask for?

Roberto Fontanarossa

Confident and stylish, with a vibrant cultural scene and a lively nightlife, **ROSARIO** dominates the whole region. With a little over one million inhabitants, it is Argentina's third biggest city – Córdoba just beats it for second place. However, Rosario likes to see itself as a worthy rival to Buenos Aires, 300km southeast – in some ways it is a far smaller version of the capital, but without the hordes of foreign visitors or the political clout. Geographically the comparison certainly holds: Rosario is a flattish riverside city and major **port**, lying at the heart of a vital agricultural region. Its cobbled streets lined with handsome buildings and leafy trees – both with a tendency to flake – manage to be decadent and dynamic at the same time. Unlike Buenos Aires, however, whose back has until recently been firmly to the water, Rosario has always enjoyed a close relationship with the **Río Paraná**; the attractive riverfront area runs for 20km along the city's eastern edge, flanked by parks, bars and restaurants and, to the north, popular beaches. One of its main attractions is the splendidly unspoilt series of so-called "**delta islands**" with wide sandy beaches, just minutes away from the city by boat. Packed with locals during the sweltering summers that afflict the region, they give Rosario the feel of a resort town, despite the city's little-developed tourist industry.

Rosario may not have any of the impressive ecclesiastical and colonial architecture of, say, Salta or Córdoba. However, as the legacy of its late nineteenth-century wealth, it does boast some particularly handsome examples of rather more worldly constructions. You can see some of Argentina's finest turn-of-the-century **architecture** here, with an eclectic spread of styles ranging from English chalets to Catalan Modernism. The last decades of the twentieth century saw the city stagnate somewhat, but the new millennium has seen a rash of architectural and art projects, such as the **Museo de Arte Contemporáneo**, housed in a conspicuously converted grain silo on the riverside. In terms of traditional sightseeing, Rosario has a handful of conventional museums and galleries, notably the excellent **Museo de Bellas Artes J.B. Castagnino** and the **Museo Histórico Provincial**, both in the city's major green space, the **Parque de la Independencia**. Its most famous sight, nationally at least, is the monolithic **Monumento a la Bandera**, a 70m marble paean to the Argentine flag.

The city's most famous son is **Che Guevara**, one of the twentieth-century's most powerful icons, who was born in an apartment block on the corner of Santa Fe and Urquiza. Other **Rosarino celebrities** include leading artists Antonio Berni and Lucio Fontana, three of Argentina's most popular singers – Fito Páez, Juan Carlos Baglietto and Litto Nebbia – and the late cartoonist Roberto Fontanarrosa, whose most famous creation was the luckless gaucho Inodoro Pereyra. Rosario's other key cultural icons are sporting, including local boy Lionel Messi, who began his international soccer career here at **Newell's Old Boys** – one of the city's two major soccer teams along with **Rosario Central**: allegiances to these two teams divide the city with a fervour possibly greater than that provoked in the capital by River Plate and Boca Juniors.

Some history

Unusually for a Hispano-American city, Rosario lacks an official founding date. Having slowly grown up around a simple chapel, built in the grounds of an estancia in the late seventeenth century and dedicated to the **Virgen del Rosario**, the original settlement became known as La Capilla del Rosario. Despite its strategic location as a port for goods from Córdoba and Santa Fe provinces, early growth was slow: as in the whole region, Rosario's progress was hindered by Buenos Aires' stranglehold on the movement of trade between the interior and foreign markets through blockades of the Río Paraná. After 1852 when river traffic was freed up, Rosario was finally set on course for expansion and the city's population ballooned from 3000 in 1850 to 23,000 in 1869, boosted further when the **Central Argentine Railway**, owned and largely financed by the British, was completed in 1870, providing a link to Córdoba. By 1895, Rosario was Argentina's second city, with 91,000 inhabitants – many of them immigrants attracted by the promise of the by now flourishing port, giving the city its other soubriquet, "**Hija de los Barcos**" (Daughter of the Ships). By the early twentieth century, the city had an important banking district populated by representatives from the world's major financial institutions, and a growing number of industries. Like Buenos Aires, Rosario also had its sleazy side, one that won it another nickname, the "Chicago of the South": during the late nineteenth and early twentieth centuries, the city was claimed to be a centre of white slave traffic with a notorious zone of **prostitution** known as the Barrio de Pichincha.

As in the rest of the country, the latter half of the twentieth century saw a period of intense political conflict and a steady decline in Rosario's fortunes. Towards the end of the century the city suffered one of the country's highest unemployment rates, but the municipality's social policies, based on decentralized power, and the post-crisis turnaround, have helped to mitigate its potentially dangerous effects. The first few years of the new millennium have seen Rosario once again become a vital link between its hinterland's rejuvenated farmland (producing beef, dairy goods, soya, wheat and maize) and the outside world. Tourism, both domestic and international, is also on the rise, catered to by a constantly improving set of hotels and even Latin America's biggest casino. To the casual visitor, at least, the city looks like a boomtown.

Arrival and information

Rosario's **airport** lies around 10km northwest of the city centre, along the RN-9 (T0341/451-3220). There is no bus service to the centre from the airport – the half-hour taxi ride will cost around $40.

Long-distance buses arrive at Rosario's clean and user-friendly **Terminal de Omnibus Mariano Moreno**, twenty blocks west of the city centre, at Santa Fe and Cafferata (T0341/437-3030). An information kiosk there (daily 9am–7pm) can provide you with a list of hotels and a map. At the terminal you can buy a magnetic card (*tarjeta magnética*) used instead of cash on the city's local buses – walk one block north along Cafferata to catch buses #116 or #107 to the centre from the corner with San Lorenzo. Otherwise, plenty of taxis pull up outside the front entrance, and will set you back only $15 or so to the city centre.

There's a good **tourist information office** (ETUR) down by the riverfront, on the corner of Avenida Belgrano and Calle Buenos Aires (daily 9am–7pm; T0341/480-2230, Wwww.rosarioturismo.com). They produce an informative map covering most of the city, together with accommodation and restaurant lists. Note that many of Rosario's attractions have different winter (usually mid-March to mid-Nov) and summer (mid-Nov to mid-March) hours; both are included in the text, but it's always worth checking ahead, especially if you arrive on the cusp.

Accommodation

Rosario's **accommodation** has improved as the city has grown in stature, and there are now decent options available at all budgets, with discounts often possible at weekends. There are a growing number of **youth hostels** in the city, including

ROSARIO

Río Paraná

PICHINCHA

EATING & DRINKING
Alma	17
Bruno	15
Café de la Opera	16
Cairo	11
Club Español	12
Davis	1
Escauriza	4
Espacio Once	18
Gringo's	3
Pampa	13
Pasaporte	10
Piluso	6
Pobla del Mercat	7
La Sede	9
Señor Arenero	2
Victoria	8
El Viejo Balcón	5
Wembley	14

ACCOMMODATION
Anamundana	I
Guesthouse	
Benidorm	H
Boulevard	C
Esplendor Savoy	E
Garden	A
Hostel de Pichincha	B
Nuevo Imperio	D
La Paz	F
Río Grande Apart	G
Hotel	

0   500 m

Casa del Tango

Isla de los Inventos

Parque de España

Complejo Cultural Parque de España

Parque Nacional de la Bandera

Museo Municipal de Arte Decorativo

Mercado de Pulgas del Bajo

Palacio de los Leones

Monumento a la Bandera

Catedral de Rosario

Estación Fluvial

Palacio del Correo

Teatro El Círculo

Museo Municipal de Bellas Artes Juan B Castagnino

Jardín Francés

Aguas Danzantes

Jardín de los Niños

Museo Histórico Provincial Dr. Julio Marc

Newells Old Boys Football Stadium

Parque de la Independencia

Parque Urquiza

Complejo Astronómico Municipal

MACRo (200m) & ◆ ①   ◀ Bridge to Victoria, Balneario La Florida, ②, ③ & ④

◀ Airport, RN-9, Córdoba & Santa Fe

◀ Granja de la Infancia (7km)

▶ Monumento al Che Guevara

▶ RN-9 & Buenos Aires

Bus Terminal

Hostel de Pichincha, at Av Francia 241 (℡ 0341/439-6798, ⓦ www.pichinchahostel .com.ar; $35 per person; ❸), with bright, airy rooms and dorms, regular *asados* and bike tours. Better still is 🏃 *Anamundana Guesthouse*, at Montevideo 1248 (℡ 0341/424-3077, ⓦ www.anamundanahostel.com; $40 per person; ❸), an attractive guesthouse/hostel run by friendly ex-backpacker Ana, with beautiful stained-glass windows and polished wooden floors, as well as clean dorms with comfortable beds and air conditioning.

Benidorm San Juan 1049 ℡ 0341/421-9368, ⓦ www.hotelbenidorm.com.ar. Airy, clean and modern rooms, all with external windows, a/c and TV. Rates include breakfast and parking. ❹

🏃 **Boulevard** San Lorenzo 2194 ℡ 0341/440-4164, ⓦ www.hotelboulevard.com.ar. Great B&B in a converted 1920s villa on the majestic Boulevard Oroño. Rooms share a bathroom, except for the bridal suite, which has its own. ❹–❺

🏃 **Esplendor Savoy** San Lorenzo 1022 ℡ 0341/429-6007, ⓦ www .esplendorsavoyrosario.com. Rosario's *belle époque* Savoy hotel has been given a respectful makeover by the Fën group, creating a beautiful boutique hotel that incorporates many of its original features, including the marble staircases, chandeliers and the crowning cupola, where you can sit and contemplate the street scene below. ❼

Garden Callao 45 ℡ 0341/437-0025, ⓦ www .hotelgardensa.com. An attractive modern hotel in a quiet area of town. Rooms have large,

comfortable beds, a/c and cable TV, and rates include breakfast, parking and use of a swimming pool. Spacious bar area. ❺

Nuevo Imperio Urquiza 1264 ℡ 0341/448-0091, ⓦ www.hotelimperio.com.ar. A bland 1970s construction grafted on to a venerable old hotel (part of the stunning but dilapidated Moorish interior survives but is not in use). A spotless, if slightly overpriced, place with decent rooms (facilities include cable TV and a/c), a bar and restaurant and a pool. ❺

La Paz Cda Barón de Mahuá 36 ℡ 0341/421-0905, ✉ lapazhotel@hotmail.com. Plain but adequate rooms with TV and private bathroom, some with balconies. Prices include breakfast. ❹

🏃 **Río Grande Apart Hotel** Dorrego 1261 ℡ 0341/424-1144, ⓦ www.riograndeapart .com.ar The best of the city's *apart-hotels*, with bright, roomy suites in a smart, renovated building in a fairly quiet part of the city. Outstanding buffet breakfasts, reliable internet and a safe garage. ❻

The City

Though Rosario is a large city, stretching for over 20km along the Río Paraná, most points of interest lie within a fairly compact area and – with the exception of excursions to the city's popular *balneario*, **La Florida**, to the north, and to the island beaches, to the south – there is seldom any need to take public transport. It's an easy city to find your way around, too, with streets following an exceptionally regular grid pattern, and the river itself making a useful reference point. Rosario's main square is the quiet **Plaza 25 de Mayo**, where you'll find the post office, the cathedral and the **Museo Municipal de Arte Decorativo Firma y Odilo Estévez**. One block east lies the **Monumento a la Bandera**, which faces the city's main riverside avenue, Avenida Belgrano. The southern end of Avenida Belgrano leads to **Parque Urquiza**, popular with joggers and walkers in the evening and home to the city's astronomical observatory.

South and west of Plaza 25 de Mayo lies Rosario's main commercial and shopping district, centred on the pedestrianized streets of San Martín and Córdoba. Beyond Calle Corrientes, Córdoba is known as the **Paseo del Siglo**, a stretch of street that is home both to some of Rosario's best-preserved architecture and to the city's most upmarket shops and bars. The Paseo del Siglo ends at **Bulevar Oroño**, an elegant boulevard fringed with palms and plane trees, dissected by a cycle path and lined with seigniorial French-style villas, mostly now converted into clinics and offices; it runs south towards Rosario's oasis of a main park, the **Parque de la Independencia**, where you will find some of the city's main **museums**.

Plaza 25 de Mayo and around

Constructed on the site of the first modest chapel built to venerate the Virgen del Rosario, **Plaza 25 de Mayo** sits on the edge of the city, near where it slopes down to Avenida Belgrano and the river. The plaza itself is a pleasantly shady space laid out very formally around its central marble monument, the **Monumento a la Independencia**. Around the square lie a number of grand public buildings, including the imposing **Palacio del Correo** on the corner of Córdoba and Buenos Aires and, on the northeast corner, the terracotta-coloured Municipal Palace, also known as the **Palacio de los Leones**, in reference to the majestic sculptured lions that flank the main entrance.

South of the Palacio lies the **Catedral de Rosario** (Mon–Sat 9am–12.30pm & 4.30–8.30pm, Sun 8am–1pm & 5–9.30pm), a late nineteenth-century construction in which domes, towers, columns and pediments are mixed to particularly eclectic effect. Inside, there's a fine Italianate altar carved from Carrara marble and, in the crypt, the colonial wood-carved image of the Virgin of Rosario, brought from Cádiz in 1773.

At Santa Fe 748 you'll find the **Museo Municipal de Arte Decorativo Firma y Odilo Estévez** (Wed–Fri 3–8pm, Sat & Sun 10am–4pm; free). Housed in a fantastically ornate mansion, whose facade reflects the early twentieth-century fashion for heavily ornamental moulding, the museum exhibits the collection of the building's former occupants, the Estévez family, Galician immigrants who made their fortune by growing *mate*. It's a stunning display – every inch of the interior is furnished and ornamented with objects seemingly chosen to exemplify the wealth and taste of the owners, from Egyptian glassware and tiny Greek sculptures to Flemish tapestry and Limoges porcelain, via pre-Columbian ceramics and Spanish ivory figures. There's a small but impressive **painting collection**, too, including *Portrait of a Gentleman* by French Neoclassicist Jacques Louis David and a Goya portrait, *Doña Maria Teresa Ruiz de Apodaca de Sesma*, with strikingly piercing black eyes.

Monumento a la Bandera

Your first sight of the **Monumento a la Bandera** (aside from its picture on the ten-peso note) is likely to be through the gap between the cathedral and the Palacio de los Leones, from where the Pasaje Juramento, lined with marble figures by the great sculptress Lola Mora (see box opposite), leads down to the monument itself. Finished in 1957 under the direction of architect Ángel Guido, the Monumento a la Bandera is basically a huge allegorical sculpture based on the idea of a ship (representing Argentina) sailing towards a glorious future. General Manuel Belgrano "created" the flag in the city in 1812, and Rosario enjoys the official title of "Cuna de la Bandera" (Cradle of the Flag). The country's major Flag Day celebrations are held at the monument on June 20 each year.

Physically, it is divided into three sections: the so-called **Propileo**, a kind of temple-like structure within which burns an eternal flame commemorating Argentines who have died for their country; the **Patio Cívico**, a long, shallow rectangular flight of stairs leading away from the Propileo; and, looming above everything, the **central tower** – a massive 70m block of unpolished marble whose coarse lines seem particularly inappropriate in a city otherwise distinguished for its graceful architecture – though you might say they are in keeping with American novelist Waldo Frank's description of Rosario as "vital and crude, tough and tender". It's worth taking the lift to the top of the tower (daylight hours; $2), from where there's a commanding **view** of the river and the city. After dark, the whole monument is lit and the central tower bathed in azure and white light, looking not unlike a giant branch of Ikea.

Lola Mora

Dolores Mora Vega de Hernández – better known as **Lola Mora** – was born on November 17, 1866, at El Tala, a tiny village in Salta Province very close to the Tucumán border. She completed her studies in Italy and took to working in **marble**, a medium used for much of her prolific oeuvre of statues and monuments. In addition to works in various towns and cities around the country, she is best known for her invaluable contribution to the Monumento a la Bandera in Rosario (see p.286); the magnificent Nereidas fountain adorning the Costanera Sur in Buenos Aires (see p.100); and the voluptuous set of allegorical figures – Peace, Progress, Justice, Freedom and Labour – intended for the National Congress building (see p.93) but never placed there, as they were considered too shocking. Instead the five naked forms can be admired at the Casa de Gobierno in Jujuy (see p.344). Hailed as the country's foremost **sculptress**, Lola had a tragic life, losing her parents at an early age, enduring a turbulent marriage and facing social rejection owing to her bohemian lifestyle and her predilection for portraying shapely female forms (leading to comparisons with Camille Claudel). Towards the end of her life, she suffered from ill health and psychological problems. She died in poverty, on June 7, 1936, shortly after reconciliation with her husband after seventeen years of estrangement and only a few months after the national government agreed to grant her a pension.

Below the tower, there's a **crypt** dedicated to the creator of the flag, General Belgrano, and, below the Propileo, there's the rather pointless and pompous **sala de banderas**, in which flags of all the American countries are exhibited, together with the national flower, the national anthem, the national shield and a sample of earth.

The Costanera

Stretching over 20km from north to south, Rosario's **Costanera**, or riverfront, is one of the city's most appealing features, offering numerous green spaces and views over the Río Paraná. You'll find this area's most central park, the **Parque Nacional de la Bandera**, a narrow wedge of grass lining the river, just to the east of the Monumento a la Bandera. At the southern end of the park lies the **Estación Fluvial** from where regular boat services run to the river islands (see p.282, p.290). Every Saturday and Sunday evening around Av Belgrano 500, which runs past the western edge of the park, there is a flea market, the **Mercado de Pulgas del Bajo**, where you can browse through a selection of crafts, antiques and books. The park merges to the north with the **Parque de España**, where a cultural and exhibition centre, the **Complejo Cultural Parque de España**, has been imaginatively installed above some old nineteenth-century tunnels.

Fifteen blocks south of the Parque Nacional de la Bandera – follow Avenida de la Libertad, which climbs the bluff just south of the Monumento – lies **Parque Urquiza**, a small park popular for an evening jog or stroll. The park is also home to Rosario's astronomical observatory, the **Complejo Astronómico Municipal** (☎0341/480-2533), which also has a planetarium and an experimental science museum (Sat & Sun 5–8pm).

Around 8km north of the centre, Rosario's most popular mainland beach, **Balneario La Florida** (bus #101 from Rioja) is packed on summer weekends, and has bars, restaurants and shower facilities. At the southern end of the *balneario* you'll find the **Rambla Catalunya** and Avenida Carrasco, lined with glitzy bars, smart restaurants and see-and-be-seen nightclubs that are the summertime focus of Rosario's famed *movida*.

Kids' Rosario

Rosario's city government has a justified reputation for progressiveness, and one of its most positive achievements is the provision of entertainment for children, a rarity in Argentina. Everywhere you go in the city you see children's playgrounds, kids' menus and entertainment aimed at smaller people, although most of this takes place at the weekend. One of the best initiatives is the **Isla de los Inventos** (Fri–Sun 2–7pm; $3), housed in the stunning former central train station at Corrientes and Wheelwright. Literally the "Island of Inventions", it features a series of interactive exhibits based on Rosario and its history – such as a contraption representing fluvial navigation on the Río Paraná – plus workshops where visitors can help assemble toys. Adults will enjoy some of the more abstract sections, such as one dedicated to infinity, and may need to hold toddlers' hands when they enter the magical dark chamber that comes to life to explain the history of the universe since the Big Bang.

Inside the **Parque de la Independencia** (see below), the former zoo is another kids' attraction, the **Jardín de los Niños** ("Children's Garden") mostly aimed at youngsters aged 4 and above (Fri–Sun 1–6pm; free). An ingenious theme park whose only (strictly non-commercial) theme is enabling young people to discover everyday phenomena such as sound, mystery, flight and balance, it is adventurous but safe and great fun.

There are two museums aimed at children: a hands-on experimental **science museum** at the observatory (see p.287), and the privately run **Museo de los Niños** in Shopping Alto Rosario (Tues–Sun 2–8pm; $9–12), which leads children around a play version of a town, albeit one with a commercial flavour.

Finally, the **Granja de la Infancia** – "Youngsters' Farm" – is some way out of the centre at Avenida Perón 8100 (Tues–Fri 9am–5pm, Sat & Sun 10am–6pm; $3). Aimed at urban youth who think chickens are born oven-ready and have never seen a real-life goat or capybara, it is so well designed that even the most field-wise kids get something out of it and, like all the other child-targeted venues, it will keep grown-ups entertained for a while too.

Parque de la Independencia

Dissected by various avenues and containing several museums, a football stadium – Newell's Old Boys, known affectionately as "El Coloso" – and a racetrack, the **Parque de la Independencia** feels like a neighbourhood in itself. The park was inaugurated in 1902 and is an attractively landscaped space with shady walkways and beautifully laid-out gardens such as the formal **Jardín Francés**, just west of the main entrance on Bulevar Oroño. Just south of the entrance there is a large lake which is the setting for a rather kitsch but not unattractive spectacle known as the **Aguas Danzantes** (literally the "dancing waters"), a synchronized fountain display complete with coloured lights and music (Wed–Sun 8–11pm). Parque de la Independencia can easily be reached on foot from the city centre – it's a particularly attractive walk along the Paseo del Siglo and the Bulevar Oroño, or you can take buses #129 and #123 from Rioja.

Museo Municipal de Bellas Artes Juan B. Castagnino

At Avenida Pellegrini 2202, which runs through the Parque de la Independencia, you'll find the **Museo Municipal de Bellas Artes Juan B. Castagnino** (Mon & Wed–Fri 2–8pm, Sat & Sun 1–7pm; $4), regarded as the country's most important fine arts museum after the Museo de Bellas Artes in Buenos Aires. The museum has two permanent collections: European painting from the fifteenth to the twentieth centuries, with works by Goya, Sisley and Daubigny, among others; and Argentine painting with examples from major artists such as Spilimbergo and Quinquela

▲ Parque de la Independencia, Rosario

Martín, plus Antonio Berni and Lucio Fontana, both born in Rosario. The museum, arranged on two floors with large, well-lit rooms, also puts on some excellent temporary exhibitions – it's well worth looking out for exhibitions featuring local artists, who are producing some of Argentina's most interesting contemporary work.

Museo Histórico Provincial Dr Julio Marc

West of Parque de la Independencia's lake sits the **Museo Histórico Provincial Dr Julio Marc** (Tues–Fri 9am–5pm, Sat & Sun 2–6pm; $1), a large and well-organized museum. Despite its name, it's not just a provincial museum but has a vast and splendid collection of exhibits spanning the whole of Latin America. Among its most notable collections are those dedicated to **Latin American religious art**, with a stunning eighteenth-century silver altar from Alto Peru, which was used for the Mass given by Pope John Paul II when he visited the city in 1987, and some fine examples of polychrome works in wood, wax and bone, representing the famed Quiteña School (named after the capital of Ecuador). There's also an important collection of **indigenous American ceramics**, including some valuable musical pieces known as whistling glasses (*vasos silbadores*) from the Chimú culture of northern Peru and some well-preserved and delicate textiles. Colonial-era furniture is also well represented – look for the beautifully worked travel desk featuring carvings of conquistadores and native Americans.

Museo de Arte Contemporáneo de Rosario (MACRo)

West of the northern reaches of the elegant Bulevar Oroño lies the former red-light district, the Pichincha. This barrio has undergone earnest gentrification in recent years and is now home to trendy bars, fashionable restaurants and, above all, antique shops, the latter mostly clustered along Avenida Rivadavia. At the far end of the boulevard, on the waterfront, set among the verdant Parque Sunchales, is an unmissable hulk of a building, looking like a row of upturned giant liquorice allsorts. Once a grain silo belonging to the Davis family, it has been turned into one of the country's most promising museums of contemporary art, the **Museo de Arte Contemporáneo de Rosario**, or **MACRo** (Thurs–Tues: summer

Monumento al Che Guevara

Acknowledgement of Rosario's most famous son, the revolutionary **Ernesto "Che" Guevara**, has been a long time in coming; compared to with Cuba, where Che is a hero of gigantic proportions, the Argentine authorities have seemed rather embarrassed about him, and it took until 2008 for a monument to him to be erected in his hometown. The bronze statue was unveiled to commemorate what would have been his 80th birthday, but even then, it was funded by thousands of small donations from around the world rather than the government, though they did contribute the space – an out of the way, rather forlorn plaza on 27 de Febrero and Laprida, twelve blocks east of Parque de la Independencia. The statue itself depicts a larger-than-life though not, in truth, very lifelike Che striding purposefully, mounted on a concrete plinth covered in suitably socialist graffiti.

4–10pm; rest of year 2–8pm; $4; ⓦwww.macromuseo.org.ar). The most striking aspects of the museum are its exterior, especially the huge silo cylinders painted in vibrant pink, purple and azure shades, and its riverside location – both the top-floor viewpoint and the Perspex lift-shaft leading to it offer fine views of the majestic Paraná. The exhibitions are mostly dedicated to up-and-coming local and national artists, but even if the art leaves you cold the museum is worth a visit for the building, location and excellent café-restaurant, *Davis* (see p.291), where you can enjoy watching boats, barges and bits of vegetation float past.

The Alto Delta islands

Known as the **Alto Delta**, the low-lying **islands** off Rosario's "coast" in fact fall under the jurisdiction of the neighbouring province, Entre Ríos. Like the islands of the Tigre Delta in Buenos Aires (see p.156), they host subtropical vegetation fed by sediment from the Upper Paraná River. The Alto Delta is far less developed than Tigre, however. With the exception of the more remote island of **Charigüé**, where there is a small settlement with its own school, police station and a handful of restaurants, the islands are largely uninhabited.

Boat trips and accommodation possibilities in the Delta shift with every season, so it's worth dropping in to the tourist office on the riverfront to ask about what's available. One long-established trip is a two-hour **river cruise** on the sightseeing boat, *Ciudad de Rosario* (Sat & Sun: winter 2.30pm & 5pm; summer 5pm & 7.30pm; $19; ⓣ0341/449-8688). Passenger boats also run to the various islands throughout the week, with regular services from November to March, from 9am to dusk; out of season, services are less frequent. Bike Rosario (see Listings, p.292) runs kayak excursions on the river, while the English-speaking Rosario Sail (ⓣ0341/156-289287, ⓦwww.rosariosail.com.ar) offers sailboat trips. All boats depart from the Estación Fluvial (ⓣ0341/447-3838, ⓦwww.lafluvialrosario.com.ar).

There are currently two places to **stay** on the islands. One is *Puerto Pirata*, on a nameless island opposite the Granadero Baigorria area of town (ⓣ0341/153-037156, ⓦwww.paradorpuertopirata.com.ar; ❸ including lunch and transfer), which rents out *cabañas* and has a good bar and restaurant with great views over the river from its terrace and long strip of beach. The other is the *Complejo del Francés* (ⓣ0341/155-083284; ❹–❺) on Isla La Invernada, where there are attractive rustic-style as well newer, more luxurious *cabañas* and a bar. *Aldo Traslados* at the Estación Fluvial ferries passengers back and forth ($20 return).

If you fancy just spending a day swimming or sunbathing, head for **Vladimir**, just south of the Estación Fluvial, where there are good beaches and a couple of snack bars; be warned, though, that the sun can be very fierce and there is little or no shade.

Eating and drinking

Rosario has plenty of **restaurants** to suit all budgets, both in the city centre and along the Costanera. In addition to pasta, pizza and *parrillada*, there are some dazzlingly adventurous places that easily rival the best in the capital, as well as a number of excellent fish restaurants specializing in *boga*, *dorado* and *surubí*. The city has always excelled in a **bar culture** – there are so many stylishly revamped bars around the city centre that you're spoilt for choice when it comes to drinking. The best spots for bar-hopping are just north of the centre, roughly between Santa Fe and Avenida Belgrano, and to the west, in the Pichincha, centred on an oblong formed by calles Ricchieri, Suipacha, Salta and Güemes.

Restaurants

Alma Montevideo 2394 ℡0341/449-2397. Quiet, toned-down place in a charming corner house, all done in soothing lime-green and pastel shades, with mellow music, laidback service and interesting fusion fare – try the rabbit stuffed with bacon or the sucking-lamb tajine. Relatively expensive.

Bruno Ovidio Lagos 1599. Long-established, family-run Italian restaurant serving excellent home-made pasta. Closed Mon.

Club Español Rioja 1052. Friendly restaurant housed in a beautiful old building with stunning decorative glass ceilings and an astonishingly elaborate facade. Simple daily menu includes a main course, dessert and wine and soda. Sun lunch times are popular for Spanish specialities such as paella and tortilla.

Davis Blv Oroño s/n. Named for the silo that was converted into the fabulous MACRo museum, this waterside restaurant enjoys an incredible location. The food is adventurous – pork in stout and mustard sauce, or a platter of Paraná river fish – and the ambience lively.

Escauriza Paseo Ribereño and Escauriza. Highly regarded *parrilla* specializing in fish, on the river front near the access to the Victoria road bridge. Surubi, boga and dorado are on the menu as well as more conventional meat, and the prices are very reasonable.

Pampa Moreno 1206. Elegant tables in a trendy restaurant with a consciously industrial look, bare brickwork and all. Food is more conventional, though some dishes have a twist, such as the signature turkey, mozzarella and nut sorrentinos.

Pobla del Mercat Salta 1424 ℡0341/447-1240. A wine club and gourmet grocery with a smart restaurant attached. Attentive service, an impressive wine list and all manner of culinary wonders – from the fish carpaccio to the peach tart – make this one of the top restaurants in the city.

Señor Arenero Av Carrasco 2568. Big glitzy restaurant specializing in fish, in the popular Rambla Catalunya area; prices are above average.

Victoria San Lorenzo and Pte Roca. Old-fashioned corner café-bar and restaurant with a sober wooden interior and tables on the pavement. Good-value *menú ejecutivo* with a main dish such as pork chops, a dessert and drink. Closed Sun lunch.

El Viejo Balcón Wheelwright and Italia. One of the city's best *parrillas*, serving up all the usual cuts at an attractive riverside location. Moderate prices.

Wembley Av Belgrano 2012 ℡0341/481-1090. Busy upmarket restaurant opposite the port. Daily specials such as salmon with capers though the most successful dishes are the more simply executed grilled river fish or *parrillada*.

Cafés and bars

Café de la Ópera Laprida and Mendoza 787 ℡0341/421-9402156-422024. Beautiful old-fashioned café adjoining the Teatro El Círculo, serving specials like tarragon chicken, along with pasta, omelettes and salads; or just have a coffee and a slice of date tart. Also hosts lively musical or cabaret events on Fri and Sat from 10pm.

Cairo Sarmiento and Santa Fe. A Rosarian institution, the high ceilinged *Cairo* fleshes out its claim to be a literary cafe with a library at the back and theatrical looking velvet drapes; it's also well known in town for being where the great cartoonist Roberto Fontanarossa came to work. As well as full blown meals, there is a huge cocktail menu and a *mate* bar serving Argentina's favourite brew.

Espacio Once Av de la Libertad 10. This large café on the southern Costanera is a popular early-evening pit-stop for Rosarinos on their way back from a walk around Parque Urquiza. The outside tables are good for a spot of people-watching.

Gringo's Av Carrasco 2765. Popular summer bar along the Rambla Catalunya and a good place to pick up free invites for one of the area's clubs. Vast outside seating area and a range of beers, cocktails and fast food.

Pasaporte Maipú and Urquiza. Stylish bar with outside tables on a pleasant corner down near

the riverfront. Coffee, alcoholic drinks and a large selection of filled crepes. Board games available.
Piluso Alvear and Catamarca. Pleasing wood-panelled bar on an attractive corner in Pichincha. Good range of beers and also fruity non-alcoholic drinks.

La Sede San Lorenzo and Entre Ríos. Elegant and rather literary bar in a fabulous Art Nouveau building – a favourite meeting-place for Rosario's artistic celebrities. Theatrical/cabaret evenings.

Nightlife and entertainment

Rosario is noted for its nightlife, **la movida**, but its **clubs** can be a little disappointing and in summer, when all the action moves to the Rambla Catalunya, a beachfront avenue at the northern end of town, you're limited to one or two very popular but faceless mega-discos, whose names but not character change with the seasons. You'll be far better off if you check out one of the city's popular *milongas*, a more authentic experience: Rosario has a hard core of **tango** enthusiasts – who dance a slightly showier version of the tango than Porteños – and most nights of the week there is something going on.

Berlín Pje Zabala 1128, between the 300 block of Mitre and Sarmiento. Regular cabaret and musical events from Thurs to Sun at this popular bar.

Casa del Tango Av Arturo Illia 1701 ☎0341/449-4666, ⊛www.la casadeltangorosario.com. Popular tango *cena show* in a converted railway building near the beachfront (Wed–Sat).

Las Chirusas ☎0341/155-832255, ⊛www .milongaschirusas.com.ar. Rosario *milonga*, currently taking place on Tues at 10pm at Mano a Mano Artes, Ov. Lago 790, and on Sun from 10pm at *Café de la Flor*, Mendoza 862.

Gotika City Club Mitre 1739, ⊛www.gotikacityclub .com.ar. A loft, three bars and a garden are all features at the city's main gay disco, with regular shows and events.

Madame Brown 3126. This megaclub aimed at the over-25s claims to be the biggest in Argentina. Fri & Sat only.

Peña La Amistad Maipú 1121 ☎0341/447-1037. A good spot to listen to folk music, especially *chamamé* and other regional styles. Snacks such as empanadas and tamales are served. Fri and Sat from 11pm.

Teatro El Círculo Laprida 1235 ☎0341/448-3784 ⊛www.teatro-elcirculo.com.ar. Rosario's best known theatre has an extensive programme of plays, music, opera and dance; check the website for full listings.

Vudú Patio de la Madera, Av Santa Fe. Located next to the bus terminal, this big club plays a slightly incongruous mixture of latin, pop and trance and attracts a trendy crowd. Closed during the summer season.

Listings

Airlines Aerolíneas Argentinas/Austral, Santa Fe 1410 ☎0341/424-9332 and at the airport ☎0341/451-1470; Lan Chile, San Lorenzo 1116 ☎0341/424-8205; Sol ☎0810/444-4765.
Laundry Mitre 1723.
Post office Correo Central at Buenos Aires and Córdoba, on Plaza 25 de Mayo.

Tours For bicycle tours, as well as bike or kayak rental, contact Bike Rosario at Zeballos 327 ☎0341/155-713812, ⊛www.bikerosario.com.ar. English and French spoken.
Travel agent ASATEJ, Shopping Del Siglo piso 2, Córdoba 1643 ☎0341/425-6002.

Victoria

Since a stunning road **bridge** ($9 toll for cars, valid both ways, so keep the ticket) across the Río Paraná was inaugurated in 2003, the somnolent little market town of **VICTORIA**, 122km southeast of Paraná, has been cajoled into life. Founded by immigrants from northern Italy and the Basque country, it has been brought physically much closer to Rosario, 58km southwest – and seems to relish its prospects as an up-and-coming holiday resort, with a new casino and a thermal baths complex. The RN-11 Paraná–Gualeguaychú road bypasses the town to the north, while Avenida

Costanera Dr Pedro Radio skirts round the southern edge, following the contours of the riverbanks, where summer tourists flock to bathe along the sandy beaches. Centred on an alluring main square, its mostly unpaved streets, forming a regular grid, are lined with a number of fine neocolonial buildings in varying states of repair that reward aimless wanderings. Look out for a local architectural feature, the highly ornate late nineteenth-century **wrought-iron grilles** (*rejas*) that adorn many of the town's doors and windows. On the square itself you should focus on the **cathedral**, or **Templo Parroquial** – an Italianate nineteenth-century pile that looks dreadful outside but conceals some fabulously delicate frescoes, especially those depicting the four Evangelists, with their pronounced Pre-Raphaelite style – and the adjacent wedding cake of a **municipalidad**, whose exotic eccentricity marries well with the palm fronds and other subtropical vegetation in the plaza, where you'll find the usual collection of statues, benches and a bandstand, plus stalls selling handicrafts.

Victoria's main tourist attraction is the **Abadía del Niño Dios** (guided visits daily at 10am and 2pm; free), home to Latin America's oldest Benedictine foundation, dating from 1899. The modern monastery and cheerfully designed church are certainly worth seeing, and include the chance to hear the monks singing Gregorian chant. The highlight for most visitors, however, is the excellent shop selling delicious, and mostly healthy, products, true to the Benedictine tradition, ranging from unusual jams and bee products to liqueurs and cheeses. The abbey sits alongside the main RN-11 artery, between the turn-off to the Rosario bridge and the town proper.

Practicalities

Victoria's little **bus terminal** is halfway between the main northern entrance and the central plaza, just four blocks north of the latter, at Junín and L.N. Alem. The helpful little **tourist office** (daily 8am–8pm; ☎03436/421885, ⓦwww.turismovictoria .com.ar) is conveniently situated at the northern access, on the corner of main drag 25 de Mayo and Bulevar Sarmiento. The best **accommodation** option is the smart *Hotel Sol* (☎03436/424040, ⓦwww.hotelsolvictoria.com.ar; ❽), which is also the casino – the spacious, well-appointed rooms are extremely comfortable, and there is a fine dining room and swimming pool, with views down to the river. Otherwise *Hotel Casablanca* (☎03436/424131, ⓦwww.hotelcasablancavictoria.com; ❺) is a hospitable medium-sized establishment at Bulevar Moreno s/n, in the southern neighbourhood of Barrio Quinto Cuartel, with large, slightly kitsch rooms, a beautiful garden and swimming pool, plus ample parking space. Lower down the budget scale is *Residencial Los Altos* (☎03436/15-615537, ⓦwww.los-altos.com.ar; ❹), on the RN-11 near the abbey; it also has a pool and pleasant rooms and gardens. Otherwise ask at the tourist office for details of estancias in the nearby countryside offering *ecoturismo* rooms.

Enjoy Victoria's slow pace of life down on the riverfront over a lengthy *parrilla*, such as that offered by the restaurant *Fontanarrosa*. Alternatively, head for the *Jockey Club*, L.N. Alem 91, one block north of the central square, for simple but tasty fish dishes, though the pasta is not so great. For decent, drinks and snacks, try *Plaza Bar*, at the corner of San Martín and Sarmiento.

Santa Fe

Capital of its namesake province and an important commercial centre for the surrounding agricultural region, **SANTA FE** lies 475km north of Buenos Aires, along the banks of the Río Paraná. A sizeable city of about 400,000 inhabitants, Santa Fe is of interest mainly as a stopover – although even on those terms the city loses out to the nearby and more appealing cities of Rosario and Paraná. Apart from a particularly hot and humid climate in summer, owing to its low-lying riverside location, Santa Fe's main handicap is a rather sprawling and disjointed layout that makes getting to and from the city's modest attractions a bit of a slog.

Though Santa Fe is one of Argentina's oldest settlements – it was founded in 1573 by Juan de Garay in **Cayastá**, 80km north, and then moved to its current site in 1660 after repeated Indian attacks – careless development has made for a rather scruffy city in which unremarkable modern buildings largely overshadow the few remnants of a fine architectural heritage. What is left is largely grouped around the city's **centro histórico**, where there are a handful of sights worth visiting, notably the seventeenth-century **Iglesia y Convento de San Francisco**. The city's **port area** has been given a smart revamp, with a hotel in a converted grain silo, casino, shops and boat trips attracting visitors.

Santa Fe is linked to Entre Ríos' provincial capital, Paraná (see p.297), by the **Túnel Subfluvial Uranga-Sylvestre Begnis**, better known as "Hernandarias", which runs for nearly 3km under the Río Paraná.

Arrival and information

Santa Fe's **airport** is at Sauce Viejo, 7km south of the city along the RN-11 (☎0342/475-0386). The local bus marked "L" or "aeropuerto" runs between the airport and Calle San Luis in the city centre (45min). The **bus terminal** is on the corner of Avenida Belgrano and Hipólito Yrigoyen (☎0342/455-3908), just northeast of the town centre and within walking distance of most accommodation.

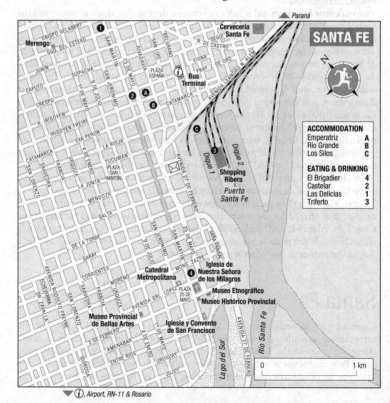

The main **tourist office** (Mon–Fri 7am–8pm, Sat & Sun 8am–8pm; ℡0342/457-4124) is in the bus terminal. Don't expect much, though the staff should at least be able to provide you with a map. At the weekends, **tours** of the city are possible from the vantage point of a somewhat incongruous red London bus (Sat & Sun 4pm; $10; ℡0342/483-1036), departing from dock one in the port area.

Accommodation

Mostly business-oriented and overpriced, Santa Fe's **hotels** are uninspiring, with some horrid budget options in the immediate vicinity of the bus terminal that are best avoided. There are a few exceptions, however, including *Los Silos,* at Dique 1, Puerto Santa Fe (℡0342/450-2800, Ⓦwww.hotellossilos.com.ar; ❼), a luxury hotel in an enormous former grain silo, complete with bar, swish rooms with fantastic views and a very high rooftop pool. The *Río Grande,* at San Jerónimo 2586 (℡0342/450-0700, Ⓦwww.hotel-riogrande.com.ar; ❼), has less character but its comfortable rooms are spotless, with cable TV, safe and air conditioning; there's a good buffet breakfast and the staff are courteous. The run-down *Emperatriz Hotel,* at Irigoyen Freyre 2440 (℡0342/453-0061, Ⓔemperatrizhotel @arnet.com.ar; ❸), is the best budget option, housed in a 1920s, Mudéjar construction – combining Moorish and Gothic features – with arched wooden doors and a tiled interior; all rooms come with private bathroom, but some may find the hotel lacking in cleanliness.

The City

Santa Fe doesn't actually sit on the Río Paraná, but at the western extremity of a series of delta islands, which separate it from the city of Paraná. Ships enter Santa Fe's important **port**, the most westerly along the Paraná, via an access channel; the port itself has been given a makeover in recent years and is fast becoming the tourist focus of Santa Fe, as far as such a modest city can have one. The Río Santa Fe borders the southern end of the city, running north to feed into the **Laguna Setúbal**, a large lake east of the city, and bordered by the city's lively Costanera, which runs for 5km or so from north to south.

Santa Fe's mostly modern **downtown** area is centred on busy Calle 25 de Mayo, lined with shops and *confiterías*. The quieter **centro histórico**, where you will find the majority of Santa Fe's older buildings, lies ten blocks south of Tucumán and is centred on **Plaza 25 de Mayo**. This is the most interesting area to explore on foot and you could while away an afternoon moving between its museums and churches.

Plaza 25 de Mayo and around

Like the rest of the city, Santa Fe's main square, the **Plaza 25 de Mayo**, is an architecturally disjointed kind of place, with the styles of its surrounding buildings leaping from colonial through French Second Empire to nondescript modern. The square is somewhat unusual in having two churches. On the north side stands the rather stark white **Catedral Metropolitana** (daily 8am–8pm), originally built in the mid-eighteenth century but subsequently modified to give it a simple Neoclassical facade crowned with domed and majolica-tiled bell towers. Little remains of the original building except the massive studded wooden entrance doors. On the east side of the square is the **Iglesia de Nuestra Señora de los Milagros**, its pleasingly simple and typically colonial facade looking rather overwhelmed by the more modern constructions around it. Built between 1667 and 1700, it is the oldest church in the province; look inside to see the fine carvings produced by Guaraní in the Jesuit Missions – most notably the impressive Altar Mayor, produced in Loreto.

On the southeastern corner of the square you'll find the **Museo Histórico Provincial Brigadier General Estanislao López** (Tues–Fri 8.30am–noon and 4–8pm, Sat & Sun 5.30–8.30pm; ℡0342/457-3529, Ⓦwww.museohistorico-sfe .gov.ar; free). Housed in a cool late-colonial family house, the museum's collection comprises furniture, paintings, silverwork, religious icons and everyday items from the seventeenth century. Its most notable items are carvings from the missions and paintings from the Cusco School.

Museo Etnográfico y Colonial Juan de Garay

One block east of the main plaza, at 25 de Mayo 1470, is the **Museo Etnográfico y Colonial Juan de Garay** (Tues–Fri 8.30am–noon & 3.30–8.30pm, Sat & Sun 5.30–8.30pm; ℡0342/457-3550; free). The bulk of the museum's well-organized and coherently displayed collection comprises pieces recovered from the site of **Santa Fe La Vieja** at Cayastá. The most commonly recovered pieces were *tinajas*, large ceramic urns – many of them in a surprisingly complete state considering they spent around three hundred years underground – and delicate amulets in the form of shells or the *higa*, a clenched fist symbol, used to ward off the evil eye. There's also a fine collection of **indigenous ceramics** with typical zoomorphic forms ranging from birds – especially parrots – and bats, to capybaras, cats and snakes.

Iglesia y Convento de San Francisco

One block south of Plaza 25 de Mayo, at Amenábar 2557, lies the **Iglesia y Convento de San Francisco** (Mon–Fri 8am–noon & 3.30–6.30pm, Sat & Sun 8am–noon & 5.30–6.45pm). Built in 1676, the church is notable for its incredible solid but rustic construction: the walls are nearly two metres thick and made of adobe, while the stunning and cleverly assembled interior **ceiling** was constructed using solid wooden beams of Paraguayan cedar, *lapacho*, *algarrobo* and *quebracho colorado* held together not with nails but with wooden pegs. The intricate dome at the centre of the church is a particularly impressive example of the application of this technique and also has a rather light-hearted touch: at the centre a beautifully carved pinecone is suspended. Of the various icons around the church the most notable is that of **Jesús Nazareno**, immediately to your left as you enter. The beautifully detailed image was produced by one of Spain's most famous *imagineros*, or religious image makers, Alonso Cano, in 1650. It was presented to the church by the Queen of Spain when the city was moved from Cayastá, to show sympathy for the repeated Indian attacks.

One of the strangest relics in the church is found in the sacristy, a simple table scored by claw marks and known as the *mesa del tigre* ("the tiger's table"). According to a gory tale, in 1825 a jaguar – the word *"tigre"* often means a jaguar in Latin America – was washed up by a flood and sought refuge in the sacristy. It was eventually shot in a small room off the convent cloisters, but not before it had attacked and killed three monks.

Puerto Santa Fe

Lying just to the southeast of the city centre where the Paraná forks towards Laguna Setúbal, the old dock area, **Puerto Sante Fe**, is being enthusiastically developed. Its two **diques** (docks) are now home to a casino and upmarket hotel, housed in a giant former grain silo (see p.295), while the nearby warehouses have been converted into a smart, relatively tasteful shopping centre, with some good fish restaurants. Catamaran trips leave from dock one to explore the local waters at weekends (Sat & Sun 11am, 3.30pm & 5.45pm; $30; ℡0342/456-4381).

Eating, drinking and nightlife

Cuisine-wise, Santa Fe is famous in Argentina for two things - *alfajores merengo* and beer. An *alfajor merengo* is a particularly tempting version of Argentina's favourite cake, coated in crispy, white sugar frosting and produced in the city for more than 150 years; they can be bought from *Merengo* at Santiago del Estero 3623. Excellent beer, meanwhile, is brewed at the *Cervecería Santa Fe*, one of South America's largest breweries (free guided visits are possible with prior booking on ☎0342/450-2201). Locals ask for a *liso* – a draught lager served in a straight glass. A good place to try one is in *Las Delicias*, on the corner of San Martín and Hipólito Yrigoyen, a traditional *confitería* serving good sandwiches and cakes.

Santa Fe also has plenty of **restaurants**, mostly within a few blocks of San Martín, though few really stand out. One which does is the stylish *El Brigadier*, San Martín 1670, housed in an old colonial building with a fine selection of well-prepared fish (both fresh- and saltwater) and meat. Alternatively, *Castelar*, at the far end of the shopping centre in dock one at Puerto Santa Fe, is done out in soothing dark wood and tiles and serves a good value set meal at lunchtime; it also has an attached *bodega*, where you can try and buy wine.

Santa Fe's liveliest **bars** are found around the intersection of San Martín and Santiago del Estero, all with tables on the pavement and a fun atmosphere on summer evenings – try *Triferto*, San Martín 3301.

Paraná

Lying 30km southeast of Santa Fe, and linked to it by the **Túnel Subfluvial Uranga-Sylvestre Begnis**, better known as "Hernandarias", **PARANÁ** is far more appealing than its cross-river neighbour. Favoured by a gentle hilly terrain and a handsome, pedestrian-friendly riverfront area, the city is a pleasant place to chill out for a day or two. In addition to some fine sandy **beaches**, it has a particularly attractive park, the **Parque Urquiza**, whose shady walkways and thick vegetation provide welcome respite in the summer. Paraná's most famous landmark is its imposing, heavily Neoclassical **cathedral**, which dominates the city's main square. On another fine square, the Plaza Alvear, the **Museo Histórico Martiniano Leguizamón** has a well-presented section on the history of the region and a more than usually interesting collection of *criollo* silverwork. Sadly, the city's best museum, which showcased a comprehensive collection of *mate* paraphernalia, has closed down, though the collection remains in the city and may re-emerge at some point, so it's worth checking with the tourist office for an update.

Like Rosario, Paraná lacks a true **foundation** date: the area was simply settled by inhabitants from Santa Fe, who regarded the higher ground of the eastern banks of the Paraná as providing better protection from Indian attack. The city was declared provincial capital in 1822 and leapt to prominence as capital of General Urquiza's short-lived Confederación Argentina between 1854 and 1861, when the city's major public buildings were constructed. Like most of Argentina, Paraná had its most significant period of growth in the late nineteenth century when the city received thousands of European immigrants. Today, Paraná's population of around 250,000 makes it the largest city in Entre Ríos Province.

Arrival and information

Paraná's confusing **Terminal de Omnibus** is at Av Ramírez 2550, around nine blocks east of central Plaza 1 de Mayo (☎0343/431-5053); in the middle of it, a

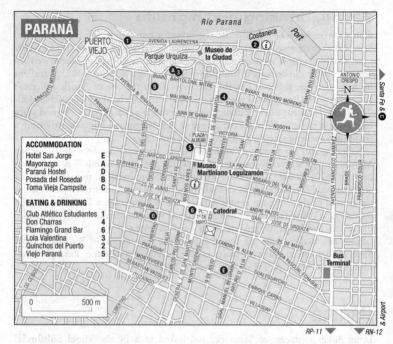

PARANÁ

Río Paraná

PUERTO
VIEJO

AVENIDA LAURENCENA

Costanera

Port

Parque Urquiza

Museo de
la Ciudad

N

Santa Fe & G

ACCOMMODATION
Hotel San Jorge   E
Mayorazgo   A
Paraná Hostel   D
Posada del Rosedal   B
Toma Vieja Campsite C

EATING & DRINKING
Club Atlético Estudiantes 1
Don Charras   4
Flamingo Grand Bar   6
Lola Valentina   3
Quinchos del Puerto   2
Viejo Paraná   5

Museo
Martiniano Leguizamón

Catedral

Bus
Terminal

0   500 m

& Airport

RP-11

RN-12

helpful bus-information-cum-tourist-office (daily 8am–2pm & 4–8pm) offers accommodation lists and maps. The central **tourist office** is at Buenos Aires 132 (daily 8am–8pm; ☎0343/423-0183 or 0800/555-9575).

Accommodation

Paraná's **hotels** are slightly more appealing than Santa Fe's, although choice is limited, particularly at the budget end, with those in the vicinity of the bus terminal too costly to justify staying in such a dreary area. However, Paraná does boast a good **youth hostel** – a truly wonderful place in a converted townhouse: ⚕ *Paraná Hostel*, at Andrés Pazos 159 (☎0343/455-0847, ⓦwww.paranahostel .com.ar; US$11 per person; ❸), which has dorms and doubles with TV, plus a laundry, fully equipped kitchen and extensive library. Otherwise, the pick of the cheaper places is *Hotel San Jorge,* at Belgrano 368 (☎0343/422-1685, ⓦwww.sanjorgehotel.com.ar; ❸), a lovely old building with tiled floors, a small garden and kitchen facilities. *Posada del Rosedal*, at Santiago del Estero 656 (☎0343/422-3148, ⓦwww.posadadelrosedal.com.ar; ❹–❺), is a welcoming guesthouse, with just three neat rooms and an enticing garden filled with flowers and birdsong, while Paraná's most luxurious hotel is the *Mayorazgo* (☎0343/423-0333, ⓦwww.hjmayorazgo.com.ar; ❽), towering over the Costanera at Avenida Etchevere and Miranda; now run by the Howard Johnson chain, it has two swimming pools as well as great views over the river. The best place to **camp** is *Toma Vieja*, around 4km northeast of the centre, at the end of Avenida Blas Parera (☎0343/433-1721; $16 per tent plus $2 per person), a huge site with several swimming pools and views over the Paraná. Hot showers and electricity are provided and there's a grocery store just down the road. Bus #5 goes to *Toma Vieja* every hour from the terminal.

The City

While Paraná is a pleasant place to wander round – though at night the poor street lighting can be a hazard – there aren't any major sights, and the city is probably best treated as a place to take a bit of a break. The main square is the **Plaza 1° de Mayo**, ten blocks inland. The single most outstanding building here is the **cathedral**, built in 1887. It's a superficially handsome if somehow rather awkward Neoclassical edifice distinguished by an intense blue brick-tiled central dome and rather exotic, almost Byzantine bell towers.

Pedestrianized Calle San Martín leads to Plaza Alvear, three blocks north, on the southwestern corner of which, at Buenos Aires 285, you'll find the mostly well-organized **Museo Histórico de Entre Ríos Martiniano Leguizamón** (Tues–Fri 8am–12.30pm & 3–8pm, Sat 9am–noon & 5–7pm, Sun 9am–noon; $1; ℡0343/431-2735). The upper floor is devoted to the history of Entre Ríos Province from pre-Columbian times to the present day. The informative panels are sometimes more interesting than the objects themselves, which are often notable mainly for their illustrious owners – they include such highlights as a 1976 Julio Iglesias LP and a wheelbarrow used by builders of the railways. Downstairs, however, there's an excellent collection of *criollo* silverwork. Among the more interesting pieces are vicious-looking spurs known as *lloronas* – *llorar* means "to cry", and it's debated whether they were thus called for the sound they made when the horse was moving or for the fact that they made the animal "cry blood". There's also a fine collection of gaucho *facas*, or knives, with inscriptions such as "do not enter without cause nor leave without honour". Look out, too, for the beautifully crafted *yesqueros*, elaborate precursors of the cigarette lighter formed by a stone and chain contraption – the last two creating a spark to light the tinder – made out of materials as diverse as silver and the tail of an armadillo.

Flanking Paraná's riverside, the **Parque Urquiza** is a park created on land donated by General Urquiza's widow. It is on a fairly narrow but hilly stretch of ground which slopes up from Avenida Laurencena, Paraná's Costanera, to the higher ground of the

▲ Swimmers before a race, Paraná beach

city. Designed, like so many of Argentina's parks, by landscape gardener Charles Thays, it's particularly attractive and verdant, traversed by serpentine walkways and with great views over the river, but the area is best avoided at night. At its western end, there's a picturesque little neighbourhood called the **Puerto Viejo**, distinguished by its winding cobbled streets and handsome old-fashioned residences.

The real hub of Paraná life on summer evenings, the **Costanera** itself, is lined with a handful of bars and restaurants and some good public **beaches**; you can also become a member for the day of various clubs, giving you access to the smartest beaches and facilities such as swimming pools and showers. For guided **boat tours** of the river and kayak rental, try La Baxada (℡0343/154-763443).

Eating, drinking and nightlife

There are enough decent **places to eat** to keep you happy for a day or two in Paraná. You'll find a couple of excellent fish restaurants and *parrillas* down by the river, notably *Club Atlético Estudiantes*, at the western end of the Avenida Costanera (℡0343/421-8699), and the highly rated if pricey *Quinchos del Puerto*, in a rustic thatched construction at the corner of Avenida Laurencena and Santander (reservations advised at summer weekends; ℡0343/423-2045). Near Parque Urquiza at Mitre 302 (℡0343/423-5234), *Lola Valentina* serves up enormous and tasty river fish dishes – try the *dorado* in a rich cream and spring onion sauce. For a traditional *parrilla*, *Don Charras*, at Avenida Uranga 1127, has excellent meat but also throws fish on the barbecue too. Several kilometres west of the Puerto Viejo, in a splendid riverside setting at Avenida Estrada 3582, *Rio Abajo* is the place to be seen in Paraná; specializing in fusion cuisine, fish, pasta and cocktails, its tropical decor and large terraces fill up with the city's young and beautiful throughout the summer.

For **drinks and snacks** in the city centre try the welcoming and classic *Viejo Paraná* with pavement tables on the corner of Buenos Aires and Rivadavia, or the very upmarket *Flamingo Grand Bar* on the corner of San Martín and Urquiza.

Estancias of Corrientes Province

En route between Paraná and Corrientes are a couple of outstanding **estancias** that take in guests – often providing horse rides or hands-on experiences of genuine ranch life. You cannot just turn up on spec but must book ahead; sometimes they will arrange for you to be picked up at the nearest town, airport or bus terminal, even if you have your own car – often the lengthy approach roads are impassable other than by 4WD.

Near the small town of Esquina some 250 km north of Paraná, 🖈*Estancia La Rosita* (℡011/4312-6448, 🖳www.estancialarosita.com.ar; ⬤ full board), lies among huge pastures dotted with ever-changing lakes and marshes, and is very much a working estancia, with lots of cattle and horses – galloping is a definite option. The house is an agreeable low-rise farmstead, with shady galleries and a noble dining room, while the guest rooms are simple and homely. Alicia Cometta de Landgraf runs the place with her sons, who are avid polo players – take a look at the impressive pitch even if you never get to see or participate in a game. An Australian tank swimming pool and barbecue facilities are added attractions; the food is authentic *criollo*.

A few kilometres north of Esquina, off the road to Corrientes, *Estancia Buena Vista* (℡011/4815-9305, 🖳www.estanciabuenavista.com.ar; ⬤ full board, 20 percent discount for Rough Guide readers) is another traditional working estancia, with large numbers of cattle and sheep but specializing in game, which can be sampled here at dinner. Run by a Swiss Argentine, Sara Röhner, and her German-born husband, the estancia combines a high level of comfort with old-fashioned *correntino* hospitality. The German-style teas are memorable.

Corrientes

Sensual, sultry, subtropical and sitting on a bend in the Río Paraná, **CORRIENTES** is one of the region's oldest and most attractive cities, founded in 1588 as an intermediary port along the river route between Buenos Aires and Asunción. Its charm is derived largely from the number of traditional *correntino* buildings in its crumbling – but very handsome – centre, based around the **Plaza 25 de Mayo**. These Neocolonial edifices, with overhanging roofs supported on wooden posts, are interspersed with more elaborate late nineteenth-century Italianate architecture. Corrientes' modest museums, most notably the original **Museo de Artesanía**, where you can see fine examples of the province's distinctive crafts, are given added appeal by being housed in these traditional buildings, and its central streets make it a pleasant place to just wander around for a day or two. If you visit from November to February, though, be aware that both temperatures and humidity can be very high. As a result, locals take the siesta very seriously, not emerging from indoors until dusk on the hottest days: if you must hit the streets on a summer afternoon, head for Corrientes' attractive **Costanera**, curving for 2.5km around the northwest of the city centre where native *lapacho* trees, with exquisite pink blossom in spring, provide a welcome bit of shade – though mosquitoes like it here, too.

Corrientes is linked to Resistencia, the capital of Chaco Province, 20km to the west, via the Puente General M. Belgrano, a suspension bridge across the Río Paraná. Like many other cities in the region, Corrientes has an important **carnival**, held throughout January and February until Mardi Gras in the Corsódromo – a kind of open-air stadium specially constructed for the festival. A more locally authentic affair, though, is the **Festival del Chamamé**, a celebration of the region's most popular folk music with plenty of live music and dancing, held on the second weekend in December.

Arrival and information

Corrientes' **Aeropuerto Fernando Piragine Niveyro** (☎03783/458340) lies 10km northeast of the city, along the RN-12. The **bus terminal** (☎03783/442149) is around 4km southeast of Plaza 25 de Mayo, along one of the city's main access roads, the Avenida Maipú. Various local buses, including the #103, run between the terminal and the centre, or a taxi will cost around $20. Corrientes' **tourist office** (daily 7am–9pm) is down on the Costanera, where it meets Pellegrini, but is one of the country's least helpful and worst equipped – you'll probably find your hotel reception a more useful source of information. Look out too for the little booklets given out in hotels and stores that, alongside advertising, provide maps and what's on guides.

Accommodation

A new hostel and two fantastic boutique hotels have greatly improved the choice of accommodation on offer in Corrientes. The town's first hostel is the *Bienvenida Golondrina* on La Rioja 455 (☎03783/435316; $55–65 per person), with fairly ordinary dorm rooms: the pricier ones have air conditioning. The building, however, is very pleasant – a restored nineteenth-century house with original tiled floor and ceiling frescoes, and walls painted soothing lilac – and the friendly staff can help arrange river excursions. There are also some cheaper hotels around the bus terminal but – unless you are literally just spending a night in transit – this area is too far away from anything. The city's particularly

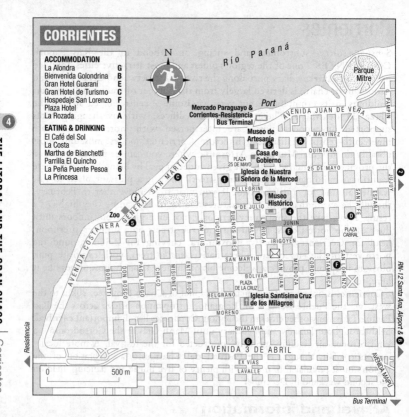

CORRIENTES

ACCOMMODATION
La Alondra	G
Bienvenida Golondrina	B
Gran Hotel Guaraní	E
Gran Hotel de Turismo	C
Hospedaje San Lorenzo	F
Plaza Hotel	D
La Rozada	A

EATING & DRINKING
El Café del Sol	3
La Costa	5
Martha de Bianchetti	4
Parrilla El Quincho	2
La Peña Puente Pesoa	6
La Princesa	1

hot and humid summers make air conditioning almost a necessity – though a shady room with a good fan can be acceptable. There's a good **campsite**, with showers, electricity and barbecue facilities around 10km northeast of town at Laguna Soto, on the way to Santa Ana (see p.265). Local bus #109 from the terminal goes there every ten minutes or so, taking about 45 minutes.

La Alondra 3 de Abril 827
☎03783/430555, ⊛www.laalondra
.com.ar. Truly original small hotel in a converted family house, with a library, reception and restaurant/bar stacked with antique travel trunks, chandeliers, globes, leather chairs and mahogany bookshelves. The rooms are decorated in a similar *belle époque* style, though in a nod to modernity they also have a/c and flatscreen TVs. ❽
Gran Hotel Guaraní Mendoza 970
☎03783/433800, ⊛www.hguarani.com.ar. The doyen of Corrientes' hotels, this is a business-oriented establishment in a modern glass-fronted building, with an inviting pool and bar area. There are several categories of rooms ranging from standard to VIP and two categories of suites; all have a/c and cable TV. ❺

Gran Hotel de Turismo Entre Ríos 650
☎03783/429112, ⊛www.ghturismo.com.ar. A quaintly old-fashioned place (Graham Greene stayed here in the 1960s) in a good location down by the Costanera. The rooms are showing their age a bit as is the very noisy a/c, but there's a great outdoor pool. Rates include breakfast. ❺
Hospedaje San Lorenzo San Lorenzo 1136
03783/421740. One of the best of the cheaper places to stay, friendly *San Lorenzo* offers basic, well-kept rooms on a quiet central street. Fans and private bathrooms. ❷
Plaza Hotel Junín 1549 ☎03783/466500,
⊛www.hotel-corrientes.com.ar. The *Plaza* overlooks the animated Plaza Cabral and is a shiny modern block blessed with a refreshing pool and bright rooms but noisy a/c. ❻

La Rozada Placido Martinez 1223
☎03783/433001, ✆www.larozada.com.ar.
Beautifully furnished hotel, with local artworks and
harmoniously blended features of the original
1890s building giving the place character. The
larger suites are duplexes with proper kitchens; the
classic rooms are quite a bit smaller, but still
elegant, with great views over the Paraná. ⑥

The City

Corrientes is reasonably compact: all the major points of interest lie within the streets
north of Avenida 3 de Abril, which runs east–west through the city towards Puente
General Belgrano. The whole of this approximately triangular area is bordered to the
northwest by the **Avenida Costanera General San Martín**. There are two centres: the
centro histórico, with **Plaza 25 de Mayo** at its heart, lies to the north and is where you'll
find most of Corrientes' historic buildings and museums, while the less interesting
Centro Comercial is focused on Plaza Cabral, ten blocks southeast of Plaza 25 de Mayo
and Corrientes' main pedestrianized shopping street, Calle Junín.

Plaza 25 de Mayo

An old-fashioned leafy square surrounded by some of Corrientes' most striking
buildings, **Plaza 25 de Mayo** encapsulates the city's sleepy subtropical ambience.
The square lies one block south of the Costanera, to which it is linked by the
narrow streets of Buenos Aires and Salta, the former in particular lined with fine
examples of late nineteenth-century architecture. One of the most striking
buildings on the square itself, the pink **Casa de Gobierno**, on the eastern side, was
constructed in 1886 in the ornate Italianate style that replaced many of the older,
colonial buildings at the end of the nineteenth century. Particularly attractive are
the delicate filigree window grilles, best admired on the building's northern wall,
along Fray José de la Quintana. At the southern end of the square, the nineteenth-
century **Iglesia de Nuestra Señora de la Merced** (daily 7am–noon & 4–8pm)
houses a handsome hand-carved wooden retable, or altar screen, with twisted
wooden pillars and rich golden inlay work.

Museo de Artesanía

On the corner of Fray José de la Quintana and Salta, you'll find the **Museo de
Artesanía** (Mon–Fri 7am–noon & 4–7pm; free) and the craft workshops, or
talleres. The museum is housed within a typical colonial Corrientes building; a
low, whitewashed residence constructed around a central patio flanked by a
gallery, providing shade from the fierce summer sun. Inside you'll find a selection
of local crafts, including fine examples of leather, ceramics and basketwork.
Perhaps the most intriguing pieces, sold by craftsmen working in the workshops
within, are the carvings of San La Muerte (literally "Saint Death"). These solemn
little skeletons, carved of wood, gold or bone are carried around – or, in the case
of the smallest figures, inserted under the skin – to ensure the bearer a painless
death; they're a typical example of the popular cults, many of them inherited from
the Guaraní, which coexist in Corrientes with profound Catholic beliefs.

Iglesia Santísima Cruz de los Milagros

Seven blocks south of Plaza 25 de Mayo is the **Iglesia Santísima Cruz de los
Milagros** (daily 9am–noon), at the southern end of the Plaza de la Cruz. Both the
square and the church – an austere Italianate construction dating from 1897 – are
named after Corrientes' first cross, brought by the Spaniards on the city's founding
in 1588. The cross gained its epithet, the "Cross of Miracles", when, according to
legend, it proved impervious to native attempts to destroy it with fire. A piece of
the original cross is preserved as part of the altar within the church.

The Costanera

Corrientes' attractively maintained riverside avenue, the **Avenida Costanera General San Martín**, runs from the small **Parque Mitre**, at the northern end of the city, as far as the Puente General Belgrano. Lined with fine examples of native trees, it's a lovely spot on summer evenings, when the heat dissipates a little and locals leave the cool refuge of their homes to pack its promenades for a jog or a stroll, or simply sit sipping *mate* or *tereré* on stone benches – but be prepared to share the experience with persistent mosquitoes. Just to the west of Parque Mitre, you'll find the port buildings and the **Mercado Paraguayo** – a standard fixture in northern Argentine cities – selling all manner of cheap imported Paraguayan goods, from shoes to stereos. Beyond here, the wide avenue sweeps southeast, with various panoramic points jutting out over the river, from where there are views to the flat Resistencia "coast".

Eating, drinking and nightlife

The best of Corrientes' rather poor choice of **restaurants** is ☆ *La Princesa*, at Buenos Aires 628, with a stylish ambience in an attractively converted Neocolonial house. It's not in line for any gastronomic awards but the cuisine is relatively innovative for these parts, including dishes such as fish in an Asian-style sauce, or meat with fresh fruit, and is well prepared, at moderate prices; late at night you can dance to jazz and bossa nova. Along the Costanera, you'll find a number of good *parrillas*, including *La Costa*, at the junction with Junín. The restaurant at *La Alondra* (see p.302) is popular with well-heeled locals, and unusually for Argentina (let alone Corrientes) does a Sunday brunch. Snacks and coffees are on offer at the wonderfully kitsch and extremely popular *confitería*, *Martha de Bianchetti*, at Mendoza and 9 de Julio. For a more traditional café-bar atmosphere, head for *El Café del Sol*, at Rioja 708.

A popular **nightlife** option is a chamamé show held at various restaurants; chamamé (see Contexts, p.622) is perhaps Argentina's most infectious folk music, a lively danceable rhythm punctuated by a rather bloodcurdling cry, known as the *sapucay*. *Parrilla El Quincho*, on Av Juan Pujol and Pellegrini, and *La Peña Puente Pesoa*, at the intersection of the RN-12 with Avenida P. Ferrer (the continuation of Avenida 3 de Abril), both do a very reasonable *tenedor libre parrilla* and live chamamé shows on Fridays and Saturdays from about 10pm.

The Gran Chaco

One of Argentina's forgotten corners and poorest regions, the **GRAN CHACO** is a land of seemingly unending alluvial plains, with areas of arid thornscrub in the dry west, and subtropical vegetation and palm savannah in the humid east. It has little in the way of dramatic scenery, no impressive historical monuments and few services for the visitor, but if you have a special interest in **wildlife** or like to get far away from the gringo trail you will find it rewarding, provided you avoid the blistering heat of summer. In the sizeable sectors not yet cleared for agriculture, it harbours an exceptional diversity of **flora and fauna** (see box, p.305), making it worth your while to break your journey for a day or two as you cross the region.

Birdwatchers fare best: more than three hundred bird species have been recorded in the dry Chaco; and anglers come from all over the world in search of fish such as the *dorado*.

Wet Chaco scenery is mostly found near the **river systems** of the **Río Paraguay** and the **Río Paraná**, where the rainfall can be as high as 1200mm a year, causing heavy flooding at times. It is characterized by palm savannahs, patches of jungle and plantations of sugar cane, soya and fruit. Narrow strips border the main rivers that cross the region from west to east: the Río Pilcomayo and the Río Bermejo, which, after a fairly energetic start in the Bolivian highlands, grow weary with the heavy load of sediment they carry by the time they reach the Chaco plains. They meander tortuously, frequently change course, and sometimes lose their way entirely. In some places they dissipate into swamps called *esteros* or *bañados*, or **lagoons** that can become saline in certain areas owing to high evaporation. Rainfall diminishes the further west you travel from the Paraná and Paraguay rivers and the habitat gradually alters into dry Chaco scenery, typified by dense **thornscrub** that is used to graze zebu-crossbreed cattle, but cleared in those areas where irrigation has made it possible to cultivate crops such as cotton.

This zone was known to the conquistadors as **El Impenetrable**, less because of the thornscrub than for the lack of water, which only **indigenous groups** seemed to know how to overcome. Indeed, Formosa and Chaco provinces still have one of

Wildlife viewing in the Chaco

The main reason for visiting the Chaco is to see its varied and fascinating **wildlife**. Despite the vast lists of elusive, endangered mammals given in the region's tourist literature, though, only the very luckiest or most patient observers will see a **jaguar**, maned wolf, giant armadillo or *mirikiná* (nocturnal monkey). The surest bet for seeing any animals is to hire the services of one of the region's few but excellent **tour operators**; recommendations are listed in a separate box on p.309.

In the northeast corner of Santiago del Estero Province, the **Parque Nacional Copo** is the best remaining chunk of prime dry Chaco left in the country and the only area of protected land in the Argentine Chaco big enough to provide a sustainable habitat for some of the region's most threatened wildlife, including the elusive **Wagner's peccary**. Giant and honey anteaters also inhabit the park, as do the threatened Crowned Eagle, the Greater Rhea and the King Vulture. Frequently parched, it's a huge expanse of approximately 1140 square kilometres, with 550 square kilometres of provincial reserve attached to the west.

The edges of the woodland patches of the **Parque Nacional Río Pilcomayo**, to the north of Formosa city, can be great for glimpsing the larger mammals, including giant anteaters, honey anteaters, peccaries, deer, three types of monkey and pumas. Capybara, the two species of cayman, and even tapir live in the wetter regions of the park. Jaguars are believed to be extinct here, but the maned wolf can, very occasionally, be found – indeed, this park offers one of your best chances of seeing one. Almost three hundred species of **birds** have been recorded here, including the **Bare-faced Curassow** and **Thrush-like Wren**, both highly endangered in Argentina.

The **Complejo Ecológico** (daily 8am–7.30pm; ☏03732/424284; $5), on the RN-95 near **Presidente Roque Sáenz Peña**, however, is really the best place for guaranteed viewing of the endangered beasts of the Chaco, including the maned wolf, jaguar, puma, tapir, honey anteater, bare-faced curassow, giant anteater and giant armadillo. This zoo fulfils an important educational role in an area where ecological consciousness is sometimes acutely lacking. Poorly funded, it nonetheless does an excellent job at rescuing, releasing or housing wounded or impounded specimens that are the victims of road traffic accidents, fires, illegal hunting and unscrupulous animal trading.

the most numerous and diverse indigenous populations in the country, including the Komlek, who are members of the Guaraní group and make a living from manual labour and crafts such as basket-weaving and pottery; and the Wichí, who still rely on hunter-gathering for their economic and cultural life but also sell beautifully woven yica bags made of a sisal-like fibre.

When to go

The Gran Chaco records some of the highest **temperatures** anywhere in the continent from December to February, often reaching 45°C or more. At these times, the siesta becomes even more sacred and people take to drinking chilled *tereré*. The best times to see wildlife are in the early morning or late afternoon and the best time of year to visit is from June to September: although night frosts are not unknown in June and July, daytime temperatures generally hover in the agreeable 20–25°C bracket. Moreover, the deciduous trees lose their leaves, so you've more chance of seeing wildlife. The **rainy season** generally lasts from October to May but violent downpours are possible throughout the year. For outdoor activities arm yourself with insect repellent, sunscreen and a hat, especially in summer; and make sure you have plentiful drinking water supplies.

Chaco Province

The **easternmost strip of Chaco Province**, along the Paraná and Paraguay rivers, is the heartland of the wet Chaco. Most of the original forests and swamps have fallen victim to agricultural developments, dedicated to the production of beef cattle and crops such as fruit, soya and sugar cane. The main highway through this region is the **RN-11**, which connects Santa Fe with **Resistencia**, the starting point for trips along the RN-16 to **Parque Nacional Chaco** and the interior of the province.

▲ Indigenous woman, Chaco Province

Resistencia

RESISTENCIA is Chaco Province's sprawling administrative capital, with nearly half a million inhabitants, and the principal gateway to the Gran Chaco. Despite its commercial importance and lack of colonial architecture, the city is a pleasant enough place; it has a feeling of spaciousness about it and is known for the outstanding friendliness of its inhabitants.

The city's nickname is "Ciudad de las Esculturas" ("City of Sculptures"), owing to over two hundred outdoor statues scattered throughout town. The man behind this use of art to instil civic pride, Aldo Boglietti, also founded a remarkable cultural centre called the **Fogón de los Arrieros**, at Brown 350 (daily 8am–noon & 9pm–midnight; $5). Its name means "The Drovers' Campfire", and it's where artists came to meet, share their particular art form and then continue their journey. You can come during the day to look round the eclectic mix of paintings and sculptures left behind by visiting artists, but it's more fun in the evening, when you can have a drink or empanada at the cosy bar. Best of all, try to catch one of the **events** – concerts, poetry recitals and the like – staged once or twice a week in the main salon or, weather permitting, the patio.

Resistencia also has a couple of modest museums. The **Museo del Hombre Chaqueño**, near the main plaza at Arturo Illia 655 (daily 8am–noon & 5–9pm; free), has a clearly presented collection detailing provincial history, with information on the region's pre-Columbian cultures – before the arrival of the Spanish, the Gran Chaco was a melting pot of indigenous cultures from across the continent. The museum's highlights include models of figures from Guaraní mythology and beautiful nineteenth-century silver *mate* gourds. A more extensive archeological and ethnographical collection is housed in the **Museo de Antropología**, further southeast at Las Heras 727 (Mon–Fri 9am–noon & 4–8pm; free); it displays objects recovered from the ruins of the failed sixteenth-century settlement of Concepción del Bermejo, the only serious attempt by the Spanish to colonise this area of hostile terrain and equally hostile natives.

The best place in the Chaco to purchase crafts made by the area's indigenous groups is the **Fundación Chaco Artesanal**, Pellegrini 272 (Mon–Fri 8am–1pm & 4–8pm, Sat & Sun 9am–noon & 5–8pm; ☎03722/459372), a smart, nonprofit outlet which sells items such as Wichí pottery, Komlek basketware and graceful *palo santo* crucifixes.

Practicalities

The **bus terminal** (☎03722/461098) is at the junction of avenidas Malvinas Argentinas and MacLean, 4km southwest of the main square Plaza 25 de Mayo. A *remise* from here to the centre costs around $15. There is a small **tourist information** kiosk on the Plaza 25 de Mayo (Mon–Fri 7.30am–12.30pm; ☎03722/458291), and you can get a *remise colectivo* to Corrientes ($3.50) from the south side of the plaza at Alberdi.

Most of the town's **accommodation** is well located, within four blocks of the main square. Knocking spots off the competition, the *Amerian Hotel Casino Gala* at J.D. Perón 330 (☎03722/452400, ⓦwww.hotelcasinogala.com.ar; ⓪), in a converted Neoclassical building, has comfortable and enormous rooms that are all effectively suites, a glorious swimming pool and an efficient spa offering massages and foot-rubs. The *Hotel Covadonga* at Güemes 200 (☎03722/444444, ⓦwww .hotelcovadonga.com.ar; ⓪) is a well-run if more old-fashioned place with smart rooms and comfy beds, while *Hotel Colón*, at Santa María de Oro 143 (☎03722/422861, ⓔhotelcolon@gigared.com; ④), is a decent enough budget place, with pleasant albeit poorly lit rooms.

"El Chaco" and the Campo del Cielo meteors

An estimated five thousand years ago an asteroid shattered on impact with the earth's upper atmosphere, sending huge chips of matter plummeting earthwards, where they fell on a 15km band of the Chaco. This cataclysmic spectacle and the subsequent fires that would have been triggered must have terrified the locals. When the Spanish arrived in South America, the Komlek called the area *Pigüen Nonraltá* – or Field of the Heavens – Campo del Cielo in Spanish. They venerated the "stones from the sky", whose surface, when polished, reflected the sun. Mysterious legends reached Spanish ears, arousing an insatiable curiosity for anything that smacked of precious metal, and even sparking illusions of the fabled City of the Caesars, a variant of the El Dorado myth. In 1576, Hernán Mexía de Miraval struggled out here hoping to find gold but, instead, he found iron. The biggest expedition of all came in 1783, when the Spanish geologist and scientist Miguel Rubín de Celis led an expedition of two hundred men to find out if the **Mesón de Fierro** – a 3.5m long curiosity and the most famous of the **meteors** – was in fact just the tip of a vast mountain of pure iron. When they dug below, they found only dusty earth. The latitude was recorded, but since there was no way of determining its co-ordinate of longitude, the Mesón de Fierro was subsequently lost – it's probable that the indigenous inhabitants reburied their "sunstone".

The largest of the meteorites you can see today, **"El Chaco"**, has been reliably estimated to weigh 33,700kg, a strong contender for the second biggest in the world (the biggest, almost twice the size, is in Namibia). El Chaco and the Campo del Cielo (ⓦ www.campodelcielo.com.ar) both lie in the southwestern corner of Chaco province, 15km south of the town of Gancedo, in the Reserva Natural Pigüen N'onaxá

Resistencia has a very poor choice of **restaurants**, with the best option being *Kebon*, at Güemes and Don Bosco (closed most of Jan): it has a tasteful ambience and serves well-cooked classics and tasty river fish. Alternatively, you could try one of the pizzerias on Perón, between Belgrano and Alberdi, or the passable restaurant at the *Amerian*. For **nightlife**, the bar at *El Fogón* (see p.307) is excellent for a friendly conversation or one of its first-rate events; or catch a folklore show at the *Peña Nativa Martín Fierro*, 9 de Julio and Hernández (ⓣ03722/423167; Fri from 9pm), where they also serve empanadas and *parrilla* meals. *Don Angelo*, Güemes 183, is a café-cum-bar, with a varied choice of beers, whose sedate ambience is ideal for chatting.

Parque Nacional Chaco

The paved **RN-16** shears straight through Chaco Province, northwest from Resistencia, clipping the northeastern corner of Santiago del Estero Province, before reaching Salta Province; it's the route taken by all trans-Chaco buses. Much of the land has been cleared to plant bananas, while *caranday* palms grow in the drier land between streams and reed- and lily-beds. Dedicated naturalists can spend a few days trying to track down the region's fauna in the **PARQUE NACIONAL CHACO** in the province's humid east. Within easy striking distance of Resistencia, the park conserves a mix of threatened wet- and semi-dry Chaco habitat around the banks of the Río Negro. In quick succession, you can pass from riverine forest to open woodland, palm savannah and wetlands. Its 150 square kilometres are too restricted a space to provide a viable habitat for the largest Chaco predator, the jaguar, but plenty of mammals still inhabit the park, even if your chances of seeing them are slight. Birdlife, however, is plentiful and easy to spot.

Practicalities

The turn-off to the park is 56km west of Resistencia along the RN-16, from where the paved RP-9 heads 40km north to Capitán Solari, 6km from the park headquarters. There are regular buses from Resistencia to Solari, from where you can pick up a *remise* to the park. The park has a camping area with toilets, fire pits and electricity, but there's no **food** to buy, and little in Solari, so bring supplies.

A board by the park headquarters displays the trails, which are also marked on a pamphlet available from the *guardaparques*. A good introduction to the park is the well-shaded, nature-trail loop that leads from a suspension bridge behind the park headquarters (1.5km). But the most popular walk is the one to the lookouts at the ox-bow lagoons of **Laguna Carpincho** and **Laguna Yacaré** (6km), with a deviation to see an enormous *quebracho*, El Abuelo, which is an estimated five hundred years old. A longer walk (9km) is to **Laguna Panza de Cabra**, a swamp choked with lilac-bloomed *camalote* waterlilies and offering excellent birdwatching opportunities.

Formosa Province

Formosa Province is dominated by its eponymous **capital city**, at its eastern end and second in importance to Resistencia in the Argentine Chaco; it's really a base for visiting the province's wildlife – but not in the height of summer. To the north are the nasty border town of Clorinda, best avoided; the internationally significant wetland site of **Parque Nacional Río Pilcomayo**, on the border with Paraguay; and the Paraguayan capital, Asunción, effectively the historical and spiritual nerve centre of the whole Gran Chaco. For those set on seeing deepest Argentina, the aptly named **El Impenetrable** poses a real challenge – the weather, bad roads and virtually nonexistent infrastructure being the main obstacles. The **Bañado La Estrella** is a remote wetland that rewards the most intrepid and determined with fine birdlife, but go on an organized tour to make it worthwhile.

Formosa city

The city of **FORMOSA**, the provincial capital, seems as though it has been pressed flat by the heat: few buildings rise above a single storey and many exhibit the grey mouldy stains of subtropical decay. Situated on a great loop in the Río Paraguay, it acts as a **port** for the entire province. Not a particularly attractive place, despite its name (an archaic form of *hermosa*, "beautiful"), it's given a pink

---

Tours in the Gran Chaco

The logistics of **visiting the parks and reserves** in the Gran Chaco region, and Formosa Province in particular, are complicated to say the least. Argentina's hottest climate, poorest roads and most inaccessible terrain are likely to frustrate even the most adventurous of travellers. Signposts are erratic and wildlife lurks where you least expect it. You will certainly need a helping hand if you are to get the most out of the Chaco and you will be best off going on an **organized tour** with a reputable company. **Aventura Formosa**, Paraguay 520, Formosa (☏03717/433713, ✉fiznardo@hotmail.com), has extremely reliable tours run by an experienced local guide with a tremendous in-depth knowledge of the region, its geography, wildlife and culture. **El Jabiru** (☏03715/432435, ✇www.eljabiru.com.ar) does bird-watching trips into the Bañado de la Estrella and other trips in Formosa, including to the Parque Nacional Río Pilcomayo; English spoken.

facelift when the *lapacho* trees flower in September, the best time to see it. Graham Greene, in *Travels With My Aunt*, wrote that "there was a pervading smell of orange petals, but it was the only sweet thing about Formosa", for him "an ignoble little town".

The main commercial district is concentrated within a block or two either side of the **Avenida 25 de Mayo**, east of the Plaza San Martín. The **Casa de la Artesanía**, a nonprofit organization based at San Martín and 25 de Mayo (Mon–Sat 8am–noon & 4–8pm), is the best outlet for the province's indigenous crafts. It stocks a good selection of Wichí *yica* bags, Pilagá woollen carpets, tightly woven Komlek basketwork, plus *palo santo* carvings and *algarrobo* seed jewellery. A block inland from here, on the corner of 25 de Mayo and Belgrano, is the pink, hacienda-style **Museo Histórico** (Mon–Fri 8am–7.30pm; free), housed in the former residence of General Ignacio Fotheringham, the Southampton-born first governor of what was then Formosa Territory. It is an eclectic and poorly organized collection, and exhibits include a stuffed Swiss bear and Komlek artefacts, plus information on early exploration of the region.

Practicalities

Arriving in Formosa from the southwest, you'll be welcomed by **La Cruz del Norte**, a white Meccano-style cross that's a common reference point. The **bus terminal** is to the east of here on Avenida Gutnisky, a multi-laned thoroughfare that changes its name to Avenida 25 de Mayo before it reaches the Plaza San Martín, the start of the town centre and nearly 2km from the terminal. There's a small **tourist office** on Plaza San Martín, at Uriburu 820 (Mon–Fri 8am–noon & 4–8pm; ☏03717/425192), which can help with accommodation in the province, including a handful of tourism estancias.

There's little in the way of decent budget **accommodation** in town. The best option of all is the *Asterión* (☏03717/452999, ⓦwww.asterionhotel.com.ar; ◉), on the RN-11 just before you reach the Cruz del Norte roundabout when arriving from Resistencia; the hotel's name comes from a Borges short story about the Minotaur, and you will find a small collection of Borges memorabilia on display in the lobby. As for the rooms, they are bright, spacious and appealingly decorated, with an ethnic touch, and all the facilities are impeccable, from the safe garage to the shady swimming pool. Alternatively, *Casa Grande*, at González Lelong 185 (☏03717/431612, ⓦwww.casagrandeapart.com.ar; ◉), is an attractive little complex whose well-equipped rooms have kitchenettes. Its facilities include a pool and garden, massages and a gym, plus one of the best restaurants for miles, *Mirita*, which specializes in delicious fish dishes and has a very decent wine list.

Parque Nacional Río Pilcomayo

The 519-square-kilometre **PARQUE NACIONAL RÍO PILCOMAYO** was created in the 1950s to protect some of the best remaining subtropical wet Chaco habitat. Extensive areas are subject to spring and summer flooding, whereas in the winter months it is prone to droughts. The park is protected under the international Ramsar Convention – designed to protect the planet's key wetland ecosystems – and its biological diversity was safeguarded by a concerted and largely successful campaign in the 1990s to get rid of most of the semi-wild cattle left by former settlers. In addition to swampy wetlands, it conserves some remnant gallery forest along the Río Pilcomayo, and large swathes of savannah studded with copses of mixed woodland.

The best times to **visit the park** are sunset and dawn, when it's cooler and you stand a better chance of seeing the wildlife. The park has **two entrances** – to the

Estero Poí and the more compact Laguna Blanca sectors – both within striking distance of **Laguna Blanca**, a village 52km west of Clorinda. The **national park administration office** (Mon–Fri 7am–4pm; ☎03718/470045), for information and permits, is on the RN-86 at the entrance to the village.

The turn-off to **Estero Poí** lies 2km from Laguna Blanca village in the direction of Clorinda, from where 9km of dirt road leads to the *guardaparques'* house. An interpretation trail runs from a bush campsite through the adjacent scrub, and within easy walking distance is a pair of swamps, dominated by the attractive *pehuajó* reed with its banana-palm leaves, along with bulrushes, horsetails and the mauve-flowered waterlilies. Further into the park lie swathes of savannah grassland and the gallery forest of the Río Pilcomayo – good for spotting wildlife.

At Naick Neck, 12km east of Laguna Blanca village, a dirt track (5km) leads to the **Laguna Blanca Sector**. Next to the *guardaparques'* dwelling is a pleasant free **campsite**, shaded by *algarrobos* and palms, with drinking water and showers; bring all your own food supplies. From behind the toilet block, there's a 300m **nature trail** where you have a good chance of seeing howler monkeys, while an excellent boardwalk from the campsite takes you 500m through reedbed marshland to lookout points and a 10m **tower** on the shore of the shallow lagoon itself. If you swim here, wear shoes so the piranhas don't snack on your toes. There are excellent opportunities for **birdwatching** here, especially at dawn.

El Impenetrable

The straight RN-81 runs northwest of Formosa through an area so difficult to enter it has been dubbed **El Impenetrable**. For those with a specialist interest in wildlife – especially birdlife – the route gives access to the **Bañado La Estrella**, a fascinating wetland near Las Lomitas, 300km from Formosa. Otherwise, avoid it: if you want to cross the Chaco region, take the much faster the RN-16 from Resistencia.

Buses pass regularly in both directions (north to Tartagal and Pocitos; south to Embarcación, Jujuy and Salta) and can be flagged down. **Driving times** on unsealed roads in this area of the world are dependent on rainfall. Many vehicles can't negotiate the mud, and the ones that do often take far longer than they would in good conditions (if in doubt, call the Vialidad Provincial in Formosa; ☎03717/426040 or 426041).

Bañado La Estrella

As you head west, the scenery becomes drier scrub with some virulently green wetland. The land is mainly used for grazing cattle and goats, but charcoal is also produced – witness the roadside ovens. About 45km north of the village of Las Lomitas, on unsealed RP-28, is the **Bañado La Estrella**, a huge swathe of wetland swamp in the central northern part of the province, fed by the waters of the Río Pilcomayo, a river that dissipates into numerous meandering channels.

The RP-28 crosses the Bañado by means of a long causeway (*pedraplén*), usually just beneath the water line. The scenery looks like a Dalí painting: tree skeletons (known as *champales*) swaddled in vines, as if the floodwaters had once covered them and then receded, leaving them snagged with weed; beneath their branches shines the mirror-smooth blue water, dotted with rafts of lilac-flowered *camalote* waterlilies. If you are lucky you might even get to see members of the **Pilagá community**, an indigenous people that number about five thousand, fishing for *sábalo* with spears; note they are generally reluctant to be photographed, especially without permission.

Travel details

Buses

Colón to: Buenos Aires (hourly; 5hr 30min); Corrientes (2 daily; 10hr); Gualeguaychú (8 daily; 2hr); Paraná (9 daily; 5hr); Santa Fe (6 daily; 6hr).

Corrientes to: Buenos Aires (6 daily; 12hr); Córdoba (1 daily; 14hr); Posadas (9 daily; 5hr); Puerto Iguazú (1 daily; 10hr); Resistencia (hourly; 30min); Rosario (5 daily; 10hr).

Formosa to: Buenos Aires (7 daily; 14hr); Corrientes (10 daily; 3hr); Jujuy (1 daily; 14hr); Posadas (1 daily; 6hr); Puerto Iguazú (1 daily; 10hr); Resistencia (15 daily; 2hr); Salta (1 daily; 14hr); Santa Fe (5 daily; 10hr).

Gualeguaychú to: Buenos Aires (hourly; 3hr 30min); Colón (8 daily; 2hr); Corrientes (3 daily; 12hr); Paraná (7 daily; 5hr); Rosario (4–5 daily; 8hr); Santa Fe (5 daily; 6hr).

Mercedes to: Buenos Aires (10 daily; 10hr); Colonia Carlos Pellegrini (2 daily; 4hr); Corrientes (10 daily; 3hr); Posadas (3 daily; 4hr); Resistencia (6 daily; 3hr 30min).

Paraná to: Buenos Aires (hourly; 7hr); Corrientes (3 daily; 8hr); Posadas (7 daily; 10hr); Puerto Iguazú (3 daily; 14hr); Rosario (2 hourly; 3hr); Santa Fe (every 20min; 50min).

Posadas to: Buenos Aires (hourly; 14hr); Corrientes (9 daily; 5hr); El Soberbio (7 daily; 4hr); Formosa (1 daily; 7hr); Puerto Iguazú (hourly; 6hr); Resistencia (hourly; 5hr 30min); Rosario (5 daily; 15hr); San Ignacio (9 daily; 1hr).

Puerto Iguazú to: Buenos Aires (7 daily; 14hr 30min–19hr); Córdoba (2 daily; 22hr); Corrientes (1 daily; 10hr); Posadas (hourly; 6hr); Rosario (2 weekly; 18hr); San Ignacio (hourly; 5hr).

Resistencia to: Buenos Aires (hourly; 12hr 30min– 14hr); Corrientes (hourly; 30min); Formosa (hourly; 2hr 15min); Posadas (hourly; 5hr); Puerto Iguazú (1 daily; 10hr); Santiago del Estero (3 daily; 10–11hr).

Rosario to: Buenos Aires (2–3 hourly; 4hr); Córdoba (hourly; 6hr); Corrientes (5 daily; 10hr); Posadas (5 daily; 15hr); Puerto Iguazú (1 daily; 18hr); Resistencia (hourly; 8–10hr); Salta (9 daily; 16hr); Tucumán (hourly; 12hr); Victoria (5 daily; 1hr 20min).

Santa Fe to: Buenos Aires (hourly; 6hr); Córdoba (hourly; 5hr); Posadas (8 daily; 14hr); Puerto Iguazú (2 daily; 20hr); Resistencia (hourly; 7hr); Rosario (hourly; 2hr 20min).

El Soberbio to: Posadas (7 daily; 4hr).

Flights

Corrientes to: Buenos Aires (1 daily; 1hr 30min).
Formosa to: Buenos Aires (1 daily; 1hr 50min).
Posadas to: Buenos Aires (2 daily; 1hr 30min).
Puerto Iguazú to: Buenos Aires (3–5 daily; 2hr).
Resistencia to: Buenos Aires (3 daily; 1hr 40min).
Rosario to: Buenos Aires (1–6 daily; 1hr).
Santa Fe to: Buenos Aires (1–4 daily; 1hr).

The legendary Ruta 40

Argentines fondly refer to the RN-40, or Ruta 40, the country's longest road, as La Cuarenta – The Forty. Stretching from Cabo Virgenes, the southernmost point of the Argentine mainland, to northernmost Ciénaga, on the Bolivian border, it's more than just a highway. Like Route 66 in the US, the road has its own ethos – it has inspired songs, been the subject of books and caused arguments. Whatever you do, don't steer clear of Ruta 40 – it's as central to a visit to Argentina as a football match or a *milonga*.

A long and winding road

La Cuarenta runs a staggering 5224km from the tip of **Patagonia** to **Bolivia** – the distance from Amsterdam to Afghanistan. Partly to make it more attractive for tourists, the road's **itinerary** has been changed over the years. Ruta 40 now starts at the ocean at **Cabo Vírgenes** and winds north through eleven provinces, past twenty national parks and across 24 major rivers, before reaching the altiplano. There it breaks a record: the dizzying **Abra de Acay**, at 5061m, is the highest point on a national road anywhere in the world.

Although sections of the route are relatively busy, notably around Bariloche and between Mendoza and San Juan, most of La Cuarenta runs through Argentina's magnificent **open spaces**, seldom more than 100km from the majestic peaks of the **Andes**. Many visitors are drawn by the road's rugged mystique – a result of its inaccessibility and frequently poor condition – while others are put off for the same reason. Over half its length is currently **tarmacked** but it looks as if the Argentine government's pledge to pave the entire road by the end of 2010 will be honoured – albeit a few years late.

Lighthouse, Cabo Vírgenes ▲

Andean landscape, Santa Cruz province ▼

The south

Between a navy lighthouse at **Cabo Vírgenes**, La Cuarenta's starting point, and Chos Malal, in Neuquén Province, the road zigzags across the **Patagonian steppe**, a barren, windswept expanse thickly blanketed with snow during the winter. Consider splurging at **Estancia Lagos del Furioso**, in Santa Cruz (see p.550), where you'll find glorious views, excellent fishing and every creature comfort.

The midlands

North of Neuquén Province, Ruta 40 enters the **Cuyo**, Argentina's western midlands. It meanders through little-visited **La Payunia**, in Mendoza Province (see p.412), a land of rosy lava and ebony gorges, deep karstic caves and flamingo-flecked lagoons, before passing near **Laguna Diamante** (see p.401). A visit to this all-but-inaccessible lagoon rewards the adventurous – enjoy a picnic on the banks of a crystalline brook as you admire the silhouette of Volcán Maipo. Further north, in La Rioja Province, the road skirts sunny valleys and hugs the **Cuesta de Miranda** (see p.429), a serpentine corniche winding through polychrome mountains that contrast with the verdant vegetation along the riverbanks below.

▲ Cuesta de Miranda

▼ Horses along the Ruta 40 near Cachi

The north

Mostly dirt track, La Cuarenta's last – and highest – stretch cuts through the historic Northwest. Rippling hills, herds of goats and crumbling adobe houses are typical sights here. For a top-notch poncho, stop off at **Belén**, in Catamarca (see p.366–7) – local methods of weaving have been maintained in this highland village since pre-Hispanic times. You'll also want to stop in **Cachi** (see p.336), for a photo of the surrounding snow-topped sierras and valleys, where fields blaze red with drying paprika peppers in the autumn. Just before Ruta 40 reaches Bolivia, it is spanned by the mighty **La Polvorilla** viaduct (see p.334). It may look like something out of a model town in all the tourist brochures, but this fabulous feat of engineering is impressive whether you chug across it in the Train to the Clouds or look up at it from the road below.

▼ La Polvorilla viaduct

4WD plying the Ruta 40 ▲

Bikers en route to Rio La Leona ▼

Hitting the road

By far the best way to approach Ruta 40 is to **hire a vehicle and drive yourself** – it's worth investing in a 4WD, even for the paved sections. Special care is required, though, especially further south where strong crosswinds and poorly maintained gravel (*ripio*) roads make it extremely easy to flip over. Driving on gravel is much like driving on snow – fine in a straight line but difficult on bends or when braking. To keep safe, stick to the Highway Code and follow this **advice**:

▶▶ On unpaved sections, follow the most recently used tracks and never exceed 70km/hr (you'll often creep along at 40km/hr).

▶▶ Slow down and move as far right as possible when approaching an oncoming vehicle to avoid windscreen or headlight damage.

▶▶ Overtake with caution – dust and stones thrown up will obscure visibility.

▶▶ Go downhill in a low gear – the rear will skid if you go too fast.

▶▶ Slow down in strong winds, especially crosswinds – in a high-clearance 4WD the wind may get underneath – and be careful opening doors, as they can be wrenched from their hinges.

▶▶ Give help if you see someone has broken down: offering to give them a lift or taking a message to the next town could be vital.

▶▶ Refuel whenever you see a pump – the next may be hundreds of kilometres away.

▶▶ Take plenty of provisions with you (especially drinking water), plus warm clothing in case you are stranded overnight.

▶▶ Always allow more time than you need to get from A to B, as the distances are huge.

5

The Northwest

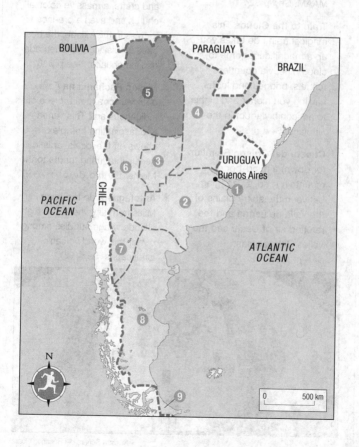

CHAPTER 5

Highlights

✳ **Incan mummies**
Controversially displayed in hi-tech fridges, three impeccably preserved Incan children, discovered up a lofty volcano, can be seen in the Northwest's best museum, MAAM. See p.324

✳ **Train to the Clouds** This magical train ride takes you up a magnificent gorge to cloud nine, via countless tunnels, bridges and loops, hauling you higher and higher to an iconic viaduct in the altiplano. See p.334

✳ **Cuesta del Obispo** Spiral up (or down) a mind-boggling mountain road, zigzagging between the sultry plains of the Valle de Lerma and the rarefied air of Cachi and the Valles Calchaquíes. See p.335

✳ **Vineyards of Cafayate** Try fruity cabernet sauvignons, earthy malbecs and heady torrontés at the world's highest wineries. See p.338

✳ **Tilcara** You'll find charming hotels, an abundance of arts and crafts, a massive colonial church and even a pre-Incan fortress in this village, the best base for visiting the Quebrada de Humahuaca. See p.348

✳ **Museo Pachamama** *Folie de grandeur* or a masterpiece of indigenous art? This varied and fascinating complex shows off the locals' artistic genius in a fitting tribute to the Mother Earth deity. See p.365

✳ **Antofagasta de la Sierra** Miles from anywhere, this high-altitude village huddles among out-of-this world volcanic landscapes. See p.371

▲ Nuestra Señora del Rosario, Tilcara

The Northwest

Argentina's **Northwest** (El Noroeste Argentino – NOA – or "El Norte") is infinitely varied: ochre deserts where flocks of llamas roam, charcoal-grey lava flows devoid of any life form, blindingly white salt flats and sooty-black volcanic cones, pristine limewashed colonial chapels set against striped mountainsides, lush citrus groves and emerald-green sugar plantations, impenetrable jungles populated by peccaries and parakeets. The Northwest is also the birthplace of Argentina – a Spanish colony thrived here when Buenos Aires was still an unsteady trading post on the Atlantic coast. One of the colonial cities, **Salta**, is indisputably the region's tourism capital, with some of the country's best hotels, finest architecture and a well-earned reputation for hospitality. From here, you can meander in a northwesterly direction up the enchanting **Quebrada del Toro** on a safari or on the **Tren a las Nubes** (Train to the Clouds), one of the world's highest railways. Alternatively, you can head due northeast across the subtropical lowlands, where jungle-clad **cloudforests**, or *yungas*, poke out of fertile plains into the raincloud that gives them their name. These habitats are a birdwatcher's paradise.

To Salta's northwest huddles boot-shaped Jujuy Province, one of the federation's poorest and remotest, shoved up into the corner of the country against Chile and Bolivia, where in the space of a few kilometres humid valleys and soothingly green jungles give way to the austere, parched altiplano (or *puna*), home to flocks of flamingoes, herds of llamas and very few people. **San Salvador de Jujuy**, the slightly oddball provincial capital, cannot rival Salta for its amenities or architectural splendours, but it's the best starting-point for exploring the many-hued **Quebrada de Humahuaca**.

Further south, snaking mountain roads scale the verdant **Cuesta del Obispo** and the stark but vividly coloured **Quebrada de Cafayate** from Salta to the **Valles Calchaquíes**, dry, sunny dales along which high-altitude vineyards somehow thrive, particularly around the airy regional capital of **Cafayate**. Whereas Salta and Jujuy have a well-established international tourist industry, the provinces to the south remain far less known. Domestically the provinces of Tucumán and Catamarca are dismissed as poor, dull backwaters with more than their fair share of political, social and economic woes, and there is a certain amount of truth in that analysis. That said, the city of **San Miguel de Tucumán** – the region's biggest urban centre by far – has an addictively lively atmosphere. Tucumán – proudly calling itself the "Garden of the Nation" – may be one of Argentina's smallest provinces, but it does contain some real treasures, including the impressive pre-Inca ruins at **Quilmes**, the marvellous museum dedicated to the Pachamama, or Earth Mother, at **Amaicha**, and the dramatic mountain scenery around **Tafí del Valle**, where the trekking opportunities are endless.

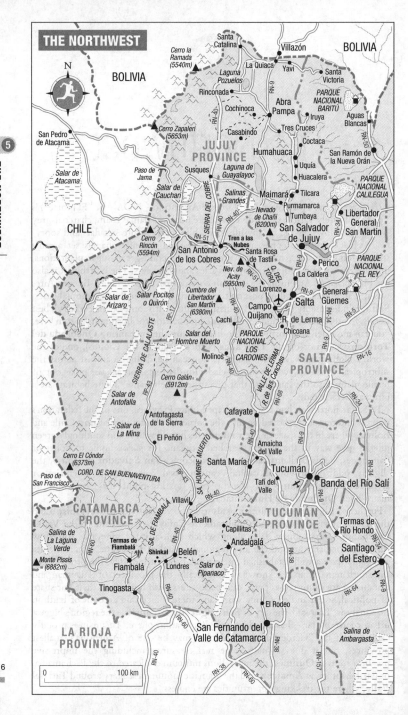

THE NORTHWEST

N

BOLIVIA

Santa Catalina

Cerro la Ramada (5540m)

Villazón

BOLIVIA

La Quiaca   Yaví

Laguna Pozuelos

Santa Victoria

Rinconada

PARQUE NACIONAL BARITÚ

San Pedro de Atacama

Cerro Zapaleri (5653m)

Cochinoca

Abra Pampa

Iruya

Aguas Blancas

Casabindo

Tres Cruces

Coctaca

San Ramón de la Nueva Orán

Salar de Atacama

JUJUY PROVINCE

Humahuaca

Uquía

Paso de Jama

Susques

Laguna de Guayalayoc

Huacalera

PARQUE NACIONAL CALILEGUA

Salar de Cauchari

Salinas Grandes

Maimará

Tilcara

CHILE

Nevado de Chañi (6200m)

Purmamarca

Tumbaya

Libertador General San Martín

Cerro Rincón (5594m)

Tren a las Nubes

Santa Rosa de Tastil

San Salvador de Jujuy

Perico

SIERRA DEL COBRE

San Antonio de los Cobres

Nev. de Acay (5950m)

La Caldera

PARQUE NACIONAL EL REY

Salar de Arizaro

Salar Pocitos o Quirón

Cumbre del Libertador San Martín (6380m)

San Lorenzo

Salta

General Güemes

Cachi

Campo Quijano

R. de Lerma

Salar del Hombre Muerto

Chicoana

SIERRA DE CALALASTE

PARQUE NACIONAL LOS CARDONES

Molinos

SALTA PROVINCE

Salar de Antofalla

Cerro Galán (5912m)

VALLE DE LERMA
R. de las Conchas

Salar de La Mina

Antofagasta de la Sierra

Cafayate

Cerro El Cóndor (6373m)

El Peñón

Amaicha del Valle

CORD. DE SAN BUENAVENTURA

Paso de San Francisco

Santa María

Tucumán

Banda del Río Salí

Salina de La Laguna Verde

CATAMARCA PROVINCE

Villavil

Tafí del Valle

Monte Pissis (6882m)

SA. DE FIAMBALÁ

Hualfin

TUCUMÁN PROVINCE

Termas de Fiambalá

Capillitas

Termas de Río Hondo

Shinkal

Belén

Andalgalá

Santiago del Estero

Fiambalá

Londres

Salar de Pipanaco

Tinogasta

El Rodeo

LA RIOJA PROVINCE

San Fernando del Valle de Catamarca

Salina de Ambargasta

0   100 km

5

THE NORTHWEST

Equally impressive are the eternally snowy peaks that give their name to the Nevados del Aconquija, the natural border with neighbouring Catamarca Province, where a plethora of picturesque villages, each more isolated than the previous, reward patient visitors with rural hospitality, wondrous natural settings and some fabulous handmade crafts: **Belén** and **Londres** stand out. Even more awe-inspiring than Quilmes, the less-publicized pre-Columbian remains at **Shinkal**, near Londres, look almost more Maya than Inca, with their well-preserved pyramids and symbolic temples, whose real purposes have so far defied the archeologists. Try and make it all the way to **Antofagasta de la Sierra**, an amazingly out-of-the-way market town set among rock and lava formations and reached via some of the emptiest roads in the country.

Be aware that summers can be steamy in the valleys, making large cities like Tucumán unbearable, whereas in July and August night-time **temperatures** around Antofagasta are bitterly low, so your first purchase there will probably be an alpaca-wool poncho.

Salta and around

SALTA, historic capital of one of Argentina's biggest and most beautiful provinces, easily lives up to its well-publicized nickname of *Salta la Linda* (Salta the Fair), thanks to its festive atmosphere, handsome buildings and dramatic setting. In a region where the landscape and nature, rather than the towns and cities, are the main attractions, Salta is the exception. Fifteen hundred kilometres northwest of Buenos Aires, at the eastern end of the fertile Valle de Lerma, nationally famous for its tobacco plantations, and bounded by the Río Vaqueros to the north and Río Arenales to the south, the city is squeezed between steep, rippling mountains; at 1190m above sea level, it enjoys a relatively balmy climate. In recent years, Salta has become the Northwest's undisputed tourist capital, and its top-quality services include a slew of highly professional tour operators, some of the region's best-appointed hotels and liveliest youth hostels and a handful of very good restaurants. In addition to a cable car and a tourist railway, its sights include the marvellous Neoclassical **Iglesia San Francisco**, and a raft of excellent **museums** dedicated to subjects as varied as pre-Columbian culture, anthropology, local history and modern art. A generous sprinkling of well-preserved or well-restored **colonial architecture** has survived, giving the place a pleasant homogeneity and certain charm.

San Lorenzo, a self-contained suburb of Salta only fifteen minutes west, enjoys a slightly cooler mountain climate and is awash with lush vegetation, making it alluring for both visitors and locals who want to escape from the big city, especially in the summer.

Some history

Governor Hernando de Lerma of Tucumán, who gave his name to the nearby valley, founded the city of Salta on April 16, 1582, following the instructions of Viceroy Toledo, to guarantee the safety of anyone entering or leaving Tucumán itself. The site was chosen for its strategic mountainside location, and the streams flowing nearby were used as natural moats. In 1776, the already flourishing city was made capital of a huge intendencia that took in Santiago del Estero, Jujuy and even the southern reaches of modern Bolivia, becoming one of the major centres in the viceroyalty. From 1810 to 1814 it was the headquarters of the Ejércitos del Norte and for the following seven years was where General Güemes posted his anti-royalist forces, creating the now traditional red-and-black-poncho uniform for his gaucho militia. However, once Buenos Aires became the capital of the young country, Salta went into steady decline, missing out on the rest of the country's mass immigration of the mid- and late nineteenth century; the railway didn't arrive here until 1890. A belated urban explosion in the 1920s and 1930s has left its mark on the predominantly Neocolonial style of architecture in the city. Since the turn of the millennium, Salta has joined the ranks of Argentina's

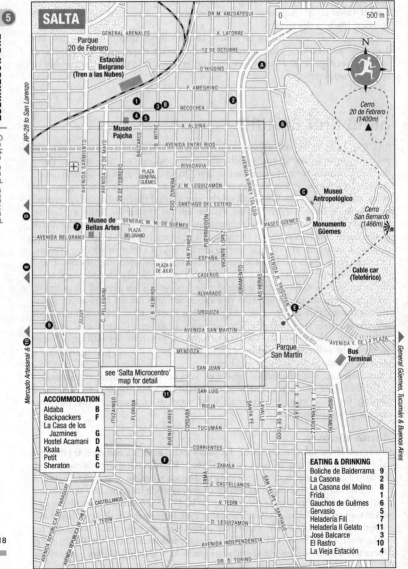

▲ RN-9 to Jujuy

SALTA

0   500 m

N

Parque 20 de Febrero

Estación Belgrano (Tren a las Nubes)

Museo Pajcha

Cerro 20 de Febrero (1400m) ▲

Museo Antropológico

Cerro San Bernardo (1466m) ▲

Monumento Güemes

Museo de Bellas Artes

Cable car (Teleférico)

Parque San Martín

Bus Terminal

see 'Salta Microcentro' map for detail

ACCOMMODATION

Aldaba	B
Backpackers	F
La Casa de los Jazmines	G
Hostel Acamani	D
Kkala	A
Petit	E
Sheraton	C

EATING & DRINKING

Boliche de Balderrama	9
La Casona	2
La Casona del Molino	8
Frida	1
Gauchos de Güemes	6
Gervasio	5
Heladería Fili	7
Heladería Il Gelato	11
José Balcarce	3
El Rastro	10
La Vieja Estación	4

◀ Mercado Artesanal & ⑩

General Güemes, Tucumán & Buenos Aires ▶

▼ RN-68 to Chicoana, Cachi, Cafayate, Airport & ⑥

fastest growing and most dynamic metropolises, and its increased wealth can be seen in the remarkable sophistication of its inhabitants and the services they share with visitors.

Arrival, information and city transport

Salta's **Martín Miguel de Güemes International Airport** (☏0387/424-2904) is in El Aybal, about 10km southwest of the city centre, along the motorway-like RN-51. Buses #8A and 6 run between the airport and central Avenida San Martín; a taxi will set you back about $30. AirBus (☏0387/431-5327 or 156-832897) takes you to the city centre for $15. Buses from all across the region and throughout the country use the modernized **bus terminal** at Avenida Hipólito Yrigoyen (☏0387/401-1143), just east of the Parque San Martín, five blocks south and eight east of central Plaza 9 de Julio. Bus #5 links the bus terminal with the **train station**, at Ameghino 690, via Plaza 9 de Julio, though the only passenger train serving Salta these days is the privately run tourist train, *Tren a las Nubes/del Sol* (see box, p.334).

The excellent and dynamic **provincial tourist office** at Buenos Aires 93 (Mon–Fri 8am–9pm, Sat & Sun 9am–8pm; ☏0387/431-0950, Ⓦwww.turismosalta .gov.ar) dispenses a free map and extensive accommodation information; some staff members speak English. Awash with useful brochures and leaflets but otherwise rather less impressive, despite its new location in a converted Neoclassical building, is the **city tourist office** at Caseros 460 (daily 8am–9pm; ☏0387/421-6285).

You're unlikely to need any sort of city transport, given the compactness of downtown Salta, but **taxis** (with red and black livery) are plentiful and cheap.

Accommodation

As you might expect of such a regional hub, Salta has a wide variety of **places to stay**, everything from five-star international hotels to a handful of exquisite boutique hotels to several lively youth hostels, plus plenty of decent middle-range hotels and good-value *residenciales* in between. If you'd rather avoid the city, you'll also find a number of excellent accommodation options in nearby San Lorenzo (see p.331), only fifteen minutes from the city centre, plus a good many **fincas** and **estancias** (see box, p.332) in the surrounding countryside, offering accommodation that ranges from the modestly comfortable to the plain luxurious, plus all kinds of pursuits and other services. Salta's enormous municipal **campsite**, *Casino* (☏0387/423-1341), in the Parque Municipal 3km south of the centre, is a little noisy but well equipped, with a huge swimming pool, hot showers, *balneario* and supermarket. The #13 bus runs there from Calle Jujuy.

Central Salta

The accommodation listed below is marked on the Salta Microcentro map on p.321.

Altos de Balcarce Balcarce 747 ☏0387/431-5454, Ⓦwww.altosdebalcarce.com.ar. Despite its location on Salta's liveliest night-time street, this first-rate, professionally run hotel is safe and quiet. The fine rooms are decorated with traditional touches, the public areas are bright and appealing and there is a pleasant swimming pool. **⑦**

Bloomer's Bed and Brunch Vicente López 129 ☏0387/422-7449, Ⓦwww .bloomers-salta.com.ar. The five suites around a colonial patio – all with mod cons like flat-screen TVs – ooze charm. Run by a British–Peruvian couple, this B&B serves brunch rather than breakfast, is welcoming, comfortable and brightly decorated. **⑤–⑥**

Caseros 44 Caseros 44 ☏0387/421-6761, Ⓦwww.caseros44bandb.com.ar. Homely little B&B just like a private house. All the rooms have ceiling fans and en-suite bathrooms, and there's internet access. **⑤**

Design Suites Pasaje Castro 215 ☏0387/439-5962, Ⓦwww.designsuites.com. Housed in the carefully renovated Palacio Usandivaras, a 1913 mansion with a rather ugly modern adjunct. Inside it is all modern art and minimalism, with the best suites in the old palace, also home to a top-rate restaurant lorded over by Gonzalo Doxandabarat, now established as Salta's favourite chef. ❾

Elena Buenos Aires 256 ☏ 0387/421-1529. This tried and tested institution, an old-fashioned Spanish-run guesthouse, has large dowdy bedrooms with en-suite bathrooms around a leafy patio like a little bit of Andalucía. ❸

El Lagar 20 de Febrero 877 ☏ 0387/421-7943, ✉ ellagar@arnet.com.ar. A Neocolonial boutique hotel with an exquisite art collection. It's exclusive but not snobbish, and is undoubtedly one of the most tastefully appointed hotels in the region, though some of the installations are a little old-fashioned. There is a fine pool to relax in or by, and breakfast is served in a wood-panelled dining room. Reservations required. ❽

🏃 **Legado Mítico** Mitre 647 ☏ 0387/422-8786, ⓦ www.legadomitico.com. Wonderfully inviting themed hotel in a well-located converted townhouse – each of the huge, sumptuously decorated rooms is named after a figure of regional importance such as a writer, a gaucho or the member of an indigenous tribe. ❾

Marilian Buenos Aires 176 ☏ 0387/421-6700, ⓦ www.hotelmarilian.com.ar. Professionally run, attractively decorated central hotel with both heat and a/c, a decent *confitería* and room service. It has an *apart-hotel* branch (❺) at España 254 and also runs a low-budget hostel. ❻

Regidor Buenos Aires 10 ☏ 0387/431-1305, ⓦ www.hotelregidor.com. Charming place with character, a rustic *confitería* and very pleasant rooms. Rooms overlooking the square tend to be noisy. ❹

🏃 **Solar de la Plaza** Leguizamón 669 ☏ 0387/431-5111, ⓦ www.solardelaplaza .com.ar. Definitely one of the classiest acts in the city, *Solar* is housed in a converted Neocolonial mansion with beautifully furnished, large rooms, rooftop pool, professional service and outstanding buffet breakfast featuring delicious local products. ❽

Terra Oculta Córdoba 361 ☏ 0387/421-8769, ⓦ terraoculta.com. Popular hostel with table tennis, internet, a video room and double rooms (❹). Dorm beds $60–70.

Out of the centre

The accommodation listed below is marked on the Salta map on p.318.

Aldaba Mitre 910 ☏ 0387/421-9455, ⓦ www .aldabahotel.com. A wonderful boutique hotel

with six rooms, each with its own decor and style, including lots of crisp white linen, antique furniture and attention to detail. The owners, golf fans, can arrange for guests to visit Salta's course. ❻

Backpackers Buenos Aires 930 ☏ 0387/423-5910, ⓦ backpackerssalta.com. The facilities at the city's veteran hostel are not great but there's a very friendly, international atmosphere and a strong tendency to have fiestas. You might also want to try one of the other hostels in the same group (see website). Double rooms (❸) as well as cramped dorms costing $60 per person.

La Casa de los Jazmines RN-51 Km11, La Merced Chica, near Salta airport ☏ 0387/431-5454, ⓦ www.houseofjasmines.com. The House of Jasmins is a colonial house tastefully transformed into a luxury lodge with discreet service. It has just seven suites and a scattering of private dining areas. The food and wine are memorable, making it just the place for a romantic treat. ❽

🏃 **Finca Valentina** RN-51 Km11, La Merced Chica, near Salta airport ☏ 0387/154-523490, ⓦ www.finca-valentina.com.ar. Some way out of Salta, but conveniently close to the airport – great for early departures – this delightful modern finca is run by an utterly stylish couple from Milan who combine flair (Valentina is an architect) with professional know-how (Fabrizio is an economist). A handful of charming rooms set among a green park near wonderful walking and riding country. Memorably delicious food, too. ❽

🏃 **Kkala** Las Higueras 104 ☏ 0387/439-6590, ⓦ www.hotelkkala.com.ar. Fabulous new boutique hotel in Tres Cerritos, a well-heeled barrio close to the centre but far from the hustle and bustle. The enticing rooms are beautifully furnished while the views from the hotel, its pool/deck and homely public areas are stunning. ❽

Petit Hipólito Yrigoyen 225 ☏ 0387/421-3012, ✉ petit_hotel@ciudad.com.ar. Good service and plush rooms. From the swimming pool, café terrace and the rooms at the back you get wonderful mountain views. ❺

Sheraton Avenida Ejercito del Norte 330 ☏ 0387/432-3000, ⓦ www.sheraton.com/salta. Although part of the international chain, this impeccably run hotel, shoved up against the hillside in a slightly awkward location, has real personality – the decor is unmistakably northwestern, based on Andean rugs and indigenous masks. There's a handsome pool, a fine restaurant and a decent gym. ❾

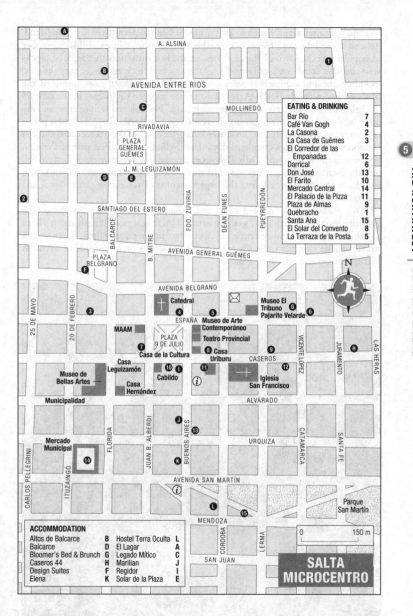

EATING & DRINKING

Bar Río	7
Café Van Gogh	4
La Casona	2
La Casa de Guëmes	3
El Corredor de las Empanadas	12
Darrical	6
Don José	13
El Farito	10
Mercado Central	14
El Palacio de la Pizza	11
Plaza de Almas	9
Quebracho	1
Santa Ana	15
El Solar del Convento	8
La Terraza de la Posta	5

ACCOMMODATION

Altos de Balcarce	B	Hostel Terra Oculta	L
Balcarce	D	El Lagar	A
Bloomer's Bed & Brunch	G	Legado Mítico	C
Caseros 44	H	Marilian	J
Design Suites	F	Regidor	I
Elena	K	Solar de la Plaza	E

SALTA MICROCENTRO

The City

Salta's central square, **Plaza 9 de Julio**, is one of the country's most harmonious, especially since it was spruced up in the early years of the new millennium. Surrounded on all four sides by graceful, shady *recovas*, or arcades, under which several café terraces lend themselves to idle people-watching, it's a great place to while away an hour or two. The well-manicured central part of the square is a collection of palms and tipas, fountains and benches, plus a quaint late nineteenth-century bandstand. Around it stand the city's Neoclassical **cathedral**, the snow-white **Cabildo**, a number of popular cafés and two of the city's newest and best **museums**. A couple of blocks west huddle some well-preserved eighteenth- and nineteenth-century houses, including the immaculately whitewashed Casa Arías Rengel, now home to the **Museo Provincial de Bellas Artes**. Two of the most striking sights in the city are the **Iglesia San Francisco**, an extravagant piece of Neocolonial architecture, and the more subdued but equally imposing **Convento de San Bernardo**. All of these places of interest are concentrated in the square kilometre or so of the microcentro and can comfortably be seen in a couple of days. The liveliest and trendiest part of the city, however, is the area around **Calle Balcarce**, especially north of Avenida Entre Ríos, near the Estación Belgrano; arts and crafts are on sale in the evenings and on weekends, and this is also where you'll find the largest number of restaurants, bars, discos and folk-music venues.

Heavy traffic and the related noise and exhaust pollution are something of a growing problem in Salta but **getting around** on foot is not difficult and it's hard to get lost, since the grid system is almost perfect in the microcentro; north–south streets change name at Calle Caseros; east–west streets on either side of avenidas Virrey Toledo and Hipólito Yrigoyen.

▲ Plaza 9 de Julio, Salta

Earthquakes and the Fiesta del Milagro

No earthquake as destructive as those that flattened the cities of Mendoza in 1861 and San Juan in 1944 has struck the Northwest region of Argentina within recent history, but this part of the country lies along the same fault line that was responsible for that seismic activity and is prone to occasional tremors, some of them violent. The **Nazca plate**, beneath the eastern Pacific, and the **South American plate**, comprising the whole continent, are constantly colliding – a continuation of the tectonic activity that formed the Andean cordillera. To make matters worse, the Nazca plate is subducting – nudging its way beneath the landmass – an action that accounts for the abundance of **volcanoes** along the range; some of them are extinct, others lie dormant, but none in the Northwest is very active. Nonetheless, frequent **earthquakes** of varying strength (but mostly mild for geological reasons) rock Northwest Argentina, accounting for the repeated displacement of many settlements and the absence of colonial architecture in some.

Salta still thanks its lucky stars for **El Milagro**, the legend according to which two sacred images have spared the city the kind of destruction caused by seismic disasters. An image of **Christ** and another of the **Virgin Mary** were found floating in a box off the coast of Peru in 1592, exactly a century after the Americas were discovered by Columbus, and somehow ended up in Salta. Precisely one century later, on September 13, 1692, a series of tremors began to shake the city, damaging some public buildings and houses. During that night, a priest named José Carrión dreamed that if the images of Christ and Mary were paraded through the streets for nine days the earthquakes would stop and Salta would be spared forever. Apparently it worked and, ever since, the **Fiesta del Milagro** has been a major event in the city's calendar. Festivities and religious ceremonies starting on September 6 reach a climax on September 15, when the now-famous images, which are kept in the cathedral, are paraded through the city's streets in a massive, solemn but colourful procession.

The cathedral

Towering over the northern side of the Plaza 9 de Julio at España 537, and mirrored in the innocuous plate-glass building next door, the brightly painted **cathedral** dates from 1882, the city's third centenary year. It's an Italianate Neoclassical pile of the kind found all over the region, with some well-executed interior frescoes – the one of the Four Apostles around the cupola is particularly fine. Inside, and immediately to the left of the entrance, is the grandiose Panteón de los Héroes del Norte, where local liberator General Güemes is buried. The Capilla del Señor del Milagro and Capilla de la Vírgen del Milagro, at the far end of the left and right aisles respectively, house the sacred images that are the centrepieces of major celebrations every September (see box above).

Museo de Arte Contemporánea (MAC)

Housed on the first floor of a handsomely renovated Neocolonial building on the northeast corner of Plaza 9 de Julio, the outstanding **Museo de Arte Contemporánea** (MAC; Tues–Sat 9am–8pm, Sun 4–8pm; $2) – all sleek white walls and dark parquets – puts on exhibitions of mainly local artists, from up-and-coming wannabes straight out of art school to more established local names, who are often given shows of their own. Painting dominates but sculpture, video and photography are also often on display.

Museo El Tribuno Pajarito Velarde

Two blocks east of the MAC, at Pueyrredón 106 and España, the curious **Museo El Tribuno Pajarito Velarde** (Mon–Fri 10.30am–2pm & 3.30–6pm, Sat

10am–2pm; $4) was the home of a colourful local personality, Guillermo Velarde Mors (born 1895), who died in his magnificent wooden bed here in 1965. Nicknamed "Pajarito" ("little bird"), this controversial bohemian was born into a wealthy, influential family, then worked in turn as a lawyer, journalist and banker, but retired from his last job, at the Banco Provincial de Salta, at the age of 37 to create a kind of arts club. While promoting artists, writers and musicians, especially local folk singers and groups, at a time when they lacked social kudos, he also went out of his way to cause scandals – he particularly liked provoking the nuns who ran the girls' school opposite his house. Respected as a great patron of the arts, he was also marginalized by local society, owing to his outlandish lifestyle – he never married, had lots of affairs and his music sessions often degenerated into drunken orgies. Crammed full of his fascinating belongings – including a hat donated by an admiring Carlos Gardel (two tangos were composed in Pajarito's honour) – this humble adobe house is a fitting tribute to both an original local character and the history of Salta's socio-cultural life in the twentieth century. The mischievous curator, Carol, delights in shocking visitors with some of Pajarito's prize trinkets, several of which are in dubious taste, but unfortunately her lively explanations are in Spanish only.

Museo de Arqueología de Alta Montaña (MAAM)

In an attractive Neo-Gothic building on the western side of the plaza, at Mitre 77, the **Museo de Arqueología de Alta Montaña** (MAAM; Tues–Sun 11am–7.30pm; $30; Ⓦwww.maam.org.ar) is the one museum in Salta that you should not miss. It was specially created to present to the public the discovery of the so-called **Llullaillaco Children**, one of the most important archeological finds ever made in Argentina. In 1999, three naturally mummified Inca children were uncovered by an expedition of mountaineers and scientists on top of **Volcán Llullaillaco**, due west of Salta on the Chilean border and 6740m above sea level. They are a 6-year-old girl, visibly struck by lightning some time after her burial, her hair arranged in two small braids and with a metal plaque as an adornment (which attracted the lightning); a teenage girl whose face was painted with a red pigment and who had small fragments of coca leaves above her upper lip; and a 7-year-old boy wearing a white feather ornament tied around his head. Their incredibly well-preserved corpses – all three lived around 1490 AD – were at first kept in a university laboratory in the city while tests on their tissue and other remains were completed. They are now shown, one at a time, in specially refrigerated cases and the effect is startling.

The jury is still out as to whether it is sacrilegious to display the bodies in a public museum: the decision to do so provoked a furore, including demonstrations by representatives of local indigenous groups, so bear in mind that this is a sensitive issue. Certainly the fainthearted will want to skip the room where they are shown, as expressions of fear are clearly shown on their young faces – the children were sacrificed to the Inca deities, possibly in a fertility ceremony or as an offering to the gods of the sun and moon. They were probably knocked out with a blunt weapon (so their bodies were not rendered imperfect by wounds) and then left to die of the lack of oxygen and the extreme cold.

Over a hundred **artefacts**, part of the remarkably intact treasure trove buried with the children at the end of the fifteenth century, are on display in the museum's other rooms, where the temperature and humidity are kept artificially low – bring something warm to wear. The exhibit is both scientific and didactic, including a video about the expedition, displays of textiles and the like, but it is no musty old-fashioned museum. The ground-floor bookshop is prime hunting ground for souvenirs, mostly of very high quality, while the marvellous **cafeteria**, offering local specialities, is open daily from 9am to 10pm.

Cabildo (Museo Histórico del Norte)

Opposite the cathedral, on the southern side of the plaza at Caseros 549, stands the white-facaded **Cabildo**. Originally built in the early seventeenth century, it took on its current appearance in the late eighteenth, when the city became capital of the *intendencia*. It underwent a facelift that left its slightly lopsided structure – the two rows of graceful arches don't quite tally – essentially intact in the middle of the twentieth century, over a hundred years after it ceased to be the colonial headquarters. It now houses the highly eclectic **Museo Histórico del Norte** (Tues–Fri 9am–6pm, Sat & Sun 9am–1.30pm; $5, free Wed until 9.30am), whose collections range from coins and eighteenth-century paintings to wooden saints and archeological finds to wonderful horse-drawn carriages parked in the cobbled courtyards, among them an elegant nineteenth-century hearse. Of the religious art in the first two rooms, the moving *San Pedro de Alcántara*, by eighteenth-century Altoperuvian artist Melchor Pérez de Holguín, stands out. Excellent temporary exhibitions, usually of regional art, are staged in the beautifully restored building, but the superb views across the plaza from the upper-storey verandah alone make a visit worthwhile.

Around the Museo de Bellas Artes Arías Rengel

More colonial and Neocolonial buildings are clustered in the few blocks to the west of Plaza 9 de Julio. Just 100m west of the Cabildo, at La Florida 20, is the **Museo Provincial de Bellas Artes Arías Rengel** (Mon–Sat 9am–7.30pm; $2). The pedestrianized street allows you an unrestricted view of its brilliant white facade, with an elaborate arched doorway and handsome green door. Erected towards the end of the eighteenth century, and virtually intact, albeit well restored, it's the finest viceregal building left in the city. The home of Sergeant-Major Félix Arías Rengel, who conquered the Argentine Chaco and had the house built, it has splendid patios, full of lush trees and plants, while the fine interior details include verandahs, banisters and rafters of red *quebracho* timber.

Occasionally putting on regional or national art exhibitions, the museum houses the city's rich fine art collection, ranging from paintings from Cusco to twentieth-century sculpture. Highlights are a *St Matthew* of the **Cusqueña School**, the eighteenth-century polychrome *Asunción de la Virgen* from the Jesuit missions, the large painting *The City of Salta*, painted in 1854 by Giorgio Penutti, and some fine engravings by nineteenth-century artists Basaldúa, Spilimbergo and Quinquela Martín.

Contrasting effectively with the pristine museum building is the **Casa Leguizamón** next door, at Caseros and La Florida. Constructed at the beginning of the nineteenth century for a rich merchant, it's painted a deep raspberry pink, and its plain two storeys are set off by fine detailing, a delicate wrought-iron balcony and zinc gargoyles. A few steps south is the **Municipalidad**, whose unusual twelve-columned oval patio is worth investigating, while opposite, at La Florida 97, is the **Casa de Hernández**, a typical Neocolonial corner house with a chamfered angle. Built around 1870, with a delightful patio at its heart, it now houses the **Museo de la Ciudad** (Mon–Fri 9am–1pm & 4–8.30pm, Sat 9am–1pm & 5–8.30pm; free), a collection of artefacts and documents tracing the city's history.

Casa Uriburu

Calle Caseros, a busy thoroughfare leading east from the southern side of Plaza 9 de Julio, takes you past a number of striking Neocolonial buildings and a fine late eighteenth-century house built to a simple design and with one of the most charming patios in the city: the **Casa Uriburu**, at Caseros 417. Now containing a museum of period furniture and Uriburu memorabilia (Tues–Fri 9.30am–6pm,

Sat 9am–1.30pm; $5), it was once home to the influential Uriburu family, who produced two presidents of Argentina. The most impressive room is undoubtedly the reconstructed kitchen, with its polished copper and earthenware pots.

Iglesia San Francisco

Further east still, at the corner of Caseros and Córdoba, and taking up a whole block, stands a city landmark and one of the most beautiful religious buildings in the country, the **Iglesia y Convento San Francisco**. Built between 1750 and 1850 by architect **Luigi Giorgi**, it's an extravaganza of Italianate Neocolonial exuberance, displaying a textbook compliance with architectural principles combined with clever idiosyncrasies. The first thing that strikes you is the colour: pure ivory-white columns stand out from the vibrant ox-blood walls, while the profuse detailing of Latin inscriptions, symbols and Neoclassical patterns is picked out in braid-like golden yellow. The church's most imposing feature is its slender **campanile**, towering over the low-rise Neocolonial houses of downtown Salta and tapering off to a slender spire. The highly elaborate **facade** of the church itself, behind a suitably austere statue of St Francis in the middle of the courtyard, is lavishly decorated with balusters and scrolls, curlicues and pinnacles, Franciscan inscriptions and the order's shield, but the most original features are the organza-like **stucco curtains** that billow down from each of the three archways, nearly touching the elegant wrought-iron gates below. Inside, the decoration is subdued, almost plain in comparison, but the most eye-catching elements are the three eighteenth-century Portuguese-style jacaranda-wood **armchairs** behind the altar. The **cloisters** of the convent sometimes shelter exhibitions of local arts and crafts. If you can, do go on a **guided tour** ($2; Spanish only), which will also get you into the fascinating Museo de Arte Sacro (Mon–Sat 9.30am–1pm & 3–7pm) – where the surprising archeological section features a perfect terracotta Etruscan head dating from the fourth century BC.

Museo Antropológico Juan Martín Leguizamón and Cerro San Bernardo

Starting three blocks north of the Iglesia San Francisco, and five east, across Avenida Hipólito Yrigoyen, tree-lined **Paseo Güemes** is the main thoroughfare of a leafy, well-to-do barrio crammed with later Neocolonial houses; it climbs up towards a bombastic **monument** of General Güemes, Salta's local hero. Surrounded by a grove of eucalyptus, the bronze equestrian statue, dating from 1931, is decorated with bas-reliefs depicting the army that defended newly independent Argentina from several last-ditch invasions by the Spanish. Immediately behind it, where the streets begin to slope up the lower flanks of the mountain, is the modern **Museo Antropológico Juan Martín Leguizamón** at Ejército del Norte and Ricardo Sola (Mon–Fri 8am–7pm, Sat 10am–6pm; $3). The varied collection could be better presented, and most of the explanations in Spanish are sketchy and inaccurate, but many of the items on display are worth seeing. One highlight is another well-preserved **mummy** found on **Volcán Llullaillaco** (see p.324), also bearing signs that it may have been a human sacrifice, while the centrepiece of the extensive ceramics collection is a set of finds from Tastil (see p.333), along with a petroglyph known as the **Bailarina de Tastil**, a delightful dancing figure painted onto rock, removed from the *pukará*, or pre-Columbian fortress, to the safety of a glass case. A well-executed reconstruction of a pre-Columbian burial urn shows how the local climate preserved textiles and wood in perfect condition for centuries. Finally, the section on festivals and **carnival** includes photographs of celebrations in Iruya (see p.353) and displays examples of the so-called *máscaras de viejo*, the old-man **masks** worn during the ceremonies there, along with the distinctive Chané masks, animal and bird heads made of *palo borracho* wood and the grotesque carnival masks from Oruro in Bolivia.

Immediately behind the museum a steep path zigzags up the overgrown flanks of **Cerro San Bernardo** (1458m), but you might prefer to take the **teleférico**, or cable car, from the base station on Avenida Hipólito Yrigoyen, between Urquiza and Avenida San Martín, at the eastern end of Parque San Martín (daily 10am–7.30pm; $20 each way, $6 for children). The smooth cable-car gondolas take you to the summit in less than ten minutes, and from them and the small garden at the top you can admire panoramic **views** of the city and the snowcapped mountain range to the west. A **café** with a terrace serves drinks and simple meals.

Museo de Bellas Artes

Four blocks west and one north of the central Plaza 9 de Julio, the **Museo de Bellas Artes**, Belgrano 992 (Mon–Fri 10am–8pm, Sat 11am–7pm; $5), was inaugurated in December 2008 in the landmark Casona Usandivaras, an Art Nouveau mansion standing majestically at the corner of Avenida Sarmiento. Its eleven beautifully restored rooms house a rich patrimony, covering a wide range of provincial art history, ranging from pre-Hispanic to contemporary.

Museo de Arte Étnico Americano Pajcha

Proof that the lively Balcarce district is not all about eating and drinking, the **Museo de Arte Étnico Americano Pajcha**, 20 de Febrero 838 (Mon–Sat 10am–1pm & 4–8pm, closed Sun except during Holy Week, the whole of July and Sept; $10; ⓦ www.museodearteetnico.com.ar), is a strong contender for the best museum of American ethnic art in the country. The result of the lifelong work of Liliana Madrid de Zito Fontán, a local ethnologist, this magnificent collection is arranged thematically and geographically in seven rooms, each with its own music. Native Argentine art and handicrafts loom large, but there are many outstanding items from all over South America, along with some beautiful photographs. Painting, textiles, religious objects (Christian and pre-Columbian) and wooden articles represent all the main ethnic groups; the silver jewellery crafted by the Mapuche of Chile and Andean ceramics are undoubtedly the highlights. There is also a fine example of a *pajcha*, an Inca offering tray with several compartments, looking not unlike an ancient muffin-mould. A selection of contemporary crafts is on sale at the reception, and there's also an excellent café on site.

Eating, drinking and entertainment

Salta has plenty of **eating** places to suit all pockets, ranging from simple **snack bars** where you can savour the city's famous **empanadas** to a growing number of classy **restaurants** where people dress smartly for dinner. The most traditional **cafés** huddle together around the Plaza 9 de Julio, while the city's many lively **peñas**, informal folk-music clubs mainly found in the Northwest, also serve food and drink. Calle Balcarce and the surrounding area towards the train station are firmly established as the hub of Salta's nightlife, focused on a row of bars, *peñas* and restaurants along Balcarce itself. People go to see and be seen – and have a good time in the process. The world-class **Teatro Provincial** on the Plaza 9 de Julio (ⓦ www.culturasalta.gov.ar) is a beautifully renovated masterpiece with aplush interior: it's home to one of Argentina's best regarded classical orchestras, the Sinfónica de Salta, which attracts leading musicians from around the world, and also hosts theatre, dance and folklore concerts.

Restaurants

Don José Urquiza 484. Cheap and cheerful restaurant serving up home cooking in a laidback atmosphere; the paintings on the walls are Don José's too.

Frida Balcarce 935. Stylish and fairly pricey restaurant serving Argentine and other Latin American dishes, though the links with Ms Kahlo and her native Mexico are rather tenuous.

Gervasio Balcarce 892. Rustic and reasonably priced restaurant serving regional specialities and a variety of fish and meat dishes – with good local wine.

José Balcarce Mitre and Necochea. José López presides over the kitchen at this charming – if slightly costly – Neocolonial corner restaurant and uses regional products like quinoa and grain amaranth (another Andean cereal) to accompany llama; also try llama carpaccio or, for the less adventurous, the steak and roast potatoes.

Plaza de Almas Pueyrredón 6. Lively, happening joint open all day – mainly to sell crafts and clothes – and until very late to feed and make merry. Salads, kebabs and stir-fries to tempt all palates and all budgets, plus live music in the patio, weather permitting.

Quebracho Virrey Toledo 702. One of the best restaurants in the city, with reliable if predictable food, plus fish – unusual for Salta – all at reasonable prices.

Santa Ana Mendoza 208. An elegant but fairly pricey establishment serving international cooking, which makes a change from the usual *locro* and *humitas*.

El Solar del Convento Caseros 444 ☎0387/421-5124. Elegant surroundings, classical music and a free glass of champagne set the tone for this high-class but not so expensive restaurant, serving juicy steaks and with an excellent wine list.

La Terraza de la Posta España 476. A moderately priced family *parrilla*, ideal for children, with no-nonsense traditional food, such as *locro* and *humitas*, as well as tender steaks and the usual desserts.

Cafés and bars

Bar Río Plaza 9 de Julio. A traditional bar, with fewer tourists than most around the square, despite the inexpensive drinks.

La Casona Virrey Toledo 1017, and at 25 de Mayo and Santiago del Estero. Both branches, open round the clock, churn out a never-ending supply of empanadas, including the best cheese pasties in town.

El Corredor de las Empanadas Caseros 117. Pleasant decor and a large patio are the settings for outstanding empanadas, *humitas*, tamales and other Northwestern dishes.

El Farito Caseros 509, Plaza 9 de Julio. Tiny empanada joint, dishing out delicious piping-hot cheese and meat pasties all day long.

Heladería Fili Av Güemes 1009. In a handsome Art Deco building, one of the two best ice-cream places in town.

Heladería Il Gelato Buenos Aires 606. The other of the two excellent ice-cream parlours in Salta.

Mercado Central La Florida and San Martín. A number of small stalls serving all the local fare at very low prices; great for a lunch-time snack.

El Palacio de la Pizza Caseros 427. It lives up to its name, with the best pizzas in Salta by far. Also good empanadas.

Van Gogh Plaza 9 de Julio. The best coffee in town, excellent cakes, quick meals, appetizing snacks and the local glitterati are the attractions, plus live music late at weekends.

Peñas

Boliche de Balderrama San Martín 1126 ☎0387/421-1542. One of the most popular *peñas*; well known as a bohemian hangout in the 1950s, nowadays it's a more conventional place, attracting tourists and local folk singers alike. Some nights an additional charge is added to the bill for the music.

La Casa de Güemes España 720. A mellow atmosphere combines with decent food and spontaneous music-making starting at midnight at the earliest.

La Casona del Molino Luis Burela and Caseros 2500 ☎0387/434-2835. Empanadas, *locro*, *guaschilocro*, tamales, *humitas*, sangria and improvised live music much later on, all in a handsomely restored Neocolonial mansion.

Gauchos de Güemes Av Uruguay 750 ☎0387/421-0820. One of the more touristy *peñas*, but it's still worth a try. Delicious food but be prepared for a music charge on top.

El Rastro San Martín 2555. One of the least known and therefore most authentic of all the *peñas salteñas*, with outbreaks of spontaneous guitar in between large helpings of *locro*.

La Vieja Estación Balcarce 885 ☎0387/421-7727. Modern *peña* in one of the city's trendiest streets, dishing out food, draught beer and music shows nightly.

A number of outfits offering a wide variety of highly professional **tours**, **expeditions** and other **activities** in the Northwest region are based in and around Salta city. The following is a selection of the best.

Clark Expediciones Mariano Moreno 1950, San Lorenzo ☎0387/497-1024, Ⓦwww.clarkexpediciones.com. Supremely experienced and professional team that specializes in bird-watching trips in Northwest Argentina, to Calilegua and El Rey national parks, to the Laguna de los Pozuelos and further afield (Chile, Bolivia, Paraguay and Brazil, plus other parts of Argentina). Based at the *Hostería Selva Montana*, San Lorenzo.

DM Norte Argentino Alvarado 203 ☎0387/422-9515, Ⓔcbearzi@conniebearzi .com.ar. Excellent outfit centred on the luxury estancia at Colomé but able to fix up all manner of services and bookings, from hotels and car hire to full-blown tours and safaris. Connie is worth her weight in gold. English spoken.

Marina Turismo Caseros 489 ☎0387/431-2097, Ⓦwww.marina-semisa.com.ar. One of the most professional outfits in the region, Marina's friendly and dynamic team will bend over backwards to get you a vehicle (and driver-guide, should you need one), find a guided excursion, book your hotel, change your flight or even just give you useful tips about where to eat, sleep or drink. English spoken.

MoviTrack Buenos Aires 28 ☎0387/431-6749, Ⓦwww.movitrack.com.ar. Offers the "Safari a los Nubes", a fun and adventurous way of discovering the Quebrada del Toro; there's an optional extension via the Quebrada de Humahuaca, in a special vehicle giving all passengers panoramic views. In addition to safaris to Cachi, Quilmes and Cafayate, and day-trips to Molinos and Tilcara, they also arrange an outing to Iruya and a five-day expedition to San Pedro de Atacama, Chile.

Norte Trekking Los Juncos 173 ☎0387/436-1844 or 156-832543, Ⓔfede @nortetrekking.com. Federico Norte and his experienced team can take you on a safari into the *puna*, on a two-day trip to the Valles Calchaquíes or to the Parque El Rey. Also also organizes longer tours to the Atacama Desert, Chile.

Salta Rafting Buenos Aires 88, local 13 ☎0387/401-0301, Ⓦwww.saltarafting.com. Highly professional, youthful team of operators specializing in rafting on the Río Juramento, southeast of the city: also offers kayaking, horseriding and mountain-biking.

Socompa Balcarce 998, 1st floor ☎0387/416-9130, Ⓦwww.socompa.com. Excellent operator working out of Salta (and connected with the *Finca Valentina*, see p.320) but specializing in the Puna Catamarqueña.

Tailored Expeditions Ⓦwww.tailoredexpeditions.com.ar. Internet-based tour company specializing in tailor-made tours – with native English-speakers as guides – of the Argentine Northwest for very small groups with emphasis on culture, leisure and luxury.

Tastil Caseros 468 ☎0387/431-0031, Ⓦwww.turismotastil.com.ar. Professionally run but mostly routine trips to the Salinas Grandes, Humahuaca, Cafayate, the cloudforest national parks, Laguna de Pozuelos and even as far as Chile. Expect to waste lots of time collecting and dropping off passengers and not much English in the commentary.

Turismo San Lorenzo Juan Carlos Dávalos s/n, San Lorenzo ☎0387/492-1757, Ⓦwww.turismosanlorenzo.com. As well as a variety of San Lorenzo trips, this outfit also offer tours of the whole region on horseback, on foot or by bike, ranging from $70 for a trek through the Quebrada de San Lorenzo to $600 for overnight trips to Iruya and the Quebrada de Humahuaca.

5

THE NORTHWEST

Listings

Airlines Aerolíneas Argentinas at the airport
☏0387/424-1185, and at Caseros 475
☏0387/431-1331; Andes, España 478
☏0387/437-3514-19; LAN ☏0810-9999526;
Lloyd Aéreo Boliviano, at the airport ☏0387/424-
1181, and at Caseros 529 ☏0387/431-0320.
Banks and exchanges Banco de la Nación, Mitre
151; Masventas, España 610. There's nowhere
reliable to change travellers' cheques, but there are
plenty of ATMs around town.
Car rental Marina Turismo, Caseros 489
☏0387/431-2097, ⊛www.semisa-marina.com.ar.

Consulates Bolivia, Mariano Boedo 32
☏0387/422-3377; Paraguay, Mariano Boedo 38.
Internet access There are *locutorios* all around
the city offering reasonably priced internet and
phone services.
Laundry Tía Maria, Av Belgrano 236; Laverap,
Santiago del Estero, 363.
Post office Deán Funes 170.
Taxis Remises Sol ☏0387/431-7317, or Balcarce
☏0387/421-3535 or 431-5142.
Tour operators See box, p.329.

San Lorenzo

Just 11km northwest of Salta along the RP-28, little **SAN LORENZO** is part dormitory town, part retreat for many Salteños, appreciated for its spotlessly clean ceibo-lined avenues and patrician villas. Plentiful walking and riding opportunities, a private nature reserve, an excellent range of **accommodation** and a couple of very good restaurants all make it an ideal alternative to staying in downtown Salta.

It's a pleasant one- to two-hour walk up the **Quebrada de San Lorenzo**, a rocky gorge down which a stream flows, sometimes forming falls and pools; the walk

ACCOMMODATION
Cabañas del Sol	A
Casa de Campo Arnaga	B
Eaton Place	D
Hostería Los Ceibos	E
Hotel Cerros de San Lorenzo	C
Posada Don Numas	F

EATING & DRINKING
Confitería Don Sanca	2
El Duende de la Quebrada	1
Lo de Andrés	3

Reserva del Huaico

SAN LORENZO

THE NORTHWEST | Salta and around

takes you through unspoilt woodland to the foot of the hulking mountains that form a natural barrier behind the village. Another enticing stroll can be taken through the **Reserva del Huaico** (daily 8am–6pm, by prior appointment only; ℡0387/497-1024 or 154-449521, ✉huaico1790@gmail.com), a nature reserve set up to protect the native forest and its endogenous flora and fauna (especially its birds); the exploration of its trails culminates at a viewpoint from where you can take in the whole valley to Salta city and beyond.

Buses run at regular intervals from central Salta to the Camino de la Quebrada, just before the gorge, stopping along Avenida San Martín and Juan Carlos Dávalos.

Accommodation

Even if you don't have your own transport, it's worthwhile bedding down for the night in the calm fresh air of San Lorenzo, with accommodation ranging from the basic and rustic to the positively luxurious. Some of these lodgings are located outside the village itself, but the staff at these places can arrange transport to and from the city and/or the airport for those who need it.

Cabañas del Sol RP-28 Km11.5 ℡0387/492-2072, ⊛www.saltacabanasdelsol.com.ar. Wonderful complex of *cabañas*, some of them right down by the riverside, in a fabulous rural setting some way out of San Lorenzo; ideal for anyone who wants to have self-catering accommodation. ❺

Casa de Campo Arnaga Aniceto la Torre, on the road to Lesser ℡0387/492-1478, ✉arnaga @arnet.com.ar. This wonderfully located handsome Basque-style patrician home drips with old-world charm and Salta's new-world colonial tradition. The slightly old-fashioned rooms are comfortable and the mountain views breathtaking. ❻

🏃 **Eaton Place** Av San Martín 2457 ℡0387/492-1347, ⊛www.eatonplace .todowebsalta.com.ar. As the name hints, this exquisite hotel – whose English-speaking owner has a collection of antiques that reflect his impeccable taste – is inspired by London mansions, though what townhouse in Belgravia boasts a palm-lined driveway? The plush rooms, classy service, dreamy swimming pool, toothsome food and marvellous grounds make this a plum choice. ❻

Hostería Los Ceibos 9 de Julio and España ℡0387/492-1675 or 492-1621, ⊛www .hlosceibos.com.ar. This relatively modest *hostería* in an attractive Neocolonial building has clean if uninspiring rooms, a swimming pool and other sports facilities. ❹

Hotel Cerros de San Lorenzo Joaquín V. Gonzales s/n, Loteo los Berros ℡0387/492-2500, ⊛www .cerrosdesanlorenzo.com.ar. Built in a fabulous Neocolonial style around a shady patio; the rooms are commodious and most attractive, and the bathrooms modish. The high location makes for breathtaking views. ❻

🏃 **Posada Don Numas** Pompilio Guzmán 1470 ℡0387/492-1918, ⊛www .donnumas.com.ar. This home-from-home posada boasts twelve spacious rooms with modern bathrooms, ultra-friendly service, two swimming pools, a fully equipped spa (saunas, massages, gym) and a prime setting affording mountain views. The breakfast, complete with home-made cakes and pies, will keep you going all day, but other simple meals or *asados* are offered on request. ❺

Eating and drinking

San Lorenzo's best **restaurant** by far is 🍴 *Lo de Andrés*, in a shocking pink galleried building with a large terrace, at Juan Carlos Dávalos and Gorriti (℡0387/492-1600); the extensive menu includes unforgettable empanadas, delicious *locro*, home-style *cazuela de cabrito*, fresh trout (best simply grilled, rather than smothered in sauce) and excellent pasta, with friendly service to boot. Just along the road, at Juan Carlos Dávalos 1450, is *Confitería Don Sanca*, a charming place serving delicious food, including a very good stab at tea. Further uphill, at the entrance to the Quebrada, *El Duende de la Quebrada*, at Juan Carlos Dávalos 2309, is an attractive rustic construction, with seemingly endless wooden balconies overlooking the stream; it serves very decent fare, with emphasis on local specialities, plus cakes, teas, coffees, juices and the like.

Salta and, to a lesser degree Jujuy, are provinces with a very long colonial history, which has left behind many **estancias** (traditional ranches), known locally as *fincas*, some of which now offer rooms to guests. Estancia stays are a wonderful way of combining rest – and sometimes even luxury – with a chance to get to know locals, tune in to nature and experience *criollo* customs and farming activities.

Remote *Finca Puerta del Cielo* (☎0387/156-840400 or 0387/492-1757; ❼ full board) is up in the Andean foothills not far from the city of Salta. Reachable only on horseback, though, it's a difficult place to get to, but rewarding once you are there. It's famous for its round-the-bonfire *asados*. You need to book your stay (1–3 nights) through a tour operator, such as Turismo San Lorenzo in San Lorenzo (see p.329).

Finca Santa Anita (☎0387/490-5050 or 431-3858, ⓦwww.santaanita.com.ar; ❻) is in the Valle de Lerma, 75km south of Salta by the RN-68, near Coronel Moldes, on the west bank of the huge Embalse Cabra Corral reservoir. As well as swimming in the pool or taking organized horse rides, you can watch tobacco being processed and visit the tobacco museum on the premises.

Between Chicoana and Rosario de Lerma, along the RP-33, is the oddly named *Finca Los Los* (☎0387/431-7258; ❻), where the food's excellent and the welcome very friendly, but make sure you book ahead if you want to stay – note that they close from Christmas until the end of January. Otherwise, you can enjoy a *día de campo* (day of farm activities, horse rides, lunch and tea) for $200 per person. The *finca* sits among superb parkland and the rooms are charming, and there is a small collection of archeological finds as an added attraction.

Another historic tobacco farm, *El Bordo de las Lanzas* (ⓦwww.estanciaelbordo .com; US$220 per person full board), at Rivadavia s/n near General Güemes, 80km northeast of Salta, can be reached via the RN-9 to Jujuy and then a side road that heads north from the village of Cobos; it is an early seventeenth-century house and maintains its colonial structures but with all modern conveniences – the furniture and artefacts come from Jesuit missions in the Northwest, Peru and Bolivia.

Commanding stunning mountain views through a huge picture window just outside the mountain village of Cachi (see p.336) is luxurious *Finca El Molino* (☎03868/491094 or 0387/421-9368; ❽). The very comfortable rooms are mostly located in a purpose-built annexe but the delicious meals are served in an aristocratic dining room. The small vineyards now produce remarkable high-altitude wines, made in the state-of-the-art bodega.

Finca Los Lapachos (☎0388/491-1291, ✉lapachos@jujuytel.com.ar; ❼ full board) sits along the RP-42 near the village of Perico, fairly close to Jujuy airport. It's definitely the place if you're looking for charm, luxury, peace and quiet and an authentic *finca* experience, with horseriding and a beautiful swimming pool. The Leach family, who call this place home, are extremely hospitable and related to the British settlers who set up the regional sugar industry; booking ahead is recommended.

Quebrada del Toro

Whether you travel up the magnificent **Quebrada del Toro** by train – along one of the highest railways in the world (see box, p.334) – in a tour operator's jeep, in a rented car or, as the pioneers did centuries ago, on horseback, the experience will be unforgettable, thanks to the gorge's constantly changing dramatic mountain scenery and multicoloured rocks. It is named after the **Río Toro**, normally a meandering trickle, but occasionally a raging torrent and as bullish as its name suggests, especially in the spring. The road and rail track swerve up from the tobacco fields of the Valle de Lerma, southwest of Salta, through dense thickets of ceibo, Argentina's national tree, ablaze in October and November with their fuchsia-red spring blossom. Both go past **Santa Rosa de Tastil**, with its two museums, and **Tastil**, with its pre-Colombian site, on to the dreary but strategic mining settlement of **San Antonio de los Cobres** (see below).

Many tour operators in Salta (see box, p.329) offer **tours by road**, some of which shadow the train for much of the way, offering passengers the chance to photograph the handsome locomotive and wave at it frantically, expecting passengers to reciprocate. Alternatively, operators such as Clark Expediciones (see box, p.329) can meet you off the train when it stops at Polvorilla Viaduct, and guide you around the altiplano in a jeep; you miss out on the return train journey and the folk show (a possible blessing) but get the best of both worlds – the train ride up in daylight plus a chance to explore the area more independently. MoviTrak runs the most popular jeep safari excursions up the Quebrada del Toro, often combined with a return leg down the Quebrada de Humahuaca (see box, p.329).

Santa Rosa de Tastil and Tastil

If you are travelling by road, the minute village of **Santa Rosa de Tastil** is worth a quick stop for its tiny **Museo del Sitio** (Tues–Fri 10am–6pm, Sat & Sun 10am–2pm; $2), set beneath the gorge's cactus-clad rocks. It contains a fine pre-Inca mummy and miscellaneous finds from nearby excavations, including arrowheads, plus some fine paintings of the region. A short distance away is the newer **Museo Regional Moisés Zerpa** (same times and entrance fee), furnished and decorated like a traditional local house, complete with cooking utensils, ceramics and textiles.

If you're lucky, the curator of both museums might also take you around the pre-Inca site, signposted 3km west, at **TASTIL** proper. The well-restored remains of one of the region's largest pre-Inca towns, it was inhabited by some three thousand people in the fourteenth century AD. The **mirador**, on once-fortified heights commanding fabulous valley and mountain views, overlooks the clearly terraced farmland from which the people of Tastil eked out a living.

San Antonio de los Cobres and around

A major regional crossroads at a dizzying 3775m above sea level, **SAN ANTONIO DE LOS COBRES** is the small, windswept "capital" of an immense but mostly empty portion of the altiplano, rich in minerals, as its name ("of the coppers") suggests, and little else, except some breathtaking **scenery**. The **Salinas Grandes**, to the north of San Antonio de los Cobres, are among the continent's biggest salt flats, a huge glistening expanse surrounded by brown mountains, snow-peaked volcanoes and sparse pasture.

Most people only ever see San Antonio de los Cobres from its train station – the Tren a las Nubes (when it is up and running) makes a short stop here on its way back down to the plains, during which the blue and white Argentine flag is hoisted and the national anthem played. You won't be missing much if you don't hop off: the town's low houses (many of them built by the borax and lithium mining firms for their workforce in a highly utilitarian style), dusty streets and lack of vegetation make for a rather forlorn little town, not especially inviting and displaying few signs of the wealth generated by the valuable metals running in rich veins through the nearby mountains. **Overnight stays** can be accommodated at the *Hostería de las Nubes*, at Caseros 441 (℡0387/490-9059; ◐); it's fairly basic but the plumbing and central heating work and **meals** are fine. Otherwise, there are a

The Train to the Clouds

Travelling through the Quebrada del Toro gorge on the Tren a las Nubes, or **Train to the Clouds**, is an unashamedly touristic experience. Having been out of service on and off for a while, the train began seriously again in 2009, run by a consortium of three local companies.

Clambering from the station in Salta (it never exceeds 35 km/hr) to the magnificent Meccano-like **La Polvorilla Viaduct**, high in the altiplano, the smart train – with a leather-upholstered interior, shiny wooden fittings, spacious seats, a dining car, a post office and even altitude-sickness remedies – was originally built to service the borax mines in the salt flats of Pocitos and Arizaro, 300km beyond La Polvorilla. The viaduct lies 219km from Salta, and on the way the train crosses **29 bridges** and **twelve viaducts**, threads through **21 tunnels**, swoops round two gigantic **360° loops** and chugs up **two switchbacks**. La Polvorilla, seen on many posters and in all the tour operators' brochures, is 224m long, 64m high and weighs over 1600 tonnes; built in Italy, it was assembled here in 1930. The highest point of the whole line, just 13km west of the viaduct, is at Abra Chorrillos (4475m). Brief stopovers near La Polvorilla, where the train doubles back, and in San Antonio de los Cobres, allow you to stretch your legs and meet some locals, keen on selling you llama-wool scarves and posing for photos (for a fee). Folk groups and solo artists interspersed with people selling arts, crafts, cheese, honey and souvenirs galore help while the time away on the way down, when it's dark for the most part.

The train leaves (and returns to) Salta's Ferrocarril Belgrano station several times a week during Holy Week and in July and August, with a less frequent service from March to June and from September to November. **Tickets** cost US$120–140 and should be reserved in advance at Ⓦwww.trenalasnubes.com.ar. The **Ferrocarril Belgrano** station in Salta is at Ameghino 690, ten blocks north of the central Plaza 9 de Julio, and can be reached by buses #5 and #13 from downtown, the bus terminal and the campsite.

number of places that cannot really be recommended. The police next to the train station can give you news about the state of the road and any weather hazards.

El Quebracho runs a twice-daily **bus service** between Salta and San Antonio; there are also services onwards to San Pedro de Atacama (Chile) via the Paso de Jama.

Salinas Grandes

Northwards from San Antonio de los Cobres, the re-routed RN-40 starts its final, partly surfaced, run towards the northernmost reaches of Argentina, and the border settlement of Ciénaga, more than 200km away. The RP-75 branches off 21km from San Antonio, eventually leading to Abra Pampa via Casabindo (see p.354) – 130km north – over very difficult terrain but through eerily dramatic altiplano scenery, well worth exploring if you have plenty of time (and fuel supplies), while the main RN-40 route veers northwest to Susques (see p.348). Where it crosses into Jujuy Province, 60km further on, you're treated to views of the snow-peaked Nevado de Chañi (6200m), an extinct volcanic cone poking above the brown slopes of the stark range where the Río Toro has its thaw-fed source, in the east. To the north stretches the glistening expanse of the aptly named **Salinas Grandes** (also accessible from Purmamarca, Jujuy Province, via the fabulous Cuesta de Lipán; see p.347) one of the country's biggest salt flats and certainly the most impressive, ringed by mountains on all sides and beneath almost perennial blue skies. This huge rink of snow-white crystals, forming irregular octagons, each surrounded by crunchy ridges, crackling like frozen snow under foot, acts as a huge mirror. The salt, shimmering in the nearly perpetual blazing sunshine, often creates cruel water mirages, though there are in fact some isolated pools of brine where small groups of flamingoes and ducks gather. This is a likely place for spotting vicuñas and llamas, too, flocks of which often leap across the road to reach their scrawny, yellow pastureland, or *tola*, on either side of the RN-40.

Valles Calchaquíes

Named after the Río Calchaquí, which has its source in the Nevado de Acay (at over 5000m) near San Antonio de los Cobres, in the north of Salta Province, and joins the Río de las Conchas, near Salta's border with Tucumán, the **Valles Calchaquíes** are a series of beautiful highland valleys that enjoy over three hundred days of sunshine a year, a dry climate and much cooler summers than the lowland plains around Salta. The fertile land, irrigated with canals and ditches that capture the plentiful snowmelt from the high mountains to the west, is mostly given over to vineyards – among the world's highest – that produce the characteristic torrontés grape. The scenery is extremely varied and of an awesome beauty, constantly changing as you make your way along winding mountainside roads. Organized tours from Salta squeeze a visit into one day, stopping at the valleys' main settlement, the airy village of **Cafayate**, for lunch. However, by far the most rewarding way to see the Valles Calchaquíes is under your own steam, by climbing the amazing **Cuesta del Obispo** (go in the morning before clouds hide the views), through the **Parque Nacional Los Cardones**, a protected forest of gigantic *cardón* cacti, to the picturesque village of **Cachi**; then follow the valley south through some memorable scenery via **Molinos** and **San Carlos**, on to **Cafayate**, where plentiful accommodation facilitates a stopover. The scenic road back down to Salta through the **Quebrada de Cafayate**, or Cuesta de las Conchas, snakes past some incredible rock formations, optimally seen in the late afternoon or early evening light. All along the valleys, you'll see typical *casas de galería*: long, single-storey houses, some with a colonnade of rounded arches, others decorated with pointed ogival arches or straight pillars.

Regular **public transport** to Salta and Tucumán makes travelling around the valleys straightforward even without your own vehicle, though it is less frequent in the northern reaches around Cachi. **Organized tours** from Salta are your best bet if you have no transport of your own and don't have time to wait for buses.

Up to Cachi

The northern Calchaquí settlement of Cachi sits 170km southwest of Salta: to get there you go along the partly sealed RP-33, a scenic road that squeezes through the dank Quebrada de Escoipe, before climbing the dramatic mountain road known as the **Cuesta del Obispo**, 20km of hairpin bends, offering views of the rippling Sierra del Obispo. These fabulously beautiful mountains, blanketed in olive-green vegetation and heavily eroded by countless brooks, are at their best in the morning light; in summer, cloud and rain descends in the afternoon and evening storms can make the road impassable. A good place to stop before negotiating the steep, meandering climb is the rudimentary *Hostería El Maray*, where you can have a delicious snack, tea or coffee. About 60km from Chicoana, just before you reach the top of the *cuesta*, a signposted track leads south down to the **Valle Encantado**, 4km away; this is a fertile little valley, set around a marshy lagoon, that becomes a riot of colour in September and October, when millions of wild flowers burst into bloom, but it makes for a rewarding detour all year round; its cool temperatures and delightfully pastoral scenery make it a good place for a short rest, especially if you're driving. Foxes, vizcachas and other small animals are often spotted here. Back on the main road, 1km further on, is the **Abra Piedra del Molino**, a narrow mountain pass at 3347m, marked by the mysterious "millstone" that gives the pass its name; nobody knows how this perfectly circular stone got here, but the idea that it is a discarded millstone is probably apocryphal.

Some 20km west of the Abra Piedra del Molino, where the road forks to the left – an uninteresting shortcut to Seclantás and the RN-40 – the RP-33 continues straight northwards, cutting through the **Parque Nacional Los Cardones**, an official reserve recently set up to protect the forest of *cardón* cacti that covers the dusty valley and creeps up the arid mountainside, mingled with the parasol-like *churquis* and other spiny trees typical of desert regions; there's no *guardería* and you can wander as you like among the gigantic cacti, many of them more than five metres tall. *Cardones* grow painfully slowly, less than a couple of millimetres a year, and their wood has been excessively exploited for making furniture and crafts and for firewood; it's now protected, so don't remove any specimens. Part of this road, known as the **Recta Tin-Tin**, 10km of straight-as-a-die roller-coaster track, is well known for its optical illusion – the lie of the valley makes it look as though you're climbing when in fact you're going down (heading in this direction that is). At the tiny village of **Payogasta**, where the RP-33 joins the RN-40, you have a choice of roads. You can either head north to explore the furthest reaches of the Valles Calchaquíes, with dramatic high mountains on either side and beguiling desert-like scenery accompanying you all along the rough track to La Poma, 40km north; or, especially if time is short or night is drawing in, you can head straight south for **Cachi**.

The picturesque village of **CACHI**, 2280m above sea level, is overshadowed by the permanently snowcapped **Nevado del Cachi** (6380m), whose peak looms only 15km to the west. The village is centred around the delightful Plaza Mayor, shaded by palms and orange trees. On the north side of the plaza stands the much-restored **Iglesia San José**, with its plain white facade, fine wooden floor and unusual cactus-wood altar, pews and confessionals. On the east side, in a Neocolonial house around an attractive whitewashed patio, is the **Museo Arqueológico Pío Pablo Díaz** (Mon–Sat 8.30am–6.30pm, Sun 10am–1pm; $2), displaying a run-of-the-mill collection of locally excavated items. Apart from that, there's little in the way of sights in Cachi; it's simply a place to wander, investigating the various local crafts, including ponchos and ceramics, or climbing to the **cemetery** for wonderful mountain views and a panorama of the pea-green valley, every arable patch of which is filled with vines, maize and capsicum plantations. Further afield, the scenic tracks to **Cachi Adentro** and **La Aguada**, each 6km west of the village, lead from the end of Calle Benjamín Zorrilla and take you through fertile farmland where, in late summer (March–May), the fields are carpeted with drying paprika peppers, a dazzling display of bright red that features in many postcards on sale in the region.

Practicalities

Buses from Salta (and local buses from various villages) arrive very close to the main plaza, where there is a helpful **information office** in the municipalidad (Mon–Fri 8am–9pm, Sat & Sun 9am–3pm & 5–9pm; ℡03868/491053, @www .cachionline.com.ar); the staff should be able to find you guides to take you up into the surrounding mountains.

In a converted convent, *La Merced del Alto* (℡03868/490030, @www .lamerceddelalto.com; ⑥) is Cachi's most comfortable **accommodation**; set in lush gardens with a pool and a spa, it enjoys outstanding views of the surrounding countryside, and has a very decent bar and restaurant serving top-notch breakfasts. A distant second is hill-top *Hostería ACA Sol del Valle*, nearer the village proper at Avenida del Automóvil Club Argentino s/n (℡03868/491105, Ⓦwww.soldelvalle.com.ar; ❼); it has a swimming pool with a view and a passable restaurant. Nearby *Hostal El Cortijo* (℡03868/491034, Ⓦwww.elcortijohotel.com; ❻), in a colonial house at the bottom of the hill, is incredibly good value, with its unusual native-style decor combined with sophisticated Neocolonial furnishings and very attentive service. Welcoming *Hotel Llaqta Mawka* (℡03868/491016, Ⓔhostal_llaqta_mawka@hotmail .com; ❹), at Ruíz de los Lanos s/n, has made a concerted effort to respect local building and decoration customs and techniques and offers interesting tours of the immediate region. *Hospedaje Nevado de Cachi*, also on Ruíz de los Llanos (℡03868/491004; ❷), is a good budget place to stay, with basic rooms and curious cactus-wood furniture but erratic hot water.

A reliable **place to eat** is the basic *El Jagüel*, on Avenida General Güemes (℡03868/491135), which serves memorable *locro* and empanadas. *Luna Cautiva* in Pasaje Borja, at the corner of Suárez, and the *Confitería del Sol*, on the main square at Ruíz de los Llanos s/n, are more upmarket, with more atmosphere and serve a range of classic Argentine dishes and local specialities such as goat. For real espresso coffee and all manner of snacks, charming little *Oliver*, on the main square just along from the *Confitería del Sol*, has no rivals.

From Cachi to Cafayate

The mostly unsealed RN-40 from Cachi to Cafayate takes you along some stupendous corniche roads that wind alongside the Río Calchaquí itself, offering views on either side of sheer mountainsides and snowcapped peaks. It's only 180km from one town to the other, but allow plenty of time as the narrow track slows your progress and you'll want to stop to admire the views, take photographs and visit the picturesque valley settlements en route, oases of greenery in an otherwise stark landscape. **Molinos**, 60km south of Cachi, lies a couple of kilometres west of the main road, in a bend of the Río Molinos, and is worth the side-trip for a peek at its lovely adobe houses and the eighteenth-century **Iglesia de San Pedro Nolasco**, currently undergoing restoration; the expansive facade, topped with two sturdy turrets, is shored up with props. Opposite, in the refurbished Finca Isasmendi, the eighteenth-century residence of Nicolás Severo de Isasmendi, the last royalist governor of Salta, is the beautiful *Hacienda de Molinos* (℡03868/494094, Ⓦwww.haciendademolinos.com.ar; ❼–❽), a rural inn with eighteen enchanting rooms, some with four-poster beds, set around a marvellous patio.

Just beyond tiny Angastaco, the already impressive scenery becomes even more spectacular: after 10km you enter the surreal **Quebrada de las Flechas**, where the red sandstone cliffs form a backdrop for the flinty arrowhead-like formations on either side of the road that give the gorge its name. For 10km, weird rocks like desert roses dot the landscape and, beyond the natural stone walls of **El Cañón**, over 20m high, the road squeezes through **El Ventisquero**, the "wind tunnel".

The oldest settlement in the valley, dating from 1551, is picturesque **San Carlos**, 35km further, straddling the RN-40; it's a wine-growing village and the several bodegas welcome visitors at all times, but do not provide proper guided visits. The nineteenth-century **Iglesia San Carlos Borromeo** has interior walls decorated with naive **frescoes** depicting the life of St Charles Borromeo himself. The last stretch of the road to Cafayate threads its way through extensive **vineyards**, affording views of the staggeringly high mountains – many of them over 4000m – to the west and east.

5

The Cafayate vineyards

While Mendoza and, increasingly, San Juan are the names most associated with wines from Argentina, supermarkets and wine shops around the world are selling more and more bottles with the name **Cafayate** on their labels. These **vineyards**, which are some of the highest in the world, at around 1700m, are planted with the malbec and cabernet varieties for which Mendoza is justly famous, but the local speciality is a grape thought to have been brought across from Galicia: the torrontés. The delicate, flowery white wine it produces, with a slight acidity, is the perfect accompaniment for the regional cuisine, but also goes well with fish and seafood. You can try some excellent samples and see how the wine is made at one of the many bodegas in and around Cafayate, where tastings and wine sales round off each tour (Spanish only). Bodegas Domingo Hermanos, Etchart, La Banda, Don David and Finca Las Nubes open their doors every weekday and sometimes at weekends too (daily usually 9am–1pm & 3–7pm).

Cafayate

The sprawling village of **CAFAYATE** is nearly 190km south of Salta, via the RN-68 at its junction with the RN-40; the latter is called Avenida Güemes within the village limits, the Río Chuschas in the north and the Río Loro Huasi in the south. The self-appointed capital of the Valles Calchaquíes and the main settlement hereabouts, it's also the centre of the province's wine industry and the main tourist base for the valleys, thanks to its plentiful, high-quality accommodation, and convenient location at a crossroads between Salta, Cachi and Amaicha (see p.365). Though not that big, it's nonetheless a lively, modern place, originally founded by Franciscan missionaries who set up *encomiendas*, or Indian reservations with farms attached, in the region. However, apart from exploring the surroundings on foot, by bike or on horseback, or tasting wine at the bodegas (see box above), there's not actually a lot to do here. The late nineteenth-century **Iglesia Catedral de Nuestra Señora del Rosario** dominates the main plaza but is disappointingly nondescript inside, while the **Museo de Arqueología Calchaquí**, one block southwest, at Calchaquí and Colón (Mon–Fri 11.30am–9pm, Sat 11.30am–3pm; free), comprises one room piled with **ceramics** of the Candelaria and Santamaría cultures, including some massive urns, followed by another room cluttered with *criollo* antiques and curios. Two blocks south of the plaza, at avenidas Güemes and Chacabuco, is the feeble **Museo de la Vid y del Vino** (daily 8am–8pm; $2), a motley collection of wine-related relics and photographs, in a defunct winery. About 2km south, on the RN-40 to Santa María, you'll find the workshop and salesroom of one of the region's finest artisans, Oscar Hipaucha. He sells wonderfully intricate wood and metal boxes, made of *quebracho*, *algarrobo* and copper, at justifiably high prices. Way up to the north of the town, the Cristofani ceramic workshop makes elegant urns but most tend to be too big to make practical souvenirs.

Arrival and information

Frequent **buses** from Salta and less frequent ones from Cachi, via Molinos, plus daily services from Tucumán via Amaicha (see p.365) arrive at the cramped terminus just along Belgrano, half a block east of the plaza, or sometimes deposit passengers wherever they want to get off in the village. A kiosk (daily 8am–9pm) on the plaza dispenses **information** about where to stay, what to do and where to rent bikes or hire horses.

▲ Vineyard, Cafayate

Accommodation

You'll have little trouble finding a room except during the popular, but not very exciting, **folk festival**, the Serenata Cafayateña, held on the first weekend of Lent. The range extends from the humblest *residencial* to a couple of truly memorable establishments. Be warned that there have been reports of theft and other unpleasant experiences at a number of places in the village – to our knowledge there have been none concerning our recommendations.

Casa de la Bodega RN-68 Km18.5
℡ 03868/421555, Ⓦ www.casadelabodega.com.ar.
Off the road to San Carlos that branches off the Quebrada road (RN-68), but only 15min from Cafayate, this sumptuous wine boutique hotel has only eight rooms, some of which are giant suites; the decor, comfort, service and, of course, the wine are all top-notch. ❽

El Hospedaje Camila Quintana de Niño and Salta
℡ 03868/421680, Ⓔ elhospedaje@nortevirtual
.com. Great little *hospedaje* that boasts a swimming pool in its grounds – a charming Neocolonial house, with comfortable rooms. If you are looking for somewhere even less costly, ask about their *Colonial* annexe where a dorm bed costs $50. ❸

Hospedaje El Portal de las Viñas Nuestra Señora del Rosario 165 ℡ 03868/421098. Traditional *hospedaje* just off the main square – large rooms sleeping up to four, with en-suite bathrooms. ❹

Hostal del Valle San Martín 243
℡ 03868/421039, Ⓔ hostaldelvalle@nortevirtual
.com. Wonderful family-run B&B in an impeccably clean house. Rooms are comfortable but the highlight is a top-floor conservatory set aside for reading, listening to music and admiring the

all-round views. Home-made jams served at breakfast. ❸–❹

Hostel Ruta 40 Av Güemes 178 ℡ 03868/421689,
Ⓦ www.hostel-ruta40.com. Look for the handsome yellow front just a block south of the main plaza. This is the best hostel in Cafayate, without a doubt – dorm beds go for just $60 and there are some decent doubles (❸) too.

Hotel Asturias Av Güemes 154 ℡ 03868/421328,
Ⓔ asturias@infonoa.com.ar. This centrally located hotel with a northern Spanish facade has a swimming pool, a reliable restaurant and tasteful rooms decorated with beautiful photographs of the region. ❻–❽

🏃 **Hotel Killa** Colón 47 ℡ 03868/422254,
Ⓦ www.killacafayate.com.ar. Only a block from the central plaza, this splendid hotel is charming, comfortable and incredibly classy – it successfully combines Neocolonial elegance with rustic cosiness; some of the upstairs rooms have dream-like views of the surrounding mountains. There is a fair-sized pool. ❻–❽

🏃 **Hotel Los Patios de Cafayate** RN-40 and RN-68 ℡ 03868/421747, Ⓦ www
.starwoodhotels.com. Handwoven carpets,

chandeliers, colonial tapestries, native textiles and local arts and crafts all give this beautiful Sheraton-group hotel a feeling of luxury. This is enhanced by the beautiful swimming pool and the fabulous spa, housed in a modern annexe and offering wine and grape massages. The rooms will make you feel like a local aristocrat for a day. ⑨

Hotel Portal del Santo Silverio Chavarría 250 ☎03868/422500, ⓦwww.portaldelsanto.com.ar. New hotel built in a Neocolonial style – note the arched galleries. The handsome rooms are well equipped, with mini-bars and cable TV, while breakfasts are delicious and generous, using

home-made products. There's a swimming pool with jacuzzi. ⑥

Hotel Los Sauces Calchaquí 62 ☎03868/421158, ⓔlossauces@arnet.com.ar. A pleasant, modern hotel, only a couple of blocks from the central plaza, with attractively decorated rooms looking onto a garden – avoid those facing the noisy street – and a bright *confitería* where a copious breakfast is served. ⑦

Hotel Villa Vicuña Belgrano 76 ☎03868/422145. Picturesque, slightly quirky hotel in a mustard-yellow Neocolonial house right next to the bus terminal. The rooms are delightful, as is the central patio where you can have breakfast or tea, weather permitting. ⑥–⑦

Eating and drinking

The choice of **eating** establishments is more limited than for lodging. Reliable – and popular, so grab tables while you can – El Rancho, at Güemes and Toscano, on the southern flank of the main plaza, specializes in regional cooking, as does the much frequented and well-priced *Carreta de Don Olegario* on the east side. *Baco* at Avenida Güemes (N), at the corner of Rivadavia, is a pleasant bistro-style joint serving good traditional food. The ice creams at *Heladería Miranda*, on Avenida Güemes half a block north of the plaza, are outstanding: try the wine sorbets, both the cabernet and torrontés.

Quebrada de Cafayate

The RN-68 forks off the RN-40 only 2km north of Cafayate, north of the Río Chuschas, before heading across fertile land, some of it given over to vineyards. It soon begins its winding descent, following the Río de las Conchas through the **QUEBRADA DE CAFAYATE** north to the Valle de Lerma and onwards to Salta. The gorge is seen at its best on the way down, in the mellow late afternoon or early evening light; organized tours aim to take you down this way and you should follow suit if travelling under your own steam. Leave plenty of time, as once in the gorge you'll be tempted to make several stops, to admire the views and take pictures. At the northernmost part of the gorge you enter an invariably windy stretch, where you're better off inside your vehicle unless you want to be sandblasted. One positive result of frequent sandstorms, though, is the formation of wonderful sand dunes, **Los Médanos**, like gigantic piles of sawdust by the road. This is where the canyon proper begins, and the road snakes its way down alongside the riverbed. The majestic Sierras de Carahuasi – the northernmost range of the Cumbres Calchaquíes – loom behind as a magnificent backdrop, while in the foreground rock formations have been eroded and blasted by wind and rain to form buttresses, known as **Los Castillos**, or "the castles", and a huge monolith dubbed **El Obelisco**. The reds, ochres and pinks of the sandstone make it all look staggeringly beautiful. Further on, **La Yesera**, or "chalk quarry", is actually a strange group of eerily grey and yellow rocks exposed by millions of years of erosion, while a monk-like figure, skulking in the cliff-side, has earned the name **El Fraile**. Just off the road, about 50km from Cafayate, two semicircular ravines carved in the mountainside are called **La Garganta del Diablo** (Devil's Throat) and **El Anfiteatro**, while the animal-like figure nearby is **El Sapo** (Toad). Still passing through delightful scenery, you leave the stupendous canyon, spiked with cacti, behind you to enter the forested valley bottom. Halfway between Cafayate and Salta, a convenient stopoff is provided by the excellent 🖈 *Posta de Las Cabras*, where in addition to the goat's cheese suggested by its name, you can sample all kinds of local delicacies, buy fine crafts, or just have a cup of coffee. From La Viña, 100km northeast of Cafayate and just south of Embalse Cabra Corral, the enormous reservoir serving Salta, it's another 90km or so to the city, along the relatively busy RN-68.

San Salvador de Jujuy

Just over 90km north of Salta by the direct and scenic but rather slow RN-9, **SAN SALVADOR DE JUJUY** – Jujuy for short – is a tranquil place and, at 1260m above sea level, enjoys an enviably temperate climate. It is the capital of the federation's most remote mainland province, a small but intensely beautiful patch of land, ostensibly having more in common with next-door Chile and Bolivia than with the rest of Argentina, and little with Buenos Aires, nearly 1600km away. Dramatically situated, Jujuy lies in a fertile natural bowl, with the spectacular multicoloured gorge of the **Quebrada de Humahuaca** (see p.345), a major reason for heading in this direction, immediately north. The Cerro de Claros (1704m) and Cerro Chuquina (1987m) loom just to the southeast and southwest, and the city is wedged between two rivers, the Río Grande and Río Chico or Xibi Xibi, both bone dry for most of the year. In *The Old Patagonian Express* (1978), Paul Theroux wrote that Jujuy "looked peaceful and damp; just high enough to be pleasant without giving one a case of the bends; it was green, a town buried, so it seemed, in lush depthless spinach". The riverbeds, overgrown with lush vegetation though certainly not spinach, only add to the rather abandoned appearance, while the city's outskirts spill along the riversides, sometimes in the form of shantytowns.

Despite, or perhaps because of, its location, Jujuy lacks the buzz of Salta and Tucumán, and good hotels are few and far between. Scratch the lacklustre surface, though, and you'll unearth some real treasures, among them one of the finest pieces of sacred art to be seen in Argentina, the **pulpit** in the **cathedral** – and the interior of **Iglesia San Francisco** is almost as impressive. A day or two in this slightly strange "world's end" kind of place will probably suffice; you'll soon want to start exploring the rich hinterland, its polychrome gorges and typical altiplano villages of adobe houses. Jujuy is also the ideal springboard for visiting the most accessible of the three cloudforest national parks, **Calilegua** (see p.357), as well as the less accessible and utterly remote **Baritú** (see p.359).

Some history

Jujuy was founded, after a couple of early false starts thwarted by attacks by indigenous peoples, on April 19, 1593. Earthquakes, the plague and further sackings, culminating in the Calchaquí Wars, all conspired to hamper the city's growth during the seventeenth and eighteenth centuries and have deprived it of any of its original buildings. Even after the famous **Jujuy Exodus** ordered by General Belgrano at the height of the Wars of Independence – on August 23, 1812, he ordered the whole of the city's population to evacuate the city, which was then razed to the ground to prevent its capture by the royalist commander – Jujuy continued to bear the brunt of conflict, sacked by the royalists in 1814 and 1818. It then remained a forgotten backwater throughout the nineteenth century, and the railway did not reach it until 1903. Since the 1930s, its outskirts have spilt across both rivers and begun to creep up the hillsides, and it now has a sizeable immigrant population, mostly from across the Bolivian border to the north. The

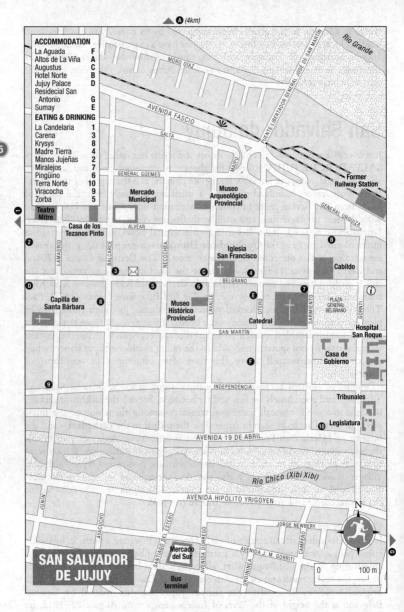

province – and therefore the city, which lives off the province's agricultural production – have traditionally grown rich on sugar and tobacco, with a little copper and lead mining thrown in, but earnings from all these products have declined in recent years and forced farmers to diversify into other crops, including fruit and vegetables. Tourism may be the solution for the city's economic woes but so far has been exploited only half-heartedly, with very little state assistance.

Arrival and information

Jujuy's **airport**, Dr Horacio Guzmán (℡0388/491-1109), is over 30km southeast of the city, along the RN-66 near Perico. TEA Turismo (℡0388/423-6270 or 156-857913) runs a shuttle service to and from the city centre for $20, while the **taxi** fare is around $60. The rudimentary **bus terminal**, at Iguazú and Avenida Dorrego (℡0388/422-6299), just south of the centre, across the Río Chico, serves all local, regional and national destinations, and also runs a service to Chile. There's a **left-luggage** facility at the terminal. For basic **tourist information**, head for the Dirección Provincial de Turismo (Mon–Fri 7am–9pm, Sat & Sun 8am–8pm; ℡0388/422-8153, ℗www.turismo.jujuy.gov.ar), at the northeastern corner of central Plaza General Belgrano.

Accommodation

Apart from two excellent **campsites** near the city – *Los Vertientes* (℡0388/498-0030) and *El Carmen* (℡0388/493-3117) – Jujuy's limited but decent accommodation covers the range from squalid *residenciales*, best avoided, to a couple of top-notch **hotels**. In between are one or two decent hotels and a few inexpensive *pensiones*. Some 25km outside the city, but conveniently close to the airport, is an outstanding **finca**, or ranch, *Finca Los Lapachos* (see box, p.332).

La Aguada Otero 170 ℡0388/423-2034. Wonderful B&B with large, stylish rooms and lots of attention to detail – the owner is an architect. The family is a mine of information about Jujuy and its surroundings. **⑤**

Hotel Altos de la Viña Pasquini López, La Viña ℡0388/426-1666, ℗www.hotelaltosdelavina .com.ar. On the heights of La Viña, 4km northeast of the city centre, this successfully refurbished hotel, with large, comfortable rooms and a shady garden, commands fabulous views of the valley and mountains. Shuttle service to and from downtown. **⑦**

Hotel Augustus Belgrano 715 ℡0388/423-0203, ℗www.hotelaugustus.com.ar. Extremely friendly place, with clean rooms, spacious bathrooms and good breakfasts. Snack bar serves delicious sandwiches and *lomitos*. **⑤**

Hotel Jujuy Palace Belgrano 1060 ℡0388/423-0433. One of the two top-range hotels actually in central Jujuy, this one has the edge in terms of stylish decor and charm. Professionally run, with a pleasant restaurant. **⑥**

Hotel Norte Alvear 444 ℡0388/424-0903. Boutique hotel in a converted *pension*: eight sumptuous rooms, with crisp linens and great bathrooms (the executive suites have a jacuzzi), around a fabulous Neocolonial patio; wonderful restaurant, too. **⑦**

Hotel Sumay Otero 232 ℡0388/423-5065. By far the nicest lower-range hotel, it's roomy, comfortable, and very popular, so book ahead. Can be noisy. **③**

Residencial San Antonio Lisandro de la Torre 993 ℡0388/422-5998. Small, modern and very close to the bus terminal – the only non-squalid place in the vicinity. **②**

The City

Jujuy is the most Andean of all Argentina's cities: much of its population is descended from indigenous stock, mostly mestizos, with a considerable influx of Bolivian immigrants in the last couple of decades. It's not a conventionally beautiful city, but the central streets have a certain atmosphere – near the market, women in bright shawls with their babies strapped to their backs huddle in groups and whisper in Quichoa. Most of the city's main sights are near **Plaza General Belgrano**, at the eastern extremity of the compact microcentro. Planted with orange trees, it was the colonial settlement's central square or Plaza Mayor and is still the city's hub, partly occupied by craftsmen, mainly potters, displaying their wares.

Casa de Gobierno

Plaza General Belgrano is dominated to the south by the **Casa de Gobierno** (Mon–Fri 9am–noon & 4–8pm; free) with its extremely Gallic-looking slate mansard roof, where the national flag donated to the city by General Belgrano, as a tribute to the Exodus, is proudly guarded. In the grounds of the government house, dotted around the building, stand five large **statues** by renowned sculptress **Lola Mora** (see box, p.287). Representing Peace, Progress, Justice, Freedom and Labour, the set was originally designed for the Congreso Nacional in Buenos Aires, inaugurated in 1906, but the reactionary federal government vetoed the project and had the statues dumped in a store room. Luckily Jujuy's government at that time was less intransigent and in 1915 it appointed Lola Mora as the city's director of parks and squares, in order to erect the statues in their present position.

The cathedral

On the west side of the plaza stands Jujuy's late eighteenth-century **cathedral** (Mon–Fri 7.30am–1pm & 5–9pm, Sat & Sun 8am–noon & 5–9pm), topped by an early twentieth-century tower and extended by an even later Neoclassical atrium. The exterior is unremarkable, but the interior, a layer of painted Bakelite concealing the original timber structure, is impressively naive: a realistic mock-fresco of sky and clouds soars over the altar, while above the nave is a primitive depiction of the ceremony in which Belgrano awarded the Argentine flag to the people of Jujuy. Two original doors and two confessionals, Baroque masterpieces from the eighteenth century, immediately catch the eye, thanks to their vivid red and sienna paint, picked out with gilt, but the undisputed highlight – and the main attraction of the whole city – is the magnificent **pulpit**. Decorated in the eighteenth century by local artists, it easily rivals those of **Cusco**, its apparent inspiration, with its harmonious compositions, elegant floral and vegetable motifs and the finesse of its carvings. Its various tableaux in gilded, carved wood, gleaming with an age-old patina, depict subjects such as Jacob's ladder and St Augustine along with biblical genealogies from Adam to Abraham and David to Solomon. One curiosity is the error in the symbols of the four **apostles**: Matthew and John are correctly represented by a human figure and an eagle respectively, but Mark, symbolized by a bull, and Luke, by a lion, are the wrong way round.

Iglesia San Francisco

Not of quite the same calibre as the cathedral's, but very striking nonetheless, is the Spanish Baroque **pulpit** in **Iglesia San Francisco**, two blocks west of the plaza at Belgrano and Lavalle; also inspired by the pulpits of Cusco and almost certainly carved by craftsmen in eighteenth-century Bolivia, it drips with detail, with a profusion of little Franciscan monks peeking out from row upon row of tiny columns, all delicately gilded. Although the church and separate campanile are built to the traditional colonial Franciscan design, in a Neo-Baroque style, the church was built in the 1930s.

Eating, drinking and nightlife

Jujuy is no gastronomic paradise but its **restaurants** will give you more than enough variety between local specialities and *parrilladas*. Apart from a couple of snazzy **bars**, sometimes hosting musicians, the nightlife is confined to a couple of out-of-town **discos** and the beautiful Italian-style theatre and opera house, **Teatro Mitre**, at Alvear 1009 (℡0388/442-2782). Its gleaming white exterior and plush interior are the result of recent refurbishment; plays and classical concerts are regularly staged here, and are often of a high standard.

La Candelaria Alvear 1346. This very stylish *parrilla*, ten blocks or so out to the west of the city, offers you mountains of meat until you burst. Heavenly desserts, too.

Carena Balcarce and Belgrano. Mellow *confitería*, serving snacks and acting as a community centre – concerts, seminars and group meetings are held here.

Krysys Balcarce 272. Trout is the speciality on an otherwise not very inventive meat-dominated menu, but the service is impeccable.

🏃 Madre Tierra Belgrano 619. Delightful, airy vegetarian lunch-only spot with an unbeatably low-priced menu. Even if you're not a vegetarian, though, you'll find the fresh salads, meatless empanadas and delicious fruit juices a great change from the meat overdose, and you can stock up on all manner of goodies for a picnic. Closed Sun.

🏃 Manos Jujeñas Senador Pérez 379. Absolutely fabulous Northwestern food, including memorable *locro* and delicious empanadas, accompanied by jugs of honest wine and, from time to time, by live folk music. Incredibly friendly service too. Closed Sun lunch & Mon eve.

Miralejos Sarmiento 268. Classic Northwestern gastronomy at its best in this popular place, with a few tables out on the plaza.

Pingüino Belgrano 718. This is Jujuy's finest *heladería*, scooping out delicious ice cream by the bucketful; every flavour imaginable.

Terra Norte 19 de Abril 475. Specializing in trout from nearby Yala – considered the best in the region – this smart restaurant also acts as a *confitería*; try the trout ravioli.

🏃 Viracocha Independencia and Lamadrid. Unusual dishes like llama in dark beer sauce, or smoked llama ravioli, plus delicious classic Andean fare – lots of quinoa and native potatoes – make this one of the top eateries in Jujuy.

Zorba Belgrano and Necochea. Reasonably priced Greek food – feta salads, moussaka, *pastitsio* and stuffed vine leaves – along with Argentine favourites and delicious sandwiches in a bright, modern venue with a real buzz that would not look out of place in Kolonaki.

Listings

Airlines Aerolíneas Argentinas, at the airport ☎0388/422-1373, and at Belgrano 1053 ☎0388/422-2575; LAB, Güemes 779 ☎0388/423-0699.

Banks and exchanges Quilmes, Belgrano 902; for exchange and travellers' cheques: Masventas, Balcarce 223 (Mon–Fri 8am–1.30pm & 5–8pm). Several ATMs dotted around.

Consulate Bolivia (the most helpful in the Northwest), Av Senador Pérez and Independencia.

Internet access Telecentro, Güemes and La Madrid.

Laundry Laverap, Belgrano 1214.

Post office Belgrano, between Necochea and Balcarce.

Telephones Telecom, Belgrano and Lavalle.

Tour operators TEA, Belgrano 775 ☎0388/423-6270. Well-run tours into Quebrada de Humahuaca and Puna Jujeña, plus smaller circuits near the city.

Quebrada de Humahuaca

Although the intense beauty of the **Quebrada de Humahuaca** gorge features so often in tourist literature, posters and coffee-table books that some of the surprise element is taken away, a trip along it is nonetheless an unforgettable and moving experience. Stunning, varied scenery is on display all the way up from the valley bottom, just northwest of San Salvador de Jujuy, to the namesake town of **Humahuaca**, 125km north of the provincial capital. Here, in addition to some decent accommodation and a monument or two, you will also find an outstanding cultural centre that includes a surprisingly good cinema. While most day-trips along the gorge from Jujuy (and Salta) take you up and down by the same route, the RN-9, you're actually treated to two spectacles: you'll have your attention fixed on the western side in the morning, and on the eastern flank in the afternoon, when the sun lights up each side respectively and picks out the amazing geological features: polychrome strata, buttes and mesas, pinnacles and eroded crags. What's more, the two sides are quite different, the western mountains rising steeply, often striped with vivid colours, while the slightly lower, rounded range to the east is for the most part gentler, more mellow, but just as colourful.

Most (day) tours organized out of Jujuy and Salta only go as far as Humahuaca and then head back, but this still gets you two tracking-shot views of multicoloured mountains, the highlight of which is the photogenic **Cerro de los Siete Colores**, overhanging the picturesque village of **Purmamarca**. From Purmamarca a dramatic side road leads across splendid altiplano landscapes, via pretty little **Susques**, to the Chilean border at the Paso de Jama, high in the Andes. Purmamarca has enough accommodation options to make it a possible stopover, especially if you are forging on towards Chile, but most of the lodgings are on the expensive side. Further up the gorge, just outside the village of **Maimará** and overlooked by oyster-shaped rock formations in the mountainside, is one of the region's most photographed cemeteries. Two-thirds of the way to Humahuaca, the small town of **Tilcara** is worth lingering in, if only for its beautiful pre-Inca fortress, or *pukará*; Tilcara boasts the best range of lodgings and eateries in the whole area, plus an interesting archeological museum. Between Tilcara and Humahuaca, in the little village of **Uquía** is one of the finest churches along the gorge; in these parts the typical chapel design is utterly simple, a plain whitewashed facade, sometimes embellished with an arch, and a single squat tower, usually acting as a campanile; many retain their straw roofs.

Beyond Humahuaca, the RN-9 crosses bleak but stunningly beautiful altiplano landscapes all the way up to La Quiaca on the Bolivian border, nearly 2000m higher yet only 150km further on. A side road off the RN-9 climbs to the incredibly isolated and highly picturesque hamlet of **Iruya**, if you really want to get off the beaten track. The whole of the RN-9 and some of the side roads are accessible by regular **buses** from Jujuy, many of them also serving Salta.

Tumbaya

As you climb the first stretch of the Quebrada beyond Yala, you soon leave the subtropical forest behind and enter an arid, narrow valley, gouged out by the Río Grande. Some 47km from Jujuy, you come to **TUMBAYA**, a tiny village with a handsome colonial church, the first of many along the Quebrada; the **Iglesia de Nuestra Señora de los Dolores y Nuestra Señora de la Candelaria** houses some fine colonial art, including a painting of *Nuestra Señora La Aparecida*, another of *El Cristo de los Temblores*, and a *Jesús en el Huerto*. Originally built at the end of the eighteenth century, it was partially rebuilt after two earthquakes in the nineteenth century and restored in the 1940s; its design is typical of the Quebrada, a solid structure clearly influenced by the Mudéjar churches of Andalucia. The domed campanile is particularly elegant.

Purmamarca

About 13km north of Tumbaya, the region's main trans-Andean route, the RN-52, forks off to the left, heading northwest towards Susques and the Chilean border. Lying 4km to the west of the RN-52, the tiny, picturesque village of **PURMAMARCA**, at the base of the gorge of the same name, is no longer quite as peaceful and quiet as it was, due to an increase in traffic resulting from stronger trading links with Chile. The main square is still a haven of tranquillity, though, flanked to the south by a pretty seventeenth-century church, the **Iglesia Santa Rosa de Lima**, built to the typically plain, single-towered design of the Quebrada, and a huge *algarrobo* tree that is claimed to be a thousand years old. At the northeast corner of the plaza, the four graceful arches of the **Cabildo** (daily 10am–noon & 5–7pm; free) embellish its otherwise simple white facade. The real attraction, though, is the famous **Cerro de los Siete Colores**, a dramatic bluff of rock overlooking the village. The mountain's candy stripes range from pastel beiges and pinks to orangey ochres and dark purples, though you may not be able to make out all seven of the reputed shades. A signposted route marked "Los Colorados", following an irrigation canal, takes you round the back of the village for the best views of the polychrome mountainside. There is a helpful little **tourist information office** (daily 8am–8pm) on the main plaza. Frequent **buses** to Tilcara, Humahuaca and Jujuy leave from a block east of the main square.

Accommodation

Casa de Adobe RN-52 Km4 ☎0388/490-8003, ⓦwww.casadeadobe.com.ar. A small set of hyper-luxurious *cabañas*, affording magnificent mountain views and with a terrific display of good taste and technological progress. Gorgeous materials and textiles, plus plasma-screen TVs with international satellite channels. ❻

Hospedaje El Viejo Algarrobo Salta s/n ☎0388/490-8286, ⓔelviejoalgarrobo@hotmail .com. A cosy *hospedaje* named after an ancient *algarrobo* tree (sadly destroyed by lightning in a freak storm in 2009) behind the church, with small but adequate rooms. ❸

Hostal La Posta de Purmamarca Pantaleón Cruz s/n ☎0388/490-8029, ⓦwww.postadepurmamarca .com.ar. Sturdy wooden beds in a white room – not exactly luxury but good value and in a great central location. ❺

Hostería del Amauta Salta s/n ☎0388/490-8043, ⓦwww.hosteriadelamauta.com.ar. Oozing with charm, this well-designed *hostería* has a selection of rooms impeccably decorated with soft linens, local timber and wrought-iron detailing. Breakfasts are delicious, healthy and copious. ❼

Hotel La Comarca RN-52 Km3.8 ☎0388/490-8001, ⓦwww.lacomarcahotel.com.ar. In a stunning setting with unbeatable views of the coloured mountains, this stylish adobe-and-stone complex has twelve huge rooms, four *cabañas* sleeping four, two houses (for four to six persons) and a presidential suite, plus a beautiful heated pool, a mini-spa and a top-rate gourmet restaurant (open to non-residents) with a cellar worth visiting alone. ❽

Hotel Manantial del Silencio RN-52 Km3.5 ☎0388/490-8080, ⓦwww.hotelmanantial.com.ar. This delightful, convent-like Neocolonial building in a large parkland a short distance out of the village houses small but comfortable rooms. The restaurant varies in quality, the swimming pool is unheated and the service leaves a lot to be desired, but as the pioneer boutique hotel in the area it has its merits. ❽

Residencial Bebo Vilte Salta s/n and Rivadavia ☎0388/490-8038. A classic B&B that still offers some of the best inexpensive rooms in the village. ❹

Residencial Zulma Salta s/n ☎0388/490-8023. This cosy, basic little *residencial* is the nicest of the lowest-budget options. ❸

Eating and drinking

There are various places to eat and have a drink or a coffee near the central plaza. Next to the Cabildo, *La Posta* serves simple meals, snacks and drinks, and sells local crafts, in a rich red-ochre walled building. A short way from the church is the area's best **restaurant** by far, *Los Morteros*, at Salta s/n (closed Mon); the gourmet food, using the region's excellent natural produce, including goat's cheese empanadas and chicken fricassee with broad beans and quinoa, is served in a classy decor, adorned with traditional textiles and other crafts. On Mondays, when it is closed, fall back on the excellent restaurant at *La Comarca* hotel. Alternatively, try *Sabor a Tierra* at Lavalle and Sarmiento, which serves snacks, pasta and regional dishes.

Cuesta de Lipán and Susques

Leading west from Purmamarca, the RN-52 follows the Río Purmamarca, quickly climbing up the remarkable zigzags of the **CUESTA DE LIPÁN**, one of the most dramatic roads in the region. This road heads towards the Chilean border at Paso de Jama crossing some of the country's most startling landscapes – barren steppe alternating with crinkly mountains, often snow-peaked even in the summer. Some 30km west of Purmamarca, just after the Abra de Potrerillos pass, you reach the road's highest point, at nearly 4200m, and enter majestic altiplanic landscapes: ahead you have open views to gleaming salt-flats and to the north, beyond the valley of the Río Colorado, the shallow, mirror-like **Laguna de Guayatayoc** glistens in the sun. Beyond the junction with the RN-40, which runs north–south from San Antonio de los Cobres (see p.333) to Abra Pampa (see p.354), the pastures on either side of the road are home to considerable communities of vicuña. Where the road snakes between the **Cerro Negro** and the valley of the Río de las Burras, through the **Quebrada del Mal Paso**, it crosses the Tropic of Capricorn several times, before reaching Susques, some 180km from Purmamarca.

A minute but wonderfully picturesque village, formerly belonging to Chile, **SUSQUES** is now where the Argentine customs point is located; expect lengthy clearance procedures, especially if coming from Chile. While waiting, take a look at the sumptuous church, with its delicate thatched roof and rough adobe walls, like those of all the houses in the village, and the naive frescoes on the inside. **Accommodation** in Susques really boils down to three options: the very basic but clean *Hostería Las Vicuñitas* (℡03887/490207; ❷), serving simple food and located close to the village centre; *Hostería El Unquillar* (℡03887/490210 or 0388/425-5252; ❺), a gorgeous adobe house, blending into the environment, with a cosy sitting room, comfortable rooms and excellent cuisine, a couple of kilometres out on the RN-52 towards Chile; or slightly further out of the village towards the Paso de Jama, well-run *Hostal Pastos Chicos* (℡0388/423-5387, Ⓦwww .pastoschicos.com.ar; ❹). Conveniently next to the fuel station, its rooms are perfectly adequate and the restaurant is cosy.

Pullman (℡0388/422-1366) runs **buses** from Salta, via Jujuy, Purmamarca and Susques, to San Pedro de Atacama and on to Antofagasta, Iquique and Arica, in Chile, twice a week, leaving Salta at 7am and arriving at San Pedro in the evening.

Maimará

From Purmamarca, the RN-9 continues north, climbing through the Quebrada de Humahuaca past coloured mountainsides, ornamented with rock formations like organ-pipes or elephants' feet with painted toes. One highly photogenic sight, conveniently visible from the main road, is the extraordinary cemetery at **MAIMARÁ**, 75km from Jujuy; a honeycombed mountain of a graveyard, surrounded by rough-hewn walls and covered with a jumble of centuries-old tombs of all shapes and sizes, crowned with bouquets of artificial flowers and rickety crosses, it appears even bigger than the village it serves. Behind it, the rock formations at the base of the mountain resemble multicoloured oyster-shells. The multiple shades of creams and reds, yellows and browns have earned the rocks the name La Paleta del Pintor ("the artist's palette"). Maimará isn't the most happening place in the Quebrada, but if you choose to stay your best bet is *Hostal Posta del Sol* (℡0388/423-5387, Ⓦwww.pastoschicos.com.ar; ❹), at Rodríguez and San Martín, which has a number of very smart, simply decorated rooms.

Tilcara

Only 5km further along the RN-9 you are treated to your first glimpse of the great pre-Inca *pukará*, or fortress, of **TILCARA**. Just beyond it is the side road off to the village itself. At an altitude of just under 3000m and yet still dominated by the dramatic mountains that surround it, this is one of the biggest settlements along the Quebrada and the only one on the east bank; it lies just off the main road, where the Río Huasomayo runs into the Río Grande. The pleasant, easy-going village is always very lively, but even more so during **Carnival**; like the rest of the Quebrada, it also celebrates **El Enero Tilcareño**, a religious and popular procession and feast held during the latter half of January (good to avoid if you dislike crowds and have not booked accommodation well ahead), as well as **Holy Week**, and **Pachamama**, or the Mother Earth festival, in August, with remarkable festivities, wild games, all manner of

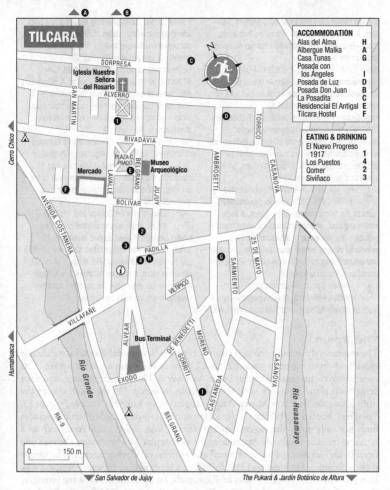

TILCARA

▼ San Salvador de Jujuy

The Pukará & Jardín Botánico de Altura ▼

music, noisy processions and frenzied partying. Frequent **buses** from Humahuaca and Jujuy stop at the terminal along Avenida Alvear.

Accommodation

Thanks to a number of recent additions, mostly of a luxurious nature, Tilcara is not short of **places to stay**, including a couple of the region's best **youth hostels**, though prices tend to reflect the area's growing popularity. *El Jardín* (☎0388/495-5128) is Tilcara's main **campsite**, well run and in an attractive riverside location 1km northwest of the village.

Alas del Alma Padilla 437 ☎0388/495-5572, ⓦwww.alasdelalma.com. Extremely comfortable adobe-and-stone *cabañas* sleeping two or four, done out in an appealing traditional style with local textiles and ceramics, conveniently located at the entrance to the village. ⑥

Albergue Malka San Martín s/n ☎0388/495-5197, ⓦwww.malkahostel .com.ar. An outstanding, rather upmarket youth hostel, 400m up a steep hill, east of Plaza Alvarez Prado, commands sweeping views, is extremely comfortable and serves excellent breakfasts. The friendly owner runs treks and 4WD tours in the area. A dorm bed costs $60 including breakfast; there are also doubles (⑤) and *cabañas* sleeping three to ten persons.

Casa Tunas Padilla 765 ☎0388/154-045784, ⓦwww.casatunas.com.ar. Simple house with whitewashed walls, antique furniture and a lot of charm; half board is an option. ❸

Posada con los Ángeles Gorriti s/n ☎0388/495-5153, ⓦwww.posadaconlosangeles.com.ar. Heavenly hotel, as the name intimates, built around an idyllic courtyard, with a quirky but attractive architectural style decor, charming rooms, great views and tip-top service. ❻

🏃 **Posada de Luz** Ambrosetti and Alverro ☎0388/495-5017, ⓦwww.posadadeluz .com.ar. Panoramic views up the valley, a large swimming pool, original architecture and a friendly welcome are just some of the assets of this wonderful posada, where each tastefully furnished and decorated room has its own cachet. Book well ahead as it fills up quickly. ❻

🏃 **Posada Don Juan** Lavalle s/n ☎0388/495-5422, ⓦwww.posadadonjuan .com.ar. Wonderful semi-detached units, each with

a small terrace, spaced evenly around a fine park affording marvellous views of Tilcara and its surroundings. Simple, tasteful decor, excellent breakfasts and professional staff. ❺

La Posadita La Sorpresa s/n ☎0388/154-4729997, ⓦwww.laposadita.com.ar. A marvellous newcomer in a similar style to its "mother", *Posada de Luz*; the bright airy rooms have huge picture windows that look over to the coloured mountains to the west. ❹

Residencial El Antigal Rivadavia and Belgrano ☎0388/495-5020, ⓔelantigaltilcara@yahoo .com.ar. A basic but decent *residencial* with a picturesque tearoom that doubles as a bar in the evening; all the beds now have proper sprung mattresses. ❹

🏃 **Tilcara Hostel** Bolívar 166 ☎0388/495-5105, ⓦwww.tilcarahostel.com. This hostel has established a good reputation for safety, cleanliness and comfort in its dorms ($55 per person) and doubles (❷). It has a pleasant common room, barbecue facilities (the village market is just next door, for supplies) and the owners organize local excursions.

The Town

The impressively massive colonial church, **Nuestra Señora del Rosario**, stands one block back from the main square, Plaza C. Alvarez Prado, on a smaller square of its own; *cardón* cactus replaces timber in the doorway and interior furnishings, while the beige walls blend agreeably with the mountain backdrop. On the south side of the main plaza, you'll find the **Museo Arqueológico** (daily 9am–12.30pm & 2–6pm; $5, Tues free); housed in a beautiful colonial house, the well-presented collection includes finds not only from the region but also from Chile, Bolivia and Peru, such as a mummy from San Pedro de Atacama, anthropomorphic Mochica vases, a bronze disc from Belén and assorted items of metal and pottery, of varying interest. The simple patio is dominated by three menhirs, including a very tall one, depicting Simpson-like humanoid figures, from the *pukará* of Rinconada, far up in the north of the province. Keep your ticket to visit the local **pukará** (daily 9am–6pm; $5, Tues free) and the **Jardín Botánico de Altura**, both a kilometre or so southwest of the plaza. The University of Buenos Aires has long been working on the pre-Columbian fortress, one of the region's most complex, with row upon row of family houses built within the high ramparts. It has reconstructed, with considerable success and expertise, many of the houses, along with a building known as La Iglesia or "church", thought to have been a ceremonial edifice, no doubt used for sacrifices. The whole magnificent fortress is spiked with a grove of cacti and, with the backdrop of imposing mountains on all sides, it affords marvellous panoramic views in all directions. The garden, in the lee of the *pukará*, is an attractively landscaped collection of local **flora**, mostly cacti, including the hairy *cabeza del viejo* ("old man's head") and equally hirsute "lamb's tail" varieties. There are fabulous views of the *pukará* from its stone paths.

Eating and drinking

As well as the hotel restaurants and bars, there are a number of different possibilities for **meals** or a **drink** in Tilcara. *Pacha Mama*, Belgrano 590, prepares reliable regional fare, as does *Sivviñaco*, an ultra trendy joint that puts on live music most nights, at Belgrano and Padilla. An excellent place for a coffee, a snack or a more elaborate meal, such as a hearty *locro* – plus top-rate breakfasts – is *Qomer*, right on the central plaza at Rivadavia 225. Another ideal place for good food and some excellent folk music is the appealing *El Nuevo Progreso 1917*, on the smaller plaza opposite the church at Lavalle 351. For a special meal, in exceptionally beautiful surroundings, with handsome photos on the walls, ⅄ *Los Puestos*, at the corner of Belgrano and Padilla, rules supreme: the varied menu features tender grilled llama, mouthwatering empanadas, juicy *humitas* and succulent pasta.

Uquía

After a short, steep climb beyond the side road from Tilcara, the RN-9 levels off and crosses the Tropic of Capricorn – marked by a giant sundial monument built in the 1980s and meant to align with the noon shadow at the solstice, but curiously installed at the wrong angle by mistake – one kilometre south of **Huacalera**, a tiny hamlet dominated by its seventeenth-century chapel. The road then climbs past Cerro Yacoraite, a polychrome meseta to the west, streaked with bright reds and yellows, to picturesque **UQUÍA**, just over 100km north of Jujuy. Also set against a vivid backdrop of brick-red mountains and surrounded by lush *quebrachos*, behind a delightful square, is the seventeenth-century **Iglesia de San Francisco de Paula**, with its separate tower integrated in the churchyard wall, all painted pristine white, except the smart green door. Inside, the simple nave directs your gaze to the fine **retable**, the original, with its little inset painted canvases. Nine beautiful and unusual **paintings**, also from the seventeenth century, line the walls; these are unique to Collao, Alto Peru, and depict warrior-like *ángeles militares*, or angels in armour, holding arquebuses and other weapons. Formerly they numbered ten, but one went missing while they were being exhibited in Buenos Aires, where the remaining nine were restored, excessively to some tastes – they seem to have lost their centuries' old patina. If the church is closed – which is likely – ask around for the old lady who keeps the key, apparently the three-hundred-year-old original.

There are two **places to stay**: In the village, at Belgrano and Lozano, is the delightful *Hostal de Uquía* (☏03887/490508, ⓦwww.hostaldeuquia.com.ar; ⑤), with a big homely sitting room, done out in colonial pink, and fine dining room. *Hosteria Huasadurazno* (☏0388/154-398457; ⑤) is set back slightly from the RN-9, about 1km north of the village; its bright rooms, some with bath, are arranged along a traditional galleried house, and delicious meals, using home-grown vegetables, are served to order. After Uquía, along the final stretch before Humahuaca, you have views to the east of some very high mountains: Cerro Zucho (4995m), Cerro Santa Bárbara (4215m) and Cerro Punta Corral (4815m).

Humahuaca

The main town in the area, **HUMAHUACA**, 125km north of Jujuy, spills across the Río Grande from its picturesque centre on the west bank. Its enticing cobbled streets, lined with colonial-style or rustic adobe houses, lend themselves to gentle ambling – necessarily leisurely at this altitude, a touch below 3000m. Most organized tours arrive here for lunch and then double back to Jujuy or Salta, but you may like to stay over, and venture at least as far as the secluded village of **Iruya**; Humahuaca is also an excellent springboard for trips up into the desolate but hauntingly beautiful landscapes of the altiplano or **Puna Jujeña**.

Most tours to and around the town aim to deliver you at the beautifully lush main square at midday on the dot, in time to see a kitsch **statue of San Francisco**

Solano emerge from a niche in the equally kitsch tower of the whitewashed **Municipalidad**, give a sign of blessing, and then disappear behind his door. A crowd gathers, invariably serenaded by groups of folk musicians; the saint repeats his trick at midnight to a smaller audience. On the western side of the square, and far more impressive, is the **cathedral**, the Iglesia de Nuestra Señora de la Candelaria y San Antonio, built in the seventeenth century and much restored since. Within its immaculate white walls is a late seventeenth-century retable, and another on the north wall by Cosmo Duarte, dated 1790, depicting the Crucifixion. The remaining artworks include a set of exuberantly Mannerist paintings called the *Twelve Prophets*, signed by leading Cusqueño artist Marcos Sapaca and dated 1764. Looming over the church and the whole town is the controversial **Monumento a la Independencia**, a bombastic concoction of stone and bronze, built in the 1940s by local artist Ernesto Soto Avendaño. Triumphal steps lead up to it from the plaza, but the best thing about it is the view across the town and valley to the mountainside to the east. The twenty-metre high monument is topped by a bronze statue of an Indian in a ferociously warrior-like pose. Behind it, and far more appealing, framed by two giant cacti, is an adobe tower decorated with a bronze plaque, all that remains of the Iglesia Santa Bárbara, whose ruins were destroyed to make way for the monument.

Buses from Jujuy, Salta, La Quiaca and Iruya arrive at the small bus terminal a couple of blocks southeast of the main square, at Belgrano and Entre Ríos. If you're travelling by car, be prepared for the local boys who will approach you at the RN-9 turn-off and offer to guide you. They'll show you around for a small tip, but speak only Spanish.

Accommodation

The range of **accommodation** in Humahuaca is not so extensive and is less upmarket than in Tilcara, but the variety is certainly greater than in Purmamarca. Many people tend to prefer staying in Tilcara, as it is at considerably lower altitude, but Humahuaca is still lower down than, say, La Quiaca or Iruya. A couple of the best options are some way from the village centre, across the Río Grande, in the Barrio Medalla Milagrosa, but if you call ahead they will come and collect you from the bus terminal.

Hospedaje Kuntur Wasi Santa Fe 520 ℡03887/421337, ✉kunturwasi@argentina.com. The rustic stone exterior is matched by a rustic stone interior, but the rooms are comfortable, albeit a little offbeat in design. The excellent restaurant is open only to patrons. ❸

Hostal Azul Barrio Medalla Milagrosa ℡03887/421596, ⓦwww .hostalazulhumahuaca.com.ar. The excellent-value rooms are a little cramped but exquisitely decorated and built around a tranquil patio (only the facade is blue), according to traditional techniques. The bread and jams served at breakfast are home-made. ❹

Hostal Inti Sayana La Rioja 83 ℡03887/154-099806, ⓦwww.intisayanahostal.com.ar. Lively, clean little hostel that organizes all kinds of cultural events – mostly music and dance. Some of the larger rooms ($200) sleep up to five persons. ❹

Hostería Solar de la Quebrada Santa Fe 450 ℡03887/421986, ⓦwww.solardelaquebrada .com.ar. Gorgeous *hostería* with fabulous views,

six stylishly appointed rooms with excellent mattresses on the beds and appealing, bright decor. ❻

Posada El Sol Barrio Medalla Milagrosa ℡03887/421466, ✉elsolposada@imagine.com.ar. Fun little posada that doubles up as a youth hostel charging $55 for a dorm bunk; otherwise there are neat doubles (❸) and larger rooms, too. The house is built of adobe brick with a straw roof, and the atmosphere is young, with lots of guitar-centred evenings.

Residencial Humahuaca Córdoba 401 and Corrientes ℡03887/421141. Conveniently located right next to the bus terminal, this homely *residencial* has very reasonable doubles, triples, quadruples and even quintuples. Breakfast is served in the *confitería* and there is a sunny patio. ❸

Eating and drinking

The best restaurant in town is the enticing 🍴 *Casa Vieja*, on Buenos Aires at the corner with Salta; its rustic interior belies some very fine cooking, with the emphasis on Andean ingredients, and the stage is regularly graced by leading folklore singers and musicians. There's also delicious, plentiful regional food accompanied by live folk music – albeit aimed at tour groups – at the *Peña de Fortunato Ramos*, at San Luis and Jujuy, though you can have a more authentic experience – and delicious fare based on llama and quinoa – at *El Rosedal*, Buenos Aires 175. The 🍴 *Bar del Tantanakuy*, up at Salta 370, serves regional dishes, wines and real espresso coffee and holds literary, artistic and musical events, and in its marvellous little projection room it screens non-blockbuster films by the likes of Orson Welles and Wong Kar Wai.

Iruya

Just 25km due north of Humahuaca along the RN-9, the RP-13 forks off to the northeast, crosses a couple of oases and stony riverbeds before winding up a stunningly beautiful narrow valley, and then down again to **IRUYA** via a dramatic corniche road along which you wonder how two buses can pass each other – yet they somehow manage. The point where you cross the border into Salta Province is the Abra del Cóndor pass, at a giddying and often gale-blown 3900m. The Andean hamlet fits snugly into the side of the valley of the Río Iruya, in the far northern corner of Salta Province, and its fortified walls, steep cobbled streets, whitewashed houses and timeless atmosphere, accentuated by the rarefied air – at an altitude of 2780m – alone make it worth a visit. You certainly feel a long way from the hectic streets of Jujuy or Salta – especially since the whole place is reminiscent of certain Greek island villages, transposed to an Andean landscape. On the first Sunday of October, its beautiful little **Iglesia de Nuestra Señora del Rosario y San Roque** – a typical Quebrada chapel built to the by now familiar Mudéjar design – is the focal point for a wonderfully picturesque festival, half-Catholic, half-pre-Columbian, culminating in a solemn procession of weirdly masked figures, some representing demons. Of all the Northwest's festivals, this is the most fascinating and mysterious. The only really decent **place to stay**, should you want to soak up this otherworldly atmosphere, is the comfortable but overpriced *Hostería de Iruya* (☎03887/156-29152; ❺–❻), where the food is agreeable. You can also ask around for rooms for rent, though comfort is minimal and many houses suffer from damp. Two or three Empresa Mendoza **buses** (☎03887/421016 or 156-829078) a day make the at least three-hour trip from Humahuaca.

Up to the Puna Jujeña

Due north of Humahuaca and the turn-off to tiny Iruya, the RN-9 begins its long winding haul up into the remote **altiplano** of northern Jujuy, known as the **Puna Jujeña**; this is a fabulously wild highland area of salt flats, **lagoons** speckled pink with flamingoes and tiny hamlets built of mud-bricks around surprisingly big Quebrada-style chapels. Some 30km north of Humahuaca, the RN-9 enters the **Cuesta de Azul Pampa**, a dramatic mountain pass peaking at 3730m and offering unobstructed views across to the huge peaks to the east. Past the bottleneck of the Abra de Azul Pampa, where fords along the road sometimes freeze, causing extra hazards, the road winds along to the bleak little mining town of **Tres Cruces**, where there's a major *gendarmería* post – personal and vehicle papers are usually checked. Nearby, but out of sight, are some of the continent's biggest deposits of

▲ Espina del Diablo

lead and zinc, along with silver mines, while overlooking the village is one of the strangest rock formations in the region, the so-called **Espinazo del Diablo**, or "Devil's Backbone", a series of intriguingly beautiful stone burrows, clearly the result of violent tectonic activity millions of years ago, ridged like giant vertebrae. This road continues all the way to the Bolivian border at **La Quiaca** – an ideal base for visiting the remote corners of the province, such as **Yavi**, and its superb colonial church, and **Laguna de los Pozuelos**, with its sizeable wildfowl colony. On the way you pass through the crossroads village of **Abra Pampa**, from where you can branch off to visit the picturesque villages of **Cochinoca** and **Casabindo**, with their fine churches and colonial art treasures.

Abra Pampa and around

ABRA PAMPA, a forlorn village of llama herdsmen living in adobe houses amid the windswept steppe, 80km north of Humahuaca, lives up to its former name of Siberia Argentina. This really isn't a place that you'd choose to spend the night, but should you need to, pick from one of the rather spartan **residenciales**: *Cesarito*, at Senador Pérez 200 (③03887/491001; ②), the better of the two, and *La Coyita*, at Fascio 123 (③03887/491052; ②). Due southwest, the rough surfaced RP-11 follows the Río Miraflores to **Casabindo**, nearly 60km away, a tiny unspoilt village dwarfed by its huge church. Nicknamed La Catedral de la Puna, the **Iglesia de la Asunción** houses a collection of Altoperuvian paintings of *ángeles militares*, or angels in armour, similar to those in Uquía (see p.351). The church itself was built in the late eighteenth century to a Hispano-Mexican design and its several chapels are the theatre of major celebrations on August 15, the **Feast of the Assumption**, when plume-hatted angels and a bull-headed demon lead a procession around the village, accompanied by drummers. The climax of the festival is a bloodless *corrida*, a colonial custom known as the **Toreo de la Vincha**. The bull, representing the Devil, has a rosette hung with coins stuck on his horns and the Virgin's "defenders" have to try and remove it. Coca leaves and fermented maize are buried in another ceremony on the same day, as an offering to Pachamama, the Earth Mother, in a fusion of pre-Christian and Christian rituals; these are among the most fascinating and colourful of all the Northwest's festivals and well worth catching if you're here at the right time. The only **place to stay** in Casabindo is the very rudimentary *Albergue Casabindo* (☎03887/491126; ❶).

Cochinoca is another unspoilt village, 22km along a numberless dirt track heading in a westerly direction from Abra Pampa. Its nineteenth-century church, **Iglesia de Nuestra Señora de la Candelaria**, shelters some fine colonial paintings and a magnificent retable. The alabaster windows were rescued from the colonial church destroyed in a major earthquake in the mid-nineteenth century, as was the *Lienzo de la Virgen de la Almudena*, an oil painting depicting the construction of the original building, put up on the same site in the late seventeenth century. Both Casabindo and Cochinoca are very hard to reach – there's no public transport – but are great destinations if you're looking to get well off the beaten track.

La Quiaca and around

LA QUIACA, the largest settlement in the Puna Jujeña, almost 165km north of Humahuaca, is a border town that has seen better days. Immediately to the north, the river of the same name, gushing through a deep gorge, forms the natural frontier with Bolivia; on the other side of it the twin town of Villazón thrives on cross-border trade, while La Quiaca stagnates because its shops are losing trade to cheaper stores in Bolivia. Although there's simply nothing to do here, except get used to the altitude – 3445m – and perhaps plan your trip into Bolivia, its accommodation makes it a possible base for exploring this furthest corner of Argentina. La Quiaca livens up a little on the third and fourth Sundays of October, when the **Manca Fiesta**, also known as the Fiesta de la Olla, or cooking-pot festival, is staged; ceramists and other artisans show off their wares, while folk musicians put on concerts. The best **place to stay** is the well-run *Hostería Munay Tierra de Colores*, at Belgrano 51 (☎03885/423924, Ⓦwww.munayhotel.jujuy.com; ❸), which has pleasant rooms in a modern building and a safe garage. This is followed at a distance by the simple but clean *Hotel de Turismo*, two blocks southeast of the bus terminal at Siria and San Martín (☎03885/422243, Ⓔhotelmun@laquiaca.com.ar; ❸), while *Residencial Cristal*, at Sarmiento 539 (☎03885/422255; ❷), has very basic rooms leading off a stark courtyard, and serves decent food at low prices. The only **restaurant** worth trying is the *Casola* at the southwestern corner of the Plaza Independencia, specializing in pasta and *parrillas*.

Yavi

The RP-5 also leads east from La Quiaca, ostensibly to an airport that has yet to materialize. Across the rolling Siete Hermanos mountain range, 17km away along this road, sits the charming altiplanic village of **YAVI**, with sloping cobbled streets, adobe houses and a splendid working flour mill. From a mirador at the top of main drag Avenida Senador Pérez, to the north of the village, you have a panoramic view, taking in the dilapidated but attractive eighteenth-century **Casa del Marqués de Tojo**, the erstwhile family home of the region's ruling marqués, the only holder of that rank in colonial Argentina; the house, on the Plaza Mayor, is a museum of sorts with erratic opening hours (in theory daily 9am–1pm & 2–6pm; $5). A motley collection of artefacts and junk, such as the bedstead used by the last *marqués*, is arranged in various rooms around a fabulous patio shaded by a willow and an elm. Next to it is the village's seventeenth-century church, **Iglesia de Nuestra Señora del Rosario y San Francisco** (Mon 3–6pm, Tues–Fri 9am–noon & 3–6pm, Sat & Sun 9am–noon). Behind its harmonious white facade – ask around for the lady who keeps the key, she won't always be there at the hours posted at the entrance – is one of the region's best-preserved colonial interiors, lit a ghostly lemon-yellow by the unique wafer-thin onyx-paned windows. Some of the church's treasures were stolen during the border conflict with Chile – when *gendarmes* left the village to guard Argentine territory – and were recently traced to a private collection in the US. The ornate Baroque pulpit, three retables decorated with coloured wooden statuettes of saints and a fine sixteenth-century Flemish oil painting that must have been brought here by early colonizers, look wonderful in the simple white nave.

Apart from a couple of grimly basic *hospedajes*, there are two recommendable **places to stay**, both offering half board, which is just as well, as there are no restaurants to speak of. The better of the two is *Hostería Pachama* right at the entrance to the village, Senador Pérez s/n (☏03887/490508; ❸), though the ultra-simple, plain rooms come as a disappointment after the appealing decor of the main building; they can concoct a basic but tasty meal if required, served in an attractive dining room. If it is full then you'll have to stay at the rundown *Hostería de Yavi*, at Güemes 222 (☏03887/423235, ⓦwww.pachamahosteria.net; ❸); the rooms are OK but not especially attractive, and the service can be shoddy. You can also **camp** across the *acequia* (irrigation channel) from the church, but the site has no facilities. Guides – ask at the *Hostería de Yavi* – can take you to local attractions, such as pre-Columbian petroglyphs and cave-paintings in the nearby mountains; the petroglyphs are nothing special but the walk there, through stunning countryside, is worthwhile. La Quiaqueña runs frequent **buses** from La Quiaca, or you could try and hitch a lift from the market.

The cloudforest national parks: El Rey, Calilegua and Baritú

A trio of the Northwest's cloudforests, or *yungas* – areas of dense jungle draped over high crags that thrust out of the flat, green plains of lowlands on either side of the Tropic of Capricorn – are protected by national park status. The biggest of the three, the **Parque Nacional Calilegua**, is also the most accessible and best developed – it's the pride and joy of Jujuy Province – and within easy reach of San Salvador de Jujuy, though it might be better to stay in nearby **Libertador General San Martín**. **Parque Nacional El Rey**, in Salta Province, is much closer to the provincial capital, but its access roads are sometimes impassable after the heavy seasonal rains. Slightly smaller than Calilegua, **Parque Nacional Baritú**, away to the north in a far-flung corner of Salta Province, is the hardest to get to, and therefore even less spoilt, than either of the other two national parks; the small town of **San Ramón de la Nueva Orán** can act as a springboard for getting there. The microclimates of all three *yungas* are characterized by clearly distinct dry and wet seasons, winter and summer, but relatively high year-round precipitation. The peaks are often shrouded in cloud and mist, keeping most of the varied plant life lush even in the drier, cooler months. They are worth a visit for the dramatic scenery alone, though the incredibly varied fauna that lives amid the dense vegetation is perhaps the main attraction.

Parque Nacional El Rey

PARQUE NACIONAL EL REY straddles the borders of Salta and Jujuy provinces, nearly 200km by road from the city of Salta, from where it can be quickly reached, though heavy rains can sometimes make the route impassable. Covering 400 square kilometres of land once belonging to Finca El Rey near the provincial border with Jujuy, the national park (9am–dusk; free) perches at an average of 900m above sea level and nestles in a natural horseshoe-shaped amphitheatre, hemmed in by the curving **Crestón del Gallo** ridge to the northwest, and the higher crest of the **Serranía del Piquete**, to the east, peaking at around 1700m. A fan-shaped network of crystal-clear brooks, all brimming with fish, drains into the Río Popayán. The handsome **toucan** (*Ramphastos toco*) is the park's striking and easily recognizable mascot, but other birdlife abounds, totalling over 150 species. Despite this, it is not that easy to see birds here; however, the park is the best place in the region for spotting tapirs, peccaries and wild cats.

Public transport to the park is nonexistent and through traffic very slight, so visiting the park without your own transport is quite difficult – an organized trip is the best option. Norte Trekking (see box, p.329) can take you on an informative and enjoyable safari to the park; equally professional Clark Expediciones (see box, p.329) specializes in natural history and bird-watching trips here. If you do plan to come under your own steam, make sure you have a 4WD. The park's only access road is the RP-20, branching left from the RP-5, which in turn leads eastwards from the RN-9/34, near the village of Lumbrera halfway between Metán and Güemes. **Guardaparques** at the entrance can advise you on how to get around in your vehicle. The only **accommodation** option is to pitch your tent in the clearing in the middle of the park. A road of sorts follows the **Río La Sala**, while more marked trails through the park are currently being planned to add to the two-hour climb from the rangers' station to **Pozo Verde**, a lakelet coloured green by lettuce-like *lentejas de água*, and a nearby pond where birds come to drink.

Parque Nacional Calilegua

Spread over 760 square kilometres, just south of the Tropic of Capricorn, in a province better known for its arid mountains, multicoloured valleys and parched altiplanic landscapes, the **PARQUE NACIONAL CALILEGUA** sticks up above rich fertile land that is home to some of the country's biggest sugar farms. It's the setting for amusing anecdotes in Gerald Durrell's book *The Whispering Land*; his tales of roads cut off by flooding rivers can still ring true but his quest for native animals to take back to his private zoo cannot be imitated – the park's rich flora and fauna (see Contexts, p.612) are now strictly protected by law. The land once belonged to the Leach brothers, local sugar barons of British origin, whose family donated it to the state to turn it into a national park in the 1970s. This was a shrewd business move: sugar plantations need a lot of clean water and the only way to keep the reliable supplies which run through the park free of pollution, uncontrolled logging and the general destruction of the fragile ecosystem was through the state regulations that come with national park status.

The **park entrance** (daily 9am–6pm; free) is at Aguas Negras, 120km from Jujuy city via the RN-34. At **Libertador General San Martín** take the RP-83, which climbs to **Valle Colorado**, and is paved as far as Aguas Negras. Libertador General San Martín is an uninviting little town, dominated by the huge Ledesma industrial complex – the world's biggest sugar refinery – and usually referred to as Libertador or LGSM on signs, but is a possible stopover base for visiting the park. Cars can make it along the main road, punctuated by numerous viewpoints, some offering splendid panoramas, as far as the **Mesada de la Colmenas**, near the other rangers' headquarters, but a 4WD will be required beyond here – the road continues its climb to the highest point, at 1700m, marked by the **Abra de las Cañas** monolith. You should certainly walk off the beaten track, well away from noisy trucks, if you want to have the slightest chance of spotting any of the wildlife. Trekking around Calilegua takes time and it's a very good idea to spend a night or two in the park. Morning and late afternoon are the best times to see animals and birds by streams and rivers. Seven trails of varying length and difficulty have been hacked through the dense vegetation, and it's worth asking the rangers for guidance – there aren't any maps.

The summits of the **Serranía de Calilegua**, marking the park's northwestern boundary, reach heights of over 3300m, beyond which lies grassland and rocky terrain. The trek to the summit of Cerro Amarillo (3320m) takes three days from the park entrance; the nearby shepherds' hamlet, **Alto Calilegua**, is certainly worth a visit. From the tiny settlement of San Francisco within the park it's even possible to link up with **Tilcara** (see p.348), a four-day trek; some of the organized trips arranged in Salta and Tilcara itself, including horse rides, offer this amazing chance to witness the stark contrast between the verdant jungle and the desiccated uplands.

Practicalities

At the park entrance, you'll find the ranger's house (the *intendencia* is in the town of **Libertador General San Martín**), definitely worth a visit before you head in, for maps and extra information about the park; general **tourist information** about the area can be obtained at Confianza Turismo, Avenida Libertad 350 in Libertador (T03886/424527, Econfianza@cooplib.com.ar). **Accommodation outside the park** is also in Libertador. Offering top-notch service and excursion possibilities is the plush *Posada del Sol* (T03886/424900, Wwww.posadadelsoljujuy .com.ar; ⑤), with inviting rooms arranged around an attractive courtyard and swimming pool, hidden away at Los Ceibos and Pukará. A little cheaper and rather less appealing, but clean enough, is the *Hotel Los Lapachos*, at Entre Ríos 400 (T03886/423790; ④). Alternative accommodation is available at the *Complejo Termal Aguas Calientes* spa resort (T0388/156-50699; ③), 30km northeast of Libertador along the RP-1, which turns eastwards off the RN-34 past the straggly village of Caimancito. Near the banks of the Río San Francisco in a bucolic setting, it offers excellent meals and clean rooms, camping or the opportunity to splash around in the various curative mineral pools for the day. Barring the mosquitoes (bring repellent), this is an excellent place to rest, conveniently near Calilegua in an area rich in trails and scenery. Alternatively, try the *Portal de Piedra* at nearby Villa Monte (T0388/156-820564; ④), across the eastern border of Salta Province: gaucho traditions, fine countryside walks and excellent wildlife-spotting are its attractions, with the emphasis firmly on ecotourism. The best **places to eat** in the area are in Libertador: *Del Valle*, at Entre Ríos 793, is a restaurant serving plain but well-cooked meals at reasonable prices, while ⅄ *La Yapa*, at Victoria 698, is an excellent *parrilla*.

Buses from Salta stop at Libertador's terminal on Avenida Antartida Argentina, 200m east of the RN-34. Buses for Valle Grande pass through the park, leaving the terminal early in the morning, returning late at night – times vary – but you could also contact the *intendencia* (T03886/422046, Epncalilegua@cooperlib .com.ar) to find out whether any timber trucks are going towards the park at a time convenient for you; there's no problem hitching a lift if there are. Buses from Salta to San Ramón de la Nueva Orán sometimes stop at the *Club Social San Lorenzo*, near the park entrance, but otherwise hitching might well be the only way to get that far; the RN-34 is a busy route. Announce yourself to the rangers at the park entrance, 8km from the RN-34; nearby a camouflaged **campsite**, with basic facilities, has been cleared ($7 per person). For the time being, it's the only practical way of being **on site** early enough in the morning or late enough at dusk to be assured of spotting wildlife

– though the voracious insects may deter you. If you get as far as **Valle Grande**, you could stay at either of the village's extremely basic **accommodation** options: *Albergue San Francisco* (no phone; ❷) or *Albergue Valle Grande* (☎03886/461000; ❷).

Like the other two parks, Calilegua should be visited in **spring** or **autumn**, as the summer months – December to March or April – can see sudden cloudbursts cut off access roads and make paths much too slippery for comfort. At all times bring **insect repellent** since mosquitoes and other nasty bugs are also plentiful and virulent, especially in the warmer months and in particular around Aguas Negras. You may wish to visit the park on an **organized tour**; TEA (see p.345) can get you here and fix up accommodation, while Clark Expediciones (see box, p.329) regularly runs expert bird-watching safaris to the park.

Parque Nacional Baritú and San Ramón de la Nueva Orán

Located in an isolated corner of northeastern Salta Province, the all but inaccessible **Parque Nacional Baritú** is one of the country's least visited national parks. Baritú's mascot is the red **yunga squirrel** (*ardilla roja*), but you will find most of the cloud-forest animal life here, enjoying the relative seclusion. In addition to the typical flora (see p.612), the virgin vegetation includes large numbers of the impressive **tree-fern**, a dinosaur of a plant surviving from the Palaeozoic era, whose scaly trunk and parasol of fronds can reach five or six metres in height; they are hard to see, however, preferring the densest parts of the forest for their habitat. Less pleasant is the *maroma*, a parasite that ungratefully strangles its host tree to death.

A poor road, usually cut off in the rainy season, runs for 30km west from the customs post at Aguas Blancas on the Bolivian border, 50km north of **SAN RAMÓN DE LA NUEVA ORÁN**, a rather grandiose name for an insignificant little town (it's usually shortened to Orán), and enters the park at the rangers' post known as **Sendero Angosto**, on the Río Pescado. Though of little interest in itself, Orán is the ideal base for visiting Baritú. **Accommodation** ranges from the fairly luxurious *Hotel Alto Verde*, at Pellegrini 671 (☎03878/421214, ✆hotelaltoverde @arnet.ar; ❸), boasting air conditioning in all rooms and a fair-sized swimming pool, to the *Crillon*, at 25 de Mayo 225 (☎03878/421101; ❸), and *Colonial*, on Pizarry Colón (☎03878/421103; ❸): both are basic but have clean bathrooms and decent rooms. It may be more convenient to stay at **Los Toldos**, on the way into the park, where you will find the ranger's house and maybe some *cabañas* to rent.

Covering 720 square kilometres, the park has a geography that is complicated by a maze of *arroyos* and largely impervious high mountains: the steep Las Pavas and Porongal ranges both exceed 2000m while the park's southern reaches are dominated by the **Cerro Cinco Picachos**, at nearly 2000m. The lack of public transport and on-the-spot facilities combined with the challenging terrain all but rule out individual travel and hardly any tour operators based in nearby towns seem interested in taking you there. If you're really determined, contact Hugo Luna, at 9 de Julio 430 in Orán, or an operator such as TEA, in Jujuy (see p.345), or Clark Expediciones, in Salta (see box, p.329).

San Miguel de Tucumán

In the humid valley of the Río Salí, in the eastern lee of the high Sierra de Aconquija, **SAN MIGUEL DE TUCUMÁN** (or simply **Tucumán**) is Argentina's fourth largest city, 1190km northwest of Buenos Aires and nearly 300km south of Salta by the RN-9. It hasn't changed much, it seems, since Paul Theroux was here in 1978 and wrote, in *The Old Patagonian Express*, that it "was thoroughly European in a rather old-fashioned way, from the pin-striped suits and black moustaches of the old men idling in the cafés or having their shoes shined in the plaza, to the baggy, shapeless school uniforms of the girls stopping on their way to the convent school to squeeze – it was an expression of piety – the knee of Christ on the cathedral crucifix"; it still looks a bit like a European city caught in a time warp.

The capital of a tiny but heavily populated sugar-rich province, Tucumán is by far the biggest metropolis in the Northwest, the region's undisputed **commercial capital** and one of the liveliest urban centres in the country, with a thriving business centre, bustling, traffic-choked downtown streets, a youthful population and even a slightly violent undercurrent, by Argentine standards. Tucumán certainly has a boisterous image, perhaps partly since it's Argentina's rugby capital, but its confidence has been trimmed over the past two or three decades by municipal political and economic crises – and the city seems to have taken longer than the rest of the country to recover from the turmoil of 2001.

Some history

Originally founded in 1565 by Diego de Villarroel, Tucumán's first home was near the town of Monteros, 50km southwest of the present city, but mosquitoes proved an intolerable nuisance, and the settlement was moved to its current drier spot in 1685. The etymology of the name Tucumán is something of a mystery – it is probably a corruption of the Quichoa for "place where things finish", a reference to the abrupt mountains that loom above the fertile plains, but may have been derived from the Kana word *yukuman* meaning "welling springs". For a while, the city flourished and its name was applied to a whole region of Spanish America corresponding to southern Bolivia and the northwestern quarter of today's Argentina. Soon, though, the city was eclipsed by Salta and Córdoba, whose climates were found to be more bearable. Then came its moment of glory, on July 9, 1816, when the city hosted a historic Congress of Unitarist politicians at which Argentina's independence from Spain was declared. British investment and climatic conditions favoured Tucumán's sugar industry, and most of the city's wealth, built up around the end of the nineteenth century, accrued from this "white gold". A slump in international sugar prices and shortsighted over-farming have now forced local sugar growers to branch out into alternative money earners, such as tobacco and citrus fruit. Tucumán has become the world's biggest lemon-producing area, but also grows mandarins, grapefruit and kumquats. With a climate similar to that around Santa Cruz de la Sierra in Bolivia, much of the area has also been given over to growing blueberries and strawberries – with large numbers of Bolivian workers helping local farmers at harvest time.

Arrival, information and city transport

Tucumán's international **airport**, Aeropuerto Benjamín Matienzo (℡0381/426-4906), is 9km east of the centre of town; a **taxi** will cost about $30. Tucumán is quite fog-prone and flights are sometimes inconveniently re-routed as far away as Santiago del Estero. Tucumanos are justifiably proud of their modern and efficient **bus terminal** (℡0381/422-2221), at Brígido Terán 350, six blocks east and two south of Plaza Independencia. It has sixty wide-berthed platforms, a shopping centre ("Shopping del Jardín") and supermarket, restaurants, bars, post office, telephone centres, left-luggage and even a hairdresser – but no working ATMs: try the supermarket for cash withdrawals. Most **city buses** run between the centre and the bus terminal, and you'll need a token for each trip, on sale at all kiosks. Trains still run to and from Buenos Aires via Santiago del Estero from the **train station**

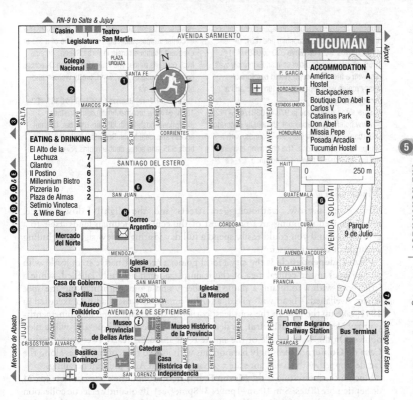

(℡0381/431-0725) at Catamarca and Corrientes. **Tourist information** is available at the provincial office at 24 de Septiembre 484 (Mon–Fri 7am–1pm & 5–9pm, Sat & Sun 9am–1pm & 5–9pm), on Plaza Independencia. The branch at the **bus station** (same hours) can sometimes scrape a map together.

Accommodation

Rather than stay in the city, especially in the unbearable summer heat (Nov–March), you may well prefer to do as the locals do and **stay** in the cooler heights of Tafí del Valle (see p.363) or near the archeological site of Quilmes (see p.366). Downtown Tucumán has a wide selection of **hotels**, but the quality is poor – you're better opting for one of the boutique hotels in leafy Yerba Buena. In town, many mid-range hotels are conveniently clustered around the central Plaza Independencia, but even they are shoddily run and overpriced. At the budget end, you can choose from a number of decent **residenciales** and a couple of excellent **youth hostels**.

Catalinas Park Hotel Av Soldati 380 ℡0381/450-2250. Rather bland and aimed mainly at the conference and business market, but worth trying, nonetheless, for its fine location overlooking Parque 9 de Julio, large roof-top pool, saunas and all mod cons; rates are cut at weekends. ➐
Hostel Backpackers Laprida 456 ℡0381/430-2716, ℮backpackerstucuman@hotmail.com.

Excellent hostel situated in a beautiful Neocolonial townhouse. Dorm beds $45, and some double rooms (➌).
Hotel América Santiago del Estero 1064 ℡0381/430-0810. Hotel well known for its bar, but it also has smart rooms, with bright bathrooms. ➍
Hotel Boutique Don Abel Guemes 35 ℡0381/425-1230. Handsome small hotel in Yerba Buena, with an

attractive garden; the rooms are aptly named after precious gems such as sapphire and ruby. ⑥–⑧

Hotel Carlos V 25 de Mayo 330 ☎0381/431-1666, ⓦwww.hotelcarlosv.com.ar. Extremely well run, with a friendly reception and comfortable, classy rooms with reproduction furniture and a decent restaurant. ⑥

Missia Pepe Av Aconquija 978 ☎0381/425-1120, ⓦwww.hotelmissiapepe.com. Unusually decorated suburban bungalow in stunning grounds, with a fine pool, in Yerba Buena. The charming owners will lay on dinner If booked In advance. ⑥–⑦

Posada Arcadia Guemes 480 ☎0381/425-22140, ⓔcontacto@posadaarcadia.com.ar. One of a trio of excellent boutique hotels in Yerba Buena, *Arcadia* lives up to its name. The four rooms have Quechua names meaning beauty, wind, pretty woman and blooming. ⑤–⑦

Tucumán Hostel Buenos Aires 669 ☎0381/420-1584, ⓦwww.tucumanhostel.com. Another exceptional hostel with kitchen-use, bar, internet access and local tours. Breakfast included. Dorm beds $35, and some double rooms (②).

The City

Despite its narrow, traffic-clogged streets and the slightly down-at-heel pedestrianized shopping area northwest of the centre, Tucumán lends itself to a gentle stroll and you could easily spend a full day visiting its few sights, including a couple of decent museums.

Plaza Independencia is the city's focal point; a grove of native trees jostle with orange trees in the central area of the main plaza, each helpfully labelled, while a large pool with a fountain, a statue to Liberty and a monolith marking the spot where Avellaneda's head was spiked, after his opponent Rosas had him executed in 1841, take up the rest. In the southeast corner of the square is the mid-nineteenth-century Neoclassical **cathedral**, its slender towers topped with blue-and-white tiled domes. On the western side of the square is the imposing, early twentieth-century **Casa de Gobierno**, pleasingly harmonious with its two rows of porticoes along the facade, topped with an elegant slate mansard roof, and Art Nouveau detailing.

Much more interesting is the **Museo Folklórico**, around the corner at Avenida 24 de Septiembre (Tues–Sun 10am–1pm & 3–8pm; free). Its quaintly eclectic collection is housed in a beautiful Neocolonial house and ranges from *mate* ware and textiles, including the typical local lace, known as "randas", to an exquisite set of traditional musical instruments, including the little banjos or *charangos* made of mulita shell – a small species of armadillo – and *bombo* drums made of cardón (cactus wood).

Two blocks south of the cathedral, at Congreso 151, is the **Casa Histórica de la Independencia** (Mon–Fri 10am–6pm, Sat & Sun 1–7pm; $5; free guided tours hourly in the morning). Behind the gleaming white facade, between two grilled windows and mock-Baroque spiralling columns, the mighty *quebracho* doors lead into a series of large patios, draped with bougainvillea, jasmine and tropical creepers. This is where Argentina declared its independence from Spain and its first Congress was held. Most of the patrician house was demolished in the late nineteenth century – this replica was completed in the 1940s. Now a national monument, it contains a fine collection of armour, furniture, paintings, silverware and porcelain, while a rather kitsch but nonetheless interesting sound-and-light show in Spanish (daily 8.30pm; closed Thurs; $10, tickets on sale shortly before each performance) re-enacts the story of how the country gained its independence.

Eating, drinking and nightlife

There are plenty of places to **eat**, some trendy bars and cafés in downtown, especially along Calle 25 de Mayo, and a number of **nightspots** mostly located in the chic neighbourhood of **Yerba Buena**, three or four kilometres west of the centre, on slightly higher ground. **Discos** change name and location at the drop of a hat, so ask around.

El Alto de la Lechuza 24 de Septiembre 1199. One of the oldest *peñas*, or traditional music venues, in the country – there's great improvised music in an ancient building where the empanadas are particularly succulent. It's busy till late every day Wed–Sun.

Cilantro Monteagudo 541. Fusion food and an excellent wine list at this highly regarded – and very fashionable – restaurant. Leave room for dessert and one of the delicious liqueurs on offer. Closed Sun dinner.

Millennium Bistró Av Aconquija 1702, Yerba Buena. A popular, trendy pre-disco restaurant, bar and tearoom all rolled into one, with fashionable decor, in the cool heights of suburban Yerba Buena.

Pizzeria Io Salta 602. Vying for the best pizza award, this place bakes its pizzas in a wood oven and shows more than usual imagination with the toppings.

Plaza de Almas Maipú 791. Popular place where locals flock to see the latest art exhibition, or just have a drink among friends. It also serves sandwiches, pizzas and other simple dishes.

Il Postino Córdoba 501 and 25 de Mayo. A reliable pizzeria that also serves good pasta, in a laidback atmosphere.

Setimio Vinoteca & Wine Bar Santa Fe 512. As the full name suggests, this pricey place takes its wine seriously – either sample it by the glassful with a hearty *picada* or enjoy the braised lamb and other fine dishes with a bottle of top-quality malbec or syrah.

Listings

Airlines Aerolíneas Argentinas, 9 de Julio 110 ☏ 0381/431-1030.

Exchange Noroeste Cambios, San Martín 771.

Internet access *Locutorios* all around the city offer internet services.

Laundry Lavadero 25, 25 de Mayo 950.

Post office 9 de Julio and Córdoba.

Tafí del Valle, Amaicha and Quilmes

Some of the Northwest's finest scenery is within easy reach of Tucumán. Nothing can provide a more startling contrast than the steep ascent from the steamy lowlands, through the tangled mossy jungle of the Selva Tucumana, up to **Tafí del Valle** amid the bare mountains of the Sierra del Aconquija. An unusual museum, at **Amaicha**, and a restored pre-Inca fortress, at **Quilmes**, are the two main attractions in the far west of Tucumán Province, at the southern end of the Valles Calchaquíes, on the other side of the sierra. While these can all be visited on classic day-trips from Tucumán, you may wish to stay over in Tafí.

Tafí de Valle

TAFÍ DEL VALLE, 128km west of Tucumán by the RP-307 – which turns off the RN-38 at Acheral, 42km southwest of the provincial capital – makes an ideal alternative stopover to Tucumán itself, especially in the summer when the city swelters, or a cool day-trip. The dramatic journey lifts you out of the moist lowlands of eastern Tucumán Province, emerald-green sugar plantations as far as the eye can see, up through the tangled mass of **Selva Tucumana** – ablaze with blossom from September to December – to the dry steppe of the highland valley that gives Tafí its name. As the RP-307 snakes up steep jungle-clad cliffs, it offers fewer and fewer glimpses of the subtropical plains way below, where the sugar fields look increasingly like paddyfields and the individual trees of the citrus orchards resemble the dots of a pointillist painting. At 2000m, the road levels off and skirts the eastern bank of **Dique la Angostura**, a large reservoir; the often-snowy peak of extinct volcano **Cerro Pelao**, 2680m, is mirrored in the lake's still surface. If you head in a westerly direction towards Potrerillo along the RP-355, a signposted turning to El Mollar brings you to the **Parque de los Menhires**, where a number of engraved **monoliths**, deceptively Celtic-looking in appearance – but in fact the work of the Tafí tribes who farmed the area around two thousand years ago – have been planted haphazardly in a field. They used to be scattered decoratively on an exposed hill overlooking the lake at La Angostura, but weathering and graffiti led the authorities to move the historic standing stones to a safer, but not aesthetically pleasing, location.

From the turn-off to Potrerillo, the RP-307 continues north to reach Tafí del Valle itself, a sprawling village in the western lee of the Sierra del Aconquija, and sandwiched between the Río del Chusquí and the Río Blanquita, both of which flow into the Río Tafí and then into the reservoir. Although blue and sunny skies are virtually guaranteed year-round, occasionally thick fog descends into the valley in the winter, making its alpine setting feel bleak and inhospitable. While Tafí is a favourite weekend and summer retreat for Tucumanos – the average temperature is 12°C lower than in the city – there's very little to do here except explore the surrounding mountains and riverbanks, but the trekking is very rewarding. Popular trails go up **Cerro El Matadero** (3050m; 5hr), **Cerro Pabellón** (3770m; 4hr), **Cerro Muñoz** (4437m; one day) and **Mala-Mala** (3500m; 8hr); go with a guide, as the weather is unpredictable. The town's main streets, lime-tree-lined Avenida San Martín, and avenidas Gobernador Critto and Diego de Rojas (Av Perón on some maps), converge on the semicircular plaza, around which most of the hotels, restaurants, cafés and shops are concentrated. Across the Río Tafí, 1km from the Plaza, the **Capilla Jesuítica de la Banda** (Mon–Fri 10am–6pm, Sat & Sun 9am–noon; $2; guided tours), is a late eighteenth-century Jesuit building now housing archeological finds, mostly ceramic urns, from nearby digs, plus some items of furniture and modest paintings from the colonial period. Famous for its delicious cow's and goat's cheese, available at small farms and stalls all around the town, Tafí holds a lively **Fiesta Nacional del Queso**, with folk music and dancing and rock bands, in early February.

Arrival and information

Buses from Tucumán, Santa María and Cafayate arrive at the terminal on the corner of avenidas San Martín and Gobernador Campero (☎03867/421025). Information can just about be gleaned from the **tourist office** on the southeastern edge of the main square (☎03867/421020, ⑩www.tafidelvalle.com), though you may find *La Cumbre* hostel (see below) more useful.

Accommodation

Accommodation in Tafí is plentiful, and often very good, ranging from a very comfortable hostel to luxurious lodgings offering haute cuisine. Rooms can get booked up at weekends in the summer, and during the cheese festival (early Feb) will be like gold dust. There is a campsite, *Los Sauzales* (☎03867/421084), at Los Palenques on the banks of Río El Churqui.

Estancia Las Carreras RP-325 Km13 ☎03867/4214732, ⑩www.estancialascarreras.com. Rather a way from the village centre, this traditional Jesuit estancia is very much a family-oriented place. Guests have contact with farm animals, dogs and horses; there's a cheese dairy on the premises; and the rooms are large and beautifully decorated, with lots of locally produced textiles. **⑥**

Estancia Los Cuartos Juan Calchaquí ☎03867/421444, ⑩www.estancialoscuartos.com. A truly *criollo* estancia experience – you can even visit for the day (including lunch and horse ride, for $200) – at this traditional family home conveniently located right next to the bus terminal. There are

seven charming rooms in the long galleried *casco* or in a more recent extension. **⑥**

Hospedaje Celia Correa Belgrano 443 ☎03867/421170. The pick of the budget options, it has basic but en-suite rooms. **❸**

Hostel La Cumbre Av Presidente Perón 120 ☎03867/421768, ⑩www.lacumbretafidelvalle .com. Tafí's hostel – highly recommended – is in a Neocolonial house built on two floors around a bright patio, all painted yellow; it doubles up as a de facto information office, much better than the official one, plus an adventure travel tour company, Yungas. **❷**

Hostería ACA Sol del Valle San Martín and Gobernador Campero ☎03867/421027,

@ tafi@soldelvalle.com.ar. This well-refurbished institution is excellent value, with bright, clean and comfortable rooms. There is also a very good restaurant on the premises. ❻

Hostería Castillo de Piedra La Banda s/n ☎03867/421199. This fabulously professional place is a quaint stone mock castle on the outside, but has designer rooms on the inside, with exquisite furnishings, great views, a swimming

pool, a sauna and, above all, a gourmet restaurant – call ahead if you are not staying at the *hostería* but want to come for a meal. ❽–❾

Hostería Huayra Puca Los Menhires 71 ☎03867/421190, @www.huayrapuca.com.ar. Unpretentious place with characterful, spacious, centrally heated rooms, soothing decor, unobjectionable artwork and a fine bar/ *confitería*. ❻

Eating and drinking

The best **places to eat**, apart from the wonderful restaurant at the *Castillo de Piedra* (call ahead to book; ☎03867/421199), are *El Portal de Tafí*, on Avenida Diego de Rojas; *La Rueda*, on Avenida Gobernador Critto; and *Rancho de Félix*, at avenidas Diego de Rojas and Belgrano, south of the plaza; they all serve local dishes plus *parrilladas* in a cosy alpine atmosphere. *El Parador Tafinista*, on the corner of avenidas Gobernador Critto and Diego de Rojas, dishes up hefty portions of pasta and grilled meat. For scrumptious coffees, teas, cakes, scones and, above all, *alfajores*, head for *El Blanquito*, a fabulous tearoom with outside tables on the road towards Amaicha.

Amaicha

To get to the village of **AMAICHA**, take the RP-307, which zigzags northwards from Tafí, offering views of the *embalse* and the mountains – but be warned that low cloud often persists here, so you might be penetrating a blanket of thick fog instead – and heaves you over the wind swept pass at Abra del Infiernillo (3042m). From here, the road steeply winds back down, along the banks of the Río de Amaicha. It takes you through arid but impressive landscapes thickly covered with a forest of *cardón* cacti, with the Cumbres Calchaquíes to the east and the Sierra de Quilmes ahead of you, until you reach Amaicha itself. The peaceful, nondescript little place livens up during the **Fiesta de la Pachamama** in carnival week, when dancers and musicians lay on shows while locals put on a kind of pre-Columbian Passion Play, acting the roles of the different pagan deities, including Pachamama, or Mother Earth. Along with a number of small eateries serving delicious *locro*, the *Casa de Piedra* is open for meals year-round; it also sells local crafts.

Just 200m along the road from the village centre, near the junction with the RP-357, is the splendid **Museo Pachamama** (daily 8.30am–1pm & 2–6pm; $10). The brainchild of local artist Héctor Cruz, it's actually several museums rolled into one, and it's worth a look to see the structure itself, built around fabulous cactus gardens and incorporating eye-catching stone mosaics, depicting llamas, pre-Hispanic symbols and geometric patterns. Each large room in turn displays an impressive array of local archeological finds, the well-executed reconstruction of a mine along with impressive samples of various precious and semi-precious ores and minerals extracted in the area, plus paintings, tapestries and ceramics from Cruz's own workshops, to modern designs inspired by pre-Columbian artistic traditions.

Beyond Amaicha, the RP-307 veers westwards before running south to Santa María, in Catamarca Province, from where you can travel down to Belén (see p.366), whereas the RP-357, a straight well-surfaced road, takes you northwest for 15km to the RN-40, which heads north along the west bank of the Río Calchaquí towards Quilmes (see p.366) and Cafayate (see p.338). The regular **buses** from Tafí to Quilmes and Cafayate will drop you off by Amaicha's museum.

Quilmes

Just 3km north of the RP-357/RN-40 junction, 15km north of Amaicha, is the westward turn-off to the major pre-Inca **archeological site** of **Quilmes**, one of the most extensively restored in the country. **Buses** to Cafayate running along the RN-40 will drop you at the junction, leaving you with the 5km trek along the dusty side road to the site (daily 9am–dusk; $10). Inhabited since the ninth century AD, the settlement of Quilmes had a population of over 3000 at its peak in the seventeenth century, but the whole Quilmes tribe was punished mercilessly by the Spanish colonizers for resisting evangelization and enslavement. Walls and many buildings in this terraced **pukará**, or pre-Columbian fortress, have been thoroughly, if not always expertly, excavated and reconstructed, and the overall effect is extremely impressive, especially in the morning light, when the mountains behind it are illuminated from the east and turn bright orange. The entrance fee also entitles you to visit the site **museum**, which contains some items found here, such as ceramics and stone tools, and displays more expensive modern crafts by local artist Héctor Cruz (p.365).

Belén and Londres

Mysteriously overlooked by most visitors – no doubt because of its relative inaccessibility by public transport – Catamarca Province becomes utterly spectacular as you leave behind the populated eastern valleys and climb towards the lonely **altiplano**. Across the barrier of the Sierra de Ambato from the dull provincial capital lies a magical landscape of dazzling **salt flats**, rugged highland scenery and small hamlets whose inhabitants harvest walnuts, distil fabulously grapey *aguardiente* or weave rugs and ponchos for a living. Two historic villages, **Belén** and **Londres**, serve as useful halts and are worth a longer stop if you're venturing further into this dramatic outback; only the former has any decent accommodation to speak of.

Belén

The region's main settlement of **BELÉN** is squeezed between the Sierra de Belén and the river of the same name. Olive groves and plantations of capsicum – paprika-producing peppers (*pimentones*) – stretch across the fertile valley to the south. A convenient stopover, Belén offers the area's best accommodation and a couple of restaurants, and it's also a base for **adventure tourism**, including trekking and horse riding. And since Belén promotes itself as the **Capital del Poncho** you might like to visit the many excellent *teleras*, or textile workshops, dotted around the town; they also turn out beautiful blankets and sweaters made of llama, vicuña and sheep's wool, mostly in natural colours. The wool is sometimes blended with walnut bark, to give the local cloth, known as *belichas* or *belenistos*, its typical rough texture. As for **festivals**, every January 6 a pilgrimage procession clambers to a huge statue of the Virgen de Belén, overlooking the town from its high vantage point to the west, the Cerro de la Virgen.

On the western flank of its main square, **Plaza Presbítero Olmos de Aguilera**, shaded by whitewashed orange trees and bushy palms and ringed by cafés and ice-cream parlours, stands the Italianate **Iglesia Nuestra Señora de Belén**, clearly inspired by the cathedral in Catamarca and designed and built by Italian immigrants at the beginning of the twentieth century. Its brickwork is bare, without plaster or decoration, lending it a rough-hewn but not displeasing look. Housed on the first floor of a rather grim commercial arcade, at San Martín and Belgrano, half a block from the main square, the

Rhodochrosite

Rhodochrosite is a semi-precious stone, similar to onyx but unique to Argentina. It is mined only from a generous seam in the Capillitas mine, to the north of Andalgalá in Catamarca Province. Known popularly as the Rosa del Inca – and believed by the indigenous people to be the solidified blood of their ancestors – rhodochrosite is reminiscent of Florentine paper, with its slightly blurred, marble-like veins of ruby red and deep salmon-pink, layered and rippled with paler shades of rose-pink and white. Its rarity has made it Argentina's unofficial **national stone**. Much of it is sold in Buenos Aires, in luscious blocks suitable as paperweights or book-ends, or worked into fine, expensive jewellery, or into animal and bird figures, many of them kitsch.

Museo Provincial Cóndor Huasi (Tues–Sat 8am–noon & 4–8pm; $2) has one of the country's most important collections of **Diaguita** artefacts, but is poorly laid out. The huge number of ceramics, and some bronze and silver items, trace the Diaguita culture through all four archeological "periods": the Initial Period, 300 BC–300 AD, is represented by simple but by no means primitive pieces, often in the shape of squashes or maize-cobs; in the Early Period (Cóndor Huasi and Ciénaga; 300–550 AD), anthropomorphic and zoomorphic ceramics dominate, including naive representations of llamas and pumas; the Middle or Aguada Period, 650–950 AD, produced some of the museum's most prized pieces, such as a ceramic jaguar of astonishing finesse; and the Late Period, from 1000 AD onwards, includes the so-called Santa María culture, when craftsmen produced large urns, vases and amphoras decorated with complex, mostly abstract geometric patterns, with depictions of snakes, rheas and toads. There are a few Inca artefacts, too.

Practicalities

Regular but infrequent **buses** from Catamarca city, Salta and Santa María arrive at the corner of Sarmiento and Rivadavia, near the museum. For **tourist information** ask at the municipalidad, one block to the east. The best **place to stay** in the region is relative newcomer ⚘ *Hotel Belén* (℡03835/461501, ⊛www.belencat.com.ar; ❹), part of a large complex that includes a convention centre and a games room-cum-cybercafé at Belgrano and Cubas – rooms are divided into Sullka (small) and Suma (large), but both are decorated in pristine white, with dark wood furnishings and amusing ethnic bathrooms, with lots of stone and ceramic tiling; there is also a clean hostel-style dorm ($15 per person without breakfast, $20 with breakfast). *Hotel Samai*, Urquiza 349, one block east and south of the main square (℡03835/461320; ❸), is clean, and warm in winter (fans cool it enough in the summer), but certainly not luxurious. In the unlikely event that it's full, try the very basic *Hotel Gómez*, at Calchaquí 213 (℡03835/461388; ❷). Most of the **restaurants** cluster around the main square. A classic favourite is *Parrillada El Único*, housed in a rustic hut at Sarmiento and General Roca, one block north of the church. It serves excellent empanadas and does a great *locro*. However, it is now outdone by the fabulous ⚘*1900*, at Belgrano 390, a couple of blocks away towards the *Hotel Belén*; smart waiters serve up lovingly prepared lunches and dinners in a cheery brightly coloured decor – try the huge *bife de chorizo* with cheese and a potato tortilla plus the earthy house wine.

Londres

Fifteen kilometres west of Belén and even more charming, with partly crumbling adobe houses and pretty orchards, **LONDRES** lies 2km off the RN-40 along a winding road that joins its upper and lower towns, on either side of the Río Hondo, a usually dry river that peters out in the Salar de

Pipanaco. Known as the Cuna de la Nuez, or Walnut Heartland, the town celebrates the **Fiesta de la Nuez** with folklore and crafts displays during the first few days of February. Londres de Abajo, the lower town, is centred on Plaza José Eusebio Colombres, where you'll find the simple, whitewashed eighteenth-century **Iglesia de San Juan Bautista**, in front of which the walnut festival is held. The focal point for the rest of the year is Londres de Arriba's **Plaza Hipólito Yrigoyen**, overlooked by the quaint **Iglesia de la Inmaculada Concepción**, a once lovely church in a pitiful state of repair but noteworthy for a harmonious colonnade and its fine bells, said to be the country's oldest. As yet, there's no accommodation in the town, but ask around, just in case someone has a room to let.

Londres' humble present-day aspect belies a long and prestigious history, including the fact that it's Argentina's second oldest "city" (*ciudad*), founded in 1558, only five years after Santiago del Estero. **Diego de Almagro** and his expedition from Cusco began scouring the area in the 1530s and founded a settlement which was named in honour of the marriage between Philip, heir to the Spanish throne, and Mary Tudor: hence the tribute to the English capital in the village's name. Alongside the municipalidad, on the wall of which is a quaint fresco testifying to the town's glorious past, is the small but interesting **Museo Arqueológico** (Mon–Fri 8am–1pm; $5), displaying ceramics and other finds from the impressive **Shinkal ruins**. The ruins themselves lie 5km west (daily Dec–April 9am–1pm & 4–7pm; May–Nov 10am–5pm; $10); just follow the well-signposted scenic road, next to the Iglesia de la Inmaculada Concepción. Amazingly intact, though parts of it are over-restored in a zealous attempt to reconstruct the fortress, it was the site of a decisive battle in the **Great Calchaquí Uprising** (see box, p.370). After Chief Chelemín cut off the water supplies to Londres and set fire to the town, forcing its inhabitants to flee to La Rioja, he was captured and had his body ripped apart by four horses. Shinkal gives you an insight into what Diaguita settlements in the region must have looked like: splendid steps lead to the top of high **ceremonial mounds**, with great views of the oasis and Sierra de Zapata.

▲ Shinkal ruins

The Puna Catamarqueña

The altiplano of northwestern Catamarca Province, known as the **Puna Catamarqueña** (*puna* is the Quichoa word for altiplano, a word of Spanish coinage), stretches to the Chilean border and is one of the remotest and most deserted, but most outstandingly beautiful parts of the country. **Antofagasta de la Sierra**, a ghostly town of adobe-brick miners' houses and whispering womenfolk, is far flung even from Catamarca city in this sparsely populated region, but the tiny **archeological museum** is worth seeing for its fantastic mummified infant. Dotted with majestic ebony volcanoes and scarred by recent lava-flows, with the Andean cordillera as a magnificent backdrop, the huge expanses of altiplano and their desiccated vegetation are grazed by hardy yet delicate-looking **vicuñas** while **flamingoes** valiantly survive on frozen lakes. This is staggeringly unspoilt country, with out-of-this-world landscapes, and a constantly surreal atmosphere, accentuated by the sheer remoteness and emptiness of it all; the trip out here is really more rewarding than the destination, **Antofagasta**, which is primarily a place to spend the night before forging on northwards, to San Antonio de los Cobres in Salta Province (see p.333), or doubling back down to Belén. As you travel, look out for *apachetas*, little cairns of stones piled up at the roadside as an offering to the Mother Goddess, Pachamama, and the only visible signs of any human presence. Although a **bus** shuttles back and forth between Catamarca and Antofagasta twice a week, the surest way to get around is by 4WD, along the RP-43, one of the quietest roads in Argentina; it's quite possible not to pass another vehicle all day. Take all the necessary precautions including plenty of fuel, and don't forget warm clothing as the temperature can plummet several degrees below freezing at night in July. The best way to explore this difficult region is with the Salta-based Socompa tours (see p.329), which also runs the *hostería* in El Peñón, a good alternative to staying in Antofagasta, where accommodation is limited.

In **Hualfín**, a tiny village where RP-43 branches northwestwards from the RN-40, 60km north of Belén, you can find rooms for rent, if you need **accommodation**, but most people use Hualfín as their last **fuel stop** before the long haul to Antofagasta de la Sierra; provisions can also be bought here. The village itself is famous for its paprika, often sprinkled on the delicious local goat's cheeses, and a fine **colonial church**, dedicated to Nuestra Señora del Rosario and built in 1770; ask for the key at the municipalidad to see the pristine interior adorned with delicate frescoes. Hualfín was also the birthplace and stronghold of Chelemín, the Calchaquí leader who spearheaded the Great Uprising in the 1630s (see box, p.370). **Thermal springs** with rudimentary facilities, and slightly better ones 14km north at **Villavil**, are open from January to April only.

Up to Antofagasta de la Sierra

Between **Corral Quemado** and **Villavil**, the first stretch of the RP-43 to Antofagasta de la Sierra, all of 200km from Hualfín to the northwest, takes you through some cheery if understated countryside, planted with vines and maize, with feathery acacias and tall poplars acting as windbreaks, and dotted with humble mud-brick farmhouses. Potentially treacherous fords at Villavil and, more likely, at **El Bolsón**, 10km further on, are sometimes too deep to cross even in a 4WD, especially after spring thaws or summer rains; you'll either have to wait a couple of hours for the rivers to subside or turn back. Just over 70km from the junction at Hualfín, the road twists and climbs through the dramatic **Cuesta de Randolfo**, hemmed in by rocky pinnacles and reaching an altitude of 4800m before corkscrewing back down to the transitional plains. The good news is that from here to Antofagasta the road is now paved.

5

The Calchaquí wars

After the European invasions of this region in the late sixteenth and early seventeenth centuries, the indigenous tribes who lived along the **Valles Calchaquíes**, stretching from Salta Province in the north, down to central Catamarca Province, steadfastly refused to be evangelized by the Spanish invaders and generally to behave as their aggressors wanted; the region around Belén and Londres proved especially difficult to colonize. Even the Jesuits, usually so effective at bringing the "natives" under control, conceded defeat. The colonizers made do with a few *encomiendas*, and more often *pueblos*, reservations where the Indians were forced to live, leaving the colonizers to farm their "own" land in peace. After a number of skirmishes, things came to a head in 1630, when the so-called **Great Calchaquí Uprising** began. For two years, under the leadership of **Juan Chelemín**, the fierce cacique of Hualfín, natives waged a war of attrition against the invaders, sacking towns and burning crops, provoking ever more brutal reactions from the ambitious new governor of Tucumán, Francisco de Nieva y Castilla. Eventually Chelemín was caught, drawn and quartered, and various parts of his body were put on display in different villages to "teach the Calchaquíes a lesson", but it took until 1643 for all resistance to be stamped out, and only after a network of fortresses was built in Andalgalá, Londres and elsewhere.

War broke out once more in 1657, when the Spanish decided to arrest "El Inca Falso", also known as Pedro Chamijo, an impostor of European descent who claimed to be Hualpa Inca – or Inca emperor – under the nom de guerre of **Bohórquez**. Elected chief at an impressive ceremony attended by the new governor of Tucumán, Alonso Mercado y Villacorta, amid great pomp and circumstance, in Pomán, he soon led the Calchaquíes into battle, and Mercado y Villacorta, joined by his ruthless predecessor, Francisco de Nieva y Castilla, set about what today would be called ethnic cleansing. Bohórquez was captured, taken to Lima and eventually garrotted in 1667, and whole tribes fell victim to genocide: their only remains are the ruins of Batungasta, Hualfín and Shinkal, near Londres. Some tribes like the **Quilmes**, whose settlement is now an archeological site near Amaicha (see p.366), were uprooted and forced to march to Buenos Aires. Out of seven thousand Quilmes who survived a long and distressing siege in their *pukará*, or fortress, despite having their food and water supplies cut off, before being led in chains to Buenos Aires, where they were employed as slaves, only a few hundred were left. These few remaining survivors, however, were sadly wiped out in a smallpox epidemic at the end of the eighteenth century.

Along this flat section, you're treated to immense open views towards the dramatic crags of the Sierra del Cajón, to the south, and the spiky rocks of the Sierra Laguna Blanca, to the north. Impressive white **sand dunes**, gleaming like fresh snow against the dark mountainsides, make an interesting pretext for a halt. Down in the plain, the immense **salt lakes** stretch for miles and this is where you'll probably spy your first **vicuñas** – the shy, smaller cousins of the llamas with much silkier wool – protected by the **Reserva Natural Laguna Blanca**. All along this road, with photogenic ochre mountains as backdrops, whole flocks of vicuñas graze off scrawny grasses, less timid than usual, perhaps because the flocks are so big and they feel the safety of numbers. You'll also see nonchalant llamas and shaggy alpacas and, if you're very fortunate, the ostrich-like suris or ñandús, before they scurry away nervously. You could make a short detour to visit the shores of **Laguna Blanca** itself, a shallow, mirror-like lake fed by the Río Río and home to thousands of teals, ducks and **flamingoes**; it's clearly signposted along a track off to the north. A few kilometres on, the road then climbs steadily again up the often snow-streaked Sierra Laguna Blanca to reach the pass at **Portezuelo Pasto Ventura** (4000m), marked by a sign: this is the entrance to the altiplano, or *puna* proper. From here you have magnificent panoramas of the Andes, to the west, and of the great volcanoes of northwestern Catamarca, plus your first glimpse of wide-rimmed **Volcán Galan** (5912m), whose name means "bare mountain" in Quichoa. It's an incredible geological feature: some 2,500,000 years ago, in a cataclysmic eruption, blasting over 1000 cubic kilometres of material into the air, its top was blown away, leaving a hole measuring over 45km by 25km, the largest known crater on the Earth's surface, or in the solar system as locals like to boast.

Intriguing **El Peñón**, 135km from Hualfín, is the first altiplano settlement you reach along RP-43: just a few gingerbread-coloured adobe houses,; a good *hostería*, run by Socompa tours (see p.329); some proud poplar trees; and an apple orchard, surprising given the altitude. The village nestles in the **Carachipampa Valley**, which extends all the way to the Cordillera de San Buenaventura, to the southwest, and its striking summit **Cerro El Cóndor** (6000m), clearly visible from here in the searingly clear atmosphere. Soon the chestnut-brown volcanic cones of **Los Negros de la Laguna** come into view, a sign that you're in the final approaches to Antofagasta. One of twin peaks, **La Alumbrera** deposited enormous lava flows when it last erupted, only a few hundred years ago. The huge piles of visibly fresh **black pumice** that it tossed out, all pocked and twisted, reach heights of ten metres or more. Just before Antofagasta, the road swings round **Laguna Colorada**, a small lake often frozen solid and shaded pink with a massive flock of altiplanic flamingoes which somehow survive up here.

Antofagasta de la Sierra and around

Perched 3440m above sea level, 260km north of Belén, **ANTOFAGASTA DE LA SIERRA** lies at the northern end of a vast, arid plain hemmed in by volcanoes to the east and south, and by the cordillera, which soars to peaks of over 6000m, a mere 100km over to the west. With a population of under a thousand it exudes a feeling of utter remoteness, while still managing to exert a disarming fascination. It's a bleak yet restful place, an oasis of tamarinds and green alfalfa fields in the middle of the *meseta altiplánica* – a harsh steppe that looms above the surrounding altiplano. Two rivers, Punilla and Las Paitas, meet just to the south, near the strange volcanic plug called **El Torreón**, adopted as the town's symbol. Named after the Chilean port-city, this is a tough town with a harsh climate, where night temperatures in midwinter drop well below freezing, accompanied by biting winds and a relentless sun during the day: its name means "home of the Sun" in the language of the Diaguita. Salt, borax and various minerals and metals have been mined in the area for centuries and Antofagasta has the hardy feel of a mining town, but most of its people are now subsistence farmers and herdsmen, scraping a living from maize, potatoes, onions and beans or rearing llamas and alpacas, whose wool is made into textiles. The people here are introverted and placid, hospitable but seemingly indifferent to the outside world.

The best views of the immediate surroundings can be enjoyed from the top of the Cerro Amarillo and Cerro de la Cruz, two unsightly mounds of earth that look like part of a huge building-site and dominate the town's humble streets of small mud-brick houses. The **Cerro de la Cruz** is the destination of processions held to honour Antofagasta's patron saints, St Joseph and the Virgin of Loreto, from December 8 to 10. In another sombre ceremony, the town's dead are remembered on November 1 and 2, when villagers file to and from the cemetery before a feast, talking in whispers so as not to disturb the spirits. And every March the town comes to life, for the **Feria Artesanal y Ganadera de la Puna**, a colourful event attended by craftspeople and herdsmen from all over the province. The only tourist attraction in the town is the beautifully presented **Museo Arqueológico** (Mon–Fri 8am–6pm; $2), recently created primarily to house a perfectly preserved, naturally mummified baby, found in the mountains nearby and believed to be nearly two thousand years old; surrounded with jewels and other signs of wealth, suggesting the child belonged to a ruling dynasty, it exerts a morbid fascination. The museum's other exhibits, few in number but of extraordinary value, include an immaculately preserved pre-Hispanic basket, the pigment colouring and fine weave still intact.

The **bus** from Catamarca will drop you in the main street. Apart from rooms in private houses, the only **accommodation** is near the municipalidad, at the basic but scrupulously clean and much improved *Hostería de Antofagasta* (☎03835/471001; ❹), where you can also **eat**. **Fuel** can be bought at inflated prices from the pump opposite the municipalidad, so it's better to fill up before making this trip. Antofagasta has no tourist office; for visiting the immediate and farther-flung surroundings ask at the municipalidad for the town's most experienced guides, Catalino Soriano, Antolín Ramos and Jesús Vásquez.

Around Antofagasta de la Sierra

The mostly unsealed and sometimes very bumpy RP-43 (in Catamarca Province, becoming RP-17 in Salta Province) leads north from Antofagasta to **San Antonio de los Cobres** (see p.333), 330km away via Caucharí. Antofagasta could therefore be visited as part of a gigantic loop, taking in vast, lonely yet dramatically memorable tracts of Salta and Catamarca provinces, but allow plenty of time and take far more provisions and fuel supplies than you think you'll need – in other words reckon on two or three days' food and several jerry-cans of petrol in reserve. The same road leads to the desolate, disorientingly mirage-like landscapes of the great **Salar del Hombre Muerto salt flats**, 75km to the north of Antofagasta and best explored using the services of a *baqueano*, or guide. **Cerro Ratones** (5252m) and Cerro Incahuasi (4847m) form a breathtaking backdrop to the bright whiteness of the flats.

Within easy excursion distance of Antofagasta are a number of archeological and historical sites, such as the ruins at **Campo Alumbreras**, 5km south, and **Coyparcito**, 3km further away. The pre-Columbian **pukará**, or fortress, on the flanks of the Alumbrera volcano, a few kilometres south of Antofagasta, and nearby **petroglyphs** (mostly depicting llamas and human figures) are also worth a visit; you'll definitely need the services of a guide to find them, and for the necessary explanations to make a visit worthwhile, but they are all open to the public at all times and no entrance fee is charged. Ask at Antofagasta's museum for archeological information and guided visits. The abandoned onyx, mica and gold **mines** in the region are another interesting attraction, while long treks on mule-back are the only way of seeing **Volcán Sufre** (5706m) on the Chilean border. If you want quieter recreation than climbing mountains or scrambling through disused mines you might try a day's **trout fishing** at **Paicuquí**, 20km north of Antofagasta. In the crystal-clear streams you can catch delicious rainbow trout.

Travel details

Buses

Jujuy to: Buenos Aires (hourly; 20hr); Córdoba (10 daily; 13hr); Humahuaca (hourly; 3hr); La Quiaca (hourly; 7hr); Purmamarca (hourly; 1hr 15min); Resistencia (1 daily; 14hr); Salta (hourly; 1hr 30min); Tilcara (hourly; 2hr); Tucumán (10 daily; 5hr 30min).
Salta to: Buenos Aires (hourly; 18hr); Cachi (2 daily; 5hr); Cafayate (7 daily; 3hr); Córdoba (10 daily; 12hr); Jujuy (hourly; 1hr 30min); Resistencia (1 daily; 13hr); Tucumán (10 daily; 4hr).

Tucumán to: Buenos Aires (10 daily; 15hr); Córdoba (6 daily; 8hr); Jujuy (10 daily; 5hr 30min); Salta (10 daily; 4hr); Tafí del Valle (6 daily; 3hr).

Flights

Jujuy to: Buenos Aires (3 daily; 2hr 10min); Salta (1 daily; 20min).
Salta to: Buenos Aires (6 daily; 2hr); Jujuy (1 daily; 20min).
Tucumán to: Buenos Aires (6 daily; 1hr 50min).

6

Mendoza, San Juan and La Rioja

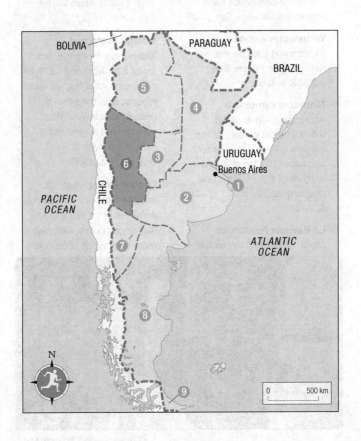

CHAPTER 6 # Highlights

✳ **Mendoza city** Argentina's wine capital has a lot to offer, from top-class dining to a vibrant nightlife. See p.378

✳ **Bodega Salentein** Who said the Dutch can't make wine? This "Wine Cathedral" is one of the continent's most impressive wineries. See p.391

✳ **Whitewater rafting** Exhilarating trips on the region's feisty rivers See p.393 & p.405

✳ **Mountain climbing** If Aconcagua – one of the world's tallest peaks – is too crowded, then take your tent and ropes to Mercedario or another of the Andes' great challenges. See p.398, p.401 & p.422

✳ **La Payunia** A secluded region of ancient volcanoes, dark and rust-red lava flows, and photogenic guanacos. See p.412

✳ **Flour mills of Jáchal** Part of Argentina's industrial heritage, these intriguing adobe mills are located near one of San Juan's many oasis towns. See p.425

✳ **Ischigualasto and Talampaya** The pride and joy of San Juan and La Rioja provinces – the first an eerie moonscape, the other an unsurpassable Wild West canyon with mighty red sandstone walls. See p.427 & p.430

✳ **Laguna Brava** Head up into the strikingly-coloured cordillera of La Rioja to see flamingos on this wild, high-mountain lagoon. See p.432

▲ Oak wine barrels at Bodega Salentein

6

Mendoza, San Juan and La Rioja

Argentina's midwestern provinces of **Mendoza**, **San Juan** and **La Rioja** stretch all the way from the chocolate-brown pampas of **La Payunia**, on the northern borders of Patagonia, to the remote highland steppes of the **Reserva Las Vicuñas**, on the edge of the altiplano, more than a thousand kilometres to the north. Extending across vast, thinly populated territories of bone-dry desert, they are dotted with vibrant oases of farmland and the region's famous **vineyards**: the sophisticated metropolis of **Mendoza**, one of Argentina's biggest cities, is the epicentre of the country's blossoming wine – and wine tourism – industry, while the two smaller provincial capitals, **San Juan** and **La Rioja**, continue to be quiet backwaters by comparison.

More than towns and cities, though, the area's dynamics are about its highly varied **landscapes** and **wildlife**. In the west of the provinces loom the world's loftiest peaks outside the Himalayas, culminating in the defiant **Aconcagua**, whose summit is only a shade under 7000m. Ranging from these snowy Andean heights to totally flat pampas in the east, from green, fertile valleys to barren volcanoes – including the world's second-highest cone, extinct **Monte Pissis** – the scenery also includes two of the country's most photographed national parks: the sheer red sandstone cliffs of **Talampaya** and the moonscapes of **Ischigualasto**. All this provides a backdrop for some of Argentina's best opportunities for **extreme sport** – from **skiing** in exclusive **Las Leñas**, to whitewater rafting, rock-climbing, and even the ascent of Aconcagua or the **Mercedario** and **Tupungato** peaks.

European settlers have wrought changes to the environment, bringing the grape vine, the Lombardy poplar and all kinds of fruit trees with them, but the thousands of kilometres of irrigation channels that water the region existed long before Columbus "discovered" America. Pumas and vicuñas, condors and ñandús, plus hundreds of colourful bird species inhabit the thoroughly unspoilt wildernesses of the region, where some of the biggest known dinosaurs prowled millions of years ago. Countless flowering **cacti** and the dazzling yellow *brea*, a broom-like shrub, add colour to the browns and greys of the desert in the spring.

Mendoza, San Juan and La Rioja provinces make up three quarters of a region known as **El Nuevo Cuyo**, and you will often see the words *Cuyo* and *Cuyano* here, particularly in names of travel companies. The etymological origins of the word *cuyo* are not entirely clear, but it probably comes from the native Huarpe

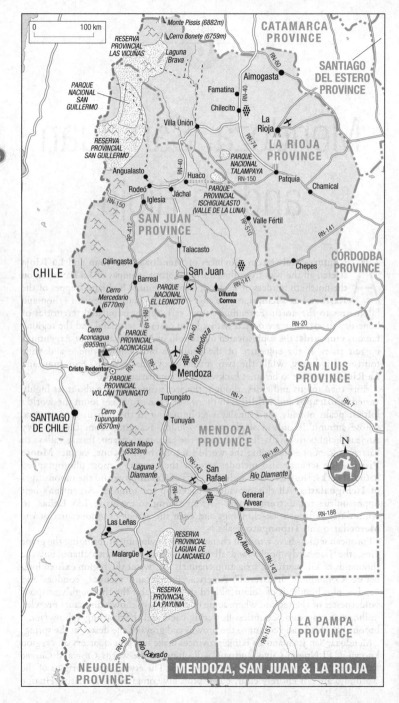

MENDOZA, SAN JUAN & LA RIOJA

word *xuyu*, meaning riverbed. The area has strong historical ties with Chile, and the accent in much of the region reflects this – with, for example, the "-ll" and "-y" being pronounced as the "y" in yellow, as it is in Chile, rather than the "sh" sound you hear in Buenos Aires.

Mendoza Province

The southern half of El Nuevo Cuyo is taken up by **Mendoza Province**, the self-styled Tierra del Sol y del Buen Vino, the "land of sunshine and good wine". Within its borders are enough attractions to occupy a whole holiday, including some of the country's most dramatic **mountain landscapes**, where you can try a host of adventure pursuits, from kayaking to hang-gliding. The charms of its lively capital city, **Mendoza**, can satisfy yearnings for creature comforts after treks, climbs into the Andes or a day of whitewater rafting. Although Mendoza Province shares many things with San Juan and La Rioja – bleak wildernesses backed by snow-peaked mountains, remarkably varied flora and fauna, an incredibly sunny climate prone to sudden temperature changes and pockets of rich farmland mainly used to produce beefy red wines – it differs in the way it exploits all these assets. At the national level Mendoza leads the way in **tourism** just as it does in the **wine industry**, combining professionalism with enthusiasm plus a taste for the alternative or avant-garde. The two industries come together for Mendoza city's nationally famous **Fiesta de la Vendimia**, or Wine Harvest Festival, held in early March, a slightly kitsch but exuberant bacchanalia at which a carnival queen is elected from candidates representing every town in the province.

For travelling purposes Mendoza Province can be divided into three sections, each with its own base. The north, around the capital, has the country's biggest concentration of vineyards and top-class **wineries**, clustered around **Maipú** and **Luján de Cuyo**, while the scenic **Alta Montaña** route races up in a westerly direction towards the high Chilean border, passing the mighty **Cerro Aconcagua**, an increasingly popular climbing destination. Not far to the southwest are the much more challenging **Cerro Tupungato** (6570m) and the remote **Laguna Diamante**, a choppy altiplanic lagoon in the shadow of the perfectly shaped **Volcán Maipo**, which can only be visited from December to March. Central Mendoza is focused on the laidback town of **San Rafael**, where you can taste more wine, and from where several tour operators offer whitewater rafting trips along the nearby **Cañon del Atuel**, or rivers like the Sosneado and **Diamante**. If you've always wanted to ski or snowboard in July, try the winter sports resort at **Las Leñas**, where you'll be sharing pistes with South America's jet-set. The third, least-visited section of the province wraps around the southern outpost of **Malargüe**, a final-frontier kind of place promoting itself as a centre for nature, scientific discovery and adventure. Within easy reach are the **Laguna de Llancanelo**, home to an enormous community of **flamingos**, the charcoal-grey and rust-red lava deserts of **La Payunia** and the karstic caves of **Caverna de las Brujas**. The province's dull eastern fringe bordering San Luis Province can be missed.

Tourism is so well developed in the province it's possible to visit virtually all of these places by **public transport** or on tours from Mendoza and other towns. However, to see them at your own pace and have many of them to yourself, consider renting a vehicle, preferably a 4WD, since many of the roads are, at best, only partly sealed.

Mendoza and around

MENDOZA is a mostly low-rise city, spread across the wide valley of the Río Mendoza, over 1000km west of Buenos Aires and less than 100km east of the Andean cordillera – whose perennially snowcapped peaks are clearly visible from downtown. Its airy microcentro is less compact than that of most comparable cities, partly because the streets, squares and avenues were deliberately made wide when the city was rebuilt in the late nineteenth century (see p.379), to allow for evacuation in the event of another major earthquake. Another striking feature is that every street is lined by bushy sycamore and plane trees – providing vital shade in the scorching summer months, they are watered by over 500km of *acequias*, or irrigation ditches, which form a natural, outdoor air-cooling system. Watch out, though, when you cross the city's streets, as the narrow gutters are up to a metre deep and often full of gushing water, especially in the spring when the upland snows melt.

Argentine wine

Argentina is now the world's fifth largest wine producer (after Italy, France, Spain and the US), with three-quarters of the country's total production coming from **Mendoza** province, focused on Maipú and Luján de Cuyo in the south of the city. **San Rafael**, **La Rioja** and **San Juan** are also major wine-growing centres.

Many wine experts would agree that Argentina's vintages are improving rapidly as a result of both a domestic market that's fast becoming more discerning and the lure of exports. **Table wines** still dominate, often sold at the budget end of the market in huge, refillable flagons called *damajuanas*, and sometimes marketed under usurped names such as *borgoña*, or burgundy, and chablis. Younger Argentines often only drink wine on special occasions, plumping for lighter **New Wave** wines such as Chandón's **Nuevo Mundo**. Many upmarket restaurants offer extensive wine lists including older vintages – but beware of exorbitant corkage charges. Commonly found bodega names to look for include **Chandón, Graffigna, Navarro Correas, Salentein, Finca Flichmann** and **Weinert**.

Although the most attractive wineries to visit are the old-fashioned ones, with musty cellars crammed with oak barrels, some of the finest vintages are now produced by growers using the latest equipment, including storage tanks lined with epoxy resin and computerized temperature controls. They tend to concentrate on making varietal wines, the main grape varieties being riesling, chenin blanc and chardonnay, for whites, and pinot noir, cabernet sauvignon and malbec, for reds – the reds tend to be better than whites. **Malbec** is often regarded as the Argentine grape par excellence, giving rich fruity wines, with overtones of blackcurrant and prune that are the perfect partner for a juicy steak. The latest trend is for a balanced combination of two grapes: for example, mixing malbec for its fruitiness and cabernet for its body, while toning down the sometimes excessive oakiness that used to characterize Argentine wines. Growers have also been experimenting with varieties such as tempranillo, san gervase, gewürztraminer, syrah and merlot, and very convincing sparkling wines are being made locally by the *méthode champenoise*, including those produced by Chandón and Mumm, the French champagne-makers.

The city has an attractive park and one or two museums that are worth visiting, but most people come to Mendoza principally to do a **wine-tasting tour** at the many **bodegas** in or near the city (see box opposite). Mendoza's leading restaurants serve seafood from the Pacific coast and delicious, fresh produce, all accompanied by the outstanding local wines. Within easy reach to the south of the city are two small satellite towns, **Luján de Cuyo** and **Maipú**, where, in addition to the majority of the region's wineries, you'll find a couple more interesting museums, one displaying the paintings of Fernando Fader – a kind of Argentine Van Gogh – and the other focusing on the wine industry. And, in a very different vein, the city also acts as a base for some of the world's most thrilling **mountain-climbing** opportunities.

Some history

Mendoza started out as part of the **Spanish colony of Chile**. In 1561 García Hurtado de Mendoza, captain-general of Chile, sent over an expedition led by Pedro del Castillo to establish a colony from which to "civilize" the indigenous Huarpe; Castillo named the town he founded after his boss. Soon flourishing, Mendoza continued to be ruled from across the Andes, though its isolation enabled it to live a life of its own. The extensive network of pre-Hispanic **irrigation canals** was exploited by the colonizers, who planted **vineyards** that soon became South America's most productive. By 1700, the city's merchants were selling wine to Santiago, Córdoba and Buenos Aires. After the Viceroyalty of the River Plate was created in 1777, Mendoza was incorporated into the huge **Córdoba Intendencia**. Mendocinos are still proud of the fact that San Martín's Army of the Andes was trained in their city before thrashing the Spanish royalist troops at the Battle of Maipú, Chile, in 1818.

Once Argentina gained its independence, however, Mendoza began to suffer from its relative isolation, stagnating by the mid-nineteenth century. Worse was to come, though: as night fell on March 20, 1861, three hundred years after the city's founding, an **earthquake** smashed every building in Mendoza to rubble, and some four thousand people, a third of the population, lost their lives. It's believed to have been one of the worst ever to have hit South America in recorded history, an estimated 7.8 on the Richter scale. Seismologists now believe that the epicentre lay right in the middle of the city, explaining why the damage was so terrible and yet restricted in radius. Pandemonium ensued, God-fearing Mendocinos seeing the timing – the city's anniversary and Eastertide – as double proof of divine retribution. Remarkably, a new city was quickly built, overseen by the French urban planner **Ballofet**, who created wide streets, open squares and low buildings for the new-look Mendoza. The city's isolation ended soon afterwards, with the arrival of the railway in 1884. The earth continues to shake noticeably at frequent intervals, but all construction in modern Mendoza is designed to be earthquake resistant.

Gran Mendoza (or "Greater Mendoza"), with a population of close to one million, includes the city centre – home to around 150,000 people – plus leafy suburbs such as **Chacras de Coria** and **Las Heras**, and industrial districts, such as Godoy Cruz. Wine, petrochemicals, a thriving university and, more recently, **tourism** have been the mainstays of the city economy.

Arrival, information and city transport

Officially called Aeropuerto Internacional Ing. Francisco J. Gabrielli, but known popularly as "Plumerillo" after the suburb where it's located, Mendoza's modern and efficient **airport** (℡0261/520-6000 ext 101) is only 7km north of the city centre, just off the RN-40. **Taxis** and *remises* are in plentiful supply, or **buses**

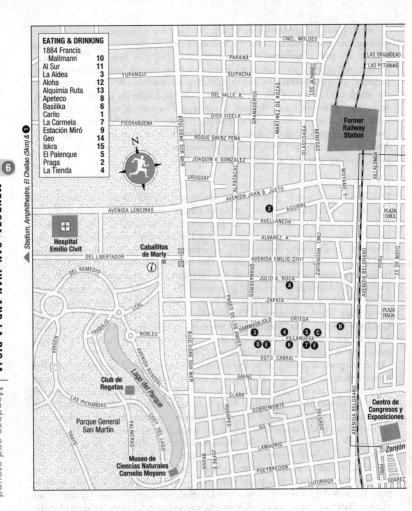

EATING & DRINKING

1884 Francis Mallmann	10
Al Sur	11
La Aldea	3
Aloha	12
Alquimia Ruta	13
Apeteco	8
Basilika	6
Carilo	1
La Carmela	7
Estación Miró	9
Geo	14
Iskra	15
El Palenque	5
Praga	2
La Tienda	4

#6/63 can also take you downtown; for information, ask at the Atención al Cliente office. Heading back to the airport, be sure to catch a bus that has an "Aeropuerto" sign in the windscreen.

Mendoza's very busy **bus station** (℡0261/431-5000) is slightly drab, but has plenty of facilities, including a small **tourist office** (7am–10pm). There are buses to and from just about everywhere in the country, plus Santiago de Chile, Lima and Montevideo. It's due east of the microcentro, on the edge of the suburb of Guaymallén, at the corner of avenidas Gobernador Videla (usually referred to as the Costanera) and Acceso Este (RN-7); this is less than 1km from the city centre but if the walk is too much, the "Villa Nueva" trolley-bus ($1.40) is a cheaper alternative to a taxi.

The main **tourist office** (Mon–Fri 8am–9pm, Sat & Sun 9am–9pm; ℡0261/413-2101 or 420-2800, ⓦwww.turismo.mendoza.gov.ar) is at San Martín 1143, a building that was previously the Jockey Club; this is also the place to obtain Aconcagua climbing permits (see p. 400). Another city **tourist office** is at Edificio

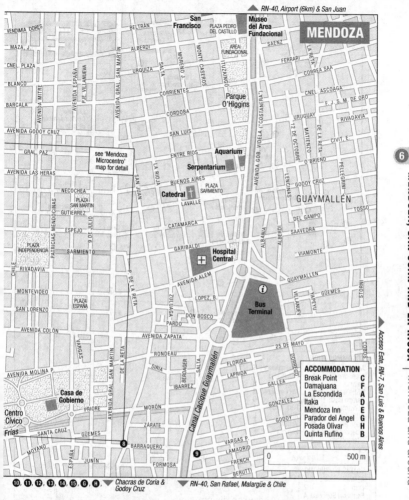

MENDOZA

6

MENDOZA, SAN JUAN AND LA RIOJA | Mendoza and around

Acceso Este, RN-7, San Luis & Buenos Aires

see 'Mendoza Microcentro' map for detail

Parque O'Higgins

Aquarium

Serpentarium

Catedral ✝

Hospital Central ✚

ⓘ

Bus Terminal

Casa de Gobierno

Centro Cívico

Frías

ACCOMMODATION

Break Point	C
Damajuana	F
La Escondida	A
Itaka	D
Mendoza Inn	E
Parador del Angel	G
Posada Olivar	H
Quinta Rufino	B

0 — 500 m

⑩, ⑪, ⑫, ⑬, ⑭, ⑮, Ⓖ, Ⓗ, ▼ *Chacras de Coria & Godoy Cruz*   ▼ RN-40, San Rafael, Malargüe & Chile

Municipal, 9 de Julio 500 (Mon–Fri 8.30am–1.30pm; ☎0261/449-5185), as well as one in the satellite town of Luján de Cuyo (see p. 393) at Sáenz Peña 1000 (Mon–Fri 8.30am–6pm, Sat & Sun 10am–4pm; ☎0261/498-1912).

The tourist office also runs guided walks with themes such as history or religion – ask for the latest timetable and a number of tour operators run half-day **city tours** (see "Listings", p.393). For finding your own way around, there are **buses** and **trolley-buses** – the latter mostly serving the inner suburbs plus the bus station. They have a complex numbering system, with a logic that escapes most people; study the map displayed at each stop. You pay a flat $1.40 fare for both – no change given – except for much longer distances such as the airport.

Accommodation

Mendoza is very well off for places to stay, with more than enough beds for its needs, except during the Fiesta de la Vendimia in early March. It has several

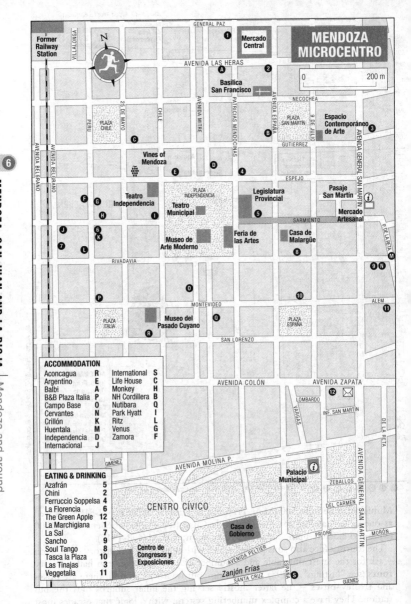

MENDOZA MICROCENTRO

0   200 m

ACCOMMODATION

Aconcagua	R	International	S
Argentino	E	Life House	C
Balbi	A	Monkey	H
B&B Plaza Italia	P	NH Cordillera	B
Campo Base	O	Nutibara	Q
Cervantes	N	Park Hyatt	I
Crillón	K	Ritz	L
Huentala	M	Venus	G
Independencia	D	Zamora	F
Internacional	J		

EATING & DRINKING

Azafrán	5
Chini	2
Ferruccio Soppelsa	4
La Florencia	6
The Green Apple	12
La Marchigiana	1
La Sal	7
Sancho	9
Soul Tango	8
Tasca la Plaza	10
Las Tinajas	3
Veggetalia	11

luxurious **hotels**, including branches of top-class international chains, as well as over a dozen **youth hostels** (dorms range in price from $30–60), plus a couple of **B&Bs**. In the middle range are countless nondescript but decent smaller hotels. At the higher end, particularly interesting options are **bodega hotels** or **posadas**, many of which are in the swish suburbs of Chacras de Coria and Maipú. The quiet, suburban location of these bodega hotels does mean that unless you have your own car you may be more or less limited to the delights the bodega has to offer. Always book bodega accommodation ahead, and let your hosts know if you don't have your own transport, as they will usually pick you up from Mendoza city or airport.

If you haven't got anything booked, the best street to head for is Arístides Villanueva (usually referred to as Arístides), three blocks south and four blocks west of the Plaza Independencia – it's packed with both hostels and more upmarket options. You can also ask at the tourist office for their list of rooms to rent in private houses. Campers should make for the heights of El Challao, 6km northwest, where **campsite** *El Suizo* (℡0261/444-1991, Ⓦwww.campingsuizo.com.ar) sits among shady woods on Avenida Champagnat. It has a swimming pool, a small restaurant and even an open-air cinema; tent pitches and *cabañas* (both ❶) are available. **Bus** #110 runs out to El Challao from the corner of Salta and Avenida Além.

Hostels

Break Point Av Arístides Villanueva 241 ℡0261/423-9514, Ⓦwww.breakpointhostel .com.ar. At the heart of the city's *movida* zone, this hostel offers free internet, all kinds of tours, a large TV lounge and a small pool. An added bonus is the excellent-value *parrilla*. The private rooms (❹) are particularly good value for solo travellers.

Campo Base Mitre 946 ℡0261/429-0707, Ⓦwww.campobase.com.ar. The youth hostel traditionally preferred by Aconcagua climbers, as the owners organize their own treks. Clean, friendly and very laidback, with lots of barbecues, parties and general fun, though some of the dorms are slightly cramped. One double room (❸). If it's full, try its sister hostel, *Mendoza Inn*, at Arístides Villanueva 470 (℡0261/420-2486; ❸).

Damajuana Arístides Villanueva 282 ℡0261/425-5858, Ⓦwww.damajuanahostel.com.ar. Airy hostel in one of the city's main nightlife areas. One of its best features is the garden, with its decent-sized pool. Organizes tours. One double room with shared bathroom (❹).

Independencia Mitre 1237 ℡0261/423-1806, Ⓦwww.hostelindependencia.com.ar. Nicely located in an attractive townhouse near the plaza of the same name, this has a fully equipped kitchen, a games room, a patio, one double room (❷) and a triple, in addition to pleasant dorms. The staff organize bodega tours and treks.

International España 343 ℡0261/424-0018, Ⓦwww.hostelmendoza.net. The best-established of all the hostels, with a bright patio, welcoming ambience, small dorms with private bathroom and an excellent kitchen; the staff can also fix you up with tours and sports activities in the whole region. Its *El Carajo* bar is a popular meeting-place, and there's an *asado* cook-out most Fri. Private rooms available (❷).

Itaka Av Arístides Villanueva 480 ℡0261/4239793, Ⓦwww.itakahouse.com. Fun and friendly newcomer with pretty patio and garden, above-average kitchen facilities and a small pool. Dorms and doubles (❹).

Life House Gutiérrez 565 ℡0261/420-4294, Ⓦwww.lifehouse.com.ar. Two-, four- and six-bed rooms with their own bath, decent kitchen, barbecue area and small swimming pool, at this friendly if rather neglected hostel. ❷

Monkey Hostel Sarmiento 681 ℡0261/423-1148, Ⓦwww.monkeyhostel.com. Clean, friendly and central hostel with a small pool and bar. Staff can help you organize tours. Dorms ❷, double room ❸

B&Bs and hospedajes

Bed and Breakfast Plaza Italia Montevideo 685 ℡0261/423-4219, Ⓦwww.plazaitalia.net. Genuine, English-speaking B&B in a comfortable family house with en-suite rooms, a/c and a delicious breakfast; parking. Also organize wine tours. ❼

La Escondida Julio A. Roca 344 ℡0261/425-5202, Ⓦwww.laescondidabb.com. Wonderfully welcoming B&B in a quiet residential part of the city, with a superb swimming pool at the end of a long garden; rooms are extremely comfortable. ❺

Quinta Rufino Rufino Ortega 142 ℡0261/420-4696, Ⓦwww.quintarufinohostel.com.ar A converted house in a quiet neighbourhood, with pleasant en-suite rooms; friendly staff. ❸

Zamora Perú 1156 ℡0261/425-7537, Ⓦwww .hotelzamora.netfirms.com. A Neocolonial villa with clean rooms around a leafy patio; ask for the room with a roof terrace. Also rooms with four or five beds, and group discounts available. Popular with Aconcagua climbers. ❸

Hotels

Aconcagua San Lorenzo 545 ℡0261/520-0500, Ⓦwww.hotelaconcagua.com. Professionally run modern hotel, with small but comfortable rooms with TV and mini-bar; it's worth paying an extra $20 for a room with a glorious mountain view. A swimming pool and sauna are welcome facilities. ❼

Argentino Espejo 455 ☎0261/405-6300, ⊛www
.argentino-hotel.com. Shiny place on the Plaza
Independencia aimed squarely at the foreign tourist
dollar, with ultra-stylish rooms, a gym, swimming
pool and attentive service. **❼**

Balbi Av Las Heras 340 ☎0261/423-3500,
⊛www.hotelbalbi.com.ar. Hotel with old-fashioned
decor, a lavish reception space, huge breakfast area
and large rooms. Swimming pool and terrace. **❻**

Cervantes Amigorena 65 ☎0261/520-0400,
⊛www.hotelcervantes.com.ar. Traditional-style,
comfortable three-star hotel. Has one of the best
hotel restaurants in town, the *Sancho* (see p.392). **❼**

Crillón Perú 1065 ☎0261/429-8494, ⊛www
.hcrillon.com.ar. An above-average three-star hotel,
the *Crillón* has efficient service. Bathrooms are well
kept, although showers are rather cramped. **❼**

Huentala Primitivo de la Reta 1007
☎0261/4200766, ⊛www.huentala.com. Trendy new
four-star boutique hotel with stylish lobby and rooms,
pool and a French restaurant, *Chimpay Bistro*. **❽**

🏃 **Internacional** Sarmiento 720 ☎0261/425-
5606, ⊛www.hinternacional.com.ar. The
best in this class in Mendoza, this hotel has
understated, tasteful furnishings in spacious a/c
rooms. A swimming pool and parking are two
further assets. **❻**

NH Cordillera España and Gutiérrez ☎0261/441-
6464, ⊛www.nh-hotels.com. Jazzy hotel, one of
the nicest of the Spanish chain in Argentina, with
professional reception service, sleek rooms,
agreeable bathrooms; plus a gym, sauna and
swimming pool. **❼**

Nutibara Av Mitre 867 ☎0261/429-5428,
⊛www.nutibara.com.ar. Rather dated but
comfortable hotel, with large rooms, a/c, cable TV
and efficient room service, plus a gym and
swimming pool. **❼**

Parador del Angel Jorge Newbery 5418, Chacras
de Coria ☎0261/4962201, ⊛www
.paradordelangel.com.ar. A handsome guesthouse
built around a century-old adobe house. The
owners are keen art collectors and share their
exquisitely decorated home and peaceful garden
with great sense of hospitality. **❸**

Park Hyatt Chile 1124 ☎0261/441-1234,
⊛www.mendoza.park.hyatt.com. The most central
of Mendoza's luxury hotels, this modern block is
located on the site of the *Plaza Hotel* where Perón
and Eva once stayed. Apart from the much vaunted
casino, facilities include a luxurious spa, a large
pool, the stylish *Uvas* cocktail bar and *Bistro M*, one
of the classiest restaurants in the city. Rooms are
spacious, with luxurious bathrooms. **❾**

Posada Olivar Besares 978, Chacras de Coria
☎0261/4960061, ⊛www.posadaolivar.com. Set in

fine grounds giving an insight into the typical
chacras (smallholdings) that gave this leafy
Mendoza suburb its name, this friendly posada
combines simplicity with comfort. There is a large
pool in the garden. **❻**

Ritz Perú 1008 ☎0261/423-5115, ⊛www
.ritzhotelmendoza.com. This place tries very hard
to look British, and partly succeeds with its chintz
furnishings and plush fitted carpets. Rooms have
a/c. **❻**

Venus Perú 1155 ☎0261/423-8930, ⊛www
.granhotelvenus.com. A good-value, central option
that's modern and clean, if lacking personality.
Parking available. **❹**

Bodega accommodation

🏃 **Cavas Wine Lodge** Costa Flores s/n, Alto
Agrelo ☎0261/4106927, ⊛www
.cavaswinelodge.com. Impeccably designed luxury
lodge near Luján de Cuyo. Each of the fourteen
individually designed rooms comes with its own
wooden deck, pool and circular terrace with
unobstructed views of the cordillera. The final
Bacchanalian touch is a red-wine spa bath in an
ancient tub; this and other wine-based spa
treatments, such as a crushed malbec scrub, can
be booked by non-guests, too. **❾**; US$120 for just
the bath.

Club Tapiz Pedro Molina s/n, Maipú ☎0261/496-
4815, ⊛www.tapiz.com.ar. Affiliated with Bodega
Tapiz in Maipú, *Club Tapiz* has seven tastefully
appointed rooms in a renovated villa dating from
1890, as well as a spa, pool, gaucho-style *pulpería*
bar and its own gourmet restaurant, *Terruño*,
surrounded by a vineyard. **❾**, breakfast included.

Finca Adalgisa Pueyrredón 2222, Chacras de Coria
☎0261/496-0713, ⊛www.fincaadalgisa.com.ar.
Small *finca* (ranch) now geared more towards
tourism than wine production, though still with its
own vineyard. The attractive rooms are in an annexe
with a jasmine-covered verandah running alongside,
there's a swimming pool among the vines. **❾**

Posada Salentein RP-89 and E. Videla, Tunuyán
☎02622/429090, ⊛www.bodegasalentein.com
/bodega/posada/english/index.html. A posada
belonging to the Salentein winery, which can also
be visited on a tour (see p.391). **❾**; horseriding
tour and a wine tasting included.

Tupungato Divino Ruta 89 and Calle Los
Europeos ☎0261/156014424, ⊛www
.tupungatodivino.com.ar. A beautifully located hotel,
surrounded by young vines, and with fabulous
Andean views. Its rooms blend rustic charm with
eye-catching modernity, and the outstanding food
served in the restaurant complements the fine
wines made at the nearby bodegas. **❾**

The City

Mendoza's sights are few and far between – much of its interest lies in its wide avenues, lively plazas and green parks. The centre of the urban layout is the **Plaza Independencia**, the size of four blocks. Near its corners lie four orbital squares, **Plazas Chile**, **San Martín**, **España** and **Italia**, each with its own distinctive character. Museums are not Mendoza's forte, but the **Museo del Pasado Cuyano**, which offers an insight into late nineteenth-century life for the city's richer families, is worth a visit, as is the **Museo de Ciencias Naturales y Antropológicas**, a wideranging natural history museum. The latter sits in the handsomely landscaped **Parque General San Martín**, which slopes up a hill to the west of the microcentro and commands views of the city and its surroundings. One of the country's finest green spaces, it's also the venue for the city's major annual event, the **Fiesta de la Vendimia**, held every March. The ruins of colonial Mendoza's nucleus, where it was founded between the Guaymallén and Tajamar canals to the northeast of the present-day centre, have been preserved as the **Área Fundacional**, where there's another small museum. The most impressive sight in the whole city, however, is the historic **Bodega Escorihuela** (see p. 390), the beautiful **winery** in Godoy Cruz, a southern suburb.

Mendoza has the most complicated **street-name system** of any city in Argentina. Streets that run north–south keep the same name from end to end, but those that run west–east have up to four names within the city limits alone. From west to east, names change at Avenida Belgrano, Avenida San Martín and Avenida Gobernador R. Videla, the latter running along the Guaymallén canal, the city's eastern boundary. Beyond it lies the residential suburb of Guaymallén, itself divided into several districts, where you'll find the bus terminal, a cluster of budget accommodation, a number of restaurants and a couple of wineries. On all street signs is a useful number telling you how many blocks you are from the city's point zero, at San Martín and Sarmiento; 100 (O) means one block west, 500 (N) five blocks north. Paseo Sarmiento, a busy pedestrian precinct lined with loads of shops and cafés with terraces, joins Plaza Independencia, the city's centre-point, to Avenida San Martín.

For an overview of the city, to get your bearings and to enjoy unobstructed views towards the Andes, preferably in the morning when the mountains are lit by the rising sun, take a lift up to the **Terraza Mirador**, on the roof of the **Palacio Municipal**, 9 de Julio 500 (Mon, Wed & Fri 8.30am–1pm, Tues, Thurs & Sat 8.30am–1pm & 4–7pm; free).

Plaza Independencia

Four blocks in size, **Plaza Independencia** lies at the nerve-centre of the city and at the crossroads of two of Mendoza's main streets, east–west Avenida Sarmiento and north–south Avenida Mitre. It's modern Mendoza's recreational and cultural focus, planted with shady acacias and magnolias and bustles with life both during the day and on summer evenings. It is also the setting for festivals, concerts and outdoor cinema-screenings, and a crafts fair is held here at weekends. During remodelling in 1995, monumental fountains, backed by a mosaic mural depicting the story of Argentina's independence, were installed. Just west of the central fountains stands a seventeen-metre-high steel structure, dating from 1942, on which a mass of coloured lights form the national coat of arms at night.

Just north of the square, on the corner of Sarmiento, is the site of the illustrious 1920s **Plaza Hotel**, famous because the Peróns stayed here soon after first meeting in San Juan; it is now the Hyatt's five-star luxury establishment (see "Accommodation", p.384). Next door is the Neoclassical facade of the **Teatro Independencia**, one of the city's more traditional playhouses, while, over on the eastern side of the plaza, is the grim **Legislatura Provincial**.

Plaza España

The small plaza that lies a block east and a block south of Independencia's southeast corner, called Plaza Montevideo until 1949, is now known as **Plaza España**. It's the most beautiful of all Mendoza's plazas – its benches are decorated with brightly coloured Andalucian ceramic tiles, and the paths are lined with luxuriant trees and shrubs. Although Mendoza's population is of overwhelmingly Italian origin, the city's old, traditional families came from Spain, and they had the square built in the late 1940s. The mellow terracotta flagstones, picked out with smaller blue and white tiles, and the lily ponds and fountains set off the monument to the Spanish discovery of South America, standing at the southern end of the plaza. It comprises a *zócalo* or brightly tiled pedestal, decorated with scenes from *Don Quixote* and the Argentine gaucho epic *Martín Fierro*, along with Columbus's "discovery" and depictions of missionary work. At the centre of the plinth stand two female statues: one is a Spanish noblewoman clasping a book, the other a mestiza (part Spanish, part native American) woman, a Mendocina, holding a bunch of grapes. Dancing and folk music take place here on October 12, the **Día de la Raza**, a celebration of mestizo culture.

Plaza Italia and Museo del Pasado Cuyano

Four blocks west of Plaza España's northwest corner along Calle Montevideo – an attractive street lined with plane trees and picturesque Neocolonial houses with brightly coloured facades – is **Plaza Italia**. A monument on the south side of the square is a bronze statue of the mythical Roman wolf feeding Romulus and Remus, next to a marble pillar. The main monument in stone and bronze, to its west, represents La Patria – The Motherland – flanked by a statue of an Amerindian and a Roman philosopher. A frieze running around the monument, showing scenes of building, ploughing and harvesting, is a tribute to the Italian immigrants whose labour helped build the country. In November, the park blazes with the bright red flowers of its tipas, and during the week leading up to the Fiesta de la Vendimia in March, the plaza hosts the **Festa in Piazza**, a big party at which stalls representing every Italian region serve their local culinary specialities. The climax is an extravagant fashion parade.

▲ Plaza España, Mendoza

Half a block east of the plaza is the **Museo del Pasado Cuyano** (Mon–Fri 9am–12.30pm; $2), at Montevideo 544. It's the city's history museum, housed in part of an aristocratic late nineteenth-century mansion, the Quinta de los Civit. The adobe house, built to resist earthquakes, belonged to the family of Francisco Civit, governor of Mendoza, and his son Emilio, who was a senator and was responsible for many of Mendoza's civic works, including the great park. It contains a large amount of San Martín memorabilia and eighteenth-century furniture, artworks and weapons, all rescued from the earthquake rubble. The most valuable exhibit, in the chapel, is a fifteenth-century polychrome **wooden altarpiece**, with a liberal dose of rosy cherubim that somehow turned up here from Sant Andreu de Socarrats in Catalonia.

Plaza San Martín

The square to the northeast of Plaza Independencia is the relatively nondescript **Plaza San Martín**; it's dominated by an early twentieth-century statue of General San Martín on a horse, looking towards the Andes, which he crossed with his army to defeat the Spanish. Near the plaza's northwest corner is the city's only church of note, the **Basílica de San Francisco**, one of the first buildings to go up after the 1861 quake. Its Belgian architect modelled it on Paris's Église de la Trinité, but part of the structure had to be demolished after another earthquake in 1927, leaving the church looking a bit truncated. It's venerated locally, as some members of San Martín's family are buried in simple tombs inside. A special chamber up the stairs next to the altar (Apr–Oct Tues–Sat 7.45am–5pm, Sun 9am–6.30pm; Nov–Mar Mon–Sat 9am–noon; free) contains a revered image of Our Lady of Carmen, the patron saint of the Army of the Andes, along with San Martín's stylish rosewood staff, with a topaz hilt and a silver tip – it, too, has the status of a religious relic among the people of Mendoza.

The surrounding district is Mendoza's "**City**", or financial district, whose opulent banks and insurance-company offices, most built in a "British" style, are among the city's most impressive buildings. Both the Banco de Galicia and the Banco de la Nación were built in the 1920s and 1930s, the city's heyday, as was the ex-Banco de Mendoza, lying on the eastern side of Plaza San Martín, diagonally opposite the basilica. The latter now houses the **Espacio Contemporáneo de Arte** (Mon–Sat 9am–1pm & 4–9pm, Sun 4–9pm; free), worth a look for both its contemporary art exhibitions, its tasteful arts and crafts shop, and the eight-sided lobby crowned with a huge stained-glass cupola.

Área Fundacional

The **Museo del Área Fundacional**, at Alberdi and Videla Castillo (Tues–Sat 8am–7pm, Sun 3–8pm; $2), is built on the Plaza Mayor, where the city was originally founded, 1km northeast of Plaza Independencia. The modern building houses an exhibition of domestic and artistic items retrieved from the rubble after the mammoth earthquake of 1861. It's built over part of the excavated colonial city foundations, which you can peer at through a glass floor. The exhibition relates the story of Mendoza's foundation and development before and after the great disaster. Nearby, across landscaped Plaza Pedro del Castillo, named for the city's founder, are the eerie ruins of the colonial city's Jesuit temple, popularly but erroneously known as the Ruinas de San Francisco.

Parque General San Martín

Just over 1km due west of Plaza Independencia by Avenida Sarmiento, on a slope that turns into a steep hill overlooking the city, **Parque General San Martín** is one of the most beautiful parks in the country, although you're advised not to visit after dark. As well as large areas of open land, used for impromptu football matches and picnics, its four square kilometres are home to the main football stadium, the amphitheatre where the finale of the Fiesta de la Vendimia is staged, a meteorological observatory, a monument to the Army of the Andes, a rowing lake, a tennis club, a hospital, the university campus, the riding club, an agricultural research centre, several restaurants, Mendoza's best jogging routes, a rose garden and an anthropological museum – in short, a city within the city.

It was first created in 1897 by French botanist and landscape artist, **Charles Thays** (see box, p.113). It contains over fifty thousand trees of 750 varieties, planted, among other reasons, to stop landslides from the Andean foothills. The aristocratic Avenida de los Plátanos and Avenida de las Palmeras, lined with tall plane trees and Canary Island palms, and the romantic Rose Garden, with its five hundred rose varieties and arbours of wisteria, are popular walks.

The main entrance is through magnificent bronze and wrought-iron gates, topped with a rampant condor, at the western end of Avenida Emilio Civit. They were not, as a popular legend would have it, ordered for Ottoman Sultan Hamid II, who couldn't pay the bill; the crescent motif in their fine lace-like design, which lead to the apocryphal anecdote, was simply a fashionable pattern at the time. The gates were actually ordered by city authorities in 1910 to celebrate the country's centenary, and were made by the McFarlane ironworks in Glasgow. A road open to traffic runs westwards from here, skirting the northern edge of the park after going round the Caballitos de Marly, an exact reproduction in Carrara marble of the monumental horses in the middle of Paris's Place de la Concorde. From here you can rent a bike, take a horse and cart or catch a bus to the park's furthest points. A short walk southwest of the entrance, near the northern shores of the rowing lake, the recently restored **Fuente de los Continentes** is a dramatic set of sculptures meant to represent the diversity of humankind, and a favoured backdrop for wedding photographs.

A good 2km west of the entrance you'll find the city's **zoo** (Tues–Sun 9am–5pm; $8; ☎0261/428-1700), one of the best in the country for its variety of animals and, more to the point, for the conditions in which they are kept. It's a landscaped forest of eucalyptus, *aguaribay* and fir trees, built into the lower slopes of the Cerro de la Gloria, from which also you get sweeping views of the city.

Another popular destination is the top of the Cerro de la Gloria, where there's an imposing 1914 monument to the Army of the Andes, the **Monumento al Ejército Libertador**. All cast in bronze, a buxom, winged *Liberty*, waving broken chains, leads General San Martín and his victorious troops across the cordillera. Around the granite plinth are bronze friezes depicting more picturesque scenes: the anti-royalist monk Luis Beltrán busy making weapons for the army, and the genteel ladies of Mendoza donating their jewellery for the good cause – these "Patricias Mendocinas", after whom a city street is named, were rumoured to have been particularly excited by the presence of so many soldiers billeted in the city; babies and infants sadly watch their valiant fathers head off to battle.

At the southern tip of the park's one-kilometre-long, serpentine rowing lake, in its southeastern corner, is the **Museo de Ciencias Naturales y Antropológicas** (Tues–Fri 8am–1pm & 2–7pm, Sat & Sun 3–7pm; $2; ☎0261/428-7666). Built in the 1930s to imitate the shape of a ship's bridge by local architects who introduced German Rationalism to Argentina, the museum is a series of mostly private collections of stuffed animals, ancient fossils, indigenous artefacts and mummies. The most interesting exhibits are a female mummy discovered at over 5000m in the Andes – along with a brightly coloured shawl – shrunken heads from Ecuador and fossils or skeletons of dinosaurs unearthed near Malargüe in southern Mendoza.

Fiesta de la Vendimia

Mendoza's main festival is the giant **Fiesta de la Vendimia**, or Wine Harvest Festival, which reaches its climax during the first weekend of March every year. Wine takes over the city and the tourist trade shifts into high gear. On the Sunday before the carnival proper (the last Sun in Feb), the *Bendición de los Frutos*, or Blessing of the Grapes, takes place, in a ceremony involving the bishop of Mendoza. During the week leading up to the grand finale, events range from folklore concerts in the *centro cívico* to Italian food and entertainment in the Plaza Italia. On Friday evening is the **Vía Blanca**, a parade of illuminated floats through the central streets, while on Saturday it's the *Carrusel*, when a carnival parade winds along the same route, each department in the province sending a float from which a previously elected beauty queen and her entourage of runners-up fling local produce, ranging from grapes and flowers to watermelons and packets of pasta, into the cheering crowds lining the road. On Saturday evening, the *Acto Central* is held in an amphitheatre in the Parque San Martín; it's a gala performance of song, dance and general kitsch-o-rama, hosted by local TV celebs, eventually leading up to a drawn-out vote – by political leaders representing each department in the province – to elect the queen of the festival. The same show is re-run, minus the election, and therefore less tedium, on Sunday evening. The spectacle costs millions of pesos and is a huge investment by the local wine-growers, but as it's attended by some 25,000 people it seems to be financially viable. The organizers boast that it's the biggest such festival in South America and one of the most lavish wine-related celebrations in the world. For more information contact the city's tourist office (see p.380).

Eating, drinking and nightlife

Mendoza is the prosperous capital of Argentina's western region, and the produce grown in the nearby oases is tip-top; as a result, the city's many, varied and often highly sophisticated **restaurants** and **wine bars** are usually full, and serve some of the best food and drink in the country. Its **bars** are lively and it has a well-developed café-terrace culture, with Avenida Arístides Villanueva, to the west of the centre, a hotspot; **nightlife** is also vibrant, and is mostly concentrated in outlying places such as El Challao, to the northwest, and Godoy Cruz and fashionable Chacras de Coria to the south.

Restaurants

1884 Francis Mallmann Belgrano 1188, Godoy Cruz ☎0261/424-2698, ⓦwww.1884restaurante.com.ar. This ultra-chic wine bar and award-winning restaurant with fashion-model staff, swish decor and crystal wine-glasses – rare in Argentina – is considered one of the country's finest. It is next to the Bodega Escorihuela, and serves its fine wines with a balanced menu that includes Patagonian lamb, trout from Malargüe and plums from General Alvear.

Azafrán Sarmiento 765 ☎0261/429-4200. A deli-cum-restaurant with an excellent cellar, colourful decor and delicious food – specialities include smoked venison ravioli – plus home-brewed beer; portions are a bit on the miserly side, though.

Basilika Av Arístides Villanueva 332. One of the best pizzerias in the city, dishing up an array of toppings on delicious crusts until the early hours.

There's also a giant screen showing football matches on Sun. Closed Mon & Tues.

La Carmela Av Arístides Villanueva 298. Great, no-fuss Argentine cooking with a menu that changes daily, speedy service and an attractive outdoor seating area from which to watch the lively Arístides streetlife.

Don Mario 25 de Mayo 1324, Guaymallén. An institutional *parrilla* in the neighbourhood of Guaymallén (east of the city centre), frequented by Mendocino families in search of comforting decor and an old-fashioned *parrillada*.

La Florencia Sarmiento 698 esq Perú. A no-nonsense *parrilla* that's popular with tourists and locals alike. Sit inside or streetside, and check out their extensive wine list.

La Marchigiana Patricias Mendocinas 1550 ☎0261/423-0751. This is *the* Italian-Argentine restaurant in the city, run by the same

There are dozens of **wineries** in the **Mendoza area** that are open to visitors. The easiest way to visit bodegas is on a **tour** organized by an agency in Mendoza (see "Listings", p.393). A typical half-day trip visits two or three bodegas, while a full day visits five or six and includes lunch; full-day trips are better value. Wine enthusiasts willing to splurge should contact Grapevine (☏0261/429-7522, ⊛www.thegrapevine-argentina.com), which does a range of small group "premium" tours led by native English speakers who are also expert tasters; lunch is included.

Alternatively you can rent a car and **drive** yourself; using **public transport** only works if you're planning on seeing a limited number of bodegas. Another option is to rent a **bike**, but always double check the bike, take an emergency number in case of punctures, and ask which routes are the safest as it's no rural idyll – some busy roads have bike lanes, but on others you are exposed to industrial traffic. In Maipú, try the friendly Bikes and Wines, at Urquiza 1606 (☏0261/410-6686, ⊛www.bikesandwines.com); or Maipu Bikes, Urquiza y Gómez, (☏0261/487-3311, ℮maipubikes@gmail.com).

If you're going under your own steam, call ahead to check times, to book a visit and to ask for an English-speaking guide, if necessary. The bodegas are concentrated in **Guaymallén**, in **Maipú** (see p.394) and in **Luján de Cuyo** (see p.393). For transport to Maipú and Luján de Cuyo, see the respective town accounts. Buses referred to below stop at the Mendoza bus terminal or along Avenida San Martín.

Some visits and tastings are **free**, but you're pointedly steered to a sales area at the end (cash only; surcharge for the best tipples). Try and see different kinds of wineries, ranging from the old-fashioned, traditional bodegas to the highly mechanized, ultra-modern producers; at the former you're more likely to receive personal attention and get a chance to taste finer wines.

Bodega tours

Chandón Agrelo 5507, Luján de Cuyo ☏0261/490-9966, ℮visitorcenter@chandon.com.ar. A modern bodega, somewhat lacking in character but impressive all the same, with excellent wine-tasting. The tours start with a video and end up at the salesroom. English or premium-tasting tours should be requested ahead. Bus #380. Tours Feb–Mar & July Mon–Fri 9.30am–4.30pm, Sat 9.30am–12.30pm; rest of year Mon–Fri 10.30am–4pm.

Domaine St Diego Franklin Villanueva 3821, Maipú ☏0261/499-0414, ℮juanmendoza@sinectis.com.ar. Small producer, specializing in cabernet sauvignon. One of the more intimate wineries in the region, giving visitors the chance to try good-quality wines after an hour in the vineyards and an hour in the bodega. Tours (limited to six people) Mon–Fri 9am–5pm, Sat 9am–2pm; reserve 24hr ahead.

Escorihuela Belgrano 1188 and Presidente Alvear, Godoy Cruz ☏0261/424-2744. Just 2km south of Mendoza's city centre, this historic bodega, founded in 1884, is to reopen in late 2010. It is famous for its enormous barrel from France, housed in a cathedral-like cellar. The sumptuous buildings include huge vaulted storage rooms stacked with aromatic casks and a gourmet restaurant, *1884 Francis Mallmann* (see p.389). Tours Mon–Fri 9.30am–12.30pm & 2.30–3.30pm.

Giol ("La Colina de Oro") Ozamis 1040, Maipú ☏0261/497-2592. A wonderfully old-fashioned place, with its fair share of antique barrels – including one of the biggest in South America – alongside the Museo Nacional del Vino y la Vendimia. Bus #160. Tours Mon–Sat 9am–6.30pm, Sun & public holidays 11am–2pm.

El Lagar Carmelo Patti San Martín 2614, Luján de Cuyo ☏0261-4981379. Known as "El maestro del vino", local personality Carmelo has been working in the wine trade since 1971. His enthusiasm and knowledge make him one of the best wine guides in the area (Spanish only). Visits are informal, but call ahead to arrange a mutually convenient time.

Lagarde San Martín 1745, Luján de Cuyo ☎0261/498-0011, ⓦwww.lagarde .com.ar. Lagarde is a major producer, and well worth visiting. There's also an impressive vintage car exhibition and a gourmet restaurant on this enormous site. Tours Mon–Fri 10am–noon & 2.30–3.30pm, Sat 10am–12.30pm; $15 to taste three wines.

Luigi Bosca San Martín 2044, Luján de Cuyo ☎0261/498-1974, ⓦwww.luigibosca .com.ar. One of the best-known wine brands in Argentina, Luigi Bosca appears on many of the agency-run trips. The professional guides are keen to emphasize the family credentials of the winery, but it all feels a bit too neat and commercial. Tours Mon–Fri 10.30am & 3.30–5pm, Sat noon.

Nieto Senetiner Guardia Vieja, Ruta Panamericana, Chacras de Coria ☎0261/498-0315, ⓦwww.nietosenetiner.com.ar. Some of Argentina's finest wines are produced by this traditional winery. The 12.30pm tour can be followed by a delicious lunch (reserve in advance). Tours Mon–Sat 10am–12.30pm & 3pm; $20.

Norton RP-15, Perdriel, Luján de Cuyo ☎0261/488-0480, ⓦwww.norton.com.ar. A prize-winning producer, making top-class if slightly old-fashioned wines, but well worth the visit. Also has a restaurant. Bus #380. Tours must be reserved in advance: Mon–Sat 9am–4.30pm; $10 or $30.

🏃 **Salentein** RP-89 and E. Videla, Tunuyán ☎02622/423550, ⓦwww .bodegasalentein.com. One of the most beautiful wineries in the country. Visiting this magnificent state-of-the-art building, known as the "Cathedral to Wine", makes for a memorable experience; the wines are also outstanding. Tours daily 11am–3pm (English); $10.

San Felipe ("La Rural") Montecaseros s/n, Coquimbito, Maipú ☎0261/497-2013. This magnificent traditional bodega stands among its own vineyards and has its own small museum. An interesting contrast with some of the more urban wineries. Bus Linea 10 #171, #172 or #173. Free hourly tours (bilingual) Mon–Sat 9am–noon & 2–5pm.

Santa Ana Roca and Urquiza, Villa Nueva, Guaymallén ☎0261/421-1000, Ⓔavivas@bodegas-santa-ana.com.ar. One of the closest good bodegas, near the city centre, with an enchanting mix of old-style and ultra-modern. Tours are especially friendly; English spoken. Bus #20. Tours Mon–Fri 9.30am–noon & 2.30–5pm.

Viña El Cerno Moreno 631, Coquimbito, Maipú ☎0261/ 481-1567, ⓦwww .elcerno.com.ar. One of the most satisfying boutique wineries, in a small traditional country house with a tiny vineyard. The malbec and chardonnay are delicious and the tour highly personalized and enthusiastic. Does *parrilla* lunches noon–5pm ($50pp). Tours Mon–Sat 10am–5pm, and weekend tours (Spanish only) can be arranged; $15.

Weinert San Martín 5923, Chacras de Coria ☎0261/496-0409, ⓦwww .bodegaweinert.com.. One of Argentina's oldest and best wine producers, with an enormous antique barrel still in use, a fabulous cellar and mud and cane buildings – characteristic of the area's indigenous population – used to provide the perfect temperature for fermentation. Tasting tours are family-friendly, with grape juice on hand for the kids. Tours Mon–Fri 9am–12.30pm & 2.30–4.30pm, Sat 10am–12.30pm & 2.30–3.30pm.

family for decades. For a reasonable price you can eat fresh *caprese* salad, have delicious cannelloni and finish with one of the best tiramisus in the country.

El Patio de Jesús María Viamonte 4961, Chacras de Coria. Well-known and respected classic *parrilla* out in Chacras. There are also other branches in the city, such as at the junction of Av Arístides Villanueva and Boulogne sur Mer.

Praga L. Aguirre 413 ☎0261/425-9585. Top-quality culinary venue, with understated decor, delicately prepared fish and seafood, a fitting wine list and impeccable service. Book ahead.

La Sal Belgrano 1069 ☎0261/420 4322. Striking surroundings, great music – including jazz – and impeccable service are all pluses at this outstanding downtown restaurant where the rotating menu is an experience in itself – save room for the desserts. Everything is accompanied by amazing wines as recommended by the staff. International and Argentine contemporary cuisine. Prices range from moderate to expensive.

Sancho Amigorena 65. Conventional meals such as *milanesas* and steaks, together with pasta and fish dishes, are on offer at this smart institutional establishment with an appealing patio seating area.

Tasca la Plaza Montevideo 117. Intimate little bistro, or *tasca*, conveniently located on the Plaza España and serving appropriately Hispanic fare, including tapas, along with sangría and good wines; charming service.

Las Tinajas Lavalle 38. Good-value *tenedor libre* in the city centre. The food quality is a cut above the usual all-you-can-eat establishments – there's an excellent *asado* and heaving salad bar.

Veggetalia Além 43 ☎0261/15-625-0355. This agreeable vegetarian restaurant serves a wide variety of well-prepared food by the kilo. Closed Sun.

Bars and cafés

La Aldea Av Arístides Villanueva 495. A lively pub-style bar that does great sandwiches.

Apeteco San Juan and Barraquero. A city institution, this pre-club bar used to be called *El Rancho*, and still hosts "El Rancho" nights on Wed – an essential stop on a Wed night out.

Chini Av España and Las Heras. One of the best ice-cream parlours in the city, with dozens of flavours.

Ferruccio Soppelsa Branches at Emilio Civit esq Belgrano, Espejo 299 plus elsewhere in and around the city. This chain of *heladerías*, run for years by the same Italian family, is guaranteed to give you enough calories to last you to the top of Aconcagua.

El Palenque Av Arístides Villanueva 287. A *pulpería*-style bar with bags of old-fashioned pampas atmosphere and a range of empanadas and wines; popular with the city's youth.

Soul Tango Rivadavia and 9 de Julio. Fun little café that plays both soul and tango music, as the name suggests, and hosts occasional tango classes and live bands.

La Tienda Av Arístides Villanueva 341 ☎0261/423-6050. Smart modern café and resto-bar serving uncomplicated snacks until 2am, plus cocktails till later, to an eclectic mix of popular Latin and Western hits.

Vines of Mendoza Espejo 567 ⓦwww .vinesofmendoza.com. Not a bar as such, but rather a sophisticated wine-tasting room in the city centre. The friendly and knowledgeable staff can recommend wines to try and bodegas to visit, and also make the necessary reservations – it's an ideal starting point for anyone thinking of heading off on the viniculture trail.

Nightclubs

Aloha Ruta Panamericana s/n, Chacras de Coria. Extremely fashionable club playing Argentine rock music, frequented by a 30s crowd. Open Fri–Sun, but best on Sat.

Al Sur Ruta Panamericana s/n, Chacras de Coria. Sat night electronica.

Alquimia Ruta Panamericana s/n, Chacras de Coria. Restaurant-bar-club with disco on one floor, varied electronica on another and patios at which to eat throughout. One of the most popular places to dance the night away on Fri and Sat.

Carilo Av Champagnat s/n, El Challao. The über-fashionable club during the summer season (Sept–March), spinning house and techno.

Estación Miró Ejército de los Andes 656, Dorrego, Guaymallén. The city's main gay nightclub, open every weekend night, although Sun is the best night to go. Cocktails, shows and even an alternative Fiesta de la Vendimia in March.

Geo San Martín Sur 576, Godoy Cruz. Trendy club playing a mix of electronica, rock and reggaeton. Open Thurs–Sat.

Iskra San Martín Sur 905, Godoy Cruz. Varied mix of rock, reggaeton and dance music for a young crowd, most of whom are in their late teens and 20s. Open Thurs–Sat.

Listings

Airlines Aerolíneas Argentina and Austral, Paseo Sarmiento 82 ⊕0261/ 420-4101, and at the airport ⊕0261/448-7065; LAN España 1002 ⊕0261/448-7387 or 0810-9999-526; United, Espejo 183 1st floor ⊕0261/423-4683.

Banks and exchange Banex, Av San Martín 1190; Boston, Necochea 165; Citibank, Av San Martín 1092; Banco Mendoza, Av España 1340; Banco de la Nación, Necochea 101. ATMs everywhere.

Bike rental Bikes and Wine, 25 de Mayo 981 ⊕0261/410-6686; City Bike, San Martín 1070 ⊕0261/423-2103.

Car rental Alamo, Primitivo de la Reta 928 ⊕0261/429-3111; Avis, Primitivo de la Reta 914 ⊕0261/429-6403; Budget, Primitivo de la Reta 923 ⊕0261/425-3114; Localiza, Primitivo de la Reta 936 ⊕0261/429-6800. Also branches at airport.

Consulates ⓦwww.ccmdz.consul.org.ar; Bolivia, M. Lemos 635 ⊕0261/423-0413; Brazil, Perú 789 ⊕0261/423-0939; Chile, Belgrano and Liniers ⊕0261/425-5024; Ecuador, Francisco Moyano 1587 ⊕0261/429-6416; France, Houssay 790 ⊕0261/429-8339; Germany, Montevideo 127 ⊕0261/425-6539; Italy, Necochea 712 ⊕0261/520-1400; Peru, Huarpes 629 ⊕0261/429-9831; Spain, Agustín Alvarez 455 ⊕0261/425-3947; UK/Netherlands, Av Boulogne Sur Mer 889, 6th floor ⊕0261/425-2823.

Internet access WH at Sarmiento 219, Colón 136 and Las Heras 61.

Laundry Lavasec Colón 470 ⊕0261/423-8866.

Police Tourist police, San Martín 1143 ⊕0261/413-2135 or in Maipú ⊕0261/15-502-0277.

Post office San Martín and Colón.

Taxis Mendocar ⊕0261/423-6666; Radiomóvil ⊕0261/445-5855; Radiotaxi ⊕0261/430-3300; Veloz del Este ⊕0261/4239090.

Tour operators Popular tours include ones to wine bodegas, Alta Montaña and Villavicencio. Mountain-bike tours in the foothills and whitewater rafting on the Río Mendoza are also possible. Many operators also offer longer trips to La Payunia, Cañon del Atuel, Talampaya and Ischigualasto, but Malargüe, San Rafael, San Agustín de Valle Fértil and Villa Unión are much closer bases for these. Try Argentina Rafting, Primitivo de la Reta 992 (⊕0261/429-6325, ⓦwww.argentinarafting.com); Aymará, 9 de Julio 1023 (⊕0261/420-4304 or 2064, ⓦwww.aymara.com.ar); Campo Base Adventures and Expeditions, Peatonal Sarmiento 229 (⊕0261/425-5511, ⓦwww.campobase.com.ar); Cata, Las Heras 601 (⊕0261/425-1750); El Cristo, Espejo 228 (⊕0261/429-1911, ⓦwww.turismo-elcristo.com.ar); Mendoza Viajes, Sarmiento 129, which offers wine tours (⊕0261/438-0480, ⓦwww.mdzviajes.com.ar); and Sepean, Primitivo de la Reta 1088 (⊕0261/420-4162, ⓦwww.sepean.com). Argentina Mountain, Lavalle 606, San José, Guaymallén (⊕0261/431-8356, ⓦwww.lagunadeldiamante.com), offering trips to places like Laguna Diamante and Tupungato.

Luján de Cuyo

Immediately south of Mendoza are two satellite towns, the first of which, sitting where the Guaymallén Canal meets the Río Mendoza, is **LUJÁN DE CUYO**. Lying just west of the Ruta Panamericana, or the RN-40, it's part residential, part industrial, with a huge brewery and some of the city's major **wineries**. The northern district, known as **Carrodilla**, 7km south of downtown Mendoza, is an oasis of the colonial city that survived the 1861 earthquake. Here you'll find the **Iglesia de la Carrodilla** (Mon–Fri 10am–noon & 4–8pm; free), usually included in the city's wine tours. Built in 1840, it's now a museum of seventeenth- and eighteenth-century religious art as well as the parish church. The naive frescoes depict scenes of grape harvesting, and the church's main relic, is an oakwood statue of the Virgin and Child, star of the religious processions that precede Mendoza's Fiesta de la Vendimia. Artistically, the finest exhibit is the moving *Cristo de los Huarpes*, an exceptional piece of mestizo art carved out of *quebracho* wood in 1670 by local indigenous craftsmen.

The western district of Luján de Cuyo is **Chacras de Coria**, a leafy suburb of European-style villas, golf courses, bodegas and several new, upmarket hotels. It's also full of outdoor *parrillas*, bars and nightclubs, frequented at weekends and in the summer by affluent Mendocinos. On its eastern edge, in a rural area called

Mayor Drummond, at San Martín 3651, is Mendoza's **Museo Provincial de Bellas Artes Emiliano Guiñazú**, also known as the **Casa de Fader** after Fernando Fader (see p.227), the artist who decorated the interior (Tues–Fri 8.30am–7pm, Sat & Sun 3–8pm; $2). It's housed in a grandiose red sandstone villa, which was built at the end of the nineteenth century for Emiliano Guiñazú, an influential landowner and socialite, in a style influenced by Art Nouveau, and is set off by a luxuriant garden of cacti, cypresses, magnolias and roses, among which you will find Neoclassical marble statues. Having heard that Fader had been to art school in France, Guiñazú commissioned him to decorate the house interior. Fader's **Impressionistic murals** – especially appealing are the frescoes of tropical vegetation painted on the walls of the bathroom, alongside Art Nouveau tiles – are the main attraction here. His paintings also dominate the museum's collection of nineteenth- and early twentieth-century Argentine art. Temporary exhibits are staged from time to time. Bus #200 from downtown Mendoza or the bus terminal runs to Luján de Cuyo.

Maipú

The self-styled "Cuna de la Viña", or birthplace of the grapevine, **MAIPÚ**, lying some 15km southeast of Mendoza via the RN-7, is the city's other small satellite town. Founded in 1861 by the Mercedarian monks Fray Manuel Apolinario Vásquez and Don José Alberto de Ozamis as a new site for the earthquake-levelled Mendoza, it quickly became the centre of wine-making in the region, and is where many of the city's **wineries** are located today (see box, pp.390–391). The wine-growing district, to the north of the town's centre, is called Coquimbito, where vineyards alternate with dusky olive groves. The large Bodega La Rural at Montecaseros is where you'll find Mendoza's **Museo del Vino** (Mon–Sat 9am–6pm, Sun 10am–1pm; $1; ☎0261/497-7763), a summary explanation of the region's wine industry housed in a fabulous Art Nouveau villa, with elegant fittings and detailing, including some delicate stained glass – the venue far outstrips the contents. **Buses** #150, #151, #170, #172, #173 and #180 all go to Maipú, taking slightly different routes from downtown Mendoza; once there, you can rent bikes for exploring the area at Urquiza 2288 (☎0261/497-4067).

Alta Montaña

The Andean cordillera, including some of the world's tallest mountains, loom a short distance west of Mendoza, and its snow-tipped peaks are visible from the city centre almost all year round, beyond the picturesque vineyards and fruit orchards. Even if you've come to the region for the wine, you'll want to head up into the hills before long: the scenery is fabulous, and skiing, trekking and highland walks are all possible, or you can simply enjoy the views on an organized excursion.

The so-called **Alta Montaña Route** – the RN-7 – is also the international highway to Santiago de Chile, via the upmarket Chilean ski resort of Portillo, and one of the major border crossings between the two countries, blocked by snow only on rare occasions in July and August. If you're in a hurry to get to or from Santiago, try to travel by day, to see the stunning scenery in the area. However, if you've more time to explore, possible stop-offs along the RN-7 include the pretty village of **Potrerillos** and **Vallecitos**, a tiny ski resort that caters for a younger crowd than exclusive Las Leñas (see p.406). As the road climbs further up into the mountains it passes another village, **Uspallata**, and then a variety of colourful

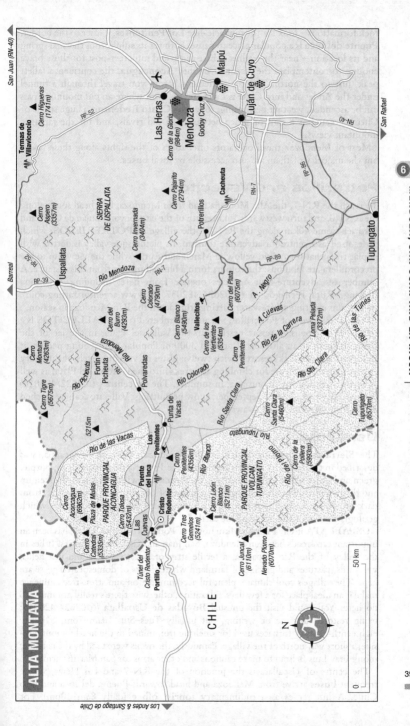

ALTA MONTAÑA

San Juan (RN-40)

San Rafael

Barreal

Los Andes & Santiago de Chile

Maipú

Luján de Cuyo

Las Heras

Mendoza

Godoy Cruz

Cerro Higueras (1741m)

Termas de Villavicencio

Cerro de la Gloria (984m)

Cacheuta

RP-52

RP-52

RP-82

RP-39

RP-86

RN-7

RN-7

RN-40

RN-89

Cerro Aspero (3357m)

SIERRA DE USPALLATA

Cerro Pajarito (2794m)

Potrerillos

Uspallata

Tupungato

Cerro Invernada (3404m)

Río Mendoza

Cerro Montura (4263m)

Cerro Tigre (5675m)

Río Picheuta

Fortín Picheuta

Río Mendoza

Cerro del Burro (4293m)

Polvaredas

Río Colorado

Cerro Colorado (4790m)

Cerro Blanco (5490m)

Vallecitos

Cerro de los Vertientes (5354m)

Cerro del Plata (6075m)

A. Negro

A. Cuevas

Cerro Penitentes

Río de la Carrera

Loma Pelada (3372m)

Río de las Tunes

Río Sta. Clara

Punta de Vacas

5215m

Río de las Vacas

Los Penitentes

Río Santa Clara

Cerro Santa Clara (5460m)

Cerro Tupungato (6570m)

PARQUE PROVINCIAL ACONCAGUA

Plaza de Mulas

Cerro Aconcagua (6962m)

Cerro Catedral (5335m)

Cerro Tolosa (5432m)

Las Cuevas

Puente del Inca

Cristo Redentor

Túnel del Cristo Redentor

Portillo

Cerro Penitentes (4356m)

Cerro Tres Gemelos (5241m)

Cerro León Blanco (5211m)

Río Blanco

Río Tupungato

PARQUE PROVINCIAL VOLCÁN TUPUNGATO

Río del Plomo

Cerro de la Pollera (5993m)

Cerro Juncal (6110m)

Nevado Plomo (6070m)

CHILE

N

50 km

0

rock formations – look for the pinnacle-like **Los Penitentes**. Closer to the border, **Puente del Inca** is a popular place to pause, both for its sulphurous thermal spring and its location – near the trailhead, base camp and muleteer-post for those brave enough to contemplate the ascent of mighty **Aconcagua**, the continent's tallest peak, just to the north. The last settlement before you travel through a tunnel under the Andes and into Chile is **Las Cuevas**, from where an old mountain pass can be ascended, weather permitting, to see the **Cristo Redentor**, a huge statue of Christ, erected as a sign of peace between the old rivals, and for the fantastic mountain views.

Most of Mendoza's travel operators offer tours of the sights along these roads, but the majority of them are also accessible by local **buses**.

Potrerillos and Vallecitos

To reach the RN-7, the Alta Montaña road from Mendoza, first head south along the RN-40, and turn westwards 15km south of the city, beyond Luján de Cuyo and Perdriel. Some 40km along the RN-7 is the village of **POTRERILLOS**, which styles itself as a centre for adventure tourism. Its picturesque valley is dotted with poplar trees that turn vivid yellow in March and April, while the views up to the precordillera are fabulous: the colours form a blurred mosaic from this distance. A number of adventure-tour agencies operate from here, including Argentina Rafting, Ruta Perilago s/n (T02624/482037, Wwww.argentinarafting.com), which runs exciting **whitewater rafting** trips down the Río Mendoza in season.

Some 25km west of Potrerillos, via an unnumbered track, **VALLECITOS** is a relatively inexpensive resort nestling in the Valle del Plata, in the lee of the Cerro Blanco, at an altitude of around 3000m. Popular with young people, it functions as a small ski resort – with twelve pistes of varying levels of difficulty – in winter and as a base for climbing and treks into the Cordón del Plata, as well as acclimatization for Aconcagua, in summer. The ski centre (T02622/488810) is open daily from July to September, snow permitting. Vallecitos can be reached easily from Mendoza, 80km away.

Uspallata

The **Sierra de Uspallata**, which blocks Mendoza's view of Aconcagua, was described in the 1830s by Charles Darwin in the *Voyage of the Beagle*: "Red, purple, green and quite white sedimentary rocks, alternating with black lavas broken up and thrown into all kinds of disorder, by masses of porphyry, of every shade, from dark brown to the brightest lilac. It really resembled those pretty sections which geologists make of the inside of the earth."

USPALLATA itself, a village 54km north of Potrerillos by the RN-7, has been an important crossroads between Mendoza, San Juan and Chile for centuries. It lies in the valley of the Río Uspallata, a fertile strip of potato, maize and pea fields, vineyards, pastures and patches of farmland where flocks of domesticated geese are kept. The village's cool climate, plentiful accommodation and stress-free ambience make it an ideal place for a few days' relaxation; otherwise there's really not much to do here. You could visit the unusual **Bóvedas de Uspallata** (T02624/420045; being restored at time of writing, but usually Tues–Sun 10am–7pm; $1), late eighteenth-century furnaces used for smelting iron mined in the nearby mountainside, a short way north of the village. Famously, the ovens were used by the patriotic monk Fray Luis Beltrán to make cannons and other arms for San Martín's army.

The centre of Uspallata is the junction of the RN-7 and Las Heras, where frequent **buses** arrive from Mendoza and head towards Puenta del Inca and into Chile. A hut serves as a rudimentary **tourist office** (daily 8am–10pm). For

somewhere to stay, nearby at Las Heras 240 is *Hotel Viena* (☎02624/420046; ③), with simple rooms, private bath and cable TV. Closer to the junction, with nicer rooms – albeit with hard beds – enormous modern bathrooms and a *confitería*, is *Hostal Los Cóndores* (☎02624/420002, ⓦ www.loscondoreshotel.com.ar; ⑤); the buffet breakfast is excellent, and they also offer horseriding and treks into the nearby mountains. Some way south, lying just off the RN-7, is the more luxurious *Hotel Valle Andino* (☎02624/420095, ⓦ www.hotelvalleandino.com; ④), which has spacious rooms, tennis courts and a pleasant sitting room, and offers full board for $30 more. *Café Tibet*, near the junction, serves good coffee in a very imaginatively stylized Tibetan temple (in homage to the movie *Seven Years in Tibet*, some of which was shot here). The best **place to eat** is *Lo de Pato*, 1km south of the junction; it's a popular stopoff for coach trips and buses to and from Chile, but despite the frequent crowds the food is tasty, especially the trout.

Up to Los Penitentes

From Uspallata, the RN-7 swings round to the west and rejoins the Río Mendoza, whose valley it shares with the now-disused rail line all the way to its source at Punta de Vacas. The road follows an ancient Inca trail; several mummified corpses have been found in the mountains to the south and are displayed in Mendoza at the Museo de Ciencias Naturales y Antropológicas (see p.388). The scenery is simply fantastic: you pass through narrow canyons, close by the Cerro del Burro (4293m) and the Cerro División (4603m) to the south, with the rugged ridges of the Cerros del Chacay culminating in the Cerro Tigre (5700m) to the north. Stripes of different coloured rock – reds, greens and yellows caused by the presence of iron, copper and sulphur – decorate the steep walls of the cordillera peaks, while the vegetation is limited to tough highland grass and *jarilla*, a scruffy, gorse-like shrub gathered for firewood. The road climbs a gentle slope, slips through a series of tunnels, takes you through the abandoned hamlet of Polvaredas and past the police station at Punta de Vacas, at 2325m above sea level; the public customs post is further on at Los Horcones.

Some 65km from Uspallata is the small ski resort of **LOS PENITENTES**, or more properly Villa Los Penitentes (☎0261/428-3601, ⓦ www.penitentes.com). The "penitents" in question are a series of strange pinnacles of rock, high up on the ridge atop Cerro Penitentes (4356m), towering over the small village of typical, brightly coloured ski resort buildings to the south. The pointed rocks are thought to look like cowled monks, of the kind that traditionally parade during Holy Week in places such as Seville – hence the name. The resort's 25 pistes vary from nursery slopes to the black "Las Paredes", with most of the runs classified as difficult and the biggest total drop being 700m. The modern ski lifts also run at weekends in the summer, so you can enjoy the fabulous mountain and valley views from the top of Cerro San Antonio (3200m); the fissured peak looming over it all is the massive Cerro Leña (4992m).

As well as a ski school, a ski rental shop, a supermarket and a hospital, the resort (☎02624/420110) offers several types of **accommodation** during the ski season. In addition to a number of *apart-hotels* run by the resort, there's also the extremely comfortable *Hostería Los Penitentes* (☎0261/420-2137; ⑦), usually booked by the week; or the rather basic *Ayelén Hotel de Montaña* (☎02624/420229, ⓦ ayelenpenitentes.com.ar; ⑦) and its sister hostel, the *Hostería Ayelén* (②), which can be booked by the night. A modest but still pleasant alternative are the *cabañas* run by Gregorio Yapurai (☎0261/430-5118; $89 per person); or bed down at the dormitories in *Campo Base Penitentes* (☎0261/427-1641; $35 per person, or US$15 half board). The horseshoe-shaped La Herradura building houses both a *confitería* and a disco for après-ski.

Puente del Inca

Just 6km west of Los Penitentes is **PUENTE DEL INCA**, a compulsory stop for anyone heading along the Alta Montaña route. At just over 2700m, this natural **stone bridge** is an impressive sight, featuring on many a postcard. Formed by the Río de las Cuevas, it nestles in an arid valley, overlooked by majestic mountains; just beneath the bridge are the remains of a once sophisticated spa resort, built in the 1940s but swept away by a flood. The ruins, the bridge itself and the surrounding rocks are all stained a nicotine-yellow by the very high sulphur content of the warm waters that gurgle up nearby. Stalls sell souvenirs here, including all kinds of objects that have been left to petrify and yellow in the mineral springs: shoes, bottles, hats, books, ashtrays and statues of the Virgin Mary have all been treated to this embellishment, and are of dubious taste, but the displays make for an unusual photograph. Only 4km west of Puente del Inca is the dirt track that heads into the Parque Nacional Aconcagua.

There are only two possibilities for **accommodation**, both popular with Aconcagua climbers: the relatively luxurious *Hostería Puente del Inca* (☎02624/420266; ❻ with half board); and the *Refugio La Vieja Estación* (no phone; ❶), which has basic bunk beds and shared bath.

Aconcagua

At 6962m – or 6959m according to some maps – **CERRO ACONCAGUA** is the highest peak in both the western and southern hemispheres, or outside the Himalayas. Its glacier-garlanded summit dominates the Parque Provincial Aconcagua, even though it is encircled by several other mountains that exceed 5000m: cerros Almacenes, Catedral, Cuerno, Cúpula, Ameghino, Güssfeldt, Dedos, México, Mirador, Fitzgerald, La Mano, Santa María and Tolosa, some of which are easier to climb than others, and many of which obscure views of the great summit from most points around. The five glaciers that hang around its faces like icy veils are Horcones Superior, Horcones Inferior, Güssfeldt, Las Vacas and Los Polacos.

Aconcagua may be the highest Andean mountain, but for many mountain purists, it lacks the morphological beauty of Cerro Mercedario to the north or Volcán Tupungato to the south; it's also not as difficult a climb to the summit as some of the other Andean peaks. Nevertheless, ever since it was conquered by the Italian–Swiss mountaineer Mathias Zurbriggen in 1897 – after it had been identified by German climber Paul Güssfeldt in 1883 – Aconcagua has been one of the top destinations in the world for expeditions or solo climbs. In 1934, a Polish team of climbers made it to the top via the Los Polacos glacier now named after them; in 1953, the southwest ridge was the route successfully taken by a local group of mountaineers; and in 1954, a French team that had successfully conquered Cerro Fitz Roy made the first ascent of Aconcagua up the south face, the most challenging of all – Plaza Francia, one of the main base camps, is named after them. In recent years, Aconcagua has become a major attraction for less experienced mountaineers, and of the seven thousand-odd people who try to reach the summit every year, about half make it.

Although **climbing** Aconcagua is technically less demanding than climbing-many lower-altitude peaks, it is still a challenge to be taken seriously. Fitness, patience and acclimatization are key, and, unless you're fairly experienced at high-altitude treks, you shouldn't even consider going up; despite what the agencies may tell you, both independent climbers and people climbing as part of organized treks often end up turning back. The two biggest obstacles are coping with the altitude and the cold – temperatures can plummet to -40°C at night even in the summer – and fickle weather is also a major threat. Expeditions always descend when they see milky-white clouds shaped like the lenses of eye-glasses, known as *el viento blanco*, which announce violent storms. On average, some two people a year die trying to climb Aconcagua. Frostbite and altitude sickness are the main health hazards, but proper precautions can usually prevent both. Allow two to three weeks for an expedition, since you should acclimatize at each level, and take it easy throughout the climb; many of the people who don't make it to the top fail because they try to rush. Given the huge amount of supplies needed to make the ascent most people invest in a mule.

Of the three **approaches** – south, west or east – the western route from the Plaza de Mulas (4230m) is the most accessible and most used, and is known as the Ruta Normal. Very experienced climbers take either the Glaciar de los Polacos route, with its base camp at Plaza Argentina, reached via a long track that starts near Punta de Vacas, or the very demanding south face, whose Plaza Francia base camp is reached from Los Horcones, branching off from the Plaza de Mulas trail at a spot called Confluencia (3368m). For more details of the different routes, advice on what to take with you and how to acclimatize, consult the Aconcagua website (Ⓦwww.aconcagua.com.ar). For more specialist information, especially for serious climbers who are considering one of the harder routes, the best publication is R.J. Secor's *Aconcagua, A Climbing Guide* (1994).

The origins of the name Aconcagua are not entirely clear, although it probably comes either from the Huarpe words *Akon-Kahuak* ("stone sentinel") or from the Mapuche *Akonhue* ("from the beyond"). That it was a holy site for these and/or other native peoples is evidenced by the discovery in 1985 of an Inca mummy – now in the Museo del Área Fundacional, Mendoza (see p. 387) – on the southwest face. Found at an altitude of 5300m, the presence of the mummy shows that ceremonies, including burials and perhaps sacrifices, took place at these incredible heights.

Practicalities

Unless you are arranging everything through a tour operator, the first place you need to go is the **Dirección de Recursos Naturales Renovables** (Mon–Fri 8am–6pm, Sat & Sun 9am–1pm; ℡0261/425-2090, Ⓦwww.aconcagua.mendoza.gov.ar),

▲ Trekking with donkeys at Aconcagua

located on the first floor of Mendoza's main tourist office at Avenida San Martín 1143. This is where you must apply for the compulsory permits to enter the Aconcagua reserve. For foreign trekkers these cost from $75 for a single day's access to as high as $2000 for a twenty-day permit to climb to the summit in winter. Argentine nationals pay much lower fees. The main climbing season runs from mid-November to mid-March; January is the most popular month, and therefore most expensive, as it coincides with Argentine summer holidays and is when the weather is usually most settled.

To get to either Los Horcones or Punta de Vacas, you can take the twice-daily **buses** from Mendoza, or hop off a through bus headed to Santiago de Chile. It's definitely preferable, though, whether trekking or climbing, to go with local guides on an **organized trip**, if only because of the treacherous weather. Several outfits in Mendoza specialize in tours, which cost around US$2500 per person plus US$600 each for equipment rental and permits. These include Aconcagua Trek, at Barcala 484 (℡0261/429-5007, ⓦwww.aconcaguatrek .com); Aconcagua Xperience, at Avenida Mitre 1237 (℡0261/423-1806, ⓦwww.aconcagua-xperience.com.ar); Campo Base Expeditions, at Pt Sarmiento 229 (℡0261/425-5511, ⓦwww.campobase.com.ar & www .cerroaconcagua.com); Aymará Viajes, at 9 de Julio 1023 (℡0261/420-2064); and Fernando Grajales (℡0261/428-3157, ⓦwww.grajales.net), where you can also hire mules if climbing independently. The only possible **places to stay** near the base camps are at Puente del Inca (see p.398) or at Las Cuevas (see below).

Las Cuevas and Cristo Redentor

It's just 15km from Puente del Inca, via the customs post at Los Horcones, to **LAS CUEVAS**, the final settlement along the Alta Montaña road before the **Túnel Cristo Redentor** – a toll-paying tunnel under the Andes into Chile (open 24hr; passport and vehicle documents required; no perishable foods or plant material allowed into Chile). At 3112m, Las Cuevas is a bit of a ghost town, a feeling enhanced by the rather grim Nordic-style stone houses, one of which houses a *confitería*, *Nido de Cóndores*, which serves decent hot food and snacks. The *Hostel Arco de la Cuevas*, an attractive stone building arching over the RN-7, is popular with Aconcagua climbers (℡0264/420185, ⓦwww.arcodelascuevas.com.ar; dormitory $50 per person or a double with en-suite bathroom; ❹). It also has a restaurant.

From January to March, but usually not for the rest of the year because of snowfalls or frost, you can drive up the several hairpin bends to the **Monumento al Cristo Redentor**, an eight-metre-high, six-tonne statue of Christ as the redeemer. It was put here in 1904 to celebrate the so-called May 1902 Pacts, signed between Argentina and Chile, under the auspices of British King Edward VII, to determine once and for all the Andean boundary between the two countries. Designed by Argentine sculptor Mateo Alonso, the statue was made from melted-down cannons and other weapons, in a reversal of Fray Luis Beltrán's project a hundred years before (see p.396). Nearby is a disused Chilean customs post – the Paso de la Cumbre, no longer used by international traffic. The views towards Cerro Tolosa (5432m), immediately to the north, along the cordillera and down into several valleys, are quite staggering; make sure you have something warm to wear, though, as the howling winds up here are bitterly cold. When the road is open, most Alta Montaña tours bring you up here as the grand finale to the excursion; would-be Aconcagua conquerors often train and acclimatize by clambering to the top on foot.

South of Mendoza

The cordillera south of Mendoza city contains two remote and little visited but stunning provincial parks – the fabulous **Parque Provincial Tupungato**, 80km southwest from Mendoza and dominated by the soaring volcano of the same name, and the **Reserva Provincial Laguna Diamante**, with a turquoise altiplanic lake, the **Laguna Diamante**, at its heart. The latter is a further 140km southwest of Tupungato and only open during the summer; both are well worth the effort it takes to reach them.

Tupungato and Parque Provincial Tupungato

Now that Aconcagua has become almost a victim of its own success, anyone looking for a challenging mountain trek with fewer people crowding the trails and paths should head for the better-kept secret of Cerro Tupungato, an extinct volcano peaking at 6570m. Its hulking cone dominates the **PARQUE PROVINCIAL TUPUNGATO**, which stretches along the Chilean border to the south of the RN-7 at Puente del Inca, but is most accessible from the town of **TUPUNGATO**, reached from Mendoza via the RN-40 and the RP-86. The virgin countryside within the park is utterly breathtaking, completely unspoilt and unremittingly stark.

There's little to see in the small market town, but this is where you can contract guides to take you to the top of the mighty volcano; ask at the *Hotel Turismo* (see below), which also acts as the town's **tourist office** (daily 9am–6pm). You'll need plenty of time as the treks last between three and fifteen days, depending on how long you're given to acclimatize at each level – the longer the better. Calculate on US$1000 per person. Apart from the companies recommended for Aconcagua, which also arrange tours to Tupungato (see p.393), check out Rómulo Nieto at the *Hostería Don Rómulo*, at Almirante Brown 1200 (T 02622/489020, W www .donromulo.com.ar; ❸). Not only does he arrange reasonably priced tours, but you can stay here in the small, plain but comfortable rooms. Alternatively, you could **stay** at the *Hotel Turismo*, Avenida Belgrano 1066 (T 02622/488007; ❸), which is a little more spacious, with more modern bathrooms and a full-board option. There's also a very decent **campsite** on Calle La Costa, with barbecue facilities and clean toilets and showers. The best **place to eat** is *Pizzeria Ilo*, at Belgrano and Sargento Cabral, which serves up an excellent margarita and delicious home-made pasta. **Buses** run fairly regularly from Mendoza, arriving at Plaza General San Martín.

Reserva Provincial Laguna Diamante

Some 220km southwest of Mendoza, **LAGUNA DIAMANTE** is the destination of one of the least-known but most unforgettable excursions in the area. The source of the Río Diamante, the lake is so called because the choppy surface of its crystalline waters suggests a rough diamond. One reason for its relative obscurity is that weather conditions make it possible to reach Laguna Diamante only from mid-December to the end of March. At Pareditas, 125km south of Mendoza by the RN-40, take the reliable, unsealed the RP-101, which forks off to the southwest; the drive is one marvellous panoramic view of the Andean precordillera, following Arroyo Yaucha through fields of gorse-like *jarilla* and gnarled *chañares*, affording views of the rounded summits of the frontal cordillera, before entering the Cañón del Gateado, through which the Arroyo Rosario flows past dangling willows. At another fork in the road, 20km on, take the right fork to the Refugio Militar General Alvarado, the entrance to the **Reserva Provincial Laguna Diamante**. Here, you'll catch your first sight of **Cerro Maipo** (5323m), the permanently snowcapped volcano that straddles the frontier, some 4000m above sea level. Nestling beneath the Cordón del Eje, a majestic range of dark ochre rock, and towered over by the snow-streaked Maipo opposite – a perfect cone worthy of a Japanese woodcut – this ultramarine lake is constantly buffeted into white horses by strong breezes and its waves noisily lap the springy, mossy banks. The silence is broken only by the howl of the wind. Rangers at the **guardería**, which you pass on the final approach to the lagoon, can offer some information on the reserve and its wildlife, and appreciate the chance to share a *mate*.

No public transport reaches this remote spot, so you'll need a 4WD. Some tour agencies also come; try Nicolás García at Argentina Mountain, Lavalle 606, San José, in Guaymallén, Mendoza (℡0261/431-8356 or 15-555-3103, Ⓦwww.lagunadeldiamante.com), who offers day-trips from Mendoza ($350 per person), as well as longer horse treks and climbs up Maipo and Tupungato. You may also be able to pick up a tour from San Rafael, which is closer. Since it's in an area under military control, near a strategic point on the Chilean border, take your passport.

San Rafael and around

The small city of **SAN RAFAEL** is the de facto capital of central Mendoza Province; around 230km south of Mendoza via the RN-40 and the RN-143, it's a kind of mini-Mendoza, complete with wide avenues, irrigation channels along the gutters and scrupulously clean public areas. The town was founded in 1805 on behalf of Rafael, Marqués de Sobremonte – hence the name – by militia leader Miguel Telles Meneses. Large numbers of Italian and Spanish immigrants flocked here at the end of the nineteenth century, but the so-called Colonia Francesa expanded further when the railway arrived in 1903. Favoured by French immigrants during the nineteenth century, San Rafael built its prosperity on vineyards, olives and fruit, grown in the province's second biggest oasis. In all, there are nearly eighty wine **bodegas** in San Rafael department, most of them tiny, family-run businesses, some of which welcome visitors. Tourism has been a big money-spinner over the past couple of decades, especially since adventure tourism has taken off. The **Cañon del Atuel**, a short way to the southwest, is a great place for gentle whitewater rafting, or you can try the much more challenging, dramatic **Río Diamante**. If exploring the southern parts of the province, there's more choice of accommodation in San Rafael than in Malargüe, although the latter still makes a far more convenient base.

Arrival and information

San Rafael's small **airport**, with daily flights to Buenos Aires, is 5km west of the town centre, along the RN-143 towards Mendoza. There are no buses, but taxi rides into town won't break the bank ($15). The **bus terminal** – buses arrive here from Mendoza, Malargüe, San Juan and places further afield – is central, wedged in between calles Almafuerte and Avellaneda, at Coronel Suárez. It's surrounded by shops and cafés and has its own tourist information kiosk (Mon–Fri 9am–2pm). The city's main **tourist office** is at the corner of avenidas Hipólito Yrigoyen and Balloffet (daily 8am–9pm; ℡02627/424217, Ⓦwww.sanrafaelturismo.gov.ar).

SAN RAFAEL

ACCOMMODATION
Camping El Parador	L
Cerro Nevado	E
Hostel Puesta del Sol	K
Jardin	G
Kalton	F
Millalén	J
Regine	I
San Rafael	B
Tonin	A
Tower Inn	D
Trotamundos	H
Vecchia Terra	C

EATING & DRINKING
Daikin Disco	5
La Fusta	4
La Fusta II	7
Jockey Club	1
Nina	3
El Restauro	2
Sociedad Anónima	6
Tienda del Sol	8
La Zona	9

RP-156 & General Alvear

RN-143 to Malargüe, Museo de Historia Natural &

Airport, RN-143 to Mendoza & Bianchi Champagnes

Accommodation

San Rafael has no shortage of **places to stay**, ranging from basic refuges to luxurious *apart-hotels*. One extremely good value option is to rent the house (sleeps eight) for self-catering groups at Avenida Moreno 634, (℡02627/429801 or 15-537298; ❹). It has a private swimming pool, garden and parking. The best **campsite** hereabouts is *Camping El Parador* (℡02627/420492; tents ❶, *cabañas* ❹), set in an attractive wooded location on the Isla Río Diamante, 6km south of the centre; it has excellent facilities.

Cerro Nevado Hipólito Yrigoyen 376 ℡02627/428209, @www.cerronevadohotel.com.ar. This spotless place has a pleasant restaurant, but avoid the streetside rooms, as they can be noisy. ❸

🏃 **Hostel Puesta del Sol** Deán Funes 998 ℡02627/434881, @www.complejopuesta delsol.com. One of the most stunning hostels in the country, with modern facilities, a huge swimming pool amid landscaped grounds, and a lively atmosphere. It's 2.5km from the terminal – $8 in a *remise*. $25 per person; double room ❸

Jardín Hipólito Yrigoyen 283 ℡02627/434621, @www.hoteljardin.com.ar. Very comfy rooms, all en suite, arranged around a lush patio shaded by an impressive palm tree. ❹

Kalton Hipólito Yrigoyen 120 ℡02627/430047, @www.kaltonhotel.com. Typical mid-range town hotel near the bus station, with well-kept, albeit unremarkable, rooms. ❻

Millalén Ortíz de Rosas 198 ℡02627/422776, @ricardoloparco@hotmail.com. Modern hotel with pleasantly understated rooms, sparkling bathrooms and unfussy decor. ❸

Regine Independencia 623 and Colón ℡02627/421470, @www.hotelregine.com.ar. Rooms are well furnished and charming, while the rustic dining room serves reliably good food; there's a beautiful garden and a small pool. ❹

San Rafael Coronel Day 30 ℡02627/430125, @www.hotelsanrafael.com.ar. Another of San Rafael's comfortable mid-range hotels; this one has a bar, reception with log fire and cable TV in the rooms. ❺

Tonin Pellegrini 330 ℡02627/422499, @www .sanrafael-tour.com/tonin. Very pleasant, good-value rooms with modish stainless-steel washbasins in gleaming bathrooms. ❹

Tower Inn Hipólito Yrigoyen 774 ℡02627/427190, @www.towersanrafael.com. This sandy-hued tower of stone and plate glass may be a bit of an eyesore, but the interior is comfortable and well run, and a large swimming pool, spa, gym and patio bar make it San Rafael's only four-star hotel. ❽

Trotamundos Barcala 300 ℡02627/432795, @www.trotamundoshostel.com.ar. A rather cramped hostel that's popular with young Argentines, and conveniently located for the bus station if you're just passing through town. ❷

Vecchia Terra Castelli 23 ℡02627/424169, @www.vecchiaterra.com.ar. A high quality *apart-hotel* with apartments for up to 6 people. Luxuriously fitted out throughout, with modern kitchens and great showers. Better value for money than the Tower, although lacks the pool. ❻

The City

San Rafael has a flat, compact centre that lends itself to a gentle stroll, but otherwise there aren't any sights to speak of – the town is essentially a base for visiting the surrounding area. The main drag, with most of the shops and hotels, is a continuation of the RN-143 from Mendoza, called **Avenida Hipólito Yrigoyen** west of north–south axis **Avenida General San Martín** and **Avenida Bartolomé Mitre** to the east. Streets change name either side of both axes.

To fill an hour or so, take a taxi or a bus marked "Isla Diamante" from Avenida Hipólito Yrigoyen. Isla Diamante is a large island 6km south of the town centre, in the middle of the river of the same name, and is home to the **Museo de Historia Natural** (Mon–Fri 8am–1pm & 3–8pm, Sat & Sun 8am–8pm; $1). Among masses of bedraggled stuffed birds, moth-eaten foxes and lumps of rock, you'll find some fabulous pre-Columbian ceramics, the best of which are statues from Ecuador; there's also a small collection of crafts from Easter Island and some particularly fine ceramics from northwestern Argentina. You'll also see a mummified child dating from 40 AD and a gorgeous multicoloured leather bag decorated with striking, very modern-looking geometric designs, found in the Gruta del Indio in the Cañon del Atuel.

The city is also an excellent base for **rafting** with the Cañon del Atuel (see p.406) being the most sedate option. More challenging experiences are available with rapids as tough as Grade IV–V in season, such as the Río Sosneado (booked through Bruni Aventura, Avenida Balloffet 98 ℡02627/423790, Ⓦwww.bruniaventura.com.ar; season Dec–Feb, minimum of four people, $550 per person); and one- or multi-day adventures down the splendid and rarely visited canyon of the **Río Diamante**, or the Río Grande (Exoticandes Expediciones, San Luis 336 ℡02627/445415 or 15-407602, Ⓦwww.exoticandes.com; season Dec–Feb, minimum 5 people; prices from US$150 per person).

Eating, drinking and nightlife

Good **restaurants** and **bars** are few and far between, but one or two stand out. In addition, there are a couple of decent bars and **discos** out of town towards the west.

Daikiri Disco Hipólito Yrigoyen 3177. New, large club that's the place to go out in the city on Friday night, with a sizeable garden area and outside bars.

La Fusta Hipólito Yrigoyen 538. By far the town's best *parrilla*, serving succulent steaks, full *parrilladas* and local wines at very reasonable rates.

La Fusta II Hipólito Yrigoyen and Beato Marcelino Champagnat. Sister restaurant to the above, in ultra-modern surroundings with fine decor and a large terrace.

Jockey Club Belgrano 330. Good old-fashioned service and hearty food, with a good-value *menú turista* at lunch time.

Nina San Martín and Olascoaga. Very smart cocktail bar doubling as a café and tearoom.

El Restauro Chile and Salas. Friendly service and creative, interesting but inexpensive cuisine using local ingredients such as trout at this new, ample restaurant.

Sociedad Anónima Hipólito Yrigoyen 1530. This bar is one of San Rafael's more trendy options – and a great place to people-watch.

Bodegas in and around San Rafael

Though Mendoza is undeniably Argentina's wine capital, **San Rafael's** wineries are among the finest in the country. Several open their doors willingly to visitors, although tours are more informal than in Mendoza and often don't run at set times; don't be surprised if no one speaks English. Some of the best include:

Champañera Bianchi Hipólito Yrigoyen s/n ℡02627/435353. An interesting contrast with its old downtown bodega, this ultra-modern sparkling wine-production unit, housed in a postmodern steel and glass building, is 4km west of the town centre. Excellent sparkling wines made according to the *méthode champenoise*. Twenty-minute tours Mon–Sat 9am–noon & 2–5pm. English spoken.

Jean Rivier Hipólito Yrigoyen 2385 ℡02627/432675, Ⓦwww.jeanrivier.com. Friendly small winery, founded by Swiss winemakers; their tip-top wines include an unusual cabernet sauvignon–fer blend. Delicious chardonnays, too. Mon–Fri 8–11am & 3–6.30pm, Sat 8–11am.

Simonassi Lyon 5km south of San Rafael, at Km657 of RN-143, at Rama Caida ℡02627/430963, Ⓦwww.bodegasimonassi.com. Family-run, prize-winning winery, in an attractive farmhouse. Guided visits Mon–Fri 8am–5pm, but phone an hour in advance to reserve.

Suter Hipólito Yrigoyen 2850 ℡02627/421076, Ⓔturismo@sutersa.com.ar. Slightly mechanical guided visits every 30min, but you're given a half-bottle of decent wine as a gift. Traditional-style winery. Mon–Sat 9am–5pm; free.

Tienda del Sol Hipólito Yrigoyen 1663. Trendy,
postmodern resto-bar, serving seafood and pasta
dishes alongside cocktails and other drinks, at
slightly inflated prices.

La Zona Deán Funes 1000. Hip dance club,
popular on Sat nights.

Cañon del Atuel

The **CAÑON DEL ATUEL** is one of San Rafael's main attractions, a beautifully
wild canyon linking two man-made lakes along the Río Atuel, to the southwest of
the town. Visits begin at the reservoir furthest away, the **Embalse del Nihuil**,
reached along the winding RN-144 towards Malargüe, up the Cuesta de los
Terneros to the 1300-metre summit, which offers great views of the valley below;
and then via the RP-180, which forks off to the south. The lake lies 92km
southwest of San Rafael. The partly sealed RP-173 then squeezes in a northeasterly
direction through a narrow gorge whose cliffs and rocks are striped red, white and
yellow, contrasting with the beige of the dust-dry mountainsides. Wind and water
have eroded the rocks into weird and often rather suggestive shapes that stimulate
the imagination: tour guides attach names like "the Nun" or "the Toad" to the
strange formations. The road then passes a couple of dams, attached to power
stations, before swinging round the other reservoir, the **Embalse Valle Grande**.
Sticking out of these blue-green waters are more strange rock formations, one of
which does indeed look like the submarine its nickname suggests. From the high
corniche roads that skirt the lakeside you are treated to some grand views of the
waters, dotted with kayaks and other boats, and the mountains beyond.

At the northern end of the reservoir you'll find two *confiterías*, which serve decent
snacks and drinks. Near here starts the stretch of the Río Atuel used for
whitewater rafting. Raffeish, at RP-173 Km35, Valle Grande (☎02627/436996
or 15-409089, ⓦwww.raffeish.com.ar), is the most reliable and ecologically
conscious operator, and has an office here. Trips last an hour, along an easy stretch
for beginners, or a couple of hours or more, taking in a tougher Grade II section
of the river; take a change of clothes as you get soaked. The scenery along the way
is pleasantly pastoral along the more open parts and staggeringly beautiful in the
narrower gorges. Further downstream, Hunuc Huar is a wonderful crafts
workshop (daily 9.30–1pm & 4–9pm) run by an indigenous family, specializing in
fine ceramics, set in an idyllic garden.

San Rafael is only 25km away from the canyon by RP-173, but unless you have
your own transport, you'll have to get here on an **organized tour**: try Risco
Viajes, Avenida Hipólito Yrigoyen 284, in San Rafael (☎02627/436439, ⓦwww
.riscoviajes.com). The upmarket *Hotel Valle Grande* (☎02627/155-80660, ⓦwww
.hotelvallegrande.com; ◍), with all kinds of sports facilities and a fine swimming
pool, is a good place to **stay**, though it can get very crowded during the summer
months; the hotel also has four-bed *cabañas* for rent ($440 plus $60 per person)
that can sleep up to seven.

Las Leñas

To Argentines, **LAS LEÑAS** means chic: this is where the Porteño jet set come to
show off their winter fashions, to get photographed for society magazines and to
have a good time. **Skiing** and **snowboarding** are only part of the fun – as in all
exclusive winter resorts, the *après-ski* is just as important as the snow conditions.
More seriously, many ski champions from the northern hemisphere head down
here during the June to October season, when there's not a lot of snow in the US

or Europe; the Argentine, Brazilian and South American skiing championships are all held here in August, while other events include snow-polo matches, snow-rugby, snow-volleyball and fashion shows. But even though Las Leñas is a playground for the rich and famous, it's possible to visit without breaking the bank; you could stay in the least expensive accommodation, or overnight elsewhere nearby, such as in Los Molles or Malargüe (see p.410). Las Leñas is also trying to branch out into **summertime adventure travel**, such as mountain-biking, rafting and horseriding, making the most of its splendid upland setting and pleasant daytime temperatures. Note that the resort is completely **closed** down, however, from March to May and October to the end of December.

The road to Las Leñas heads due west from the Mendoza to Malargüe section of the RN-40, 28km south of the crossroads settlement of El Sosneado. It climbs past the ramshackle spa resort of Los Molles, and the peculiar **Pozo de las Animas**, a set of two huge well-like depressions that make for a diverting photo stop (scheduled bus services don't stop, and they can't be seen from the road). Caused by underground water erosion, each is several hundred metres in diameter, with a pool of turquoise water in the bottom. The sand-like cliffs surrounding each lake have been corrugated and castellated by the elements, like some medieval fortress, and the ridge dividing the two looks in danger of collapse at any minute. The resort lies 50km from the RN-40, a total of nearly 200km southwest of San Rafael. If you are booked at the resort, look to get a transfer from Malargüe airport (once weekly charter flight from Buenos Aires, June to mid-Sept, US$500 return), Mendoza or San Rafael; or during the ski season you can take the daily **buses** run by Iselín and CATA from Mendoza, a seven-hour journey (US$20 one way), or the daily public bus or agency transfers from Malargüe. Otherwise you need your own transport.

Accommodation

All **accommodation** booking in Las Leñas is organized centrally through Las Leñas resort, whose office is in Buenos Aires at Bartolomé Mitre, 4th floor (T011/4819-6000, W www.laslenas.com). Usually booked as weekend, or eight-day packages, all the hotels below are within tramping distance of the slopes and cost around US$250 per person per night (half board & ski passes included) in the peak weeks of July and August, though prices tend to drop by some fifty percent at either end of the season. They're all rather functional in their aesthetic. More economical options are the "dormy houses", *Laquir*, *Lihuén*, *Milla* and *Payén*, chalets grouped at the edge of the village that can sleep up to five and have simple kitchens and bedrooms.

Hotels

Acuario A very comfortable option close to the lifts. ⑨

Aries Much further away from the central village, and therefore rather quieter, than the other hotels. Decent rooms, a lobby bar, modern gym and impeccable service. ⑨

Club de la Nieve Housed in an Alpine-style chalet, with its own reasonable restaurant and spacious, functional rooms. A tad cheaper than the other options. ⑨

Piscis The resort's most luxurious hotel, with piste views from many rooms and its own equipment for rent; also has a heated swimming pool with a questionable carbon footprint (half indoors, half outdoors), plus jacuzzis and saunas. ⑨

Virgo Hotel Large, elegant rooms, a heated pool and spa, and a restaurant with panoramic views of the slopes. ⑨

The resort

Las Leñas is no Gstaad or St Moritz: it's a purpose-built **resort** built at an altitude of 2200m, with excellent **skiing** and **snowboarding** – when there is enough snow – and a breathtaking backdrop of craggy mountain-tops, of which Cerro Las Leñas is the highest (4351m) and Cerro Torrecillas (3771m) the most daintily pinnacled. The whole area covers more than 33 square kilometres, with 28 pistes, ranging from several gentle nursery slopes to a couple of sheer black runs; cross-country and off-piste skiing are also possible.

Experienced skiers will want to head direct for **El Marte** lift, the only one which accesses the harder runs, but be aware that this is often closed due to the resort's characteristic high winds, which can be a source of some frustration. Contact the Ski School for information about off-piste excursions into the area's impressive **back-country** (from $500 per person for a half day). Nature is, of course, unpredictable, but **August to early September** is probably your best bet for serious powder, as well as for lower winds (and prices) and thinner crowds. Lessons are available in several languages, including English. The equipment-rental service (next to the *Hotel Acuario*) is pricey, as are the lifts – day passes cost around $135–210, depending on the season – though many hotels offer discounts on these as part of packages. Your ski pass includes cover for getting you off the mountain in the event of an accident on piste, but only as far as the resort's medical centre. An early start to the day definitely pays off – the slopes are relatively empty, as many people are recovering from all-night partying.

Eating and drinking

For **eating** at the ski village, there's the *confitería* and popular meeting-place *Innsbruck*, which serves beer and expensive snacks on its terrace with piste views. *La Roca* is an on-piste snack bar with Tex-Mex food, while *Olimpos*, accessible by the Minerva chairlift, serves lunch. *La Cima* is a pizzeria by day and a more chic *parrilla* restaurant by night, and the *Hotel Piscis'* luxury restaurant, *Cuatro Estaciones*, is the place to be seen for dinner. Rather more informal, if still expensive, and serving delicious, huge-portioned fondues and raclettes with the best Argentine white wines, is *El Refugio*, in the central Pirámide building. Apart from Hotel Piscis' casino, for until-dawn **nightlife** – which tends to be dominated by under-25s – you have a choice between *Urban* (Sun & Wed only) and *Ufo Point*.

▲ Skiing at Las Leñas

Malargüe and around

MALARGÜE is a laidback town 186km south of San Rafael by the RN-144 and the RN-40. The biggest settlement in the far southern portion of Mendoza Province, it's less of a destination in itself, and more – like San Rafael – a base for exploring the prime tourist sites in this region. It's more conveniently located for most of these than San Rafael, although it has less choice of middle and upper-end accommodation.

The town is within day-trip distance of the black and red pampas of **La Payunia**, a nature reserve where flocks of guanacos and ñandús roam over lava flows. Far nearer – and doable as half-day outings – are some remarkable underground caves, the **Cueva de la Brujas**, and **Laguna Llancanelo**, a shining lagoon flecked pink with flamingos and crammed with other aquatic birdlife. You could also consider staying here in order to go skiing at **Las Leñas**, 77km away (see p.406).

Arrival and information

Buses from Mendoza and San Rafael stop at the bus terminal at Esquibel Aldao and Avenida General Roca, six blocks south and two west of central Plaza San Martín, but will also drop off and collect passengers at the plaza en route. Malargüe's excellent **tourist office** (daily 8am–10pm; ☎02627/471659, ⓦwww .malargue.gov.ar), in a fine rustic building on the RN-40 by the Parque de Ayer, four blocks north of the plaza, has loads of information on what to see and do, and on places to stay, tour operators and fishing in nearby rivers. It also issues the Malargüe Card, which can be used at various businesses around town to get discounts.

The town's **tour operators**, which offer excursions to places like Laguna Llancanelo, La Payunia, and Caverna de las Brujas, are generally of a high standard, but there is a lot of political infighting between them, and most are linked to a particular hostel, so deal direct with the agency of your choice. Check out Karen Travel, at Avenida San Martín 54 (☎02627/470342, ⓦwww.karentravel.com.ar), which has a long pedigree in the area; Huarpes del Sol, at San Martín 85 (☎02627/472764 or 15557878 155-84842, ⓦwww.huarpesdelsol.com.ar); and Choique, at San Martín y Rodriguez, 1st floor (☎02627/470391, ⓦwww .choique.com). Prices range from $50 for the 90-minute transfer to Las Leñas, to $220 for a day-trip to La Payunia (minimum four people). In the ski season, there's a daily public bus service to Las Leñas – best to buy tickets from the terminal the night before; ask if they'll pick you up from your hotel. **Ski equipment**, including snowboards, can be rented from a number of outlets along Avenida San Martín, including Aires de Libertad or Fuera de Pista at #129 (☎02627/472430), which has a good range of skis. It makes sense to rent gear in Malargüe rather than at Las Leñas – it's cheaper and you'll avoid the queues, but try to avoid travelling with a second pair of footwear that you can't pop in a daypack as lockers at Las Leñas are expensive. Kitting yourself out fully will cost some US$25–50 a day, depending on the quality of skis; and rental shops are open late.

Accommodation

The range of **accommodation** in Malargüe is expanding with every year, though higher-end options are still limited. Additionally, twice a year (in March and Nov), what decent options there are get packed out with physicists, who come for an international convention on the Pierre Auger experiment (see p.411). You get a fifty percent discount on a Las Leñas ski pass if you stay at least two nights in Malargüe during the season, but the benefits of this are cancelled out by the fact you have to rent your equipment at Las Leñas, which is more expensive. You can **camp** at

Reliving Alive

In 1972, a group of young **rugby players from Uruguay** caught the attention of the world after they survived an **air crash** and over two months of brutal subzero temperatures in the Andes, at a place on the Argentine–Chilean border in the mountains west of the Cerro Sosneado and Río Atuel, now called the **Glaciar de la Lágrimas** (glacier of tears). The students survived by consuming snow and their colleagues' corpses and fashioning sleeping bags from the insulation in the plane's tail, before two of them finally made it west over the mountains and alerted the Chilean authorities, who had long since given them up for dead. Their incredible story was told in the 1993 movie *Alive* and the documentary *Alive: 20 Years Later*. It is now possible to **visit the site** of the crash, where parts of the plane are still scattered. Some may find the idea macabre, and getting there is obviously no walk in the park – count on at least three days of trekking and horseriding through the snow, although you'll also get to take a unique hot bath in the warm blue waters bubbling up out of the ground at the ruins of the old *Hotel Sosneado*. Tours are run by Risco Viajes in San Rafael (see p.406) or with guides from Malargüe – such as Karen Travel (see p.409).

Camping Polideportivo, at Capdeval and Esquibal Aldao (℡02627/470691; ❶), or in a wonderful setting at Castillos de Pincheira, 27km southwest of town. There are also a couple of good options some 6km to the south of town, off the stretch of the RN-40 known as the Prolongación Constitución Nacional: the delightful, cosy *Seu Sek*, at Colonia Pehuenche 1, Finca 82 (℡02627/15587890, Ⓦwww.seusek .com.ar; ❷), which is full of rural character; or the youth hostel *Eco Hostel*, at Finca 65 (℡02627/470391 or 154-02439, Ⓦwww.hostelmalargue.net; $40 per person).

Hotels and hostels

El Capitán hostel Telles Meneses 897
℡02627/471534, Ⓦwww.hostelelcapitan.com.
Decent, family-run hostel eight blocks from the bus terminal. $40 per person.
Cisne ℡02627/471350 at Civit and Villegas.
Clean, functional hotel in the centre of town. ❺
City Avenida Rufino Ortega 158 (℡02627/471151,
Ⓦwww.hostelmalargue.net. Dorms $35 per person, attractive double and triple bedrooms (❸).
Kathmandú Hostel Saturnino Torres
121℡02627/15414899, Ⓦwww.hostel-kathmandu
.com.ar. A basic but homely place whose owner is very helpful, half a block from Plaza San Martín. $40 per person in dorms.
Maggio Hotel Manuel Ruibal 592,

℡02627/472496, Ⓦwww.maggiohotel.com.ar.
The most pristine mid-range option with large, well-furnished rooms in a contemporary style. ❻
Nord Patagonia Fray Inalicán 52
℡02627/471151, Ⓦwww.vallesaventura.com.ar.
Pleasant, compact hostel right on the main square. ❸
Río Grande ℡02627/471589,
Ⓔhotelriogrande@rucared.com.ar. Friendly owners, a choice between decent but very plain rooms and more commodious, tastefully decorated ones, and a restaurant serving delicious food. ❻
Rioma Fray Inalicán 68 ℡02627/471065,
Ⓔhotelrioma@rucared.com.ar. Reasonable, if rather nondescript, hotel in the centre of town. ❹

The Town

The core of the town lies on either side of the RN-40, called Avenida San Martín within the town's boundaries, a wide, rather soulless avenue along which many of the hotels are located, as well as a couple of cafés, the bank and telephone centres. **Plaza General San Martín** is the focal point, with its benches shaded by pines and native trees, but it's nothing to get excited about. The town is extremely easy to find your way around, although it's fairly spread out.

Its handful of attractions are clustered together at the northern reaches, beyond the built-up area. Malargüe's pride and joy is the fine little **Centro de Convenciones y Exposiciones Thesaurus** (daily 10am–8pm; free; ℡02627/470027), subtly plunged underground in the middle of the garden. Its postmodern design, incorporating some fine workmanship, is certainly impressive for a town of this size. The centre also houses an art gallery with small exhibition rooms linked by corridors, intended to echo a cave's labyrinth. The centre complements the **Observatorio Pierre Auger** (guided visits Mon–Fri 5pm; free; Ⓦ www.auger.org.ar), opposite at San Martín Norte 304, part of a fascinating twenty-year astrophysics project to measure the mysterious ultra-high-energy cosmic rays that bombard Earth. A grid of 1600 cream-coloured water tanks serving as particle detectors have been placed 1.5km apart across an area of the pampas fifteen times the size of Buenos Aires – look out for them as you drive into town. It makes hunting for a needle in a haystack seem like child's play: only one such particle is likely to hit a square kilometre of the Earth's surface per century.

Heading back into town you pass the **Museo Regional** (daily 9am–1pm & 4–9pm; free). The four-room display in a neatly refurbished building includes objects as varied as ammonites, guanaco leather, clay pipes for religious ceremonies, jewellery and dinosaur remains. A new annexe to the museum houses Mi Viejo Almacén, a store selling local artisan goods.

Eating and drinking

For a delicious *parrilla*, it's well worth the walk to *La Cima* at Avenida San Martín 886 where the RN-40 enters town from the north (Ⓣ 02627/472583). Otherwise try the restaurant in the *Hotel Río Grande*, over the road. For the best trout, head out of town to El Dique, 8km west of Malargüe, where at the *Cuyam-Co* trout farm (Ⓣ 02627/15661917) you can catch your own fish. It is then perfectly cooked and served with an excellent local rosé; book ahead and note that the kitchen closes around 10pm.

Reserva Faunística Laguna de Llancanelo

The **RESERVA FAUNÍSTICA LAGUNA DE LLANCANELO** makes an easy half-day trip from Malargüe. It's an internationally-recognised RAMSAR wetland, with large populations of waterfowl year round, although you'll find the greatest concentrations in spring and summer, as many species come here to nest. On windless days, the shallow saline lagoon's mirror-still waters in the middle of a huge dried-up lakebed make for a fantastic sight. You'd be very unlucky not to spot flocks of flamingos, at times so huge that whole areas of the lake's surface are turned uniformly pink. Other species of birds include black-necked swans, several kinds of duck, grebe and teal, gulls, terns and curlews. Parts of the reserve are out of bounds all year, and access to others is restricted to non-critical seasons. The park is patrolled by *guardaparques*, and it is best to go on an organized tour from Malargüe, as you'll get more out of visiting the lagoon with someone who knows the terrain and the fauna. Preferably come very early in the morning or in the late afternoon and evening, when the light is fabulous and the wildfowl more easily spotted. Access to the reserve is via the RP-186, which branches east off the RN-40 some 20km south of Malargüe; it's then another 20km to the reserve entrance, near the shallow cavern known as the Cueva del Tigre.

Caverna de las Brujas

The **CAVERNA DE LAS BRUJAS** is a marvellous cave that plunges deep into the earth, just 73km southwest of Malargüe, 8km off the RN-40 along a marked track. The road climbs over the scenic **Cuesta del Chihuido**, which affords fantastic views of the Sierra de Palauco to the east, in a region of outstanding beauty enhanced by sparse but attractive vegetation. This area is covered by a thick layer of marine sedimentary rock, through which water has seeped, creating underground cave systems. The name Caverna de las Brujas literally means "witches' cave", and local legends say that it was used as a meeting-place for sorcerers. Las Brujas is a karstic cave, filled with rock formations, including some impressive **stalactites and stalagmites**; typically they have been given imaginative names such as "the Virgin's Chamber", "the Pulpit" and "the Flowers". Water continues to seep inside, making the walls slippery, as if they were awash with soapsuds. Although the tourist circuit is only 260m long and never descends more than 6m below the surface, the experience is memorable.

The *caverna* lies within a provincial park, and a small *guardería* stands nearby; ask here for the key to the padlocked gates that protect the grotto. It's compulsory to enter with a guide, and again the best option is to go on an organized tour from Malargüe ($70 per person plus $30 entrance each, minimum 5 people). Wear good walking shoes and take a sweater – the difference in temperature between inside and out can be as much as 20°C – and a pocket torch, though miners' helmets are also supplied; a highlight inside the cave is experiencing the total darkness by turning out all lights and getting used to the spooky atmosphere.

La Payunia

The highlight of any trip to southernmost Mendoza Province, yet overlooked by most visitors because of its relative inaccessibility, **LA PAYUNIA**, protected by the Reserva Provincial La Payunia, is a fabulously wild area of staggering beauty, sometimes referred to as the Patagonia Mendocina. Dominated by Volcán Payún Matru (3690m), and its slightly lower inactive neighbour Volcán Payún Liso, it is utterly unspoilt apart from some remnants of old fluorite and manganese mines plus some petrol-drilling derricks, whose nodding-head pump-structures are locally nicknamed "guanacos", after the member of the llama family they vaguely resemble in shape. Occasionally, you will spot real guanacos, sometimes in large flocks, standing out against the black volcanic backdrop of the so-called **Pampa Negra**. This huge expanse of lava in the middle of the reserve was caused by relatively recent volcanic eruptions, dating back hundreds or thousands of years rather than millions, as is the case of most such phenomena in the region. "Fresh" trails of lava debris can be seen at various points throughout the park, and enormous boulders of igneous rock are scattered over these dark plains, also ejected during the violent volcanic activity. The only vegetation is flaxen grass, whose golden colour stands out against the blackened hillsides. Another section of the reserve is the aptly named **Pampa Roja**, where reddish oxides in the lava give the ground a henna-like tint. The threatening hulk of Volcán Pihuel looms at the western extremity of the reserve – its top was blown off by a particularly violent explosion that occurred when the mountain was beneath the sea.

To visit the park, take one of the excellent day-trips run by Karen Travel in Malargüe (see p.409). If you plan to drive there independently, you'll need a 4WD and a good map. You must also take a guide with you – ask in the travel agencies or tourist office in Malargüe. You can also stay at the lovely eco-conscious **accommodation**, *Kiñe* (☎02627/155-88635 or 02627/471344, ⊛www.kinie.com.ar; from $250 per person per night full board; trips extra), in a basic but comfortable little farmstead at the remote hamlet of La Agüita, on RP-186 in the northeast corner of the reserve. In addition to simple but tasty meals the friendly family also lays on treks in the mountains and horse rides across plains full of guanacos. There is no public transport to *Kiñe* but the owners will pick you up in Malargüe (consult in advance for transfer costs if not arriving in your own vehicle).

San Juan and La Rioja

San Juan and La Rioja provinces share some memorable countryside, with range after range of lofty mountains alternating with green valleys of olive groves, onion fields and vineyards. Forming the northern half of Argentina's midwestern region, they're often regarded as the poorer cousins, in every sense, of Mendoza Province; and often give the impression of being resigned to backwater status. The provinces' **bodegas**, for example, continue to take a back seat to those of Mendoza and San Rafael, even though their wine can be just as good and they export much of their grape harvest to Mendoza's wineries. **Tourism** has not fully got off the ground here. Transport services are sometimes below par, and public transport tends to radiate out of the provincial capitals, making it frustratingly difficult to engineer tourist circuits – for those, you'll need your own transport, preferably a 4WD. But as long as you see this as a challenge rather than an obstacle, you can still enjoy the breathtaking scenery. The small southeastern corner of the region should be bypassed or given short shrift, however: it's a horrendous, flat area of dusty gorse and drab salt-flats.

To say that both provinces are sparsely inhabited is a gross understatement: outside the capital, La Rioja's population density barely reaches one inhabitant per square kilometre, while San Juan, where the equivalent ratio is around three, is on average half as densely populated as Mendoza Province. Leaving the cities behind to scout around the outback, you'll experience a real sense of setting off into uncharted territory. Some unpaved roads peter out into tracks barely passable in the hardiest jeep, and the weather conditions can be inclement – bakingly hot in summer, mixed with sudden downpours that can flood roads and sweep bridges away; in winter, you can be beset unpredictably by blizzards. However, this inhospitable nature does offer up fantastic opportunities for alternative tourism, such as 4WD trips or hiking.

About halfway between the dizzy heights of the Andean cordillera – many of its peaks exceeding 6000m along this stretch – and the tediously flat *travesías* in the easternmost fringe of both provinces, rises the **precordillera**, lower than the main range but still a respectable 4000m or more above sea level. Club-sandwiched between it and the two rows of cordillera – known as main and frontal ranges, a geological phenomenon unique to this section of the Andes – are successive chains of valleys. The higher ones over 1500m above sea level are known as the *valles altos*, of which the **Valle de Calingasta** is an outstanding example.

The two provinces have four natural parks. The highly inaccessible **Parque Nacional San Guillermo** in San Juan Province adjoins the **Reserva Provincial Las Vicuñas** across the boundary in La Rioja; respectively, they give you a sporting chance of spotting wild pumas and vicuñas, along with a host of other Andean wildlife, amid unforgettable landscapes. Further east are the provinces' star attractions: **Parque Nacional Talampaya**, with vertiginous red cliffs that make you feel totally insignificant and – only 70km south – its contiguous, unidentical twin, **Parque Provincial Ischigualasto**, more commonly referred to as the Valle de la Luna, an important dinosaur graveyard in a highly photogenic site.

San Juan and around

Some 165km north of Mendoza and nearly 1150km northwest of Buenos Aires, the city of **SAN JUAN** basks in the sun-drenched valley of the Río San Juan, which twists and turns between several steep mountain ranges. Understandably, the city revels in its pet name, Residencia del Sol. In some of its barrios it has

6

SAN JUAN

▲ RN-20 to Difunta Correa, Airport & **K**

◀ San José de Jáchal

▲ Antigua Bodega 1929 & Museo Bodega Graffigna

RN-40 to Mendoza & Museo Arqueológico ►

EATING & DRINKING

Abuelo Yuyi	7
Aptko	4
Aruba	1
Baró & De Sánchez	6
Bonafide	5
Freud Café	9
Hostal de Palito	3
Las Leñas	10
Maloca	2
Rigoletto	11
Soychú	8

ACCOMMODATION

Albertina	H
Alhambra	D
Alkázar	C
América	J
Gran Hotel Provincial	E
Jardín Petit	A
El Refugio	B
San Francisco	F
Suizo	G
Viñas del Sol	K
Zonda Hostel	I

Bus Terminal

BARRIO MITRE

Museo Histórico

Bus Stop ★

BARRIO JUAN XXIII

Convento de Santo Domingo

Catedral

Museo Casa de Sarmiento

Mercado Artesanal

Museo de Ciencias Naturales

Museo de Bellas Artes

Parque de Mayo

Former Railway Station

VILLA RIPOLL

N

0   250 m

The zonda effect

San Juan, like the rest of the Cuyo, though even more so, is prone to the **zonda**, a legendary dry wind that blows down from the Andes and blasts everything in its path like a blowtorch. It's caused by a **thermal inversion** that arises when wet, cold air from the Pacific is thrust abruptly up over the cordillera and suddenly forced to dump its moisture, mostly in the form of snow, onto the skyscraper peaks before helter-skeltering down the other side into the deep chasm between the Cordillera Principal and the precordillera, which acts like a very high brick wall. Forced to brake, the zonda rubs against the land like tyre-rubber against tarmac, and the resulting friction results in **blistering temperatures** and an atmosphere you can almost see. Mini-tornadoes can sometimes also occur, whipping sand and dust up in clearly visible spirals all along the region's desert-like plains. The Cuyo's answer to the *Föhn*, mistral or sirocco, ripping people's nerves to shreds, the zonda is one of the world's nastiest meteorological phenomena. Although it can blow at any time of year, the zonda is most frequent in the winter months, particularly August, when it can suddenly hike the temperature by ten to fifteen degrees in a matter of hours.

rained only a couple of times over the past decade, and the provincial average is less than 100mm a year. When it does rain, it's usually in the form of violent storms, as savage as the *zonda* wind that occasionally stings the city and shortens people's tempers (see box above). All this sunshine – more than nine hours a day on average – and the generally mild climate quickly ripen the sweetest imaginable grapes, melons and plums, irrigated by pre-Columbian canals and ditches, that have helped the city and its mainly Spanish and Middle Eastern immigrant population to prosper over the years. But nature is also a foe: periodic tremors, some of them alarmingly high on the Richter scale, remind Sanjuaninos that they live along one of the world's most slippery seismic faults; the Big One is dreaded as much here as in California but, as they do there, people just live their lives, trusting the techniques used in the construction of the city's newer buildings.

One of South America's strongest ever recorded earthquakes flattened the city in 1944 and as a result the city has hardly any buildings more than half a century old. It's modern and attractive, but San Juan is also quite conservative compared with its much bigger rival Mendoza. Around a third of a million people live in Greater San Juan, but in the compact microcentro everyone seems to know everyone else. Broad pavements, grand avenues and long boulevards shaded by rows of flaky-trunked plane trees lend the city a feeling of spaciousness and openness. Although none of the sights amounts to much, San Juan is a comfortable starting-point for touring some of the country's finest scenery. Destinations close to the city include an **archeological museum** in the southern suburbs and the mind-bogglingly grotesque pilgrim site of **Difunta Correa**, to the east.

Some history

The city was founded by the Spanish aristocrat Juan Jufré as San Juan de la Frontera on June 13, 1562 during an expedition from Santiago de Chile, and since then it has had a persistently troubled history. In 1594, the settlement was washed away by floods, and in 1632 it was again destroyed, this time in attacks by natives. The following year an uprising by the indigenous inhabitants was brutally put down; seventeen were hanged on the Plaza Mayor as an example. In the middle of the nineteenth century, San Juan found itself at the heart of the country's civil war when its progressive leader, Dr Antonino Aberastain, was assassinated by federalist troops. In 1885 the arrival of the railways heralded a change to San Juan's backwater status, as Basque, Galician and Andalucian immigrants began arriving.

Like Mendoza, the city has had terrible luck with seismic shocks: several violent earthquakes struck the city in the 1940s, but the strongest of all, reaching around 8.5 on the Richter scale, hit San Juan on January 15, 1944. It flattened the city and killed more than ten thousand people; during a gala held in Buenos Aires to raise funds for the victims shortly afterwards, a relatively unknown army officer, Juan Domingo Perón, met an equally obscure actress, Eva Duarte.

Arrival and information

Las Chacritas **airport**, small but functional, is 12km east of the city, just off the RN-20 (℡0264/425-4133); there are plenty of taxis and *remises* to the centre ($25). The city's user-friendly **bus station**, with regular services all over the province, region and country, is twelve blocks east of the central Plaza 25 de Mayo, at Estados Unidos 492 sur (℡0264/422-1604 or 5147). The extremely helpful main **provincial tourist office** is at Sarmiento 24 sur (Mon–Fri 7.30am–8pm, Sat & Sun 9am–8pm; ℡0264/421-0004, Ⓦwww.turismo.sanjuan.gov.ar).

Accommodation

San Juan has a limited selection of luxury **hotels**; and a whole crop of middling ones that are nothing special but pleasant enough. For those on a tighter budget, there are also a handful of generally clean **hostels** and *residenciales*. Campers should head west to either Zonda's campsite, *Camping Municipal Rivadavia* (℡0264/433-2374 or 1756 or 1993; ❶), on the RP-12 opposite the racetrack, with a swimming pool and very decent facilities, or Ullum's *Camping El Pinar* (℡same as Camping Municipal Rivadavia; ❶) within the grounds of the Parque Sarmiento, along the RP-14 just before the Dique Nivelador. Set amid a refreshing wood of pines, cypresses and eucalyptus, it has a bathing area, a canteen and well-kept facilities.

Hotels & hostels

Albertina Mitre 31 este ℡0264/421-4222 or 422-5442, Ⓦwww.hotelalbertina.com. Tastefully decorated, comfortable rooms in a refurbished hotel on the main square. ❹

Alhambra General Acha 180 sur ℡0264/421-4780, Ⓦwww.alhambrahotel.com.ar. Medium-sized rooms, each with bath, in this well-run establishment with friendly staff. ❹

Alkázar Laprida 84 este ℡0264/421-4965/8, Ⓦwww.alkazarhotel.com.ar. One of San Juan's few luxury hotels; although on the impersonal side, it does have extremely smart rooms, with ultra-modern bathrooms and sweeping views across the city, and a swimming pool in the grounds. ❻

América 9 de Julio 1052 este ℡0264/421-4514, Ⓦwww.hotel-america.com.ar. Agreeable, traditional, small hotel. Popular, so call ahead to reserve. All rooms have an en-suite bathroom. ❸

Gran Hotel Provincial José Ignacio de la Roza 132 ℡0264/422-7501, Ⓦwww.granhotelprovincial.com. An old-fashioned hotel with old-fashioned polite service, right at the centre of San Juan, a few steps from the Plaza 25 de Mayo. ❻

Jardín Petit 25 de Mayo 345 este ℡0264/421-1825, Ⓦwww.jardinpetithotel.com.ar. Small,

functional rooms with bath, and a bright patio overlooked by the breakfast room. ❹

El Refugio Ramón y Cajal 97 norte and San Luis ℡0264/421-3087, Ⓔelrefugio@uolsinectis.com.ar. Attractive, professionally run *apart-hotel*, with car park, a refreshing little pool, and tastefully decorated duplex apartment-like rooms, with kitchenettes, bright bathrooms and breakfast served in the room or outside. ❺

San Francisco Av España 284 sur ℡0264/422-3760, Ⓦwww.nuevo-sanfrancisco.com.ar. Very reliable place, with smart rooms, new bathrooms and friendly service. ❸

Suizo Salta 272 sur ℡0264/422-4293. An odd mixture, with a rather chaotic entrance and twee bedrooms, in an Swiss style; good value, though. ❷

Viñas del Sol RN-20 and General Roca ℡0264/425-3922, Ⓦwww.viniasdelsol.com.ar. Very comfortable hotel, one of San Juan's newest, between the city and the airport. There's a nice swimming pool. ❺

Zonda Hostel Caseros 486 sur ℡0264/4201009, Ⓦwww.zondahostel.com.ar. San Juan's new youth hostel offers clean dorm rooms ($30 per person) and a small garden, with breakfast included – whenever you want it. Doubles from ❷

The City

The total area of San Juan city is extensive but easy to find your way around, as the grid is fairly regular and the streets don't change name. In all directions from the point zero, the inter-section of Calle Mendoza and Avenida San Martín, the cardinal directions are added to the street name; for example, Avenida Córdoba oeste (west) or este (east), or Calle Tucumán norte (north) or sur (south). **Plaza 25 de Mayo** is the city centre, surrounded by terraced cafés and shops. The controversial **cathedral**, too modern for many tastes, on the northwest edge of the plaza, has a 50m brick campanile, built in the 1960s, that takes its inspiration from the tower of St Mark's in Venice. You can climb or take the lift almost to the top of the **bell tower** (daily 9.30am–1pm & 5–9.30pm; $3) – which plays the national anthem on special occasions – for panoramic views.

Two blocks west and one north, opposite the tourist office, is the city's most famous historical site, the **Museo Casa de Sarmiento** (Tues–Fri 9am–7pm, Mon & Sat 9am–2pm, Sun 10am–7pm; $5; guided tours every 30min, some in English) at Sarmiento 21 sur. The house where Sarmiento, Argentine president and Renaissance man, was born on February 15, 1811, was only slightly damaged in the 1944 earthquake, thanks to its sturdy adobe walls and sandy foundations, and has since been restored several times, to attain its present gleaming state – for the Sarmiento centenary in 1911 it was declared a national historic monument, Argentina's first. Check out their website for news of events planned for the bicentenary in 2011 (ⓦ www.casanatalsarmiento.gov.ar). It's a beautiful, simple whitewashed house built around a large patio, with a neat fig tree. The rooms contain an exhibition of Sarmiento relics and personal effects, plenty of portraits and signs of sycophancy, echoed by the gushing commentary of the guides who steer you round.

Of San Juan's several other museums, only three have any potential whatsoever. The fine arts collection, the **Museo de Bellas Artes Franklin Rawson**, was being moved to a planned site near the Parque de Mayo in the west of the city at the time of writing (no scheduled date for reopening). The **Museo Histórico Provincial Agustín Gnecco**, at General Paz 737 este (Tues 9am–1pm & 6–9pm, Wed, Fri & Sat 9am–1pm, Thurs 9am–7pm; free), contains a rather motley collection of antiquities, including coins and lots of nineteenth-century furniture. The **Museo de Ciencias Naturales** (daily 9am–1pm; free), meanwhile, housed in the former train station at avenidas España and Maipú, contains an exhibition focusing on the remarkable **dinosaur skeletons** unearthed at Parque Provincial Ischigualasto (see p.427), and features models showing how the dinosaurs may have looked. You can also see the lab where the finds are analysed.

The most notable bodega to visit is the **Bodega Graffigna**, now incorporating a wine museum – the **Museo Santiago Graffigna**, at Colón 1342 norte (Mon–Sat 9am–5.30pm, Sun 10am–4pm; free; ☎0264/421-4227; bus #12A from Avenida Libertador San Martín, $1.40). Located in a beautiful brick reconstruction of the pre-quake winery, it still produces red and white wines, among the best in the province. The displays use audiovisual techniques to give a guided tour (English included), and are a tribute to the Graffigna family, who went on producing wine despite major setbacks, not least the 1944 quake. The company is now owned by the French drinks company Pernod Ricard.

Museo Arqueológico Profesor Mariano Gambier

Some 6km south of San Juan centre, the **Museo Arqueológico Profesor Mariano Gambier**, on the RN-40 between Progreso and Calle 5 in the Rawson neighbourhood (Mon–Fri 8am–8pm, Sat 10am–6pm; $3; ☎0264/424-1424), is worth the trek: take a taxi if you don't have your own transport. Don't be put off by its (possibly temporary) location in an industrial warehouse – inside, the highly academic presentation, by San Juan University, takes you through the pre-history and history of the provinces' cultures, from the so-called Cultura de la Fortuna (10,000–6000 BC), of which there are just a few tools as evidence, to the Ullum-Zonda civilization of the Huarpe people, whose land was invaded first by the Incas in the fifteenth century and then by colonizers from Chile in the sixteenth. A number of digs near the city of San Juan have uncovered a treasure of ceramics and domestic items from the latter, well displayed here. The museum's highlight, though, is a set of mummified bodies dating from the first century BC through to the fifteenth century AD, with the most impressive of all discovered in 1964 at over 4500m in the cordillera, in northern San Juan Province. Kept in an antiquated fridge is **La Momia del Cerro el Toro**, probably the victim of an Inca sacrifice; the body is incredibly well preserved, down to her eye lashes and leather sandals. Other items worth a mention are a two-thousand-year-old carob-wood **mask**, some fine **basketwork** coloured with natural pigments and ancient ponchos with geometric patterns. All the exhibits are labelled in Spanish and English.

Eating, drinking and nightlife

San Juan has a wide range of **places to eat**, including one of the region's best vegetarian restaurants, as well as plenty of pizzerias, *parrillas* and *tenedor libre* joints. Most of the best places are in the western, residential part of the city, near the Parque de Mayo. **Café** life is all part of the *paseo* tradition, imported lock, stock and barrel from Spain, but later in the evening most Sanjuaninos entertain themselves in their gardens, round a family *asado*. There are also a couple of decent **discos**, mostly in the outskirts.

Restaurants

Abuelo Yuyi Av José Ignacio de la Roza and Urquiza. The most popular pizzeria in town, offering delicious thick-crust pies with a variety of toppings.

Baró and **De Sánchez** Rivadavia 55 & 61 oeste respectively. Two of San Juan's most fashionable restaurants, under the same ownership: the first serving tasty Italian food; the second a chic belle-époque-style restaurant which serves imaginative contemporary cuisine and displays a connoisseur's selection of books, albums and CDs, many of which are for sale. Good value lunch-time menus.

Hostal de Palito Av Circunvalación 284 sur. This is one of the best *gastronomic restaurants* in town, with a wide selection of international dishes and a delightful garden terrace.

Las Leñas Av San Martín 1670 oeste. Cavernous dining room often packed with large parties; delicious meat.

Maloca Del Bono 321. Off-beat place with psychedelic decor, Latino music and a range of Mexican tacos, Colombian *arepas* and Cuban rice dishes, plus tropical cocktails.

Rigoletto Paula A. de Sarmiento 418 sur. Cosy atmosphere and friendly service, as well as delicious pizzas and pasta.

Soychú Av José Ignacio de la Roza 223 oeste. Delightful vegetarian restaurant serving fabulous dishes, in a bright, airy space; office workers flock here to take food away, so come early.

Bars, cafés and nightclubs

Aptko Av San Martín 1369 oeste. Not terribly aesthetically appealing, but still the city's trendiest night spot, where San Juan's affluent youth come to be seen, chat and dance the night away to a mixed soundtrack, dominated by house. Fri & Sat nights.

Aruba Rioja and Maipú. Disco with a bar and *confitería* attached, playing salsa and Latin rhythms.

Bonafide Plaza 25 de Mayo, esq Mendoza y Rivadavia. A bustling meeting place for the city's movers and shakers near the cathedral. Part of an upmarket café chain famous for its chocolate and decent strong coffees.

Freud Café Plaza 25 de Mayo. An establishment on the eastern side of the main square; coffee, drinks, lots of gossip and football chat.

El Santuario de la Difunta Correa

The most unusual site around San Juan lies some 65km east of the city: **EL SANTUARIO DE LA DIFUNTA CORREA** (W www.visitedifuntacorrea .com.ar) is both a repellent and an intriguing place and one of the most concrete

As legend would have it, during the Civil War in the 1840s, a local man named Baudilio Correa was captured, taken to La Rioja and killed; his widow Deolinda decided to walk to La Rioja with their baby boy to recover Baudilio's corpse. Unable to find water she dropped dead by the roadside, where a passerby found her, the baby still sucking from her breast. Her grave soon became a holy place and lost travellers began to invoke her protection, claiming miraculous escapes from death on the road. The story of the widow Correa is believed to be Amerindian in origin but has been mingled with Catholic hagiography in a country where the borderline between religion and superstition can often be very faint. The **Difunta Correa** – *difunta* meaning deceased – is now the unofficial saint of all travellers, but especially bus- and truck-drivers, and thousands of people visit the shrine every year, over 100,000 of them during Holy Week alone, many of them covering part of the journey on their knees; national truck-drivers' day in early November also sees huge crowds arriving here. Some people visit the shrine itself – where a hideous statue of the Difunta, complete with sucking infant, lies among melted candles, prayers on pieces of paper and votive offerings including people's driving licences, the remains of tyres and photographs of mangled cars from which the occupants miraculously got out alive – while others just deposit a bottle of mineral water on the huge collection that is creeping along like a small-scale replica of the Perito Moreno glacier (see p.530).

examples of how Amerindian legends and Roman Catholic fanaticism have melded together into one belief. All around Argentina you'll come across mini-Difunta shrines, sometimes little more than a few bottles of mineral water heaped at the roadside – and easily mistaken for a particularly bad bout of pollution. But the original shrine is here. To get here from San Juan, head east on the RN-141. Past the suburbs, the landscape turns into desert-like plains, complete with sand dunes; to the north the reddish Sierra Pie de Palo ripples in the distance, relieving the monotony. Suddenly, in the middle of nowhere, amid its own grim complex of hotels, *confiterías* and souvenir shops and on top of a small hill, is Argentina's answer to Lourdes. Regular **buses** to Vallecito stop here, but unless you're really curious, it's only worth the short stop you get on the bus route from San Juan to La Rioja, or if you're travelling under your own steam between San Juan and Ischigualasto (see p.427).

Valle de Calingasta

In the west of San Juan Province is the marvellous, fertile **VALLE DE CALINGASTA** – a bright green strip of land around 90km west as the crow flies of the city of San Juan, on the other side of the Sierra del Tontal range, but reached by a long road detour. Its major settlement of interest is **Barreal**, a pleasant, laidback little town set amid fields of alfalfa, onions and maize, with a stupendous backdrop of the sierra, snowcapped for most of the year. Barreal's environs are home to the **Complejo Astronómico El Leoncito**, one of the continent's most important space observatories, and the clay flats of the **Barreal del Leoncito**, used for wind-cart championships. To the east of town is a series of mountains, red, orange and deep pink in colour, known aptly as the **Serranías de las Piedras Pintadas**. To the southwest of Barreal, the RP-400 leads to the tiny hamlet of Las Hornillas, the point of departure for adventurous treks and climbs to the summit of **Cerro Mercedario** (6770m), said by many mountaineers to be the most satisfying climb in the cordillera in this region. In the sedate town of **Calingasta** itself, north of Barreal, the main sight is a fine seventeenth-century **chapel**.

Since the closure of the old RP-12, the main paved route from San Juan is to drive north along the RN-40 to Talacasto, then take the RP-436 for 23km, and branch left to Calingasta at the main RN-149 junction.

Barreal

The small oasis town of **BARREAL**, set alongside the Río Los Patos, 1650m above sea level, at the southern extreme of the Valle de Calingasta, is a fast up-and-coming, friendly place which makes a great base for adventure tourism in the surrounding area. It enjoys a pleasant climate, and the views to the west, of the cordillera peaks, including the majestic **Cerro Mercedario**, El Polaco, La Ramada and Los Siete Picos de Ansilta, seen across a beautiful plain, shimmering with onion and maize fields, are superb. Barreal makes a good base if you want to conquer **Mercedario** – one of the Andes' most challenging yet climbable mountains. To the east you can climb up into the coloured mountains, or up to the **Cima del Tontal**, which affords one of the most famous of all views of the cordillera, as well as panoramas across to San Juan city.

Accommodation

Barreal has a surprisingly wide choice of excellent **accommodation**. As this is spread out over a couple of kilometres – some of it on the northern and southern approaches into town – ask the bus driver to drop you as close to your lodging as possible.

Hotels and hostels

Cabañas Doña Pipa at Mariano Moreno s/n
℡0264/8441004, ⊛www.cdpbarreal.com.ar. Rents out cabins (❸ for up to 5 people) in pleasant grounds and has a simple hotel annexe (❷).
Cabañas Kummel Presidente Roca s/n
℡0264/8441206, ⓔcabaniaskummel@infovia .com.ar. A good option with friendly owners who are very knowledgeable about the area and can also help arrange trips. Sleeps up to seven people. ❻
Eco Posada El Mercedario Avenida Presidente Roca esq Los Enamorados ℡0264/155090907 or 155114522, ⊛www.elmercedario.com.ar. A lovingly restored adobe farmhouse, with high, cane ceilings, swept brick floors and wood-fired stoves in the rooms, which are all tastefully themed around famous Argentine women. There's a homely restaurant, and the owner runs 4WD tours. ❹
Hostel Barreal Avenida San Martín s/n
℡0264/8441144 or 154157147 or 154393129, ⓔhostelbarreal@hotmail.com. An excellent and restful hostel whose owner organizes rafting trips on the Río Los Patos. ❷
Hostel Don Lisandro Avenida San Martín s/n
℡0264/155059122 or 154393129, ⊛www .donlisandro.com.ar. A well-equipped, wonderfully

sociable hostel set in attractive grounds where there's also space for tents. ❷

🥾 Posada de Campo La Querencia 4km south from the main plaza on Calle Florida ℡0264/154364699, ⊛www.laquerenciaposada .com.ar. Charming, appealingly designed rooms with fabulous views of open country – it's worth paying a little extra for the west-facing ones, looking towards the cordillera. Breakfasts are irreproachable, as is the friendliness of the welcome. ❻

🥾 Posada Don Ramón 8km north of the village on Avenida Presidente Roca ℡0264/154040913, ⊛www.posadadonramon .com.ar. All of the huge rooms are designed to maximize the splendid panoramic views of the cordillera, including Aconcagua and Mercedario. Lie back in your bathroom jacuzzi – or the swimming pool – and enjoy. The place is luxuriously, if simply, furnished, and has a lovely bodega stocked with organic Sanjuanino wines. The proprietor also owns and guides for Fortuna Viajes (see p.421). ❻
Posada San Eduardo Avenida San Martín s/n
℡0264/8441046. Large, simple rooms set around an old, wisteria-lined colonial-style patio. Its restaurant serves well-cooked, if a little unimaginative, food, and there's a garden pool. ❺

The Town

The central square, **Plaza San Martín**, is the focal point, at the crossroads of Avenida Presidente Roca and General Las Heras. **Buses** from San Juan stop here, and there's a helpful **tourist office** (Mon–Fri 9am–9pm, Sat & Sun 9am–midnight).

For **trips** in the surrounding area try Fortuna Viajes (℡0264/4040913, ⓦwww
.fortunaviajes.com.ar), which organizes treks and climbs, including that of
Mercedario (US$3500 per person for a 12-day expedition from Barreal, all-
inclusive except food; 2 people minimum). The offices for Parque Nacional El
Leoncito (see below) are at Cordillera Ansilta s/n (℡0264/8441240).

Eating and drinking

There are fewer good places **to eat** than to stay in Barreal. The best place by far is
El Alemán, at Belgrano s/n (℡0264/8441193; closed Mon), where huge servings
of sauerkraut, smoked hams and slabs of pork are served with well-prepared
vegetables and German-style beer in a bucolic setting – follow signs from the
Posada San Eduardo. The owners also rent *cabaña* accommodation. Otherwise try
the restaurant in the Posada El Mercedario (see Accommodation, p.420).

Around Barreal

Immediately south of Barreal along the western side of the RN-149 is a huge flat
expanse of windswept, hardened clay, the remains of an ancient lake, known as the
Barreal del Leoncito, the Pampa del Leoncito, or simply the Barreal Blanco.
Measuring 14km by 5km, this natural arena, with a marvellous stretch of the
cordillera as a background, is used for **wind-car** championships (*carrovelismo* in
Spanish) – the little cars with yacht-like sails have reached speeds of over 130km/
ph here; contact Sr. Rogelio Toro in Barreal if you want to have a go
(℡0264/156717196, Ⓔdontoro.barreal@gmail.com; main season Nov–Dec;
$200 for 2hr with an instructor).

Some 15km or so further south along this road is a turn-off eastwards up into
the **Parque Nacional El Leoncito**, which is symbolized by the suri, or Andean
rhea. Up on nearby hills are two space **observatories**, among the most
important in the world because of the outstanding meteorological conditions
hereabouts – averaging more than 320 clear nights a year. About 12km up this
track is the park entrance (open 24hr daily, information 8am–6pm): announce
your presence to the *guardaparques*. You then go up a narrow canyon, past a
colonial estancia building, to the huge white dome of the **Complejo
Astronómico El Leoncito**, at an altitude of over 2500m, and with fabulous
views of the valley and the cordillera (℡0264/8441088, ⓦwww.casleo.gov.ar;
visits 10am–noon, 3–5.30pm; $10; visits not permitted for people under 4 or
over 70; no wheelchair access). Inaugurated in 1986, this observatory was built
to resist earthquakes registering 10 or higher on the Richter scale, an absolute
necessity in this area of violent seismic activity. The primary telescope weighs
some 40 tonnes and its main 2.15m diameter mirror has to be replaced every two
years. The guided tour, led by enthusiastic staff members (English spoken), takes
you through the whole process; take warm clothing as the inside is kept cold.
Night visits, with food and lodging, are sometimes allowed: call or email at least
24hr in advance (℡0264/4213653 ext 123, Ⓔkdominguez@casleo.gov.ar), and
turn up for 5pm.

Off a turn-off 3km back down the track is the more modest-looking **Estación
Astronómica Dr Carlos U. Cesco** (daily 10am–noon & 4–6pm; $20; ⓦwww
.oafa.fcefn.unsj-cuim.edu.ar), where the staff will also be only too happy to show
you the visitors' centre and explain the observatory's work. You can also make
night visits: either simply turn up at 7.30pm for a visit that will last to about 11pm
or call them in advance to reserve a night's accommodation (℡02648/441087; $80
per person with breakfast, dinner $30 extra). You actually get to use telescopes;
take a torch and warm clothing.

Frustratingly, there are no public buses south from Barreal or the national park along the RN-149 – still mostly unpaved on this stretch – to Uspallata in Mendoza Province (see p.396). The scenic RP-400 strikes out in a southwesterly direction from Barreal to **Las Hornillas**, over 50km away. This tiny hamlet is inhabited mostly by herdsmen and their families amid pastureland and gorse scrub and is effectively the base camp for the mighty **Mercedario**, which looms nearby. If you want to climb this difficult but not impossible mountain, regarded by many as the most noble of all Argentina's Andean peaks, contact Fortuna Viajes in Barreal (see p.421). The nearby rivers are excellent for fishing for trout; ask at the tourist office in Barreal.

The mountainsides to the immediate east of Barreal, accessible by clear tracks, are a mosaic of pink, red, brown, ochre and purple rocks, and the so-called **Cerros Pintados**, or "Painted Mountains", live up to their name. Among the rocky crags, tiny cacti poke out from the cracks, and in the spring they sprout huge wax-like flowers, in translucent shades of white, pink and yellow, among golden splashes of broom-like *brea* shrubs. About 8km north of Barreal, another track heads eastwards from the main road, climbing for 40km past some idyllic countryside inhabited only by the odd goatherd or farming family, to the outlook atop the **Cima del Tontal**, at just over 4000m. To the east there are amazing views down into the San Juan valley, with the Dique de Ullum glinting in the distance, or west and south to the cordillera, where the peak of Aconcagua and the majestic summit of the Mercedario are clearly visible.

Calingasta

CALINGASTA itself is a peaceful place, 37km north of Barreal; its only attraction apart from its idyllic location is the seventeenth-century **Capilla de Nuestra Señora del Carmen**, a simple whitewashed adobe building, with an arched doorway and a long gallery punctuated by frail-looking slender pillars. The bells are among the oldest in the country and the iron and wooden ladder leading onto the roof is a work of art, too. **Accommodation** in town consists of a choice between two basic but clean places in the centre: *Hotel Calingasta* (☎02648/421220; ③) and *Hospedaje Nora* (☎02648/421027, ⓔ calingasta22 @hotmail.com; ③), which has cable TV and car parking. From Calingasta it's 125km along the RP-412 north to Iglesia, along a dry valley, through the occasional ford, with the Sierra del Tigre to the east and the Cordón de Olivares providing stupendous views to the west. No public transport runs on this stretch.

Valle de Iglesia

The **VALLE DE IGLESIA** is named after one of its main settlements, **Iglesia**, a sleepy village of adobe houses. It is a fertile valley separated from the Valle de Calingasta by the dramatic Cordón de Olivares range of mountains. You can get there directly from San Juan via the RN-40, which forks off to the northwest at Talacasto, some 50km north of the city. From there a mountain road, the RP-436, joins up with the RN-149 heading north. From Calingasta you can get to Iglesia direct along the rugged, unsealed RP-412. More interesting than Iglesia itself are the small market town and windsurf hangout of **Rodeo** to the northeast, along the RN-150, and further north still, the idyllic village of **Angualasto**, along the dirt track that leads to one of the country's most recent national parks, **San Guillermo**, the place in Argentina where you are most likely to spot pumas in the wild.

Rodeo and around

The RN-150 arches round the pleasant, easy-going market town of **RODEO**. To visit the town, turn off onto its main street, Santo Domingo. This leads to the Plaza de la Fundación and the town's **tourist office** (daily 8am–9pm; ℡02647/493193). Opposite the plaza – quite unexpectedly – you'll find a rasta-inspired restaurant and bar *La Surfera*, the local chill-out spot for **windsurfing** and **kitesurfing** dudes who come from afar to take advantage of the superb, consistent winds on the local reservoir – the **Dique Cuesta del Viento** (season Oct–April). An excellent place to base yourself if you're keen on joining the windsurfistas for real is the *Hostel Rancho Lamaral* in an atmospheric breezy farmstead, set a short walk from the reservoir's northeastern shore (℡0264/156601197, ⓦwww .rancholamaral.com; $10 in a *remise* from town; $40 dorm bed, double room ❷). The owner and staff exude a highly positive vibe: they give lessons, and will help sort you out with rental gear.

More luxurious accommodation can be found in town at the *50 Nudos* posada (℡011/155-7033743, ⓦwww.50nudos.com; ❺). Some 2.5km from the plaza at the town's northernmost end is the **Finca El Martillo**, (daily 9am–6pm; ℡02647/493019, ⓔelmartillo@sinectis.com.ar). You can buy all kinds of wonderful local produce here, including herbs, fresh and preserved fruit and excellent jam and honey. Ask about the eight-bed *cabaña* at the *finca* nearby (❸). Rodeo hosts one of the region's major folk festivals in the first weekend of February, the **Fiesta de la Manzana y la Semilla**, when you can try local specialities, such as empanadas and *humitas*, and watch dancing and musical groups in the Anfiteatro, just off Santo Domingo at the heart of the town.

North of Rodeo, you can head off towards Angualasto and the Parque Nacional San Guillermo (see below), while to the east the RN-150 takes you to Jáchal (see p.424); it is an impressive, winding cliff-side road that follows the stark valley of the Río Jáchal.

Angualasto and Parque Nacional San Guillermo

From Rodeo, the RP-407 heads north, cutting through a ridge of rock and sloping down into the valley of the Río Blanco. The little village of **ANGUALASTO**, which has preserved a delightful rural feel, seemingly detached from the modern world, is set among rows of poplars, fruit orchards and small plots of maize, beans and other vegetables. It is proud of its little **Museo Arqueológico Luis Benedetti** (daily 8am–8pm), whose tiny collection of mostly pre-Columbian finds includes a remarkable four-hundred-year-old mummified corpse, found in a *tumbería*, or burial mound, nearby. To the north the road follows the Río Blanco valley, fording it once – often impossible after spring or summer rains or heavy thaws – to the incredibly remote hamlets of Malimán and **El Chinguillo**, where the Solar family's delightful farmhouse (no phone; ❷) provides the only **accommodation** in the area, as well as delicious empanadas and roast lamb. This is the entrance to San Guillermo, in a beautiful valley surrounded by huge dunes of sand and mountains scarred red and yellow with mineral deposits.

The **Reserva Provincial San Guillermo**, in the far northern reaches of San Juan Province, was the first region in the country to be declared a **UNESCO Biosphere Reserve**, in 1980. Part of the Provincial Reserve, on great heights to the west of the Río Blanco valley, later attained national park status, in 1998: the **PARQUE NACIONAL SAN GUILLERMO**. The Parque Nacional is home to a huge variety of wildlife. Guanacos and vicuñas abound, along with suris or ñandús, eagles, condors, several different kinds of lizards, foxes and all kinds of waterfowl, including flamingos, which match the seams of jagged pink rock that run along the mountainsides like a garish zip-fastener. Above all, this is a part of Argentina where if you stay for a number of days you stand an extremely good chance of a spotting a puma – a very rare occurrence elsewhere in the country. For some reason the pumas living here are less shy of humans and often approach vehicles; treat these powerful and potentially dangerous creatures with caution. The highest peaks, at well over 5000m, are permanently snowcapped, and the high altitude of the park's roads – as high as 3700m – affects some visitors.

Visiting requires advance preparation – the park is isolated and the weather can be capricious. You'll need at least three days, and must register with the **park office** on the western outskirts of Rodeo on Calle La Colonia (Mon–Fri 7am–2pm; ☎02647/493214, ✉sanguillermo@apn.gov.ar). You will require a 4WD and a guide (roughly $200 a day), as negotiating the fords can be dangerous, plus you'll have to travel with at least one other vehicle in case of breakdown. Make sure you travel with adequate clothing, fuel and supplies. Motorcycles and horses are not allowed. Registered guides include Alberto Ramírez (☎0261/156581527) and Ramón Ossa (☎0264/8441004; book as far in advance as possible). By end of 2010, you should be able to overnight in bunkbeds in the planned *Refugio Agua del Godo* in the centre of the park (bring suitably warm bedding; free).

San José de Jáchal and around

The sleepy little town of **San José de Jáchal** is most famous for a handful of nineteenth-century flour mills scattered about attractive farmland immediately north of the town, in a landscape rather like that of North Africa.

From Jáchal you can head northeast for 145km on the **RN-40** to **Villa Unión**, in La Rioja Province (see p.429). You squeeze along the Cuesta de Huaco, a mountain road with magnificent views of the arid valleys to the north. From Huaco the road runs through the Río Bermejo valley, bone dry for most of the time but suddenly flooding after storms. Beware of the many deep fords (*badenes*) along the road; if they are full of water, wait for the level to drop before attempting to cross; even when dry they can rip tyres if taken too fast.

San José de Jáchal

The small town of **SAN JOSÉ DE JÁCHAL** (usually called simply Jáchal) lies in the fertile valley of the Río Jáchal, 155km due north of San Juan by the RN-40; it's also 45km due east of Rodeo via the scenic RN-150 (see p.423). The town was founded in the seventeenth century on the site of a pre-Columbian village. Destroyed in a severe earthquake in 1894, the town was rebuilt using mud-bricks in an Italianate style, with arched facades and galleried patios, focused on the Plaza San Martín.

Jáchal itself isn't much to write home about, but it makes for a convenient stopover. There's a helpful **tourist office** on the plaza at San Juan 133 (daily 7am–9pm; ☎02647/42003); ask here for updates on which flour mills are open for visits. They'll also help sort out a *remise* for a tour of the mills (one recommended driver is Jorge Saleme at Rivadavia 525, ☎02647/420736). If you have a moment to spare, visit the astonishingly eclectic **Museo Arqueológico Prieto** (☎02647/420298 to arrange visit), at 25 de Mayo 788 oeste, signposted along the RN-150. It is a motley collection of all manner of odds and ends, but among the curios are some fine pre-Columbian artefacts, painstakingly collected and displayed by a local who handed it all over to the police. During the first fortnight in November, the town stages the **Fiesta de la Tradición**, a festival of folklore, feasts and music.

Buses from San Juan stop at the terminal seven blocks southeast of the main plaza. A few **accommodation** possibilities exist, the best of which is the *Hualta Picum Apart-Hotel*, at Sarmiento 749 (☎02647/420774; ④) with spacious, well-furbished apartments for up to eight people. Otherwise, there's the idiosyncratic *Plaza Hotel*, at San Juan 545 (☎02647/420256; ②), which offers rather run-down rooms with or without bath. A decent place to eat is *Tata Viejo*, at Calle San Martín e/ Echegaray y General Paz, which offers hearty, inexpensive food, although service is unexceptional.

North of Jáchal, the RN-40 suddenly swerves to the east and the road continuing straight ahead, the RP-456, cuts through Jáchal's rural northern suburbs amid bucolic farmland, used to grow wheat, maize, alfalfa and fruit. With the stark mountain backdrop of the Sierra Negra to the east, Sierra de la Batea to the north and Cerro Alto (2095m) to the west, this dazzlingly green valley, dotted with adobe farmhouses, some of them with splendid sun-faded wooden doors, looks like the parts of Morocco in the lee of the Atlas. Canals and little ditches water the fields, using snow melt from the cordillera and precordillera, as rain is rare here. In the nineteenth century, a number of **flour mills** were built, and they are now rightly recognised as historic monuments. Their beige or whitewashed walls, wonderfully antiquated machinery and enthusiastic owners or managers make for a memorable visit; always offer guides a tip if shown around. **El Molino del Alto** (also called El Molino de García) is the best, as it is fully functioning, and – if he's around – the passion of Dionício Pérez, the manager, is a joy to behold (Spanish only). Also worth visiting if you can find the charming owner is the **Molino de Sardiña** (no longer in operation) at the corner of calles Maturrango and Mesias, just to the south of El Molino del Alto.

Huaco

Back on the RN-40, the road hugs the Sierra Negra, before skirting the Dique Los Cauquenes reservoir. Then you enter the Cuesta de Huaco, a narrow mountain road accurately described as a place "where the reddish dawn lingers on the even redder clay of the mountainside". Those words were sung by deep-voiced crooner **Buenaventura Luna**, real name Eusebio de Jesús Dojorti Roco, who was a highly popular star in the 1940s and 1950s, and is buried in nearby **HUACO**. This small village, shaded by *algarrobos* and eucalyptus, is no more than a cluster of mud-brick houses, but just before you get to the village you pass a splendid adobe **flour mill**, similar to those north of Jáchal. Built in the nineteenth century, it belonged to the Docherty family, descendants of an Irishman who fought in the British army that invaded Buenos Aires, was captured and decided to settle in Argentina; Buenaventura Luna was one of their descendants. The *Hostería Huaco* on the main through road is an airy adobe-style building with a garden that offers pleasant rooms (☎0264/4219528 or 154579003; ②).

Parque Provincial Ischigualasto and Parque Nacional Talampaya

San Juan and La Rioja provinces boast two of the most-photographed protected areas in the country, which together have been declared a UNESCO World Heritage Site, as the only place on the Earth's surface where you can see all stages of the Triassic geological era, which witnessed the emergence of the first dinosaurs. In San Juan is **Parque Provincial Ischigualasto**, better known as Valle de la Luna – Moon Valley – because of its out-of-this-world landscapes and apocryphal legends. The province has jealously resisted repeated attempts to turn it into a national park, and the authorities are doing a good job of providing easy access and looking after the fragile environment. While he was in office, President Menem, on the other hand, made sure that his native province of La Rioja got its first national park: **Parque Nacional Talampaya**, best known for its giant red sandstone cliffs, which are guaranteed to impress even the most jaded traveller. It's also the country's best example of desert *monte* scrub – a vulnerable ecosystem with rare fauna and flora, and the only habitat endemic to Argentina.

While you can visit both parks in the same day from either **Villa Unión** in La Rioja (see p.429) or the more appealing town of **San Agustín de Valle Fértil** in northeastern San Juan Province, you can get more from the parks by splitting your visits; Talampaya especially merits a longer visit. In many ways it is wise to go to Talampaya in the morning, when the sun lights up the coloured rocks and illuminates the canyon, whereas Ischigualasto is far more impressive in the late afternoon and at sunset in particular. Avoid the gruelling day-trips offered from San Juan, or even La Rioja. You can visit Ichigualasto in your own vehicle, but you'll need to join a tour to visit Talampaya. Doing the trip by public transport is complicated and not advised.

San Agustín de Valle Fértil

Set among enticing landscapes some 250km northeast of San Juan by the RN-141 and the RP-510, the oasis town of **SAN AGUSTÍN DE VALLE FÉRTIL** is the best base for visiting Parque Provincial Ischigualasto, about 80km to the north, via Los Baldecitos. It's built around a mirror-like reservoir, the Dique San Agustín just up in the hills – cacti and gorse grow on its banks, and a small peninsula juts artistically into the waters. The town prospered in the nineteenth century thanks to the gold, iron and quartz mines and marble quarries in the mountains nearby, but it has now turned to tourism as its source of income, to supplement meagre farm earnings. The fertile valley that gives it its name – sometimes it's referred to simply as "Valle Fértil" – is a patchwork of maize fields, olive groves and pasture for goats and sheep – and the local cheese and roast kid are recommended.

Arrival and information

Buses from San Juan and La Rioja arrive at the terminal at Santa Fe and Entre Ríos. The **tourist office** (daily 7am–midnight; ☎02646/420104) on Plaza San Agustín is extremely helpful and can fix you up with guides and transport both to Ischigualasto and to other less dramatic sites in the nearby mountains, including pre-Hispanic petroglyphs. For tours to Ischigualasto, contact Paula Tour at Tucumán s/n (☎0264/6420096 or 154-032674, ⓦwww.paula-tour .com.ar). They organize a number of circuits in the park, including night-time ones around the time of full moon. You'll need to reserve an English-speaking guide in advance ($50 extra). They also offer tours of the town, the wider province, and Talampaya – the latter often in combination with the Runacay agency in Villa Unión (see p.429).

Accommodation

There are a number of cheap *pensiones* and hostels downtown, not far from the bus terminal. The best campsite is also within walking distance: the well-kept *Camping Valle Fértil*, at the lower end of the road leading up to the *Hostería Valle Fértil* and ran by the *hostería*.

Hotels and hostels

Campo Base Valle de la Luna Tucumán and San Luis ☏ 02646/420063, ⊛ www.hostelvalledelaluna .com.ar. A good youth hostel which can help organize tours in the area. ❷

Eco Hostel Mendoza s/n, half a block from the plaza ☏ 02646/420147 or 154-154830. There's nothing specifically "eco" about it apart from the name, but it's nevertheless a decent option. Tango and Spanish lessons available. ❷

Fatme Rivadavia s/n, three blocks from the plaza ☏ 02646/420014, ✉ fatmehotel@yahoo .com.ar. Clean and friendly place with very reasonably priced rooms. ❷

Hostería Valle Fértil Rivadavia, seven blocks from the plaza ☏ 02646/420015, ⊛ www.alkazarhotel .com.ar/vallefertil). Comfortable, three star with a decent restaurant, specializing in casseroled kid, and good, if cramped, rooms – the more expensive ones with lake views. ❹

Posada Los Olivos Santa Fe s/n ☏ 02646/420115, ⊛ www.posadalosolivos.alojar .com.ar. Offering decent hostel accommodation, and a spacious wood-beamed patio restaurant area. ❷

Rustico Cerro del Valle Santa Fe s/n, over the road from the bus terminal ☏ 0264/6420202 or 154369123, ⊛ www.cerrodelvalle.com.ar. Comfortable rooms, a fine garden pool, hospitable owners and fun dogs. ❹

Eating and drinking

One of the best restaurants in town is *A lo de Pepe*, at Rivadavia and Sarmiento, an intimate little place that serves a fine *parrilla*. *El Serranito*, by the bus terminal, cooks up cheap and tasty *milanesas* and snacks.

Parque Provincial Ischigualasto

Some 80km north of Valle Fértil, the **PARQUE PROVINCIAL ISCHI-GUALASTO**, also known as the Valle de la Luna, or Moon Valley, is San Juan's most famous feature by far. Covering nearly 150 square kilometres of desolate but astonishingly varied terrain, it can be visited only in a vehicle – either your own or that of a tour operator. For paleontologists, Ischigualasto's importance is primarily as a rich dinosaur burial ground: two of the world's very oldest species of dinosaurs, the diminutive *Euraptor lunesis* and *Herrerasaurus ischigualastensis*, both dating back some 230 million years, were found here, among many others. The park is also a joy for geologists, as most strata of the 45-million-year Triassic era are on plain view. However, the majority of visitors come simply to admire the spectacular lunar landscapes that give the park its popular nickname, and the much publicized and alarmingly fragile rock formations – some have already disappeared, the victims of erosion and the occasional flash floods that seem to strike with increasing frequency. **Cerro El Morado** (1700m), a barrow-like mountain that according to local lore is shaped like an Indian lying on his back, dominates the park to the east. A segmented row of rocks is known as El Gusano (the Worm); a huge set of vessel-like boulders is known as El Submarino; a sandy field dotted with cannon-ball-shaped stones is dubbed the Cancha de Bolas (the Ball-court). One famous formation, painfully fragile on its slender stalk, is El Hongo (the Mushroom), beautifully set off against the red sandstone cliffs behind.

The park is in a desert valley between two ranges of high mountains, the Sierra Los Rastros to the west and Cerros Colorados to the east. As witnessed by the mollusc and coral fossils found in the cliffsides, for a long time the whole area was under water. Over the course of millions of years the terrain has been eroded by wind and water, and sections built of volcanic ash have taken on a ghostly greyish-white hue. A set of red sandstone mountains to the north acts as a perfect backdrop to the paler stone formations and clay blocks, all of which are impressively illuminated in the late evening. Another of the park's attractions is its wealth of flora and fauna. The main plant varieties are the native broom-like *brea*, three varieties of the scrawny *jarilla*, both black and white species of *algarrobo*, the *chañar*, *retamo* and *molle* shrubs and four varieties of cactus. Animals that you are likely to spot here include

▲ Parque Provincial Ischigualasto

European hares, Patagonian hares, the vizcacha, the grey fox, armadillos and small rodents, plus several species of bat, frog, toad, lizard and snake. Condors and ñandús are often seen, too, while guanacos may be spotted standing like sentinels atop the rocks, before scampering off.

The main driving tour follows a set **circuit**, beginning in the more lunar landscapes to the south. Panoramic outlook points afford stunning views of weird oceans of hillocks. These are the typical moonscapes, but they look uncannily like the famous landscapes of Cappadocia, with their Gaudiesque pinnacles and curvaceous mounds. The whole tour takes at least a couple of hours to be done at all comfortably. But be warned that sudden summer storms can cut off the tracks for a day or two, in which case you may not be able to see all the park.

Park practicalities

The **guardería** (daily: Oct–Mar 8am–5pm last entrance; Apr–Sept 9am–4pm last entrance; you must leave by dusk; ℡02646/491100; $40) lies at the entrance to the park, along a well-signposted lateral road off the RP-510 at Los Baldecitos. There is no camping or accommodation and most people stay at either Villa Unión or, preferably, Valle Fértil. At the entrance, an excellent **museum** exhibits some wonderful stories of forensic paleontology, unravelling some curious examples of dinosaur death (Spanish only); plus a restaurant and handicraft stalls. You'll be assigned a *guardaparque* – many of whom only speak Spanish – who will accompany your convoy. Convoys leave every hour, and at busy times (eg Jan–March) can sometimes involve more than thirty vehicles. If you're seeking more solitude, arrive very early or late in the day; big convoys can also generate a lot of dust and considerably reduce the time you get to spend at each stop. The optimal time of day for visiting the park is in the mid- to late afternoon, when the light is the most flattering. That way you also catch the mind-boggling sunsets that illuminate the park, turning the pinkish orange rock a glowing crimson, which contrasts with the ghostly greyish white of the lunarscapes all around.

Apart from the main vehicle circuit (which you can also arrange to do at night around full-moon time), there are a couple of other options: a **mountain bike** circuit or a **trek** to climb Cerro El Morado (contact an agency in Valle Fértil, such as Paula Tour, see p.426). In 2012, the RN-150 that skirts the park's southern boundary is due to join up Los Baldecitos with San José de Jáchal (see p.424), which would make a much-needed tourist circuit possible, providing an alter-native route to Villa Unión. But don't hold your breath on the timing.

Villa Unión

The small town of **VILLA UNIÓN**, in the parched Valle de Vinchina, 120km northeast of Huaco, isn't much to write home about, but is fast developing as a convenient base for tours to Parque Nacional Talampaya 70km south, but also to the staggeringly desolate Reserva Provincial Las Vicuñas, wrapped around the beautiful Laguna Brava (see p.432), over 150km northwest. The town, formerly called Hornillos, received its name in the nineteenth century in recognition of the hospitality of its people towards peasants thrown off a nearby estancia by the ruthless *estancieros*.

A popular trip from Villa Unión is east along the RN-40, over the 2025m mountain pass that crosses the Sierra de Famatina and down the fabulous **Cuesta de Miranda**, a sinuous, parapet-like mountain road, on towards Sañogasta and the old mining town of Chilecito. The Río Miranda snakes through a deep gorge, hemmed in by multicoloured cliffs and peaks, striped red, green, blue and yellow with oxidized minerals and strata of volcanic rock. Agencies like Runacay do tours, or you can catch the local Ivanlor buses that travel once a day in each direction. From Chilecito, buses continue to La Rioja.

Arrival and information

The town is essentially strung out along the main RN-76, with services including an ATM, an obliging **tourist office** on the main square, Plaza San Martín s/n (daily 8am–10pm; ☎03825/470543), and a growing number of places to stay and eat. A couple of blocks east is the new **bus station**, serving La Rioja, Chilecito and planned routes to Valle Fértil and Huaco. The **park office** for Talampaya (Mon–Fri 7am–2pm; ☎03825/4703567, ⓦwww.talampaya.gov.ar) is at San Martín 150, half a block from the plaza, while Coop Transporte Talampaya (☎03825/15662086) runs transfers to the park, as well as a couple of circuits within it. *Runacay* is a first-rate travel agency, located on the main plaza at Hipólito Irigoyen esq J.V. González (☎03825/470368, ⓦwww.runacay.com). They run a variety of tours, prime among them being their walking tours of Talampaya (including a night-time option around full moon), but also other Talampaya options and adventure trips into the cordillera, such as to Laguna Brava. Tours are available in English, French and Portuguese.

Accommodation

As with many Argentine towns, the accommodation is spread out on the town and its approach roads, so get the bus driver to drop you off as close to where you're staying. The less expensive options can be found in town, while the most luxurious accommodation is a couple of kilometres to the south of town on the RN-76, near the RN-40 junction.

Hotels and hostels

Cañon de Talampaya RN-76 ☎03825/470753, ⓦhotelcanontalampaya.com. Modern, earth-toned rooms, restaurant and a swimming pool. Owned by Rolling Travel, who run minibus circuits in Talampaya. ❺

Hospedaje Doña Gringa Nicolás Dávila 103 ☎03825/470528. Tiny but very clean rooms, a leafy patio and a laidback atmosphere. ❷
Hostel Laguna Brava Honorato Guerrero e/. Alem e Independencia ☎0261/155913559. Andalucian style villa with dorms ($35). Doubles from ❷

Noryanepat, Joaquín V. González 150 ☎03825/470133. Just about acceptable rooms with cramped bathrooms; one block east of the main plaza. ❹

Pircas Negras RN-76 ☎03825/470611, ⓦwww .hotelpircasnegras.com. Smart rooms, parking and a passable restaurant, although service can be sloppy. ❻

Eating and drinking

The best place to **eat** out is atmospheric *La Palmera*, a couple of kilometres south of town by the junction of the RN-40 and the RN-76, where they do fabulous *asados*, including chivito, to be washed down with their fine selection of local wines. Service is excellent, and the decor is authentically *riojano* rustic - even if the puma and wild cat pelts might not be to everyone's taste. There's also a nice new café by the church, on the northeast corner of the main plaza, at San Martín y Hipólito Irigoyen.

Parque Nacional Talampaya

The entrance to **PARQUE NACIONAL TALAMPAYA** is 55km down the RN-76 from Villa Unión, and then along a signposted road to the east. Coming from the south, it's 93km north of Ischigualasto and 190km from Valle Fértil. The park's main feature is a wide-bottomed canyon flanked by 180m-high, rust-coloured sandstone cliffs, so smooth and sheer that they look as if they were sliced through by a giant cheese-wire. Another section of the canyon is made up of rock formations that seem to have been created as part of a surreal Gothic cathedral. Added attractions are the presence of several bird species, including condors and eagles, as well as rich flora and some pre-Columbian petroglyphs. The park's name comes from the indigenous people's words *ktala* – the locally abundant *tala* bush – and *ampaya*, meaning dry riverbed.

Talampaya's cliffs appear so frequently on national tourism promotion posters and in coffee-table books, you think you know what you're getting before you arrive. But no photograph really prepares you for the belittling feeling you have when standing at the foot of a massive rock wall, where the silence is broken only by the wind. Even the classic shots of orange-red precipices looming over what looks like a toy jeep, included for scale, don't really convey the astonishment. The national park, covering 215 square kilometres, was created in 1997 to protect the canyon and all its treasures. Geologically it's part of the Sierra Los Colorados, whose rippling mass you can see in the distance to the east. The sandstone cliffs were formed at the beginning of the Triassic period, nearly 250 million years ago, and have gradually been eroded by torrential rain and various rivers that have exploited geological faults in the rock, the reason why the cliffs are so sheer.

Just south of the entrance to the canyon, huge sand dunes have been swept up by the strong winds that frequently howl across the Campo de Talampaya to the south. The higgledy-piggledy rocks at the foot of the cliffs host a gallery of white, red and black **rock paintings**, made by the Ciénaga and Aguada peoples who inhabited the area around a thousand years ago. The pictures include animals such as llamas, suris and pumas, a stepped pyramid, huntsmen and phallic symbols, and the nearby ink-well depressions in the rock are formed by decades of grinding and mixing pigments. There is a huge *tacu*, or carob tree, here, thought to be more than one thousand years old. Inside the canyon proper, the so-called **jardín botánico**, or more accurately the *bosquecillo* – thicket, – is a natural grove of twenty or so different native cacti, shrubs and trees. They include *algarrobos*, *retamos*, *pencas*, *jarillas* and *chañares*, all labelled; occasionally grey foxes and small armadillos lurk in the undergrowth and brightly coloured songbirds flit from branch to branch. Nearby, and clearly signposted, is the **Chimenea** (chimney), also known as the

6

Cueva (cave) or the Canaleta (drainpipe), a rounded vertical groove stretching all the way up the cliff-side; guides revel in demonstrating its extraordinary echo, which sends condors flapping.

Rock formations in the canyon have been given imaginative names, mostly with a religious slant, but many of them do fit. **El Pesebre** (Crib) is a set of rocks supposed to resemble a Nativity scene, and appropriately nearby are **Los Reyes Magos**, the Three Kings, one of them on camel-back. A cluster of enormous needles and pinnacles is known as **La Catedral** – the intricate patterns chiselled and carved by thousands of years of erosion have been compared variously with Albi cathedral or the facade of Strasbourg cathedral, both built of a similar red sandstone. A set of massive rock formations is known as **El Tablero de Ajedrez**, or the Chessboard, complete with rooks, bishops and pawns, while a 53m-high monolith, resembling a cowled human figure is El Cura, the priest, or El Fraile, the monk, depending on whom you ask. **El Pizarrón**, or the Blackboard, is fifteen metres of flat rock-face of darker stone etched with more suris, pumas, guanacos and even a seahorse – suggesting that the peoples who lived here a thousand years ago had some kind of contact with the ocean.

Park practicalities

The park's **main entrance**, located a few kilometres down a well-signposted turn-off from the RN-76 at the Puerta de Talampaya (daily May–Sept 8.30am–5.30pm; Oct–April 8am–6pm; $25 entrance; no phone, Ⓦ www.talampaya .gov.ar), has been sympathetically designed and has a restaurant and a good little shop. Most visitors come here on an **organized tour** but if you don't mind the walk, you could get a bus to drop you off on the main road. The closest accommodation to the park is in the village of **Pagancillo**, 27km north of the park entrance, which is served by a local bus from Villa Unión. You can pitch a tent at the basic **campsite** (Ⓣ 03825/470397; ❶) here, but bear in mind that it's often windy and can get extremely cold at night. There's also a *confitería* serving simple, reasonably priced snacks and small meals.

Private vehicles are not allowed into the park, so if you arrive here under your own steam you must choose between various **guided tours**. These should generally be arranged in advance, especially at busy times. Rolling Travel (Ⓣ 03825/470397 or 0351/5709909, Ⓦ www.talampaya.com) operates the two most commonly travelled **vehicle circuits** inside Talampaya, leaving roughly hourly, with the last tour of the day leaving an hour or so before the park's closure. Both circuits visit the main points of interest – the shorter is 2.5 hours and the longer 4.5 hours. Runacay (see p.429) offers a variety of excellent **walking circuits**, which enable you to avoid congested minibuses and explore the park at a much more sedate pace, as well as getting into some of its lesser-known recesses. The local Cooperativa de Transporte Talampaya (Ⓣ 03825/15662086, Ⓦ www.turismoentalampaya.com.ar) offers transfers from Villa Unión, plus tours to the Ciudad Perdida and Cañon Arco Iris sectors of the park. **Mountain bike tours** are also possible – enquire at the entrance or contact the park guides' association (Ⓣ 03822/15508816, Ⓔ sergiolei_guiatur @hotmail.com), but you need your own transport. Bring sun cream, headgear and water. Avoid Easter if possible, when the park is at its busiest; the middle of the day in the height of summer, when it can be unbearably hot; and the day after a storm, when the park closes because of floods. The zonda wind can also cause the park to close. In midwinter, it can be bitterly cold. The best time of day by far to visit is soon after opening, when the dawn light deepens the red of the sandstone.

Reserva Provincial Las Vicuñas

The **RESERVA PROVINCIAL LAS VICUÑAS** is nearly 150km northwest of Villa Unión, via the RN-76 and then a numberless track that twists and turns to the park's central feature, the wild and shallow **Laguna Brava**. The main attractions are fabulous altiplanic scenery – most of the terrain is at over 4000m – the magnificent, strikingly coloured mountainous backdrops and the abundant wildlife, mainly vicuñas, as the name suggests. Large flocks of this smaller cousin of the llama graze on the reserve's *bofedales*, the typical spongy marshes watered by trickles of run-off that freeze nightly. The best time to visit is in spring and autumn, since summer storms and winter blizzards cut off roads and generally impede travel. On the way to the reserve you pass through **Villa San José De Vinchina**, 65km north of Villa Unión, a nondescript village near which are six large, low circular mounds. Made of a mosaic of pink, white and purple stones, these mysterious **Estrellas de Vinchina** form star-shapes and are thought to have had a ceremonial purpose for the pre-Columbian indigenous people of the area, perhaps serving as altars. Otherwise head on through the Quebrada de la Troya, a magnificent striped canyon, into the Valle Caguay, dominated by the majestic cone of Volcán Los Bonetes. From here the road is best negotiated in a 4WD – in any case it is wise to visit the reserve on an organized tour from Villa Unión (see p.429). You'll need to pull off the main road into **Alto Jagüe** to show your passport at the checkpoint and pay the park entrance fee ($15 per person plus $10 for the vehicle; ☎03825/15440879; don't forget to check back in when leaving the park so they know you're safe).

The track heads through to the southern banks of the Laguna Brava, a deep blue lake 17km by 10km, whose high potassium-chloride levels make it undrinkable. When it's blowing a gale, huge waves can be whipped up; when there is no wind, the mirror-like waters reflect the mountains behind. Behind stretches a panorama of 6000m peaks, including the enormous Pissis – the second highest volcano in the world (now believed to be 6793m instead of the commonly cited measurement of 6882m). Other lakes in the reserve are the smaller Laguna Verde – a green lake as its name suggests – and the Laguna Mulas Muertas, often covered with pink flamingos, Andean geese and other wildfowl. There's no public transport, no *guardería* and nowhere to stay: just you and the wilds.

La Rioja and around

LA RIOJA – or Todos los Santos de la Nueva Rioxa, as it was baptized at the end of the sixteenth century – is an indolent kind of town, built in a flat-bottomed valley, watered by the Río Tajamar, and nearly 1200km northwest of Buenos Aires and 517km northeast of San Juan. It is not a sightseers' city, but you can find enough to occupy a full day if passing through. Among the highlights are two of the country's best **museums** of indigenous art, one archeological and the other with a folkloric slant. It is best visited in the spring (Oct–Nov), when the jacaranda trees are abloom, and the city is perfumed by the blossom of orange trees that have earned it the much-bandied sobriquet "Ciudad de los Naranjos". In spite of the plentiful shade of this luxuriant vegetation, the blistering summer heat is refracted off the brutally arid mountains looming to the west and turns the city, notoriously one of the country's hottest, virtually into a no-go zone even for its hardy inhabitants. Whatever you do, avoid the midsummer, when temperatures can get up to 45°C. At all times the place has a rough and ready, Wild West edge to it, and the heat seems to make people tetchy even when they've had their institutional siesta

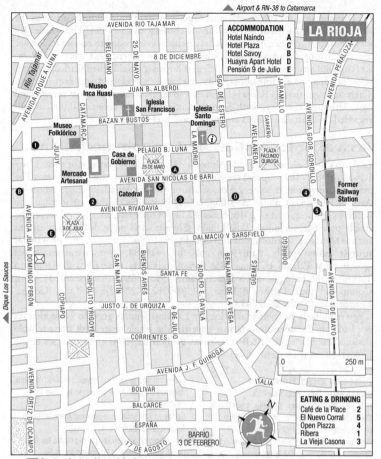

ACCOMMODATION
Hotel Naindo — A
Hotel Plaza — C
Hotel Savoy — B
Huayra Apart Hotel — D
Pensión 9 de Julio — E

LA RIOJA

AVENIDA RIO TAJAMAR

8 DE DICIEMBRE

BELGRANO

25 DE MAYO

SGO. DEL ESTERO

JARAMILLO

AVENIDA PEÑALOZA

AVENIDA ROQUE A LUNA

Río Tajamar

JUAN B. ALBERDI

Museo Inca Huasi

CATAMARCA

Iglesia San Francisco

BAZAN Y BUSTOS

Iglesia Santo Domingo

ⓘ

AVELLANEDA

CARRENO

AVENIDA GDOR. GORDILLO

Museo Folklórico

JUJUY

Casa de Gobierno

PELAGIO B. LUNA

LA MADRID

PLAZA 25 DE MAYO

Ⓐ

PLAZA FACUNDO QUIROGA

Mercado Artesanal

AVENIDA SAN NICOLAS DE BARI

Ⓒ

Ⓓ

Catedral

Former Railway Station

Ⓑ

2

Catedral

3

AVENIDA RIVADAVIA

4

5

AVENIDA JUAN DOMINGO PERÓN

PLAZA 9 DE JULIO

Ⓔ

DALMACIO V SARSFIELD

DORREGO

Dique Los Sauces

SAN MARTIN

BUENOS AIRES

SANTA FE

ADOLFO E. DAVILA

BENJAMIN DE LA VEGA

GÜEMES

AVENIDA 1 DE MAYO

HIPOLITO YRIGOYEN

COPIAPO

JUSTO J. DE URQUIZA

9 DE JULIO

CORRIENTES

AVENIDA J. F. QUIROGA

0   250 m

ITALIA

AVENIDA ORTIZ DE OCAMPO

BOLIVAR

BALCARCE

ESPAÑA

17 DE AGOSTO

BARRIO 3 DE FEBRERO

N

EATING & DRINKING
Café de la Place — 2
El Nuevo Corral — 5
Open Piazza — 4
Ribera — 1
La Vieja Casona — 3

San Juan, San Luis, Córdoba & Bus Terminal (2km)

6

MENDOZA, SAN JUAN AND LA RIOJA | La Rioja and around

– everything shuts down from 1pm to 5pm. Yet La Rioja is not without its fashionable boutiques and cafés, and the city's chic business people in sharp suits love to strut along the tree-lined streets, clutching mobile phones that chirp in competition with the omnipresent and vociferous cicadas.

Some history

La Rioja came into being on May 20, 1591 when the governor of Tucumán, Juan Ramírez de Velasco, a native of La Rioja in Castile, founded the city in its strategic valley location. Today's main Plaza 25 de Mayo coincides exactly with the spot he chose. Ramírez de Velasco had set out on a major military expedition to populate the empty spaces of the Viceroyalty and subdue the native Diaguitas, who had farmed the fertile oasis for centuries. La Nueva Rioxa, the only colonial settlement for leagues around, soon flourished and Ramírez de Velasco felt justified in boasting in a letter that it was "one of the finest cities in the Indies".

From it, mainly Franciscan missionaries set about fulfilling Ramírez de Velasco's other aim of converting the native peoples. Their convent and that of the Dominicans, one of the oldest in Argentina, both miraculously survived the earthquake that flattened most of the old colonial city in 1894. The whole city was rebuilt, largely in a Neocolonial style that was intended to restore its former glory, but long decades of neglect by the central government were to follow. La Rioja did not even benefit as much as it hoped it would when Carlos Menem, scion of a major La Rioja wine-producing family was elected president in 1990. There are signs that La Rioja is beginning to diversify away from its agricultural base, although the city, with a current population of about 150,000, is still regarded by most Argentines as a rather arid backwater.

Arrival, information and accommodation

La Rioja's small **airport**, Vicente Almandos Almonacid, is 7km east of town along RP-5 (℡03822/462160), and the only transport from it into town is by *remise*. The new **bus terminal** is some 2.5km south of the central Plaza 25 de Mayo, at Avenida F.O. de la Colina s/n (℡03822/468459 or 425453; the tourist office here is due to be completed in 2010; buses #2 or #8 to centre, $1.50), and serves the whole province, including Villa Unión, Chilecito and more distant destinations such as Mendoza, Córdoba, Catamarca and Salta. In the city centre, the **provincial tourist office** (daily 8am–9pm; ℡03822/426384, Ⓦwww.turismolarioja.gov.ar) is at Pelagio B. Luna 345. If you only have time for a day tours to Talampaya or Ischigualasto, contact Ramón Pio Molina (℡03822/15315674); Corona del Inca, Pelagio B Luna 914 (℡03822/422142); or Terra Riojana, Lamadrid 93 (℡03822/420423).

You're unlikely to want to stay long in La Rioja, but it's good to know that it's not badly off for **accommodation**, covering the whole range with a few reliable options. Enquire about B&B-style **casas de familia** (❷–❸), the best bet at the budget end, at the tourist office.

Hotels and hostels

Huayra Apart Hotel Rivadavia 283
℡03822/464053, Ⓦwww.huayraaparthotel.com.
Good value, spruce apartments for up to five people, with deals for single occupancy. ❺

Naindo at San Nicolás de Bari and Joaquin Victor Gonzalez ℡03822/470700, Ⓦwww
.naindoparkhotel.com. Sparkling new, five-star luxury hotel with comfortable if characterless rooms and its own restaurant, decent-sized pool and bar. ❽

Plaza at San Nicolás de Bari and 9 de Julio ℡03822/425215. Everything is squeaky clean, almost clinically so, but the rooms are smart and the roof-top pool and terrace enjoy views of the

cathedral and mountains beyond. Its well-located *confitería* is one of the places to be seen in La Rioja. ❻

Savoy at San Nicolás de Bari and Avenida Roque A. Luna ℡03822/426894, Ⓦwww
.hotelsavoylarioja.com.ar. Unimaginative neutral decor, but friendly and the rooms are quite spacious, with decent bathrooms. ❹

Pensión 9 de Julio Copiapó 197
℡03822/426955. Your best bet for basic, budget accommodation. The leafy patio gives some atmosphere and the rooms are cramped but acceptably clean. Streetside rooms are extremely noisy at weekends. ❷

The City

La Rioja's microcentro really is small and all the places of interest are grouped around the two main squares, Plaza 25 de Mayo, and, two blocks west and one south, Plaza 9 de Julio. On the west side of the former is the striking white Casa de Gobierno, built in a Neocolonial style with a strong Andalucian influence, which contrasts with the **Catedral San Nicolás de Bari** (daily 8am–9pm) on the south of the plaza. This Neoclassical hulk of a church, built at the beginning of the twentieth century in beige stone, with a huge Italianate cupola, Neo-Gothic campaniles and Byzantine elements in the facade, is primarily the sanctuary for a locally revered relic: a seventeenth-century walnut-wood image of St Nicholas of Bari, carved in Peru (kept locked in a side room; to see it, ask in the cathedral for the key).

One block north of Plaza 25 de Mayo, at 25 de Mayo and Bazán y Bustos, is the **Iglesia San Francisco** (daily 9am–noon & 5–9pm) itself, an uninspiring Neoclassical building visited by St Francisco Solano, who played a key role in the sixteenth century converting the local indigenous population. The stark cell where he stayed, containing only a fine statue of the saint and a dead orange tree, said to have been planted by him, is treated as a holy place by Riojanos. Another block north is the **Museo Arqueológico Inca Huasi** (Tues–Fri 9am–1pm & 4-8pm, Sat 9am–1pm; $2), set up in the 1920s by a Franciscan monk who was interested in the Diaguita culture – rather ironic, considering that the Franciscan missionaries did all they could in the seventeenth century to annihilate it. One of the pieces of art on display is a quite hideous seventeenth-century painting of the conversion of the Diaguita people by St Francisco Solano, but the rest of the exhibition is a fabulous collection of **Diaguita ceramics** and other pre-Columbian art. The dragon-shaped vase near the entrance is around 1200 years old; another later piece, inside one of the dusty cases, is a pot with an armadillo climbing it, while fat-bellied vases painted with, among other things, phalluses and toads – symbols of fertility and rain – line the shelves. The current director is striving to give a more pre-Christian context to the collection while not offending the friars.

Far more impressive is the **Museo Folklórico**, at Pelagio B. Luna 811 (Tues–Fri 9am–1pm & 5–9pm, Sat & Sun 9am–1pm; $2). In the display on local mythology, a set of beautiful terracotta statuettes representing the various figures brings to life the whole pantheon, such as Pachamama, or Mother Earth, and Zapam-Zucum, the goddess of children and the carob tree – she has incredibly elongated breasts the shape of carob-pods. Zupay is the equivalent of the Devil, while a series of characters called Huaira personify different types of wind. The museum also contains a reconstruction of a nineteenth-century Riojano house. Opposite, on the corner of Pelagio B. Luna and Catamarca, is one of the region's best **crafts markets** (Tues–Fri 8am–noon & 4–8pm, Sat & Sun 9am–1pm); the *artesanía*, all of it local, is of high quality, especially the regional *mantas*, or blankets.

One block east of Plaza 25 de Mayo, the **Iglesia Santo Domingo** (daily 9am–noon & 5–9pm), at Pelagio B. Luna and Lamadrid, is the only building of interest to have survived the 1894 earthquake; it's one of the oldest buildings in Argentina, dating from 1623. The extremely long, narrow, white nave is utterly stark, apart from a fine altar decorated with seventeenth-century statuary, as is the simple whitewashed facade – but the carob-wood doors, carved by Indian craftsmen in the late seventeenth century, are a fine example of **mestizo art**.

Eating and drinking

Not as hard up as it sometimes likes to make out, La Rioja has a gaggle of reasonable **places to eat**, most clustered along Avenida Rivadavia towards the old train station. Two pizzerias stand out: *Ribera*, on the corner of Avenida Perón and Pelagio B. Luna, with decades of tradition but a polished, fresh setting with attractive wooden tables; and *Open Piazza*, a pub-bar at the corner of Rivadavia and F. Quiroga, with a summer terrace, men-in-black waiters and decent music – plus a good range of toppings. *La Vieja Casona*, at Rivadavia 427, is probably La Rioja's best *parrilla*, serving outstanding meat and delicious home-made pasta, with a wine list from local bodegas. It faces competition from a newer, trendier rival, *El Nuevo Corral*, right next to the train station. *Café de la Place*, at Rivadavia and Hipólito Yrigoyen, is one of the most strategically located places to have a **drink** or snack – the service is a bit nonchalant, and the decor is resolutely late 1990s, all brushed metal and diffused lighting.

Travel details

Buses

La Rioja to: Buenos Aires (6 daily; 14hr); Catamarca (20 daily; 2hr); Chilecito (4 daily; 3hr); Córdoba (hourly; 6hr 30min); Salta (21 daily; 10hr); San Juan (17 daily; 6hr); Valle Fértil (3 weekly; 4hr); Villa Unión (4 daily; 4hr).
Malargüe to: Las Leñas (June–Sept daily; 1hr 15min); Mendoza (6 daily; 4–5hr); San Rafael (10 daily; 2hr 30min).
Mendoza to: Buenos Aires (15 daily; 13hr); Córdoba (25 daily; 9–10hr); General Alvear (10 daily; 4hr 30min); La Rioja (16 daily; 8hr 30min); Las Leñas (June–Sept 2 daily; 5hr); Los Penitentes (3 daily; 4hr); Malargüe (8 daily; 4–5hr); Neuquén (12 daily; 12hr); Río Gallegos (1 daily; 40hr); Salta (9 daily; 19hr); San Rafael (hourly; 3hr 15min); San Juan (hourly; 2hr 20min); San Luis (hourly; 3hr 40min); Santiago de Chile (12 daily; 6–7hr); Uspallata (7 daily; 2hr); Valparaíso, Chile (5 daily; 8hr 30min).
San Agustín de Valle Fértil to: La Rioja (3 weekly; 4hr); San Juan (3 daily; 3hr 30min–4hr) .
San Juan to: Barreal (2 daily; 5hr); Buenos Aires (13 daily; 16hr); Córdoba (5 daily; 8hr 30min);

Huaco (daily; 3hr); La Rioja (7 daily; 6hr); Mendoza (hourly; 2hr 20min); Rodeo (daily; 3hr); Salta (5 daily; 16hr); (San Agustín de) Valle Fértil (3 daily; 4hr); San José de Jáchal (6 daily; 2hr 15min); San Rafael (2 daily; 5hr 30min).
San Rafael to: Buenos Aires (4 daily; 13hr); General Alvear (3 daily; 1hr 20min); Las Leñas (June–Sept 3 daily; 2hr 40min); Malargüe (2 daily; 2hr 30min); Mendoza (hourly; 3hr 15min); Neuquén (2 daily; 12hr); San Juan (2 daily; 5hr 30min); San Luis (2 daily; 3hr).
Villa Unión to: Chilecito (daily; 4hr 30min); La Rioja (4 daily; 4hr); Patquía (4 daily; 3hr); Vinchina (4 daily; 1hr).

Flights

La Rioja to: Buenos Aires (daily except Sat; 1hr 40min).
Mendoza to: Buenos Aires (4 daily; 1hr 50min); Córdoba (1–2 daily; 1hr 20min); Rosario (1–2 daily; 2hr 40min); Santiago (2–3 daily; 55min).
San Juan to: Buenos Aires (2 daily; 1hr 40min).
San Rafael to: Buenos Aires (daily; 1hr 50min).

Bariloche and the Lake District

BOLIVIA

PARAGUAY

BRAZIL

5

4

6

3

URUGUAY
Buenos Aires

1

2

CHILE

PACIFIC
OCEAN

7

ATLANTIC
OCEAN

8

N

9

0   500 km

CHAPTER 7 # Highlights

* **Bariloche** The region's principal town and leading resort boasts an international ambience and plenty of amenities – plus it has some of the most handsome Lake District landscapes right on its doorstep. See p.440

* **Lake District beer** The El Bolsón and Blest breweries serve a variety of highly drinkable real ales from palest *rubia* to dark stout. See p.461, p.447 & p.461

* **Seven Lakes Route** Seven lakes and more – this breathtakingly scenic route swings past at least a dozen meres whose waters range from deep ultramarine to delicate turquoise. See p.458

* **La Trochita** This much loved steam-train ride was the final destination of Paul Theroux's *The Old Patagonian Express* – follow his example and take a trip down the memory tracks. See p.466

* **Volcán Lanín** Climb the slopes of a woodcut-perfect volcano that reigns over its namesake national park – or just admire the views from a peaceful lakeside vantage point. See p.484

* **Giant dinosaurs** Gawp up at some of the biggest dinosaur remains ever found or check out a clutch of unique titanosaur eggs – all within reach of Neuquén city. See p.490

* **Patagonian wine** Visit one of the most southerly vineyards in the world, sample award-winning wines and even stay overnight amid the vines. See p.491

▲ La Trochita

Bariloche and the Lake District

Argentina's **Lake District** – the northwestern wedge of Argentine Patagonia – is a coffee-book-cover land of picture-perfect glacial lakes surrounded by luxuriant forests, jagged peaks and extinct volcanoes. Not so long ago it was a wilderness controlled by indigenous peoples but the undisputed modern capital, **Bariloche**, now sees annual invasions of Argentine and foreign holiday-makers. Thanks to excellent transport links, they descend on the town in droves year-round for the fresh air and outdoor adventures. According to the tourist literature, their supposed lure is the alpine flavour of this "Argentine Switzerland" – a moniker borne out to some extent thanks to the Mitteleuropa-like setting, wooden chalet architecture and the region's breweries, dairies and chocolate shops. Yet the real attraction is the sheer unspoilt beauty of the goliath **Parque Nacional Nahuel Huapi**, the grandfather of all Argentina's national parks, packed with enough trekking and other outdoor activities to last any enthusiast weeks rather than days.

North of Bariloche is the upmarket resort of **Villa La Angostura**, and the stunning **Seven Lakes Route**, while to the south is the more alternative resort of **El Bolsón** and the splendid **Parque Nacional Los Alerces**, home to more fabulous lakes and ancient alerce trees. Further south still lurk a trio of curiosities: **Butch Cassidy's cabin,** the Welsh settlement of **Trevelin** and the historic railway at **La Trochita**.

In the less visited northern swathes of the Lake District the main hub is family-oriented **San Martín de los Andes**, Bariloche's nearest regional rival, with an admirable lakefront location. Both it and neighbouring **Junín de los Andes** – renowned nationwide for its angling and hunting opportunities – are perfect bases for exploring the rugged **Parque Nacional Lanín**, whose focus is **Volcán Lanín**, a conical peak popular with mountaineers. **Neuquén**, the namesake capital of Argentina's only palindromically named province, is a pleasant enough city to relax in or sort out some practicalities but its indisputable draw has to be the nearby treasure trove of giant dinosaur fossils, earning it the nickname of **Dinosaur Paradise**. In recent years vines have been planted with considerable success in the desert-like areas to the north and east of the city; **wineries** with dramatic names like Valle Perdido "lost valley" and Bodega del Fin del Mundo "winery at the end of the world" have started making fabulous semillons and syrahs that you can go and taste on the premises.

The Southern Lake District

Bariloche is one of those places that Argentines always tell you not to miss, the kind of hype that can easily lead to disappointment. Europeans familiar with the Alps – or North Americans or New Zealanders used to similar scenery – are unlikely to travel thousands of miles to see a simulacrum of Switzerland. Yet the city is undeniably worth the trip because it is the main base for visiting the stunningly pristine landscapes of the **southern Lake District**, unspoilt in a way that nowhere in Europe can match. The magnificent **Parque Nacional Nahuel Huapi**, to which Bariloche is the major gateway, rewards **trekkers** of all degrees of stamina and hardiness with a highly developed infrastructure of trails and refuges. Those who prefer the comfort of admiring scenery from a tour bus or boat have plenty of choices as well: two popular land circuits, the **Circuito Chico** and **Circuito Grande**, plus a pair of recommended lake excursions from nearby **Puerto Pañuelo**, to **Isla Victoria** and **Puerto Blest**.

Just over the provincial border into Neuquén, the self-consciously chic resort of **Villa La Angostura** attracts the more moneyed travellers looking to escape city stress without sacrificing urbane creature comforts. A hop away from its glossy-magazine architecture is the **Parque Nacional Los Arrayanes**, with a grove of namesake *arrayán* trees, cinnamon-barked myrtles some of which are up to six hundred years old. More dramatic is the **Seven Lakes Route**, a gorgeous drive northwards past a dozen or so mountain lakes and lakelets of stunning beauty.

Heading down towards Patagonia proper, another hiking base, **El Bolsón**, acts as an alternative hangout to Bariloche, with a quieter, partly hippy tradition that sets it completely apart from its larger, more commercial neighbour. In the north-western corner of Chubut province, the action is centred around **Esquel**, the low-key starting point for discovering the splendid **Parque Nacional Los Alerces**, home to more fabulous lakes and, as the name suggests, the best place to see cypress-like *alerce* trees, some of which make the oldest *arrayanes* look like babies. Nearby **Cholila**'s claim to fame is **Butch Cassidy's cabin**, more of a curiosity than a monument, but you can learn more about Cassidy and his gang plus the life of pioneers in northern Patagonia at a fabulous new museum, at **Leleque**. Engaging **Trevelin** still preserves its Welsh roots in the form of a museum housed in a disused flour mill, traditional tearooms and an annual Eisteddfod. Another highlight of the Lake District's southernmost tip is a ride on the legendary **La Trochita**, an old steam train that rattles and hoots its way through the steppe on a precarious narrow-gauge track.

Bariloche

The holiday capital of the Argentine South, **SAN CARLOS DE BARILOCHE**, or **Bariloche**, as it is nearly always called, rests up against the slopes of Cerro Otto, behind which rear the spire-tipped crests of the Cerro Catedral massif. Everything in Bariloche faces the mesmerizing Lago Nahuel Huapi, one of the scores of lakes that give the region its name, but something went massively wrong with the urban planning – the main road artery was built along the shore, severing the centre from the town's best feature. The **Parque Nacional Nahuel Huapi** (see pp.448–459), the prime reason for winging your way here, surrounds the town and you'll want to head out to discover its many treasures as soon as possible.

The town's lifeblood is tourism, with getting on for a million visitors arriving annually. This is a place of secular pilgrimage for the nation's students, who flood here in January and February on their summer breaks, plus coachloads of young Israelis, here simply because they have heard about it from other Israelis. None of these necessarily comes in search of the true mountain experience, but they often end up having one, pushed out of town by the inflated high-season prices of hotels and clubs. In winter, it's specifically the nearby **ski resort** of Cerro

Catedral that draws the crowds. For five days in August, Bariloche celebrates the **Fiesta Nacional de la Nieve**, with ski races, parades and a torch-lit evening descent on skis to open the season officially, as well as the election of the Reina Nacional de la Nieve, or Snow Queen.

At peak times, in particular, the excesses of commercialization and crowds of tourists may spoil your visit. Nevertheless, the place does offer remarkably painless access to many beautiful and genuinely wild sections of the Andean cordillera, and out of season (May–June or Sept–Nov) the town is still big enough to retain some life of its own.

Some history

Before the incursions of the Mapuche and Spanish, the area was the domain of indigenous tribes, whose livelihood largely depended on the lake and trade with their western, Mapuche, counterparts. The discovery of their mountain passes (the name Bariloche is derived from a native word meaning "people from beyond the mountains") became an obsession of early Spanish explorers in Chile, many of whom were desperate to hunt down the wealth of the mythical City of the Caesars. Knowledge of the passes' whereabouts was a closely guarded secret until the 1670s. The history of the non-autochthonous presence in the region really began when the Jesuit **Nicolás Mascardi** was dispatched by the Viceroy to found a **mission** around that time. The natives put paid to Mascardi and his successors and, in 1717, the mission was abandoned. The local indigenous groups took one Jesuit introduction more to their hearts than Christianity: the apple (*manzana*). Used for cider, wild apples became so popular that the region's Mapuche tribes became known as **Manzaneros**.

Modern Bariloche has its roots in the arrival of German settlers from southern Chile in the early twentieth century, but was tiny until the creation of the national park in 1937. In recent decades, the population has skyrocketed, and the town is now a major urban centre, though the homogeneity of its original alpine-style architecture has sadly been swamped by a messy conglomerate of high-rise apartment blocks.

Arrival and information

Bariloche's **airport** (℡02944/426162) is 14km east of town. A shuttle bus run by Del Lago Turismo meets most flights and ferries passengers to the company's central office at Villegas 222 (℡02944/430056). There are always *remises* hanging around, or you can take local bus #72, which runs every two hours (7am–10pm). The main **bus terminal** is next door to the **train station**, 3km east of the city centre along Avenida 12 de Octubre (RN-237). The best local buses for the centre are #10, #20 or any bus marked "Catedral" (every 15–20min; 10min; $1.50). In town, buses to the terminal leave from Elflein and Quaglia.

The **tourist office**, in the centro cívico, operates a queuing system in summer (daily 9am–9pm; ℡02944/429850, Ⓦwww.barilochepatagonia.info or www .bariloche.com). It keeps a list of available accommodation, including *casas de familia*. A few blocks south is the **Intendencia of the Parque Nacional Nahuel Huapi**, at Avenida San Martín 24 (summer Mon–Fri 8am–8pm, Sat–Sun 9am–8pm; winter daily 9am–3pm; ℡02944/423111), which should be your first point of call if you are planning a visit to the park. A block behind is the **Club Andino Bariloche**, at 20 de Febrero 30 (Jan & Feb daily 9am–1pm & 4–8.30pm; rest of year weekdays only same hours; ℡02944/527966, Ⓦwww.clubandino .org), which can offer more detailed information on trekking routes.

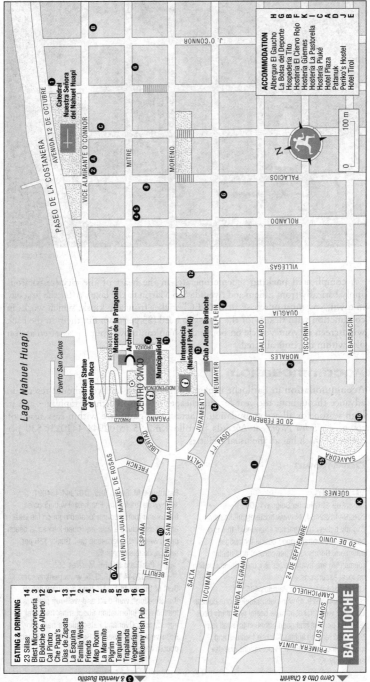

EATING & DRINKING

23 Sillas	14
Biest Microcervecería	3
El Boliche de Alberto	12
Cal Pintxo	6
Che Papa's	1
Días de Zapata	13
La Esquina	11
Familia Weiss	2
Friends	4
Map Room	7
La Marmite	5
Pilgrim	8
Tarquinho	15
Trapalanda	9
Vegetariano	16
Wilkenny Irish Pub	10

ACCOMMODATION

Albergue El Gaucho	H
La Bolsa del Deporte	G
Hospedería Tito	B
Hostería El Ciervo Rojo	F
Hostería Güemes	K
Hostería La Pastorella	I
Hostería Piuké	C
Hotel Plaza	A
Pataruk	D
Periko's Hostel	J
Hotel Tirol	E

Lago Nahuel Huapi

Puerto San Carlos

Catedral
Nuestra Señora
del Nahuel Huapi

Equestrian Statue
of General Roca

Museo de la Patagonia

Archway

CENTRO CÍVICO

Municipalidad

Intendencia
(National Park HQ)

Club Andino Bariloche

N

0   100 m

BARILOCHE

7

443

▲ Cerro Otto & Chairlift

▲ 8 Avenida Bustillo

▲ 3 Avenida Bustillo

▲ Cerro Otto & Chairlift

▲ Skiers at Bariloche

A complicated **parking** scheme operates in the heart of the city (restrictions apply basically from Elflein and Avenida San Martín to the lake). After the first day in town, you must purchase an "ALTEC" sticker from any kiosk, which works in conjunction with tickets for the time you need ($5 per day). Fix them in the back windscreen of your vehicle on both sides. You can move your car as often as you like within the time allotted.

Accommodation

Accommodation in Bariloche is plentiful but pricey, and you should reserve in advance throughout the year for the cheaper options, which fill rapidly – and in high season for all accommodation. There is one **campsite** within easy reach of town: *La Selva Negra*, at Avenida Bustillo Km2.95 (℡02944/441013; $30 per person), which has all the usual facilities.

Downtown

Hostels

Albergue El Gaucho Belgrano 209
℡02944/522464, ⓦwww.hostelelgaucho.com.
Slightly rickety backpacker stronghold, this is a basic but essentially good option for budget travellers. Dorms ($45 per person) and double rooms (④) are available, as is excellent information on local excursions.

La Bolsa del Deporte Palacios 405
℡02944/423529, ⓦwww.labolsadeldeporte.com.ar.
Excellent wooden cabin-style hostel with thirty beds ($50 per person) and good attention to detail (eg bunk-bed reading lights). Kitchen facilities and internet access available. Reservations one day ahead only. ④

Patanuk J.M. Rosas 585 ℡02944/434991,
ⓦwww.patanuk.com. Fun hostel with doubles, triples and roomy dorms located right on the lake; amenities include a well-equipped kitchen, a beach deck, wi-fi and a barbecue grill. Bunks $55 per person, double rooms ④

Periko's Hostel Morales 555
℡02944/522326, ⓦwww.perikos.com.
Best of the youth-hostel-type accommodation, this excellent, well-built and well-run place is loaded with information about trips. Its travel agency arm, Overland Patagonia, is next door. Reserve well in advance. Bunks $45 per person, double rooms ④

Hotels

Hospedería Tito Vice Almirante O'Connor 745 ⊤02944/435241. The decor is unintentionally retro, but *Tito* is clean and pleasant with a good location just east of the action. One of the better budget hotels in town. **❹**

Hostería El Ciervo Rojo Elflein 115 ⊤02944/435241, ⓦwww.interpatagonia.com /elciervorojo/index.html. More pink than *rojo*, but nevertheless a tastefully remodelled and centrally located townhouse which successfully fuses modest old-style charm with modern comforts. Continental breakfast is included in the price and discounts are offered for stays of more than one night. **❻**

Hostería Güemes Güemes 715 ⊤02944/424785, ⓕ435616. One of the best budget options in town sits on a tranquil side street with a prize-winning garden. The owner was a tourist guide for 45 years and has an in-depth knowledge of the the surroundings. A spacious living room with a central coal fire makes for cosy winter evenings. **❺**

Hostería La Pastorella Av Belgrano 127 ⊤02944/424656, ⓦwww.lapastorella.com.ar. Tasteful French decor gives this place a homely feel. Rooms are tidy and spacious but lack the charm of the rest of the hotel. There's a small tranquil garden and a sauna for relaxing. **❻**

Hostería Piuké Beschtedt 136 ⊤02944/423044. Despite having a name that could easily be mispronounced, this is an attractive chalet-style hotel with flowery gardens just a block from the cathedral. Rooms are simple but comfortable and breakfast is included. **❺**

Plaza Vice Almirante O'Connor 431 ⊤02944/424100, ⓦwww.hotelplazabariloche .com.ar. Nothing flashy, but good value for its lakeside location and a simple breakfast is included, served in the dining room with panoramic views over the lake and cathedral. Popular with students, particularly in the winter. **❺**

Tirol Libertad 175 ⊤02944/426152, ⓦwww .hoteltirol.com.ar. Ideally located a block from the centro cívico, this is a modern but tastefully decorated hotel. Rates include breakfast served in a dining room with stunning lake views – the huge glass windows will shield you from any cold wind blowing from the lake. **❻**

Around the lake

Avenida Bustillo runs for 25km along the lakeshore to Puerto Pañuelo and is packed, at least for the first dozen kilometres, with bungalows and cabins, some of which have sensational lake views, though most of which have been gentrified in the worst possible taste; below is a small selection of some of the best, along with one or two places to stay a little farther afield.

Aldebaran Av Bustillo Km 20, 4 ⊤02944/448678, ⓦwww.aldebaranpatagonia.com. Named after one of the brightest stars in the night sky, this hotel stands out for its stunning lakeside location at the entrance to the Península de San Pedro, its spacious understated rooms and the original decor, which continues the astronomical theme without demanding stratospheric prices. All rooms enjoy breathtaking views of the mountains and lake. **❾**

Arelauquen Lodge Ruta 82, 8km from junction with Av Bustillo ⊤02944/467150, ⓦwww .arelauquen.com. Set amid parkland and a golf course near the shores of Lago Gutiérrez, this Portuguese-owned hotel in the Pestana Group is an exceptional upmarket option. Fine mountain views with tasteful and original decoration and an excellent restaurant. **❾**

Cabañas del Arroyo Av Bustillo Km 4050 ⊤02944/442082, ⓦwww.delarroyo.com.ar. Comfortable and functional cabins, with well-equipped kitchens, in a convenient location, situated over the *arroyo* (brook) that gives them their name, providing natural cooling on hot summer days. **❼**

Casco Av Bustillo Km 11.5 ⊤02944/463131, ⓦwww.hotelelcasco.com/es. Belonging to one of the country's leading art dealers, this fabulous hotel, whose grounds are lapped by the lake's waters, is like staying in a private art gallery – indeed, the mouthwatering works, mostly by native artists of the highest calibre, are on sale. Every detail refers back to this arty theme, without becoming heavy-handed; even the cocktails at the bar are inspired by specific painters and their palettes. **❾**

La Cebra Av Bustillo Km7 ⊤02944/461390, ⓦwww.lacebrabungalows.com. One of the first bungalows to be built along Av Bustillo and still among the best, with its own beach and sensational scenic views. **❼**

Charming Luxury Lodge and Private Spa Hua Huan 7549, Av Bustillo Km 7.5 ⊤02944/462889, ⓦwww.charming-bariloche.com. The name says it all: it is charming and luxurious, and each room has its own private spa, with jacuzzi, sauna, steam bath, aromatherapy and chromotherapy. It is pricey, though, with rooms starting at US$330. **❾**

Estancia Peuma Hue Entrance RN-40 Km
2014 towards El Bolsón ☎02944/457349,
ⓦwww.peuma-hue.com. Aptly named (it means
"place of dreams" in Mapudungun), Peuma Hue is
idyllically located at the head of the sapphire Lago
Gutiérrez, and offers supreme comfort, exquisite
and well-balanced food and the possibility of
kayaking, horseriding, birdwatching, walking or just
lapping up the beauty of the place. There is even
an ecumenical chapel within the fabulous grounds,
and the owner and staff are supremely helpful and
friendly. ❾

Hostería Lonquimay Lonquimay 3672, Barrio
Melipal ☎02944/443450. Nicely appointed chalet-
style hotel with an intimate feel not far from the Cerro
Otto chairlift. Take bus #10 to Av Bustillo Km3.8. ❺
Llao Llao Av Bustillo Km28 ☎02944/448530,
ⓦwww.llaollao.com. One of Argentina's most
famous hotels, designed and built (twice) by
Alejandro Bustillo along the lines of an enormous
Canadian cabin; see p.451 for further details.
Excellent views and services, including indoor
and outdoor pools, a golf course and even a
presidential suite. ❾

The Town

Bariloche's focal point is the **centro cívico**, a set of buildings constructed out of timber and the local greenish-grey stone, resolutely facing the lake. Dating from 1939, it's a noble architectural statement by Ernesto de Estrada, who collaborated with Argentina's most famous architect, Alejandro Bustillo (after whom the main lakeside avenue is named), in the development of an alpine style that has come to represent the region. In the centre of the main plaza, around which these buildings are grouped, stands a graffiti-strewn equestrian **statue** of General Roca, whose horse looks suitably hang-dog after the Campaign of the Desert. People bring Saint Bernards along, often with the obligatory cask around their necks, in readiness for photo opportunities at a small price. The pavement is adorned with painted white scarves, symbols of the Madres de la Plaza de Mayo (see p.91) and the names of local *desaparecidos*. Of the plaza's attractions, the most interesting is the **Museo de la Patagonia** (Mon & Sat 10am–1pm, Tues–Fri 10am–12.30pm & 2–7pm, closed Sun; $5), which also rates as one of the very best museums on things Patagonian, from wildlife to modern history. Look out for the caricature of Perito Moreno as a wet nurse guiding the infant Theodore Roosevelt on his trip through the Lake District in 1913. Superb, too, are the engraved Tehuelche tablet stones that experts speculate may have been protective amulets, Aónik'enk painted horse hides and playing cards made of guanaco skin, one of the Mapuche's famous lances and Roca's own uniform. Informative booklets are on sale, but only the one on the Campaign of the Desert is translated into English – ask about guided tours.

On the lakeshore to the east of the museum is the Bustillo-designed **Catedral Nuestra Señora del Nahuel Huapi**, whose attractive stained-glass windows illustrate Patagonian themes such, as the first Mass held by Magellan – the oppression of the indigenous peoples is clearly evident.

The town's **beach** is narrow but pleasant enough and the views are predictably spectacular, but the water is cold even in summer. If you want to swim there is a wonderful **outdoor pool** nearby at the Albergue Deportivo Municipal (Mon–Sat noon–8pm, Sun 1–8pm; $2) which offers a similar experience without the chill.

Eating

Bariloche has a large and excellent selection of places to **eat**, ranging from cheap diners to expensive gourmet restaurants. Most are within walking distance of the centre. Calle Mitre is also lined with stores selling local specialities such as chocolate – including penguins and St Bernard dogs – smoked trout, ice cream and *alfajores*.

23 Sillas 20 de Febrero 40. This is one of the few places where vegetarians can eat almost without fear. Keenly priced wholegrain sandwiches, fresh fruit juices and other dishes (including some with meat) will tempt anybody looking to detox.

El Boliche de Alberto Villegas 347 ☏ 02944/431433 and Av Bustillo 8800 ☏ 02944/462285. The juiciest and largest (and not the priciest) *parrillas* in town: prepare to gorge yourself. Also runs a pasta restaurant under the same name at Elflein 49 for a respite from meat.

Cal Pintxo Mitre 633 ☏ 02944/456888. Spanish-style tapas bar with a good selection of seafood dishes at reasonable prices. The beer on tap is also cheap by Bariloche standards, and there is live music at weekends.

Dias de Zapata Morales 362 ☏ 02944/423128. Mexican-run Mexican restaurant, so you are guaranteed the real deal. Portions are large, moderately priced and of high quality, and you can even choose your spice level from mild to mind-blowingly hot.

La Esquina Urquiza and Perito Moreno. Corner by name and corner café by nature, this popular local haunt is a good place to have a drink and while away the time with a newspaper or book at outdoor tables sheltered from the summer sun.

Familia Weiss Palacios and O'Connor ☏ 02944/435789. A perennial hit with visitors, especially for its *cievro a la cazadora* (venison in a creamy mushroom sauce) or *picada* selection of smoked specialities. Moderate prices. Open 8–3am.

Friends Mitre and Rolando. Open 24hr in summer, *Friends* is well suited for night owls with the munchies. Burgers, pizzas and beers and spirits are served, all at competitive prices.

La Marmite Mitre 329 ☏ 02944/423685. Not a bargain by any means, the intimate, old-fashioned *Marmite* is nonetheless worthwhile for its regional and Swiss specialities, especially its fondues. Closed Sun lunch.

Tarquinino 24 de Septiembre and Saavedra. In a tasteful lodge with trees growing through its roof, this *parrilla*, with succulent chunky *bifes de lomo*, is a popular local haunt that doesn't hit the wallet too hard.

Vegetariano 20 de Febrero 730 ☏ 02944/421820. If you've had your fill of *parrillas* this restaurant will provide relief. Vegans beware though – most dishes contain egg and dairy products, and there are also fish dishes.

Drinking and nightlife

With the constant influx of Argentine students mixing with an onslaught of thirsty backpackers, Bariloche has a lively *movida*. **Bars** are scattered around town but the majority of the action is in the area between Elflein and the waterfront. However, drinking can be expensive – plan on spending about a third more than elsewhere in Argentina in the trendiest bars, while many discos charge $50-plus entry fee for non-Argentines. The two best-known **discos** in town, both are at the western end of J.M. de Rosas, are *Roket*, a futuristic dance club, and *Grisu* for Latin and pop music.

Blest Microcervecería Av Bustillo Km11.6 ☏ 02944/461026. This microbrewery has an excellent selection of very good home-made brews – their potent strawberry beer is worth sampling as are all the ales. It also serves moderately priced meals, mostly with a Germanic flavour. Open noon–1am daily.

Che Papa's John O'Connor 33. A relaxed, bohemian hangout, this is a cosy and friendly little bar that's a hit with Che Guevara fans.

Map Room Urquiza 248. Run by a US and Argentine ex-backpacker couple, this restaurant-bar is packed with memorabilia from their extensive travels. The food is good too, and very reasonably priced. Closed Sun.

Pilgrim Palacios 167 ☏ 02944/421686. Owned by the same folk as *Blest*, the *Pilgrim* has an equally fine selection of beer, serves burgers and more and boasts a good atmosphere to boot.

Trapalanda España 322. One of the few bars in Bariloche with a terrace and beer garden, this bar is rapidly turning into a travellers' hangout. The fresh fruit cocktails are delicious.

Wilkenny Irish Pub San Martín 435 ☏ 02944/424444. Standard wannabe Irish bar with happy hour on selected drinks each night 7–9pm. This is the most famous party pub in Patagonia – drinks are not cheap.

Listings

Airlines Aerolíneas Argentinas, Mitre 185
☎02944/423234 or 422144 at airport; LADE,
Villegas 480 ☎02944/423562.

Banks and exchange Bank hours vary depending
on season: April–Nov 9am–2pm; Dec–March
8am–1pm. Banco de la Nación, Mitre 178; Banco
Francés, San Martín 336; Banco de Galicia, Moreno
77; Cambio Sudamericana, Mitre 63.

Car rental Avis, Av San Martín 162 ☎02944/431648;
Bariloche, Moreno 115 ☎02944/427638; Budget,
Mitre 106 ☎02944/429999.

Laundry Patagonia, Palacios 191.

Post office Moreno 175 (Mon–Fri 8.30am–1pm &
4–7pm, Sat 9am–1pm).

Taxis Usually some hanging around the centro
cívico and main shopping streets. Dina Huapi
☎02944/468136; Patagonia Remise
☎02944/443700.

Telephone Several along Mitre, including Telecom,
Mitre and Quaglia (8.30am–midnight).

Travel agencies and tour operators Most of the
following offer a variety of excursions, including
rafting, fishing and boat trips: Alternativa Patagonia,
Quaglia 262 (☎02944/430845, @anorana
@bariloche.com.ar); Del Lago Turismo, Villegas 222
(☎02944/430056); Turisur, Mitre 219
(☎02944/426630); Catedral Turismo, Palacios 263
(☎02944/423918, @transita@bariloche.com.ar).
Mountain-bike rental is available from Dirty Bikes,
Vice Almirante O'Connor 681 (☎02944/425616).
For steam-train trips from Bariloche to Perito
Moreno see ⊛www.trenhistoricovapor.com.ar. For
kayaking through Senzalimiti ⊛www.slimiti.com.
For Rafting Aguas Blancas (⊛www.aguasblancas
.com.ar) book through local travel agents.

Parque Nacional Nahuel Huapi

The main goal of any trip to Bariloche is to see the natural wonders contained within the **PARQUE NACIONAL NAHUEL HUAPI,** the doyen of the Argentine national park system. Protecting a glorious chunk of the Andean cordillera and its neighbouring steppe, its origins lie in a grant of seven thousand hectares of land made by Dr Francisco P. Moreno (known as "Perito" Moreno, "perito" meaning "expert") to the national government in 1903 on the condition that it was safeguarded for the enjoyment of future generations. It has since grown a hundredfold in size.

Most of the park falls within the watershed of the immense **Lago Nahuel Huapi**, an impressive expanse of water that can seem benign one moment and a froth of seething whitecaps the next. Of glacial origin, it's 557 square kilometres in area, but highly irregular in shape with peninsulas, islands and attenuated, fjord-like tentacles that sweep down from the thickly forested border region. The lake's name comes from the Mapudungun (Mapuche tongue) for Isle (*huapi*) of the Tiger (*nahuel*) and refers to the jaguars that once inhabited regions even this far south. Rainfall is heaviest by the border with Chile, especially in places such as Puerto Blest and Lago Frías – the nucleus of the land donated by Moreno – where over 3000mm fall annually. This permits the growth of Valdivian temperate rainforest and individual species such as the *alerce*, here at the northernmost extent of its range in Argentina. Other species typical of the sub-Antarctic Patagonian forests also flourish: giant *coihues*, *lengas* and *ñire* among others.

A second important habitat is the high alpine environment above the tree line (upwards of 1600m), including some summits that retain snow all year. The dominant massif of the park is an extinct volcano, **Cerro Tronador**, whose three peaks (Argentino at 3410m; Internacional at 3554m; and Chileno at 3478m) straddle the Argentine–Chilean border in the south. Glaciers slide off its heights in all directions, though all are in a state of alarmingly rapid recession. The "thundering" in its Spanish name is not meteorological or volcanic, but refers to

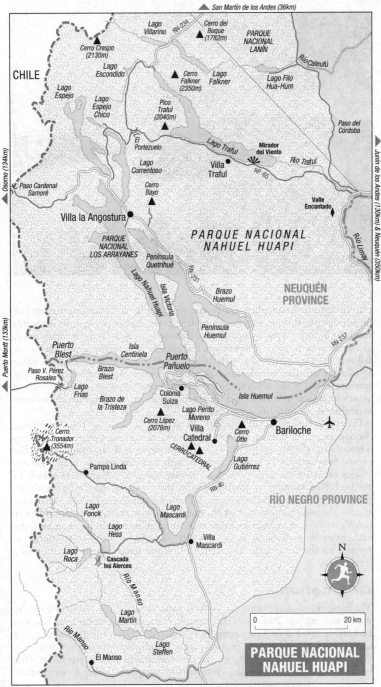

San Martín de los Andes (36km)

Lago Villarino

Cerro del Buque (1782m)

PARQUE NACIONAL LANÍN

Río Caleufú

RN 234

Cerro Crespo (2130m)

Lago Escondido

CHILE

Cerro Falkner (2350m)

Lago Falkner

Lago Filo Hua-Hum

Lago Espejo

Pico Traful (2040m)

Lago Espejo Chico

Paso del Córdoba

El Portezuelo

Lago Traful

Mirador del Viento

Río Traful

Osorno (134km)

Lago Correntoso

Villa Traful

RP 65

Paso Cardenal Samoré

Cerro Bayo

Junín de los Andes (130km) & Neuquén (350km)

Valle Encantado

Villa la Angostura

PARQUE NACIONAL LOS ARRAYANES

PARQUE NACIONAL NAHUEL HUAPI

NEUQUÉN PROVINCE

Río Limay

Península Quetrihué

RN 231

Lago Nahuel Huapi

Isla Victoria

Brazo Huemul

Puerto Montt (133km)

Península Huemul

RN 237

Puerto Blest

Isla Centinela

Puerto Pañuelo

Paso V. Pérez Rosales

Brazo Blest

Isla Huemul

Lago Frías

Brazo de la Tristeza

Colonia Suiza

Cerro Tronador (3554m)

Cerro López (2076m)

Lago Perito Moreno

Villa Catedral

Cerro Otto

Bariloche

CERRO CATEDRAL

Lago Gutiérrez

Pampa Linda

RN 40

RÍO NEGRO PROVINCE

Lago Fonck

Lago Mascardi

Lago Hess

Villa Mascardi

N

Lago Roca

Cascada los Alerces

Río Manso

Lago Martín

0   20 km

Lago Steffen

El Manso

Río Manso

PARQUE NACIONAL NAHUEL HUAPI

El Bolsón (55km) & Esquel (222km)

▲ Lago Nahuel Huapi

the echoing roar heard when vast chunks of ice break off its hanging glaciers and plunge down to the slopes below. Rainfall decreases sharply as you move eastwards from the border. Cypress woodland typifies the transitional semi-montane zone, and at the eastern side of the park you find areas of arid, rolling steppe. Snow can fall as late as December and as early as March at higher altitudes: it's not advisable to hike certain trails outside the high season. Average temperatures are 18°C in summer and 2°C in winter. The strongest winds blow in spring, which is otherwise a good time to visit, as is the calmer autumn, when the deciduous trees wear their spectacular late-season colours.

The park has abundant **birdlife**, with species such as the Magellanic Woodpecker, the Green-backed Firecrown, the ground-dwelling Chucao Tapaculo and the Austral Parakeet. You'll hear mention of rare **fauna** such as the *huemul* (see box, p.455) and the *pudú*, though you have only a slightly greater chance of seeing them than you do of spying Nahuelito, Argentina's answer to the Loch Ness monster. Animals that make their home in the steppe regions of the park (guanaco, rheas and foxes) are more easily seen. Of the non-native species, the most conspicuous are the **red deer** (*ciervo colorado*) and the **wild boar** (*jabalí*), introduced by hunt-loving settlers. In an effort to cull their numbers, the authorities issue shooting permits, which continue to serve as a source of revenue for the park – expect to see roast boar and venison carpaccio on many a local menu.

Orientation

The most visited sites within the **central zone**, around Lago Nahuel Huapi, lie within easy reach of Bariloche. The numerous **excursions** available from here can be roughly divided into two categories, land and water, with the town's travel agents offering more or less identical packages and prices, though in some cases you may prefer to do it at your own pace on public transport or by private car. One of the excursions heads to **Isla Victoria**, the elongated, thickly forested island northwest of the city. The central zone also embraces the "park within a park", **Parque Nacional Los Arrayanes**, on the Península Quetrihué (see p.457), which can be visited from the exclusive upmarket resort of **Villa La Angostura** (see p.455). At the western end of Brazo Blest, the outpost of **Puerto Blest** is surrounded by some of the park's most impressive forest. A short and scenic trail connects it with the north side of the bay, where a stepped walkway leads up past the **Cascada Los Cántaros**, a series of waterfalls in the forest. A dirt road runs south for 3km to Puerto Alegre at the northern end of tiny Lago Frías, with a launch crossing the lake daily to Puerto Frías: from here you can cross to Chile or hike south across the Paso de las Nubes towards the **southern zone**. It is in the south where you'll find most of the longer and more mountainous treks, either around **Cerro Catedral** or **Pampa Linda**.

The **zone to the north** of Lago Nahuel Huapi, bordering on the Parque Nacional Lanín, centres around **Lago Traful**. Its big attraction is the Seven Lakes Route (see box, pp.458–459). *Guardaparques* stationed at points along the route are helpful when it comes to recommending day-treks in their particular sectors. The *Guía Sendas & Bosques de Lanín y Nahuel Huapi* is a very useful **guide** (in Spanish only) and comes with two reasonably reliable maps (1:200,000) of the region.

From Bariloche, In addition to those listed above, see also the "Trekking in Parque Nahuel Huapi" box, pp.452–453.

Circuito Chico

The most popular, if not the most exciting, excursion from Bariloche is the short **Circuito Chico**, a 65km road course that follows Avenida Bustillo westwards. You could join one of the organized tours (4hr; see "Listings", p.448) or visit the highlights on public transport. **Buses** leave from the terminal and from Moreno and Rolando: #20 for Puerto Pañuelo and *Llao Llao* (hourly 8am–9pm) and #10 or #11 for Colonia Suiza (every 20min 4am–11pm).

The first ten or so kilometres of the circuit are underwhelming. Although the lake views are great, they are accompanied by a steady stream of twee boutiques, hotels, restaurants, workshops and factory outlets for cottage industries. It's great for buying regional produce – you can get everything from woollen sweaters to preserves, smoked trout and meats, ceramics, chocolates and wood-carvings – but for very little else.

The circuit's best sights lie along its westernmost stretch. Before you reach **Puerto Pañuelo** – where boats depart for excursions to the Isla Victoria (see p.454), the Bosque de los Arrayanes (see p.457) and Puerto Blest (see p.454) – you pass a tiny chapel, the **Capilla San Eduardo**, on the left-hand side. Built with cypress and tiled with *alerce* shingles, it was designed by Estrada under the supervision of Bustillo. Across from the chapel is the imposing **Llao Llao**, one of Argentina's most famous hotels (T02944/448530; see p.451). From below, it looks like a carbuncle set on top of a verdant knoll, though Alejandro Bustillo's alpine design strangely improves the closer you get. The original building burnt down in 1939, less than a year after completion, in a closed-season blaze caused by an inattentive housekeeper. The forests were plundered again, and the hotel reopened in 1940. State-owned until 1991, it is now owned by a private company and can be visited as part of a **guided tour** (booking essential; free). The sensational views are worth a hike up alone, but for guests facilities include an indoor pool, gym, tennis courts and a fine restaurant – *Los Césares* – with superbly cooked regional cuisine. The restaurant is open in the evenings to non-guests – reservations are a must.

Trekking in Parque Nacional Nahuel Huapi

To say **Parque Nacional Nahuel Huapi** is an ideal destination for **trekking** would be a sizeable understatement. Myriad spectacular trails lace the park, though its principal trekking region is the sector southwest of Bariloche, where the two foremost points of interest are **Cerro Catedral** and the **Pampa Linda** area, southeast of Cerro Tronador. An impressive network of well-run **refuges** ($40–50 per person) makes trekking that much more appealing: you'll need to bring a sleeping bag, but can buy **meals** and basic supplies en route. In high season, refuges and trails in the more popular areas can get very busy, so carry a tent with you. There are authorized **camping sites**, but you need to get a camping **permit** from the *intendencia* or any *guardaparque* in order to use them; the park has suffered a series of devastating **fires** in recent years, so restrictions have tightened up as regards free camping and you must now carry your own stove for cooking. Before departure it is obligatory to fill out a *registro de trekking* at the *guardaparque* station on entering the park and to check out again before leaving.

The **trekking season** is basically between December and March, but you should always heed weather conditions (Ⓦwww.accuweather.com has forecasts) and come prepared for unseasonal snowfalls. Check in advance with the *guardaparques* to find out which refuges are open. As a rule, trails or *sendas* to refuges are well marked; the high-mountain trails (*sendas de alta montaña*) are not always clearly marked, though, while the less-frequented paths (*picadas*) are not maintained on a regular basis, and close up with vegetation from time to time. Before you set out, you should also visit the Club Andino Bariloche, at calle 20 de Febrero 30 in Bariloche. Their information office and shop is in the wooden hut alongside the main building (Jan & Feb daily 9am–1pm & 4–8.30pm, rest of year weekdays only; Ⓣ02944/527966, Ⓦwww.clubandino.org or www.activepatagonia.com.ar). They sell a series of trekking **maps**: the standard one is the *Carta de Refugios, Sendas y Picadas* (1:100,000), which has been expanded into three larger-scale (1:50,000) maps. These are useful and include stage times, but the route descriptions are in Spanish only, and not all topographical details are accurate. A newer *Infotrekking* map, compiled from satellite images, is better but may not have all the trails marked. CAB also sells a slim volume, *Infotrekking de la Patagonia* by Diego Cannestraci, which has good route descriptions for those who can read Spanish.

The wildest scenery of the circuit is found along the road that runs through the forested stretch beyond *Llao Llao*. Four kilometres beyond the hotel a track heads north to **Villa Tacul**, where you'll find a pretty sandy beach. There are also a couple of short forest walks, one around Cerro Llao Llao, the other between *Llao Llao* and **Lago Escondido**. The latter walk brings you to **Mirador López**, which overlooks the deep blue waters of Nahuel Huapi and offers excellent views of **Cerro Capilla** (2167m). At nearby Bahía López you'll find the *Alun Nehuen* hotel, at Avenida Bustillo Km32 (Ⓣ02944/448005, Ⓦwww.alunnehuenbariloche .com.ar; Ⓞ), a lakeside hotel with spectacular views that offers big discounts in the low season. The last point of call on the circuit is **Colonia Suiza**, originally settled by Swiss immigrants. There's nothing particular to see here, but it's a good place for gorging yourself on Sunday lunch. The local speciality is *curanto*, traditionally prepared in a pit with hot stones: try *Curanto Emilio Goye* (Wed & Sun lunch only; reservations on Ⓣ02944/448250) with all manner of meat and veg.

Circuito Grande

The **Circuito Grande** is a 240km loop that leads east out of Bariloche on the RN-237 past the incredible rock formations of the **Valle Encantado** ("Enchanted Valley"). Here you'll see pine forests lining the steep valley outcrops and stone fingers pointing skywards while the blue waters of the Río Limay flow below. The

In the **Cerro Catedral** area, popular one- or two-day hikes include ones to **Refugio Frey**, which can be reached by a gentle ascent up the valley or by taking the ski lift to Refugio Lynch and then a rocky traverse (medium difficulty). Follow the ridge heading southwest picking up the red paint blotches on the rocks – after an hour or more the trail forks left on a steep descent to Refugio Frey, while the right fork leads to Refugio San Martín. From here the standard descent is to the northeast, along the course of the Casa de Piedra stream.

In the **Pampa Linda** sector there are a number of day-treks and longer possibilities. Very popular is the hike to **Refugio Otto Meiling**, above even the summer snowline and with spectacular views of Cerro Tronador, where you can stay or camp. Much less frequented is the trek to **Refugio Tronador**, also with mountain vistas. You'll need a permit from both the Pampa Linda *guardaparque* and the nearby *gendarmaría*, since the trek takes you into Chile before doubling back into Argentina. There are no services at Refugio Tronador, and many prefer to overnight near the Chilean *carabineros* and make a day-hike to Refugio Tronador, returning to Pampa Linda the third day.

At Pampa Linda there's **accommodation** at *Hostería Pampa Linda* (☏ 02944/490517, ⓦ www.hosteriapampalinda.com.ar; closed May and June; ⑩) which offers half- and full-board options, or the *refugio* next door. Nearby there's also upmarket *Hotel Tronador*, at the northwestern end of Lago Mascardi (☏ 02944/441062, ⓦ www .hoteltronador.com; Nov–April; ⑨ full board). **Campsites** ($35 per person) are at all major destinations: *Lago Roca* near the Cascada Los Alerces; *Los Rápidos* (☏ 02944/461861) and *La Querencia* (☏ 02944/520665) at Lago Mascardi; and *Pampa Linda* or the camping *libre* site opposite. Check with the *intendencia* in Bariloche as to the current status of other authorized sites.

A useful Transportes RM **bus** connects Bariloche to Pampa Linda, leaving from outside the Club Andino Bariloche (summer daily 8.30am, returning 5pm; get tickets in advance). A Vía Bariloche bus goes to Paraje El Manso at the extreme southwest corner of the park, by the park boundary (buy tickets from company office at Mitre 321).

Río Traful joins the Río Limay at Confluencia, 70km from Bariloche. Here the RN-237 continues on towards Neuquén while the RP-65 turns northwest towards Villa Traful. At the junction is a service station and, from a good vantage point above the other shore, *Hostería Gruta de las Vírgenes* (☏ 02944/426138, ⓦ www .glvpatagonia.com.ar; ⑨), which can put you in contact with fishing guides. Take the RP-65 towards Lago Traful (see p.458), soon after which, at El Portezuelao pass, the circuit joins the northern section of the Ruta de los Siete Lagos (see box, pp.458–459) near Lagos Correntoso and Espejo, and then returns southwards to Bariloche via Villa La Angostura (see p.455). Alternatively, you could turn right when you meet the Ruta de los Siete Lagos and head to San Martín de los Andes (see p.473). Returning from there to Bariloche you can take either the Paso del Córdoba (a return trip of 360km) or the paved route via Junín (460km).

Renting a car (see "Listings", p.448) is the ideal way in which to do the Circuito Grande, though you could also take a full-day guided tour – ask at the tourist office – or agree on an itinerary and price with a taxi-driver.

Cerro Catedral

Some 20km south of Bariloche is **Cerro Catedral**, named after the Gothic steeples of rock that make up its craggy summit (2405m). In summer, the village of **Villa Catedral**, at the foot of the bowl, is the starting-point for a couple of fantastic treks up and around Cerro Catedral, though you could just take a cable car and then a chairlift to reach Refugio Lynch near the summit (1870m; 10am–5.30pm). Views from here and from the ridge above are superb, and you just might catch a glimpse of condors. Experienced hikers can follow the ridge southwest; it later forks either to Refugio San Martín or to Refugio Frey. From here an easy descent leads back to Villa Catedral (see box, pp.452–453).

In winter (July is the busiest month), the village becomes the main **ski resort** (Ⓦwww.catedralaltapatagonia.com). Cerro Catedral boasts comfortable lifts and excellent access to the après-ski in Bariloche. There are 67km of runs in all, some with descents of up to 4km in length. Buses (marked "Catedral") leave from Moreno 470 in Bariloche to Villa Catedral; alternatively, you could take a half-day organized trip to the village (4hr 30min).

Lagos Gutiérrez and Mascardi and Cerro Tronador

The RN-258 heads south from Bariloche past handsome **Lago Gutiérrez** to the southernmost point on **Lago Mascardi**, where a dirt road strikes west around the lakeshore and you must pay a $30 park entrance fee. Further along, at Los Rápidos (where there's an organized campground), the road forks, and you can go west along the southern Río Manso to Lago Hess and Cascada de los Alerces or north towards **Pampa Linda**. The latter route has terrific views of the glaciers on **Cerro Tronador**. Both roads here become single-track, necessitating a timetable for travelling in each direction. To Cascada de los Alerces, you can drive east to west 8–10.15am, returning 11.15am–1pm. After 2pm the road is open to traffic in both directions. For Cerro Tronador, you can enter 10.30am–2pm and return 4–6pm, after which the road reverts to double direction. Tours increasingly miss out the Cascada de los Alerces fork and waterfall – a 20m plunge of white water that is said to resemble a seated nineteenth-century lady with her dress spread out.

Organized trips take you past Pampa Linda as far as the Ventisquero Negro lookout, a moraine-encrusted glacier and offshoot of Glaciar del Manso on the upper slopes of Cerro Tronador. You may also have time for the short walks to the fifty-metre-high Saltillo de las Nalcas or Garganta del Diablo and there are plenty of hiking options from Pampa Linda (see box, pp.452–453). Day-tours are run by several travel agents, with some also offering the possibility of a boat trip on Lago Mascardi, though you should consult about availability at the tourist office in advance.

Isla Victoria and Puerto Blest

A very popular boat trip within the park heads to **Isla Victoria** from **Puerto Pañuelo** (see p.451; daily 10.30am–5.30pm or 2–7pm; transfer and park entrance fees not included), where there are rock paintings, beaches and a chairlift to Cerro Bella Vista with the requisite stunning views. The boat continues north to the Parque Nacional de los Arrayanes.

Equally worthwhile, and much less crowded, is the boat-and-bus excursion to **Puerto Blest** in the western fringes of the Parque Nacional Huapi, which takes in lake vistas along the way and starts with a 75-minute boat trip from Puerto Pañuelo. A minibus continues the trip to the shores of Lago Frías, with its peppermint-coloured waters. During the early morning and late afternoon you can see condors gathering at their nearby roost. Returning to Puerto Blest, the boat crosses the channel to dock on the north shore after which there is a forty-minute stroll to the stepped Cascada Los Cántaros waterfall.

Villa La Angostura

Spread along the northern lakeshore of Nahuel Huapi, **VILLA LA ANGOSTURA** has grown enormously in the past decade, capitalizing on the Lake District's surging popularity. The settlement originally swelled owing to its proximity to the trout-fishing at Río Correntoso, one of the world's shortest rivers, but today caters mostly to upper-end tourists, with whole new areas of wooded hills giving way to luxury hotels, cabins and spas. The almost ubiquitous and somewhat forced log-cabin architecture gives the town a clichéd feel, rather like a mountain village theme park, and may not be to everyone's taste. There is some top-notch accommodation, however, and even some budget options, though these are in a minority; this is a place to show off designer outdoor wear rather than trudge around with a rucksack.

For those not into fly-fishing or luxury lodges, the main reason for visiting Villa La Angostura is that it provides the only land access to **Parque Nacional Los Arrayanes** (see p.457) plus a couple of useful boat trips that save you time if not money. The park is reached by crossing the isthmus at **La Villa**, a 3km-long peninsula west of the centre – the old harbour. In winter, there's skiing on the slopes of **Cerro Bayo**, 10km east from the centre, while in summer you can get good views from the summit; you can hike up but you'll need a guide – ask at the tourist office. Another good local hike (or short drive) is to **Mirador Belvedere** and Cascada Inacayal, a delightful waterfall, both along the southeast shore of Lago Correntoso.

Arrival, orientation and information

The town sprawls along the lakeside and is split into six barrios; the two most northerly – **Villa Correntoso** and **Epulaufquen** – overlook Lago Correntoso. You pass through the two southerly barrios, **Las Balsas** and **Puerto Manzano**, on the approach from Bariloche. The town centre is known as **El Cruce** and west of here is **La Villa**, which provides access to the park. The RN-231 is known as Avenida Arrayanes as it transects the town; everything you are likely to need during your stay is concentrated in a 200m stretch between Boulevard Nahuel Huapi and Cerro Bayo. The **bus station** (℡02944/494961) is just off Avenida Arrayanes at Avenida

The huemul (Hippocamelus bisculus)

If you spend any time in the Argentine Lake District it won't be long before you hear talk of the almost legendary **huemul**. This little deer, which stands 1m at the shoulder, was declared a "National Monument" in 1996 in response to an alarming decline in population. A secretive denizen of high Patagonian forests, it once played an important role in the livelihood of indigenous groups who relied on it for food and often depicted it in cave paintings. The arrival of the Europeans and their firearms had disastrous consequences for the remarkably tame species, and there are even tales about them being killed with knives after having been approached to a few metres. With the increasing destruction of their forest habitat, their numbers declined rapidly and today only an estimated six hundred remain in Argentina. Your best chance of glimpsing one is in winter, when harsh weather may drive them down to lower altitudes and more open areas in search of food. One of the likeliest locations to spy a huemul is near Playa El Francés on the northeastern shore of Lago Futaleufquen in the Parque Nacional Los Alerces – but even there you'll need luck on your side.

The *huemul* shows a series of adaptations to its tough environment, possessing a thick, dense coat to protect against the cold and short strong legs that help it gain a foothold on rocky slopes. They are also remarkably good swimmers, and can cross lakes and rivers with ease.

Siete Lagos, with the **tourist office** opposite (daily summer 8am–10pm; winter 9am–8.30pm; ☎02944/494124, ⓦwww.villalaangostura.gov.ar), which can help find accommodation if you haven't made reservations in advance. Empresa 15 de Mayo (☎02944/495104) runs seven daily buses between La Villa and El Cruce (last return 8.45pm), while a **city tour** leaves from the bus station daily at 2.30pm (☎02944/495251). You can **hire kayaks** and **bikes** from Aventura Maxima at the port building on Playa Mansa (☎02944/495545). **Fishing** can be organized through Bananafly, at Avenida Arrayanes 282 (☎02944/494634) and **horseriding** with Cabalgatas Correntoso, at Cacique Antriao (☎02944/15510559).

Accommodation

The most affordable **accommodation** tends to be in El Cruce, with more upmarket choices in the northern and southern suburbs – prices increase as the lake view improves. There are a few decent **hostels**, the best and most central of which is the modern and tastefully designed *Hostel La Angostura*, two blocks from the bus station at Barbagelata 157 (☎02944/494834, ⓦwww.hostellaangostura.com.ar; $60 per person), which has four- to six-bed dorms, two double rooms (④) and a pleasant communal area. The most convenient **campsite** is *Camping Unquehué* (☎02944/494103; $35 per person), 500m west of the bus terminal at Avenida Siete Lagos 727. *Camping Cullunche* (☎02944/494160; $30 per person) is closest to the **port**, 2km down Boulevard Quetrihue, a signposted northwest turn-off from Boulevard Nahuel Huapi in Barrio La Villa.

Las Balsas Bahía Las Balsas s/n ☎02944/494309, ⓦwww.lasbalsas.com. Part of the Relais et Chateaux group, Las Balsas epitomizes Angostura, renowned for its sybaritic qualities: beautiful rooms, a relaxing spa and a perfect location, though the restaurant is disappointing. ⑧

Correntoso Av Siete Lagos 4505 ☎02944/156-19728, ⓦwww.correntoso.com. Overlooking Río Correntoso, the settlement's original fishing lodge, dating from 1917, was completely renovated before reopening in 2003. Making the most of its spectacular setting, the *Correntoso*'s historic charm, created by abundant natural light and highly tasteful decor, mixes well with its modern services, which include a herbal spa and gourmet restaurant. ⑨

La Escondida Av Arrayanes 7014 ☎02944/475218, ⓦwww.hosterialaescondida .com.ar. Exquisite hostería lounging in sumptuous grounds that slope down to the lakeside, where a

heated pool, loungers, kayaks, boats and even beds beckon. The rooms, named after typical Argentine game, are stylish in an understated fashion; each enjoys breathtaking views and is distinctly decorated and furnished. ⑦

Hostel del Francés Lolog 2057 ☎02944/155-64063, ⓦwww.lodelfrances.com.ar. A beautiful cabin with lake views and double rooms with wooden bathrooms 4km from the tourist office. ⑥

Rio Bonito Tora Topa 260 ☎02944/494110, ⓔriobonito@ciudad.com.ar. This spotlessly clean and pleasant *residencial* offers airy rooms, among the cheapest in town. ⑤

🏃 **Verena's Haus** Los Taiques 268 ☎02944/494467, ⓔverenashaus @infovia.com.ar. White, wooden-clad and homely establishment run with tender loving care. The breakfasts are excellent, with a selection of home-made breads, cakes and jams. Children under 12 not permitted. ⑥

Eating and drinking

Most of Villa La Angostura's **restaurants** are located along a two-hundred-metre stretch of the RN-231 in El Cruce. Prices are high by Argentine standards – don't expect much change from $100 per head for a full meal with wine – and the gentrification can be a bit over the top, but the quality of food is generally good.

Asador Loncomilla Arrayanes 176 ☎02944/155-59442. With high wooden ceilings hung with Spanish-style hams, this is an excellent place for a meat feast, particularly Patagonian lamb.

🍺 **La Encantada** Belvedere 69 ☎02944/495436. Great home-brewed beer and wood-fired artisanal pizzas served in a well-appointed cabin. Popular with locals – a sure sign that the prices are keener.

Estancia La Esperanza Av Siete Lagos next to bus station ⓉⒽ02944/488281. Excellent *parrilla* with meat brought fresh from the estancia of the same name. Also a good reasonably priced *menú del día*.

Hub Arrayanes 256 ⓉⒽ02944/495700. Trendy bar-restaurant with imaginative variations on a typically Patagonian theme. Live music some nights.

Lado Sur "Los Amigos" Los Taiques 55. The tables here have views over the restaurant's beautiful garden. Dishes include reasonably priced (by Angostura standards) wild boar and venison.

La Macarena Arrayanes 44 ⓉⒽ02944/494248. Set in an attractive "gingerbread house" building, *La Macarena* serves an evocatively named set of dishes such as "Sublime Bambi" and "Pasión por Ella".

Parque Nacional Los Arrayanes

A national park within another national park, **PARQUE NACIONAL LOS ARRAYANES** was specially created to protect the world's best stand of myrtle woodland, the **Bosque de los Arrayanes**, at the far tip of the Península Quetrihué, the narrow-necked peninsula jutting out from Barrio La Villa. Quetrihué, in Mapudungun, means "place of the *arrayanes*", and the peninsula is a legacy from the glaciation of the Pleistocene era, as its rock proved more resilient to erosion than that which surrounded it. It is now covered with forests of *coihue*, *radal* and uncommon species such as *palo santo* (different from the species found in the Chaco), which sports rich, glossy foliage and an ashy grey bark. These forests provide cover for native fauna such as Des Mur's Wiretail.

The **arrayán**, a member of the myrtle family, is a slow-growing tree characterized by flaky, cinnamon-coloured, paper-like bark and amazing spiralling trunks, which look rather like barley-sugar church columns. It can reach heights of up to 15m and live for three hundred years (although some specimens here may be as much as six hundred years old), and it only grows close to cool water. The canopy of the *arrayán* is made up of delicate glossy clusters of foliage, and in late summer it flowers in dainty white blossoms, with the edible blue-black berries maturing in autumn.

The Bosque can be reached by hiking or cycling from La Villa (12km one way), or by boat from La Villa or Bariloche. Last entry into the park is at 2pm if arriving by land or 4.30pm if arriving by boat. Boulevard Nahuel Huapi terminates in La Villa with the stretch that connects the two bays on either side of the peninsula's narrow neck: **Bahía Mansa** ("Peaceful Bay"), on the eastern side, is where you'll find the **Intendencia** (daily 8am–8pm; ⓉⒽ02944/494152) of the park and the Puerto Angostura **jetty** for boats to the Bosque; and **Bahía Brava** ("Wild Bay") on the western side, which is used only by fishing boats. The park **entrance** ($30) is halfway between the two.

If you're **hiking**, count on a five- to six-hour return trip. Start early (the park opens at 8am) to enjoy the wildlife of the peninsula and avoid most of the crowds. The first twenty minutes, when you climb steeply to the lookout, is by far the hardest part. If you go by mountain bike (3–4hr return trip), you'll have to push it up this initial section but you should be able to get to the myrtle forest before the first boat arrives. Greenleaf (ⓉⒽ02944/494004) runs three daily **catamaran excursions** year-round (10.30am, 2pm and 5pm). In January and February they get very busy, so book in advance. The Bosque is open till 7pm and there's a *guardaparque* post and a *cafetería* here.

When seen from the lake, the Bosque doesn't look much different from the surrounding forest – it's when you're underneath the canopy that its magic envelops you. The much-told story that Walt Disney took his inspiration for the forest scenes in *Bambi* from this enchanted woodland is apocryphal (he actually took it from photographs of birch forests in Maine), but that doesn't much matter as the place certainly does have a fairytale feel, as you walk around

The classic **Ruta de los Siete Lagos** ("Seven Lakes Route") connects **Villa La Angostura** with **San Martín de los Andes** (see p.473) in spectacular fashion, passing through forested valleys and giving access to many more than the eponymous seven lakes, which are lagos Nahuel Huapi, Espejo, Correntoso, Escondido, Villarino, Falkner and Machónico. You'll also pass several fishing spots – buy permits before setting off (from tourist offices, YPF stations or campsites). The route is mostly paved, but be warned that the unsealed section – between Lago Espejo and Lago Villarino – can get extremely dusty, especially in summer. El Ko-Ko and Albus run daily bus services along the route between Villa La Angostura and San Martín. Many agencies in San Martín offer trips along the route, including 7 Lagos Turismo, at Gral Roca 826 (☎02972/427877), and Chapelco Turismo, San Martín 876 (☎02972/427550). Birdwatching tours are available with AvesPatagonia (☎02972/422022, ⓦwww.avespatagonia.com.ar), and fishing with Fly-fishing 3x (☎02972/422216). See also travel operators in Bariloche, listed on p.448.

Soon after leaving Angostura, the paved RN-231 crosses Río Correntoso, famous for its fishing and, at barely 250m long, one of the planet's shortest rivers; the road then skirts the northernmost tip of **Lago Nahuel Huapi**, by far the largest lake on the route. Beside the T-junction where you turn into the RN-234, the winding road that takes you all the way to San Martín, is tidy, cosy *Hostería Lago Espejo* (☎02944/494583; mid-Dec to Easter; ⓪), with well-appointed rooms and fantastic views; the beach bar and restaurant are open to non-residents. You quickly sight **Lago Espejo** ("Looking-glass" lake), renowned as the warmest and smoothest (hence the name) lake hereabouts. Alongside the Seccional Espejo *guardaparque* post is a free campsite, by a beach that's good for swimming. Just before the *guardaparque*'s house is another campground, with spacious pitches and a beach, while opposite is an easy forest trail (30min) through the woods to an isolated spot on the western shore of magical **Lago Correntoso**. Beyond here you trace Lago Correntoso's northern shores and pass the excellent *Hostería Siete Lagos* (no phone, reservations on ☎02944/494218; $45 per person). The cabin is the home of one of the area's original indigenous families who, apart from lodging, offer *tortas fritas*, meals and provisions, and run the lakeshore campground. After the road swings sharply north you'll reach the RP-65 turn-off via the Portezuelo pass to Lago Traful (see below). You then pass through a magnificent valley with sheer cliffs towering over 600m. It's worth stopping at the signposted track to a series of five waterfalls known collectively as Cascadas

the 600m **boardwalk** at your leisure while the contorted corkscrew trunks creak against each other in the breeze and the light plays like a French Impressionist's dream.

Lago Traful

A popular destination for trout and salmon fishermen, **LAGO TRAFUL** is a pure, intense blue, like a pool of liquid Roman glass. It's best accessed along the RP-65, which follows its entire southern shore, with the most beautiful approach from the Ruta de los Siete Lagos (see box above), crossing the pass of El Portezuelo and heading through the **Valle de los Machis** (with its majestic *coihue* trees), beneath the heights of Pico Traful (2040m).

Midway along the lake on the RP-65 is **Villa Traful**, a loose assemblage of houses spread out along several kilometres of the shoreline. Five kilometres east of the village on the RP-65 is a particularly impressive lookout point: the **Mirador Pared del Viento** (or Mirador del Traful), a precipitous rock-face with superb views over the azure waters 75m below.

Ñivinco. Reaching them involves an easy 2km walk through *ñire* and *caña colihue* forest, but you'll get your feet (and possibly knees) wet when you ford the river.

Further north is pint-sized **Lago Escondido**, the most enchanting of all the lakes, hiding its emerald-green charms demurely in the forest. Before crossing the limpid waters of Río Pichi Traful, you pass through Seccional Villarino (8am–8pm), where the *guardaparque* will give you information on recommended walks, such as the trek up Cerro Falkner. Some 2km down a bumpy track is a pleasant fisherman's campsite on the Brazo Norte (northern arm) of Lago Traful.

About halfway along the route, *Hostería Lago Villarino* (℡02972/427483; closed April–Oct; ⑥) is a 1940s lodge with characterful rooms and cosy fireplaces, and bungalows for up to six people. There are excellent horseriding possibilities in the vicinity, and it's possible to rent mountain bikes and fishing boats. A four-hour trail to the summit of Cerro Falkner, which has views of Volcán Lanín, starts about 150m from the *hostería*. Continuing north you come to the eastern point of **Lago Villarino**, a popular place for fishing, with Cerro Crespo (2130m) as a picturesque backdrop and a free lakeside campground. On the other side of the main road, **Lago Falkner** is a perennial favourite of fishermen, sitting at the foot of **Cerro Falkner** (2350m). The beautiful lakeside *Camping Lago Falkner* has a small shop, toilets and showers ($15 per person). Just to the north of Lago Falkner you pass Cascada Vulliñanco, a 20m waterfall to the west of the road.

Well into Parque Nacional Lanín, the next landmark you come to is the excellent and beautifully located *Refugio Lago Hermoso* (℡02972/425290 or 02944/155-69176, ⓦwww.refugiolagohermoso.com; open Nov–Easter), offering B&B, half-board and full-board stays in a charming rustic lodge with double, triple and quadruple rooms (⑥) as well as horseriding, canoeing and fishing. A short detour west from the junction here leads to Lago Hermoso itself, where you'll find the *Lago Hermoso* campsite (mid-Dec to Feb; $20 per person), which sells provisions and has showers. Just a few metres further on is the basic *Refugio Winka Mawida* (no phone, ⓦhwinkamawida.tripod.com/id2.html; summer only) with one twelve-bed dorm ($60 per person) and a three-person *cabaña* (⑤). Back on the RN-234 you then skirt the eastern shore of **Lago Machónico** and, in the final meanders of the route, you pass through handsome *ñire* and *coihue* woods. Make sure you stop at the Mirador de Pil Pil to take in the superb panorama of mighty Lago Lácar, whose waters lap San Martín de los Andes, the route's northern terminus.

Set back from the village's main jetty, a **guardaparque post** (daily 9am–8pm; ℡02944/479033) can provide you with information on local hikes – register with them before setting out. Trekking options include hikes to various waterfalls, climbing **Cerro Negro** behind the village (1999m; 7–9hr) or making a trip to **Laguna Las Mellizas** on the northern side of the lake to see indigenous rock paintings. You'll need to hire a boat for the fifteen-minute crossing, preferably with a driver who can also guide you through the multiple tracks to the paintings (5hr return); the *Hostería Villa Traful* (see below) can often put you in contact with someone. To the east of the village, near the YPF **fuel station**, is the **tourist office** (daily 9am–9pm; ℡02944/479099). As well as advising on accommodation, they sell fishing permits and have information on fishing guides.

The village's only **hotel** as such is homely *Hostería Villa Traful* (℡&℻02944/479005; ⑥; closed Easter to mid-Nov), which also rents out cabins all year for up to four people ($300 per cabin). *La Vulcanche* (℡02944/494015, ⓦwww.vulcanche.com) is a pleasant budget **hostel** with dorm rooms ($60 per person) and a **campsite** ($25) in addition to double rooms (④) and good-value cabins ($250 for 4 people). *Camping Costa Traful*, near the tourist office

(℡02944/479049, ⊛www.interpatagonia.com/costatraful; $25 per person), also has cabins (Ⓒ). More scenic is the free *Paloma Araucana* site (no facilities), by the foot of the Mirador Pared del Viento. Ten kilometres out of town to the west is another lakeshore campsite: *Cataratas* has only basic services ($15 per person; closed Feb to mid-Nov) but is near a beautiful waterfall.

In Villa Traful a popular tearoom and **restaurant**, *Ñancú Lahuen* (℡02944/479017), serves high-quality chocolates and cakes, as well as pasta and trout. Turismo Traful (no phone) runs half-day trips to the Valle Encantado (see p.335), **boat excursions** and **horseriding**. The latter can also be done with Eco Traful (℡02944/479139, Ⓔecotraful@yahoo.com.ar). Mountain **bikes** can be rented at Del Montaña, signposted off the main road.

El Bolsón

The 123km trip southwards along the RN-258 from Bariloche to **EL BOLSÓN** offers yet more stunning mountain and lake views. Just inside Río Negro province and set in the bowl of a wide, fertile valley, hemmed in by parallel ranges of mountains, El Bolsón is a thriving tourist centre with numerous trekking opportunities close at hand. It was Latin America's first town to declare itself nuclear free and an "ecological municipality". Owing to the claim that the jagged peak of the nearby **Cerro Piltriquitrón** is one of the earth's "energy centres", El Bolsón became a popular hippy hangout in the 1960s, and while it's a bit more commercial these days, the laidback atmosphere persists. In summer it's particularly popular with young Argentine backpackers, since it's far easier on the wallet than nearby Bariloche. Spiritual life in El Bolsón is cosmopolitan, and you'll find Buddhist temples as well as a variety of practitioners of alternative paths. Unsurprisingly, UFOs and spirits (*duendes*) are also said to stop off regularly, being guaranteed an especially sympathetic reception on the last Saturday of February, when the town's main party, the **Fiesta del Lúpulo** (Hops Festival), is held. It celebrates the harvest of an important local crop (and in particular the heady brew made from it), with music in the main square and an enjoyable, well-lubricated atmosphere. The **Olimpiadas Agrarias** (Farm Olympics) is another offbeat festival worth checking out, occurring over four days in mid-February, with ox races and other oddities. More refined, the town's **Jazz Festival** (⊛www.elbolsonjazz.com.ar) is held over a long weekend in early December. Also worth visiting is the **crafts market** (Tues, Thurs & Sat) on the **Plaza Pagano**, famous throughout the Lake District for the quality of its merchandise, including locally brewed beers. A small **ornithological museum** (daily 8am–3pm; $5) two blocks east of the plaza, on Saavedra and Feliciano, features over one hundred exhibits of stuffed Patagonian birds.

East of town, on the wooded slopes of **Cerro Piltriquitrón** (2260m), is another unconventional and interesting site – the **Bosque Tallado** (Sculpted Forest) – 31 tree stumps carved by local craftsmen into a variety of fascinating and often grotesque figures. You'll need to take a taxi to the base of the Cerro, but there is a forty-minute uphill walk before you get there. If dairy products float your boat, head to Humas (Mon–Fri 9am–1pm & 3–9pm, Sat 9am–1pm) on Camino los Nagales, signposted from Avenida San Martín north of the plaza. Here you can learn all about the making of organic yogurt, cheese and ice cream on one of the two daily guided tours (10am & 12.30pm)

Arrival and information

Arriving from the north, the RN-258 is called Avenida Sarmiento; its southern end is called Avenida Belgrano. These two converge on the ACA fuel station in the centre of town on **Avenida San Martín**, the town's backbone. Local **buses** drop you off at their respective offices, most of which are on or just off Avenida Sarmiento. On the north side of the plaza, at the corner of San Martín and Roca, is the useful **tourist office** (Mon–Sat 8am–11pm, Sun 9am–11pm; ☏02944/492604, ⊛www.bolsonturistico.com.ar), with the **post office** opposite (Mon–Fri 8.30am–1pm). If you come in a car it's worth filling your tank – fuel is cheaper in El Bolsón than in nearby localities. **Taxis** can be hard to find, though, and should be booked in advance: try Remises Patagonia (☏02944/493907). Fran's Remises (☏02944/493041) offers return services to local attractions such as Cascada Escondida and Bosque Tallado.

Accommodation

El Bolsón has no shortage of **accommodation** choices, particularly the more inexpensive variety, many of which are within walking distance of Plaza Pagano. Leafy *La Chacra* **campsite**, at Belgrano 1128 (☏02944/492111; $12 per person), is close to the centre, less than fifteen minutes' walk down the RN-258 towards Esquel.

Albergue Gaia 7km north of the centre ☏02944/492143, ⊛www.alberguegaia.com.ar. A stellar hostel, the airy, ecologically minded *Gaia* boasts laundry facilities, a swimming pool and a kitchen. Take a Transporte Urbano bus to Km118 on the RN-258. ❷

Albergue El Pueblito ☏02944/493560, ⊛www .elpueblitohostel.com.ar. The well-run, HI-affiliated *El Pueblito* is 4km north of the centre. Take a Transporte Urbano bus or a taxi to get there. ❶

Cabañas Paraiso at access to Cerro Piltriquitrón ☏02944/492766, ⊛www.cabaniaparaiso.com.ar. Ideally located for the Bosque Tallado.

Well-equipped cabins for up to six people. The staff can organize rafting, trekking and horseriding excursions. ❺

Hosteria Valle Nuevo 25 de May and Berutti ☏02944/492087. Small but clean, bright rooms with stunning mountain views. Well maintained (and renovated in 2009) with excellent customer care – there are even fire escapes. ❺

La Posada de Hamelín Granollers 2179 ☏02944/492030, ⊛www.posadadehamelin .com.ar. In town, *La Posada de Hamelín* is in a lovely brick building with hops growing up the walls and adobe interiors to some rooms. ❺

Eating, drinking and nightlife

El Bolsón is one of the few towns in Argentina where finding vegetarian **food** is not a problem. The valleys around are chock-a-block with *chacras* or smallholdings that produce organic vegetables, and fruits and berries for jams or desserts; local honey and cheeses are also good. *Calabaza*, at San Martín 2518, offers some appetizing vegetarian dishes, including cheese *milanesas*, and maintains a pioneering feel; it doesn't overcharge either. Next door, at *Cerro Lindo*, you'll find an imaginative menu that includes rabbit and wild boar, though the prices reflect the higher quality. For the less adventurous, *Boulevard*, at the corner of San Martín and Hube, has a relaxed atmosphere and does superb pizza at bargain rates. Next to the tourist office, *Jauja* (☏02944/492448) is a Patagonian restaurant, ice-cream parlour and artisanal chocolate shop all in one; the ice cream, especially the red fruits flavours, is fantastic.

The in-crowd tend to hang out at *Dos Ruedas* on San Martín, while those preferring a quieter **drink** go across the road to the more chilled *Boulevard* or a scattering of open-air, summer-only bars around the plaza. There are a couple of discos – *Barr* and *Insomnia* – on Dorrego a block north of Plaza Pagano. *El Bolsón Brewery* (Mon–Sat 9am–midnight, Sun 10am–10pm; ⊛www.cervezaselbolson.com) is outside town at Km124 on the main road north. Here the aficionado owner serves up a variety of beers, including fruity brews (an acquired taste, but if you like the similar ales from Belgium, you'll love these). Free guided tours of the brewery are given on Tuesday, Thursday and Saturday afternoons.

Trekking and other outdoor activities

The Club Andino Piltriquitrón (CAP; daily 9am–9pm mid-Dec to Easter ⓣ02944/492600), at Roca and Sarmiento, can guide you through **trekking** possibilities in the area, most of which consist of considerable ascents – they will also mind your bags for you for a small fee. Among the most popular is the **Cerro Hielo Azul Circuit** (4–6hr), which brings you high enough to present glacier vistas. Further north you can make side treks to less visited areas of **Cerro Dedo Gordo** (4–5hr) and **Los Laguitos** (6–8hr). To the south, the hike to *Refugio Cerro Lindo* (5–7hr) takes in the lake of the same name with beautiful blue waters encased by sheer cliffs. Another interesting, relatively gentle hike to **Cajón Azul** (4–5hr) starts from the same point as Dedo Gordo and passes an excellent *refugio* that serves hot food. The Cajón (gorge) itself is an opening one metre wide and forty metres deep; the Río Azul roars through the bottom. CAP sells a Spanish-language guidebook, *Ingreso a los Refugios*, detailing local hikes.

Local tour operators offer a variety of excursions and day-trips, most incorporating a mix of horseriding, trekking, rafting and boating. Particularly good is Grado 42, at Avenida Belgrano 404 (ⓣ02944/493124, ⓦwww.grado42.com), which offers tours to the Bosque Tallado and Butch Cassidy's cabin near Cholila.

Cholila and around

Sitting amid prairie grasslands, 3km east of the junction of the RP-71 and the RP-15, the hamlet of **CHOLILA**, with its spectacular backdrop of savage peaks, seems to belong in the American West. The area's main tourist attraction lies 12km north of the village itself along the RP-71 towards Leleque. When you reach the police commissionaire's white house (with Argentine flag flying) at El Blanco, turn left down the track towards *La Casa de Piedra* teahouse. Fifty metres down this lane, there's a basic sign for Cabañas Butch Cassidy (with a confusing arrow); jump the fence and head parallel to the RP-71. After 200m you'll see a cluster of three buildings among trees ahead. This is the site of the **cabin** of **Butch Cassidy**, who fled incognito to this isolated area at the start of the twentieth century with his partner, the **Sundance Kid**, who also lived here for a short while with his beautiful gangster moll, **Etta Place**. The buildings were already in a lamentable state of repair when Bruce Chatwin (*In Patagonia*) visited in the 1970s and were about to collapse when the local authorities finally set about restoration in 2007 – overdoing the job, to some tastes; the site is nevertheless of utmost interest for Wild West fans.

Cholila's **bus terminal** is on the main square (ⓣ02945/498173). Comfortable, roomy **lodging** is available at tranquil *Hostería El Trebol*, 2.7km from the terminal along the RP-15 (ⓣ02945/498055, ⓦwww.interpatagonia/hosteriatrebol/; ❺), which offers a half-board option. From Cholila, you can continue southwest through a glorious lush valley hemmed in by snowcapped mountains towards the northern gate of Parque Nacional Los Alerces (see p.470). Before the park entrance at Villa Lago Rivadavia, 16km from Cholila, there are a number of good-quality, good-value cabins for rent including *Cabañas Carrileufú* (ⓣ02944/527851, ⓦwww.cabcarrileufu.com.ar; ❺) and *Cabañas Wanalen* (ⓣ02945/498174, ⓦwww.cabanaswanalen.com.ar; ❹).

Leleque

A couple of kilometres off the RN-40 along a track that leads eastwards from the RP-15 turn-off to Cholila, **LELEQUE** is an estancia lying within the Benetton

▲ Horse riders at Cholila

estate, one of the largest private properties in the country. The only part of the estancia open to the public is the fabulous **Museo Leleque** (Thurs–Tues: Jan & Feb 11am–7pm; March, April, July, Aug, Oct & Dec 11am–5pm; ℡02945/455151; $5), housed in a beautifully restored outbuilding. The handsome exhibits spread over four rooms trace the history of the indigenous peoples, local pioneers and the relations between them by means of a collection of memorabilia collected by the late Pablo Korscheneweski, born in Odessa in 1925. The highlight, though, is the *boliche* – a typical rural inn combined with general store and canteen, where you can have a drink and something to eat while admiring a set of remarkably well-preserved old bric-a-brac. Save some money for the excellent museum catalogue.

Esquel and around

Heading south beyond Cholila and Leleque you'll notice a distinct change in the scenery, as the lush pine forests are replaced by drier terrain that is home to the stunted *meseta*-style vegetation more typical of Patagonia proper. Some 90km south of the Cholila/Leleque turn-off, **Esquel**, the main town in the area, is a starting-point for visits to **Parque Nacional Los Alerces**, as well as a scattering of Welsh villages of which **Trevelin** is the most appealing. This is also the stage through which the steam train **La Trochita**, one of the region's most enduring attractions, plies its trade.

Esquel

For a place so close to exuberant Andean forests, **ESQUEL**, 180km south of El Bolsón, is surprising for the aridity of its setting. Enclosed in a bowl of dusty ochre mountains, it is a stark contrast to Bariloche and El Bolsón. The town itself is

Butch Cassidy, Etta Place and the **Sundance Kid** were fugitives together in the Argentine frontier town of Cholila between the years 1901 and 1906, as attested by both the Pinkerton Agency and provincial records of the time. Butch and Sundance had begun to grow weary of years of relentless pursuit, and had heard rumours that Argentina had become the new land of opportunity, offering the type of wide-open ranching country they loved, and where they could live free from the ceaseless hounding of Pinkerton agents.

It appears that, at first, the *bandidos* tried to go straight, even living under their real names – Butch as "George Parker" (an old alias derived from his name at birth, Robert Leroy Parker), and Etta and Sundance as Mr and Mrs Harry Longabaugh – and in this they succeeded, for a while at least. They were always slightly distant from the community and were evidently viewed as somewhat eccentric, yet decent, individuals. Certainly no one ever suspected they had a criminal past.

Various theories are mooted as to why the threesome sold their ranch in such a rush in 1907, but it seems as though the arrival of a Wild Bunch associate, the murderous Harvey "Kid Curry" Logan, following his escape from a Tennessee jail, had something to do with it. The robbery of a bank in Río Gallegos in early 1905 certainly had the hallmarks of a carefully planned Cassidy job, and a spate of robberies along the cordillera in the ensuing years have, with varying degrees of evidence, been attributed to the *bandidos norteamericanos*.

What happened to Cholila's outlaws next is a matter of conjecture. Etta returned to the US, putatively because she needed an operation for acute appendicitis, but equally possibly because she was pregnant, as a result of a dalliance with a young Anglo–Irish rancher. The violent deaths of Butch and Sundance were reported in Uruguay, and in several sites across Argentina and Bolivia. The least likely scenario is the one depicted by Paul Newman and Robert Redford in the famous 1969 Oscar-winning film. Bruce Chatwin in his classic *In Patagonia* proposes that the Sundance Kid was shot by frontier police in Río Pico, south of Esquel. Countless books have been written on the trio, including *In Search of Butch Cassidy*, by Larry Pointer, and most recently *Digging Up Butch and Sundance*, by Anne Meadows.

pretty drab and uninteresting – most people make the trip to access the nearby **Parque Nacional Los Alerces** (see p.468), with the trip on *La Trochita* (see box, p.466) as the next biggest attraction. If you're looking to kill some time in town, the **Museo de Arte Naif**, next to the post office on Avenida Alvear, hosts a display of pictures by local artists, charmingly child-like in their simplicity.

Some 13km northeast of Esquel is the **skiing** centre of **La Hoya** (@www .interpatagonia.com/lahoya/index.html), which often has snow lasting into mid-October. It has nine lifts, is good for powder and is promoted as a low-key family centre with moderately challenging pistes.

Arrival and information

The town's **airport** (@02945/451676) is 19km east of the centre; you can take a *remise* to town or a minibus run by Gales al Sur, who have a kiosk at the bus terminal (@02945/455757). The stylish **bus terminal** (@02945/451566) is on the main boulevard, **Avenida Alvear**, at no. 1871, about 1km from the town centre, while the *La Trochita* **train station** (see box, p.466) is at Roggero and Brun, nine blocks northeast of the terminal. The excellent **tourist office**, just past the post office, at Alvear and Sarmiento (daily Jan & Feb 7am–11pm; March–Dec 8am–10pm; @02945/451927, @www.esquel.gov.ar), operates a number system; get one as soon as you walk in. They can help you find accommodation if you haven't reserved.

Accommodation

There's a wide range of **accommodation** in town from a backpacker hostel to a couple of top range options, as well as cabins, most of which are two or three kilometres from the centre. Outside summer (Dec–Feb) and the skiing season (July & Aug) you'll get large discounts. The best **campsite** within easy reach of town, *Millalen*, Avenida Ameghino 2063 (☏02945/456164), has cabins (④) and a small camping area with individual pitches ($25 per person).

Canela Los Notros s/n ☏02945/453890, ⓦwww.canelaesquel.com.ar. Veronica and Jorge run a fabulous British-style B&B in a pleasant residential area a short way out of town. The tastefully decorated rooms are extremely comfortable, the house is charming – as are the hosts – and the breakfast will keep you up and running all day. ⑥

El Hogar del Mochilero Roca 1028 ☏02945/452166. Cheap but cheerful, and particularly popular with Argentine backpackers, *El Hogar* is much as you would expect from a hostel with dorm rooms and a camping area adjacent. ①

Hostería Angelina Alvear 758 ☏02945/452763. This comfortable, family-run *hostería* is modern with stone-clad walls and a fountain. Ask for a room at the back, as the front can be a bit noisy. ⑥

Hostería Cumbres Blancas Av Ameghino 1683 ☏02945/455100, ⓦwww.cumbresblancas .com.ar. A classy motel feel pervades this upmarket establishment. Large airy rooms come with free internet connection and safe, and there's a sauna and "Scottish shower" (lateral water jets). ⑧

Ibai Ko Mendi Rivadavia 2965 ☏02945/451503, ⓦwww.ibaikomendi .com.ar. Extremely attractive wood and stone cabins, plus delightful rooms in the main *hostería* building, all set in a tranquil complex that includes a pool and spa. ⑥

Lago Verde Volta 1081 ☏02945/452251, ⓦwww.patagonia-verde.com.ar. Peaceful and welcoming guesthouse (its family also runs the Patagonia Verde travel agency) with clean rooms

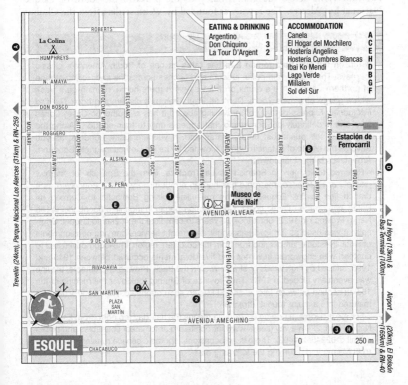

EATING & DRINKING
Argentino	1
Don Chiquino	3
La Tour D'Argent	2

ACCOMMODATION
Canela	A
El Hogar del Mochilero	C
Hostería Angelina	E
Hostería Cumbres Blancas	H
Ibai Ko Mendi	D
Lago Verde	B
Millalen	G
Sol del Sur	F

ESQUEL

La Colina

ROBERTS
HUMPHREYS
N. AMAYA
DON BOSCO
ROGGERO
A. ALSINA
R. S. PEÑA
9 DE JULIO
RIVADAVIA
SAN MARTÍN
PLAZA SAN MARTÍN
AVENIDA AMEGHINO
CHACABUCO

MOLINARI
DARWIN
PERITO MORENO
BARTOLOME MITRE
BELGRANO
25 DE MAYO
GRAL. ROCA
SARMIENTO
AVENIDA FONTANA
ALBERDI
ALTE. BROWN
VOLTA
PJE. URRUTIA
A. BRUN
URQUIZA

Estación de Ferrocarril

Museo de Arte Naif
AVENIDA ALVEAR

Trevelin (24km), Parque Nacional Los Alerces (31km) & RN-259

La Hoya (13km) & Bus Terminal (100m)
Airport (20km), El Bolsón (165km) & RN-40

0   250 m

465

overlooking a rose garden. Reserve in advance in high season. ❹

Sol del Sur 9 de Julio 1086 ⓣ02945/452189, Ⓦhttp://hsoldelsur.com.ar. A dependable mid-range choice, with standard, comfortable rooms and amenities (TV and fridge). Breakfast is included. ❻

Eating and drinking

It can be frustratingly difficult to find somewhere to eat in Esquel. Most **restaurant** owners close several days a week, shut in the afternoon, go off on long holidays in the summer and, when they are open, take last orders at midnight. If all else fails, there is a supermarket at Avenida Fontana and Sarmiento, where you can buy supplies to tide you over. One reliable restaurant is the decent *Don Chiquito* at Avenida Ameghino 1641 (ⓣ02945/450035), which serves tasty Italian food in a cosy atmosphere, though it gets packed in high season. Alternatively *La Tour d'Argent* at San Martín 1063 (ⓣ02945/454612; closed Tues in low season) offers cheap and filling menus of pastas and chicken, as well as a more adventurous, appetizing à la carte selection that includes trout with a variety of sauces. The best **bar** in town is in the *Hotel Argentino*, at 25 de Mayo 862 (ⓣ02945/452237).

Trevelin and around

The main Welsh settlement along the Andes (most of the Welsh towns in Patagonia are closer to the ocean), **TREVELIN** is a small, easy-going place that retains a pioneering feel, with several low brick buildings characteristic of the late nineteenth century and early twentieth. Lying 24km south of Esquel, it has beautiful views across the grassy valley to the peaks in the south of Parque Nacional Los Alerces. The town was founded by Welsh settlers from the Chubut

---

La Trochita: The Old Patagonian Express

A trip on the **Old Patagonian Express** rates as one of South America's classic journeys. The steam train puffs, judders and lurches across the arid, rolling steppe of northern Chubut, like a drunk on the well-worn route home, running on a track with a gauge of a mere 75cm. Don't let Paul Theroux's disparaging book *The Old Patagonian Express* put you off: travelling aboard it has an authentic Casey Jones aura and is definitely not something that appeals only to train-spotters. Along the way you'll see guanacos, rheas, maras and, if you are lucky, condors, as you traverse the estate of Estancia Leleque, owned by Italian clothes magnate Benetton, Argentina's biggest landowner.

Referred to lovingly in Spanish as **La Trochita**, from the Spanish for "narrow gauge", or *El Trencito*, the route has had an erratic history. It was conceived as a branch line to link Esquel with the main line joining Bariloche to Carmen de Patagones on the Atlantic coast. Construction began in Ingeniero Jacobacci in Río Negro Province in 1922, but it took 23 years to complete the 402km to Esquel. Originally, it was used as a mixed passenger and freight service, carrying consignments of wool, livestock, lumber and fruit from the cordillera region. The locomotives had to contend with snowdrifts in winter, and five derailments occurred between 1945 and 1993, caused by high winds or stray cows on the track. Proving unprofitable, the line was eventually closed in 1993. The Province of Chubut took over the running of the 165km section between Esquel and El Maitén soon afterwards, and *La Trochita* has matured into a major tourist attraction.

For most people, a ride on *La Trochita* means the half-day trip north from Esquel to Nahuel Pan, 22km away (see Ⓦwww.latrochita.org.ar for latest timetables and prices or call ⓣ02945/451403). There is an occasional sporadic service running the 165km to El Maitén and returning the following day.

Valley following a series of expeditions to this region that began in 1885 with a group led by Colonel Fontana of the Argentine army and John Evans. Its Welsh name means "village of the mill", and the vital **flour mill**, a stalwart brick structure dating from 1918, now forms the main museum in town, the **Museo Regional Molino Andes** or **El Viejo Molino** (daily 11am–6pm; $4). Well worth a visit, it displays clothing of the original colonists and even a combine harvester from circa 1900. By the entrance is a fascinating group photo of the 1902 plebiscite when the whole colony had to vote on whether it wanted to be Chilean or Argentine: those who want to know more should read *Down Where the Moon Is Small* by Richard Llewellyn, which is evocative in its recreation of the early years of the Welsh community here.

Another worthwhile attraction is **La Tumba de Malacara**, 200m northeast of the plaza (daily 4.30–7.30pm; $15), where Clery Evans, granddaughter of the village's founder John Evans, relates the origins of the settlement (knowing Spanish helps). In the garden is the **grave** of her granddad's faithful horse, El Malacara – who leapt heroically down a steep scarp to save his master from the same grisly fate that befell his companions. They had been killed by enraged Mapuche warriors who, following an atrocity committed against their tribe during the Campaign of the Desert, were bent on reprisals against any Europeans. The house attracts a steady stream of Bruce Chatwin pilgrims, as the story features in his classic travelogue, *In Patagonia* (see p.624).

The town's Welsh heritage is evoked in the celebration of a minor **Eisteddfod** (two days in the second week of October), and two **casas de té**, the better one being *Nain Maggie*, at Perito Moreno 179 (daily 3–10.30pm; ℡02945/480232): the teahouse is named after owner Lucia Underwood's grandmother, who was born in Trelew, came to Trevelin in 1891 and died in the town ninety years later at the age of 103.

Practicalities

The RN-259 from Esquel arrives at the octagonal Plaza Coronel Fontana at the north end of town, where you'll find the **tourist office** (daily 9am–8pm; ℡02945/480120). Gales Al Sur, Av Patagonia 186 (℡02945/480427, ⓦwww .galesalsur.com.ar), runs excursions to Los Alerces national park, horseriding trips and a full-day whitewater rafting trip on Río Corcovado; it also has **internet** access and public **telephones** available.

Although cabins are springing up on the outskirts there's not a lot of **accommodation** in town. Among the best is snug *Hostal Casaverde* (℡02945/480091, ⓦwww.casaverdehostel.com.ar; ❹), HI-affiliated and with laundry and kitchen facilities and a privileged view from its little hilltop up Los Alerces; it's off Avenida Fontana, five to ten minutes' walk from the plaza. *Ruca Ñancú*, John Daniel Evans and San Martín (℡02945/480427; ❺), is family-run, clean and spacious. Owner Alec Byrne is also a tour operator. *Hotel Estefania*, Perito Moreno s/n next to *Nain Maggie* (℡02945/480148; ❺; closed Sept & Oct), has inexpensive rooms for up to five and also serves meals. *Oregón*, on San Martín eight blocks south of the plaza (℡02945/480408, ⓦwww.oregontrevelin.com.ar; ❺), has good *cabañas* with a kitchen in an orchard. For those with **tents**, *Camping El Chacay* (℡02945/15681827; $25 per person), near the south end of San Martín – turn left one block beyond *Oregón* restaurant (see opposite) – with showers and a shop, has a rural feel and a decent view of the hills. Contact Gales Al Sur travel agency to take you to Refugio Wilson, in the countryside 7km away. This open-plan, cabin-style **refuge** has bunk-beds (with your own sleeping bag; ❶), or you can camp, as well as helpful advice on interesting hikes in the valley's foothills; concerts and other shows are held here on weekends.

The alerce (Fitzroya cupressoides)

Similar in appearance to the Californian redwood, the **alerce**, or Patagonian cypress, can reach heights of 57m and is one of the four oldest species of tree in the world. To the Mapuche it is *lahuán*, meaning "long-lived" or "grandfather", and the oldest specimens are an estimated four thousand years old. They grow in a relatively narrow band of the central Patagonian cordillera, on acidic soils by lakes and only in places where the annual rainfall exceeds 3000mm, so are more common on the wetter Chilean side of the Andes than in Argentina. Growth is extremely slow (0.8–1.2mm a year), and it takes a decade for a tree's girth to gain 1cm in diameter – though the trunk may eventually reach 3m across.

From the late nineteenth century onwards, the *alerce* was almost totally logged out by pioneers: the reddish timber is not eaten by insects and does not rot, so was highly valued for building, especially for roof shingles. Other uses included musical instruments, barrels, furniture, telegraph poles and boats. In Argentina, the only trees to survive the forester's axe were the most inaccessible ones, or those like El Abuelo, a titanic millennial specimen whose wood was bad in parts. In Argentina, a few stands exist north of Los Alerces, in Parque Nacional Lago Puelo and the Lago Frías area of Nahuel Huapi, and the trees that remain are generally well protected.

Restaurant choices are extremely limited but if it's a slap-up *parrilla* you want, head to *Oregón*, near the southern exit of the village at San Martín and Laprida. For a drink, *Zweli*, at Fontana and Perito Moreno, offers cold beers and an authentic taste of local life.

Parque Nacional Los Alerces

Established in 1937, the huge **PARQUE NACIONAL LOS ALERCES** protects some of the most biologically important habitats and scenic landscapes in the region. Its superb lakes are famous for both their rich colours and their fishing, while most have a backdrop of sumptuous forests that quilt the surrounding mountain slopes. In the northeast of the park these lakes form a network centred on **lagos Rivadavia**, **Menéndez** and **Futalaufquen**, whose waters drain south to the dammed reservoir of **Embalse Amutui Quimei**, and from here into the Río Futaleufú (also called Río Grande). The western two-thirds of the park up against the Andes are off-limits, being designated a "strict scientific reserve".

Though less spectacular than many of the region's mountains, some of the peaks along the two-thousand-metre ranges that divide the park are dramatic nonetheless, with rock colorations and cracked and craggy summits rising to 2300m in the **Cordón Situación** in the southeast. **Cerro Torrecillas** (2253m), in the north of the park, has the only glacier, but patches of snow can last into mid-summer on the upper peaks, where you'll also spot some remarkable high-altitude cloud formations.

The vegetation changes considerably as you move east from the Chilean frontier into the area affected by the rain shadow cast by the cordillera. Near the border, rainfall exceeds 3000mm a year, enough to support the growth of dense **Valdivian temperate rainforest** (*selva valdiviana*) and, most interestingly, the species for which the park is named: the **alerce**. The ground is dominated by bamboo-like *caña colihue*, while two species of flower are everywhere: the orange or white-and-violet *mutisias*, with delicate spatula-like petals, and the *amancay*, a golden-yellow lily growing on stems 50cm to 1m high. In contrast, the eastern margin of the park

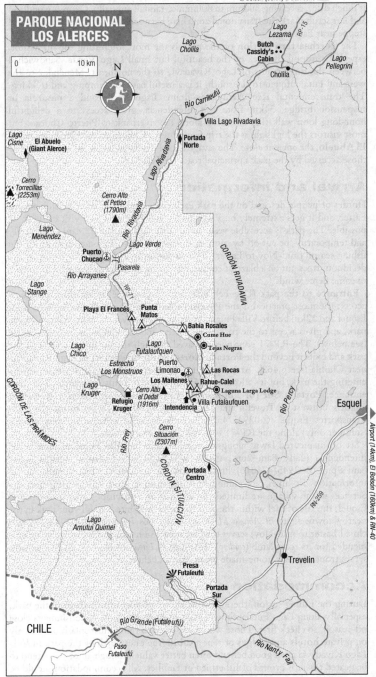

PARQUE NACIONAL
LOS ALERCES

0 — 10 km

N

Lago
Cholila

Lago
Lezama

Butch
Cassidy's
Cabin

Lago
Pellegrini

RP-15

Cholila

Río Carrileufú

Villa Lago Rivadavia

Portada
Norte

Lago
Cisne

El Abuelo
(Giant Alerce)

Cerro
Torrecillas
(2253m)

Cerro Alto
el Petiso
(1790m)

Río Rivadavia

Lago
Menéndez

Lago Verde

Puerto
Chucao

Pasarela

CORDÓN RIVADAVIA

Río Arrayanes

Lago
Stange

RP-71

Playa El Francés

Punta
Matos

Bahía Rosales
Cume Hue

Lago
Chico

Lago
Futalaufquen

Tejas Negras

Puerto
Limonao

Las Rocas

Estrecho
Los Monstruos

Los Maitenes

Rahue-Calel

Lago
Kruger

Cerro Alto
el Dedal
(1916m)

Laguna Larga Lodge

CORDÓN DE LAS PIRÁMIDES

Refugio
Kruger

Intendencia

Villa Futalaufquen

Esquel

Río Frey

Cerro
Situación
(2307m)

CORDÓN SITUACIÓN

Río Percy

Airport (14km), El Bolsón (160km) & RN-40

Lago
Amutui Quimei

Portada
Centro

RN-259

Presa
Futaleufú

Trevelin

Portada
Sur

CHILE

Río Grande (Futaleufú)

Río Nanty Fall

Paso
Futaleufú

7

BARILOCHE AND THE LAKE DISTRICT

is much drier, receiving 300mm to 800mm of rainfall annually. Cypress woodland and *ñire* scrub mark the transitional zone here between the wet forests and the arid steppe near Esquel.

The **northeastern section** of the park is the most interesting for the visitor, especially around the area of the beautiful but small **Lago Verde**. Sandwiched between the three giants of Lago Rivadavia to the northeast, Menéndez to the west and Futalaufquen to the south, it is a useful base for camping and trekking. The transcendental **Río Arrayanes** drains Lago Verde and a **pasarela** or suspension bridge, 34km from the intendencia, gives access to a delightful hour-long loop walk that takes you along the riverbank to Puerto Chucao. For most visitors the highlight is the trip from Puerto Chucao across Menéndez to see **El Abuelo**, the ancient *alerce*. The savage Lago Rivadavia area is the least visited of those accessed by the park's principal road, the RP-71.

Arrival and information

Hordes of people descend on the park each year, most from late November until Easter, and it gets extremely busy in January and February – so visit off-peak, if possible. The park is accessible year-round, although the RP-71 can, albeit rarely and temporarily, be cut off by snow, and most accommodation closes outside the fishing season (mid-Nov to Easter). The **autumn** months are perhaps best, as the deciduous trees put on a blaze of colour, but spring is also very beautiful, if subject to some fierce winds.

Entrance to the park (Dec–Feb $20, rest of year free) is via three points of access: the most practical is the **Portada Centro** (or "central gate"; 33km from Esquel and 12km before Villa Futalaufquen), which serves the central sector of the park, and gives access to the park headquarters and the useful information centre (see below). The RP-71 continues unpaved through the northeast corner of the park and exits it beyond the **Portada Norte**, by the headwaters of Lago Rivadavia near Cholila (see p.462). Arriving by the latter route is the most scenic way of entering the park, but it's a long way (55km) to the information centre. The third entrance, **Portada Sur (or Futaleufú)**, is in the southeast corner of the park, 14km southwest of Trevelin and 12km before the dam. To get round the park, Transportes Esquel (℡02945/453429) runs a useful twice-daily **bus** service (summer only) along the RP-71 between Esquel and Cholila.

Set on manicured lawns alongside the bus stop in **Villa Futalaufquen** is the intendencia (daily 8am–2pm; ℡02945/471020) and **visitors' centre** (daily 8am–9pm; ℡02945/471015), lurking amid fine araucarias, which supplies useful information on hikes, accommodation and fishing, and sells fishing permits. Services in the village are limited and all food and provisions are far cheaper in Esquel; the sale of fuel within the park has been prohibited, so fill your tank in the nearby towns first. *El Abuelo Monje* on Calle Los Retamos (℡02945/471029; closed Easter to mid-Nov) serves the best **meals** in town, and is especially recommended for its roast lamb (*cordero*). Tearoom *El Lugar del Lago* on Calle Corcolen serves trout and sells home-made bread, jam and cheese.

Accommodation

During the fishing season, there's a wide choice of **accommodation** in the park, especially along Lago Futalaufquen's eastern shore, but most establishments close off-season, so check first. Those who don't want to camp must splash out heavily on private **hotels** and **lodges** or rent a **cabin** (the ones north of the park in Villa Lago Rivadavia are a good bet and often better value), though all of these tend to be geared towards groups of fishermen or families. All accommodation should be reserved in advance, especially in summer. *Los Maitenes* (☎02945/451006; $25 per person; closed Easter to mid-Nov) is the closest **campsite** to Villa Futalaufquen (400m from the intendencia) and is generally good, although packed. On the other side of the road before the Río Desaguadero, *Rahue-Calel* is quieter, but doesn't front the lake ($18 per person). Of the free sites, avoid *Las Lechuzas* and head for lakeside *Las Rocas* (about 2km from the intendencia), which is cleaner, quieter and smaller, though more exposed. At Km21, *Punta Matos* is a small free site with excellent views and fine swimming, while nearby *Playa El Francés*, also free, has a good beach.

Complejo Bahía Rosales ☎02945/471044, ⓦwww.bahiarosales.alojar.com.ar. Roughly 14km from the *intendencia*, this complex includes a campsite with a shop and hot water ($25 per person); it rents out bikes, kayaks and horses and is the starting point of a boat trip to Lago Kruger. It also has twelve cabins for four people with kitchen facilities. ❹

Hostería Cume Hue ☎02945/453639. This pretty white house on the eastern shore of Lago Futalaufquen is popular with anglers and offers full-board packages. The delicious teas include home-made scones and fabulous jams made with local fruit ❼

Laguna Larga Lodge ☎02322/402231, ⓦwww.lagunalargalodge.com. Impeccably run by Andrés, an enthusiastic sports fisherman and lover of excellent wine and fine dining – hence the top-rate restaurant and enticing cellar – this secluded fishing lodge set on the shore of the attractive Laguna Larga is well worth the slightly difficult trip to get here (make sure you ask for clear directions when you book. ❾

Tejas Negras ☎02945/471012, ⓔtejasnegras @infovia.com.ar. Essentially a tearoom – serving memorable meriendas – it also has attractive cabins for rent all year round, which sleep up to four people comfortably. ❼

El Abuelo

The most popular excursion in the park is the lake trip ("Safari Lacustre") to the far end of Lago Menéndez's northern channel to see **El Abuelo** ("The Grandfather", also named *El Alerzal*), a gigantic *alerce* 2.2m in diameter, and 57m tall. This magnificent tree is an estimated 2600 years old, making it a sapling when Pythagoras and Confucius taught, but at the end of the nineteenth century it almost became roof shingles: only the fact that settlers deemed its wood rotten inside saved it from the saw. To see it you need to take a **boat trip**, the earliest leaving at 10am from Puerto Limonao, 3km north of the *intendencia*, with another from Puerto Chucao at noon, halfway round the Lago Verde/Río Arrayanes trail loop that starts at the *pasarela*. The earlier sailing crosses Lago Futalaufquen and goes down Río Arrayanes to Puerto Mermoud followed by a thirty-minute walk across the isthmus to meet up with the noon sailing at Puerto Chucao. The excursion is guided, but in Spanish only; if you want an English translation, you'll need to organize a tour from Esquel rather than just turn up at the pier. Either way, you should book in advance – boats are generally full in peak season and go only when demand is sufficient in low season. Both boats are run by Brazo Sur (☎02945/471008, ⓦwww.brazosur.com.ar/safari.htm).

On the ninety-minute trip across the pristine blue waters of **Lago Menéndez** you get fine views of the Cerro Torrecillas glacier, which is receding fast and may last only another seventy years. To get to El Abuelo, a three-kilometre trail takes you through dense Valdivian temperate rainforest (*selva valdiviana*), a habitat distinguished from the surrounding Patagonian forests by the presence of different layers to the canopy, in addition to the growth of lianas, epiphytes, surface roots and species more commonly found in Chile. Here a mass of vegetation is engaged in the eternal struggle of the jungle: height equals light. In addition to the *alerces*, look out for fuchsia bushes and *arrayanes* (see p.457). Despite its name **Lago Cisne** is no longer home to any Black-necked Swans; they were wiped out by mink.

Trekking in the park

There are 130km of **public trails** in the park, which are generally well maintained and marked at intervals with red spots. As always, you are required to **register** with the nearest *guardaparque* before setting off (remember to check back in afterwards), and some treks – such as El Dedal – are not recommended in winter or for those under 10 years old. In times of drought, some trails are closed, while others (including El Dedal) can only be undertaken with a guide. Bring plenty of water, sun protection, and adequate clothing as the weather changes rapidly and unseasonal snowfalls occur in the higher regions. Insect repellent is worthwhile, especially after several consecutive hot days in December and January, as that's when the fierce horseflies (*tábanos*) come out.

The most difficult part of the pastoral 500m **Pinturas Rupestres** circuit is the spring-loaded gate at the beginning. You pass eroded indigenous geometric designs painted about three thousand years ago on a hulk of grey rock that's surrounded by *caña colihue* and *maitén* trees; the lookout from the top of the rock affords a fine view. Longer walks include the **Cinco Saltos**, **El Cocinero** and **Cerro Alto El Petiso** in the north of the park, which is best accessed from Lago Verde and provides sterling vistas of the northern lakes. Another worthwhile trip is to the *hostería* and campsite at the southern end of **Lago Krugger**. This can be reached in a fairly stiff day's trekking, returning the same way or by launch the next day (cost depends on number of passengers). However, it's better to make it into a three- or four-day excursion. You can break the outward-bound trek by putting up a tent by the beautiful beach at Playa Blanca (about 8hr from the intendencia), but you must have previously obtained permission at the visitors' centre. Fires are strictly prohibited and there are no facilities.

The **El Dedal Circuit** is one of the most popular and convenient hikes in the park. It involves some fairly stiff climbs but you'll be rewarded with excellent panoramic views – ask the *guardaparque* about guides. Calculate on taking some six to seven hours (4hr up and 2–3hr down). Take the "Sendero Cascada" (which runs up behind the visitors' centre) for approximately 35 minutes through thick *maitén* and *caña colihue*, then take the signposted right-hand branch where the path forks. Further up, you enter impressive mature woodland. Approximately two hours into the walk, you climb above the tree line into an area of open, flattened scrub on the hilltop. From here you have a panoramic view of the scarified, rust-coloured **Las Monjitas** range opposite. If it's *tábano* (horsefly) season, though, you'll want to keep moving rather than enjoy the view. Climb up to the ridge and follow this northwest towards the craggy El Dedal massif above you. Up here you'll see delicate celeste and grey-blue *perezia* flowers, and possibly even condors. Do not follow the crest too far up though: look out for a short right-hand traverse after some 300m. The path then levels off for 100m. Below you is gorgeous **Lago Futalaufquen**, whose turquoise body is fringed, in places, by a frill of Caribbean-blue shallows. Bear left across a slight scoop of a valley, and you'll come to the lip of an impressive, oxide-coloured glaciated cwm (valley). From here, follow the thirty-degree slope down into the bowl. The path up the other side of the cwm is difficult to make out: follow the paint blotches, choosing the pale, broad band of scree and make the tiring scramble up the top of the ridge, which overlooks the *Hostería Futalaufquen* and Puerto Limonao. From the ridge, a poor path leads up left to the summit of **Cerro Alto El Dedal** (1916m), about forty minutes away; don't attempt it in poor weather. Descending from the ridge, it's about ninety minutes to the road by the port's prefectura and then another half-hour back to the *intendencia*.

The Northern Lake District and Neuquén

Shaped like a fishtail, **Neuquén Province** can be divided into three geographical parts, the northernmost being a transitional zone segueing into the Cuyo. The easternmost swathe, where the tail would join the fish, is focused on the provincial capital, **Neuquén**, a pleasant enough town with decent hotels and access to two major attractions, **dinosaur sites** and **wineries**. The region's prehistoric legacy can be witnessed in the museum at nearby **Villa El Chocón** and at a handful of other sites, while some successful young wineries producing delicious wines are also within easy reach of the provincial capital.

The southern-pointing tip of the tail more closely resembles the southern Lake District (indeed part of the Parque Nacional Nahuel Huapi lies within its territory): a string of glacial lakes, fast-running rivers and brooks, tree-clad mountainsides all bristling with Andean flora and fauna. Here the peaceful resort of **San Martín de los Andes**, Bariloche's main regional rival, is the big draw, offering good accommodation and eating options, panoramic views and lakeside relaxation as well as more strenuous activities such as skiing or trekking. Nearby **Junín de los Andes** is firmly on the international angling map – be sure to taste the local trout even if fishing is not your thing. Much of the habitat around here is preserved in the wonderful **Parque Nacional Lanín**, centred on the extinct **Volcán Lanín**, a mountaineers' paradise. This fairytale snowcapped cone of 3776m is reflected in **lagos Huechulafquen** and **Paimún**, a sumptuous brace of lakes not far from Junín. For unbeatable outdoor experiences check out the **Pehuenia Circuit** and its trio of stunning lakes northwest from slow-paced **Aluminé**: you can choose between mountain-biking, rafting and horseriding, or just hike along rewarding trails through woodland of utmost beauty.

San Martín de los Andes and around

Nestled between mountains on the eastern shores of jewel-like Lago Lácar, the relaxing resort of **San Martín de los Andes is** an excellent base for exploring much of Parque Nacional Lanín (see p.480). The northern terminus of the famous **Ruta de los Siete Lagos** (see box, pp.458–459), San Martín is Neuquén Province's most-visited destination by far (easily outdoing Villa La Angostura, see p.455, and the capital) and gets very busy indeed in the high mid-summer and mid-winter seasons.

San Martín de los Andes

The southern belle of Argentine towns, **SAN MARTÍN DE LOS ANDES** consists of chalets and generally low-key architecture set in a sheltered valley at the eastern end of **Lago Lácar**. There's a sandy, if often windy, beach on the lake's shores, and in spring, the introduced broom (*retama*) daubs the scenery on the approach roads a sunny yellow. Expansion has been rapid, but – with the exception of the hideous derelict *Hotel Sol de Los Andes* that overlooks town – by no means as uncontrolled. Whereas the larger rival resort of Bariloche caters to the young

SAN MARTÍN DE LOS ANDES

0   250 m

N

Mirador Bandurrias ◄

CARLOS WEBER

TRES DE CABALLERIA

ASUNCION FOSBERY

JOSE CALDERON

RUDECINDO ROCA

PERITO MORENO

GENERAL ROCA

**La Pastera
Museo del Che**

National
Park Office

PLAZA
SAN
MARTÍN

**Museo de
los Primeros
Pobladores**

PLAZA
SARMIENTO

AV. SAN MARTÍN   **1 2**

5

GENERAL VILLEGAS

I

H   **3**   **4**

6

8

Bus
Terminal

GABRIEL OBEID

J   **K**

ALMIRANTE BROWN

7

9

ANTU-HUE

Laco
Lácar

Mirador
Arrayán

TTE. CNEL PEREZ

BELGRANO

ELORDI

SARMIENTO

CAPITAN DRURY

MARIANO MORENO

JUEZ DEL VALLE

CORONEL DIAZ

CORONEL ROHDE

RIVADAVIA

MISIONERO MASCARDI

TENIENTE RAMAYON

CACIQUE CURRUHINCA

◄ Bariloche, Cerro Chapelco & RN- 234

Junín & Chapelco Airport ►

EATING & DRINKING

La Barra	9
Casino Magic	6
La Costa del Pueblo	7
Experience	8
Kawen	5
Ku	3
Pulgarcito	1
El Quincho	2
Taco's	4

ACCOMMODATION

ACA Camping	E
Amigos de la Naturaleza	F
Aparthotel Cascadas	K
Camping Lolen	G
Hostel Secuoya	B
Hostería Hueney Ruca	J
Hostería Laura	D
Hostería Las Lucarnas	C
Hotel Caupolicán	H
Hotel Intermonti	I
Puma	A

party crowd, San Martín attracts a more sedate type of small-town tourism, aimed at families and professionals rather than students and backpackers. **El Trabún** (meaning the "Union of the Peoples") is the main annual **festival**, held in early December on the Plaza San Martín. Local and Chilean musicians hold concerts (predominantly folklore), and mighty bonfires are lit at the corners of the square to prepare delicious *asados* of lamb and goat.

Arrival and information

Chapelco Airport (☎02972/427636; open only during the skiing season, usually June–Aug) lies 25km away in the direction of Junín de los Andes. Caleuche minibuses connect the airport with the town (☎02972/422115 or 425850 for hotel pick-up), or you can take a *remise*. The **bus terminal** is scenically located in the southwest of town, across the road from Lago Lácar and the **pier**. Nearly everything you need is found along avenidas Roca and San Martín, or the parallel Villegas.

On the Plaza San Martín, the **tourist office** (daily 8am–10pm; ☎02972/427347, ⓦwww.smandes.gov.ar) will lend a hand if you can't find a room in high season. The **Intendencia of Parque Nacional Lanín** (Mon–Fri 8am–3pm; ☎02972/429106, Ⓔlanin@apn.gov.ar) is on the opposite side of the plaza – it should be your first stop if you are planning on trekking. It also sells fishing permits, as do all the fishing shops in town. Aquaterra, at Villegas 795, rents out camping equipment.

Accommodation

During the peak summer and skiing seasons you should **reserve rooms** as far in advance as possible. If you haven't, the tourist office keeps a daily list of vacancies, though you may find these choices limited. Some hotels have three or four price brackets, with the ski season often more expensive than summer. Out of season, room prices can be as much as halved.

Of the **hostels** in the northwest of town, the most established is the small, well-scrubbed and modern *Puma*, at Fosbery 535 (℗02972/422443, ℮puma@smandes .com.ar; $60 per person), with a couple of double rooms (④), kitchen and washing facilities. Better is the new *Secuoya*, at Rivadavia 411 (℗02972/424485, ⊛www .hostelsecuoya.com.ar; $80 per person), which has some double rooms (⑥) and is modern, safe and friendly. For **camping**, there's a choice of three sites, though none offers facilities in winter: the *ACA* site, at Avenida Koessler 2175 (℗&℉02972/429430; $45 per person), is popular with families; *Amigos de la Naturaleza* (℗02972/426351; $25 per person) is about 7km out on the road to Junín; while *Camping Lolen* ($20 per person) is a lakeside site with superb views, run by the Curruhuinca Mapuche community – it's 4km southwest of town, 1km off the RN-234 at Km78 and down a very steep track to Playa Catritre.

Aparthotel Cascadas Obeid 859 ℗02972/420133, ⊛www.apartcascadas.com.ar. Great value, aesthetically pleasing six-person *cabañas* (⑧) on a quiet street with superb facilities for the price. Includes a heated pool, hydromassage and PC with internet connection in every cabin. Double rooms (⑥) also available.

Caupolicán San Martín 969 ℗02972/427658, ⊛www.interpatagonia.com/caupolican. Fancy three-star hotel in the centre of town with a range of facilities, including a sauna and a living room with log fire. ⑦

Hostería Hueney Ruca Obeid and Coronel Pérez ℗02972/421499, ⊛www.hueneyrucahosteria .com.ar. Spacious and airy with attractive minimalist decor and modern bathrooms. Some rooms accommodate up to five people and breakfast is included in the price. ⑥

Hostería Laura Mascardi 632 ℗02972/427271. Simple but pleasant with airy rooms. Among the cheaper places in town in summer. ⑤

Hostería Las Lucarnas Coronel Pérez 632 ℗02972/427085, ℮laslucarnas @smandes.com.ar. The best of the cheaper spots, *Las Lucarnas* boasts excellent, spacious rooms in a family-run, central but tranquil place. ⑤

Intermonti Villegas 717 ℗02972/427454, ⊛www.hotelintermonti.com.ar. Functional, comfortable, well-lit rooms in an excellent location a block from the main plaza and surrounded by eating options. ⑥

The Town

There is little to do in town itself apart from bar-hopping, sunning yourself on the small beach by the lake or popping into the tiny **Museo de los Primeros Pobladores** (Mon–Fri 10.30am–1.30pm & 5.30–8.30pm, Sat 10am–1pm; free) on the main square. There is an interesting (Spanish only) guided tour of its exhibits on the Mapuche and skiing.

If you can muster the energy, drag yourself away from the bars to visit the two compelling *miradores*, both within easy walking distance of the centre. Mirador Bandurrias (named after the buff-necked ibis) is 3km along the northeast shore of Lago Lácar and has marvellous views along its length. Take the bridge across Arroyo Pocahullo (meaning "place of seagulls" in Mapuche) on Calle Juez del Valle and head left past the water treatment plant. The path divides and subdivides through cypress and oak woods, but keep heading more or less northwest until you reach the lookout. Alternatively, Mirador Arrayán is 3km in the other direction and overlooks the town, with good mountain views. From the lakeshore, the road forks, with the RN-234 heading right towards Bariloche while a smaller left fork climbs above the town. Follow this road past *Hotel Sol de los Andes*, after which it becomes a dirt track. There's another fork, right this time following the signs, leading to the *mirador*. If you can't face the climbing, the town's tour bus – an old red London double-decker – leaves from Plaza San Martín and goes as far as the *Hotel Sol de los Andes*.

A historical curiosity is **La Pastera Museo del Che** (Wed–Mon noon–6pm; $5; Ⓦwww.lapastera.org.ar), at the corner of Sarmiento and Roca. Behind a whitewashed wall is a simple building where Che Guevara spent a night or two at the end of January 1952 during his first trip across South America – later immortalized in *The Motorcycle Diaries*. Well restored, perhaps overly so, it now functions as a community and cultural centre with regular poetry recitals and music performances. The permanent exhibit is a tribute to Che and includes a bale of hay, on which the future freedom fighter apparently slept during his stay here.

Eating, drinking and nightlife

There's a good selection of places to **eat** in town, most staying open past midnight but closing between 3pm and 7.30pm. **Nightlife**, however, is limited; options include *Casino Magic*, at Villegas and Elordi (2pm–4am), which has a dated, 1970s feel but is good for cheap eats late at night, and *Experience* nightclub, at Elordi 950, open daily in season and playing a wide mix of music.

La Barra Brown and Costanera ☎02972/425459. A superb wood-cabin restaurant on the lakeside. Patagonian specialities (not always that cheap) are the order of the day and the wine list is extensive. Artisanal pasta and stone-baked pizza will appeal to those who have had enough of trout and lamb.

La Costa del Pueblo Costanera at Villegas ☎02972/429289. With good, if slightly obscured lake views, *La Costa del Pueblo* is an excellent place to grab a snack while waiting for a bus. The food is abundant and cheap.

Kawen Villegas 624 ☎02972/429242. Arab restaurant and *parrilla*. It's not cheap but portions are large, the food is different and the desserts are particularly tasty.

Ku San Martín 1053 ☎02972/427039. This moderately priced restaurant offers a varied menu that includes *parrillas* and pastas as well as regional trout, venison and wild boar dishes in a rustic setting decorated with wine barrels and bottles.

Pulgarcito San Martín 461 ☎02972/427081. Inexpensive home-made pasta a couple of blocks from Plaza San Martín.

El Quincho Rivadavia 815 and San Martín ☎02972/422564. Classy wood-cabin restaurant offering traditional Argentine and Patagonian dishes, including the inevitable *parrilla*. The walls are adorned with gaucho artefacts.

Taco's San Martín 1100 ☎02972/429444. A good place for budget travellers serving cheap and filling pizzas and pasta.

Lago Lácar and around

Southwest of San Martín, **LAGO LÁCAR** ("lake of the sunken city"), which lies entirely within the Parque Nacional Lanín (see p.480), is best explored by combining boat or road trips with the odd hike. The unsurfaced RP-48 runs for 46km along the northern shore of Lácar and the adjoining **Lago Nonthué** to **Hua-Hum**, at the far western end of Nonthué. On the way, 13km from San Martín, is the trailhead for an excellent two-hour hike up **Cerro Colorado** (1774m). You'll go towards a broad V-shaped valley, then along the banks of a stream – a steep climb with views of the valley and lake below.

Around 3km from Hua-Hum is the **Paso Hua-Hum**, one of the most enjoyable of the Andean routes through to Chile, open all year round and leading towards the town of Villarrica. Following the Río Hua-Hum northwest brings you to the slender, gorgeous Lago Pirehueico, which can be crossed only by **car ferry** (timetable changes frequently; check Ⓦwww.sietelagos.cl or call ☎0056/63 1971585). A bus service run by Lofit (☎02972/422800) connects San Martín with the ferry three times a week (2hr) and there are various campsites along the route. Alternatively, Chapelco Turismo in San Martín, San Martín 876 (℡02972/427550, Ⓦwww.chapelcoturismo.com) offers twelve-hour day-trips crossing Lago Pirehueico into Chile, looping north past Termas de Liquiñe, Pucón or Huilo Huilo and returning to San Martín.

To the southeast of Hua-Hum, 12km by dirt track, is the *guardaparque*'s post at **Lago Queñi**. The area around this lake is one of the wettest places in Parque Nacional Lanín, and is covered with Valdivian temperate rainforest and dense thickets of *caña colihue*. The star attraction here is the enchanting **Termas de Queñi** – unadorned hot springs, set in lush forest near the southern tip of the lake. Late September to early May is generally the best time to visit the springs: register with the *guardaparque*, and you can **camp** just past the post, on the other side of Arroyo Queñi. You can walk to the springs on an easy route from the campsite (1hr).

From San Martín's pier you can take a **boat excursion** to Hua-Hum and back (leaves 12.30pm, returns 8pm; some English-speaking guides). Hourly ferries also leave the pier on the hour (last boat 7pm) for the beautiful, sheltered bay at **Quila Quina**, an incongruous mix of agricultural smallholdings of the Curruhuinca Mapuche community and holiday homes on the southern shore of Lago Lácar. You can also reach the settlement by signposted dirt road off the RN-234. There's a beach and walks in the area, including a two-day trek to the western end of Lago Lácar at **Pucará**.

Junín de los Andes and around

Set in a dry, hilly area of the steppe at the foot of the Andes to the northeast of San Martín, **JUNÍN DE LOS ANDES** is aptly named – Junín means "grassland" in the Aymara language. It's a relaxed town popular with fishermen, largely owing to the rivers in the region that teem with trout. Though not as aesthetically attractive as its bigger neighbour, San Martín de los Andes (see p.473), Junín is immensely likeable, lacking the trappings of a tourist town and the high prices that generally accompany them. It is also better placed for making trips to the central sector of Parque Nacional Lanín (see p.484), especially if you plan to climb Volcán Lanín itself, or to explore the **Lago Huechulafquen** area. A good time to visit is mid-February, when the **Fiesta del Puestero**, with gaucho events, folklore music in the evenings, *artesanía* and *asados*, takes place.

Arrival and information

Chapelco **airport** (open during the skiing season, usually June–Aug; ℡02972/427636) lies halfway between Junín and San Martín and is shared by the two towns. There are no facilities for arrivals, though a small tourist office does open to meet incoming flights. You'll need to take a *remise* into town; try El Rápido (℡02972/491666). The RN-234, called Boulevard Rosas/Roca (rather confusingly) for the stretch through Junín, cuts across the western side of town. Nearly all you'll need lies to the east, including the **bus terminal** (℡02972/492038), one block over at Olavarría and F.S. Martín. Continue east along Olavarría for two blocks and turn right (south) for one block along Calle San Martín to reach the pleasant main square, Plaza San Martín, the hub of the town's activity. Diagonally opposite, at Padre Milanesio and Coronel Suárez, is the **tourist office** (daily 8am–9pm; ℡02972/491160, Ⓦwww.junindelosandes.gov.ar). Almost next door

Calling themselves the people (*che*) of the earth (*Mapu*), the **Mapuche** were, before the arrival of the Spanish in the sixteenth century, a loose confederation of tribal groups who lived exclusively on the Chilean side of the cordillera. The aspiring conquistadors knew them as Araucanos, and so feared their reputation as indomitable and resourceful warriors that they abandoned attempts to subjugate them and opted instead for a policy of containment. Encroachments into Araucania sparked a series of Mapuche migrations eastwards into territory that is now Argentina, and they soon became the dominant force in the whole region, their cultural and linguistic influence spreading far beyond their territories.

By the eighteenth century, four major Mapuche tribes had established territories in Argentina: the **Picunche**, or "the people of the north", who lived near the arid cordillera in the far north of Neuquén; the **Pehuenche**, or "the people of the monkey puzzle trees", dominant in the central cordillera; the **Huilliche**, or "the people of the south" (also called Manzaneros; see p.442), of the southern cordillera region based around Lago Nahuel Huapi; and the **Puelche**, or "the people of the east", who inhabited the river valleys of the steppe. These groups spoke different dialects of **Mapudungun**, a tongue that belongs to the Arawak group of languages. Lifestyles were based around a combination, in varying proportions, of nomadic hunter-gathering, rearing livestock and the cultivation of small plots around settlements of *rucas* (family homes that were thatched usually with reeds). Communities were headed by a *lonco*, or cacique, but the "medicine-men", or *machis*, also played an influential role.

The arrival of the Spanish influenced Mapuche culture most significantly with the introduction of **horses and cattle**. Horses enabled tribes to be vastly more mobile, and hunting techniques changed, with the Mapuche adopting their trademark lances in lieu of the bow and arrow. As importantly, the herds of wild horses and cattle that spread across the Argentine pampas became a vital trading commodity.

Relations between the Mapuche and the Hispanic *criollos* in both Chile and Argentina varied: periods of warfare and indigenous raids on white settlements were

---

on the Paseo Artesanal is Parque Nacional Lanín's **information office** (Mon–Fri: summer 8am–9pm; winter 8–5pm; ☏02972/492748).

Banco de la Provincia, at San Martín and Lamadrid, has an **ATM** and changes Amex travellers' cheques while Andina at Cap. Drury 876 is a good palce to change money; there are a couple of **telephone** offices that also provide **internet** on the main square. The **post office** is at Don Bosco and Coronel Suárez (Mon–Fri 8.30am–1pm & 4–7pm, Sat 9am–1pm). Alquimia, Milanesio 840 (☏02972/491355, ⓦwww.alquimiaturismo.com.ar), is a helpful **travel agency** that sells flights and organizes professional day-tours in the region, including one to lakes Huechulafquen and Paimún with a visit to a Mapuche community; they specialize in adventure tourism, such as climbing Lanín (see box, p.484) and rafting on the Río Aluminé, and rent climbing equipment.

Accommodation

Junín's **hotel** tariffs rise somewhat in summer, when it's worth reserving in advance. There are some good places on the main road but often the best bet is to head for the streets east of the plaza. A pair of decent **campsites** on an island in the Río Chimehuín can be accessed from the eastern extreme of Ginés Ponte, a few blocks from the centre. Both offer similar, shady pitches: the larger and

interspersed with times of relatively peaceful coexistence. By the end of the eighteenth century, the relationship had matured into a surprisingly symbiotic one, with the two groups meeting at joint *parlamentos* where grievances would be aired and terms of trade regulated. Tensions increased after Argentina gained its independence from Spain, and the Mapuche resisted a military campaign organized against them by the dictator Rosas in the early 1830s, but they were finally crushed by Roca's Campaign of the Desert in 1879. The military humiliation of the Argentine Mapuche nation was completed with the surrender, in 1885, of Valentín Sayhueque, dynastic head of the Manzaneros. Following that, Mapuche communities were split up, forcibly relocated and "reduced" onto reservations, often on some of the most marginal lands available.

Nevertheless, today the Mapuche remain one of Argentina's **principal indigenous peoples**, with a population of some forty thousand divided among communities dotted around the provinces of Buenos Aires, La Pampa, Chubut, Río Negro and, above all, Neuquén. Most families still earn their livelihood from mixed animal farming, but increasingly, Mapuche communities are embarking on tourist-related ventures. These include opening campsites; establishing points of sale for home-made cheese or *artesanía* such as their fine woven goods, distinctive silver jewellery, ceramics and wood-carvings; offering guided excursions; or receiving small tour groups.

Today Mapuche culture is not as visibly distinct in Argentina as it is in Chile – you will not find elderly women dressed day-to-day in old-style traditional outfits in Argentina. Political organization is also less developed; nevertheless, the Mapuche are one of Argentina's best-organized indigenous groups. The **Nguillatún** – a religious ritual which aimed to root out evil and ensure good harvests – is still practised in some Argentine Mapuche communities. After decades of being in steep decline, there is some evidence too that there may be a reawakening of interest in such ceremonies. The *rehue* (Mapuche altar) at Ñorquinco (see p.486), for example, stood neglected between 1947 and 2000, when the first Nguillatún in fifty years was held, attended by Mapuche delegations from both sides of the border.

cheaper of the two is *La Isla* (☎02972/492029; $20 per person). The other, *Camping Laura Vicuña* (☎02972/491149; $25 per person), also has small apartments for four or five people (④–⑤).

Albergue la Casa de Aldo y Marita 25 de Mayo 371 ☎02972/491042, ⓔlacasade maritayaldo@hotmail.com. Rustic dormitory-style accommodation in a traditional fishing lodge down by the river ($34 per person). The owner is a fishing guide and smokes his own trout and cheese at the on-site smoker.

Aparthotel Alina Gines Ponte 80 and Félix San Martín ☎02972/492636, ⓔapartalina@hotmail .com. Close to the bus terminal and ideal for small groups, with rooms and cabins for four to six people, but no double rooms. Tours can be arranged, and yoga and massages are also on offer. $250–350 per person.

Cabañas Las Bandurrias Lanín s/n ☎02972/491295, ⓦlasbandurriasjunin.blogspot .com. Two delightful cabins set in extensive

grounds in Jardines del Chimehuín, a quiet residential area of town. $250 per person.

Complejo Caleufu Travel Lodge J Roca 1323 ☎02972/492757, ⓦwww.caleufutravellodge .com.ar. Motel-style travel lodge on the main road, run by a fun-loving couple who lived in California for years – they have a true sense of hospitality and an equally great sense of humour, though watch out for the strict set of rules posted in every room. ⑤

Hostería Chimehuín Coronel Suárez and 25 de Mayo ☎02972/491132, ⓦwww .interpatagonia.com/hosteriachimehuin. A rare gem, it combines excellent value with a cottage-like setting among well-tended gardens, and engenders great loyalty from its regular guests, especially fishing aficionados. A fine home-made breakfast is included in the price. Book well ahead in summer. ⑤

Residencial Marisa J.M. Rosas 360 ⓣ&ⓕ02972/491175, ⓔresidencialmarisa @jedeandes.com.ar. The best of the budget options and just around the corner from the bus terminal, this residencial is a neat, amiable place, and not too noisy, despite having some rooms that face the main road. ③

The Town

The few sites of interest in Junín are all within a couple of blocks of **Plaza San Martín**, and can be seen in an hour or two. The **Paseo Artesanal** on the east side of the square is a cluster of boutiques selling a selection of crafts, among which Mapuche weavings figure heavily. More Mapuche artefacts and some dinosaur bones can be seen at the tiny **Museo Mapuche**, at Ginés Ponte 541 (Mon–Fri 9am–1pm & 2.30–7pm; free), while opposite stands the imposing, alpine-style tower of the **Santuario de la Beata Laura Vicuña**, also called by its old name of the Iglesia Nuestra Señora de las Nieves. Splendid in its simplicity, it is dedicated to the beatified Laura Vicuña, and rates as the most refreshingly original church in southern Argentina. Its airy, sky-blue interior is suffused with light, and its clean-cut lines are tastefully complemented by the bold use of panels of high-quality Mapuche weavings, with strong geometric designs and natural colours. Laura Vicuña, born in Santiago de Chile in 1891, studied in Junín and died here, aged just 13, in 1904. As a rather macabre touch, one of her vertebrae resides in an urn at the entrance to the sanctuary.

Trout-fishing is a popular pastime along the river, a short walk of six blocks east from the terminal along Olavarría. A humpbacked bridge crosses the fast-flowing waters here to a pleasant **park**, enjoyed by picnicking families in summer.

Eating and drinking

There are a cluster of *parrillas* and other **eateries** on the plaza. The largest of these is ⚹ *Ruca Hueney* (ⓣ02972/491113), a local institution whose speciality is unforgettably delicious trout as (be sure to try it); it also offers some tasty Lebanese dishes and takeout options. Alternatively, *El Preferido de Junín* (ⓣ02972/491322), a block north of the square at Lamadrid 260, is an attractive wood-panelled *parrilla* with some outdoor tables. *Roble Bar*, Ginés Ponte 331, is the town's most happening **pub**, and serves a *menú del día* at lunch and burgers, etc, in the evenings. *La Morocha*, in Costanera, is a **disco** worth trying in high season (Fri & Sat).

Parque Nacional Lanín

Formed in 1937, **PARQUE NACIONAL LANÍN** (ⓦwww.parquenacionallanin .gov.ar) protects 420 square kilometres of Andean and sub-Andean habitat that ranges from barren, semi-arid steppe in the east to patches of temperate Valdivian rainforest pressed up against the Chilean border. To the south, it adjoins its sister park, Parque Nacional Nahuel Huapi (see pp.448–459), while it also shares a boundary with Parque Nacional Villarrica in Chile.

The park's raison d'être and geographical centrepiece – the cone of **Volcán Lanín** – rises to 3776m and dominates the entire landscape. The park's other trump card is the **araucaria**, or monkey puzzle tree (see box below), which grows as far south as Lago Curruhue Grande, but is especially prevalent in the northern sector of the park, an area known as the **Pehuenia region** (see p.486). As well as the araucaria, other tree species endemic to the park are the *roble pellí* and the *raulí*,

▲ Volcán Lanín

both types of deciduous *Nothofagus* southern beech. Parque Lanín also protects notable forests of *coihue* and, in the drier areas, cypress. Flowers such as the *arvejilla* purple sweet pea and the introduced lupin abound in spring, as does the flame-red *notro* bush. Fuchsia bushes grow in some of the wetter regions.

As for **fauna**, the park is home to a population of *huemules*, a shy and rare deer (see box, p.455). *Pudú*, the tiny native deer, and pumas are present, but rarely seen: you're more likely to glimpse a coypu, a grey fox or two species introduced for hunting a century ago, the wild boar and the red deer, which roam the semi-arid steppes and hills of the east of the park. Birdwatchers will want to keep an eye out for the active White-throated Treerunner, a bizarre bird with an upturned bill adapted for removing beech nuts, while the acrobatic Thorn-tailed Rayadito is another regional speciality.

The whole park can be covered in snow from May to October, and it can snow in the higher mountain regions at almost any time of year. The **best time to visit** is in spring (especially Oct–Nov) or autumn (March to mid-May), when the deciduous trees adopt a spectacular palette, particularly in the Pehuenia area. Trekking is possible between late October and early May, although the season for some of the higher treks is shorter, usually from December to March. January and February see an influx of Argentine holidaymakers, but in general it is less crowded than Nahuel Huapi even in high season. If you want to hike and can read Spanish, the *Guía Sendas & Bosques de Lanín y Nahuel Huapi* is very useful. Two reasonably reliable maps (1:200,000) accompany the guide.

The volcano, and the central sector of the park around lakes Huechulafquen, Paimún and Tromen are best accessed from Junín de los Andes, while the park's southernmost reaches, already touched on in the box on the Siete Lagos route (p.458), and the area around Lago Lácar (see p.476) are best visited from San Martín – or, indeed, as part of the Siete Lagos circuit.

Lago Huechulafquen and around

The RP-61 branches west off the RN-234 just north of Junín de los Andes, entering Parque Nacional Lanín and skirting the shores of **LAGO HUECHULAFQUEN**.

The araucaria, or monkey puzzle tree

The distinctive and beautiful **araucaria** (*Araucaria araucana*), more commonly known as the **monkey puzzle tree**, is one of the world's most enduring species of trees. It grows naturally only in the cordillera of Neuquén Province and at similar latitudes in Chile, where it favours impoverished volcanic soils at altitudes between 600m and 1800m. This prehistoric survivor has been around for more than one hundred million years.

Araucarias grow incredibly slowly, though they can live for over **1000 years**. Young trees grow in a pyramid shape, but after about a hundred years they start to lose their lower branches and assume their trademark umbrella appearance – mature specimens can reach 45m in height. Their straight trunks are covered by panels of thick bark that provide resistance against fire. The female trees produce huge, head-size cones filled with up to two hundred fawn-coloured pinenuts called *piñones*, some 5cm long, and rich in proteins and carbohydrates.

Known to the Mapuche as the *pehuén*, the tree was worshipped as the daughter of the moon. Legend has it that there was a time when the Mapuche, though they adored the *pehuén*, never ate its *piñones*, believing them to be poisonous. This changed, however, during a terrible famine, when their god, Ngüenechén, saved them from starvation by sending a messenger to teach them both the best way of preparing these nutritious seeds (roasting them in embers or boiling), and of storing them (burying them in the earth or snow). *Piñones* became the staple diet of tribes in the area (principally the Pehuenche, named after their dependence on the tree), and have been revered by the Mapuche ever since.

On the first stretch of this road are a couple of sights that are easily visited in a few hours with your own vehicle. Just 4km from the junction is the **Centro de Ecologia Aplicada de Neuquén** (Mon–Fri 9am–1pm), which undertakes studies of regional fauna and has a trout farm that raises fish for restocking the area's rivers. A few kilometres further on is the **Escuela Granja San Ignacio** (Sept–May Mon–Fri 8am–2pm), a charming initiative where pupils take you on a guided tour of the school and offer you jams and honey that they produce themselves.

When you arrive at the park gate, you will be charged $30 entrance (note that all other routes into or through the park are free) and have to fill in a *registro de trekking* (trekking register). The park's largest lake, Huechulafquen is an enormous finger of deep blue water extending into the steppe, its northern shores black with volcanic sand. The mouth of the Río Chimehuín, at the lake's eastern end, is a notable fly-fishing spot, and on the north shore, between Km47 and Km60, there are plenty of places to **camp**, with no fewer than fifteen sites with varying facilities run by the Raquithué and Cañicul Mapuche communities. *Bahía Cañicul* ($25 per person) is about halfway along the lake at Km54, and has good, secluded pitches on top of the peninsula but basic toilets. As you get further into the park the sites become gradually busier.

At the western end of the lake is the settlement and jetty of **Puerto Canoa**, where you can look up at the fantastic, crevassed **south face** of Volcán Lanín. From Puerto Canoa, a fun **boat trip** plies a circuit that includes lakes Huechulafquen, Paimún and Epulafquen, where you'll see the solidified lava river of Volcán Achen Ñiyeu. At Puerto Canoa, there is **accommodation** at *Hostería Huechulafquen* (T&F02972/427598; ⑤), a snug fishing lodge in full view of Lanín. Its **restaurant** is open to the public. Just beyond is more expensive *Hostería Paimún* (T02972/491211, Wwww.interpatagonia.com/hosteriapaimun/index .html; ⑧) in another delightful spot on the shore of Lago Paimún. In summer, Co-op Litran (T02972/492038) operates four daily bus services between Lago Huechulafquen and Junín de los Andes, or you can take a taxi to Puerto Canoa.

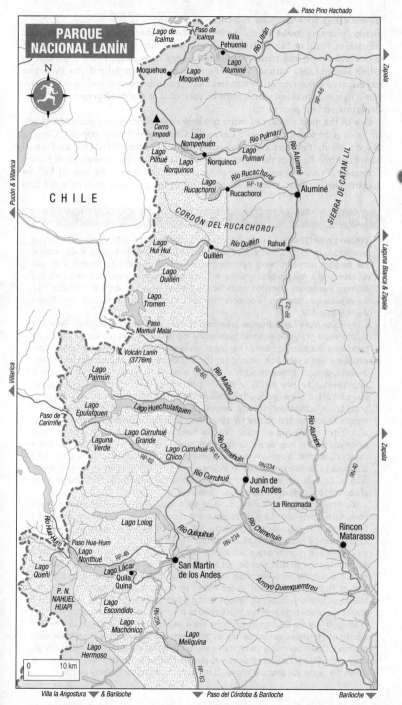

PARQUE
NACIONAL LANÍN

CHILE

Paso Pino Hachado

Lago de Icalma
Paso de Icalma
Villa Pehuenia

Río Litrán

Moquehue
Lago Moquehue
Lago Aluminé

Zapala

Cerro Impodi

Lago Pilhué
Lago Nompehuén
Lago Norquinco
Ñorquinco
Río Pulmarí
Lago Pulmarí
Río Aluminé

Río Rucachoroi
Lago Rucachoroi
RP-18
Rucachoroi
Aluminé

RP-46

Pucón & Villarica

CORDÓN DEL RUCACHOROI

SIERRA DE CATAN LIL

Lago Hui Hui
Quillén
Río Quillén
Rahué

Lago Quillén

Laguna Blanca & Zapala

Lago Tromen
Paso Mamuil Malal

Volcán Lanín (3776m)

RP-60
Río Malleo
Río Aluminé

Zapala

Villarica

Lago Paimún
Lago Epulafquen
Lago Huechulafquen
Laguna Verde
Lago Curruhué Grande
Paso de Carirriñe
Lago Curruhué Chico
Lago Curruhué
RP-62
RP-61
Río Chimehuín
Río Currhué
RN-234
Río Aluminé

Junín de los Andes
La Rinconada
RN-40

Lago Lolog
Río Quilquihué
RN-234
Río Chimehuín
Rincon Matarasso

Río Hua-Hum
Paso Hua-Hum
Lago Nonthué
RP-48
San Martín de los Andes
Arroyo Quemquemtreu

Lago Queñi
Lago Lácar
Quila Quina

P. N. NAHUEL HUAPI
Lago Escondido
RN-234
Lago Machónico
Lago Meliquina
RP-63

Lago Hermoso

0   10 km

Villa la Angostura ▼ & Bariloche   Paso del Córdoba & Bariloche   Bariloche ▼

Before planning **treks** in the park you should check thoroughly with park officials in Junín or San Martín. Make sure your map is new – this is an area of active volcanoes, and trails and refuges change constantly. Do not attempt to climb Volcán Lanin without a guide (see box below), especially if you are not an experienced mountaineer. Before trekking, remember that it is obligatory to fill out a *registro de trekking*, which must be presented at the *guardaparque* post before departure and on your return.

One of the most popular of many trekking possibilities within striking distance of Junín is the four-hour hike to **Cerro del Chivo**, which starts opposite *Camping Bahía Cañicul*. It's a steep climb and you'll need to concentrate not to lose the trail above the tree-line, but the views are spectacular. From the *guardaparque* in Puerto Canoa there's another good, if somewhat arduous, day-hike to the **base of Volcán Lanín**. The last forty minutes are steep and there's no water source for the final

Climbing Lanín

Volcán Lanín (3776m) – meaning "choked himself to death" in Mapudungun – is now believed to be extinct. It is a good mountain to climb: easy to access, it also retains the balance between being possible for non-expert climbers to ascend while still representing a real physical challenge. The most straightforward route is from Lago Tromen; the heavily glaciated south face is a much fiercer option that's suitable only for experienced climbers. For more information, consult the national park office in Junín (see p.478).

The route **from Lago Tromen** takes two to three days in good weather. There is a slight danger of altitude sickness towards the top (see p.61) and you must have a fairly good level of fitness to attempt the climb, especially if you go for the two-day option, which involves a very tiring second day that includes the summit push and a complete descent. Group climbing through an agency is possible: a good one to book with is Alquimia in Junín (see p.478), or else the park offices (@lanin@apn.gov.ar) can email you a list of authorized guides. They also rent out all the essential mountaineering gear: good boots, waterproof clothing, helmet, ice axe, crampons, torch (or, better still, a miner's headlamp) and cooker. UV sunglasses, high-factor sunblock, matches and an alarm clock are likewise essential. Optional items are gaiters (especially in late summer when you have to negotiate volcanic scree), black bin liners (for melting snow in sunny weather), candles, a two-way radio and emergency whistle. You are unlikely to need a compass or climbing rope, but an incense stick will help to counter pungent refuge odours. *La Guía Verde* (on sale locally) comes with a reasonable map and an aerial photo with the climbing route superimposed.

You'll need to register for the climb at the Lago Tromen **guardaparque's office** (daily 8am–6pm), and the *guardaparque* will check that you have all the equipment listed above. If permission is granted you'll need to start the climb by 1pm at the latest. It will be necessary to acclimatize for a night in one of the three refuges on the mountain. The *guardaparque* will assign one to you, and will try to accommodate your preference. In high season, get to Tromen early, as all refuges might otherwise be full (about fifty people in total). The first refuge that you reach following the main trail is, **Refugio RIM**, which sleeps fifteen to twenty people, though it is not the lowest altitudinally. Its big advantage is that it has meltwater close by (Jan & Feb; if climbing outside high summer, you'll need to melt snow for water anyway). You may prefer to try for the **CAJA**, further up the slope, especially if you plan to make the final ascent and total descent in one day, as this saves you half an hour's climb in the early morning. CAJA sleeps six comfortably and up to ten at a squeeze. The **BIM** refuge, down from RIM via a second path, has pleasant tables and chairs, but is the lowest down the slope. It's also the largest of the three, sleeping up to thirty people.

hour. You can take a short detour to the waterfall at Cascada El Saltillo from *Camping Piedra Mala* at Km64, where there's space to pitch a tent. Beyond is the Río Paimún, which is currently the furthest point you can hike before you'll have to back-track to Puerto Canoa.

An excellent two-day option for losing the crowds is to cross the narrows linking the two lakes at La Unión near Puerto Canoa (there's normally a rowing-boat service) and head along the south shore of Lago Paimún. Initially, you strike inland skirting round the southern slopes of Cerro Huemules (1841m) before reaching the lake again mid-way along its length at **Don Aila**, where you can camp.

Aluminé and the Pehuenia Circuit

Northwards from Junín, the **RP-23** runs mostly parallel to the turbulent waters of the Río Aluminé, carving through arid rocky gorges, before continuing on to Lago Aluminé and Villa Pehuenia (see pp.486–487) and the groves of araucaria trees along the river's upper reaches. To the east, parallel with the valley, lies the **Sierra de Catan Lil**, a harsh and desiccated range that's older and higher than the nearby stretch of the Andes.

Aluminé

ALUMINÉ itself is a small but growing riverside town with a gentle pace of life. For a week in March it celebrates the **Fiesta del Pehuén** to coincide with the Mapuche harvest of *piñones*, with displays of horsemanship, music and *artesanía*. Its main claim to fame, though, is as a summer **rafting centre**: organized trips are run by *Servicio Amuyén*, General Villegas 348 (T&F02942/496368). A branch road heads west from the village to Rucachoroi and (28km away) the *guardaparque* post. There is no public transport heading that way; you'll need to book a taxi (T02942/496397 or 496200) or inquire at local travel agent Mali Viajes (T02942/15-662984) about group transport – their office is just off the plaza.

Practicalities

Aluminé's **bus terminal** (T02942/496041) is on Avenida 4 de Caballería. Albus runs two daily services on a circuit from Zapala, via Aluminé to Villa Pehuenia, and back to Zapala again. Only one overnight service runs the reverse route, though Mali Viajes organize day-trips to Villa Pehuenia. From the bus terminal it's half a block to the Plaza San Martín, where you'll find the **tourist office**, Cristian Joubert 326 (daily 8am–10pm; T02942/496001, W www.alumine.gov.ar). *Hotel Pehuenia*, at the junction of the RP-23 and Capitán Crouzeilles (T&F02942/496340, 6), is a resort **hotel** a little out of place in the otherwise rustic village. Its rooms are comfortable, if a little twee, and some have river views. The hotel rents out mountain bikes and arranges horseriding. *Hostería Aluminé*, opposite the tourist office at Cristian Joubert 336 (T02942/496174, F02942/496347; 4), is a clean, straightforward ex-ACA hotel, though it's a bit pricey for single travellers. The adjacent **restaurant**, *La Posteria del Rey*, is a good place to try a sort of *piñones* paté, while imaginative home-made pastas are the house speciality. More basic but better value is *Hostería Nid-Car*, at Cristian Joubert 559 (T02942/496131; 5), which also serves meals. Cheaper still is the pleasant **campsite**, *La Anita* (T02942/496158; $25 per person), 2km from the southern entrance to town. Aluminé also has a **fuel station** and a **bank** with ATM.

The Pehuenia Circuit

The area around Villa Pehuenia, north of Aluminé, is one of the least developed yet most beautiful parts of the Argentine Lake District. This "forgotten corner" of Mapuche communities, wonderful mountain lakes, basalt cliffs and araucaria forests has largely escaped the commercial pressures found further south in the park system, although locals and recent settlers are fast waking up to its potential and tourists are arriving in ever-increasing numbers. However, infrastructure links are still fairly rudimentary, and having your own transport is a boon – otherwise, you'll need to take a taxi, as there is almost nothing in the way of public transport. One of the most popular routes is the **Pehuenia Circuit**, which links **Villa Pehuenia** on the northern bank of Lago Aluminé with tiny **Moquehue**, at the southwest tip of the lake of the same name, and passes along **Lago Ñorquinco**, which forms the northernmost boundary of the Parque Nacional Lanín. Most people finish or start the circuit in **Aluminé**.

The lack of convenient road routes acts as an encouragement to **trek**: there is great potential in the area around Moquehue and Ñorquinco, but local politics and unreliable weather mean you should carefully discuss your plans and route with local *guardaparques* or, even better, take a guide who knows the area. Remember that it is obligatory to register your departure with a *guardaparque* before setting out and clock in your arrival at the other end. If it's not safe, you will be refused permission to trek. The terrain is also ideal for **mountain-biking**, and there's tremendous scope for other outdoor activities here as well, such as **horseriding** and **rafting** through the scenic gorge of the Río Aluminé.

Villa Pehuenia

Set among araucaria trees on the shores of pristine Lago Aluminé, **VILLA PEHUENIA** is a splendid, fast-growing holiday village. *Cabañas* are the boom industry here, springing up in both the main part of the village and on the lumpy, tree-covered peninsula that juts into the lake's chilly waters. High-season prices start around $400 for up to eight people. To the north is **Volcán Batea Mahuida**, a mountain that has a minuscule Mapuche-run ski resort and a picturesque crater lake.

The well-informed **tourist office** (summer 9am–9pm; winter 10am–6pm; ☏02942/498011, ⓦwww.villapehuenia.gov.ar) is at Km11 on the main road to Aluminé. From here it is 700m to the commercial centre – a cluster of buildings selling food and other provisions. If you're walking around town, note that there are no street names and that the map provided by the tourist office lacks distinguishing features. You can also take a taxi; try *Remise Pehuenia* (☏02942/498033).

Camping Lagrimitas (☏02942/498003; $30 per person plus $5 per tent; US$250 for apartments sleeping five or six people) has some fantastic, tranquil pitches beneath araucarias by the lakeshore. The higher-end **accommodation** is on the peninsula, a picturesque twenty-minute walk from the main village. The best lodging is at the luxurious ⚜ *Posada La Escondida* (☏02942/156-91166, ⓦwww.posadalaescondida .com.ar; ❽), on the west coast of the peninsula, where the suite-like rooms all have their own sun decks. *Cabañas Caren* (☏02942/155-801227, ⓦwww.cabanascaren .com.ar; ❾) rents out well-designed luxury cabins with a fully equipped kitchen for up to five people ($350 per person), though there is a minimum stay of five nights. Nearby is the excellent *Hostería La Serena* (☏02942/156-65068, ⓦwww .complejolaserena.com.ar; open Dec–April only; ❾), a well-designed, rustic hotel with wonderful views and *cabañas* for up to eight people ($300 per person).

Following the road that runs by the side of the tourist office and then branches left at the lake brings you to a cluster of **eating options** – besides the hotel restaurants there is little else on the peninsula. Try *Anhedonia* (☏02942/156-69846) for fondue, or *Iñaki* (☏02942/498047), which has more of a pub-type atmosphere.

Moquehue and around

Villa Pehuenia is connected to the pioneer village of **MOQUEHUE** by an unsurfaced road (15km) that runs around the northwestern shores of **Lago Moquehue**, Lago Aluminé's sibling. The two lakes are joined at La Angostura by a twenty-metre-wide, five-hundred-metre-long channel of captivating turquoise waters. There is no public transport to Moquehue – you'll need to have your own car or organize a taxi from Villa Pehuenia.

A loose conglomeration of farmsteads set in a broad pastoral valley at the southwestern end of its lake, Moquehue is overlooked on both sides by splendid ranks of rugged, forested ranges and **Cerro Bella Durmiente**, so named because the summit supposedly looks like the profile of a sleeping beauty. As yet, there's none of the contrived feel that comes from an excess of holiday-makers, and most residents have deep roots here. There is also no electricity in the village, though some places have generators. The *Hostería Bella Durmiente* (℡02942/496172, ⊛www.bdurmientemoquehue.com.ar; closed June–Aug, reserve in advance in Jan; minimum three nights; ❺) is a wonderfully authentic, wood-built guesthouse with camping ($25 per person) and commanding vistas of the scenery. There is another **campsite**, *Camping Trenel* (℡02942/156-64720; $20 per person), at the southeast corner of the lake on a slightly raised area with glorious views. Owner Fernando López is a well-known hiking guide in the area.

Unguided **hiking** around Moquehue has created local political problems, with landowners complaining that hikers ignore private-property signs and are causing damage to the countryside. While the effects of hiking are probably exaggerated, the depth of feeling is not, and the tourist office strongly recommends all hikers be accompanied by an authorized guide. Once you've organized a guide (available through LM Aventura; ℡02942/156-64705), one of the best day-hikes takes you around the southeastern shores of **Lago Moquehue**, through land belonging to the **Puel Mapuche** community. The trail leads past several Puel farmsteads as well as diminutive, secluded lakes, including Cari Laufquén, and beautiful woodland of *ñire*, *radal*, *notro*, araucaria and *coihue*.

However, there are also some excellent local walks that you can do independently: one short leg-stretch (35min one way) leads to an attractive **waterfall** in mystical mixed araucaria woodland; a slightly longer option is the hike up **Cerro Bandera** (2hr one way), with excellent views to Volcán Llaima. Alternative **outdoor activities**, such as lake excursions, mountain-biking, trekking, etc, can all be arranged through Mundo Creativo in Moquehue (℡02942/156-66654).

Central and northern Neuquén

Central and northern Neuquén Province is an area of desert-like *meseta* and steppe, home to Argentina's most important reserves of natural gas and petroleum and a major exporter of thermal and hydroelectric energy. **Neuquén**, the eponymous provincial capital, is a likeable city and a good base for visiting the area's dinosaur-related attractions (see box, p.490): the village of **El Chocón** has a world-class paleontology exhibit and some truly remarkable dinosaur footprints *in situ* by the turquoise-hued Embalse Ezequiel Ramos Mexía reservoir, while in **Plaza Huincul** you can see bones from the largest dinosaur ever discovered, the *Argentinosaurus huinculensis*. Further north at **Lago Barreales** you can watch paleontologists in action, while at **Rincón de los Sauces**, in the extreme north of the province, the world's first fossilized dinosaur eggs were unearthed. Wine buffs will be more interested in the region's award-winning **wineries** a short way north of Neuquén – you can even stay at one and sleep above the cellars.

Neuquén

The bustling provincial capital of **NEUQUÉN** sits at the confluence of the rivers Neuquén and Limay, whose waters unite to become the Río Negro. With a population of a quarter of a million or so, this plains metropolis functions as the commercial, industrial and financial centre of the surrounding fruit- and oil-producing region. It's a surprisingly attractive and friendly place to pass a day or two, with a couple of museums as good as any other in the region.

Arrival, information and city transport

Neuquén is a major transport nexus for the whole region. Its modern **bus terminal,** 3.5km east of the city centre on the RN-22, is regarded as one of the best in the country; it's styled along airport lines (bags come through on a conveyor belt and passengers have to check in to platforms). El Ko-Ko runs a bus service to the centre every fifteen minutes; buy tickets from Kiosk 39 before boarding. Alternatively, you can take a **taxi.** Neuquén's **airport** (℡0299/444-0448) is 5km west of town off the RN-22. Indalo runs a bus to the city centre; it departs from the main road in front of the airport every twenty minutes (pay on the bus). To use Neuquén's other city buses, you must buy a ticket in advance from marked kiosks scattered throughout the city.

▲ Chañar & Wineries

NEUQUÉN

ACCOMMODATION
Belgrano	B
Hotel El Cortijo	C
Residencial Inglés	D
Suizo	A

Obelisk

Museo Gregorio Alvarez

Parque Central

Disused Railway Line

Sala de Arte Emilio Saraco

Malvinas Monument

Museo Paraje Confluencia

Museo Bellas Artes

EATING & DRINKING
1900 Cuatro	3
La Birra	5
Cafeteria Marrones	4
Franz y Peppone	2
La Nonna Francesca	1
Rosignano	6

Bus Station

Airport

0   100 m

There are tourist information booths at both the airport and the bus terminal, but the main **tourist office** (daily 7am–11pm; ☎0299/442-4089, ⓦwww.neuquentur.gov.ar) is at Félix San Martín 182, two blocks east of Avenida Olascoaga. It is a mine of information on the whole province.

Accommodation

Hotels in Neuquén are busy even during the week, so it's well worth booking in advance. Several unspectacular though centrally located mid-range places are clustered around avenidas Olascoaga and Argentina – a simple breakfast is generally included in the price. The nearest **campsite** is *Camping Las Araucarias*, 13km from the centre along the RN-22 towards Plotier ($35 per person); take a *remise* from the centre.

Belgrano Rivadavia 283 ☎0299/448-0612. This agreeable hotel with wooden chalet exterior is probably the best value for money at the lower end of the price range. ❸

Hotel El Cortijo Tierra del Fuego 255 ☎0299/442-1795. Decent mid-range option just off the Parque Central. Heated rooms are clean and well maintained, if a little plain, and are arranged around small sunny courtyards. ❺

Residencial Inglés Félix San Martín 534 ☎0299/442-2252. A fallback budget choice, with clean but dated and slightly tatty rooms. Marginally the cheapest in town, and the garden with a vine is quite pleasant. ❷

Suizo Carlos Rodríguez 167 ☎0299/442-2602, ⓦwww.hotelsuizo.com.ar. Good value higher-end option with bright, stylish rooms for up to four people, all with mini-bar and spacious bathroom. The reception area plays on the Swiss-chalet theme, but this is a classy and modern hotel. ❻

The Town

You'll find everything you need in the **microcentro**, which comprises the area north of the RN-22, three blocks on either side of the central boulevard. The centre of life in town is the vast **Parque Central**, bisected by an old railway line and home to four free museums (all Tue–Fri 10am–8pm, Sat–Sun 4pm–8pm), three of which are housed in abandoned railway buildings. From west to east these are: the **Museo Gregorio Álvarez**, San Martín and Misiones, which contains several works by the local sculptor for whom the museum was named, as well as a small display on Patagonian history; the **Sala de Arte Emilio Saraco**, an old cargo shed featuring temporary exhibitions by local artists; the **Museo Paraje Confluencia**, which specializes in the city's history; and, the pick of the bunch, the **Museo Nacional de Bellas Artes**, at the southeast corner of the park. The permanent exhibition here features examples from all the major European art movements and works by all the great Argentine masters; the most valuable painting is *La Última Copla*, by the great Valencian artist, Joaquín Sorolla. Adjacent to the museum is an impressive **monument to the fallen** of the Malvinas/Falklands campaign of 1982 – the names of the dead are poignantly displayed on a glass wall that overlooks the serene fountain.

Eating and drinking

Neuquén's best places to **eat** and **drink** are scattered around Avenida Argentina between San Martín and Roca, where there are a number of pool bars and pizzerias in addition to more upmarket restaurants.

1900 Cuatro On the first floor of the *Hotel Del Comahue*, Av Argentina 377 ☎0299/443-2040. Serves eclectic and imaginative foreign dishes and appetizing meals, though the overall ambience is somewhat formal and staid, and prices are predictably high.

La Birra Santa Fe and Independencia ☎0299/443-4344. Housed in a beautiful warehouse-style building with Hollywood-themed interior, this restaurant serves an international menu and the food is superb – and not that expensive.

Since 1988, the area around Neuquén has become a hotbed of dinosaur fever, with paleontologists uncovering **fossils** of both the largest herbivorous sauropod and the largest carnivorous dinosaur ever found. As you cross the Neuquén environs en route for the sites of discovery it is easy to imagine dinosaurs roaming the stunted plains and pterodactyls launching themselves into the air from the imposing cliff-faces.

On the banks of the picturesque Embalse Ezequiel Ramos Mexía hydroelectric reservoir, 79km southwest of Neuquén along the RN-237, the little oasis of **Villa El Chocón** is home to the **Museo Municipal Ernesto Bachmann** (daily 8am–9pm; $2) where you can see a virtually complete, hundred-million-year-old skeleton of *Giganotosaurus carolinii*, discovered 18km away in 1993. This fearsome creature puts even *Tyrannosaurus rex* in the shade: it measured a colossal 13m long (its skull alone accounting for 1.8m), stood 4.7m tall and weighed an estimated eight tonnes. Cono Sur runs buses to El Chocón from the Neuquén bus terminal, but getting there and back in one day can be difficult, as departure and return times are inconvenient. If you find yourself stranded, the **tourist office** (✆0299/490-1230; 8am–7pm) at the entrance to town can help you find family **accommodation** if necessary.

Three kilometres further south along the RN-237, a left turn-off leads another 2km down to the shores of Embalse Ezequiel Ramos Mexía. Here, at the northwest corner of the lake, is the **Parque Cretácico**, where you'll find some huge, astonishingly well-preserved **dinosaur footprints**. Not realizing what they were, fishermen once used them as barbecue pits. The footprints resemble those of a giant rhea, but were probably left by an iguanadon – a ten-metre-long herbivore – or some kind of bipedal carnivore. Other kidney-shaped prints are of four-footed sauropods, and smaller prints were probably left by 3m-long theropods.

Plaza Huincul, just over 110km west of Neuquén along the RN-22, is where the region's petroleum reserves were discovered in 1918. Memorabilia from those pioneering days is displayed at the **Museo Carmen Funes** on the main street (Mon–Fri 9am–7.30pm, Sat & Sun 9am–8.30pm; $2), though you'll find it impossible to concentrate on petroleum with the full-size reconstruction of *Argentinosaurus huinculensis* looming in the hangar next door. Walking between the legs of this beast – 40m long, 18m high and weighing 100 tonnes – is a bit like walking under a jumbo jet. The only fossils of this giant beast that have been found are the pelvis, tibia, sacrum and some vertebrae – the reconstruction of the rest of the animal is based on educated guesswork. From Neuquén, the easiest way to Plaza Huincul is on the Zapala bus from the terminal (Centenario, El Petróleo or Cono Sur hourly).

Heading northwest from Neuquén approximately 90km along the RP-51 or the RP-7 brings you to the shores of **Embalse Cerros Colorados**, where you can watch paleontologists at work on the **"Dino Project"** at Lago Barreales (✆0299/154-048614, ⊛www.proyectodino.com.ar). Considered a "complete ecosystem of the Mesozoic era", the project, overseen by the University of Comahue, gives you the chance to help with the excavation. The most important finds are displayed at the on-site museum.

Further afield, 250km northwest of Neuquén along the RP-8, the isolated town of **Rincón de los Sauces** is home to the **Museo Argentino Urquiza** (Mon–Fri 8am–6pm; ✆0299/488-6643), whose collection features the only known fossils of a titanosaurus, including an almost complete specimen. What makes the trip worthwhile, however, are the fossilized set of titanosaur eggs from nearby Auca Mahuida: the first set of **dinosaur eggs** ever to be found, they are approximately 14cm in diameter and have thin, porous shells through which the embryonic dinosaurs are thought to have breathed.

Cafeteria Marrones Av Argentina 125 ☎0299/442-5489. Despite the plush interior and bow-tied waiters, this café-bar-restaurant is surprisingly affordable. Ten different varieties of coffee will keep the caffeine junkie happy.

Franz y Peppone 9 de Julio and Belgrano ☎0299/448-2299. Next door to *La Nonna Francesca* and on a similar theme, though aimed more squarely at those on a backpacker's budget.

La Nonna Francesca 9 de Julio 56 ☎0299/430-0930. Pizza, pasta and all things Italian in this atmospheric if slightly pricey trattoria. Large portions mean you won't go hungry.

Rosignano Independencia and Buenos Aires. Hugely popular deli and takeout joint (there's no room for eating in) packed with office workers at lunch time. Varied and inventive menu includes fish, vegetarian offerings and grilled meats.

Chañar and the wineries

The RP-7 follows the mighty Río Neuquen northwestwards from Neuquen across alluvial plains whose fertile lands feed the city with all manner of fruit and vegetables, while a series of reservoirs provides it with much needed water. Artificial oases have been created in the desert-like terrain just west of tiny **SAN PATRICIO DEL CHAÑAR** (or **Chañar**), 41km from Neuquén, to support some of the country's newest and finest vineyards, producing highly palatable whites and reds, using grape varieties such as semillon and malbec.

A handful of outstanding have sprung up in the region and four can be visited, in some cases free of charge, as part of the local **Ruta del Vino**, or wine route. After leaving Chañar in the direction of Añelo, heading along the RP-7, watch out on the right-hand side for the numbered lanes (*picadas*). Number 6 leads off towards **Bodega Valle Perdido**, a state-of-the-art winery that is also a luxury **hotel** (☎011/6091-7777, Ⓦ www.valleperdido.com.ar; Ⓞ), in a majestic building. The rooms are spacious and extremely comfortable, while the impressive public areas are decorated and furnished with panache. In addition to checking out the fabulous cellars and tasting a variety of wines (visits Mon, Wed and Fri, 11am and 7pm; US$40 includes a free bottle of wine), you can make use of the wine spa and pool (with water, not wine), or lunch or dine at the top-rate restaurant, drinking the house wines, of course.

The next *picada*, no. 7, strikes off in the direction of **Bodega Familia Schroeder** (☎0299/4435917, Ⓦwww.familiaschroeder.com), where one-hour tours with tastings (hourly; Mon–Fri 9am–5pm, Sat & Sun 10.30am–5.30pm; $15) include a visit to the "dinosaur cellar". The vineyard also has a reputed restaurant-bar, open daily for lunch.

Picada 12 leads to the dramatically named **Bodega del Fin del Mundo** ("Winery at the end of the world") – so called because these wineries are in close competition with one or two in New Zealand for the title of the world's most southerly vineyard. For the hourly tours (Tues–Fri 10am–4pm, Sat & hols 10am–5pm; free) it is best to reserve ahead (☎0299/4424040, Ⓦwww.bodegadelfindelmundo .com), which can also be done at the winery's Neuquén office at Juan B Alberdi 87, 1st floor.

Finally, *Picada* 15 is the approach to **Bodega NQN** (☎0299/4897500, Ⓦwww .bodeganqn.com.ar), which also has an excellent if pricey restaurant-bar on the premises, *Malma* (☎0299/4897600); there is a set menu on weekdays and à la carte lunch at weekends. "Malma", meaning "pride" in Mapudungun, is also the name of the winery's flagship range of red and white varietals, such as pinot noir and sauvignon blanc. The bodega also offers hour-long tours (Mon–Fri 9am–1pm & 2–4pm; Sat, Sun & hols 10.30am-4.30pm; free) with a tasting and, of course, a chance to buy.

Travel details

Buses

The major bus companies operating in this region are: Albus (⊛ www.albus.com.ar), Andesmar (⊛ www.andesmar.com.ar), Cruceros del Norte (⊛ www.crucerosdelnorte.com.ar), El Valle (⊛ www.elvalle.com.ar), Via Bariloche (⊛ www.viabariloche.com.ar) and Via TAC (⊛ www.viatac.com.ar).

Aluminé to: Villa Pehuenia (3 daily; 1hr–1hr 30min).

Bariloche to: El Bolsón (14 daily; 2hr); Buenos Aires (7 daily; 23hr); Córdoba (2 daily; 22hr); Esquel (5–6 daily; 4hr 30min); Junín de los Andes (1 daily; 4hr); Mendoza (daily; 18hr 45min); Neuquén (12 daily; 5hr 30min–6hr); Puerto Madryn (daily; 14hr); Salta (2 daily; 39hr); San Martín de los Andes (2 daily; 6hr); Trelew (daily; 13–16hr); Villa La Angostura (3 daily in summer; 1hr); Villa Traful (daily–4 weekly; 1hr 45min–2hr 30min).

El Bolsón to: Bariloche (14 daily; 2hr); Esquel (6 daily); Lago Puelo (5–10 daily; 30min).

Cholila to: El Bolsón (daily; 1hr 40min–2hr); Esquel (3 daily or 5 weekly depending on season; 2hr 30min–3hr 45min).

Esquel to: Bariloche (15 daily; 4hr 30min); El Bolsón (15 daily; 2hr 30min); Cholila (3 daily or 5 weekly depending on season; 2hr 30min–3hr 45min); Trevelin (hourly Mon–Fri, every 2hr Sat–Sun; 30min).

Junín de los Andes to: Aluminé (3 weekly; 3hr); Buenos Aires (7 daily; 20hr); San Martín de los Andes (9 daily; 1hr).

Lago Puelo to: El Bolsón (5 daily; 30min); Cholila (2 weekly; 2hr 45min).

El Maitén to: El Bolsón (daily; 1hr); Esquel (4 weekly).

Moquehue to: Neuquén (3 weekly; 5hr 30min); Villa Pehuenia (5 weekly; 40min).

Neuquén to: Bariloche (21 daily mainly am; 5hr 30min–6hr); Buenos Aires (hourly; 15hr–16hr 30min); Córdoba (7 daily; 18hr 30min); Mendoza (8 daily; 12hr–12hr 30min); Moquehue (1 daily; 5hr 30min); San Juan (3 daily; 12hr–12hr 30min); San Martín de los Andes (8 daily; 6hr); Villa Pehuenia (2 daily; 5hr).

San Martín de los Andes to: Bariloche (3 daily; 6hr); Junín de los Andes (hourly; 1hr); Villa La Angostura (2 daily; 2hr 30min).

Trevelin to: Esquel (every 1–2hr; 30min).

Villa La Angostura to: Bariloche (approximately hourly; 1hr); San Martín de los Andes (5 daily; 2hr 30min).

Villa Pehuenia to: Aluminé (3 daily; 1hr–1hr 30min); Moquehue (5 weekly; 30min); Neuquén (3 weekly; 5hr).

Villa Traful to: Bariloche (daily; 1hr 45min–2hr 30min).

Flights

Bariloche to: Buenos Aires (6–8 daily; 2hr); Córdoba (1 daily; 2hr); Esquel (5 weekly; 30min); Mendoza (1 daily; 1hr 30min); Puerto Madryn (2 weekly; 3hr); Trelew (2 weekly; 1hr 15min).

Chapelco to: Buenos Aires (daily during skiing season; 2hr).

Esquel to: Bariloche (5 weekly; 1hr); Buenos Aires (Wed–Fri 1–2 daily; 3hr); Trelew (Wed–Fri 1–2 daily; 2hr).

Neuquén to: Buenos Aires (3 daily; 1hr 35min); Puerto Madryn (1 weekly; 4hr 30min); Trelew (1–2 daily; 5hr); Ushuaia (1 daily; 7hr 30min–8hr 30min).

Patagonia

CHAPTER 8

Highlights

✳ **Whale-watching** Grab close-up views of imperial whales off the Península Valdés. See p.505

✳ **Welsh experience** Argentina's most traditional Welsh village. See p.512

✳ **Magellanic penguins** See tens of thousands of these comical birds waddling around their major nesting sites – the biggest is at Punta Tombo. See p.513

✳ **Petrified forests** Phenomenally preserved fossilized logs and trunks are scattered over the lunar landscapes of central Patagonia – the two best sites are at Jaramillo and near Sarmiento. See p.516 & p.555

✳ **Parque Nacional Los Glaciares** The legendary Glaciar Perito Moreno – dominates any visit to southern Patagonia, with world-class trekking in the Fitz Roy sector a close second. See pp.528–531

✳ **Estancias of Santa Cruz** Experience Patagonian hospitality on these legendary working ranches – real farms with huge acreages, delicious food and down-to-earth comfort. See p.545

✳ **Asados** Succulent lamb cooked over an open fire defines Patagonia almost as much as the horizon-defying terrain and relentless gales. See p.546

✳ **Cueva de las Manos Pintadas** Wonder at rock art executed hundreds or thousands of years ago, dramatically sited in the heart of a scenic canyon. See p.552

▲ Baleen whale breaching, Península Valdés

Patagonia

"Why then, and this is not only my particular case, does this barren land possess my mind? I find it hard to explain...but it might partly be because it enhances the horizons of imagination."

Charles Darwin

An immense land of arid steppe, seemingly stretching into infinity, **Patagonia** is famed for its adventures and adventurers, for marvellous myths and fabulous facts. Its geographical immensity is paralleled only by the size of its reputation – which itself has taken on legendary proportions, thanks partly to writers such as Chatwin, Hudson, Theroux and Darwin himself. As a region of extremes, it has few equals in the world: from the biting winds that howl off the **Hielo Continental Sur** (Southern Patagonian Icecap) – the planet's largest area of permanent ice away from the poles – to the hearthside warmth of old-time Patagonian hospitality; from the lowest point on the South American continent, the **Gran Bajo de San Julián**, to the savagely beautiful peaks of the **Fitz Roy massif**; from the mesmerizingly sterile plains along the coastline to the astoundingly rich **marine fauna** that thrives and breeds just off shore.

One of southern Argentina's principal arteries, the **RN-3**, stretches from the capital all the way down to austral **Río Gallegos**. The highlight of this Atlantic fringe of Patagonia is the wildlife, most notably at the nature reserve of **Península Valdés**, famous for its **whale-watching**, but also at **Punta Tombo**, the continent's largest **penguin** colony. Further south, in Santa Cruz Province, colonies of sea birds perch on spectacular porphyry cliffs at **Puerto Deseado** and playful Commerson's dolphins frolic in the *ría*, or estuary, just outside the town. This coastal area was key in defining the Patagonian pioneering spirit: Welsh settlers landed on a beach just south of Península Valdés, at what is now the resort town of **Puerto Madryn**, and gradually ventured into the **Lower Chubut Valley**. You can explore their cultural legacy in settlements such as **Gaiman** and **Trelew**.

The second main road running through Argentine Patagonia is the famous – and partly unpaved – the **RN-40** ("Ruta 40"), which starts at Cabo Vírgenes, the most southerly point of mainland Argentina and hugs the Andean backbone most of the way all the way up to the country's northerly tip. Some of the destinations in this western fringe are difficult to reach without your own transport (and not always that easy with it) but it is along or close by this route that you'll find Argentine Patagonia's hallmark features: a slew of impressive national parks brimming with wild beauty, a series of great mountain lakes, the finest spit-roast lamb *asados* and some unique skies. The Cañon of Río Pinturas is home to one of Argentina's most famous archeological sites, the **Cueva de las Manos Pintadas**, with its striking, age-old rock art; to the west two beautiful, wind-whipped **lakes, Posadas and Pueyrredón**, lie in a seldom-visited area in the lee of stately San Lorenzo peak.

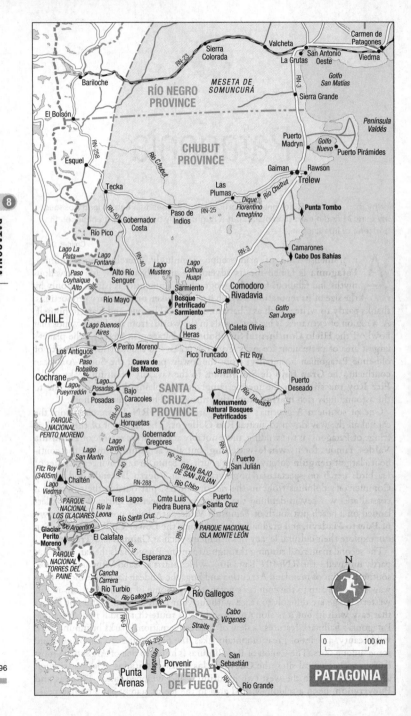

PATAGONIA

Further north is an outstanding geological curiosity, the **Bosque Petrificado Sarmiento**, a beguiling collection of ancient fossilized trees, while to the south stretches the wilderness of **Parque Nacional Perito Moreno**, one of the most inaccessible – and, consequently, untouched – of Argentina's national parks, with some excellent hiking trails.

The region's climax is reached, however, with two of the country's star attractions: the trekkers' and climbers' paradise of the **Fitz Roy** sector of **Parque Nacional Los Glaciares**, accessed from the laidback village of **El Chaltén**; and the patriotically blue-and-white hues of craggy **Glaciar Perito Moreno**, one of the world's natural wonders, within easy reach of the tourist hotspot of **El Calafate**.

Some history

For over ten thousand years, before the arrival of European seafarers in the sixteenth century, Patagonia was exclusively the domain of nomadic **indigenous tribes**. It was Magellan who coined the name "Patagonia" (see p.517) on landing at the **Bahía San Julián**. The tales related by these early mariners awed and frightened their countrymen back home, mutating into myths of a godless region where death often struck hard.

Two centuries of sporadic attempts to colonize the inhospitable coastlands only partially ameliorated Patagonia's unwholesome aura. In 1779, the Spanish established **Carmen de Patagones**, which managed to survive as a trading centre on the Patagonian frontier. In doing so, it fared considerably better than other early settlements: **Puerto de los Leones**, near Camarones (1535); **Nombre de Jesús**, by the Magellan Straits (late 1580s); **Floridablanca**, near San Julián (1784); and **San José** on the Península Valdés, all failed miserably, the latter crushed by a Tehuelche attack in 1810 after braving it out for twenty years. Change was afoot, nevertheless. In 1848, Chile founded Punta Arenas on the Magellan Straits, and in 1865, fired by their visionary faith, a group of **Welsh Nonconformists** arrived in the Lower Chubut Valley. Rescued from starvation in the early years by **Tehuelche** tribespeople and Argentine government subsidies, they managed to establish a stable agricultural colony by the mid-1870s.

In the late nineteenth century, Patagonia changed forever with the introduction of **sheep**, originally brought across from the Islas Malvinas/Falkland Islands. The region's image shifted from one of hostility and hardship to that of an exciting frontier, where the "white gold" of wool opened the path to fabulous fortunes for pioneer investors. The transformation was complete within a generation: the plains were fenced in and roads were run from the coast to the cordillera. Native populations were booted out of their ancestral lands, while foxes and pumas were poisoned en masse to make way for gigantic estancias. By the early 1970s, there were over sixteen million sheep grazing the fragile pastures on over a thousand of these ranches. Later, the region's confidence and wealth blossomed further with the discovery of oil, spurring the growth of industry in towns such as **Comodoro Rivadavia**.

Plummeting international wool prices and desertification, though, eventually brought sheep farming to its knees, with the final blow being the eruption of Volcán Hudson in 1991, which buried immense areas of grazing land in choking ash. To make matters worse, the oil industry also went through a massive downturn and shed thousands of jobs.

The corner has since been turned, however, and today the picture is far from bleak. Although there are hundreds of abandoned estancias in Santa Cruz alone, the Patagonian economy is once again booming – wool prices have been steadily rising owing to rocketing demand in emerging economies and a worldwide interest in a return to natural fibres. Perhaps more importantly for the region's economic future, **tourist** numbers are also rising sharply, as visitors come looking for a wild experience in an almost mythical land. This swelling interest has helped rekindle regional pride to the point where locals boast of being NYC – Nacido y Criado ("Born and Bred") – in Patagonia.

The RN-3 coastal route

A journey along the seemingly endless RN-3 road, with a few detours just off it, offers many opportunities – albeit at great distances from one another – to marvel at magnificent wildlife; nowhere is this easier or more rewarding than at the world-class reserve of **Península Valdés**, best accessed from the seaside town of **Puerto Madryn**. In addition you can check out Patagonia's fascinating Welsh legacy in the villages of the Lower Chubut Valley near **Trelew**, while nature lovers will want to see the huge Magellanic penguin colony at **Punta Tombo**. The long trip can be broken up with stopovers in a trio of typical austral ports, **Puerto Deseado**, **Puerto San Julián** and **Puerto Santa Cruz**, each with its own wealth of marine wildlife and historical associations. A short way south of the last of these three, **Monte León**, the country's newest national park – and the first to be created on the coast – is well worth a visit even if the marvellous estancia in its midst is beyond your budget. With your own transport, you could also fit in a side-trip to the curious petrified forests of the **Monumento Natural Bosques Petrificados**, or the **Bosque Petrificado Sarmiento** (see p.555), closer to the Ruta 40 but accessible from the coast, too. The end of the road – and seemingly the end of the world – is reached at workaday **Río Gallegos**, a jumping-off point for travelling on to Tierra del Fuego or for starting a journey northwards along the RN-40.

Puerto Madryn

Sprawling along the beautiful sweep of the Golfo Nuevo, Argentina's self-styled diving capital, **PUERTO MADRYN**, is the gateway to the ecological treasure trove of Península Valdés; indeed, the superb **Ecocentro** (see p.500), just east of town, makes a great introduction to the area's abundant marine life. Though Puerto Madryn was where the Welsh first landed in Patagonia in 1865, little development took place until the arrival of the railway from Trelew two decades later, when it began to act as the port for the communities in the Lower Chubut Valley. With the explosion of tourism in recent years, Madryn has undergone rapid growth, and the town's small permanent population swells exponentially during the summer months.

Arrival and information

Madryn's **airport** handles the odd LADE flight plus three Andes flights a week (in the summer the latter link up with various major destinations around the country as well as Buenos Aires); either take a *remise* into town ($35) or call Aitue (☎02965/15272444) for a minibus ($25 per person). Most air travellers to the region, however, arrive at Trelew, 65km south (see p.510); minibuses shuttle passengers to Madryn and will

PUERTO MADRYN

Muelle Cmte Luis Piedra Buena

Peninsula Valdés (100km)

Playa Doradilla (17km)&

Museo Oceanográfico

Bus Terminal

Monumento al Indio Tehuelche (4km), Ecocentro & Punta Loma (19km)

BOULEVARD ALMIRANTE GUILLERMO BROWN

AVENIDA RAWSON
JULIO A. ROCA
25 DE MAYO
MITRE
MARCOS A. ZAR
SAN MARTÍN
GOBERNADOR MAÍZ
M.T. DE ALVEAR
J.B. JUSTO
RECONQUISTA
VILLEGAS
SAN LUIS
ROSALES
CHACO
COLÓN
BOUCHARD
PIEDRABUENA
SAN LORENZO
CORRIENTES
MISIONES

PLAZA SAN MARTÍN

H. YRIGOYEN
R.S. PEÑA
28 DE JULIO
BELGRANO
9 DE JULIO
SARMIENTO
AVENIDA GALES
ALBARRACÍN
ESTIVARIZ
MORENO
RIVADAVIA
ALEM
PERLOTTI
PIERO
HERNÁNDEZ
BELGRANO
ACORAZADO

GENERAL MOSCONI
G. FONTANA
NECOCHEA
ESPORA
INDEPENDENCIA
O'HIGGINS
LAPRIDA
BOLIVAR
H. YRIGOYEN
PALAZZO
MIMOSA
EXUPERY

RUTA NACIONAL 3

0   200 m

ACCOMMODATION

El Gualicho	H
Hostel International Puerto Madryn	E
Hostería Casa de Pueblo	D
Hostería Solar de la Costa	A
Hostería Torremolinos	G
Hotel Bahía Nueva	C
Posada del Madryn	B
Residencial Jo's	I
El Retorno Hostel	F

EATING & DRINKING

Ambigú	2
Caccaros	4
El Clásico	7
Estela	6
Havanna	3
Margarita	2
Mar y Meseta	5
Mr Jones	8
Plácido	1
Taska Beltza	10
La Vieja Esquina	9

Trelew (65km)

drop you off at any central address ($35). Much of what you'll need in Madryn lies within three blocks in any direction of the first-rate **tourist office**, at Julio Roca 223 (April to mid-Dec Mon–Fri 7am–9pm, Sat & Sun 8am–9pm; mid-Dec to March Mon–Fri 7am–11pm, Sat & Sun 8am–11pm; ☎02965/453504 or 452148, ⓦwww.madryn.gov.ar), where you can get good maps, leaflets in English, and a list of independent guides who speak foreign languages.

Diving trips that take in the area's offshore wrecks and abundant marine life are available through numerous outfits – expect to pay around $200 per excursion. The experienced Madryn Buceo, on Boulevard Brown by the third roundabout in Balneario Nativo Sur (☎02965/155-64422, ⓦwww.madrynbuceo.com) has English-speaking instructors teaching a range of courses starting from $200 (diving with sea lions costs $500), while Scuba Duba, Boulevard Brown 893 (☎02965/452699, ⓦwww.scubaduba.com.ar), is another worthwhile option. **Mountain bikes** can be rented from Vernadino Club Mar, Boulevard Brown 860. There are a couple of good bike excursions within easy reach of town: north along the old Puerto Pirámides road to Playa Doradilla (17km from Madryn), where you can often see whales late in the afternoon between June and September, and to the sea-lion colony at Punta Loma (19km in other direction; $15).

Accommodation

Madryn has a wide range of **accommodation** with appealing discounts available off season; high season (Oct–Dec), when prices jump significantly, is the best time for whale-watching. There are two **campsites** near the Monumento al Indio

Tehuelche (see box opposite), round the bay (Linea #2 from the bus terminal or the main plaza will take you to within easy walking distance): *Automóvil Club Argentino* (T 02965/452952; $35 per person) and *Camping Luz y Fuerza*, beside Ecocentro (T 02965/457047; $18 per person).

Bahia Nueva Roca 67 T 02965/451677. Smart, red-brick hotel on the seafront, with standard rooms – try to get one of the few with an ocean view – an extensive library, ample buffet breakfasts and covered parking. ⑤

El Gualicho Marcos Zar 480 T 02965/454163, W elgualicho.com.ar. Fantastic hostel with a lovely garden and welcoming staff who arrange tours and diving trips. Has a good range of private rooms (⑤) and four-, six- and eight-bed dorms ($50), each with breakfast included. Bike rental available.

Hostel International Puerto Madryn 25 de Mayo 1136 T 02965/474426. Calm, clean hostel with a mixture of shared and en-suite doubles (③) and bungalows (three, four or five people). It has kitchen and laundry facilities, plus a pleasant garden with a barbecue area. Closed May–Sept. Bungalows $30 per person.

Hostería Casa de Pueblo Roca 475 T 02965/472500, W www.madryncasadepueblo.com.ar. Housed in one of the town's early buildings, this attractive seafront hotel maintains a pioneering yet homely feel. Bedrooms – overlooking either the internal garden or the sea – are cosy, and there's a lovely little first-floor terrace. Price includes breakfast. ⑤

Hostería Solar de la Costa Brown 257 T 02965/458822, W www.solardelacosta.com. Popular beachfront hotel at the eastern end of town, with tastefully furnished rooms – the doubles have good-sized beds – overlooking the Golfo Nuevo. Serves a decent buffet breakfast. Private parking. ⑤

Hostería Torremolinos Marcos Zar 64 T 02965/453215. Modern, intimate and stylish, with tasteful wooden interiors. Only five rooms, so book in advance in season. ⑤

Posada del Madryn Abraham Matthews 2951 T 02965/474087, W www.la-posada.com.ar. Stylish posada in a lovely setting. Compact rooms are bright, while the large living areas have a touch of the design hotel about them. Breakfast is served in a glass-fronted annexe overlooking the spacious garden. ⑥

Residencial Jo's Bolivar 75 T 02965/471433. Cosy little guesthouse run by a charming couple. Good prices for singles, but a fair walk from the centre of town. ③

El Retorno Mitre 798 T 02965/456044, W www.elretornohostel.com.ar. Attractive place whose white-washed exterior is mirrored by the spick-and-span rooms – four-, six- and eight-bed dorms ($40–50) and en-suite doubles (③) – heated bathrooms and spotless communal areas. Kitchen and laundry facilities, barbecue, table tennis and bike rental.

The Town

Early in the morning, the **Golfo Nuevo** can be as still and glassy smooth as a lake, while at sunset there's a glorious view of the wide arc of the gulf back to the lights of town from the **Monumento al Indio Tehuelche**. Four kilometres south along the beach at **Punta Cuevas**, the statue marks the centenary of the arrival of the Welsh (see box, p.510), and stands in homage to the Tehuelche (see box opposite), without whose help the settlement would probably have failed. Just before it sits the three-metre-square foundations of the very first houses built by the pioneers, right above the high-water mark.

Round the headland past the monument is Madryn's prime attraction, the excellent **Ecocentro**, at Julio Verne 3784 (March–Aug Mon & Wed–Sun 3–7pm; Sept–April Mon & Wed–Sun 9am–7pm, though hours can vary so check beforehand; $32; T 02965/457470, W www.ecocentro.org.ar), reachable on Linea #2 from the bus terminal. An interactive museum set up to promote respect and understanding for marine ecosystems, it also houses a stunning life-size model of the orca Mel, famous for catching sea-lion pups and returning them to the shore unharmed. Be sure to go up the tower as well, to relax on one of the comfy sofas while enjoying panoramic views of the bay.

North of town, at D. Garcia and Menéndez, is the rather staid **Museo Oceanográfico y de Ciencias Naturales** (Mon–Fri 9am–7pm, Sat 3–7pm; $10).

Once spread throughout much of Patagonia, the **Tehuelche**, whose name, meaning "brave people", is derived from the language of the Chilean Araucanian groups, actually consisted of three different tribes – the Gününa'küna, Mecharnúek'enk and Aónik'enk – each of whom spoke a different language but shared common bonds of culture. Great inter-tribal parliaments were held occasionally to discuss trade or common threats to the community, but any alliances formed would be temporary and shifting, and sporadic warfare occurred between the different tribes.

The Tehuelche's **nomadic culture** – centred on the hunting of rhea and guanaco, the skins of which they used to build shelters (*toldos*) – had probably existed for well over three thousand years by the time Magellan and the first Europeans landed on Patagonian soil, but contact with Europeans soon brought change. By 1580, Sarmiento de Gamboa had reported use of the horse by the Tehuelche around the Magellan Straits, and by the early eighteenth century the animal had become integral to Tehuelche life. Inter-tribal contact and intermarriage became more regular, and hunting techniques evolved, with **boleadoras** and lances increasingly preferred to the bow and arrow. The *boleadora* consisted of two or three stones wrapped in guanaco hide and connected by long thongs made from the sinews of rheas or guanacos. Whirled around the head, these were thrown to ensnare animals at close quarters. *Boleadoras* are the main physical legacy of Tehuelche culture in today's Argentina.

Tehuelche **religious beliefs** recognized a benign supreme god (variously named Kooch, Maipé or Táarken-Kets), but he did not figure greatly in any outward devotions. In contrast, the malign spirit, **Gualicho**, was a much-feared figure, the regular beneficiary of horse sacrifices and the object of shamanistic attentions; today, this spiritual legacy is recognized not just in Argentina, but also elsewhere in South America. The main divine hero was **Elal**, the being who created man, gave him fire and established the sacred relationships that exist both between the sexes and between man and beasts.

The decline of **Tehuelche civilization** came fast: in 1870, the Victorian adventurer George Musters estimated that there were 1500 Tehuelche in Patagonia; a 1931 census in the province of Santa Cruz (home to the greatest population of Tehuelche) recorded only 350. Wars with the *huincas* (white men) were catastrophic – above all, Julio Roca's Conquest of the Desert in 1879 – and were exacerbated by inter-tribal conflicts between Tehuelche groups themselves and with the Araucanians. Contact with *huinca* civilization, even when conducted peacefully led to severe problems: disease wiped out whole tribal groups, while alcohol abuse led whites to replace one misconception (that of the "noble savage") with another (the "moral delinquent"), enabling them spuriously to justify attempts to settle ancestral Tehuelche lands as part of a greater plan to "civilize the *indio*".

Following the capitulation of the last rebel group to Roca in December 1884, the remaining Tehuelche were pushed into increasingly marginal lands. Guanaco populations plummeted and Tehuelche life became one of dependency. Many found the closest substitute to the old way of life was to join the estancias that had displaced them as *peón* shepherds. In this way, they were absorbed into the rural underclass. Whereas Mapuche customs and language have managed, tenuously, to survive into the twenty-first century, Tehuelche populations fell below that imprecise, critical number that is necessary for the survival of a cultural heritage. The last speaker of Gününa'küna died in 1960. The Aónik'enk language can be spoken, at least partially, by fewer than a dozen people.

It's not in the same league as Ecocentro, but the location – in the elegant, turreted Chalet Pujol – is grand and you can feel a whale's baleen and view relics from Welsh pioneering days in addition to more sombre photos of sea-lion massacres.

Eating and drinking

Like many of the Atlantic harbours, Puerto Madryn is known for its seafood, and there are several beachfront **restaurants** that serve nothing else, including the town speciality, *arroz con mariscos* – a variant of paella usually containing prawns, squid and clams.

Ambigú Roca and R.S. Peña. Good Spanish-style ham and melon, but the pizzas – arguably the best in town – are the real draw at this tasteful, warehouse-style spot. Prices are moderate.

Caccaros Roca 385. Stylish but unpretentious waterfront bistro with terrace seating and good tunes on the stereo. The moderately priced menu includes seafood and meat dishes, plus simpler sandwiches.

El Clásico 28 de Julio and 25 de Mayo. Large portions of affordable pasta and meat or a good-value *menú del día*, served in a fun café that's popular with locals.

Estela R.S. Peña 27. Warm, down-to-earth diner that prepares a juicy *parrilla* mixed grill for two that won't break the bank. Closed Mon.

Havanna Roca and 28 de Julio. Relaxed central café/bar with a sea view, serving tasty *alfajores* to accompany the best espresso in town. Open till 2am Fri & Sat.

Mar y Meseta Roca 485 ☎02965/458740. Enjoy imaginative *raciones* such as prawns in champagne or rabbit in chocolate sauce in the stylish dining room or out on the seafront terrace – though the luxury doesn't come cheap.

Margarita Roca and R.S. Peña. An attractive place to enjoy a pre- or post-dinner drink – most people

plump for one of the potent cocktails. Live music on Thurs.

Mr Jones 9 de Julio 116. Buzzing little keenly priced eatery, immensely popular with locals and young gringos alike. Most of the diners – who fill up the wooden benches and spill out onto the streetside tables – are here for the delicious *picada* (cold meat and cheese platters).

Plácido Roca 506 ☎02965/455991. Elegant, intimate and relatively pricey restaurant, directly overlooking the Golfo Nuevo: it serves fine seafood, including delicious prawn kebabs with sweet-potato mash, and (cheaper) home-made pasta dishes. There's an excellent Argentine wine list. Open till 1am.

Taska Beltza 9 de Julio 345 ☎02965/474003. Unquestionably the best seafood restaurant in town, and very good value for money. Ask for the daily special, or sample a few Basque tapas, followed by a mouthwatering *merluza* and washed down with a chilled chablis. Closed Mon.

La Vieja Esquina Mitre and R.S. Peña. Choice *asados* and great pasta – at prices that won't shock most diners – prepared in a big corrugated building surreally decorated with hundreds of melted wine bottles and old typewriters.

Listings

Airlines Aerolíneas Argentinas, Roca 427 ☎02965/471463; LADE, Roca 117 ☎02965/451256.

Banks Plenty of ATMs, including at Banco de la Nación, 9 de Julio 117; Banco del Chubut, 25 de Mayo 154.

Car rental Fiorasi Roca 165 ☎02965/456300; Localiza, Roca 536 ☎02965/456300.

Laundry Servicios de Lavandería Morenas, Sarmiento and Marcos Zar. Closed Sun.

Taxis Gales ☎471100; Patagonia ☎458300.

Tour agents Dozens of agencies organize day-trips to the Península Valdés, all charging around $170 (plus $45 entrance fee; whale-watching extra): some of the best run are Tito Bottazzi, Boulevard Brown and Martín Fierro (☎02965/474110, ⊛www.titobottazzi.com); Argentina Vision, Roca 536 (☎02965/451427, ⊛www.argentinavision.com); Cuyun Co, Roca 165 (☎02965/451845, ⊛www.cuyunco.com); and Nievemar, Roca 549 (☎02965/455544, ⊛www.nievemartours.com.ar).

Península Valdés

PENÍNSULA VALDÉS, a sandy-beige, treeless hump of land connected to the mainland by a 35-kilometre isthmus, is one of the planet's most significant marine reserves, winning deserved UNESCO World Heritage status in 1999. It was beautifully evoked by Gerald Durrell in *The Whispering Land*: "It was almost as if

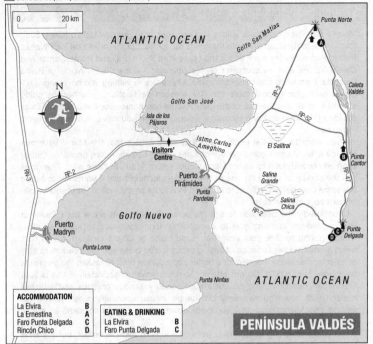

PENÍNSULA VALDÉS

ACCOMMODATION
La Elvira	B
La Ernestina	A
Faro Punta Delgada	C
Rincón Chico	D

EATING & DRINKING
| La Elvira | B |
| Faro Punta Delgada | C |

▼ Trelew (17km)

the peninsula and its narrow isthmus was a cul-de-sac into which all the wildlife of Chubut had drained and from which it could not escape." No description, however, prepares you for the astonishing richness of the marine environment that surrounds it – most notably the **southern right whales** that migrate here each year to frolic in the waters off the village of **Puerto Pirámides** – nor the immense animal colonies that live at the feet of the peninsula's steep, crumbly cliffs.

The first attempt to establish a permanent settlement here was made in 1779 by Juan de la Piedra, who constructed a fort on the shores of the Golfo San José. A small number of settlers tried to scrape a living by extracting salt, but the colony was abandoned in 1810 after attacks by the local Tehuelche; an extremely limited salt-extraction industry exists to this day in the salt pans at the bottom of Argentina's second deepest depression, the **Salina Grande**, 42m below sea level, in the centre of the peninsula. However, it is nature tourism that's the pot of gold now, with **Punta Delgada**, **Punta Cantor** and **Punta Norte**, along with **Caleta Valdés** bay, providing some of the best opportunities on the continent for viewing marine mammals such as elephant seals and sea lions.

The road to the peninsula

The reserve entrance ($5 per vehicle plus $45 per person; pay at the toll-booth) is halfway along the isthmus, 43km from Madryn. Some 22km further, you pass a signposted turn-off north that takes you 5km to the lookout point for the **Isla de los Pájaros** (Bird Island), a strictly controlled area where access is only permitted for the purposes of scientific research. From the shore, telescopes enable you to view sea birds in the nesting colonies 800m away. The most active months are

Visiting Península Valdés

Many people see Península Valdés in a day **tour** from Puerto Madryn (see p.502), following a fairly standard route that visits the lookout point for Isla de los Pájaros, Puerto Pirámides (where a whale trip costs from $60 extra) and Punta Cantor and Caleta Valdés and – depending on the operator – either Punta Norte or Punta Delgada. Be sure to find out exactly what sights you're visiting and how long you'll get in each place (most tours stay 1hr at each destination), whether the guide speaks English and the size of the group (some companies use large buses). Tours are long (10–12hr) so bring picnic provisions, though you can buy lunch in Puerto Pirámides.

If you want to visit the peninsula independently, note that the Mar y Valle **bus service** links Madryn with Puerto Pirámides (daily 9.30am, return 6pm; 1hr 15min; Jan/Feb second departure from Madryn 5pm, return 11am; $17 one way). This gives you the choice of going on one or two whale-watching trips, if you want to return the same day, but it's difficult to get from Pirámides to the rest of Península Valdés without your own wheels.

Undoubtedly the best way to see the peninsula is to **rent a car** from Trelew or Puerto Madryn, allowing you to decide how long you want to spend wildlife-watching, and to time your arrival at Punta Norte or Caleta Valdés for high tide, when there's the best chance of seeing orcas; it also gives you the freedom to stay at an estancia, recommended for a better appreciation of what makes the peninsula so special (see p.502). Do not attempt to rush, however, especially if this is your first experience of driving on unsurfaced roads – serious crashes and fatalities happen with alarming regularity on the peninsula, especially after rain. When renting, check what happens if you break down or have a minor accident, as rescue bills can be hefty.

The whale-watching season runs from mid-June to mid-December, but the **best time to visit** the peninsula is from September to November, when elephant seals are also active, the penguin colonies have returned to breed and, if you're lucky, you stand a chance of seeing orcas cruising behind the spit at Caleta Valdés.

between September and March, when you can spot egrets, herons, waders, ducks, cormorants, gulls and terns. Just past the turn-off is the **Centro de Interpreta-ciones** (daily 8am–8pm; free), poor by comparison with Madryn's Ecocentro, but with some interesting old photos and the skeleton of a young southern right whale that washed up at Caleta Valdés.

Be warned not to collect your own shellfish in the area, because of the possibility of periodic **red-tide** outbreaks; all shellfish served in restaurants is safe for consumption.

Puerto Pirámides

At the end of the asphalt road, 105km from Madryn, lies the tiny settlement of **Puerto Pirámides**, named after the pointed cliff at the mouth of the bay. This is *the* place for whale-watching: between June and mid-December the nearby waters are temporarily home to the most famous of all the peninsula's visitors, the **southern right whale**. Few experiences beat the thrill of watching these massive animals approaching your boat, breaching (leaping out of the water) or jutting their tails above the surface as they dive to feed. There are also good **diving** opportunities for humans (see p.505), with some trips attracting the attention of sea lions and whales, though it's officially illegal to dive with whales; locals refer euphemistically to "*excursiones especiales*". You can walk to the **sea-lion colony** (Jan is the best time) at Punta Pirámides, 5km round the headland to the northwest.

Arrival and information

With only three streets, the village's orientation is straightforward: the main one you come in on, Avenida de las Ballenas, runs parallel to the beach, with two perpendicular streets descending to the water – the shorter, busier Primera Bajada and the much longer Segunda Bajada. There's **tourist information** on Primera Bajada (daily 8am–6pm; open until 8pm Jan–Feb; ℡02965/495048), and a Banco del Chubut **ATM** a short way along Las Ballenas. There's a good range of **accommodation**, but book ahead in January and February when hordes of tourists arrive for a seaside-cum-partying experience, and throughout the whale-watching season (June–Dec). Some places close shop in the early winter months (May and sometimes June). The huge **campsite** in the centre of the village can get severely overcrowded in the height of summer, but it does have showers and direct access to the beach (℡02965/15200521; $15 per person).

Accommodation

Bahía Ballenas Av de las Ballenas s/n ℡02965/474110, ⓦwww.bahiaballenas .com.ar. Excellent little hostel with a snug lounge, two tidy dorms and some of the cleanest bathrooms you'll see; the owners run the Tito Bottazzi agency (see box below) and offer guests discounts on their tours. Breakfast included. ❷

Hostería ACA Av de las Ballenas s/n ℡02965/495004, ⓦwww.motelacapiramides.com. Clean, spacious motel with rather uninspired rooms, some with sea views. ❼

Hostería Ecológica del Nomade Avenida de las Ballenas s/n ℡02965/495044, ⓦwww .ecohosteria.com.ar. Eight gorgeous minimalist rooms in a handsome house that emphasizes environmental friendliness: the staff are ultra-friendly and the home-made breakfasts delicious. Big discounts offered for stays of two nights or more. ❽

La Posta Avenida de las Ballenas at corner with 1a Bajada ℡02965/495036, ⓦwww .lapostapiramides.com.ar. Staggered line of great-value, if rather plain, apartments that come with kitchenette and cable TV. Breakfast included. ❹

Excursions from Puerto Pirámides

In season (June to mid-Dec), you are almost guaranteed to come within a few metres of a southern right whale. If you're here towards the end of the season, there will be fewer specimens and you'll have to go farther out to sea to spot them, but you're also likely to see mothers with calves. Outside these dates, boat trips generally spot dolphins and sea lions. During the whale-spotting season, half a dozen reliable and professional companies offer regular daytime (1hr 30min; $60–75) and "sunset" (2–3hr; $120–150) **whale-watching** trips into the Golfo Nuevo: Hydrosport (℡02965/495065, ⓦwww.hydrosport.com.ar), Tito Bottazzi (℡02965/495050, ⓦwww.titobottazzi.com) and Whales Argentina (℡02965/495015, ⓦwww.whalesargentina.com.ar) are all on Primera Bajada; Jorge Schmid (℡02965/495012, ⓦwww.puntaballena.com.ar) and Peke Sosa (℡02965/495010, ⓦwww.pekesosa.com.ar) are both on Segunda Bajada; while excellent newcomer Southern Spirit (ⓦwww.southernspirit.com.ar) is marked by a model whale on Las Ballenas at the top of Primera Bajada. Services vary little, but check what type of boat you'll be using; the semi-rigid inflatable zodiacs allow you to get closer to the animals, but bounce more in rough waters. Remember, though, that boat operators are meant to observe strict regulations about keeping a respectful distance from the cetaceans; the whales, especially the young, are highly inquisitive, however, and will often come up close or even plunge beneath the boat.

For **diving**, Buceo Aventura (℡02965/495031) has decent equipment and friendly staff, as does Patagonia Scuba (℡02965/495030); both charge around $250 per dive. Patagonian Brothers Expeditions on Avenida de las Ballenas (℡02965/1541 6843, ⓦwww.patagoniaexplorers.com) runs excellent guided small-group **kayak** trips in both gulfs, from half-day paddles to nine-day expeditions.

Las Restingas Primera Bajada s/n
℡02965/495101, Ⓦwww.lasrestingas.com. The
most upmarket place in town in a unique location

on the beach. Most of the bright airy rooms have
wonderful sea views, so you might even do some
whale-spotting from your own bedroom. ⑨

Eating and drinking

🏃 La Estación Opposite the petrol station.
One of the best bars in Patagonia with a
cosy ambience, laidback vibe and mix of old-time
memorabilia and rock iconography. It also serves
great home-made pastas and other delicious,
keenly priced food.

Hostería The Paradise Avenida de las Ballenas on
corner with 2a Bajada. Regarded as Puerto
Pirámides' best restaurant thanks to its fresh but
expensive seafood dishes and a varied wine list.

Piedra Guacha, Avenida de las Ballenas. In a
beautiful, relatively old building serves excellent
seafood, including a tremendous fish stew at very
reasonable prices.

Las Restingas Primera Bajada s/n. A close rival
to Hostería The Paradise, with fabulous views of
the bay. It serves imaginative seafood dishes,
fine wines and delicious pudding, but is fairly
pricey – reckon on at least $100 per person with
a lower-range wine.

Punta Pardelas and Punta Delgada

Just outside Puerto Pirámides, it's worth taking the short road down to **Punta Pardelas**, a delightful little spot right on the shore of Golfo Nuevo, from where you can often get spectacular close-up sightings of southern right whales as they make their way along the coast. From here, it's another 70km to **Punta Delgada**, at the southeasterly tip of the peninsula, past the pinky-white salt deposits of the **Salina Grande** and **Salina Chica** depressions. Punta Delgada itself is a headland topped by a lighthouse, part of the attractive *Faro Punta Delgada* **hotel** (℡02965/471910, Ⓦwww.puntadelgada.com; ⑨ including excellent three-hour tour of nearby elephant-seal colony; closed April–July); perched on the cliff and buffeted by winds, it's an extremely atmospheric place to stay. The area affords excellent opportunities to view **sea lions** and, in high season, **elephant seals**. However, it is private property, and can only be visited on tours run by Argentina Vision (see p.502), who own the *Faro Punta Delgada*. Independent travellers are allowed to stop, but will need to buy lunch at the hotel's restaurant in order to access the beach on a short guided tour (1pm, 2pm & 3pm; free).

Just southwest of Punta Delgada, a short gravel road (signposted) leads to more superb **accommodation** at 🏃 *Estancia Rincón Chico* (℡02965/471733, Ⓦwww .rinconchico.com.ar; ⑨ full board including excursions; closed Easter to mid-Aug), an estancia that blends traditional Patagonian architecture with attractively furnished modern rooms. Food served in the handsome dining room is simple but delicious, while the lobby and living room are decorated with bric-a-brac, such as stranded whale-bones. The highlight of any stay is a guided visit to the large colonies of marine wildlife (up to 3500 sea lions and 10,000 elephant seals) that gather on the estancia's private beach. You can also hire bikes to explore the steppe and admire the cliff-top ocean views.

Punta Cantor and Caleta Valdés

Heading north along the coast from Punta Delgada, a string of beaches bustles with marine mammals. **Punta Cantor**, mid-way up the peninsula, is a colony of seven thousand elephant seals at the foot of a high cliff. Walk down the cliff face of sedimentary deposits and fossilized oysters (around a million years old) to the ridge just above the beach – don't try to climb down onto the beach, however, as it is strictly off limits. The best time to visit is from late September until early November, when the bull elephant seals fight for females – a display of bloodied

Although diverse and significant populations of birds and terrestrial mammals exist on **Península Valdés**, it is the **marine mammals** here that are of particular interest. Pride of place goes to the **southern right whale** (*Ballena franca austral*), which comes to the sheltered waters of the Golfo Nuevo and Golfo San José to breed. Weighing up to 50 tonnes and measuring up to 18m in length (the females are larger than the males), these gentle leviathans are filter-feeders, deriving nutrients from the plankton they sift from the seas with their baleen plates. Once favoured targets for the world's whalers – they were the "right" whales to harpoon, as they were slow, yielded copious quantities of oil and floated when killed – they have now been declared a National Natural Monument, and are protected from the moment they enter Argentine territorial waters. This foresight has enabled the present tourist industry to develop, reinforcing the economic value of keeping these creatures alive; their charming curiosity – a trait that once put them in danger – now makes them one of the most enjoyable cetaceans to view in the wild.

The **killer whale**, or orca, is not in fact a whale at all, but the largest member of the dolphin family – it displays the high levels of intelligence we associate with such creatures, if not their cuteness. This is amply demonstrated in their unique hunting behaviour at Caleta Valdés and Punta Norte, where orcas storm the shingle banks, beaching themselves in order to snap up their preferred prey: baby sea lions and young elephant seals. Male killer whales have been known to measure over nine metres, and weigh some eight tonnes, although the ones off Valdés do not reach these sizes; females are not quite as long and weigh considerably less. The dorsal fin on an adult male is the biggest in the animal kingdom, measuring 1.8m – the height of an average man – and its size and shape is one of the factors used to identify individual orcas, along with the shape of the saddle patch and colour variations; 23 have been tracked off Punta Norte. If you want to know more, contact Fundación Orca (℡02965/454723, ⓦwww.fundorca.org.ar), a Madryn-based scientific organization dedicated to the study of this creature.

Sea lions (*Lobos marinos*) were once so numerous on the peninsula that 20,000 would to be culled annually for their skins and blubber – a figure that equals the entire population found here today, even after almost thirty years of protection. They are the most widely distributed of the Patagonian marine mammals and their anthropomorphic antics make them a delight to watch. It's easy to see the derivation of the name when you look at a 300-kilogram adult male, ennobled by a fine yellowy-brown mane.

As animals go, few come into the league of the southern **elephant seal** (*Elefante marino*), a creature so large that Noah made him swim. Península Valdés is their only continental breeding ground and, the only place you're ever likely to see them in the all-too-evident flesh. Weighing some three tonnes and measuring four to five metres, bull elephant seals mean business. Though the average size of a harem for a dominant male ranges between ten and fifteen females, some superstud tyrants get greedy. One macho male at Caleta Valdés infamously amassed 131 consorts, fighting off love rivals in the process. October is the best month to see these noisy clashes of the titans, but be prepared for some gore, as tusk wounds are inevitable. Adult females, a fifth of the size of the vast males, are pregnant for eleven months of the year, giving birth from about mid-September. Pups weigh 40kg at birth, but then balloon on their mother's rich milk to weigh 200kg after only three weeks. The elephant seal's most remarkable attribute, however, is as the world's champion deep-sea diving mammal. Depths of over a thousand metres are not uncommon, and it is reckoned that some of these animals have reached depths of 1500m, staying submerged for a (literally) breathtaking two hours.

▲ Elephant seals, Caleta Valdés

blubbery bulk. During the rest of the year, you will hear snorts and sneezes, see stretches yawns and scratching and the odd fatty quiver like a waterbed being slapped, but otherwise the animals are content just to sleep.

Two kilometres north is a viewpoint over the shifting curves of the shingle spits of **Caleta Valdés** – from September to November, orcas may be spotted entering the *caleta*, or bay behind the spit, at high tide – and there's a colony of Magellanic penguins 3km further on. This road is also one of the best for sighting *maras*, *choiques*, skunks and other terrestrial wildlife.

For **accommodation** there's *La Elvira*, a rather ugly modern block with somewhat attractively rustic rooms, near the Punta Cantor turn-off (℡02965/474248, Ⓦwww.laelvira.com.ar; $740 full board including excursions; closed April–Aug); the restaurant's cheap, buffet-style food is popular with tour groups.

Punta Norte

Wild **Punta Norte**, the northernmost point of the peninsula, is famous for the **orca attacks** on baby sea lions that occur there during March and early April. In a spectacle rivalling anything in the natural world, the eight-tonne orcas beach themselves at up to 50km per hour and attempt to grab a pup; most efforts are unsuccessful, and an orca will sometimes settle for a snack of penguin. Attacks usually occur with the high tides – if you're so inclined, check with the Centro de Interpretaciones (see p.504) for times and plan your arrival to coincide with the hour either side of high tide to stand the best chance of witnessing one. These aside, the sight of ominous black dorsal fins of a pod of killer whales cruising just off the coast is thrilling enough. Serious photographers can buy an expensive permit to descend to the beach (contact the Secretaria de Turismo in Rawson ℡02965/481113, Ⓔinfo@chubutur.gov.ar), but the general viewing area can be as good a vantage point as any.

On the slope above the beach there's a **café** where the personable owner prepares filling snacks, as well as an interesting **visitors' centre and museum** (free); inside, you can identify the distinguishing features of the different individual orcas. You can also **stay** up here, at the characterful but pricey *La Ernestina* (☎02965/471143, ⓦwww.laernestina.com; US\$420 full board including drinks and excursions), whose excellent location, right on the beach, makes it a favourite haunt of wildlife photographers.

Trelew and Gaiman: the Welsh heartland

If you're coming to Chubut Province looking for Argentina's answer to Snowdonia, think again. Not only is there not a mountain in sight, but also the **Welsh**, like the Tehuelche before them, have been absorbed almost seamlessly into Argentina's diverse cultural identity. Under the surface, though, there remain vestiges of their pioneering culture and a real pride in both the historical legacy – evident in the number of fine **Welsh chapels** dotted across the farmlands of the **Lower Chubut Valley** – and the current cultural connection that goes well beyond the touristy trappings.

Halting Welsh is still spoken by some of the third- or fourth-generation residents in the main towns of **Trelew** and **Gaiman**, even if it isn't the language of common usage, and whereas it once seemed doomed to die out, the tongue now appears to be enjoying a limited **renaissance**. In municipal schools today, young students have the option to study the language of their forebears: a team of **Welsh teachers** works in Chubut, and **cultural exchanges** with Mam Cymru are thriving – two or three pupils are sent annually from Chubut to Welsh universities and numerous delegations from different associations ply across the Atlantic. It's not all one way either: scholars have come from Wales to study the manuscripts left by pioneers and seek inspiration from what they pronounce to be the purity of the language that was preserved in Patagonia.

Airport (5km), Puerto Madryn (65km) & Comodoro Rivadavia (370km) ▼

In July 1865, after two months at sea, 153 **Welsh** men, women and children who had fled Britain to escape cultural and religious oppression disembarked from their clipper, the *Mimosa*, and took the first steps into what they believed was to be their Promised Land. Here they planned to emulate the Old Testament example of bringing forth gardens from the wilderness, but though the land around the Golfo Nuevo had the appearance of Israel, its parched harshness cannot have been of much comfort to those who had left the green valleys of Wales. Fired by Robert FitzRoy's descriptions of the Lower Chubut Valley, they explored south and, two months later, relocated – a piecemeal process during which some groups had, in the words of one of the leading settlers, Abraham Matthews, to live off "what they could hunt, foxes and birds of prey, creatures not permitted under Mosaic Law, but acceptable in the circumstances".

The immigrants were mostly miners or small merchants from southeast Wales and had little farming experience. Doubts and insecurities spread, with some settlers petitioning the British to rescue them, but when all avenues of credit seemed closed, vital assistance came from the Argentine government by way of provisions and substantial monthly subsidies. And despite initial mistrust of the **Tehuelche**, the Welsh learned survival and hunting skills from their native neighbours, which proved invaluable when the settlers' sheep died and the first three harvests failed. By the early 1870s, 44 settlers had abandoned the attempt, and sixteen had died, but optimists pointed to the fact that ten new settlers had since arrived, and 21 Welsh-Argentines had been born into the community. They decided to stick it out.

With increasing awareness of irrigation techniques, the pioneers began to coax their first proper yields from the Lower Chubut Valley, and recruitment trips to Wales and the US brought a much-needed influx of new settlers in 1874, the year in which Gaiman (see p.512) was founded. Yet the best indicator of the settlement's progress was the international recognition received when samples of barley and wheat grown in Dolavon returned from major international expositions in Paris (1889) and the US (1892) with gold medals in their respective categories. The village's flour mill, built in the 1880s, still works.

Trelew

The medium-sized town of **TRELEW** – its Welsh name means the "village of Lewis", in honour of Lewis Jones, its founder – is home to a couple of excellent museums, while its good transport connections make it a convenient base from which to explore the surrounding Welsh settlements of the **Lower Chubut Valley** and, to the south, the famous penguin colony at **Punta Tombo**. The only downside is the lack of particularly appealing accommodation – nearby Gaiman has a far better selection.

Arrival and information

Trelew's **airport** (which also serves Puerto Madryn) is 5km northeast of town; there's a Banco de Chubut **ATM** and a simple **tourist office** counter that opens for flight arrivals. Several car-rental agencies serve the airport, though you'll get a better deal in Trelew itself; *remises* into town cost $20. The **bus terminal** is within easy walking distance of the town centre; regular buses run to Gaiman, Dolavon and Rawson. The helpful main **tourist office** is at San Martín and Mitre (Mon–Fri 8am–8pm, Sat & Sun 9am–9pm; ☏ 2965/426819, ⓦ www.trelewpatagonia .gov.ar); the staff can provide you with a good leaflet on the various Welsh chapels of the Lower Chubut Valley.

Accommodation

With the exception of the historic *Hotel Touring Club*, Trelew's **hotels** are rather mundane. The nearest **campsite** is *Camping Patagonia* (☎02965/15406907; $15 per person), 12km southeast of town along Ruta 7.

Galicia 9 de Julio 214 ☎02965/433802, ⓦwww .hotelgalicia.com.ar. Has a grand entrance and a lavish lobby but the rooms, while perfectly comfortable, are on the small side. ❻

Hotel Libertador Rivadavia 31 ☎02965/420220, ⓦwww.hotellibertadortw.com.ar. Another large, rather old-fashioned establishment, but the rooms are clean and the staff efficient and friendly. ❻

Hotel Rayentray San Martin 101 ☎02965/434702, ⓦwww.cadenarayentray.com.ar. The most upmarket option in town (though that

isn't saying much), with larger than normal rooms and a range of facilities, including a top-floor swimming pool. ❼

Hotel Touring Club Fontana 240 ☎02965/425790, ⓦwww.touringpatagonia .com.ar. Charming if slightly faded Art Deco historic monument (Butch Cassidy and the Sundance Kid once stayed here), with airy, spacious rooms, fronted by a tremendous high-ceilinged bar (see below). ❹

The Town

Trelew rose to prominence after the completion, in 1889, of the rail link to Puerto Madryn, which allowed easy export of the burgeoning agricultural yields. The railway has since disappeared, but the old station, on 9 de Julio and Fontana, is now home to the **Museo Regional Pueblo de Luis** (Mon–Fri 8am–8pm, Sat & Sun 2–8pm; $5). One of two fine museums in Trelew, it does a good job of tracing the area's **Celtic** history and also explores the coexistence of the Welsh and the Tehuelche as well as the eisteddfod (traditional annual Welsh) festivals. Across the road is the excellent modern **Museo Paleontológico Egidio Feruglio (MEF)**, Fontana and Lewis Jones (April–Aug Mon–Fri 10am–6pm, Sat & Sun 10am–8pm; Sept–March daily 9am–8pm; $23; ⓦwww.mef.org.ar), one of South America's most important paleontological collections, which sets out to describe "300 million years of history" and contains beautifully preserved clutches of dinosaur eggs and skeletons from the region, including a 95-million-year-old argentosaurus, one of the world's largest dinosaurs. Ask for an English guided tour (45min; free), if you need one.

Trelew's urban centrepiece is its fine main square, the **Plaza Independencia**, with flourishing trees and an elegant gazebo, built by the Welsh to honour the centenary of Argentine Independence; in September/October each year, the leafy plaza becomes the focus for the most important of the province's **eisteddfodau**, when two prestigious awards are made: the *Sillón del Bardo* (The Bard's Chair), for the best poetry in Welsh, and the *Corona del Bardo* (The Bard's Crown), for the best in Spanish.

Eating and drinking

Most of Trelaw's **eating** and **drinking** options are close to the main square. You can stock up on food for day-trips at several **supermarkets** around town, including the Hiper Norte at Rivadavia and 9 de Julio.

Comedor Universitario Luis Llana Opposite the Museo Regional on Rivadavia. Simple but filling local fare at student prices. Open 10am–8pm.

La Eloisa Belgrano 351. A smart, formal restaurant, which, despite the impressive *asado* in the window, also does a good seafood à la carte menu. Prices range from moderate to expensive. Open 7am–3am.

Nouveau Chateau Vieux 25 de Mayo and A.P. Bell ☎02965/425247. Fine Patagonian dining – lamb, rabbit and the like – and even finer wines in its atmospheric 1920s building. Prices match the quality.

Touring Club Fontana 240. Characterful *confitería* and bar with touches of grandeur, offering *milanesas* – or something a little stronger from the terrifying array of dusty bottles lining the 1920s bar. Open 6.30am–midnight.

El Viejo Molino Avenida Gales 250. Excellent meat and fish dishes, including a novel *tabla de ahumados* (a mixed platter of smoked cold cuts), served in an old mill setting. The prices, like the venue, are at the upper end.

Listings

Airlines Aerolíneas Argentinas, 25 de Mayo 33 ☎02965/420170; LADE, 1st floor bus terminal ☎02965/435740.

Banks Banco del Chubut, Rivadavia and 25 de Mayo; Banco de la Nacion, Fontana and 25 de Mayo.

Taxis Outside bus terminal, or call ☎02965/420404 or 424445.

Tour agencies In season (Sept–March), several agencies run half-day tours to the penguin colony at Punta Tombo ($150 plus $35 entrance fee), and full-day tours that also take in a Welsh tea in Gaiman and Commerson's dolphin-watching in nearby Playa Unión ($250 plus $35 entrance fee and $50 tea). Recommended outfits include Alcamar Travel, San Martín 146 (☎02965/421213, ⓦwww.argentinapatagonia.com.ar); Explore Patagonia, Roca 297 (☎02965/437860); and Nievemar Tours, Italia 98 (☎02965/434114, ⓦwww.nievemartours.com.ar).

Gaiman

West of Trelew is the broad Lower Chubut Valley, a fertile ribbon of land amid some barren steppe, thanks to the Río Chubut, which flows through here from the Andes. The river derives its name from the Tehuelche word *"chupat"*, meaning clean or transparent. The Welsh began using the Chubut to irrigate the valley in 1867, and it was dammed a hundred years later to ensure a more predictable flow to the farm plots, while also generating electricity for industrial development around Trelew. A string of well-maintained **Welsh chapels** (*capillas galesas*) line the Chubut, including – just south of Trelew – the Capilla Moriah; dating from 1880 it's the oldest in Argentina and many of the original settlers are buried in its cemetery. The small towns along the river's route are all charming and, though you won't exactly hear Welsh spoken in the streets, the legacy of pioneering times is detectable.

The town of **GAIMAN**, 16km west of Trelew along the RN-25, sits amid lush pastures and poplar trees that – in clement weather, at least – form a landscape more like a Monet watercolour than typical Patagonia. It's a pleasant place and the most eminently "Welsh" of the area's settlements, as manifested in the numerous tearooms (*casas de té*), various monuments to the settlers, and its mini-**eisteddfodau** in mid-September and the first week of May.

You can spend a pleasant hour or two taking in the village's various sights: the handsome brick **Capilla Bethel** from 1913, next to its late nineteenth-century predecessor; the squat stone **Primera Casa** (First House), dating from 1874, and looking as if it had been transplanted from Snowdonia; the appealing little plaza with its early bust commemorating Christopher Columbus; the old train station that now houses the **Museo Histórico Regional** (Tues–Sun 3–7pm; $3), with exhibits relating to the trials of pioneer life; and you can even walk through the abandoned 300-metre-long **railway tunnel** near the tourist office.

For all its Celtic heritage, Gaiman's most surprising monument has nothing whatsoever to do with tradition, Welsh or otherwise. **Parque El Desafío** ("The Challenge Park"; Mon–Wed 3–7pm, Thurs–Sun 9am–1pm & 3–7.30pm; $10), at Almirante Brown 52, is a backyard where tens of thousands of **tin cans and plastic bottles** have been recycled and reincarnated. It's the work of Joaquín Alonso (who died at a ripe old age in 2007), dubbed by the local media as the Dalí of Gaiman. His fabulous constructions, such as the tower he erected "in homage to myself", stand alongside ironic mockeries of modern consumerist society.

Gaiman's Casas de Té

The highlight of a visit to Gaiman is working your way through a mountain of cakes over afternoon tea at a **casa de té**, some of which are owned and run by descendants of the original Welsh settlers. Open daily (around 2–7pm) they all serve similar arrays of cake, toast, scones and home-made jams ($40–50 per person); the most traditional component is the *torta negra* (dark fruit cake), originally a wedding gift to be eaten on a couple's first anniversary. Ivy-clad *Ty Nain*, Avenida Yrigoyen 283, is one of the most authentic, and bang in the centre, next to the plaza; take your tea surrounded by the owners' collection of tea- and Welsh-related artefacts. The warm welcome guests receive at *Plas y Coed*, Michael D. Jones 123, is mirrored in the generous portions served there, while at nearby *Ty Cymraeg*, Abraham Matthews 74, a descendant of the pioneers serves tea in the original family home.

Practicalities

Buses from Trelew stop at the corner of Rivadavia and Belgrano, one block up from the main drag, Avenida Eugenio Tello; a **taxi** for the same trip will cost around $40. The helpful **tourist office** (Mon–Sat 9am–8pm, Sun 11am–7pm; ⓣ02965/491571, ⓔinformes@gaiman.gov.ar) is located at Belgrano 574.

If you intend **to stay**, try the *Plas y Coed* on Avenida. Yrigoyen 320 (ⓣ02965/15697069, ⓦwww.plasycoed.com.ar; ④). The owners have done a good job of recreating the homely atmosphere that pervaded their original property – the first teahouse in Gaiman – just around the corner, and there's a spacious living room for guests; it also serves a huge, high-calorie breakfast. The *Hostería Gwesty Tywi*, at Chacra 202 (ⓣ02965/491292, ⓦwww.hosteria-gwestywi.com.ar; ④), is a clean, perfumed B&B whose owners speak Welsh and English, while the larger *Ty Gwyn*, 9 de Julio 147 (ⓣ02965/491009; ⑤), has compact wood-floored rooms with partial views of the Río Chubut. *Yr Hen Ffordd* ("The Old Way"), Michael D. Jones 342 (ⓣ02965/491394, ⓦwww.yrhenffordd.com.ar; ③) is a good budget option, but could do with a bit of a face-lift. There's also a **campsite**, *Los Doce Nogales* ($15 per person), across the river to the southeast, near the *Tŷ Té Caerdydd* teahouse.

For a more substantial meal than tea and cakes, *Gwalia Lân*, an inviting **restaurant** on the corner of Jones and Avenida Tello (Tues–Sat 12.30–3pm & 7.30pm–midnight, Sun 12.30–3pm), serves delicious pizzas, pasta and meat dishes, or try *El Angel*, at Rivadavia 241 (ⓣ02965/491460; evenings only, closed Thurs), which is essentially someone's home, so ring in advance.

Punta Tombo and Cabo Dos Bahías

Two of Chubut Province's main attractions are the coastal reserves of **Punta Tombo,** home to half a million penguins, and **Cabo Dos Bahías**, with its sizeable colony of sea lions. Punta Tombo lies 107km south of Trelew, and is easily reached on a day-excursion from here or from Gaiman. At 260km from Trelew, Cabo Dos Bahías is too far to reach within a day, but you can stay on site, albeit in fairly basic lodgings.

Punta Tombo

Punta Tombo is by far the largest single colony of penguins on the continent, with a population of more than half a million birds; it is also one of the most commercialized. The noise from these black and white **Magellanic penguins** – slightly less glamorous versions of the larger king and emperor penguins, the yellow-throated

The Magellanic penguin

The word "penguin", some maintain, derives from Welsh *pen gwyn* (white head), a name allegedly bestowed by a Welsh sailor passing these shores with Thomas Cavendish in the sixteenth century. In fact, **Magellanic penguins** don't have white heads and it's far more likely that the name comes from the archaic Spanish *pingüe*, or fat. The birds were a gift to the early mariners, being the nearest equivalent at that time to a TV dinner.

Though they're not exactly nimble on land, in water these birds can keep up a steady 8km an hour, or several times that over short bursts. An adult bird stands 50 to 60cm tall and weighs a plump 4–5.5kg. Birds begin arriving at their ancestral Patagonian nesting sites – which can be up to 1km from the sea – from late August, and by early October nesting is in full swing. Parents share the task of incubation, as they do the feeding of the brood once the eggs start to hatch, in early November. By early January, chicks that have not been preyed upon by sea birds, foxes or armadillos make their first sorties into the water. During the twenty-day February moult, the birds do not swim, as they lose their protective layer of waterproof insulation; at this time, penguin sites are awash with fuzzy down and sneezing birds. In March and April, they begin to vacate the nesting sites. Although little is known of their habits while at sea, scientists do know that the birds migrate north, reaching as far as the coast off Rio de Janeiro, 3000km away.

birds that have so successfully cornered the brand image – is immense; it's quite an experience to wander around this scrubland avian metropolis amid a cacophony of braying, surrounded on all sides by waddling, tottering birds. The penguins nest behind the stony beach in scrapes underneath the bushes, with a close eye on approaching strangers. Get too close and they'll indicate their displeasure by hissing or bobbing their heads from side to side like a dashboard dog – respect these warning signals, and remember that a penguin can inflict a good deal of pain with its sharp bill.

The **reserve** ($35; pay at the gate) is open between September and late March although late **November** to **January** is probably the best time to visit, as there are plenty of young chicks. The penguins are most active in the morning and early evening; tour agencies run morning trips from Trelew, allowing around one and a half hours with the birds. The nearby countryside is an excellent place to see **terrestrial wildlife**, such as guanacos, *choiques*, skunks, armadillos and *maras*.

Cabo Dos Bahías

The remote coastal reserve of **Cabo Dos Bahías** ($25; pay at the gate), stuck out on a headland 30km from the tiny fishing village of **Camarones**, is home to another 55,000 Magellanic penguins plus a colony of sea lions from August to April. Tame herds of guanacos are abundant in the park, which also has healthy populations of *choique* and *mara*. There is a **restaurant** at Caleta Sara, a small bay reached by taking the left fork shortly after the reserve entrance, where there is also basic but clean **accommodation** in converted five-metre-long freight containers ($20 per person); you can also pitch your tent for free by the *Club de YPF*. In Camarones, 72km off the RN-3 down the paved RP-30, there is decent enough accommodation at the pleasant *Viejo Torino* near the harbour (℡0297/496-3003; ⓞ), or try the *Bahía del Sueño* cabins on the left as you approach the village (℡0297/496-3007; $300 for a four-person cabin).

Note that **buses** from Trelew reach only as far as Camarones (Mon, Wed & Fri 8am; returns same day 4pm; 3hr); you'll have to rely on bagging a lift from someone in Camarones to the park.

The coast of Santa Cruz Province

The stretch of the RN-3 south of Cabo Dos Bahías encompasses some pretty dreary towns, not least the oil-hub of **Comodoro Rivadavia** – a dire place best avoided, though it does have a useful airport and other services such as car rental. While this section of eastern Patagonia must claim some of most desolate scenery in Argentina, there are some natural gems threaded along it: the **Ría Deseado estuary** at **Puerto Deseado**, with its handsome porphyry cliffs and marvellous opportunities to view dolphins and penguins at close quarters; the tremendous trunks of fossilized araucaria monkey puzzles in the **Monumento Natural Bosques Petrificados**; and **Puerto San Julián**, a historic town with access to one of the most conveniently situated penguin colonies in Patagonia. Farther south you could also break the excruciatingly long distances of largely uneventful coastline into more manageable chunks by stopping at **Comandante Luis Piedra Buena**, known for its fishing, or **Parque Nacional Monte León**, Argentina's first coastal national park, in which a century-old estancia offers some of the area's finest lodgings.

Puerto Deseado and around

Avoiding grim Caleta Olivia, the first place worth visiting in Santa Cruz Province (albeit entailing a hefty detour) is easy-going **PUERTO DESEADO**, a straggly but engaging fishing and naval port on the flooded estuary, or *ría*, of the Río Deseado. Some spectacular coastal scenery and a couple of remarkable colonies of marine wildlife are within sight of town, most dramatically along the **estuary** itself. The town owes its name to the English privateer Thomas Cavendish, who baptized it **Port Desire**, in honour of his ship, when he put in here in 1586. Later expeditions had less success, and a sunken caravel from 1770, the *Swift*, was discovered in the port in 1982 – the **Museo Regional Mario Brozoski**, by the seafront (Mon–Fri 8am–3pm, Sat & Sun 3–5pm; free), displays items brought up from the ship, including gallon gin bottles. Modern-day Puerto Deseado, however, was shaped more by the Ferrocarril Nacional Patagónico, a cross-country cargo route that ran northwest to Las Heras; the town's fine, porphyry-coloured former train station, opposite the Salesian college, operated as the route's terminus from 1911 until 1979 and now functions as the **Museo de la Estación del Ferrocarril** (Mon–Sat 4–7pm; free), housing train memorabilia.

Practicalities

Buses connect the town with Comodoro Rivadavia and Río Gallegos, via Caleta Olivia, but Deseado's **bus terminal** is inconveniently sited at the far end of town. Try to disembark in the centre or, if leaving town, flag down the bus as it passes along Avenida España. The main **tourist office** is at San Martín 1525 (daily April–Oct 9am–4pm; Nov–March 9am–9pm; ☎0297/487-0220, ⓦwww.turismo .deseado.gov.ar). There's an **ATM** at the Banco Santa Cruz, San Martín 1056, and several **internet** and **phone** places on the corner of San Martín and Alte Brown.

The best **accommodation** is at *Hotel Los Acantilados* (☎0297/487-2167, ⓔacantour@pdeseado.com.ar), occupying the bluff at España and Pueyrredón as you enter the town, though the smart *confitería* at the entrance far outdoes the rooms in terms of style. Some of the comfortable superior rooms on the upper storey have estuary views (⑥), while the good value rooms facing the town (⑤) can get very noisy when there's a "night-time" show on in the downstairs bar. Cheaper options include *Isla Chaffers*, a very clean and welcoming hotel in the centre, on San Martín and Moreno (☎&ⓕ0297/487-2246; ⑤), and friendly *Residencial Los*

Olmos, Gob. Gregores 849 (℡&℉0297/487-0077; ❹), meticulously well kept with good-value rooms.

Always full of locals, the most popular **restaurant** in town is *El Pingüino*, Piedrabuena 958 (℡0297/4871399; closed Sun); the *platos del día* are excellent value, and there is a good fish and *parrilla* selection, though the service can get stretched at times. Better still, and open for Sunday lunch, *Lo de Armando*, (℡0297/4871399; closed Sun eve) at San Martín and Sarmiento, is smarter and friendlier, offering hearty home cooking. For Sunday dinner, you may need to fall back on the *confitería* in the *Hotel Los Acantilados*.

Ría Deseado

Stretching 45km inland from Puerto Deseado is the **RÍA DESEADO**, an astonishing sunken river valley, which, unlike most other estuaries on the continent, is flooded by the sea, like a shallow fjord. Opposite the town, its purple cliffs are smeared with guano from five species of **cormorant**, including the dapper, morning-suited Grey Cormorant (*cormorán gris*), whose dull-coloured body sets off its yellow bill and scarlet legs. These birds are seen in few other places, and nowhere else will you get such a sterling opportunity to photograph them. The estuary also hosts several penguin colonies, small flocks of dazzling white Snowy Sheathbills (*palomas antárticas*), a colony of sea lions and an estimated fifty playful and photogenic **Commerson's dolphins** (*toninas averas*); the undisputed stars here, these beautiful creatures torpedo through the water to rollick in bow waves just feet from boats.

Darwin Expediciones, based beside the Gipsy dock on the approach to town (℡0297/156-247554, ⓦwww.darwin-expeditions.com), runs three excellent **boat trips** around the Ría Deseado and, if the tide is high, up the **Cañadón Torcida**, a narrow and steep-sided channel of the estuary, dolphin-spotting on the way to **Isla de los Pájaros**, where passengers can disembark and observe the birdlife – dominated by Magellanic penguins – at close hand (departs 10am & 3pm; 2hr; $140); to **Isla Pingüino**, one of the few places outside Antarctica where the punkish Rockhopper Penguin (*pingüino de penacho amarillo*) can easily be spotted (departs early morning, weather permitting; 6hr; $400); and a trip up the estuary to the scenic **Miradores de Darwin**, retracing the scientist's 1833 journey and stopping to look at wildlife en route (departs 10am; 6hr; $400). Charming owners Javier and Ricardo also tailor trips to demand and will run excursions to see the rare fur seals at Cabo Blanco, 90km north of Puerto Deseado, as well as to the Monumento Natural Bosques Petrificados, a couple of hours due west by dirt roads (see below).

Monumento Natural Bosques Petrificados

The **MONUMENTO NATURAL BOSQUES PETRIFICADOS** (aka Jaramillo; daily: April–Sept 10am–5pm; Oct–March 9am–8pm; free) lies 50 km down a branch road leading west off the RN-3, 80km south of the turn-off to Puerto Deseado. The **fossilized tree trunks** here are strangely beautiful, especially at sunset, when their jasper-red expanses soak up the glow, as though they're heating up from within. The sheer magnitude of the trunks is astonishing, too, measuring some 35m long and up to 3m across. The primeval Jurassic forest grew here 150 million years ago – 60 million years before the Andean cordillera was forced up, forming the rain barrier that has such a dramatic effect on the scenery we know now. In Jurassic times, this area was still swept by moisture-laden winds from the Pacific, allowing the growth of araucaria trees. A cataclysmic blast from an unidentified volcano flattened these colossi and covered the fallen trunks with ash. The wood absorbed silicates in the ash and petrified, later to be revealed when erosion wore down the supervening strata.

Surrounding the trunks is a bizarre **moonscape** of arid basalt *meseta*, dominated by the 400-metre-tall **Cerro Madre e Hija** (Mother and Daughter Mount). A two-kilometre trail, littered by shards of fossilized bark as if it were a woodchip path through a garden, leads from the park office past all the most impressive trunks, while the small **museum** has displays of some fascinating fossils such as the araucaria pinecones.

Puerto San Julián

The small port of **PUERTO SAN JULIÁN**, just off the RN-3 some 260 km south of the turn-off to Puerto Deseado, is another convenient place to break the long journey down to Río Gallegos. This barren town, rich in historical associations owing to its shingle-banked **bay**, was once one of the few safe anchorages along the Patagonian coast. Today, there's little visible evidence of the port's history apart from a replica of Magellanes' ship the *Victoria* moored along the *costanera*, but it's a good place to go on one of various **tours**, including a highly recommended trip to view the **marine life** of the bay. The penguins here live closer to human settlement than at any other site in the south, and are not afraid to assert ancestral privilege – indeed, local radio has been known to put out appeals to remove penguins from the town hall.

One of the few traces of the past to be preserved, right in what passes for the town's main square, went unobserved for many years, until someone noticed that a paving slab he'd just walked on had been walked on before – by a dinosaur. The distinct, prehistoric prints of the **sauropod** (a crocodile-like reptile) can now be seen at the local **Museo Regional Rosa Novak** on Rivadavia and Vieytes (early March to mid-Dec Mon–Fri 9am–1pm & 2–5pm; mid-Dec to early March daily 9am–9pm; free).

Practicalities

Puerto San Julián lies 3km off the RN-3, down a straight road that becomes Avenida San Martín, the town's main artery. The **tourist office** is at San Martin and Rivadavia (Mon–Fri 7am–9pm, Sat & Sun 9am–9pm; ℡02962/452353, ⓦwww.sanjulian.gov.ar).

For **accommodation**, the breezy, recently refurbished seafront *Hostería Costanera*, 25 de Mayo 917 (℡02962/452300, ⓦwww.costanerahotel.com; ❺),

Patagonia's birthplace

Puerto San Julián can rightfully claim to be the **birthplace of Patagonia**. In 1520, during **Magellan's** stay in the bay, the very first encounter occurred between the Europeans and the "giants" of this nameless land, when, it is believed, the explorer bestowed on them the name "*patgon*" (literally "big foot") in reference to their comparatively large build. As related by Antonio Pigafetta, the expedition's chronicler: "One day, without anyone expecting it, we saw a giant, who was on the shore of the sea, quite naked, and was dancing and leaping, and singing, and whilst singing he put sand and dust on his head... When he was before us he began to be astonished, and to be afraid, and he raised one finger on high, thinking that we came from heaven. He was so tall that the tallest of us only came up to his waist... The captain named this kind of people Patagon." On Palm Sunday, April 1, 1520, Magellan celebrated the first Mass on Argentine soil, near a site marked by a cross, down by the town's port.

offers good views of the bay from its upstairs rooms, though *Hotel Bahía*, San Martín 1075 (℡02962/454028, ⓦwww.hotelbahiasanjulian.com.ar; ⑤), is more upmarket, with modern, well-furnished rooms with spacious bathrooms. Alternatively, try the moderately priced *Hostería Miramar* at San Martín 210 (℡02962/454656, ⓔhosteriamiramar.uvc.com.ar; ④), or the budget *La Casona*, on Avenida Costanera (℡02962/452434; ③), a rustic corrugated-iron house with simple rooms. The municipal **campsite** next to the bay is stony but clean (℡02962/452806; $6 per person), and gets very busy in January.

The best seafood **restaurant** in town is *La Rural*, near the Museo Regional, at Ameghino 811 (℡02962/454066; closed Tues) – aside from tasty snooks and *pejerrey*, their menu occasionally features local specialities such as seven-gill shark, elephant fish and rhea fillets – although *Naos*, at 9 de Julio and Mitre, runs it a close second. *Casa Lara*, on San Martín and Ameghino, is an excellent, informal **bar** in a historic early 1900s building.

Bahía de San Julián

The easiest tour from Puerto San Julián is also the best: a trip around **Bahía de San Julián** in a zodiac launch to see the most conveniently situated **penguin colony** in Patagonia and all manner of flying sea birds. In addition, you stand a good chance of spotting **Commerson's dolphins**, a graceful, fun-loving species that regularly play games with the boats. You'll also be taken to the protected island of **Banco Justicia** (Justice Bank) to see the cormorant colonies (home to four different species – Rock, Olivaceous, Guanay and Imperial), and other sea birds. Banco Justicia is thought by some to be where, in the sixteenth century, Magellan, and later **Francis Drake**, executed members of their crews who had mutinied while in the bay, although others maintain it was at **Punta Horca** (Gallows Point), on the tongue of land that encloses the bay, opposite the town. You're not allowed to disembark at either, though you are allowed to get off at the misleadingly named **Banco Cormorán** where there is a colony of Magellanic penguins but no cormorants.

In season (Sept–April), good-value **trips** run by Excursiones Pinocho, Costanera and 9 de Julio (depart 8am; 2hr; $120, minimum four people; ℡02962/454600, ⓦwww.pinochoexcursiones.com.ar) leave from next door to *Muelle Viejo* on the seafront, with English commentary from volunteer biologists. The best time for seeing dolphins and cormorants is December to Easter, especially early on, though the guide will always give a scrupulously honest appraisal of your chances.

Comandante Luis Piedra Buena

Even the most ardent devotee of steppe scenery might be finding the RN-3 a trifle tiring by now. Around 50km south of Puerto San Julián, the desolate monotony is lifted briefly by the **Gran Bajo de San Julián**, whose Laguna del Carbón – 105m below sea level – is the lowest point in the entire South American continent. It's another 70km from here to **COMANDANTE LUIS PIEDRA BUENA**, a sleepy town 1km off the RN-3, with little to detain visitors unless you've come specifically for the world-class **steelhead trout fishing** (licences available at the municipalidad, Avenida Gregorio Ibañez 388, just down from the bus terminal). The town is named after naval hero Piedra Buena, who was famed for his gentlemanly ways and determination to assert Argentine sovereignty in the south. In 1859, he made **Isla Pavón** (the island in the jade-coloured Río Santa Cruz) his home, building a diminutive house, from which he traded with the local Aónik'enk Tehuelche. You can visit a bare reconstruction of the house, the **Casa Histórica Luis Piedra Buena** (if closed, ask at the campsite next door for the key; free).

Accommodation is limited to the well-kept *El Alamo*, at Lavalle 8 (☎02962/497249; ➋), with a *confitería*, and the clean but basic *Huayén*, at Belgrano 321 (02962/497265; ➋).

Parque Nacional Monte León

Beyond Piedra Buena, the Patagonian plateau continues with unabating harshness for some 250km to Río Gallegos. An early detour, 33km out of Piedra Buena, leads to the **PARQUE NACIONAL MONTE LEÓN** (Ⓦwww .monteleon-patagonia.com), Argentina's first coastal national park. Created in October 2004 on land donated by two conservation NGOs, the magnificent 627-square-kilometre reserve encompasses sweeping cliffs, rocky islands and picturesque bays and, between September and April, the waters are awash with wildlife, including sea-lion and penguin colonies (the fourth largest in Argentina) and three types of cormorant. The rugged cliffs that dominate the landscape are indented with vast caverns and rock windows – at low tide, you can walk out to **Isla Monte León**, a steep-sided islet chock-a-bloc with cormorants. Check first with the *guardafauna* office, 7km north of the park entrance on the RN-3 for tide schedules; you also have to register here before entering the park and even if you choose not to hire a guide (they have a list) it is worthwhile asking about what there is to see and how to get there. There are wild beaches and a **campsite** (mid-Nov to mid-April) with drinking water and a toilet-cum-shower block, plus an enticing *confitería*. However, if your budget will stretch, the best place to stay in the park is at the glorious *hostería* in the former estancia homestead; it offers a taste of classy but simple, isolated country life in large rooms with wooden floors, fireplaces and old-fashioned bathrooms; reservations must be made in advance through their Buenos Aires office (☎011/4621-4780, Ⓦwww .monteleon-patagonia.com; ➒; closed April–Oct).

Río Gallegos

With its harsh climate and no-nonsense commercial feel, provincial capital **RÍO GALLEGOS** – 246km south of Piedra Buena – is not the kind of place where you want to stay for long, though there are a couple of little museums and a handful of attractive early twentieth-century buildings. The reason why a lot of people come to Gallegos is for its incredible **fly-fishing**: along with the Río Grande in Tierra del Fuego (see p.580), the **Río Gallegos** (the town's namesake river) is the haunt of some of the biggest **brown trout** anywhere in the world. Get a licence from the provincial tourist office, and take a guide and a camera, for the glory shot.

Arrival and information

The **airport** is 7km west of town, though there are no buses to the town centre – a taxi will cost around $30: bizarrely, there are direct buses from the airport to El Calafate, some 300km away.

From the **bus terminal**, near the edge of town on the RN-3, it's best to take a taxi 2km into the centre; alternatively, buses #1 or #12 will drop you on Avenida Roca in the heart of town. Gallegos has two main **tourist offices** in the centre, both extremely helpful and efficient: the provincial office, at Roca 863 (Mon–Fri 9am–6pm, Sat 10am–4pm; ☎02966/438725), and the municipal office, at Roca and Córdoba (Mon–Fri 8am–8pm; ☎02966/436920, Ⓔturismo@riogallegos .gov.ar). The municipal office also has a tiny booth in the bus terminal (daily: May–Nov 8am–8pm; Dec–April 7am–9pm; ☎02966/442159).

Accommodation

Accommodation in Río Gallegos is mostly within walking distance of the centre, and can get busy so it's worth arriving early or booking ahead.

Colonial Urquiza and Rivadavia 212 ℡02966/422329. A pleasant budget choice, not far from the centre, and good for singles ($100). Rooms have shared bathrooms. ❸

Nevada Zapiola 480 ℡02966/425990. Excellent-value hotel with friendly owners, though you'll have to fight past the enormous plants at the front door. The slightly pricier, en-suite rooms are worth the money for the extra space – in both the bedroom and the bathroom. ❸

Patagonia Fagnano 54 ℡02966/444969, Ⓦwww.hotel-patagonia.com. Undoubtedly the smartest hotel in town, catering more for business people than tourists, this brand new hotel has comfortable rooms, a spa and a good restaurant. ❻

Sehuén Rawson 160 ℡02966/425683, Ⓦwww.hotelsehuen.com. Its bright, modern rooms have en-suite bathrooms with a bath and good shower, at reasonable prices. ❹

El Viejo Miramar Roca 1630 ℡02966/430401, Ⓔhotelviejomiramar@yahoo.com.ar. Small family-run *hostería* with clean if rather petite and gloomy rooms. Off-street parking. ❺

The Town

The provincial capital is a bustling centre of commerce for the region, and the main shopping thoroughfare, **Avenida Roca**, is the focus of city life; outdoor clothing and other gear costs far less here than in the tourist hubs such as El Calafate, so stock up here if you're off trekking. The attractive main square, **Plaza San Martín**, is marked by a fine equestrian **statue** of General San Martín and the quaint white and green Salesian **cathedral**, Nuestra Señora de Luján (open daily with restrictions during mass), a classic example of a pioneer church made from corrugated iron, and originally built in 1899 with a labour force composed of displaced indigenous Tehuelche.

The **Museo de Los Pioneros**, in the city's oldest house, on the corner of Alberdí and Elcano (daily 10am–7.30pm; free), gives an insight into life in the region at the beginning of the twentieth century, with curators playing ancient, crackly discs on a 1904 Victrola. The eclectic **Museo Regional Provincial Padre Jesús Molina**, San Martín and Ramón and Cajal 51 (Mon–Fri 10am–7pm, Sat & Sun 11am–7pm; free), hosts temporary exhibitions of contemporary art, along with displays of Tehuelche artefacts, dinosaur remains and impressive reconstructions of Pleistocene mammals; there's also a weaving workshop selling woollens.

Eating and drinking

Most **eating and drinking** options open daily for lunch from noon to 3pm, and then again between about 7.30pm and midnight.

Club Británico Roca 935. Well-priced and imaginative food, such as *pulpo en escabeche* (marinated octopus), served in formal style. A port of call for Bruce Chatwin, it has more than a hint of a gentleman's club about it and is still the favoured hangout for the declining community of those with British descent.

El Horreo Roca 862 ℡02966/426462. An attractive, sophisticated place in the historic Sociedad Española building, with an original Spanish-inspired menu and fairly high prices. Open till 1am.

 Laguanacazul Lista and Sarmiento ℡02966/444114. The best restaurant in Gallegos, where the stylish setting is bettered only by the food: fresh Patagonian cuisine – both lamb and seafood – that varies with the season but is never short of excellent, though the prices do reflect this. The selection of wines is equally impressive.

Puesto Molino Roca 854. Buzzing, high-quality pizzeria with a busy wood-fired oven and communal wooden tables.

RoCo Roca 1157 ℡02966/420203. A fine, moderately priced, and consequently popular, *parrilla* with large servings of *lomo*, and a refreshingly wide selection of salads.

It takes the best part of a day to travel overland from Río Gallegos to Río Grande (see p.580), the first major town in **Argentine Tierra del Fuego**, a tedious journey that involves crossing two borders and the **Magellan Straits**; you might well consider flying. At the **Monte Aymond border crossing** (April–Oct 9am–11pm; Nov–March 24hr), 67km south of Gallegos, formalities are fairly straightforward, but don't try to bring fresh vegetables, fruit or meat products into Chile, as they'll be confiscated. On the **Chilean** side, the road improves and heads to **Punta Arenas**, **Puerto Natales** and, down a turning at Kimiri Aike, 48km from the border, **Tierra del Fuego**. This road, the RN-257, takes you to **Punta Delgada** and the Primera Angostura (First Narrows) of the Magellan Straits. The **ferry** that plies across them leaves from 7am to midnight, making the thirty-minute crossing roughly every 40min (ⓦwww.tabsa.cl /Eng/Html/PrimeraAngostura; CH$1600 per person, CH$14,000 for a car). As early mariners found, the currents here can be ferocious, but they're unlikely to be as disruptive to your plans as they were to sea-goers in the past – only in extreme weather does the ferry not leave. While crossing history's most famous straits, look out for Commerson's dolphins. Heading for **Ushuaia**, the road then traverses Chilean Tierra del Fuego to the border settlement of San Sebastián (April–Oct 9am–11pm; Nov–March 24hr), 80km from Río Grande. Check times carefully, as there may be a time difference between the Argentine and Chilean sides. **Buses** depart regularly from Río Gallegos for Punta Arenas (5hr), Río Grande (8hr) and Ushuaia (13hr); ferry crossings are included in the fare.

Much of the landscape between Gallegos and **El Calafate** is gale-blasted steppe, though there is the odd oasis, plus fabulous views of the austral Andes including the baroque peaks of Torres del Paine on the Chilean side in clear weather. There are two main routes: the more scenic but far longer the **RN-40**, which passes several crossing points into the far south of Chile as it curves round the southwesternmost reaches of Argentina; and the quicker, more direct the **RP-5**, the "busiest" of the roads that cross the deep south of Santa Cruz Province – in the early twentieth century this journey took up to six weeks by ox-cart, but you can now do it in less than four hours by bus and around three by car. About halfway along the RP-5 route is tiny **La Esperanza**, where you can **refuel** and **eat**, and, if it's too late to push on, **stay** at the only hotel (☎02902/499200; ❷). Regular buses run from Río Gallegos to El Calafate along the RP-5 (4hr).

Parque Nacional Los Glaciares

Declared a UNESCO World Heritage Site in 1981, the wild expanse of **Parque Nacional Los Glaciares** is a huge chunk of magical terrain shoved up against the Andes in the southwest corner of Santa Cruz Province. It encompasses a range of contrasting environments from enormous glaciers that ooze down from the heights of the gigantic Hielo Continental Sur ice cap to thick, sub-Antarctic woodland of deciduous *lenga* and *ñire*, and evergreen *guindo* and *canelo*; and from savage, rain-lashed, unclimbed crags to dry, billiard-table Patagonian *meseta*

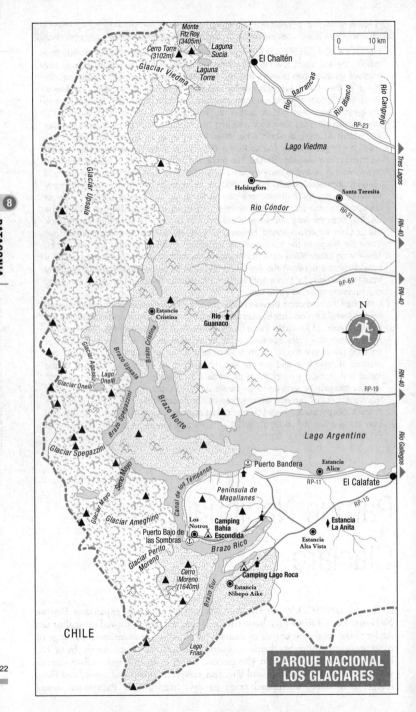

Monte
Fitz Roy
(3405m)

Cerro Torre
(3102m)

Laguna
Sucia

Laguna
Torre

Glaciar Viedma

El Chaltén

Río Barrancas

Río Blanco

Río Cangrejo

RP-23

Lago Viedma

▶ Tres Lagos

Helsingfors

Santa Teresita

RP-21

Río Cóndor

▶ RN-40

Glaciar Upsala

RP-69

▶ RN-40

Estancia
Cristina

Río
Guanaco

N

Glaciar Agassiz

Glaciar Onelli

Lago
Onelli

Brazo Cristina

Brazo Upsala

Brazo Norte

RP-19

▶ RN-40

Glaciar Spegazzini

Brazo Spegazzini

Seno Mayo

Lago Argentino

▶ Río Gallegos

Puerto Bandera

Estancia
Alice

El Calafate

RP-11

Glaciar Mayo

Glaciar Ameghino

Península de
Magallanes

Canal de los Témpanos

RP-15

Los
Notros

Camping
Bahía
Escondida

Estancia
La Anita

Puerto Bajo de
las Sombras

Brazo Rico

Estancia
Alta Vista

*Glaciar Perito
Moreno*

Cerro
Moreno
(1640m)

Camping Lago Roca

Estancia
Nibepo Aike

Brazo Sur

CHILE

Lago
Frías

0   10 km

**PARQUE NACIONAL
LOS GLACIARES**

stretching as far as the eye can strain. Most people will visit only the two sightseeing areas: the southern sector, around **Glaciar Perito Moreno**, one of the planet's most famous glaciers; and the **Fitz Roy** sector in the north for its superb trekking. Serving as bases for these two areas are, respectively, the villages of **El Calafate**, in the **south**, and **El Chaltén**, in the **north**, both lying just outside the boundary of the park itself, but catering well to a burgeoning influx of outdoor enthusiasts from the world over.

El Calafate

The overriding reason to visit **EL CALAFATE** is to make it your base for seeing **Glaciar Perito Moreno** and the other world-class attractions that occupy the southern sector of **Parque National Los Glaciares** (see box, p.529) – these make it one of Argentina's most-visited tourist destinations and a world class attraction. The main sites cluster around **Lago Argentino**, the largest of all exclusively Argentine lakes, and the third biggest in all South America, with a surface area of 1600 square kilometres – it's so deep that its temperature remains almost constant at 8°C year round (it's fed by melting glaciers). Catch it on a cloudy day and you could be looking at a tarnished expanse of molten lead, while when the weather is brighter the lake soaks up the light of the Patagonian sky to reflect a glorious hue of polarized blue. Most of Lago Argentino is surrounded by harsh, rolling steppe, but the scenery becomes infinitely more interesting around its western tendrils: transitional scrub and southern beech woodland press up on its shores, and the impressive snowcapped mountains (many well over 2000m) that fringe the **Hielo Continental Sur** rear up behind.

Until the mid-1980s, El Calafate was little more than a single street with a handful of hostels and hotels, but now there are dozens of places to stay with more being built to accommodate tens of thousands of annual visitors. The resulting space and labour shortage has led to considerable inflation, which you will find reflected in accommodation and restaurant prices, while the town has a bloated feel, sprawled in the shadow of its eponymous mountain. Much money has been visibly invested in development, not least because this is the fiefdom of President Cristina Fernández and her ex-President husband, local lad Néstor Kirchner.

The best **times to visit** are spring and autumn (Nov to mid-Dec & Mar–Apr), when there's a nice balance between having enough visitors to keep services running but not too many for the place to seem overcrowded. If you're planning to arrive any time outside winter (when access can be hard and many places are closed any way), you're advised to book accommodation, flights and car rental (especially if you want a 4WD) well in advance.

Arrival and information

Calafate's international **airport** lies 22km east of town; taxis run into town ($80) or you can take the Aerobus ($15). All **buses** stop at the terminal on Avenida Julio Roca, on the hillside one block above the main thoroughfare, Avenida Libertador, to which it's connected by a flight of steps. The main **tourist office** is in a handsome new building a short way up Coronel Rosales, a side street leading off Avenida San Martín just before the bridge (daily 8am–10pm; ℡02902/491090, ⓦwww.elcalafate.gov.ar); it has a list of hotels with daily availability and can help you track down a room in a *casa de familia* if everywhere else is full. There is also a useful branch office (same hours) in the bus terminal. The **national park information office**, Libertador 1302 (Mon–Fri

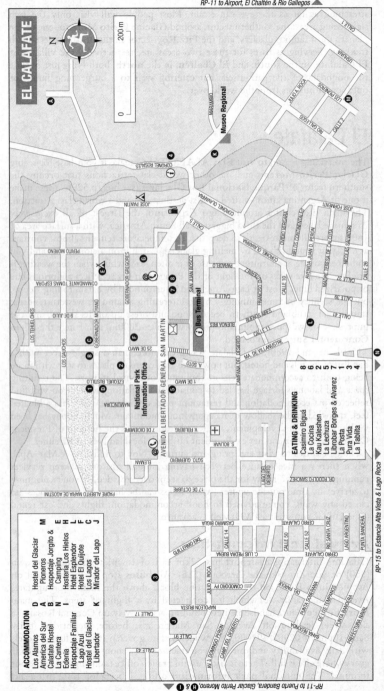

EL CALAFATE

N

0   200 m

8

PATAGONIA

Museo Regional

Bus Terminal

National Park
Information Office

ACCOMMODATION

Los Alamos	D	Hostel del Glaciar
America del Sur	A	Pioneros M
Calafate Hostel	B	Hospedaje Jorgito &
La Cantera	N	Camping
Edenia	I	Hostería Los Hielos H
Hospedaje Familiar		Hotel Esplendor L
Lago Azul	G	Hotel El Quijote F
Hostel del Glaciar		Los Lagos C
Libertador		Mirador del Lago J

EATING & DRINKING

Casimiro Biguá	8
La Cocina	6
Kau Kaleshen	2
La Lechuza	5
Librobar Borges & Alvarez	7
La Posta	1
Pura Vida	3
La Tablita	4

RP-15 to Estancia Alta Vista & Lago Roca ▶

RP-11 to Puerto Bandera, Glaciar Perito Moreno ▲

The calafate bush

Calafate, the indigenous name for what is known in English as the box-leaved barberry (*Berberis buxifolia*), is Patagonia's best-known plant. The bushes are protected by vindictive thorns, and the wood contains a substance known as *berberina*, which possesses medicinal properties and is used as a textile dye. From late October onwards, the bushes are covered with exquisite little bright yellow flowers. Depending on where they're growing, the berries mature between December and March. Once used by the indigenous populations for dye, they're nowadays often employed in delicious ice creams, appetizing home-made preserves or as a filling for *alfajores*. Remember the oft-quoted saying: "*Él que come el calafate, volverá*" ("Eat calafate berries and you'll be back").

8am–7pm, Sat & Sun 9.30am–7pm; ℡02902/491545, ✉apnglaciares@cotecal .com.ar), has some maps and sells fishing licences. The town's biggest festival, the **Festival del Lago Argentino**, takes place in the week leading up to February 15, with music and a free *asado* on the final day.

Accommodation

Outside high season (Jan–Feb & Easter) **accommodation** prices are considerably reduced and all but the top-end hotels become affordable. **Camping** options include the pleasant *Camping Municipal*, at José Pantín s/n (℡02902/493422; $15 per person), with restaurant and sparkling shower block, conveniently located one block behind the YPF station at the entrance to town; and *Jorgito Camping*, at Gob. Moyano 943 (℡02902/491323; $16 per person), in the owner's garden. There's also rural **camping** at Lago Roca (℡02902/499500; $20 per person, two- and four-bed cabins ❺; restaurant and bike hire) and a busy **campsite**, *Bahía Escondido* (℡02902/493053; $23 per person, book in advance in Jan) near the Glaciar Perito Moreno, as well as the **luxury hotel** *Los Notros* (see p.526). If you don't want to stay in town, try one of several nearby **tourist estancias**; the office of *Estancias de Santa Cruz*, at Libertador 1215 (℡02902/492858, ❿www.estanciasdesantacruz .com), has leaflets on the many estancias in the area and throughout the province (see box, p.545), plus maps, and can take reservations.

Hostels and hospedajes

América del Sur Puerto Deseado s/n ℡02902/493525, ❿www.americahostel.com.ar. Well-designed, spacious and friendly place with sensational views of Lago Argentino. Knowledgeable owners can help organize a wide range of trips. Four-bed dorms and doubles have under-floor heating. Free shuttle bus into centre. Dorms $60, rooms ❺

Calafate Hostel Gob. Moyano 1226 ℡02902/492450, ❿www.calafatehostels.com. Huge but friendly cabin-style hostel with kitchen, big living room and internet. Accommodation is in four-bed dorms, with or without bathrooms ($60 per person), and doubles (❺) – prices include breakfast. Open all year.

Hospedaje Familiar Lago Azul Perito Moreno 83 ℡02902/491419. In the family home of the charming Echeverría couple, two of Calafate's original settlers, who have been putting up visitors in their spick-and-span rooms for decades. Open all year. $40 per person.

Hospedaje Jorgito Gob. Moyano 943 ℡02902/491323. Simple, bright and clean rooms (shared bathrooms only) in a long-running *hospedaje*; the eponymous owner also offers camping in his garden (see above). Use of kitchen and living room. $50 per person.

Hostel del Glaciar Libertador Av Libertador 587 ℡02902/491792, ❿www.glaciar.com. Run by the same family as *Pioneros* below, in an attractive building closer to town, and appealing to a slightly older clientele. Same services as its sister hostel, though dorms – set around an internal courtyard – are more spacious and have en-suite bathrooms. Superior double rooms are exactly that. Central heating throughout. Dorms $60, rooms ❻

Hostel del Glaciar Pioneros Los Pioneros 255 ☎02902/491243, ⓦwww.glaciar.com. Opened in 1987, this is Calafate's original hostel, and by far the largest in town. Multilingual, friendly staff, decent restaurant, cheap laundry, bright, three- four- and six-bed dorms, excellent en-suite rooms – from singles to quads – kitchen facilities, free internet access and bargain lunchboxes all make *Glaciar Pioneros* great value. They also run their own travel service, including recommended alternative trips to Glaciar Perito Moreno and two-day El Chaltén glacier trekking. Dorms $50, rooms ④–⑤

Hotels

Los Alamos Gob. Moyano and Bustillo ☎02902/491144, ⓦwww.posadalosalamos.com. One of the most luxurious of the town's hotels, modestly posing as a posada, but with the feel of a village complex. It has wood-panelled rooms (those in the new part are bigger than those in the old), with bright bathrooms, an excellent restaurant, gardens, tennis court and even a Lilliputian golf course. ⑨

La Cantera Calle 306 173 ☎02902/495998, ⓦwww.lacantera-calafate.com.ar. Enjoying tremendous views of Lago Argentino, tastefully furnished rooms are set in a beautiful dark-wood cabin and have huge beds, designer couches and plush bathrooms. There's also a sizeable balcony scattered with comfy loungers. ⑨

Edenia Manzana 642, Punta Soberana ☎02902/497021, ⓦwww.edeniahoteles .com.ar. Impressive, professionally run new hotel with great bay views – the out-of-way location is compensated for by a regular minibus service to the centre and the fact that you are the last to be collected in the morning on glacier tours. The rooms are bright and simply decorated, while the excellent hotel restaurant and bar mean you don't have to trek into town in the evening. ⑧

Esplendor Perón 1143 ☎011/5217-5700, ⓦwww.esplendorelcalafate.com. Sharp boutique hotel on the hill that overlooks town. The rather forbidding exterior belies a light, sun-filled interior: a huge lobby – complete with antler chandeliers – a minimalist bar-restaurant, and rustically cool bedrooms awash in the colours of the Patagonian steppe. Corner suites (US$400) have 270-degree views of El Calafate and Lago Argentino. Free shuttle bus into town every 30min. Disabled access. Closed June to mid-Aug. ⑨

Hostería Los Hielos René Favaloro 3968 ☎02902/492965, ⓦwww.hosterialoshielos.com. Stylishly rustic hotel, scenically located near the shores of Bahía Redonda, 2.5km west of town. The light, attractive en-suite bedrooms have bay-window views across Lago Argentino – as does the snug living room, where you can thumb through the hotel's small library in front of an open fire. The attached restaurant has its own *asado* pit, and there's a spa with sauna. Very helpful reception. Price includes a fresh buffet breakfast. ⑨

Los Lagos 25 de Mayo 120 ☎02902/491170, ⓦwww.loslagoshotel.com.ar. Extremely welcoming, family-run spot that's among the most affordable of the hotels with private bathrooms. Pleasant rooms, which benefit from the quiet location, are on the larger side, particularly the plusher ones in the new extension. Price includes breakfast. ⑥

Mirador del Lago Libertador 2047 ☎02902/493176, ⓦwww.miradordellago.com.ar. Attractively built hotel with cosy rooms and plush decor – the breakfasts are generous and there is a very good if fairly pricey restaurant, *Bahía*. ⑧

Los Notros 80km west of El Calafate, in Buenos Aires ☎011/4814-3934, ⓦwww.losnotros.com. The only hotel right up close to the Glaciar Perito Moreno (and with views of its left flank), it is named after the plant with striking scarlet blossom seen throughout the region in summer. Tastefully designed "rustic" wooden lodge built on private land within the park, with an excellent (if expensive) restaurant serving regional specialities. Much cheaper if you book in advance: check the online offers on two- to four-day all-inclusive packages. Closed June to mid-Sept. ⑨ full board; at peak times US$1030 per person for a minimum two-night stay with meals, excursions and other extras included.

El Quijote Gregores 1155 ☎02902/491017, ⓦwww.quijotehotel.com.ar. Excellently sited and modern hotel catering to tour groups. The double and triple rooms come with minibar and TV but are on the small side. Breakfast (included) is served next door at the hotel's appropriately named restaurant, *Sancho*. Closed May–Sept. ⑨

Estancias

Alice also known as *El Galpón del Glaciar* ☎02902/491793, ⓦwww.estanciaalice.com.ar. *Alice*, on the way to Puerto Bandera, 22km west of El Calafate, is nice enough, a welcoming homestead in a beautiful area, but high numbers of day-trippers may take off some of the charm. It also has an office in town, at Libertador 1015, that books excursions to see agricultural displays such as sheep-shearing. Closed May–Sept; minimum two-night stay. ⑨

Alta Vista 35km west of El Calafate on the RP-15 ☎02902/491247, ⓦwww.hosteriaaltavista.com.ar. One of the more exclusive and expensive of the Santa Cruz tourist estancias, catering to those seeking discretion and peace. Airy, intimate rooms have tasteful, restrained decor; the service is non-intrusive and professional; and there's a delightful garden filled with lupins. The excellent restaurant serves simple, classically prepared regional cuisine. Closed May–Sept. ❾ full board including excursions.

🏃 Cristina ☎02902/491034 or in Buenos Aires ☎011/4814-3934, ⓦwww.estanciacristina.com. Superbly located estancia hidden at the end of remote Bahía Cristina, accessible only by boat. Top-notch accommodation – in spacious, homely rooms with peak-framed views across the surrounding *meseta* – is part of a two-day package, which includes a boat trip to Glacier

Upsala and hiking or horseriding excursions. Can also be visited on a day-trip to Upsala (see p.532). Closed June to mid-Sept. ❾ full board including boat transfer and excursions.

🏃 Nibepo Aike ☎02966/422626, ⓦwww .nibepoaike.com.ar. Beautiful farmhouse dating from early last century set in a stunning valley south of Lago Roca, 60km from El Calafate. Delicious meals are prepared with home-grown produce; it's also a great place to try traditional lamb *asado*. Excellent hiking and horseriding options. Minimum two-night stay. Closed May– Sept. ❽ half board.

The Town

Once a primitive staging post between the area's estancias and Río Gallegos, El Calafate is now a hotchpotch of neo-pioneer architecture designed to appeal solely to tourists – and, in the shape of the shiny new casino, to gamblers. Though not unpleasant, its main street is crowded with garish souvenir shops and in January and February, in particular, the place is invaded by everyone and their grandmother who come to marvel at the Glaciar Perito Moreno, some 80km away. For anyone emerging from a journey along the isolated RN-40, arriving in Calafate can seem like coming to suckle at Mammon's very breast; if you've flown in from Buenos Aires, you'll be surprised at just how modest and dusty the place is. Apart from shopping or eating, and planning your visits, there's little to do in the town itself. The small **Museo Regional** (Mon–Fri 8am–7pm; free) in the Dirección de Cultura, Libertador 575, has the standard collection of pioneer family photos plus some indigenous artefacts, but isn't particularly inspiring.

Eating and drinking

Most **restaurants** are clustered along or within a block of Avenida Libertador; with a few exceptions, prices are high by Argentine standards. Surprisingly the choice of **bars** and late night hangouts is limited – perhaps because everyone has to get up so early for the excursions.

Restaurants

🏃 Casimiro Biguá Grill & Rotisserie Libertador 963. Upmarket designer joint serving fine cuts of prime Argentine beef and succulent Patagonian lamb in a slick but congenial

atmosphere. It has English-speaking waiters and one of the best wine lists in town, including 250 vintages from Argentina alone; while the prices near international levels, eating here is an experience. There are two other branches along Libertador, one,

Excursions from El Calafate

Few people allow for more time in El Calafate than it takes to see the big-name glaciers (see pp.528–532), but there are other **excursions** worth checking out if you're around for longer. The Cerro Frías agency at Libertador 1857 (☎02902/492808, ⓦwww.cerrofrias.com) runs twice-daily **trekking**, horseriding or **4WD trips** (all day or in the evening) to **Cerro Frías** ($170–195 including barbecue lunch or dinner), from which there are stunning views, weather permitting, of both Monte Fitz Roy to the north and Torres del Paine in the south. Calbagatas del Glaciar (☎02902/495447, ⓦwww.cabalgatasdelglaciar.com; book through Cal Tur, see p.529) offers recommended **horseriding** trips to Glaciar Perito Moreno and Lago Roca ($250 including lunch), as well as two-day trips to Paso Zamora, at the border with Chile.

at no. 993, specializing in barbecued meat, and the other, at no. 1359, serving mainly pasta.

La Cocina Libertador 1245. Cosy diner with a mouthwatering list of savoury pancakes and pastas but understaffed – the stressed waiters sweat to cover the room. From 7pm. Closed Tues.

La Lechuza Libertador and Primero de Mayo. Not to be confused with their branch on Espora that specializes in *panchos*, this deservedly popular place serves up a huge range of pizzas from its wood-fired oven, plus make-your-own salads and family-sized meat sandwiches.

La Posta In the grounds of *Los Alamos* hotel ☎02902/491144. Spacious dining room overlooking a manicured setting. Exotic inter-national menu, with an inventive range of sauces and sympathetic use of local ingredients – the rolled lamb with rose-hip sauce is excellent. There's a well-chosen selection of Argentine wines, but prices are high.

Pura Vida Libertador 1876. The young owners provide traditional food with a modern touch in an A-frame cabin. Hearty stews and good vegetarian choices, such as baked pumpkin with corn, at reasonable prices make this a place not to be missed. Evenings only. Closed Wed.

La Tablita Cnel. Rosales 28 ☎02902/491065. Legendary *asador*,

deservedly popular with locals and tour groups alike, who come here to gorge on delicious, serious-sized lamb or beef grills (the mixed *parrilla* could feed a small army); all are served with suitable dignity even though waiters are often rushed off their feet. Sides are fairly expensive but the massive mains are good value – don't eat all day before dining here. Closed Wed lunch & June–Aug.

Cafés and bars

Casablanca Libertador 1202. Buzzing café that serves some of the best coffee in town, as well as cool draught beer and tasty *lomitos*. Extensive jazz play-list. Open until 1am.

Kau Kaleshen Gob. Gregores 1256. Charming but expensive *casa de té* frequented by locals and visitors alike and devoting itself to speciality coffees and home-made cakes. Open daily 5–10pm.

Librobar Borges y Alvarez Libertador 1005. Small café-bar that makes a relaxing spot from which to watch the comings and goings down on Avenida Libertador or pour over the extensive selection of local-interest books crammed onto overstacked shelves. There's a good range of coffees, and cocktails are served in the evenings.

Listings

Airlines Aerolíneas Argentinas, 9 de Julio 57 ☎02902/492814; LADE, Roca 1004 ☎02902/491262.

Banks and exchange Several ATMs including the Banco de la Nacion, Libertador 1133, and Banco de Santa Cruz, Libertador 1285. Thaler, 9 de Julio, exchanges all major international and South American currencies.

Bike rental HLS, Buenos Aires 173 ☎02902/493806, ⊛www.travesia.sur.com.ar.

Bus connections Freddy Representaciones in the bus terminal (☎02902/492127,

(Ⓔfreddy@cotecal.com.ar) has forensic knowledge of national bus routes and timetables.

Car rental Dubrovnik, Padre Agostini 147 ☎02902/496222; Localiza, Libertador 687 ☎02902/491398; Servi Car, Libertador 695 ☎02902/492301; Wagen, Libertador 1341 ☎02902/492297.

Laundry Lava Andina, Cmte. Espora 88 (daily 9am–1pm & 4–9pm).

Post office Libertador 1133.

Taxis Cóndor, 25 de Mayo 50 ☎02902/491655.

Glaciar Perito Moreno and the southern sector of the park

The exalted glaciers in the **southern sector** of the Los Glaciares national park attract huge numbers of visitors from all over the world and it takes a bit of planning to find the magic and avoid the crowds. The three hotspots in the southern sector of the park are: the easy-to-reach and not-to-be-missed **Glaciar Perito Moreno**, which slams into the western end of the **Península de Magallanes**; **Puerto Bandera**, from where boat trips depart to Glaciar Upsala and the other northern glaciers that are inaccessible by land; and, to the south down the RP-15, the much less-visited **Lago Roca** and the southern arm of Lago Argentino, the **Brazo Sur**.

Park entrance for the Glaciar Perito Moreno and Upsala trips is $75 per day for foreigners, which you must pay at the respective gates, but the Lago Roca area is free. Within the boundaries, be especially aware of the dangers of fire – an area of forest near Glaciar Spegazzini that burnt in the 1930s still hasn't even remotely recovered. **Mammals** in the park include the *gato montés* wildcat, pumas and the endangered *huemul*, although you are highly unlikely to see any of these owing to their scarcity and elusive nature. There is plenty of enjoyable **flora** on display, though, such as the ubiquitous *notro* (*Embothrium coccineum*, known in English as the Chilean firebush or firetree), with its flaming red blooms between November and March. Commonly seen **birds** include the majestic black and red Magellanic Woodpecker (*carpintero patagónico*).

Getting to the Glaciar Perito Moreno

Most people visit the **Glaciar Perito Moreno** on guided day-**tours**, which are offered by virtually all agencies in El Calafate and allow for around four hours at the ice face, the minimum required fully to appreciate the spectacle, and cost around $150, plus the park entrance fee of $75 a day. Rather than having a fixed point of departure, companies tend to drive round town collecting passengers from hotels; to avoid having to get up much earlier than you need to, try to arrange that you're the last pick-up (not always possible) or go to the office yourself just before the bus leaves. The trips with *Hostel del Glaciar Pioneros* (see p.526), Chaltén Travel (Libertador 1174 ☏02902/492212, ⓦwww.chaltentravel.com) and Rumbo Sur (Libertador 960 ☏02902/492155, ⓦwww.rumbosur.com.ar) are recommended for their knowledgeable, friendly guides and time spent at the glacier.

If you don't want to be restricted to a tour, note that Cal Tur runs a twice-daily **bus service** ($40 each way) departing at 8am and 3pm and returning 1pm and 8pm. If you get the 8am departure you'll probably be among the first to arrive at the glacier – it's worth the effort to beat the crowds and glimpse the early morning sun shining on the west-facing snout. Equally, the 3pm departure returns after most tours have long gone, but arrives at the glacier after the boat trips (see p.531) stop running. Alternatively, you could hire a **remise taxi** ($300 or so, including four-hour wait at the glacier).

The other option is to **rent a car** (around $300/day) and drive along the lesser-used RP-15 towards Lago Roca or along the paved RP-11. The **RP-15** is unsurfaced but by far the most picturesque. About 30km from El Calafate, the road passes historical Estancia Anita, the scene of one of Patagonia's most grisly episodes: in 1921, 121 men were executed here by an army battalion that had been sent to crush a rural strike and the related social unrest; a monument by the roadside commemorates the victims. Turn right just after the tourist estancia of *Alta Vista* (see p.526), and then left after another 12km to the park's main entrance.

The second route, along the **RP-11**, heads straight down Avenida Libertador and along a paved road that lines the lakeshore, passing the tourist estancia *Alice* (see p.526) before dropping down to the park's main entrance; the right turning here, down the RP-8, leads to Puerto Bandera (see p.532), for boat trips to Upsala and other glaciers.

The **park's main entrance** (24hr; $75) is as you enter the peninsula, and the trees nearby are a favourite evening roost of the rabble-rousing austral parakeet (*cachaña*), the most southerly of the world's parrots. From here it's a forty-minute drive (a little more than 30km) past picnic spots, a campsite and the exclusive *Los Notros* hotel (see p.526) to the boardwalks in front of the glacier. The *ripio* (gravel) road is poor and very dusty in hot weather, but traversable by any family car; arrive early and/or leave late to avoid the inevitable congestion.

Glaciar Perito Moreno

Though both water-based, Argentina's two greatest natural wonders couldn't offer a starker contrast: the sub-tropical waterfalls at Iguazú and the immense pack ice of the **GLACIAR PERITO MORENO** (also called Ventisquero Perito Moreno). It's not the longest of Argentina's glaciers – nearby Glaciar Upsala is twice as long (60km) – and whereas the ice cliffs at its snout tower up to 60m high, the face of Glaciar Spegazzini can reach heights double that. However, such comparisons prove irrelevant when you stand on the **boardwalks** that face this monster. Perito Moreno has a star quality that none of the others rivals.

The glacier zooms down off the icecap in a great motorway-like sweep, a jagged mass of crevasses and towering, knife-edged seracs almost unsullied by the streaks of dirty moraine that discolour many of its counterparts. When it collides with the southern arm of Lago Argentino, the **Canal de los Témpanos** (Iceberg Channel), the show really begins: vast blocks of ice, some weighing hundreds of tonnes, detonate off the face of the glacier with the report of a small cannon and come crashing down into the waters below. These frozen depth charges then surge back to the surface as icebergs, sending out a fairy ring of smaller lumps that form a protecting reef around the berg, which is left to float in a mirror-smooth pool of its own.

Along with the virtually inaccessible Pío XI in Chile, Perito Moreno is one of only two **advancing glaciers** in South America, and one of the very few on the planet, at a rate of about 7cm a day in winter. Above all, the glacier became famous for the way it periodically pushes right across the channel, forming a massive dyke of ice that cut off the Brazo Rico and Brazo Sur from the main body of Lago Argentino. Isolated from their natural outlet, the water in the *brazos* would build up against the flank of the glacier, flooding the surrounding area, until eventually the pressure forced open a passage into the canal once again. Happening over the course of several hours, such a **rupture** is, for those lucky enough to witness it, one of nature's most awesome spectacles. The glacier first reached the peninsula in 1917, having advanced some 750m in fifteen years, but the channel did not remain blocked for long and the phenomenon remained little known. This changed in

▲ Glaciar Perito Moreno

1939, when a vast area was flooded and planes made a futile attempt to break the glacier by bombing it. In 1950, water levels rose by 30m and the channel was closed for two years; in 1966, levels reached an astonishing 32m above their normal level. The glacier then settled into a fairly regular cycle, completely blocking the channel approximately every four years or so up to 1988; after that there was a sixteen-year gap until the more recent ruptures in 2004 and again in March 2006, when, during the night, tonnes of ice crashed from the face of the glacier into the chilly waters below.

That said, it's more likely you'll have to content yourself with the thuds, cracks, creaks and grinding crunches that the glacier habitually makes, as well as the wonderful variety of **colours of the ice**: marbled in places with streaks of muddy grey and copper-sulphate blue, while at the bottom the pressurized, de-oxygenated ice has a deep blue, waxy sheen. The glacier tends to be more active in sunny weather and in the afternoon, but early morning can also be beautiful, as the sun strikes the ice cliffs.

Practicalities

The park infrastructure was designed to support only a fraction of the two thousand or so tourists who visit the glacier daily and authorities are under pressure from El Calafate businesses to double the boardwalks and expand eating facilities. Currently, there are just a couple of **cafés** (which have the only toilet facilities). With the wind coming off the ice, the temperature at the glacier can be a lot colder than in El Calafate, so take extra clothes. Do not stray from the boardwalks: many deaths have been caused by ricocheting ice or wave surges.

An excellent way of seeing the ice face from another angle is to take one of the hour-long **boat trips** that chug along near the towering heights of the ice wall: Safari Náutico heads to the southern face from Puerto Bajo de las Sombras (daily departures every hour 10.30am–3.30pm; $50), while Moreno Fiesta runs a similar trip to the northern side from near the ranger's house 2km before the boardwalks (daily departures every hour 10.30am–2.30pm; $60).

For an even closer look, you can **walk on the glacier** with Hielo y Aventura, Libertador 935 (T02902/492205, Wwww.hieloyaventura.com), which organizes daily "Mini Trekking" trips (depart El Calafate at 8am; 1hr 30min on the ice; $400 plus park entrance fee) and longer, more demanding "Big Ice" excursions (departs 7am; 4hr on the ice; $500 plus park entrance fee), which include a boat trip across to the glacier. This is **ice-trekking**, not ice-*climbing* (try El Chaltén for that): you do not need to be a peak-bagging mountain man to do it. You'll be issued crampons, but bring sunglasses, sun cream, gloves and a packed lunch, and wear warm, weatherproof clothes.

Upsala, Spegazzini, Onelli and Agassiz glaciers

Glaciar Upsala is the undisputed heavyweight of the park, between 5km and 7km wide, with a sixty-metre-high snout and a length of 60km. It's still South America's longest glacier, despite massive retrocession over the last decade or so, and covers a total area three times larger than that of metropolitan Buenos Aires. Upsala played an important role in consolidating Argentine claims to its Antarctic territory – expedition teams used to acclimatize by living for months in a base on the glacier.

Navigating **Brazo Upsala** is a highlight in itself, though trips here are often cancelled due to the increasing number of **icebergs** that bob, grind and even turn occasional flips around you. As any good student of the *Titanic* will know, for every one part of iceberg above the surface, it has six to seven parts below, which gives an idea of the tremendous size of these blocks. Even in flat light, the icy blues shine as if lit by a neon strip-light – an eerie, incredible, cerulean glow.

Glaciar Spegazzini is many visitors' favourite glacier, with an imposing ice cascade to the right and the most dizzying snout of all the glaciers in the park (between 80 and 135m high). The **Onelli** and **Agassiz glaciers** are less impressive – but beautiful nonetheless – and are reached by an easy eight-hundred-metre walk to **Laguna Onelli**, a chilly lake dotted with small bergs. The walk itself is likely to appeal only to those who haven't had the opportunity to see Patagonian forest elsewhere, since the beauty of these woodlands is not enhanced by the presence of up to three hundred day-trippers.

Practicalities

Boat trips to see the Upsala, Spegazzini and Onelli glaciers are run from **Puerto Bandera** by René Fernández Campbell, Libertador 867 (℡02902/49115, ⊛www .fernandezcampbell.com.ar), using a fleet of superb modern catamarans and launches. When the weather's fine, the full-day excursions (8.30am–5.30pm; $295 plus park entrance fee) are definitely an unforgettable experience; when it's rough, they can be memorable for the wrong reasons – if badly affected by motion sickness, take precautionary seasickness tablets. Be sure to dress in warm, waterproof and windproof clothing, and take your own food since prices on board are high. Before booking, remember that your scope for refunds is limited: the weather has to be exceptionally foul for the trip to be cancelled entirely, and the company fulfils its legal obligations if only one main part of the trip is completed; in windy weather especially, icebergs can block the channels, with Brazo Upsala being particularly prone. That said, the company is highly professional and tries hard to complete itineraries: in the event of cancellation, you will be offered a refund or a passage the next day. In recent years, Upsala has been frequently inaccessible and the tour takes you down to the Perito Moreno glacier instead – this is worth bearing in mind before you splash out on a separate boat trip at the Perito Moreno site.

A rather more expensive excursion, but one where you get to **stay overnight near the glaciers**, is "The Spirit of the Glaciers", run by Mar Patag (in Buenos Aires ℡011/5031-0756, ⊛www.crucerosmarpatag.com); the two-day trip aboard a brand new vessel takes in close-quarter views of the Upsala and Spegazzini glaciers – as well as Glacier Perito Moreno – anchoring at Puerto las Vacas, off the Brazo Spegazzini, for the night (July–May; US$600 full board, guided activities and transfers).

Alternatively, the long day-trip run by *Estancia Cristina* (book through their El Calafate office, 9 de Julio 69 ℡02902/491133, ⊛www.estanciacristina.com) is one of the few ways of gaining access to the central sector of the park and the windswept, desolate **Bahía Cristina** area. Boats visit Glacier Upsala (breakfast on board) before heading up Bahía Cristina to the isolated estancia (see p.527), a favoured point of entry for explorers of the icecap, including Padre de Agostini and Eric Shipton, the famous mountaineer and explorer of the 1960s. Lunch is at the estancia followed by a choice of excursion: 4WD, horseriding or the recommended moderate trek to the Upsala lookout (May–Sept; $380 per person, plus transfer to/from Puerto Bandera and park entrance fee ($75).

Lago Roca

Overshadowed by the nearby glaciers, **Lago Roca**, a southern branch of Lago Argentino, tends to be frequented mainly by keen fishermen. Lying 52km from El Calafate, it offers good horseriding and trekking possibilities in stunning areas of open woodland and among the neighbouring hills of the Cordón de los Cristales. It also has examples of rock art dating back three thousand years, which can be seen along a signposted trail to the left of the main road just before Lago Roca campsite (see p.525); from here, you can continue the four-hour hike to the summit of Cerro Cristales, with fine views of Torres del Paine to the south.

Cal Tur runs **buses** to Lago Roca (Wed & Fri–Mon leaving El Calafate at 8.30am, returning 6pm; $75), while a *remise* from town costs about $250. Alternatively, you can take a day-trip with Leutz Turismo, Libertador 1341 (daily 9.30am; $200; ℡02902/492316, ⓦwww.leutzturismo.com.ar), which visits Estancia Anita and includes lunch at Lago Roca and a visit to the *Nibepo Aike* estancia (see p.527). You can arrange to return another day and stay at either of the above.

El Chaltén

EL CHALTÉN, 90km west of the RN-40 and 220km north El Calafate, has undergone a convulsive expansion since it was established in 1985 in a (successful) attempt to claim the area from Chile. Today, it's a thriving tourist centre showing regrettable signs of uncontrolled development: whereas some hotels have been built in a style sympathetic to their surroundings, others would look more at ease in the beach resort of Mar del Plata. That said, the atmosphere in the village is extremely pleasant and relaxed, with a friendly mix of Argentines and foreign visitors of all ages, and a particular appeal for younger, more adventurous backpackers.

Rearing up on the opposite bank of the **Río de las Vueltas** is the curiously stepped, dark-grey cliff face of **Cerro Pirámide**, while you can glimpse the tips of the park's most daunting peaks, **Fitz Roy** and **Cerro Torre**, from the southern and eastern fringes of the village. In terms of specific sights, there is only the classically uncluttered alpine **chapel** on the western edge of the village. Built by Austrian craftsmen with Austrian materials, it's a fitting memorial to the climbing purist Toni Egger (see box, p.541), as well as to others who have lost their lives in the park.

Arrival and information

Unless you ask otherwise, **buses** will drop you off at their offices or at hotel terminals: Cal Tur start and finish at the *Fitz Roy Inn*; Chaltén Travel at the *Albergue Rancho Grande*; and TAQSA and Los Glaciares from their offices on M.M. Güemes 68 and San Martín, and Lago del Desierto, respectively. Cal Tur, Chaltén Travel and TAQSA run daily services in season to El Calafate, while

La Leona, a historic wayside inn

En route from El Calafate to El Chaltén, by a huge new bridge over the Río La Leona, stands one of the RN-40's original inns, **Hotel La Leona** (ⓦwww .laleonacountrylodge.com). It's a wonderfully atmospheric place (despite heavy restoration) worth stopping at for a slice of home-made lemon meringue or apple pie or maybe just a tea or coffee; they also sell crafts and useful maps. You could try your hand here at the **juego de la argolla**, an old gaucho drinking game where you take turns to land a ring that's attached by a string to the ceiling over a hook mounted on the wall opposite: the first person to succeed wins a drink – try one of the **typical gaucho tipples**, such as sweet *caña ombú* or *caña quemada*.

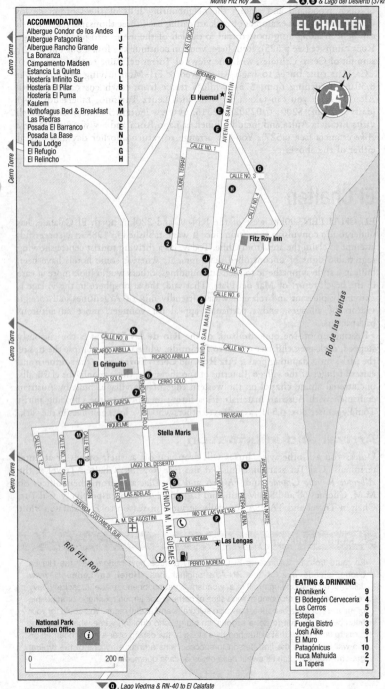

Monte Fitz Roy ▲ / ▲ Ⓐ, Ⓑ & Lago del Desierto (37km)

EL CHALTÉN

◀ Cerro Torre

◀ Cerro Torre

◀ Cerro Torre

◀ Cerro Torre

ACCOMMODATION
Albergue Condor de los Andes	P
Albergue Patagonia	J
Albergue Rancho Grande	F
La Bonanza	A
Campamento Madsen	C
Estancia La Quinta	Q
Hostería Infinito Sur	L
Hostería El Pilar	B
Hostería El Puma	I
Kaulem	K
Nothofagus Bed & Breakfast	M
Las Piedras	O
Posada El Barranco	E
Posada La Base	N
Pudu Lodge	D
El Refugio	G
El Relincho	H

El Huemul ★

Fitz Roy Inn

Río de las Vueltas

El Gringuito

Stella Maris

Río Fitz Roy

National Park
Information Office ℹ

0 — 200 m

PATAGONIA

8

534

EATING & DRINKING
Ahonikenk	9
El Bodegón Cervecería	4
Los Cerros	5
Estepa	6
Fuegia Bistró	3
Josh Aike	8
El Muro	1
Patagónicus	10
Ruca Mahuida	2
La Tapera	7

▼ Ⓠ, Lago Viedma & RN-40 to El Calafate

Los Glaciares' buses leaves three times a week (Tues, Thurs & Sat). In the summer months, a daily service runs to Perito Moreno and Los Antiguos: Itinerarios y Travesías, at Perito Moreno 152, heads north on even dates, Chaltén Travel on odd.

The **national park visitors' centre** (8am–6pm; ☎&℻02962/493004), less than 1km south of the village, is a necessary point of call; helpful volunteers advise visitors of the park's regulations. Inside are wildlife exhibits, a message board and a useful information book for climbers, all of whom must register here, as should anyone planning to stay at the Laguna Toro refuge and campsite to the south. Fishing licences can be purchased at the desk, or in the Mercado Artesanal in the village. The helpful **tourist office** and the **post office** are in the Comisión de Fomento, at M.M. Güemes 21 (March–Nov Mon–Fri 9am–6pm; Dec–Feb daily 8am–8pm; ☎02962/493011, ✉comfomelchalten@yahoo.com.ar). There are no **banks** or official money-changing facilities in El Chaltén, though some restaurants will change US dollars: there is an ATM, but it's often empty, so bring plenty of cash.

Accommodation

As a rule of thumb, the **accommodation** in El Chaltén's centre has better views of the mountains, while the places on and around Avenida San Martín are more upmarket. The high prices are partly due to the short season – most places close between Easter and October – and in high season (Dec–Feb), especially January, you should **book well in advance**. Scenic *Campamento Madsen*, at the Fitz Roy trailhead north of town, is the best of the free **campsites**. It has no showers and only one latrine; you should only use fallen wood for fires. Two of the best paying sites in town are *El Refugio*, at San Martín s/n (☎02962/493221; $20 per person; closed May–Sept), next to the Río de las Vueltas, with 24-hour hot showers and barbecue facilities; and *El Relincho*, at San Martín s/n (☎02962/493007; $20 per person; closed May–Sept). Alternatively, *La Bonanza* ($20 per person), 8km north of town on the RP-23 to Lago del Desierto, is a charming place right next to the Río de las Vueltas, where trees offer some shelter from the wind.

Excursions from El Chaltén

Casa de Guias, on Avenida Costanera del Sur (☎02962/493118), provides **guides** for the Parque Nacional Los Glaciares' numerous day-treks (from $50 per person) and also runs one-day **rock-climbing** workshops. Local legend Gabriel "Rapa" Rapaport, is the rep for top-rate operator ⛰Camino Abierto, at San Martín s/n (☎02962/493043, ⓦwww.caminoabierto.com/patagonia), offering a range of **tours and treks** in the area for beginners and experienced mountain fans. The excellent ⛰Fitz Roy Expediciones, at Lionel Terray 212 (☎02962/493017, ⓦwww.fitzroyexpediciones.com.ar), managed by another legendary climber, Alberto del Castillo, organizes **trekking on Glaciar Torre** (teaching basic ice-climbing techniques; $500) and even more demanding and expensive (as much as US$3000) five- to nine-day expeditions onto the Hielo Continental Sur for experienced trekkers. Patagonia Magica, on San Martín (☎02962/493066, ⓦwww.patagoniamagica.com), runs **mountain-bike trips** from Lago del Desierto back to El Chaltén, while Rodolfo Guerra, near *Rancho Grande* (☎02962/493020), can arrange **horseriding** excursions outside the park boundaries (horses are not permitted inside the park). South of El Chaltén, **boat trips** across Lago Viedma to **Glaciar Viedma** and mini-trekking near its flanks ($400 with transfer) are run by Patagonia Aventura, on Güemes (☎02962/493110).

Hostels and B&Bs

Albergue Condor de los Andes Río de las Vueltas s/n ☎02962/493101. Excellent, cosy hostel with welcoming staff, four en-suite double rooms (⑤) including breakfast, and an inviting sitting area. Closed April–Sept. Dorms $60.

Albergue Patagonia San Martín 392 ☎02962/493019, ⓦwww.elchalten.com /patagonia. The most homely of the YHA-affiliated hostels, run by a hard-working, genial crew (English spoken). Has heated dorms and twin rooms with shared bathrooms, plus cooking facilities, a cheap laundry service, a book exchange, bike hire and a snug living room. The staff can make excursion and transport reservations and are a good source of local travel information. Breakfast is included in the price for the rooms, but not for dorm guests, and is served in *Fuegia Bistró*, the hostel's good little restaurant next door (see opposite). Closed April–Sept. Dorms $50, rooms ⑤

Albergue Rancho Grande San Martín 724 ☎02962/493005, ⓔrancho@cotecal.com.ar. Large, well-oiled operation with clean, clinical four-bed rooms and en-suite doubles and triples. It has a lively bar-restaurant area (meals served 6am–midnight), kitchen facilities, left luggage, internet and a good laundry service. It's also the agent for Chaltén Travel buses. Closed Easter–Oct. Dorms $60, rooms ⑤

Nothofagus Bed & Breakfast Hensen and Riquelme ☎02962/493087. As the name would suggest, wood features prominently in the interior of this welcoming B&B. The good-value, sun-washed double rooms come with or without bathroom, and there's delicious home-made bread at breakfast. Closed May–Aug. ⑤

Hotels

Hostería Infinito Sur Riquelme 208 ☎02962/493325, ⓦwww.infinitosurelchalten.com. Handsome new establishment with nine stylishly decorated rooms in a fine modern building affording breathtaking views of the Fitz Roy peak. Impeccably run, with wholesome breakfasts. ⑨

Hostería El Puma Lionnel Terray 212 ☎02962/493095. Run by Alberto del Castillo (of Fitz Roy Expediciones; see box, p.535), this excellent, upper-end accommodation was designed with mountaineers in mind. Warm, softly lit rooms are stylishly rustic, with wooden flooring throughout, and there's a tremendous open fireplace in the cosy reading lounge. Price includes breakfast. Closed April–Sept. ⑨

Kaulem Av Antonio Rojo and Arrua ☎02962/493251, ⓦwww.kaulem.com.ar. Just four plush doubles and a tastefully decorated living room offering fine views in this bijou new hostería. Full American breakfast. ⑨

Posada El Barranco Lionel Terry and Calle 2 ☎02962/493006, ⓦwww.posadaelbarranco.com. Charming joint Argentine–Kiwi-run bed and breakfast with beautiful rooms plus a self-contained cabin ($400 for four people). Attractive stone work on the outside and clean lines and smart furniture on the inside. ⑦

Posada La Base Hensen 16 ☎02962/493031, ⓦwww.elchaltenpatagonia.com.ar. Some of the best-value rooms (singles, doubles and triples) in El Chaltén, several with mountain views. Its owners are hospitable, and it has shared kitchen facilities (one for every two rooms), cheap laundry and free video showings in the attic sitting room. Closed May–Sept. ⑤

Pudu Lodge Las Loicas 97 ☎02962/493365, ⓦwww.pudulodge.com. This friendly, modern hotel with hospitable bilingual staff may be farthest from the village centre but it is closer to some of the best trekking, which can be arranged by the lodge's charming owner, Gabriel "Rapa" Rapaport , an experienced mountaineer and rep for tour operator Camino Abierto (see above). The spacious rooms and private bathrooms are done out in a pleasing contemporary style and the copious breakfasts are delicious. ⑨

Out of town

Estancia La Quinta 5km south of town off the RP-23 ☎02962/493012, ⓦwww.estancialaquinta .com.ar. A working cattle ranch in a lovely location whose thoroughly modern refurbishment belies its considerable history – the owner's wife was born in the estancia. Rooms (some of which accommodate disabled travellers) are neat and compact, there's a peaceful lounge with views across the valley and beautifully home-cooked local dishes are served in the 100-year-old *casco*. Transfer from/to El Chaltén. Price includes buffet breakfast. Closed May–Sept. ⑨

Hostería El Pilar 15km north of town on the RP-15 ☎02962/493002, ⓦwww .hosteriaelpilar.com.ar. Charming, old-fashioned corrugated metal *casco*, delightfully decorated in period style. Rooms are snug and peaceful, the homely living room has a wood-burning stove and home-made pies are served in the tearoom, which has an enviable view of Fitz Roy. There is a neat little garden and the owner is a knowledgeable guide. Transfer from/to El Chaltén. Price includes breakfast. Closed April–Sept. ⑧

Eating and drinking

El Chaltén has several very good **restaurants** (although prices are fairly high), as well as a growing number of great little **bars** in which to ease your aches and pains at the end of the day. Most hotels and restaurants make up **lunchboxes** for day-treks.

Ahonikenk Güemes 23. No-nonsense little place dishing up pasta, pizza and simple dishes at relatively low prices for the location.

El Bodegón Cervecería San Martín s/n. Excellent microbrewery whose crisp, clean pilsners provide relief after a day on the trail. Genial staff and the occasional music session add greatly to the convivial atmosphere.

Los Cerros San Martín s/n ☏ 02962/493182. Delicious two- or three-course meals are thoughtfully presented and skilfully served in this pricey hotel restaurant, which specializes in Patagonian fare, particularly lamb and trout dishes. The views – spectacular panoramas of the Río de las Vueltas – are equally impressive, visible through wall-length windows.

Estepa Cerro Solo and Antonio Rojo. Warm, welcoming restaurant-bar in an adobe-style building lying in the shadow of Fitz Roy. Good selection of lamb dishes, as well as hearty calzones and pizzas from the wood-fired oven. Bar open until 1am.

Fuegia Bistró San Martín 493. Located in the *Albergue Patagonia*, and deservedly popular with the hostel's clientele. Serves a decent, moderately priced range of Patagonian-influenced meat dishes, as well as one or two interesting vegetarian options.

Josh Aike Lago Desierto 104. Charming little *chocolatería* in a two-storey wood cabin with stand-out views of Fitz Roy from the upstairs window seat. Fresh orange juice, coffee, cakes and, of course, chocolate – home-made and in a mouthwatering variety of flavours. The bittersweet hot chocolate is worth the visit alone.

El Muro San Martín 912. The name, "The Wall" comes from the climbing wall on its exterior – inside you can build up your trekking calories with a range of tasty offerings like lamb chops with red fruit, though service can be slow at times.

Patagónicus Güemes and Madsen. Terrific range of fine pizzas – the best in town – served up at chunky wooden tables in a social, friendly atmosphere.

Ruca Mahuida Lionel Terray 104 ☏ 02962/493018. Tiny cabin that's home to the most imaginative and, with only six tables, exclusive dining in El Chaltén. The menu – the largest in town – covers regional and international dishes, including surprising options such as venison ragout and vegetarian risotto. Sheepskin-covered benches complete the homely ambience. Moderate prices for the region.

La Tapera Av Antonio Rojo s/n. Welcoming log cabin with ultra-friendly service, and a menu featuring tasty and filling dishes (much needed after a long day in the park) as well as tapas (hence the name). The wine list is excellent and make sure you eave room for the unusual but lip-smacking house pudding, mint pancakes.

Fitz Roy and the northern sector of Parque Nacional Los Glaciares

The locally vaunted claim that the northern sector of **Parque Nacional Los Glaciares** is Argentina's trekking paradise is fully justified, and the closer you get to the mountains, the clearer their grandeur becomes. One of the beauties of the park is that those with limited time, or not in peak fitness, can still make worthwhile **day-walks** using El Chaltén as a base. The shortest of these walks is to **Chorrillo del Salto**, a plunging twenty-metre waterfall, framed by a moss-green cliff and adorned by the skeletons of drowned *lenga* trees, ten minutes off the RP-23, 3km past *Campamento Madsen* north of town.

For those who enjoy camping, the quintessential three-day **Fitz Roy/Cerro Torre loop** at the centre of the park makes a good option, and can be done in either direction. The advantage of going anticlockwise is that you avoid the steep climb up to Lagunas Madre y Hija and you have the prevailing wind behind you

Blanketing massive expanses of Parque Nacional Los Glaciares, the **Hielo Continental Sur** (Southern Patagonian Icecap) is the largest body of ice outside the poles. Estimates vary as to exactly how big it is but most studies put the figure at around 17,000 square kilometres, some seventy percent of which is in neighbouring Chile. What is certain is that it is suffering from the effects of global warming. In 2003, the journal *Science Magazine* published a report claiming over sixteen cubic kilometres of ice was melting annually; Greenpeace puts the figure at 42 cubic kilometres annually, or "enough to fill 10,000 large football stadiums".

when returning to El Chaltén. However, the biggest gamble is always what the weather will be like around Cerro Torre, so if this unpredictable peak is visible on day one, you might like to head for it first. The longer interlocking circuit to the north will add at least another two days.

Adequate outdoor clothing is essential in the park at all times of the year, as snowstorms are possible even in midsummer. Note that there is a **ban on lighting campfires** in the park, so if you need your food hot, make careful use of gas stoves; **horses** are no longer allowed in the park, either, owing to the damage they were doing to the terrain but some operators now use environmentally friendly **llamas** as pack animals for treks. The best trekking **map** available is the 1:50,000 *Monte Fitz Roy & Cerro Torre* published by Zagier & Urruty, on sale in town, which includes a 1:100,000 scale map of the Lago del Desierto area. The informative *Trekking in Chaltén and Lago del Desierto* by Miguel A. Alonso is also good.

The Fitz Roy sector

The northernmost section of Parque Nacional Los Glaciares, the **Fitz Roy sector**, contains some of the most breathtakingly beautiful mountain peaks on the planet. Two concentric jaws of jagged teeth puncture the Patagonian sky with the 3405m incisor of **Monte Fitz Roy** at the centre of the massif. This sculpted peak was known to the Tehuelche as El Chaltén, "The Mountain that Smokes" or "The Volcano", owing to the almost perpetual presence of a scarf of cloud attached to its summit. It is not inconceivable, however, that the Tehuelche were using the term in a rather more metaphorical sense to allude to the fiery pink colour that the rock walls turn when struck by the first light of dawn. Francisco Moreno saw fit to name the pagan summit after the evangelical captain of the *Beagle*, who, with Charles Darwin, had viewed the Andes from a distance, after having journeyed up the Río Santa Cruz by whaleboat to within 50km of Lago Argentino. Alongside Monte Fitz Roy rise **Cerro Poincenot** and **Aguja Saint-Exupéry**, while set behind them is the forbidding needle of **Cerro Torre**, a finger that stands in bold defiance of all the elements that the Hielo Continental Sur hurls against it.

El Chaltén to Laguna Capri, Campamento Poincenot and Laguna de los Tres

The trek from **El Chaltén to Laguna de los Tres** (13km; 3–4hr; 750m ascent), at the very foot of **Monte Fitz Roy**, is one of the park's most scenic trails, and can be hiked either as a return trip or part of the Fitz Roy/Torre loop. The starting point for this classic hike is the house overlooking *Camping Madsen*, at the northern end of Avenida San Martín. The path is clearly indicated, climbing up through the wooded slopes of Cerro Rosado and Cerro León, until the scenery opens out with views of Fitz Roy. After heading up alongside the ravine of the Chorillo del Salto, you come to a turn-off left (1hr–1hr 30min from El Chaltén), which leads after ten minutes to the **campsite** at **Laguna Capri** – there are great views, but the site is rather exposed to the winds, and water from the lake should be boiled or treated. Better, if you have the time, to push on down the main path, crossing one stream just past the turn-off to Laguna Madre, and another brook, the Chorrillo del Salto, until you reach **Campamento Poincenot** (1hr–1hr 15min from the Laguna Capri turn-off), named after one of the team of French climbers who made the victorious first ascent of Fitz Roy in 1952. According to the official story, Poincenot drowned while trying to cross the Río Fitz Roy before the assault on the mountain even took place, although another rumour hinted that this was no accident, but the work of a cuckolded estancia owner, enraged by his wife's infidelities with the dashing Gallic mountaineer. The campsite covers a sprawling area, set among *lenga* and *ñire* woodland on the eastern bank of the Río Blanco. Choose your spot well and you won't need to get out of your tent to see the rosy blaze of dawn on the cliffs of Fitz Roy.

From *Campamento Poincenot*, follow the crisscrossing paths to the wooden bridge that spans the main current of the Río Blanco. A second, makeshift bridge takes you to the far bank, from where the path heads up through the woods, passing the refuges of the **Río Blanco campsite** (intended for the use of climbers), before pushing on

▲ Monte Fitz Roy and Laguna de los Tres

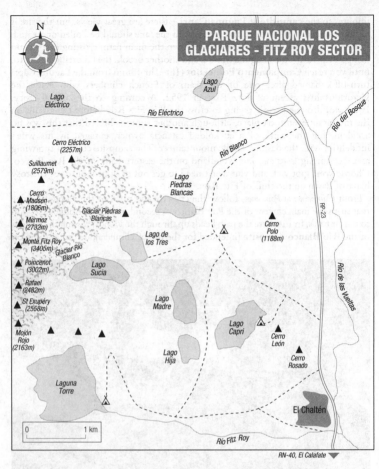

Lago Azul

Lago Eléctrico

Río Eléctrico

Río del Bosque

Cerro Eléctrico (2257m)

Río Blanco

Suillaumet (2579m)

Lago Piedras Blancas

Cerro Madsen (1806m)

Glaciar Piedras Blancas

RP-23

Mermoz (2732m)

Lago de los Tres

Cerro Polo (1188m)

Monte Fitz Roy (3405m)

Glaciar Río Blanco

Poincenot (3002m)

Lago Sucia

Río de las Vueltas

Rafael (2482m)

Lago Madre

St Exupéry (2558m)

Lago Capri

Cerro León

Mojón Rojo (2163m)

Lago Hija

Cerro Rosado

Laguna Torre

El Chaltén

0   1 km

Río Fitz Roy

RN-40, El Calafate

past the tree line. The next section is tough going as the eroded path ascends a steep gradient, but mercifully it's not long before you come to the top of the ridge, cross a boggy meadow and then climb the final hurdle: a moraine ridge that hides a breath-taking panorama – perhaps the finest in the entire park – on the other side.

You now stand in the cirque of the rich, navy-blue **Laguna de los Tres** (1hr–1hr 15min from *Campamento Poincenot*) fed by a concertinaed glacier and ringed by a giant's crown of granite peaks, including Aguja Saint-Exupéry (named after Antoine de Saint-Exupéry, who drew on his experiences as a pioneer of Patagonian aviation when writing the minor classic, *Vol de Nuit*), Cerro Poincenot, Fitz Roy and a host of other spikes. Round the small rocky outcrop to the left for even more impressive views: this ridge separates the basins of Laguna de los Tres and Laguna Sucia, some 200m below the level of the first lake. The **Glaciar Río Blanco**, hanging above Laguna Sucia, periodically sheds scales of ice and snow, which, though they look tiny at this distance, reveal their true magnitude by the ear-splitting reports they make as they hit the surface of the lake. Retrace your steps and follow the path on the western (right-hand) bank of the Río Blanco (40min from the *Río Blanco* campsite).

The Cerro Torre controversy

Even members of the French team that first ascended Fitz Roy in 1952 thought that summitting **Cerro Torre** was an impossible task. The altitude wasn't the problem – at 3102m, it wouldn't reach even halfway up some Andean peaks – neither was the type of rock it was made out of – crystalline igneous diorite is perfect for climbing. Rather, it was the shape and the formidable weather: a terrifying spire dropping sheer for almost 2km into glacial ice, battered by winds of up to 200kph and temperatures so extreme that ice more than 20cm thick can form on rock faces. Not only that, but the peculiar glaciers – "mushrooms" of ice – which build up on the mountain's summit often shear off, depositing huge blocks of ice onto climbers below.

The Italian alpinist **Cesare Maestri** became the first to make a serious attempt on the summit. In 1959, he and Austrian climber **Toni Egger** worked their way up the northern edge. Caught in a storm, Egger was swept off the face and killed by an avalanche. Maestri somehow made it to the bottom, and announced that he had **conquered the summit** with Egger. The world, however, demanded proof, something that Maestri could not furnish – the camera, he claimed, lay entombed with Egger.

Angered by the doubters, Maestri vowed to return. This he did, in 1970, and it was clear that he meant business. Among the expedition equipment lay his secret weapon: a compressor weighing over 150kg for drilling bolts into the unforgiving rock. Torre couldn't resist in the face of such a determined onslaught, and Maestri's expedition reached the summit, making very sure that photos were snapped on top. A stake had been driven through Torre's Gothic heart.

Or had it? The climbing world was riven by dispute. Were Maestri's tactics in keeping with the aesthetic code of climbing or had the use of a machine invalidated his efforts? Did this represent a true ascent? On top of this, Maestri's photos revealed that although he had reached the top of the rock, he had not climbed the ice mushroom – the icing that topped the cake. The monster would not lie down and die.

Enter **Casimiro Ferrari**, another Italian climber. Using guile where Maestri had favoured strong-arm tactics, Ferrari sneaked up on the beast from behind, from the Hielo Continental Sur. In the space of two days, Ferrari achieved his goal, and, elatedly, his team brought down photos of them atop the summit, ice mushroom and all.

So, almost thirty years on, who does the climbing community take as the first to conquer the mountain? Toni Egger's body was recovered in 1975, but no camera was found with him (he is now commemorated in the name of a jagged peak alongside Cerro Torre and a simple chapel in El Chaltén). The compressor drill used by Maestri in 1970 still hangs near the top, a testament to his subjection of the mountain. And, despite the controversy at the time, the bolts drilled by Maestri are used to this day, forming the most common route to the summit.

Nevertheless, this irony is a bittersweet triumph for Maestri, who feels he has been cursed. In the 1990s, he reputedly voiced his hatred for the mountain, claiming that he wanted it razed to the ground. History has added its own weight to that of the doubters. The mountain has been scaled by routes of tremendous technical difficulty by modern climbers with modern equipment, culminating in the Slovenians Silvo Karo and Janez Jeglic's ascent of the south wall in 1988. It wasn't until 2005 that a team of climbers manage to climb the route that Maestri claimed he and Egger took in 1959.

Lagunas Madre y Hija trail

From *Campamento Poincenot*, there are two other trails: one crosses the Río Blanco and follows its western bank northward towards the Río Eléctrico and Piedra del Fraile (see p.543), while the path from **Campamento Poincenot to Campamento De Agostini** (6km; 2–3hr; 100m descent), at the eastern end of Laguna Torre, leads past **Lagunas Madre y Hija** (Mother and Daughter Lagoons);

to do this, you'll need to double back towards Laguna Capri a little way, before finding the signposted route.

Walk due south of the campsite to the Chorrillo del Salto and follow the stream's eastern bank until you see a signpost directing horseriders left and hikers right. Take the right turning, which leads across a little bridge, and follow the boardwalk as it curves east to the turn-off to Laguna Madre, less than five minutes away. The route past the two lagoons makes for gentle walking and is easy to follow, pushing through knee-high bushes, and after a few hundred metres rising to and passing through the young forest to avoid the swampy ground for the most part. Look out for Upland Geese (*cauquenes*), which like to graze by the lakeshore. The path curls round to the right, squeezing between the far end of Laguna Hija and Laguna Nieta (Granddaughter Lagoon), and continues through mixed pasture and woodland before coming to the lip of the valley of Río Fitz Roy. Here, the path descends the steep slope and, if you look to your right, you may get your first glimpses of Cerro Torre through the *lenga* forest. Emerging from the trees, the slope levels out and you link up with the path from El Chaltén to *Campamento De Agostini* (see below), a forty-minute walk away.

El Chaltén to Campamento De Agostini and Laguna Torre

The most scenic route from **El Chaltén to Laguna Torre** (10km; 2hr 15min–3hr; 250m ascent), the silty lake in which – on perfect days – the imposing peak of **Cerro Torre** (3102m) is reflected, is reached by turning off Avenida San Martín by Viento Oeste and picking up the marked path at the base of the hill. This path climbs past the eerie skeleton of a large *lenga* tree (now a monument to the dangers of cigarettes), on to some rocks used by climbers for bouldering, and then weaves through hilly country before arriving, after an hour, at a viewpoint where, weather permitting, you'll catch your first proper view of Cerro Torre.

The path subsequently levels out along the Río Fitz Roy valley, in whose ragged stands of southern beech you're likely to come across wrens and the Thorn-tailed Rayadito, a diminutive foraging bird. A signposted turn-off on the right leads to Lagunas Madre y Hija (see above), which you'll need to return to if hiking the central circuit in clockwise fashion. This path soon starts to climb a steep, wooded hillside, before levelling out, running along the right-hand (eastern) side of the shallow lakes and continuing on to *Campamento Poincenot* (1hr 30min–2hr 15min from turn-off).

Sticking on the trail towards Laguna Torre, the path climbs to another viewpoint, before dropping down onto the valley floor – covered here in puddles that, in good weather, mirror Cerro Torre. You'll see an area that burned in 2003, apparently due to a discarded cigarette. The last section crosses a hill in the middle of the valley and a small stream before coming to blustery *Campamento De Agostini*, the closest **campsite** to the mountain for trekkers. Occupying a beautiful wooded site on the banks of the Río Fitz Roy, it also acts as the base camp for climbers and can get very busy (especially in Jan), so plan accordingly. The only good views of Cerro Torre from the campsite are from a rocky outcrop at the back of the wood, where there's one extremely exposed pitch. Otherwise, follow the path alongside the river, which brings you after about ten minutes to the moraine at the end of **Laguna Torre**. On top of the moraine, you can gaze at the granite needles of Cerro Torre, **Aguja Egger** (2900m) and **Cerro Standhardt** (2800m). Here, too, you'll find a **cable crossing** of the river, used by climbers that go ice-trekking on **Glaciar Torre**. Although it looks easy enough to cross without a harness, be warned: a girl drowned here in 1998 while attempting to do just that – gusts of wind can be sudden and fierce.

You can get closer to the mountain by walking for forty minutes along the path that runs parallel to the northern shore of Laguna Torre to the **Mirador Maestri** lookout point, passing en route an expedition hut that contains moving commemorative dedications to climbers who never quite succeeded in their attempts on the various peaks (note that this is not a recognized camping spot). The *mirador* provides superb views of Cerro Torre and Cerro Grande, and the incredible peak-dotted ridge that runs between them.

Río Eléctrico, Piedra del Fraile and beyond

The area to the north of Fitz Roy, just outside the national park, makes for rewarding trekking and can be linked to the Fitz Roy/Torre circuit. Although much of this is private land, you are welcome as long as you observe the same regulations stipulated by the park and camp only in designated sites.

To get to the start of the trek from the **RP-23 to Piedra del Fraile** (6km; 1hr 45min–2hr 15min; 80m ascent), take a Las Lengas or El Huemel **minibus** bound for Lago del Desierto (daily 7am, 8.30am & 3pm; $30) and get off right next to the bridge over the **Río Eléctrico**, a tempestuous river; this saves having to struggle for five to six hours against the prevailing winds that sweep down the valley from the north. The path starts to the left of the bridge, although its first section is imperilled every time the river is in spate. Soon you peel away from the river and, following the fairly inconspicuous cairns, cross the flat gravel floor of the Río Blanco valley. On the other side of the valley, the path joins the one heading south to Laguna Piedras Blancas and *Campamento Poincenot* (see p.539). Rather than turn south, aim right of the ridge ahead, into the valley of the Río Eléctrico, where you enter an enchanting, sub-Antarctic woodland, interspersed with grassy glades. Cross a brook and fifteen minutes further on you come to a gate in a ragged fence, followed shortly by another gate in another, equally dishevelled, fence. From the second gate, head right, towards the Río Eléctrico, and follow its bank. After approximately 35 minutes' gentle walk, you emerge from the woodland to be greeted with a terrific view of **Glaciar Marconi**; Piedra del Fraile is just five minutes' further on.

At **Piedra del Fraile**, you'll find the *Los Troncos refugio* and campsite ($14 per tent), scenically set alongside the swift-flowing Río Eléctrico and sheltered by a vast erratic boulder – the *piedra* of the name. The *fraile* (friar or priest) was Padre de Agostini (1883–1960), a Salesian priest who was one of Patagonia's most avid early mountaineers and explorers, and who lends his name to the campsite at Laguna Torre (see p.542). He was the first person to survey the area, and chose this site for his camp. There is a day-use *refugio* with kitchen and possibly the hottest shower in Patagonia. The cosy restaurant hut serves doorstep wedges of toasted sandwiches, unpretentious but filling meals, and chocolate and alcohol.

Two worthwhile treks lead from here, though you'll be charged $20 to continue your journey on through private land: the first, from **Piedra del Fraile to Glaciar Marconi** (10km return; 5hr–6hr 30min return; 35m ascent), takes you to the foot of the glacier, fording the Río Pollone and passing through the blasted scenery on the southern shore of Lago Eléctrico. There are fine views of the northern flank of Fitz Roy, especially from the Río Pollone valley, but be warned that the trail is unmarked once you cross the river; keep tight to the shore of Lago Eléctrico as it curves right, then continue due north past *Campamento La Playita*, following the Río Eléctrico Superior upstream to Laguna Marconi and its glacier. Glaciar Marconi itself sweeps down off the **Hielo Continental Sur** (see box, p.538), and forms the most frequently used point of access for expeditions heading onto this frigid expanse, by way of the windy **Paso Marconi** (1500m).

The second hike, from **Piedra del Fraile to the Paso del Cuadrado** (6km return; 7–9hr return; 1200m ascent), involves a much more difficult climb and should only be attempted by those with comprehensive mountaineering experience. From the camp, cross the small stream on the south side, walk through a wood and strike towards the gap between two streams, to the right of the wooded hillside. The path zigzags steeply up, though eventually levels out. After one-and-a-half to two hours, you pass an oddly shaped boulder with a tiny pool just above it and then the path peters out further up, once it reaches the scree. From here on you must make your own course, keeping the main stream to your right. When you reach the terminal moraine of the glacier, ford the river and work your way around the right-hand side of the col, two to two-and-a-half hours from the boulder. Cross the exposed area of rock on your right and then make the tiring thirty-minute climb up the snow to the pass, which is not immediately obvious but lies in the middle of the ridge. Expect a ferocious blast of wind at the top of Paso del Cuadrado (approximately 1700m), but hold onto your headgear and look out at one of the most dramatic views you're likely to come across in Patagonia. Weather permitting, you'll be able to see Fitz Roy's north face, across to the steeple of Cerro Torre, and down, across deeply crevassed glaciers, to the peaks of Aguja and Cerro Pollone, named after Padre de Agostini's home village in the Italian Alps.

Piedra del Fraile to Campamento Poincenot

You can head back east from **Piedra del Fraile to Campamento Poincenot** (11km; 3hr–3hr 30min; 200m ascent) to join up with the Fitz Roy/Torre loop. The path follows the Vallé Río Blanco south but can be difficult to pick up due to a number of false trails created by meandering cattle. On leaving the woods and emerging into the valley plain of the Río Blanco, head back towards the RP-23 until you reach a stream (about 20min). Turn right and follow its course until you see a faint path that heads south along the tree line. After about half an hour, you enter back into the national park and eventually pick up the line of under-ambitious cairns that mark the path: follow these until you come to the confluence of the Piedras Blancas stream and Río Blanco.

This area is strewn with chunks of granite. It's worth making a short detour right (west) up this valley, scrambling across the boulders to see the **Glaciar Piedras Blancas** tumbling into its murky lake, backed by a partial view of Fitz Roy (20–30min one way). Otherwise, ford the Piedras Blancas stream a little way up from where it meets the Río Blanco and cross the moraine dump to regain the trail. From this point, it's less than an hour's walk along the deteriorated if fairly easy path to *Campamento Poincenot* (see p.539).

The RN-40 and the Cordillera

The western boundary of Argentine Patagonia and the border with Chile are formed by the southern reaches of the Cordillera de los Andes, the world's longest mountain chain. These peaks are the feature that draws most visitors to this part of the country, luring them along with a ring of beautiful lakes and a national park, albeit not as famous or as breathtaking as Los Glaciares. The nationally renowned

In many people's minds, Argentina is composed of a vast patchwork of immense *latifundias* presided over by their *estanciero* owners. Although this image is no longer entirely true, landowning is still deeply embedded in the national consciousness, and an opportunity to stay at an **estancia** provides an excellent glimpse into this important facet of Argentine culture. Indeed, a stay on one of these farmsteads can be a holiday destination in itself. In the sheep-farming province of Santa Cruz a group of estancia owners runs the **Estancias de Santa Cruz** (ⓦwww.estanciasdesantacruz.com), which can make reservations at their estancias and produces an excellent booklet detailing them all, available from the head office at Suipacha 1120, Buenos Aires Capital Federal (ⓣ011/43253098), or the office in El Calafate at Libertador 1215 (ⓣ02902/4928580). The best of their estancias are listed in the relevant sections of the guide.

RN-40 (Ruta Cuarenta", often simply called "La Cuarenta" – for more about this emblematic highway, see *The legendary Ruta 40* colour section) zigzags up this mountainside swathe of inland Patagonia; indeed it hugs the Andes all the way from the southern tip of the mainland to the Bolivian border in the far north of the country. Most access roads for visiting the region run west from the RN-40: to the wild trekking areas around lakes Posadas and Pueyrredón and into Parque Nacional Perito Moreno. The main exceptions are the major archeological site of the Cueva de las Manos Pintadas, which lies in the canyon of **Río de las Pinturas**, just to the east of the RN-40; and the interesting oasis town of **Sarmiento**, a pioneer town and a very useful stop-over for anyone travelling farther up to the Lake District.

From November to the end of March, Andes Patagónicos (Mitre 125, Bariloche ⓣ02944/426809) operates a **bus** service along the RN-40 between Bariloche and Perito Moreno, from where Chaltén Travel (ⓦwww.chaltentravel.com) and Itinerarios y Travesías (El Chaltén ⓣ02962/493088) continue the trip to El Chaltén and El Calafate. The journey gives a good picture of the immensity of Patagonia, though it takes two long days (each about 13hr) without stopping to see the mountains or meet the locals.

Alternatively, and to truly appreciate the mystique of the area, you could **drive** yourself. The RN-40 is just about passable in a normal sedan – if it doesn't rain, and if you don't mind having to drive at 30kph along some sections for fear of crunching the undercarriage. Although the government is steadily tarmacking the road, large sections are still *ripio*: the worst stretches are between Tres Lagos and Bajo Caracoles (which is partly tarmacked); and between Perito Moreno and Río Mayo (the southernmost section was being upgraded in early 2010). They require careful negotiating but add greatly to the sense of adventure; for more on driving techniques see *The legendary Ruta 40* colour section.

The scenery in this region is predominately dry and flat, though some slopes are densely cloaked in southern beech woods, with a narrow fringe of scrubland separating forest from steppe. It's in these areas that you stand your best chance of seeing the region's outstanding **fauna**: condors, and perhaps even a puma or a highly endangered huemul. As for **flora**, the brush looks dreary and anonymous for the better part of the year. Some bushes liven up considerably in the spring, however, not least the thorny calafate, which blooms with a profusion of delicate yellow flowers, and the *lengua de fuego* with its gloriously bright orange flowers like clam shells. The RN-40 also passes harsh meseta, blasted rocky outcrops, patches of desert and the occasional river valley, usually accompanied by boggy pasture and lined in places with emerald-green willows and poplars. Here you'll find the few people who live along the route, where old traditions (like the open-air *asado*), gaucho clothes and an unhurried pace still reign.

The RN-40 north to Parque Nacional Perito Moreno

The taste of things to come, the paved RN-40 heading north-eastwards from the El Chaltén turn-off is desolate and remote: the minuscule and rather depressing settlement of **TRES LAGOS**, 35km to the north, is little more than a road junction (unpaved tracks lead off the RN-40, west towards the Andes and east into the heart of the steppe) but it does have a few services for the traveller, useful in emergencies: a free municipal **campsite**, shaded by cherry trees along a small stream; a couple of tyre-repair places (*gomerías*); and a supermarket. If you need to stay, *Huentru Niyeu*'s has small *cabañas*, just past the campsite (☏02962/495006; $45 per person).

The next 340km stretch of the RN-40, between Tres Lagos and Bajo Caracoles, is the most rugged of all. High crosswinds can make driving hazardous, so always keep your speed under control and take breaks. There are virtually no fuel stations along this part of the route, and you should carry enough fuel for several hundred kilometres of motoring (ie invest in a jerry can or two) if you plan to make any side-trips. Journeys are now speedier thanks to the excellent tarmac section between the junction near Estancia La Verde –where you can make a detour to tiny **Gobernador Gregores** some 70km away for fuel and some basic accommodation – and **Las Horquetas**, the hamlet from which a road leads to the Parque Nacional Perito Moreno. Both tourist estancias in or near the national park – Estancia Menelik and Estancia La Oriental – sell petrol and diesel, but the former is often out and the latter's supply is intended for guests only; they will, however, help out in an emergency.

Parque Nacional Perito Moreno

Extreme isolation means that, despite being one of Argentina's first national parks to be created, the **PARQUE NACIONAL PERITO MORENO** is also one of its least visited. Though replete with glorious mountains and beautiful lakes, this is not a "sightseeing" park like Nahuel Huapi or Los Glaciares. The bulk of the park's forested mountain scenery lies in its western two-thirds, which are reserved for **scientific study**, meaning that most of the area accessible to the public consists of arid steppe. Although visitor numbers are increasing annually, the park still offers a solitude that few other places on the continent can match.

You can see much of the park by car in a day or two, but could equally spend much longer trekking through the starkly beautiful high pampas, past virulently colourful lakes and near the imperious snowcapped hulk of San Lorenzo – and still miss out on many of its hidden wonders. In the absence of humans, **wildlife** thrives here. Guanacos can be seen at close quarters, while the luckiest visitors may glimpse a puma (or at least its tracks), or an endangered *huemul*, of which about one hundred are thought to live in the park. Condors are plentiful as is other **birdlife** including the Chilean flamingo, black-necked swans and the powerful black-chested Buzzard Eagle (*águila mora*). One of the park's most biologically interesting features is its **lakes**: the ones here have never been stocked with non-endemic species – native fish are protected and no fishing is allowed.

Park practicalities

Reached by a ninety-kilometre *ripio* spur road, which joins the RN-40 just west of Las Horquetas, the park is **open year round** but can be cut off by snow, sometimes for weeks on end; the weather changes moods like a spoilt child. Temperatures are bracing all year, and can drop to −25°C in winter, lower with wind chill.

Without your own transport, **getting to the park** is expensive: visitors to *La Oriental* (see below) can arrange a pick-up from the RN-40 ($400 or so unless someone from there happens to be making the journey). A *remise* from Gobernador Gregores, where there is a national park office at San Martín 882 (Ⓣ02962/491477, Ⓔperitomoreno@apn.gov.ar), will charge around $600, though don't rely on finding one willing to go all that way. Alternatively, the RN-40, a tour agency based in Comodoro Rivadavia (Ⓣ0297/446-5337, Ⓦwww.ruta-40.com) visits the national park on one of its RN-40 itineraries.

On arrival, you'll need to register at the park **administration building** (daily 8am–8pm), 5km inside the park. You'll also be given a welcoming talk and leaflets

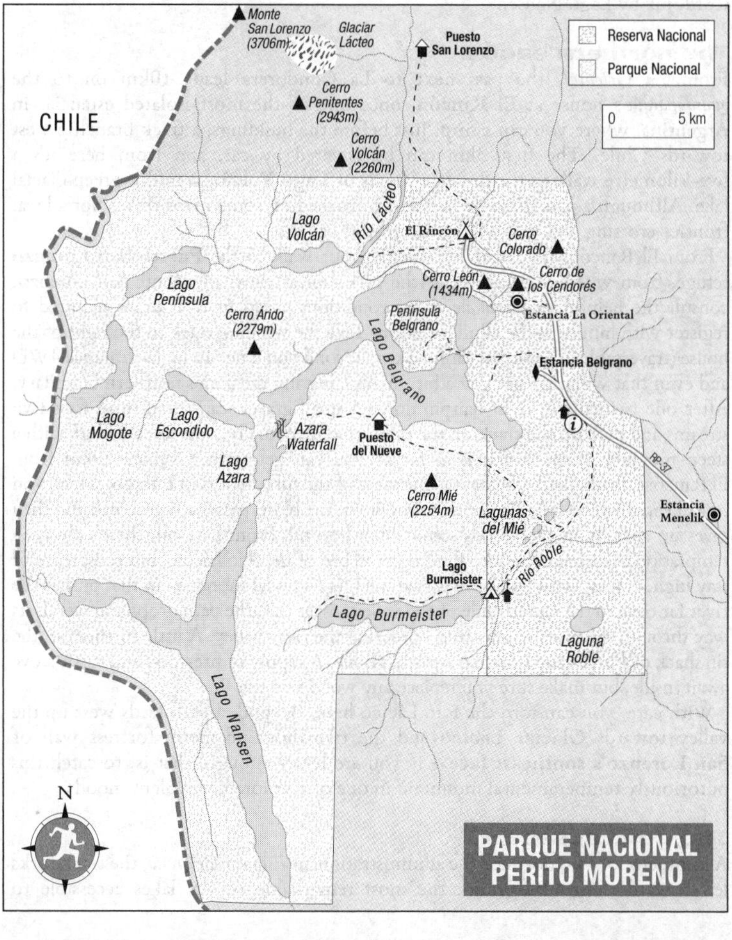

Monte San Lorenzo (3706m)
Glaciar Lácteo
Puesto San Lorenzo
Reserva Nacional
Parque Nacional
0 5 km
CHILE
Cerro Penitentes (2943m)
Cerro Volcán (2260m)
Lago Volcán
Río Lácteo
El Rincón
Cerro Colorado
Cerro León (1434m)
Cerro de los Cendorés
Estancia La Oriental
Lago Península
Cerro Árido (2279m)
Península Belgrano
Lago Belgrano
Estancia Belgrano
Lago Mogote
Lago Escondido
Azara Waterfall
Puesto del Nueve
Lago Azara
RP-37
Cerro Mié (2254m)
Lagunas del Mié
Estancia Menelik
Ruta 40
Lago Burmeister
Río Roble
Laguna Roble
Lago Nansen
N
PARQUE NACIONAL PERITO MORENO

on the trails and wildlife (some in English); there are creative educational displays in the small museum. Apart from water, there are no facilities.

The best **place to stay** is the homely ℐ *Estancia La Oriental*, a beautifully sited working estancia, looking out across the northern curl of Lago Belgrano about 7km north of the administration (in Buenos Aires ℡011/5237-4043, Ⓦwww .estanciasdesantacruz.com; ❸ half board; closed April–Oct). The owner cooks simple but hearty food and often serves delicious scones for breakfast: the facilities here for camping ($75 per tent) are clean and sheltered and the horseriding is fantastic. An equally scenic option, 10km outside the park, off the RP-37, is *Estancia Menelik* (in Buenos Aires ℡011/4836-3502, Ⓦwww.cielospatagonicos .com; ❾ full board; closed April to mid-Oct), an English-style *casco viejo*, most of whose cosy, wood-floored rooms have views across the steppe. There is also a sixteen-bed refuge with hot water and firewood (US$25 per person).

Otherwise, there are **refugios** at Puesto del Nueve and Puesto San Lorenzo, and a couple of basic, free **campsites** – in great locations at Lago Burmeister and El Rincón. If you are heading for any of these, you must register first at the administration office. Note that it is strictly illegal to cross into Chile at Paso Cordoniz by Lago Nansen.

The northern sector

From *La Oriental*, the pass next to La Condorera leads 10km on to the *guardaparque*'s house at **El Rincón**, once one of the most isolated estancias in Argentina, where you can **camp**. Just before the buildings, a track branches west towards Chile. The first 3km can be covered by car, and from here it's a five-kilometre walk to the desolate shores of **Lago Volcán**, a milky-green glacial lake. Although a pass (Paso de la Balsa) is marked on some maps this is not a legal frontier crossing and you will be detained if caught.

From El Rincón, it's a stiff five- to six-hour walk to the **Puesto San Lorenzo** refuge, from where you can access the park's finest views of Monte San Lorenzo; consult the helpful *guardaparque* about conditions ahead first. You are required to register with him or at the administration. Take the winding track to the right of the house (traversable in a normal car for 5km; beyond you'll need a high-clearance 4WD and even that will only get you a bit further), leaving the park's northern boundary. After one particularly tight hairpin down a small gravel scarp, you must ford two streams and pick up the track on the other side. Eventually, you reach a bluff with a steep moraine scarp, which is as far as you can get with a vehicle (9km from El Rincón). From here, you have a fine view of the turbulent **Río Lácteo**, which you must keep on your left. The track drops down the bluff, passes a windbreak and then gives up entirely in the woods some 200m beyond. From here on, there's always a temptation to drop down onto the flat gravel bed of the Río Lácteo, but resist this and stay high, at least until you have passed the huge alluvial moraine fan that pushes the river far over to the eastern side of the valley. After this, the path drops and wends its way through the marshy grassland bordering the river valley. A little further on, the tin shack of Puesto San Lorenzo is easily visible. A supply of firewood and rustic stove await inside, but make sure you replace any wood you use.

With care, you can ford the Río Lácteo here. Beyond, a path leads west up the valley towards **Glaciar Lácteo** and the two-thousand-metre fortress wall of **San Lorenzo's southeast face** – if you are lucky enough, that is, to catch this notoriously temperamental mountain in one of its more benevolent moods.

The central sector

A kilometre or two north of the administration, at *Estancia Belgrano*, the track forks left towards **Lago Belgrano**, the most remarkable of the lakes accessible to visitors, with one of the most intensely gaudy turquoise colours anywhere in Patagonia. After 8km you reach the scrub-covered **Península Belgrano**; a leaflet is available from administration for a self-guided two-hour circular trail through the *mata negra* bushes, detailing the behaviour of its graceful guanaco inhabitants. Look out for the mounds of guanaco dung at the animals' communal toilets, and the piles of bones pumas have left behind. Although it only takes three to four hours to walk to the other side, you can **camp** on the peninsula allowing more time to take in the beauty – or worry about the predators.

A longer hike of two to three days can be made south of Lago Belgrano, accessed on a path that cuts through the Lagunas del Mié, but you must ask permission from park administration first to use the old shepherd's refuge, **Puesto del Nueve**, as a base. From here, you can visit the ten-metre waterfall that drains Lago Belgrano and explore the region around beautiful **Lago Azara**, where you stand a slim chance of finding footprints or traces of *huemules*, the endangered Andean deer that is the park's symbol. You may cook on the small stove in the refuge, but should replace all firewood used.

Back on the main track, heading north from *Estancia Belgrano*, you reach the well-marked turn-off to *Estancia La Oriental*, which lies on the edge of a tranquil valley (see p.548). About 3km further north, on the other side of the valley, stands **Cerro de los Cóndores**, a cliff face stained by great white smears, indicating the presence of condors' nests. About thirty of the giant birds use the *condorera* regularly. To gain a similar perspective, you can climb nearby **Cerro León** (1434m; 4hr return), which affords excellent views of the heartland of the park.

Bajo Caracoles, Posadas and the lakes

From the Parque Nacional Perito Moreno turn-off, the RN-40 swings north across more desolate steppe – the Pampa del Asador to the west at least affords occasional glimpses of the cordillera as relief – to the tiny crossroads settlement of **Bajo Caracoles**. This stretch of the road is currently being paved, leading to slight changes in the route. From Bajo Caracoles an unpaved road leads west to the larger village of **Posadas**, which has better facilities, especially accommodation, and is the base for visiting the turquoise **Lago Posadas**, and the stunning lapis lazuli **Lago Pueyrredón**, set among splendid landscapes and famed their fishing. The lakes are separated by the narrowest of strips of land, the arrow-straight **La Península**, which looks for all the world like a man-made causeway. It was actually formed during a static phase of the last Ice Age, when an otherwise retreating glacier left an intermediate dump of moraine, now covered by sand dunes, which cut shallow Lago Posadas off from its grander neighbour. Most places of interest around the lakes are accessible only to those with their own vehicle.

Bajo Caracoles

Just short of 110km north of the side road to Parque Nacional Perito Moreno, nondescript **BAJO CARACOLES** is only useful as a transport hub (with buses to Posadas: Tues around 8pm) or for **refuelling** (the first reliable petrol stop north of Gobernador Gregores, or Tres Lagos). If you are in need of **accommodation**, the friendly *Hostel Ruta 40* (ⒺHostel_ruta40@hotmail.com; ❸) has dinky rooms, and serves keenly priced evening meals. Alternatively, the overpriced *Hotel Bajo Caracoles* (☏02963/490100; ❹) has an equally overpriced shop, a café, a **public phone** and a couple of simple rooms. You are far better off, however, staying in nearby Posadas or forging on to Perito Moreno, possibly staying at one of the estancias on the way.

Posadas

The area's main village, a loosely grouped assemblage of modern houses, is listed on some maps as **Hipólito Yrigoyen** (or even, confusingly, as **Lago Posadas**), but locals use the old name of **POSADAS**, which it shares with the neighbouring lake. Three kilometres south of town, the low, rounded wedge of **Cerro de los Indios** lies beneath the higher scarp of the valley. Bruce Chatwin's description of this rock in *In Patagonia* is unerring: "a lump of basalt, flecked red and green, smooth as patinated bronze and fracturing in linear slabs. The Indians had chosen the place with an unfaltering eye for the sacred."

Indigenous **rock-paintings**, some almost ten thousand years old, mark the foot of the cliff, about two-thirds of the way along the rock to the left. The well-known depiction of a "unicorn" – now thought to be a *huemul* – is rather faded; more impressive are the wonderful concentric circles of a hypnotic labyrinth design. The red blotches high up on the overhangs appear to have been the result of guanaco hunters firing up arrows tipped in pigment-stained fabric, perhaps in an ancient version of darts. However, the site's most remarkable feature is the polished shine on the rocks, which really do possess the patina and texture of antique bronze. There's also no fence screening off the engravings and paintings here, leaving the site's magical aura uncompromised.

Practicalities

There are a couple of decent places to **stay**: *Los Pioneros*, shortly after you enter the village (☎02963/490209; ④), has tiny but tidy rooms, while the more established *La Posada del Posadas* (☎02963/490250, ⓦ www.delposadas.com.ar) has both an old hotel ($40 per person), with shared bathrooms around a courtyard, and a set of smart bungalows further towards Lago Posadas (⑥ including breakfast), with modern fittings and comfortable beds in rooms sleeping two or three people. The owners of *La Posada*, Pedro and Susana Fortuny, run the village's best **restaurant**, serving two-course Mediterranean-style meals, and have excellent knowledge of local hikes and fishing. The village has a **fuel** station, a public telephone and little else. El Guraño **buses** leave for Bajo Caracoles and Perito Moreno once a week (Tues around 7pm). Five kilometres east of Posadas, the beautiful RP-41 runs north towards the Chilean border at Paso Roballos, and Los Antiguos, though spring floods mean that it is usually only passable from mid-December to March.

Lago Posadas

Do not try to drive around the south shore of **Lago Posadas**, even though a road is marked on many maps: cars can easily get bogged down near the Río Furioso. Instead, take the route running around the north shore, which passes through a zone of blasted, bare humps, crisscrossed by lines of *duraznillo* bushes. Known as **El Quemado** (The Burnt One), it's one of the most ancient formations in Argentina, dating back 180 million years to the Jurassic age, and there are spectacular contrasts between minerals such as green olivina sandstone and porphyry iron oxides. One of the best places **to stay** hereabouts is at the beautifully located, luxurious *Estancia Lagos del Furioso* at the southern end of La Península (in Buenos Aires ☎011/4812-0959, ⓦ www.estanciasdesantacruz.com; ⑨, minimum two-night stay; closed Easter–Oct). Purpose-built as a hotel, it doesn't provide the agrotourism opportunities of a working estancia, but the corresponding comforts are obvious: well-designed bungalows blanketed from the wind by a pocket of poplars, a sauna and an airy communal dining room where freshly prepared cuisine of an international standard is served, complemented by panoramic views of Lago Posadas and the Río Furioso canyon.

Lago Pueyrredón and the Río Oro Valley

Ambitious engineers have somehow managed to squeeze a dirt road between the southern shore of pristinely beautiful **Lago Pueyrredón** and the hills that press up against it, without having to resort to tiresome infill projects. This precarious arrangement is compromised only by the occasional spring flood (Sept is the worst month).

Just past the neat bridge over the **Río Oro**, a track wends its way up the mountainside and past the magnificent purple chasm of the **Garganta del Río Oro**. Fourteen kilometres from *Lagos del Furioso* are the *Estancia Suyai* **cabins** (℡02963/490242, ⓦsuyaipatagonia.com.ar; closed April–Sept; ❼) and **camping** ($25 per person), set on a stunningly beautiful peninsula jutting out into the lake. Beyond the campsite, the track deteriorates and the Río Oro is normally only crossable by 4WD.

Further on, the road rises through the wild foothills of **Monte San Lorenzo** and towards the snowline. This is private land, and crossing the border here is illegal; climbers intending to ascend San Lorenzo from the Chilean side should cross over to Cochrane at one of the legitimate border posts further north and tackle the mountain from Padre de Agostini's base camp, owned by the mountain guide, Luís Soto de la Cruz. Alternatively, contact Pedro Fortuny (of *La Posada de Posadas*; see p.550), who can help organize an expedition up San Lorenzo ($1000 per person for four people). The best **maps** of the area are those from the Instituto Geográfico Militar in Buenos Aires (see p.65: #4772-27 *Cerro Pico Agudo* and #4772-33 y 32 *Lago Belgrano*).

Perito Moreno and around

With a little over four thousand inhabitants, **PERITO MORENO** is the biggest town in this part of the world, which shows just how thinly populated the region is. Lying 130km north of Bajo Caracoles, it's a typically featureless, spread-out Patagonian settlement whose main interest is as a base for excursions to places such as the **Cueva de las Manos Pintadas**, some 120km south. When there is enough water, Black-necked Swans and flamingoes pass their time at the free wildlife refuge in town, the **Laguna de los Cisnes**.

Perito Moreno practicalities

The **bus terminal** is just north of town on the RP-43, by the **fuel** station; from here, cross the road and walk down Avenida San Martín to reach the town centre in about ten minutes. Chaltén Travel **buses** stop outside the *Hotel Belgrano*, at the far end of San Martin, en route between Bariloche and El Chaltén, while El Guraño buses for Bajo Caracoles (Tues around 5–6pm) leave from *Hotel Santa*

Tours from Perito Moreno

English-speaking Harry Nauta of Guanacóndor, at Perito Moreno 1087 (℡02963/432303, ✉jarinauta@yahoo.com.ar), runs a variety of trips to the **Cueva de las Manos Pintadas**, the best of which includes a three-hour walk down into the spectacular canyon floor ($150). He also runs a recommended tour to **Arroyo Feo** ("Ugly Stream"; $160), another area of great beauty and archeological interest, 70km south of town; with its dramatic narrow canyon and important nine-thousand-year-old cave-paintings, it offers a wilder alternative to the Cueva de las Manos. From December, Nauta also runs three-day trips ($500) that take in the **RP-41**, a scenic road that skirts striking Monte Zeballos. Zoyen Turismo, at San Martín and Saavedra (℡02963/432207, ⓦwww.zoyenturismo.com.ar), runs similar tours.

Cruz, three blocks west of San Martín, at Belgrano 1565. It is a useful stopover if you need to **change money** – the Banco de Santa Cruz at San Martín 1493 has an **ATM** – or stock up on **food**, at one of several *panaderías* lining San Martin. The **tourist office** is at San Martín and Gendarmería Nacional (daily 7am–11pm; ☎02963/432732), and there's **internet** at CTC, Perito Moreno 1062, and a *locutorio* at San Martin 1730.

Accommodation in town is neither good value nor abundant, with the best being the comfortable, smart hotel *Austral* at San Martín 1386 (☎02963/432538; ⑤), or the homely *Posada del Caminante* at Rivadavia 937 (☎02963/432204; ③), which has large, pleasant rooms and a relaxing communal area. The sociable municipal **campsite** ($15 per tent) lies on the shore of Laguna de los Cisnes, at Mariano Moreno and Paseo Julio A. Roca: it also has a couple of small, six-person **cabins** for rent ($20 per person) – the cheapest option in town for those with a sleeping bag but no tent. Funds permitting, however, you're better off heading 30km south of town to *Estancia Telken* (☎02963/432079, ⑩www.estanciasdesantacruz.com; ⑧ with breakfast; closed May–Sept), one of the best estancias to give a taste of what it means to live on a working ranch; you can **camp**, go birdwatching at Laguna del Clarke or reconnoitre the extensive land on horseback.

None of Perito Moreno's **restaurants** is particularly special, but *Patagones* restaurant-bar, at San Martín and Mitre, has filling home-made burgers and a good taste in rock music, while *Nono's*, at 9 de Julio and Saavedra, dishes up a decent pizza.

Cueva de las Manos Pintadas

The landscape between Perito Moreno and Bajo Caracoles best embodies most people's concept of Patagonia – sparsely populated and at times empty lands stretching to the horizon. Why most people venture to these parts at all is to see the magnificent **Cueva de las Manos Pintadas** (Cave of the Painted Hands), one of South America's finest examples of rock-paintings and listed as a UNESCO World Heritage Site. It can be approached either by road along a sidetrack just north of Bajo Caracoles, or, better, by walking or riding up the canyon it overlooks, the impressive **Cañón de Río Pinturas**.

From the canyon rim, it's a spectacular two-hour **walk** to the cave-paintings. The path drops sharply to the flat valley bed, and continues to the right of the snaking river, nestling up against rock walls and pinnacles that display the region's geological history in bands of black basalt, slabs of rust-coloured sandstone and a layer of sedimentary rocks that range in hue from chalky white to mottled ochre. Bring binoculars for viewing the finches and birds of prey that inhabit the canyon, plus food, water, a hat and sunscreen.

At the point where the course of the Río Pinturas is diverted by a vast rampart of red sandstone, you start to climb the valley side again to reach the road from Bajo Caracoles and the **entrance building** to the protected area around the paintings (daily 9am–7pm; $50), where there's a modest display. Unfortunately, some parts of the site have been tarnished by tourists etching modern graffiti on the rock – hence the fence that now keeps visitors at a distance – and you can only access the cave accompanied by a *guardaparque* on a **guided walk** (1hr; June–Sept on demand, Oct–May every 90min).

The *cueva* itself is less a cave than a series of overhangs: natural cutaways at the foot of a towering 90m cliff face overlooking the canyon below, a vantage point from which groups of Palaeolithic hunter-gatherers would survey the valley floor for game. Despite the rather heavy-handed fence that now frames them, the collage of black, white, red and ochre **handprints**, mixed with gracefully flowing vignettes of guanaco hunts, still makes for an astonishing spectacle. Of the 829 handprints, most are male, and only 31 are right handed. They are all "negatives", being made by placing the hand on the rock face, and imprinting its outline by blowing pigments through a tube. Interspersed with these are human figures, as well as the outlines of puma paws and rhea prints, and creatures such as a scorpion.

The earliest paintings were made by the **Toldense** culture and date as far back as 11000 BC, but archeologists have identified four later cultural phases, ending with depictions by early Tehuelche groups – notably geometric shapes and zigzags – from approximately 1300 AD. The significance of the paintings is much debated: whether they represented part of the rite of passage for adolescents into the adult world, and were thus part of ceremonies to strengthen familial or tribal bonds, or whether they were connected to religious ceremonies that preceded the hunt will probably never be known. Other tantalizing mysteries involve theories surrounding the large number of heavily pregnant guanacos depicted, and whether these herds were actually semi-domesticated. One thing is for certain: considering their exposed position, it is remarkable how vivid some of the colours still are – the colours were made from the berries of *calafate* bushes, earth and charcoal, with guanaco fat and urine applied to create the waterproof coating that has preserved them so well.

Practicalities

To get to the paintings, take the turn-off just to the north of Bajo Caracoles, a rough 45km stretch of *ripio* leading to a car park, 600m from the entrance building. Alternatively, you can take a **tour** from Perito Moreno (see above), some of which involve walking up through the canyon. If you want **to stay**, the *Estancia La Cueva de las Manos* (also known as Los Toldos; ℡02963/432730 or in Buenos Aires ℡011/4901-0436, Ⓦwww.estanciasdesantacruz.com; ❽; closed May–Oct) is a functional building 7km up a well-signed side track off the RN-40, serving good meals with kitchen facilities for guests too. The *cueva* actually lies on land owned by the estancia, which teems with horses, guanacos and rheas, and they can organize **horse rides** and **hikes** there as well as **transport** to the canyon rim. They

▲ Cueva de las Manos Pintadas

also run 4WD trips to the *cueva* as well as to nearby Charcamata, a similar rock-art site. Note that any visit to the paintings from the estancia side involves negotiating a steep and difficult climb down to the river valley and up again.

Sarmiento and the Bosque Petrificado

Heading north from Perito Moreno, the RN-40 has undergone some major rerouting, and the first stretch has been paved, while the particularly rough section immediately south of Río Mayo should be fully tarmacked by 2011. The RN-40 now heads northeast from Río Mayo to meet the newly upgraded RN-26 at a junction 70km west of Sarmiento, the first real town you reach if you travel up the whole RN-40 from El Calafate. A rough-and-ready but not unappealing pioneering settlement with a couple of worthwhile attractions, Sarmiento can also be reached along the RN-26 from Comodoro Rivadavia, 150km to the east. Cutting through hilly steppe country covered in duraznillo bushes, this road provides ample evidence of the country's oilfields, with the nodding heads of hundreds of oil wells relentlessly probing the ground. Just over 30km south of Sarmiento, a well-tended site allows you to see in situ one of the best preserved examples in the country of a petrified forest, the Bosque Petrificado Sarmiento. Beyond the RN-26 intersection, the (paved, but badly potholed) RN-40 heads northwest again, crossing some particularly bleak Patagonian pampa, towards Tecka and, eventually, Esquel (see p.463) in the Argentine Lake District.

Sarmiento

With a population of more than ten thousand inhabitants, the market town of **SARMIENTO** (or Colonia Sarmiento) is irrigated by waters from the Río Senguer and the sizeable lakes it feeds, **Lago Colhué Huapi** and **Lago Musters**, the latter named after a nineteenth-century English adventurer, Captain George Chaworth Musters, who put it on the map. Both lakes, shining royal blue on sunny days, are home to large numbers of birds, including flamingos. The irrigation supports a strong farming community (try and be around for the cherry blossom in early October or the fruit harvest in December), originally founded by the Welsh, with an influx of Lithuanians and **Boers**, who fled here after the Boer War and soon took to the strenuous task of farming in relatively hostile conditions. In addition to agriculture, the town services a large military presence (this is border country), though tourism is relatively underdeveloped despite the vicinity of the petrified forest (see below).

In town, the outdoor **Parque Paleontológico** on Perito Moreno (ask at the tourist office for the hourly guided visits; $8), with its convincing replicas of dinosaurs whose remains have been found in the area, makes for a slightly scary theme park that's good for children. The excellent **Museo Regional Desiderio Torres**, housed in the old train station round the corner at 20 de Junio (daily 9am–7pm; $8), is also worth a visit for its sizeable collection of indigenous artefacts and well-explained displays of weavings by the Mapuche (see p.478) and Tehuelche (see p.501), plus dinosaur bones and other fossils. Part of the museum is given over to the town's pioneering immigrant communities, including some fascinating photos. The tourist office can provided details about about visits to three local *chacras* or **market gardens** (Labrador, San José and San Cayetano), which are especially interesting during the cherry season. The season for **trout fishing**, regionally renowned, is November to April, but you'll need a permit ($350 per week) from the tourist office. Finally, if you're here over the second weekend in February, don't miss the three-day **Festival Provincial de Doma y Folklore**, with horse-taming in the afternoon and folk concerts in the evening, at the Club Deportivo on the RN-26.

Practicalities

Sarmiento's main street, initially Avenida Regimiento de Infantería, later becoming Avenida San Martín, runs off the RN-26 at a right angle. **Buses** pull into the terminal at the far end, at San Martín and Avenida 12 de Octubre. The **tourist office** (daily: April to mid-Dec 8am–8pm; mid-Dec to March 8am–11pm; ☎0297/489-8220, ⓦ wwwcoloniasarmiento.gov.ar) is at Pietrobelli 388, and has a useful tourist map of the town centre and surrounding region. The Banco Chubut at San Martín 756 has an **ATM**.

For **accommodation**, by far the best option is ♨ *Chacra Labrador*, about 8km west of town on the RN-26 at km 146.5 (☎0297/489-3329, ⓦ www .hosterialabrador.com.ar; ❻). The congenial owners of English, Boer and Dutch origins (English, German and Dutch spoken) have modelled their farmhouse on a British-style B&B, with four charming rooms on a sixty-hectare estancia. Dinner can be provided for guests and they can arrange guided tours to the petrified forests. In town, the best of a poor bunch is *Hotel Ismar*, at Patagonia 248 (☎0297/489-3293; ❸), which has clean, basic rooms off a courtyard occupied by noisy oil workers' trucks. *Camping del Búlgaro* is the most attractive of the town's **campsites**, set among a strand of poplars on the shores of Lago Musters (☎0297/489-3114, ⓔelbulgaro@coopsar.com.ar; $15); there's a small shop selling provisions on site.

In a gastronomic desert (unless you're staying at *Chacra Labrador*), *Parrilla La Tranquera*, at the corner of Estrada and San Martín (closed Mon), is as good as **dining** gets despite its bland outward appearance.

Bosque Petrificado Sarmiento

Two kilometres from the centre of town, a clearly signposted gravel track off the RN-26 leads 30km to the **BOSQUE PETRIFICADO SARMIENTO** (daily April–Sept 9am–6pm; Oct–March 9am–9pm; $20). Here, perfectly preserved 65-million-year-old trunks are randomly strewn across a near-lunar setting with a stunning purple-and-orange cliff backdrop. The petrified forest – formed by mineral-rich water permeating the wood over hundreds of thousands of years, effectively turning the trees into stone – has parallels with the Monumento Natural Bosques Petrificados in Santa Cruz Province (see p.516), but its bands of "painted desert" soils are more striking and erosion processes are much more visible here. Traversing the two-kilometre circuit is rather like walking around a sawmill, the ground covered by splinters of bark and rotten wood that chink under foot, except that these woodchips are Mesozoic. The highlight is a famous and much photographed chunk of **hollow fossilized log** that looks like nature's take on a giant drainage pipe.

Remises from the town will run you to the park and back for around $120 including a ninety-minute wait; ask at tourist office if you want a guide. Take water, sunscreen and hats as the sun can be very strong, as can the winds. There are toilets in the park but no other services.

Travel details

Buses

Some services do not operate out of season (Easter–Sept), above all along and around the RN-40, while others are severely curtailed.

Bajo Caracoles to: Perito Moreno (every Tues; 2hr); Posadas (every Tues; 2hr).

Camarones to: Trelew (3 weekly; 3hr).

Comandante Luis Piedra Buena to: Comodoro Rivadavia (4 daily; 6hr 30min–8hr); Puerto San Julián (4 daily; 1hr 30min); Río Gallegos (6 daily; 3hr).

El Calafate to: El Chaltén (9–10 daily; 4hr); Perito Moreno (daily in summer; 13hr); Río Gallegos (4–5 daily; 4hr–4hr 30min); Río Turbio (2 daily; 4hr); Ushuaia (via Chile; Mon–Sat daily; 18hr).

El Chaltén to: El Calafate (9–10 daily; 4hr); Lago del Desierto (3 daily; 1hr); Los Antiguos (daily in summer; 13hr); Perito Moreno (daily in summer; 13hr).

Gaiman to: Trelew (11–18 daily; 25–35min).

Perito Moreno to: Bajo Caracoles (every Tues; 2hr); El Calafate (daily in summer; 13hr); El Chaltén (daily in summer; 13hr); Los Antiguos (5–9 daily; 50min); Posadas (every Tues; 4hr).

Posadas to: Bajo Caracoles (every Tues; 2hr); Perito Moreno (every Tues; 4hr).

Puerto Madryn to: Bariloche (1–3 daily; 9hr); Buenos Aires (13–14 daily; 18hr); Carmen de Patagones (6 daily; 6hr); Puerto Pirámides (1–2 daily; 1hr 15min); Río Gallegos (5–7 daily; 16–19hr); Trelew (hourly; 1hr).

Puerto Pirámides to: Puerto Madryn (1–2 daily; 1hr 15min); Trelew (daily in summer; 2hr 45min).

Puerto San Julián to: Comandante Luis Piedra Buena (4 daily; 1hr 30min); Río Gallegos (hourly; 4–5hr); Trelew (5 daily; 10hr 30min).

Río Gallegos to: El Calafate (10–12 daily; 3hr 30min–4hr 30min); Puerto Madryn (7 daily; 18–19hr); Puerto San Julián (hourly; 4–5hr); Río Grande (via Chile; 6 weekly; 13hr);Trelew (4 daily; 15–16hr); Ushuaia (via Chile; 1–2 daily; 13hr).

Río Turbio to: El Calafate (2 daily; 4hr); Río Gallegos (4 daily; 5hr).

Sarmiento to: Comodoro Rivadavia (5 daily; 2hr 15min); Esquel (1–2 daily; 6hr).

Trelew to: Bariloche (3 daily; 13hr); Buenos Aires (11 daily; 19–21hr); Camarones (3 weekly; 3hr); Esquel (daily; 8hr 30min); Gaiman (11–18 daily; 25–35min); Puerto Madryn (hourly; 1hr); Puerto Pirámides (daily; 2hr 45min); Puerto San Julián (5 daily; 10hr–11hr 30min); Río Gallegos (4 daily; 15–16hr).

Ferries

Punta Delgada to: Bahía Azul, across the Magellan Straits (every 40min, no crossings at low tide; 30min).

Flights

Comodoro Rivadavia to: Buenos Aires (1–3 daily; 2hr); Perito Moreno (Mon; 1hr); Río Gallegos (2 daily; 1hr 15min); Trelew (daily; 45min).

El Calafate to: Bariloche (1–2 daily; 2hr); Buenos Aires (2–4 daily; 3hr); Río Gallegos (4 weekly; 50min); Ushuaia (2–3 daily; 1hr 10min).

Puerto Madryn to: Buenos Aires (daily; 2hr); Ushuaia (irregular; 2hr). *See also* Trelew.

Perito Moreno to: Comodoro Rivadavia (Mon; 1hr).

Río Gallegos to: Buenos Aires (2–3 daily; 3hr); Comodoro Rivadavia (2 daily; 1hr 15min); El Calafate (daily; 50min); Río Grande (twice weekly; 1hr 15min); Ushuaia (daily 55min).

Trelew to: Buenos Aires (3–4 daily; 1hr 50min); Comodoro Rivadavia (daily; 45min); Ushuaia (irregular; 2hr).

9

Tierra del Fuego

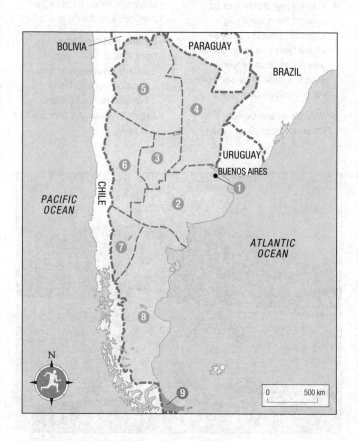

BOLIVIA

PARAGUAY

BRAZIL

URUGUAY

BUENOS AIRES

PACIFIC
OCEAN

CHILE

ATLANTIC
OCEAN

N

0   500 km

CHAPTER 9 # Highlights

* **Arriving at Ushuaia by plane** The town's dramatic location – wedged between the tail-end of the Andes and the Beagle Channel – makes this a landing to remember. See p.563

* **Fresh king crab** Plucked straight from the Beagle Channel, *centolla* appears on all the best menus in Ushuaia, and is delicious served in soups, baked in its shell or simply grilled. See p.569

* **Wildlife in the Beagle Channel** Spot albatrosses and sea lions, terns and whales as you brave the elements in this stunningly beautiful waterway. See p.570

* **Parque Nacional Tierra del Fuego** Parakeets and hummingbirds are some of the surprising inhabitants of this precious forestland. See p.572

* **Estancia stays** Get away from it all at charming *Estancia Rivadavia*, or get a taste of working life on a Fuegian farm at historic *Estancia Viamonte*. See p.578 & p.580

▲ Upland geese at Parque Nacional Tierra del Fuego

9

Tierra del Fuego

cross the Magellan Strait from mainland Patagonia, **TIERRA DEL FUEGO** is a land of windswept bleakness, whose settlements seem to huddle with their backs against the elements: cold winters, cool summers, gales in the spring, frost in the autumn. Yet this remote archipelago, tucked away at the foot of the South American continent, exercises a fascination over many travellers. Some look to follow in the footsteps of the region's famous explorers, such as navigator Ferdinand Magellan, naturalist Charles Darwin or more recently, author Bruce Chatwin. Others just want to see what it's like down here, at the very end of the world.

Though comprising a number of islands, it's more or less the sum of its most developed part, **Isla Grande**, the biggest island in South America. Its eastern section, roughly a third of the island, along with a few islets, belongs to Argentina – the rest is Chilean territory. The major destination for visitors is the Argentine city of **Ushuaia**, a year-round resort on the south coast. Beautifully located, backed by distinctive jagged mountains, it is *the* base for visiting the tremendous **Beagle Channel**, rich in marine wildlife, and the wild, forested peaks of the **Cordillera Darwin**. With the lakes, forests and tundra of **Parque Nacional Tierra del Fuego** just 12km to the west, and historic **Estancia Harberton**, home to descendants of Thomas Bridges, an Anglican missionary who settled here in 1871, a short excursion from the city, you could easily spend a week or so in the area.

Lago Fagnano, and the village of **Tolhuin** at its eastern end, is the main focus of the island's central area, which is of considerably greater interest than the windswept plains and scrubby *coirón* grasslands in the north. The southeastern chunk of Isla Grande, **Península Mitre**, is one of Argentina's least accessible regions, a boggy wilderness with low scrub and next to no human habitation, while, to its east, lies the mysterious **Isla de los Estados**, known in English as Staten Island. It is an extremely difficult area to visit, even more than the great white continent of **Antarctica**, which can be reached from Ushuaia – at a price.

The majority of the region's visitors arrive during the summer (Dec–Feb), when places such as Ushuaia can get very busy. The best **time to visit** is between late March and the end of April, when the mountains and hills are daubed with the spectacular autumnal colours of the *Nothofagus* southern beech. Springtime (Oct to mid-Nov) is also beautiful, if rather windy. For **winter sports**, you need to head for Ushuaia between June and August; the area is good for cross-country skiing, especially around Sierra Alvear, though the downhill facilities are best suited to beginners and intermediates. The **climate** here is generally not as severe as you may expect given the latitude, and temperatures rarely reach the extremes of mainland continental areas of Patagonia, though you'll need to be prepared for blizzards and icy winds at any time of year.

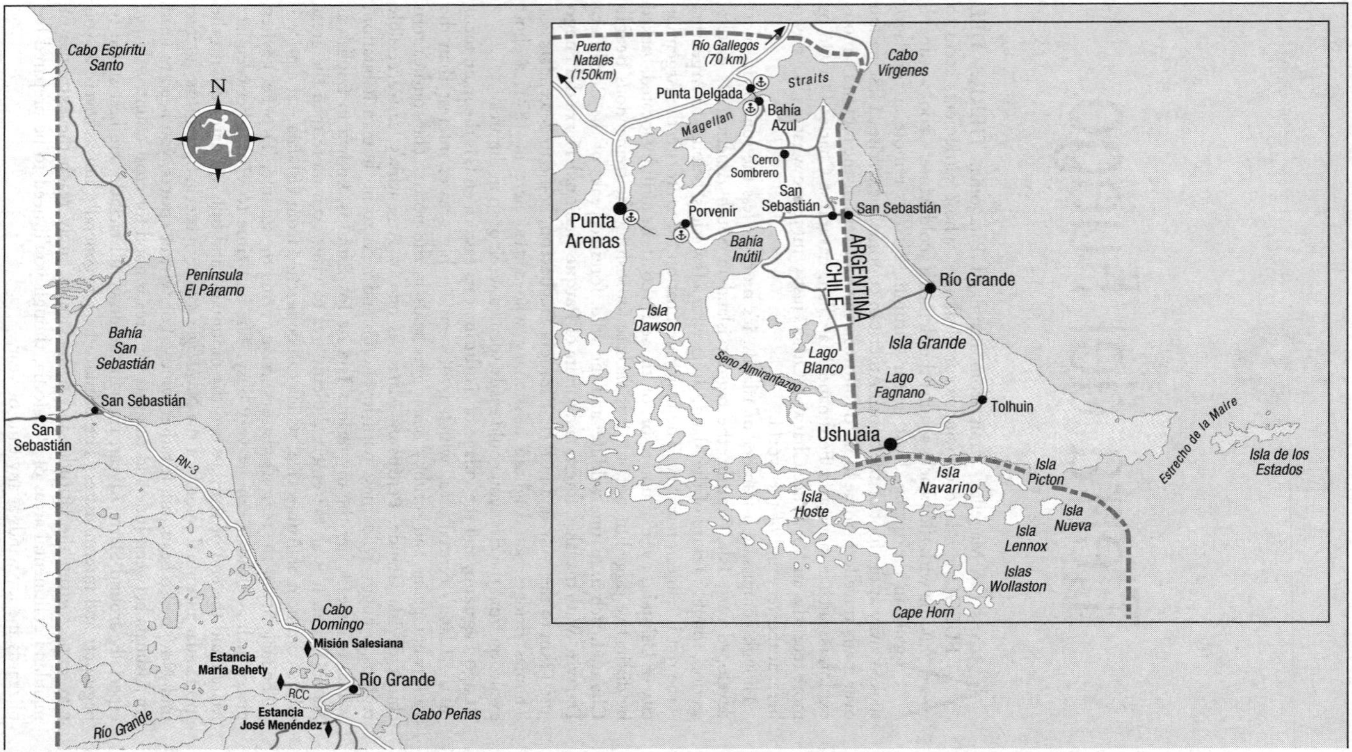
Cabo Espíritu Santo
N
Península El Páramo
Bahía San Sebastián
San Sebastián
San Sebastián
RN-3
Cabo Domingo
Misión Salesiana
Estancia María Behety
RCC
Río Grande
Estancia José Menéndez
Río Grande
Cabo Peñas
Puerto Natales (150km)
Río Gallegos (70 km)
Cabo Vírgenes
Straits
Punta Delgada
Bahía Azul
Magellan
Cerro Sombrero
San Sebastián
San Sebastián
Punta Arenas
Porvenir
Bahía Inútil
ARGENTINA
CHILE
Río Grande
Isla Dawson
Isla Grande
Lago Blanco
Seno Almirantazgo
Lago Fagnano
Tolhuin
Ushuaia
Estrecho de la Maire
Isla de los Estados
Isla Picton
Isla Navarino
Isla Hoste
Isla Nueva
Isla Lennox
Islas Wollaston
Cape Horn

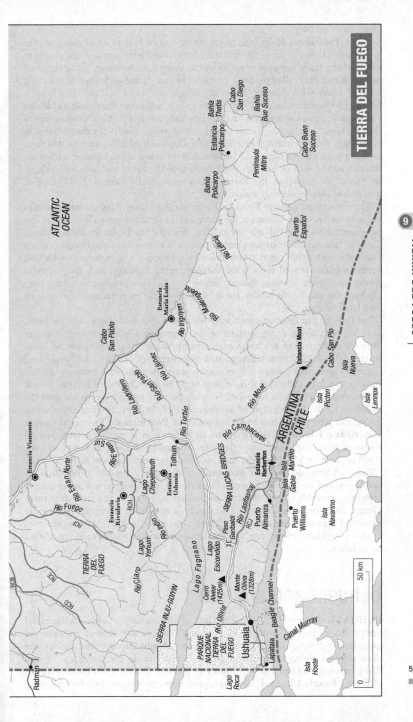

TIERRA DEL FUEGO

In 1520, **Ferdinand Magellan**, in his attempt to be first to circumnavigate the globe, sailed through the straits that were later named after him and saw clouds of smoke rising from numerous fires lit by the indigenous Selk'nam along the coast of Isla Grande. He called the land Tierra del Humo ("Land of Smoke"); it was the king of Spain who thought Tierra del Fuego, or "Land of Fire", much more poetic. Early contact between indigenous groups and other **European explorers** was sporadic from the sixteenth century onwards, but this changed dramatically in the latter half of the nineteenth century, with tragic results for the indigenous population. When FitzRoy came here in the *Beagle* in the 1830s, an estimated three to four thousand Selk'nam and Mannekenk were living in Isla Grande, with some three thousand each of Yámana and Kawéskar in the entire southern archipelago. By the 1930s, however, the Mannekenk were virtually extinct, and the other groups had been effectively annihilated.

White settlement came to Tierra del Fuego in three phases. Anglican **missionaries** began to catechize the Yámana in the south, and Thomas Bridges established the first permanent mission on Ushuaia Bay in 1871. From the late 1880s, the Italian Roman Catholic Salesian Order began a similar process to the north of the Fuegian Andes. From the mid-1890s came a new colonizing impetus: the inauspicious-looking northern plains proved to be ideal **sheep-farming** territory, and vast *latifundias* sprang up. Croat, Scottish, Basque, Italian and Galician immigrants, along with Chileans from across the border, arrived to work on the estancias and build up their own landholdings.

The issue of that international border has been a contentious one over the years, as it has been along other sections of the Argentina–Chile boundary. Frontier disputes at the end of the nineteenth century required the arbitration of Great Britain, who in 1902 awarded Argentina the eastern half of Tierra del Fuego; land squabbles were still going on over eighty years later, the two countries almost coming to war in 1984 over three islands in the Beagle Channel. This time it took the intervention of Pope John Paul II, who, possibly to even things up, gave the islands to Chile. A cordial peace has reigned since. In 1991, the Argentine sector gained full provincial status and is known as the **Provincia de Tierra del Fuego, Antártida e Islas del Atlántico Sur**. Its jurisdiction is seen to extend over all southern territories, including the Islas Malvinas/Falklands Islands (see box, p.601), which lie 550km off the coast, and the Argentine segment of Antarctica.

Today, Tierra del Fuego's **economy** is dependent on the production of petroleum and natural gas, fisheries, forestry and technological industries such as television assembly plants, attracted to the area by its status as a duty-free zone. Luxury items are comparatively cheap, but basic items such as food are much more expensive than in other parts of the country, owing to the huge distances involved in importing them. Hopes run high for the fast-expanding tourist industry centred on Ushuaia.

Ushuaia and around

USHUAIA, the provincial capital and hub of tourism for the whole of Tierra del Fuego, lies in the far south of Isla Grande. Dramatically situated between the mountains – among them **Cerro Martial** and **Monte Olivia** – and the sea, the town tumbles, rather chaotically, down the hillside to the encircling arm of land that protects its bay from the southwesterly winds and occasional thrashing storms of the icy **Beagle Channel**. Ushuaia is primarily a convenient base for exploring the rugged beauty of the lands that border the channel, a historically important sea passage, but be warned that it exploits tourism to the full – prices vary between high and astronomical. Puerto Williams lies just across the channel, on the southern (Chilean) side of the straits, and there are other trips as well: to historic **Estancia Harberton**, to a small penguin colony, and to nearby **Parque Nacional Tierra del Fuego**. In winter, there's decent skiing in the **Sierra Alvear** region north of town; in warmer seasons, it's also good for **trekking**.

Every year on June 21 – the longest night of the year – the **Bajada de Las Antorchas** takes place, with the darkness celebrated by a torchlit ski descent of Cerro Martial's slopes, traditionally opening the season. Daylight lasts from about 9am until 4pm at this time of year.

Some history

In 1869, Reverend Waite Stirling became Tierra del Fuego's first white settler when he founded his **Anglican mission** among the Yámana here; the city takes its name from the Yámana tongue, and means something akin to "bay that stretches towards the west". Stirling stayed for six months, before being recalled to the Islas Malvinas/Falklands Islands to be appointed Anglican bishop for South America. Thomas Bridges, his assistant, took over the mission in 1871, after which Ushuaia began to figure on mariners' charts as a place of refuge in the event of shipwreck. A modest **monument** to the achievements of the early missionaries can be found where the first mission stood, on the south side of Ushuaia Bay, and is reached by the modern causeway southwest of the town centre.

In 1884, Commodore Augusto Lasserre raised the Argentine flag over Ushuaia for the first time, formally incorporating the area into the Argentine Republic. From 1896, in order to consolidate its sovereignty and open up the region to wider colonization, the Argentine state established a **penal colony** here. Forced convict labour was used for developing the settlement's infrastructure and for logging the local forests to build the town, but the prison had a reputation as the Siberia of Argentina and Perón closed it in 1947.

Nowadays, Ushuaia has a quite different reputation: the most populous, and popular, town in Tierra del Fuego, it depends largely on its thriving **tourist** industry, capitalizing on the beauty of its natural setting. You'll soon catch on that this is the world's most southerly resort, allowing you to amass claims to fame galore – golf on the world's most southerly course, a ride on the world's most southerly train, and so on. Ushuaia has plenty of sites worthy of a visit on their own merits, but unfortunately tourism has been allowed to develop with scant regard for the unique character of the town, and has changed it almost beyond recognition in the last decade. At certain moments you can still get a sense of the other-worldliness that used to make Ushuaia special, but if you are coming expecting a Chatwin-esque frontier town, you will be disappointed.

Arrival and information

The modern international **airport**, Malvinas Argentinas, is 4km southwest of town; there's no public transport to the city, and a **taxi** to the centre costs around $15. **Buses** – to Estancia Harberton, Parque Nacional Tierra del Fuego and other nearby attractions, as well as long-distance services to Río Grande and beyond – arrive and depart from the car park on seafront Avenida Maipú, at the corner with Juan Fadul.

The main commercial street, **Avenida San Martín**, runs parallel to and one block uphill from Maipú; at no. 674, you'll find the **tourist office** (Mon–Fri 9am–10pm, Sat & Sun 9am–8pm; ℡02901/432001, ⓦwww.turismoushuaia.com). Its

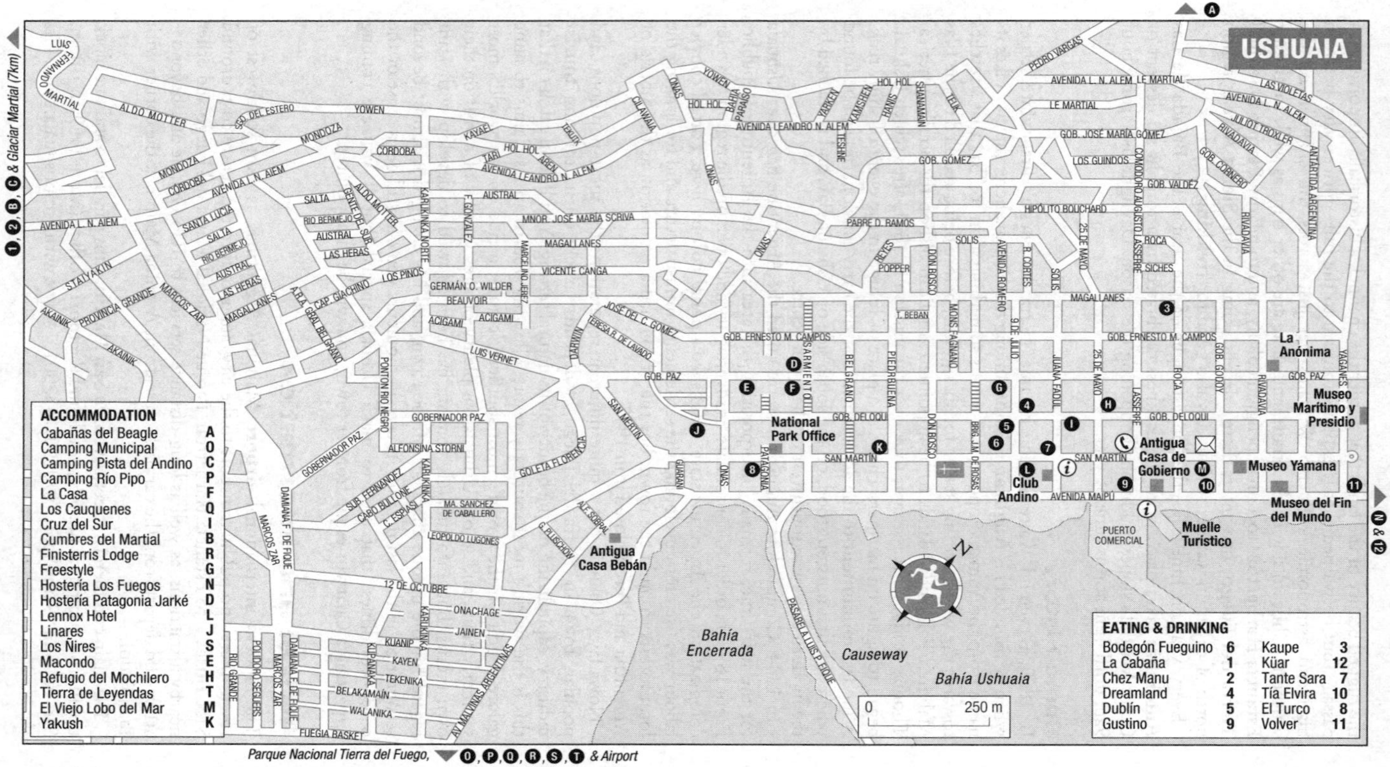

USHUAIA
A
1, 2, B, C & Glaciar Martial (7km)
N & 12
Parque Nacional Tierra del Fuego, O, P, Q, R, S, T & Airport
La Anónima
Museo Marítimo y Presidio
Museo Yámana
Museo del Fin del Mundo
Antigua Casa de Gobierno
Club Andino
National Park Office
Antigua Casa Bebán
Muelle Turístico
Puerto Comercial
Bahía Encerrada
Causeway
Bahía Ushuaia
Pasarela Luis P. Fique
Av. Malvinas Argentinas
Avenida Maipú
San Martín
Gob. Deloqui
Gob. Paz
Gob. Ernesto M. Campos
Magallanes
Avenida Leandro N. Alem
0 250 m
N
ACCOMMODATION
Cabañas del Beagle A
Camping Municipal O
Camping Pista del Andino C
Camping Río Pipo P
La Casa F
Los Cauquenes Q
Cruz del Sur I
Cumbres del Martial B
Finisterris Lodge R
Freestyle G
Hostería Los Fuegos N
Hostería Patagonia Jarké D
Lennox Hotel L
Linares J
Los Ñires S
Macondo E
Refugio del Mochilero H
Tierra de Leyendas T
El Viejo Lobo del Mar M
Yakush K
EATING & DRINKING
Bodegón Fueguino 6
La Cabaña 1
Chez Manu 2
Dreamland 4
Dublín 5
Gustino 9
Kaupe 3
Küar 12
Tante Sara 7
Tía Elvira 10
El Turco 8
Volver 11

well-informed, friendly staff have lots of info on what you can visit in the region, and they can help you find accommodation. They'll even frank your passport with an "End of the World" stamp.

Two other **information kiosks** operate in summer: one at the Muelle Turístico (daily 9am–6pm) and another at the airport, opening when flights arrive. Serious trekkers and climbers should contact the **Club Andino Ushuaia**, at Fadul 50 (Mon–Sat 10am–1pm & 3–7pm; ☎02901/422335), which can advise on longer treks outside the normally visited areas of the Parque Nacional Tierra del Fuego and put you in touch with qualified guides. Registering here or at the tourist office before embarking on any trek or climb is optional but advisable.

Accommodation

Ushuaia has a wide range of **hotels** and a number of **hostels**, many of which are clustered along the first four streets parallel to the bay. Nonetheless, most manage to get booked up in the height of summer, and have become increasingly expensive. The most attractive options tend to be up the mountainside on the road to Glaciar Martial or west towards the national park; some of these have occasional shuttle buses running to town and back but you're still bound to need taxis ($15–25) from time to time. Be aware that hotels in Tierra del Fuego are the main culprits when it comes to charging **higher rates for non-residents**, often as much as three times more – in such cases, we have quoted the non-resident rate.

The nearest **campsite** to the centre is the well-equipped *Camping Pista del Andino*, at Alem 2873 (☎02901/435890, ⦿www.lapistadelandino.com.ar; $22 per person), at the base of the Club Andino skiing piste (free transfer from the centre). *Camping Municipal*, 8km from the centre, near the Tren del Fin del Mundo train station, is basic (no showers) but free.

Hostels and B&Bs

La Casa Gob. Paz 1380 ☎02901/423202, ⦿www.silviacasalaga.com.ar. A thoroughly inviting and distinctive B&B – it was designed by its architect owner – with fantastic views from the breakfast room. The six bedrooms share three bathrooms. Closed June–Sept. ❹

Cruz del Sur Gob. Deloqui 636 ☎02901/434099, ⦿www.xdelsur.com.ar. One of the better unofficial youth hostels in town, with a good kitchen and a laidback lounge area. Dorms are on the small side but are clean and each has a view. Breakfast included in the price. Dorms $50

Freestyle Gob. Paz 866 ☎02901/432874, ⦿www.ushuaiafreestyle.com. Delightful place that is part boutique hotel, part hostel, with spacious four- and six-bed dorms, personable en-suites in the attached Alto Andino Urban Lodge and swish bathrooms. There's a beanbag-filled TV room, and the relaxing top-floor lounge enjoys superb views across the bay. Breakfast included. Dorms $60, rooms ❻

Linares Gob. Deloqui 1522 ☎02901/423594, ⦿www.hosterialinares.com. Welcoming B&B in a cosy, split-level house with sterling views of the Beagle Channel. There's free Wi-Fi and a decent breakfast. ❼

Refugio del Mochilero 25 de Mayo 231 ☎02901/436129, ⦿www.refugiodelmochilero .netfirms.com. A dark but friendly hostel, in a central location, with several kitchens, laundry facilities and internet access. Dorms are spacious but bare; clean doubles have good bathrooms. Other amenities include cable TV, free coffee and *mate*. Dorms $40, rooms ❸

Yakush San Martín and Piedrabuena ☎02901/435807, ⦿www.hostelyakush.com.ar. High-ceilinged hostel with a location in the centre of town – the breakfast room overlooks busy San Martín – and a couple of good communal areas: an attic lounge room and a backyard with panoramic views. Breakfast included. Dorms $50.

Cabañas, hosterías and hotels

Cabañas del Beagle Las Aljabas 375 ☎02901/432785, ⦿www.cabanasdelbeagle.com. Self-contained cottages beautifully constructed in local stone and wood, with floor-to-ceiling windows that make the most of their lofty location. Original fireplaces add to the cosiness, and there's under-floor heating throughout. Continental breakfast and transfer from/to airport included. ❼

Los Cauquenes Reinamora, 7km out of town towards Parque Nacional Tierra del Fuego ☎011/4735-2648, ⊛www.loscauquenesushuaia.com.ar. Luxury wood-framed resort-style hotel at the far edge of Ushuaia, right on the Beagle Channel – the channel-facing rooms are so close the sound of the waves lulls you to sleep. Entry to the spa, with a gorgeous indoor/outdoor pool and hot tub, is included in the price for guests; non-guests can pay $200 to use the facilities for the day. Tariffs are US$295 for the mountain view, US$354 for the channel view. ❾

Cumbres del Martial Luis Martial 3560 ☎02901/424779, ⊛www.cumbresdelmartial.com.ar. Situated by the glacier chairlift, this excellent hotel combines its fabulous position, which affords amazing views of the city and the Beagle Channel, with tasteful charm, enticing decor and modern amenities, such as jacuzzis and smart bathrooms. ❾

Finisterris Lodge Monte Susana, Ladera Este ⊛www.finisterrislodge.com. Not so much a hotel as the opportunity for you and a loved one to hole up in your own log cabin, up on a hillside far from the madding crowd. The owner – who built the two-storey cabañas himself using local materials such as lenga wood – will take you skiing and arrange excursions for you but with your own log fire, sauna, jacuzzi and incredible view of the bay you probably won't want to leave the cabin. US$600 per night, including transfers. ❾

Hostería Los Fuegos Perito Moreno 4960 ☎02901/430884, ⊛www.hosterialosfuegos.com. Truly charming hostería set among lenga woods on the banks of the Río Olivia, on the far eastern outskirts of town; the warm, rustic rooms are sympathetically decorated, scrumptious teas are served in the teahouse and the highly personable owner is full of good advice. ❽

Hostería Patagonia Jarké Sarmiento 310 ☎02901/437245, ⊛www.hosteriapatagoniaj.com. Bright, rambling, timber-and-glass building, enthusiastically bedecked by the congenial owner.

The majority of the cosy rooms enjoy stunning views across the bay. ❽

Lennox Hotel San Martín 776 ☎02901/436430, ⊛www.lennoxhotel.com.ar. Smart boutique hotel, with the emphasis on rustic chic. Rooms are large and extremely comfortable – those at the front have mountain views from their balconies – and breakfast is taken directly overlooking the Bahía Ushuaia. Popular with Antarctic expeditions. ❾

Macondo Gob. Paz 1410 ☎02901/437576, ⊛www.macondohouse.com. Elegant little hotel creatively designed by its welcoming Barcelona-born owner. The seven minimalist doubles see plenty of natural light and have attractive stoneware bathrooms, and there are good vistas from the tasteful corner living room. The video room doubles as a kids' play area. ❼

Los Ñires Av de los Ñires 3040 ☎02901/445173, ⊛www.nires.com.ar. Quality mid-range place that has fewer frills but is not significantly different to its more luxurious neighbours on the town outskirts. Cosy rooms with large windows give lots of light and views over the mountains or channel; good restaurant too. ❼

Tierra de Leyendas Tierra de Vientos 2448 ☎012901/443565, ⊛www.tierradeleyendas.com.ar. Charming couple Maria Paz and Sebastian have created an equally charming hostería, with country-style decor in its five rooms and guest-only restaurant, and lots of nice touches to give it a real sense of a local place, without stinting on comfort. Airport transfer included in price. ❽

El Viejo Lobo del Mar Gob. Godoy 98 ☎02901/424850, ⊛www.hotelelviejolobodemar.com. Centrally located apart-hotel for up to three people, with neat apartments that contain bedroom, living room, bathroom and simple kitchen. There are a couple of nearby supermarkets where you can buy supplies, and breakfast is included. Discounts available if you pay in advance. ❽

The City

The best place to start wandering around Ushuaia is down by the pier, the **Muelle Turístico**, where an **obelisk** commemorates Augusto Lasserre's ceremony to assert Argentine sovereignty in this part of the world. Overlooking the sea from the other side of the street is the late nineteenth-century **Antigua Casa de Gobierno** (daily 9am–8pm; $20) at Maipú 465. This stately building was originally the governor's house and then used by local government and, later, the police. It was restored in 2003 to reflect its original use and you can wander around to get an idea of how the wealthy would have lived in Ushuaia's early years. The ticket also allows you entry to the small, worthwhile **Museo del Fin del Mundo** (same hours), further along at Maipú and Rivadavia, with exhibits on the region's history and wildlife, including the polychrome figurehead of the *Duchess of Albany*, an English ship wrecked on the eastern end of the island in 1883, and a rare example of a Selk'nam–Spanish dictionary written by a Salesian missionary.

You can visit the former **prison**, now home to the **Museo Marítimo y Presidio** (daily 10am–8pm; $50; free guided visits in Spanish at 11.30 and 18.30), two blocks further along the front and two more inland, at Yaganes and Gobernador Paz. This houses a motley collection of exhibits, the best of which are the meticulous scale-models of famous **ships** from the island's history in the maritime section as you first enter. The prison building itself, though, is the main draw, an example of the panopticon style popularized by English philosopher Jeremy Bentham, its wings radiating out like spokes from a half-wheel, most of which have now been opened to the public. The cells in wing four are complete with gory details of the notorious criminals who occupied them, and details of prison life, with informative panels in Spanish and English. The most celebrated prisoner held here was early twentieth-century anarchist Simón Radowitzsky, whose miserable stay and subsequent brief escape in 1918 are recounted by Bruce Chatwin in *In Patagonia*. Upstairs, fairly dry displays tell something of Antarctica and the history of its exploration. Wing three has been given over to an art museum and a gift shop (Mon–Sat 2–8pm), while wing two houses an art gallery of dubious quality and more exhibits and photos of early Ushuaia and its maritime history. Finally, wing one, which has not been restored and contains no exhibits at all, is in many ways the most interesting – the unheated and bare cells with peeling walls are quite spooky, and give something of an idea of what it must have been like to have been locked up or working here.

Ushuaia's other museum is the **Museo Yámana**, a charming little place in a converted house at Rivadavia 56 (daily 10am–8pm; $18) that charts the arrival of pre-Columbian and European settlers in the archipelago. Beautiful dioramas give an idea of the native habitats and way of life, but the displays go rather easy on the European colonists; excellent descriptions in Spanish and English, though, more than validate its claim to be an interpretation centre.

It's worth popping into the **Antigua Casa Bebán**, at the southwestern end of town at Maipú and Plüschow, a lovely pavilion-style place with a steep roof and ornamental gabling that was prefabricated in Sweden in 1913. It hosts exhibitions

Winter sports around Ushuaia

In order to boast that you have been to the end of the world to **ski** or **snowboard**, you'll need to visit between late May and early September – June to August are the most reliable months. The majority of runs are for beginners and intermediates, but several companies, such as Gotama Expediciones (℡02901/15605301, ⒲www .gotama-expediciones.com) offer guided back-country skiing for the more advanced. Equipment rental is reasonable and there are a couple of downhill (*esquí alpino*) pistes close to Ushuaia: the small Club Andino, 3km from town, and the more impressive one up by Glaciar Martial, 7km behind town. Better runs are to be had, however, in the Sierra Alvear, the resorts of which are accessed from the RN-3 (see p.577). These include the modern Cerro Castor centre (⒲www.cerrocastor.com), 27km from town, with 15km of pistes in runs, including a few black ones, up to 2km long.

The Sierra Alvear is also an excellent area for **cross-country** skiing (*esquí de fondo* or *esquí nórdico*). In addition, there are several winter-sports centres (*centros invernales*) along the **Valle Tierra Mayor** where you can try out snowmobiles, snowshoes, ice-skating and dogsled trips (*trineos de perros*), including Altos del Valle (see p.577) and Nunatak (see p.577). Bear in mind that winter this far south entails short days, and it can be bitterly cold.

▲ Ushuaia harbour

of photos and artwork, as well as occasional films (daily 10am–8pm; free), and is the venue for the **Ushuaia Jazz Festival** every November. Finally, for first-rate views of the Beagle Channel and the islands of Chile, you can head to the hanging (and fast receding) **Glaciar Martial**, 7km behind town; walk up the steep Luis Martial road, or take a bus from the Muelle Turístico ($20 return), and then climb or take the **chairlift** ($30) from behind the *Cumbres del Martial*. During the winter, Glaciar Martial offers the closest decent skiing to Ushuaia (see box, p.567).

Eating, drinking and nightlife

The city centre has plenty of places to **eat** or grab a coffee, but increasingly the locales in this part of town are turning into tourist traps. You'll get better quality food at better value – and, often as not, breathtaking views into the bargain – if you move around a bit. The quality of cuisine in Ushuaia has rocketed in recent years and there are several places where you can splash out on a memorable meal and sample the local gastronomic pride, *centolla* (king crab). **Prices** in Ushuaia are high by Argentine standards, but don't vary much – *centolla*, for instance, costs around $90 pretty much everywhere, while seafood pasta is around $60. Places that are particularly cheap or pricey are noted in the individual listings. With tourists to cater to round the clock, many of Ushuaia's restaurants open daily at 8am and close at around midnight; again, exceptions are noted.

Eating

La Cabaña Luis Martial 3560. Part of the *Cumbres del Martial* complex, this cosy mountain cabin serves tea, cakes, chocolate and delicious selections of cheese and smoked cold cuts in earnestly alpine style.
Chez Manu Luis Martial 2135 ☎02901/432253. Stunning panoramic views from huge windows and

gourmet French food using local produce – *centolla*, of course, plus fish, melt-in-the-mouth lamb and seafood – make this one of the city's most sought-after dining spots, though it is a bit expensive. Daily noon–3pm & 8pm–midnight.
Gustino Maipú and Lasserre ☎02901/430003. Smart restaurant attached to the *Hotel Albatros*, with full-length-window views of the Beagle

Channel, where you can wash down creative regional dishes with a glass of *vino* from the most comprehensive wine cellar in town.

🏃 **Kaupe** Roca 470 ⊤02901/422704. *Kaupe*'s service is friendly, the food delicious and the decor unpretentious, in what is just a family home with a fabulous view (the tables are packed in together). Seafood is the star; try the sea bass in black butter sauce with capers. Reservations essential; prices above average.

Tante Sara San Martín 175. Popular *confitería* and *panadería*, which does a fine line in fresh, oven-baked baguettes and rolls, in addition to simple coffees and teas.

Tía Elvira Maipú 349 ⊤02901/424725. Long-running Ushuaia classic with simple decor and views over the channel, *Tía Elvira* specializes in fresh seafood, including excellent mussels and delicious *centolla*, and offers a respectable list of Argentine wines. Daily noon–3pm & 7–11.30pm.

El Turco San Martín 1410. Local favourite, serving hearty portions of pizza, home-made pasta and empañadas by the dozen with good-humoured service. Closed Sun lunch.

Volver Maipú 37. The usual seafood menu at the usual prices, but the portions are generous and cooked well. *Volver* is an Ushuaia original and the place is dripping with character and bric a brac, from faded newspaper cuttings to old tango shoes on the wall to a lifesize statue of Che – it's virtually a museum in itself. Daily noon–3pm & 7.30pm–midnight.

Drinking and nightlife

Bodegón Fueguino San Martín 895. A convivial place, its sheep-skin-covered benches packed with young gringos appreciating the home-brewed beer, interesting – and tasty – *picada* menu and good-value pasta dishes. Closed Mon.

Dreamland 9 de Julio and Deoqui. Wood-cabin club with a good bar and a beanbag-filled corner for chilling in between DJ (mainly house) sets. Open from 3pm.

Dublín 9 de Julio 168. In theory, an Irish pub, serving good draught beer and Irish whiskey, its buzzing atmosphere attracting locals and gringos alike – but apart from the Guinness adverts, there isn't much in the way of Hibernian trappings.

🏃 **Küar** Perito Moreno 2232. Set in an attractive stone-and-timber building right on the seafront, on the road out towards Río Grande, this youthful bar-restaurant has stupendous views and a blazing fire, as well as fish and pasta dishes and its own delicious home-brewed pale ale, amber ale and dark porter.

Listings

Airlines Aerolíneas Argentinas, Maipú and 9 de Julio ⊤02901/436338; DAP, 25 de Mayo 64 ⊤02901/31110; LADE, San Martín 542 ⊤02901/421123; Aeroclub Ushuaia ⊤02901/421717, ⓦwww.aeroclubushuaia.org.ar.

Banks and exchange Banco Tierra del Fuego, San Martín and Roca; Banco de la Nación, San Martín 190. There's a *casa de cambio* at San Martín 880.

Car rental Cinco Estrellas, 9 de Julio 128 ⊤02901/436709, ⓦwww.5estrellasrentacar.com.ar; Crossing Patagonia, Maipú 857 ⊤02901/430786, ⓦwww.crossingpatagonia.com; Localiza, Sarmiento 81 ⊤02901/437780, ⓦwww.localiza.com. Most companies do not permit you to take your rental car out of the Argentine part of the island. Roads are fairly reliable from Oct to early May; outside this period, carry snow chains and drive with caution.

Consulate Chile, Jainén 50 ⊤02901/430909 or 910.

Hospital Maipú and 12 de Octubre ⊤02901/421439 or 1278; emergencies ⊤107.

Laundry Qualis, Güiraldes 568.

Pharmacy Andina, San Martín 638.

King crab

The undisputed emperor of crustaceans, the **centolla** (king crab) has spindly legs that can measure over a metre from tip to tip, but the meat comes from the body, with an average individual yielding some 300g. The less savoury practice of catching them with traps baited with dolphin or penguin meat has almost been stamped out by the imposition of hefty fines by both Chilean and Argentine authorities, but despite controls on size limits, they are still subject to rampant over-fishing. Canned king crab is served off season, but is bland and not worth the prices charged; frozen *centolla* is only slightly better, so always make sure it is fresh.

Police Deloqui 492 ☏02901/421773;
emergencies ☏101.
Post office San Martín and Godoy.
Shopping Renata Rafalak, Piedrabuena 51. The
eponymous owner makes some of the finest craft
items in southern Patagonia, her specialities
being reproductions of the bark masks worn by
the Selk'nam and Yámana in their Hain and Kina
initiation ceremonies.

Supermarkets La Anonima, Gob. Paz and
Rivadavia, also at San Martín and Onas.
Taxis Carlito's ☏02901/422222.
Travel agents All Patagonia, Juan Fadul 40
☏02901/433622, ⓦwww.allpatagonia.com;
Canal, 9 de Julio 118 ☏02901/437395,
ⓦwww.canalfun.com; Rumbo Sur, San Martín
350 ☏02901/421139, ⓦwww.rumbosur.com.ar.

Beagle Channel

No trip to Ushuaia is complete without a voyage on the legendary **Beagle Channel**, the majestic, mountain-fringed sea passage south of the city. Most **boat excursions** start and finish in Ushuaia, and you get the best views of town looking back at it from the straits. Standard trips visit Isla Bridges, Isla de los Pájaros and Isla de los Lobos, looping around Faro Les Eclaireurs, sometimes erroneously called the Lighthouse at the End of the World – that title belongs to the beacon at the tip of Isla de los Estados – on their way back. On boat trips, look out for **sea birds** such as the Black-browed Albatross, the thick-set Giant Petrel, Southern Skuas and the South American Tern, as well as **marine mammals** such as sea lions, Peale's dolphin (with a grey patch on its flank) and the occasional minke whale.

Boats depart from the **Muelle Turístico**, where you'll find agents' booking huts: recommended vessels include the *Barracuda*, offering good-value, informative tours (daily 3pm; 3hr; $120), and the long-running *Tres Marías* (daily 10am & 3pm; 4hr; $150, including hot drinks), a quiet motorized sailboat, whose trip includes trekking on Isla "H" to see Yámana shell middens. There are lots of other trips of a similar length in various size boats available, but bear in mind the large catamarans make it harder to see wildlife close up.

For an alternative perspective, Ushuaia Divers (☏02901/444701, ⓦwww .ushuaiadivers.com.ar) runs **diving** trips into the channel to look for king crabs and sea lions among the seaweed forests.

Estancia Harberton and around

Estancia Harberton is Patagonia's most historic estancia, an ordered assortment of whitewashed buildings on the shores of a sheltered bay (daily 10am–7pm; $30; no phone). Though Harberton is assuredly scenic, it's the historical resonance of the place that fleshes out a visit: this farmstead – or more particularly the family that settled here – played a role out of all proportion to its size in the region's history. It was built by Reverend Thomas Bridges, the man who authored one of the two seminal Fuegian texts, the *Yámana–English Dictionary*, and was the inspiration for the other, Lucas Bridges' classic, *Uttermost Part of the Earth*. Apart from being a place where scientists and shipwrecked sailors were assured assistance, Harberton developed into a sanctuary of refuge for groups of Yámana and Mannekenk.

Today the estancia is owned by Tommy Goodall, a great-grandson of Thomas Bridges, and is open to **guided tours** that take in the copse on the hill, where you learn about the island's plant life, authentic reconstructions of Yamaná dwellings, the family cemetery and the old shearing shed. Housed in a building at the entrance to the farmstead is an impressive marine-mammal museum, **Museo Acatushún** (same hours as house; $15, plus estancia entrance fee; ⓦwww.acatushun.com), which displays the remains of all the main families of such animals – whales, dolphins, seals and the like – found in the surrounding waters.

Harberton is **accessed** via the **RCj** branch road, whose turn-off is 40km northeast of Ushuaia on the RN-3. Around 25km from the turn-off, you emerge from the forested route by a delightful lagoon fringed by the skeletons of *Nothofagus* beeches, and can look right across the Beagle Channel to the Chilean town of Puerto Williams. A few hundred metres beyond here the road splits: take the left-hand fork heading eastwards across rolling open country and past a clump of **flag trees**, swept back in exaggerated quiffs by the unremitting wind. The estancia is a further 10km beyond the turn-off, 85km east of Ushuaia.

Practicalities

You can stay the night at Harberton, though the **accommodation** (© estanciaharberton@gmail.com; reservations essential) is hardly luxurious or inexpensive: choose between the old *Shepherd's House*, which has two triple rooms with private bath, a small shared kitchenette and a large porch (US$120 per person); and the old *Cook's House*, with a double room and another bedroom with bunk beds, a rustic bathroom, kitchenette and dining/sitting room (US$90 per person). The stay includes an extended tour and breakfast; dinner is available for an extra US$25. Alternatively, you could stay at one of the estancia's three **campsites**: all are free, but you must first register at the *Mánacatush* tearoom and obtain a permit. Food-wise, you can enjoy delicious tea and cakes at the **tearoom** or a simple lunch.

A number of companies run **buses** from Ushuaia to Harberton (1hr 30min), which can be booked direct at the Muelle Turístico. Alternatively, you can visit the estancia as part of a Beagle Channel tour with *Canoero* (daily 9.30am; $270; outward by boat, return by land) or *Tolkeyen* (Mon, Wed & Fri 9.30am, $240; outward and return by boat), both of whom have booths at the Muelle Turístico.

Isla Martillo

While at Harberton you can cross to the Reserva Yecapasela on **Isla Martillo**, the only island in the Beagle Channel that **penguins** call home – biologists think it's because the softness of the soil is perfect for their burrowing, and the sea currents in which they feed lead here, too. There are two species – Magellanic, the same species but a different group from the larger colony in Punta Tombo (see p.513), and the orange-beaked sub-Antarctic Gentoo. The only operator allowed to land boats on

▲ Magellanic penguins in the Beagle Channel

the island is *Piratour* (☎02901/424834), which has half-day bus and boat trips that depart from Ushuaia via Harberton but don't really visit the estancia ($250). If you want to tour the estancia too, you can get there under your own steam and buy a boat-only ticket with *Piratour* (twice daily; $210) but places on the boat fill quickly, so it's advisable to book at least a day ahead at *Piratour*'s kiosk at the Muelle Turístico.

RCJ beyond Harberton

Beyond Harberton, the RCj runs for forty spectacular kilometres – accessible only with your own transport – to **Estancia Moat**, past the famous islands that guard the eastern mouth of the Beagle Channel: **Picton**, **Nueva** and **Lennox**. These uninhabited atolls have a controversial past, with both Chile and Argentina long claiming sovereignty over them. The track comes to an end at a naval outpost, beyond which Península Mitre (see p.580) stretches to Cabo San Diego, at the far tip of Tierra del Fuego.

Parque Nacional Tierra del Fuego

PARQUE NACIONAL TIERRA DEL FUEGO, a mere 12km west of Ushuaia, is the easiest to access of southern Argentina's national parks. Protecting 630 square kilometres of jagged mountains, intricate lakes, southern beech forest, swampy peat bog, sub-antarctic tundra and verdant coastline, the park stretches along the frontier with Chile, from the Beagle Channel to the **Sierra Inju-Goiyin** (also called the Sierra Beauvoir) north of Lago Fagnano, but only the southernmost quarter of this is open to the public, accessed via the RN-3 from Ushuaia. Fortunately, this area contains much of the park's most beautiful scenery, if also some of the wettest – bring rain gear.

The quarter is broken down into three main sectors: Bahía Ensenada and Río Pipo in the east, close to the station for the Tren del Fin del Mundo; Lago Roca further west; and the Lapataia area south of Lago Roca, which includes Laguna Verde and, at the end of the RN-3, Bahía Lapataia. You can get a good overview of the park in a day, but walkers will want to stay two to three days to appreciate the scenery and the **wildlife**, which includes birds such as Magellanic Woodpeckers

Antarctica

Ushuaia lies 1000km north of **Antarctica**, but is still the world's closest port to the white continent – and most tourists pass through the town to make their journey across Drake's Passage, the wild stretch of ocean that separates it from South America. The grandeur of Antarctica's pack ice, rugged mountains and phenomenal bird and marine life will leave you breathless: whales, elephant seals, albatrosses and numerous species of penguins are just some of the species you can hope to see. Regular **cruise ships** depart from November to mid-March and most cruises last between eight and 22 days, some stopping at the **South Atlantic islands** (Islas Malvinas/Falklands, South Georgia, the South Orkneys, Elephant Island and the South Shetlands) en route. These trips are generally very expensive (at least US$4500). Occasionally you can get last-minute discounts in Ushuaia, especially on the newest ships, which are less likely to sell out their berths, though don't expect much in the way of bargains. Ushuaia's **Oficina Antártica** at the Muelle Turístico (☎02901/430015) has details of current sailings and can advise on what each trip involves; otherwise, try contacting Antarpply, at Gob. Paz 633 (☎02901/436747, Ⓦwww.antarpply.com), or Quark Expeditions (Ⓦwww.quarkexpeditions.com).

(*carpintero patagónico*), condors, Steamer Ducks, Kelp Geese – the park's symbol – and Buff-necked Ibises; and mammals such as the guanaco, the rare southern sea otter (*nutria marina*), the Patagonian grey fox and its larger cousin, the native Fuegian red fox, once heavily hunted for its pelt.

The park is also one of southern Argentina's easiest to walk around, and offers several relatively unchallenging though beautiful **trails** (*sendas*), many of which are completed in minutes rather than hours or days; the best is arguably the scenic Senda Costera (Coastal Path) connecting Bahía Ensenada with Lago Roca and Bahía Lapataia. The spectacular climb up Cerro Guanaco from Lago Roca is comparatively tough, though hardened trekkers will find sterner physical challenges in the Sierra Valdivieso and the Sierra Alvear (see p.577). Obey the signs warning you to refrain from collecting shellfish – which are sometimes affected by poisonous red tide – and light fires only in permitted campsites, extinguishing them with water, not earth.

Park practicalities

The commonest and cheapest way to **access the park** is along the good dirt road from Ushuaia. A $50 entrance fee must be paid at the main park gate, payable in addition to any bus, boat or train tickets; they should be able to provide with you a simple map of the park's trails here, as well as some bumpf on its attractions. Virtually all travel agencies in Ushuaia offer **tours** of the park ($140, plus entrance fee); most last four hours and stop at the major places of interest, including Bahía Lapataia. If you want to get off and walk, take one of the regular **buses** (depart daily 9am–6pm, return 10am–7pm from the Muelle Turistico; $50 return) that stop at various points in the park.

You can also get to the park on the world's most southern railway, the **Tren del Fin del Mundo** (9.30am, noon & 3pm; 40min; $90 one way; ☏02901/431600,

Ⓦwww.trendelfindelmundo.com.ar), which chugs its way through woodland meadows and alongside the Río Pipo to the park station, 2km from the main gate. Used to transport wood in the days of the penal colony, it's now little more than a tourist toy train, and you'll still need to get a bus to the main station, 8km west of Ushuaia on the road to the national park ($30 return).

There are also limited **boat** services running to the park from Ushuaia, usually going to Bahía Lapataia as part of a combined boat and bus tour of the area – enquire at the Muelle Turístico.

There are four main areas for **camping** in the park: the two nearest the entrance, *Río Pipo* and *Bahía Ensenada*, are free, but you're better off heading to Lago Roca and Laguna Verde, in the more exciting western section of the park. *Camping Lago Roca* sits near picturesque Lago Roca, where it bottlenecks into the Río Lapataia (Ⓣ02901/433313, Ⓦwww.confiterialagoroca.com.ar; $18 per person), and is the only one with services, including hot showers and a shop; there is also a new *refugio* here (dorm beds $40). The free sites further south, on the Archipiélago Comoranes – *Camping Las Bandurrias*, *Camping Laguna Verde* and *Camping Los Cauquenes* – just about edge it for beauty, though, set on grassy patches of land encircled by the Río Ovando, with lawn-like pitches kept trim by the resident rabbits.

Río Pipo and Bahía Ensenada

North of the train terminus is the pleasant wooded valley of Cañadón del Toro, through which runs the **Río Pipo**. A gentle 4km walk along an unsealed road brings you to *Camping Río Pipo* (see above), and a couple of hundred metres on you come to an attractive **waterfall**. Although a through route north from here to Lago Fagnano is marked on some old maps, the area is now off limits and you will be fined if caught there. If you're heading from Río Pipo back south to Bahía Ensenada, a more interesting alternative to walking between the two by road is to take the fairly demanding **Senda Pampa Alta** (5km; 1hr 30min), which is signposted off west on the way back to the train-station crossroads. This offers fine views from a lookout over the Beagle Channel as it crosses the RN-3 towards Bahía Lapataia 3km west of the crossroads, and then drops to the coast on a poor path through thick forest.

Bahía Ensenada, 2km south of the crossroads, is a small bay with little of intrinsic interest. It does, however, have the jetty for boats to Bahía Lapataia and Isla Redonda, and is the trailhead for one of the park's most pleasant walks, the excellent **Senda Costera** (6.5km; 3hr). The route affords spectacular views from

Tierra del Fuego's surprising avian residents

Parrots and hummingbirds are two types of birds most visitors to South America quite naturally associate more with the steamy, verdant jungles of the Amazon than the frigid extremes of Tierra del Fuego. Nevertheless, don't go jumping to conclusions, as you can see both in the Parque Nacional Tierra del Fuego. The unmistakably garrulous **Austral Parakeet** is the world's most southerly parrot, inhabiting these temperate forests year-round. The Selk'nam christened it *Kerrhprrh*, in onomatopoeic imitation of its call. Once upon a time, according to their beliefs, all Fuegian trees were coniferous, and it was *Kerrhprrh* who transformed some into deciduous forests, painting them autumnal reds with the feathers of its breast. The tiny **Green-backed Firecrown** is the planet's most southerly hummingbird, and has been recorded – albeit rarely – flickering about flowering shrubs in summer. Known to the Selk'nam by the graceful name of *Sinu K-Tam* (Daughter of the Wind), this diminutive creature was, curiously, believed by them to be the offspring of *Ohchin*, the whale, and *Sinu*, the wind.

the Beagle Channel shoreline and takes you through dense coastal forest of evergreen beech, Winter's bark and *lenga*, some of their branches clad in *barba de viejo* (old man's beard), a hanging lichen that gives the trees a rather sorrowful appearance. Look out, too, for the *pan de Indio* (Indian bread), a bulbous orange fungus that clusters around the knots of branches. On the way, you'll pass grass-covered mounds that are the ancient campsite **middens** of the Yámana – these are protected archeological sites and should not be disturbed.

Lago Roca

Two kilometres after the Senda Costera rejoins the RN-3, a turn-off to the right takes you across the lush meadows of the broad Río Lapataia to **Lago Roca** and its campsite. Just past the campsite buildings, which include a *confitería* that serves warming drinks and cakes, there's a car park. From here, the gentle **Senda Hito XXIV** (8km return; 3hr) hugs the lake's northern shore and heads through majestic *lenga* forest to the Chilean border. This is a particularly good trail from which to spot the red-headed **Magellanic Woodpecker** – most people hear it before they see it, hammering away at trees. Do not attempt to cross the border: it is under regular surveillance and you may be arrested if you try to do so.

A more spectacular but much more demanding trek is the tough climb up 970m-high **Cerro Guanaco** (8km return; 7hr), the mountain ridge on the north side of Lago Roca. From here, the **views** of the angular landscape are superb: the swollen finger of Lago Roca, flanked by the spiky ridge of Cerro Cóndor, with the jagged Cordillera Darwin beyond; to the east, Ushuaia and its airport; and to the north, a vertiginous cliff plunges down to the Cañadón del Toro. Best of all, however, are the views to the south: the tangle of islands and rivers of the Archipiélago Cormoranes; Lapataia's sinuous curves; the Isla Redonda in the Beagle Channel; and across to the Chilean islands, Hoste and Navarino, separated by the Murray Channel. On a clear day, in the distance beyond the channel, you can make out the Islas Wollaston, the group of islands whose southernmost point is Cape Horn.

Note that the weather on Cerro Guanaco can turn capricious with little warning at any time of year, so bring adequate clothing, even if you set out in glorious sunshine.

The Lapataia area

The absorbing Lapataia area is accessed by way of the final 4km stretch of the RN-3, as it winds south from the Lago Roca junction, past **Laguna Verde**, and on to **Lapataia** itself, on the bay of the same name. This is one of the most intriguing sections to explore: a kind of "park within a park". In the space of a few hours, you can take a network of short trails past an incredible variety of scenery, including peat bogs, river islets, wooded knolls and seacoast. A few hundred metres past the Lago Roca junction, you cross the Río Lapataia – over a bridge that's a favoured haunt of Ringed Kingfishers (*martín pescador grande*) – onto the **Archipiélago Cormoranes** (Cormorant Archipelago). Signposted left off the road here is a short circuit trail, the **Paseo de la Isla** (600m), a delightful walk through tiny, enchanting humped islets.

Next you pass **Laguna Verde**, which is actually a sumptuous, sweeping bend of the Río Ovando, and makes a lovely setting for the two campsites here, *Camping Laguna Verde* and *Camping Los Cauquenes* (see p.574). From Laguna Verde, it's only 2km to Lapataia, but there are several easy nature trails along the way, which you can stroll along in half an hour or so, allowing time to stop and study the signs with ecological and botanical information (in Spanish). Paseo Mirador (1km) takes you down to Bahía Lapataia via an impressive lookout over the bay; **Paseo del Turbal**

(2km) takes you on a walkway across the peat bogs; and the **Senda Castorera** passes a **beaver dam**. You stand a good chance of spotting these rodents – which now number nearly fifty thousand – if you arrive in the early morning or at dusk.

The RN-3 comes to its scenic end – marked by a much-photographed sign – at Lapataia on the **Bahía Lapataia**. For some this is not just the end of the RN-3, but the end of the entire Pan-American Highway – around a mere 49,958km from Prudhoe Bay, Alaska. Deriving its name from the Yámana for "forested cove", Lapataia is a serenely beautiful bay studded with small islets. Near the car park here is the **jetty** where boats arrive from Ushuaia.

Central and northern Tierra del Fuego

The second-largest settlement in Tierra del Fuego, **Río Grande** is also the only town of significance in Isla Grande's **central** and **northern** sector. The sterile-looking plains that surround it harbour fields of petroleum and natural gas that generate millions of dollars of wealth annually, with huge quantities of gas transported each year to Ushuaia and as far away as Buenos Aires. North of town, the RN-3 runs through monotonous scenery towards San Sebastián, where you cross the border into Chile or continue north on a dead-end route to the mouth of the Magellan

Puerto Williams and Cape Horn

Nestled in a small bay on the north shore of **Isla Navarino** on Chile's side of the border, 82km due east and ever so slightly south of Ushuaia along the Beagle Channel, is **Puerto Williams**. "Williams" is something of a thorn in Argentina's toe, since despite all the publicity and hype about Ushuaia being **the most southerly town in the world**, that dubious privilege actually belongs to Puerto Williams. Founded as a military outpost and officially the capital of Chilean Antarctica, the town looks tranquil and idyllic on a fine day, with colourful roofs surrounded by the jagged peaks of Los Dientes. Though the settlement can easily be seen from the RN-3, actually **getting there** from Argentina is a bureaucratic headache, meaning that companies that do the trip are few and expensive. At the time of writing the only company operating boats across the channel to Puerto Williams was Zenit Explorer at Fadul 126 (☎02901/433232, ⓦwww.zenitexplorer.com.ar; 1hr 30min; $500 each way). Aeroclub Ushuaia (see Listings, p.569) operates small planes that fly loops without landing over Puerto Williams and the surrounding area (1hr; US$120); in the past they have landed there and may do so again, so it's worth enquiring. Otherwise, you could cross the land border with Chile (see box, p.582) and make your way there from Punta Arenas. **Accommodation** in Puerto Williams is mostly basic but reasonable – try simple but warm *Hostal Pusaki*, at Piloto Pardo 222 (☎61/621116, ⓔpattypusaki@yahoo.es; ④), where use of the kitchen is free and delicious meals are laid on for overnight guests.

Having come this far south, many travellers like to go the whole hog and "round the Cape", erroneously translated into Spanish as *Cabo de Hornos* ("Ovens Cape"). Ask around in Puerto Williams – SIM travel agency (ⓦwww.simexpeditions.com) on the main plaza is a good place to start – about **boat trips** to the most southerly point of the world's landmass, barring Antarctica. Weather permitting, you disembark on a shingle beach, climb a rickety ladder and visit the tiny Chilean naval base, lighthouse and chapel; there's not much to do otherwise and it's all quite desolate. DAP (ⓦwww.aeroviasdap.cl) runs **flights** from Punta Arenas, which make a loop over the headland and return without landing, or which land at Puerto Williams. These air excursions treat you to incredible views of Isla Navarino and the Darwin peaks, but, again, weather is a vital factor.

Straits at Cabo Espíritu Santo. On the way to Río Grande from Ushuaia, the RN-3 winds up to **Paso Garibaldi**, where you have majestic views over **Lago Escondido**, and then bypasses **Tolhuin**, crossing the woodland scenery of the central region. This stretch is marked by a string of *ripio* branch roads, the **rutas complementarias**, which wiggle away from the RN-3; those headed west take you to a couple of fine estancias, and those headed east into the **Península Mitre**, the windswept land that forms Isla Grande's desolate tip.

One of the northern region's principal tourist draws is its world-class **trout-fishing**, especially for sea-running brown trout, which on occasion swell to weights in excess of 14kg. The river, also named Río Grande, currently holds five of the fly-fishing world records for brown trout caught with various breaking strains of line. The mouths of the Río Fuego and Río Ewan can also be spectacularly fruitful, as can sections of the Malengüeña, Irigoyen, Claro and Turbio rivers and lakes Yehuin and Fagnano.

Ushuaia to Paso Garibaldi and the Sierra Alvear

The road from Ushuaia to **Paso Garibaldi** wends its way north and east through dramatic forested scenery, with great views of the valleys and savage mountain ranges that cross the southern part of the island. Many activity centres and refuges have sprung up along the route, primarily to cater to **winter-sports** enthusiasts, though they often also make excellent bases for adventurous **trekking** or horse-riding. Above all, the rugged, serrated peaks of the **Sierra Valdivieso** and **Sierra Alvear ranges** make ideal bushwhacking territory. If rough-hiking independently, consult the Club Andino in Ushuaia (see p.565) and arm yourself with a copy of Zagier & Urruty's *Ushuaia Trekking Map*, but do not underestimate the need for orienteering skills or the unpredictable nature of the weather: blizzards can hit at any time. You must also be prepared to get thoroughly soaked when crossing bogs and streams, but you'll be rewarded by the sight of **beaver dams** up to two and a half metres high, as well, in all probability, as their destructive constructors.

Heading northeast from Ushuaia, the RN-3 curls up around the foot of **Monte Olivia** and heads into the **Valle de Tierra Mayor**, a popular area for winter sports and a good spot for trekking in the Sierra Alvear. One of the first centres you come across, 18km out from Ushuaia, is Altos del Valle, a breeding centre for baying huskies (sled rides available) that offers rustic **accommodation** in a *refugio* (©gatocuruchet@hotmail.com). The *refugio* marks the start of a relatively clear trail to attractive **Laguna Esmeralda** (4.5km; 2hr), where you can camp, and a more challenging hike to **Glaciar Alvear** (another 3.5km; 2hr 30min), which feeds the lake below. A kilometre beyond Altos del Valle is the excellent Nunatak (T 02901/430329, W www.nunatakadventure.com), a sports centre offering husky rides and snowmobile trips in the winter and trekking in the summer, among other activities. Ask about their tough but fascinating guided trek to **Lago Ojo del Albino** (10hr; guide, crampons and food included). Several companies in Ushuaia run **buses** to Altos del Valle and Nunatak, leaving town daily from 9am until 1pm, returning between 2 and 6pm ($40 return).

Lago Fagnano and Tolhuin

Cresting the **Paso Garibaldi** some 45km out of Ushuaia, the RN-3 descends towards **Lago Escondido**, the first of the lowland lakes, accessible via a 4km branch road to the north, before heading alongside the southern shore of

LAGO FAGNANO. This impressive lake, also called Lago Kami from its Selk'nam name, is flanked by ranges of hills, and straddles the Chilean border at its western end. Most of its 105km are inaccessible to visitors, apart from dedicated anglers who can afford to rent a good launch. Travelling along the RN-3 as it parallels the lake, you'll see several sawmills, denoted by their squat, conical brick chimneys, used for burning bark.

Near the eastern end of Lago Fagnano, the road splits: the left fork is the more scenic, old, unsealed RN-3 route, which cuts north across the lake along a splendid causeway; the right is the RN-3 bypass, the more direct route to **TOLHUIN**, the region's oddest little town. Created in the 1970s, Tolhuin was designed to provide a focus for the heartland of Isla Grande – indeed, the name means "heart-shaped" in Selk'nam – but as a place of unassuming houses that hangs together with little focus, it has an artificial commune-like feel. It does, however, make a useful halfway point to break the journey – as most buses do – between Ushuaia and Río Grande.

Practicalities

Daily **buses** from Ushuaia to lakes Escondido and Fagnano leave at 10am and 2pm, and return at 2pm and 6pm ($120 return). For accommodation, head to the eastern end of Lago Fagnano to windy *Camping Hain del Lago* (℡02964/15-603606), which has *cabañas* ($200) and a **campsite** ($15 per person), or adjacent *Cabañas Khami* (℡02964/15566045, ⓦwww.cabaniaskhami.com.ar; ❼ for up to 6 people), with snug log cabins intended primarily for fishermen. Ushuaia–Río Grande buses stop in Tolhuin at the quirky 🍴 *Panadería La Unión*, a bakery and **restaurant** that acts as the hub of village life, selling delicious breads and other goodies.

Tolhuin to Río Grande: the RN-3 and the rutas complementarias

The main route between Tolhuin and Río Grande is the fast, paved RN-3, but if you have the time it's worth exploring one or more of the unsealed **rutas complementarias** (RC) that branch off it – alphabetized roads that provide access to the heartland of Argentine Tierra del Fuego but are only really accessible to those with their own transport. Dotted around this inhospitable land are some hospitable **estancias**, worth the journey for the authentic experience of seeing a working Fuegian farm, or for the opportunity to gallop on horses across the steppe.

The RCh and RCf loop

The **RCh**, which branches off the RN-3 22km north of Tolhuin, and the connecting **RCf**, which joins the RN-3 some 10km south of the bridge over the Río Grande, form a 120km loop that passes through swathes of transitional Fuegian woodland and grassy pasture-meadows (*vegas*) populated by sheep. Along RCh you'll see cone-shaped Mount Yakush and pyramid-like Mount Atukoyak to the south before the road joins the RCf by **Lago Yehuin**, a popular fishing locale and a good place for spotting **condors**, which nest on Cerro Shenolsh between the lake and its shallow neighbour, **Lago Chepelmut**. Just off the RCh is the upmarket 🍴 *Estancia Rivadavia* (℡02901/492186, ⓦwww.estanciarivadavia.com; ◑), a hospitable boutique hotel with delightful rooms, where you can ride horses and trek across the estancia's 160 square kilometres of land, which include the deep azure waters of Lago Yehuin and Lago Chepelmut.

The lands at the end of the earth were home to several distinct societies before the arrival of the Europeans. In 1580, Sarmiento de Gamboa became the first European to encounter the **Selk'nam**, one of the largest groups. He was impressed by these "Big People", with their powerful frames, guanaco robes and conical headgear. It was not long before their war-like, defiant nature became evident, though, and a bloody skirmish with a Dutch expedition in 1599 proved them to be superb fighters. Before the arrival of the Europeans, Selk'nam society revolved around the hunting of **guanaco**, which they relied on not just for meat – the skin was made into moccasins and capes, the bones were used for fashioning arrowheads and the sinews for bowstrings. Hunting was done on foot, and the Selk'nam used stealth and teamwork to encircle guanacos, bringing them down with bow and arrow, a weapon with which they were expert.

The other sizeable group was the **Yámana** (Yaghan), a sea-going people living in the channels of the Fuegian archipelago. Their society was based on tribal groups of extended families, each of which lived for long periods aboard their equivalent of a houseboat: a canoe fashioned of *lenga* bark. Out on the ocean, work was divided between the sexes: the men hunted seals from the prow while the women – the only ones who could swim – took to the icy waters, collecting shellfish with only a layer of seal grease to protect them from the cold. When not at sea, the Yámana stayed in dwellings made of *guindo* evergreen beech branches, building conical huts in winter (to shed snow), and more aerodynamic dome-shaped ones in the summer (when strong winds blow). Favoured campsites were used over millennia, and, at these sites, **middens** of discarded shells would accumulate in the shape of a ring, since doors were constantly being shifted to face away from the wind.

The arrival of European settlers marked the beginning of the end for both the Selk'nam and Yámana. To protect colonists' **sheep farms in the late nineteenth century**, hundreds of miles of wire fencing were erected, which the Selk'nam, unsurprisingly, resented, seeing it as an incursion into their ancestral lands; however, they soon acquired a taste for hunting the slow animals, which they referred to as "white guanaco". For the settlers, this was an unpardonable crime, representing a drain on their investment. The Selk'nam were painted as "barbarous savages" who constituted an obstacle to settlement and progress, and isolated incidents of attack and retaliation soon escalated into bloody conflict. Reliable sources point to bounty hunters being paid on receipt of grisly invoices, such as a pair of severed ears. The assault on Selk'nam culture, too, was abrupt and devastating, led by the "civilizing" techniques of the **Salesian missions**, who "rehoused" them in their missions. By the late 1920s there were probably no indigenous Selk'nam living as their forefathers had done and when pure-blooded Lola Kiepje and Esteban Yshton passed away in 1966 and 1969, respectively, Selk'nam culture died with them.

Meanwhile, the arrival of settlers in 1884 triggered a **measles epidemic** that killed approximately half the estimated one thousand remaining Yámana. Damp, dirty clothing – European castoffs given by well-meaning missionaries – increased the risk of disease. Missionaries promoted a shift to sedentary agriculture, but the consequent change of diet, from one high in animal fats to one more reliant on vegetables, reduced the Yámana's resistance to the cold, further increasing the likelihood of disease. Outbreaks of scrofula, pneumonia and tuberculosis meant that by 1911 fewer than one hundred Yámana remained. Abuela Rosa, the last of the Yámana to live in the manner of her ancestors, died in 1982. Nevertheless, a few Yámana descendants still live near Puerto Williams on Isla Navarino.

RCa and Península Mitre

Some 40km north of Tolhuin, the most beautiful of the central *rutas complementarias* – the **RCa** – branches east through golden pastureland towards the coast and the knobbly protrusion of **Cabo San Pablo**. A wonderful panorama stretches out from the south side of Cabo San Pablo, encompassing the wreck of the *Desdémona*, grounded during a storm in the early 1980s – at low tide, you can walk out to the ship – but the area is mainly of interest to fishermen. Beyond the cape, the road continues for 17km through wetlands and burnt-out "tree cemeteries" and past the odd beaver dam to the *Estancia Fueguina*, from where you'll need a high-clearance 4WD to progress any further.

The public track eventually fizzles out at *Estancia María Luisa*, 18km further on, just beyond which run the famous fishing rivers, Irigoyen and Malengüeña. This is the beginning of the **Península Mitre**, the bleak toe of land that forms the southeastern extremity of Tierra del Fuego. This semi-wilderness – primarily swampy moorland and thickets fringed by rugged coastal scenery – was once the territory of the indigenous Mannekenk, whose presence is attested to by old shell middens. Before the 1850s, the only white men who came ashore were sailors and scientists, such as FitzRoy and Darwin, as well as shipwreck victims; the remains of many wrecks line the shore, including the late nineteenth-century *Duchess of Albany*, near **Bahía Policarpo**. Apart from a few gauchos, the peninsula is now effectively uninhabited, and the only way to explore the area is on guided **horse-riding** excursions with Centro Hípico Ushuaia (☎02901/1556-8278, ⑩www .centrohipicoushuaia.com.ar), which runs eight-day trips down the Costa de los Naufragios, from *Estancia María Luisa* to *Estancia Policarpo* and back.

Estancia Viamonte and the RCb to Chile

Heading north along the RN-3 from the RCa turn-off leads, after some 37km, to the extremely atmospheric *Estancia Viamonte* (☎02964/430861, ⑩www .estanciaviamonte.com; ⑧ full board; closed April–Oct). Established against the odds by Lucas Bridges with the help of his Selk'nam friends – and still run by his descendants – this is one of the island's most historic farms and figures prominently in his epic work, *Uttermost Part of the Earth*. The rooms are simple but thoughtfully furnished and the welcome warm; it's a great place to gain a real insight into life on a working estancia – farm activities are included in the price.

The scenery north of *Estancia Viamonte* undergoes an abrupt transition, from scraggly clumps of Fuegian woodland to the forlorn, bald landscape of the steppe. South of the town of Río Grande, a few kilometres before you cross the Río Grande itself, you pass the turn-off for the **RCb**, worth detouring along for 1km to see the tiny village of **Estancia José Menéndez**, whose shearing shed is emblazoned by the head of a prize ewe, its face obscured by an over-effusive wig of curls. The estancia was founded as Estancia Primera Argentina in 1896 by sheep magnate Menéndez. The most notorious of its first managers was a hard-drinking Scotsman by the name of MacLennan, who earned himself the sobriquet of "Red Pig" for taking pleasure in gunning down the Selk'nam. The RCb continues across the steppe for 70km to the Chilean frontier at **Radman**, where there's a little-used **border crossing**, known as Bella Vista (Nov–March 8am–9pm), which allows access to Lago Blanco, an excellent fishing destination, as well as providing an alternative route west to Porvenir in Chile.

Río Grande

RÍO GRANDE is a drab, sprawling city that grew up on the river of the same name as a port for José Menéndez's sheep enterprises. The treacherous tides along this stretch of the coast can reach over 15m at the spring equinox, and low tide exposes a shelf of mud flats better for sea birds than boats. The port, therefore, has virtually ceased to exist, having been superseded by the vastly superior one at Ushuaia. And in spite of the people's friendliness, the atmosphere here is as flat as the landscape: it's a place to pass through quickly, unless you're a trout fisherman, in which case it's a functional starting-point for exploring the region's fruitful rivers – the wonderful **Monumento a la Trucha**, a statue of a giant brown trout on the RN-3, leaves you in little doubt about what the town is famous for. The only sight worth visiting hereabouts is the **Misión Salesiana Nuestra Señora de la Candelaria**, a mission turned agricultural school 11km north of town, whose museum traces attempts to convert the local Selk'nam. If you're looking to kill time, you might consider taking a **city tour**, a convenient way of visiting the town's scattered subsidiary sites that are otherwise awkward to reach, including the **Estancia María Behety**, one of the island's largest and oldest sheep-farming establishments, dating from 1897, 17km due west of town along the RCc.

Practicalities

Buses drop passengers off at the new terminal at Finocchio and Obligado, four blocks from the main avenue, San Martín. Mantiel (℡02901/421366) runs minivans between Ushuaia and Río Grande that will pick up and drop off door-to-door ($70). The helpful provincial **tourist office** is on Plaza Almirante Brown, at Rosales 350 (Dec–March Mon–Fri 9am–8pm, Sat & Sun 2–9pm; April–Nov Mon–Fri 9am–5pm; ℡02964/431234, ⓦwww.riogrande.gov.ar). **Fishing licences** and information on fishing can be obtained from the Asociación de Pesca con Mosca at Montilla 1040. For **city tours** contact Shelk'nam Viajes, Belgrano 1122 (℡02964/426180).

Accommodation in Río Grande, catering mostly to anglers with big pockets, is generally overpriced. The most comfortable option is the restful *Posada de los Sauces*, at El Cano 839 (℡02964/432895, ⓦwww.posadadelossauces.com.ar; ❼), across the road from the bus terminal, with well-decorated rooms, a relaxed lounge bar and an appealing *á la carte* restaurant. *Albergue Turístico Argentino*, at San Martín 64 (℡02964/420969, ⓔhotelargentino@hotmail.com; dorms $50 with shared bath, $65 private bath), is the best budget option, an amicable hostel with kitchen facilities and an airy dining area.

The best spot to grab something to **eat** is *La Nueva Colonial*, at Belgrano and Laserre, a popular spot where the convivial owner spoons out large portions of home-cooked pasta with hearty sauces. There is also the inevitable *parrilla* – *Los Troncos* at Islas Malvinas 998 serves fish and barbecued meat dishes, accompanied by a salad buffet bar.

Misión Salesiana Nuestra Señora de la Candelaria

Eleven kilometres north of the centre of Río Grande on the RN-3 stands the **Misión Salesiana Nuestra Señora de la Candelaria**, a collection of whitewashed buildings grouped around a modest but elegant chapel. Río Grande's first mission, it was founded in 1893 by two of Patagonia's most influential Salesian fathers, Monseñor Fagnano and Padre Beauvoir, but their first township burnt down in 1896, and was relocated to its present site. Originally, it was built with the purpose of catechizing the island's Selk'nam, but in effect it acted as part refuge and part prison, since local sheep magnates would round up the indigenous peoples on their land and pay the Salesians for their "conversion". In 1942, with virtually no Selk'nam remaining, the mission became an agricultural school, a role it has retained to this day. The **Museo Monseñor Fagnano** (Mon–Sat 9.30am–2.30pm & 3–7pm, Sun 3–7pm; ℡02964/430667; $5) is in the building to the left of the chapel as you enter the compound. There's a medley of exhibits on local flora and fauna but more interesting are the homages to Don Bosco, the founder of the Salesian movement, among which you'll find some first-rate Fuegian indigenous items and a kerosene-lit projector that was used to entertain, and no doubt indoctrinate, the Selk'nam. Across the road is a fenced **cemetery** with some vandalized tombs of Salesian fathers and unmarked crosses indicating Selk'nam graves, testaments to a culture that had been completely depersonalized. To reach the mission from town, take the Línea B **bus** "Misión" from Avenida San Martín (hourly; 25min; $2).

Border with Chile and into Patagonia

If you're planning on heading north into Patagonia via land, you'll need to cross first into Chilean Tierra del Fuego and then across the **Magellan Straits** that separate Isla Grande from Patagonia. The main land **border crossing** between the Chilean and Argentine halves of the island is at **San Sebastián**, in the north of the island. The respective customs posts (April–Oct 7am–1am; Nov–March 24hr) are several hundred metres apart, some 15km west of the Argentine village of the same name. Formalities are straightforward, if somewhat lengthy at times. There is also a smaller border post at Bella Vista. You may not take any fresh fruit, meat or dairy products into Chile, and Argentine officers sometimes reciprocate. Once into Chile, you can either continue to the town of Porvenir, where a long (2hr) and irregular crossing connects direct with Punta Arenas, or head to Bahía Azul, where there is a shorter (30min) and much more frequent crossing to Punta Delgada, although these ferries can't operate at low tide and involve a longer drive afterwards if you're planning to head further into Chilean Patagonia. Buses depart most days from Ushuaia or Río Grande to Punta Arenas and other destinations in Patagonia, but their schedules change accord to the ferry timetable and time of year, so you should enquire ahead.

North to San Sebastián and the Chilean border

North of the Misión Salesiano rears **Cabo Domingo**, and beyond that, the unforgiving plains of Patagonian shingle begin again, dotted by shallow saline lagoons that sometimes host feeding flamingoes. The RN-3 is paved as far as the **San Sebastián border post**, 82km north of Río Grande (see box above), on the bay of the same name. The Bahía San Sebastián itself is famous for its summer populations of migratory waders and shore birds and is a vital part of the **Hemisphere Reserve for Shorebirds**, designed to protect migratory birds along the coasts and interior wetlands of the Americas. Oil companies operate in the area, and access is therefore restricted, but there are some birdwatching spots on the mud flats at Río Grande. Spare a thought for birds such as the Hudsonian Godwit (*becasa de mar*) and the Red Knot (*playero rojizo*): they've travelled over 17,000km to get here.

Travel details

Below are the summer season timetables; out of season, services are reduced drastically.

Buses

Río Grande to: Porvenir (irregular; 5hr); Punta Arenas (Mon–Sat daily; 9hr); Río Gallegos (Mon–Sat daily; 10hr); Tolhuin (11–15 daily; 1hr 30min); Ushuaia (12–16 daily; 3hr 30min).
Tolhuin to: Río Grande (11–15 daily; 1hr 30min); Ushuaia (11–15 daily; 1hr 30min).
Ushuaia to: El Calafate (Mon–Sat daily; 18hr); Puerto Natales (4 weekly; 16hr); Punta Arenas (daily except Tues; 12hr); Río Gallegos (1–2 daily; 13hr); Río Grande (12–16 daily; 3hr 30min); Tolhuin (11–15 daily; 1hr 30min).

Flights

Río Grande to: Buenos Aires (daily; 3hr 30min).
Ushuaia to: Buenos Aires (Ezeiza and Aeroparque; 9–12 daily; 3hr 30min); El Calafate (twice daily; 1hr 10min); Punta Arenas (3 weekly; 1hr); Río Gallegos (4 daily; 55min); Trelew (4 daily; 2hr).

Contexts

Contexts

History

rgentina's past might best be summed up as "chequered". The modern nation is a product of Spanish colonialism and immigration from all corners of Europe and the Middle East during the late nineteenth and early twentieth centuries. Relatively little of its pre-Columbian civilizations has survived, other than archeological finds, though there is more of an indigenous influence on present-day Argentine culture than initially meets the eye. After independence, Argentina repeatedly took one step forward to progressive democracy and two steps back into corrupt lawlessness. Twentieth-century Argentina produced its fair share of international icons – with Evita and Che Guevara leading the way, followed closely by Maradona – and was often in the news for the wrong reasons. The country experienced a series of military dictatorships, including that of the late 1970s, whose widespread campaign of state-sponsored terror came to be known as the Dirty War. That regime eventually collapsed in 1983, in part due to the Falklands/Malvinas fiasco. Argentina again hit the international headlines for the wrong reasons when social unrest and recession lurched into chaos in late 2001. In 2003, Néstor Kirchner became president, overseeing an economic recovery and a period of relative calm. And in 2007, his wife, Cristina Fernández de Kirchner, became the country's first woman to be elected head of state.

Pre-Columbian Argentina

The earliest records for human presence in the territory that is now Argentina can be dated back to around 10,000 BC. Over the millennia that preceded the arrival of Europeans, widely varying cultures developed. From around 4000 BC, distinct nomadic cultures like that of the **Yámana** (see box, p.579) emerged in the Fuegian archipelago. Other groups, such as the **Guaraní** peoples of the subtropical northeast, evolved semi-nomadic lifestyles dependent on hunter-gathering and slash-and-burn agriculture.

The most complex cultures emerged, however, in the **Andean northwest**, where sedentary agricultural practices developed from about 500 BC. Irrigation permitted the intensive cultivation of crops like maize, quinoa, squash and potatoes and this, combined with the domestication of animals like the llama, facilitated the growth of rich material cultures. The most important early sedentary culture was the **Tafí**, whose people sculpted intriguing stone menhirs. Later, this period saw the development of Catamarca's **Condorhuasi** culture, renowned for its distinctive, beautifully patterned ceramics. From about 600 AD, metallurgical technologies developed, and bronze was used for items such as ceremonial axes and chest-plates, perhaps best by the **Aguada** civilization, also centred on Catamarca. The increasing organization of Andean groups after 850 AD is demonstrated by the appearance of fortified urban settlements. Three important **Diaguita** cultures emerge: Sanagasta, Belén and **Santa María**, whose overlapping zones of influence stretched from Salta to San Juan, and which are notable for their painted ceramics, anthropomorphic funeral urns and superb metalwork.

Trade networks vastly increased once the area came under the sway of pan-Andean empires: first that of Bolivia's great city, **Tiahuanaco**, which probably influenced Condorhuasi culture; and, from 1480, that of the **Inca**, who incorporated the area

CONTEXTS | History

585

into Kollasuyo, their southernmost administrative region. Incredibly well-preserved finds, such as **three ritually sacrificed mummies** at the summit of 6739m Cerro Llullaillaco – the world's highest archeological discovery (see p.324) – are helping to reveal the extent of this influence in terms of customs, religion and dress.

In the early sixteenth century, before the arrival of Europeans, Argentina's **indigenous population** was probably around half a million, an estimated two-thirds of whom lived in the Northwest. Other relatively densely settled areas included the central sierras of Córdoba and San Luis, where the **Comechingones** and the Sanavirones lived. The Cuyo region was home to semi-sedentary Huarpe, while south and east of them lived various Tehuelche tribes (see p.501), often referred to generically by the Spanish as Pampas Indians or, further south, Patagones. Tierra del Fuego was inhabited by Selk'nam and Mannekenk, as well as Yámana (see p.579). The Gran Chaco region was home to many nomadic groups, including Chiriguano, Lule-Vilela, **Wichí** and groups of the Guaycurú nation, like the Abipone and Qom. The northeastern areas of El Litoral and Mesopotamia were inhabited by Kaingang, Charrúa and Guaraní.

The first group to encounter the Spanish were probably the nomadic **Querandí** of the Pampas region. They lived in temporary shelters and hunted guanaco and rhea with *boleadores* (lassos with heavy balls attached). Though they put up determined resistance to the Spanish for several decades, their culture was eliminated during the subsequent colonial period – a fate shared by many others.

Early Spanish settlement

In 1516, Juan Díaz de Solís, a Portuguese mariner in the employ of the Spanish Crown, led a small crew to the shores of the River Plate in the search of a trade route to the Far East. He was killed by either the Querandí or the Charrúa, who inhabited what is now Uruguay. Another brief exploration of the region was made in 1520 by **Ferdinand Magellan**, who continued his epic voyage south to discover the famous straits that now bear his name, and the next significant expedition to this part of the world was made by an explorer of Italian descent, **Sebastian Cabot** (see box below).

Cabot – Argentina's unwitting baptizer

Explorer **Sebastian Cabot** reached the River Plate in 1526 and built a small, short-lived fort near modern Rosario. He misleadingly christened the river the Río de la Plata ("River of Silver"), after finding bullion and believing there to be deposits nearby. Ironically, the metal had probably been brought here by a Portuguese adventurer, Aleixo Garcia. In 1524, Garcia had reached the eastern fringes of the Inca empire, but was killed with his Andean booty on his return journey.

Cabot's silver had its most lasting legacy in the word "Argentina" itself, which derives from the metal's Latin name, **argentum**. Its first recorded use was in a Venetian atlas of the New World produced in the middle of the sixteenth century. Martín del Barco Centenera, a member of a later expedition, published an epic poem in 1602 called *La Argentina*. The name also appeared in Ruy Díaz de Guzmán's 1612 book *Historia del descubrimiento, población y conquista del Río de la Plata* (History of the discovery, population and conquest of the River Plate), where he referred to the territory as Tierra Argentina, or "Land of Silver". However, "Argentina" was not adopted as the name of the Republic until the middle of the nineteenth century.

In 1535, Pedro de Mendoza was authorized by the Spanish Crown to colonize the River Plate in an effort to pre-empt Portuguese conquest. In February 1536, he founded Buenos Aires, naming it Ciudad de la Santísima Trinidad y Puerto de Santa María de los Buenos Ayres, after the sailors' favourite saint, the provider of fair winds. However his plans soon went awry, as it proved impossible to subjugate the local nomadic Querandí. Mendoza was forced to send Pedro de Ayolas upstream to find a more suitable site for settlement, and in August 1537, Ayolas founded **Nuestra Señora de la Asunción del Paraguay** (Asunción). Mendoza died at sea on the way back to Spain, and authority for the colony devolved to Domingo de Irala, who, after almost constant struggle with the Querandí, finally ordered the evacuation of Buenos Aires in 1541. By this time, Spanish interest in colonizing this area of the world had decreased significantly anyway, mainly as a result of **Pizarro**'s spectacular conquest, in 1535, of Inca Peru.

From 1543, the new Viceroyalty of Peru, with its capital at Lima, was given authority over all of southern Spanish South America. The northwest region of Argentina was first tentatively explored in the mid-1530s, but the impulse for colonizing this region really came with the discovery, in 1545, of enormous **silver deposits** in **Potosí**, in Alto Peru (modern-day Bolivia). This led to the establishment of the **Governorship of Tucumán**, covering a region embracing most of today's Northwest. Conquistadors crossed the Andes seeking to press the locals into labour and find other overland routes to the Potosí mines. Francisco de Aguirre founded Santiago del Estero, Argentina's earliest continually inhabited town, in 1553, while other settlements were established at Mendoza (1561), San Juan (1562), Córdoba (1573), Salta (1582), La Rioja (1591) and San Salvador de Jujuy (1593).

Meanwhile, the Spanish in Asunción sent an expedition under the command of Juan de Garay down the River Paraná, founding Santa Fe in 1573 and **resettling Buenos Aires** in 1580 – this time, for good. Settlers benefited from one vital legacy of the Mendoza settlement – the feral **horses and cattle** that had multiplied in the area. Few then realized the significance these animals would have on most of Argentina's future.

Colonial developments

Buenos Aires and its surrounds were largely overlooked by the Spanish Crown until the late eighteenth century. Direct trade with Spain from the River Plate was prohibited from 1554, and all imported and exported goods traded via Lima, which restricted growth of the port, but encouraged **contraband** imports. The potential of the Governorship of the River Plate was limited: there was no market in pre-industrial Europe for agricultural produce, and the indigenous populations could not easily be yoked into the **encomienda** system of forced labour. It was the Society of Jesus – the Jesuits – that effectively pioneered Spanish colonization of this region (see box, p.588).

More important than the River Plate at this point was the Governorship of Tucumán. The *encomienda* system was more effective here and in the central Córdoban sierras, as they were more densely settled. Though some trade from this area was directed towards Buenos Aires, the local economy was run so as to provide the Potosí mine with mules, sugar, cotton textiles and wheat. Indigenous resistance to the colonizers erupted on occasion, as with the Diaguita rebellion of 1657, which was actually led by a Spanish rebel, Pedro Bohórquez. The rebellion was brutally crushed in 1659 and survivors were displaced from their ravaged communities and forcibly resettled as workers on haciendas. By the

The Jesuit missions

The **Jesuits** first arrived in the region of the upper Paraná during the late sixteenth century, initially prospering under the protection of the Crown. The first **missions** to the Guaraní were established in the upper Paraná from 1609 (see box, p.266). Though the Jesuits tried to evangelize other parts of the country over the next 150 years, it was in the subtropical Upper Paraná where they had their greatest success. After raids in the region by roaming **Portuguese slavers** in the 1630s, the Jesuits established their own indigenous militias for protection. Thereafter, Jesuit activity thrived: there were as many as thirty missions here by the beginning of the eighteenth century. The Guaraní who lived in the missions had the benefit of Jesuit education and skills, and were exempt from forced labour in silver mines, but this was no earthly paradise: coercion and violence were not unknown, and epidemics periodically ravaged these communities.

In the seventeenth century, the Crown revoked its tax concessions to the Jesuits, forcing their communities to enter the colonial economy. They did so with vigour, exporting **yerba mate** (see box, p.263), sugar and tobacco. However, their success aroused jealousy. Some missions housed more than 4000 indigenous people and this **monopolization of labour**, together with the economic and political influence of the Jesuits in Córdoba (see box, p.217), stirred the resentment of nearby settlers. In the 1720s, secular settlers rebelled, urging the Crown to curb the domination of the Jesuits. In and around Asunción and Corrientes, they subjected Jesuit communities to **raids**, and other acts of violence. Though it survived that threat, the mission experiment succumbed soon afterwards, a victim of power politics in Europe, lobbying from interests bent on exploiting native labour and **King Carlos III**'s perception that the existence of a powerful Jesuit community was a threat to secular royal authority. In 1767, he ordered the **Jesuits' expulsion** from all Spanish territories, an order carried out the following year. The remaining communities were subsequently entrusted to the Franciscans, whose mismanagement led to their being plundered and to many Guaraní being led away to slavery.

second half of the eighteenth century, demand for labour from both Potosí and the towns of Tucumán was so great that it led to the importation of **black slave labour**. It is estimated that by 1778 one in ten of Tucumán's regional population was a slave, while well over a quarter were of pure indigenous blood. Racial divisions were strongly demarcated, and the rights of whites to control land and political offices were reinforced by a dress code and a weapons ban for the non-white castes.

As with Tucumán, the economies of Buenos Aires, Santa Fe, Entre Ríos and Corrientes engendered strife with the native peoples. Mounted raids by indigenous tribes from the Gran Chaco, such as the Abipone, terrorized the northeastern provinces well into the eighteenth century, and Buenos Aires, dependent on its round-ups of wild cattle (*vaquerías*) for its **hide and tallow industries**, frequently came into conflict both with groups of Tehuelche and, increasingly from the eighteenth century, Mapuche (Araucanians). These peoples relied on the same feral cattle and horses, driving vast herds of them to the northern Patagonian Andes for the purpose of trading with Chileans, both white settlers and other indigenous groups. The seventeenth and eighteenth centuries also saw the emergence and apogee of **gauchos**, nomadic horsemen, often of mestizo origins, who roamed in small bands and lived off the wild herds of livestock.

The Viceroyalty of the River Plate

By the late eighteenth century, the British controlled the Caribbean and were blocking the Lima sea routes, so the establishment of another route to Potosí became vital. The River Plate seemed the logical choice, and the growing value of Buenos Aires as a market and strategic post gained the recognition of the Spanish Crown, which, in 1776, made it the capital of the new **Viceroyalty of the River Plate**, whose jurisdiction included Alto Peru (modern Bolivia), Paraguay and the Governorship of Montevideo. Commercial restrictions were gradually loosened, and trade permitted with ports in Spain and Spanish America, but the Crown still clung to its monopoly on colonial commerce, prohibiting the sale of silver to foreign powers.

Tensions between **monopolist traders** and those who advocated **free trade** were becoming entrenched. Thanks to the European wars of the late eighteenth century the Crown was forced to further loosen its control, and in 1797, allowed its colonies to trade with neutral countries. To the dismay of monopolists, cheap European manufactures flowed freely into Buenos Aires courtesy of contraband merchants. Monopolists trading on the traditional Cádiz route suffered, and exports to Spain plummeted. It became increasingly difficult to reinstate restrictions, and attempts to do so caused anger among merchants, such as **Manuel Belgrano**, who argued for free trade with all nations, but not rebellion against the Crown. Although the ideas of the French Revolution and the American Declaration of Independence circulated among Buenos Aires' elite, there was not yet any significant revolutionary feeling against Spain. The **British**, however, caught wind of the commercial tensions in Buenos Aires, and, mistakenly interpreting them as revolutionary, **invaded** the city in 1806 (see box, below).

Other changes in the economy of Buenos Aires became increasingly apparent during the Viceroyalty. Rich merchants (*comerciantes*) helped finance the growth of **estancias** (ranches) in the province, a shift away from the earlier practice of *vaquerías* – Wild West-style cattle round-ups. By the end of the eighteenth century, these estancias had become highly profitable enterprises.

The British invasions

In **June 1806**, a force of 1600 men led by **General William Beresford** stormed into Buenos Aires hoping to assert British imperial control over the entire Viceroyalty. The Viceroy, the **Marqués de Sobremonte**, fled the city, and the remaining Spanish authorities grudgingly swore allegiance to the British Crown. Among the ordinary inhabitants, though, there was a sense of offended honour at the way such a tiny force had been allowed to overrun the city's defences.

The locals regrouped under a new commander-in-chief, the French-born **Santiago Liniers**, and ousted their invaders during the **Reconquista** of August 12. Undaunted, the British captured Montevideo, from where they launched a second assault on a better-prepared Buenos Aires in July 1807. This battle led to the surrender of the British and came to be known as **La Defensa**, a name imbued with the bravura of Liniers' hastily assembled militia, whose cannon- and musket-fire peppered the enemy, while women poured boiling oil from the tops of the city's buildings on the hapless British soldiers.

The May revolution and independence

One consequence of the victory over the British was to make the people of Buenos Aires aware of the extent to which they could manage their own affairs and how little they could rely on the viceregal authorities. This was the first time that they had fought in unison against a foreign invader and in certain sectors the feeling of pride carried over into a stance of defiance against the monarchy.

In 1808, **Napoleon Bonaparte's troops** invaded the Iberian Peninsula. Napoleon forced the rival Spanish Bourbon kings – Carlos IV and his son, Ferdinand VII – to **abdicate**, and installed his own brother, Joseph Bonaparte, on the throne. This had massive repercussions in the Latin American colonies, ushering in two decades of upheaval. A new viceroy, **Viscount Balthasar de Cisneros** – appointed by a Spanish junta in Seville loyal to the imprisoned Ferdinand VII – was unable to curb tensions between peninsular Spanish and creole elites, and parallel tensions between various trading interests. The authority of Cisneros was fatally undermined in 1810, when news came through of the fall of Seville to French troops. On May 25 of that year, supporters of self-government gathered in front of the Cabildo in Buenos Aires, with some accounts claiming they wore sky-blue and white ribbons, the colours that were later to make up the **Argentine flag**. Inside, Cisneros was ousted and the **Primera Junta** sworn in. However, deposition of the viceroy and the establishment of self-government did not necessarily mean advocating republicanism. The new authority continued to proclaim loyalty to the deposed Ferdinand VII, although in reality this was a convenient fudge that allowed people of many different persuasions to unite.

The Primera Junta was headed by **Cornelio Saavedra**, who believed in sharing power with the provinces. Other members of the Junta, including Belgrano and **Mariano Moreno**, were avowed free-trade enthusiasts, intent on bringing the rest of the territory under the control of Buenos Aires. Moreno's views came to represent what was to be the position of the **Unitarists** (or **Azules** – "Blues") who favoured centralism, while Saavedra's contained the first seeds of the ideas of **Federalists** (the **Colorados** or Rojos – "Reds"), promoting the autonomy of the provinces within the framework of a confederation. This dispute was to dominate nineteenth century Argentine politics, causing bitter division and **civil war**. While the Junta's internal disputes prevented unity in Buenos Aires, the May Revolution also failed to mark a clean break from the motherland. Royalists under the leadership of Martín de Alzaga continued to press for the return of a viceroyalty.

As Unitarist and Federalist interests continued to battle for control of the capital, clashes between pro-royalist forces and pro-independence forces flared up across the old viceroyalty. After 1810, in the interior these struggles saw the emergence of Federalist **caudillos**, powerful local warlords. They recruited – or, rather, press-ganged – militias from among the slaves, indigenous peoples and gauchos of the countryside. Back in Buenos Aires, the royalist factions were effectively crushed by 1812, and a *criollo* front led by **José de San Martín** (see box, p.591), the Sociedad Patriótica, sought full emancipation from foreign powers.

Two congresses were convened to discuss the future of the former viceroyalty, but these were dominated by Unitarists and failed to produce a cohesive plan for the country. However, at the second, held on **July 9, 1816** in the city of Tucumán, the independence of the **United Provinces of the River Plate** was formally

It's impossible to stay for even a short time in Argentina without coming across the name of national hero **José de San Martín** – he's as ubiquitous as Washington in the US or de Gaulle in France, and has countless villages, barrios, streets, plazas, public buildings and even a mountain named after him, as well as innumerable statues in his honour. He's often simply referred to as **El Libertador** (The Liberator) and is treated with saint-like reverence. It's ironic, therefore, that he didn't even take part in the country's initial liberation from the Spanish Crown, that he actually helped to free Chile – Argentina's traditional rival – and that he spent the last 23 years of his life in self-imposed exile in France. Even this last fact is celebrated, though, with streets and whole barrios named after **Boulogne-sur-Mer**, the northern French town where he died on August 17, 1850. A slightly larger-than-original replica of his Parisian mansion, Grand Bourg, built on the edge of leafy Palermo Chico, is now the Instituto Sanmartiniano, a library-cum-study-centre given over to research into the great man.

San Martín was born into a humble family – he was the son of a junior officer – in 1778 in the former Jesuit mission settlement of Yapeyú, Corrientes Province. He was packed off to the academy in Buenos Aires and then to military school in Spain, and later served in the royal army, taking part in the Spanish victories against the Napoleonic invasions in 1808–11. He even lived in Westminster for a few weeks at the end of 1811. He returned to his homeland soon afterwards, and assisted in training the rag-bag army that was trying to resist Spain's attempt to cling onto its South American empire. After replacing Manuel Belgrano as leader of the independence forces in 1813, he became increasingly active in politics, as a conservative, and attended the Tucumán Congress in 1816. He then formed his own army, known popularly as the **Ejército de los Andes**, basing himself in Mendoza, where he was governor for several years, and in San Juan. From there he crossed the Andes and obliterated royalist troops at Chacabuco, thereby **freeing Chile** from the imperialist yoke – though his friend and comrade-in-arms Bernardo O'Higgins got most of the credit – finally mopping up the remaining royalist resistance at Maipú in 1818, before moving on to Lima, Peru.

San Martín was not at all interested in personal political power, but was in favour of setting up a constitutional monarchy in the emerging South American states. In 1821, he signed the so-called Punchanca agreement with the viceroy of Peru to put a member of the Spanish royal family on the Peruvian throne, but the royalists did not respond and, ultimately, he declared Peru's independence on July 12, 1821. Unable to hold the country together in the face of royalist resistance, he called upon **Simón Bolívar**, the liberator of Venezuela, to come to his assistance. The only meeting between the two occurred in Guayaquil, Ecuador, in 1822. Bolívar's radical republican ideals clashed with San Martín's conservative mindset, and, though no one knows what exactly was said in this encounter, San Martín opted to withdraw from Peru. Frustrated by a nascent Argentina that was neither the new-style kingdom he yearned for nor the democratic modern nation-state Bolívar had advocated, but, instead, a patchwork of disunited provinces led by brutish *caudillos*, San Martín took off to **France**. He never returned to Argentina during his lifetime, and, in his self-imposed exile, he slipped into obscurity; all this changed after his death, however, and the national hero's bodily remains were repatriated later that century. He now lies buried in Buenos Aires' Metropolitan Cathedral, where his tomb is a national monument (see p.92). His death is commemorated every year with a national holiday on the Monday nearest to August 17.

declared, a title first adopted by Buenos Aires in 1813. The date, July 9, has since come to be recognized as Argentina's official **independence day**.

Later that year, San Martín led five thousand men across the Andes to attack the Spanish in Chile, in one of the defining moments of Latin America's struggle against its colonial rulers. During this time, he was assisted in the north by another hero of Argentine independence, **Martín Miguel de Güemes**, an anti-royalist, Federalist *caudillo* whose gaucho army eventually liberated Salta. Though *caudillos* such as Güemes were in favour of independence, many resented the heavy taxes imposed to fund the struggle for autonomy, and tensions remained high. Men like López and Ramírez defeated the attempt to impose a Unitarist constitution in 1819.

Caudillismo and civil war

The 1820s began with infighting among *caudillo* groups. In 1826, **Bernardino Rivadavia**, a Unitarist admirer of European ideals, became the first outright president of what was then called the United Provinces of South America. He proposed a new constitution, which was rejected by the provinces, who objected to the call for dissolution of their militia and the concession of land to the national government. At the same time, conflict with Brazil over Uruguay led to a blockade of the River Plate and caused a financial crisis. These two issues brought Rivadavia's presidency to its knees by 1827. The bitter Unitarist/Federalist fighting that ensued only ceased when a *caudillo* from Buenos Aires, **General Juan Manuel de Rosas**, emerged victorious (see box, p.593). In 1829, he became governor of Buenos Aires, with power over the newly titled Confederation of the River Plate or Argentine Confederation.

The creation of Argentina

The thirty years that followed the defeat of Rosas saw the foundations laid for the **modern Argentine state**. Economic expansion and the triumph of Unitarism ensured the conditions for the boom that followed. Buenos Aires was finally to emerge from its struggles with the provinces and territorial conquest began in earnest, resulting in the subjugation of the most important of the unconquered indigenous groups: those of the south.

Urquiza's attempt to establish a constitution sympathetic to Federalist interests foundered when Buenos Aires proved unwilling to renounce its privileged trading terms or submit to his rule. The province refused to approve the **1853 constitution**, which led to the creation of two republics: one in Buenos Aires and the other, the Argentine Confederation, centred on Entre Ríos and headed by Urquiza. This situation changed in 1861, when the governor of Buenos Aires, **Bartolomé Mitre**, defeated Urquiza. The 1853 constitution was then, with a few significant amendments, ratified by Buenos Aires, and the basic structure of Argentine government was set. In 1862, Mitre was elected the first president of the new **Argentine Republic**. Constitutional provisions included ending trade restrictions throughout the country and promoting the colonization of the interior, one result of which was the small Welsh settlement in Patagonia (see box, p.510).

Mitre aimed for the rapid **modernization** of the country, focusing particularly on the capital. His achievements included the creation of a national army and postal system, and the expansion of a **railway network**. These initiatives were financed by foreign investment from Britain, which contributed the capital to

General Juan Manuel de Rosas, one of the most controversial figures of Argentine history, was born into an influential cattle-ranching family, and was respected by his gauchos for his riding skills and personal bravery. He was an avowed Federalist, but his particular brand of Federalism had more to do with opposing intellectual Unitarism, with its gravitation towards foreign, European influence, than it did in respecting provincial autonomy per se. As it turned out, his platform was more about centralizing power in his own province, Buenos Aires.

He left office at the end of his term in 1832 but returned as dictator in 1835 as the country teetered on the brink of fresh civil war after the assassination of an ally of his, the *caudillo* of La Rioja, **Juan "Facundo" Quiroga**. For seventeen years Rosas ruthlessly consolidated power using the army and his own brutal police force, the **Mazorca**. The Mazorca used a network of spies and assassins to keep resistance in check. During this time, many opponents and intellectuals fled to Uruguay and Europe.

Rosas sought to improve his network of **patronage** through the expansion of territories available for farming in the Pampas. His **Desert Campaign** of 1833 against the indigenous peoples was the precursor to Roca's genocidal Conquest of the Desert of the late 1870s (see p.594). The vast landholdings that Rosas dealt out to "conquerors" ensured he retained powerful allies.

However, Rosas managed to alienate many of the interior provinces by not permitting free trade along the Paraná, by increasing taxes on provincial trade and by allowing the import of cheap foreign produce, such as French wine, into Buenos Aires. Rosas' bloody regime was brought to an end in 1852, at the Battle of Caseros. Defeat came at the hands of a one-time ally, the powerful *caudillo* governor of Entre Ríos, **Justo José de Urquiza**, who was backed by a coalition of interests that desired free trade on the Paraná, including the Brazilians, British and French. After defeat, Rosas left for England to become a farmer in Southampton, where he died in 1877.

C

CONTEXTS | History

build railways, and by greater export earnings, the result, particularly, of the important expanding trade in **wool**. The other significant event of Mitre's presidency was the **War of the Triple Alliance** (1865–70), a conflict that had its origins in the expansionist ambitions of Paraguay and disputes over navigation rights in the Paraná and River Plate. In it, Argentina allied with Uruguay and Brazil to defeat Paraguay, though much of the fighting, some of it farcical yet brutal, was left to the Brazilians, whose military ineptitude resulted in a prolonged campaign. Argentina secured control of the upper Paraná and the territory (now Province) of Misiones.

The end of the war overlapped with the presidency of **Domingo Sarmiento**, the man most identified with the drive to "Europeanize" Argentina in the nineteenth century. Sarmiento was an opponent of *caudillismo* and famous for pillorying the likes of Rosas. He believed that they represented a "barbaric" era in Argentine history, and that their legacy impeded the country from adopting contemporary North American and European notions of progress and civilization. These theories of progress impacted heavily on the remaining indigenous populations of Argentina, as they sponsored those who believed in "civilizing the Indian", and helped underpin the doctrine of the so-called "Generation of the Eighties" (the 1880s) who subscribed to imposing the nation-state by force. Sarmiento is also remembered for his highly ambitious **education policy** and for encouraging European immigration on a grand scale.

The Conquest of the Desert

With the near disappearance of wild herds of livestock and the movement of settlers into the Pampas, Mapuche and Tehuelche groups found it increasingly difficult to maintain their way of life. Indigenous raids – called **malones** – on estancias and white settlements became more frequent, and debate raged in the 1870s as to how to solve the "Indian Problem". Two main positions crystallized. The one propounded by Minister of War **Alsina** consisted of containment, and aimed at a gradual integration of the indigenous tribes. The second, propounded by his successor, **General Julio Roca**, advocated uncompromising conquest and subjugation – Argentina could then concentrate on territorial expansion to the south. Indeed, the likes of Roca believed that was where the future of the Argentine nation lay.

Roca led an army south in 1879, and his brutal **Conquest of the Desert** was effectively over by the following year, leaving over 1300 indigenous dead and the whole of Patagonia open to settlement. Roca swept to victory in the 1880 presidential election on the back of his success. He believed strongly in a highly centralized government and consolidated his power base by using the vast new tracts of land as a system of patronage. With the southern frontier secure, he could, from the mid-1880s, back campaigns to defeat indigenous groups in the **Gran Chaco**, and thus stabilize the country's northern frontier with Paraguay.

Social and economic change: 1850–1914

Agriculture and infrastructure continued to expand, benefiting from massive British investment. The first **railway**, built in 1854, connected Buenos Aires to the farms and estancias in its vicinity. By 1880, the railway network carried over three million passengers and over one million tonnes of cargo, and between 1857 and 1890, nearly 10,000km of track were built. **Wool production** became such a strong sector of the economy in the second half of the nineteenth century that sheep outnumbered people, thirty to one. The rise in the number of sheep farms – small, privately owned or rented family concerns – saw the growth of a strong middle class in the provinces. Also transforming the countryside was the boom in **export crops** such as wheat, oats and linseed. Another development of importance was the invention of **refrigerator ships** in 1876, which enabled Argentina to start exporting meat to the urban centres of Britain and Europe. In Buenos Aires and other areas, the age of **latifundismo** had begun as huge tracts of land were bought up by Argentine speculators hoping to profit by their sale to railway companies. In the interim period they were rented out to sheep farmers and sharecroppers.

At the same time, European immigration to Argentina was rising. Significant numbers of French people arrived in the 1850s, followed later by groups of Italians, Swiss and Germans. Many came in search of land but settled for work either as sharecroppers in estancias or as shepherds, labourers and artisans. Between 1880 and World War I, six million **immigrants** came to Argentina. Half of these were Italians and a quarter Spaniards, while other groups included French, Portuguese, Russians, Ottoman subjects (mostly Syrians and Lebanese), Irish and Welsh. In 1895, immigrants represented nearly one-third of the population of

Buenos Aires city, which had grown from 90,000 in 1869 to 670,000 in 1895. This convulsive influx caused occasional resentment, particularly during periods of economic depression, which were usually sparked by events abroad. Growth depended largely on foreign investment and the country was susceptible to slumps like the one that affected Britain in the 1870s, prompting occasional debate about **protectionism**. Immigrant participation in politics was not encouraged, and few took up Argentine citizenship on arrival, because citizens were obliged to perform military service. Generally, though, immigrants were welcomed as part of the drive towards economic expansion and colonization of the countryside.

The age of Radicalismo

By the early years of the twentieth century, pressure for political change was increasing. Power still rested in the hands of the landed and urban elite, a tiny minority, leaving the rapidly expanding urban professional and working classes unrepresented. From 1890, a new party, the **Radical Civic Union** (Unión Cívica Radical or UCR), agitated for reform but was excluded from power. A sea change came with the introduction of **universal manhood suffrage** and secret balloting in 1912 by reformist conservative president, Roque Sáenz Peña. In 1916, this saw the victory of the first Radical president, **Hipólito Yrigoyen**, ushering in thirteen unbroken years of Radicalism, under him and his associate, **Marcelo T. de Alvear**. After World War I, economic growth picked up again, with the expansion of manufacturing industries, but its benefits were far from equally distributed. Confrontations between police and strikers in Buenos Aires led to numerous deaths in the **Semana Trágica** – or Tragic Week – of 1919. This was followed by the 1920–21 **workers' strikes** in southern Patagonia. Most strikers were immigrant peón farmhands from the impoverished Chilean island of Chiloe but there were also a few labour activists, Bolsheviks and anarchists. A first strike in 1920 was sparked by the fact that peones had been unable to cash in or exchange the tokens with which they were paid by sheep barons. The protest expanded to include a raft of other grievances concerning working rights and conditions, and more extreme factions latched onto what was, at root, a fairly conservative phenomenon. Shaken, estancia owners promised to arrange payment, but when this was not forthcoming, a second strike was unleashed, this time releasing more in the way of pent-up anger and frustration. Incidents of **violent lawlessness** were used by opponents of the strike to panic the authorities, now better prepared, into **brutal repression**. The final tragedy came with the massacre in cold blood of 121 men by an army battalion at Estancia Anita. Later, the Radicals introduced social security and pro-labour reforms.

By the end of the 1920s, Argentina was the **seventh-richest nation in the world**, and confidence was sky-high. Britain remained the country's major investor and market – as revealed in a confidential report by Sir Malcolm Robertson, ambassador to Argentina, in 1929: "Argentina must be regarded as an essential part of the British Empire. We cannot get on without her, nor she without us." This was a nation that people predicted would challenge the United States in economic power. Within a few decades, however, Argentina had fallen to the status of a Third World state. The loss of this golden dream of prosperity has haunted and perplexed the Argentine conscience ever since. The decline in status was not constant, but the **world depression** that followed the Wall Street Crash of 1929 marked one of the first serious blows. The effects of the crash and the collapse of export markets left the Radical regime reeling and precipitated a **military takeover** in 1930 – an inauspicious omen of events later in the century. The military restored power to the oligarchic elite, who ruled through a succession of coalition governments that gained a reputation for fraud and electoral corruption. By the late 1930s, the value of the manufactured goods overtook that of agriculture for the first time. Immigration continued apace, with one important group being Jews fleeing persecution in Germany.

The rise and fall of Perón

Another major watershed of the twentieth century was the rise of **Juan Domingo Perón**, a charismatic military man of relatively modest origins who had risen through the ranks during the 1930s to the status of colonel. The outbreak of **World War II** had repercussions in Argentina, though it stayed neutral: a split developed in the armed forces, with one faction favouring the Allies and a larger one, the Axis powers.

Perón's involvement with politics intensified after a **military coup** in 1943, in which the army replaced a conservative coalition government that had come to be seen as self-serving and which was veering towards a declaration of support for the Allies. Perón was appointed Secretary for Labour, and he used this minor post as a platform to cultivate links with trade unions. His popularity alarmed his military superiors, who arrested him in 1945. However, this move backfired: Perón's second wife, **Evita** (see box, p.597) helped to organize mass demonstrations that secured his release, generating the momentum that swept him to the **presidency** in the 1946 elections. His first term in government signalled a programme of radical social and political change, but his philosophy of government, known as Peronism, defies easy definition (see box, p.598).

Controversy surrounds many aspects of Perón's regime. Dissident opinion had no place in his scheme: these years were marked by a **suppression of the press**, increasingly heavy-handed control over institutions of higher education and the use of violent intimidation. Though it is unclear to what extent he was personally involved, Perón's apparent willingness to provide a haven for Nazi refugees has also done little for his or Argentina's international reputation. Adolf Eichmann was one of the most notorious war criminals to settle here and, much more recently, Erich Priebke was extradited from Bariloche to Italy to face trial for atrocities committed in wartime Rome. A recent report has revealed that fewer Nazis actually fled to Argentina than was thought, listing the number as 180, most of whom were Croats, not Germans – though others suggest that various regimes including Carlos Menem's (see p.603) had records relating to this period destroyed.

In 1949, Perón secured a constitutional amendment that allowed him to run for a **second term**. Though he won by a landslide in the 1951 elections, his position was severely weakened by the death of Evita, who had been a principal political asset. It was becoming clear that his administration, and the cult of personality that had swept him to power and fed his reputation, was losing political impetus. He faced dissent within the army, resentful at what they saw as the subordination of their role during Evita's lifetime. He had also incited the wrath of the powerful Catholic Church, whose privileges he had attacked. In addition, his successful wealth-redistribution policies had alienated wealthy sectors of society while raising the expectations of the less well-off – expectations that he found increasingly difficult to fulfil. Agriculture had been allowed to stagnate in favour

Evita Perón

Evita Perón, in true rags-to-riches style, began life humbly. She was born **María Eva Duarte** in 1919, the fifth illegitimate child of Juana Ibarguren and Juan Duarte, a landowner in the rural interior of Buenos Aires. She was raised in poverty by her mother, Duarte having abandoned the family before Evita reached her first birthday. At the age of 15, she headed to the capital to pursue her dream of becoming an actress, and managed to scrape a living from several minor roles in radio and TV before working her way into higher-profile leading roles through the influence of well-connected lovers. Her life changed dramatically in 1944 when she met Juan Perón. She became his mistress and married him a year later, shortly before his election to the presidency.

As First Lady, Evita was in her element. She championed the rights of the working classes and underprivileged poor, whom she named her **descamisados** ("shirtless ones"), and immersed herself in populist politics and programmes of social aid. In person, she would receive petitions from individual members of the public, distributing favours on a massive scale through her powerful and wealthy instrument of patronage, the Social Aid Foundation. She played the role of the devoted wife, but was, in many ways, a pioneering feminist of Argentine society, and has been credited with assuring that women were finally granted suffrage in 1947. She yearned to legitimize her political role through direct election, but resentment among the military forced her to pull out of running for the position of vice-president to her husband in the election of 1951.

Another role she revelled in was that of **ambassador** for her country, and she captivated a star-struck press and public during a 1948 tour of post-war Europe, during which she was granted an audience with the Pope. Hers was the international face of Argentina, dressed in Dior and Balenciaga, which assuredly compounded the jealousy of Europhile upper-class women at home. She was detested by the Argentine elite as a vulgar upstart who respected neither rank nor customary protocol. They painted her as a whore and as someone who was more interested in feeding her own personality cult than assisting the *descamisados*. Evita, for her part, seemed to revel in antagonizing the oligarchic establishment, whipping up popular resentment towards an "anti-Argentine" class.

Stricken by **cancer of the uterus**, she died in 1952, at the age of only 33. Her death was greeted with mass outpourings of grief never seen in Argentina before or since. Eight people were crushed to death in the crowds of mourners that gathered, and over two thousand needed treatment for injuries. In death, Evita led an even more rarefied existence than she had in life. After the military coup of 1955, the military made decoy copies of her **embalmed corpse** and spirited the original away to Europe, all too aware of its power as an icon and focus for political dissent. There followed a truly bizarre series of burials, reburials and even allegations of necrophilia, before she was repatriated in 1974, during Perón's third administration and, later, afforded a decent burial in Recoleta Cemetery. To this day, Evita retains saint-like status among many traditionalist, working-class Peronists, some of whom maintain altars to her. Protests and furious graffiti greeted the casting of Madonna, fresh from a series of pornographic photo shoots, to portray her in the Alan Parker film musical, *Evita*. For many, this was sacrilege – an insult to the memory of the most important woman of Argentine history.

of industrial development, resulting in inflation and economic recession. Against a background of strikes and civil unrest, factions within the military rebelled in 1955, with the tacit support of a broad coalition of those interests that Perón had alienated. In the **Revolución Libertadora**, or Revolution of Liberation, Perón was ousted from power and went into **exile**.

Defining Peronism

Perón's brand of fierce **nationalism**, combined with an authoritarian cult of the leader, bore many of the hallmarks of Fascism. Nevertheless, he assumed power by overwhelming democratic vote, and was seen by the poor as a saviour. Perón's scheme involved a type of "corporatism" that offered genuine improvements to the lives of the workers while making it easier to control them for the smooth running of the capitalist system. Perón saw strong **state intervention** as a way of melding the interests of labour and capital, and propounded the doctrine of **justicialismo**, or social justice, which soon began to be identified as **Peronism**. His administration passed a comprehensive programme of social welfare legislation that, among other things, granted workers a minimum wage, paid holidays (often at specially built hotels) and pension schemes, and established house-building programmes.

Perón also supported nationalization and **industrialization**, in an attempt to render Argentina less dependent on foreign capital. One of the most significant acts of his administration was, in 1947, to nationalize the country's railway system, compensating its British owners to the tune of £150 million. In so doing, he also capitalized on popular anti-British sentiment, which had been fostered over preceding generations during a period of disproportionate commercial influence wielded by the tiny class of British farming and industrial oligarchs. Nevertheless, some believe that he paid over the odds for outdated stock.

Military governments and guerrilla activity: 1955–73

The initial backlash against Peronism was swift: General Aramburu banned it as a political movement, Peronist iconography and statues were stripped from public places and even mention of his name was forbidden. There followed eighteen years of alternate military and short-lived civilian regimes that lurched from one crisis to another. Civilian administrations were dependent on the backing of the military, which itself was unsure of how to align itself with the Peronist legacy and the trade unions. Much of the 1960s was characterized by economic stagnation, strikes, wage freezes and a growing disillusionment of the populace with the government. Throughout this time, Perón hovered in the background, in exile in Spain, providing a focus for opposition to the military.

In 1966, a **military coup** led by General Juan Carlos Onganía saw the imposition of austerity measures to stabilize the economy, and repression to keep a tight rein on political dissent. This was not without consequences, and, in the city of radical politics, Córdoba, tension eventually exploded into violence in May 1969. In what has become known as the **Cordobazo**, left-wing student protesters and trade unionists sparked off a spree of general rioting that lasted for two days, and left many people dead and the authorities profoundly shaken. Onganía's position became less and less tenable and, with unrest spreading throughout the country and an economic crisis that provoked devaluation, he was deposed by the army.

It was about this time that society saw the emergence of **guerrilla** organizations, which crystallized, over the course of the early 1970s, into two main groups: the People's Revolutionary Army (Ejército Revolucionario del Pueblo or **ERP**), a movement committed to radical international revolution in the style of Trotsky or

Che Guevara; and the **Montoneros**, a more urban movement that espoused revolution on a more distinctly national model, extrapolated from left-wing traits within Peronism. Multinationals, landed oligarchs and the security forces were favoured Montonero targets.

The return of Perón and the collapse of democracy

By 1973, the army seemed to have recognized that its efforts to engineer some sort of national unity had failed. The economy continued to splutter, guerrilla violence was spreading and incidences of military repression were rising. Army leader General Lanusse decided to risk calling an election, and in an attempt to heal the long-standing national divide permitted the Peronist party – but not Perón himself – to stand. Perón, then living in Spain, nominated a proxy candidate, **Héctor José Cámpora**, to stand in his place. Cámpora emerged victorious in the June elections and forced a reluctant military to allow Perón himself to return to stand in new elections.

By this time, Perón had come to represent all things to all men. Left-wing Montoneros saw themselves as true Peronists – the natural upholders of the type of Peronism that championed the rights of the *descamisados* and freedom from imperialist domination. Likewise, some members of conservative landed groups saw him as a symbol of stability in the face of anarchy. Any illusion that Perón was going to be the balm for the nation's ills dissipated before touchdown at Ezeiza International Airport. Like a group of unsuspecting wives assembled to greet a secret polygamist, his welcoming party dissolved into a violent melee, with rival groups in the crowd of 500,000 shooting at each other. It's not known how many people died in the fracas; the total is thought to be in three figures, though the official figure is 25.

Cámpora resigned and handed power to a stand-in, who called new elections in September 1973. Perón was allowed to stand this time and as his running mate he chose his third wife, María Estela Martínez de Perón, a former dancer from La Rioja, commonly known by her stage name, **Isabelita**. They had met at a night club in Panama (where Perón was first exiled), in circumstances that were later the cause of much speculation, lived together in Venezuela and then in Spain, where they married.

Perón was 78 and his health was failing; though he won the elections with ease, his third term lasted less than nine months, ending with his death in July 1974. Power devolved to Isabelita, who became the world's first woman president. She managed to make a bitterly divided nation agree on at least one thing: her regime was a catastrophic failure. Rudderless, out of her depth and with no bedrock of support, Isabelita clung increasingly desperately to the advice of her Minister for Social Welfare, José López Rega, a shadowy figure who had been Perón's private secretary and who became known as the "Wizard", even being compared to Rasputin. Rega's prime notoriety stems from having founded the much-feared right-wing **death squads** (the Triple "A", or Alianza Argentina Anticomunista) that targeted intellectuals and guerrilla sympathizers. The only boom industry, it seemed, was corruption, and with hyperinflation and spiralling violence, the country was set to enter a dark phase in its history.

Totalitarianism: the Proceso, or Dirty War

The long-expected **military coup** finally came on March 24, 1976 (now commemorated every year as a national holiday). Ousted President Isabelita Perón was imprisoned and later returned to exile in Spain. Under **General Jorge Videla**, a military junta initiated what it termed the Process of National Reorganization (usually known as the **Proceso**), which is more often referred to as the Guerra Sucia, or **Dirty War**. In the minds of the military, any attempt to combat opposition through the normal judicial process was sure to result in failure, so there was only one response to it: an iron fist. The constitution was suspended, and a campaign of systematic violence backed by the full apparatus of the state was unleashed. In the language of chauvinistic patriotism, they invoked the Doctrine of National Security to justify what they saw as part of the war against international Communism. These events were set against the background of **Cold War politics**, and the generals received covert CIA support. Apart from guerrillas and anyone suspected of harbouring guerrilla sympathies, those targeted included liberal intellectuals, journalists, psychologists, Jews, Marxists, trade unionists, atheists and anyone who, in the words of Videla, "spreads ideas that are contrary to Western and Christian civilization".

The most notorious tactic was to send hit squads to make people "disappear". Once seized, these **desaparecidos** simply ceased to exist – no one knew who had taken them or where they had gone. In fact, the *desaparecidos* were taken to secret detention camps – places like the infamous **Navy Mechanics School** (ESMA), now a national memorial – where they were subjected to torture, rape and, usually, execution. Many were taken up in planes and thrown, drugged and weighted with concrete, into the River Plate. Most victims were between their late teens and thirties, but no one was exempt, even pregnant women and the handicapped. Jacobo Timerman, in *Prisoner Without a Name, Cell Without a Number*, an account of his experiences in a torture centre, gives an insight into the mind of one of his interrogators, who told him: "Only God gives and takes life. But God is busy elsewhere, and we're the ones who must undertake this task in Argentina."

In the midst of this, the armed forces had the opportunity to demonstrate the "success" of their regime to the world, by hosting the **1978 football World Cup**. Though victory of the Argentine team in the final stoked national pride, few observers saw this as a reflection of the achievements of the military. Indeed, the event backfired on the military in other ways. The vast expense of hosting the tournament compounded the regime's economic problems. In addition, it provided a forum for human-rights advocates, including a courageous group called the **Madres de Plaza de Mayo** (see box, p.91), to bring the issue of the *desaparecidos* to international attention. The Madres of the Plaza de Mayo were one of the few groups to challenge the regime directly, organizing weekly demonstrations in Buenos Aires' central square. Their protests continued until January 2006, when their leader said that they no longer had an enemy in the Casa Rosada.

A slight softening of Videla's extremist stance came when **General Roberto Viola** took control of the army in 1978 and then the presidency of the junta in 1981, but he was forced out later the same year by hardliners under **General Leopoldo Galtieri**. The military's grip on the country, by this time, was nonetheless increasingly shaky, with the economy in recession, skyrocketing interest rates and the first mass demonstrations against the regime since its imposition in 1976. Galtieri, with no other cards left to play, chose April 2, 1982 to play his trump: **an**

A historical dispute: the Falkland Islands/Islas Malvinas

The islands known to the British as the **Falklands**, and to Argentines as **Las Malvinas,** lie some 12,500km from Britain and 550km off the coast of Argentina. Disputes have raged as to who first discovered them, but the first verifiable sighting comes from a Dutch sailor in 1600. In 1690, Captain John Strong discovered the strait that divides the two major islands in the group, and christened the archipelago the "Falkland Islands", after Viscount Falkland, the commissioner of the British Admiralty at the time.

French sailors from St Malo made numerous expeditions to the islands from 1698, naming them the **Iles Malouines**, from which derives the Argentine name "Malvinas". The first serious attempt at settlement came when a French expedition established a base at Port St Louis in 1764. A year later, claiming ignorance of the French settlement, a party of British sailors settled **Port Egmont**, and claimed the islands for George III. The Spanish also believed they had legal title to the area, dating from the 1494 papal treaty that divided the Americas between Spain and Portugal. Reluctant to come to blows with an ally, the French negotiated a settlement, and, in 1767, Port St Louis was surrendered to Spain. In 1774, the British were persuaded to abandon their colony (although not, they would later maintain, their claims to sovereignty).

In 1820, the newly independent Argentine federation asserted what it saw as its right to inherit the sovereign Spanish title to the islands. This was not, initially, contested by the British, but in the late 1820s Britain started to make noises about reasserting its sovereignty claim. The Argentine federation, paralysed by internal disputes, was powerless to prevent Britain from establishing a base on the islands, and its colony developed significantly after the founding, in 1851, of the **Falkland Islands Company** and with the beginnings of serious commercial exploitation such as sheep farming and whaling. By 1871, eight hundred people were living in Port Stanley.

In April 1982 General Galtieri saw the opportunity to divert attention away from his junta's failed policies (see p.600) by organizing a military campaign to "liberate" the islands. The British had been making preparations for the scrapping of its only naval presence in the South Atlantic, and Galtieri made a serious misjudgement in believing Britain would acquiesce in the face of an invasion. Following the arrival of a **British task force**, the conflict was short. The struggle was unequal: poorly equipped Argentine teenagers on military service were expected to combat professional paratroopers. In the worst atrocity of the war, the *General Belgrano* was torpedoed outside the British-imposed naval exclusion zone, leading to the death of hundreds – an event that is still viewed with considerable bitterness by many Argentines.

More than 900 people perished in the 74-day conflict, and negotiations on the sovereignty issue were set back decades. At the time of the invasion, the islands were essentially a forgotten British colony that had long suffered a dearth of development and were being gradually integrated into the Argentine economic sphere. This stopped abruptly with the war.

In some ways, old wounds are healing – in 2009, after years of wrangling, relatives of the Argentine war dead were allowed to visit the islands to dedicate a war memorial to their fallen. But in others, the issue of sovereignty remains a major obstacle. Britain says there can be no negotiations on sovereignty until the Falkland Islanders so wish and there are occasional flare-ups in rhetoric, such as when British exploration companies began drilling for oil in the Falklands waters in 2010. Both sides, however, insist that the countries are friendly and that any future moves will take place via diplomatic and peaceful channels.

invasion of the Falkland Islands, or Islas Malvinas as they are known to Argentines. Nothing could have been more certain to bring a sense of purpose to the nation, and the population reacted with delight. This, however, soon turned to dismay when people realized that the British government was prepared to go to war. The Argentine forces were defeated by mid-June (see box above).

The military had proved themselves incapable of mastering politics and disastrous stewards of the economy, and now they had suffered ignominious failure doing what they were supposed to be specialists at: fighting. Perhaps the only positive thing to come out of this futile war was that it was the final spur for Argentines to throw off the shackles of the regime. While the junta prepared to hand over to civilian control, **General Reynaldo Bignone**, successor to Galtieri, issued a decree that pronounced an amnesty for all members of the armed forces for any alleged human rights atrocity.

Alfonsín and the restoration of democracy

Democracy was restored with the elections of October 1983, won by the Radical **Raúl Alfonsín** – the first time in its four decades of existence that the Peronist party had been defeated at the polls. Alfonsín, a lawyer much respected for his record on human rights, inherited a precarious political panorama. He faced two great challenges: the first, to build some sort of national concord; and the second, to restore a shattered economy, where inflation was running at over 400 percent and the foreign debt was over US$40 billion. In the midst of this, he solved a politically sensitive border dispute with Chile over three islands in the Beagle Channel – **Picton, Nueva and Lennox**. Papal arbitration had awarded the islands to Chile, but Alfonsín ensured, in 1984, that a public referendum approved this.

The issue of prosecuting those responsible for crimes against humanity during the dictatorship proved an intractable one. Alfonsín set up a **National Commission on Disappeared People** (CONADEP), chaired by the respected writer Ernesto Sábato, to investigate the alleged atrocities. Their report, *Nunca Más* – or "Never Again" – documented nine thousand cases of torture and disappearance, although human rights groups believe the actual figure for the number of deaths during the Dirty War is closer to thirty thousand. It recommended that those responsible be brought to **trial**. Those convicted in the first wave of trials included the reviled Videla, Viola, Galtieri, and Admiral Emilio Massera, one of the most despised figures of the junta. All were sentenced to life imprisonment.

Military sensibilities were offended by the trials: defeat in the South Atlantic War had discredited them but they could still pose considerable danger to the fragile democracy and Alfonsín decided he couldn't risk full confrontation. In 1986, he caved in to military pressure and passed *Punto Final*, or "End Point", legislation, which put a final date for the submission of writs for human rights crimes. However, in a window of two months, the courts were flooded with such writs, and, for the first time, the courts indicted officers still in active service.

Several short-lived uprisings forced Alfonsín to pull back from pursuing widespread prosecutions. In 1987, the **Law of Due Obedience** (*Obediencia Debida*) was passed, granting an amnesty to all but the leaders for atrocities committed during the dictatorship. At a stroke, this reduced the number of people facing charges from 370 to fewer than fifty. This incensed the victims' relatives, who saw notorious Proceso torturers escape prosecution, including the "Angel of Death", **Alfredo Astiz**, who attained international notoriety for the brutal murder of two French nuns and a young girl.

Alfonsín managed to secure some respite regarding the economy by restructuring the national debt and, in 1985, introducing a platform of stringent austerity measures, which were angrily received by many sectors of the population. The government deemed measures – named the **Plan Austral** in reference to the new currency that was introduced – to be essential, with inflation running at over a thousand percent annually. The country continued to be crippled by **hyperinflation**, however, even after the introduction of a second raft of belt-tightening measures, the *australito*, in 1987. The inflationary crisis turned to meltdown in 1989, when the World Bank suspended all loans: many shops remained closed, preferring to keep their stock rather than selling it for a currency whose value disappeared before their eyes. In supermarkets, purchasers would have to listen to the tannoy to hear the latest prices, which would often change in the time it took to take an item from the shelf to the checkout. Elections took place in 1989, but, with severe **civil unrest** breaking out across the country, Alfonsín called a state of emergency and stood down several months early, handing control to his elected successor, **Carlos Saúl Menem**. This was the first time since 1928 that power had transferred, after a free election, from one civilian government to another.

Menem's Presidency: 1989–99

The 1990s were dominated by Peronist leader **Carlos Menem** – the son of Syrian immigrants – and were characterized by radical reforms and controversy. Menem had been governor of La Rioja at the outbreak of military rule in 1976 and he had spent most of the dictatorship in detention. His **Justicialist Party** (*Partido Justicialista* or PJ) was Peronist in name but – once elected in 1989 – he was to embark on a series of sweeping **neo-liberal reforms**.

His first major achievement was to destroy **inflation**. Backed by international finance organizations, Menem and his finance minister, **Domingo Cavallo**, introduced the Convertibility Plan (*Plan de Convertibilidad*), which pegged a new currency (the Argentine peso, worth 10,000 australes) at parity with the US dollar, and guaranteed its value by prohibiting the Central Bank from printing money it couldn't cover with federal reserves. Inflation fell to an annual rate of eight percent by 1993 and remained in single figures throughout the 1990s.

Menem also abandoned the Peronist principle of state ownership and the dogma of state intervention. His presidency saw the **privatization** of all the major utilities and industries: electricity, gas, telephones, Aerolíneas Argentinas and even the profitable YPF, the state-owned petroleum company, were sold off. Investment came primarily from European, mainly Spanish and French, corporations, and the sales often benefited individuals rather than the state. Free-market development policies also saw the cessation of all Federal railway subsidies in 1993 and the introduction of massive **public spending cuts**. In 1995, many regional trade barriers fell, as a consequence of the full implementation of the **Mercosur** trading agreement, creating a **free-trade block** of Southern Cone countries – Brazil, Argentina, Uruguay and Paraguay, with Chile and Venezuela developing close ties later on. Unemployment rates rocketed and acute financial hardship resulted in strikes and sporadic civil unrest, as more people fell beneath the bread line.

One thing about Menem's brand of Peronism that stayed faithful to the original was his style of government. A cavalier **populist**, Menem never stopped trying to develop the "cult of the leader". He modelled his image, mutton-chop sideburns and all, on that of provincial *caudillos* such as Facundo Quiroga, the La Rioja warlord of the 1830s. Not known for his modesty, he preached austerity while developing a penchant for the life of a playboy.

The president increasingly became associated with trying to rule by **decree**. One of the most controversial aspects of this policy was the issuing of executive amnesties in 1989 to those guilty of atrocities during the 1970s. Although the amnesty included ex-guerrillas, public outrage centred on the release of former members of the junta, including all the leading generals. To Menem it was the pragmatic price to pay to secure the military's cooperation; to virtually all the rest of the country, it was a flagrant moral capitulation. His apparent failure to launch a serious investigation into two terrorist attacks that targeted the **Jewish community** in 1992 and 1994 (see box, p.96) also showed him in a very poor light.

In August 1994, he secured a **constitutional amendment** that allowed a sitting president to stand for a second term, though the mandate was reduced from six years to four. The voters, trusting Menem's economic record, elected him to a second term the following year.

Human rights issues continued to surface. One of the most important developments was the start of a campaign to prosecute those guilty of having "**kidnapped**" babies of *desaparecidos* born in detention, in order to give them up for adoption to childless military couples. Recognition of this crime, not covered by Alfonsín's Punto Final legislation, resulted in the successful interrogation and detention of many leading members of the old junta, including Videla and Massera. In the mid-1990s, the armed forces acknowledged their role in the atrocities of the dictatorship, making a **public apology** – a symbolic act that was followed by similar repentance by the Catholic Church.

Austerity measures seemed to apply to anyone not in government, and foreign debt continued to balloon. When, at the beginning of 1999, Brazil's currency lost half of its value, the government had to resist acute pressure to devalue the peso. Convertibility held, but Menem announced that Argentina ought seriously to consider the "**dollarization**" of the economy – an issue that would have had severe ramifications on national pride.

As the end of his second term approached, Menem mooted the possibility of running for a third consecutive term of office, shenanigans which helped alienate the populace from his Justicialist Party and contributed to the defeat of its eventual candidate, Eduardo Duhalde, in 1999. Duhalde was emphatically beaten by **Fernando De la Rúa**, the Córdoba-born mayor of the city of Buenos Aires, who headed up the **Alianza**, a coalition of the Radicals (UCR), of which he was leader, and **FREPASO**, itself a coalition party of left-wingers and disaffected Peronists.

The De la Rúa government: hope followed by disaster

Known for his stolid reliability rather than his charisma – he admitted to being as dull as ditch water – De la Rúa was a complete contrast to his predecessor. On taking office in 1999 he seemed to represent the **fiscal and moral probity** that Argentines, tired of the excesses of the Menem administration, felt their country – already starting to show signs of its worst-ever recession – needed. Once in charge, though, the Alianza coalition was hit by severe infighting, and public spending cuts forced by economic strictures led to large-scale demonstrations.

By early 2001, De la Rúa had already appointed his third finance minister – bringing back Domingo Cavallo. Menem's erstwhile finance minister announced an unrealistic "zero deficit" drive to meet stiff IMF targets and protect convertibility, but the country still wasn't pulling out of recession, with industrial production and exports dismally low owing to the phoney exchange rate, unemployment rising rapidly and financial confidence on the wane. Then, in the national elections of October 2001, the Peronists gained control of both houses of Congress. Soon afterwards private depositors began to pull their money out of banks, afraid the peso-dollar peg would be abolished. Under severe pressure to abandon convertibility and devalue the peso, Cavallo stood firm. In early December 2001, in a desperate bid to avoid devaluation and stop the cash drain from banks, he announced restrictions severely limiting access to private deposits, including salaries. This measure, known as the **corralito**, or "playpen", riled Argentines of all classes, though the wealthiest managed to get their money out in dollars and into accounts abroad. To cap it all, shortly afterwards, the IMF announced the withdrawal of support on grounds of lack of confidence that Argentina could meet its targets.

On December 13, a general strike was staged against the *corralito* by the Peronist-controlled unions and acts of looting were reported in Greater Buenos Aires, a Peronist bastion. Despite De la Rúa's announcement of a state of emergency to deal with the crisis, on the evening of December 19 tens of thousands of protestors bashing pots and pans (the first of many noisy "**cacerolazos**", or saucepan protests) marched on the Plaza de Mayo. Although the police dispersed the huge crowd, more demonstrations took place the following day. De la Rúa found himself politically isolated, while brutal police efforts to clear the Plaza de Mayo and halt **demonstrations** in other cities ended in a bloodbath, with at least 25 people dead nationwide. De la Rúa left office ignominiously, fleeing the Casa Rosada by helicopter.

The interregnum

After a series of farcical, short-lived appointments, Congress finally opted for **Eduardo Duhalde**, the former Peronist presidential candidate defeated by De la Rúa in 1999, who was sworn in on January 1, 2002. He heavily **devalued the peso** within days and then spent most of the year trying to negotiate a new agreement with the IMF to avoid a humiliating default with international lending agencies. After militant jobless groups known as *piqueteros* (see box below) clashed with police, leaving two people dead, in June 2002 he announced early **presidential elections** at some time in 2003, promising that he and his colleagues would not stand for office.

Piqueteros and cartoneros – the tougher side of Argentine life

Piqueteros – "picketers" – came to prominence in the late 1990s and especially around the time of the 2001 crisis, staging often violent protests outside the houses of former junta members or banks and businesses, blockading roads and major access points to cities, in order to draw attention to social injustices such as job losses, poor working conditions or hospital closures. They've become a feature of Argentine life, with some pickets being organized on the spur of the moment in response to specific grievances, and other groups being linked to political movements – mainstream or otherwise.

A new phenomenon for the new millennium, the **cartonero**, is now a common sight on the streets of the capital. *Cartoneros* are poor people who effectively act as semi-official refuse recyclers. They rummage through garbage bags, salvaging paper and cardboard to sell for scrap value. The sight of whole families, including young children, sorting out rubbish on the city pavements, does not exactly make for a good image and is an ongoing challenge faced by the authorities.

Once the worst of the crisis had subsided, Duhalde's unflappable finance minister, **Roberto Lavagna**, was credited with calming financial markets, avoiding hyperinflation and stabilizing the US dollar exchange rate at just over three pesos, after a peak of nearly four. He also reached a short-term agreement with the IMF and, by early 2003, signs of economic recovery – in particular, increased exports – began to show. The downside to this was a **sharp rise in poverty** across the country, as the price of basic products and imports soared.

The Peronists failed to unite ahead of the 2003 elections, and warring factions fielded three separate contenders: former presidents Menem and Rodríguez Saá (who'd been head of state for only a matter of days at the height of the 2001 crisis) and Duhalde's protégé, **Néstor Kirchner**, who enjoyed a narrow lead in opinion polls. Memories of the disastrous De la Rúa administration meant that none of the opposition parties seemed likely to oust the Peronists from power. In the event, **Menem** came first, with just under a quarter of the vote, with Kirchner going through to the second round, only a couple of percentage points behind. But, as the runoff approached, opinion polls unanimously suggested that only three voters in ten would back Menem – who withdrew from the race to avoid a crushing defeat and, it was said, to deprive Kirchner of an overwhelming mandate.

Kirchner: into the new millennium

The omens weren't auspicious when Néstor Kirchner took power. The political and economic situation he inherited was still grave. And few had real confidence that Kirchner – a lacklustre public speaker who had previously been the governor of the relatively uninfluential province of Santa Cruz – had the skills or support to instigate a real recovery. However, against the odds, he grew to be a surprisingly powerful force in Argentine politics. Since 2003, he and his wife, **Cristina Fernández de Kirchner** (see box, p.608), have come to dominate the country to an extent that some Argentines talk of a "penguin" takeover. Kirchner, often known simply as **"K"** – easier on the tongue than his Swiss–German surname – is nicknamed "Pingüino", both for his bird-like appearance and his Patagonian origins.

Kirchner emerged as one of a new generation of left-leaning **South American leaders**, set on forging regional independence and interdependence, strengthening

The 2010 bicentennial

On May 25, 1810, locals gathered in Buenos Aires' Plaza de Mayo to demand the withdrawal of the Spanish viceroy and to form the **Primera Junta**, the first move in throwing off the yoke of Spanish rule and creating an independent nation.

In 1910, the centennial anniversary was cause for great celebration. In its first hundred years Argentina had gone from being a fairly small colonial backwater to one of the world's richest countries, still in the throes of an unprecedented immigration and building boom, bursting with confidence, and destined for great things on the world stage. Several foreign nations gifted statues and other monuments, many of which are still standing in Buenos Aires, including the Torre Monumental (Britain; see p.111) and the Monumento de los Españoles (Spain; see p.126).

A century further on, Argentina hasn't exactly lived up to that heady promise. Nevertheless, the bicentenary will see grand celebrations throughout the country, along with – doubtlessly – endless reflection. For more information see @www .bicentenario.gov.ar.

Mercosur, limiting the influence of multinationals, defying the IMF and largely thumbing his nose at Washington.

He oversaw an astonishing revival in the Argentine economy. The devalued peso provided a platform for Argentina's export sector to flourish, and from 2003, the country registered one of the world's highest **GDP growth rates** (averaging over eight percent a year through to 2007). The hard-nosed Kirchner hammered out favourable settlements with the majority of Argentina's international creditors, and succeeded in paying back the IMF billions of dollars in defaulted loans. Joblessness figures started to drop, dipping below ten percent for the first time in a decade in 2007. Argentina also had a string of record years for **international tourism**, matched with huge numbers of Argentine holiday-makers forced to discover their own country due to the newly unfavourable exchange rate.

As tax revenues swelled, Kirchner – who describes himself as an opponent of neoliberal capitalism – was able to honour many of his election pledges, namely to reverse years of spending cuts in the education, welfare and public-service sectors. Acute **poverty** was reduced, although it remains widespread – witness, for example, the *cartoneros* on the streets of the capital (see box, p.605). Skilful macroeconomic management was certainly a factor, but the government was also lucky as, for example, commodity and agriculture prices (especially **soya**) reached all-time highs.

All of this helped make Kirchner the most popular resident of the Casa Rosada for years, with an approval rating at times as high as eighty percent. A man seldom seen in a suit and tie, he was initially seen as down-to-earth, although the presidential couple was criticized for making too many flights to their home base of Santa Cruz in the official presidential jet. Further criticism was levelled at him from within his own, still-divided Peronist party, not least because he never mentioned the Peróns by name. His response was that he focuses on the social justice aspect of **justicialismo**, rather than looking to specific personalities and the past. He also risked the wrath of sections of his party, as well as the military, by repealing the **amnesty laws** that had made it impossible to prosecute members of the military regime who had committed human rights atrocities. Moreover, he closed the **Escuela Mecánica de la Armada** (Navy Mechanics School) so it could be turned into a monument to the dictatorship, and excluded some Peronist politicians with a dubious past from a memorial ceremony for the disappeared.

However, not all was plain sailing. The government faced an upsurge in the number of violent **crimes** in the capital and other large cities – some of them directly involving corrupt police officers. Critics accused the government of massaging inflation figures, via the state statistical office, **INDEC**. And a couple of high profile financial scandals hit his administration in 2007: a finance minister had to resign after a stash of cash was found in the toilet next to her office (she claimed it was a loan from her brother to buy a house); and a Venezuelan businessman who had arrived on a plane chartered by the Argentine government was stopped by Argentine customs carrying a suitcase of US$800,000 in undeclared money (opponents alleged it was from Hugo Chávez's government, destined to help Kirchner election funds – something both the Argentine and Venezuelan government denied).

Nevertheless, Kirchner's term was seen as a success. Rather than running for a second term in 2007, he stepped aside for his wife, **Cristina Fernández de Kirchner** (see box, p.608) to run as the candidate of their Frente para la Victoria (Victory Front, or FPV). She swept to a resounding victory in the first round of the presidential election.

Cristina Fernández de Kirchner

Cristina Fernández de Kirchner – commonly known simply as Cristina – has become Argentina's most high-profile female politician since Evita. She was born in 1953 in La Plata, and began a career of political activism while studying law there in the 1970s. She met Néstor Kirchner through politics, and after they married, moved to his native **Santa Cruz Province**, where they practised law and began their political careers. She served several terms as a representative of Santa Cruz province in the national Congress; and then as a senator for the province of Buenos Aires. In 2003, she became the country's First Lady – or, as she preferred it, "First Female Citizen". Glamorous and extremely photogenic, she has a forthright manner and a sharp tongue – in the early years of her husband's presidency she famously scowled (rather than smiled) at cameras.

Her popularity with the working classes and her high-profile **ambassadorial trips** to Europe and the US – together with a fashionable wardrobe – led to inevitable comparisons with **Evita**. She famously said in a newspaper interview – perhaps tongue-in-cheek – that she would replace Evita in history because she is both more intelligent and more beautiful. She has taken a firm and progressive stand on issues such as human rights (especially justice for the victims of the dictatorship), equality, combating anti-Semitism and the need for Latin America to assert itself on the world stage.

As for the comparisons with Evita, more serious observers tend to liken her instead to **Hillary Clinton** – another clever, tough politician not afraid to make enemies. But in another press interview Cristina dismissed that too, saying that Hillary only became a force in national politics because she was married to Bill. She, on the other hand, is very much her own boss. And, unlike Hillary, she won her tilt at the top job.

Fernández de Kirchner's administration has been involved in a series of bruising political battles. In 2008, she was forced to back down in a major dispute with farmers over attempts to raise export taxes on agricultural produce. Her administration successfully expropriated US$26 billion in private pension funds, to the consternation of foreign investors. And in 2009, she managed to drive legislation through Congress that aimed to encourage plurality of the media, although opponents – above all voices in the powerful *Clarín* media group – fought the legislation, maintaining that it was an attack on the free media that aimed to stifle legitimate dissent.

Although Latin America was not as hard hit by the global recession of 2009 as many countries, it has not been entirely unscathed – Argentina's economy grew less than one percent in 2009. Suddenly, Argentina was once again faced with the prospect of raising money on skeptical international financial markets to keep levels of public spending high – the same markets that had been burned by Argentina's massive debt default during the 2001 crisis.

The Kirchners suffered defeat in the mid-term elections of 2009, with their governing coalition losing its majority in both houses of Congress. Néstor Kirchner failed in his attempt to be elected as a member of the lower house of the national Congress for Buenos Aires Province, and stood down as Justicialist party leader.

The Kirchner gloss seems to be wearing thin with some sectors of society. They face allegations of nepotism – Néstor's sister has been a minister in both administrations – and questions have been raised over the extent to which the Kirchners' personal declared assets have risen since they've been in power.

When Néstor stood aside in 2007, it was generally assumed he would run again for the presidency at the end of his wife's term in 2011, and that he would stand a good chance of winning. That prospect no longer seems so certain, even if it's still far too early to write off Argentina's governing double-act.

Environment and wildlife

Argentina's natural wonders are some of its chief joys. Its remarkable diversity of habitats, ranging from subtropical jungles to sub-antarctic icesheets, is complemented by an unexpected juxtaposition of species: parrots foraging alongside glaciers, or flamingoes surviving bitter sub-zero temperatures on the stark Andean altiplano. Though the divisions are too complicated to list fully here, we've covered Argentina's most distinctive habitats, along with the species of flora and fauna typical to each.

Despite the protection afforded by a relatively well-managed national park system, the country's precious environmental heritage remains under threat. As ever, by far and away the most pressing issue is **habitat loss**. The chaco is a good case in point. Previously, the lack of water in the *Impenetrable* was the flora and fauna's best asset. Nowadays, climate change has seen rainfall levels increase, and irrigation projects are fast opening up areas to settlement and agriculture, with a poorly controlled exploitation of mature woodland for timber or charcoal and **land clearance** (*desmonte*) for crops such as cotton. Forestry in other areas of the country – notably Misiones and Tierra del Fuego – is worrying as well, although the provincial government in Misiones is making efforts to protect its threatened Paraná forest – a habitat that's been decimated over the border in Brazil and Paraguay. **Hydroelectric projects** in the northeast have destroyed valuable habitats along the Uruguay and Paraná rivers, and **overfishing** has also severely depleted stocks in the latter. The phenomenal rise of **genetically modified soya** production in Argentina has also alarmed environmental campaigners. While genetic modification does not provoke the same "Frankenstein food" outcry as in Europe, there is concern about the effects of monoculture on the country's biodiversity.

That said, **environmental consciousness** is slowly gaining ground (especially among the younger generation). Greenpeace is self-financing in Argentina, with thousands of paying members; the national parks system is expanding with the help of international loans; and committed national and local pressure groups such as the Fundación de Vida Silvestre and Asociación Ornitológica del Plata (both based in Buenos Aires) and Fundación Orca (based in Puerto Madryn) are ensuring that ecological issues are not ignored.

Pampas grassland and the espinal

The vast alluvial plain that centres on Buenos Aires Province and radiates out into eastern Córdoba, southern Santa Fe and northeast La Pampa provinces was once pampas grassland, famous for its clumps of brush-tailed *cortadera* grass. However, its deep, extremely fertile soil has seen it become the agricultural heart of modern Argentina, and this original habitat has almost entirely disappeared, transformed by cattle grazing and intensive arable farming. It's still possible to find a few vestiges of marshlands and grasslands, such as the area of tall *stipa* grassland around Médanos, southwest of Bahía Blanca.

Once, these plains were the home of **pampas deer** (*venado de las pampas*), but today only a few hundred individuals survive, mainly in Samborombón and Campos del Tuyú in Buenos Aires Province. The deer is easily identified by its three-pronged antler. The **coypu** (*coipo*) is a large rodent commonly found in the region's wetlands, especially in places like the Paraná Delta. The great vizcacha dens (*vizcacheras*) described in the nineteenth century by famous natural history writer W.H. Hudson have all but disappeared, but you may see an endemic bird named after the writer, Hudson's Canastero, along with **Greater Rheas**, **Burrowing Parrots** (*loro barranquero*), and **Ovenbirds** (*horneros*). Named after the domed, concrete-hard mud nests they build on posts, Ovenbirds have always been held in great affection by gauchos and country folk.

Bordering the pampas to the north and west, across the centre of Corrientes, Entre Ríos, Santa Fe, Córdoba and San Luis provinces, is a semicircular fringe of **espinal woodland**, a type of open wooded "parkland". Common species of tree include **acacia** and, in the north, the **ceibo**, Argentina's national tree, which in spring produces a profusion of scarlet blooms.

A habitat found only in Argentina is the so-called **monte scrub** from the arid intermontane valleys that lie in the rainshadow of the central Andes. It runs from northern Patagonia through the Cuyo region and as far north as Salta Province, and is best seen in La Rioja's Talampaya national park. Monte scrub is characterized by thorny *jarilla* bushes, which flower yellow in spring. In the Andean foothills and floodplains of the Mendoza region, much desert monte has been irrigated and replaced with vineyards.

Mesopotamian grassland

The humid Mesopotamian grasslands extend across much of Corrientes and Entre Ríos provinces and into southernmost Misiones. Here you will find *yatay* palm savannah and some of Argentina's most important **wetlands**, most notably the Esteros de Iberá and the Parque Nacional Mburucuyá, which make for some of the country's most productive nature safaris.

The wetlands have a remarkable diversity of birdlife, including numerous species of ducks, rails, ibises and herons. Some of the most distinctive species are the **Wattled Jacana** (*jacana*); the **Southern Screamer** (*chajá*), a hulking bird the size of a turkey; the **Scarlet-headed Blackbird** (*federal*); **Roseate Spoonbills** (*espátula rosada*); the **Rufescent Tiger Heron** (*hocó colorado*); and **Jabirus** (*yabirú*), the largest variety of stork, measuring almost 1.5m tall, with a bald head and shoe-horn bill. Up above fly **Snail Kites** (*caracoleros*), which use their bills to prise freshwater snails from their shells.

In the shallow swamps, among reedbeds and long grasses, you will find the **marsh deer** (*ciervo de los pantanos*), South America's largest native deer, with multi-horned antlers. One of the most common wetland animals is the **capybara** (*carpincho*), the world's biggest rodent, weighing up to 50kg. **Reptiles** include the **black cayman** (*yacaré negro*), which grows up to 2.8m in length, and is the victim of illegal hunting; and snakes like the *lampalagua* **boa** (up to 5m in length) and the *curiyú* **yellow anaconda** (which can grow over 3m), both of which are non-poisonous, killing their prey by constriction.

Subtropical Paraná forest

Subtropical Paraná forest (*Selva Paranaense*) is Argentina's most biologically diverse ecosystem, a dense mass of vegetation that conforms to most people's idea of a jungle. The most frequently visited area of Paraná forest is Parque Nacional

Iguazú, but it is also found in patches across the rest of Misiones, and parts of northeast Corrientes. It has over two hundred tree species, including the **palo rosa** (one of the highest canopy species, at up to 40m); the **strangler fig** (*higuerón bravo*); the **lapacho**, with its beautiful pink flowers; and the **Misiones cedar** (*cedro misionero*), a fine hardwood species that has suffered heavily from logging. Upland areas along the Brazilian border still preserve stands of **Paraná pine**, a type of rare araucaria monkey puzzle related to the more famous species found in northern Patagonia. Lower storeys of vegetation include the wild **yerba mate** tree, first cultivated by the Jesuits in the seventeenth century; the **palmito** palm, whose edible core is exploited as palm heart; and endangered prehistoric **tree ferns**. Festooning the forest are lianas, mosses, ferns and epiphytes, including several hundred varieties of **orchid**.

More than five hundred species of bird inhabit the Paraná forest, and you stand a good chance of seeing the **Toco Toucan** (*tucán grande*), with its bright orange bill. Rarities include the magnificent **Harpy Eagle** (*harpía*) and the **Bare-faced Curassow** (*muitú*).

This part of the country is one of the few places you just might see the highly endangered **jaguar** (*yaguareté* or *tigre*). Weighing up to 160kg, this beast is the continent's most fearsome predator. The beautiful **ocelot** (*gato onza*) is similarly elusive and almost as endangered, having suffered massive hunting for its pelt during the 1970s.

The wet chaco

The habitat described as wet chaco is found in the eastern third of Chaco and Formosa provinces and the northeast of Santa Fe. It consists of small patches of gallery forest (not unlike the Paraná forest) growing by rivers and ox-bow lakes; savannah grasslands studded with *caranday* palms; "islands" of mixed scrub woodland (*isletas de monte*); and wetland environments similar to the Mesopotamian grasslands. The key tree species is the **quebracho colorado chaqueño**, one of Argentina's four *quebracho* species, whose name means "axe-breaker" in Spanish, though it has always been valued more for its tannin than for its hard wood. It can reach the height of 24m, and the most venerable specimens can be anything from 300 to 500 years old. Another common tree species is the intriguing **crown of thorns** (*espina corona*), with dramatic spikes jutting out from its trunk. On the savannahs, graceful **caranday** palms (*palmares*) reach heights of up to 15m. They are extremely resilient, surviving both flooding and the regular burning of the grasslands to stimulate new growth for cattle pasture.

The wetland swamps are often choked with rafts of **camalote**, a waterlily with a lilac flower, or with the large pads of another distinctive waterlily, the *flor de Irupé*, whose name comes from the Guaraní word for "plate on the water".

The birdlife of the wet chaco is similar to that of the Mesopotamian swamps. You're likely to see the **Greater Rhea** (called *suri* in this region); **Fork-tailed Flycatchers** (*tijereta*); **Monk Parakeets** (*cotorras*), which build huge communal nests in *caranday* palms; **Red-legged Seriemas** (*chuña de patas rojas*), long-legged roadrunner-type birds; and two birds that are trapped for the pet trade – the **Red-crested Cardinal** (*cardenal común*), and the **Turquoise-fronted Amazon** (*loro hablador*), an accomplished ventriloquist parrot.

One of the most beautiful, and rarest, animals in the wet chaco is the solitary, nocturnal **maned wolf** (*aguará guazú*). To this day it is persecuted for fear that it's a werewolf (*lobizón*), and the legend that its glance can kill a chicken hardly endears it to farmers. The coppery auburn beast, standing almost a metre tall, actually eats birds' eggs, armadillos, rodents and fruit. A curious-looking denizen of the region is the **giant anteater** (*oso hormiguero*). It has poor eyesight, but its sense of smell is forty times better than humans'. It breaks open termite mounds with its claws, and scours them out with its tongue. In the trees you may see **black howler monkeys** (*carayá* or *mono aullador negro*), one of South America's biggest primates; the black-capped or **tufted capuchin** (*caí*); and the tiny, endangered **mirikiná** (*mono de noche*), the world's only nocturnal monkey.

The dry chaco

The dry chaco refers to the parched plain of thorn scrub that covers most of central and western Chaco and Formosa provinces, northeastern Salta and much of Santiago del Estero. To early explorers and settlers, much of this area was known simply as the **Impenetrable** for its aridity. The habitat was once more varied, but deforestation and the introduction of cattle have standardized the vegetation. Everything, it seems, is defensive: the *vinal* shrub, for instance, is dreaded by riders for its brutal spikes, up to 20cm long. In places, there is a dense undergrowth of **chaguar** and **caraguatá**: robust, yucca-like plants that the Wichí process to make fibre for their *yica* bags.

The tallest trees in the dry chaco are the *quebrachos*, notably the **quebracho colorado santiagueño**, exploited for tannin. Several other species also reach imposing heights, such as the two types of **carob tree**, the *algarrobo blanco* and *algarrobo negro*. Perhaps the hardest wood is that of the endangered, slow-growing **palo santo** (meaning "holy stick"). Its fragrant, green-tinged wood can be burnt as an insect repellent. Finally, the **palo borracho** (or *yuchán*) is the most distinctive tree of all, with a bulbous, porous trunk to store water; the tree protects itself, especially when young, with rhino-horned spikes.

Commonly associated with dry-chaco habitat are birds like the **Black-legged Seriema** (*chuña de patas negras*); and the noisy **Chaco Chachalaca** (*charata*). The dry chaco is home to forty percent of Argentina's mammal species. An estimated two hundred **jaguars** hang on here. Less threatened are the **puma** and the **Geoffroy's cat** (*gato montés*). One of three species of native Argentine wild pig, the famous **Chacoan peccary** (*chancho quimilero*) was thought to be extinct until rediscovered in Paraguay in 1975, and later in a few isolated areas of the Argentine dry chaco. Another high-profile living fossil is the nocturnal **giant armadillo** (*tatú carreta*). Weighing as much as 60kg, a full-grown one is strong enough to carry a man.

The yungas

Yungas is the term applied to the subtropical band of the Argentine Northwest that lies between the chaco and the Andean precordillera, from the Bolivian border through Jujuy, Salta, Tucumán and into Catamarca. Abrupt changes of altitude give rise to radical changes in the flora here, creating wildly different ecosystems. All are characterized by fairly high year-round precipitation, but have distinct seasons, with winter being drier. The lowest altitudes are home to transitional woodland and lowland jungle (*selva pedemontana*), up to about 600m. Most of the trees and shrubs in these lower levels are deciduous and have showy blossoms: jacaranda, *palo blanco* and *amarillo*, *lapacho* and the **ceibo**. Much of this forest has been hard hit by clearance.

Above 600m starts the most famous *yungas* habitat, the **montane cloud-forests** (*selva montaña* or *nuboselva*), best seen in the national parks of Calilegua, Baritú and El Rey. The *selva montaña* is split into two categories, with true cloudforest growing in the altitude band from 1000m to 2200m. These forests form a gloomy canopy of tall evergreens – dominated by laurels and acacia-like tipas at lower levels, and *yunga* cedars, *horco molle*, *nogal* and myrtles higher up – beneath which several varieties of cane and bamboo compete for sunlight. The tree trunks are covered in moss and lichen; lianas hang in a tangle; epiphytes and orchids flourish; and bromeliads, heliconias and succulents all add to the dank atmosphere.

More than three hundred varieties of **bird** inhabit the *yungas* forests. Species include the **Toco Toucan**; the rare **Black-and-chestnut Eagle** (*águila poma*); the **King Vulture** (*jote real*), with a strikingly patterned head; **Red-faced Guans** (*pava de monte común*); numerous varieties of **hummingbird**; **Mitred** and **Green-cheeked parakeets** (*loro de cara roja* and *chiripepé de cabeza gris* respectively); and the **Torrent Duck** (*pato de los torrentes*).

Like the flora, the **fauna** in the *yungas* changes with altitude. The streams are favourite haunts of crab-eating **raccoons** (called *mayuatos* here). Other mammals found close to the water include South America's largest native terrestrial mammal, the **Brazilian tapir** (*tapir*, *anta* or *mboreví*). The strange **tree-porcupine** (*coendú*) clambers around the canopy with the help of its tail, while the **three-toed sloth** (*perezoso*) depends on its sabre-like claws for locomotion. Felines are represented by **jaguars**, **margays**, **pumas** and **Geoffroy's cats**, but you will be lucky to see anything other than their tracks. This also applies to the most famous regional creature of all: the **taruca**, a stocky native Andean deer. Traditionally hunted by locals, it was brought to the brink of extinction in Argentina and is now one of only three animals protected by the status of Natural Monument. It grazes in small herds just below the tree line in winter, and on high rocky pastures such as those above Calilegua in summer.

The puna

The pre-*puna* and higher **puna** of the Andean Northwest encompass harsh, arid habitats that range from *cardón* cactus valleys to bleak altiplanic vegetation. Pre-*puna* habitat usually refers to the sparsely vegetated rocky gullies and highland meadows (*prados*) of the cordillera, and is found at altitudes of 2000m to 3500m. The most distinctive Pre-*puna* plant is the **cardón cactus** (also called *pasakán*), which indigenous folklore holds to be the reincarnated form of ancestors.

The *puna* is found above 3400m, and is characterized by spongy wetlands (*bofedales*) around shallow high-mountain lagoons and sun-scorched flat altiplano pastures. On the higher slopes, you'll find a type of rock-hard cushion-shaped prehistoric moss called **yacreta** that grows incredibly slowly – perhaps a millimetre a year – but lives for hundreds of years. It has been heavily exploited – partly for medicinal teas, but mainly because it is the only fuel found at these altitudes.

Of the fauna, birds are the most prolific; you can see all three varieties of **flamingo** – Andean, Chilean and James' – wading or flying together, especially on the banks of Laguna de los Pozuelos. The Lesser Rhea (*ñandú petizo*, *choique* or *suri*), a flightless bird, is shy and will sprint away from you. Look out for **Giant Coots** (*gallareta gigante*) and its rare relative, the **Horned Coot** (*gallareta cornuda*), **Puna**

Plovers (*chorlito puñeno*), **Andean Geese** (*guayata*), **Andean Lapwings** (*tero serrano*), and all kinds of grebes, teals and ducks.

The animals most people associate with the Andean *puna* are the four species of South American camelids, especially the **llama**, a domesticated species. The local people use llamas as beasts of burden, as well as for meat and wool. The other domesticated camelid is the slightly smaller **alpaca**, which produces finer wool. You're only likely to see them in the Antofagasta de la Sierra area.

The two other South American camelids are both wild. The short-haired antelope-like **guanaco** inhabits a wide area, from the northwest *puna* to the mountains and steppe of Tierra del Fuego. Listen for their eerie, rasping call. The guanaco population is still relatively healthy, although it is hunted for its meat and skin. The guanaco's diminutive cousin, the **vicuña**, is the most graceful, shy and – despite its appearance – hardy of the four camelids, capable of living at the most extreme altitudes. It's usually found between 3500m and 4600m, as far south as northern San Juan Province, although the biggest flocks are in Catamarca Province. Hunting brought them to the brink of extinction, but protection measures have helped ensure that their numbers have risen to safe levels. This has allowed a carefully monitored experiment in Jujuy's Valle Calchaquíes, whereby their valuable fur (the second finest natural fibre in the world after silk) is exploited on a sustainable commercial level.

Other mammals spotted in the *puna* include **vizcachas**, looking like large rabbits with long, curly tails; and – if you're lucky – **pumas**, which have an extensive range in Argentina but are rarely seen.

Patagonian steppe

Typified by brush scrub and wiry *coirón* grassland, the Patagonian steppe (*estepa*) covers the greatest extent of any Argentine ecosystem. This vast expanse of semi-desert lies south of the pampas and east of the Andean cordillera. Vegetation is stunted by gravelly soils, high winds and lack of water, except along rivers, where you find marshlands (*mallines*) and startlingly green willows (*sauces*). Just about the only trees, apart from the willows, are non-native Lombardy poplars, planted to shelter estancias.

Much of the scrubby brush is composed of monochrome *mata negra*, but in places you'll come across the resinous, perfumed *mata verde*, or the ash-grey *mata guanaco*, which blooms with dazzling orange flowers. You'll also see spiky **calafate** bushes, and *molle* – one of the largest bushes, covered with thorns and parasitic galls.

Your best chance of sighting some of the steppe's key species is in places such as Chubut's Península Valdés and Punta Tombo. **Guanacos** abound here. Look out too for the **mara** (Patagonian hare), the largest of Argentina's endemic mammals. This long-legged rodent, the size of a small dog, is becoming ever rarer. The **grey fox** (*zorro gris*) is regularly found around national park gates, waiting for scraps thrown by tourists. *Pichi* and *peludo* **armadillos** are often seen scampering across the plains. More regularly, they are spotted at the side of the road, being eaten by scavengers like the **Southern Crested Caracara** (*carancho*) or a **Chimango Caracara** (*chimango*).

Another characteristic bird of prey is the Black-chested Buzzard-Eagle (*águila mora*), a powerful flier with broad wings and splendid plumage. The classic bird of the steppe, though, is the Lesser or Darwin's Rhea (*ñandú petiso* or *choique*). These ashy-grey birds lay their eggs in communal clutches. The Patagonian **Sierra Finch** (*fríngilo patagónico*) is an attractive yellow and slate-grey bird often found near humans, as is the **Rufous-collared Sparrow** (*chingolo*). On lagoons and lakes, you'll find the **Black-necked Swan** (*cisne de cuello negro*). Also look out for **Chilean Flamingoes**; the endangered **Hooded Grebe** (*macá tobiano*), endemic to Santa Cruz; the **Great Grebe** (*huala*); four types of *chorlito* seedsnipes; **Upland Geese** (*cauquén* or *avutarda*), which migrate as far north as Buenos Aires Province; **Buff-necked Ibises** (*bandurrias*), ambling around in small bands, honking, as they probe wetland pastures with their curved bills; and the **Southern Lapwing** (*tero*), a bird that mates for life and whose plaintive cries and insistent warning shrieks will be familiar to trekkers.

Patagonian cordillera forests

The eastern slopes of the Patagonian cordillera are cloaked in forests of **Nothofagus southern beech**. Two species run from northern Neuquén to Tierra del Fuego: the **lenga** (upland beech) and the **ñire** (lowland or antarctic beech). In autumn both species turn a variety of hues. Associated with *lenga* and *ñire* are three intriguing plant species: false mistletoe (*farolito chino*), a semi-parasitic plant; verdigris-coloured **lichen beards** (*barba del indio* or *toalla del indio*); and **llao llao** tree fungus, also called *pan de indio* ("Indian's bread"). The *llao llao* produces brain-like knots on trunks and branches that are beloved of local artisans.

The next most prominent tree species are two related evergreen beeches, the **coihue** and the **guindo**, found mainly in Tierra del Fuego. Both have fairly smooth bark and laurel-green leaves and grow only in damp zones near lakes or, in Tierra del Fuego, by the shores of the Beagle Channel.

One of Argentina's most remarkable trees, the **araucaria monkey puzzle**, grows in central Neuquén on volcanic soils. But the most diverse type of forest in the region is the rare **Valdivian temperate rainforest** (*selva Valdiviana*), found in patches of the central Patagonian Andes from Lanín to Los Alerces, usually around low passes where rainfall is heaviest. Another tree species found only in the central Patagonian Lake District is the mighty **alerce**, or Patagonian cypress, which resembles a Californian redwood and is one of the world's oldest and grandest species.

The understorey of the forests is dominated in most places by dense thickets of a bamboo-like plant, **caña colihue**. The most stunning shrub, if you catch it in bloom (late spring or autumn), is the **notro firebush** (or *ciruelillo*). Of forest flowers, two of the most brightly coloured are the **amancay**, a golden-orange lily, and the yellow **lady's slipper** (*zapatilla de la Virgen*), whose blooms bob on delicate stems in spring.

Many of the birds that inhabit the steppe are also found in the cordillera. Typical woodland species include the world's most southerly parrot, the **Austral Parakeet** (*cachaña* or *cotorra*); the **Green-backed Firecrown** (*picaflor rubí*); the hyperactive **Thorn-tailed Rayadito**; and two birds that allow you to get surprisingly close – the **Magellanic Woodpecker** (*carpintero negro gigante*), and the **Austral Pygmy Owl** (*caburé*). Finally, if any bird has a claim to symbolizing South America, it's the **Andean Condor**. With eyesight eight times better than a human's, and the longest wingspan of any bird of prey, it's the undisputed lord of the skies from Venezuela to Tierra del Fuego. Until fairly recently, this imperious bird was poisoned and shot. It's now protected in Argentina, with a stable population.

The principal predator of cordillera mammals is the **puma**. Though chances are that a puma will sight you and make itself scarce well before you sight it, there are extremely infrequent cases of attacks on humans. In the highly unlikely event of being faced with an aggressive puma, do not run, but make yourself appear as big as possible, and, facing it at all times, back off slowly, shouting loudly.

Perhaps the most endangered creature is the **huemul** (see p.455), a thick-set native deer, of which fewer than two thousand remain. It is a relative of the *taruca* of the northwestern Andes, and has likewise been named a Natural Monument. Almost as endangered is the **pudú**, the world's smallest deer, measuring 40cm at the shoulder. It has small, single-pointed horns, and is difficult to spot, as it inhabits the dense undergrowth of the central cordillera forests.

Introduced species include the European **red deer** (*ciervo colorado*) and **wild boar** (*jabalí*), both of which have reached plague proportions in some parts of the central Lake District. The **beaver** (*castor*), introduced to Tierra del Fuego in an attempt to start a fur-farming industry, has had devastating effects on the environment. Year-round, no-limits hunting has been permitted to combat this public enemy. Other non-native species have had deleterious effects too: **muskrats** (*ratas almizcleras*); European **hares** (*liebres*) and **rabbits** (*conejos*); and the **mink** (*visón*), the principal threat to the southern river otter, or *hullin*.

The Atlantic seaboard

Argentina has 4725km of **Atlantic coastline**, comprising three main types of habitat. From the mouth of the estuary of the Río de la Plata to just south of Buenos Aires Province, the shoreline is mainly flat, fringed by dunes, sandy beaches and pampas grass. South of Viedma begin endless stretches of Patagonian cliffs (*barrancas*), broken in places by gulfs and estuaries, but largely devoid of vegetation. The third type of coastline is found south of Tierra del Fuego's Río Grande, where you see, in succession, patches of woodland, bleak moorland tundra and the southern beech forests of the Beagle Channel.

Several coastal areas, notably those of the Bahía San Antonio, Bahía San Sebastián and the Estuario del Río Gallegos, have been integrated into the Western Hemisphere Shorebird Reserve Network, designed to protect migrant waders across the Americas. Birds like the **Hudsonian Godwit** (*becasa de mar*) and the **Red Knot** (*playero rojizo*) migrate from Alaska as far as Tierra del Fuego – over 17,000km. Other coastal species are **Magellanic Penguins** (*pingüino magallánico*), whose major continental breeding colony is at Punta Tombo; **Chilean flamingoes**; and the **South American Tern** (*gaviotín sudamericano*). At Puerto Deseado, you can see all four different types of **cormorant** (*cormorán*) including the Blue-eyed (*imperial*) and the Red-legged Cormorant (*gris*). Look out for the dove-like **Snowy Sheathbill** (*paloma antártica*); and several types of duck, including the **Crested Duck** (*pato juarjual* or *crestón*) and the flightless **Steamer Duck** (*quetro no volador* or *alacush*). On the open sea, especially in the far south, you stand a good chance of seeing **Black-browed Albatrosses** and **Giant Petrels**.

Península Valdés is the main destination for marine fauna. Its twin bays, Golfo Nuevo and Golfo San José (Latin America's first marine park), are where as much as a quarter of the world's population of **southern right whales** (*ballena franca austral*) breed annually. The peninsula also hosts a forty-thousand-strong and growing colony of **southern elephant seals** (*elefante marino*). Other sightings might include **sea lions** (*lobos del mar*), found in colonies along the whole Atlantic coast, and possibly even a **killer whale** (*orca*). Further down the coast at Cabo Blanco, you can see the endangered **fur seal** (*lobo de dos pelos*); while Puerto Deseado and San Julián are fine places to catch the piebald **Commerson's dolphins** (*toninas overas*). Sea trips on the Beagle Channel offer a slim chance of seeing **minke whale**, or even perhaps an endangered **marine otter** (*nutria marina* or *chungungo*).

Music

With the obvious exception of **tango**, Argentina's music has a fairly low international profile. True to its image as the continent's odd man out, the country has a tradition that doesn't quite fit the popular concept of "Latin American" music: there is little of the exhilarating tropical rhythms of, say, Brazil, nor is there much of the pan-pipe sound associated with Andean countries. Within Latin America, however, Argentina is famed for its rock music, known simply as **rock nacional** – a term which embraces an eclectic bunch of groups and musicians, from the heavy rock of Pappo, to the sweet poppy rock of Fito Páez, to ska- and punk-influenced Los Fabulosos Cadillacs. Folk music, known as **folklore** in Argentina, is also popular throughout the country and provides a predominantly rural counterpoint to the essentially urban tango.

Tango

The great Argentine writer Jorge Luis Borges was a tango enthusiast and something of a historian of the music. "My informants all agree on one fact," he wrote. "The Tango was born in the brothels." Borges' sources were a little presumptuous, perhaps, for no one can exactly pinpoint **tango**'s birthplace, but it certainly had roots in Buenos Aires. Early tango was a definitively urban music: a product of the melting pot of European immigrants, *criollos*, blacks and natives, drawn together when the city became the country's capital in 1880. Tango was thus forged from a range of musical influences that included Andalucían flamenco, southern Italian melodies, Cuban habanera, African candombé and percussion, European polkas and mazurkas, Spanish contradanse and, closer to home, the *milonga* – the song of the gaucho. In this early form, tango became associated with the bohemian life of bordello brawls and *compadritos* – knife-wielding, womanizing thugs. By 1914 there were over one hundred thousand more men than women in Buenos Aires, and machismo and violence were part of the culture. Men would dance together in cafés and bars, practising new steps and keeping in shape while waiting for their women, often the *minas* of the bordellos. Their dances tended to have a showy yet predatory quality, often revolving around a possessive relationship between two men and one woman. In these surroundings, the *compadrito* danced the tango into existence.

The original **tango ensembles** were trios of violin, guitar and flute, but around the end of the nineteenth century the **bandoneón**, the tango accordion, arrived from Germany, and the classic tango orchestra was born. The box-shaped button accordion, now inextricably linked with Argentine tango, was invented around 1860 in Germany to play religious music in organless churches, and was reworked as the *bandoneón*.

In Argentina, an early pioneer of the instrument was **Eduardo Arolas**, remembered as the "Tiger of the Bandoneón". He recognized its immediate affinity with the tango – indeed, he claimed it was an instrument made to play tango, with a deep melancholy feeling that suited immigrants. It is not, however, an easy instrument to play, demanding a great deal of skill, with its seventy-odd buttons each producing one of two notes depending on whether the bellows are being compressed or expanded.

Vicente Greco (1888–1924) is credited as the first bandleader to standardize the form of a tango group, with his **Orquesta Típica Criolla** of two violins and two *bandoneones*. There were some larger bands but the instrumentation remained virtually unchanged until the 1940s.

First tango in Paris

By the first decade of the twentieth century, the tango was an intrinsic part of the popular culture of Buenos Aires, played on the streets by organ grinders and danced in tenement courtyards. Its association with whorehouses and the low-down Porteño lifestyle, plus its saucy, sometimes obscene and fatalistic lyrics, didn't endear it to the aristocratic families of Buenos Aires, though, and they did their best to protect their children from the new dance, but it was a losing battle.

A number of upper-class playboys, such as poet and writer **Ricardo Güiraldes**, enjoyed mixing with the *compadritos* and emulating their lifestyle – from a debonair distance. It was Güiraldes who, on a European grand tour in 1910, was responsible for bringing the dance to Europe. The following year Güiraldes gave an impromptu performance in a Paris salon to a fashionable audience, for whom tango's risqué sexuality ("the vertical expression of horizontal desire", as one wag dubbed it) was highly attractive. Despite the local archbishop's admonition that Christians should not in good conscience tango, they did, and in large numbers. And, once it was embraced in French salons, its credibility at home greatly increased. Back in Argentina, from bordello to ballroom, everyone was soon dancing the tango.

And then came **Rudolph Valentino**, a charismatic Hollywood star whose image tango fitted to a T. A tango scene was added to his latest film, *The Four Horsemen of the Apocalypse* (1926): dressed in a gaucho's wide trousers, Valentino danced with a carnation between his lips and a whip in his hand. The scene was the hit of the film, and, travesty though it was, it meant the dance was now known all over the world. Tango classes and competitions were held in Paris, and tango teas in England, with young devotees togged up as Argentine gauchos. Even the greatest tango singer of all time, **Carlos Gardel**, when he became the darling of Parisian society, and later starred in Hollywood films, was forced to perform dressed as a gaucho. To this day, this image remains many people's primary perception of tango.

Tango's golden age

Back in Argentina, in the 1920s, the tango moved out of the cantinas and bordellos and into cabarets and theatres, entering a classic era under bandleaders like **Roberto Firpo**, **Julio de Caro** and **Francisco Canaro**. With their *orquestas típicas* they took the old line-up of Vicente Greco (two *bandoneones*, two violins, a piano and flute) and substituted a double bass for the flute, thereby adding sonority and depth. It was during this period that some of the most famous of all tangos were written, including Uruguayan **Gerardo Hernán Matos Rodríguez's** *La Comparsita* in 1917.

Early **tango-canciónes** (tango songs) used the language of the ghetto and celebrated the life of ruffians and pimps. **Angel Villoldo** and **Pascual Contursi** introduced the classic lyric of a male perspective, placing the blame for heartache firmly on the shoulders of a fickle woman. In its **dance**, tango consolidated a contradictory mix of earthy sensuality and middle-class kitsch. It depended on an almost violent and dangerous friction of bodies, which collided often in a passion that seemed controlled by the dance itself.

Carlos Gardel

Carlos Gardel (1887–1935) was – and still is – a legend in Argentina. He was a huge influence in spreading the popularity of tango round the world, and came to be seen as a symbol of the fulfilment of the dreams of poor Porteño workers.

In Argentina, it was Gardel above all who transformed tango from an essentially low-down dance form to a song style popular among widely differing social classes. Everything about Gardel – his suavity, his arrogance and his natural machismo – spelt tango. The advent of radio, recording and film all helped his career, but nothing helped him more than his own voice – a voice that was born to sing tango and which became the model for all future singers of the genre.

His arrival on the scene coincided with the first period of tango's golden age and the development of *tango-canción* in the 1920s and 1930s. During his life, Gardel recorded some nine hundred songs and starred in numerous films, notably *The Tango on Broadway* in 1934. He was tragically killed in an air crash in Colombia at the height of his fame, and his legendary status was confirmed. His image is still everywhere in Buenos Aires, on plaques and huge murals, and in record-store windows, while admirers pay homage to his life-sized, bronze statue in Chacarita cemetery (see p.127).

After Gardel, the split between the **evolutionists**, who wanted to develop new forms of tango, and the **traditionalists**, who thought it was fine as it was, became more pronounced. Bands, as elsewhere in the world during this period, became larger, in the mode of small orchestras, and a mass following for tango was enjoyed through dance halls, radio and recordings until the end of the golden age around 1950.

The second golden age

As an expression of the working classes, the progression of the tango has inevitably been linked with social and political developments in Argentina. The music declined a little in the 1930s as the army took power and suppressed what was seen as a potentially subversive force, but it enjoyed a second golden age with the rise of Perón and his emphasis on nationalism and popular culture. By the late 1940s Buenos Aires was a city of five or six million, and each barrio boasted ten or fifteen amateur tango orchestras, while the established orchestras played in the cabarets and nightclubs in the city centre. Sometime in this era, however, tango began to move away from working class and into middle class and intellectual milieus. It became a sort of collective reminiscence of a world that no longer existed – essentially nostalgia.

In the 1950s, with the end of Peronism and the coming of rock 'n' roll, tango slipped into the shadows once again.

Astor Piazzolla and tango nuevo

Astor Piazzolla dominates the recent history of tango, much as Carlos Gardel was the key figure of its classic era. From 1937, Piazzolla played second *bandoneón* in the orchestra of the master Aníbal Troilo, where he developed his feel for arrangements. (The first *bandoneón* takes the melody, and the second *bandoneón* the harmony.)

Troilo left Piazzolla his *bandoneón* when he died, and Piazzolla went on to ensure that tango would never be the same again. Piazzolla's idea was that tango could be a serious music to listen to, not just for dancing, and for many of the old guard this was a step too far. As he explained: "Musicians hated me. I was taking the old tango away from them. The old tango, the one they loved, was dying. And they hated me, they threatened my life hundreds of times. They waited for me outside my house, two or three of them, and gave me a good beating. They even put a gun at my head once." In the 1970s, Piazzolla was out of favour with Argentina's military regime and he and his family moved to Paris, returning to Argentina only after the fall of the junta. His influence, however, had spread, and his experiments – and international success – opened the way for other radical transformations.

Chief among these, in 1970s Buenos Aires, was the fusion of **tango-rockero** – tango rock. This replaced the flexible combination of *bandoneón*, bass and no drums, as favoured by Piazzolla, with a rock-style rhythm section, electric guitars and synthesizers. It was pioneered by **Litto Nebbia**, whose album, *Homage to Gardél and Le Péra*, is one of the most successful products of this fusion, retaining the melancholy of the traditional form in a rock format. Tango moved across to jazz, too, through groups such as the trio **Siglo XX**, while old guard figures like **Roberto "Polaco" Goyeneche** and **Osvaldo Pugliese** kept traditional tango alive.

These days in Argentina, the tango scene is a pretty broad one, with rock and jazz elements along with the more traditional sound of acoustic groups. There is no shortage of good *tangueros* and they know each other well and jam together often. Big tango orchestras, however, are a thing of the past, and tango bands have returned to their roots, to an intimate era of trios, quartets and quintets – a sextet is serious business. Two of the best sextets, the **Sexteto Mayor** and **Sexteto Berlingieri**, joined together in the 1980s to play for the show *Tango Argentino*, and subsequent shows which revived an interest in tango across Europe and the US. The Sexteto Mayor, founded in 1973 and starring the virtuoso *bandoneonistas* **José Libertella** and **Luís Stazo**, is one of the best tango ensembles in Argentina today.

In a more modern idiom, singers like **Susana Rinaldi** and **Adriana Varela** are successfully renovating and recreating tango, both at home and abroad. They are names to look out for along with *bandoneonistas* **Osvaldo Piro**, **Carlos Buono** and **Walter Ríos**; singer **José Angel Trelles**; and **Grupo Volpe Tango Contemporáneo**, led by Antonio Volpe.

Latterly, tango is enjoying an upsurge of popularity in Argentina and other parts of the world. Young bohemians such as Buenos Aires' Parakultural outfit, and the Bajofondo Tango Club, which successfully melds tango with drum 'n' bass and other forms of electronic music, are once again reinventing tango for a new generation.

Discography

Tango can often be found in the world-music section of major record stores throughout the globe, most commonly in collections of variable quality aimed at dancers, closely followed by the works of Carlos Gardel and Astor Piazzolla. A worldwide mail-order service is offered by the Buenos Aires' tango store Zivals, accessed through their website ⊛ www.tangostore.com.

The following recordings offer a good introduction to tango's major stars, both old and new.

The Rough Guide to Tango and **The Rough Guide to Tango Nuevo** With tracks from twenty of the greatest tango musicians – from Gardel and Piazzolla to more contemporary artists – *The Rough Guide to Tango* is one of the best introductions to the genre, while the *Tango Nuevo* disc features nineteen tracks from contemporary figures such as Adriana Varela and Juan Carlos Caceres.

Carlos Gardel *20 Grandes Éxitos*. One of the best of the innumerable collections of Gardel's finest recordings, packed with his unmistakable renderings of iconic classics such as *El día me quieras*, *Volver*, *Caminito* and *Cuesta Abajo*.

Roberto Goyeneche *Maestros del Tango*. A superb compilation of hits from one of tango's most beloved characters; includes his classic interpretations of *Malena*, the seductive *Naranjo en Flor* and the wonderful *Sur*, an elegy to the south of Buenos Aires, tango's true home.

Tita Merello *La Merello.* Classic compilation by one of tango's early and most famous female stars, including her own composition, the bittersweet *Se dice de mí.*

Astor Piazzolla *Noches del Regina.* The master of modern tango interprets classics such as the polemical *Cambalache* and the inimitable *Balada para un loco.* For his most characteristic, avant-garde compositions, check out *Adios Nonino,* titled after perhaps his most famous composition, or *A Rough Guide to Astor Piazzolla,* a compilation of his best tracks.

Edmundo Rivero *En Lunfardo.* The charismatic singer interprets classic tangos such as *El Chamuyo* and *Atentí, Pebeta,* infused with Buenos Aires' street slang, *lunfardo.*

Sexteto Mayor *Trottoirs de Buenos Aires.* This largely instrumental album of classic tangos by Argentina's premier tango ensemble is thrilling, with Adriana Varela unleashing her husky voice on four songs. Unashamedly emotional and utterly convincing.

Aníbal Troilo *Obra Completa.* Known affectionately as "pichuco", *bandoneonista* Aníbal Troilo led one of Argentina's most successful tango orchestras and composed many classics such as *Sur* and *Barrio de Tango.* His trademark *Che, bandoneón,* with lyrics by one of tango's great poets, Homero Manzi, is a sweet, sad elegy to the *bandoneón* itself.

Adriana Varela *Maquillaje.* One of tango's most successful contemporary singers, offering a very distinctive, throaty interpretation of classic tangos and compositions by *rock nacional* superstars Fito Páez and Litto Nebbia.

Text courtesy of Jan Fairley, with a discography by Lucy Phillips

Rock nacional

Listened to passionately throughout the country, Argentina's homegrown rock music – known simply as **rock nacional** – has something for just about everyone among its numerous charismatic performers.

Rock nacional began to emerge in the 1960s with groups such as **Almendra**, one of whose members, **Luis Alberto Spinetta**, went on to a solo career and is still one of Argentina's most successful and original musicians, and **Los Gatos**, who in 1967 had a massive hit with the eloquent *La Balsa* and two of whose members – Litto Nebbia and Pappo – also went on to solo careers. From a sociological point of view, though, the significance of *rock nacional* really began to emerge under the military dictatorship of 1976–83. At the very beginning of the dictatorship, there was an upsurge in rock concerts, during which musicians such as **Charly García**, frontman of the hugely popular **Serú Girán** and now a soloist, provided a subtle form of resistance with songs such as *No te dejes desanimar* (Don't be discouraged), which helped provoke a collective sense of opposition among fans. It wasn't long, however, before the military rulers clamped down on what it saw as the subversive atmosphere generated at such concerts. The government issued recommendations that stadium owners should not let their premises be used for rock concerts, and by the end of the 1970s many bands had split up or gone into exile.

By 1980, cracks had begun to appear in the regime and a subtle freeing-up of the public sphere began. In December 1980, a concert by Serú Girán attracted sixty thousand fans to La Rural in Palermo: led by Charly García, the fans began to shout, in full view of the television cameras "no se banca más" (We won't put up with it anymore).

By 1982 the rock movement was a loudly cynical voice, creating massively popular songs such as **Fito Páez**'s self-explanatory *Tiempos difíciles* (Difficult times), Charly García's *Dinosaurios*, whose title is a clear reference to the military rulers and *Maribel* by Argentina's finest rock lyricist, Spinetta, dedicated to the Madres de Plaza de Mayo. After the dictatorship ended, rock returned to a more apolitical role, typified by the lighthearted approach of 1984's most popular group, **Los Abuelos de la Nada**. One of the founding members of Los Abuelos, **Pappo**, went on to a solo career in heavy rock, appealing to a predominantly working-class section of society who felt that their lot had improved little with democracy; Pappo's music seemed to sum up their frustrations. One of the most popular groups of the 1980s was **Sumo**, fronted by charismatic **Luca Prodan**, an Italian raised in the UK who had come to Argentina in an attempt to shake off his heroin addiction. Sumo made sometimes surreal, noisy, reggae-influenced tracks, expressing distaste for the frivolous attitudes of Buenos Aires' upper-middle-class youth on tracks such as *Rubia tarada* (Stupid blonde). Luca Prodan ultimately died of a heroin overdose in 1987, but is still idolized by Argentine rock fans.

Like Sumo, the strangely named and massively popular **Patricio Rey y sus Redonditos de Ricota** (literally: Patricio Rey and his little balls of ricotta) made noise with enigmatic tracks such as *Aquella vaca solitaria cubana* (That solitary Cuban cow), often touching on the dissatisfactions felt by many young Argentines in the aftermath of the dictatorship. Another success story of the 1980s and 1990s – albeit in a very different vein – was **Fito Páez**, whose 1992 album *El Amor después del amor*, with its sweet melodic tunes – one of them inspired by the film *Thelma and Louise* – sold millions throughout Latin America. One of Argentina's most original bands also emerged in the 1980s – **Los Fabulosos Cadillacs**, with their diverse and often frenetic fusion of rock, ska, dub, punk and rap. An irreverent and ironic sense of humour often underlies their politicized lyrics, all belted out by their charismatic, astringently voiced lead singer, Vincentico, and backed up with a tight horn section and driving Latin percussion. Their classic album is *El León* (1992), on which you'll find their most famous anthem, *Matador*, a savage indictment of the military dictatorship.

Rock nacional's most enduring figures are still Charly García – whose wild exploits fill the pages of gossip magazines – and other old timers such as Fito Paéz, Los Fabulosos Cadillacs, León Gieco and Luis Alberto Spinetta. Standout newcomers to the scene – who regularly play in the country – include the internationally popular "sonic rock" band **Babasónicos**; experimental **Catupechu Machu**; punky **Attaque 77**; **Las Pelotas**, incorporating former Sumo members; melodic indie rockers **Los Estelares**; and the tropical rock sound of **Bersuit Vergarabat**.

Chamamé, cuarteto and folklore

Tango aside, Argentine music is mostly rooted in the rural dance traditions of the countryside, an amalgam of Spanish and immigrant Central European styles with indigenous music. Many of these dances – *rancheras, milongas, chacareras* and more – are shared with the neighbouring countries of Chile, Peru and Bolivia, while others like **chamamé** are particularly Argentine. Argentina's Amerindian roots are explored by Atahualpa Yupanqui, which grew new shoots in the politicized *nueva canción* (new song) movement.

Chamamé

Chamamé is probably Argentina's most popular roots music. It has its origins in the rural culture of Corrientes – an Amerindian area that attracted nineteenth-century settlers from Czechoslovakia, Poland, Austria and Germany. These immigrants brought with them Middle European waltzes, mazurkas and polkas, which over time merged with music from the local Guaraní Amerindian traditions, and African rhythms from the music of the region's slaves. Thus emerged chamamé, a music of poor rural mestizos, many of whom looked more Indian than European, and whose songs used both Spanish and the Indian Guaraní languages.

Chamamé's melodies have a touch of the melancholy attributed to the Guaraní, while its history charts the social, cultural and political relationships of mestizo migrants. Until the 1950s, it was largely confined to Corrientes, but during that decade many rural migrants moved to Buenos Aires, bringing their music and dances with them. Chamamé began to attract wider attention – in part, perhaps, because it was a rare folk dance in which people dance in cheek-to-cheek embrace.

The essential sound of chamamé comes from its key instrument – the large **piano accordion** (on occasion the *bandoneón*). It sweeps through tunes which marry contrasting rhythms, giving the music an immediate swing. Its African influences may have contributed to the music's accented weak beats so that bars blend and swing together. The distinctive percussive rhythms to the haunting, evocative melodies are the music's unique, compelling feature.

Argentina's reigning king of chamamé is **Raúl Barboza**, an artist who has also notched up a certain degree of success in Europe. Barboza's conjunto features a typical chamamé line-up of one or two accordions, a guitar and *guitarrón* (bass guitar). Perhaps one of the best-known chamamé artists internationally is **Chango Spasiuk**, an Argentine of Ukrainian heritage, who has been successful in producing a sort of chamamé-rock crossover, with a more modern feel that still preserves the music's essence.

Cuarteto

The Argentine dance style known as cuarteto first became popular in the 1940s. Named after the original **Cuarteto Leo** who played it, its line-up involved a solo singer, piano, accordion and violin, and its dance consisted of a huge circle, moving counter-clockwise, to a rhythm called *tunga-tunga*. In the 1980s it underwent a resurgence of interest in the working-class "tropical" dancehalls of Buenos Aires, where it was adopted alongside Colombian *guarachas*, Dominican merengue and Latin salsa. It slowly climbed up the social ladder to reach a middle-class market, notching up big record sales. The most famous contemporary singer of cuarteto is **Carlos "La Mona" Jiménez**.

Folklore

In a movement aligned to *nueva canción*, dozens of folklore singers and groups emerged in the 1960s and 1970s – their music characterized by tight arrangements and four-part harmonies. The big *nueva canción* star was **Mercedes Sosa**, who sadly passed away in 2009; other leading artists of these decades included the group **Los Chalchaleros**, guitarist **Eduardo Falú**, and **Ariel Ramírez**, notable for his *zambas* and Creole Mass. In more recent years groups have come through experimenting and re-evaluating the folk dance traditions, including the *zamba*, a national dance that involves the couple taking slow steps back and forth while waving handkerchiefs. Among this new wave are **Los Trovadores**, **Los Huanca Hua** and **Cuarteto Zupuy**. The best place to see folklore music is at the annual **Cosquín national folklore festival** (see p.221), which has been a fixture since the 1960s.

Books

A rgentina's 95 percent literacy rate is one of the highest in the world and its many bookshops, especially the splendidly monumental ones in Buenos Aires, are a reflection of the considerable interest in what is written in both Argentina and the outside world. There are a fair number of books about Argentina available in English, ranging from academic publications to travelogues. In Argentina itself, there are many coffee-table books produced that focus on subjects such as Patagonia, gauchos and indigenous peoples. These vary in quality, but generally consist of pretty, glossy photos interspersed by rather dubious text. Novels in English are available from specialist sellers in Buenos Aires (see p.147 for stockists), though if you're looking for specific books, such as the works listed below, your best bet is to get a copy before you depart. Most can be tracked down fairly easily via the internet – Amazon (⑨www.amazon.co.uk or ⑨www.amazon .com) is a good starting point. The term o/p denotes that a book is currently out of print, but is still generally available through secondhand bookstores or the internet.

A ⚘ preceding a title means that it is highly recommended.

Travel

⚘ **Bruce Chatwin** *In Patagonia*. For many travellers, this is *the* Argentine travel book – in fact, the book that broke the mould for travel writing in general. Written in the 1970s, it's really a series of self-contained tales (most famously of the Argentine adventures of Butch Cassidy and the Sundance Kid) strung together by their connection with Patagonia. This idiosyncratic book has even inspired a "Chatwin trail", although his rather cold style and literary embellishments on the region's history have their detractors too.

Bruce Chatwin and Paul Theroux *Patagonia Revisited* (o/p), published in the US as *Nowhere is a Place* (o/p). The two doyens of Western travel writing combine to explore the literary associations of Patagonia. Wafer-thin and thoroughly enjoyable, this book throws more light on the myths of this far-flung land than it does on the place itself.

Miranda France *Bad Times in Buenos Aires* (o/p). Despite the title and the critical (some might say patronizing) tone, this journal penned during the

height of the Menem era brings Porteños to life, and you can't help feeling the author secretly loves the place. Highlights include a near-miss with Menem's toupee.

Che Guevara *The Motorcycle Diaries*. Ernesto "Che" Guevara's own account of his epic motorcyle tour around Latin America, beginning in Buenos Aires and heading south to Patagonia and then up through Chile. Che undertook the tour when he was just 23 and the resulting diary is an intriguing blend of travel anecdotes and an insight into the mind of a nascent revolutionary. The 2004 movie version, starring Gael García Bernal as Che, has done its part to inspire a new generation to read the book and pin up a Che poster.

George Chaworth Musters *At Home with the Patagonians*. The amazing 1869 journey of Musters as he rode with the Aónik'enk from southern Patagonia to Carmen de Patagones, becoming in the process the first outsider to be accepted into Tehuelche society and the first white man to traverse the region south to north. This book is our prime source for information on the Tehuelche, and gives a portrait of a culture about to be exterminated.

Paul Theroux *The Old Patagonian Express*. More tales about trains by the tireless cynic. In the four chapters on Argentina, which he passed through just before the 1978 World Cup, he waxes lyrical about cathedral-like Retiro station and has a surreal dialogue with Borges.

A.F. Tschiffely *Tschiffely's Ride*. An account of a truly adventurous horseback ride – described as the "longest and most arduous on record ever made by man and horse" – made by Tschiffely from Buenos Aires to Washington DC in the 1920s and providing an insight into rural Argentina at the time. A similar equestrian journey was made in contemporary times by Marianne du Toit, who has published an account of her adventures called *Crying with Cockroaches*.

History, politics and society

Rita Arditti *Searching for Life*. The story of the *abuelas* (grandmothers) of the Plaza de Mayo and their long-running investigation into the whereabouts of the hundreds of children who disappeared during the Dirty War, many given to military families for adoption. A moving yet positive account of the grandmothers' ongoing search, which remains a controversial issue in the country.

Paul Blustein *And the Money Kept Rolling In (and Out); Wall Street, the IMF, and the Bankrupting of Argentina*. The definitive account of the Argentine economic crisis of 2001. *Washington Post* journalist Blustein contends that, though Argentina's fate was always in the hands of its politicians, the IMF worsened the situation by indulging their emerging market "poster child" long beyond the point when the debt burden had become unsustainable, while the unrestricted flows of the global finance market had their role to play, too. Authoritative, and a cracking read.

Lucas Bridges *The Uttermost Part of the Earth*. Returned to publication in 2007, the genius of this classic text on pioneering life in Tierra del Fuego in the late nineteenth century lies less in its literary attributes than in the extraordinary tales of an adventurous

young man's relationship with the area's indigenous groups, and the invaluable ethnographic knowledge he imparts about a people whose culture was set to disappear within his lifetime.

Jimmy Burns *The Hand of God*. A compelling read in which Anglo-Argentine journalist Burns charts the rise and fall of Argentina's bad-boy hero of football, Diego Maradona. Burns also wrote *The Land that Lost its Heroes*, a thoroughly researched account of the Falklands/Malvinas conflict.

Uki Goñi *The Real Odessa*. This is the definitive account of the aid given by Perón (and the Vatican) to Nazi war criminals; hundreds infamously settled in Argentina. The Argentine government and Peronist party in particular has done little to address its previous sheltering of these men – indeed, Goñi finds evidence that incriminating documents were being burnt as late as 1996.

Naomi Klein *The Shock Doctrine*. The author of anti-globalization bible *No Logo* looks at the social and economic fallout of Friedmanite extreme free market policies in Argentina and beyond. Provides useful context to events of the last thirty years, albeit as seen through a certain filter. Look out also for her documentary film *The Take* about grassroots activism in the wake of Argentina's 2001 financial crisis.

Daniel K. Lewis *The History of Argentina*. Reasonably brief, chronological account of the country's history. Strongest and most detailed on the Perón years and their aftermath.

John Lynch *San Martín: Argentinian soldier, American hero*. The first English-language biography of modern times of José de San Martín, arguably the greatest of all Latin American heroes, who led the continent's independence stuggle against Spain in the nineteenth century. Lynch is a major Latin American scholar; his numerous books on the region also include essential biographies nineteenth-century dictator Rosas and of San Martín's brother-in-arms Simón Bolívar.

Gabriella Nouzeilles and Graciela Montaldo (eds) *The Argentina Reader*. Compendium of essays and stories on Argentina's history and culture, with the majority of the pieces written by Argentines. An excellent starting point for further reading, though a bit hefty for lugging around.

Domingo F. Sarmiento *Facundo, or Civilization and Barbarism*. Probably the most influential of all books written in Latin America in the nineteenth

century, this essay defines one of Argentina's major cultural peculiarities – the battle between the provinces seeking decentralized power and a sophisticated metropolis more interested in what is going on abroad than in its vast hinterland. Written in the form of a fictional biography of a gaucho thug named Facundo Quiroga, it attacks the arbitrary rule of provincial strongmen such as Rosas, Sarmiento's arch-enemy.

Richard W. Slatta *Gauchos and the Vanishing Frontier*. Scholarly work that is the perfect cerebral accompaniment to the coffee-table tomes sold on the subject. Slatta charts the rise, fall and rise again of the gaucho, his lifestyle, his maltreatment by the upper classes and the myths that grew around him.

Jacobo Timerman *Prisoner Without A Name, Cell Without A Number*. First-person memoir that recounts the terrors of Argentina's Dirty War from the point of view of a prisoner who survived. See also *Buenos Aires Herald* editor Andrew Graham Yool's *State of Fear*, an account of this darkest of times told through the eyes of a journalist living through and reporting on it, and Horacio Verbitsky's *Confessions of an Argentine Dirty Warrior*, the memoir of a naval officer who was involved in the horrific practice of pushing drugged prisoners out of planes over the River Plate.

Nature and wildlife

Charles Darwin *The Voyage of the Beagle*. Very readable account of Darwin's famous voyage, which takes him through Patagonia and the pampas. Filled with observations on the flora, fauna, landscape and people (including the dictator Rosas) that Darwin encounters, all described in the scientist's methodical yet evocative style.

Gerald Durrell *The Whispering Land*. A lighthearted read detailing Durrell's observations while animal-collecting in Peninsula Valdés, the Patagonian steppe and the *yungas*. Enduring good value, despite what now comes across as a colonial tone: his capacity for making animals into characters is unsurpassed. See also *The Drunken Forest* (o/p), about his trip to the Chaco.

W.H. Hudson *Far Away and Long Ago*. A nostalgic and gently ambling portrait of childhood and rural tranquillity in the Argentine pampas in Rosas' time. An early environmentalist, the author regrets the expansion of agriculture and the destruction of habitat variety in the pampas in the course of his lifetime. In the US it is out of copyright and can be downloaded free at ⓦwww.gutenberg.org.

Martín R. de la Peña and Maurice Rumboll *Birds of Southern South America and Antarctica*. A useful companion for even the non-specialist birdwatcher. It would benefit from some indication of frequency and a few illustrations could do with more detail, but overall thoroughly recommended.

The arts

Shirley Brooks *Argentina Cooks!* Comprehensive collection of recipes from around Argentina. While the idea of digging an *asado* fire pit in the back garden or spending hours over a bubbling vat of *dulce de leche* may seem a little daunting, this comprehensive recipe book gives you no excuse not to have a bash at making your own *empanadas* or *alfajores*.

Simon Collier (ed) *Tango! The Dance, the Song, the Story*. A glossy coffee-table book with a lively account of the history of tango and its key protagonists, well illustrated with colour and black-and-white photos.

Dereck Foster & Richard Tripp *Food and Drink in Argentina*. Foster has been the *Buenos Aires Herald*'s food and drink columnist for forty years, and in this slim and useful guide, co-authored with Richard Tripp, he provides both general information to whet the appetite of first-time visitors and a detailed pictorial glossary to enable veteran travellers to tell *medialunas* from *moñitos*.

Alberto Manguel *With Borges*. Accomplished Argentine writer Manguel recounts the time as a young man he spent reading to Borges. Absolutely charming essay, with the kind of gentle humour, subtle poetry and sharp insights into Buenos Aires life that characterize the great man's own work.

Fiction

César Aira *The Hare* (o/p). A witty novel about an English naturalist in nineteenth-century Argentina by Borges' literary heir, a truly prolific and original writer at the forefront of contemporary Argentine literature.

Roberto Arlt *The Seven Madmen* (o/p). Until his tragically early death, Roberto Arlt captured the lot of the poor immigrant with his gripping, if idiosyncratic, novels about anarchists, whores and other marginal characters in 1920s Buenos Aires. *The Seven Madmen* is the pick of his works – dark and at times surreal, it's filled with images of the frenetic and alienating pace of urban life as experienced by the novel's tormented protagonist, Remo Erdosain.

Jorge Luis Borges *Labyrinths*. Not only Argentina's greatest writer, but one of the world's finest and most influential. His prose is highly original, witty and concise; rather than novels, he introduces his ideas through short stories and essays – ideal for dipping into – and *Labyrinths* is a good introduction to these, with selections from his major collections. It includes many of his best-known and most enigmatic tales, including *Library of Babel*, an analogy of the world as a never-ending library.

🏃 **Julio Cortázar** *Hopscotch*. Cortázar is probably second only to Borges in the canon of Argentine writers and *Hopscotch* is a major work, published in the 1960s. In this fantastically complex book, Cortázar defies traditional narrative structure, inviting the reader to "hop" between chapters (hence the name), which recount the lives of a group of friends in Paris and London.

Nathan Englander *The Ministry of Special Cases*. Jewish-American writer Englander set his 2007 novel in Argentina in the 1970s, with the backdrop of the Dirty War and the plot centering on the disappearance of a teenage son. The observations of Argentine society are astute, the story wry, compelling, and tragic in equal measures – not unlike the country itself.

Graham Greene *The Honorary Consul*. A masterful account of a farcical kidnapping attempt that goes tragically wrong. Set in the city of Corrientes and dedicated to Argentine literary doyenne Victoria Ocampo, with whom Greene spent time in San Isidro and Mar del Plata.

🏃 **Ricardo Güiraldes** *Don Segundo Sombra*. A tender and nostalgic evocation of past life on the pampas, chronicling the relationship between a young boy and his mentor, the novel's eponymous gaucho. Written in 1926, some decades after the gaucho era had come to a close, it was a key text in changing the image of the Argentine cowboy from that of a violent undesirable to a strong, independent man with simple tastes, at the heart of Argentina's national identity.

José Hernández *Martín Fierro*. The classic gaucho novel – actually a verse of epic proportions, traditionally learnt by heart by many Argentines. Written

as a protest against the corrupt authorities, it features a highly likeable gaucho outlaw on the run, who rails against the country's weak institutional structures and dictatorial rulers. Its rhyming verse and liberal use of gaucho lingo make translation difficult; one version is the classic Walter Owen translation from the 1930s, available in Argentine bookshops.

🏃 **Tomás Eloy Martínez** *The Perón Novel* and *Santa Evita* (both o/p). Darting between fact and fiction, Tomás Eloy Martínez intersperses his account of the events surrounding Perón's return to Argentina in 1973 with anecdotes from his past. The companion volume *Santa Evita* recounts the morbid and at times farcical true story of Evita's life and – more importantly – afterlife, during which her corpse was hijacked and smuggled abroad.

Manuel Puig *Kiss of the Spiderwoman*. Arguably the finest book by one of Argentina's most original twentieth-century writers, distinguished by a style that mixes film dialogue and popular culture with more traditional narrative. Set during the 1970s dictatorship, this is an absorbing tale of two cellmates, worlds apart on the outside but drawn together by gay protagonist Molina's recounting of films to his companion, left-wing guerrilla Valentín.

Horacio Quiroga *The Decapitated Chicken and Other Stories*. Wonderful if sometimes disturbing gothic tales of love, madness and death. Includes the spine-chilling "Feather Pillow", in which the life is slowly sucked from a young bride by a hideous blood-sucking beast, found engorged after her death within her feather pillow.

Colm Toibin *The Story of the Night*. A moving tale of a young Anglo-Argentine trying to come to terms both with his sexuality and existential dilemmas in the wake of the South Atlantic conflict, and getting caught up in an undercover plot by the CIA to get Carlos Menem elected president.

Language

Language

Argentine Spanish

You'll find at least a decent smattering of Spanish very useful in Argentina. English-speakers are not uncommon, especially in big cities, but they are not ubiquitous and Argentines are appreciative of visitors who make the effort to communicate in **castellano**, or Spanish. A good pocket **dictionary** is a vital accessory but if you really want to refine your grasp of the language, a comprehensive grammar such as *A New Reference Grammar of Modern Spanish* by John Butt and Carmen Benjamin is a worthwhile investment.

Argentine Spanish is highly distinctive, especially the unmistakable Porteño accent, characterized by a musical lilt and peppered with colloquialisms, betraying the strong Italian influence, as does the irresistible tendency to gesticulate. Beyond the River Plate region (in or close to the capital), certain regional variations take hold, though most rules of pronunciation, grammar and vocabulary apply for the whole country. Nowhere in Argentina will you hear the Iberian lisp in words like *cerveza* ("beer" – pronounced "sehr-bessa"). What really sets the local lingo apart, though, is the unique pronunciation of y/ll in words such as *yo* ("I/me") and *llave* ("key") as "zh" (the English equivalent is the "s" in "treasure"): "zho", "zhabe". A notable grammatical difference is the use of *vos* as the second-person pronoun ("you" singular), in place of *tú*, with correspondingly different verb endings – eg *vos sabés* = "you know", instead of *tú sabes*. *Ustedes* is always used as the second-person plural pronoun (the plural of "you"); *vosotros* and its derivatives are unheard of. The use of *"che"* (used when addressing someone; it loosely translates as "hey mate") in particular is so much identified with Argentina that other Latin Americans sometimes refer to Argentines as *"Los Che"*. The word was most famously applied as a nickname of Ernesto Guevara, who was popularly and universally known as "Che" Guevara.

Pronunciation

The Spanish pronunciation system is extremely phonetic – in other words spelling follows rigid rules, unlike English that seems to make them up as it goes along. Sounds in no two languages are exactly alike – be aware in particular that Spanish tends to be more fluid, less clearly enunciated and less staccato than English – but the following are examples of letters that are pronounced in a radically different way in (Argentine) Spanish and English. By the way, an (acute) accent written on a vowel denotes emphasis or stress – otherwise the tonic accent nearly always falls on the last syllable but one.

c is like the "ss" before E and I, like "k" elsewhere.

g is like the ch in "loch" before E and I, like "g" (as in "got") elsewhere.

h is silent, except after C when the two letters combine to make "ch" as in "Chile".

j is like the "ch" in "loch" or closer to an aspirate H.

ll is like the "s" in "pleasure", except in Corrientes and Misiones where it is pronounced "li" as in "pavilion". LL is like the "s" in "pleasure": *ella* sounds like "pleasure" (British pronunciation) without the "pl". In the northeast this word sounds like "ell-ya".

ñ is pronounced "ni" as in "onion". Ñandú is pronounced "nyandOO".

r is trilled as in Italian or Scots; RR or R at the beginning of a word is doubly trilled (in parts of central and northwestern Argentina this sound is more like a "sh": *rosa* ("rose") and *barrio* ("district/neighbourhood").

s is always soft as in "sign", never like a Z and not slushy as in much of Spain.

u after G and Q is silent. Miguel, the name, is "Mig-el", not "Mig-well".

v is basically pronounced like a B, though softened to a sound closer to English V in between two vowels: eg *Eva*.

y as a consonant (e.g. in *yacaré* – "alligator") is like the "s" in "pleasure", even in Corrientes and Misiones. Y meaning "and" is an example of "y" as a vowel: it is pronounced like the "y" in "city".

z is a soft "ss" sound, never hard like an English Z: *zorro* (fox) sounds a little like the English word "sorrow".

Useful vocab

Essentials

yes, no	sí, no	yesterday	ayer
please, thank you	por favor, gracias	nothing, never	nada, nunca
where, when	dónde, cuándo	entrance, exit	entrada, salida
what, how much	qué, cuánto	pull, push	tire, empuje
here, there	acá, allá	Australia	Australia
now, later	ahora, más tarde/luego	Canada	Canadá
open, closed	abierto/a, cerrado/a	England	Inglaterra
with, without	con, sin	Great Britain	Gran Bretaña
good, bad	bueno/a, malo/a	Ireland	Irlanda
big	grande	New Zealand	Nueva Zelanda
small	chico/a (pequeño/a is used less)	South Africa	Sudáfrica
		United Kingdom	Reino Unido
more, less	más, menos	United States	Estados Unidos
a little, a lot	poco, mucho	Scotland	Escocia
very	muy	Wales	Gales
today, tomorrow	hoy, mañana		

Greetings and responses

hello, goodbye (adiós is used for goodbye, but is more formal)	hola, chau	how are you?	¿cómo está(s)? ¿cómo anda/andás?
		(very) well, thanks	(muy) bien gracias
		excuse me	(con) permiso
good morning	buen día	sorry	perdón, disculpe
good afternoon	buenas tardes	cheers!	¡salud!
good night	buenas noches		
see you later	hasta luego		

Useful phrases and expressions

Note that when two verb forms are given, the first corresponds to the familiar *vos* form and the second to the formal *usted* form.

I (don't) understand	(No) entiendo	the toilet	el baño
Do you speak English?	¿Hablás inglés?/¿habla inglés?	I want a (return) ticket to...	Quiero un pasaje (de ida y vuelta) para...
I (don't) speak Spanish	(No) hablo castellano	Where does the bus for...leave from?	¿De dónde sale el micro para...?
My name is...	Me llamo...	What time does it leave?	¿A qué hora sale?
What's your name?	¿Cómo te llamás?/¿cómo se llama (usted)?	How long does it take?	¿Cuánto tarda?
I'm British/	Soy británico/a	far, near	lejos, cerca
...English	...inglés(a)	I want/would like...	quiero/quería...
...American	...estadounidense/ norteamericano/a	Is there a discount for students?	¿Hay descuento para estudiantes?
...Australian	...australiano/a	Is there hot water?	¿Hay agua caliente?
...Canadian	...canadiense	Do you have...?	¿Tiene...?una
...Irish	...irlandés(a)	a (single, double) room with two beds	habitación (single/ doble) con dos camas-
...Scottish	...escocés(a)	with a double bed	con cama matrimonial
...Welsh	...galés(a)	with a private bathroom	con baño privado
...a New Zealander	...neocelandés/a		
...South African	...sudafricano(a)	with breakfast	con desayuno
What's the Spanish for this?	¿Cómo se dice en castellano?	It's for one person /one night /two weeks	Es para una persona/ una noche/dos semanas
I'm hungry	Tengo hambre	How much is it?	¿Cuánto es/Cuánto sale?
I'm thirsty	Tengo sed		
I don't feel well	No me siento bien	It's too expensive	Es demasiado caro
What's up?	¿Qué pasa?	Do you have anything cheaper?	¿Hay algo más barato?
I don't know	No (lo) sé	Is there a discount for cash?	¿Hay descuento por pago en efectivo?
What's the time?	¿Qué hora es?	Is camping allowed here?	¿Se puede acampar aquí?

Hotels and transport

Is there a hotel/	¿Hay un hotel/banco cerca (de aquí)?
How do I get to...?	¿Cómo hago para llegar a...?
Turn left/right	Doblá/doble a la izquierda/derecha
On the left/right	A la izquierda/derecha
Go straight on	Seguí/siga derecho
One block/two blocks	Una cuadra, dos cuadras
Where is...?	¿Dónde está...?
the bus station	la terminal de omnibus
the train station	la estación de ferrocarril

Numbers, days and months

0	cero
1	uno/una
2	dos
3	tres
4	cuatro
5	cinco
6	seis
7	siete
8	ocho
9	nueve

10	diez	70	setenta
11	once	80	ochenta
12	doce	90	noventa
13	trece	100	cien/ciento
14	catorce	200	doscientos/as
15	quince	1000	mil
16	dieciséis	1,000,000	un millón
17	diecisiete	2008	dos mil ocho
18	dieciocho	Monday	lunes
19	diecinueve	Tuesday	martes
20	veinte	Wednesday	miércoles
21	veintiuno	Thursday	jueves
30	treinta	Friday	viernes
40	cuarenta	Saturday	sábado
50	cincuenta	Sunday	domingo
60	sesenta		

An Argentine menu reader

Basics

aceite de maíz	corn oil
aceite de oliva	olive oil
agregado	side order or garnish
ají	chilli
ajo	garlic
almuerzo	lunch
arroz	rice
azúcar	sugar
carta/menú	menu
cena	dinner
comedor	diner or dining room
copa	glass (for wine)
cuchara	spoon
cuchillo	knife
cuenta	bill
desayuno	breakfast
guarnición	side dish
harina	flour
huevos	eggs
lata/latita	can or tin
manteca	butter
mayonesa	mayonnaise
menú del día	set meal

mermelada/dulce	jam
mostaza	mustard
pan (francés)	bread (baguette or French stick)
pimentón dulce	paprika
pimienta	pepper
plato	plate or dish
queso	cheese
sal	salt
sanduich	sandwich (usually made with very thinly sliced bread: sanduich de miga)
servilleta	napkin
taza	cup
tenedor	fork
vaso	glass (for water)
vegetariano	vegetarian
vinagre	vinegar

Culinary terms

parrilla	barbecue
asado	roasted or barbecued; un asado is a barbecue
a la plancha	grilled

ahumado	smoked	chorizo (blanco)	meaty sausage (not spiced like Spanish *chorizo* – *chorizo colorado*)
al horno	baked/roasted		
al natural	canned (of fruit)		
al vapor	steamed		
crudo	raw	corazón	heart
frito	fried	criadillas	testicles
picante	hot (spicy)	hígado	liver
puré	puréed or mashed potatoes	lengua	tongue
		mollejas	sweetbreads (thymus gland)
relleno	stuffed		
		mondongo	cow's stomach

Meat (carne) and poultry (aves)

		morcilla	blood sausage
bife	steak	orejas	ears
bife de chorizo	prize steak cut	patas	feet or trotters
cabrito	goat (kid)	riñones	kidneys
carne vacuna	beef	sesos	brains
cerdo	pork	tripa gorda	tripe (large intestine)
ciervo	venison	ubre	udder
codorniz	quail		

Typical dishes (platos)

conejo	rabbit		
cordero	lamb	arroz con pollo	a kind of chicken risotto
chivito	kid or goat		
chuleta	chop	bife a caballo	steak with a fried egg on top
churrasco	grilled beef		
fiambres	cured meats – hams, salami, etc	bife a la criolla	steaks braised with onions, peppers and herbs
filete	fillet steak		
jabalí	wild boar	brochetas	kebabs
jamón	ham	carbonada	a filling meat stew
lechón/cochinillo	suckling pig	cazuela de marisco	a seafood casserole
lomo	tenderloin steak	cerdo a la riojana	pork cooked with fruit
milanesa	breaded veal escalope	fainá	baked chickpea dough traditionally served with pizza
oca	goose		
paletilla	shoulder of lamb		
panceta	Italian-style bacon	guiso	basic meat stew
pato	duck	locro	stew based on maize, beans and meat, often including tripe
pavo	turkey		
pebete	sandwich in a bun or bread roll		
		matambre relleno	cold stuffed flank steak (normally filled with vegetables and hard-boiled eggs, and sliced; literally means "stuffed hunger killer")
pollo	chicken		
ternera	grass-fed veal		
tocino/beicon	bacon		

Offal (achuras)

bofes	lights (lungs)		
chinchulines	small intestine	matambrito	pork, often simmered in milk until soft

milanesa napolitana	breaded veal escalope topped with ham, tomato and melted cheese
milanesa de pollo	breaded chicken breast
mondongo	stew made of cow's stomach with potatoes and tomatoes
pastel de papa	shepherd's pie
provoletta	thick slice of provolone cheese grilled on a barbecue
puchero	a rustic stew, usually of chicken (*puchero de gallina*), made with potatoes and maize or whatever vegetable is to hand
vittel tonné	the Argentine starter par excellence: slices of cold roast beef in mayonnaise mixed with tuna

Fish (pescado)

abadejo	cod
atún	tuna
boga	large, flavoursome fish caught in the Río de la Plata
caballa	mackerel
corvina	sea bass
dorado	a large freshwater fish, with mushy flesh and loads of bones
lenguado	sole
lisa de río	oily river fish
manduví	river fish with delicate, pale flesh
manguruyú	oily river fish (best grilled)
merluza	hake
pacú	firm-fleshed river fish
pejerrey	popular inland-water fish
pirapitanga	salmon-like river fish
sábalo	oily-fleshed river fish
salmón	salmon

surubí	kind of catfish
trucha (arco iris)	(rainbow) trout
vieja	white, meaty-fleshed river fish

Seafood (mariscos)

camarones	shrimps or prawns
cangrejo	crab
centolla	king crab
mejillones	mussels
ostras	oysters
vieira	scallop

Vegetables (verduras)

aceitunas	olives
acelga	chard (like spinach but tougher and more bitter)
albahaca	basil
alcauciles	artichokes
apio	celery
arvejas	peas
aspárragos	asparagus
berenjena	aubergine/eggplant
berro	watercress
cebolla	onion
champiñon	mushroom
chauchas	runner beans
choclo	maize or sweetcorn
chucrút	sauerkraut
coliflor	cauliflower
ensalada	salad
espinaca	spinach
garbanzo	chickpea
habas	broad beans
hinojo	fennel
hongos (silvestres)	(wild) mushrooms
lechuga	lettuce
lentejas	lentils
morrón (dulce/ rojo/verde)	(sweet/red/green) pepper
palmito	palm heart
palta	avocado
papa	potato
papas fritas	chips/French fries
papines	small potatoes eaten whole

perejil	parsley
pimiento	green pepper
poroto	bean
puerro	leek
remolacha	beetroot
rúcula	rocket
tomate	tomato
tomillo	thyme
zanahoria	carrot
zapallito	gem squash – small green pumpkins that are a favourite throughout the country, usually baked stuffed with rice and meat
zapallo	pumpkin

Fruit and nuts (fruta y frutos secos)

almendra	almond
almíbar	syrup
ananá	pineapple
arándano	cranberry/blueberry
avellana	hazelnut
banana	banana
batata	sweet potato
castaña	chestnut
cayote	spaghetti squash
cereza	cherry
ciruela (seca)	plum (prune)
damasco	apricot
dátiles	dates
durazno	peach
frambuesa	raspberry
frutilla	strawberry
higo	fig
lima	lime
limón	lemon
maní	peanut
manzana	apple
melón	melon
membrillo	quince
mora	mulberry
mosqueta	rose hip
naranja	orange
nuez	walnut
pasa (de uva)	dried fruit (raisin)

pera	pear
pomelo (rosado)	(pink) grapefruit
quinoto	kumquat
sandía	watermelon
uva	grape(s)
zarza mora	blackberry

Desserts (postres)

arroz con leche	rice pudding
budín de pan	bread pudding
crema	custard or cream
dulce	sweet in general; candied fruit or jam
dulce de leche	thick caramel made from milk and sugar, a national religion (see box, p.42)
ensalada de fruta	fruit salad
flan	crème caramel
helado medialuna	ice cream
(dulce/salado)	(sweet/plain) croissant-like pastry, more like the Italian "cornetto"
miel (de abeja)	honey
miel (de caña)	molasses
panqueque/crepe	pancake
sambayón	zabaglione (custard made with egg yolks and wine, a popular ice-cream flavour)
torta	tart or cake
tortilla/tortita	breakfast pastry

Drinks (bebidas)

agua	water
agua mineral (con gas/sin gas)	mineral water (sparkling/still)
aguardiente	brandy-like spirit
botella	bottle
cacheteado	Coke and red wine spritzer (very popular in Córdoba)
café (con leche)	coffee (with milk)
cerveza	beer
champán	sparkling wine, usually Argentine, or champagne

chocolate caliente /submarino	hot chocolate (often a slab of chocolate melted in hot milk, served in a tall glass)	lata	can
		leche	milk
		licuados	juice-based drinks or milkshakes
chopp	draught beer	liso	small draught beer (Litoral)
cortado	espresso coffee "cut" with a little steaming milk (similar to macchiato)	mate cocido	infusion made with mate, sometimes heretically with a tea bag
Fernet (branca)	Italian-style digestive drink, popularly mixed with Coke (the gaucho drink par excellence)	sidra	cider
		soda	fizzy water
		té	tea
gaseosa	fizzy drink	vino (tinto/blanco /rosado)	wine (red/white/rosé)
jugo (de naranja)	(orange) juice		

Argentine idiom and slang

Anyone who has learnt Spanish elsewhere will need to become accustomed to the specific vocabulary in Argentina, as a familiarity with Argentine equivalents will certainly smooth things along. Many words for foodstuffs, especially fruit and vegetables, are not the same in Argentina as in other Spanish-speaking countries – you will find many of them in the Argentine menu reader (see p.634).

Though few terms used in Spain are actually taboo in Argentina, there is one major exception, which holds for much of Latin America. The verb **coger**, used in Spain for everything from "to pick up" or "fetch" to "to catch (a bus)", is never used in this way in Argentina, where it is the equivalent of "to fuck". In Argentina use *tomar* (to take) as in *tomar el colectivo* (to catch the bus) or *agarrar* (to take hold of or grab) as in *agarrá la llave* (take the key). Less likely to cause problems, but still one to watch, is **concha**, which in Spain is a perfectly innocent word meaning "seashell", but in Argentina is usually used to refer to the female genitals; the words *caracol* or *almeja* are always used instead for shells and Argentines never tire of finding the Spanish woman's name Conchita (short for Inmaculada Concepción) hilarious (it sounds like "little cunt").

Colloquial speech in Argentina, particularly in Buenos Aires, is extremely colourful, and it's good fun to learn a bit of the local lingo. There's a clear Italian influence in some words. Many colloquial expressions and words also derive from an Italian-influenced form of slang known as *lunfardo*, originally the language of the Buenos Aires underworld (hence the myriad terms in *lunfardo* proper for police, pimps and prostitutes). There's also a playful form of speech, known as **vesre**, in which words are pronounced backwards (*vesre* is the word for *revés* – reverse, backwards); a few of these words, such as *feca* (coffee from *café*), have found their way into everyday speech. Though these expressions will sound odd coming from the mouth of a less-than-fluent foreigner, knowing a few of them will help you get the most out of what's being said around you. *Lunfardo* is also an important part of the repertoire of tango lyrics. Another feature to listen for is the widespread use of the prefix "re-", to mean "really" or "totally". *Re-lindo/a* means really good-looking; *re-malo/a* means really bad. *Reconstra-* is even stronger: something that is *recontra-barato* means it is on sale at a rock-bottom price.

Words listed below that are marked with an asterisk (★) should be used with some caution as they are very familiar; those marked with a double asterisk (★★) denote strong language and are best avoided until you are really familiar with local customs or know the person who are speaking to won't be offended.

afanar	to rob★	chata	pick-up truck★
almacén	grocery shop/store	chico/a	small (also boy/girl)
auto	car (coche is rarely used)	chorro	thief★
		chupar	to drink (alcohol)★
bancar	to put up with★; no me lo banco ("I can't stand it/him")	colectivo	bus
		combi	small minibus that runs urban bus routes
bárbaro/a	great!	copado	cool, good★
barra brava	(group of) hardcore football fans	despelote	mess★
		estancia	farm, traditionally with huge areas of land
birome	biro/ballpoint pen	faso	cigarette★
birra	beer★	feca	coffee★
boliche	nightclub; also sometimes bar/store/shop in rural areas	fiaca	tiredness/laziness★, eg tengo fiaca ("I can't be bothered")
boludo/pelotudo	idiot (equivalent to prat, jerk etc)★★	forro	condom/idiot★★
		gamba	leg★
bombachas	knickers	gaucho	typical Argentine "cowboy" or rural estancia worker
bombilla	straw-like implement, usually of metal, used for drinking mate from a gourd		
		gil	idiot★
bondi	bus	guita/plata	money★
bronca	rage★, as in me da bronca ("he/she/it makes me angry")	hinchapelotas	irritating person★★
		laburar	to work★
cana	police officer (cop)★	lapicera	pen
cancha	football stadium	living	living room
canchero	sharp-witted, (over) confident, cool	luca	one thousand★ (pesos)
		mamado	drunk★ (un mamado★★ means a blow-job)
cartera	handbag/purse		
carpa	tent	mango	mango; peso★/monetary unit as in no tengo un mango ("I don't have a penny")
cataratas	waterfalls, usually used to refer specifically to Iguazú Falls		
caudillo	regional military or political leader, usually with authoritarian overtones	manyar	to eat★
		mate	strictly the mate gourd or receptacle, but used generally to describe the national "tea" drink
chabón	boy/lad★		
chamuyo	conversation/chat★		
chancho	ticket inspector★	medias	socks
chanta	braggart, unreliable person★	micro	long-distance bus

639

milico	member of the military*
mina	woman/girl*
morfar	to eat*
negocio	shop (in general)
nene/la nena	child
onda	atmosphere/character, as in *tiene buena onda* ("there's a good atmosphere" or "she's good-natured")
palo	one million (pesos)*; un *palo verde* is a million US dollars (greenbacks)
pato	Argentine national sport; similar to handball on horseback
patota	gang*
pedo (estar en)	fart** (to be drunk*)
pendejo	kid (mostly used derogatorily)**
petiso	small, also small person
pibe	kid
pinta	"it looks good"; *la pinta* means appearance, as in *tiene pinta* or *tiene buena pinta*

piola	cool, smart
pollera	skirt
pucho	cigarette*
quilombo	mess*
remera	T-shirt
subte	Buenos Aires' underground railway
suéter	sweater
tacho	taxi (*tachero* is taxi driver)
tano/tana	Italian**
tapado	coat (usually woman's)
telo	short-stay hotel where couples go to have sex*
tereré	drink composed of yerba *mate* served with wild herbs (*yuyos*) and ice-cold water or lemonade/orange juice
trucho	fake, phoney
vereda	pavement
vidriera	shop window
vieja/viejo/viejos	mum/dad/parents*
zafar	to get away with*

Travel store

Travel

Andorra The Pyrenees, Pyrenees & Andorra Map, Spain
Antigua The Caribbean
Argentina Argentina, Argentina Map, Buenos Aires, South America on a Budget
Aruba The Caribbean
Australia Australia, Australia Map, East Coast Australia, Melbourne, Sydney, Tasmania
Austria Austria, Europe on a Budget, Vienna
Bahamas The Bahamas, The Caribbean
Barbados Barbados DIR, The Caribbean
Belgium Belgium & Luxembourg, Bruges DIR, Brussels, Brussels Map, Europe on a Budget
Belize Belize, Central America on a Budget, Guatemala & Belize Map
Benin West Africa
Bolivia Bolivia, South America on a Budget
Brazil Brazil, Rio, South America on a Budget
British Virgin Islands The Caribbean
Brunei Malaysia, Singapore & Brunei [1 title], Southeast Asia on a Budget
Bulgaria Bulgaria, Europe on a Budget
Burkina Faso West Africa
Cambodia Cambodia, Southeast Asia on a Budget, Vietnam, Laos & Cambodia Map [1 Map]
Cameroon West Africa
Canada Canada, Pacific Northwest, Toronto, Toronto Map, Vancouver
Cape Verde West Africa
Cayman Islands The Caribbean
Chile Chile, Chile Map, South America on a Budget
China Beijing, China, Hong Kong & Macau, Hong Kong & Macau DIR, Shanghai
Colombia South America on a Budget
Costa Rica Central America on a Budget, Costa Rica, Costa Rica & Panama Map
Croatia Croatia, Croatia Map, Europe on a Budget
Cuba Cuba, Cuba Map, The Caribbean, Havana
Cyprus Cyprus, Cyprus Map
Czech Republic The Czech Republic, Czech & Slovak Republics, Europe on a Budget, Prague, Prague DIR, Prague Map
Denmark Copenhagen, Denmark, Europe on a Budget, Scandinavia
Dominica The Caribbean
Dominican Republic Dominican Republic, The Caribbean
Ecuador Ecuador, South America on a Budget
Egypt Egypt, Egypt Map
El Salvador Central America on a Budget
England Britain, Camping in Britain, Devon & Cornwall, Dorset, Hampshire and The Isle of Wight [1 title], England, Europe on a Budget, The Lake District, London, London DIR, London Map, London Mini Guide, Walks In London & Southeast England
Estonia The Baltic States, Europe on a Budget
Fiji Fiji
Finland Europe on a Budget, Finland, Scandinavia
France Brittany & Normandy, Corsica, Corsica Map, The Dordogne & the Lot, Europe on a Budget, France, France Map, Languedoc & Roussillon, The Loire, Paris, Paris DIR, Paris Map, Paris Mini Guide, Provence & the Côte d'Azur, The Pyrenees, Pyrenees & Andorra Map
French Guiana South America on a Budget
Gambia The Gambia, West Africa
Germany Berlin, Berlin Map, Europe on a Budget, Germany, Germany Map
Ghana West Africa
Gibraltar Spain
Greece Athens Map, Crete, Crete Map, Europe on a Budget, Greece, Greece Map, Greek Islands, Ionian Islands
Guadeloupe The Caribbean
Guatemala Central America on a Budget, Guatemala, Guatemala & Belize Map
Guinea West Africa
Guinea-Bissau West Africa
Guyana South America on a Budget
Holland see The Netherlands
Honduras Central America on a Budget
Hungary Budapest, Europe on a Budget, Hungary
Iceland Iceland, Iceland Map
India Goa, India, India Map, Kerala, Rajasthan, Delhi & Agra [1 title], South India, South India Map
Indonesia Bali & Lombok, Southeast Asia on a Budget
Ireland Dublin DIR, Dublin Map, Europe on a Budget, Ireland, Ireland Map
Israel Jerusalem
Italy Europe on a Budget, Florence DIR, Florence & Siena Map, Florence & the best of Tuscany, Italy, The Italian Lakes, Naples & the Amalfi Coast, Rome, Rome DIR, Rome Map, Sardinia, Sicily, Sicily Map, Tuscany & Umbria, Tuscany Map, Venice, Venice DIR, Venice Map
Jamaica Jamaica, The Caribbean
Japan Japan, Tokyo
Jordan Jordan
Kenya Kenya, Kenya Map
Korea Korea
Laos Laos, Southeast Asia on a Budget, Vietnam, Laos & Cambodia Map [1 Map]
Latvia The Baltic States, Europe on a Budget
Lithuania The Baltic States, Europe on a Budget
Luxembourg Belgium & Luxembourg, Europe on a Budget
Malaysia Malaysia Map, Malaysia, Singapore & Brunei [1 title], Southeast Asia on a Budget
Mali West Africa
Malta Malta & Gozo DIR
Martinique The Caribbean
Mauritania West Africa
Mexico Baja California, Baja California, Cancún & Cozumel DIR, Mexico, Mexico Map, Yucatán, Yucatán Peninsula Map
Monaco France, Provence & the Côte d'Azur
Montenegro Montenegro
Morocco Europe on a Budget, Marrakesh DIR, Marrakesh Map, Morocco, Morocco Map,
Nepal Nepal
Netherlands Amsterdam, Amsterdam DIR, Amsterdam Map, Europe on a Budget, The Netherlands
Netherlands Antilles The Caribbean
New Zealand New Zealand, New Zealand Map

DIR: Rough Guide **DIRECTIONS** for short breaks

Available from all good bookstores

ROUGH GUIDES

NOTES

Small print and
Index

A Rough Guide to Rough Guides

Published in 1982, the first Rough Guide – to Greece – was a student scheme that became a publishing phenomenon. Mark Ellingham, a recent graduate in English from Bristol University, had been travelling in Greece the previous summer and couldn't find the right guidebook. With a small group of friends he wrote his own guide, combining a highly contemporary, journalistic style with a thoroughly practical approach to travellers' needs.

The immediate success of the book spawned a series that rapidly covered dozens of destinations. And, in addition to impecunious backpackers, Rough Guides soon acquired a much broader and older readership that relished the guides' wit and inquisitiveness as much as their enthusiastic, critical approach and value-for-money ethos.

These days, Rough Guides include recommendations from shoestring to luxury and cover more than 200 destinations around the globe, including almost every country in the Americas and Europe, more than half of Africa and most of Asia and Australasia. Our ever-growing team of authors and photographers is spread all over the world, particularly in Europe, the US and Australia.

In the early 1990s, Rough Guides branched out of travel, with the publication of Rough Guides to World Music, Classical Music and the Internet. All three have become benchmark titles in their fields, spearheading the publication of a wide range of books under the Rough Guide name.

Including the travel series, Rough Guides now number more than 350 titles, covering: phrasebooks, waterproof maps, music guides from Opera to Heavy Metal, reference works as diverse as Conspiracy Theories and Shakespeare, and popular culture books from iPods to Poker. Rough Guides also produce a series of more than 120 World Music CDs in partnership with World Music Network.

Visit www.roughguides.com to see our latest publications.

Rough Guide credits

Text editors: James Rice, Mandy Tomlin, Hazel Meek, David Leffman
Layout: Ankur Guha
Cartography: Maxine Repath
Picture editors: Ed Steer, Nicole Newman
Production: Louise Daly
Proofreader: Susannah White
Cover design: Nicole Newman, Dan May, Chloë Roberts
Photographer: Greg Roden
Editorial: London Andy Turner, Keith Drew, Edward Aves, Alice Park, Lucy White, Jo Kirby, James Smart, Natasha Foges, Róisín Cameron, Lara Kavanagh, Emma Traynor, Emma Gibbs, Kathryn Lane, Monica Woods, Mani Ramaswamy, Harry Wilson, Lucy Cowie, Alison Roberts, Eleanor Aldridge, Ian Blenkinsop, Joe Staines, Matthew Milton, Tracy Hopkins, Ruth Tidball; **Delhi** Madhavi Singh, Lubna Shaheen, Jalpreen Kaur Chhatwal
Design & Pictures: London Scott Stickland, Dan May, Diana Jarvis, Mark Thomas, Sarah Cummins, Emily Taylor; **Delhi** Umesh Aggarwal, Ajay Verma, Jessica Subramanian, Pradeep Thapliyal, Sachin Tanwar, Anita Singh, Nikhil Agarwal, Sachin Gupta

Production: Rebecca Short, Liz Cherry, Erika Pepe
Cartography: London Ed Wright, Katie Lloyd-Jones; **Delhi** Rajesh Chhibber, Ashutosh Bharti, Rajesh Mishra, Animesh Pathak, Jasbir Sandhu, Karobi Gogoi, Swati Handoo, Deshpal Dabas, Lokamata Sahu
Online: London Faye Hellon, Jeanette Angell, Fergus Day, Justine Bright, Clare Bryson, Aine Fearon, Adrian Low, Ezgi Celebi; **Delhi** Amit Verma, Rahul Kumar, Narender Kumar, Ravi Yadav, Debojit Borah, Rakesh Kumar, Ganesh Sharma, Shisir Basumatari
Marketing & Publicity: London Liz Statham, Jess Carter, Vivienne Watton, Anna Paynton, Rachel Sprackett, Laura Vipond;
New York Katy Ball; **Delhi** Aman Arora
Digital Travel Publisher: Peter Buckley
Reference Director: Andrew Lockett
Operations Assistant: Becky Doyle
Operations Manager: Helen Atkinson
Publishing Director (Travel): Clare Currie
Commercial Manager: Gino Magnotta
Managing Director: John Duhigg

Publishing information

This fourth edition published October 2010 by
Rough Guides Ltd,
80 Strand, London WC2R 0RL
11, Community Centre, Panchsheel Park, New Delhi 110017, India
Distributed by the Penguin Group
Penguin Books Ltd,
80 Strand, London WC2R 0RL
Penguin Group (USA)
375 Hudson Street, NY 10014, USA
Penguin Group (Australia)
250 Camberwell Road, Camberwell, Victoria 3124, Australia
Penguin Group (NZ)
67 Apollo Drive, Mairangi Bay, Auckland 1310, New Zealand
This paperback edition published in Canada in 2010. Rough Guides is represented in Canada by Tourmaline Editions Inc., 662 King Street West, Suite 304, Toronto, Ontario, M5V 1M7
Cover concept by Peter Dyer.

Typeset in Bembo and Helvetica to an original design by Henry Iles.

Printed in Italy by L.E.G.O. S.p.A, Lavis (TN)
© Danny Aeberhard, Andrew Benson, Rosalba O'Brien and Lucy Phillips 2010
Maps © Rough Guides
No part of this book may be reproduced in any form without permission from the publisher except for the quotation of brief passages in reviews.
664pp includes index
A catalogue record for this book is available from the British Library
ISBN: 978-1-84836-521-6

The publishers and authors have done their best to ensure the accuracy and currency of all the information in **The Rough Guide to Argentina**, however, they can accept no responsibility for any loss, injury, or inconvenience sustained by any traveller as a result of information or advice contained in the guide.

1 3 5 7 9 8 6 4 2

Help us update

We've gone to a lot of effort to ensure that the fourth edition of **The Rough Guide to Argentina** is accurate and up-to-date. However, things change – places get "discovered", opening hours are notoriously fickle, restaurants and rooms raise prices or lower standards. If you feel we've got it wrong or left something out, we'd like to know, and if you can remember the address, the price, the hours, the phone number, so much the better.

Please send your comments with the subject line "Rough Guide Argentina Update" to ©mail @roughguides.com. We'll credit all contributions and send a copy of the next edition (or any other Rough Guide if you prefer) for the very best emails.

Have your questions answered and tell others about your trip at ®www.roughguides.com

Acknowledgements

Danny Aeberhard wishes to thank: Paula García Celis of Mendoza for her letter; Alejandro Tello & Chloe of Runacay in Villa Union; Manuel Barrios in La Rioja; Ivanlor; Dionicio Pérez for his uncommon enthusiasm in Jáchal; Jorge Saleme; Adriana Rizzetto of PN San Guillermo; Mario Riveros Alvarez of Paula Tour; Mauro of Don Lisandro plus Jorge, Analía and the mighty "Goyo" for a great night in Barreal; Manuel Octavio, Hernán & Cote for the *buena onda* at the Rancho Lamaral; Amanda Savedra & Santiago Cara in Malargüe; Manuel Uranga & El Pingüino at Las Leñas. Also thanks to James and Hazel for a considerate edit and Ed for his photo selection. Friends at the Argentine embassy: Javier Figueroa & Alessandra Viggiano, Carolina Pérez Colman, Santi Villalba & Javier Pedrazzini. Mark & Ale Pearman and Laurita Devoto & Jorge Martene with their respective families. To the whole Kojnover family – Kely, Anselmo, Silia, Raúl Alvarez and David – without whom Argentina simply wouldn't be the same; and above all to my gorgeous partner, Britta Jaschinski, for her passion and support throughout.

Andrew Benson wishes to thank: hoping I haven't forgotten anyone, all my friends around Argentina, especially Eugenio, Josefina and her family, Ricardo, Patricia and Mauricio (al porvenir!), and Constanza (for everything!); Rubén and his parents; Gustavo and everyone who extended their customary but still much appreciated hospitality in Buenos Aires; Jackie and Peter for being patient companions, sharing the rough and the smooth, the driving and the wine; Marjan for some whistlestop driving,

loyal company and lasting friendship; Pascale for her enormous help; my wonderful hosts all around Patagonia and the Lake District for their hospitality, with a special mention for Carolina, Verónica and Agustín; Soraya for her fabulous cooking and for the fun times in Tafí and Santiago de Compostela; Mercedes and Paz for their great generosity; Rosalba for her great work, support and friendship; Danny for his helpful tips and sharp eye; James for quiet perseverance and a very helpful approach; and Fernando for his encouragement and humour.

Rosalba O'Brien wishes to thank: Isobel and Juliana at Destino Argentina; Romina in Iguazú; Charlie Adamson; Ana in Rosario; all at La Alondra; Rodrigo at Las Pizarras; Jess; Irene; the gentleman manning Victoria's tourist office; Andrew; James and David at Rough Guides; my family in San Nicolás – Amalia, Sebastian and Mimi – and of course as always Esteban and Arwen.

Ed Stocker and Clemmy Manzo wish to thank: Ariel Bustos for all his help, advice and impressive knowledge of Córdoba's history; Tomás Torrado at Córdoba tourist board; Luciana Salaün; Kevin and Louisa Begg at Los Potreros; Virginia and Mikael at Oh La La in Mina Clavero; Leandro Laffon at Emtur Mar del Plata; James Rice at Rough Guides HQ in London; plus all the friendly strangers we asked for tips along the way. And lastly each other for being great travel companions and staying calm under pressure, despite one wobbly moment in Cerro Colorado!

Readers' letters

Thanks to all the readers who have taken the time to write in with comments and suggestions (and apologies if we've inadvertently omitted or misspelt anyone's name):

Patrick Augustine, Cristina Becker, Victoria Bennett, Melissa Calderwood, Ciara Cassidy, Mayra Decastelli, Olwen Golden, Isabel Heim Vadis, Rob Laber, Gavin May, Erik Moerch, Nad Mylvaganam, Jessica Rossell, Anne Sargent, Dawn Smallwood, S Stokes, Luca Toscani, Edith Werner.

Photo credits

All photos © Rough Guides except the following:

Introduction

Tango dancers, Buenos Aires © Julian Finney/ Getty

Iguazú Falls © Photolibrary Tucuman © Florian von der Fecht

Gaucho's belt buckle © Barnabas Bosshart/ Corbis

Wine bar, Finca Adalgisa hotel, Mendoza © Photolibrary

Cerro Torre, Los Glaciares National Park, Patagonia © Photolibrary

Southern right whale, Península Valdés © blickwinkel/Alamy

Lake Belgrano, Perito Moreno National Park © Javier Etcheverry/ Alamy

Things not to miss

01 Aconcagua © Enrique Marcarian/Corbis

02 El Carnaval del Pais, Gualeguaychu © Enrique Marcarian/Corbis

03 Laguna Iberá, Esteros del Iberá, Corrientes © Aurora Photos/Alamy

04 Quebrada de Humahuaca © Hemis /Alamy

05 Glaciar Perito Moreno © Florian von der Fecht

06 Cliff face, Talampaya National Park © Nick Baylis /Alamy

07 Mendoza wine bar © Yadid Levy/Corbis

09 Gravestones in La Recoleta Cemetery, Buenos Aires © Aurora Photos/Alamy

10 Iguazú Falls with rainbow © Dennis Cox/Alamy

11 Snowboarding © LOOK Die Bildagentur der Fotografen /Alamy

12 Local handicrafts hanging in shop in Cafayate © Jonathan Gordon/Alamy

13 Dinosaurs in Patagonia, Villa El Chocon, Neuquen © Etcheverry Images/Alamy

14 Volcán Lanin © Jason Friend Photography/ Alamy

15 Maned wolf © Terry Whittaker/Alamy

16 Capilla de Candonga, Córdoba © Florian von der Fecht

17 *Asado* © Danita Delimont/Alamy

18 Hiker on trail in Andes © Michael Lewis/Corbis

19 Young southern elephant seals © Theo Allofs/ Corbis

20 Ushuaia © Buena Vista Images/Getty

21 Fishing Boat on Lago Espejo, Nahuel Huapi National Park © Robert Harding/Alamy

22 San Telmo © Etcheverry Images/Alamy

23 Close view of a guanaco © Pablo Caridad / Alamy

24 Football © Sean Gallup/Getty

25 Rounding up sheep on horseback, Patagonia © Jon Crwys-Williams/Alamy

26 Tigre village on Paraná Delta © Hemis/Alamy

27 A gaucho on horseback rounding up cattle in The Pampas © ImageState/Alamy

28 Cueva de los Manos Pintadas © Hubert Stadler/Corbis

The legendary Ruta 40 colour section

Signpost on Ruta 40 © Florian von der Fecht

Lighthouse, Cabo Vírgenes © Florian von der Fecht

Andean landscape, Santa Cruz province © Florian von der Fecht

Cuesta de Miranda © Photolibrary

Horses along the Ruta 40 near Cachi © Photolibrary

La Polvorilla viaduct © Javier Etcheverry/Alamy

4WD plying the Ruta 40 © Javier Etcheverry/ Alamy

Bikers en route to Rio La Leona © Javier Etcheverry/Alamy

Criollo culture colour section

Bowl of *locro* © Eduardo Pucheta/Alamy

An *asado* © Etcheverry Images/Alamy

Mate gourd and straw (bombilla) © Etcheverry Images /Alamy

A gaucho facón © Michel Friang/Alamy

Men watching *jineteadas* at the Fiesta de la Tradición © Etcheverry Images/Alamy

Gaucho in traditional attire, drinking *mate* © Marco Simoni/Robert Harding

A gaucho foreman selects horses for work © Christopher Pillitz/Alamy

Rounding up sheep on an estancia near El Calafate © Jeremy Hoare/Alamy

Horseman, San Antonio de Areco © Etcheverry Images/Alamy

Black & whites

p.74 Boca Juniors soccer fans © Marcos Brindicci/Corbis

p.90 Changing guards ceremony at Casa Rosada © Yadid Levy/Alamy

p.122 Exhibition Hall, Museo de Arte Latinoamericano © Demetrio Carrasco/DK

p.130 Traditional folk dancing © Stefano Paterna/ Alamy

p.152 Beach at Pinamar © photolibrary

p.164 Preparing fossils © Louie Psihoyos/Corbis

p.182 Fiesta de la Tradición © ARGENTINA-PHOTO/Alamy

p.188 Basilica de Nuestra Señora De Luján © Sarah Murray/Masterfile

p.200 Cathedral and Cabildo, Córdoba © Getty

p.219 Jesuit estancia de Santa Catalina © Arco Images GmbH/Alamy

p.222 Ex-hotel Edén Hotel in La Falda city © A. Parada/Alamy

p.229 Museo Ernesto Che Guevara © Emiliano Rodriguez/Alamy

p.240 Ruins of San Ignacio Mini © Jordi Cami/ Alamy

p.247 El Carnaval del Pais © Enrique Marcarian/ Corbis

p.257 Capybaras © Joe McDonald/Corbis

ROUGH GUIDES

SMALL PRINT

SMALL PRINT

Index

Map entries are in colour.

INDEX